Heads of States and Governments

Heads of States and Governments

A Worldwide Encyclopedia of Over 2,300 Leaders, 1945 through 1992

by

HARRIS M. LENTZ III

McFarland & Company, Inc., Publishers
Jefferson, North Carolina, and London

British Library Cataloguing-in-Publication data are available

Library of Congress Cataloguing-in-Publication Data

Lentz, Harris M.
    Heads of states and governments : a worldwide encyclopedia of
2,300 leaders, 1945 through 1992 / by Harris M. Lentz III.
      p. cm.
    Includes index.
    ISBN 0-89950-926-6 (lib. bdg. : 50# alk. paper) ∞
    1. Heads of state — Biography.   2. Statesmen — Biography.
3. History, Modern — 20th century — Biography. I. Title.
D412.L46 1994
920.02 — dc20   94-13310
                                                  CIP

Manufactured in the United States of America

McFarland & Company, Inc., Publishers
 Box 611, Jefferson, North Carolina 28640

To my mother,
Helene Z. Lentz,
for her invaluable assistance,

my sister,
Nikki Lentz Walker,
for her support,

and Nina Heffington and Kent Nelson,
for their encouragement and advice

Contents

Acknowledgments

I would like to thank the many individuals and institutions that assisted with this work by supplying me with information, reading my material, and encouraging my completion of this project. They include Ernest Staes, Consul General of Belgium, the Swiss Consulate, the Embassy of Romania, Marja Guercin, Secretary of Public Affairs at the Embassy of Finland, Indra de Silva, Information and Cultural Officer of the Embassy of the Democratic Socialist Republic of Sri Lanka, former Prime Minister Steingrímur Hermannsson of Iceland, the Embassy of the Republic of Korea, Dario Suro, Minister Plenipotentiary of the Embassy of the Dominican Republic, Patricio Powell, the Secretary for Cultural Affairs at the Embassy of Chile, President Václav Havel of the Czech Republic, former President Léopold Sédar Senghor of Sierra Leone, former King Michael of Romania, Prince Norodom Sihanouk of Cambodia, H.R.H. King Hassan II of Morocco, Tony Pruitt, Bobby Mathews, Bruce Lyons, Joy Martin, Jennifer Habecker, Maggie Trafford, Donna Raburn, Katy Miller, Ronda Billingsley, Tammy Mathews, Jean Purdy, Meredith Looney, Carla Clark, Louis and Vickie Berretta, Andy and Missy Branham, Anne and Monte Taylor, Scott Graves, Paul and Sam Geary, Mark Heffington, Bill and Cheryl Dabbs, Wade DeHart, Kimberley Lord, Jackie Mabry, Anne Hall, Mickey Alderson, Athenee and Brian Morris, Mike and Janet Jewell, Bill and Jennifer McAnally, Mary Linder, Nadoline Miller, Janette Campbell, Jimmy Walker, Betty Dean Lundeman, Sid Cromwell, Doy L. Daniels, Jr., LaVelle Sorrell, Terry Mitchell, Deborah Neeley, Billie Dickey, Kim Brown, Larry Taubert, Ursula Hannaford, Mickey Martin, Rosa Burett, Bill Wood, Greg and Angela Bridges, John Hoffman, State Technical Institute Library, Memphis State University Library, Memphis and Shelby County Public Libraries, Fred P. Gattas Co., and Beretta's Spike & Rail.

Preface

The world has gone through numerous changes since the end of World War II. Over half of the nations that exist today have gained their independence since 1945. During this period over 2,300 individuals have ruled the various nations of the world. I hope the information found on the following pages helps to give the reader some insight into the history of individual nations through the lives of their leaders. One may find few common threads among these men and women. Some were regarded as international statesmen, others were little more than common thugs. Some brought to their countries peace and prosperity, others took their homelands to the brink of destruction. Some pursued power from an early age, others reluctantly accepted the role of leadership when it was thrust upon them. Some served in office for over half a century, others held power for less than a day. Some remained prominent and powerful leaders throughout their lives, others vanished into the footnotes of history. Some completed their terms of office peacefully, others were ousted, exiled, or murdered. All of them have made some impact on their own nation and therefore have influenced the world at large.

In compiling this book I have included all heads of state and government of independent nations from the conclusion of World War II in 1945 through the end of 1992. I have also chosen to include all such persons who took office on or after January 1, 1945, even if they were no longer serving at the end of the war. They are generally viewed as being strongly linked to the postwar period with which this book is concerned, and their inclusion seems necessary.

I have included all countries that had independent governments during the period of time covered. Acceptances in the United Nations and other international agencies and diplomatic recognition by other nations were major criteria in the inclusion of a country. Areas that were controlled by a separatist movement (e.g., Biafra, Western Sahara, Somaliland) were not included where a central government continued to claim control over the contested area. Information on those areas can generally be found within the entries of the country that the separatist regions are a part of. The republics of Serbia and Montenegro were also not given a separate entry,

1

as they are still considered to be a part of what remains of Yugoslavia. I have chosen to include the independent homelands carved from South Africa (e.g., Transkei, Venda, Ciskei), despite the lack of formal recognition by other governments. I have not included colonies or areas that have yet to be granted independence (e.g., Puerto Rico, Northern Ireland, Palau), though I have included some information on preindependence leaders of former colonies that have gained their independence. Nations that were created after the cutoff date of December 31, 1992—the Czech Republic and Slovakia, for example—are not a part of this book.

I have endeavored to include all elected, appointed, hereditary, or proclaimed leaders of the countries included. Typically a monarch, president, or military junta leader is considered the head of state, while a prime minister, premier, or chairman of the council of ministers would be considered the head of government. In some countries, particularly in the former Communist bloc, the chairman of the Communist party was the preeminent political figure in the country. Often, but not always, he held one of the other positions as well. Nevertheless, I have included these individuals in the book. On a few occasions the most powerful figure in the country does not hold a usual position or title that represents his status (e.g., the Ayatollah Khomeini of Iran, Deng Xiaoping of China, and generals Torrijos and Noriega of Panama). These individuals will also be found in this book. I have also included interim presidents for most nations. These were typically individuals who held the office briefly between terms of elected presidents. Their entries are often brief. Most "acting presidents" are not included, however; in many countries an acting president takes over whenever the head of state is unable to perform his duties—often including when the president is simply traveling out of the country. These individuals have virtually no impact on the government. I have included only a handful of acting presidents who took their office because of the physical incapacity of the president.

The countries are listed alphabetically by the English-language name by which they are most commonly known, with the full name (if different) and full local-language name listed as well. Some nations have changed names during the years covered in this volume. The entries are listed under the current name of the country (e.g., Sri Lanka rather than Ceylon), though the previous names of the countries are indicated directly under the country heading. Some nations have ceased to exist during the period of time covered in the book, having been absorbed by other countries. The leaders of these former nations will be found listed under the country's name before its absorption (e.g., German Democratic Republic, Republic of Vietnam, West Indies Federation).

Place names mentioned within individual entries are located within the countries being discussed unless otherwise indicated. I have generally used the current name of cities and towns within an entry (e.g., St. Petersburg for Leningrad, Nizhny Novgorod for Gorky). I have used earlier place names within an entry for reasons of clarity when necessary (e.g., Saigon rather than Ho Chi Minh City in the entry for the Republic of Vietnam).

Other countries have emerged from the division of nations found in this book, the most prominent example being the Soviet Union. The Soviet leaders will be found under that listing, while separate country entries will be found for the currently independent nations which were once Soviet Republics (e.g., Russia, Ukraine, Georgia, Kazakhistan, etc.).

The name of the country is followed by a brief geographical and historical description. The biographical entries then follow with heads of state listed in chronological order by term of office. They are followed by heads of government. When an individual has served multiple terms of office, his biographical entry will be found following his earliest listed term. Subsequent terms of office will refer the reader to the leader's first entry.

The entries of the leaders included give biographical information, including dates of birth and death, where possible. I have also tried to include pertinent information concerning political careers and important events that occurred during the subjects' terms of office. In all cases I have tried to resolve conflicting information as accurately as possible. I have attempted to use the most common spelling of names of individuals and locations included in the book, consulting *The New York Times,* the *Encyclopaedia Brittanica,* the *Times of London* and the *International Who's Who* as primary sources for spelling and diacritical marks. I have also relied upon official government information from the individual countries included in regard to this matter.

Whenever possible I have verified facts included in this book from a minimum of two sources, though it was sometimes necessary to rely on biographical information from a single reliable source on the more obscure leaders included. I consulted a myriad of sources in the compilation of the information found in this book, including newspapers, encyclopedias, histories, and biographies. My research also included contact with the embassies and governments of many of the countries included in this work, and in some cases I directly contacted individual heads of state and members of their families to determine accurate biographical information.

I have attempted to make this book as comprehensive and as easy to use as possible. My hope is that what follows will be of interest to the casual reader as well as of value to researchers.

Bibliography

BOOKS

Abrahamian, Ervand. *Iran Between Two Revolutions.* Princeton, NJ: Princeton University Press, 1982.

Adams, Michael, ed. *The Middle East.* New York: Facts on File, 1988.

Afghanistan: A Country Study. Washington, DC: U.S. Government Printing Office, 1986.

Akbar, M. J. *Nehru: The Making of India.* London: Viking, 1988.

Alam, Asadollah. *The Shah and I.* New York: St. Martin's, 1992.

Algeria: A Country Study. Washington, DC: U.S. Government Printing Office, 1986.

Ali, Tariq. *The Nehrus and the Gandhis: An Indian Dynasty.* London: Hogarth Press, 1985.

Alisky, Marvin. *Historical Dictionary of Peru.* Metuchen, NJ: Scarecrow, 1979.

Ameringer, Charles D. *Don Pepe: A Political Biography of Jose Figueres of Costa Rica.* Albuquerque, NM: University of New Mexico Press, 1978.

Amirsadeghi, Hossein. *Twentieth Century Iran.* New York: Holmes and Meier, 1977.

Anthony, John Duke. *Historical Dictionary of the Sultanate of Oman and the Emirates of Eastern Arabia.* Metuchen, NJ: Scarecrow, 1976.

Appiah, L. H. Ofosu, ed. *Dictionary of African Biography.* 2 vols. New York: Reference Publications, 1977.

Archer, Jules. *The Dictators.* New York: Bantam, 1968.

Arvil, Pierre. *Politics in France.* Baltimore: Penguin, 1969.

The Australian Encyclopedia. Sydney, Australia: Grolier Society of Australia, 1983.

Ayany, Samuel G. *A History of Zanzibar.* Nairobi: East Africa Literature Bureau, 1970.

Ayling, S. E. *Portraits of Power.* New York: Barnes and Noble, 1961.

Azimi, Fakhreddin. *Iran: The Crisis of Democracy, 1941–1953.* New York: St. Martin's, 1989.

Bangladesh: A Country Study. Washington, DC: U.S. Government Printing Office, 1989.

Bartke, Wolfgang. *Who's Who in the People's Republic of China.* Armonk, NY: M. E. Sharpe, 1981.

Bhutto, Benazir. *Daughter of Destiny.* New York: Simon and Schuster, 1989.

Bidwell, Robin. *The Two Yemens.* Boulder, CO: Westview Press, 1983.

Bizzaro, Salvatore. *Historical Dictionary of Chile.* Metuchen, NJ: Scarecrow, 1972.

Boorman, Howard L., ed. *Biographical Dictionary of the Republic of China.* New York: Columbia University Press, 1967.

Bork, Albert W., and George Maier. *Historical Dictionary of Ecuador.* Metuchen, NJ: Scarecrow, 1973.

Brace, Richard M. *Morocco Algeria Tunisia.* Englewood Cliffs, NJ: Prentice-Hall, 1964.

Briggs, Donald C., and Marvin Alisky. *Historical Dictionary of Mexico.* Metuchen, NJ: Scarecrow, 1981.

Brown, Archie, ed. *The Soviet Union: A Biographical Dictionary.* New York: Macmillan, 1991.

Bullock, Alan, and R. B. Woodings, eds. *Twentieth Century Culture.* New York: Harper & Row, 1983.

Burki, Shahid Javed. *Pakistan Under Bhutto, 1971–1977.* New York: St. Martin's, 1980.

Burma: A Country Study. Washington, DC: U.S. Government Printing Office, 1983.

Burrowes, Robert D. *The Yemen Arab Republic: The Politics of Development, 1962–1986.* Boulder, CO: Westview Press, 1987.

Buttinger, Joseph. *Vietnam: A Dragon Embattled.* New York: Frederick A. Praeger, 1967.

Carroll, Raymond. *Anwar Sadat.* New York: Franklin Watts, 1982.

Castagno, Margaret F. *Historical Dictionary of Somalia.* Metuchen, NJ: Scarecrow, 1975.

Chandler, David P. *A History of Cambodia.* Boulder, CO: Westview Press, 1983.

Cheng, Peter. *A Chronology of the People's Republic of China.* Totowa, NJ: Rowman and Littlefield, 1972.

Columbia Encyclopedia. Morningside Heights, NJ: Columbia University Press, 1950.

Colvin, Lucie G. *Historical Dictionary of Senegal.* Metuchen, NJ: Scarecrow, 1981.

Creedman, Theodore S. *Historical Dictionary of Costa Rica.* Metuchen, NJ: Scarecrow, 1977.

Crosby, Cynthia A. *Historical Dictionary of Malawi.* Metuchen, NJ: Scarecrow, 1980.

Crozier, Brian. *South-East Asia in Turmoil.* Baltimore: Penguin, 1978.

Davis, Robert H. *Historical Dictionary of Colombia.* Metuchen, NJ: Scarecrow, 1977.

Decalo, Samuel. *Historical Dictionary of Chad.* Metuchen, NJ: Scarecrow, 1977.

————. *Historical Dictionary of Dahomey.* Metuchen, NJ: Scarecrow, 1975.

————. *Historical Dictionary of Niger.* Metuchen, NJ: Scarecrow, 1979.

————. *Historical Dictionary of Togo.* Metuchen, NJ: Scarecrow, 1976.

Delpar, Helen, ed. *Encyclopedia of Latin America.* New York: McGraw-Hill, 1974.

De Silva, K. M. *A History of Sri Lanka.* London: Hurst, 1989.

Dickie, John, and Alan Rake. *Who's Who in Africa.* London: African Development, 1973.

Diederick, Bernard, and Al Burt. *Papa Doc: The Truth About Haiti Today.* New York: Avon, 1969.

Egypt: A Country Study. Washington, DC: U.S. Government Printing Office, 1991.

Encyclopaedia Britannica. Chicago: Encyclopaedia Britannica, various editions.

Encyclopedia of Asian History. New York: Scribner's, 1988.

Farouk-Sluglett, Marion, and Peter Sluglett. *Iraq Since 1958.* London: KPI, 1987.

Flemion, Philip F. *Historical Dictionary of El Salvador.* Metuchen, NJ: Scarecrow, 1972.

Foray, Cyril Patrick. *Historical Dictionary of Sierre Leone.* Metuchen, NJ: Scarecrow, 1977.

Gailey, Harry A. *Historical Dictionary of the Gambia.* Metuchen, NJ: Scarecrow, 1975.

Galindez, Jesus de. *The Era of Trujillo.* Tucson, AZ: University of Arizona Press, 1973.

Gardinier, David E. *Historical Dictionary of Gabon.* Metuchen, NJ: Scarecrow, 1981.

Gerteiny, Alfred G. *Historical Dictionary of Mauritania.* Metuchen, NJ: Scarecrow, 1981.

Gleijeses, Piero. *The Dominican Crisis: The 1965 Constitutionalist Revolt and American Intervention.* Baltimore, MD: Johns Hopkins University Press, 1978.

Grant, Bruce. *Indonesia.* Australia: Penguin, 1967.

Gregorian, Vartan. *The Emergence of Modern Afghanistan.* Stanford: Stanford University Press, 1972.

Grotpeter, John J. *Historical Dictionary of Swaziland.* Metuchen, NJ: Scarecrow, 1975.

————. *Historical Dictionary of Zambia.* Metuchen, NJ: Scarecrow, 1979.

Hahn, Lorna. *Historical Dictionary of Libya.* Metuchen, NJ: Scarecrow, 1981.

Hale, Julian. *Ceausescu's Romania.* London: Harrap, 1972.

Halebsky, Sandor, and John M. Kirk, eds.: *Cuba: Twenty-Five Years of Revolution, 1959-84.* New York: Praeger, 1985.

Haliburton, Gordon. *Historical Dictionary of Lesotho.* Metuchen, NJ: Scarecrow, 1977.

Hanifi, M. Jamil. *Historical Dictionary of Afghanistan.* Metuchen, NJ: Scarecrow, 1976.

Harvey, Robert. *Portugal: Birth of a Democracy.* New York: St. Martin's, 1978.

Heath, Dwight B. *Historical Dictionary of Bolivia.* Metuchen, NJ: Scarecrow, 1972.

Hedrick, Basil C., and Anne Hedrick. *Historical Dictionary of Nepal.* Metuchen, NJ: Scarecrow, 1972.

————. *Historical Dictionary of Panama.* Metuchen, NJ: Scarecrow, 1970.

Heggoy, Alf Andrew. *Historical Dictionary of Algeria.* Metuchen, NJ: Scarecrow, 1981.

Heinl, Robert Debs, Jr., and Nancy Gordon Heinl. *Written in Blood: The Story of the Haitian People 1492-1971.* Boston: Houghton-Mifflin, 1978.

Hilton, Ronald, ed. *Who's Who in Latin America.* 2 vols. Stanford: Stanford University Press, 1971.

Holden, David, and Richard Johns. *The House of Saud.* New York: Holt, Rinehart and Winston, 1981.

Holt, David K., and M. W. Daly. *The History of the Sudan.* London: Longman, 1988.

Hopwood, Derek. *Syria, 1945-1986.* London: Unwin Hyman, 1988.

Imperato, Pascal James. *Historical Dictionary of Mali.* Metuchen, NJ: Scarecrow, 1977.

India: A Country Study. Washington, DC: U.S. Government Printing Office, 1986.

The International Who's Who. London: Europa, various editions.

Ionescu, Ghita. *Communism in Rumania, 1944-62.* London: Oxford University Press, 1964.

Iran: A Country Study. Washington, DC: U.S. Government Printing Office, 1989.

Iraq: A Country Study. Washington, DC: U.S. Government Printing Office, 1990.

Jordan: A Country Study. Washington, DC: U.S. Government Printing Office, 1991.

Kalck, Pierre. *Historical Dictionary of the Central African Republic.* Metuchen, NJ: Scarecrow, 1980.

Karnow, Stanley. *Vietnam: A History.* New York: Viking, 1983.

Keddie, Nikki R. *Roots of Revolution: An Interspective History of Modern Iran.* New Haven: Yale University Press, 1981.

Kim, Joungwon A. *Divided Korea: The Politics of Development 1945-72.* Cambridge: Harvard University Press, 1975.

Kinross, Lord. *Ataturk.* New York: William Morrow, 1965.

Kolinski, Charles J. *Historical Dictionary of Paraguay.* Metuchen, NJ: Scarecrow, 1973.

Kousoulas, D. George. *Modern Greece: Profile of a Nation.* New York: Scribner's, 1974.

Kurian, George. *Historical Dictionary of India.* Metuchen, NJ: Scarecrow, 1976.

Kurtz, Laura S. *Historical Dictionary of Tanzania.* Metuchen, NJ: Scarecrow, 1978.

Kurzman, Dan. *Ben-Gurion: Prophet of Fire.* New York: Simon and Schuster, 1983.

Langley, Lester D. *Central America: The Real Story.* New York: Crown, 1985.

Langville, Alan R. *Modern World Rulers: A Chronology.* Metuchen, NJ: Scarecrow, 1979.

Laos: A Country Study. Washington, DC: U.S. Government Printing Office, 1985.

Lebanon: A Country Study. Washington, DC: U.S. Government Printing Office, 1989.

Lentz, Harris M., III. *Assassinations and Executions: An Encyclopedia of Political Violence, 1865-1986.* Jefferson, NC: McFarland, 1988.

Levine, Robert M. *Historical Dictionary of Brazil.* Metuchen, NJ: Scarecrow, 1979.

Levine, Victor T. *The Cameroon Federal Republic.* Ithaca: Cornell University Press, 1971.

Lewis, Paul H. *Paraguay Under Stroessner.* Chapel Hill: University of North Carolina Press, 1980.

Lewis, Paul H., and Roger P. Nye. *Historical Dictionary of Cameroon.* Metuchen, NJ: Scarecrow, 1974.

Levy, Felice, comp. *Obituaries on File.* 2 vols. New York: Facts on File, 1979.

Lewis, Bernard. *The Emergence of Modern Turkey.* London: Oxford University Press, 1968.

Lewytzkyj, Borys, and Juliusz Stroynowski, eds. *Who's Who in the Socialist Countries.* New York: Saur, 1978.

Libya: A Country Study. Washington, DC: U.S. Government Printing Office, 1989.

Lineberry, William P. *East Africa.* New York: Wilson, 1968.

Liniger-Goumaz, Max. *Historical Dictionary of Equatorial Guinea.* Metuchen, NJ: Scarecrow, 1979.

Lipschutz, Mark R., and R. Kent Rasmussen. *Dictionary of African Historical Biography.* Chicago: Aldine, 1978.

Livermore, H. V. *A New History of Portugal.* Cambridge: Harvard University Press, 1966.

Lobban, Richard. *Historical Dictionary of Guinea-Bissau.* Metuchen, NJ: Scarecrow, 1979.

Lunt, James. *Hussein of Jordan.* New York: William Morrow, 1989.

Lux, William. *Historical Dictionary of the British Caribbean.* Metuchen, NJ: Scarecrow, 1975.

McFarland, Daniel Miles. *Historical Dictionary of Upper Volta.* Metuchen, NJ: Scarecrow, 1978.

McLintock, A. H., ed. *An Encyclopedia of New Zealand.* Wellington, New Zealand: Owen, 1966.

Malaysia: A Country Study. Washington, DC: U.S. Government Printing Office, 1985.

Malhotra, Inder. *Indira Gandhi.* London: Hodder and Stoughton, 1989.

Mansor, Menahem, ed. *Political and Diplomatic History of the Arab World, 1900-1967.* 7 vols. Washington, DC: NCR/Microcard Editions, 1972.

Maring, Ester G., and Joel M. *Historical Dictionary of the Philippines.* Metuchen, NJ: Scarecrow, 1973.

_____. *Historical Dictionary of Burma.* Metuchen, NJ: Scarecrow, 1973.

Martin, Phyllis. *Historical Dictionary of Angola.* Metuchen, NJ: Scarecrow, 1980.

Mays, Stanley. *Makarios: A Biography.* New York: St. Martin's, 1981.

Meir, Golda. *My Life.* New York: Putnam, 1975.

Metraux, Guy S., and Francois Crouzet. *The New Asia.* New York: New American Library, 1965.

Meyer, Harvey K. *Historical Dictionary of Honduras.* Metuchen, NJ: Scarecrow, 1976.

_____. *Historical Dictionary of Nicaragua.* Metuchen, NJ: Scarecrow, 1972.

Moore, Richard E. *Historical Dictionary of Guatemala.* Metuchen, NJ: Scarecrow, 1973.

Moreno, Jose A. *Barrios in Arms: Revolution in Santo Domingo.* Pittsburgh: University of Pittsburgh Press, 1970.

Ogot, Bethwell A. *Historical Dictionary of Kenya.* Metuchen, NJ: Scarecrow, 1981.

Okelly, John. *Revolution in Zanzibar.* Nairobi: East African Publishing House, 1967.

Olson, James S., ed. *Historical Dictionary of the Spanish Empire, 1402-1975.* New York: Greenwood, 1992.

O'Toole, Thomas. *Historical Dictionary of Guinea.* Metuchen, NJ: Scarecrow, 1978.

Pakistan: A Country Study. Washington, DC: U.S. Government Printing Office, 1984.

Palmer, Alan. *The Facts on File Dictionary of 20th Century History.* New York: Facts on File, 1979.

Parsa, Misagh. *Social Origins of the Iranian Revolution.* New Brunswick: Rutgers University Press, 1989.

Parsons, Anthony. *The Pride and the Fall, Iran 1974-1979.* London: Jonathan Cape, 1984.

Perlmutter, Amos. *Israel: The Partitioned State.* New York: Scribner's, 1985.

_____. *The Life and Times of Menaghem Begin.* Garden City, NY: Doubleday, 1987.

Perusse, Roland I. *Historical Dictionary of Haiti.* Metuchen, NJ: Scarecrow, 1977.

Petran, Tabitha. *Syria.* New York: Praeger, 1972.

Pluvier, Jan. *South-East Asia from Colonialism to Independence.* London: Oxford University Press, 1974.

Pollo, Stefanaq, and Arben Puto. *The History of Albania.* London: Routledge and Kegan Paul, 1981.

Prouty, Chris, and Eugene Rosenfeld. *Historical Dictionary of Ethiopia.* Metuchen, NJ: Scarecrow, 1981.

Rasmussen, R. Kent. *Historical Dictionary of Rhodesia/Zimbabwe.* Metuchen, NJ: Scarecrow, 1979.

Richmond, J. C. B. *Egypt 1798–1952*. London: Methuen, 1977.

Riley, Carroll L. *Historical Dictionary of Saudi Arabia*. Metuchen, NJ: Scarecrow, 1972.

Riviere, Lindsay. *Historical Dictionary of Mauritius*. Metuchen, NJ: Scarecrow, 1982.

Rose, Leo E., and John T. Scholz. *Nepal: Profile of a Himalayan Kingdom*. Boulder, CO: Westview, 1980.

Rose, Norman. *Chaim Weizmann: A Biography*. New York: Viking, 1986.

Rudolph, Donna K., and G. A. Rudolph. *Historical Dictionary of Venezuela*. Metuchen, NJ: Scarecrow, 1971.

Sharma, Jagdish Saran. *India Since the Advent of the British: A Descriptive Chronology*. Delhi, India: Chand, 1970.

Shimoni, Yaacov, and Evyatar Levine, eds. *Political Dictionary of the Middle East in the 20th Century*. New York: Quadrangle, 1974.

Shreshtha, Kusum. *Monarchy in Nepal*. Bombay: Popular Prakashan, 1984.

Simon, Reeva. *Iraq Between the Two World Wars*. New York: Columbia University Press, 1986.

Singapore: A Country Study. Washington, DC: U.S. Government Printing Office, 1991.

Singhal, Damodar P. *Pakistan*. Englewood Cliffs, NJ: Prentice-Hall, 1972.

Sisson, Richard, and Leo E. Rose. *War and Secession: Pakistan, India, and the Creation of Bangladesh*. Berkeley: University of California Press, 1990.

Skidmore, Thomas E. *The Politics of Military Rule in Brazil 1964–85*. New York: Oxford University Press, 1988.

Smith, Harold. *Historical Dictionary of Thailand*. Metuchen, NJ: Scarecrow, 1976.

Spencer, William. *Historical Dictionary of Morocco*. Metuchen, NJ: Scarecrow, 1980.

Spuler, Bertold, C. G. Allen, and Neil Saunders. *Rulers and Governments of the World*. 3 vols. London and New York: Bowker, 1977.

Sri Lanka: A Country Study. Washington, DC: U.S. Government Printing Office, 1985.

Stempel, John D. *Inside the Iranian Revolution*. Bloomington: Indiana University Press, 1981.

Stevens, Richard P. *Historical Dictionary of Botswana*. Metuchen, NJ: Scarecrow, 1975.

Stewart, Donald E. J. *Historical Dictionary of Cuba*. Metuchen, NJ: Scarecrow, 1981.

Stewart, John. *African States and Rulers*. Jefferson, NC: McFarland, 1989.

Storry, Richard. *A History of Modern Japan*. Baltimore: Penguin, 1968.

Taylor, Sidney, ed. *The New Africans*. New York: Putnam, 1967.

Thailand: A Country Study. Washington, DC: U.S. Government Printing Office, 1989.

Theroux, Paul. *The Happy Isles of Oceania*. Norwalk, CT: Easton Press, 1993.

Thomas, Hugh. *The Spanish Civil War*. New York: Harper and Row, 1961.

Thompson, Virginia, and Richard Adloff. *Historical Dictionary of the Congo (Brazzaville)*. Metuchen, NJ: Scarecrow, 1974.

Tsoucalas, Constantine. *The Greek Tragedy*. Baltimore: Penguin, 1969.

Tunney, Christopher. *A Biographical Dictionary of World War II*. New York: St. Martin's, 1972.

Turkey: A Country Study. Washington, DC: U.S. Government Printing Office, 1988.

Voll, John. *Historical Dictionary of the Sudan*. Metuchen, NJ: Scarecrow, 1978.

Webster's Biographical Dictionary. Springfield, MA: Merriam, various editions.

Weinstein, Martin. *Uruguay: The Politics of Failure*. Westport, CT: Greenwood, 1975.

Weinstein, Warren. *Historical Dictionary of Burundi*. Metuchen, NJ: Scarecrow, 1976.

Werlich, David P. *Peru: A Short History*. Carbondale and Edwardsville, IL: Southern Illinois University Press, 1978.

Whitfield, Danny J. *Historical Dictionary of Vietnam*. Metuchen, NJ: Scarecrow, 1976.

Who's Who in Switzerland. Geneva: Nagel, 1966.

Who's Who in the World. Chicago: Marquis Who's Who, various editions.

Wiedner, Donald L. *A History of Africa South of the Sahara*. New York: Vintage, 1962.

Wilbur, Donald Newton, ed. *The Nations of Asia*. New York: Hart, 1966.

Willis, Jean L. *Historical Dictionary of Uruguay*. Metuchen, NJ: Scarecrow, 1974.

Wilson, A. Jeyaratnam. *Politics in Sri Lanka, 1947-73*. New York: St. Martin's, 1974.

Wint, Guy, ed. *Asia Handbook*. London: Anthony Blond, 1965.

Wise, L. F., and E. W. Egan. *Kings, Rulers and Statesmen*. New York: Sterling, 1967.

Woddis, Jack. *Introduction to Neo-Colonialism*. New York: International, 1972.

Wright, Ione, and Lisa M. Nekhom. *Historical Dictionary of Argentina*. Metuchen, NJ: Scarecrow, 1978.

Wyatt, David K. *Thailand: A Short History*. New Haven: Yale University Press, 1984.

Yao Ming-Le. *The Conspiracy and Death of Lin Biao*. New York: Knopf, 1983.

Young, Jordan M. *Brazil 1954-64: End of a Civilian Cycle*. New York: Facts on File, 1972.

PERIODICALS

Annual Register of World Events (London), 1945-1991.

Current Biography (New York), 1940-1993.

Encyclopaedia Britannica Book of the Year (Chicago), 1945-1993.

Facts on File (New York), 1940-1993.

Memphis Commercial Appeal (Memphis), 1945-1993.

Memphis Press Scimitar (Memphis), 1945-1983.

Newsweek (New York), 1950-1993.

Time (New York), 1945-1993.

Times of London (London), 1950-1992.

Washington Post (Washington, DC), 1948-1992.

The World Almanac (New York), 1948-1993.

Heads of States
and Governments

Afghanistan, Islamic Republic of

(De Afghanistan Islami Jamhuriat)

Afghanistan is a landlocked country in southwestern Asia. It was granted independence by Great Britain in August of 1919.

HEADS OF STATE

MOHAMMED ZAHIR SHAH (King, November 8, 1933–July 17, 1973). Mohammed Zahir Shah was born in Kabul on October 30, 1914. His father, Mohammed Nadir Shah, had been proclaimed king of Afghanistan in October of 1929, following the overthrow of King Amanullah the previous December. Zahir was educated in France and attended the Kabul Infantry School. In 1931 he married Princess Houmairah Begum.

Mohammed Zahir Shah was minister of education when he succeeded his father after Nadir's assassination on November 8, 1933. The 19-year-old king, with the advice and support of his uncle and prime minister, Sardar Hashim Khan, continued his father's programs of modernization and reform. During the 1930s Zahir largely depended on the financial support of Germany for these projects, though Afghanistan remained neutral during World War II. Following Germany's defeat, the United States began providing financial assistance. Zahir survived a short-lived revolt led by followers of former king Amanullah Khan in 1945. Two years later Afghanistan began a long-standing dispute with Pakistan, following the latter country's independence from Great Britain. Zahir's brother-in-law and cousin, Mohammed Daud Khan, became prime minister and reduced the king's power to that of a figurehead in September of 1953. Two years later the dispute with Pakistan accelerated when Daud demanded the creation of an independent state on the Afghan-Pakistan border. Violent clashes resulted in the closure of the Khyber Pass for several months until diplomatic intervention by the Soviet Union and the Western powers succeeded in temporarily easing tensions between the two countries. During the 1950s and 1960s, Zahir managed to balance Afghanistan between the Soviet Union and the United States and gained financial aid from both world powers. In March of 1963 Zahir dismissed his powerful brother-in-law as prime minister. The following year he approved Afghanistan's first written constitution, which allowed a limited parliamentary democracy. Afghanistan's border dispute with Pakistan was also eased with the restoration of diplomatic relations. Zahir's rule was threatened during the late 1960s by outbreaks of civil disorder arising from demands for an increase in democratization. A drought also added to the country's financial woes. The king managed to remain in power until July 17, 1973, however. Zahir was in Italy for health reasons when he was ousted by his former prime minister, Mohammed Daud Khan, who eliminated the monarchy and proclaimed Afghanistan a republic. Following his ouster, Zahir lived modestly in exile near Rome. He continued to receive monthly financial support from the Afghanistan government until Daud's overthrow in 1978, when the former king was stripped of his citizenship. He made few public statements during his exile, though he was reportedly considered as a possible compromise leader of his country during the insurrection against the Soviet-backed administrations that followed Daud. Zahir's citizenship was restored in 1991.

MOHAMMED DAUD KHAN (President, July 17, 1973–April 27, 1978). Mohammed Daud Khan was born in 1909 in Kabul. He was educated in Kabul and Paris. In 1932 he was appointed governor of the province of Kandahar by his uncle, King Nadir Shah. Daud also married the king's daughter, Zarmina. Following Nadir's assassination in 1933, Daud became governor and commander in chief of Afghanistan's Eastern Province, and in 1937 he became commander in chief of the central armed forces. Daud remained a powerful force in the military until 1946, when he was appointed ambassador to France. Four years later he returned to Kabul as minister of defense. Daud succeeded Shah Mahmud Khan as prime minister on September 7, 1953. As prime minister, Daud actively sought the financial support of the Soviet Union while maintaining Afghan neutrality. For ten years Daud ruled Afghanistan virtually alone, as he reduced King Zahir's role to that of a figurehead. The king was finally able to remove Daud as prime minister on March 10, 1963, by promoting a constitution which made it illegal for a member of the royal family to serve in the government. Daud remained in Kabul, though his relationship with the king was strained. On July 17, 1973, Daud took advantage of the absence of King Zahir from the country for medical reasons and ousted his cousin in a military coup. Daud abolished the monarchy and assumed the posts of president and prime minister. He successfully put down several coup attempts in 1973 and 1974, though economic difficulties in the country continued to escalate. The president was also faced with opposition from the powerful Muslim Brotherhood. Daud survived another

coup led by former military officers in November of 1976. The following year Daud called a meeting of the Grand National Assembly, which had not met for four years, to approve a new constitution giving greater powers to the president. There was an outbreak of domestic violence following the murder of a prominent Afghan Communist leader in April of 1977. Daud began a crackdown on Communists following a period of rioting and demonstrations against his regime. Daud was overthrown and killed on April 27, 1977, during a coup led by the Afghan Communist party and segments of the military loyal to the air force chief of staff.

NUR MOHAMMAD TARAKI (President, April 30, 1978–September 15, 1979). Nur Mohammad Taraki was born in 1917 in the Ghazni Province of Afghanistan. He worked in Bombay, India, in the late 1930s, where he became a follower of Mahatma Gandhi. In the late 1940s he began working in minor positions for the Afghan government and was stationed at Afghanistan's embassy in the United States in the early 1950s. Taraki, a noted writer and Marxist intellectual, founded the Maoist Khalq, or Masses, party in 1963 in opposition to King Zahir Shah. The party divided with the ascension of the Daud regime in 1973, with the pro-Soviet Parcham, or Banner, party faction supporting Daud. Taraki remained a leading opponent of the Daud regime and served several jail sentences for his views. He became secretary-general of the People's Democratic party when the two rival factions of the Khalq reunited in 1977. On April 27, 1978, Taraki was a leader of a bloody coup which overthrew and killed President Daud. Three days later Taraki was named president and prime minister of the new Soviet-backed government. Taraki relinquished the post of prime minister to Hafizullah Amin on March 27, 1979, following a major revolt by conservative Muslim tribesmen opposed to the Marxist regime. Taraki's Soviet advisors favored the ouster of the brutal Amin as prime minister, but their plan backfired when Amin instead overthrew Taraki on September 16, 1979. The new government announced that Taraki died of an undisclosed illness on October 9, 1979, though it was later revealed that Taraki had died of gunshot wounds at the time of his ouster.

HAFIZULLAH AMIN (President, September 16–December 27, 1979). Hafizullah Amin was born on August 1, 1929, in Paghman, Afghanistan. Amin reportedly attended Columbia University in the United States. He later joined Taraki's Khalq party in the 1960s and was active in the coup which overthrew the regime of Mohammed Daud Khan in April of 1978. Amin was named foreign minister in Taraki's new Marxist government. On March 27, 1979, Amin became Taraki's prime minister and was responsible for the brutal repression of Muslim insurgents in the provincial Afghan capital of Herat. Continuing religious and civil disorders in Afghanistan resulted in a buildup of Soviet military support for the besieged Afghan regime. Amin ousted and killed Taraki on September 16, 1979, and took control of the government. The Amin government proved even more unpopular than its predecessor as rebels advanced throughout the country. Amin survived as president for a little over three months. He was ousted and killed on December 27, 1979, in a Soviet-backed coup which installed Babrak Karmal as the new Afghan leader.

BABRAK KARMAL (President, December 27, 1979–November 10, 1986). Babrak Karmal, the son of a prominent Afghan army general, was born in Kabul in 1929. He became active in leftist politics while a student at Kabul University. In 1949 he began serving a

five-year prison sentence for his Communist activities. After his release from jail, Karmal received a legal degree and served in the Ministry of Planning in the late 1950s and early 1960s. In 1965 he was elected to the National Assembly as a member of the pro-Communist Khalq party. He served as an outspoken opponent of the government until the Assembly was abolished in 1973. In 1973 Karmal broke with the Taraki-Amin leadership of the Khalq party and founded the Parcham, or Banner, party. Karmal's faction was considered more pro-Soviet and supported Mohammed Daud Khan's ouster of the monarchy. In 1977 Karmal reunited with his rivals in the People's Democratic party when Daud abolished all political parties. On April 27, 1978, Daud was ousted by a Marxist-led military coup, and Karmal was named vice president and deputy prime minister in the new Taraki government. The partnership of the Khalq and Parcham parties disintegrated shortly thereafter, and in July, Karmal was appointed ambassador to Czechoslovakia. In September, while still in Prague, Karmal was purged by the government and ordered to return to Kabul to stand trial. He remained in exile in Eastern Europe for the next year. Following Amin's coup against Taraki in September of 1979, a Soviet-led invasion of Afghanistan took place in December, and Amin was ousted and killed. Karmal was then installed as president and prime minister on December 27, 1979. The Muslim rebellion continued during Karmal's presidency, and Soviet military activity increased. On June 11, 1981, Karmal relinquished the post of prime minister to his ally, Sultan Ali Keshtamand. The Soviets became increasingly disillusioned with Karmal's inability to quell the Afghan civil war, and on May 4, 1986, he was replaced as leader of the People's Democratic party by Mohammed Najib. Karmal remained as a figurehead president of the Revolutionary

Council until November 24, 1986, when he retired to Moscow. Karmal returned to Afghanistan in June of 1991 and reportedly died in a plane crash near Kabul on June 21, 1992.

HAJI MOHAMMAD CHAMKANI (President, November 24, 1986–September 30, 1987). Haji Mohammed Chamkani was born in 1947. He was a tribal leader from the Paktia Province in Eastern Afghanistan. Chamkani, a non–Communist, served as vice president of the Revolutionary Council. He succeeded Babrak Karmal in the largely ceremonial position of president of the Revolutionary Council on November 24, 1986. He remained in that position until he was replaced by Mohammed Najib on September 30, 1987.

SAYID MOHAMMED NAJIB (ULLAH) (President, September 30, 1987–April 16, 1992). Najib, a member of the Pashtun tribe, was born in 1947 in Afghanistan's Paktia Province near Pakistan. His father was a banker, and Najib, then called Najibullah, was raised in Kabul. Najib, nicknamed the "Ox," joined the Communist party while studying medicine at the University of Kabul in 1965. He joined the Parcham wing of the Communist party and was arrested on several occasions for his political activities. Najib became a member of the ruling Revolutionary Council after the overthrow of Mohammed Daud in 1978. Shortly afterwards the Taraki government began a purge of Parcham members and named Najib as ambassador to Iran. He then went into exile in Eastern Europe. Following the overthrow of the Khalq regime of Hafizullah Amin in December of 1979, Najib returned to Afghanistan to become leader of the Afghan secret police, or KHAD. Najib's successes in this position impressed the Soviets to the extent that he was named to replace Babrak Karmal as general secretary of the People's Democratic party on May 4, 1986. Najib assumed the post of president of the Revolutionary Council on September 30, 1987, and on November 30 he was elected president of Afghanistan under a new constitution. Najib proved a more popular figure with Afghan religious leaders than his predecessors, and the intelligence network he supervised while head of the KHAD helped to secure more support of tribal leaders in the ongoing civil war. Nevertheless, the violence continued as Najib sought a political solution to the Islamic guerrilla war. Pressure for a settlement increased following the withdrawal of Soviet troops in February of 1989. Najib survived several coup attempts in early 1990, including one led by his defense minister, Shahnawaz Tanai, in March of 1990. In June, Najib founded a new political party in Afghanistan, the Homeland party, in an effort to win mass support for his government. The new party was primarily composed of his Communist allies and did little to improve his popularity. Najib was forced to resign in April of 1992 as the rebels advanced on the capital. He took refuge in the United Nations compound in Kabul on April 16, 1992. The Islamic government that succeeded him attempted to have him turned over to the government to stand trial for war crimes.

SIBGHATULLAH MOJADIDI (President, April 28, 1992–June 28, 1992). Sibghatullah Mojadidi was born in 1926. He was a moderate Islamic scholar and leader of the Afghan National Liberation Front. He had served as leader of a rebel government in exile in 1989. The government had collapsed due to conflicts among rival factions. Mojadidi was chosen as a compromise choice to serve as Afghanistan's interim president on April 28, 1992. He sought to have his term extended beyond the interim period, but was unable to gain the support needed to do so. He turned the government over to Burhanuddin Rabbani on June 28, 1992.

BURHANUDDIN RABBANI (President, June 28, 1992–   ). Burhanuddin Rabbani was born in 1939. He served as the leader of the Jamiat-e-Islami, or Islamic Afghan Association, one of the strongest guerrilla factions in Afghanistan. He was chosen by the Supreme Council to serve as president and took office on June 28, 1992. Fighting continued in Afghanistan between the rival guerrilla organizations. The government was also threatened by Iranian-backed Shi'ite Muslims and the fundamentalist Islamic party.

HEADS OF GOVERNMENT

SARDAR MOHAMMED HASHIM KHAN (Prime Minister, November 8, 1933–May 14, 1946). Sardar Mohammed Hashim Khan, the son of Muhammad Yusof Khan, was born in 1884. Hashim joined his brother, Mohammed Nadir Shah, in exile in France in 1926. Hashim returned to Afghanistan with his brother in 1929 to raise an army to defeat the brigand chief Bacha Sakao, or Habibullah Khan, who had seized control of Afghanistan. Following their victory, Nadir Shah became king of Afghanistan, and Hashim was named a member of the Council of Ministers. Following Nadir's assassination in September of 1933, Hashim was named prime minister on November 8, 1933. He was the virtual ruler of Afghanistan during the early years of the reign of his nephew, Mohammed Zahir Shah. Hashim was responsible for restoring the orthodox and conservative way of life that former King Amanullah's reformations had threatened. Hashim remained as prime minister and Zahir's chief advisor until his retirement for health reasons on May 14, 1946. Hashim died in Kabul on October 26, 1953, at the age of 69.

SARDAR MAHMUD SHAH KHAN GHAZI (Prime Minister, May 14, 1946–September 7, 1953). Sardar Mahmud Shah Khan Ghazi was born in 1888. He served as minister of war in the cabinet of his brother, Mohammed Nadir Shah, after Nadir gained the Afghan throne in 1929. Mahmud was instrumental in securing the throne for his nephew, Mohammed Zahir Shah, following Nadir's assassination in 1933. Mahmud remained as minister of war until he succeeded another brother, Hashim, as prime minister on May 19, 1946. He was considered more progressive than his predecessor and initiated a number of reforms during his term of office. Mahmud served in this position for seven years until Mohammed Daud Khan became prime minister on September 7, 1953. Mahmud died at the age of 71 on December 27, 1959, in northern Afghanistan.

MOHAMMED DAUD KHAN (Prime Minister, September 7, 1953–March 10, 1963). *See entry under Heads of State.*

MOHAMMED YUSUF (Prime Minister, March 10, 1963–October 29, 1965). Mohammed Yusuf was born in Kabul on January 21, 1917. He served as minister of mines and industries before being named prime minister and minister of foreign affairs by King Zahir on March 10, 1963. Yusuf was instrumental in drafting a new Afghan constitution which did not allow members of the royal family to serve in the government. He remained in office until he was dismissed on October 29, 1965. He was appointed ambassador to West Germany in 1966 and served until 1973. Yusuf retired from political activity and went into exile in Germany following the overthrow of King Mohammad Zahir Shah.

MOHAMMED HASHIM MAIWANDWAL (Prime Minister, November 1, 1965–November 1, 1967). Mohammed Hashim Maiwandwal was born on March 12, 1921. In the 1940s he edited and wrote for several Afghanistan newspapers. In 1949 he was named press secretary to the Afghan government. The following year he was appointed advisor to the king. During the 1950s Maiwandwal served as ambassador to Great Britain and to Pakistan, and from 1958 to 1963, he was ambassador to the United States. He succeeded Mohammed Yusuf as prime minister on November 1, 1965. During his tenure as prime minister, Maiwandwal was noted for his policies of modernization and liberalization of the government. He had completed a second five-year plan of development and had started a third when he resigned for reasons of health on November 1, 1967. Maiwandwal was the leader of the Progressive Democracy movement when he was arrested on September 20, 1973, on charges of conspiring to overthrow the government of President Mohammed Daud Khan. He died in prison on October 1, 1973, reportedly having hanged himself with his necktie in his prison cell.

NOOR AHMAD ETAMADI (Prime Minister, November 1, 1967–May 17, 1971). Noor Ahmad Etamadi was born on February 22, 1921, in Khandahr. He was educated at Kabul University and joined the Foreign Ministry in 1946. He was named deputy foreign minister in 1963 and was appointed ambassador to Pakistan the following year. Etamadi served as foreign minister in the Maiwandwal government from 1965 and succeeded Maiwandwal as prime minister on November 1, 1967. Etamadi continued his predecessor's policies of modernization, but was often frustrated in his attempts by a poor relationship with the Parliament. He announced his resignation on May 17, 1971, but remained in his position until the con-

firmation of his successor on June 9, 1971. Etamadi remained in the government and served as ambassador to Italy in 1971, to the Soviet Union in 1973, and to Pakistan from 1976 to 1978. He was arrested following the overthrow of the regime of Mohammed Daud Khan in 1978 and was reportedly executed in August of 1979.

ABDUL ZAHIR (Prime Minister, June 9, 1971–September 25, 1972). Abdul Zahir was born in Laghman on May 3, 1910. He attended medical school in the United States, where he graduated from Johns Hopkins University. He returned to Afghanistan in 1943 to serve as chief doctor in the Kabul Municipal Hospital until 1950. Zahir served in the Ministry of Health from 1950 and became minister in 1955. In 1958 he was appointed ambassador to Pakistan, and he served there until 1961, when he was elected president of the Parliament. From 1964 to 1965 he was deputy prime minister and minister of health. Zahir was named ambassador to Italy in 1969 and was serving in that capacity when he was appointed to succeed Etamadi as prime minister, an office he assumed on June 9, 1971. Zahir had better success than Etamadi in securing cooperation from the Parliament for his programs, including legislation designed to help lower-income Afghanistanis. Afghanistan was faced with a major famine in 1972, and Zahir was criticized for the government's inability to cope with the crisis. He resigned his office on September 25, 1972, though he retained his position until December, when his government lost a parliamentary vote of confidence. He died on October 21, 1982.

MOHAMMAD SHAFIQ (Prime Minister, December 1972–July 17, 1973). Mohammad Shafiq was born in Kabul on May 30, 1924. He was employed by the Justice Ministry in 1957 while serving as a professor of international law at Kabul University. From

1963 to 1964 he served as the deputy justice minister and was influential in writing the 1964 Afghanistan Constitution. Shafiq was appointed ambassador to Egypt in 1968 and served in that position until he was named foreign minister in 1971. He was appointed prime minister in December of 1972 and served until July 17, 1973, when he was ousted with King Zahir Shah by a military coup led by Mohammad Daud Khan. Shafiq was imprisoned by the Daud government until 1976, when he was put under house arrest. He was rearrested following the overthrow of Daud in 1978 and was executed by the new government shortly thereafter.

MOHAMMED DAUD KHAN (Prime Minister, July 17, 1972–April 27, 1978). *See entry under Heads of State.*

NUR MOHAMMED TARAKI (Prime Minister, April 30, 1978–March 27, 1979). *See entry under Heads of State.*

HAFIZULLAH AMIN (Prime Minister, March 27–December 27, 1979). *See entry under Heads of State.*

BABRAK KARMAL (Prime Minister, December 27, 1979–June 11, 1981). *See entry under Heads of State.*

SULTAN ALI KESHTAMAND (Prime Minister, June 11, 1981–May 26, 1988). Sultan Ali Keshtamand was born in 1937. A Shi'ite Muslim and Communist, Keshtamand was a leading figure in the Parcham party and a close ally of President Babrak Karmal. He was a member of the Supreme Military Council when he succeeded Karmal in the position of prime minister on June 11, 1981. Keshtamand served as leader of the government until May 26, 1988. He again served as prime minister from February 21, 1989, until May 8, 1990, when he was named first vice president of Afghanistan. Keshtamand was ousted from office in February of 1991 and went briefly into exile in the Soviet Union. He returned to Afghanistan in July of 1991 and resumed his political activities.

MOHAMMAD HASSAN SHARQ (Prime Minister, May 26, 1988–February 20, 1989). Mohammad Hassan Sharq was born in Anardara in the Farah province of Afghanistan in 1926. He attended military school and received a medical degree from the University of Kabul. He served as an assistant to Mohammad Daud Khan when Daud was prime minister from 1953 until 1963. Sharq then remained out of government service until Daud's overthrow of King Mohammed Zahir Shah in 1973. Sharq was appointed first deputy prime minister in the new government. He was appointed ambassador to Japan in 1977, but was recalled following the overthrow of Daud in 1978. Sharq was named by the Karmal government to be ambassador to India in 1980 and served there until 1986. The following year he was appointed minister of refugee repatriation and deputy prime minister. Although he was not a Communist party member, he was named prime minister on May 26, 1988. Sharq was promoted by the Soviets as a possible leader of a coalition government of national reconciliation. He attempted to reach a settlement with the opponents of the regime and invited former King Mohammed Zahir Shah and other exile leaders to personal meetings. He met with little success in this regard and resigned the office of prime minister on February 20, 1989, when the Supreme Military Council for the Defense of the Homeland took control of the government's economic, political, and military policy.

SULTAN ALI KESHTAMAND (Prime Minister, February 21, 1989–May 8, 1990). *See earlier entry under Heads of Government.*

FAZAL HAQ KHALIQYAR (Prime Minister, May 8, 1990–April 16, 1992). Fazal Haq Khaliqyar was born in Herat in 1934. After studying economics at Kabul University, he worked in government service. He served as governor of the Baghlan Province in 1971 and was subsequently deputy minister of finance until 1972. He served as first deputy minister of finance until the overthrow of the government of Mohammed Daud Khan in 1978. Khaliqyar remained in the new government as an advisor to the Ministry of Finance. In 1985 he was again appointed deputy minister of finance, and later that year he was named minister of state for financial affairs, a position in which he served until 1987. The following year he was appointed governor of Herat Province. Khaliqyar remained in that position until he was named prime minister by President Najib on May 8, 1990. He left office when President Najib's government collapsed on April 16, 1992.

ABDUL SABUR FARID KUHESTANI (Prime Minister, July 6, 1992–August 15, 1992). Abdul Sabur Farid Kuhestani was a deputy to rebel fundamentalist leader Gulbuddin Hekmatyar. He was selected as prime minister in an interim government on July 6, 1992, and served until August 15, 1992.

Albania, Republic of

(Republika e Shqipërisë)

Albania is a country in southeastern Europe. It was granted independence from Turkey on November 28, 1912.

HEADS OF STATE

ENVER HOXHA (President, November 10, 1945–January 13, 1946). Enver Hoxha was born to a poor Muslim family in Gjirokaster, Albania, on October 16, 1908. He attended the French school at Korce on a scholarship and went to France to study at Montpellier University in 1930. When he lost his scholarship the following year, he moved to Paris, where he became involved with the French Communist Party. While in Paris, Hoxha also wrote a series of articles about Albania for the Communist newspaper *L'Humanité*. Hoxha began working for the Albanian Consulate in Brussels, Belgium, in 1934, but he lost his position when it was learned that he had written articles critical of the government of King Zog I. Hoxha returned to Albania and accepted a teaching position at his old school in Korce. He remained active in Communist activities and was arrested for conspiracy in early 1939. He was released from prison prior to the Italian invasion of Albania on April 7, 1939. Hoxha then moved to Tirana, Albania's capital, where he engaged in anti-Fascist activities. Hoxha founded the Albanian Communist party in 1941 and edited the party newspaper. He was sentenced to death in absentia by the Italian regime when his activities were exposed. Hoxha was also a leader of the National Liberation Front (FNC), a Communist Resistance group which fought against the Italian and German occupation forces. Hoxha was named prime minister and army commander in chief in the provisional government formed in October of 1944. The following year Hoxha became Albania's first postwar president on November 10, 1945, in a government recognized by the Allied powers. The new government proclaimed Albania a people's democracy early the next year. At this time Hoxha relinquished the Communist party leadership to Gen. Koci Xoxe and the presidency to Omer Nisani. Hoxha began the arduous task of rebuilding his war-torn country. As foreign minister, minister of defense, and head of government, Hoxha agitated for war reparations from Italy and for Albania's entry into the United Nations. His attempts were rebuffed by the United States and Great Britain, who had earlier withdrawn official recognition of his government. Albania's support for the Communist guerrillas during the civil war in Greece in the late 1940s further aggravated relations with the West. Albania's friendly relationship with its other neighbor, Yugoslavia, also ended during the Stalin-Tito feud of 1948. Hoxha replaced Xoxe, a Tito supporter, as first secretary of the Communist party, now called the Albania Party of Labor, on October 6, 1948. Hoxha resigned as prime minister on July 20, 1954, having given up the Foreign Ministry the previous year. He continued to rule Albania as leader of the Communist party. Albania was finally allowed into the United Nations in 1955. The Albanian government was considered one of the most brutal and repressive in the world. All religious activities were outlawed in the country, and Hoxha crushed any opposition in a ruthless fashion. Albania maintained a good relationship with the Soviet Union until the death of Stalin in 1953. The relationship between the two countries rapidly deteriorated in the post-Stalin period, however, and all ties were broken in 1961. Hoxha's regime then became closely tied with the Chinese government, but this alliance also soured after the death of Chairman Mao Tse-tung in 1976. Hoxha, who was the author of nearly 40 books, suffered

from ill health in the early 1980s. He relinquished most of his duties to President Ramiz Alia in 1984. Hoxha died in Tirana of heart failure brought on by a diabetic condition on April 11, 1985.

OMER NISHANI (President, January 13, 1946–July 23, 1953). Dr. Omer Nishani (Nisani) succeeded Enver Hoxha as president of the Presidium of the Council of Ministers on January 13, 1946, in Albania's postwar government. Nishani, a democratic nationalist, had served as leader of the Anti-Fascist Council of National Liberation during World War II. He retained the largely ceremonial position of president until July 23, 1953, when the Council of Ministers was abolished. Gen. Hadji Lechi replaced him as head of state.

HADJI LECHI (President, July 23, 1953–November 22, 1982). Hadji Lechi (Lleshi) was born in 1913. He was active in the Communist Party during World War II and fought with the Resistance against the Italians and the Germans. He served as a member of the Albanian provisional government in 1944 and served as minister of the interior until 1946. On July 23, 1953, Lechi was named to replace Omer Nisani as Albania's president. He remained as Albania's head of state for nearly twenty years until he was replaced by Ramiz Alia on November 22, 1982.

RAMIZ ALIA (President, November 22, 1982–April 3, 1992). Ramiz Alia was born in Shkoder, Albania, on October 18, 1925. He fought against the Italian occupation forces in Albania as a member of the National Liberation Movement during World War II. He became a close ally of Enver Hoxha and was elected to the Communist party Central Committee in 1948. Alia was elected to the People's Assembly two years later. In the early 1960s he was named a full member of the Albanian Politburo. He succeeded Hadji

Lechi as president on November 22, 1982, and was groomed by Hoxha as his likely successor. Alia was named first secretary of the Communist party on April 13, 1985, two days after Hoxha's death. Alia continued the repressive policies of his predecessor throughout the 1980s. Albania seemed unaffected by the wave of popular uprisings that brought other hard-line Communist governments in Eastern Europe to an end in 1989. Albania was finally forced, however, to liberalize some policies in 1990, including emigration, and opened some diplomatic channels to the West. Alia was forced to remove some hard-line members of the Politburo after widespread antigovernment demonstrations took place throughout the country. In December of 1990 he also approved the formation of political parties other than the Communists to take part in elections scheduled for the following year. Alia was reelected chairman of the Presidium of the People's Assembly on April 30, 1991. The Communist party was renamed the Socialist party in June of 1991, and in March of 1992 Alia's Socialist party was defeated by the Democratic party under Dr. Sali Berisha. Alia resigned the presidency on April 3, 1992, rather than face dismissal by the new Parliament.

SALI BERISHA (President, April 4, 1992 –). Sali Berisha was born in 1945. He was a heart surgeon and leader of the Democratic party. His party defeated the Socialist party of President Ramiz Alia in national elections on March 22, 1992. Alia subsequently resigned his office, and Dr. Berisha replaced him as president on April 4, 1992.

HEADS OF GOVERNMENT

ENVER HOXHA (Prime Minister, November 10, 1945–July 20, 1954). *See entry under Heads of State.*

MEHMET SHEHU (Prime Minister, July 20, 1954–December 18, 1981). Mehmet Shehu was born in Corush on January 10, 1913. He joined the Communist party in the 1930s and fought against the Fascists in the Spanish Civil War. Shehu fought against the Italian and German occupation forces during World War II. He became army chief of staff following the war. Shehu was an ally of Enver Hoxha, and he opposed a proposed federation between Albania and Yugoslavia. He succeeded Koci Xoxe as minister of the interior in 1948 when Xoxe was ousted following a purge of pro-Tito sympathizers in Albania. Shehu was also appointed to the Politburo and became deputy premier. When Hoxha relinquished the position of prime minister, Shehu succeeded him on July 20, 1954. He attempted to promote industry and agriculture in Albania, but the Albanian economy continued to falter after the Soviet Union, and later China, cut off economic aid. Viewed as a likely successor to Hoxha as leader of the Communist party, Shehu came into conflict with his longtime ally when he began advocating an opening of relations with the West. Shehu resigned as Albania's defense minister early in 1981, and on December 18, 1981, it was reported by the Albanian government that he had committed suicide "at a moment of nervous distress." There was some speculation that he had been executed due to his failing relationship with Hoxha.

ADIL ÇARÇANI (Prime Minister, January 18, 1982–February 22, 1991). Adil Çarçani was born in Fushe-Bardha on May 5, 1922. He joined the Communist party in 1942 and served in the Albanian army. In 1950 he was elected to the People's Assembly, and he served on the Politburo from 1961. Çarçani also served as minister of industry and mining from 1959 until 1965. He served as deputy chairman of the Council of Ministers from 1965. On January 18, 1982, he was selected by Enver Hoxha to succeed Mehmet Shehu as prime minister. Çarçani retained his position following the death of Hoxha and the rise of Ramiz Alia as Albania's leader. He left office on February 22, 1991.

FATOS NANO (Prime Minister, February 22, 1991–June 5, 1991). Fatos Thanas Nano was born in Tirana in 1952. He became deputy chairman of the Council of Ministers in January of 1991. He was the head of the Socialist party of Albania, and on February 22, 1991, he became prime minister. A general strike in June of 1991 brought down the Communist government, and Nano left office on June 5, 1991.

YLLI BUFI (Prime Minister, June 5, 1991–December 10, 1991). Ylli Bufi served as minister of foodstuff industry from 1990 until 1991 and served as minister of food and light industry and minister of nutrition in 1991. A member of the Labor party, he was selected

prime minister of Albania on June 5, 1991, following a general strike against the previous government. He was faced with resignations from his cabinet and food riots and was replaced by Vilson Ahmeti on December 10, 1991.

VILSON AHMETI (Prime Minister, December 10, 1991–April 4, 1992). Vilson Ahmeti was born on September 5, 1951. He was educated at the University of Tirana and worked as an engineer from 1973 until 1978. He was a member of the Foreign Trade Department from 1978 and was appointed deputy minister of food in 1987. Ahmeti served as minister of industry from March until June of 1991 and minister of food from June until December of 1991. He was selected by Ramiz Alia to form a government as prime minister on December 10, 1991. Ahmeti was replaced as prime minister on April 4, 1992, following the defeat of the Socialist party in national elections the previous month.

ALEXANDER MEKSI (Prime Minister, April 4, 1992–). Alexander Meksi was born in 1939. He was educated as an archaeologist. Meksi was chosen by the Democratic party to serve as prime minister on April 4, 1992.

OTHER LEADERS

ENVER HOXHA (First Secretary, Communist Party, 1941–January, 1946). *See entry under Heads of State.*

KOCI XOXE (First Secretary, Communist Party, January 1946–October 6, 1948). Koci Xoxe (Kochi Rodze) was born on May 1, 1911, in Korce. He was a leading opponent of King Zog I. He joined with Enver Hoxha in founding the Albanian Communist party during the Italian occupation of World War II. In January of 1946 Xoxe succeeded

Hoxha as first secretary of the Albanian Communist party. He also served as deputy prime minister, minister of the interior, and head of the secret police. Xoxe was a leading proponent of Albanian unification with Yugoslavia and was a follower of Yugoslavia's Marshal Tito. When Stalin broke with Tito in 1948, Hoxha took the opportunity to purge Xoxe and his supporters in Albania. Xoxe was removed from office on October 6, 1948, and was tried and convicted of anti-Soviet tendencies. He was shot on June 11, 1949.

ENVER HOXHA (First Secretary, Communist Party, October 6, 1948– April 11, 1985). *See entry under Heads of State.*

RAMIZ ALIA (First Secretary, Communist Party, April 13, 1985–June, 1991). *See entry under Heads of State.*

Algeria, Democratic and Popular Republic of

(al-Jumhuriyah al-Jaza'iriyah)

Algeria is a country on the northern coast of Africa. It was granted independence from France on July 5, 1962.

HEADS OF STATE

AHMED BEN BELLA (President, September 15, 1963–June 19, 1965). Ahmed Ben Bella was born in Marnia, a town in western Algeria, in December of 1916. After receiving an education at a French school in Marnia, Ben Bella served in the French army during World War II. He received several commendations for bravery during the war, but was turned down for a regular army commission after the war because he was a Muslim. Ben Bella became active in politics after the war and was elected to the Marnia City Council and became deputy mayor of Marnia. He joined with several pro-independence groups, including Messali Hadji's Movement for the Triumph of Democratic Liberation. He left the movement because he disagreed with their moderate views and founded the Secret Organization (SO), a revolutionary group organized to overthrow French rule. Ben Bella became its leader in 1947. He was arrested for terrorist activities in May of 1950, but served only five days in prison before he escaped to France and eventually to Cairo. In 1954 he and eight other revolutionary leaders founded the Algerian Front of National Liberation (FLN), and the revolution began in earnest in November of that year. Ben Bella served as a leading international spokesman for the Front. He was arrested by the French on October 22, 1956, when the Moroccan plane he was traveling in from Rabat to Tunis was intercepted and forced to land in Algiers. He was imprisoned in Paris and spent his time there studying revolutionary theory. When the Algerian provisional government was formed on September 19, 1958, Ben Bella was named vice premier while he was still in prison. Negotiations for a cease-fire began with the French in 1960, with Ben Bella's release a major condition for a settlement. The talks initially fell through, and in November of 1961 Ben Bella led a hunger strike which successfully gained political status for all Algerian prisoners. He was finally released on March 18, 1962, when the cease-fire agreement was concluded. On July 11, 1962, he returned to Algeria, where he advocated a one-party government. Ben Bella engaged in a feud with the more moderate Premier Ben Yussef Ben Khedda. He joined with Ferhat Abbas, a respected moderate, and Houari Boumédienne, a leader of the army, to undercut Ben Khedda's power. Ben Bella formed a political bureau which on August 2, 1962, took control of the government from the provisional officials. He was chosen as premier in the first independent Algerian government on September 26, 1962. The following year he was elected as Algeria's first president on September 15, 1963. Ben Bella was internationally recognized as a leading spokesman for the Third World, but his popularity at home waned. He had difficulty coping with the major internal problems caused by the long period of fighting. He survived, with the help of Boumédienne, several major revolts in 1963 and 1964. Ben Bella attempted to centralize power by eliminating his rivals. While planning the ouster of Boumédienne, the powerful defense minister, Ben Bella was himself removed from office in a bloodless coup led by Boumédienne on July 5, 1965. Ben Bella was imprisoned by the new regime and for 14 years remained in a small prison apartment in Algiers. While imprisoned, he married a journalist, Zohra Sellami, in 1971. After Boumédienne's death in 1978, Ben Bella was moved to the town of M'Sila, where he remained under house arrest until his release on October 30, 1980. Ben Bella went into exile first in France and then in London, where in 1985, he formed a coalition group in opposition to the ruling National Liberation Front. Ben Bella continued to be a powerful figure in Algerian politics, though he was not allowed to return to Algeria until September of 1990.

HOUARI BOUMÉDIENNE (President, June 19, 1965–December 27, 1978). Houari Boumédienne was born in Guelma to a poor farming family on August 22, 1927 (some sources vary on the date, ranging from 1925 to 1934). He was originally named Mohammed Boukharouba and chose the name he became known by during the Algerian war. He was educated at both French and Islamic schools in Algeria and attended al-Azhar University in Cairo. It was in Cairo that Boumédienne first became involved in nationalist politics, when he joined with Ahmed Ben Bella in the National Liberation Front (FLN). After the start of the Algerian revolution, Boumédienne returned to Algeria as military commander of the National Army of Liberation (ALN) and a member of the provisional government's national Parliament. Boumédienne was regarded as a leader of the Algerian nationalist army by 1960. Boumédienne and his staff were dismissed by Premier Ben Yussef Ben Khedda following Algerian independence on June 30, 1962, because Ben Khedda feared that Boumédienne might lead a military coup against the civilian government. Boumédienne joined with Ben Bella, who had been released from prison by the French following independence. Their alliance proved successful in replacing Ben Khedda's centralist government, and Boumédienne was named defense minister in the new Ben Bella regime. Boumédienne was named vice president in 1963 and supported Ben Bella during several rebellions. When Ben Bella began a purge of Boumédienne's supporters in the government in preparation for the ouster of Boumédienne himself, however, the defense minister led a bloodless military coup on June 19, 1965. Ben Bella was overthrown and imprisoned, and Boumédienne assumed leadership of the country. He was officially named president of the Revolutionary Council on July 5, 1965. Boumédienne was a remote and somewhat reclusive leader. His mixture of socialism and pragmatism was partially successful in improving the Algerian economy. He nationalized the oil and gas industry, but failed to decrease the unemployment and poverty in his country. Boumédienne became a leading advocate of Arab unity and a spokesman for Third World causes. His authoritarian rule was not seriously challenged, and he remained Algeria's leader until his death. On December 27, 1978, he succumbed to Waldenstrom's disease, a rare disorder of the blood and bone marrow, after nearly six weeks in a coma.

RABAH BITAT (President, December 27, 1978–February 9, 1979). Rabah Bitat was born in the Constantine region on December 19, 1925. He was an early Algerian revolutionist and one of the founders of the Revolutionary Committee for Unity and Action, which was instrumental in starting the Algerian War in 1954. He was captured with Ahmed Ben Bella and other Algerian nationalist leaders in October of 1956 when the plane he was traveling in was intercepted by the French. Bitat spent the next five years in prison, but was released after Algeria gained independence. Bitat then joined with Ben Bella in his successful political battle with Ben Yussef Ben Khedda and served as deputy premier from September 1962 until May 1963. He later sided with Houari Boumédienne in his ouster of Ben Bella in 1965. Bitat served as minister of state from 1965 to 1966 and minister of transport from 1966. He served on the Council of the Revolution and was president of the National Assembly when Boumédienne died on December 27, 1978. Bitat assumed the presidency on an interim basis and served until February 9, 1979, when Chadli Benjedid was selected as Algeria's new leader. Bitat then resumed his position as National Assembly president, where he remained until his retirement in 1990.

CHADLI BENJEDID (President, February 9, 1979–January 11, 1992). Chadli Benjedid was born in the village of Seabaa, near Annaba, in eastern Algeria in 1929. He served in the French army until the outbreak of the Algerian revolution, when he joined with the National Liberation Army. A close ally of Houari Boumédienne, he was selected by him to command the second military district in Oran after independence. He remained in that position during Boumédienne's presidency and maintained the strong support of the army and the loyalty of the president. When Boumédienne died on December 27, 1978, Col.

Chadli, with the backing of the army, emerged as a compromise candidate to succeed the late president. He was selected by the ruling National Liberation Front and was sworn into office on February 9, 1979. One of Chadli's first acts as president was to free Ahmed Ben Bella, the former president who had remained in prison since his ouster by Boumédienne 14 years earlier. Chadli also tried to ease tension with Morocco over the issue of the Western Sahara, where Algeria backed the Polisario Front rebels. Relations initially improved with France, but the Western Sahara question again dampened them in the early 1980s. In 1988 Chadli's government forced the Polisario Front rebels to accept a United Nations treaty for the area, and tensions in North Africa decreased. Chadli also had the difficult task of improving Algeria's economy, but met with little success. By 1988 economic conditions in the country had deteriorated to the point that rioting and violence broke out throughout the country. Agitation by Islamic fundamentalists was also blamed for the unrest. In 1990 Benjedid allowed for the return of all political exiles to Algeria. He also called for the first multiparty elections, which were held in June of 1990. The fundamentalist Muslim Front Islamique du Salut was the upset winner in the elections, further damaging Benjedid's ability to govern. The Islamic Front won another victory in the elections in January of 1992, but the ruling High State Committee suppressed the election results and forced Benjedid's resignation as president on January 11, 1992.

SID AHMED GHOZALI (Acting President, January 11, 1992–January 16, 1992). Sid Ahmed Ghozali was born in Marnia on March 31, 1937. He was educated in Paris before returning to Algeria to enter the civil service in the early 1960s. He was president of Sonatrach, Algeria's oil and gas monopoly, from 1966 until 1984. In 1987 Ghozali was appointed ambassador to Belgium. He served until 1989, when he was appointed foreign minister. From June of 1991 Ghozali served as interim premier. He became acting president following the resignation of Chadli Benjedid on January 11, 1992, and served until January 16, 1992. He was reappointed premier by the High State Council on February 22, 1992. Ghozali was replaced as premier on July 8, 1992, shortly after the assassination of President Mohamed Boudiaf.

MOHAMED BOUDIAF (President, January 16, 1992–June 29, 1992). Mohamed Boudiaf was born in M'Sila on June 23, 1919. He fought in the French army during World War II, but joined the Algerian Nationalist Movement seeking independence from France in the early 1950s. He served on the National Liberation Front (FLN) leadership council from 1954. Boudiaf was captured by the French in 1956 along with Ahmed Ben Bella and other Algerian leaders. They remained imprisoned until 1962. Boudiaf and Ben Bella disagreed over the political future of Algeria after the formation of the National Front government in 1962.

Boudiaf was imprisoned during Ben Bella's leadership and went into exile in Morocco in 1964. He remained a critic of the National Liberation Front leadership. Boudiaf returned from exile and was chosen by the High State Committee to succeed Chadli Benjedid as president on January 16, 1992. He was selected to lead a government of reconciliation following the suppression of Islamic fundamentalists in Algeria who had been successful in winning an election victory. Boudiaf led a campaign against government corruption and maintained a hard line against the radical Islamics. Boudiaf was assassinated on January 29, 1992, by machine-gun fire while speaking at a rally in Annaba designed to gain popular support for the government.

ALI KAFI (President, July 2, 1992–). Ali Kafi served as secretary-general of the National Organization of Holy Warriors, an association of veterans from Algeria's war of independence from France. Kafi was a member of the High State Committee which seized power in January of 1992. He was appointed president on July 2, 1992, by the committee following the assassination of Mohamed Boudiaf.

HEADS OF GOVERNMENT

FERHAT ABBAS (Premier, September 18, 1958–August 27, 1961). Ferhat Abbas was born in Taher on October 24, 1899. His family was closely tied to the French government, and his father was a local administrator. Abbas was educated at a French school in Philippeville, and after service in the French army, attended the University of Algiers. He received a pharmacy degree and set up shop in Setif. Abbas also began his political and literary activities in the early 1930s. Though he was regarded as a moderate, he spoke out often against the abuses of the

French colonial government. During World War II, Abbas again served in the French army, and he spent several months as a German prisoner of war in 1940. After his release Abbas continued his political activities by forming the Democratic Union for the Algerian Manifesto, a political party based on his writings, which advocated autonomy for Algeria. Abbas was elected to the French Constituent Assembly in 1946. The following year he was elected to the Algerian Assembly, where he served until 1955. Opposing a violent solution to the independence question, Abbas initially distanced himself from the National Liberation Front (FLN) after the war for Algerian independence began in November of 1954. By April of 1956 Abbas and other moderate leaders had lost hope for a peaceful settlement and joined with the FLN. When the Front formed Algeria's first provisional government in Cairo on September 19, 1958, Abbas was elected premier. He continued to advocate negotiations with the French government, now headed by Charles De Gaulle, to end hostilities. The first direct talks between the French and Algerian rebels took place in June of 1960 in Melun, France, but no settlement was reached. Abbas was subsequently replaced as premier of the provisional government by Ben Yussef Ben Khedda on August 27, 1961. Ben Khedda was considered slightly more leftist than the anticommunist Abbas. Negotiations with the French continued, and on March 18, 1962, a cease-fire was signed. This led to the establishment of the Republic of Algeria on July 3, 1962. Abbas was then elected president of the Algerian National Assembly on September 25, 1962. He served until August 13, 1963, when he resigned after a dispute with Premier Ahmed Ben Bella. In 1964 Abbas was placed under house arrest by the Ben Bella government. He was released following Houari Boumédienne's coup, but declined to serve as civilian head of state under Boumédienne. In 1976 Abbas attacked the Boumédienne government for not providing democratic institutions for the country. He was again put under house arrest and thus had little opportunity to influence Algerian political affairs. He died in Algiers at the age of 86 on December 24, 1985.

BEN YUSSEF BEN KHEDDA (Premier, August 27, 1961–August 4, 1962). Ben Yussef Ben Khedda was born in 1920. He was active in the Algerian revolution and served as a member of the Committee of Coordination and Execution. He served as minister of cultural and social affairs in the provisional government from 1958 to 1960, when he was sent as a representative to Moscow and Peking. Ben Khedda succeeded Ferhat Abbas as premier of the provisional government of the Algerian Republic on August 27, 1961. Following Algerian independence, Ben Khedda's government was challenged by Ahmed Ben Bella and other revolutionary leaders who had been released from imprisonment by the French. After a bitter political struggle, Ben Bella's group emerged victorious, and Ben Khedda left office on August 4, 1962. He was arrested in July of 1964 and spent much of the next several decades either in prison or under surveillance that limited his political activities.

AHMED BEN BELLA (Premier, August 4, 1962–June 19, 1965). *See entry under Heads of State.*

HOUARI BOUMÉDIENNE (Premier, July 5, 1965–December 27, 1978). *See entry under Heads of State.*

MOHAMMED BEN AHMED ABDELGHANI (Premier, March 8, 1979–January 22, 1984). Mohammed Ben Ahmed Abdelghani served in the National Army of Liberation and was named military commander of the Blida Region following independence. He was later commander of the Ourgla Military Region. He was a member of the political bureau of the Algerian Front of National Liberation and served as minister of the interior in Houari Boumédienne's government from 1975. On March 8, 1979, he was appointed premier in Chadli Benjedid's first government. He served until his resignation on January 22, 1984.

ABDELHAMID BRAHIMI (Premier, January 22, 1984–November 5, 1988). Abdelhamid Brahimi was born in

Constantine on April 2, 1936. He fought with the National Liberation Army during the Algerian War. He served in the Ben Bella government as representative for the province of Annaba from 1963 until 1965. After serving in several positions in the Boumédienne government Brahimi left in 1970 to teach economics at the University of Algiers until 1975. He returned to public service as minister of planning from 1979 to 1983. Brahimi was appointed premier of Algeria on January 22, 1984. During his term of office, demonstrations against Algeria's economic situation took place. Mass rioting erupted over food shortages and unemployment, and nearly 200 people were killed. Brahimi's inability to control the situation resulted in his resignation on November 5, 1988.

KASDI MERBAH (Premier, November 5, 1988–September 9, 1989). Kasdi Merbah was born in 1938. He fought with the revolution during the 1950s and was a member of the Algerian provisional government's delegation which negotiated independence from France. In 1962 Merbah was appointed director of military security, in charge of army intelligence, and he served until 1978. He was then named to the political bureau of the National Liberation Front. From 1982 to 1984 he served in the cabinet as minister of heavy industry. Merbah was moved to the ministry of agriculture in the Brahimi government in 1984. In February of 1988 he was named minister of health, and on November 5, 1988, he replaced Brahimi as premier. Merbah initiated policies that would open the way for a multiparty political system in Algeria. When he was dismissed from office by President Benjedid after less than a year, the reform-minded Merbah threatened a constitutional crisis when he initially refused to leave office. He was ultimately replaced by Mouloud Hamroche on September 9, 1989. He served as leader of the Algerian Movement for Justice and Development from 1990. Merbah was ambushed and assassinated by Muslim militants in Bordj el-Bahri, near Algiers, while returning from a coastal resort on August 21, 1993.

MOULOUD HAMROCHE (Premier, September 9, 1989–June 5, 1991). Mouloud Hamroche served as a senior presidential advisor to President Chadli Benjedid. He was named to succeed Kasdi Merbah as Algeria's premier on September 9, 1989. Hamroche resigned from the Politburo of the Algerian Front of National Liberation after the FLN suffered an electoral defeat in June of 1990. He resigned as premier on June 5, 1991.

SID AHMED GHOZALI (Premier, June 5, 1991–July 8, 1992). *See entry under Heads of State.*

BELAID ABDESALAM (Premier, July 8, 1992–). Belaid Abdesalam was born in Dehemcha in July of 1928. He was educated in Switzerland and served as an advisor to the government of Premier Ben Khedda in 1961. Abdesalam was a founder of Sonatrach, Algeria's oil and gas company, and served as its president from 1964 until 1966. He was named minister of industry and energy in 1966 and served until his appointment as minister of light industry in 1977. He left the cabinet in 1984. Abdesalam was elected Algeria's premier on July 8, 1992.

Andorra, Valleys of

(Les Vallées de'Andorra; Principado de Andorra)

Andorra is an independent principality located between France and Spain in the Pyrenees Mountains.

HEADS OF STATE

Andorra is jointly ruled by two co-princes who are the President of France and the Bishop of Urgel, Spain. The current Co-Princes are President François Mitterand of France since May 21, 1981, and Mgr. Joan Marti y Alanis, the Bishop of Urgel, since January 31, 1971. The General Council of Andorra selects a Syndic General to serve as the principalities' chief executive officer.

FRANCISCO CAYRAT (First Syndic, January 1946–December 31, 1960). Francisco Cayrat was a resident of the parish of Sant Julia de Loria. He was elected by the Andorran General Council to serve as First Syndic in January of 1946. He retained office until his retirement on December 31, 1960.

JULIÀN REIG RIBÓ (First Syndic, December 31, 1960–December 31, 1966). Juliàn Reig Ribó was born in 1913. He was a resident of the parish of Sant Julia de Loria. He was a prominent Andorran tobacco factory owner when he was selected to serve as First Syndic on December 31, 1960. He completed his second three year term on December 31, 1966. Reig Ribó was again elected as First Syndic on December 31, 1972, and was re-elected to a second term in December of 1975. He retained office until the expiration of his second term on December 29, 1978.

FRANCESC ESCUDÉ-FERRERO (First Syndic, December 31, 1966–December 31, 1972). Francesc Escudé-Ferrero was a resident of the parish of Sant Julia de Loria. He was elected to succeed Julian Reig Ribó as Andorra's First Syndic on December 31, 1966. He completed his second three year term on December 31, 1972, and relinquished office to Reig Ribó.

JULIÀN REIG RIBÓ (First Syndic, December 31, 1972–December 29, 1978). *See earlier entry under Heads of State.*

ESTANISLAU SANGRÀ FONT (First Syndic, December 29, 1978–January 4, 1982). Estanislau Sangrà Font was a resident of the parish of Les Escaldes-Engordany. He defeated Carlos Ribas Reig, the nephew of outgoing First Syndic Julian Reig Ribó, to become the first First Syndic not a resident of Sant Julia de Loria parish in over a century. Sangrà Font retained office until January 4, 1982, when a constitutional change eliminated the position of First Syndic and created the posts of Syndic General and President of Government.

FRANCESC CERQUEDA I PASQUET (Syndic General, January 4, 1982–January 12, 1990). Francesc Cerqueda i Pascuet was a resident of Sant Julia de Loria parish. He was selected as Andorra's Syndic General on January 4, 1982, following constitutional changes that created a position of President of Government. He retained office until January 12, 1990, when he relinquished the position to Josep Maria Beal Benedico.

JOSEP MARIA BEAL BENEDICO (Syndic General, January 12, 1990–

February 15, 1991). Josep Maria Beal Benedico was a resident of Sant Julia de Loria parish. He was selected as Syndic General on January 12, 1990. He retained office until February 15, 1991.

ALBERT GELABERT (Syndic General, February 15, 1991–April 12, 1992). Albert Gelabert was elected by the General Council to serve as Syndic General on February 15, 1991. He re-tained office until April 12, 1992, when he was replaced by Jordi Farras Forne following new legislative elections.

JORDI FARRAS FORNE (Syndic General, April 12, 1992–). Jordi Far-ras Forne was elected Andorra's Syndic General on April 12, 1992, following legislative elections called by Oscar Ribas Reig, the Andorran Head of Government.

HEADS OF GOVERNMENT

OSCAR RIBAS REIG (President of Government, January 8, 1982–April 30, 1984). Oscar Ribas Reig was a nephew of Juliàn Reig Ribó, Andorra's former First Syndic. Ribas Reig was named to the position of Andorra's first Presi-dent of Government by the General Council on January 8, 1982. Ribas Reig resigned from office on May 21, 1984, following a dispute with the Council over taxes. He returned to office on December 10, 1989, following legislative elections. His reformist policies resulted in a deadlock with the Council and he resigned with the Council in April of 1992. Ribas Reig returned to power in the subsequent general elections.

JOSEP PINTAT SOLANS (President of Government, May 21, 1984–Decem-ber 10, 1989). Josep Pintat Solans was a prominent member of the Andorran business community. He was selected as President of Government following the resignation of Oscar Ribas Reig on May 21, 1984. Pintat Solans retained office after general elections held in December of 1985. Pintat Solans stepped down on December 10, 1989, when Ribas Reig was returned to office.

OSCAR RIBAS REIG (President of Government, December 10, 1989–). *See earlier entry under Heads of Gov-ernment.*

Angola, People's Republic of

(República Popular de Angola)

Angola is a country in southwestern Africa. It received indepen-dence from Portugal on November 11, 1975.

HEADS OF STATE

AGOSTINHO NETO (President, No-vember 11, 1975–September 20, 1979). Agostinho Antônio Neto was born in Bengo, a small village southeast of the Angolan capital of Luanda, on Sep-tember 17, 1922. The mulatto son of a Methodist minister, Neto graduated from the Salvador Correia High School.

He later worked for the Luanda Public Health Service from 1944 until 1947. With the assistance of Rev. Ralph Dodge, a Methodist bishop, Neto received a scholarship to the University of Lisbon to study medicine. Neto's political activism began while he was abroad, and he became a noted nationalist poet. He was arrested in 1955 and was not allowed to continue his studies until 1957. The following year he received his medical degree from the University of Porto. Neto returned to Angola as a doctor in 1959. He was again arrested on June 8, 1960, by the Portuguese authorities.

A year later he was removed to Portugal's Aljube prison, where he remained until he was placed under house arrest. He escaped to Morocco in 1962, where he led the Popular Liberation Movement of Angola (MPLS), one of the three major revolutionary groups fighting the Portuguese for Angolan independence. Following a long and bitter struggle, independence for Angola was gained after a military coup replaced the Portuguese government in 1974. Neto, a Marxist, had the support of the Soviet Union in the succeeding struggle against Holden Roberto's National Front for the Liberation of Angola (FNLA) and Jonas Savimbi's National Union for the Total Independence of Angola (UNITA). Dr. Neto refused to participate in a coalition government, and with Soviet military assistance and Cuban troops, he captured the capital from his rivals and was proclaimed the first president of the People's Republic of Angola on November 11, 1975. The civil war against the rival factions, which were receiving assistance from the West and South Africa, continued throughout Neto's term of office. Despite an abundance of natural resources, the new government was virtually powerless to improve economic conditions in Angola because of continued fighting against rebel guerrillas and infighting within the government itself. Dr. Neto

died in Moscow of cancer of the pancreas on September 10, 1979.

JOSÉ EDUARDO DOS SANTOS
(President, September 21, 1979–). José Eduardo dos Santos was born in Angola on August 28, 1942. He joined with the MPLA, Agostinho Neto's revolutionary group, in 1961. He was subsequently sent to Moscow for military training, where he became a devout Marxist. Dos Santos remained a leading supporter of Neto during the war for independence and the civil war that followed. When the MPLA formed Angola's first independent government in 1975, dos Santos was named foreign minister. He retained that post until 1978 when he was appointed minister of planning. Dos Santos was named acting head of state when Neto left for Moscow for medical treatment the following year. After Neto's death on September 10, 1979, dos Santos was selected by the MPLA as president and took office on September 21, 1979. The Angolan civil war continued during dos Santos's term of office. South Africa also conducted military activities against the MPLA government, acting in concert with Jonas Savimbi's UNITA forces. After dos Santos was elected to a second five-year term as president by the MPLA in December of 1985, he began negotiations to remove Cuban troops which had been supporting his government. A cease-fire was arranged between Angola, Cuba, and South Africa in August of 1988, though the battle with UNITA rebels continued until December of 1990. At that time a tentative cease-fire agreement was reached between dos Santos's government and the rebels led by Savimbi. Free elections were held in Angola on September 29, 1992. Dos Santos was overwhelmingly re-elected president, defeating Savimbi and other minor candidates. Savimbi disputed the election results, charging fraud. His supporters protested the results violently, and threatened to renew the civil conflict.

HEADS OF GOVERNMENT

LOPO DO NASCIMENTO (Premier, November 14, 1975–December 9, 1978). Lopo do Nascimento was born in Luanda on July 10, 1940. He was a supporter of Agostinho Neto's MPLA during the war of independence and was a member of the transitional government from January to November of 1975. On November 14, 1975, he was named Angola's first premier. In 1977 Nascimento also served in the cabinet as minister of internal trade. He served in these positions until December 9, 1978, when the post of premier was abolished. Nascimento remained in the government as foreign trade minister until 1982 and was also minister of planning. He was also named to head the Angolan Fifth Military Region in 1986.

FERNANDO JOSÉ DE FRANÇA VAN DUNEM (Prime Minister, July 19, 1991–December 2, 1992). Fernando José de França van Dunem served as minister of external affairs in the 1980s. He was a member of the Popular Movement for the Liberation of Angola Worker's Party, and when the post of prime minister was reestablished on July 19, 1991, van Dunem became prime minister and minister of planning. Multiparty elections were held on September 29, 1992, and a new parliament was convened in November of 1992. Van Dunem left office on December 2, 1992.

MARCOLINO MOCO (Prime Minister, December 2, 1992–   ). Marcolino Moco was a member of President Jose Eduardo dos Santos's ruling Popular Movement for the Liberation of Angola (MPLA) party. He was elected prime minister following parlimentary elections on September 29, 1992, and took office on December 2, 1992.

Antigua and Barbuda

Antigua and Barbuda form an island country in the eastern Caribbean that received independence from Great Britain on November 1, 1981.

HEAD OF STATE

SIR WILFRED E. JACOBS (Governor-General, November 1, 1981–   ). Wilfred Ebenezer Jacobs was born on October 19, 1919. He was educated in London and became an attorney. Jacobs was appointed magistrate for Dominica in 1947 and for St. Kitts in 1952. He served as attorney-general for the Leeward Islands from 1957 until 1959 and for Antigua in 1960. He served in various other colonial offices until 1967, when he was appointed governor of Antigua. When independence was granted to Antigua and Barbuda on November 1, 1981, Jacobs began serving as the nation's first governor-general.

HEAD OF GOVERNMENT

VERE CORNWALL BIRD (Prime Minister, November 1, 1981-). Vere Cornwall Bird was born in Antigua to a poor family on December 7, 1910. His education did not proceed past elementary school, and soon after leaving school he began working with the Salvation Army. In the early 1940s Bird was instrumental in founding the Antigua Trades and Labour Union and became its president. He was elected to the Antiguan Legislative Council in 1945. He remained on the Council throughout the 1950s and formed the Antiguan Labour party with his associates from the trade unions. Bird was selected as Antigua's first chief minister in 1960 and the island's first premier in 1967. In February of 1971 Bird was defeated for reelection and George Walter succeeded him as premier. Bird was returned to office in February of 1976, and in 1980 he led negotiations with Britain which established independence for the Caribbean islands of Antigua and Barbuda on November 1, 1981. Despite some internal rivalries in the Antiguan Labour party, Bird retained the prime minister's office throughout the 1980s and was most recently reelected in March of 1989.

Argentina, (Argentine Republic)

(República Argentina)

Argentina is a country in southern South America. It received independence from Spain on July 9, 1816.

HEADS OF STATE

EDELMIRO J. FARRELL (President, February 24, 1944–June 4, 1946). Edelmiro Julian Farrell was born in Avellaneda on August 12, 1887. He began a career in the military and had risen to the rank of general when he supported the military coup that installed Pedro Pablo Ramirez as president on June 4, 1943. Farrell served as minister of war in the Ramirez administration and was later named vice president. When Ramirez was forced from office by supporters of Col. Juan Perón, Farrell, a Perón ally, assumed the presidency on February 24, 1944. The Allied powers were concerned over Argentina's pro-Axis leanings during World War II. In 1945 Farrell, under pressure from the United States, declared war on Germany and Japan as the war neared its end. Farrell remained as president until June 4, 1946, when Perón was sworn into office. Upon leaving the presidency, Farrell retired from the military and public life. He died of a heart attack in Buenos Aires on October 31, 1980, at the age of 93.

JUAN DOMINGO PERÓN (President, June 4, 1946–September 19, 1955). Juan Domingo Perón was born on October 8, 1895, at Lobos in the Buenos Aires Province of Argentina. He entered a military college in 1911 and three years later was commissioned as a lieutenant. In 1925 Perón married Aurelia Tizon. She died of cancer in 1938 at the age of 33. He served at the

Argentina Staff College from 1926 until 1929, and in 1930, after participating in the military coup that ousted President Hipolito Irigoyen, he became a professor of military history there. Perón taught until 1936, when he was stationed in Chile as military attaché. Following the June 1943 military coup in Argentina, Perón was appointed secretary of labor and welfare. The following year he was also named vice president and minister of war. He was forced to resign his posts in October of 1945 by his rivals in the military and was arrested. While Perón was imprisoned, Eva Duarte, who had just become his second wife, called for his supporters to demonstrate for his release. The Perónists rallied against the government, and Perón was freed. He immediately announced his candidacy for the presidency and was elected in February of 1946. Perón, now a general, took office on June 4, 1946. He began his administration with pledges of social reform which, with the assistance of his wife, assured him the loyalty of the peasant masses. He was also popular with the Roman Catholic church at this time and made religious instruction mandatory in national schools. Perón easily won reelection in 1951, though his popularity waned during his second term. His wife, known as Evita, was Perón's link to the Argentine peasants. She died of cancer on July 26, 1952. The following year a military rebellion was quickly quelled. Perón also broke with the Catholic church over social issues in 1954. The church then joined landowners, liberals, students, and much of the military in opposing his rule. Demonstrations against his government increased, and rioting in the streets was rampant. Perón signed a land concession for Patagonia with the Standard Oil Company in April of 1955. This act galvanized the military, who viewed the accord as an infringement by the United States on Argentine air bases. Perón survived an armed uprising by naval and air forces on June 16, 1955. He attempted to consolidate his position by arming the peasants, but another military revolt began on September 16, 1955. After three days of fighting, Perón was forced to resign his office. He left Argentina on September 19, 1955, and lived in exile in a succession of Latin American countries before settling in Madrid, Spain, in 1960. While in exile he met María Estela Martínez, known as Isabel, who was to become his third wife in 1961. Perón continued to exert considerable influence in Argentine politics. He attempted to return to the country through Brazil in 1964 but was forced to return to Spain by Brazilian authorities. After a series of unsuccessful civilian and military governments in Argentina, Perón was invited to return by President Alejandro Lanusse in November of 1972. In 1973 Héctor Cámpora, a close ally of Perón, ran for the presidency and was elected. Shortly after Cámpora took office, he resigned and new elections were called with Perón as a candidate. In September Perón was again elected president with 61 percent of the vote. On October 12, 1973, he was sworn into office with his wife as vice president. Perón, who was old and frail, had little time to implement policies. He died the following year, on July 1, 1974, of heart and kidney failure at the age of 78. He was succeeded by his wife. In 1987, in a bizarre incident, vandals robbed Perón's grave and stole his hands and sword. A ransom was demanded but the items were recovered after several weeks without the ransom being paid.

EDUARDO A. LONARDI (President, September 22–November 13, 1955). Eduardo A. Lonardi was born in the northern province of Entre Rios on September 15, 1896, of Italian-French parentage. He attended the National Military College and during the 1930s returned to teach there. In 1938 he was appointed military attaché to Chile, where he succeeded Juan Perón in that post. He was appointed commander of the Argentine General Staff headquarters in 1946. The following year he was sent to Washington as a military attaché. When General Lonardi returned to Argentina, he was put in command of the Third Army, a post he held until 1951. He was then forced to retire after criticizing President Perón's attempt to name his wife as vice president. Later that year General Lonardi was accused of being a part of a military conspiracy against the government and was jailed for eight months. General Lonardi remained an integral part of the anti-Perónist movement in the military and barely escaped arrest on several other occasions. He helped organize the rebellion that toppled Perón in September of 1955 and was named provisional president on September 22, 1955. Two months later, on November 13, 1955, he was ousted in a palace coup by the other members of the ruling junta, who accused him of trying to appease Perónists. The following month General Lonardi went to the United States for medical treatment. He returned to Buenos Aires in early March and died there of a cerebral hemorrhage on March 22, 1956.

PEDRO E. ARAMBURU (President, November 13, 1955–May 1, 1958). Pedro Eugenio Aramburu was born in Rio Cuarto, Argentina, on May 21, 1903. He attended the National Military College in Buenos Aires. He served in the army and was promoted to general staff officer in 1936. In 1939 he was sent to Paris to study armored tactics and then taught at the Superior War College. Aramburu was appointed military attaché in Rio de Janerio, Brazil, in 1951, and in December of that year, he was promoted to brigadier general by President Juan Perón. Aramburu returned to Argentina in 1953 to become director general of the Army Medical Corps.

After the military began the rebellion against Perón in September of 1955, Aramburu joined the uprising. He was named army chief of staff in the subsequent provisional government of Eduardo Lonardi. On November 13, 1955, Aramburu and other members of the junta charged Lonardi with appeasing Perónists and forced him from office. Aramburu was selected as the new provisional president. He restored the constitution of 1853, disbanded and outlawed the Perónist party, and allowed for a free press, returning the newspaper *La Prensa* to its owner, Alberto Gainza Paz. He also denationalized the national bank and instituted wage controls in an attempt to stabilize the economy. Aramburu was faced with the first major challenge to his regime on June 9, 1956, when troops led by two former Perónist generals, Juan José Valle and Raul Tanco, rebelled against the government. The rebellion was crushed, and General Valle and forty other plotters were executed by firing squad. Aramburu then made arrangements for democratic elections in which he and other members of the junta were barred from participating. In the election of 1958, Arturo Frondizi was elected by a wide margin with the support of the Perónists. General Aramburu relinquished office to Frondizi on May 1, 1958, and subsequently retired from the military. Aramburu tried for a political comeback in 1963 by running for president as the candidate for the Union del Pueblo Argentino (UDELPA) party. He fared poorly, finishing last in the six-man election. He remained a marginal figure in Argentine politics until his kidnapping by Perónist guerrillas on May 29, 1970. The terrorists were part of the Juan José Valle Montoneros Command, named after the general that Aramburu had executed in 1956. The 67-year-old Aramburu was murdered by his kidnappers on June 1, 1970, though his body was not recovered until July 16, 1970.

ARTURO FRONDIZI (President, May 1, 1958–March 20, 1962). Arturo Frondizi was born in Paso de los Libres on October 28, 1908, the thirteenth child of Italian immigrants. He was raised in Buenos Aires and attended law school at the university there. He joined the Radical party and in 1946 was elected to the Argentine House of Deputies. Frondizi became a leading opponent of President Juan Perón, and in 1951 he ran unsuccessfully for vice president on the Radical ticket. After the ouster of Perón by the military coup in September of 1955 and the subsequent banning of the Perónist party, the Radical party became the largest legal political group in the country. A split developed between Frondizi and the Radical party leader, Ricardo Balbin. Frondizi's group became known as the Intransigent Radicals and Balbin's became the People's Radicals. In the democratic election of February 22, 1958, Frondizi, who had courted the support of Perón's followers, defeated Balbin by a two-to-one margin. He was inaugurated president on May 1, 1958. In an attempt to stabilize the faltering Argentine economy, Frondizi instituted a policy of economic austerity. He also reversed his previous opposition to allowing foreign oil companies to exploit Argentina's natural resources. These decisions lost him the support of many of his followers among the Perónists and the nationalists. His party lost the 1960 congressional elections, and his government was faced with challenges from the left and the right. In March of 1962 General Raul A. Poggi led a military coup against the Frondizi government, and the president was ousted. He was succeeded by Jose Maria Guido, the President of the Senate, on March 30, 1962. Frondizi remained active in political affairs and wrote several books on the Argentine political system.

JOSE MARIA GUIDO (President, March 30, 1962–October 12, 1963). José

María Guido was born in Buenos Aires on August 20, 1910. He attended law school at the University of La Plata, where he graduated in 1940. He became involved with the Radical party and was a supporter of Arturo Frondizi. Guido served on the executive committee of Frondizi's Intransigent Radicals and was elected to the Senate in 1958. Dr. Guido was provisional chairman of the Senate when the military ousted President Frondizi on March 30, 1962. He succeeded him as the provisional president, though the military remained largely in control of the government. Guido's administration survived a naval revolt in April of 1963, and he remained in office long enough to preside over new elections in July of 1963. Arturo Illía, the People's Radical party candidate, was victorious, and Guido handed over the presidency on October 12, 1963. Dr. Guido remained involved in Argentine political affairs and briefly served in the government of Juan Perón in 1974 as an advisor in the development of the Patagonia region. He died on June 13, 1975, in Buenos Aires at the age of 64.

ARTURO ILLIA (President, October 12, 1963–June 28, 1966). Arturo Umberto Illía was born in Pergamino, Argentina, on August 4, 1900. His family were Italian immigrants. He received a medical degree from the University of La Plata and served as a medical officer of the Argentine railroad. Illía was a supporter of President Hipolito Irigoyen and lost his position with the railroad when Irigoyen was ousted by the military in 1930. Illía then became active in politics and was elected to the Provincial Senate from Cruz del Eje in 1935. He served as vice governor of Cordoba from 1940 to 1943, when he left politics for a period to practice medicine. He again became active in 1948 when he was elected by the Radical party to serve in the National Assembly. An anti-Perónist member, Illía was defeated for reelection in

1952. Following the division of the Radical party in 1955, Illía joined with Ricardo Balbin's People's Radicals in opposition to Arturo Frondizi's Intransigent Radicals. Illía served as vice-chairman until Balbin's death, when he became chairman. After the ouster of President Frondizi by the military, a new election was called for July 7, 1963. Dr. Illía led a seven-man field of candidates, but did not receive a majority vote. A coalition in the electoral college with the Conservative, Democratic Socialist, and Christian Democratic parties gave him a majority, and he was sworn into office on October 12, 1963. Illía was a personally popular leader and did his best to solve some of his nation's problems. He freed political prisoners and attempted to end foreign control over Argentina's natural resources. He also tried to stabilize the economy with efficient management, though he was frustrated by a severe drought and a shortage of beef for export. Dr. Illía was also faced with the opposition of the Perónist labor groups, who embarrassed his government on several occasions. On June 28, 1966, the military rebelled and ousted Illía in a bloodless coup. Three months later his wife of 27 years, the former Silvia Martorelli, died of cancer. Opponents of the military government attempted to use her funeral as a political event, though Illía took no part in the campaign. He remained the leader of the Radical Civic Union, though he exercised little influence during his remaining years. On January 18, 1983, he died in Buenos Aires at the age of 83 of a lung ailment.

JUAN CARLOS ONGANÍA (President, June 28, 1966–June 9, 1970). Juan Carlos Onganía was born of Basque ancestry in the province of Buenos Aires on March 17, 1914. He entered the National Military College in 1931 and rose in the ranks of the army following graduation. He remained aloof from political conspiracies during the Perón years and their aftermath and by 1959 he had risen to the rank of brigadier general. In 1962 Onganía was appointed commander of the cavalry, but he was removed from command later in the year after the regime of Arturo Frondizi was overthrown by a military coup. Onganía believed in the separation of powers and opposed military dictatorships. In August of 1962 he led a successful coup within the military and was appointed commander in chief of the army by President José María Guido. He helped ensure fair elections the following July and remained at his post in the administration of President Arturo Illía. Onganía became disillusioned with the civilian presidency and feared a resurgence of Perónism in the country. He retired from the military in November of 1965. On June 28, 1966, President Illía was ousted by a military coup, and General Onganía was called from retirement to serve as president. He tried to lead a government balanced with civilian and military members, but came into conflict with the Argentine labor unions after a series of strikes in 1967. He temporarily disbanded the unions that year. Onganía attempted to establish a government of "Participacionismo" in which labor, industry, agriculture, and other special interest groups would form committees to advise the government. The military, under General Alejandro Lanusse, disagreed with Onganía over the issue of the military's power in the government. Onganía was invited to resign from office on June 8, 1970, but when he refused he was forced into retirement the following day by a military junta composed of General Lanusse of the army, Admiral Pedro J. Gnavi of the navy, and Brig. General Juan Carlos Rey of the air force. The junta then chose General Roberto Levingston to serve as president. While in retirement, General Onganía occasionally spoke out on political issues. He was briefly jailed in 1981 for criticizing the government of General Roberto Viola.

ROBERTO M. LEVINGSTON (President, June 18, 1970–March 12, 1971). Roberto Marcelo Levingston was born on January 10, 1920, in San Luis, Argentina. He attended the National Military College and entered the Argentine cavalry upon graduation. He rose in the ranks to become chief of staff of the cavalry corps. In 1956 he was assigned to the Argentine State Intelligence Service and served as chief of intelligence under President Arturo Frondizi in the early 1960s. In September 1968 Levingston was sent as Argentina's representative to the Inter-American Defense Board in Washington, D.C. He was serving in that capacity when on June 13, 1970, he was chosen by the ruling military junta to replace deposed president Juan Carlos Onganía. Levingston returned to Argentina and was sworn in as president on June 18, 1970. He attempted to relax some of the austerity measures instituted during Onganía's rule and removed, for example, the wage-price freezes. Economic problems continued to beset Argentina, and serious rioting broke out in Cordoba in early 1971. Levingston, like his predecessor, ran into problems with the military and attempted to force Argentine strongman General Alejandro Lanusse from his position as army chief of staff on March 22, 1971. Lanusse and the leaders of the navy and air force responded by ousting Levingston, with the junta reassuming power in Argentina. Levingston attempted to regain power in October of 1971 when he was involved in a coup attempt against President Lanusse. The coup was unsuccessful, however, and Levingston was jailed.

ALEJANDRO A. LANUSSE (President, March 26, 1971–May 25, 1973). Alejandro Agustín Lanusse was born to a wealthy landowning family in Buenos Aires on August 28, 1918. He graduated from the National Military College in 1938. He served in the army during the 1940s and opposed the government of President Juan Perón. Lanusse took part in an unsuccessful military coup attempt against Perón in 1951 and was arrested. He spent four years in prison before being released after Perón's ouster in 1955. Lanusse was named commander of the presidential guard during the administration of President Eduardo Lonardi and took part in the overthrow of Lonardi later in 1955. Lanusse rose in the ranks of the military and served in various capacities during the late 1950s and early 1960s. He supported the ouster of President Arturo Illía in 1966 and was appointed commander of the army by President Juan Carlos Onganía in 1968. He was serving in this position when, as leader of a military junta, he forced Onganía's resignation on June 9, 1970. General Lanusse remained a major power in the succeeding government of President Roberto Levingston, who was also ousted by the Lanusse-led junta on March 23, 1971. Lanusse was himself sworn in as president three days later. His administration survived a coup attempt led by a tank regiment with the support of ousted President Levingston in October of 1971. In 1972 Argentina experienced several general strikes because of bad economic conditions in the country. Argentina was also beset with violence from the left and the right during Lanusse's administration. He attempted to quell the violence by calling for a democratic election to return Argentina to civilian rule. Lanusse began negotiations with the outlawed Perónist parties to insure their support in the elections called for March of 1973. Juan Perón was himself allowed to return from exile, but not to run for the presidency. Lanusse also declined to enter the election, and following the election of Perón's hand-picked candidate, Héctor Cámpora, Lanusse left office on May 25, 1973. In May of 1977 he was arrested on charges of financial corruption during his term of office, but he was released the following month.

HÉCTOR CÁMPORA (President, May 25–July 13, 1973). Héctor José Cámpora was born in Mercedes, Argentina, on March 26, 1909. He attended dental school at the National University in Cordoba. After graduating in 1934, he set up practice in San Andres de Giles. He was elected to the municipal council there in 1944. Cámpora was an early supporter of Juan Perón and was elected to the Argentine Chamber of Deputies in February of 1946. As a staunch Perónist, he was elected president of the chamber in 1948. Cámpora also served as a leader of the Perónist party until 1953, when he was appointed ambassador-at-large by President Perón. After Perón's overthrow by the military in 1956, Cámpora was arrested. He escaped the following year and spent two years in exile in Chile before returning to Argentina in 1960. Cámpora led the Justicialist party during the early 1960s. The party won impressive victories in the 1965 elections, which were subsequently annulled by the military. When General Alejandro Lanusse called for democratic elections to be held in 1973, Cámpora was named as Perón's personal representative. When Perón was not allowed to run for president himself, Cámpora was nominated, and on March 11, 1973, he received over 49 percent of the vote. He was sworn into office on May 25, 1973. His first acts as president included freeing political prisoners held in Argentina and legalizing the Communist party. Perón returned to Argentina on June 20, 1973, after a rift had developed between various Perónist factions. Cámpora resigned the presidency on July 13, 1973, paving the way for new elections to be held with Perón as a candidate. Cámpora continued to be a leading spokesman for Perón during his subsequent administration. Following the army coup which ousted Perón's widow in 1976, Cámpora was arrested. He was allowed to go into exile in Mexico in November of 1979. Cámpora died in Mexico City of cancer of the larynx on December 19, 1980.

RÁUL LASTIRI (President, July 13–October 12, 1973). Rául Alberto Lastiri was born in 1915. He was a supporter of President Juan Perón. He was serving as president of the Argentine Chamber of Deputies when he succeeded to the presidency following the resignations of President Héctor Cámpora and vice president Solano Lima on July 13, 1973. Lastiri served as interim president during new elections and remained in office until October 12, 1973, when Juan Perón was inaugurated. He died of cancer on December 12, 1978.

JUAN D. PERÓN (President, October 12, 1973–July 1, 1974). *See earlier entry under Heads of State.*

ISABEL PERÓN (President, July 1, 1974–March 29, 1976). Isabel Perón was born María Estela Martínez Cartas in La Rioja, in northeast Argentina, on February 4, 1931. She was raised in Buenos Aires, where she studied dancing. She was touring South America with the "Joe and His Ballets" dance troupe when she met General Juan Perón, the deposed dictator of Argentina, in 1955. Soon after she became Perón's personal secretary and accompanied him into exile in several South American countries before they settled in Madrid, Spain, in 1960. She married Perón in 1961 and became involved in Perónist politics. Since her husband was not allowed in the country, she served as Perón's representative in Argentina in 1964 and 1965 and was active in the support of Perónist candidates in the 1965 elections. Isabel Perón returned to Spain following the military coup in 1966. In December of 1971 she again served as Perón's representative in negotiations with President Alejandro Lanusse on upcoming elections. Juan Perón was subsequently allowed to return to Argentina, where he settled permanently on June 20, 1973, after Héctor Cámpora, the Perónist candidate, was elected president. Following Cámpora's resignation, new elections were scheduled, and Perón chose his wife to be his running mate. She was nominated for vice president on August 4, 1973, but her choice was an unpopular one with the anti-Perónist and leftist elements in Argentina. She campaigned avidly during the election, and the Peróns won on September 23, 1973. They were inaugurated on October 12, 1973. Isabel Perón assumed duties as acting head of state when her husband took ill in late 1973. She headed a state visit to Europe in June of 1974, but returned home shortly before her husband's death on July 1, 1974. She was sworn in as president and attempted to continue her husband's policies. Inflation and unemployment were on the rise during her administration, with inflation reaching an annual 500 percent increase during her term of office. Terrorist activities by left- and right-wing guerrilla groups also escalated. Isabel Perón also faced widespread criticism for corruption during her administration. Her chief advisor until July of 1975 was José López Rega, a practicing astrologer, who served as her personal secretary and social welfare minister. Rega was also the alleged leader of the Argentine Anti-Communist Alliance, a terrorist group responsible for many death-squad-style killings of leftist critics of the government. He was indicted for corruption and fled for Spain in July of 1975. That same month a general strike further weakened Isabel Perón's grip on the country. On September 13, 1975, she took a leave of absence for health reasons, and Senate President Italo Luder served as acting head of state. Despite pleas that she resign from office, Isabel Perón returned to the presidency on October 16, 1975. She survived a military uprising in December of 1975, but was ousted on March 29, 1976, by a military coup. She was arrested and spent the next five

years under house arrest. When she was released in July of 1981, she returned to Spain. Isabel Perón received a presidential pardon for most of the charges against her in 1983 and briefly returned to Argentina following the election of Rául Alfonsin the same year. She again visited Argentina during the 1988 presidential elections.

ITALO LUDER (Interim President, September 13–October 16, 1975). Italo Argentino Luder was an early supporter of Juan Perón. A lawyer, he had been instrumental in the drafting of the Perónist constitution of 1949. He also defended Perón against charges of treason following his ouster in 1955. Luder was serving as Senate president when Isabel Perón took a leave of absence for reasons of health on September 13, 1975. Luder was sworn in as acting president and immediately replaced several cabinet ministers. Luder also gave greater influence to the military during his brief term of office. He, and many others, tried to persuade Isabel Perón to resign permanently, but failed to convince her to do so. He relinquished the office back to her on October 16, 1975. Luder, a moderate, remained active in Perónist politics. He ran for president on the Perónist ticket in November of 1983, but was decisively defeated by Rául Alfonsin. Luder was later named minister of defense in the cabinet of President Carlos Saul Menem in 1989. He resigned over differences with the army chief of staff in January of 1990.

JORGE RAFAEL VIDELA (President, March 29, 1976–March 29, 1981). Jorge Rafael Videla was born on August 2, 1925, in Mercedes, Argentina. He came from an army family and entered the National Military College in 1941. After graduation he served in the war ministry and then became an instructor at the National Military College in 1948. He was stationed in Washington, D.C., in the office of the military attaché from 1956 to 1958. Videla then served as a staff officer in the Army General Command during much of the 1960s. In 1971 he was named commandant of the National Military College. Videla rose to army chief of staff in 1973 and was named commander in chief of the armed forces by Isabel Perón in August of 1975. Videla conducted a purge of Perónist army officers after his appointment and was instrumental in driving the unpopular presidential advisor José López Rega from office. He also led a vigorous antiterrorist campaign. General Videla sided with Isabel Perón during a right-wing air force coup attempt in December of 1975. He then led a military coup himself which ousted her on March 24, 1976. He was chosen by the ruling junta as the new president and was sworn into office on March 29, 1976. General Videla suspended the Congress and most political activities after taking power. He also tried to stabilize the disastrous Argentine economy by establishing a free-market economy. He survived an assassination attempt by a bomb explosion in October of 1976. Videla retired as commander in chief of the armed forces in August of 1978, but remained as president until his term expired on March 29, 1981. He was succeeded by General Roberto Viola. General Videla was later arrested and charged in August of 1984 with human rights abuses committed during his antiterrorist campaigns. He was tried and convicted, and he was sentenced to life imprisonment in December of 1985. Videla remained incarcerated until he was pardoned by President Carlos Saul Menem on December 30, 1990.

ROBERTO VIOLA (President, March 29–November 20, 1981). Roberto Eduardo Viola was born on October 13, 1924, in Buenos Aires to Italian immigrants. He joined the military and was named army chief of staff in July of 1978. In that position he helped negotiate a settlement with Chile on a major territorial dispute. He served as a member of the ruling military junta until his retirement from the military in 1979. He was selected by the junta to succeed President Jorge Videla, and he took office on March 29, 1981. Viola was unable to halt the growing economic recession, and he further aggravated the military by freeing Isabel Perón and conducting meetings with banned political parties. The junta feared that President Viola might try to restore a civilian government. On November 20, 1981, Viola suffered from a heart ailment and was temporarily replaced by General Horacio Tomás Liendo, the interior minister, as interim president. On December 11, 1981, the ruling junta announced that Viola had resigned for reasons of health, though it appeared obvious that he had been forced from office. He was succeeded by army leader General Leopoldo Galtieri. Viola later was arrested and tried for human rights abuses after civilian government was restored in 1983. He was convicted and sentenced to 17 years in prison in December of 1985. Viola remained in prison until he was pardoned by President Carlos Saul Menem on December 30, 1990.

HORACIO TOMÁS LIENDO (Interim President, November 20–December 11, 1981). Horacio Tomás Liendo was born in Dordoba on December 17, 1924. He was educated at the National Military College and became a career military officer. He rose through the ranks to major in 1959, colonel in 1970, and general in 1980. Liendo served in the cabinet of the military government as minister of labor from 1976 until 1979. He served as chief of staff of the armed forces from 1979 until 1981, when he was appointed minister of the interior in the cabinet of President Roberto Viola. On November 20, 1981, Liendo became acting head of state when President Viola suffered from a heart ailment. When Viola officially resigned from office on December 11, 1981, Liendo also resigned as interior minister and interim president.

LEOPOLDO GALTIERI (President, December 22, 1981–June 17, 1982). Leopoldo Fortunato Galtieri was born on July 15, 1926, in Caseros, a suburb of Buenos Aires. He entered the National Military College and studied civil engineering. He rose through the ranks and became brigadier general in 1972, shortly before his appointment as chief of staff for logistics and finance in the army. During the 1970s Galtieri was active in the army's antiterrorist campaigns against leftist guerrillas. On January 1, 1980, Galtieri succeeded General Roberto Viola as army chief of staff. He and the other members of the ruling junta forced Viola from the presidency in December of 1981, and Galtieri took over as president on December 22, 1981. He also remained as army chief of staff. In an attempt to gain public support for his administration, Galtieri invaded the Falkland Islands, off the coast of Argentina. The Falklands were claimed by Great Britain, and the Argentine invasion prompted a military response from the British. The initial Argentine military successes met with great approval by the Argentine public, but after several months of heavy fighting the British succeeded in recapturing the island. Argentina surrendered on June 15, 1982. Two days later Galtieri resigned his positions after widespread criticism of the military's defeat. He was replaced as army chief of staff by General Cristino Nicolaides and was temporarily succeeded as interim president by his interior minister, Maj. General Alfredo Oscar Saint-Jean. Galtieri was arrested in 1983 and was tried the following year for human rights abuses and his conduct during the Falkland War. He was acquitted of the human rights charges in December of 1985, but was convicted of incompetence in conducting the war and sentenced to twelve

years in prison. He was released from prison in October of 1989.

ALFREDO OSCAR SAINT-JEAN (Interim President, June 18–July 1, 1982). Alfredo Oscar Saint-Jean was a career army officer. He served in the cabinet of President Leopoldo Galtieri and was interior minister when Galtieri was forced to resign following Argentina's defeat by the British in the Falkland War. Saint-Jean was sworn in as interim president on June 18, 1982. He served until July 1, 1982, when he was replaced by General Reynaldo Bignone.

REYNALDO BIGNONE (President, July 1, 1982–December 10, 1983). Reynaldo Benito Antonio Bignone was born in Moron, a town west of Buenos Aires, on January 21, 1928. He attended the National Military College and later the Superior War College. He served as secretary-general of the army during the late 1970s, and in December of 1980 he was named commander of military institutes. Bignone subsequently retired from the armed forces. He was selected by army chief of staff Lt. General Cristin Nicolaides to succeed President Leopoldo Galtieri as president following the defeat of Argentina by Great Britain in the Falkland War. The selection of the former army general met with objections from the navy and air force chiefs, who resigned from the ruling junta in protest. Bignone continued the military government's free-market economic policies and began preparations for elections and a return to civilian rule. He presided over the general elections held in October of 1983 and left office on December 10, 1983, when Raúl Alfonsin was sworn in. Bignone was arrested in January of 1984, but was released without trial in June of 1984.

RAÚL ALFONSIN (President, December 10, 1983–July 8, 1988). Raúl Ricardo Alfonsin Foulkes was born in

Chascomus, in Buenos Aires province, on March 13, 1926. He attended the National Military College, but instead of joining the army he attended the University of Buenos Aires, where he received a law degree in 1950. He joined the Radical Civic Union party and was elected town councillor in Chascomus in 1950. In 1963 Alfonsin was elected to the National Congress, and two years later he was selected as the provincial president of the Radical party. Alfonsin broke with the president of the Radical party, Ricardo Balbin, in 1972 over the issue of conciliation with the military and Perónists, and he founded the Renovation and Change faction. Alfonsin was a severe critic of military rule, and when Balbin died in 1982, Alfonsin reunited the two factions. He was nominated by the Radical party for the free elections called for October 30, 1983, and defeated Italo Luder, the Perónist candidate, with 52 percent of the vote. His inauguration was moved up a month, and he was sworn into office on December 19, 1983. Alfonsin reduced the power of the military in Argentina and also repealed a law passed earlier in the year granting amnesty to members of the military who conducted human rights violations during the antiterrorist campaigns from 1973 to 1982. Nine former junta members, including three ex-presidents, were charged and tried during Alfonsin's term of office. Relations with Great Britain over the Falkland Islands remained strained, and the Argentine economy continued to plague the new government. Alfonsin was faced with two general strikes in 1987 and three unsuccessful military uprisings – in April 1987, December 1988, and January 1989. Alfonsin was not allowed by law to seek reelection, and the candidate of the Radical party was defeated in the elections of May 14, 1989. Alfonsin resigned his office on July 8, 1989, and was succeeded by Perónists Carlos Saul Menem. He remained president of the Radical party.

CARLOS SAUL MENEM (President, July 8, 1988–). Carlos Saul Menem was born in Anillaco, in the northwest Argentine province of La Rioja, on July 2, 1930. Menem was of Syrian ancestry and was raised a Sunni Moslem, though he later converted to Roman Catholicism. Menem was a supporter of Juan Perón and formed a Perónist youth group in 1955. He was briefly jailed following Perón's overthrow. He received a law degree from Cordoba University in 1958 and became affiliated as legal advisor to the General Labor Confederation, a Perónist trade union. In 1966 Menem married Zulema Fatimah Yoma. The couple were separated on several occasions during the 1980s. Menem was elected governor of La Rioja in 1973. When the military overthrew Perón's widow, Isabel, in 1976, Menem was jailed. He remained in prison or internal exile until 1981. He was elected governor of La Rioja again in 1983 and in 1987. Menem defeated Antonio Cafiero, president of the Perónist Justicialist party, for the nomination for the presidency and defeated Eduardo Angeloz, the candidate of the ruling Radical party, in the general elections held on May 14, 1989. President Raúl Alfonsin resigned from office five months earlier than scheduled, and Menem was inaugurated president on July 8, 1989. In a move unpopular with many Argentinians, Menem tried to appease the military by pardoning many of the officers tried for human rights abuses during the previous administration. In early 1990 Menem was also beset with domestic scandal when his estranged wife barricaded herself in the presidential palace and he was forced to have her removed by the police. Worsening economic conditions and strike threats by major unions also plagued Menem throughout 1990. He often consulted with leading members of the opposition in an attempt to govern by consensus to settle Argentina's problems.

Armenia, Republic of

(Hayastani Hanrapetutyun)

Armenia is a country in western Asia. It became an independent nation following the breakup of the Soviet Union on December 25, 1991.

HEADS OF STATE

LEVON TER-PETROSYAN (President, October 16, 1991–   ). Levon Ter-Petrosyan was born in 1945. He was the leader of the Armenian National Movement and was elected to succeed S. K. Tonoyan as chairman of the Supreme Soviet in August of 1990. In September of 1991 a large majority voted to support full independent status for Armenia. Ter-Petrosyan was elected the first president of the Republic of Armenia on October 16, 1991. Armenia joined the Commonwealth of Independent States in December of 1991. Armenia subsequently engaged in a war with neighboring Azerbaijan. Ter-Petrosyan survived a vote of no confidence over the war issue on August 17, 1992.

GAGIC G. ARUTYUNYAN (Premier, November 1991–   ). Gagic Garushevich Arutyunyan was born in 1948. He was the former chairman of the Armenian Communist party Central Committee. In 1990 he resigned from the Communist party to join the Nationalist opposition. Arutyunyan served as deputy chairman of the Armenian Supreme Soviet from 1990 until 1991. He was elected vice president of Armenia on October 16, 1991, and was selected as chairman of the Council of Ministers the following month.

Australia, Commonwealth of

Australia is a continent lying between the Pacific and Indian oceans. It was granted independence from Great Britain on January 1, 1901.

HEADS OF STATE

PRINCE HENRY, DUKE OF GLOU-CESTER (Governor-General, January 30, 1945–January 30, 1947). Henry William Frederick Albert of the House of Hanover, later Windsor, was born on March 31, 1900, the third son of King George V and Queen Mary of Great Britain. Prince Henry entered Eton in 1913 and Sandhurst in 1918. He embarked on a career in the army and rose to the rank of major in the 10th Royal Hussars. He was created Baron Culloden, Earl of Ulster, and Duke of Gloucester in 1928. He received a royal promotion to major general in 1936 following the death of his father and the abdication of his eldest brother, the Duke of Windsor. During World War II, Prince Henry served as a liaison officer with the British Expeditionary

Forces. He was wounded in France near the end of the war. On November 16, 1943, he was appointed by his brother, King George VI, to the honorary position of governor-general of Australia, though he did not take office until January 30, 1945. He retired as the king's representative to Australia on January 30, 1947. Prince Henry was created a field marshal in 1955. He died at the age of 74 in his home, Barnwell Manor, in Northamptonshire, on June 10, 1974.

SIR WILLIAM JOHN McKELL (Governor-General, January 30, 1947–January 1, 1953). Sir William John McKell was born on September 26, 1881, in Pambula, New South Wales, Australia. He was active in labour organizations in his youth and in 1917 was elected to the New South Wales Parliament as a Labour member. He studied law and served as minister of justice from 1920 to 1922. McKell also served as a member of the government from 1925 to 1927 and from 1930 to 1932. In 1939 he was elected leader of the Labour party. He was elected premier of New South Wales in 1941. McKell was reelected in 1944 and was serving his second term when he was recommended by Prime Minister John Chifley for the position of governor-general. Despite some opposition, McKell assumed the position on January 30, 1947. He served fairly and impartially during his term of office and was knighted in 1951. He retired on January 1, 1953. McKell later served as a representative to the Malayan Constitutional Commission from 1956 to 1957. He spent his retirement as a successful farmer in New South Wales. McKell died on January 11, 1985, in Sydney, at the age of 93.

VISCOUNT SLIM (Governor-General, January 1, 1953–February 1, 1960). William Joseph Slim was born in Bristol, England, on August 6, 1891. He joined the army in 1914 and saw action in World War I, being wounded

twice. In 1919 Slim joined the Indian army and served there for 20 years. He had risen to the rank of brigadier general by the start of World War II. After seeing action in the Sudan and Iran, he was transferred to Burma in 1942, where his jungle warfare experience from India served him well. He commanded the First Burma Corps during their retreat from the Japanese to India. Early in 1944 Slim, now commanding the 14th British Army, repulsed the Japanese from India. He was knighted that year, and in January of 1945 his forces recaptured Rangoon, the capital of Burma. Slim was widely considered one of the finest British generals to serve during the war. In 1948 he was named chief of the Imperial General Staff and was named field marshal the following year. He remained in that position until 1952, when he was nominated by Australian prime minister Robert Menzies to the post of governor-general. Slim was sworn into office on January 1, 1953. He proved an extremely popular governor-general, and his term was prolonged for two years before his retirement on February 1, 1960. He was created a viscount the same year. During the 1960s he served as director of several industries, and in 1964 he was appointed governor and constable of Windsor Castle. Viscount Slim died in London on December 14, 1970, at the age of 79 after suffering a stroke.

VISCOUNT DUNROSSIL (Governor-General, February 1, 1960–February 3, 1961). William Shepherd Morrison was born August 10, 1893, in Torinturk, Argyll, Scotland. He was educated at Edinburgh University and served in the Royal Field Artillery during World War I. He began a legal career in 1923 and in 1929 was elected as a Conservative member of Parliament representing Circencester and Tewkesbury. In 1936 Morrison was appointed minister of agriculture in the cabinet of Prime Minister Stanley Baldwin. He was appointed food minister in 1939, at the start of World War II, and was responsible for wartime rationing. He served as postmaster general from 1940 until his appointment as minister of town and country planning in 1943. Morrison remained in the cabinet until the Labour party defeated the Conservatives in the election of 1945. He remained in Parliament and in 1951 was elected Speaker of the House of Commons. He retired in 1959 and was named 1st Viscount Dunrossil of Vallaquie in the Isle of North Uist and County of Inverness by Queen Elizabeth II. In September of 1959 Viscount Dunrossil was nominated by Prime Minister Robert Menzies to serve as governor-general of Australia. He took office on February 1, 1960, but his term was cut short on February 3, 1961, by his death from a heart attack at the age of 67 in Canberra.

VISCOUNT DE L'ISLE (Governor-General, April 10, 1961–September 22, 1965). William Philip Sidney De L'Isle was born in London on May 23, 1909. He studied economics at Eton and Cambridge and served in the army in France, Belgium, and Italy during World War II. He was a Conservative member of Parliament representing Chelsea in 1944 and 1945. In 1951 De L'Isle was named secretary of state for air, and he served until 1955. In 1956, on the death of his father, he was created 6th Baron De L'Isle and Dudley. From 1958 to 1961 he served as an executive at Schwepps, Ltd. He was appointed to replace Viscount Dunrossil as governor-general of Australia and was sworn in on April 10, 1961. He served until his retirement on September 22, 1965. Viscount De L'Isle later served on the board of various corporations and from 1976 to 1984 was president of the British Heart Foundation. He died on April 6, 1991.

LORD CASEY OF BERWICK (Governor-General, September 22, 1965–April 30, 1969). Richard Gardner Casey was born in Brisbane, Australia, on August 29, 1890. He was educated at Cambridge and fought during World War I. Following the war, he joined the Australian Conservative party and was a member of Parliament from 1931 to 1940. He was named Australian ambassador to the United States in 1940 and remained there until 1942, when he was appointed British minister of state in the Middle East in the British war cabinet. In 1944 Casey was appointed governor of Bengal, India, and served there until 1945. He served in the Australian cabinet from 1949 as minister of works and housing. In 1951 he was named Australian foreign secretary. Casey held that position until 1960, when he was the first Australian to be created baron. He was appointed governor-general on September 22, 1965. During his tenure he helped organize the Southeast Asia Treaty Organization (SEATO). He remained governor-general until his retirement on April 30, 1969. Lord Casey was in an automobile accident in September of 1974, and his health deteriorated. He died of pneumonia in Melbourne on July 17, 1976, at the age of 85.

SIR PAUL HASLUCK (Governor-General, April 30, 1969–July 11, 1974). Paul Meernaa Caedwalla Hasluck was born in Freemantle, Perth, Australia, on April 1, 1905. He was educated at the University of Western Australia and upon graduation embarked on a career as a journalist. He later became a history professor and wrote several books about Australian history and the aborigines. In 1941 he joined the Foreign Ministry and was named to the Australian delegation to the United Nations in 1946. On April 28, 1946, Hasluck became the first Australian permanent representative to the United Nations and served on the UN Atomic Energy Commission. In 1949 he was elected to the Australian House of Representatives as a Liberal party member from Curtin, West Australia. He subsequently served in the cabinet as minister of territories from 1951 to 1963, minister of defense from 1963 to 1964, and foreign minister from 1964 to 1969. Hasluck was a leading candidate for prime minister in 1968, but was narrowly defeated. He was appointed governor-general on April 30, 1969, and served till the end of his term on July 11, 1974. Hasluck also wrote several historical books about Australia including *The Government and the People* (1951, 1970) and *Diplomatic Witness: Australian Foreign Affairs 1941–1947* (1980). Hasluck died in Perth on January 9, 1993.

SIR JOHN KERR (Governor-General, July 11, 1974–December 8, 1977). John Robert Kerr was born in Sydney on September 14, 1914. He studied law at Sydney University, and after serving in World War II, he was on the South Pacific Commission from 1946 to 1948. He had a distinguished legal career and in 1966 was named to the judiciary. Kerr was appointed chief justice of the Supreme Court in New South Wales in 1972 and was named lieutenant governor of New South Wales in 1973. He served in both of these positions until his appointment as governor-general on July 11, 1974. On November 11, 1975, Kerr dismissed the government of Prime Minister Gough Whitlam over the issue of Whitlam's deferment of a budget appropriations bill. Malcolm Fraser was named the new prime minister, and Kerr's decision was ratified by a popular election in December of 1975. Nevertheless, the unprecedented interference by the governor-general in Australian politics remained a center of controversy until Kerr's resignation on December 8, 1977, before the end of his term. Though retired from public life, Kerr continued to defend his decision to fire Whitlam, saying the prime minister should have called for new elections or resigned, thus avoiding the subsequent crisis. In January of 1991

Kerr was hospitalized for a brain tumor. He died two months later on March 24, 1991, at the age of 76.

SIR ZELMAN COWAN (Governor-General, December 8, 1977–July 29, 1982). Zelman Cowan was born in Melbourne on October 7, 1919. He was educated at the University of Melbourne and Oxford University and served in the navy during World War II. In 1947 he was sent to West Germany as a consultant to the military government there. Cowan then embarked on a distinguished career in education, serving as the dean of the University of Melbourne Law School from 1951 to 1966. He held other academic posts at the University of New England and the University of Queensland until his appointment to succeed Sir John Kerr as governor-general on December 8, 1977. He had been knighted the previous year. Cowan served until the end of his term on July 29, 1982, when he resumed his academic career at Oxford University in England.

SIR NINIAN MARTIN STEPHEN (Governor-General, July 29, 1982–February 26, 1989). Ninian Martin Stephen was born near Oxford, England, on June 15, 1923. He was educated in London and Switzerland and at the University of Melbourne, where he studied law. He served in the army during World War II and commenced his legal career in 1949. In 1970 Stephen was appointed to the Victoria Supreme Court. He was knighted in 1972 and was also named a justice on the High Court of Australia that year. He served there until July 29, 1982, when he was named governor-general. Stephen retired from that position on February 16, 1989. He subsequently served as chairman of the National Library of Australia and ambassador for the environment.

WILLIAM "BILL" HAYDEN (Governor-General, February 16, 1989–   ). William George Hayden was born in

Brisbane, Queensland, on January 23, 1933. He attended the University of Queensland. After graduation he worked as a police constable. He was elected a Labour member of Parliament from Oxley in 1961. Hayden served in the Labour government of Prime Minister Gough Whitlam as minister of social security from 1972 to 1975. In 1977 he was chosen as leader of the Labour party in opposition, and he was narrowly defeated for prime minister in 1980. In 1983, when a Labour government was restored, he served as foreign minister until 1988. Hayden was appointed governor-general on February 16, 1989.

HEADS OF GOVERNMENT

JOHN J. CURTIN (Prime Minister, October 7, 1941–July 6, 1945). John Joseph Curtin was born at Creswick, in Victoria, Australia, on January 8, 1885. Leaving home at an early age, he worked in various odd jobs before becoming affiliated with the Victoria Timber Workers Union in 1911. From 1917 to 1928 he was editor of the trade union paper *Westralian Worker*. Curtin was elected to Parliament as a Labour member from Freemantle in 1928. He was defeated for reelection in 1931, but regained his seat in 1934. The following year he became leader of the opposition Labour party. He served in that position until he was elected to succeed Arthur Fadden as prime minister and minister of defense on October 7, 1941. Shortly after his election, Japan bombed Pearl Harbor, and Curtin began preparations for a possible Japanese invasion of Australia. Curtin increased war production and worked closely with the United States and General Douglas MacArthur during the war. He suffered a heart attack in November of 1944 and died of a heart ailment at the age of 60 in Canberra on July 6, 1945.

FRANCIS M. FORDE (Prime Minister, July 6–13, 1945). Francis Michael Forde was born in Mitchell, Queensland, on July 18, 1890. He studied electrical engineering and taught school before entering Parliament as a Labour representative from Capricornia in 1922. He was first named to a cabinet in 1929 and served as minister for trade and customs from 1931 to 1932. Forde was deputy prime minister and minister for the army from 1941 to 1946. In April of 1945 Forde led the Australian delegation to the United Nations Conference in San Francisco. He was acting prime minister of Australia from April 30, 1945, following the illness of John Curtin. Upon Curtin's death on July 6, 1945, Forde was appointed prime minister by the governor-general, the Duke of Gloucester, and he served less than a week until July 13, 1945. He remained deputy prime minister in the government of Joseph Chifley until he lost reelection to his Parliament seat in 1946. From 1946 until 1953 Forde was Australian high commissioner in Canada. He returned to Australia and was again elected to Parliament in 1955, though he was narrowly defeated for reelection two years later. Forde then retired to a suburb of Brisbane, where he remained until his death on January 28, 1983.

JOSEPH B. CHIFLEY (Prime Minister, July 13, 1945–December 19, 1949). Joseph Benedict Chifley was born in Balthurst, New South Wales, on September 22, 1885. He worked with the New South Wales Railway and became a leader of the Federated Union of Locomotive Engineers. Chifley was elected to represent Macquarie in Parliament on the Labour party ticket in 1928. The following year he was named minister of defense. He lost reelection in 1931 and was named a member of the Royal Commission on Monetary Banking Systems while out of office. Chifley returned to Parliament in 1940 and served as treasurer in the government of prime minister John Curtin from October of 1941. He also served as acting prime minister when deputy prime minister Francis M. Forde was out of the country during Curtin's illness. Curtin died on July 6, 1945, and Chifley defeated Forde for the leadership of the Labour party on July 13, 1945. He was subsequently sworn in as prime minister. Chifley also remained treasurer in the new government. One of the major proposals of his government was the nationalization of Australian banks. Though the legislation authorizing this move was passed, it was declared unconstitutional. The Labour party was defeated in the elections of 1949, and Chifley remained party leader in opposition. He suffered a heart attack in 1950, and on June 13, 1951, he died suddenly in Canberra at the age of 65.

SIR ROBERT MENZIES (Prime Minister, December 19, 1949–January 25, 1966). Robert Gordon Menzies was born on December 20, 1894, in Jeparit in Victoria County. He was educated at Wesley College in Melbourne and received a law degree from the University of Melbourne. He began practicing law and was soon elected to the Victorian Legislative Council. From 1929 to 1934 Menzies served in the state assembly from Nunawading and was attorney general for Victoria from 1932 to 1934. In 1934 he was elected to Parliament representing Kooyong. He served as attorney general in the government of Prime Minister Joseph Lyons from 1935 and was named deputy leader of the United Australia party the same year. In April of 1939 Lyons died in office, and Menzies was selected to succeed him. The next year the United

Australia party won a one-seat majority in Parliament. As prime minister, Menzies declared war on Germany and began preparations to change Australia over to a wartime production and economy. Menzies was forced to resign on August 29, 1941. He remained in the government of Arthur Fadden as minister of defense coordination until the Labour party, under Joseph Curtin, came to power in October of 1941. Following his term as prime minister, Menzies dissolved the coalition United Australia party and formed the Liberal party. On December 19, 1949, Menzies was again chosen as prime minister in the coalition government of the Liberal and County parties. A supporter of free enterprise, Menzies avidly pursued foreign investments and succeeded in vastly increasing Australia's industrialization. Menzies was also an anti-Communist who committed Australian troops to fight in the Korean War. He helped negotiate the ANZUS treaty, which militarily allied Australia with New Zealand and the United States. In 1954 Australia also joined SEATO. Menzies also was a supporter of the United States policy in Vietnam. He was knighted by Queen Elizabeth II in March of 1963. Menzies retired from office on January 25, 1966. He suffered a series of strokes from 1968 and was confined to a wheelchair three years later. He died after a long illness in Sydney on May 14, 1978, at the age of 83.

HAROLD E. HOLT (Prime Minister, January 25, 1966–December 16, 1967). Harold Edward Holt was born in Sydney on August 5, 1908. He studied law at the University of Melbourne and set up practice in Melbourne in 1933. In 1935 he was elected to Parliament on the Nationalist party ticket representing Fawkner, Victoria. He served as minister without portfolio in the government of Robert Menzies in 1939. After serving briefly in the army, he was recalled by Menzies to serve in the wartime cabinet as minister of labour and national service. After the Nationalist party defeat in the elections of 1941, he joined with Menzies to found the Liberal party. He resumed his labour and national service ministry after Menzies was returned to office in December of 1949. In this position Holt fought against Communist control of Australian trade unions. He served as minister of immigration from 1949 until 1956 and succeeded in liberalizing immigration policies. He was elected deputy leader of the Liberal party in October of 1956 and was also elected leader of the House of Representatives. In December of 1958 Holt was also appointed treasurer in the Menzies government. He succeeded the retiring Menzies as leader of the Liberal party and prime minister and was sworn into office on January 26, 1966. As prime minister, Holt increased Australian participation in the Vietnam War and focused on Asia as Australia's major international concern. Holt's party was reelected in November of 1966. The 59-year-old Holt was lost and presumed drowned on December 16, 1967, while skindiving in Port Phillip Bay by the town of Portsea.

SIR JOHN McEWEN (Prime Minister, December 19, 1967–January 10, 1968). John McEwen was born in Chiltern, Victoria, on March 29, 1900. He joined the civil service in his youth and served in the army during World War I. In 1934 he was elected to the Parliament and served in the 1937 cabinet as minister of the interior. McEwen served in subsequent cabinets as foreign minister and minister for air and civil aviation. In 1949 he was appointed minister of commerce and agriculture in the government of Robert Menzies. In 1956 he was named minister of trade and served until 1963. McEwen was elected leader of the Country party, the junior partner in the ruling government coalition, in 1958. He also became deputy prime minister

that year. McEwen served as interim prime minister after the drowning death of Harold Holt on December 19, 1967. He held the office until January 10, 1968, when he stepped down to be succeeded by the new Liberal party leader, John Gorton. McEwen retired from politics in 1971, the same year he was knighted. He died on November 21, 1980, in Melbourne after a long illness.

SIR JOHN GORTON (Prime Minister, January 10, 1968–March 10, 1971). John Grey Gorton, son of a wealthy citrus farmer, was born in Melbourne on September 9, 1911. He studied at Oxford University in England and returned to Australia in 1936. During World War II he served in the air force, and he was seriously injured and required extensive facial plastic surgery when his plane was shot down in 1942. Gorton received a medical discharge after being shot down a second time in 1944. Two years later he entered politics and was elected to the Kerang Shire Council. From 1949 to 1950 he served as its president. Gorton had joined the Liberal party in 1948 and was elected to the Federal Senate from Victoria in December of 1949. During the 1950s Gorton served as chairman of the Foreign Affairs Committee. He was appointed minister of the navy in December of 1958 and served until 1963. He also served in the Foreign Affairs Ministry as assistant to the minister from 1960 to 1963. During the 1960s Gorton also served in various other ministries, including interior and works. He was named minister of education and science in the cabinet of Prime Minister Harold Holt in December of 1966. After Holt drowned in December of 1967, Gorton was chosen on January 9, 1968, to succeed him as Liberal party leader. He was sworn in as prime minister the following day. Shortly afterwards he resigned from the Senate and was elected to the House of Representatives in the special election called to fill Holt's seat. Gorton staved off a leadership challenge led by William McMahon in November of 1969. Gorton was forced to resign the Liberal party leadership and the office of prime minister in March of 1971 after Malcolm Fraser resigned as defense minister because of a conflict with his military policies. Gorton lost a vote of confidence by the Liberal party members of Parliament and was succeeded by McMahon on March 10, 1971. He was appointed defense minister in the new McMahon government, but was forced to resign from the cabinet in August of 1971. He remained in the House of Representatives until his retirement in 1975.

WILLIAM McMAHON (Prime Minister, March 10, 1971–December 5, 1972). William McMahon was born in Sydney on February 23, 1908. He received a law degree from the University of Sydney and set up practice after graduation. During World War II he served in the army, and after his discharge, he returned to the university to earn a degree in economics. McMahon entered politics in 1949 and was elected to the Parliament on the Liberal party ticket from Lowe, New South Wales. During the 1950s he headed up various ministries, including the navy, social services, and primary industry. He was appointed to the cabinet in 1958 as minister of labour and national service, and in 1966 he was named treasurer. McMahon was elected deputy Liberal party leader when Harold Holt became prime minister in January of 1966. After Holt's death in December of 1967, McMahon was vetoed from the prime ministership by John McEwen, the interim prime minister and chairman of the Country party in the ruling coalition. He remained as treasurer in the John Gorton government until he challenged Gorton's leadership in October of 1969. He was then named foreign minister. When Gorton was forced to resign in March of 1971, McMahon

was elected party leader, and he was sworn in as prime minister on March 10, 1971. McMahon was criticized by the Labour party for following too closely the foreign policy of the United States. While McMahon did withdraw some troops in Vietnam, he also came under fire for not proceeding at a more rapid pace in the Australian disengagement in the Vietnam War. The Liberal party was defeated in the 1972 elections, and Labour party leader Gough Whitlam succeeded McMahon as prime minister on December 5, 1972. McMahon also resigned as leader of the Liberal party, though he remained in parliament until his retirement in 1982. McMahon, who had been knighted in 1977, died of cancer in Sydney on March 31, 1988.

GOUGH WHITLAM (Prime Minister, December 5, 1972–November 11, 1975). Edward Gough Whitlam, son of a prominent Australian attorney, was born in Kew, a suburb of Melbourne, on July 11, 1916. He attended Sydney University, but interrupted his education to serve in the air force during World War II. After the war he returned to the university and received a law degree. Whitlam joined the Labour party but was unsuccessful in his first several election attempts. In November of 1952 he was elected to the Parliament representing Werriwa. Whitlam's prosperous background and intellectual bearing made him an unpopular figure in Labour parliamentary circles. Through diligence and forcefulness, however, he overcame his fellow Labourites' distrust and was elected deputy party leader in March of 1960. He succeeded Arthur Caldwell as leader of the Labour party in February of 1967. After his election Whitlam attempted to reform the power structure of the party and was briefly forced to resign in April of 1968. After his return to the leadership, he campaigned vigorously against the ruling Liberal coalition. Whitlam advocated diplomatic relations with the People's Republic of China and opposed Australia's dependence on the United States in foreign policy matters. He led the Labour party to victory in December of 1972 and was sworn into office as prime minister on December 5, 1972. Whitlam also took the foreign ministry portfolio. As prime minister, Whitlam ended the military draft and began the complete withdrawal of Australian troops from Vietnam. He also supported better laws guaranteeing aboriginal land rights. Australia was faced with severe economic problems in 1975, with inflation running out of control. The government was also faced with a major scandal involving a multimillion dollar secret loan from the Saudi Arabian government. The deputy prime minister and several cabinet officials were forced to resign in the aftermath. During 1975 Whitlam also faced an economic crisis when the Australian Senate, led by the opposition Liberal party, refused to pass a budget bill, thus threatening to leave the federal government without money. In an unprecedented move, the governor-general, Sir John Kerr, dismissed Whitlam as prime minister and called for new elections. After a bitter campaign Whitlam's party was defeated and Liberal party leader Malcolm Fraser remained prime minister. Whitlam led the Labour party in opposition until December 11, 1977, when he announced his resignation after another election defeat to the Liberals. In July of 1978 Whitlam resigned from Parliament. He was appointed as Australia's representative to UNESCO in Paris in 1983, and he served as a member of the UNESCO executive board from 1985 until 1989. Whitlam also served as a member of the constitutional commission from 1986 to 1988 and was vice-chairman of the Australian National Gallery from 1987 to 1990.

MALCOLM FRASER (Prime Minister, November 11, 1975–March 11, 1983).

John Malcolm Fraser was born in New South Wales on May 21, 1930. He attended Oxford University and worked as a rancher after returning to Australia. In the 1950s he entered politics, and in 1954 he narrowly lost a parliamentary election in Wannon on the Liberal party ticket. He successfully challenged for the seat the following year and served on various parliamentary committees during the fifties and early sixties. Fraser was on the verge of retiring from politics when he was named minister of the army by Prime Minister Harold Holt in January of 1966. Fraser was a leading supporter of Australian involvement in the Vietnamese War. In 1968 he was named minister of education and science in the cabinet of John Gorton. After the elections of October of 1969, he was appointed minister of defense. Fraser resigned that position in March of 1971 during a leadership struggle with Gorton. After Gorton was replaced by William McMahon, Fraser returned to the cabinet as minister of education and science once again. In March of 1975 Fraser defeated Billy Snedden for leadership of the Liberal party. He precipitated a crisis later in the year when he stalled a budget bill in the Liberal-controlled Senate. This action resulted in the dismissal of Prime Minister Gough Whitlam by Governor-General John Kerr. Fraser was appointed interim prime minister on November 11, 1975, and after a bitter election, the Liberal party won a massive victory over the Labour party on December 13, 1975. Though Fraser's popularity diminished over the next several years due to higher taxes and a wage freeze, he called for elections on March 5, 1983, nine months earlier than required by law. The Liberals were defeated by Labour under its new leader, Bob Hawke, and Fraser turned over the prime ministership on March 11, 1983. The following day he resigned as leader of the Liberal party, and he retired from Parliament at the end of the month. In 1987 Fraser was named chairman of CARE, Australia, and in 1990 he became president of CARE International.

BOB HAWKE (Prime Minister, March 11, 1983–December 20, 1991). Robert James Lee Hawke was born on December 9, 1929, in Bordertown, South Australia. He was educated at the University of Western Australia, where he studied law. While in college, he became active in the Labour party. In 1952 he attended Oxford University in England as a Rhodes Scholar. Hawke returned to Australia in 1956 and became involved with the Australian Council of Trade Unions (ACTU). By winning wage settlement cases, he made an impact in national politics. He was defeated in a parliamentary election in 1963. In September of 1969 he succeeded Albert Monk as president of the ACTU. Hawke was a very popular national figure during the 1970s, and in 1980 he was elected to Parliament for Wills, a suburb of Melbourne. He lost a leadership battle with Billy Hayden in July of 1982. Hayden resigned as party leader on February 3, 1983, the same day Prime Minister Malcolm Fraser called for new elections, and Hawke was selected as Labour party leader. He led the party to victory in the election and succeeded Fraser as prime minster on March 11, 1983. Hawke was initially a popular prime minister and succeeded in overcoming several challenges both from the Liberal party and from members of his own party during the 1980s. In March of 1990 Hawke faced his greatest challenge at the polls by a coalition of the Liberal and National parties. In an upset victory aided by the decision of the opposition parties to replace their leadership prior to the election, Hawke remained prime minister. Hawke was challenged as Labour party leader by his treasurer, Paul Keating, in mid-1991. The initial challenge was unsuccessful, but Hawke's popularity declined as the economy slipped into a recession. Keating again challenged Hawke for party leadership and defeated him. Hawke relinquished the prime minister's office on December 19, 1991.

PAUL KEATING (Prime Minister, December 19, 1991–). Paul John Keating was born in Sydney on January 18, 1945. He was educated in Bankstown and subsequently entered politics. He was elected to the House of Representatives in 1969 and briefly served as minister for Northern Australia in 1975. Keating was a member of the Labour party and served as opposition spokesman on agriculture, minerals and energy, and treasury matters while the party was out of power between 1976 and 1983. When the Labour party was victorious in March of 1983, Keating was named federal treasurer in the government of Bob Hawke. He challenged Hawke for leadership of the Labour party in mid-1991. He was initially unsuccessful, but was able to defeat Hawke in another challenge in December. Keating replaced Hawke as party leader and prime minister on December 19, 1991.

Austria, Republic of

(Republik Österreich)

Austria is a landlocked country in central Europe. The Republic of Austria was proclaimed in November of 1918 after the breakup of the Austro-Hungarian Empire.

HEADS OF STATE

KARL RENNER (President, December 20, 1945–December 31, 1950). Karl Renner was born in Moravia on December 14, 1870. He studied law at the University of Vienna, where he joined the Social Democratic party. He was elected to the National Assembly in 1907, where he became a leader of the opposition to the Hapsburg monarchy. The Austro-Hungarian Empire was dissolved following the end of World War I, and Austria was proclaimed a republic on November 12, 1918. Renner served as chancellor and foreign minister of the first republic and signed the Treaty of St. Germain in 1919, which greatly reduced the status and power of Austria. Renner's coalition cabinet was dissolved on June 10, 1920, and he resigned as foreign minister in October of the same year. Renner was elected to the National Assembly in 1922, where he remained a member until 1934. He also served as Assembly president from 1931 to 1933. Renner was subsequently jailed by the nationalist regime of Dr. Engelbert Dollfuss during a crackdown on Socialist elements in the government. Renner was released from prison a year later when it was ruled there was insufficient evidence to hold him for treason. He remained on the political sidelines during the abortive Nazi coup d'état and assassination of Dollfuss and the subsequent unification of Austria with Hitler's Germany. Renner left Vienna during World War II and moved to Gloggnitz in Lower Austria. He participated in the anti-Nazi underground during this period. When Soviet forces occupied Austria in the spring of 1945, Renner was called upon to form a new government, which included a coalition of Social Democrats, Communists, and other small parties. The new government was approved and recognized by the Allied forces on April 29, 1945. Renner's government declared Austrian independence from Germany, and all Nazi laws were repealed. A general election was also called, and on November 28, 1945, Renner resigned as chancellor. He was then selected by the new National Assembly to serve as federal president on December 20, 1945. As president, Renner worked for the removal of occupation forces on Austrian soil. He was denounced by the Communists in 1946 because of his support for democratic institutions. Renner remained president until his death after a brief illness on December 31, 1950, at the age of 80.

THEODORE KORNER (President, May 27, 1951–January 4, 1957). Theodore Korner was born in Komorn, Hungary, on April 24, 1873. Korner attended the Hranice Military School and the Vienna Military Academy. He served in the army, where he rose to the rank of colonel during World War I. Following World War I, Korner, holding the rank of general-inspector, was appointed section chief in the Defense Ministry of the new Austrian Republic's first government. Korner subsequently joined the Social Democratic party and retired from the army in 1924. He was elected to the upper house of Parliament in 1925, where he served until the Parliament was abolished in 1934. In February of 1934 Korner was arrested by the Dollfuss government and remained imprisoned until the following year. After the German's absorption of Austria prior to World War II, Korner refused requests by the Nazis to rejoin the army. He was arrested by the Gestapo in late 1944 and remained imprisoned until the following year, when he was freed by Allied troops. Shortly thereafter Korner reentered politics and was elected mayor of Vienna. Korner began a campaign to rebuild war-torn Vienna, which remained occupied by Allied forces. On May 27, 1951, Korner was narrowly elected to succeed Karl Renner, who had died in office, as federal president. Korner suffered a stroke in July of 1956, but remained in his largely ceremonial position until his death of a heart attack in Vienna at the age of 83 on January 4, 1957.

ADOLF SCHARF (President, May 22, 1957–February 28, 1965). Adolf Schärf was born on April 20, 1890, in Nikolsburg in Lower Austria. He was raised in Vienna and became involved with the Socialist party at an early age. He attended the University of Vienna, where he received degrees in law and philosophy in 1914. Schärf served in the infantry during World War II and then resumed his activities with the Social Democratic party. He served as an assistant to the president of Parliament and in 1930 was appointed to a leadership position in the civil service. Schärf was elected to the upper house of Parliament in July of 1933, where he served until February of the following year. At that time Chancellor Dollfus abolished Parliament and arrested Schärf and other Socialist leaders. Schärf became active in the underground Socialist movement following his release. He was arrested by the Nazis on several occasions after Austria's merger with Germany in 1938. After World War II Scharf became chairman of the Socialist party and was again elected to the upper house of Parliament. Schärf was named vice-chancellor in the government of Leopold Figl in December of 1945. He remained in that position in the subsequent government of Julius Raab. Schärf was nominated by the Socialist party to succeed Theodore Korner, who had died in January of 1957, as federal president. Schärf was elected president, taking office on May 22, 1957. During his terms of office, Schärf remained an influential leader of the Socialist party and was instrumental in keeping the coalition between the Socialists and the People's party intact. He was reelected to the presidency in 1963 and served until February 28, 1965, when he died at the age of 74 in Vienna of complications from influenza and a liver ailment.

FRANZ JONAS (President, May 23, 1965–April 23, 1974). Franz Jonas was born on October 5, 1899, in Floridsdorf, a suburb of Vienna. Jonas served in the infantry in the Austro-Hungarian army during World War I. After the war he became active in the Social Democratic party and served as an official in the Vienna printer's union. Jonas was arrested during the purge of Socialists in 1935, but was acquitted of treason charges and released the following year. During World War II Jonas worked as a clerk in an engine factory. After the Allied liberation of Vienna in April of 1945, he was named to the Floridsdorf Town Council. His administrative skills in organizing the rebuilding of the war-torn city became evident, and he rose to become chairman of the council in 1946. When Theodore Korner, the mayor and governor of Vienna, was elected federal president in 1951, Jonas was selected to succeed him. As mayor, Jonas tried to reestablish Vienna as a cultural and diplomatic center for Europe. He was a popular figure and remained mayor for 14 years. He was also elected to Parliament in 1951 and served in the upper house until 1953 and thereafter was a member of the lower house. When President Adolf Schärf died in office in February of 1965, Jonas was nominated by the Socialist party to succeed him. On May 23, 1965, Jonas won a narrow victory, culminating a bitter campaign in which his lack of formal education was a major campaign issue. In April of 1971 Jonas defeated Kurt Waldheim for a second term as president. In 1974 the president's health began to decline. He was hospitalized with stomach cancer in March of 1974 and relinquished his duties as president on March 27, 1974. Jonas died of his illness in Vienna at the age of 74 on April 23, 1974.

RUDOLF KIRCHSCHLÄGER (President, July 8, 1974–July 8, 1986). Rudolf Kirchschläger was born in the village of Obermuhl in Upper Austria on March 20, 1915. During World War II he was drafted into the infantry and was seriously wounded in combat. He was employed by the Justice Department after the war and became a district judge in Vienna in the early 1950s. Kirchschläger joined the Ministry of Foreign Affairs as a legal advisor in 1954 and was active in the negotiations that resulted in a treaty with the Allied forces insuring Austrian independence and military neutrality. He remained with the foreign service and served as chief secretary to several foreign ministers, including Bruno Kreisky, the future chancellor. In the late 1960s Kirchschläger was appointed ambassador to Czechoslovakia. He was recalled from Prague in 1970 to serve as foreign minister in the Kreisky government. He was an active proponent of Austrian neutrality and attempted to maintain stability in East-West relations. Though he was not an active member of the Socialist party leadership, Kirchschläger was selected by the party to succeed Franz Jonas as president when Jonas died in April of 1974. He was elected in June of 1974 and was sworn in as federal president on July 8, 1974. Kirchschläger was reelected to a second term in the largely ceremonial position in 1980. He announced his retirement in 1986 and left office on July 8, 1986.

KURT WALDHEIM (President, July 8, 1986–July 8, 1992). Kurt Waldheim was born in St. Andra-Wordern, near Vienna, on December 21, 1918. While a law student at the University of Vienna, Waldheim was drafted into the German army near the start of World War II. He served on the Eastern front as a lieutenant, and he was wounded in action. He returned to the University of Vienna, where he earned a law degree in 1944. Though his official biography made no mention of later military service, it was later revealed that Waldheim had returned to active duty in March of 1942 and served as an intelligence officer to executed war criminal General Alexander Lohr. It was also alleged that Waldheim took part in the campaign against Yugoslavian partisans and the deportation of Greek Jews from Salonika. In addition, it was revealed that Waldheim had been listed as a possible war criminal for his activities, though the Yugoslavian government never brought him to trial. Waldheim tried to put his Nazi past behind him and joined the Foreign Ministry in postwar Austria. Waldheim was a delegate to the United Nations when Austria was admitted to that body in 1955 and was named ambassador to Canada in 1956. He returned to the Foreign Ministry in 1960 where he served as director of the political affairs division from 1962 until 1964. He was then named as Austria's ambassador to the United Nations in 1964, where he chaired several international committees. Waldheim remained at the United Nations until 1968, when he was called back to Vienna to serve as foreign minister in Josef Klaus's government. He returned to the United Nations after Klaus's People's party was defeated in the 1970 election by the Socialists. Waldheim again returned to Austria to run as the People's party nominee for federal president in the 1971 elections, but was defeated by Franz Jonas. He then returned to the United Nations, where Secretary-General U Thant of Burma had announced his retirement. Waldheim was a leading candidate to replace Thant, and though he was vetoed on two occasions by the recently admitted People's Republic of China, he eventually won the position and took office in January of 1972. Waldheim was an active secretary-general and used his office to seek compromise between the diverse interests of the East and the West, as well as the emerging Third World nations. He worked particularly hard to secure a lasting peace in the Middle East and met with some success when Israel and Egypt agreed to discuss a peace settlement after the 1973 Middle Eastern war. Waldheim's criticisms of Israeli policy, particularly in regard to Israel's raid on the Ugandan airfield at Entebbe to rescue hostages taken during a plane hijacking in 1976, made him an unpopular figure in the Jewish community. Nevertheless, he was reelected to a second four-year term as secretary-general in 1976. Waldheim was faced with international crises throughout the globe during his second term, including the Soviet invasion of Afghanistan, the civil war in Lebanon, and the seizure of the American Embassy in Iran. Waldheim's efforts met with little success in settling the world's major crises, but he remained a competent administrator whose efforts were respected by most nations. In 1980 Waldheim failed to secure a third term when the Third World nations pushed for a representative of one of their member countries as secretary-general. Waldheim was replaced by Javier Perez de Cuellar of Peru. After leaving the United Nations, Waldheim taught diplomacy at Georgetown University in Washington, D.C., for several years before returning to Austria in July of 1984. The following year he decided to seek the Austrian presidency as the nominee of the People's party. During the campaign Waldheim's wartime record came to light and caused an international outcry against the former United Nations official. In Austria the condemnation of Waldheim produced a vote of sympathy for the besieged candidate, who claimed that he had only done his duty during the war. He defeated the Socialist party nominee, Kurt Steyrer, in a run-off election on June 8, 1986. Waldheim's

victory further antagonized the international community, with Israel recalling its ambassador from Vienna and many nations, including the United States, barring the new president from visiting their capitols. In protest of the election results, the Socialist chancellor of Austria, Fred Sinowatz, resigned from office. The election and aftermath also produced a disturbing resurgence of anti-Semitism throughout the nation. Waldheim became increasingly isolated from the international community during his term of office, and very few world leaders visited Vienna. Waldheim further distanced himself from the international political mainstream by conducting negotiations for the release of hostages with Iraq's president Saddam Hussein after the Iraqi invasion of Kuwait in 1990. Waldheim completed his term and left office on July 8, 1992.

THOMAS KLESTIL (President, July 8, 1992–). Thomas Klestil was born on November 4, 1932. He was educated in Vienna and received a degree in economics. From 1959 until 1962 he served as a member of the Austrian delegation to the Organization for Economic Cooperation and Development. He was subsequently stationed at the Austrian Embassy in Washington, D.C., until 1966. Klestil returned to Austria to serve as secretary to the chancellor until 1969. He was then appointed as consul general to Los Angeles until 1974. Klestil was named Austria's representative to the United Nations from 1978 until 1982. He was then appointed ambassador to the United States. He returned to Austria in 1987 to serve in the Foreign Ministry. Klestil was the candidate of the conservative People's party for the presidency in May of 1992. He won the election by a wide margin and was sworn in as president on July 8, 1992.

HEADS OF GOVERNMENT

KARL RENNER (Chancellor, April 29–November 28, 1945). *See entry under Heads of State.*

LEOPOLD FIGL (Chancellor, November 28, 1945–April 2, 1953). Leopold Figl was born in Lower Austria in the town of Rust on October 2, 1902. He was trained as an agricultural engineer at the Vienna Agricultural High School. He joined the Lower Austrian Peasants Union and rose to director in 1933. Figl opposed the Anschluss plebiscite which united Austria and Germany. Following unification, Figl was arrested by the Nazi regime, and he was imprisoned at the Dachau and Flossenburg concentration camps from 1938 to 1943. After his release he was active in the anti-Nazi underground until he was rearrested and sent to the Mauthausen concentration camp in 1944. Figl remained there until he was freed by the Soviet Red Army during the liberation of Austria in the spring of 1945. In May of that year he was appointed secretary of state in the cabinet of Dr. Karl Renner. On November 28, 1945, leading a coalition of the People's party and Socialist party, Figl succeeded Renner as federal chancellor of the independent Austrian Republic. With the assistance of American aid, Figl presided over the economic revival of Austria and remained as chancellor following the October 1949 general elections. He withstood an attempt by the Communists to seize power during a general strike in 1951. Figl was forced by the Socialist members of his coalition government to relinquish the chancellorship, and he was succeeded by Dr. Julius Raab on April 2, 1953. Figl was named foreign minister in the Raab government on November 23, 1953. As foreign minister, Figl signed the treaty with the Allied powers in Vienna on May 15, 1955, which officially recognized Austrian independence as a military neutral. Figl resigned from the Foreign Ministry in 1959 to become the president of Parliament, a position he held until 1962, when he returned to Lower Austria as governor. Dr. Figl died of cancer in Vienna on May 9, 1965.

JULIUS RAAB (Chancellor, April 2, 1953–April 11, 1961). Julius Raab was born in St. Polten in Lower Austria on November 29, 1891. He received an engineering degree at the Vienna technical high school. During World War I he served in the army and he subsequently entered politics. He served as a member of the town council in St. Polten from 1927 to 1933. Raab was then elected to the Austrian Parliament as a member of the conservative Christian Socialist party, where he remained until Parliament was dissolved in 1934. In January of 1938 Raab was named minister of commerce and transportation in Chancellor Kurt von Schuschnigg's government. He remained in this position until Germany's occupation of Austria in March of 1938. During World War II Raab served as an engineer for a road construction firm. Following the war and Austria's liberation in 1945, Raab was a founder of the Austrian People's party. He was elected to the Parliamentary Assembly in the elections of November 1945, where he served as party leader. After serving briefly as minister of public works and reconstruction in the provisional government of Karl Renner, Raab was vetoed as a member of the postwar cabinet by the Soviets because he had served in the authoritarian von Schuschnigg government prior to the war. Instead Raab became a leader of the Austrian Economic Federation, a coalition of political and business leaders which sought to revitalize the Austrian economy. Raab was reelected to Parliament in 1949 and

1953. In 1953 Raab was also elected president of the Austrian Chamber of Commerce. He was selected to replace Leopold Figl as chancellor of Austria on April 2, 1953. Soon after becoming chancellor, Raab led a diplomatic mission to Moscow which helped bring about the treaty with the Allied powers granting Austria independence and military neutrality. Raab also was successful in improving Austria's economic stability. He remained as chancellor and party chairman until April 11, 1961, when poor health due to diabetes forced his resignation. In April of 1963 Raab's attempt at a political comeback was dashed when he was defeated in a bid to win the Austrian presidency. Raab's health continued to decline, and on January 8, 1964, he died in Vienna at the age of 72.

ALFONS GORBACH (Chancellor, April 11, 1961–April 2, 1964). Alfons Gorbach was born on September 2, 1898, in the town of Imst in Tyrol, Austria. He joined the infantry in World War I and lost a leg due to a serious injury while fighting on the Italian front. After the war Gorbach continued his education at Graz University, where he joined the faculty upon graduation. He became active in politics and joined the Christian Socialist party. Gorbach won a seat in the Graz Municipal Council in March of 1928 and was later elected to the Styrian provincial government, where he was placed in charge of education. He was a leading anti-Nazi and campaigned against the plebiscite for Austrian unification with Germany. Following the German occupation in 1938, Gorbach was arrested and sent to Dachau concentration camp, where he remained for the next five years. He was released and forced to serve as an arms plant laborer in 1943, but was rearrested in July of 1944. He was eventually freed by American troops. He returned to Austria after the liberation in the spring of 1945. Gorbach reentered

politics and became active in the new Austrian People's party. He was elected to the Austrian lower house of Parliament in November of 1945 and was selected as speaker the following month. He remained in that position until April of 1961. Gorbach replaced Chancellor Julius Raab as People's party chairman in February of 1960, and on April 11, 1961, he succeeded him as chancellor when Raab resigned due to ill health. As chancellor, Gorbach sought to maintain cordial relations with both the United States and the Soviet Union. He was replaced as the People's party chairman in 1963, following a bitter rivalry with the party faction led by Dr. Joseph Klaus. Klaus objected to Gorbach's policy of compromise with the Socialist coalition partners. Gorbach was denied a vote of confidence by the People's party in February of 1964 and resigned the chancellorship. He was succeeded by Klaus on April 2, 1964. Gorbach's political career ended the following year when he campaigned for the federal presidency, but was narrowly defeated by Franz Jonas. He retired to Graz, where he died on July 31, 1972, at the age of 73.

JOSEF KLAUS (Chancellor, April 2, 1964–April 21, 1970). Josef Klaus was born in Mauthen in the Carinthian province of Austria on August 15, 1910. Klaus attended the University of Vienna, where he received a doctorate of law in 1934. He entered politics briefly prior to the German unification with Austria. In 1939 he was drafted and he served in the infantry during World War II. Klaus was captured and remained a prisoner of war until the fall of Germany in 1945. He then returned to Austria, where he opened a law firm in Salzburg. In 1949 Klaus was elected governor of Salzburg as a member of the People's party. He served in the position until April of 1961, when he was appointed finance minister in the government of Alfons Gorbach.

Klaus produced a balanced budget as finance minister and was able to reduce taxes, despite conflicts with the Socialists in Parliament. He resigned from Gorbach's government in November of 1962, claiming the chancellor was undermining his economic plans in an attempt to appease the Socialists. Klaus challenged Gorbach at the People's party convention in September of 1963 and replaced him as party chairman. Klaus was selected by the national party on February 25, 1964, to replace Gorbach as chancellor. He was sworn into office on April 2, 1964. Klaus continued his predecessor's policy of détente with the Soviet Union, though relations deteriorated following the Soviet invasion of neighboring Czechoslovakia in the summer of 1968. On March 1, 1970, the Socialist party of Austria won a victory in the parliamentary elections, and Klaus was replaced by Bruno Kreisky as chancellor on April 20, 1970. Klaus resigned as party chairman the following month.

BRUNO KREISKY (Chancellor, April 21, 1970–May 24, 1983). Bruno Kreisky was born to a wealthy family in Vienna on January 22, 1911. He attended school in Vienna and joined the Social Democratic party while in his teens. He continued to work underground with the party after it was banned in 1934, and he was arrested in January of 1935. He was imprisoned until mid-1936. Following his release, Kreisky attended the University of Vienna, where he earned a law degree. Following the absorption of Austria by Germany in 1938, Kreisky was arrested by the Nazi regime and exiled to Sweden. He was employed there by a consumer sales cooperative and was active in assisting Austrian refugees in Sweden. Kreisky returned to Austria after the war's conclusion and joined the foreign service. In 1946 he returned to Stockholm as first secretary of the Austrian legation, where he remained until 1950. He remained in the foreign service and on

April 2, 1953, was named state secretary of foreign affairs. Kreisky was instrumental in negotiating the 1955 treaty which restored Austria's independence and guaranteed military neutrality. He was elected to Parliament in 1956 and was sent to the United Nations as a delegate in 1957. He represented Austria on the United Nations Economic Commission in Geneva in 1957 and 1958. Kreisky was named foreign minister in the coalition cabinet of Dr. Julius Raab on July 14, 1959. He remained as foreign minister until 1966. The following year he was elected chairman of the Social Democratic party and led the Socialists to victory in the parliamentary election on March 1, 1970. Kreisky was sworn in as chancellor on April 20, 1970. The following year the Socialists won an absolute majority in Parliament, and Kreisky was able to form a one-party government. His government was successful in maintaining Austria's economic prosperity and succeeded in negotiating a special relations agreement with the Common Market in 1972. Kreisky also became a leader in international diplomatic affairs, though his attempts to encourage a peaceful Middle Eastern settlement by meeting with Palestinian Liberation Organization leader Yasir Arafat and other Arab leaders were criticized by Israel. Kreisky's party remained in power in the elections in 1975 and 1979. The Socialist party lost its majority in 1983, however, and Kreisky relinquished the chancellor's office on May 24, 1983. He remained honorary party chairman until his retirement in 1987. Kreisky died of heart disease in Vienna on July 29, 1990.

FRED SINOWATZ (Chancellor, May 24, 1983–June 16, 1986). Fred Sinowatz was born in the Austrian province of Burgenland on February 5, 1929. He attended the University of Vienna and earned a doctorate in philosophy in 1953. He joined the Socialist party and was elected to the provincial Landtag in

1961. Following the Socialist victory in 1964, he became first president of the Burgenland legislature and was cultural affairs spokesman for Burgenland from 1966 to 1971. He was named to the cabinet in the Kreisky government in 1971 and served as minister of education. After the resignation of Kreisky on May 24, 1983, following the Socialist party's failure to maintain an absolute majority, Sinowatz was named chancellor of a coalition government which included the Austrian Freedom party. He subsequently replaced Kreisky as Socialist party leader in October of 1983. Sinowatz resigned as chancellor following Kurt Waldheim's defeat of the Socialist party candidate for federal president in June of 1986. He remained Socialist party chairman until May 11, 1988, when he was succeeded by Franz Vranitzky.

FRANZ VRANITZKY (Chancellor, June 16, 1986–   ). Franz Vranitzky was born in Vienna on October 4, 1937. He was educated at the Vienna College of Commerce and graduated in 1960. The following year he was employed by the Austrian National Bank, where he later became first vice president. Vranitzky resigned in 1970 to become personal assistant to Hannes Androsch, the federal minister of finance. In 1976 Vranitzky was selected deputy board chairman for Austria's largest bank, Creditanstalt Bankverein, where he remained until 1981. He then went to Osterreichische Landerbank, the nation's second largest bank, which was in serious financial difficulty. Serving as chief executive officer, Vranitzky's aggressive managerial style restored the bank's financial stability. His successes there led to his appointment as minister of finance in 1984. He brought to this job the same style he had exhibited in the banking business and succeeded in reducing the Austrian budget deficit. When Chancellor Fred Sinowatz resigned, Vranitzky was chosen to succeed him as chancellor on June 16, 1986. In September of 1986 Vranitzky dissolved the coalition government of the Socialist party and the Freedom party because of comments by the Freedom party's newly selected rightwing leader. He called for a new election, which was held on November 23, 1986. The Socialist party maintained a slight majority over the People's party, but lost seats in the Parliament. Vranitzky submitted his resignation as chancellor but was asked to stay on by President Waldheim to form another coalition government with the People's party. After forming the new government on January 21, 1987, Vranitzky began a campaign to improve Austria's economy and restore its international standing, which had suffered from revelations concerning President Waldheim's ties to the Nazis during World War II. In 1989 Austria petitioned for admission to the European Community. Following the opening of borders with Eastern European countries, Austria also was beset by an influx of refugees in 1989 and 1990 which resulted in an increase in crime and black-market activities. The Socialist-People's party coalition survived a general election in October of 1990, despite the loss of seats by the People's party, and Vranitzky remained as chancellor.

Azerbaijan Republic

(Azarbaijchan Respublikasy)

Azerbaijan is a country in western Asia. It became an independent nation following the breakup of the Soviet Union on December 25, 1991.

HEADS OF STATE

AYAZ N. MUTALIBOV (President, December 25, 1991–March 6, 1992). Ayaz N. Mutalibov was born in Baku on May 12, 1938. He worked as an engineer and joined the Communist party in 1963. He served as vice-chairman of the Council of Ministers in Azerbaijan from 1982 until 1989 and was chairman of the Council from 1989 until 1991. Mutalibov was a member of the Politburo from 1990 until 1991. He was elected president of Azerbaijan on September 8, 1991, a month after Azerbaijan had declared its formal independence. Azerbaijan joined the Commonwealth of Independent States in December of 1991. Mutalibov was forced to resign on March 6, 1992, following massive demonstrations against his government. The Parliament tried to reinstate him on May 14, 1992, but the presidential palace was taken over by the opposition Popular Front the following day. Mutalibov went into hiding, reportedly going to a heart clinic in Moscow. Criminal charges were filed against Mutalibov in November of 1992, and the Azerbaijan government requested his extradition from Russia.

YAKUB MAMEDOV (President, March 6, 1992–May 14, 1992). Yakub Mamedov was the former rector of the Institute of Medicine. He was chairman of the Parliament when Ayaz Mutalibov resigned the presidency. He succeeded Mutalibov as acting president on March 6, 1992, but was ousted by a vote of Parliament on May 14, 1992. The Parliament voted to replace him with Mutalibov, but leaders of the opposition Popular Front took over the presidential palace and installed a ruling National Council on May 19, 1992.

AYAZ N. MUTALIBOV (President, May 14, 1992–May 15, 1992. *See earlier entry under Heads of State.*

ISA GAMBAROV (President, May 15, 1992–June 7, 1992). Isa Gambarov was an orientalist member of the Azerbaijan Popular Front (APF) presidium. He served as acting president of Azerbaijan from May 15, 1992, until elections were held on June 7, 1992.

ABULFAZ ALI ELCHIBEY (President, June 7, 1992–June 18, 1993). Abulfaz Ali Elchibey was born in 1954. He was a leading anti-Communist dissident and the leader of the Azerbaijan Popular Front, which had taken control of the government on May 15, 1992. Elchibey was subsequently elected president by a wide margin. He took office on June 7, 1992. Elchibey's government faced a rebel movement that captured a quarter of the country. Elchibey fled the capital on June 18, 1993, and Geidar Aliyev, the nation's former Communist KGB chief, took executive power in Azerbaijan.

HEADS OF GOVERNMENT

HASAN HASANOV (Premier, December 12, 1991–April 7, 1992). Hasan Aziz ogly Hasanov was an official in the Communist party. He became chairman of the Council of Ministers of Azerbaijan in September of 1990 and retained his position following Azerbaijan's declaration of formal independence. Hasanov was removed from office following the ouster of President Ayaz Mutalibov on April 7, 1992.

FIRUZ MUSTAFAYEV (Premier, April 7, 1992–June 7, 1992). Firuz

Mustafayev replaced Hasan Hasanov as acting premier of Azerbaijan on April 7, 1992. He retained office until elections were held on June 7, 1992.

RAKHIM GUSEYNOV (Premier, June 7, 1992–). Rakhim Guseynov was a member of the Azerbaijan Popular Front. He was selected by the Parliament to serve as Azerbaijan's prime minister on June 7, 1992.

Bahamas, Commonwealth of the

The Bahamas is a group of islands that are located in the Atlantic Ocean, east of Florida. The islands received independence from Great Britain on July 10, 1973.

HEADS OF STATE

SIR MILO BUTLER (Governor-General, August 1, 1973–January 22, 1979). Milo Boughton Butler was born on August 11, 1906. He was educated in the United States and the Bahamas. He served in the Legislative Council and was an early leader of the Progressive Liberal party. Butler served in the cabinet as minister of labour, welfare, agriculture, and fisheries from 1968 until 1972. He was knighted in June of 1973, and on August 1, 1973, he became governor-general of the Bahamas. Butler suffered from poor health in 1976, and most of his duties were delegated to an acting governor-general. He died in Nassau after a long illness on January 22, 1979.

SIR GERALD C. CASH (Governor-General, January 22, 1979–June 25, 1988). Gerald Christopher Cash was born in Nassau on May 28, 1917. He studied law in London and returned to the Bahamas to practice in 1940. Cash also served on various public and private boards before becoming acting governor-general while Sir Milo Butler was ill from 1976 until 1978. He replaced Butler as governor-general on Butler's death on January 22, 1979. Cash retained the largely ceremonial office until June 25, 1988.

SIR HENRY TAYLOR (Governor-General, June 25, 1988–January 2, 1992). Henry Milton Taylor was born on November 4, 1903. He worked as a public school teacher before he entered politics. He was elected to the House of Assembly in 1949. Taylor was the cofounder of the Progressive Liberal party of the Bahamas and served as the party's National Chairman from 1953 until 1964. Taylor was appointed to the post of governor-general on June 25, 1988, and served until January 2, 1992.

SIR CLIFFORD DARLING (Governor-General, January 2, 1992–). Clifford Darling was selected to succeed Sir Henry Taylor as governor-general of the Bahamas on January 2, 1992.

HEADS OF GOVERNMENT

SIR ROLAND SYMONETTE (Prime Minister, January 7, 1964–January 10, 1967). Roland Theodore Symonette was born in the Bahamas on December 16,

1898. He was educated locally and became a leading construction contractor. In 1935 he was elected to the House of Assembly as a member of the United Bahamian party. Symonette served on the party's Executive Council from 1949. He was one of the leaders of the so-called "Bay Street Boys," a group of financiers who opened the Bahamas up to foreign investment, tourism, and gambling. He served as leader of the Bahamian government in the House of Assembly from 1955, and when the Bahamas gained self-rule on January 7, 1964, he served as the new nation's first prime minister. Symonette's minority white government was defeated by Lynden O. Pindling's Progressive Liberal party, and Symonette left office on January 10, 1967. He remained in the House of Assembly as leader of the Opposition until his retirement in 1977. Symonette died of cancer in Nassau on March 13, 1980.

LYNDEN O. PINDLING (Prime Minister, January 10, 1967–August 19, 1992). Lynden Oscar Pindling was born in an impoverished section of Nassau on March 22, 1930. His father ran a small grocery store, and the stable income enabled Pindling to seek an education. He attended the University of London, where he received a degree in law. Pindling returned to Nassau in 1953 and practiced law. He also became involved in politics and joined the Progressive Liberal party. In 1956 he was elected to the House of Assembly. He was instrumental in pressuring the British colonial authorities into reform-

ing election laws that gave the minority white population an unfair advantage in elections. Pindling was reelected to the House of Assembly in 1962 and became chairman of the Progressive Liberal party the following year. Great Britain granted self-rule to the Bahamas in January of 1963. The following year Pindling led his party in a boycott of the House of Assembly. His statements in the Bahamas and at the United Nations prompted the government to call for new elections. The Progressive Liberal party narrowly defeated Symonette's United Bahamian party, and Pindling was sworn in as prime minister on January 16, 1967. Pindling also served as minister of economic affairs from 1969 until 1982 and was minister of defense from 1983 until 1984. He again became minister of economic affairs from 1984. Pindling was accused of having allowed drug smugglers the use of the Bahamas as a transit point. These accusations led to the defeat of his government in the elections of 1992. He relinquished the office of prime minister on August 19, 1992.

HUBERT INGRAHAM (Prime Minister, August 20, 1992–   ). Hubert Ingraham was born in 1947. He was a former protégé of Lyndon Pindling. He went into opposition to Pindling's party and served as leader of the center-right Free National Movement. Ingraham replaced Pindling as prime minister on August 20, 1992, following the defeat of Pindling's party in the elections held the previous day.

Bahrain, State of

(Dawlat al-Bahrayn)

Bahrain is a group of islands located in the western Persian Gulf. It received independence from Great Britain on August 15, 1973.

HEADS OF STATE

SULMAN BIN HAMAD AL-KHALIFAH (Sheikh, February 1, 1941–November 2, 1961). Sulman bin Hamad al-Khalifah was born in 1894. He succeeded his father as the tenth member of the Khalifan dynasty to rule Bahrain on February 1, 1941. During his rule Bahrain grew from a poor Arab state to a wealthy and important oil-producing country. Sheikh Sulman used his country's wealth to improve his people's living conditions by building hospitals and schools and improving roads. His autocratic rule met with some criticism by younger Bahraini who wanted a more democratic form of government and greater independence from Great Britain. Sheikh Sulman died in Bahrain at the age of 67 on November 2, 1961.

ISA IBN SULMAN AL-KHALIFAH (Emir, November 2, 1961–   ). Isa ibn Sulman al-Khalifah was born in Bahrain on July 3, 1933. He was the son of Sheikh Sulman bin Hamad al-Khalifah, the ruler of Bahrain. Sheikh Isa was named heir apparent by his father in 1958. He succeeded as ruler of Bahrain upon his father's death on November 2, 1961. Bahrain was a British protected sheikhdom until August 15, 1971, when it gained complete independence. Sheikh Isa subsequently took the title of emir. Bahrain was faced with threats of disorder from Shi'ite Muslim fundamentalists following the Iranian revolution of 1979. A conspiracy involving the Iranian-backed Bahraini National Liberation Front was uncovered in December of 1981. The government also made numerous arrests following the discovery of a rebel arms cache in February of 1984. Sheikh Isa's government signed a defense cooperation agreement with the United States in October of 1991.

HEADS OF GOVERNMENT

KHALIFAH IBN SULMAN AL-KHALIFAH (Prime Minister, June 2, 1973–   ). Khalifah ibn Sulman al-Khalifah was born in 1935. He was the son of Sheikh Sulman bin Hamad al-Khalifah and the younger brother of Sheikh Isa ibn Sulman al-Khalifah, the current emir of Bahrain. Sheikh Khalifah served as president of the Administrative Council of Bahrain from 1966 until 1970. He then served as president of the State Council from January 19, 1970, until June 2, 1973, when he became his brother's prime minister.

Bangladesh, People's Republic of

(Ganaprojatantri Bangladesh)

Bangladesh is a country located in southern Asia. It received independence from Pakistan on December 16, 1971.

HEADS OF STATE

SHEIKH MUJIBUR RAHMAN (President, April 17, 1971–January 12, 1972). Sheikh Mujibur Rahman was born in Tungipara, in the Faridpur District of India, on March 17, 1920. He was the founder of the East Pakistan Muslim Students' League in the 1950s. In 1959 he was the cofounder of the Awami League, a political organization advocating autonomy for East Pakistan. Sheikh Mujib was imprisoned on several occasions during the administration of Gen. Mohammed Ayub Khan of Pakistan. In the 1970 general election, the Awami League received an overwhelming majority of votes in East Pakistan. Sheikh Mujib was arrested the following year after he initiated a campaign of noncooperation with West Pakistan. Violence erupted in East Pakistan when government troops tried to enforce martial law. At the end of the year, East Pakistan, with the assistance of India, emerged victorious in what had become a civil war. The independent nation of Bangladesh was proclaimed, and on January 12, 1972, Mujib became the first prime minister. He had great difficulty restoring order and economic stability in the war-torn country. Mujib took the office of president and began governing by executive degree on January 25, 1975. Four months later, on August 15, 1975, he and several members of his family were killed in a military coup.

SYED NAZRUL ISLAM (Acting President, April 17, 1971–January 12, 1972). Syed Nazrul Islam was born in 1925. He joined the Awami League in 1953 and became a leading advisor to Sheikh Mujibur Rahman. He served as senior vice president of the Awami League and was acting president of the Bangladesh government-in-exile during Mujib's imprisonment from April of 1971. Nazrul Islam served as minister of industry in the subsequent Mujib govern-ment. He was named vice president of Bangladesh in January of 1975. Following the overthrow of Mujib in August of 1975, he was removed from office and imprisoned. Nazrul Islam was imprisoned in Dhaka jail, where he was murdered along with other prominent political figures on November 3, 1975.

ABU SAYEED CHOWDHURY (President, January 12, 1972–December 24, 1973). Abu Sayeed Chowdhury was born in Tangail, on January 31, 1921. He was educated in Calcutta and London, where he received a degree in law in 1947. He served as a justice on the Dhaka High Court and was on the faculty of Dhaka University during the 1960s. Chowdhury was out of the country when Bangladesh declared its separation from Pakistan. He served as ambassador-at-large for the emerging nation. He returned to Bangladesh following independence and was named president on January 12, 1972. Chowdhury remained in office until December 24, 1973. He returned to government service as minister of foreign affairs in the government of Khandekar Mustaque Ahmed from August to November of 1975. Chowdhury subsequently served as his country's foreign aid coordinator in Geneva. He also became chairman of the United Nations Commission on Human Rights in 1985. Chowdhury died of a heart attack in London on August 1, 1987.

MUHAMMADULLAH (President, December 24, 1973–January 25, 1975). Muhammadullah was born in Saicha on November 21, 1921. He was educated in Dhaka and Calcutta and became a lawyer in 1950. He also joined the Awami League in 1950 and served as secretary of the East Pakistan Awami League from 1952 until 1972. Muhammadullah was elected to the

Provisional Assembly in 1970 and served as speaker of the Bangladesh Constituent Assembly from 1972 until 1973. He was Speaker of the Parliament from 1973 and succeeded Abu Sayeed Chowdhury as president of Bangladesh on December 24, 1973. He remained in office until January 25, 1975, when Sheikh Mujibur Rahman took office under a new presidential system of government. Muhammadullah remained in Mujib's cabinet as minister of land administration and land reform until Mujib's overthrow in August of 1975. He then served as vice president under Khandekar Mustaque Ahmed until November of 1975.

SHEIKH MUJIBUR RAHMAN (President, January 25, 1975–August 15, 1975). *See earlier entry under Heads of State.*

KHANDEKAR MUSTAQUE AHMED (President, August 15, 1975–November 6, 1975). Khandekar Mustaque Ahmed was born in 1918. He was a founding member of the Awami League and was active in the East Pakistani independence movement. Mustaque was elected to the National Assembly in 1970 and the following year served as foreign minister for the Bangladesh provisional government-in-exile. Following Bangladesh's independence in 1972, Mustaque joined the cabinet of Sheikh Mujibur Rahman, where he served as minister of commerce and minister of land revenue. When Mujib was assassinated on August 15, 1975, Mustaque assumed the presidency. He remained in office until November 6, 1975, when he resigned following an abortive coup led by Khalid Musharif. Mustaque broke with the Awami party in 1976 and formed the Democratic Action Committee. He was arrested shortly afterwards and remained imprisoned until 1980. Following his release, he resumed his leadership of the Democratic Action Committee.

ABU SADAT MOHAMMED SAYEM (President, November 6, 1975–April 21, 1977). Abu Sadat Mohammed Sayem was born in 1916. He was a leading lawyer in Bangladesh and served as chief justice of the Supreme Court. On November 6, 1975, he was chosen as a compromise candidate to serve as president of Bangladesh. Sayem also served as minister of defense and foreign affairs in the government. He served as chief martial law administrator until he was replaced by Ziaur Rahman in November of 1976. Sayem resigned the presidency for health reasons on April 21, 1977, and relinquished the position to Ziaur Rahman.

ZIAUR RAHMAN (President, April 21, 1977–May 30, 1981). Ziaur Rahman was born in Bogra on January 19, 1936. He joined the Pakistani army in 1953 and was commissioned two years later. He fought in the Indo-Pakistan War in 1965 and taught at the Pakistan Military Academy from 1966 until 1969. Zia soon became a supporter of the Bengali nationalist movement. He had been promoted to major at the time of East Pakistan's war for independence. He led his forces into rebellion, and in March of 1971, he proclaimed the independence of Bangladesh on a radio broadcast. He organized the First Brigade of the Bangladesh army in the fall of 1971. Following Bangladesh's independence, Zia was named army deputy chief of staff in June of 1972. He was named army chief of staff after the ouster of President Mujibur Rahman in August of 1975. He was subsequently named deputy chief martial law administrator in November of 1975. Zia also served as minister of commerce and foreign trade until 1977 and minister of finance and home affairs until 1978. He became chief martial law administrator in November of 1976. Zia became president of Bangladesh on April 21, 1977, following the resignation of Abu Sadat Mohammed Sayem. He announced plans to hold democratic elections, but was slow to fulfill his promises. He survived a coup attempt in November of 1977. In June of 1978 Bangladesh held a presidential election, and Zia retained office by a wide margin. Though Bangladesh remained one of the world's poorest nations, Zia was given credit for having brought some reforms and stability to the nation. He was assassinated in Chittagong on May 30, 1981, during a coup attempt led by Maj. Gen. Mohammad Manzur Ahmed. The coup was unsuccessful, and the leaders were killed by Zia's guards shortly after their arrest.

ABDUS SATTAR (President, May 30, 1981–March 20, 1982). Abdus Sattar was born in Dhaka in 1906. He was educated at Calcutta University, where he received a degree in law in 1929. He returned to Dhaka in 1947 and was named to the city's high court. Sattar served as East Pakistan's minister of the interior in 1956 and was named to the East Pakistan High Court the following year. He served as Pakistan's chief election commissioner during the elections of 1970. The refusal of the Pakistani government of President Mohammed Yahya Khan to abide by the election results began a war of independence in East Pakistan that resulted in the creation of Bangladesh. Sattar served in various government positions from 1972. He was named special assistant to President Ziaur Rahman in 1977. He was also appointed vice president in June of 1977. Sattar became president of Bangladesh following the assassination of President Ziaur Rahman on May 30, 1981. He was nominated by the ruling Bangladesh Nationalist party to run in the elections in November of 1981. Sattar suffered from poor health and was an inactive leader. He was deposed on March 20, 1982, in a coup led by H. M. Ershad. Sattar died in Dhaka of heart and kidney problems on October 5, 1985.

ABUL FAZAL MOHAMMAD CHOWDHURY (President, March 27, 1982–December 11, 1983). Abul Fazal Mohammad Ahsanuddin Chowdhury was born in Mymensingh in 1915. He was educated at the University of Dhaka and joined the Bengal Civil Service in 1942. He served as a regional district judge, and in 1973 he was elected to the High Court of Bangladesh. He retired from the bench in November of 1977. Chowdhury was named by General Hossain Mohammad Ershad to serve as president of Pakistan on March 27, 1982. He also served as minister of defense and planning until he was replaced by Ershad on December 11, 1983.

HOSSAIN MOHAMMAD ERSHAD (President, December 11, 1983–December 6, 1990). Hossain Mohammad Ershad was born in Rangpur on February 1, 1930. He attended the University of Dhaka and joined the Pakistani army. He served in the East Bengal Regiment until Bangladesh received its independence in 1972. Ershad was promoted to colonel the following year and rose to major general in 1975. He served as deputy chief of staff of the army from 1975 until 1978 and was chief of staff from 1978 until 1986. In March of 1982 he led the military coup against President Abdus Sattar. Ershad declared martial law and appointed himself chief martial law administrator and served as president of the Council of Ministers. He became president of Bangladesh on December 11, 1983. In October of 1986 he was again elected president. Ershad also served as minister of defense from 1986 until 1990 and minister of information from 1986 until 1988. On December 6, 1990, he resigned from office following months of demonstrations. In June of 1991 Ershad was convicted by a special tribunal for possessing illegal firearms and was sentenced to ten years in prison. He was also charged with corruption and abuse of power.

SHAHABUDDIN AHMED (President, December 6, 1990–October 10, 1991). Shahabuddin Ahmed served as chief justice of Bangladesh's Supreme Court. He was selected to serve as interim president by the two major political parties following the ouster of President Hossain Mohammed Ershad on December 6, 1990. He relinquished office to Abdur Rahman Biswas, the victor in legislative elections on October 10, 1991.

ABDUR RAHMAN BISWAS (President, October 10, 1991–). Abdur Rahman Biswas was born in 1926. He was a member of the Bangladesh Nationalist party. He served as Speaker of the House of Assembly until he was elected by the National Parliament to serve as president. He was sworn in as president on October 10, 1991.

HEADS OF GOVERNMENT

TAJUDDIN AHMED (Prime Minister, December 1, 1971–January 12, 1972). Tajuddin Ahmed was born in 1922. He was a close associate of Sheikh Mujibur Rahman prior to Bangladesh's independence. He served as prime minister of Bangladesh's first provisional government from December 1, 1971, until January 12, 1972. Ahmed was a proponent of closer ties with the Soviet Union. He fell out of favor when Sheikh Mujibur began a policy favoring the United States. Ahmed was arrested following the ouster of Sheikh Mujibur in August of 1975. He was murdered in Dhaka jail on November 3, 1975.

SHEIKH MUJIBUR RAHMAN (Prime Minister, January 12, 1972–January 26, 1975). *See entry under Heads of State.*

MOHAMMED MANSOOR ALI (Prime Minister, January 26, 1975–August 15, 1975). Mohammed Mansoor Ali was born in 1919. He was educated as a lawyer and served as president of the Pabna Lawyers Association. From 1946 until 1950 he served as vice president of the Pabna District Muslim League. He joined the Awami League in 1951 and was named to the cabinet of Ataur Rahman Khan in 1956. Mansoor Ali served as the Awami League's vice president from 1969 and subsequently served in Bangladesh's government-in-exile as finance minister. He served in various cabinet positions following Bangladesh's independence in 1971. He was named prime minister in the government of Sheikh Mujibur Rahman on January 26, 1975. Mansoor Ali was deposed with Sheikh Mujibur in a coup on August 15, 1975. He was imprisoned in Dhaka jail, where he was murdered with other high-ranking officials of the Mujib government on November 3, 1975.

ABU SADAT MOHAMMED SAYEM (Prime Minister, August 15, 1975–April 21, 1977). *See entry under Heads of State.*

ZIAUR RAHMAN (Prime Minister, April 21, 1977–March 1, 1979). *See entry under Heads of State.*

SHAH MOHAMMAD AZIZUR RAHMAN (Prime Minister, March 1, 1979–March 24, 1982). Shah Mohammad Azizur Rahman was born in Kushtia on November 23, 1925. He was general secretary of the All-India Muslim Students' Federation from 1945 until 1947. He was active in the Awami League and served as deputy leader of the Opposition in the National Assembly of Pakistan from 1965 until 1969. Following Bangladesh's independence, Rahman served in the House.

He was appointed minister of labor and industrial welfare in 1978 and served until he was named prime minister by President Ziaur Rahman on March 1, 1979. He also served in the government as minister of education. Rahman remained in office until March 24, 1982. He died in 1988.

ATAUR RAHMAN KHAN (Prime Minister, March 30, 1984–January 7, 1985). Ataur Rahman Khan was born in Balia-Dhaka on March 6, 1905. He was a member of the Awami League and was elected to the East Bengal Assembly in 1954. He served as chief minister of East Pakistan from 1956 until 1958, when he was ousted during the coup of Mohammed Ayub Khan. Rahman Khan was leader of the Bangladesh National League and served as leader of the Opposition in Parliament from 1972 until 1975. He was appointed prime minister of Bangladesh by President H. M. Ershad on March 30, 1984, and also held the position of minister of political and parliamentary affairs. He was dismissed by President Ershad on January 7, 1985.

MIZANUR RAHMAN CHOWDHURY (Prime Minister, July 9, 1986–April 27, 1988). Mizanur Rahman Chowdhury was born in Chandpur on October 19, 1928. He attended Feni College and became a teacher. In 1962 he was elected to the Pakistan National Assembly as a member of the Awami League. Chowdhury served as minister of information and broadcasting in Sheikh Mujibur Rahman's first independent government in 1972 and served as minister of relief and rehabilitation in 1973. He remained out of government until 1985, when he was appointed minister of posts and telecommunications. Chowdhury also served as general secretary of the Jatiya Dal party from 1985 until 1986 and led a minority conservative faction of the Awami League. He was named prime minister by President H. M. Ershad on

July 9, 1986. Chowdhury was replaced by Moudud Ahmed on April 27, 1988.

MOUDUD AHMED (Prime Minister, March 27, 1988–August 12, 1989). Moudud Ahmed was born in Noakhali in 1940. He attended Dhaka University and was active in the Bangladesh independence movement. In 1972 he served in the government-in-exile. Following independence, he served as a lawyer in the Bangladesh Supreme Court. Moudud Ahmed was briefly jailed during the 1974 state of emergency. In 1977 he was appointed to lead the Bangladesh delegation to the United Nations General Assembly. He was appointed to the cabinet as minister of communications in 1985 and was named deputy prime minister and minister of industries in July of 1986. Moudud Ahmed served as prime minister from March 27, 1988, until August 12, 1989. He was subsequently named vice president by President Hossain Mohammad Ershad. Moudud Ahmed was removed from office and put under house arrest following Ershad's resignation in December of 1990. He was sentenced to prison in December of 1991.

KAZI ZAFAR AHMED (Prime Minister, August 12, 1989–December 6, 1990). Kazi Zafar Ahmed was born in Cheora on July 1, 1940. He attended Dhaka University and served on the East Pakistan Students Union in the late 1950s and early 1960s. He was imprisoned in Pakistan for nationalist activities in 1963. Zafar Ahmed was active in the independence movement in 1971, and following independence, he worked with the Awami party until 1974. He was then active with the United People's party. In 1978 he was named minister of education and deputy prime minister. Zafar Ahmed served as an advisor to the president and minister of information from 1988 until 1991. He was named prime minister on August 12, 1989, and served until December 6, 1990.

BEGUM KHALEDA ZIA (Prime Minister, March 20, 1991-). Begum Khaleda Zia was born in November of 1944. She was the widow of Ziaur Rahman, who was Bangladesh's president from 1977 until his assassination in May of 1981. She served as leader of the Bangladesh National party and was elected prime minister on March 20, 1991. She also served as minister of defense from December of 1991.

Barbados

Barbados is the easternmost island in the Caribbean Sea. It received independence from Great Britain on November 30, 1966.

HEADS OF STATE

SIR JOHN MONTAGUE STOW (Governor-General, November 30, 1966–March 18, 1967). John Montague Stow was born in 1911. He served as governor of Barbados from 1959. He became Barbados's first governor-general following independence on November 30, 1966. He relinquished the position to Sir Winston Scott on March 18, 1967.

SIR WINSTON SCOTT (Governor-General, March 18, 1967–August 9, 1976). Winston Scott was born in 1900. He was a doctor who dispensed free medical care to the poor in Barbados. He was appointed Barbados's first native-born governor-general on March 18, 1967. Scott retained the largely ceremonial position until his death from a heart attack in Bridgetown on August 9, 1976.

SIR DEIGHTON LISLE WARD (Governor-General, November 17, 1976–January 9, 1984). Deighton Harcourt Lisle Ward was born in Barbados on May 16, 1909. He was educated at Harrison College and received a degree in law. Ward practiced law from 1934. He served as a member of the Barbados Legislative Council from 1955 until 1958. He was then elected to the House of Representatives of the Federation of the West Indies. Ward served until the Federation was dissolved in 1962. He was named to the High Court of Barbados the following year and served until 1976. Ward was named to succeed Sir Winston Scott as governor-general of Barbados on November 17, 1976. He relinquished his office to Sir Hugh Springer upon his retirement on January 9, 1984.

SIR HUGH SPRINGER (Governor-General, February 24, 1984–June 6, 1990). Hugh Worrell Springer was born on June 22, 1913. He was educated in Barbados and Great Britain and became a lawyer in 1939. He served as leader of the Barbados Labor party and was elected to the House of Assembly in 1940. Springer retired from politics in 1947 to join the faculty of the University of the West Indies, where he remained until 1966. He subsequently served on various public and private commissions. On February 24, 1984, he was appointed governor-general of Barbados. He retained the position until his retirement on June 6, 1990.

DAME NITA BARROW (Governor-General, June 6, 1990-). Ruth Nita Barrow was the sister of Errol W. Barrow, the first prime minister of independent Barbados. She was educated in the United States, Great Britain, and Canada and worked as a nurse in Barbados and Jamaica from 1940. She worked for various regional and international medical organizations. Barrow was president of the World Young Women's Christian Association (YWCA) from 1975 until 1983 and served as an advisor on nursing education to the World Health Organization from 1981 until 1986. She was appointed to serve as permanent representative to the United Nations in 1986. Barrow was named governor-general of Barbados on June 6, 1990.

HEADS OF GOVERNMENT

ERROL W. BARROW (Prime Minister, November 30, 1966–September 3, 1976). Errol Walton Barrow was born in St. Lucy on January 21, 1920. He served in the Royal Air Force during World War II and received a law degree in Great Britain. He returned to Barbados and was elected to the House of Assembly in 1951 as a member of the Barbados Labor party. He formed his own Democratic Labor party in 1955 and served as its chairman from 1958. His party won a majority in the 1961 elections, and on December 4, 1961, Barrow became premier of the pre-independence government. His government was dedicated to the diversification of agriculture and the encouragement of tourism. He also pursued the goal of independence for Barbados, which was achieved on November 30, 1966, with Barrow leading the government. He was a leading proponent of the pan-Caribbean movement and a cofounder of the Caribbean Community, which advocated economic cooperation in the area. Barrow's party was defeated in 1976, and he was replaced as prime minister on September 3, 1976. He remained as chairman of the Democratic Labor party and was a critic of United States intervention in the Caribbean, particularly in Grenada in 1983. Barrow was again elected prime minister on May 29, 1986. He suffered from poor health during his last year of office and died in Bridgetown on June 1, 1987.

J.M.G. "TOM" ADAMS (Prime Minister, September 3, 1976–March 11, 1985). John Michael Geoffrey Manningham "Tom" Adams was born in Spooners Hill, on September 24, 1931. He was the son of Sir Grantley Adams, who served as Barbados's first premier from 1954 until 1958 and was subsequently prime minister of the West Indies Federation until 1962. Tom Adams studied law at Oxford University in Great Britain. He worked at the BBC and as a lawyer in Great Britain before returning to Barbados in 1962. He entered politics as a member of the Barbados Labor party and became party leader in 1971. Adams led the party to victory in 1973 and succeeded Errol W. Barrow as prime minister on September 3, 1976. He also served as minister of finance and planning. He was a strong supporter of the Eastern Caribbean Security Alliance, which was backed by the United States. He also was an early backer of United States's intervention in Grenada in 1983. Adams remained prime minister until his sudden death from a heart attack in Bridgetown on March 11, 1985.

BERNARD ST. JOHN (Prime Minister, March 11, 1985–May 29, 1986). (Harold) Bernard St. John was born in Christ Church on August 16, 1931. He was educated at the University of London, where he studied law. He returned to Barbados in 1954 and joined the Barbados Labor party in 1959. St. John was elected to the Senate in 1964 and served until his election to the House of Assembly in 1966. He served as leader of the Barbados Labor party from 1970 until he was defeated for reelection in 1971. He campaigned successfully for a Senate seat and remained there until his return to the House of Assembly in 1976. St. John was appointed minister of trade, tourism, and industry in the government of Tom Adams in 1976. He was named deputy prime minister in 1985 and succeeded to the office of prime minister following the death of Tom Adams on March 11, 1985. St. John's Barbados Labor party was defeated in the elections of 1986. St. John relinquished the office of prime minister on May 29, 1986, and retired from politics.

ERROL W. BARROW (Prime Minister, May 29, 1986–June 1, 1987). *See earlier entry under Heads of Government.*

ERSKINE SANDIFORD (Prime Minister, June 1, 1987–). Lloyd Erskine Sandiford was born on March 24, 1937. He was educated in Barbados and the University of the West Indies in Jamaica. He later attended the University of Manchester in Great Britain, where he received a degree in economics. Sandiford returned to Barbados as a teacher before entering politics as an assistant to Prime Minister Errol Barrow in 1966. He was appointed to the Senate in 1967 and was named Minister of Education. He won a seat in the House of Assembly in 1971 and remained in the cabinet as minister of education, youth affairs, community development, and sport. In 1975 Sandiford was appointed minister of health and welfare, and he held this office until the Democratic Labor party was defeated in 1976. He remained in the House of Assembly as a member of the Opposition. When Barrow was returned as prime minister in 1986, Sandiford was appointed deputy prime minister and minister of education and culture. He succeeded to the office of prime minister when Barrows died on June 1, 1987. Sandiford retained office following elections in January of 1991, though the Democratic Labor party received a reduced majority.

Belarus, Republic of

(Respublika Belarus)

Belarus is a country located in eastern Europe. It was granted independence following the breakup of the Soviet Union on December 25, 1991.

HEAD OF STATE

STANISLAS SHUSHKEVICH (President, December 25, 1991–). Stanislas S. Shushkevich was born in 1934. He was a member of the Communist party and became involved in politics in 1986. He was elected a member of the Supreme Soviet in 1990. The Belorussian Soviet Socialist Republic declared its independence on August 25, 1991. Shushkevich was elected chairman of the Supreme Soviet on September 18, 1991, to succeed Nicholai Dementei. Belorussia changed its name to the Republic of Belarus following Shushkevich's election. Belarus joined the Commonwealth of Independent States in December of 1991 with Shushkevich as president.

HEAD OF GOVERNMENT

VYACHESLAV KEBICH (Premier, December 25, 1991–). Vyacheslav Kebich was born on June 10, 1936. He was appointed chairman of the Council of Ministers of Byelorussia on April 7, 1990, succeeding Mikhail Kovalev. Kebich became the first chairman of the Council of Ministers of the Republic of Belarus following independence in December of 1991.

Belgium, Kingdom of

(Royaume de Belgique)

Belgium is a country located in northwestern Europe. It was granted independence from the Netherlands on October 4, 1830.

HEADS OF STATE

LEOPOLD III (King, February 17, 1934–July 16, 1951). Leopold was born in Brussels on November 3, 1901. He was the elder son of Albert I and Princess Elizabeth of Bavaria. Albert I ascended to the Belgian throne in 1909, and Leopold became crown prince. Leopold was allowed to join the Belgian army as a private during World War I. He was sent to Eton College in England after six months of fighting on the front lines. Following the war and the completion of his education, Leopold accompanied his parents on state visits around the world. King Albert I was killed in a fall from a cliff while mountain climbing on February 17, 1934, and Leopold was proclaimed king six days later. Leopold's wife, Queen Astrid, whom he married in 1926, was killed in an automobile accident in Switzerland in August of 1935. Leopold was faced with a growing autonomy movement in the country. He also tried to pursue a policy of neutrality as World War II grew near. He withdrew Belgium from the Locarno Pact with Great Britain and France in the hopes that he could maintain peace with Germany. His hopes were in vain, as the German army invaded Belgium on May 10, 1940. King Leopold led the Belgian army in fighting against the German invaders, but was forced to surrender on May 28, 1940. He and his family were taken prisoner by the occupation forces. They were held in the palace of Laeken, where Leopold married Liliane Baels, a commoner, in 1942. The royal family was moved to Germany in March of 1944, where they remained until their liberation by United States troops the following May. Leopold's brother Charles had been appointed regent in Leopold's absence in 1944. Leopold did not return to Belgium following his release because of public criticism of his unconditional surrender to the Germans. He went to Switzerland instead, where he remained until a plebiscite was held in March of 1950 to determine if he could reclaim the throne. The vote narrowly approved Leopold's return to Belgium. He returned to Brussels on July 22, 1950, despite the continued opposition of the Walloon community. He was met with strikes, protests, and riots upon his return. In order to ease the tension his return caused, Leopold delegated many of his royal powers to his son, Baudouin, on August 11, 1950. He abdicated in favor of Baudouin on July 16, 1951. Leopold continued to live at the royal palace, Laeken, until 1959. He remained a close advisor and confidant to his son. He died after a heart attack in Brussels on September 25, 1983, at the age of 81.

CHARLES (Regent, September 20, 1944–July 22, 1950). Charles Theodore Henri Antoin Meinrad, Count of Flanders, was born in Brussels on October 10, 1903. He was the second son of Albert I, the future king of Belgium. He spent the years during World War I in England and completed his education in Belgium following the conclusion of the war. Charles was trained in the Belgian army and the British Royal Navy. He also had an interest in engineering and traveled to the United States to work with Thomas Edison in 1931. He toured the United States incognito before his return to Belgium. When Germany occupied Belgium in 1940, Charles was held with the rest of the royal family. He secretly worked with the Belgian Resistance during the war. In June of 1944 Charles's brother, King Leopold, was sent to Germany, and Charles escaped from his captors. When the Belgian government returned to Brussels following the retreat of the Germans, Charles was named regent in his brother's stead on September 20, 1944. Charles retained the regency following the end of World War II, as sentiment in Belgium was critical of King Leopold's actions during the war. Leopold was allowed to resume the throne on July 22, 1950, following a plebiscite, and Charles withdrew to his seaside home in Ostend. Charles's relationship with his family was strained by his support for Leopold's subsequent abdication. Charles lived in seclusion, sometimes painting under the name of Karel van Vlaanderen. He experienced financial difficulties in 1981 and lost most of his money after a dispute with his business advisors. He was forced to auction off many of his personal belongings. Charles died in Ostend on June 1, 1983.

BAUDOUIN (King, July 16, 1951–July 31, 1993). Baudouin Albert Charles Leopold Axel Marie Gustave was born at the Palace of Laeken on September 7, 1930. He was the oldest son of the future King Leopold. Baudouin's father ascended to the throne in 1933, and Baudouin became crown prince and duke of Brabant. Baudouin's mother, Queen Astrid, was killed in an auto accident the following year. The crown prince received a royal education, with half of his classes being held in French and the other half in Flemish. The royal family was held prisoner by the Germans following Belgium's surrender in 1940. Baudouin and his family were liberated by the Allies in May of 1945. He subsequently accompanied his father to Switzerland because of the opposition to Leopold's return to the throne. Leopold was allowed to resume the throne in 1950 on the condition that he relinquish most of his powers to the crown prince. Baudouin became prince royal of Belgium and chief of state on August 11, 1950. Leopold abdicated the throne on July 16, 1951, and Baudouin was crowned king. Baudouin was a competent and popular monarch who ruled in a low-key fashion. He remained scrupulously neutral in regard to the Walloon and Flemish factions of the country. He married Fabiola de Mora y Aragon, a member of the Spanish nobility, in 1960. Baudouin faced a constitutional crisis in April of 1989 when the Parliament passed legislation that legalized abortion. The king informed the ministers that he could not sign the bill in good conscience. The crisis was resolved when the Council of Ministers ruled that Baudouin was unable to govern. They were then able to enact the measure into law. Parliament was convened the following day, and Baudouin's royal powers were returned to him. Baudouin remained King of Belgium until his death from a heart attack on July 31, 1993, while vacationing in Motril, in southern Spain. He was succeeded to the throne by his brother, Prince Albert.

HEADS OF GOVERNMENT

HUBERT PIERLOT (Prime Minister, February 9, 1939–February 7, 1945). Hubert Pierlot was born in Cugnon on December 23, 1883. He studied law at the University of Louvair and became one of Belgium's most prominent lawyers. He served in the Belgian army during World War I and entered politics in 1919 as a member of the Catholic party. Pierlot was elected to the Senate in 1926 and was named minister of the interior in 1934. He was elected president of the Catholic party in 1936 and became minister of agriculture. He was elected prime minister on February 9, 1939, and also served as foreign minister from April of 1939 until January of 1940. Following the German invasion of Belgium in 1940, Pierlot fled to France. He made his way to London, where he set up a government-in-exile during the occupation. After the liberation in September of 1944, he returned to Brussels. When Pierlot tried to disband Resistance groups that had fought during the occupation, he faced political problems. He was forced to ban marches and public gatherings following a period of violent demonstrations. His government survived a general strike in December of 1944. Pierlot resigned on February 7, 1945, after requesting more assistance from the Allied powers. He retired from active politics and was later made a count by the Belgian government. Pierlot died in Brussels on December 13, 1963, at the age of 79.

ACHILLE VAN ACKER (Prime Minister, February 11, 1945–February 17, 1946). Achille Van Acker was born in Bruges on April 8, 1898. He served in the army during World War I and sub-sequently entered politics. He was elected to the Bruges City Council in 1926 and entered Parliament as a Socialist member the following year. Van Acker remained in Belgium during the German occupation in 1940. He served as a Resistance leader and helped to organize the Socialist party. He was appointed minister of labor and social welfare following the liberation of Belgium in September of 1944. Van Acker formed a coalition government on February 11, 1945, following the resignation of Prime Minister Hubert Pierlot. He began the task of rebuilding Belgium's damaged economy and reviving coal production. Following parliamentary elections, Van Acker resigned as prime minister on February 17, 1946. The regent asked Christian-Social party leader de Schrijver to form a cabinet, but he was unable to do so. Van Acker returned to office on March 31, 1946, when a brief government headed by Paul-Henri Spaak was unable to win a vote of confidence. Van Acker's next government was also short-lived and collapsed on July 9, 1946, over the question of prosecution of wealthy Belgians who were economic collaborators with Germany during the war. Van Acker again served as prime minister from April 22, 1954. He retained the position until his Socialist-Liberal coalition was defeated by the Social Christian party in the elections in June of 1958. He was replaced by Gaston Eyskens on June 25, 1958. Van Acker was subsequently elected Speaker of the Lower House of Parliament. He retained that position until his retirement in 1974. He died of cancer in Bruges on July 10, 1975.

PAUL-HENRI SPAAK (Prime Minister, March 11, 1946–March 20, 1946). Paul-Henri Spaak was born in Schaerbeek on January 25, 1899. He came from a wealthy and politically active family. He was captured by the Germans during World War I and spent two years in a prison camp. Spaak attended the Université Libre de Bruzelles after the war and received a degree in law. During the 1920s he joined the Socialist party and led rallies and demonstrations. He was elected to the Belgian Chamber of Representatives in 1932 and became the leader of the Socialist party's left wing. Spaak was named minister of transport and communications in 1935 and became foreign minister in the cabinet of his uncle, Paul-Emile Janson, the following year. Spaak became prime minister on May 15, 1938, and served until February 9, 1939. He was appointed foreign minister again in September of that year. During the German occupation, he escaped to London and served as foreign minister in the government-in-exile. Spaak returned to Belgium after the liberation and was named deputy premier in February of 1945. As head of the Belgian delegation to the United Nations Conference in San Francisco in April of 1945, he helped draft the UN charter. He served as the first president of the United Nations General Assembly in 1946. Spaak was asked to form a government on March 11, 1946, but resigned several days later on March 20, 1946, when a vote of confidence resulted in a tie. He was again named prime minister on March 19, 1947. Spaak agreed to the formation of a customs union between Belgium, the Netherlands, and Luxembourg that became known as Benelux. The Social Christian party secured an absolute majority in the elections in June of 1949, and Spaak relinquished the post of prime minister on June 28, 1949. He served as foreign minister in several subsequent cabinets and was instrumental in the creation of the European Common Market in March of 1957. He resigned as foreign minister in May of 1957 to serve as secretary-general of the North Atlantic Treaty Organization (NATO). Spaak resigned from NATO in March of 1961 and returned to serve Belgium as foreign minister the following month. He was a supporter of Britain's entry into the Common Market and was highly critical of France's veto of the move in 1963. He was also instrumental in easing tensions between Belgium and its former African colony, the Congo. Spaak retired as foreign minister in July of 1966 and joined an industrial firm as an international advisor. He became ill while vacationing in the Azores in July of 1972 and returned to Brussels, where he died of a kidney ailment at the age of 73 on July 31, 1972.

ACHILLE VAN ACKER (Prime Minister, March 31, 1946–July 9, 1946). *See earlier entry under Heads of Government.*

CAMILLE HUYSMANS (Prime Minister, August 1, 1946–March 19, 1947). Camille Huysmans was born in Bilsen on May 26, 1871. He studied philosophy at the University of Liege and taught briefly. He became active in the Socialist movement and served as secretary of the Socialist International from 1905 until 1922. Huysmans also began writing for Socialist newspapers prior to World War I. In 1910 he was elected to the Chamber of Deputies, and following World War I, he helped organize the Socialist party in Antwerp. He was also elected mayor of Antwerp and served as president of the Chamber of Deputies prior to World War II. During the German occupation Huysmans escaped to London. He returned to Belgium following the liberation and was called upon to form a coalition government on August 1, 1946. Huysmans's government survived until March 19, 1947. He served as minister of education in the subsequent government of

Paul-Henri Spaak. Huysmans remained active in Socialist politics for the remainder of his life. He died at the age of 96 in Antwerp on February 25, 1968.

PAUL HENRI SPAAK (Prime Minister, March 19, 1947–June 28, 1949). *See earlier entry under Heads of Government.*

GASTON EYSKENS (Prime Minister, August 10, 1949–June 8, 1950). Gaston Eyskens was born in Lierre on April 1, 1905. He was educated at the University of Louvain, as well as at universities in Great Britain, Switzerland, and the United States. He received a master's degree from Columbia University before he returned to the University of Louvain to join the law school faculty in 1931. Eyskens joined the Ministry of Labor in 1934, and he was named counselor to the Ministry of Economic Affairs in 1937. He was elected to the Parliament as a member of the Social Christian party in 1939. He was appointed to the cabinet as minister of finance in 1945. Eyskens became deputy premier in the Belgian government in 1947, and on August 10, 1949, he led a Social Christian–Liberal coalition government as prime minister. The government collapsed over the issue of the possible restoration of King Leopold to the throne of Belgium. Eyskens relinquished his position on June 8, 1950, and returned to the Ministry of Finance. He again became prime minister on June 25, 1958, following a victory by the Social Christian party in the elections. Eyskens promoted an unpopular economic austerity program in 1961, and his party was defeated in the subsequent elections. On March 27, 1961, Eyskens stepped down, again becoming finance minister. He was again called upon to form a government on June 12, 1968. Belgium was faced with a divisive problem, with the Dutch-speaking Flemish majority seeking cultural autonomy and the French-speaking Walloon minority wanting economic

decentralization. Eyskens's Social Christian–Socialist government collapsed on November 22, 1972, over the question of a constitutional amendment providing for regionalization of the country. In 1973 Eyskens became president of the Kredietbank in Brussels. He died in Louvain on January 3, 1988.

JEAN DUVIEUSART (Prime Minister, June 8, 1950–August 15, 1950). Jean Duvieusart was born in Frasnes-lez-Gosselies on April 10, 1900. He received a law degree from the University of Louvain in 1922. He entered politics and was elected mayor of Frasnes-lez-Gosselies. From 1933 until 1936 he also served on the Hainaut Provisional Council. Duvieusart was elected to the Chamber of Representatives in 1944 and was named to the cabinet as minister of economic affairs in March of 1947. He was asked to form a government by Charles, the prince regent, on June 8, 1950. Duvieusart sponsored a bill designed to end the regency and return Leopold to the Belgian throne. Upon passage of the bill, he flew to Switzerland to accompany King Leopold back to Belgium. Duvieusart subsequently resigned as prime minister on August 15, 1950. He returned to the cabinet in 1952 as minister of economic affairs and served until 1954. Duvieusart later was president of the European Parliament from 1964 until 1965. He returned to the Belgian political scene in 1968 as founder of the Walloon Rally party that advocated a Federal Belgian State. He died at the age of 77 on October 11, 1977.

JOSEPH PHOLIEN (Prime Minister, August 15, 1950–January 15, 1952). Joseph Pholien was born in Liege on December 28, 1884. He attended the University of Brussels, where he received a degree in law in 1906. His law practice was interrupted during World War I, when he fought in the Belgian army. After the war he became a prominent lawyer. Pholien was elected to the Belgian Senate as a member of the Christian Social party in 1936. He rejoined the army during the German invasion of Belgium in 1940. Following the surrender of King Leopold, Pholien drafted the document that gave legitimacy to the Belgian government-in-exile. He remained in Belgium during the occupation and worked with the Resistance. He was arrested by the Germans on several occasions and sought refuge with the Belgian underground as the war drew to a close. Pholien returned to the Senate following the liberation of Belgium. He was a supporter of the unconditional return of King Leopold to the Belgian throne. He was asked to form a government as prime minister on August 15, 1950. Pholien retained office until January 15, 1952, when he was compelled by his own party to resign because of dissatisfaction with the economic policies of his government. He returned to the Senate, where he remained until his retirement in 1961. On January 4, 1968, he died at his home in Brussels at the age of 83.

JEAN VAN HOUTTE (Prime Minister, January 15, 1952–April 22, 1954). Baron Jean Van Houtte was born in Ghent on March 17, 1907. He attended Ghent University, where he received a degree in law in 1929. He began a successful law practice, and in 1931 he also began teaching at Liege University, where he was appointed professor of economics in 1936. Van Houtte also took a similar position at the University of Ghent. In 1944 he joined the Ministry of the Interior, and in 1946 was appointed a member of the Higher Board of Finance. He held several other government positions before his election to the Belgian Senate as a member of the Christian Social Party in July of 1949. Van Houtte was named minister of finance in the cabinet of Joseph Pholien in August of 1950. Van Houtte was asked to succeed Pholien as

prime minister on January 15, 1952. The Christian Social party lost its majority in the elections of 1954, and Van Houtte relinquished his office on April 22, 1954. He returned to the cabinet as minister of finance in 1958 and served until 1961. He also served as minister of state in 1966. Van Houtte died in the early 1990s.

ACHILLE VAN ACKER (Prime Minister, April 22, 1954–June 25, 1958). *See earlier entry under Heads of Government.*

GASTON EYSKENS (Prime Minister, June 25, 1958–March 27, 1961). *See earlier entry under Heads of Government.*

THÉO LEFÈVRE (Prime Minister, April 25, 1961–June 27, 1965). Théodore Joseph Alberic Marie Lefèvre was born in Ghent on January 17, 1914. He attended the University of Ghent, where he received a law degree in 1937. He served in the Belgian army before the German occupation of the country in 1940. Lefèvre continued to fight against the Germans in the Resistance movement during the war. After the liberation of Belgium, Lefèvre was instrumental in the founding of the Social Christian party. He was elected to the Chamber of Representatives in the Belgian Parliament in 1946. He became president of the Social Christian party in 1950. Lefèvre was named minister of state in the government of Gaston Eyskens in 1958. He was asked to form a government following the elections of 1961, and he formed a coalition with the Socialist party on April 25, 1961. His government tackled a series of reforms, including the tax and social security systems. Lefèvre also tried to settle the dispute between the French- and Dutch-speaking areas of Belgium. His reform measure led to a doctors' strike in April of 1964. His coalition collapsed after the elections of 1965, and he left office on June 27,

1965. Lefèvre left politics until 1968, when he was named minister of science in the government of Gaston Eyskens. He also served as president of the European Space Conference. He lost his position in the Eyskens cabinet in 1972. Lefèvre died of cancer in Brussels at the age of 59 on September 18, 1973.

PIERRE C.J.M. HARMEL (Prime Minister, July 28, 1965–March 19, 1966). Pierre Charles José Marie Harmel was born in Brussels on March 16, 1911. He attended the University of Louvain, where he received a doctorate of law. He joined the faculty of the University of Liege as a law professor. Harmel joined the Belgian Chritian Youth Movement in the late 1930s and served as its president. He was elected to the Parliament from Liegen in 1946 and was instrumental in the formation of the Social Christian party. In 1949 he was a member of the Belgian delegation to the United Nations, and from 1949 unto 1950, he served as vice-chairman of the Belgian House of Representatives. Harmel was appointed to the cabinet as minister of national education in 1950 and served until 1954. He was appointed minister of justice in 1958 and later in the year was named minister of cultural affairs. He remained in that position until 1960, when he became minister of civil service until 1961. On July 28, 1965, Harmel became prime minister of Belgium and he served until March 19, 1966. He then served as minister of foreign affairs until 1973, when he was elected president of the Senate. He retired from the Senate in 1977.

PAUL VANDEN BOEYNANTS (Prime Minister, March 19, 1966–June 12, 1968). Paul Vanden Boeynants was born on May 22, 1919. He was educated at Saint-Michel College and was elected to the Chamber of Representatives in 1949. He was elected chairman of the Social Christian party in 1961, and on March 19, 1966, he became prime minister as the head of a coalition Social Christian–Liberal government. The major parties all lost seats in the elections of 1968, and Vanden Boeynants was unable to form a new government. He stepped down from office on June 12, 1968. He became minister of state the following year and was named minister of defense in 1972. On October 20, 1978, Vanden Boeynants formed an interim government following the resignation of Leo Tindemans. He remained as head of a caretaker government until elections could be held in 1979. On April 3, 1979, he relinquished office. He subsequently served as deputy prime minister until 1981. Vanden Boeynants was accused of tax fraud and forgery in 1986 and was given a three-year suspended sentence. He was kidnapped in January of 1989 and was held for a month until his family paid a multimillion-dollar ransom for his release.

GASTON EYSKENS (Prime Minister, June 12, 1968–November 22, 1972). *See earlier entry under Heads of Government.*

EDMOND LEBURTON (Prime Minister, January 26, 1973–January 19, 1974). Edmond Jules Isidore Leburton was born in Waremme on April 18, 1915. He attended Liege University and received a degree in social and political science. He worked with the Ministry of State Insurance before he was elected as a Socialist member of the House of Representatives in 1946. Leburton was elected mayor of Waremme the following year. In 1954 he was named to the cabinet as minister of public health, and he remained in that post until 1958. He served as minister of social security from 1961 until 1965 and served as minister of economic affairs in the government of Gaston Eyskens from 1969 until 1971. Leburton was then elected national chairman of the Socialist party. He was appointed to replace Eyskens as head of a three-party coalition government on January 26, 1973. His government resigned on January 19, 1974, following the collapse of plans for the construction of a Belgian-Iranian oil refinery. Leburton remained in the House of Representatives until 1981 and served as Speaker from 1977 until 1979.

LÉO TINDEMANS (Prime Minister, April 25, 1974–October 20, 1978). Léo Tindemans was born in Zwijndrecht on April 16, 1922. He was educated at the University of Ghent and the Catholic University of Louvain. He subsequently worked in the Ministry of Agriculture. Tindemans was elected national secretary-general of the Social Christian party in 1958. Tindemans was elected to the House of Representatives in 1961 and also served as mayor of Edegem from 1965. He was appointed to the cabinet as minister of community relations in June of 1968. Tindemans retained that position until he was named minister of agriculture in January of 1972. The government collapsed in November of 1972, and Tindemans became deputy prime minister and minister of the budget in the subsequent government of Edmond Leburton in January of 1973. When Leburton resigned in January of 1974, Tindemans was named prime minister-designate. Following the elections in March of 1974 he formed a Social Christian–Liberal minority government on April 25, 1974. He instituted a plan of economic austerity to help ease Belgium's economic problems and he received a vote of confidence in the elections of April of 1977. Tindemans reorganized his government in a four-party coalition with the Social Christian and Socialist parties and two smaller federalist parties. On October 20, 1978, he resigned because the Flemish wing of his own party refused to back his plan to divide Belgium into three linguistic regions. He served as minister of foreign affairs from 1981 until 1989, when he was elected to the European Parliament. He was elected president of the Group of European People's party in the European Parliament in 1992.

PAUL VANDEN BOEYNANTS (Prime Minister, October 20, 1978–April 3, 1979). *See earlier entry under Heads of Government.*

WILFRIED MARTENS (Prime Minister, April 3, 1979–April 6, 1981). Wilfried Martens was born in Sleidinge on April 19, 1936. He was educated at the University of Louvain, where he received a degree in law. In 1960 he began a legal practice and became politically active. Martens joined the Christian People's party in 1962 and in 1965 became an advisor to the cabinet of Prime Minister Pierre Harmel. He retained that position in the subsequent government of Paul Vanden Boeynants. From 1968 until 1972 he served in the Ministry of Community Relations. Martens was elected chairman of the Christian People's party in 1972 and won a seat in the House of Representatives two years later. On April 3, 1979, he was asked by King Baudouin to form a government as prime minister. Belgium was plagued with rising unemployment and budgetary problems in 1981. Martens proposed an economic plan which was rejected by the Socialist members of the government. Martens resigned on April 6, 1981. General elections in November of 1981 produced no clear winner, and Martens returned to lead a coalition government as prime minister on December 17, 1981. He introduced legislation designed to grant regional autonomy in Belgium but had difficulty in negotiating its passage. Martens's government collapsed in November of 1991, and he offered his resignation to King Baudouin. The king requested he remain as caretaker prime minister until a successor could be selected. Martens relinquished the office to Jean-Luc Dehaene on March 7, 1992.

MARK EYSKENS (Prime Minister, April 6, 1981–December 17, 1981). Mark Eyskens was born on April 29, 1933, in Louvain. He was the son of Gaston Eyskens, the former Belgian prime minister. He attended the Louvain Catholic University where he received degrees in law, economics, and philosophy. Eyskens also attended Columbia University in New York and received a master's degree in economics in 1957. After returning to Belgium, he joined the faculty of the Louvain Catholic University. He joined the staff of the minister of finance as an economic advisor in 1962 and remained there until 1965. Eyskens remained active in politics, and in April of 1977 he was elected to Parliament. He was named secretary of state for Flemish regional economy in October of 1976 and served until June of 1977, when he was appointed secretary of state for the budget. The following month he was also named chairman of the European Economic Community Council of Budget Ministers. In April of 1979 he was appointed minister of cooperation and development and served as minister of finance from October 1980. Eyskens was asked to replace Wilfried Martens and form a government as prime minister on April 6, 1981.

Eyskens's government was brief, and he was replaced by Martens on December 17, 1981. He remained in the new Martens government as minister of economics until November of 1985, when he again served as minister of finance. Eyskens left the cabinet in May of 1988, but returned as foreign minister in June of 1989.

WILFRIED MARTENS (Prime Minister, December 17, 1981–March 7, 1992). *See earlier entry under Heads of Government.*

JEAN-LUC DEHAENE (Prime Minister, March 7, 1992–). Jean-Luc Dehaene was born in Montpellier on August 7, 1940. He attended the University of Namur and, upon graduation, entered government service. He became a member of the Christian People's party and worked in various government offices from 1972. In 1981 he was appointed minister of social affairs and institutional reforms. In 1988 Dehaene was named deputy prime minister under Wilfried Martens and also served as minister of communications and institutional reforms. He was selected prime minister to succeed Martens on March 7, 1992.

Belize

Belize is located on the northeastern coast of Central America. It was granted independence from Great Britain on September 21, 1981.

HEAD OF STATE

DAME MINITA GORDON (Governor General, September 21, 1981–). Dame Elmira Minita Gordon holds a doctorate in sociology. She was named the first governor-general of Belize following independence on September 21, 1981, and succeeded Governor James P. I. Hennessy.

HEADS OF GOVERNMENT

GEORGE CADLE PRICE (Prime Minister, September 21, 1981–December 17, 1984). George Cadle Price was born in Belize, formerly British Honduras, on January 15, 1919. He was elected to the Belize City Council in 1947. He became a founding member of the People's United party in 1950 and served as its chairman from 1956. In 1954 Price was elected to the Legislative Council and he was elected mayor of Belize City two years later and served until 1962. He was also elected first minister in 1961 and led the delegation that negotiated self-rule from Great Britain. He became premier in 1964, and on September 21, 1981, he was elected prime minister and minister of foreign affairs. Price remained in office until his party was defeated and he was replaced on December 17, 1984. He was reelected prime minister on November 7, 1989.

MANUEL ESQUIVEL (Prime Minister, December 17, 1984–November 7, 1989). Manuel Esquivel was born in Belize City on May 2, 1940. He was educated in the United States and Great Britain. He entered politics and joined the United Democratic party in 1973. Esquivel served as chairman of the party from 1976 and was elected to the Senate in 1979. He led his party to victory and became prime minister on December 17, 1984. He retained that position until November 7, 1989, and subsequently became leader of the Opposition.

GEORGE CADLE PRICE (Prime Minister, November 7, 1989–). *See earlier entry under Heads of Government.*

Benin, Republic of

(République du Bénin)

Benin, formerly known as Dahomey, is a country located on the western coast of Africa. It was granted independence from France on August 1, 1960.

HEADS OF STATE

HUBERT MAGA (President, August 1, 1960–October 28, 1963). Hubert Coutoucou Maga was born in Parakou, in north Dahomey, in 1916. He was educated in Dahomey and at the William Ponty School in Dakar, Senegal. He returned to Dahomey to teach in 1935 and became headmaster of his school in 1945. Two years later he was elected to the Dahomey General Council, and the following year he was elected to the Grand Council of French West Africa. In 1951 Maga was selected to represent Dahomey in the French National Assembly. He allied himself with the Indépendants d'Outre Mer party, and in November of 1957 he was appointed secretary of state for labor in the government of Premier Felix Gaillard of France. He remained in that position until May of 1958. Maga joined with Sourou-Migan Apithy in rejecting Dahomey's participation in a proposed Mali Federation. He served as labor minister in Apithy's subsequent government. On May 22, 1959, he replaced Apithy as prime minister. Maga served in this position until August 1, 1960, when he became the first president of Dahomey. His first administration was marred by fiscal irresponsibility, including the construction of an extravagant presidential palace. Maga's regime was beset with protests, primarily from student and trade union groups in southern Dahomey. The internal situation in Dahomey continued to deteriorate until October 28, 1963, when General Christophe Soglo, the army commander, took control of the government. Maga was placed under house arrest in December of 1963 and was charged with embezzlement of public funds. He was not prosecuted, however, and in September of 1965 he was ordered released by President Ahomadegbé. Following General Soglo's second coup in December of 1965, Maga went into exile in Paris, where he remained for the next five years. In 1968, while still in exile, he sponsored a successful boycott of the elections scheduled by the military government. Maga was invited to return to Dahomey and participate in the elections in 1970. He won a massive victory, though the election was voided by the ruling junta. After the northern region of Dahomey threatened to secede, a government council was agreed upon. Maga, Apithy, and Justin Ahomadegbé formed a presidential council, with Maga becoming the first chairman on April 7, 1970. Maga's second presidential term was again marred by financial mismanagement, but a relatively stable economy prevented any massive protests. The government was threatened by several failed military plots, but Maga remained in office until his term expired on May 7, 1972. He then relinquished the chairmanship to Ahomadegbé. In October of 1972 the council was overthrown by a military coup led by Mathieu Kérékou,

and Maga was again arrested. He was held at a military camp in Parakou but was finally released in 1981.

CHRISTOPHE SOGLO (President, October 28, 1963–January 19, 1964). Christophe Soglo was born on June 28, 1912, in Abomey. A member of the Fon tribe, he joined the French army in 1931. He served in Morocco during World War II and fought with the Allies in southern France. Rising to the rank of lieutenant, he was appointed military advisor in the Ministry for French Overseas Territories in 1947. Soglo was promoted to the rank of captain and fought in French Indochina. He received the Croix de Guerre in 1956. Now a major, he served in Senegal until 1960, when he returned to Dahomey to serve as army chief of staff in the independent government of President Hubert Maga. On October 28, 1968, Soglo overthrew the Maga government following a period of civil disorder. He relinquished control of the government to Sorou-Migan Apithy and Justin Ahomadegbé on January 19, 1964. He was promoted to general by the new government. On November 29, 1965, Soglo ousted Apithy and Ahomadegbé because the two men were unable to govern in tandem. He then installed Tairou Congacou as president. Congacou served until December 22, 1965, when Soglo took over the reins of government himself after Congacou was unable to form a viable government. Soglo remained in power until December 17, 1967, when he was ousted in another military coup. He went into exile in France, where in 1969 he was involved in discussions that led to the return of Maga, Apithy, and Ahomadegbé to Dahomey the following year. Soglo remained in retirement in France. He died on October 1, 1983.

SOROU-MIGAN APITHY (President, January 19, 1964–November 29, 1965). Sorou-Migan Apithy was born on April 8, 1913, to a Goun family in

Porto Novo. He attended school in Dahomey and France and received a degree in accounting from the Paris National School of Economic and Social Organization. He remained in France until 1945, when he was elected to represent Dahomey in the Constituent Assembly. The following year Apithy was elected to the National Assembly, where he remained until 1958. He was a member of various political parties in France and Dahomey during his term of office. In 1951 he founded the Republican party of Dahomey and served as its chairman. Apithy was elected mayor of Porto Novo in 1956 and was elected chief minister the following year. On December 5, 1958, he became Dahomey's first provisional prime minister. His government was plagued by corruption and regional discord. Apithy was forced from office by a coalition of Hubert Maga and Justin Ahomadegbé, with Maga succeeding him as prime minister on May 22, 1959. Apithy was appointed finance minister in Maga's government in 1960 and joined with Maga to thwart the ambitions of Ahomadegbé in the elections of 1960. Apithy was elected vice president with Maga as president. While still vice president, Apithy was effectively eliminated from power by Maga in 1963, when he was sent to Europe as Dahomey's ambassador to France, Great Britain, and Switzerland. After the ouster of Maga by the military in October of 1963, Apithy returned to Dahomey. He was named president on January 19, 1964, and served in a coalition government with Ahomadegbé as vice president and head of government. The two rivals' constant infighting led to a governmental stalemate which resulted in their ouster on November 29, 1965. Apithy spent the next several years in exile in France until he returned to Dahomey to run for president in 1970. He placed a distant third in the election behind Maga and Ahomadegbé. The results of the election were nullified by

the military, and the country nearly disintegrated into civil war. An agreement was reached by the major factions in which a Presidential Council was formed with Maga, Ahomadegbé, and Apithy rotating the chairmanship. The army ousted the triumvirate in October of 1972, before Apithy received his term as chairman. Apithy was briefly detained by the new government before returning to exile in Paris. He died on December 3, 1989.

TAIROU CONGACOU (President, November 29, 1965–December 22, 1965). Tairou Congacou, a member of the Dendi tribe, was born to the royal house of Djougou. He was elected to the General Council in the early 1950s and served in the Territorial Assembly from 1952 until 1957. Following the ouster of President Hubert Maga in October of 1963, Congacou was elected president of the National Assembly. He became president of Dahomey on November 29, 1965, when General Christophe Soglo staged a military coup to oust the government of Sorou-Migan Apithy and Justin Ahomadegbé. Congacou was unable to form a functional government, and Soglo again stepped in to take power on December 22, 1965. Congacou returned to government service in October of 1968, when he was appointed president of the Social and Economic Council by President Emile Zinsou. He served in this position until Zinsou was ousted in December of 1969. Congacou remained inactive in politics and was critically injured in a car crash in Cotonou, Benin, in June of 1993. He died of his injuries three days later on June 16, 1993.

CHRISTOPHE SOGLO (President, December 22, 1965–December 17, 1967). *See earlier entry under Heads of State.*

MAURICE KOUANDETE (President, December 17, 1967–December 22, 1967). Maurice Kouandete was born in the Gaba District in northern Dahomey in 1939. He served in the French army as a career soldier and attended military schools in France. He joined the Dahomey army upon independence and was appointed commander of the Presidential Palace Guard under Christophe Soglo in 1965. Kouandete subsequently headed the Dahomey Security Services. He was transferred to the staff of Col. Alphonse Alley, the chief of staff, in 1966. Kouandete's resentment against Soglo's government culminated in his leading a coup that ousted Soglo on December 17, 1967. Kouandete was feared by southern Dahomians and was forced to turn over leadership of the interim military government to Colonel Alley on December 22, 1967. Emile Zinsou was subsequently named president, and Kouandete ousted Alley as chief of staff of the armed forces. Kouandete led another coup on December 10, 1969, and overthrew Zinsou. He was prevented from taking the presidency by other factions in the army, however. He served as head of the interim military directorate until April 7, 1970. Kouandete was then forced out of command of the army and demoted to deputy secretary general of national defense. He plotted another coup in 1972, but was instead arrested and sentenced to death. The sentence was later commuted. He was released following the coup led by Mathieu Kérékou in October of 1972 and retired from the army.

ALPHONSE ALLEY (President, December 22, 1967–August 1, 1968). Alphonse Alley was born in Bassila on April 9, 1930. He joined the French army and served in Indochina in the early 1950s. He later saw action in Morocco and Algeria. Alley entered the Dahomian army following independence in 1960 and rose to the rank of major in 1964. He was named chief of staff of the army by Christophe Soglo in 1965. Alley was briefly arrested

following the coup led by his adjutant, Maurice Kouandete. He was released shortly thereafter and became head of the military government on December 22, 1967. He relinquished power to a civilian president, Emile Zinsou, on August 1, 1968. Alley's rivalry with Kouandete culminated in Alley being removed as chief of staff and dismissed from the army. Alley was tried in 1969 for allegedly plotting against Kouandete. He was sentenced to ten years imprisonment, but was released following Kouandete's coup in 1969. He was subsequently allowed to return to the army and became secretary-general of national defense with Kouandete as his deputy. Alley was again dismissed from the army following Mathieu Kérékou's takeover of the government in 1972. Alley was again arrested in February of 1973 and sentenced to twenty years in prison for plotting against Kérékou's regime.

EMILE ZINSOU (President, August 1, 1968–December 10, 1969). Emile Derlin Zinsou was born in Ouidah on March 23, 1918. He attended the Dakar Medical School and continued his studies in France before returning to Dahomey as a physician. He entered politics in 1947 and was subsequently elected to the French National Assembly as a senator from Dahomey. Zinsou was secretary-general of the Dahomean Progressive party from 1958. Following independence, Zinsou served in the government as minister of the economy. He was later named ambassador to France and president of the Supreme Court. He served as minister of foreign affairs from 1961 to 1963 and again from 1965 to 1967. Supporters of Hubert Maga, Sorou-Migan Apithy, and Justin Ahomadegbé boycotted the elections of 1968, and the ruling military government appointed Zinsou president on August 1, 1968. He was overthrown in a coup led by Maurice Kouandete on December 10, 1969. He was a candidate for the presidency in the elections of 1970, but placed a poor fourth. Zinsou went into exile in Paris following the coup led by Mathieu Kérékou. In 1975 he was sentenced to death in absentia for plotting against the Kérékou regime. Zinsou returned to Benin following the defeat of Kérékou in the elections in March of 1991.

MAURICE KOUANDETE (President, December 10, 1969–April 7, 1970). *See earlier entry under Heads of State.*

HUBERT MAGA (President, April 7, 1970–April 7, 1972). *See earlier entry under Heads of State.*

JUSTIN AHOMADEGBÉ (President, April 7, 1972–October 26, 1972). Justin Tométin Ahomadegbé was born a prince in the Agonglo royal family in 1917 in Abomey. He was educated at the William Ponty School and studied dentistry in Dakar, Senegal. He served briefly in the French army from 1941 to 1942 and entered politics shortly after World War II. Ahomadegbé joined the Dahomey Progressive Union in 1946, but left it the following year to found the African Popular Bloc. He was also elected to the General Council in 1957 and was elected mayor of Abomey in 1958. His rivalry with Sorou-Migan Apithy for support in southern Dahomey resulted in the election of Hubert Maga as prime minister when Ahomadegbé gave him his support. Ahomadegbé briefly retired from politics in November of 1960 following an unsuccessful attempt to displace Maga. Ahomadegbé's political party was banned by Maga, and in May of 1961 Ahomadegbé was arrested on charges of plotting to overthrow the government. He received amnesty and was released from jail in November of 1962. Following the overthrow of Maga by the military in October of 1963, Ahomadegbé joined with Apithy in a coalition government. Apithy served as president and Ahomadegbé was vice

president and prime minister from January 19, 1964. The long-standing rivalry of the two leaders made the task of governing difficult. In November of 1965 Ahomadegbé attempted to orchestrate the ouster of Apithy by a vote of the assembly. The governmental stalemate that followed resulted in an army coup led by General Christophe Soglo that ousted both Ahomadegbé and Apithy. Ahomadegbé went into exile in Togo and then in France. Though out of the country, he remained active in Dahomey politics, and in 1968 he sponsored the candidacy of Dr. Basil Adjou as his stand-in in the presidential campaign. The followers of Maga and Apithy boycotted the election and Adjou was elected, but the results were nullified by the army. Two years later Ahomadegbé, Maga, and Apithy were invited to return to Dahomey and run in another election. Ahomadegbé ran second to Maga in the balloting, but the results were again annulled by the military. Following a period of discord, the triumvirate agreed to a coalition government with the three leaders serving on a Presidential Council. Maga served as first chairman of the council for a two-year term, and on April 7, 1972, he turned over the leadership to Ahomadegbé. Ahomadegbé was unpopular with the army and was stymied in making governmental decisions by Maga and Apithy. His term of office was cut short when the military staged another coup on October 26, 1972, and ousted Ahomadegbé and the council. Ahomadegbé was arrested by the new government, but was released in April of 1981. He subsequently returned to exile in France. Ahomadegbé returned to Benin following the restoration of democracy in 1991.

MATHIEU KÉRÉKOU (President, October 27, 1972–April 4, 1991). Mathieu Kérékou was born in Kouarfa on September 2, 1933. He attended military schools and joined the French army in 1960. He was transferred to the independent Dahomean army the following year. Kérékou served as aide-de-camp to President Hubert Maga from 1961 until 1962. He was promoted to the rank of captain in 1965 and was a protégé of Col. Maurice Kouandete. Following Kouandete's coup in 1969, he was promoted to major. The following year Kérékou became deputy chief of staff of the armed forces. He was instrumental in maintaining order in the army during the Presidential Council under Maga from 1970 until 1972. Kérékou led a coup against Maga's successor, Justin Ahomadegbé, on October 26, 1972. Shortly after taking power, Kérékou purged the armed forces of senior officers. He survived an attempted coup in early 1973. Relations between Dahomey and France deteriorated under Kérékou's regime. He proclaimed Dahomey a Marxist-Leninist state in 1974, and on November 30, 1975, he changed the country's name to the People's Republic of Benin. Kérékou survived numerous attempts to overthrow his government. His regime was badly shaken in 1989 following widespread strikes and protests. Kérékou renounced his former Marxist-Leninist policies and moved toward a multiparty democracy. A new constitution was drafted in February of 1990 that shifted many of Kérékou's powers as president to Nicéphore Soglo, a former dissident who was named prime minister. Soglo challenged Kérékou in presidential elections held in March of 1991, and Kérékou was soundly defeated. He relinquished his office on April 4, 1991.

NICEPHORE SOGLO (President, April 4, 1991 –). Nicéphore Soglo was born in Lome, Togo, on November 29, 1934. He was educated in Paris and returned to Benin to work in the Finance Ministry. He became director of the Finance Department in 1963. Soglo subsequently became chairman of the National Monetary Commission. Soglo was an opponent of the government of Mathieu Kérékou. Kérékou was forced to name Soglo as prime minister of Benin on March 12, 1990. Soglo was a candidate in the presidential elections in March of 1991 and defeated Kérékou by a wide margin. He was sworn into office on April 4, 1991. Soglo was faced with several unsuccessful coup attempts in 1992. He became a leading spokesman for the democratic process and economic reforms throughout Africa.

HEADS OF GOVERNMENT

SOROU-MIGAN APITHY (Prime Minister, December 4, 1958–May 22, 1959). *See entry under Heads of State.*

HUBERT MAGA (Prime Minister, May 22, 1959–August 1, 1960). *See entry under Heads of State.*

JUSTIN AHOMADEGBE (Prime Minister, January 19, 1964–November 27, 1965). *See entry under Heads of State.*

MAURICE KOUANDETE (Prime Minister, December 22, 1967–August 1, 1968). *See entry under Heads of State.*

NICEPHORE SOGLO (Prime Minister, March 12, 1990–April 4, 1991). *See entry under Heads of State.*

Bhutan, Kingdom of

(Druk-yul)

Bhutan is a country in the Himalayan Mountains in southern Asia. It was granted independence from India on August 8, 1949.

HEADS OF STATE

JIGME WANGCHUCK (King, August 21, 1926–March 30, 1952). Jigme Wangchuck was born in 1902. He succeeded his father, Sir Uggyen Wangchuck, as druk gyalpo, or "dragon king," on August 21, 1926. Bhutan remained in almost complete isolation during his reign. The country had a 1910 treaty with the British government which provided for autonomous internal control, but stipulated that British advice would be followed in regard to foreign relations. On August 8, 1949, the government of India replaced the British government as Bhutan's foreign advisor. Jigme Wangchuck remained Bhutan's leader until his death in Bomthang after a brief illness on March 30, 1952.

JIGME DORJI WANGCHUCK (King, October 27, 1952–July 21, 1972). Jigme Dorji Wangchuck was born in Bhutan in 1929. He succeeded his father as king on October 27, 1952. Jigme Dorji Wangchuck, whose name means "fearless thunderbolt master of the cosmic powers," ruled as an enlightened and reform-minded monarch. Early in his reign he freed the remaining serfs in Bhutan. He also opened up his kingdom to outside influences, including the introduction of the wheel. Jigme Dorji Wangchuck led his country into closer ties with India following the actions of the People's Republic of China

in Tibet in 1959. Bhutan closed its northern border shortly thereafter. The king suffered a heart attack in 1963 and occasionally went overseas for medical treatment. He encouraged the Bhutan National Assembly to assert its power and allowed the Assembly to pass a law empowering it to replace a monarch if two-thirds of the Assembly should warrant it. Bhutan was admitted to the United Nations in 1971. The following year the king traveled to Nairobi, Kenya, for medical treatment. He died there on July 21, 1972, at the age of 45.

JIGME SINGYE WANGCHUCK (King, July 21, 1972–   ). Jigme Singye Wangchuck was born on November 11, 1955. He was the son of King Jigme Dorji Wangchuk and Queen Ashi Kesang. He was educated in Bhutan and England. He was named crown prince and chairman of the Planning Commission of Bhutan in March of 1972. He succeeded his father to the throne on July 21, 1972. The new king continued his father's policies of modernization, despite the opposition of traditional elements in the country. He also faced the dissent of the militant Nepalese minority in Bhutan. Jigme Singye Wangchuk continued to widen Bhutan's contacts with the international community and to decrease his nation's dependence on India.

HEAD OF GOVERNMENT

JIGME DORJI (Prime Minister, 1955–April 5, 1964). Jigme Polden Dorji was born in 1919. He was appointed premier in 1955. With his brother-in-law, King Jigme Dorji Wangchuck, he succeeded in abolishing slavery and polyandry and increased Bhutan's contacts with the outside world. Shortly after Bhutan sealed off its northern border with Tibet, which was dominated by Communist China, Jigme Dorji was assassinated in Phunchholing, Bhutan, on April 5, 1964.

Bolivia, Republic of

(República de Bolivia)

Bolivia is a country in central South America. It received its independence from Spain on August 6, 1825.

HEADS OF STATE

GUALBERTO VILLAROEL (President, December 20, 1943–July 21, 1946). Gualberto Villaroel was born in 1908. He joined the Bolivian army and fought against Paraguay in the Chaco War from 1932 until 1935. Villaroel became president of Bolivia following a military coup in December of 1943. During his administration he implemented reforms that benefited the tin miners and the Bolivian Indians. His labor and land reform programs met with bitter opposition from the tin industry and land owners and resulted in a rebellion against his regime. Villaroel survived an assassination attempt on March 12, 1945. The presidential palace in La Paz was attacked by a mob on July 21, 1946, and Villaroel was thrown from a balcony and lynched from a lamppost in the Plaza Murillo below.

NESTER GUILLEN (President, July 21, 1946–August 16, 1946). Nester Guillen was born in 1890. He was the dean of the La Paz district of Bolivia's Superior Court. He was selected by leaders of the rebellion against President Villaroel to serve as interim president on July 21, 1946. Guillen relinquished the office on August 16, 1946.

TOMÁS MONJE GUTIÉRREZ (President, August 16, 1946–March 10, 1947). Tomás Monje Gutiérrez was born in Coroica in 1884. He served as deputy minister of agriculture from 1926 until 1927. He was subsequently named minister of the government and justice. From 1930 until 1936 he served as Bolivia's attorney general. Monje Gutiérrez was serving as president of the Bolivian Supreme Court at the time of President Gualberto Villaroel's murder in July of 1946. The ruling revolutionary government asked him to serve as president, but he initially declined the request. He accepted the following month and took office on August 16, 1946. Monje Gutiérrez survived an assassination attempt the following month and remained in office until March 10, 1947, when he left office following the election of a new president. He died of a heart attack in La Paz at the age of 70 on July 1, 1954.

ENRIQUE HERZOG (President, March 10, 1947–May 7, 1949). Enrique Herzog was born in 1896. He was the candidate of the Socialist Republican Union in the presidential election held in January of 1947. He won a narrow victory over Luis Fernando Guachalla and was sworn into office on March 10, 1947. Herzog's government arrested and deported many leaders of the National Revolutionary Movement. His first year as president was also plagued by numerous labor strikes. He declared a state of siege on September 18, 1947, to deal with the labor situation. Herzog's government survived several attempts to overthrow it. Herzog resigned for reasons of poor health on May 7, 1949.

MAMERTO URRIOLAGOITIA (President, May 7, 1949–May 16, 1951). Mamerto Urriolagoitia was born in 1894. He was the head of the rightist Social Republican Union party. He served as vice president under Enrique Herzog from March of 1947. When Herzog resigned the presidency on May 7, 1949, Urriolagoitia was sworn in to complete his term. The opposition National Revolutionary Movement won the elections of 1951, but Urriolagoitia turned his government over to the armed forces on May 16, 1951, rather than allow the opposition party to take power. He died in La Sucre on June 4, 1974.

HUGO BALLIVIAN ROJAS (President, May 16, 1951–April 9, 1952). Hugo Ballivián Rojas was born in 1902. He served in the Bolivian army and was a hero of the Chaco War in the 1930s. He served as leader of the ruling military junta in Bolivia following the resignation of President Mamerto Urriolagoitia. Ballivián declared a state of siege and survived several attempts to overthrow the junta. The government made plans to hold new elections, but was ousted on April 11, 1952, after a bloody three-day revolution. Ballivián subsequently went into exile in Chile.

HERNÁN SILES ZUAZO (President, April 11, 1952–April 16, 1952). Hernán Siles Zuazo was born in La Paz on March 19, 1914. He was the illegitimate son of Hernando Siles Reyes, Bolivia's president from 1926 until 1930. He graduated from the American Institute in La Paz in 1931. Siles served in the Bolivian army and fought against Paraguay during the Chaco War from 1932 until 1935. He was wounded in action and was decorated for bravery. After the war he received a law degree from San Andres University. He was elected to the Chamber of Deputies in 1940 and was a founder of the National Revolutionary Movement (MNR) in 1941. The party espoused a pro–Axis platform during World War II. Party members planned the coup that installed Gualberto Villaroel as president in 1943. Villaroel was ousted and murdered in 1946, and the subsequent military government exiled Siles and other MNR leaders. Siles went to Argentina, where he worked as a correspondent and translator for United Press. He returned to Bolivia for the election in May of 1951 and was elected vice president under Victor Paz Estenssoro. The military again seized power to prevent the MNR from taking office. Siles led a countercoup on April 11, 1952, and became provisional president until April 16, 1952, when Paz Estenssoro returned from exile to become president. Siles then served as vice president in the subsequent administration. He was elected to succeed Paz Estenssoro as president on August 6, 1956. Siles succeeded in stabilizing the economy and was able to end a crippling miners' strike. On August 6, 1960, he completed his term and left office. He served as ambassador to Uruguay from 1960 until 1963 and was ambassador to Spain from 1963 until 1964. Siles again went into exile following a military coup in 1964. He broke with Paz Estenssoro and formed the National Revolutionary Movement (MRI) following Paz Estenssoro's support of a military coup in 1972. Siles returned to Bolivia in 1978 and was the United Popular Democratic party's candidate in the presidential elections that year. The elections were halted when evidence of widespread fraud was presented. New elections were scheduled, but were delayed by a military coup led by Juan Pereda Asbun, who had been the ruling coalition's presidential candidate. After several more changes in government, new elections took place in July of 1979. Siles received the most votes, but did not gain an absolute majority. Congress was deadlocked on settling the issue of who should take office, and this impasse led to several more military coups. New elections were again held in June of 1980. Siles again received the majority of the votes, but the election was once more sent to Congress due to the lack of an absolute majority. Once again, the military stepped in to prevent Siles from taking office, and he escaped to Peru. Siles returned to Bolivia in 1982, and was again a candidate for president. He again received a majority, but this time Congress approved his election. The military relinquished power, and Siles took office on October 10, 1982. He was faced with many problems as president, including severe economic difficulties, pressure from the United States to halt the export of cocaine, and general strikes. Siles survived an attempted coup on June 30, 1984, when he was kidnapped by members of the military with connections to Bolivia's cocaine trade. When the coup failed, he was released after having been held prisoner for ten hours. Discontent over his economic record forced Siles to call for new elections a year before his term was due to expire. The election was won by Victor Paz Estenssoro. Siles relinquished office to his one-time ally, and recent political enemy, on August 6, 1985.

VICTOR PAZ ESTENSSORO (President, April 16, 1952–August 6, 1956).

Victor Paz Estenssoro was born in Tarija on October 2, 1907. He attended San Andres University, where he received a degree in law. He was employed by the Directorate of Financial Statistics in 1928. Paz Estenssoro remained in government service until 1939, when he became president of the Banco Minero de Bolivia. He was elected a deputy to the National Congress in 1940 and served as vice president of the Chamber of Deputies until 1941. He was a founder and leader of the National Revolutionary Movement (MNR) and was accused of taking part in a coup against the government in 1941. Paz Estenssoro was subsequently absolved of the charges. He led the MNR-supported coup against the government that installed Gualberto Villaroel as president on December 20, 1943. Paz Estenssoro served as finance minister in the new government. When Villaroel was ousted in July of 1946, Paz Estenssoro went into exile in Argentina. While in exile, he was elected president of Bolivia in the elections on May 6, 1951, but a military coup prevented him from taking office. A violent revolution ousted the military government in April of 1952, and Paz Estenssoro returned to Bolivia on April 15, 1952. He took office as president the following day. His administration brought about land distribution and nationalized the three largest tin mines. He also granted the right to vote to Bolivian Indians. Paz Estenssoro was succeeded by his ally, Hernán Siles Zuazo, on August 6, 1956. He served as ambassador to Great Britain during the Siles administration. In the elections of 1960, he returned to Bolivia to again seek the presidency. He was once more victorious and took office on August 6, 1960. During his second term he reached an agreement with foreign interests to reorganize the tin-mining industry. Paz Estenssoro changed the constitution so that he could seek reelection in 1964, despite protests from the opposition. Although there was a boycott of the election, Paz Estenssoro was reelected. He was soon faced with antigovernment riots and was ousted by a military coup led by his vice president, General Rene Barrientos, on November 4, 1964. He went into exile in Peru, where he taught economics at the University of Lima. Paz Estenssoro returned to Bolivia following the ouster of President Juan Jose Torres in 1971. Paz Estenssoro was a candidate in the inconclusive elections for president in 1979 and 1980 and again ran for the presidency in 1985. Though he ran second in the balloting, he was elected by Congress when no candidate received an absolute majority. He was sworn into office on August 6, 1985. As no party had a majority in the Bolivian Congress, Paz Estenssoro was forced to reach a congressional alliance with the National Democratic Action party in order to enact legislation. The financial austerity program he introduced decreased the MNR's popularity, and the party suffered in legislative elections in 1988. Paz Estenssoro completed his term of office on August 6, 1989.

HERNÁN SILES ZUAZO (President, August 6, 1956–August 6, 1960). *See earlier entry under Heads of State.*

VICTOR PAZ ESTENSSORO (President, August 6, 1960–November 4, 1964). *See earlier entry under Heads of State.*

RENÉ BARRIENTOS ORTUÑA (President, November 4, 1964–May 26, 1965 Co-President, May 26, 1965–January 4, 1966). René Barrientos Ortuña was born in Tunary on May 30, 1919. He attended the military college in La Paz, but was expelled for revolutionary activities when he joined the National Revolutionary Movement (MNR) in 1937. He subsequently joined the Bolivian air force and moved rapidly through the ranks when the MNR took

power in 1952. Barrientos was later named air force chief of staff. When President Victor Paz Estenssoro changed the constitution to run for another term of office in 1964, the military insisted that General Barrientos be his running mate. Barrientos subsequently broke with Paz Estenssoro, and following riots against the government, the latter was ousted by the military on November 4, 1964. Barrientos and General Alfredo Ovando Candia led the ruling military junta, with Barrientos shortly becoming the junta leader. Barrientos was shot and injured in an assassination attempt near Cochbamba on March 21, 1965. He accepted General Ovando Candia as copresident on May 26, 1965, and made plans for general elections. Barrientos resigned in January of 1966 to become a candidate in the scheduled elections. After defeating several opponents in the elections, he became sole president of Bolivia on August 6, 1966. Bolivia was threatened by a crippling miners strike, and Barrientos acted to settle the crisis. Leaders of the Miners' Federation, who were accused of plotting against the government, were banished under martial law. The miners returned to work under the threat of the army taking over the operations of the mines. In 1967 revolutionary Ernesto "Che" Guevara led a guerrilla uprising in Santa Cruz. Barrientos's government withstood the challenge, and Guevara was captured and executed in October of 1967. Barrientos declared a state of siege on July 22, 1968, following violent demonstrations against his administration. He installed a military cabinet until order was restored in October of 1968. Barrientos was killed in a helicopter crash while returning from a village in the Oruru Province on April 27, 1969.

ALFREDO OVANDO CANDÍA (Co-president, May 26, 1965–January 4, 1966; President, January 4, 1966–August 6, 1966). Alfredo Ovando Candía was born in Cobija on April 6, 1918. After graduating from military school in 1936, he joined the Bolivian army. He served in various military capacities, including tours of duty as military attaché in Paraguay and Uruguay. Ovando was a supporter of the National Revolutionary Movement (MNR) and was rapidly promoted once MNR leader Victor Paz Estenssoro became president in 1952. He was appointed army chief of staff in 1957 and was promoted to brigadier general in 1959. He was named commander in chief of the Bolivian armed forces in 1962. Ovando, with General René Barrientos, led the coup that ousted Paz Estenssoro on November 4, 1964. Ovando was briefly copresident with Barrientos on November 5, 1964. Following a clash between government troops and striking mine workers, Ovando again became copresident with Barrientos on May 25, 1965. Barrientos resigned in January to become a candidate in the general election later in the year, leaving Ovando as interim president. Ovando relinquished the presidency to the victorious Barrientos on August 6, 1966, and returned to serve as commander in chief of the armed forces. Ovando led the armed forces in a struggle against leftist guerrillas led by Ernesto "Che" Guevara. This action resulted in Guevara's capture and execution in October of 1967. Ovando announced his candidacy to succeed Barrientos in the elections scheduled for 1970. Barrientos was killed in a helicopter crash in April of 1969 and was succeeded by his vice president, Luis Siles Salinas. Ovando's relationship with the new president was strained and worsened when he was accused of accepting campaign contributions from the United States. Shortly thereafter, on September 26, 1969, Salinas was ousted by a military coup, and Ovando became president. During his administration, the government nationalized the United States–owned Bolivian Gulf Oil Co. Ovando resigned the presidency on October 6, 1970, in the face of a right-wing military coup led by General Rogelio Miranda. Ovando sought asylum in the Argentine embassy, and General Miranda was ousted in a left-wing countercoup the following day. Ovando subsequently returned to Bolivia. He died in La Paz following complications from stomach ulcers on January 24, 1982.

RENÉ BARRIENTOS ORTUÑA (President, August 6, 1966–April 27, 1969). *See earlier entry under Heads of State.*

LUIS ADOLFO SILES SALINAS (President, April 27, 1969–September 26, 1969). Luis Adolfo Siles Salinas was born in 1925. He was the running mate of General René Barrientos in the presidential elections in 1966 and was sworn in as vice president on August 6, 1966. He succeeded Barrientos on April 27, 1969, when the president was killed in a helicopter crash. Siles subsequently clashed with General Alfredo Ovando Candía, the commander in chief of the armed forces. Siles was ousted by Ovando in a military coup on September 26, 1969, and went into exile in Chile.

ALFREDO OVANDO CANDÍA (President, September 26, 1969–October 6, 1970). *See earlier entry under Heads of State.*

JUAN JOSÉ TORRES (President, October 7, 1970–August 22, 1971). Juan José Torres Gonzales was born in Cochabamba on March 5, 1921. He was educated at the Bolivian Military Academy and served in the Bolivian army. He was active in the military coup that gave Victor Paz Estenssoro the presidency in 1952 and he rose to the rank of colonel during his administration. Torres was named ambassador to Uruguay by Paz's successor, René Barrientos. He later served as minister of labor and social security in Barrientos's military cabinet. Torres was promoted to general and appointed chief of staff of the armed forces by Barrientos in 1967. He remained in the government as secretary-general of the Supreme Council of National Defense following Barrientos's death in a helicopter crash in 1969. He assisted General Alfredo Ovando Candía in ousting the civilian government of Luis Siles Salinas in September of 1969 and was appointed chief of the armed forces by the subsequent Ovando administration. When Ovando was forced to resign on October 6, 1970, under the threat of a right-wing military coup, Torres led a left-wing countercoup with the support of workers and students and was sworn in as president the following day. He continued the policy of nationalizing foreign businesses and supported the labor unions' call for higher wages. Torres also expelled the Peace Corps from Bolivia and had strained relations with the United States. He retained office until August 22, 1971, when his government was ousted by another right-wing military coup led by Hugo Bánzer Suárez. Torres went into exile in Peru and moved to Argentina in 1973. There he became a victim of right-wing death squads when he was kidnapped and murdered near Buenos Aires on June 2, 1976.

HUGO BÁNZER SUÁREZ (President, August 22, 1971–July 21, 1978). Hugo Bánzer Suárez was born in Santa Cruz on July 10, 1926. He was educated at the National Military Academy in La Paz and joined the Bolivian army, where he rose through the ranks. Bánzer served as minister of education in the cabinet of President René Barrientos until 1967. He subsequently served as military attaché in the Bolivian Embassy in Washington, D.C. Bánzer was recalled to Bolivia following the military coup that installed General Alfredo Ovando Candía as president in September of 1969. He was

then named director of the National Military Academy. He supported General Rogelio Miranda's right-wing coup against Candía in October of 1970 and was ousted from his post by the subsequent left-wing government of Juan José Torres on January 4, 1971. Bánzer led an unsuccessful coup against Torres on January 10, 1971, and went into exile in Argentina after the coup's failure. Bánzer was arrested when he reentered Bolivia on August 18, 1971. This touched off a rightist revolution that succeeded in ousting Torres after violent street fighting on August 22, 1971. Bánzer was released from prison and installed as president by the new military junta. His government initially had the support of the nation's two largest political parties, the National Revolutionary Movement (MNR) and the Bolivian Socialist Falange (FSB). Bánzer organized the Nationalist Popular Front to stabilize Bolivia's political and economic situation. He halted some of Torres's nationalization policies and conducted a campaign against leftist supporters of the deposed president. He declared a state of siege in November of 1972 following strikes and demonstrations against the government's economic policies. Bánzer survived numerous coup attempts during his term of office. The MNR and FSB resigned from Bánzer's government in 1974, and he named a primarily military cabinet. Bánzer scheduled presidential elections in 1978, and on December 1, 1977, he announced that he would not be a candidate for the presidency. The elections were held, but were voided after allegations of fraud on July 19, 1978. Bánzer turned over the reins of government to a military junta on July 21, 1978. He subsequently went into exile in Argentina, but returned to Bolivia in 1985 and was a candidate in the presidential elections of that year. He received the most votes in the election, but was denied an absolute majority. The election was then sent to the Bolivian Congress and Victor Paz Estenssoro was selected as president. Bánzer was again a candidate for president in the elections of 1989. The election was again sent to the Congress, where Bánzer threw his support to Jaime Paz Zamora. Bánzer remained the leader of the Nationalist Democratic Action party.

JUAN PEREDA ASBÚN (President, July 21, 1978–November 24, 1978). Juan Pereda Asbún was born in 1932. He served in the Bolivian air force and rose to the rank of general. He was nominated as the presidential candidate of the ruling coalition government in 1978. The subsequent election was marred by fraud, and Pereda requested the annulment of the results. New elections were ordered by the National Electoral Court. Pereda organized a military coup and seized power on July 21, 1978. He announced that elections would be postponed until 1980 and that he would not stand as a candidate. The military would not accept the long delay for elections and ousted Pereda in a bloodless coup on November 24, 1978.

DAVID PADILLA ARENCIBIA (President, November 24, 1978–August 8, 1979). David Padilla Arencibia was army chief of staff at the time of the coup led by General Juan Pereda Asbún. When Pereda was ousted by the military on November 24, 1978, Padilla served as leader of the three-man military junta that followed. Padilla stepped down on August 8, 1979, to allow a civilian government to take power. The subsequent government was ousted by another military coup led by Albert Natusch Busch, without the support of Padilla. Padilla was instrumental in the ouster of Natusch in November of 1979, again restoring Bolivia to civilian rule.

WALTER GUEVARA ARZE (President, August 8, 1979–November 1, 1979). Walter Guevara Arze was born in Cochabamba on March 11, 1911. He studied law at the university there until he joined the army to fight against Paraguay in the Chaco War in 1936. He joined the National Revolutionary Movement (MNR) in the early 1940s and went into exile following the military coup in 1946. After returning to Bolivia, he was elected to the Senate in 1951, but was prevented from taking office by another military coup. The military junta was ousted the following year and Guevara was named foreign minister in the subsequent government of Victor Paz Estenssoro. Guevara was expected to be MNR's candidate for president in 1960, but President Paz changed the constitution to allow himself to run for reelection. Guevara formed a splinter opposition party to Paz and was an unsuccessful candidate for the presidency in 1960. He was sent into exile following Paz's reelection. Guevara supported the military coup against Paz in 1964 and was named foreign minister in the government of René Barrientos. Guevara was appointed ambassador to the United Nations by President Hugo Bánzer Suárez in 1971. He resigned his post in 1973 and went into exile the following year. Following an amnesty, he returned to Bolivia and was an unsuccessful candidate for president in 1978. He was elected president of the Senate in August of 1979. The presidential election in 1979 resulted in a deadlock between Paz and Hernan Siles Zuazo. Guevara was chosen by Congress as a compromise candidate to be interim president. He took office on August 8, 1979, but he was ousted by Col. Alberto Natusch Busch in a military coup on November 1, 1979. Guevara was named ambassador to Venezuela in 1983. Guevara remained active in politics, leading the Authentic Revolutionary Party (PRA), a dissident faction of the National Revolutionary Movement.

ALBERTO NATUSCH BUSCH (President, November 1, 1979–November 16,

1979). Alberto Natusch Busch was born in 1927. He was a colonel in the Bolivian army when he led a coup against the interim government of President Walter Guevara Arze on November 1, 1979. He proclaimed himself president and declared a state of siege when violent street demonstrations protested his government. Natusch did not have the unified backing of the military. An agreement was reached among various factions in the military, government, and labor unions, and Natusch was removed from office on November 16, 1979. Natusch, now a general, led a coup attempt against the government of General Luis Garcia Meza in August of 1981. The coup was unsuccessful but nearly brought the country to a state of civil war and forced Garcia Meza's resignation.

LIDIA GUEILER TEJADA (President, November 16, 1979–July 17, 1980). Lidia Gueiler Tejada was born in Cochabamba in 1925. She joined the National Revolutionary Movement (MNR) in 1946 and was active in the revolution in 1952. She subsequently served as private secretary to President Victor Paz Estenssoro. She was elected to the Chamber of Deputies in 1956, but her political career was cut short by the military coup in 1964. She spent much of the next fifteen years in exile. During this period she developed a friendship with Salvador Allende Gossens, the president of Chile who was killed during a military coup in 1973. She reentered Bolivian politics in 1979 and was elected president of the Chamber of Deputies in July of that year. She was selected to serve as interim president by the Bolivian Congress on November 16, 1979, following the resignation of Colonel Alberto Natusch Busch, the leader of a coup that had ousted Walter Guevara Arze sixteen days earlier. Gueiler made plans to return Bolivia to democratic rule and replaced a number of military commanders. This move met with opposition from high-ranking

officers, including her cousin, General Luis Garcia Meza. The elections were held on schedule in June of 1980, but no candidate received an absolute majority. The Congress was scheduled to decide the outcome of the election, but General Garcia Meza, who had recently been named army commander, led a military coup and ousted President Gueiler on July 17, 1980. She subsequently went into exile in Paris. She returned to Bolivia in 1982 and was appointed ambassador to Colombia the following year, serving until 1986.

LUIS GARCIA MEZA TEJADA (President, July 18, 1980–August 4, 1981). Luis Garcia Meza Tejada was born in La Paz on August 8, 1932. He attended the military college in La Paz and joined the army where he rose to the rank of general and was in command of the Bolivian Army's 6th Division in 1980. General Garcia Meza led the right-wing military coup that ousted President Lidia Gueiler Tejada in order to prevent the selection of Hernan Siles Zuazo as president. Garcia Meza led the ruling military junta from July 18, 1980. His administration faced a growing economic crisis in the country which was worsened by international pressures to return Bolivia to a democratic state. Garcia Meza's government was also linked to international drug cartels, which brought on the hostility of the United States. Garcia survived five major coup attempts before resigning on August 4, 1981, as Bolivia stood on the brink of civil war. He returned executive power to the military junta and was replaced by General Celso Torrelio Villa the following month. General Garcia Meza was purged from his army posts during the administration of President Siles Zuazo in 1983.

CELSO TORRELIO VILLA (President, September 4, 1981–July 19, 1982). Celso Torrelio Villas was born in Sucre on June 3, 1933. He attended the military academy and entered the army, where he rose through the ranks and was promoted to general of division in July of 1981. He had served as minister of the interior in the cabinet of President Luis Garcia Meza from February until June of 1981. Subsequently, he was named commander in chief of the army. He served as a member of the ruling military junta from June of 1981, and on September 4, 1981, he replaced General Garcia as president. His administration was beset by rising economic problems and was under international pressure to combat the drug trade in Bolivia. General Torrelio made plans to return Bolivia to civilian rule and resigned from office on July 19, 1982.

GUIDO VILDOSO CALDERÓN (President, July 21, 1982–October 10, 1982). Guido Vildoso Calderón was born in 1937. Vildoso was army chief of staff and became head of the ruling military junta on July 21, 1982, following the resignation of Gen. Celso Torrelio Villas. Bolivia was beset by major strikes following the government's announcement of changes in the election laws. Brigadier General Vildoso recalled the Congress that had been elected in 1980 to choose a president. Hernán Siles Zuazo, the victor in the presidential election of that year, was selected as president, and Vildoso and the junta stepped down on October 10, 1982.

HERNÁN SILES ZUAZO (President, October 10, 1982–August 6, 1985). *See earlier entry under Heads of State.*

VICTOR PAZ ESTENSSORO (President, August 6, 1985–August 6, 1989). *See earlier entry under Heads of State.*

JAIME PAZ ZAMORA (President, August 6, 1989–). Jaime Paz Zamora was born in Cochabamba on April 15, 1939. Paz Zamora was educated in Louvain, Belgium, and entered politics upon his return to Bolivia. He founded the Revolutionary Leftist Movement following the military coup led by General Hugo Bánzer Suárez in 1971. He was arrested for antigovernment activity in 1974 and was exiled until 1979. He returned to Brazil and was an unsuccessful candidate for the vice presidency under Hernán Siles Zuazo. The Paz-Siles ticket won the election the following year, but the results were dismissed by the military. Paz Zamora was seriously injured in a plane crash in 1980 that was believed to have been an assassination attempt. He again ran for the vice presidency in October of 1982 and was elected with Siles as president. He retained that position until his term ended in August of 1985. Paz Zamora was a candidate for president in 1989. He achieved the office with the support of Hugo Bánzer Suárez's Nationalist Democratic Action party and succeeded his uncle, Victor Paz Estenssor, as president on August 6, 1989. Despite his leftist background, Paz Zamora continued to pursue his predecessor's free-market policies. He also made an effort to improve the social welfare of Bolivia.

Bophuthatswana, Republic of
(Repaboliki ya Bophuthatswana)

Bophuthatswana is made up of several discontinuous geographic areas within South Africa. It was granted independence by South Africa on December 6, 1977.

HEADS OF STATE

LUCAS MANGOPE (Chief Minister, July 1, 1972–December 6, 1977. President, December 6, 1977–February 10, 1988). Lucas Lawrence Manyane Mangope was born in Motswedi in the Tswana homeland on December 27, 1923. He was educated locally and was employed as a school teacher from 1948 until 1958. He was subsequently appointed chief councillor in the Tswana Assembly. He succeeded his father as chief of the Bahurutshe-Boo-Manyane in September of 1959. He subsequently served as vice-chairman of the Tswana Territorial Authority from 1961 until 1968. From 1968 until 1972 he served on the Executive Council as chief councillor. Bophuthatswana obtained self-government under the South African Bantu Homeland Constitution Act in 1971, and Mangope was elected chief minister on July 1, 1972. Bophuthatswana was granted independence from South Africa on December 6, 1977, and Mangope continued as the nation's leader, becoming president. Mangope was ousted by a coup led by the Bophu-thatswana defense forces on February 10, 1988. Mangope was restored to office by South African troops later that day. His government was faced with labor unrest and demonstrations demanding reincorporation with South Africa during the 1990s.

ROCKY ISMAEL PETER MALABANE-METSING (President, February 10, 1988). Rocky Ismael Peter Malabane-Metsing formed the Progressive People's party in 1987. He was chosen as president of Bophuthatswana following the coup that ousted President Lucas Mangope on February 10, 1988. Malabane-Metsing was removed from office later in the day by South African troops. He was arrested by the restored Mangope government but escaped into Zambia. The Progressive People's party was banned in 1989 and Malabane-Metsing remained in exile.

LUCAS MANGOPE (President, February 10, 1988–   ). *See earlier entry under Heads of State.*

Bosnia-Herzegovina, Republic of
(Republika Bosne i Hercegovine)

Bosnia-Herzegovina is a country located in southeastern Europe. It declared its independence from Yugoslavia on October 15, 1991.

HEADS OF STATE

ALIJA IZETBEGOVIĆ (President, December 20, 1990–   ). Alija Izetbegović was the leader of the Moslem Democratic Action party. He was elected president of Bosnia and Herzegovina on December 20, 1990, succeeding Dr. Obrad Piljak. The National Assembly adopted a "Memorandum on Sovereignty" on October 15, 1991, and a referendum on independence was successful in an election on February 29, 1992. Bosnia soon found itself in a war with the Yugoslav army and Serbian militias. Izetbegović was seized by a

Yugoslav army unit on May 2, 1992, when he returned from a peace talk in Lisbon, Portugal, sponsored by the European Communities. He was released the following day. Fighting continued amid reports that the Serbian militias were waging a genocidal campaign against Bosnian Muslims. The United Nations imposed sanctions on the Serbians, and the United States threatened military action if a peaceful settlement could not be reached.

HEADS OF GOVERNMENT

JURE PELIVAN (Premier, December 20, 1990–November 9, 1992). Jure Pelivan was a member of the Croat Democratic Union. He was appointed prime minister on December 20, 1990, and he retained office until November 9, 1992.

MILE AKMADZIC (Premier, November 9, 1992–   ). Mile Akmadzic was selected to succeed Jure Pelivan as prime minister of Bosnia and Herzegovina on November 9, 1992.

Botswana

Botswana is a country located in southern Africa. It was granted independence from Great Britain on September 30, 1966.

HEADS OF STATE

SIR SERETSE KHAMA (President, September 30, 1966–July 13, 1980). Sir Seretse M. Khama was born in Serowe on July 1, 1921. He was the son of Sekgoma Khama II, the paramount chief of the Bamangwato tribe. Sekgoma II died in 1925, and Seretse's uncle, Tshekedi Khama, assumed the regency. Seretse was educated in South Africa and Great Britain, where he studied law. While a student in London, he met his future wife, Ruth Williams. Their interracial marriage in September of 1948 was opposed by the families of both, as well as the governments of Great Britain and South Africa. Khama returned to his homeland, and in June of 1949 he was selected by the tribal council to succeed his father to the tribal throne. Great Britain rejected Khama's ascension, and he was forced into exile in England the following year.

The Bamangwato tribal chiefs remained loyal to Khama and refused to select a replacement for him when so ordered by the British High Commission in 1953. Khama was allowed to return to Bechuanaland in September of 1956 after he renounced his claim to the tribal throne. He was elected to the tribal council in 1957 and served as a member of the executive council of Bechuanaland from 1961. He formed the Bechuanaland Democratic party, a multiracial political party, in 1962. His party was successful in the 1965 elections for the National Assembly when self-government was permitted, and Khama was selected as prime minister. When Bechuanaland became the independent nation of Botswana on September 30, 1966, Khama became his country's first president. He presided over a democratic government and was reelected in October of 1969. Khama was considered a moderate and served as a mediator between black African states and the Republic of South Africa. He also supported majority rule for neighboring Rhodesia (now Zimbabwe). Khama worked to improve the educational facilities in his country and encouraged a policy of economic diversification. He remained president until his death from pancreatic cancer in Gaberone on July 13, 1980.

QUETT KETUMILE MASIRE (President, July 13, 1980–   ). Quett Ketumile Joni Masire was born in Kanye on July 23, 1925. He was educated locally and in South Africa. He worked as a journalist, and in 1958 he was elected to the Ngwaketse Tribal Council. Masire joined Seretse Khama's Bechuanaland Democratic party in 1962 and served as secretary-general. He was elected to the Bechuanaland National Assembly in March of 1965, and he was subsequently named deputy prime minister. Masire was appointed minister of finance the following year, and upon independence on September 30, 1966, he was named vice president of Botswana. He was defeated for reelection to the National Assembly in 1969, but was returned as an at-large member selected by the Assembly. Masire was reelected to the Assembly in 1974 and remained vice president until President Khama died on July 13, 1980, and he succeeded to the presidency. Relations between Botswana and South Africa became strained in the mid-1980s because of South African military incursions into the country. Masire's government was successful in maintaining Botswana's economic development, which was one of the best on the continent.

Brazil, Federative Republic of

(República Federativa do Brasil)

Brazil is a country in central and northeastern South America. It was granted independence from Portugal on September 7, 1822.

HEADS OF STATE

GETÚLIO DORNELLES VARGAS (President, November 3, 1930–October 29, 1945). Getúlio Dornelles Vargas was born in Sao Borja, Rio Grande do Sul, on April 19, 1883. He was raised on his family's cattle ranch and was educated at the Rio Pardo Military Academy. He abandoned notions of a career in the military, however, and received a law degree from the University of Porto Alegre in 1907. Two years later he was elected to the Brazilian Chamber of Deputies for a single term, and he subsequently engaged in the practice of law. Vargas returned to politics in 1919 when he was elected a state deputy. He was named minister of finance in the government of Washington Luiz in 1926 and served until 1928, when he was elected president of the state of Rio Grande do Sul. He was defeated by Julio Prestes in his bid for the presidency of Brazil on the Liberal Alliance ticket in 1930. When the government refused to seat elected members of Vargas's party in the Chamber of Deputies, he led an armed uprising against the government.

President Luiz was ousted before Prestes could take office, and Vargas became leader of the ruling military junta on November 3, 1930. In 1934 he allowed a new progressive constitution to come into effect and was elected president in the subsequent election. Three years later Vargas, announcing his program of Estado Novo (or New State), suspended the constitution and extended his term of office from four to six years. Vargas was a staunch supporter of the Allied cause during World War II and declared war on the Axis powers in August of 1942. After the war Vargas was faced with a serious economic recession in Brazil. He agreed to hold democratic elections without himself as a candidate. The army was suspicious that Vargas might renege on his commitment and acted to insure the election by deposing Vargas on October 29, 1945. He returned to his ranch in southern Brazil, where he formed the Brazil Labor party and won election to a seat in the Brazilian Senate. He remained a powerful force in Brazil during the subsequent administration of Eurico Gaspar Dutra. He returned to the national scene as a candidate for president on October 3, 1950, and won by a large margin. He was sworn in for another term on January 31, 1951. Financial mismanagement and other scandals cost Vargas much of his popularity among the people, however. On August 4, 1954, Carlos Lacerda, a leading journalist and opponent of Vargas, was the target of an assassination attempt that resulted in the death of Major Rubens Florentino Vaz of the Brazilian air force. Supporters of Vargas were implicated in the attack, and Vargas was pressured by the military to resign from the presidency. He gave in to the pressure on August 24, 1954, and turned over his office to Vice President João Café Filho. Shortly thereafter he returned to his room in the presidential palace, where he shot himself to death.

JOSÉ LINHARES (President, October 29, 1945–January 31, 1946). José Linhares was born in Baturite, Ceara, on January 28, 1886. He attended medical school at the University of Brazil and received a Bachelor of Laws degree from the University of Sao Paulo in 1908. He began a law practice soon after and in 1913 became a criminal court judge in Rio de Janeiro. In 1931 Linhares was promoted to magistrate in the Court of Appeals of the Federal District, and in 1937 he was appointed to the Supreme Court. He became the court's vice president in 1940 and chief justice in 1945. Linhares was chief justice when the army overthrew Getúlio Vargas, and, in accordance with the constitution, he succeeded Vargas as president on October 29, 1945. Linhares proceeded with plans for democratic elections in December of that year and sought to ensure that the election was waged freely and fairly. He relinquished the presidency to the victor, Eurico Gaspar Dutra, on January 31, 1946. Linhares returned to his duties on the Supreme Court, where he remained until his retirement in 1956. He died of a heart attack the following year in Rio de Janeiro, on July 26, 1957.

EURICO GASPAR DUTRA (President, January 31, 1946–January 31, 1951). Eurico Gaspar Dutra was born in Cuiaba in the state of Mato Grosso on May 18, 1885. He enlisted in the army in 1902 and was educated at military schools. A supporter of the coup that installed Vargas as head of state in 1930, he rose to the rank of full colonel the following year. He successfully defended the Vargas regime against rebels in Sao Paolo in 1932 and was promoted to brigadier general. Dutra was also made director of military aviation and in 1935 was given command of the First Military Region. In December of 1936 he was named minister of war in the cabinet of Getúlio Vargas. Dutra approved Vargas's suspension of the constitution in 1937 and remained Vargas's minister of war until August of 1945. The army led a coup against Vargas in October of 1945 when it appeared that the president was planning to cancel elections. Dutra ran in the subsequent election and, with the support of Vargas, was elected president of Brazil. He assumed office on January 31, 1946. His administration drafted a new constitution and installed strict controls on the economy. He also banned the Brazilian Communist party and broke off diplomatic relations with the Soviet Union. His programs failed to improve the economic situation or inspire confidence in the Brazilian people. Dutra was prevented by the constitution from seeking a second term, and Vargas was returned to office in the elections of 1950. Dutra relinquished the presidency on January 31, 1951, and retired from political life. He returned briefly to public life in 1964 when he announced his support for the military coup that overthrew the government of President João Goulart. Dutra died of a lung infection in Rio de Janeiro on June 11, 1974, at the age of 89.

GETÚLIO DORNELLES VARGAS (President, January 31, 1951–August 24, 1954). *See earlier entry under Heads of State.*

JOÃO CAFÉ FILHO (President, August 24, 1954–November 8, 1955). João Café Filho was born in Natal, Rio Grande do Norte, on February 3, 1899. In 1908 he became editor of the local Natal newspaper, and he worked at various opposition newspapers during the next decade. He supported the coup that installed Vargas as head of state in 1930 and became chief of police in Natal. Two years later he was injured in an assassination attempt. In 1934 Café Filho was elected to the Federal Chamber of Deputies, where he served until Vargas dissolved the Chamber in 1937. He opposed Vargas's authoritarian rule and briefly fled to Argentina

to escape arrest. He was elected to the Chamber of Deputies again in 1945 and served as floor leader for the Social Progressive party. He became the Social Progressive party's nominee for vice president in 1950, and through an arrangement with Vargas's Labor party, he was elected vice president under Vargas. When President Vargas was pressured to resign shortly before his suicide on August 14, 1954, Café Filho assumed the office of president. His first responsibility was to restore order when a number of pro-Vargas demonstrations erupted throughout the country. Café Filho was a popular president, widely viewed as an honest man who was trying his best to stabilize the economy and solve the problems of industrialization. Since the Brazilian constitution did not allow a president to succeed himself, Café Filho could not run in the elections of 1955. On November 8, 1955, he suffered a heart attack and was replaced by Chamber of Deputies Speaker Carlos Coimbra da Luz. Three days later, the military ousted Luz and installed Senate president Nereu Ramos as president. Café Filho recovered from his illness and announced his intention to resume the presidency on November 21, 1955. The Brazilian Congress blocked this move by declaring a state of siege until the inauguration of Juscelino Kubitschek. Café Filho subsequently retired from politics. He died of a heart attack in Rio de Janeiro on February 20, 1970.

CARLOS COIMBRA DA LUZ (President, November 8, 1955–November 11, 1955). Carlos Coimbra da Luz was born in 1894. He served as president of the Chamber of Deputies and was acting president of Brazil for eleven days in August of 1955 when President Café Filho was on a state visit to Portugal. Luz again was called upon to serve as president on November 8, 1955, when Café Filho suffered a heart attack. Luz was forced to flee the capital three days later when General Henrique Teixeira

Lott led a military coup against the government. The coup was designed to insure that the government did nothing to halt the inauguration of President-Elect Juscelino Kubitschek. Luz was allowed to return to Brazil on November 13, 1955, and resigned as president of the Chamber of Deputies the following day. Luz died in Rio de Janeiro on February 9, 1961.

NEREU DE OLIVEIRA RAMOS (President, November 11, 1955–January 31, 1956). Nereu de Oliveira Ramos was born in 1889. A leading Brazilian legislator, he was serving as president of the Senate when the military ousted Acting President Carlos Coimbra da Luz on November 11, 1955. In the wake of the coup, Ramos was declared acting president by the Chamber of Deputies. He remained in office until January 31, 1956, when President-Elect Juscelino Kubitschek was sworn into office. Ramos returned to the Senate, where he remained until his death. He was killed on June 16, 1958, when the twin-engine plane he was a passenger in crashed during a storm near Curitiba, in the Parana State.

JUSCELINO KUBITSCHEK DE OLIVEIRA (President, January 31, 1956–January 31, 1961). Juscelino Kubitschek de Oliveira was born in Djamantina, Minas Gerais, on September 12, 1902. He graduated from the University of Minas Gerais medical school in 1927. He interned in hospitals throughout Europe before returning to Brazil in 1929. In 1932 he was named to head the surgical division of the Minas Gerais Military Medical Corps. Kubitschek was appointed a government secretary in 1933, and the following year he was elected to the Chamber of Deputies. He served until the Chamber's dissolution in 1937 and then returned to private practice. He was elected mayor of Belo Horizonte in 1940, where his skills as an innovative city planner won him widespread praise. Kubitschek returned to the Chamber of Deputies in 1946 and traveled extensively throughout Brazil to discuss the concerns of the populace. In 1950 he was elected governor of Minas Gerais as a member of the Social Democratic party. His successes as governor led to his nomination as the Social Democrat's candidate for president in the election held in October of 1955. Kubitschek was successful in the election, and the army, fearful that his opponents would stall his inauguration, staged a coup the following month to insure the democratic process was preserved. Kubitschek took office on January 31, 1956, and shortly thereafter lifted the state of siege and press restrictions that had been in place since the coup. He proved a popular leader who did much to preserve democratic institutions in Brazil. One of his leading achievements as president was the construction of the new inland federal capital of Brasilia. Kubitschek completed his term of office and turned over the government to his successor, Jânio da Silva Quadros, on January 31, 1961. He was subsequently elected to the Senate and planned for another bid for the presidency in the elections scheduled for 1965. His plans were thwarted by a military coup in April of 1964, however. Kubitschek was stripped of his political rights by the military junta and briefly went into exile. When he returned to Brazil, he abandoned politics and began a successful career as a banker and businessman. He remained a critic of the successive military regimes until his death in an automobile accident in Rio de Janeiro on August 22, 1976.

JÂNIO DA SILVA QUADROS (President, January 31, 1961–August 25, 1961). Jânio da Silva Quadros was born in Campo Grande, Mato Grosso, on January 25, 1917. He attended the University of Sao Paulo and received a law degree in 1939. He embarked on a career as a lawyer and educator until he entered politics in 1945. Quadros joined the small Christian Democratic party and was elected to the city council in Sao Paulo in 1947. He was elected to the state legislative assembly in Sao Paulo in 1950, where he was a successful legislator. He was elected mayor of Sao Paulo in March of 1953. His success in this office led to a narrow victory in the election for governor of Sao Paulo the following year. Quadros succeeded in improving economic conditions in Sao Paulo and led a government that was generally free from corruption. Following the completion of his term in 1958, Quadros was elected to the federal Chamber of Deputies and then embarked on a world tour. He was nominated for the presidency by the Christian Democratic party, and on October 3, 1960, he defeated a field of candidates that included General Henrique Teixeira Lott, the government-backed contender. Quadros was inaugurated on January 31, 1961, and began a campaign to eliminate corruption and political abuses. He also outlawed bikinis and cockfighting and awarded a medal to Communist revolutionary Che Guevara. Considered a leftist and something of an eccentric, he was compared by *France-Soir*, a French newspaper, to "Marx — not Karl, but Harpo." Quadros resigned the presidency on August 25, 1961, after seven months in office. It was believed that he offered his resignation in the hopes that the Chamber of Deputies would give him more power to carry out land and tax reform programs. Instead the Chamber accepted the resignation, and he was succeeded by vice president João Goulart. In October of 1962 Quadros was defeated in an election for governor of Sao Paulo. He was prohibited from engaging in political activities following the military coup in April of 1964. He remained out of politics during the successive military regimes that lasted until democratic government was restored in 1985. Quadros was subsequently elected again as mayor of Sao Paulo. He died

of lung and kidney failure in a Rio de Janerio hospital on February 16, 1992.

PASCHOAL RANIERI MAZZILLI (President, August 25, 1961–September 8, 1961). Paschoal Ranieri Mazzilli was born in 1910. He served eight terms as president of Brazil's Chamber of Deputies. While holding this position, he assumed the duties of acting president on five occasions. These terms of office included from August 25, 1961 until September 8, 1961, following the resignation of President Janio Quadros, and from April 12 until April 15, 1964, following the ouster of President João Goulart. Mazzilli died on April 21, 1975.

JOÃO BELCHIOR MARQUES GOULART (President, September 7, 1961–April 1, 1964). João Belchior Marques Goulart was born in Sao Borja in Rio Grande do Sul on March 1, 1918. Known as "Jango," he received a law degree from Porto Elegre University in 1939. He then returned to his family ranch, which adjoined land owned by President Getúlio Vargas. Goulart entered politics in 1946 and joined Vargas's Brazil Labor party. He was elected to the Rio Grande do Sul state legislature, and following Vargas's reelection to the presidency in 1950, Goulart won election to the Chamber of Deputies. He was named state's secretary of justice and the interior and in 1952 became chairman of the Brazil Labor party. That year he was also named to Vargas's cabinet as minister of labor, industry, and commerce, where he unsuccessfully pushed for a 100 percent increase in the minimum wage. He remained in the cabinet until Vargas's suicide in August of 1954. The following year Goulart was elected vice president under Juscelino Kubitschek. He again ran for vice president as the running mate of Henrique Teixeira Lott in 1960. Though Lott was defeated in his bid for the presidency, a new constitution allowed for the vice president to be elected separately, and Goulart was reelected. He served as vice president until President Jânio Quadros resigned in August of 1961. Goulart, who was out of the country at the time, was the constitutional successor to the office, but the military feared his leftist leanings and led the opposition to his assuming the presidency. Goulart received widespread popular support, however, and even his political enemies supported his constitutional right of succession. Goulart returned to Brazil on September 1, 1961, and received approval to assume the presidency from the Brazilian Congress. The Congress placed some restrictions on his succession by passing a constitutional amendment that was designed to curtail presidential powers and place most of the executive powers in the hands of a prime minister. Goulart accepted the restrictions and was sworn into office on September 7, 1961. Shortly after he assumed the presidency, Goulart began a campaign to have executive power returned to the president. On January 6, 1963, a plebiscite was passed that restored Goulart's executive power. He initiated a series of populist reforms, including land reform and wage increases. His inflationary economic policies created a severe crisis in Brazil, which was aggravated when the United States cut off financial aid and loans to the country. Goulart remained an unpopular figure with the military and business interests in the country, and labor discontent and the threat of civil disorder added to his difficulties. He was ousted by a military coup in April of 1964 and fled to Uruguay on April 1, 1964, where he was granted political asylum. Goulart remained there for nine years before going into exile in northern Argentina, where he spent his remaining years as a rancher. He died of a heart attack on his ranch near Mercedes, Argentina, on December 6, 1976.

PASCHOAL RANIERI MAZZILLI (President, April 1, 1964–April 15,

1964). *See earlier entry under Heads of State.*

HUMBERTO CASTELLO BRANCO (President, April 15, 1964–March 15, 1967). Humberto de Alencar Castello Branco was born in Fortaleza, in the northwestern state of Ceara, on September 20, 1900. He was the son of a brigadier general and attended the military college in Porto Alegre. He was commissioned as a second lieutenant in 1921 and rose through the ranks, becoming a major in 1938. Castello Branco was promoted to lieutenant colonel in 1943 when he served in the Brazilian Expeditionary Force in Italy during World War II. In 1952 he was promoted to brigadier general and rose to the rank of lieutenant general ten years later. As army chief of staff, Castello Branco was a leader of the military opposition to the presidency of João Goulart. He participated in the coup that ousted Goulart on April 1, 1964. The coup leaders, under the title of the Supreme Revolutionary Command, ordered the Brazilian Congress to elect a new president to replace Acting President Ranieri Mazzilli. Castello Branco, with the support of the Supreme Revolutionary Command, was selected as president on April 11, 1964. Two days later he resigned from the military, and two days after that he was sworn in as president. Castello Branco instituted a purge of leftists in the government and restricted political activities and the press. He had some initial success in combating inflation by instituting cuts in spending and ordering new taxes. He also sponsored a new constitution which gave more power to the central government and allowed the president to rule by decree. Castello Branco's term was scheduled to end on January 31, 1966, but was extended to March 15, 1967. He yielded the presidency to his hand-picked successor, Marshal Arthur da Costa e Silva. Castello Branco was killed on July 18, 1967, when the private plane he was a passenger in collided with another aircraft while en route to Fortaleza.

ARTHUR DA COSTA E SILVA (President, March 15, 1967–October 30, 1969). Arthur da Costa e Silva was born in the town of Taquari in Rio Grande do Sul on October 3, 1902. He attended military school and joined the army as an officer candidate in 1921. He was arrested briefly in 1922 when he participated in an abortive army revolt. During his early military career he was an instructor at various army schools. Costa e Silva served with distinction as part of the Brazilian Expeditionary Force in Italy during World War II. He was active in the military coup that ousted President Getúlio Vargas in 1945. Costa e Silva rose to the rank of brigadier general in 1952 and later served as military attaché to the Brazilian Embassy in Argentina. He was promoted to major general in 1958 and in 1961 helped to put down a rebellion against President Jânio Quadros in Sao Paulo. He refused to accept the post of army chief of staff in the government of President João Goulart in September of 1961. Costa e Silva, now a marshal, participated in the military ouster of Goulart in April of 1964. In the subsequent administration of President Castello Branco, Costa e Silva served as minister of war. He announced his candidacy to succeed Castello Branco in December of 1965. The election process had been altered to allow the president to be selected by the National Congress, rather than by direct vote. Costa e Silva had the support of the government party, the National Renewal Alliance (ARENA). He was elected on October 3, 1966, and was sworn in on March 15, 1967. As president he instituted plans to develop the Amazon region. In late 1968 Costa e Silva suspended the Congress and ruled by decree, but disappointed some supporters by not acting decisively to improve the economy and crush his opponents. Costa e Silva suffered a paralytic stroke on August 31, 1969, that left him unable to perform his duties as president. The military refused to allow vice president Pedro Aleixo to succeed in a constitutional fashion and instead a three-man junta, consisting of General Aurelio de Lyra Tavares, Admiral Augusto Hamman Rademaker Grunewald, and Air Marshall Marcio de Souza e Mello, took control of the government. This situation remained in effect until October 30, 1969, when Emilio Garrastazú Médici was sworn in as president. Costa e Silva died of a heart attack in the presidential palace on December 17, 1969.

EMILIO GARRASTAZÚ MÉDICI (President, October 30, 1969–March 15, 1974). Emilio Garrastazú Médici was born in the town of Bage in Rio Grande do Sul on December 4, 1905. He attended military school in Porto Alegre and became a cadet at the Realengo Military Academy in 1927. He was promoted through the ranks to become colonel in July of 1953, when he was appointed chief of staff to Arthur da Costa e Silva. Médici was named chief of staff of the army high command in Rio de Janeiro with the rank of brigadier general in July of 1961. He was serving as commander of the National Military Academy when the military overthrew the government of President João Goulart. He was instrumental in preventing a clash between rival army troops following the coup and soon gave his support to the military government. Médici served in the Brazilian Embassy in Washington, D.C., as the military attaché from 1964 until 1966. He returned to Brazil following the election of Costa e Silva as president and resigned from the military to take the position as head of the national intelligence service. He returned to the army in March of 1969 and took command of the third military region with the rank of lieutenant general. Following Costa e Silva's disabling stroke in August of 1969, Médici was chosen by the Army High Command as its candidate to succeed him. He was confirmed by the Brazilian Congress on October 25, 1969, and took office five days later. Médici was able to show a marked improvement in the economic status of Brazil by managing an average annual growth rate of 9 percent or better. He also increased the authoritarian nature of the military regime and ordered the arrest and execution of numerous opponents of the regime. Médici completed his term of office and turned the government over to another military man, Ernesto Geisel, on March 15, 1974. Médici retired to his cattle ranch in Rio Grande do Sul. He suffered from heart problems and was hospitalized in mid-1985. On October 9, 1985, he died of kidney failure and respiratory problems in Rio de Janeiro.

ERNESTO GEISEL (President, March 15, 1974–March 15, 1979). Ernesto Geisel was born in Bento Goncalves, Rio Grande do Sul, on August 3, 1908. He graduated from the National Military Academy in 1928 and two years later participated in the coup that installed Getúlio Vargas as president. Geisel was appointed secretary-general of the Rio Grande do Norte state government in 1931 and participated in the suppression of an anti-Vargas revolt in Sao Paulo the following year. He continued to serve Vargas in various capacities in state government. He rose to the rank of major in 1943, and after attending classes at the United States Army General Staff and Command School, he was named chief of staff of the tank division at Rio de Janeiro. In this capacity Geisel was active in the military ouster of President Vargas in 1945. He served as military attaché to the embassy in Uruguay from 1947 until 1950. When he returned to Brazil, he became involved in the Cruzada Democratica, a conservative nationalist movement. Geisel continued

to rise through the ranks and served in various military capacities. He briefly headed a military cabinet under Interim President Ranieri Mazzilli following the resignation of President Jânio Quadros. He was instrumental in arranging the compromise that allowed Vice President João Goulart to succeed Quadros. Geisel was initially reluctant to take part in a military coup against Goulart, but as Brazil's economy continued to deteriorate, he joined with the military junta that ousted Goulart on April 1, 1964. Geisel headed the military cabinet under President Castello Branco and advocated measures that allowed some democratic institutions to remain intact. Geisel served as head of the Supreme Military Tribunal from 1967 until 1969, when he retired from active military duty. When President Garrastazú Médici took office in October of 1969, he asked Geisel to head Petroleo Brasileiro, Brazil's largest oil corporation. Geisel's success in this position contributed to Brazil's economic recovery during the next four years. He was selected by the military leadership to succeed Médici as president, and he was inaugurated on March 15, 1974. In November of 1974 the government-supported ARENA party suffered severe reversals in legislative elections. Geisel proceeded with plans to restore a democratic system of government in Brazil, though many felt the process was too slow. In January of 1978 Geisel announced his selection of João Baptista da Oliveira Figueiredo as his successor. Figueiredo was approved by ARENA and replaced Geisel on March 15, 1979.

JOÃO BAPTISTA DA OLIVEIRA FIGUEIREDO (President, March 15, 1979–March 21, 1985). João Baptista da Oliveira Figueiredo was born in Rio de Janeiro on January 15, 1918. He came from a military family and joined the army in 1935. Two years later he graduated from the Realengo Military Academy. Figueiredo spent much of his career in the military as an instructor of military intelligence at the Agulhas Negras Military Academy. He was active in the military coup that ousted President Goulart on April 1, 1964. Following the coup, he was promoted to colonel, and in 1966 he was given command of the Sao Paulo state security force. He soon became chief of staff to General Emilio Médici, commander of the Third Army. Figueiredo was named chief of the presidential military staff when Médici became president in 1969. Figueiredo was appointed head of the National Intelligence Service (SNI) in the subsequent administration of President Ernesto Geisel in 1974. Figueiredo was chosen by Geisel to succeed him as president, and he was approved by the electoral college on October 15, 1978. He was sworn into office on March 15, 1979. He continued the democratization process started by President Geisel, though he was beset with labor strikes early in his administration. Figueiredo also granted amnesty and restored political rights to opponents of the government who had previously lost them. President Figueiredo suffered a heart attack on September 18, 1981. Vice President Aureliano Chaves, a civilian, served as acting president until Figueiredo was able to resume office on November 12, 1981. The democratic process was slowly restored under Figueiredo with the election of a new Congress in November of 1982. Figueiredo underwent bypass surgery in the United States in the summer of 1983. In January of 1985 Brazil held its first presidential election with civilian participation in over 20 years. Tancredo Neves, the candidate of the leading opposition party, the Brazilian Democratic Movement, was elected by a large margin, but became critically ill shortly before his scheduled inauguration on March 15, 1985. Figueiredo turned over the presidency to Neves's vice president–elect, José Sarnay, on the scheduled date.

JOSÉ SARNAY (President, March 21, 1985–March 15, 1990). José Sarnay Costa was born José Ribamar Ferreira da Costa in the town of Sao Bento in Maranhao, on April 30, 1930. He received a law degree in Sao Luis, and shortly thereafter in 1950, he joined the staff of the governor of Maranhao State. He was elected to the Maranhao State Legislature in 1956 and remained in the Legislature until 1965, when he was elected governor of Maranhao State. Though Sarnay was considered an effective leader, his reelection was vetoed by President Geisel in 1969. Sarnay remained a supporter of the military government, and in 1970 he was elected to the Brazilian Senate. When democratic elections were scheduled by the government, Sarnay left the Democratic Social party in objection to their nominee, Paulo Maluf. Sarnay and others founded the Liberal Front party, which they later joined with Tancredo Neves's Brazilian Democratic Movement. Neves and Sarnay formed a coalition ticket to run for the presidency, with Sarnay as the vice presidential nominee. The ticket was overwhelmingly elected on January 15, 1985. On the eve of his inauguration, Neves fell ill and was unable to be sworn in as president. Sarnay was sworn in as acting president on March 15, 1985. Neves's condition worsened, and on April 21, 1985, he died. Sarnay automatically became president on his death. Sarnay's supporters won an overwhelming victory in local elections in November of 1986. He presided over the writing of a new constitution, which dominated the Brazilian political scene during much of his administration. Sarnay's party was defeated in the presidential elections of 1989, and he relinquished the office to his successor, Fernando Colorr de Mello, on March 15, 1990.

FERNANDO COLORR DE MELLO (President, March 15, 1990–September 29, 1992). Fernando Colorr de Mello was born in Rio de Janerio on August 12, 1949. He attended the Federal University of Alagoas, where he received a degree in economics. He began a career as a journalist and became president of his father's media interests in 1978. Soon after, Colorr became active in politics and was elected mayor of Maceio in 1979. He served until 1982, when he was elected to the Chamber of Deputies. In 1987 he became governor of Alagoas. As governor, Colorr pledged to do away with the corruption in the government, and he eliminated numerous highly paid civil servants. He was nominated for president by the National Reconstruction party, founded in March of 1989 to promote his candidacy. He campaigned on a platform to end government corruption and improve the Brazilian economy. In November of 1989 Colorr won a spot in the runoff and he was elected president the following month. He took office on March 15, 1990. One of Collor's first actions as president was to dismantle Brazil's nuclear-bomb program. He also reduced the Amazon deforestation and opened Brazil's protected markets to free trade. Brazil's economic situation deteriorated, and the nation went into a recession. Two years into his term Colorr was accused of receiving millions of dollars from a slush fund in an influence peddling scheme run by his former campaign treasurer, Paulo

Cesar Farias. Accused of gross corruption by the Brazilian Congress, Colorr was impeached on September 29, 1992. He was stripped of power while the Brazilian Senate decided whether to remove him permanently. Colorr was subsequently indicted for corruption. He resigned from the presidency on December 29, 1992.

ITAMAR FRANCO (Acting President, September 29, 1992–   ). Itamar Augusto Cautiero Franco was born on June 28, 1930. He attended the Federal University of Juiz de Fora, where he received a degree in civil engineering. He entered politics and was elected mayor of Juiz de Fora in 1967. Franco served two terms as mayor before being elected to the Senate from Minas Gerais in 1974. He was selected by Fernando Colorr de Mello to serve as his vice presidential nominee in the elections of 1989. Following Colorr's election victory in December of 1989, Franco was sworn in as vice president on March 15, 1990. He was a critic of the government's anti-inflation policies and was seldom consulted by Colorr during his term of office. Franco was named acting president following the impeachment of Colorr on September 29, 1992, and was sworn in as president following Colorr's resignation on December 29, 1992.

HEADS OF GOVERNMENT

TANCREDO DE ALMEIDA NEVES (Prime Minister, September 7, 1961–June 26, 1962). Tancredo de Almeida Neves was born in Sao Joao del Rei, in Minas Gerais, on March 4, 1910. He studied law in the state capital of Belo Horizonte and returned to his home town in 1932 to practice. He became involved in local politics, and in 1951 he was elected to the federal Chamber of Deputies. Neves served as minister of

justice in the administration of President Getúlio Vargas from 1953 to 1954. He was appointed to administer the Banco do Brasil during the administration of President Juscelino Kubitschek. Neves was instrumental in negotiating the arrangement that allowed Vice President João Goulart to succeed as president when Jânio Quadros resigned in August of 1961. Neves, as part of the arrangement, was appointed prime minister and given much of the executive power formerly held by the president. He was sworn in on September 7, 1961, but resigned the following year on June 26, 1962. Following the military coup that ousted Goulart in 1964, Neves continued to serve in the Chamber of Deputies, where he became a leading critic of the successive military governments. He was elected a senator from Minas Gerais in 1979 and became his home state's governor in 1983. When the military regime of President João Figueiredo allowed the restoration of a democratic form of government, Neves ran for the presidency as the candidate of the Brazilian Democratic Movement. He was overwhelmingly elected in January of 1985, but suffered a serious illness on the eve of his inauguration on March 14, 1985. Neves was unable to be sworn in and his vice president, José Sarnay, took office as acting president. Neves died of heart and lung complications in Sao Paulo on April 21, 1985.

AURO SOARES DE MOURA ANDRADA (Prime Minister, July 3, 1962–July 4, 1962). Auro Soares de Moura Andrada was president of the Brazilian Senate when he was selected to serve as prime minister on July 3, 1962. He was unable to form a cabinet to meet with President Goulart's approval and resigned the following day.

FRANCISCO BROCHADO DA ROCHA (Prime Minister, July 10, 1962–September 14, 1962). Francisco Brochado da Rocha was born in Porto Alegre on August 8, 1910. He was a member of the Social Democratic party. A leftist, he was nominated by President João Goulart to serve as prime minister and took office on July 10, 1962. He resigned two months later on September 14, 1962, after a series of disagreements with Congress. He died in Porto Alegre, Brazil, on September 26, 1962.

HERMES LIMA (Prime Minister, September 16, 1962–January 6, 1963). Hermes Lima was born on December 22, 1902. He served as minister of labor in the government of President João Goulart. Following the resignation of Francisco Brochado da Rocha, Lima was nominated to serve as prime minister on September 16, 1962. He also served as foreign minister in the Goulart government. Executive power was returned to President Goulart on January 6, 1963, and the position of prime minister was discontinued.

Brunei, Sultanate of

(Negara Brunei Darussalam)

Brunei is a country in southeastern Asia. It was granted independence from Great Britain on January 1, 1984.

HEADS OF STATE

OMAR ALI SAIFUDDIN (Sultan, June 3, 1950–October 5, 1967). Omar Ali Saifuddin Sa'adul Khair Waddin was born in Bandar Seri Begawan on September 23, 1916. He served as Grand Vizier and a member of the State Council during the sultanate of his brother from 1947 until 1950. He succeeded to the sultanate upon the death of his brother, Sir Ahmed Tajudin, on June 3, 1950.

The sultan ruled Brunei under a treaty of protection with Great Britain. Brunei gained great prosperity from its oil deposits and achieved one of the highest per capita incomes in the world. The sultan introduced a written constitution in 1959 when his country gained control of its internal affairs from Great Britain. With British military assistance, he survived an internal revolt in 1962 when the Brunei People's party staged an uprising. The sultan suspended the constitution in December of 1962. He rejected bringing Brunei into the new Federation of Malaya the following year. He abdicated in favor of his son, Sir Muda Hassanal Bolkiah, on October 5, 1967, but remained a leading figure in the country. He served as minister of defense following Brunei's complete independence on December 31, 1983. He retained that position until his death in Bandar Seri Begawan on September 7, 1986.

SIR MUDA HASSANAL BOLKIAH MU'IZZADIN WADDAULAH (Sultan, October 5, 1967–). Muda Hassanal

Bolkiah Mu'izzadin Waddaulah was born in Bandar Seri Begawan on July 15, 1946. He was the eldest son of Sir Omar Ali Saiffudin, Brunei's sultan from 1950. He was educated at the Victoria Institute in Malaysia and the Sandhurst Royal Military Academy in Great Britain. Muda was named crown prince and heir apparent by his father in 1961. The sultan abdicated in favor of his son on October 4, 1967. Sultan Omar remained a powerful force behind the throne, however, and advised Sultan Muda on government affairs until his death in 1986. Brunei achieved complete independence from Great Britain on December 31, 1983. The sultan also served as prime minister upon independence. He retained the Ministries of Finance and Home Affairs from 1984 until 1986, when he became minister of defense. The sultan was regarded as one of the wealthiest men in the world because of Brunei's wealth in oil. He refused to allow the formation of political parties in Brunei, despite an increase in democratic reform movements in the early 1990s.

Bulgaria, Republic of

(Republika Bulgariya)

Bulgaria is a country in southeastern Europe. It received independence from the Ottoman Empire on September 22, 1908.

HEADS OF STATE

SIMEON II (King, August 28, 1943– September 9, 1946). Simeon Borisov Saxe-Coburg-Gotha was born in 1937. He was the son of King Boris of Bulgaria and Queen Joanna. He was proclaimed King Simeon II of Bulgaria following his father's death on August 28, 1943. Simeon ruled under a regency council headed by his uncle, Prince

Cyril. Bulgaria was an ally of Germany during World War II, until the government was ousted by the anti–Fascist Fatherland Front in September of 1944. Kimon Georgiev was installed as premier and many members of the old regime, including Prince Cyril and other members of the regency council, were arrested and executed. A referendum to proclaim Bulgaria a republic was passed on September 8, 1946, and King Simeon and his mother left the country to go into exile in Egypt the following week. Simeon attended Victoria College in Alexandria and the Valley Forge Military Academy in the United States. The royal family subsequently lived in exile in Spain. Simeon returned to Bulgaria in 1990 following the collapse of the Communist regime. Residency requirements prevented him from being a candidate in the 1992 presidential election.

VASSIL KOLAROV (President, October 27, 1946–December 9, 1947). Vassil Kolarov was born in Shumen on July 16, 1877. He worked as a teacher and joined the Bulgarian Revolutionary movement in the 1890s. He was an early leader of the Social Democratic party in 1897. Kolarov received a degree in law from the University of Geneva in 1900. He returned to Belgium, where he practiced law and continued his political activities. In 1913 he was elected to the Bulgarian Parliament. Kolarov was an opponent of Bulgaria's entry into World War I as an ally of Germany and was charged with treason in 1914. He became secretary of the Bulgarian Communist party in April of 1919 and was a leader of the uprising against King Boris III in June of 1923. The uprising was unsuccessful, and Kolarov was sentenced to death for his role in it. He went into hiding and worked with the underground until 1928, when he went into exile in Moscow. Kolarov continued to serve as secretary-general of the Comintern until 1935. He served as the director of the Moscow International Agrarian Institute from 1938. Bulgaria sided with Germany during World War II. The Fatherland Front, a Resistance group, took control of the government in September of 1944 and surrendered to the Allies. Kolarov returned to Bulgaria shortly thereafter and joined the Fatherland Front. The Communists defeated the opposition Agrarian Union in the elections in November of 1945, and Kolarov was selected as president of the National Assembly the following month. The monarchy was eliminated by a plebiscite in September of 1946, and the People's Republic of Bulgaria was established. The Communists officially took over the government in the October elections, and Kolarov became provisional president on October 27, 1946. Kolarov stepped down from the presidency on December 9, 1947, following the enactment of a new constitution. He became deputy premier and foreign minister in the new government. Kolarov took over the duties of premier when Georgi Dimitrov became ill in April of 1949. Dimitrov died on July 2, 1949, and Kolarov was elected to succeed him on July 20, 1949. Kolarov retained his position until his death in Sofia on January 23, 1950.

MINCHO NEITSEV (President, December 9, 1947–May 27, 1950). Mincho Neitsev (Neichev) was born in 1888. He was educated at the Universities of Geneva, Bern, and Brussels, and received a doctorate of law degree. He joined the Communist party at an early age and served as a defense attorney in numerous trials involving Communists. On several occasions he was himself arrested and imprisoned. During World War II Neitsev organized the Fatherland Front in opposition to the pro-Axis government. When the Front took power in 1944, Neitsev was named minister of justice. He was appointed minister of education the following year. Neitsev became Bulgaria's head of state on December 9, 1947, when he was elected president of the Presidium of the National Assembly. He retained that position until he was appointed foreign minister on May 27, 1950. Neitsev was dropped from the Central Committee of the Bulgarian Communist party in March of 1954, but remained foreign minister until his death after a long illness on August 11, 1956.

GEORGI DAMIANOV (President, May 27, 1950–November 27, 1958). Georgi Damianov was born in Lopushna on September 12, 1892. He was educated in military schools and served in the Bulgarian army during World War I. In 1923 he supported the unsuccessful Communist coup against the government. When the coup failed, he fled to Yugoslavia. Damianov later went to Moscow, where he assisted Georgi Dimitrov with his work with the Comintern. He also attended a Soviet military academy and later served in the Red Army. He was involved in the formation of the International Brigade that fought the Fascists in Spain during the 1930s. Following the ouster of the pro–Axis government of Bulgaria during World War II, Damianov returned to Bulgaria. He served as minister of war in Dimitrov's government from 1946 until 1949. He was elected chairman of the Presidium of the Bulgarian National Assembly on May 27, 1950, and served as Bulgaria's head of state until his death on November 27, 1958.

DIMITER GANEV (President, January 20, 1959–April 20, 1964). Dimiter Ganev was born in 1898. He joined the Communist party in 1918, while working as a schoolteacher. He supported the unsuccessful Communist coup in 1923 and was prevented from teaching following the coup's failure. Ganev remained active in the party and became a member of the Central Committee in 1929. He subsequently worked in the underground in Romania, where he was arrested in 1935. He was released in 1940 and returned to Bulgaria. Ganev became a member of the Bulgarian Communist party Politburo in 1942. Following the war, he served as minister of foreign trade. He was relieved of his post in September of 1952 and was subsequently named ambassador to Czechoslovakia, where he served until 1954. Ganev was dropped from the Politburo following his return to Bulgaria, but was reelected to the Polit-

buro in July of 1957. He was elected chairman of the Presidium of the Bulgarian National Assembly on January 20, 1959. Ganev remained Bulgaria's head of state until his death in Sofia on April 20, 1964.

GEORGI TRAIKOV (President, April 23, 1964–July 7, 1971). Georgi Traikov was born in 1898. He joined the Peasant Movement in 1919 and was active with the Agrarian Union from 1923. He was an opponent of the pro–Axis government during World War II, and following the installation of the Fatherland Front, he became deputy chairman of the National Assembly in 1945. Traikov served as minister of agriculture from 1946 until 1949 and was first deputy prime minister from 1949 until 1964. He was elected president of the Presidium of the National Assembly on April 23, 1964. He remained Bulgaria's head of state until July 7, 1971, when the constitution replaced the Presidium of the National Assembly with a Council of State headed by Todor Zhivkov. Traikov remained Speaker of the National Assembly until his death after a long illness in Sofia on January 14, 1975.

TODOR ZHIVKOV (President, July 7, 1971–November 10, 1989). Todor Zhivkov was born in Pravets on September 7, 1911. He was educated in Sofia and joined the Communist youth league in the 1920s. He remained active in the Communist party and became party secretary for the Sofia district in 1934. Zhivkov helped to organize the Resistance movement in Bulgaria during World War II and participated in the coup that ousted the pro–Axis government in 1944. He was elected to the National Assembly in 1945 and in 1948 became a member of the Communist party Central Committee. He was an ally of Vulko Chervenkov and rose through the party ranks to become a member of the Politburo in 1951. Zhivkov succeeded Chervenkov as first secretary of the Bulgarian Communist party in March of 1954. Zhivkov remained in Chervenkov's shadow until Chervenkov was ousted as premier on April 16, 1956. Zhivkov then consolidated his power in Bulgaria and also became premier on November 19, 1962. He survived an attempted coup by political and military leaders in April of 1965. Bulgaria subsequently began a period of liberalization in its political and economic policies. Zhivkov reinstituted hard-line policies following the Warsaw Pact invasion of Czechoslovakia in August of 1968. He sponsored a new constitution for Bulgaria in 1971 that replaced the Presidium of the National Assembly with a Council of State. Zhivkov was elected president of the Council of State on July 7, 1971. He relinquished the premiership to Stanko Todorov on the same day. Zhivkov's regime was threatened by the growing reformist movement sweeping through the Eastern Bloc nations in the late 1980s. He attempted some liberalization policies but was forced to resign as president and party general secretary on November 10, 1989. Zhivkov was expelled from the party in December of 1989 and put under house arrest in January of 1990. He was charged with embezzlement, corruption, and abuse of power. After a trial that lasted 18 months, Zhivkov was convicted on September 4, 1992, and sentenced to seven years in prison.

PETAR MLADENOV (President, November 12, 1989–July 6, 1990). Petar Toshev Mladenov was born in Toshevtsi on August 22, 1936 and was educated in Sofia and Moscow. He was active in the League of Young Communists from 1963 and became first secretary of the Bulgarian Communist party in the Vidin district in 1969. He was elected to the National Assembly and served as minister of foreign affairs from 1971. Mladenov was a candidate member of the Politburo of the Central Committee from 1974 and became a full member in 1977. He succeeded Todor Zhivkov as general secretary of the Communist party Central Committee on November 10, 1989. He replaced Zhivkov as chairman of the State Council two days later on November 12, 1989. Mladenov was faced with a growing democratic movement in Bulgaria. He relinquished the party leadership to Aleksandur Lilov in April of 1990. The Communist party subsequently changed its name to the Bulgarian Socialist party. The government structure was also revamped, and on April 3, 1990, Mladenov became state president of Bulgaria. He was forced to step down from that position on July 6, 1990.

ZHELYU ZHELEV (President, August 1, 1990–). Zhelyu Zhelev was born in Veselinovo, in the Varna region, on March 3, 1935. He was educated at the University of Sofia and became a librarian in Veselinovo. He was a member of the Bulgarian Communist party until he was expelled in 1964 for writing a master's thesis critical of Lenin. Zhelev was expelled from the university and was unemployed from 1966 until 1972. He was not allowed to complete his master's degree in philosophy until 1974. Zhelev became chairman of the Union of Democratic Forces (UDF), the leading opposition party, when democratic institutions were allowed to return to Bulgaria in 1989. Though the Socialist party held a majority in the Bulgarian Grand National Assembly, the UDF held enough seats to stalemate the election of president. Rather than call for new elections, the Socialists reached a compromise and allowed the selection of Zhelev as president on August 1, 1990.

HEADS OF GOVERNMENT

KIMON GEORGIEV (Premier, September 10, 1944–November 23, 1946). Kimon Georgiev was born in Pazardzhik in 1882. He attended military school and joined the Bulgarian army. He served in the infantry during World War I and was seriously wounded in action. In the 1920s he retired from the army and entered politics. Georgiev served in several governments in the late 1920s and early 1930s. He engineered the overthrow of the government and installed himself as premier on May 19, 1934. He served until January 22, 1935 and was briefly arrested by the subsequent administration. Georgiev was an opponent of the pro-Axis government that ruled Bulgaria during World War II. He organized the Fatherland Front in opposition to the government. He succeeded in ousting the Council of Regents on September 9, 1944, and became premier the following day. The new government arranged a surrender to the Allies. Georgiev was defeated in the elections of 1946 and left office as premier on November 23, 1946. He subsequently served as foreign minister in the Communist government of Georgi Dimitrov. Georgiev retired from politics in 1952 and lived in obscurity until his death in Sofia on September 28, 1969.

GEORGI DIMITROV (Premier, November 23, 1946–July 2, 1949). Georgi Dimitrov was born in Kovachevtsi, near Radomir, Bulgaria, on June 18, 1882. He joined the Social Democratic party in 1902. When the party split the following year, Dimitrov joined the wing of the party which adhered to the philosophy of the Russian Bolshevists. He was elected a deputy in the Bulgarian National Assembly in 1913 and served until 1917, when he was arrested for sedition because of his opposition to Bulgaria's entry into World War I. In 1919 Dimitrov became the leader of the newly organized wing of the Social Democrats, now called the Bulgarian Workers' party. The following year he traveled to Russia, where he was elected to the executive committee of the Comintern. The Bulgarian Communists attempted a coup in Bulgaria in September of 1923. The attempt was unsuccessful, and Dimitrov fled into Yugoslavia. He was tried and condemned to death in absentia for his part in the overthrow attempt. He continued his activities with the Comintern and served as leader of the Balkan section while living in Vienna until 1929. Dimitrov then went to Berlin, where he was in charge of the central European section. He was arrested and charged with complicity in the burning of the Reichstag on March 9, 1933. Dimitrov was acquitted in December of that year, but remained in prison until February 27, 1934, when he went to Moscow. The following year he was named secretary-general of the Comintern, and he remained in that position until 1943. After the end of World War II, Dimitrov returned to Bulgaria. He was appointed prime minister of the Communist government on November 22, 1946. Dimitrov fell ill in April of 1949 and went to the Soviet Union for treatment. He died there, near Moscow, on July 2, 1949.

VASSIL KOLAROV (Premier, July 20, 1949–January 23, 1950). *See entry under Heads of State.*

VULKO CHERVENKOV (Premier, February 1, 1950–April 16, 1956). Vulko Chervenkov was born in Zlatitsa on August 24, 1900. He joined the Communist party in the early 1920s and was a participant in the unsuccessful Communist coup in 1923. He subsequently went into exile in Moscow, where he attended the Marx-Lenin

School. Chervenkov later served as director of the school. He returned to Bulgaria with the Soviet army following the ouster of the pro-Axis government in 1944. He was elected to the Central Committee of the Bulgarian Communist party and served as minister of culture in the subsequent Communist government. He succeeded Georgi Dimitrov, his brother-in-law, as secretary-general of the Bulgarian Communist party in 1949. Chervenkov was also elected premier on February 1, 1950. He was a supporter of Josef Stalin, and his hold on the Bulgarian Communist party diminished with Stalin's death in 1953. He relinquished the party chairmanship in March of 1954 and was ousted as Premier on April 16, 1956. Chervenkov remained in the government as deputy premier and minister of education and culture until 1962, when he was expelled from the party. He subsequently lived in obscurity, though he was rehabilitated by the party in 1969. Chervenkov died in Sofia on October 21, 1980.

ANTON YUGOV (Premier, April 17, 1956–November 19, 1962). Anton Yugov was born on August 5, 1904. He joined the Trade Union and Workers Movement in 1922 and became a member of the Bulgarian Communist party in 1928. He was trained in Moscow from 1934 until 1936, and the following year he was elected to the Party Politburo. Yugov was imprisoned in 1940, but escaped the following year. He fought with the Resistance and served as party secretary of the underground movement throughout World War II. In 1944 Yugov was named minister of the interior in the government of Kimon Georgiev. He was appointed minister of industry in 1950 and served as deputy prime minister in the early 1950s. On April 17, 1956, Yugov was named prime minister of Bulgaria. He remained in that position until November 19, 1962, when he was forced from office and expelled from the Central Committee of the Communist party.

TODOR ZHIVKOV (Premier, November 19, 1962–July 7, 1971). *See entry under Heads of State.*

STANKO TODOROV (Premier, July 7, 1971–June 16, 1981). Stanko Todorov was born in the Pernik Region on December 10, 1920. He joined the Bulgarian Communist party and was active in the Resistance movement during World War II. He was subsequently elected to the National Assembly and served as minister of agriculture from 1952 until 1958. Todorov was named deputy prime minister in 1959 and served until 1966. He became a member of the Politburo of the Communist party in 1961. He served as secretary of the Bulgarian Communist party Central Committee from 1966 until 1971. Todorov was elected chairman of the Council of Ministers, or premier, on July 7, 1971, and retained that position until June 16, 1981, when he was appointed chairman of the National Assembly. He was forced from that office in July of 1988.

GRISHA FILIPOV (Premier, June 16, 1981–March 21, 1986). Grisha Filipov was born in Kadiyevka on July 13, 1919. He was educated at Moscow University and returned to Bulgaria in 1936, where he joined the Bulgarian Communist party. He was arrested for antigovernment activities in 1941 and remained imprisoned until the pro-Axis government was ousted in 1944. Filipov subsequently served in various Communist party and government capacities. He became a member of the Communist party Central Committee in 1966 and served as secretary of the Central Committee from 1971 until 1982. He was elected to the Politburo in 1974, and on June 16, 1981, he was elected chairman of the Council of Ministers. Filipov was replaced in that position by Georgi Atanasov on March 21, 1986. He returned to the position of secretary of the Central Committee, where he served until 1989. Filipov was arrested and charged with embezzlement on July 14, 1992. He was convicted on November 3, 1992, and sentenced to ten years in prison.

GEORGI ATANASOV (Premier, March 21, 1986–February 3, 1990). Georgi Ivanov Atanasov was born in Pravoslaven on June 23, 1933. He was educated in Bulgaria and joined the Communist party in 1956. He served in various party positions and became a member of the Central Committee of the Bulgarian Communist party in 1966. Atanasov served as head of the Department of Science and Education from 1968 until 1976. He was deputy chairman of the State Planning Committee from 1980 until 1981 and was subsequently chairman of the Committee on State Control until 1984. He was elected president of the Council of Ministers on March 21, 1986. Atanasov was replaced during a restructuring of the Communist party on February 3, 1990. He was arrested on April 24, 1992, and charged with embezzlement. On November 4, 1992, he was convicted and sentenced to ten years in prison.

ANDREI LUKANOV (Premier, February 3, 1990–December 7, 1990). Andrei Karlov Lukanov was born in Moscow on September 26, 1938. He was educated in Moscow and joined the Dimitrov Young Communist League in 1957. He worked in the Bulgarian Ministry of Foreign Affairs from 1963 and was a member of the Bulgarian Communist party from 1966. From 1976 until 1986 he served as deputy chairman of the Council of Ministers and was first

deputy chairman until 1987. Lukanov served as minister of foreign economic relations from 1987 until 1990. He was named premier of Bulgaria on February 3, 1990, and served until December 7, 1990. Lukanov was arrested on July 9, 1992, and charged with misappropriating state funds.

DIMITAR POPOV (Premier, December 7, 1990–November 8, 1991). Dimitar Popov was born in 1927. He was a judge on the Sofia Municipal Court. He served as secretary of the Central Election Commission and oversaw Bulgaria's first free election in June of 1990. Popov was selected by the Parliament to serve as prime minister on December 7, 1990, following the resignation of Andrei Lukanov. Popov remained prime minister until November 8, 1991, when he was replaced by Filip Dimitrov.

FILIP DIMITROV (Premier, November 8, 1991–December 30, 1992). Filip Dimitrov was born in 1955. He was the leader of the Bulgarian Union of Democratic Forces. On November 8, 1991, he formed a government as premier. He retained office until December 30, 1992, when his cabinet lost the support of the Turkish Movement for Rights and Freedoms party.

LYUBEN BEROV (Premier, December 30, 1992–). Lyuben Berov was born in 1925. He served as an economic advisor to President Zhelyu Zhelev. He was nominated by the ethnic Turkish party, the Movement for Rights and Freedom, to be premier and was approved by the National Assembly on December 30, 1992.

OTHER LEADERS

GEORGI DIMITROV (General Secretary, 1944–July 2, 1949). *See entry*   *under Heads of Government.*

VULKO CHERVENKOV (General Secretary, 1949–March 1954). *See entry under Heads of Government.*

TODOR ZHIVKOV (General Secretary, March 1954–November 10, 1989). *See entry under Heads of State.*

PETAR MLADENOV (General Secretary, November 10, 1989–April 3, 1990). *See entry under Heads of State.*

Burkina Faso

(Upper Volta)

Burkina Faso is a country in western Africa. It was granted independence from France on August 4, 1960.

HEADS OF STATE

MAURICE YAMÉOGO (President, December 1, 1959–January 3, 1966). Maurice Yaméogo was born on December 31, 1921. He was educated locally and was elected to the Grand Council for French West Africa in 1947. He served as minister of agriculture in 1955 and minister of the interior in 1956. Yaméogo succeeded Daniel Coulibaly as president of the Council of Ministers in September of 1958, and he became the first prime minister of Upper Volta on December 11, 1958. On December 1, 1959, Yaméogo became the first president of Upper Volta. He remained as prime minister until December 8, 1960, when he took the position of president of the Council of Ministers. In 1965 Yaméogo also took the position of minister of defense. The political situation in the Ivory Coast deteriorated following Yaméogo's introduction of an economic austerity program. He was deposed by a military coup on January 3, 1966, and survived a suicide attempt later in the year. In April of 1969 he was tried for embezzlement and sentenced to five years in prison. His sentence was subsequently reduced, and he was released in August of 1970. Yaméogo was placed under a restriction order during the administration of Thomas Sankara in 1983. He was released from restriction in September of 1984.

SANGOULÉ LAMIZANA (President, January 3, 1966–November 25, 1980). Aboubakar Sangoulé Lamizana was born in Dianra in 1916. He joined the French army in 1936 and was stationed in French North Africa in the 1940s. He served as an instructor in Bambara and Paris in the late 1940s and was promoted to lieutenant in 1951. Lamizana served in the Ivory Coast and again in North Africa until Upper Volta achieved independence in 1960. He returned to Upper Volta and was named chief of the Armed Forces General Staff. Lamizana led the military coup that ousted President Maurice Yaméogo on January 3, 1966. He organized a military government and served as head of state. His government allowed elections to be held in December of 1970. Lamizana suspended the constitution and dissolved the National Assembly on February 8, 1974. He served as premier and minister of justice in the new government. Lamizana allowed new elections in April of 1978 and was reelected to the presidency the following month. He stepped down as premier on July 7, 1978, and turned over the government to Joseph Conombo. Lamizana's government was ousted in a bloodless coup led by Col. Sayé Zerbo on November 25, 1980. Lamizana was charged with corruption by the government of Thomas Sankara in 1983, but was acquitted in January of the following year.

SAYÉ ZERBO (President, November 25, 1980–November 7, 1982). Sayé Zerbo was born in Tougan in August of 1932. He joined the French army in 1950 and served in Indo-China and Algiers. In 1961 he joined the Upper Volta army as a paratrooper. Zerbo studied and taught at the local military college. In 1974 Zerbo was appointed minister of foreign affairs, and he served until 1976. On November 25, 1980, Colonel Zerbo led a coup against President Sangoule Lamizana. He served as president until he was ousted by a military coup on November 7, 1982. He was arrested in September of 1983 and was sentenced to fifteen years imprisonment in May of the following year. Zerbo was released in August of 1986.

JEAN-BAPTISTE OUEDRAOGO (President, November 7, 1982–August 4, 1983). Jean-Baptiste Ouedraogo was a major in the Upper Voltan Army Medical Corps. When a military coup led by Capt. Thomas Sankara ousted the government of Sayé Zerbo on November 7, 1982, a progressive Provisional People's Salvation Council replaced Zerbo's military government. The new government selected Major Ouedraogo as head of state. Ouedraogo dismissed Sankara as premier and moved against the more radical members of the Council in May of 1983. Ouedraogo made plans to hold democratic elections, but was ousted by Sankara and his supporters on August 4, 1983. He was detained by the new government until August of 1985.

THOMAS SANKARA (President, August 4, 1983–October 15, 1987). Thomas Sankara was born in Upper Volta on December 21, 1949. He served as a paratrooper in the Upper Voltan army and took part in the border war with Mali in 1974. He served as secretary of state for information in the government of Sayé Zerbo in 1981, but resigned in a dispute with the president. Sankara was instrumental in the coup that ousted Zerbo in November of 1982. Sankara was appointed prime minister of Upper Volta on January 10, 1983, by the ruling People's Salvation Council. He was ousted from that position by President Jean-Baptiste Ouedraogo on May 17, 1983. In May of 1983 Sankara was briefly imprisoned, and he subsequently made plans to overthrow the government. He led a company of paratroopers against Ouedraogo on August 4, 1983, and became president of the ruling National Revolutionary Council. The following year, on August 4, 1984, Sankara changed the name of Upper Volta to Burkina Faso, meaning the country of honest men. He pursued a policy of radical nationalism and sought to reduce government corruption. Sankara was overthrown in a coup led by Capt. Blaise Compaoré, his second in command, on October 15, 1987. Sankara and twelve of his aides were executed outside of the capital shortly after the coup.

BLAISE COMPAORÉ (President, October 15, 1987–). Blaise Compaoré was born in Ouagadougou on February 3, 1951. He was educated at the military college in Cameroon and joined the Upper Voltan army as a paratrooper. He resigned from the military in 1981 following the resignation of Thomas Sankara from the government of President Sayé Zerbo. When Sankara was arrested by the government of Jean-Baptiste Ouedraogo in 1983, Compaoré organized the coup that ousted the Ouedraogo government and installed Sankara as president. He served in

Sankara's government as minister of state and justice. He was second in command to Sankara when he led the coup that ousted the government and executed Sankara on October 15, 1987. Compaoré subsequently served as chairman of the ruling Popular Front of Burkina Faso and head of government. Compaoré reluctantly agreed to schedule new elections and was reelected president in December of 1991. The opposition charged that the elections were tainted by fraud. Compaoré allowed multiparty legislative elections to be held in May of 1992, and his ruling Organization for Popular Democracy-Labour Movement was victorious in the balloting.

HEADS OF GOVERNMENT

MAURICE YAMEOGO (Prime Minister, December 11, 1958–December 8, 1960). *See entry under Heads of State.*

GÉRARD KANGO OUEDRAOGA (Prime Minister, February 13, 1971–February 8, 1974). Gérard Kango Ouedraoga was born in Ouahigouya on September 19, 1925. He served in the French colonial government from 1947 and entered politics in 1952. He was elected a deputy to the French National Assembly in 1956 and formed the Democratic Voltaic Movement (MDV) the following year. Ouedraoga was also elected to the Upper Voltan National Assembly and served as minister of finance in the government of Maurice Yaméogo. Yaméogo named Ouedraoga as ambassador to Great Britain following independence in 1961. He remained there until Yaméogo was ousted in 1966. He served as an advisor to the Foreign Ministry during the subsequent military government. When elections were scheduled in 1970, Ouedraoga's party was victorious, and he became prime minister on February 13, 1971. He retained the position until the constitution was suspended and he was dismissed on February 8, 1974. Ouedraoga later served as president of the National Assembly from 1978 until 1980.

SANGOULE LAMIZANA (Prime Minister, February 8, 1974–July 7, 1978). *See entry under Heads of State.*

JOSEPH CONOMBO (Prime Minister, July 16, 1978–November 25, 1980). Joseph Issoufou Conombo was born in Kombissiri on February 9, 1917. He attended the medical school in Dakar, Senegal, and served in the French army during World War II. He returned to Upper Volta after the war and practiced medicine from 1946. In 1951 Conombo was elected to the French National Assembly, and he served as undersecretary of state for the interior in the French government from 1954 until 1955. He remained in the French National Assembly until independence was granted to Upper Volta in 1959. He was elected mayor of Ouagadougou the following year and served until 1965. Conombo was appointed director general for public health in 1966 and served until 1968. He served as minister of foreign affairs in the government of Gérard Kango Ouedraogo from February of 1971 until his resignation in December of 1973. Conombo was elected prime minister of Upper Volta on July 16, 1978. He remained in office until November 25, 1980, when the government was overthrown in a military coup led by Col. Sayé Zerbo.

SAYÉ ZERBO (Prime Minister, November 25, 1980–November 7, 1982). *See entry under Heads of State.*

THOMAS SANKARA (Prime Minister, January 10, 1983–May 17, 1983). *See entry under Heads of State.*

YOUSSOUF OUEDRAOGO (Prime Minister, June 16, 1992–). Youssouf Ouedraogo was a leading economist and former member of the cabinet of President Thomas Sankara. Following legislative elections in May of 1992, Ouedraogo was selected to assume the restored position of prime minister, and he took office on June 16, 1992.

Burundi, Republic of

(République du Burundi)

Burundi is a country in central Africa. It was granted independence from a United Nations trusteeship administered by Belgium on July 1, 1962.

HEADS OF STATE

MWAMBUTSA IV (King, December 2, 1915–July 8, 1966). Mwambutsa Bangiricenge was born in Nyabiyogi in 1912. His father, Mutaga IV, died on November 30, 1915, and Mwambutsa succeeded him as mwami, or king, of Burundi on December 2, 1915. He ruled under a regency council until August 28, 1929. Belgium administered Burundi as part of the Rúanda-Urundi territory until internal self-government was granted on January 1, 1962. Burundi received full independence on July 1, 1962. Mwambutsa survived a rebellion by members of the Hutu tribe in late 1965. He fled the country and allowed the army to deal harshly with the Hutu leaders. Mwambutsa feared another coup attempt from members of the Tutsi tribe and remained out of the country while he allowed his son, Prince Charles Ndizeye, to rule in his absence. Prince Charles dethroned his father on July 8, 1966, and became mwami until he was ousted in a military coup four months later. Mwambutsa remained in exile in Geneva, where he died on April 26, 1977.

NTARE V (King, July 8, 1966–November 28, 1966). Charles Ndizeye was born in Kitega on December 2, 1947. He was the son of Mwami Mwambutsa IV and ruled as prince regent in his father's stead when his father left the country for Europe in December of 1965. Prince Charles ousted his father on July 8, 1966, and was proclaimed Mwami Ntare V. He subsequently suspended the constitution and named Captain Michael Micombero as his prime minister. Micombero led a military coup that deposed Ntare while he was out of the country on November 28, 1966. Ntare went into exile in Zaire and later in West Germany. He was invited to return to Burundi under a pledge of safe conduct in April of 1972. Ntare was arrested when he arrived in the country and placed under house arrest in the former royal palace at Gitega. Ntare was killed by government troops there on April 29, 1972. The government claimed that the killing had been the result of supporters attempting to free Ntare during an abortive coup attempt.

MICHEL MICOMBERO (President, November 28, 1966–November 1, 1976). Michel Micombero was born in Musenga in 1940. He was a member of the Tutsi tribe and was educated locally and at the Brussels Military Academy. He returned to Burundi after independence to serve in the police. Micombero was named minister of defense in 1965 and was instrumental in preventing a coup by members of the Hutu tribe later in the year. He assisted Prince Charles Ndizeye in the overthrow of his father, Mwami Mwambutsa, in July of 1966 and was named prime minister on July 13, 1966. Micombero then deposed Charles, known as Mwami Ntare V, on November 28, 1966. Micombero declared Burundi a republic and named himself as president. He initially tried to gain the cooperation of the Hutu tribe but in October of 1969 he announced the discovery of a conspiracy against the government and began a purge and execution of Hutu leaders. The Hutu rebelled in 1972, and the repression that followed saw the death of over 100,000 Hutus. Micombero was ousted in a peaceful military coup on November 1, 1976. He went into exile in Somalia and attended the university there. Micombero died in Mogadishu, Somalia, of a heart attack on July 16, 1983.

JEAN-BAPTISTE BAGAZA (President, November 9, 1976–September 3, 1987). Jean-Baptiste Bagaza was born in Tuovou on August 29, 1946. He was educated at the Belgian military school and subsequently joined the army of independent Burundi. After rising through the ranks to lieutenant colonel, he served as chief of staff of the armed forces under President Michel Micombero. Bagaza led the military coup that ousted Micombero on November 1, 1976. He served as head of the subsequent ruling Supreme Revolutionary Council and became president of Burundi on November 9, 1976. He abolished the post of prime minister and ruled under a military government from October of 1978. Bagaza was ousted in a military coup on September 3, 1987, while he was attending a meeting of French-speaking leaders in Canada. He went into exile in Belgium and then in Libya in 1989. Bagaza was reportedly involved in an unsuccessful coup attempt in Burundi in March of 1992.

PIERRE BUYOYA (President, September 3, 1987–). Pierre Buyoya was born in 1949. He was educated at the Belgian military school and studied in France and West Germany. After his return to Burundi, he served in the army. He was a major in the Ministry of National Defense when he led the coup that ousted President Jean-Baptiste Bagaza on September 3, 1987. Buyoya subsequently became chairman of the Military Committee for National Salvation, as well as president and minister of national defense. Buyoya's regime was threatened by rebellion in Burundi's northwestern provinces in November of 1991. Buyoya survived a military coup in March of 1992 and later in the month agreed to the drafting of a new constitution which allowed multiparty elections to be held in Burundi.

HEADS OF GOVERNMENT

JOSEPH CIMPAYE (Prime Minister, January 26, 1961–September 29, 1961). Joseph Cimpaye was born in Kitega in 1932. He was educated locally and in Belgium. He returned to Burundi to work as an assistant veterinarian in 1952 and entered politics in the late 1950s. He was elected prime minister of the provisional government on January 26, 1961. Cimpaye's party was defeated by the United and National Progress party (UPRONA) later in the year, and he left office on September 29, 1961. He subsequently left politics and was employed by a Belgian airline, but served as an advisor to Prince Regent Charles in February of 1966. Cimpaye was arrested in October of 1969 and charged with complicity in a Hutu conspiracy. He was sentenced to prison the following year, but was released in an amnesty in July of 1971. Cimpaye was murdered in April of 1972 during the government repression that followed an uprising of the Hutu tribe.

LOUIS RWAGASORE (Prime Minister, September 29, 1961–October 13, 1961). Louis Rwagasore was born in Gita on January 10, 1929. He was the eldest son of Mwami Mwambutsa of Burundi. He was educated locally and in Belgium. When Rwagasore returned to Burundi in 1956, he entered politics and founded the Union and National Progress party (UPRONA). His father objected to his political career, as Rwagasore's popularity threatened the mwami's rule. Rwagasore espoused a nationalist policy that favored independence. His party was victorious in elections for the provisional government, and Rwagasore took office as prime minister on September 29, 1961. He was shot and killed two weeks later on October 13, 1961, at a local restaurant in the capital.

ANDRE MUHIRWA (Prime Minister, October 20, 1961–June, 1963). Andre Muhirwa was born in Murete in 1920. He was educated locally and worked in the colonial offices as a clerk in the early 1940s. He became chief of Buhumuza in 1944 and was selected chief in the Bweru region in 1951. Muhirwa married a daughter of Mwami Mwambutsa in 1952. He was an early member of the Union and National Progress party (UPRONA) and a strong supporter of Prince Louis Rwagasore. He served as minister of the interior in Rwagasore's government and succeeded his brother-in-law as

prime minister on October 20, 1961. Muhirwa was dismissed as prime minister in June of 1963 following a dispute with the mwami over Muhirwa's jailing of the president of the Legislative Assembly. He remained active in politics and served as vice president of UPRONA. Muhirwa served as minister of state in the government of Albin Nyamoya from April of 1964 until January of 1965. He was suspected of being involved in the assassination of Nyamoya's successor, Pierre Ngendamdumwe, in 1965. He was also a leader of the Tutsi faction that orchestrated the repression and massacre of Hutu intellectuals. Muhirwa was instrumental in the coup that deposed Mwami Mwambutsa in 1966. When Mwambutsa's successor, Ntare, was ousted by Michel Micombero later in the year, Muhirwa was imprisoned by the new government. He was released in November of 1967 and went into political retirement.

PIERRE NGENDAMDUMWE (Prime Minister, June 17, 1963–April 1, 1964). Pierre Ngendamdumwe was born in 1930. He was a member of the Hutu tribe and was educated at Lovanium University in Zaire. A supporter of Prince Louis Rwagasore, he served as minister of finance in the provisional government in 1961. He was selected to replace Andre Muhirwa as prime minister on June 17, 1963. Ngendamdumwe displeased the Mwami by establishing diplomatic relations with the People's Republic of China and was dismissed as prime minister on April 1, 1964. Ngendamdumwe was called upon to form another government on January 7, 1965. The following week he was shot and killed by Tutsi extremists in Bujumbura on January 15, 1965.

ALBIN NYAMOYA (Prime Minister, April 1, 1964–January 7, 1965). Albin Nyamoya was born in Ibuye in Ngozi Province in 1924. He was a member of the Tutsi tribe and was educated in veterinary science. He belonged to the United and National Progress party (UPRONA) and was elected to the National Assembly in 1961. A supporter of Andre Muhirwa, he served as minister of the interior in Muhirwa's government in 1961. Nyamoya was subsequently named minister of agriculture and served until the establishment of Pierre Ngendamdumwe's government in June of 1963. Nyamoya was named prime minister on April 1, 1964 and served until his dismissal by the mwami on January 7, 1965. Nyamoya was arrested later in January for suspicion of involvement in the assassination of his successor, Pierre Ngendamdumwe, but was released in March of 1965. He was again elected to the National Assembly in May of 1965 and was named minister of state the following September. He was dismissed following the ouster of Mwami Mwambutsa in July of 1966. Nyamoya was appointed general inspector in the Agriculture Ministry by the Micombero government in March of 1967 and became director general in the ministry in September of 1969. He was appointed minister of agriculture in March of 1971 and was appointed prime minister by Micombero on July 14, 1972. Nyamoya tried to promote a policy of conciliation between the Tutsi and Hutu tribes. He invited exiled Hutu leaders to return to Burundi under an amnesty, but his policies were ignored and the returning exiles were arrested and executed. Nyamoya was dismissed from office on June 6, 1973, and returned to his farm. He was named an advisor to the minister of agriculture in 1978 and worked with the Department of Livestock from 1980. Nyamoya was again elected to the National Assembly in 1982 and served on various government committees.

PIERRE NGENDAMDUMWE (Prime Minister, January 7, 1965–January 15, 1965). *See earlier entry under Heads of Government.*

PIE MASUMBUKO (Acting Prime Minister, January 15, 1965–January 25, 1965). Pie Masumbuko was born in the Muramvya region in September of 1931. He was a member of the Tutsi tribe and was educated in Belgium and France. After receiving a degree in medicine and political science, he returned to Burundi in 1961. Masumbuko was named vice premier and minister of health in the government of Pierre Ngendamdumwe in 1963. He was a member of the United and National Progress party (UPRONA) and served as permanent secretary from January of 1964. Later in the year he was named minister of health. Masumbuko served for ten days as acting prime minister following the assassination of Pierre Ngendamdumwe on January 15, 1965. He returned to the Ministry of Health until he was appointed foreign minister on July 9, 1966, following the overthrow of King Mwambutsa. He was dismissed from the cabinet following the military coup led by Michel Micombero and was named ambassador-at-large in April of 1967. Masumbuko was briefly arrested by the Micombero government in November of 1967 and again in January of 1971. He went to France in September of 1971 to work with the World Health Organization. He continued to work with the World Health Organization the following year, when he was named their representative in Chad.

JOSEPH BAMINA (Prime Minister, January 25, 1965–September 30, 1965). Joseph Bamina was born in 1925. He belonged to the Hutu tribe and attended Lovanium University. He was a member of the United and National Progress party (UPRONA) and was elected to the National Assembly in 1961. Bamina was elected to the Senate and became its president in 1965. He was selected as prime minister to succeed the assassinated Pierre Ngendamdumwe on January 25, 1965. An advocate of Hutu rights, Bamina was dismissed as prime minister on March 30, 1965, but remained prime minister in a caretaker government until September 30, 1965. He returned to the Senate to serve as president until his arrest following the abortive Hutu revolt in October of 1965. He was condemned in a mass trial and executed in Muramvya on December 15, 1965.

LÉOPOLD BIHA (Prime Minister, October 1, 1965–July 9, 1966). Léopold Biha (Bihumugani) was born in 1919. He succeeded his father, Chief Bagorikunda, as chief of the Muramvya in 1944. He served as an aide to Mwami Mwambutsa and served on the Supreme Land Council as vice president from 1954 until 1959. Biha was a founding member of the United and National Progress party (UPRONA), but left the party to serve in the interim provisional government. In August of 1961 he founded the Popular Burundi party, but was unsuccessful in a legislative bid the following month. He subsequently served as private secretary to the mwami, until he was named prime minister on October 1, 1965. Biha was seriously injured in an assassination attempt on October 19, 1965. He subsequently went to Europe to recuperate. He returned to Burundi in April of 1966 to resume his duties under Charles Ndizeye, who was ruling as prince regent. Biha was dismissed as prime minister on July 9, 1966, following the overthrow of Mwami Mwambutsa. He was subsequently arrested by the new government. Biha retired from politics following his release.

MICHAEL MICOMBERO (Prime Minister, July 13, 1966–November 28, 1966). *See entry under Heads of State.*

ALBIN NYAMOYA (Prime Minister, July 14, 1972–June 6, 1973). *See earlier entry under Heads of Government.*

EDOUARD NZAMBIMANA (Prime Minister, November 13, 1976–October, 1978). Edouard Nzambimana was born in 1946. He served in the Burundi army, where he rose to the rank of lieutenant colonel. From 1974 until 1976 he served as minister of public works, transport, and equipment in the government of Michel Micombero. He participated in the coup that ousted Micombero in November of 1976. Nzambimana was named prime minister by President Jean-Baptiste Bagaza on November 13, 1976, and served until President Bagaza abolished the position in October of 1978. Nzambimana also served as minister of planning from 1976 until 1978. He was named foreign minister in 1978 and served until 1982.

ADRIEN SIBOMANA (Prime Minister, October 19, 1988–   ). Adrien Sibomana served as governor of the Muramvya Province of Burundi. He was elected to the National Assembly, where he served as Deputy Speaker. President Pierre Buyoya restored the position of prime minister in October of 1988 in an effort to restore national unity. Sibomana was named prime minister and minister of planning on October 19, 1988.

Cambodia, State of

(Kampuchea)

Cambodia is a country in Southeast Asia on the Indochinese peninsula. It was granted independence from France on November 9, 1953.

HEADS OF STATE

NORODOM SIHANOUK (King, April 26, 1941–September 25, 1955). Norodom Sihanouk was born on October 31, 1922, and was educated at French schools in Indo-China and Paris. He was the grandson of King Sisowath and the nephew of King Sisowath Monivong. When Monivong died in April of 1941, the French preferred to have Sihanouk succeed him rather than Prince Monireth, who was first in line of succession. Sihanouk was elected to the Cambodian throne by the Royal Council under pressure from the French on April 26, 1941. During World War II Cambodia was occupied by the Japanese, and Sihanouk was virtually powerless while the country was administered by a Japanese puppet government. The Allies regained control of the country after the war, and the French colonial government was reestablished on March 4, 1946. Sihanouk promoted a new constitution which provided for a constitutional monarchy in May of 1947. He dissolved the Assembly and ruled by decree from 1950. New elections were held in 1951, and Huy Kanthoul became premier. Kanthoul was dismissed in June of 1952, and Sihanouk led a National Union government as prime minister. He negotiated with the French for Cambodian independence, but was unable to reach an agreement with the French government. He stepped down as prime minister in May of 1953 and went into exile briefly in Thailand. Sihanouk returned to Cambodia but remained in self-imposed internal exile in the hopes of pressuring an agreement from the French. When the French government agreed to transfer full sovereignty to the Cambodian people in August of 1953, King Sihanouk emerged from exile. He abdicated as king on September 25, 1955, in order to participate more fully in Cambodia's political process. He relinquished the throne to his father, Norodom Suramarit, and took the office of prime minister on October 23, 1955. Sihanouk stepped down in January of 1956, but served again as prime minister from February 29, 1956, until March 24, 1956; from September 15, 1956, until October 15, 1956; from April 9, 1957, until July 7, 1957; and from July 10, 1958, until April 12, 1960. Sihanouk's father, King Norodom Suramarit, died on April 3, 1960. Cambodia was governed by a Regency Council until June 13, 1960, when Sihanouk was selected head of state, though he chose not to take the title of king. He appointed Lt. Gen. Lon Nol, the minister of defense, to serve as prime minister in 1966. Lon Nol's conservative policies often conflicted with the more moderate views of Sihanouk. The prince was ousted in a military coup led by Lon Nol on March 18, 1970, while Sihanouk was traveling abroad. He subsequently went into exile in the People's Republic of China, where he founded the Royal Government of Khmer National Union (GRUNK), which campaigned in behalf of the Khmer Rouge rebels. The Khmer Rouge attacked the capital, Phnom Penh, in January of 1975, and the government surrendered on April 17, 1975. Sihanouk then returned to Cambodia to serve as figurehead head of state under the Khmer Rouge. On April 11, 1976, he resigned in opposition to the policies of the Khmer Rouge and was placed under house arrest. He was released in January of 1979 and returned to China, where he verbally attacked the Vietnamese-led invasion of Cambodia and the Khmer Rouge government that it replaced. In June of 1982 Sihanouk joined with the exiled Khmer Rouge and Son Sann's Khmer People's National Liberation Front to campaign against the Vietnamese-supported government of Cambodia. The Vietnamese withdrew their troops in September of 1989. The United Nations agreed to set up a Supreme National Council in August of 1990 consisting of members of the Cambodian government and leaders of the rebel alliance. Sihanouk became chairman of the council in May of 1991, and a ceasefire was put into effect. He was reestablished as Cambodia's head of state on November 20, 1991.

NORODOM SURAMARIT (King, September 25, 1955–April 3, 1960). Norodom Suramarit was born in Phnom Penh on March 6, 1896. He was the grandson of King Norodom. He was educated in Phnom Penh and in French schools in Saigon, and he married Princess Kossamak (1904-75), the daughter of King Sisowath Monivong. In 1929 he was named minister of marine, commerce, and agriculture. Norodom Suramarit served as grand counsellor to the court and chairman of the Regency Council when his son, Prince Norodom Sihanouk, was chosen as king in 1941. Norodom Suramarit acceded to the throne after the abdication of his son on Septmber 25, 1955. The following year Cambodia severed its connection with the French Union and established complete independence. Norodom Suramarit remained Cambodia's king until his death at the age of 64 in Phnom Penh after a long illness on April 3, 1960.

NORODOM SIHANOUK (Head of State, June 13, 1960–March 18, 1970). *See earlier entry under Heads of State.*

CHENG HENG (Head of State, March 18, 1970–March 10, 1972). Cheng Heng was born in 1916. He served as president of the Cambodian National Assembly and supported the ouster of Prince Norodom Sihanouk in March of 1970. Cheng Heng was chosen as provisional head of state by the Assembly and took office on March 18, 1970. He resigned on March 10, 1972, and turned the office over to Lon Nol.

LON NOL (Head of State, March 10, 1972–April 1, 1975). Lon Nol was born in the province of Preyveng on November 13, 1913. He was educated in French schools in Phnom Penh and Saigon. In 1937 he entered the civil service, and he became governor of Kratie Province after World War II. He was appointed director of the administrative service in 1949 and was commissioned in the Cambodian army as a lieutenant colonel in 1952. Lon Nol was appointed chief of staff of the military in 1955 and subsequently served as minister of defense in the government of Norodom Sihanouk. In 1961 he was promoted to lieutenant general. He became a leading advisor to Prince Sihanouk and served in the cabinet in various capacities. Lon Nol was named deputy premier in 1963 and was appointed premier on October 19, 1966. He retained his position until April 23, 1967, when he stepped down after being injured in an automobile accident. He returned to the cabinet in 1968 and served as minister of defense. Lon Nol was again named prime minister on August 13, 1969. His conservative views were often in conflict with those of Sihanouk, and he led the coup that ousted the prince as Cambodia's head of state on March 18, 1971. The monarchy was abolished in October of 1970, and Cambodia was proclaimed the Khmer Republic. Lon Nol suffered a paralytic stroke in February of 1971. He was treated in Honolulu, Hawaii, and Deputy Prime Minister Sisowath Sirik Matak served in his stead. When Lon Nol returned to Cambodia in August of 1971, he delegated many of his duties to deputy ministers. Lon Nol replaced Cheng Heng as president on March 10, 1972, and relinquished the office of prime minister the following day. His government soon became involved in a full-scale civil war against the Communist Khmer Rouge guerrillas. Lon

Nol narrowly escaped an assassination attempt on March 17, 1973, when Prince Sihanouk's son-in-law bombed the presidential palace. Another unsuccessful attempt on Lon Nol's life was made in November of 1973. The political situation in Cambodia continued to deteriorate during 1974. The Communist insurrectionists made substantial military gains, and Lon Nol became increasingly unpopular with the Cambodian people. Lon Nol was convinced to leave Cambodia on April 1, 1975. He flew to Bali with his family and then went on to Honolulu. Lon Nol settled in Fullerton, California, where he died from heart disease at the age of 72 on November 17, 1985.

SAUKHAM KHOY (Head of State, April 1, 1975–April 12, 1975). Saukham Khoy was president of the Cambodian Senate. He succeeded Lon Nol as Cambodia's interim president on April 1, 1975, after Lon Nol fled the country. Saukham Khoy left office on April 12, 1975, when the United States withdrew its diplomatic staff from Phnom Penh. He accompanied the evacuation team to a refugee camp in the United States.

SAKSUT SAKHAN (Head of State, April 12, 1975–April 16, 1975). Saksut Sakhan was minister of defense in the government of Norodom Sihanouk in the 1960s. He served in the Cambodian army and rose to the rank of lieutenant general. In March of 1975 he was named chief of staff of the army. Saksut Sakhan took control of the government on April 12, 1975, following the United States evacuation. He presided over the fall of Phnom Penh and surrendered the capital to the Khmer Rouge on April 16, 1975. He subsequently escaped from Cambodia and fled to Thailand.

NORODOM SIHANOUK (Head of State, April 17, 1975–April 11, 1976). *See earlier entry under Heads of State.*

KHIEU SAMPHAN (Head of State, April 11, 1976–January 7, 1979). Khieu Samphan was born in Svay Rieng Province in 1932. He was educated at the Univeristy of Paris, where he received a degree in economics. He returned to Cambodia in 1953 and entered politics as a member of the Popular Socialist Community, Prince Sihanouk's political party. Khieu Samphan was appointed to the government as under secretary of state for commerce. He was accused by Prince Sihanouk of being a Communist agent in 1963 and was removed from the cabinet. He was elected to the National Assembly in 1966, but vanished from Phnom Penh in April of 1967. Khieu Samphan was believed to have been murdered, but instead had joined the Khmer Rouge in opposition to the government. He reemerged in 1970 when he announced his support for the now-ousted Prince Sihanouk's national front in opposition to the government of Lon Nol. He served as deputy prime minister and minister of defense in the Royal Government of National Union (GRUNC) in exile from 1970 until 1975. Khieu Samphan also served as commander-in-chief of the Khmer Rouge High Command from 1973. He served as president of the State Presidium in the Khmer Rouge government from April 11, 1976, and retained his position until the Khmer Rouge was forced to flee Phnom Penh on January 7, 1979. He served as president of the Khmer Rouge government in exile. In January of 1980 he replaced Pol Pot as prime minister in the government, though Pol Pot was expected to retain substantial power despite his public removal from the leadership. Khieu Samphan's Party of Democratic Kampuchea (PDK) joined in a coalition government-in-exile with Prince Sihanouk and Son Sann's Khmer Serei. Khieu Samphan served as vice president in charge of foreign affairs. In November of 1991 he returned to Cambodia to serve on the Supreme National Council. He barely escaped with his life when he was attacked by an angry mob.

HENG SAMRIN (President, January 7, 1979–). Heng Samrin was born in Southeastern Cambodia in 1934. He supported the Communists in the Vietnamese civil war in the late 1950s and early 1960s. He was active in the Cambodian Communist party and fought with the Khmer Rouge against the Cambodian republican government from 1970 until 1975. Following the establishment of a Khmer Rouge government in 1975, Heng Samrin served as a brigade commander in the eastern zone of the country. He fled to Vietnam in 1977 to avoid purges being carried out by the government of Pol Pot. He returned to Cambodia the following year to lead the uprising against the Khmer Rouge government. The Vietnamese army invaded Cambodia and ousted Pol Pot's regime. Heng Samrin became chairman of the Council of State of the pro-Vietnamese government of the People's Republic of Kampuchea on January 7, 1979. He served as secretary-general of the Kampuchean People's Revolutionary party from 1981. Cambodia remained in a state of civil war, with the government involved in a guerrilla war against various opposing factions. A peace settlement was reached in the summer of 1991. The ruling party's name was changed to the Cambodian People's Party in October of 1991, and Heng Samrin was replaced as general secretary by Chea Sim. He remained chairman of the Council of State, though Prince Norodom Sihanouk assumed the title of chairman of the Supreme National Council and served as head of state.

NORODOM SIHANOUK (Head of State, November 20, 1991–). *See earlier entry under Heads of State.*

HEADS OF GOVERNMENT

SON NGOC THANH (Prime Minister, August 1945–October 15, 1945). Son Ngoc Thanh was born in 1907 in Vietnam and was educated in France. He was a leader in the Cambodian nationalist movement against the French colonial government. In 1943 he organized a Buddhist demonstration against the French and was threatened with arrest. Son Ngoc Thanh escaped to Thailand and then went into exile in Tokyo. In April of 1945 he returned to Cambodia, and he became foreign minister the following month. He sponsored a referendum on Cambodian independence in August of 1945 and assumed the function of prime minister. He declared his intentions to prevent the restoration of French rule in Cambodia. French troops landed in Phnom Penh on October 16, 1945, and Son was arrested and taken to Saigon. He was sent into exile in France, but was allowed to return to Cambodia on October 30, 1952. He continued to encourage nationalist activities. In March of 1953 when he was again threatened with arrest, he fled to a guerrilla-held area in Cambodia. Son Ngoc Thanh was named by President Lon Nol to serve as Cambodia's first minister and minister of foreign affairs on March 18, 1972. He survived an assassination attempt in August of 1972 and resigned from office on October 14, 1972. When the Khmer Rouge took control of Cambodia in 1975, Son fled to Vietnam. He was briefly arrested and reportedly died of natural causes the following year.

PRINCE SISOWATH MONIRETH (Prime Minister, 1946–1948). Prince Sisowath Monireth was born in 1909. He was the son of King Sisowath

Monivong and was first in line for succession on his father's death in 1941. He was considered too independent by the French, however, and was bypassed in favor of his cousin Prince Sihanouk. Monireth served as prime minister of Cambodia from 1946 until 1948. He was named regent following the death of King Norodom Suramarit on April 3, 1960. The Regency Council resigned on June 13, 1960, following the selection of Norodom Sihanouk as head of state. Sisowath Monireth was imprisoned with other members of the royal family when a Cambodian air force plane bombed the presidential palace, where Lon Nol was conducting a cabinet meeting on March 17, 1973.

SAMDECH PENN NOUTH (Prime Minister, September, 1948–January, 1949). Samdech Penn Nouth was born in Phnom Penh on April 1, 1906. Prior to World War II, he was an official in the French colonial service. He served as acting minister of finance in 1945 and was governor of Phnom Penh from 1946 until 1948. Penn Nouth was named prime minister by King Sihanouk in September of 1948 and served until January of 1949. He served again as prime minister from June of 1953 until October of 1955 and from January 16, 1958, until April 10, 1958. He was subsequently appointed ambassador to France, where he remained until 1960. Penn Nouth was next named prime minister on January 28, 1961 and served until September of that year. He remained a leading supporter of Prince Sihanouk and again served as prime minister from January of 1968 until August 14, 1969. He remained loyal to Sihanouk following his ouster in 1970 and accompanied him into exile in Peking. When Sihanouk returned to Cambodia as head of state in a government controlled by the Khmer Rouge rebels, Penn Nouth again accepted the prime ministership on April 25, 1975. He resigned with Sihanouk on May 11, 1976, and went into exile in Paris. He

died there at the age of 80 on May 18, 1985.

YEM SAMBAUR (Prime Minister, February, 1949–March, 1950). Yem Sambaur was a dissident member of the Democratic party. When the Democratic party received a majority of seats in elections to the National Assembly, Sihanouk selected Yem as prime minister in February of 1949. Yem encouraged independence for Cambodia and was dismissed under pressure from the French in March of 1950. Yem Sambaur served as minister of finance in the Cabinet in 1954. He was president of the National Assembly following the ouster of Norodom Sihanouk in 1971.

PRINCE SISOWATH MONIPONG (Prime Minister, March, 1950–October, 1951). Prince Sisowath Monipong was born in Phnom Penh in 1912. The youngest son of King Sisowath Monivong, he was educated in France and served in the French air force during World War II. He represented Cambodia in the signing of the Franco-Cambodian treaty in 1949. Prince Monipong served as president of the Cambodian Council of Ministers from March of 1950 until elections were held for the National Assembly in October of 1951. He subsequently served as counselor to the government. Prince Monipong was named high commissioner to France in March of 1955. He died of a heart attack in Paris on August 31, 1956.

HUY KANTHOUL (Prime Minister, October 13, 1951–June, 1952). Huy Kanthoul was a member of the promonarchist Cambodian Democratic party. The party received the majority of the seats in the National Assembly, and Huy Kanthoul was selected to serve as prime minister on October 13, 1951. He remained in office until June of 1952, when he was dismissed by Norodom Sihanouk. He was appointed ambassador to France in 1966.

DOM SIHANOUK (Prime Minister, June 1952–June 1953). *See entry under Heads of State.*

SAMDECH PENN NOUTH (Prime Minister, June 1953–November 14, 1953). *See earlier entry under Heads of Government.*

CHAN NAK (Prime Minister, November 16, 1953–November 19, 1953). Chan Nak was born on May 27, 1892. He served as privy councillor to King Sihanouk. He was appointed prime minister on November 16, 1953, following Samdech Penn Nouth's resignation over a disagreement with the king. Chan Nak also served as minister of the interior. His cabinet collapsed on November 19, 1953, following the resignation of Son Sann as vice premier, and Samdech Penn Nouth again became prime minister.

SAMDECH PENN NOUTH (Prime Minister, November 1953–January 22, 1955). *See earlier entry under Heads of Government.*

LENG NGETH (Prime Minister, January 24, 1955–October 1955). Leng Ngeth was appointed prime minister of Cambodia by King Sihanouk on January 24, 1955, following the resignation of Samdech Penn Nouth. Leng Ngeth retained the position until October of 1955, when he was succeeded by Sihanouk. He was named ambassador to the Soviet Union in June of 1956.

DOM SIHANOUK (Prime Minister, October 23, 1955–January 1956). *See entry under Heads of State.*

OUM CHHEANG SUN (Prime Minister, January 4, 1956–February 29, 1956). Oum Chheang Sun was inaugurated to replace Norodom Sihanouk as prime minister by the Cambodian Assembly on January 4, 1956. His government resigned on January 7, 1956, following demonstrations that demanded the return of Sihanouk. Sihanouk was out of the country at the time, and Oum Chheang Sun remained caretaker prime minister until his return on February 29, 1956.

NORODOM SIHANOUK (Prime Minister, February 29, 1956–March 24, 1956). *See entry under Heads of State.*

KHIM TIT (Prime Minister, April 1, 1956–July 30, 1956). Khim Tit was born in 1896. He was educated in Cambodia and joined the provincial government in 1925. He served as minister of public works from 1945 until 1956 and was minister of works and telecommunications in 1951. From 1951 until 1952 he served as governor of Kandal, and he was under-secretary of the interior from 1952 until 1953. Khim Tit was minister of defense from 1953 until 1954 and served as minister of the interior in the government of Samdech Penn Nouth from April of 1954. He was later deputy prime minister under Norodom Sihanouk. He succeeded Prince Sihanouk as prime minister upon his resignation over tax collection policies on April 2, 1956. Khim Tit resigned the office on July 29, 1956. He was appointed ambassador to the Soviet Union in 1960 and served there until the following year, when he was named ambassador to Czechoslovakia. He retained that position until 1965. Khim Tit was named Cambodia's permanent representative to the United Nations in 1970.

NORODOM SIHANOUK (Prime Minister, September 15, 1956–October 15, 1956). *See entry under Heads of State.*

SAN YUN (Prime Minister, October 25, 1956–April 9, 1957). San Yun served in the cabinet of Prince Norodom Sihanouk. He was asked to form a government by King Norodom Sura-marit on October 25, 1956. San Yun's cabinet resigned in December of 1956 following the National Assembly's censure of two of its members. Sam Yun formed a new government in January of 1957. He lost a vote of confidence on economic policy in the National Assembly in March of 1957 and was replaced by Prince Sihanouk on April 9, 1957.

NORODOM SIHANOUK (Prime Minister, April 9, 1957–July 7, 1957). *See entry under Heads of State.*

SIM VAR (Prime Minister, July 26, 1957–January 8, 1958). Sim Var was born in 1904. He was cofounder of the nationalist newspaper *Nagara Vatta* in 1936. He served in the government of Prince Norodom Sihanouk following Cambodian independence in 1954. Sim Var was minister of public works in the government of Samdech Penn Nouth from April of 1954. He remained in the cabinet until July 26, 1957, when he was selected as prime minister. His government clashed with the National Assembly over economic issues, and Sihanouk dissolved the Assembly and called for new elections. Sim Var resigned as prime minister on January 8, 1958. Prince Sihanouk refused to allow Ek Yi Oun, the president of the National Assembly, to serve as acting prime minister. Penn Nouth was named to head the government on January 16, 1958. His government lasted until April 10, 1958, when Sim Var was again appointed prime minister. He remained in office until June 22, 1958, when Prince Sihanouk formed his own government. Sim Var remained in government service. He was Cambodia's ambassador to Japan prior to the takeover of Cambodia by the Khmer Rouge in 1975. Sim Var went into exile in Paris, where he died at the age of 85 on April 21, 1990.

SAMDECH PENN NOUTH (Prime Minister, January 16, 1958–April 10, 1958). *See earlier entry under Heads of Government.*

SIM VAR (Prime Minister, April 24, 1958–June 22, 1958). *See earlier entry under Heads of Government.*

NORODOM SIHANOUK (Prime Minister, July 10, 1958–April 12, 1960). *See entry under Heads of State.*

PHO PROEUNG (Prime Minister, April 18, 1960–January 14, 1961). Pho Proeung was born in 1897. He was a member of the Cambodian Royal Council and served on the Regency Council in 1960. He was named prime minister on April 18, 1960, serving until January 15, 1961. He was appointed ambassador to France in 1962.

SAMDECH PENN NOUTH (Prime Minister, January 28, 1961–September 1961). *See earlier entry under Heads of Government.*

NORODOM SIHANOUK (Prime Minister, September 1961–August 6, 1962). *See entry under Heads of State.*

CHAU SEN COCSAL CHHUM (Prime Minister, August 6, 1962–October 5, 1962). Chau Sen Cocsal Chhum was president of the National Assembly from 1961. He served as interim prime minister following the resignation of Prince Norodom Sihanouk on August 6, 1962. He remained in office until October 5, 1962, when Sihanouk appointed his cousin, Prince Norodom Kantol, to head the government. Chau Sen Cocsal later served as Prince Sihanouk's representative on the rebel Supreme National Council from September of 1990 until July of 1991.

PRINCE NORODOM KANTOL (Prime Minister, October 6, 1962–October 19, 1966). Norodom Kantol was born on September 15, 1920. He was a cousin of Norodom Sihanouk. He was educated in Saigon, Phnom Penh, and the University of Nancy in France and returned to Cambodia to serve in the Phnom Penh municipal government. He later served in diplomatic positions in Washington, D.C., and Tokyo. Norodom Kantol was appointed prime minister and minister of foreign affairs on October 6, 1962. His government resigned in March of 1963, but the resignation was rescinded when Sihanouk threatened to call national elections. Norodom Kantol again resigned from office on December 24, 1964, but was reappointed by the National Assembly the following day. He remained prime minister until October 19, 1966, when he was replaced by Lon Nol following elections to the National Assembly. He remained a leading advisor to Prince Sihanouk and a member of the Council for the Royal Family until the ouster of Sihanouk in March of 1970. Norodom Kantol was imprisoned with other members of the royal family when a Cambodian air force plane bombed the presidential palace where Lon Nol was conducting a cabinet meeting on March 17, 1973.

LON NOL (Prime Minister, October 19, 1966–April 23, 1967). *See entry under Heads of State.*

SON SANN (Prime Minister, April 23, 1967–December 1967). Son Sann was born in Phnom Penh in 1911. He was educated in Paris and served in the colonial government. From 1946 until 1947 he served as minister of finance, and in 1949 he was vice chairman of the Council of Ministers. He was named minister of foreign affairs in 1950. The following year he was elected to the National Assembly, and he served as president of the Assembly from 1951 until 1952. Son Sann briefly served as deputy premier in the cabinet of Chan Nak in November of 1953, and his resignation brought down the Chan Nak government. In 1954 he was named governor of the Cambodian National Bank. Son Sann served as minister of state from 1961 until 1962 and was placed in charge of economy, finance, and planning in 1965. He was named prime minister on April 23, 1967, and served until December of 1967. Son Sann remained out of the government following Lon Nol's military coup in 1970. He subsequently went into exile in France, where in 1979 he became active in the Cambodian resistance to the invasion by Vietnam. He became prime minister in the Cambodian government-in-exile in 1982 and became leader of the Khmer People's National Front in 1986. Son Sann served as a member of the Supreme National Council of Cambodia from 1991. In May of 1992 he formed the Buddhist Liberal Democratic party and served as its president.

SAMDECH PENN NOUTH (Prime Minister, January 1968–August 14, 1969). *See earlier entry under Heads of Government.*

LON NOL (Prime Minister, August 13, 1969–March 11, 1972). *See entry under Heads of State.*

SISOVATH SIRIK MATAK (Prime Minister, March 11, 1972–March 13, 1972). Sisovath Sirik Matak was born on January 22, 1914. A member of the royal family, he was educated in Cambodia and served as vice-governor from 1938 until 1949. He served in the Royal Khmer Army from 1949 until 1951 and was secretary of state for national defense from 1952 until 1953. From 1954 until 1956 he served in the cabinet as minister of defense and foreign affairs, and he was minister of defense and education from 1957 until 1958. In 1962 Sirik Matak was appointed Cambodia's ambassador to the People's

Republic of China. He was promoted to lieutenant general and later became army chief of staff. He served as deputy prime minister in the government of Lon Nol from 1969. In March of 1970 Sirik Matak was instrumental in the coup that ousted his cousin, Norodom Sihanouk. He remained Lon Nol's deputy prime minister and took over most of the powers of the office of prime minister when Lon Nol suffered a stroke in January of 1971. Sirik Matak briefly served as prime minister from March 11 until March 13, 1972, when Lon Nol vacated the office to become chief of state. Sirik Matak subsequently withdrew from political life following massive student demonstrations in Phnom Penh against his participation in a new government. In March of 1973 he was placed under house arrest, but was subsequently released and asked by President Lon Nol to join the High Executive Council. Sirik Matak was captured and executed by the Khmer Rouge shortly after it took power in Cambodia in April of 1975.

SON NGOC THANH (Prime Minister, March 18, 1972–October 14, 1972). *See earlier entry under Heads of Government.*

HANG THUN HAC (Prime Minister, October 15, 1972–April 17, 1973). Hang Thun Hac was born in 1926. He was the secretary-general of the progovernment Socio-Republican party when he was chosen as prime minister on October 15, 1972. Hang Thun Hac's government resigned on April 17, 1973.

IN TAM (Prime Minister, May 11, 1973–December 7, 1973). In Tam was born on September 22, 1922. He challenged Lon Nol for the presidency in June of 1972, but was defeated. He was subsequently named as a presidential advisor in charge of reconciliation, but resigned in February of

1973 because of his inability to affect government policy. In Tam was appointed prime minister on May 11, 1973, to lead a coalition cabinet, but he was unable to gain the cooperation of some members of his cabinet and offered his resignation to President Lon Nol in October of 1973. His resignation was rejected, but the president accepted In Tam's subsequent resignation on December 7, 1973. He died in 1975.

LONG BORET (Prime Minister, December 26, 1973–April 17, 1975). Long Boret was born in 1933. He served as foreign minister in the cabinet of In Tam. He was selected to replace In Tam as prime minister on December 26, 1973. Long Boret's cabinet resigned following the murder of Cambodia's education minister in June of 1974, but Long Boret was retained as Prime Minister in the new government. He retained office until the Cambodian government surrendered to the Khmer Rouge on April 17, 1975. Long Boret refused to evacuate with other government leaders. He was captured by the Khmer Rouge and executed later in April of 1975.

SAMDECH PENN NOUTH (Prime Minister, April 25, 1975–May 11, 1976). *See earlier entry under Heads of Government.*

POL POT (Prime Minister, May 11, 1976–January 7, 1979). Pol Pot was born in Memot on May 19, 1925. He joined the Viet Minh under Ho Chi Minh in the 1940s and fought to drive the French colonial authorities out of Indochina. He joined the Cambodian Communist party in 1946 and rose to become leader of the party in 1962. During this period Pol Pot went by various aliases, including Saloth Sar and Tol Saut. He became prime minister of Cambodia on May 11, 1976, following the Communist takeover of the government. Pol Pot's government launched the massive undertaking of relocating Cambodia's city residents to rural areas. The government's policies resulted in an estimated two million deaths. Pol Pot remained in power until he was overthrown by a Vietnamese-led invasion force on January 7, 1979. He was sentenced to death in absentia for various crimes, including genocide, in August of 1979. Pol Pot commanded the Khmer Rouge guerrillas in their fight against the Vietnamese-backed government until 1985. He was officially replaced as military leader of the Khmer Rouge by Sol Sen, though he remained an influential leader of the Khmer Rouge movement. He returned to Cambodia following the establishment of a coalition government in November of 1991.

PEN SOVAN (Prime Minister, June 27, 1981–December 1981). Pen Sovan was born in 1936. He was a Vietnamese-trained member of the Cambodian Communist party. He served as vice president and minister of defense in the revolutionary government of Heng Samrin after the ouster of the Khmer Rouge regime in January of 1979. Pen Sovan was named secretary-general of the People's Revolutionary party of Kampuchea on May 29, 1981. He also served as president of the Council of Ministers from June 27, 1981. President Heng Samrin dismissed him from both positions in December of 1981.

CHAN SY (Prime Minister, February 9, 1982–December 26, 1984). Chan Sy was born in Kompong, Chhnang Province, in 1932. He joined the Viet Minh forces in Cambodia in 1950. He left the country after Prince Norodom Sihanouk's government was recognized as the sole legitimate government in Cambodia in 1954. Chan Sy joined the Communist party in 1960. Following the ouster of Sihanouk in 1970, he returned to Cambodia. He was an opponent of Pol Pot in the Communist party and was detained in 1973. Chan Sy subsequently joined the Kampuchean United Front for the National Salvation. He became deputy minister of defense in the Front's Vietnamese-backed government in 1980 and was appointed minister of defense and deputy premier the following year. On February 9, 1982, he replaced Pen Sovan as prime minister. He went to Moscow for medical treatment in December of 1984 and died from a heart ailment in a Moscow hospital on December 26, 1984.

HUN SEN (Prime Minister, January 14, 1985–). Hun Sen was born in Kompang-Cham Province in 1950. He was educated in Cambodia and joined the Khmer Rouge in 1970. He left Cambodia in 1978 to join the pro-Vietnamese Kampucheans and returned to Cambodia following the Vietnamese-supported takeover. From 1979 until 1985 he served as vice-chairman of the Council of Ministers and as foreign minister. Hun Sen succeeded Chan Sy as prime minister on January 14, 1985. Hun Sen's government continued to face guerrilla attacks from the various opposition factions. Hun Sen met with leaders of the three major resistance groups in Peking in July of 1991. An agreement was reached that allowed for the return of Prince Norodom Sihanouk as head of state in November of 1991.

Cameroon, Republic of

(République du Cameroun)

Cameroon is a country on the western coast of central Africa. It received its independence from a United Nations trusteeship administered by the French on January 1, 1960.

HEADS OF STATE

AHMADOU AHIDJO (President, May 5, 1960–November 6, 1982). Ahmadou Babatoura Ahidjo was born in Garoua on August 24, 1924. He was educated locally and worked as a radio operator before entering politics in 1946. He was elected to the Regional Assembly in 1947 and reelected five years later. In 1956 he became president of the Assembly and was elected deputy prime minister the following year. Ahidjo formed the African Union Camerounaise in 1958. He was elected prime minister of the Cameroon on February 18, 1958, and became president on May 5, 1960, following the nation's independence from France. Cameroon prospered under Ahidjo's leadership, and he was reelected president on four occasions. Ahidjo resigned the presidency on November 6, 1982, for reasons of health. He was succeeded by his prime minister, Paul Biya. The following year Ahidjo tried to regain power and was accused by President Biya of plotting against the government. Ahidjo went into exile and was tried and sentenced to death in absentia, though the sentence was later commuted. Ahidjo remained in exile in Senegal and France. He died of a heart attack in Dakar, Senegal, on November 30, 1989.

PAUL BIYA (President, November 6, 1982–). Paul Biya was born in Sangmelima on February 13, 1933. He was educated locally before attending the University of Paris, where he studied law and political science. In 1962 he returned to Cameroon and joined the Department of Development Aid. Biya was subsequently named to Ahmadou Ahidjo's cabinet as minister of national education, youth, and culture. He was appointed minister of state and secretary-general of the presidency in 1968. On June 30, 1975, he was appointed prime minister. Biya was selected to succeed Ahidjo as president when Ahidjo resigned on November 6, 1982. Problems developed between the new president and his predecessor, and Biya accused Ahidjo of plotting against him in a coup attempt in August of 1983. Ahidjo went into exile and was convicted of attempting to overthrow the government. Biya was unopposed in his reelection bid in January of 1984 and subsequently abolished the position of prime minister. He survived another attempted coup in April of 1984. Biya made efforts to democratize the Republic of Cameroon, but arrested leaders of the opposition in February of 1990 following prodemocracy demonstrations. Biya made plans to participate in a contested election for the presidency in 1993.

HEADS OF GOVERNMENT

ANDRE MARIA MBIDA (Prime Minister, May 15, 1957–February 18, 1958). Andre Maria Mbida was born in Endinding in 1917. He was educated at local Catholic mission schools and worked as a legal secretary. In 1952 he entered politics and was elected to the Territorial Assembly. He also served as a deputy in the French National Assembly from 1956. Mbida was a supporter of a gradual process of independence and of maintaining close relations with France. He became prime minister of the first Cameroon government on May 15, 1957. His government fell on February 18, 1958, and he was replaced by Ahmadou Ahidjo. Mbida went into voluntary exile in Conakry,

Guinea, the following year. After he returned to Cameroon during a political amnesty in 1960, he was reelected to the National Assembly. He refused to accept a government ministry and was arrested for conspiring against the government in 1962. Mbida remained in prison until 1965. After his release he remained out of politics. He suffered from an eye complaint and spent much of his retirement in Paris for treatment.

AHMADOU AHIDJO (Prime Minister, February 18, 1958–May 5, 1960). *See entry under Heads of State.*

CHARLES ASSALÉ (Prime Minister, May 14, 1960–October 1, 1961). Prime Minister, East Cameroon, October 1, 1961–June 1965). Charles Assalé was born in Ebolowa on November 4, 1911. He was educated locally and became active in the trade union movement in 1935. In 1951 he founded the Union des Syndicats Autonomes du Cameroun (USAC), and the following year he entered politics. Assalé was elected to the Territorial Assembly and became its treasurer in 1955. He was named minister of finance in the government of Ahmadou Ahidjo in February of 1958. He supported Ahidjo's bid for the presidency in 1960 and succeeded him as prime minister on May 14, 1960. Assalé served as prime minister of East Cameroon from October 1, 1961, until his retirement in June of 1965. He then left national politics to become mayor of his hometown of Ebolowa.

JOHN FONCHA (Prime Minister, West Cameroon, October 1, 1961–January 11, 1968). John Ngu Foncha was born in Nkwen on June 21, 1916. He was educated locally and served as a teacher from 1934 until 1956. In 1952 he was a founder of the Kamerun United National Congress (KUNC). Foncha served in the Regional Assembly in Southern Cameroons from 1954 and founded the Kamerun National Demo-cratic party (KNDP) the following year. He served as prime minister of Southern Cameroons from 1959 until 1961 and was prime minister of West Cameroon, the former British region, from October 1, 1961, until January 11, 1968. Foncha also served as vice president of the Republic of Cameroon from 1961 until 1970. He remained on the Political Bureau until 1975.

VINCENT DE PAUL AHANDA (Prime Minister, East Cameroon, June 1965–November 20, 1965). Vincent de Paul Ahanda was born on June 24, 1918. He was educated in mission schools in Yaounde and joined the civil service in 1940. He worked in various government positions until 1956, when he was elected to the Legislative Assembly. Ahanda was named to the cabinet as minister of youth, sports, and national education the following year. He was named ambassador to West Germany in 1960. He remained in Europe to serve as ambassador to Belgium and permanent representative to the European Economic Community in 1962. Ahanda returned to the Cameroons in June of 1965 to become prime minister of East Cameroon. He was replaced by Simon Tchoungi on November 20, 1965. Ahanda became director-general of the national society "Les Argiles Industrielles du Cameroun" in August of 1967 and retained that position until his death in 1975.

SIMON TCHOUNGI (Prime Minister, East Cameroon, November 20, 1965–June 2, 1972). Simon Pierre Tchoungi was born on October 28, 1916, and was educated in Dakar, Senegal. He joined the Free French forces in 1942 and remained in the army until 1946. He attended the University of Paris in 1950 and received a degree in medicine in 1956. After his return to the Cameroons, he worked in the Ministry of Public Health. Tchoungi was named to the cabinet as minister of public health and population in 1961. He retained that position until 1964, when he was named minister of national economy. He became secretary of state to the presidency in 1965. Tchoungi was selected prime minister of East Cameroon on November 20, 1965. In May of 1970 he offered his resignation, but President Ahmadou Ahidjo persuaded him to remain in his position. Tchoungi remained in office until June 2, 1972, when the federal republic was transformed into a united government. He also served as president of the Cameroon Red Cross.

SOLOMON TANDENG MUNA

(Prime Minister, West Cameroon, January 11, 1968–June 2, 1972). Solomon Tandeng Muna was born in Bamenda in 1912. He was educated locally and worked as a teacher. In the 1950s he entered politics and was elected to the House of Assembly of Nigeria. Tandeng Muna was a supporter of Dr. Nnamdi Azikiwe and was named minister of public works in 1953. He subsequently served on the Southern Cameroons Executive Council. Following a disagreement with Dr. Enderley over the issue of the Cameroon's association with the Nigerian Federation, Tandeng Muna was expelled from the cabinet. He subsequently joined the Kamerun National Democratic party (KNDP) under John Foncha. He was later named minister of trade and industry. Tandeng Muna was named minister of finance of West Cameroon following the referendum that united the East Cameroons with the Southern Cameroons in February of 1961. He served as federal minister of transport, mines, and telecommunications from October of 1961 until November of 1965. He subsequently served as federal minister of transport and postal services until January of 1968. On January 11, 1968, he was named prime minister of West Cameroon. He also became federal vice president the following month. Tandeng Muna stepped down as West Cameroon's prime minister on

June 2, 1972, when he was named minister of state.

PAUL BIYA (Prime Minister, June 30, 1975–November 6, 1982). *See entry under Heads of State.*

MAIGARI BELLO BOUBA (Prime Minister, November 6, 1982–August 22, 1983). Maigari Bello Bouba was born in Northern Cameroon. He was a Muslim and was selected by newly elected President Paul Biya to form a government on November 6, 1982. Bello Bouba retained his office until August 22, 1983, when he was dismissed following an attempted coup against Biya that allegedly involved former president Ahmadou Ahidjo. Bello Bouba went into opposition to the Biya government and became the leader of the National Union for Democracy and Progress party in 1992.

LUC AYANG (Prime Minister, August 22, 1983–January 21, 1984). Luc Ayang was named interim prime minister following the ouster of Maigari Bello Bouba on August 22, 1983. He retained office until the position of prime minister was abolished by President Paul Biya on January 21, 1984.

SADOU HAYATOU (Prime Minister, April 26, 1991–April 9, 1992). Sadou Hayatou was appointed prime minister by President Paul Biya following the reestablishment of that position on April 26, 1991. He retained office until Biya reshuffled the cabinet on April 9, 1992.

SIMON ACHIDI ACHU (Prime Minister, April 9, 1992–). Simon Achidi Achu was a member of the Cameroon People's Democratic Movement. He was appointed prime minister by President Paul Biya on April 9, 1992. Achidi Achu remained in office following a cabinet reshuffle by President Biya in November of 1992.

Canada

Canada is a country in the northern section of North America.
It was granted independence from Great Britain on July 1, 1867.

HEADS OF STATE

ALEXANDER CAMBRIDGE, EARL OF ATHLONE (Governor-General, June 21, 1940–July 31, 1945). Alexander Augustus Frederick William Alfred George was born at Kensington Palace on April 14, 1874. The son of the German Duke of Teck and Princess Mary, he was known as Prince Alexander and was educated at Eton and Sandhurst. He subsequently joined the cavalry and served in the Matabele War in Rhodesia in 1894. Prince Alexander was also active in the South African War and World War II. He turned down an appointment to serve as governor-general of Canada in 1914 in order to remain in the military. Prince Alexander took the family name of Cambridge and became known as the Earl of Athlone in July of 1917 because of the unpopular German connections of his previous name and title. From 1923 until 1930 he served as governor-general of South Africa. He was then named governor and constable of Windsor Castle. He was also selected as chancellor of London University that year. On June 21, 1940, the Earl of Athlone was named to succeed Lord Tweedsmuir as governor-general of Canada. He retained that position until July 31, 1945, when he returned to England. He remained chancellor of London University until his retirement in 1955. The Earl of Athlone died in Kensington Palace after a long illness on January 16, 1957.

VISCOUNT ALEXANDER OF TUNIS (Governor-General, April 12, 1946–February 28, 1952). Harold Rupert Leofric George Alexander was born in Castle Caledon in Country Tyrone, Ireland, on December 10, 1891. After attending the Royal Military College at Sandhurst, he joined the Irish Guards and saw active duty in France during World War I. From 1934 until 1938 he served with the Third Punjabi Regiment in India. He led the British evacuation from Dunkirk in May of 1940 and was then sent to Burma, where he led the retreat of the British forces there. Alexander then served in North Africa as British commander in the Middle East from late 1942. He was General Bernard Montgomery's commanding officer and directed the military strategy that resulted in the destruction of the Afrika Korps. Alexander also led the Anglo-American forces that captured Sicily in 1943. He was promoted to field marshal and commanded the Allied armies in Italy, where he captured Rome in June of 1944. In March of 1946 he became Viscount Alexander of Tunis, and he was appointed governor-general of Canada on April 12, 1946. Viscount Alexander retained that position until February 28, 1952. He subsequently returned to England where he was created an earl and became minister of defense in the government of Winston Churchill. He remained in the cabinet until 1954. He later served on the board of directors of Barclay's Bank. Viscount Alexander died at Slough, Buckinghamshire, at the age of 77 on June 16, 1969.

VINCENT MASSEY (Governor-General, February 28, 1952–September 15, 1959). Vincent Massey was born in Toronto on February 20, 1887. He was the brother of actor Raymond Massey. He was educated at the University of Toronto and Balliol College at Oxford and returned to the University of Toronto to teach. In 1918 he was appointed secretary of the war cabinet at Ottawa. Massey became president of Massey-Harris, his family's business, in 1921. He was appointed to W. L. MacKenzie King's cabinet as minister without portfolio in 1925, but left office shortly thereafter when he was defeated for a seat in Parliament. He was named Canada's minister to Washington in 1926, where he served until 1930. Massey returned to Canada to serve as president of the Liberal party in 1932. In 1935 he was sent to Great Britain as high commissioner and remained there throughout World War II. He retired in 1946 and returned to Canada. The following year he became Chancellor of the University of Toronto. Massey was named the first Canadian-born governor-general of Canada on February 28, 1952. His term of office was extended twice before his retirement on September 15, 1959. Massey died in London of pneumonia on December 30, 1967.

GEORGE P. VANIER (Governor-General, September 15, 1959–March 5, 1967). George Philias Vanier was born in Montreal on April 23, 1888. He was educated in Montreal and Quebec and received a degree in law in 1911. At the start of World War I, he joined the army and fought with the Canadian Van Doos unit in France. He was seriously wounded in his legs, one of which was amputated. He subsequently served as aide de camp to two of Canada's governor-generals: Lord Byng from 1921 until 1922 and Viscount Willingdon from 1926 until 1928. Vanier served overseas during the 1930s and was appointed Canada's minister to France in January of 1939. He escaped to England in a fishing boat following the German occupation of France in 1940. He returned to Canada, where he was

promoted to general and named minister to the Allied governments. Vanier was subsequently named Canada's ambassador to France. He also served as the Canadian delegate to the Paris Peace Conference in 1946 and was the Canadian delegate to the United Nations General Assembly in Paris in 1948. He retired from the army in 1953 and from the diplomatic corps in 1954. Vanier was named governor-general of Canada on September 15, 1959. He sought to retire in 1966, but was asked to remain in his position through the Canadian centennial celebration the following year. He died of a heart attack in Ottawa, before the celebration began, on March 5, 1967.

D. ROLAND MICHENER (Governor-General, April 17, 1967–January 14, 1974). Daniel Roland Michener was born in Lacombe, Alberta, on April 19, 1900. He was educated at the University of Alberta and received a Rhodes scholarship at Oxford, England. He received a degree in law and practiced corporate law. In 1945 he was elected to the Ontario legislative assembly. Michener was elected to the House of Commons in 1953 as a member of the Conservative party. He was elected Speaker of the House of Commons in 1957 and served until 1962. He was appointed Canada's high commissioner to India in 1964. Michener retained that position until April 17, 1967, when he was named to succeed George Vanier as governor-general of Canada. He completed his term of office on January 14, 1974. He died in Toronto at the age of 91 on August 6, 1991.

JULES LÉGER (Governor-General, January 14, 1974–January 22, 1979). Jules Léger was born in Saint-Anicet, Quebec, on April 4, 1913. He received a degree in law from the University of Montreal in 1933 and then went to the Sorbonne in Paris for postgraduate studies. After returning to Canada in 1938, he began a career in journalism.

Léger became editor of *Le Droit*, the Ottawa French-language newspaper. He left journalism to join the foreign service office and served as third secretary with the Canadian mission in Santiago, Chile, from February of 1943. In 1947 Léger was sent to London, where he served as first secretary in the high commissioner's office. He returned to Canada in 1949, where he worked in the Foreign Ministry. Léger was named ambassador to Mexico in October of 1953 and served until the following year. He returned to Canada, where he was named undersecretary of state for foreign affairs. In November of 1958 he was appointed as Canada's representative to the North Atlantic Treaty Organization and he served in that post until May of 1962. Léger was then named ambassador to Italy until April of 1964, when he was appointed ambassador to France. He returned to Canada in late 1968 and became undersecretary of state. He retained that position until March of 1973, when he was named ambassador to Belgium and Luxembourg. Léger was appointed governor-general of Canada in October of 1973 and took office on January 14, 1974. He suffered a stroke in June of 1974 and lost his power of speech. He had to relearn how to speak and also remained partially paralyzed in his left arm. Léger completed his term of office on January 22, 1979. He died in Ottawa after suffering another stroke on November 22, 1980.

EDWARD R. SCHREYER (Governor-general, January 22, 1979–May 14, 1984). Edward Richard Schreyer was born near Beausejour, Manitoba, on December 21, 1935. He was educated at the University of Manitoba. He became involved in politics and was elected to the Manitoba legislative assembly in 1958. Schreyer taught at St. Paul's College in Manitoba from 1962 until 1965, when he was elected to the House of Commons. He returned to Manitoba and was elected premier in a New Democratic party government in June of 1969. His party was defeated by the Conservatives in elections in October of 1977, and Schreyer became leader of the Opposition. He was nominated to become Canada's governor-general by Pierre Trudeau and took office on January 22, 1979. He completed his term of office as the queen's representative in Canada on May 14, 1984. Schreyer subsequently served as Canada's high commissioner to Australia until 1988. He then returned to teach at the University of Winnipeg from 1989 until 1991 and then at Simon Fraser University.

JEANNE SAUVÉ (Governor-General, May 14, 1984–January 29, 1990). Jeanne Sauvé was born Jeanne Benoit in Prud'homme, Saskatchewan, on April 26, 1922. She attended the University of Ottawa and the University of Paris. She married Maurice Sauve in 1948 and subsequently worked as a freelance columnist and television journalist. Sauvé was elected to the Canadian Parliament in 1972 and was named to Prime Minister Pierre Trudeau's government in 1974. Sauvé became Canada's first female Speaker of Parliament in 1980. While her appointment initially drew criticism, she served with distinction. She retained the position until 1984, when Prime Minister Trudeau appointed her to the post of governor-general. She took office on May 14, 1984, and served in the ceremonial position until January 29, 1990. Sauvé died in Montreal on January 26, 1993, at the age of 70.

RAMON HNATYSHYN (Governor-general, January 29, 1990–). Ramon John Hnatyshyn was born in Saskatoon, Saskatchewan, on March 16, 1934. He was educated at the University of Saskatchewan, where he received a degree in law. He practiced law in Saskatoon and was elected to the House of Commons in 1974 as a member of the Progressive Conservative party. Two years later he was named deputy leader of the Opposition. Hnatyshyn served as minister of state for science and technology in 1979 and was minister of energy, mines, and resources from 1979 until 1980. He held several other ministries before being appointed minister of justice and attorney general in 1986. He served in this position until 1988. Hnatyshyn was named governor-general of Canada on January 29, 1990.

HEADS OF GOVERNMENT

W. L. MACKENZIE KING (Prime Minister, October 12, 1935–November 15, 1948). William Lyon MacKenzie King was born in Kitchener, Ontario, on December 17, 1874. He attended the University of Toronto and Harvard, where he studied economics and political science. He returned to Canada in 1900 to enter the civil service amd became deputy minister of labor. King was named to the Liberal cabinet of Sir Wilfred Laurier as minister of labor in 1909 and served until the defeat of the government in 1911. He worked in private industry until the death of Sir Wilfred Laurier in 1919. King was then elected leader of the Liberal party and became prime minister on December 29, 1921, when the party achieved victory. He remained in office with the support of the Progressive party until June of 1926, when he resigned following revelations of corruption in the customs department. New parliamentary elections were called following the collapse of the succeeding Conservative government and the Liberal party was again victorious. King again became prime minister on September 25, 1926. He promoted closer relations between Canada and the United States, and his government also reduced taxes and the national debt. His unwillingness to grant federal aid to the provinces brought about a defeat for the Liberal party in the elections of 1930. He was replaced as prime minister by Conservative leader Richard Bennett on August 6, 1930. King remained leader of the Opposition until he again formed a Liberal government on October 12, 1935. He was basically an isolationist and tried to avoid Canadian commitments in Europe. He sought to increase exports and to maintain Canada's autonomy. Canada declared war on the Axis powers on September 10, 1939, shortly after the start of World War II. King called elections in 1940 and received a large majority. He sought to avoid initiating compulsory military service during the war, but was forced to do so in order to provide reinforcements. Canada also supplied food and munitions for the war effort. The Liberal party remained in power following elections in 1945, and King led Canada back to a peace-time economy. He also supported Canada's involvement in such international organizations as the United Nations and the North Atlantic Treaty Organization. King resigned as prime minister on November 15, 1948, due to ill health. He died of pneumonia at his country home in Kingsmere, Quebec, at the age of 75 on July 22, 1950.

LOUIS ST. LAURENT (Prime Minister, November 15, 1948–June 21, 1957). Louis Stephen Saint Laurent was born in Compton, Quebec, on February 1, 1882. He received a degree in law from Laval University in Quebec in 1905. He opened a successful law firm in Quebec and served as president of the Canadian Bar Association from 1930 until 1932. St. Laurent was a member of the Liberal party but refused to enter politics or accept judicial appointments prior to World War II. Prime Minister W. L. MacKenzie King's government needed strong representatives from French-speaking Canada and requested that St. Laurent join the cabinet as justice minister in December of 1941. St. Laurent reluctantly agreed to serve in the government during World War II and was elected to the House of Commons the following year. He supported compulsory military service during the war, though Quebec overwhelmingly rejected a referendum on the issue. St. Laurent was named secretary of state for external affairs in 1946. He was selected to succeed the ailing King as prime minister and leader of the Liberal party on November 15, 1948. He led the Liberal party to victory in the elections of 1949. His government proceeded with the construction of the St. Lawrence Seaway project, which subsequently became a joint effort with the United States. St. Laurent established closer economic and military ties with the United States and was an early proponent of Canada's entry into the North Atlantic Treaty Organization. He was instrumental in gaining the entry of Newfoundland as a Canadian province in 1949. He supported revisions of the Canadian constitution to remove Canada from the status of a dominion in the British Empire. St. Laurent also assured the appointment of Vincent Massey as the first native-born Canadian governor-general in 1952. The Liberal party was again successful in elections in 1953. St. Laurent's government oversaw a period of rapid growth and development of the Canadian economy. The gross national product of Canada nearly doubled under his leadership. The Liberal party lost its majority in the Parliament following elections in 1957, and St. Laurent stepped down as prime minister on June 21, 1957. He retired from politics the following year and returned to his law practice in Quebec. He died at his home in Quebec City at the age of 91 on July 25, 1973.

JOHN G. DIEFENBAKER (Prime Minister, June 21, 1957–April 22, 1963). John George Diefenbaker was born in Grey County, Ontario, on September 18, 1895. He was educated at the University of Saskatchewan, where he received a degree in political science in 1916. During World War I he saw active duty overseas as a lieutenant. Diefenbaker returned to Canada in 1917 and received a degree in law two years later. He established a law practice and gained a reputation as a successful defense attorney. Diefenbaker became active in the Progressive Conservative party and was defeated in elections to the House of Commons in 1925 and 1926. He became the leader of the Conservative party in Saskatchewan in 1936 and was elected to the House of Commons in 1940. In 1948 he was defeated for the national leadership of the Progressive Conservatives by George Drew. He continued to serve in the Parliament and was elected party leader after Drew's resignation in 1956. Diefenbaker led his party to victory against Louis St. Laurent's Liberals in elections the following year and became prime minister on June 21, 1957. In 1958 he called new elections, and his party won a landslide victory. His government encouraged the development of Canada's Arctic resources and attempted to decrease dependence on the United States. Diefenbaker was an opponent of Communism, but he refused to break relations with Fidel Castro's Cuba and supplied grain to the People's Republic of China during a famine. Diefenbaker's party lost its majority in Parliament in elections in 1962. His government lost a vote of confidence in Parliament in a dispute over defense policy the following year. Diefenbaker stepped down as prime minister on April 22, 1963. He continued to serve in Parliament as a member of the Opposition. He occasionally took unpopular positions and was one of very few members of Parliament to oppose Prime Minister Pierre Trudeau's program of bilingualism in 1969. Diefenbaker was returned to Parliament for a record-setting twelfth time in May of 1979. He died of a heart attack in Ottawa a few months later at the age of 83 on August 16, 1979.

LESTER B. PEARSON (Prime Minister, April 22, 1963–April 20, 1968). Lester Bowles Pearson was born in Newtonbrook, Ontario, on April 23, 1897. He attended the University of Toronto, but interrupted his studies to serve with a hospital unit attached to the British army in Salonika at the start of World War I. In 1917 he was promoted to corporal and was transferred to the Royal Flying Corps. Pearson returned to Canada after crashing during his first solo flight. He continued his education and entered St. John's College at Oxford University. He returned to Toronto to teach history. He entered the government in 1928 and served in the Department of External Affairs. Pearson was posted to the office of Canada's high commissioner in London in 1935. He was sent to the Canadian Embassy in Washington, D.C., in 1942 and became Canada's ambassador to the United States in 1945. In 1945 he was a member of the delegation at the organizing session of the United Nations in San Francisco. Pearson was nominated for the post of secretary-general of the United Nations, but his selection was vetoed by the Soviet Union. In 1946 he returned to Canada to become under-secretary for external affairs. He was appointed secretary of external affairs by Prime Minister W. L. MacKenzie King in 1948 and retained that position in the subsequent government of Louis St. Laurent. Pearson represented Canada at various international conferences and served as chairman of the NATO Council from 1951 until 1952. He was elected president of the United Nation's General Assembly in 1952 and served until the following year. Pearson returned to the United Nations in 1956 to lead the Canadian delegation during the Suez crisis. Israel had attacked Egypt and the Suez Canal with the support of

Great Britain and France. Pearson was instrumental in formulating a settlement of the dispute and supported a United Nations peacekeeping force being sent to the Gaza Strip. Pearson's success in arranging a temporary truce was rewarded with a Nobel Peace Prize in 1957. He was selected as leader of the Liberal party following Louis St. Laurent's resignation in 1958. Pearson led the Opposition to the government of John Diefenbaker until the Liberals won the parliamentary elections in 1963. Pearson became prime minister on April 22, 1963. His government broadened social security benefits and initiated plans for a national health service and pension program. Pearson presided over Canada's centenary celebration and Expo '67 in 1967. He also sponsored the adoption of Canada's maple leaf national flag. His government was troubled by increasing conflict between English and French-speaking Canadians, and he instituted several studies on bilingualism. Pearson retired as prime minister and Liberal party leader on April 20, 1968, and was replaced by Pierre Trudeau. He continued his involvement with international affairs and served as head of the World Bank Commission on World Economic Development in 1969. Pearson lost his right eye during an operation to remove a tumor in August of 1970. He recovered from the surgery and resumed his activities until he was stricken by illness in December of 1972. Pearson died of cancer of the liver at his home in Rockliffe at the age of 75 on December 27, 1972.

PIERRE E. TRUDEAU (Prime Minister, April 20, 1968–June 4, 1979). Joseph Philippe Pierre Ives Elliott Trudeau was born in Montreal on October 18, 1919. He attended the University of Montreal, where he received a degree in law in 1943, and continued his education at Harvard University, the University of Paris, and the London School of Economics. He subsequently embarked on a world tour that included attendance at an international economics conference in Moscow. He returned to Canada to join the faculty of the University of Montreal. Trudeau entered politics as a member of the Liberal party and was elected to the House of Commons in 1965. In January of 1966 he was named to the government of Lester Pearson as parliamentary secretary to the prime minister. Trudeau was appointed minister of justice and attorney general in April of 1967. Following Pearson's resignation, Trudeau entered the campaign to become Liberal party leader and prime minister. He was victorious at the Liberal party convention and took office as prime minister on April 20, 1968. The Liberal party increased its majority in the Parliament in general elections several months later. Trudeau's government was threatened by a growing French-Canadian separatist movement. Radical elements of the movement, Le Front de Libération de Québec (FLQ), kidnapped and murdered the provincial minister of labor, Pierre LaPorte, in October of 1970. Trudeau was an opponent of separatism and introduced programs to strengthen Canadian unity. The Liberal party lost parliamentary seats in the election of October of 1972, and Trudeau governed as head of a minority government until the Liberals regained a clear majority in elections in July of 1974. Trudeau's government reduced Canada's armed forces and initiated closer ties with Europe and the Soviet Union. The Liberal party was defeated in the elections in 1979, and Trudeau resigned as prime minister and leader of the party on June 4, 1979. The succeeding conservative government of Joe Clark collapsed after a vote of no confidence, and Trudeau remained party leader to contest elections in February of 1980. The Liberals were again victorious, and Trudeau again became prime minister on March 3, 1980. He successfully promoted a new constitution that

helped insure the rights of French-speaking Canadians. Trudeau's popularity diminished in the 1980s, however, and he announced his decision to retire in February of 1984. John Turner was elected to succeed him as Liberal party leader, and Trudeau relinquished the prime minister's office on June 30, 1984. The Liberal party was badly defeated in subsequent parliamentary elections. Trudeau left politics and entered private industry as a legal consultant.

JOE CLARK (Prime Minister, June 4, 1979–March 3, 1980). Charles Joseph Clark was born in High River, Alberta, on June 5, 1939. He attended the University of Alberta, where he became involved with the Conservative party. After receiving a degree in history in 1960, he served as national leader of the Progressive Conservative Student Federation from 1962 until 1965. Clark then taught political science at the University of Alberta until 1967. He worked as an executive assistant to Conservative leader Robert Stanfield from 1967 until 1970. Clark was elected to the House of Commons in 1972. He was elected leader of the Progressive Conservatives in 1976 and formed a government as prime minister on June 4, 1979. Clark was unable to get Parliament's approval for his budget and was forced to call new elections in February of 1980. The Liberals were returned to power, and Clark stepped down as prime minister on March 3, 1980. He remained leader of the Opposition until 1983, when he was replaced by Brian Mulroney. Mulroney led the party to victory in 1984, and Clark was named minister of external affairs in the new government. Clark retained that position until April of 1991, when he was transferred to the new cabinet position of minister for constitutional affairs.

PIERRE E. TRUDEAU (Prime Minister, March 3, 1980–June 30, 1984).

See earlier entry under Heads of Government.

JOHN TURNER (Prime Minister, June 30, 1984–September 17, 1984). John Napier Turner was born in Richmond, Surrey, England, on June 7, 1929. His family moved to Ottawa when he was three years old. Turner received a degree in political science from the University of British Columbia in 1949. He subsequently attended Oxford University under a Rhodes scholarship. After returning to Canada, he practiced law in Montreal in 1953. Turner entered politics and was elected to the House of Commons as a Liberal party member in 1962. He was named to Lester Pearson's cabinet as minister without portfolio in 1965. He was registrar general from 1967 until 1968. Turner served in several other cabinet positions before being appointed minister of justice and attorney general in 1968. He retained that position until 1972, when he was named minister of finance. In 1975 he left the cabinet, and he retired from Parliament the following year. He subsequently opened a successful law firm in Toronto. Turner returned to politics after Pierre Trudeau announced his impending resignation as leader of the Liberal party in February of 1984. Turner was elected to succeed Trudeau and took office as prime minister on June 30, 1984. The Liberal party was badly beaten in subsequent elections, and Turner was replaced as prime minister by Brian Mulroney on September 17, 1984. Turner was elected to a seat in the House of Commons in 1984 and served as leader of the Opposition during parliamentary elections in 1988, when the Liberals again were defeated. Turner was replaced as Liberal party leader by Jean Chrétien in June of 1990.

BRIAN MULRONEY (Prime Minister, September 17, 1984–). Martin Brian Mulroney was born in Baie Comeau, Quebec, on March 20, 1939. He attended Laval University in Quebec, where he received a degree in law in 1965. He established himself as a successful labor lawyer in Montreal and gained popularity as a member of the Quebec Royal Commission into Violence in the Construction Industry. He was unsuccessful in an attempt to become leader of the Progressive Conservative party in 1976 and lost to Joe Clark. Mulroney served as director and president of the Iron Ore Company of Canada from 1977 until 1983. He reentered politics in 1983 and replaced Clark as Conservative leader. He led the party to victory in elections the following year and became prime minister on September 17, 1984. Mulroney's government found it difficult to gain support for its fiscal and defense policies. The Mulroney cabinet was also beset with several scandals. Mulroney called early elections in November of 1988, and the Conservatives maintained control of the House of Commons. The Liberal-controlled Senate refused to consider the government's unpopular goods and services tax bill. Mulroney sparked a constitutional crisis in September of 1990 when he invoked a provision of the 1867 British North America Act to add Conservative members to the Canadian Senate.

Cape Verde Islands

(República de Cabo Verde)

Cape Verde is a group of islands in the Atlantic Ocean, off northern Africa. It was granted independence from Portugal on July 5, 1975.

HEADS OF STATE

ARISTIDE PEREIRA (President, July 8, 1975–March 22, 1991). Aristide María Pereira was born in Boa Vista on November 17, 1923. He was a founder of the African Party for the Independence of Guinea-Bissau and Cape Verde (PAIGC) with Amilcar Cabral in 1956. In 1960 he went into exile in the Republic of Guinea. He served as a member of the Council of War from 1965 and became secretary-general of PAIGC following Cabral's assassination in January of 1973. Cape Verde was granted independence from Portugal in 1975, and Pereira was elected president by the National People's Assembly on July 8, 1975. Pereira supported the unification of Cape Verde and Guinea-Bissau. A constitution was adopted in September of 1980, but a coup in Guinea-Bissau the following year scuttled plans for unification. Pereira subsequently created the African Party for the Independence of

Cape Verde (PAICV) in 1981. He was reelected president by the National Assembly in February of 1981 and January of 1986. Pereira stepped down as leader of PAICV in April of 1990 and announced that democratic elections would take place the following year. He was defeated in the elections in February of 1991 and relinquished office to Antonio Mascarenhas Monteiro on March 22, 1991.

ANTÓNIO MASCARENHAS MONTEIRO (President, March 22, 1991–   ). António Mascarenhas Monteiro served as president of the Cape Verde Supreme Court. He was a member of the Movement for Democracy party and won Cape Verde's first free election for president in February of 1991. Monteiro took office as president on March 22, 1991. He subsequently began a program to privatize companies that had been owned by the state.

HEADS OF GOVERNMENT

PEDRO PIRES (Prime Minister, July 15, 1975–January 28, 1991). Pedro Verona Rodrigues Pires was born in 1934. He was a major in the Cape Verde military and negotiated the independence agreement for Cape Verde and Guinea-Bissau. He was named prime minister in the independent government on July 15, 1975. Pires succeeded President Aristide Pereira as leader of the African Party for the Independence of Cape Verde (PAICV) in August of 1990. He remained prime minister until January 28, 1991, when he stepped

down following defeat of PAICV in the general election.

CARLOS VEIGA (Prime Minister, January 28, 1991–   ). Carlos Alberto Wahnon de Carvalho Veiga was a member of the Movement for Democracy party. He was appointed to lead a transitional government on January 28, 1991, following legislative elections. He remained as prime minister following the inauguration of President Antonio Mascarenhas Monteiro in March of 1991.

Central African Republic,
(République Centrafricaine)

The Central African Republic is a country in central Africa. It was granted independence from France on August 13, 1960.

HEADS OF STATE

DAVID DACKO (President, August 13, 1960–January 1, 1966). David Dacko was born in Bouchia, in the colony of Ubangi-Shari, on March 24, 1930. He was educated at a teacher's college in Brazzaville, Congo, and returned to Ubangi-Shari to be a teacher. Dacko's uncle, Barthelemy Boganda, was the leading figure of the independence movement from the French in the 1950s. Dacko was elected to the Territorial Assembly in 1957 and served as minister of agriculture on the Central African Government Council from 1957 until 1958. He was minister of the interior, economy, and trade in the subsequent provisional government led by Boganda from 1958 until 1959. When Boganda was killed in an air crash in 1959, Dacko was selected to head the pre-independence government. The Central African Republic was granted full independence the following year, and Dacko took office as the nation's first president on August 13, 1960. He attempted to eliminate opposition to his rule by banning all political parties other than his Social Evolution Movement of Black Africa (MESAN). Dacko moved to align his country with Communist governments, and he established diplomatic relations with the People's Republic of China in 1964. This action was unpopular with French business and political interests that remained powerful in the country. Dacko was ousted in a military coup led by his cousin, Jean-Bédel Bokassa, on January 1, 1966. He was put under house arrest in Bangui, where he remained until 1976. He was then released from custody and named a personal advisor to President Bokassa. When Bokassa proclaimed himself emperor later in the year, Dacko used his position to organize a coup against him. Bokassa was ousted by Dacko on September 21, 1979, while the emperor was out of the country. Dacko became president in the new government and pledged to restore civil and political liberties to the oppressed populace. He soon began to reinstitute the harsh rule of his predecessor, however, and banned political parties and arrested political opponents. Dacko narrowly won a presidential election in March of 1981. Allegations of electoral fraud resulted in violent demonstrations in the capital. Dacko was suffering from poor health and was removed from office, possibly at his own request, by General André Kolingba on September 1, 1981. He subsequently retired from active politics.

JEAN-BÉDEL BOKASSA (President, January 1, 1966–December 4, 1976). Jean-Bédel Bokassa was born in Boubangui, Oubangui-Chari Colony, in French Equatorial Africa, on February 22, 1921. Bokassa's father was a Mbaka tribal village chief. He was killed in a tribal dispute when Bokassa was six, and his mother committed suicide shortly thereafter. Bokassa was educated at Catholic missionary schools in Bangui and Brazzaville, but gave up aspirations to enter the priesthood and instead joined the French army in 1939. After the fall of France, he served in the African unit of the Free French forces and participated in the capture of the Vichy capital in Brazzaville. He remained in the French army after the war and served in Indochina, where he survived the French defeat at Dien Bien Phu in 1954 and was promoted to second lieutenant in 1956. Bokassa returned to Bangui and retired from the French army following the Central African Republic's independence in 1960. President David Dacko, Bokassa's cousin, gave him the task of creating the new nation's armed forces, and Bokassa became commander in chief of the army in 1963. The economic woes of the country and Dacko's plan to cut the military budget prompted Bokassa to lead a military coup on December 31, 1965. Bokassa ousted his cousin on January 1, 1965, and proclaimed himself president and prime minister. Bokassa tried to improve the Central African Republic's economy and instituted a plan to modernize agriculture in the country. His rule became increasingly despotic as he tried to retain power. Bokassa tried to create a cult of personality around himself, with his portraits displayed everywhere. He purged and imprisoned political opponents, outlawed strikes, and imposed strict censorship restrictions. In April of 1969 he executed his closest aide, paratroop commander Lt. Col. Alexandre Banda, on suspicion of plotting against the government. Bokassa promoted himself to full general in 1971 and had himself proclaimed president for life in March of 1972. He relinquished the position of prime minister to Elizabeth Domitien on January 2, 1975. Bokassa's domestic and foreign policies became increasingly erratic. In February of 1976 he survived an assassination attempt at the Bangui airport. He briefly embraced Islam and changed his name to Salah Addine Ahmed following a state visit by Libyan leader Muammar al-Qaddafi. Bokassa returned to Roman Catholicism when financial assistance from Libya failed to materialize. In December of 1976 Bokassa instituted a new constitution that transformed the Central African Republic into the Central African Empire. He was proclaimed Emperor Bokassa I on December 4, 1976. He staged an elaborate coronation ceremony in December of 1977 which cost his country approximately $20 million. In January of 1979 schoolchildren demonstrated against Bokassa's order that they wear new uniforms. Bokassa ordered the massacre of over 100 schoolchildren by the Imperial Guard in April of 1979. This action prompted severe international criticism of his regime. Bokassa was on a visit to Libya when he was ousted in a coup led by former president David Dacko on September 21, 1979. Bokassa went into exile in the Ivory Coast. He was tried in absentia and sentenced to death in December of 1980. Bokassa went into exile in France, but returned to the Central African Republic in October of 1986. He was arrested and tried on charges that included murder and cannibalism. He was convicted of conspiracy to murder, illegal detentions, and embezzlement in June of 1987 and was sentenced to death. The sentence was commuted to life imprisonment and hard labor in Bangui's Ngaaba Prison by President Andre Kolingba in February of 1988.

BOKASSA I (Emperor, December 4, 1976–September 21, 1979). *See previous entry for Jean-Bédel Bokassa.*

DAVID DACKO (President, September 21, 1979–September 1, 1981). *See earlier entry under Heads of State.*

ANDRÉ KOLINGBA (President, September 1, 1981–). André Kolingba was born in Bangui on August 12, 1935. He served in the French army in Indochina and Cameroon prior to the Central African Republic's independence in 1960. He later served in the army of the Central African Republic. Kolingba assisted President David Dacko in reorganizing the nation's army following the ouster of Jean-Bédel Bokassa in 1979. He was promoted to general and named chief of staff of the army on July 30, 1981. The Dacko government had declared a state of siege following civil disturbances, and Kolingba enforced the declaration. He took control of the government on September 1, 1981, as head of the Military Committee for National Recovery. He survived a coup attempt in March of 1982 and was faced with a rebellion in late 1984. In November of

1986 he promoted a new constitution that extended his rule for an additional six years. Kolingba legalized opposition parties in 1991, though he resisted efforts for multiparty elections. He relinquished his duties as prime minister on March 15, 1991. His regime was faced with a series of general strikes in August of 1992, and Kolingba agreed to conduct legislative and presidential elections in February of 1993.

HEADS OF GOVERNMENT

JEAN-BÉDEL BOKASSA (Premier, January 1, 1966–January 2, 1975). *See entry under Heads of State.*

ELISABETH DOMITIEN (Premier, January 2, 1975–April 7, 1976). Elisabeth Domitien served as vice president of the ruling Social Evolution Movement of Black Africa party (MESAN) before she was named premier in the government of Jean-Bédel Bokassa on January 2, 1975. She became the first woman to serve as Premier in an African government. Bokassa abolished Domitien's cabinet on April 7, 1976. Domitien was arrested in November of 1979 following the ouster of the Bokassa government. She was tried in February of 1980 on charges of covering up extortion committed by Bokassa.

ANGE PATASSÉ (Premier, September 5, 1976–July 14, 1978). Ange Patassé was born on January 25, 1937. He was educated at the French Equatorial College and worked as an agriculture inspector from 1959. He was named to Jean-Bédel Bokassa's cabinet as minister of agriculture in 1965. Patassé also served as minister of development in 1965. He was named minister of state for transport and power in 1969 and held various other cabinet positions until his appointment as Bokassa's premier on September 5, 1976. He was dismissed on July 14, 1978. Patassé was imprisoned in October of 1979, following the ouster of Bokassa. After his release from detention, Patassé founded the Movement for the Liberation of the Central African People (MLPC). He was an unsuccessful candidate for president in March of 1981. He went into voluntary exile in France in late 1981. In February of 1982 he returned to the Central African Republic, and he was charged with complicity in an unsuccessful coup attempt the following month. Patassé sought refuge in the French Embassy in Bangui and was later allowed to go into exile in Togo. He subsequently went into exile in France, where he remained leader of the MLPC.

HENRI MAÏDOU (Premier, July 14, 1978–September 21, 1979). Henri Maïdou was born in Bangui on February 14, 1936. He served as minister of national education, youth, sport, and arts from 1970 until 1973. He was named minister of health and social affairs in 1973 and served until 1974. He was minister of state in charge of town planning and territorial development from 1974 until 1976. Maïdou was named second deputy prime minister in 1976 and subsequently served again as minister of national education, youth, sports, arts, and culture until 1978. He was appointed premier on July 14, 1978, and served until September 21, 1979. He served as vice president from 1979 until his arrest in August of 1980. He remained imprisoned until October of 1980. Maïdou served as the leader of the Parti Republicain du Progress in 1981. He served as president of the Central African Bank from 1988 until 1991.

BERNARD AYANDHO (Premier, September 26, 1979–August 22, 1980). Bernard Christian Ayandho was born on December 15, 1930. He was named premier in the government of David Dacko on September 26, 1979, following the ouster of President Jean-Bédel Bokassa. Ayandho was dismissed on August 22, 1980, and put under house arrest. He subsequently went into private industry and served as a representative of Air Afrique in the Equatorial Region. He also served as president of the Chamber of Commerce and Industry in the Central African Republic.

JEAN-PIERRE LEBOUDER (Premier, November 12, 1980–April 4, 1981). Jean-Pierre Lebouder was born in 1944. He was educated as an agronomist in Toulouse, France. He was named minister of rural development in 1976. Lebouder served as minister of planning under Jean-Bédel Bokassa in 1978 and retained the position in the subsequent government of David Dacko. Lebouder was appointed premier on November 12, 1980, and served until April 4, 1981.

SIMON NARCISSE BOZANGA (Premier, April 4, 1981–September 1, 1981). Simon Narcisse Bozanga was born in Bangassou on December 26, 1942. He was employed by the Ministry of Foreign Affairs as director of legal studies from 1972 until 1974. He was secretary-general to the government from 1974 until 1978 and served as ambassador to Gabon from 1978 until 1979. Bozanga again served as secretary-general until 1980, when he was named minister of justice. He was appointed premier on April 4, 1981, and retained office until September 1, 1981, when President David Dacko was replaced by General André Kolingba. He subsequently went into private industry.

EDOUARD FRANCK (Prime Minister, March 15, 1991–December 4, 1992). Edouard Franck was appointed prime minister by presidential decree on March 15, 1991. Franck, who had served as General Kolingba's presidential coordinator, was replaced by Timothée Malendoma on December 4, 1992.

TIMOTHÉE MALENDOMA (Prime Minister, December 4, 1992–   ). Timothée Malendoma was born in Dekoa in 1935. He joined the French army in 1953 and served in Indochina. In 1956 he returned to Central Africa and was transferred to the Central African Army. He subsequently attended officers' training school in France. Malendoma was appointed to the cabinet as minister of economic affairs following the coup led by Jean-Bédel Bokassa in January of 1966. He remained active in the military and the government during the administrations of David Dacko and André Kolingba. Malendoma was leader of the Civic Forum party in the early 1990s. He was named prime minister by President Kolingba on December 4, 1992, following the announcement that legislative elections would be held in February of 1993.

Chad, Republic of

(République du Tchad)

Chad is a country in north central Africa. It was granted independence from France on August 11, 1960.

HEADS OF STATE

N'GARTA TOMBALBAYE (President, April 12, 1960–April 13, 1975). Françoise Tombalbaye was born in Badaya in southern Chad on June 15, 1918. He worked as a school teacher and became a leader of the Chad trade union movement in 1946. He was active in the establishment of the Chad Progressive party (PPT) in 1947. Tombalbaye was elected to the Territorial Assembly in March of 1952, though the Progressive party was defeated. The PPT received a majority of votes in the Assembly in elections in March of 1957, and Chad was granted self-government on November 28, 1958. When Progressive party leader Gabrielle Lissette was unable to form a coalition provisional government, Tombalbaye replaced him as party leader. Tombalbaye was selected as prime minister on March 24, 1959. New elections were held several months later in which the PPT increased its victory margin. Tombalbaye also became head of state when Chad received full independence on August 11, 1960. In addition, he served as minister of defense and, from February of 1961, minister of justice. Tombalbaye consolidated his power and banned all opposition parties in January of 1962. He sponsored a new constitution granting broad powers to the president in April of 1962 and was confirmed as president on April 23, 1962. His regime was faced with numerous coup attempts and rebellions. Violence erupted between the Sudanic Muslims of northern Chad and the Bantus of the south. The Chad National Liberation Front (FROLINAT) was founded in June 1966 to unite Muslim opposition to Tombalbaye's government. Tombalbaye received financial and military aid from France to fight a guerrilla war against the Muslim rebels. He later received assistance from French Foreign Legion troops. Tombalbaye also faced opposition from elements of the military.

General Félix Malloum, the commander of the armed forces, was arrested on charges of conspiring against the government in 1973. Tombalbaye initiated the Africanization of Chad in 1973, changing his first name from Françoise to N'Garta. General Noël Odingar led a military revolt against the government on April 13, 1975. Tombalbaye was killed during the revolt when machine gun and mortar fire was directed at his official residence in the capital of N'Djamena.

NOËL ODINGAR (Acting President, April 13, 1975–April 15, 1975). Noël Odingar was a general in Chad's army. He served as acting chief of staff of the armed forces in 1975, when he led the military coup that ousted and killed President N'Garta Tombalbaye on April 13, 1975. Odingar served as interim leader of the Supreme Military Council. He ordered the release of a number of political prisoners, including General Félix Malloum. Odingar relinquished the leadership of the Supreme Military Council to Malloum on April 15, 1975. Odingar remained a member of the council during Malloum's regime.

FÉLIX MALLOUM (President, April 15, 1975–March 23, 1979). Félix Malloum was born in Ft. Archambault on September 10, 1932. He attended the French military academy and served in the French armed forces. He saw action in Indochina and Algeria. Malloum joined the Chad National Army in 1961 and was promoted to colonel in 1968. He was appointed chief of the general staff in 1971 and was named commander in chief of the armed forces in 1972. Malloum was arrested by order of President N'garta Tombalbaye in July of 1973 on charges of conspiring against the government. Malloum was released from prison following the military coup that deposed and killed Tombalbaye. He became president of the Supreme Military Council on April 15, 1975. Malloum subsequently became president and premier on May 12, 1975. His government continued to be threatened by rebel guerrilla forces. He formed a coalition cabinet with Hissene Habré, one of the rebel leaders, in August of 1978. Habré's forces soon resumed fighting with Malloum's government, and Malloum was replaced by a rebel provisional government on March 23, 1979, after signing the Kano Peace Agreement.

GOUKOUNI OUEDDEI (President, March 23, 1979–April 29, 1979). Goukouni Oueddei was born in Zouar, in the Tibesti mountains, in 1944. He was the son of the Derde, the Toubou religious leader. Oueddei led the Armed Forces of the North (FAN), in opposition to the government of N'Garta Tombalbaye. He was chosen as leader of the Chad National Liberation Front (FROLINAT) over Hissene Habré in November of 1976 and received support from the Libyan government of Muammar al-Qaddafi. Oueddei continued the guerrilla war against the regime of Félix Malloum. He became president of the Provisional State Council on March 23, 1979, following negotiations between the four major combatants. A second provisional government was formed on April 29, 1979, and Oueddei was replaced by Lol Mohamed Shawa. A conference in Lagos, Nigeria, in August of 1979 was attended by representatives of eleven Chadian rebel groups and interested foreign governments. Oueddei was again named as provisional president on August 22, 1979. He formed a Government of National Transition (GUNT) in November of 1979. Fighting between rebel factions resumed in the capital in March of 1980. Libya signed a military defense agreement with the Oueddei government and assisted Oueddei's troops in driving Habré's

forces from the capital. Libya announced a decision to incorporate Chad into Libya in January of 1981, though Oueddei signed the agreement under duress. Habré's forces regrouped and again marched on the capital. The Oueddei government fell on June 7, 1982. Oueddei's troops were again defeated in battle against Habré's forces in July of 1983. Oueddei was placed under house arrest in Tripoli, Libya, in August of 1985, when his Libyan backers disapproved of his intentions of negotiating a truce with Habré. Oueddei was reportedly injured in a shootout with his Libyan captors in October of 1985. Many of Oueddei's supporters subsequently joined with Habré's forces in opposition to the Libyans. Oueddei stepped down as leader of GUNT in 1986.

LOL MOHAMED SHAWA (President, April 29, 1979–August 22, 1979). Lol Mohamed Shawa was born in 1939. He was a member of the Popular Movement of Chadian Liberation (MPLT), one of the rival guerrilla groups fighting against the government of Félix Malloum. He was chosen president of a second provisional government under the auspices of Nigeria on April 29, 1979. Further negotiations among the leading rebel factions created a third provisional government on August 22, 1979, and Goukouni Oueddei was reinstated as president. Shawa went into exile in Paris, where he remained until 1982. He then returned to Chad to serve in the government as minister of transport until 1985.

GOUKOUNI OUEDDEI (President, August 22, 1979–June 7, 1982). *See earlier entry under Heads of State.*

HISSENE HABRÉ (President, June 19, 1982–December 2, 1990). Hissene Habré was born in Faya Largeau in northern Chad in 1942. He attended a local mission school and worked for the French military government in northern

Chad from 1962. Habré continued his education in France in 1965. In 1970 he returned to Chad and served in the civil government of the town of Moussoro. President N'Garta Tombalbaye assigned Habré to negotiate with the leadership of the Chad National Liberation Front (FROLINAT), the Muslim guerrilla organization that had been waging a war against the government. Habré defected to FROLINAT in October of 1971. He joined Goukouni Oueddei's faction of FROLINAT and led the Armed Forces of the North (FAN). Tombalbaye was overthrown and killed in a military coup in April of 1975, and the rebellion continued against the government of Félix Malloum. Habré had captured the district capital of Bardai in April of 1974 and seized three Europeans as hostages. He received international attention from this action and engaged in direct negotiations with the French. He held one of the hostages for over three years, demanding arms in exchange for her release. His actions and the fear of French reprisals caused a rift between him and Oueddei. Habré was ousted from FAN and took his supporters to a base near the Sudanese border. Habré was offered the office of prime minister in the government of Félix Malloum when Oueddei's rebel forces advanced on the capital. Habré accepted, taking office on August 29, 1978. Habré's forces turned against Malloum and led an unsuccessful coup in February of 1979. Supporters of Malloum and Habré engaged in a bloody series of battles for control of the capital. The other rebel groups arrived in the capital shortly thereafter, and a Government of National Transition (GUNT) was formed. Oueddei became president on March 23, 1979, and Habré was appointed minister of defense. Rivalry between Oueddei and Habré continued, and Habré was ousted from the government in April of 1980. After Habré's forces were driven from the capital by Oueddei's Libyan backed troops, Habré reorganized his army with military support from coun-tries opposed to Libya's involvement in Chad. Habré's forces recaptured the capital on June 7, 1982, and he was named head of state on June 19, 1982. Habré formed the Chadian National Armed Forces (FANT). He received military assistance from the French when Oueddei's forces again marched on the capital, and he was able to maintain control of the government with French support. Habré also gained many of Oueddei's supporters when Oueddei broke with his Libyan sponsors and was injured in a shootout in October of 1985. Habré's combined army succeeded in defeating the Libyan forces at Ouadi Doum in north central Chad in March of 1987. A cease-fire was negotiated by the Organization of African Unity in September of 1987. Habré survived a coup attempt in April of 1989 and was challenged by the Patriotic Salvation Movement (MPS), led by Idriss Déby, in November of 1990. Déby's forces captured several major towns in Chad and advanced on the capital. Habré fled to Cameroon on December 2, 1990, and Déby entered the capital the following day. Habré's supporters led an unsuccessful invasion of Chad in December of 1991.

IDRISS DÉBY (President, December 4, 1990–   ). Idriss Déby served as a commander of the Chadian National Armed Forces (FANT) in the government of Hisene Habré. He led an unsuccessful revolt against Habré in April of 1989. Déby then led his troops across the border into the Sudan, where he continued to attack Habré's forces. He formed the Patriotic Salvation Movement (MPS), a coalition of antigovernment forces, in November of 1990. Déby's troops marched on the capital, and Habré fled into exile in Cameroon. Déby took control of the government as provisional president of the Council of State on December 4, 1990. He was confirmed as president in March of 1991. Déby survived several coup attempts in 1992 and continued with plans to hold multiparty elections in Chad.

HEADS OF GOVERNMENT

FRANÇOISE TOMBALBAYE (Premier, March 24, 1959–August 12, 1960). *See entry under Heads of State.*

FÉLIX MALLOUM (President, May 12, 1975–August 29, 1978). *See entry under Heads of State.*

HISSENE HABRÉ (Premier, August 29, 1978–March 23, 1979). *See entry under Heads of State.*

JEAN ALINGUÉ BAWOYEA (Prime Minister, March 4, 1991–May 20, 1992). Jean Alingué Bawoyea was a former president of the National Assembly. He was named by President Idriss Déby to the newly revised position of prime minister on March 4, 1991. He founded the Union for Democracy and the Republic party (UDR) in March of 1992. Alingué Bawoyea was replaced as prime minister on May 20, 1992.

JOSEPH YODOYMAN (Prime Minister, May 20, 1992–). Joseph Yodoyman was appointed prime minister on May 20, 1992, following the modification of the national charter to grant more authority to the prime minister.

Chile, Republic of

(Républica de Chile)

Chile is a country on the South Pacific coast of South America. It received independence from Spain on September 18, 1810.

HEADS OF STATE

JUAN ANTONIO RIOS (President, April 2, 1942–June 27, 1946). Juan Antonio Rios Morales was born in Canete, Arauco Province, on November 10, 1888. He received a law degree from the University of Chile in 1914 and in 1918 was elected alderman in Concepcion. He served as deputy mayor and police magistrate for Concepcion until 1921, when he was appointed consul general to Panama. In 1923 Rios was elected to the Chilean Parliament representing Arauco, Lebu, and Canete. He was elected to the Senate in 1930 and served until Congress was dissolved in 1932. He was then appointed minister of the interior in the government of President Arturo Alessandri Palma. Shortly afterwards Rios was appointed minister of justice, and he remained in this position until March of 1937. Pedro Aguirre Cerda was elected president in 1938 with the support of the Popular Front coalition. Rios's Radical party withdrew from the coalition and relations between President Aguirre Cerda and Rios were strained. Aguirre Cerda died in November of 1941, and Rios became a candidate for the presidency. On February 1, 1942, he defeated General Carlos Ibáñez del Campo, and he was sworn into office on April 2, 1942. His administration initially refused to sever diplomatic relations with the Axis powers, but diplomatic and economic pressures persuaded Rios to reverse his stance. This change of policy resulted in the inclusion of Chile as part of the

United States lend-lease program and secured new loans for the troubled economy. In October of 1945 Rios's entire cabinet resigned in protest of the president's visit to the United States. Rios was also beset by a failing economy due to a decrease in the price of copper and by labor strikes throughout the country. His health failed early in 1946, and he gave up his presidential powers to Alfredo Duhalde Vázquez, the minister of the interior, on January 17, 1946. Rios died in Santiago on June 27, 1946.

ALFREDO DUHALDE VÁZQUEZ (Acting President, January 17, 1946–August 3, 1946). Alfredo Duhalde Vázquez was born in Rio Bueno in southern Chile in 1888. His family were successful farmers, and Duhalde attended the University of Chile in Santiago, where he studied law. He served as a lieutenant in the cavalry of the Chilean army and was elected a deputy from Llanquihue in 1924. A member of the Radical party, he was later elected to represent Valdivia. In 1939 Duhalde was named ambassador to Peru, and he served as minister of defense from 1939 until 1940. He again served as minister of defense in the cabinet of President Jose Antonio Rios. In 1945 he was named minister of the interior and also served as vice president of the republic. In January of 1946 Duhalde took over the powers of the presidency when President Rios was unable to continue due to ill health. Chile suffered from continual unrest under Duhalde, though he remained as interim president until August 3, 1946, when he resigned to campaign for the presidency. He was unsuccessful in the election and resumed the role of acting president on September 6, 1946. He again resigned on October 17, 1946, and returned to the Chilean Senate, where he served until 1953.

VICENTE MERIÑO BIELECH (Acting President, August 3, 1946–September 6, 1946). Vicente Meriño Bielech was born in 1895. He attended the Valparaiso Naval Academy, and in 1930 he was named under-secretary of the navy. He served as naval chief of staff from 1934 until 1937 and was promoted to vice admiral in 1940. In 1941 Mariño led a naval mission to the United States, and in 1944 he was appointed commander in chief of the navy. He succeeded Alfredo Duhalde Vázquez as minister of the interior and vice president when Duhalde became acting president in June of 1946. Meriño assumed the powers of the presidency from August 3, 1946, until September 6, 1946, while Duhalde campaigned in the election. Meriño retired from the navy in 1947 and died in 1977.

ALFREDO DUHALDE VAZQUEZ (Acting President, September 6, 1946–October 17, 1946). *See earlier entry under Heads of State.*

JUAN A. IRIBARREN (Acting President, October 17, 1946–November 3, 1946). Juan Antonio Iribarren Cabezas was born in Vicuna in 1885. He studied law in La Serena and Santiago and became a member of the faculty of the University of Chile. He later became director of the University's law school. During the 1930s he was the legal advisor to the General Bankruptcy Court. In 1939 he was elected secretary-general of the Radical party, and he served as minister of education from 1940 until 1942 and again in 1945. In August of 1946 he was appointed minister of the interior and vice president. He briefly assumed the powers of the presidency on October 17, 1946, pending the confirmation of Gabriel Gonzaléz Videla as president on November 3, 1946. Iribarren served as chairman of the Government Mortgage Bank from 1946 until 1952.

GABRIEL GONZALÉZ VIDELA (President, November 3, 1946–November 3, 1952). Gabriel Gonzaléz Videla was born in La Serena on November 22, 1898. He studied law at La Serena and at the University of Chile, where he earned a law degree. After his return to La Serena, he practiced law until 1929. Gonzaléz was elected as a deputy to the lower house of Congress as a member of the Radical party in 1929 and represented La Serena until 1939. During his legislative career, he served as speaker of the House and chairman of the Budget and Legislation Committee. He was elected president of the Radical party in 1932. During the 1930s he served as Chile's minister to France, Belgium, and Luxembourg. In 1942 he was the Radical party candidate for the presidency, but was defeated by Juan Antonio Rios. He was appointed ambassador to Portugal later that year, and from 1942 until 1944 he was ambassador to Brazil. Gonzaléz was also Chile's representative to the United Nations conference in San Francisco following World War II. He was elected president of Chile in 1946 and took office on November 3, 1946. Leading a campaign against the Communists in Chile, he banned the party and exiled prominent leftist figures. Gonzaléz declared martial law in August of 1949 following widespread rioting and demonstrations against the government. He was able to restore political stability in the country during the remainder of his term of office. He relinquished the presidency to Carlos Ibáñez del Campo on November 3, 1952. Gonzaléz retired from politics and died in 1980.

CARLOS IBÁÑEZ DEL CAMPO (President, November 3, 1952–November 3, 1958). Carlos Ibáñez del Campo was born in Linares, Chile, on November 3, 1877. He entered the military school in Santiago in 1894 and rose to the rank of lieutenant in 1903. That year he also went to El Salvador, where he spent the next five years training the army there. Ibáñez returned to Chile in 1908 with the rank of captain. In subse-

quent years he served as section chief of the Ministry of War and director of the cavalry school. He was assigned to Paris as military attaché in 1924, but returned to Chile in September of that year to take part in a military rebellion. Ibáñez was also active in the coup d'état in January of 1925, and he was leader of the military junta that followed the coup from January 23, 1925, until March 21, 1925. He continued to serve in the government as minister of war and was appointed minister of the interior and vice president in the government of President Emiliano Figueroa Larrain in 1927. He succeeded as president when Figueroa resigned on May 4, 1927. Ibáñez's administration was plagued by severe economic problems which resulted in his overthrow on July 26, 1931. He went into exile in Argentina and remained there until 1937. Ibáñez then returned to Chile, where he ran unsuccessfully for president in 1938 and 1942. He was elected to the Chilean Senate in 1949. In 1952 Ibáñez again ran for president and gained a plurality of the popular vote. He was confirmed as president by the National Congress. Ibáñez was an admirer of Argentina's Juan Péron and attempted to instill a sense of Chilean nationalism and anti-American sentiment in the country with little success. During his term of office, it was feared that Ibáñez would revert to a dictatorial style of government, but he ruled in a conciliatory fashion. He remained in office until his term expired on November 3, 1958. He died in Santiago, Chile, of throat cancer on April 28, 1960, at the age of 82.

JORGE ALESSANDRI RODRIGUEZ (President, November 3, 1958–November 3, 1964). Jorge Alessandri Rodriguez was born in Santiago, on May 19, 1896. He was the son of Arturo Alessandri Palma, who served as Chile's president from 1920 to 1924 and from 1932 to 1938. Alessandri Rodriguez graduated from the University of

Chile in 1919 with a degree in civil engineering. He served as an engineer in the Ministry of Public Works after graduation. In 1925 he was elected to the Chamber of Deputies, representing Santiago, and he served until 1930. Alessandri then worked in the private sector, where he founded the Paper and Cardboard Manufacturing Company and served on the boards of other industries. He was appointed minister of finance in the cabinet of President Gabriel Gonzaléz Videla in August of 1948. He served for two years in that position and succeeded in balancing the federal budget and greatly improving Chile's financial standing. Alessandri reentered politics in March of 1957, when he was elected to the Senate. The following year he ran for president as an independent supported by a loose federation of parties. A right-wing conservative, he received a plurality in a five-man race which included Salvador Allende, the Socialist candidate. The National Congress ratified Alessandri's election, and he was sworn in as president on November 3, 1958. Chile was facing grave financial difficulties when Alessandri took power. He began a campaign of austere financial policies to combat inflation. He also initiated an agrarian reform program, which was passed in 1962, and expanded public works. One of Alessandri's last acts as president was to follow the accord of the Organization of American States and break diplomatic relations with Cuba. He served out his term of office and was succeeded by Eduardo Frei Montalva on November 3, 1964. Alessandri emerged from political retirement in 1970 when he again ran for the presidency as a candidate for the Unidad Popular (Popular Unity) party. Though he reportedly received covert assistance from American business interests, he was narrowly defeated on September 4, 1970, by Salvador Allende, the Socialist candidate. When Allende was deposed in a military coup led by Gen. Augusto Pinochet, Ales-

sandri initially supported the revolt. He later broke with the new government over its financial policies and its slowness to hold democratic elections. In 1985 Alessandri was hospitalized from complications from diabetes and kidney problems. He died in Santiago on August 31, 1986, at the age of 90.

EDUARDO FREI MONTALVA (President, November 3, 1964–November 3, 1970). Eduardo Frei Montalva was born in Santiago on January 16, 1911. The son of a Swiss immigrant and a Chilean mother, he attended public school at the Institute of Humanities in Santiago. He received a law degree from the Catholic University of Chile in 1933. While practising law, he remained active in Catholic youth groups and entered politics as a member of the Chilean Conservative party. Frei served as editor of *El Tarapaca*, the Uquique, Chile, daily newspaper, from 1935 until 1937. The following year he broke with the Conservatives and helped found the National Falange, a Christian Socialist party. He served as party chairman on several occasions in the early 1940s, while also teaching at the Catholic University of Chile. In 1945 Frei was named minister of roads and public works in the administration of President Juan Antonio Rios. He remained in that position in the succeeding government of President Gabriel Gonzalés Videla. After achieving much success in this position, he was elected to the Chilean Senate in 1949. In 1958 Frei made an unsuccessful bid for the Chilean presidency under the banner of the Christian Democratic party, following the merger of the National Falange and the Social Christian Conservative party. Despite his defeat, the popularity of the Christian Democratic party grew in the 1960s, and in 1964 Frei again ran for the presidency. His leading opponent was Socialist leader Salvador Allende, who favored a Cuban-styled nationalization of Chilean industries. Frei favored a policy of "Chileanization" of certain industries, including the copper mines. With the support of American business and political interests, he won the election and was sworn in as president on November 3, 1964. His domestic policies, which he promoted as "A Revolution in Liberty," including his "Chileanization" and land reform efforts, were crippled in the legislature by supporters of Allende. Frei was ineligible to run for a second term, and in the 1970 election Allende was narrowly elected president. Following Allende's ouster by a military coup in 1973, the Christian Democratic party was banned by the new government of General Augusto Pinochet. Frei remained an outspoken leader of the opposition, with his law offices serving as the unofficial headquarters of the banned political party. He accused the Pinochet regime of human rights abuses and called for a restoration of democracy. In August of 1980 Frei led opposition to a plebiscite on a new constitution proposed by the Pinochet government, but the plebiscite succeeded by a large margin. Frei was hospitalized for a hernia operation in November of 1981 and died in Santiago from complications from the surgery on January 22, 1982, at the age of 71.

SALVADOR ALLENDE GOSSENS (President, November 3, 1970–September 11, 1973). Salvador Allende Gossens was born in Valparaiso on July 26, 1908. He was educated in Talca, Valdivia, and Valparaiso before entering medical school at the University of Chile. He was arrested twice while a student because of his opposition to the dictatorship of General Carlos Ibáñez. Allende received his medical doctorate in 1932 and helped found the Socialist party the following year. In 1937 he was elected to the lower house of Congress to represent Valparaiso. He was appointed minister of health in the government of President Pedro Aguirre Cerda in September of 1939. Chile was also ravaged by a major earthquake in

1939, and Allende led the national relief effort. He remained in the Aguirre Cerda cabinet until October of 1941 and served again from December of 1941 until April of 1942. During this period he also wrote *Socio-Medical Problems of Chile*, which attacked capitalism as a leading factor contributing to the health problems of the poor. Allende returned to Congress as a member of the Senate in 1945. He became a leading figure in the Senate, where he served as vice president and then president. Allende made his first bid for the presidency in 1952, but received only a nominal amount of the vote. In 1958 he increased his vote total, but was again defeated, running second to Jorge Alessandri in a five-man race. Allende had become an admirer and friend of Fidel Castro following the Cuban revolution of 1959 and made many visits to Cuba. He again ran for the presidency in 1964, espousing a new Socialist order for Chile based on the Cuban model. This strategy proved unsuccessful, and Eduardo Frei was elected president. In 1970 Allende ran for president again as a candidate of the Popular Unity party, a coalition of Socialists, Communists, leftist Christian Democrats, and others. On September 4, 1970, Allende won a plurality in a close election against Christian Democratic nominee Radomiro Tomic and former President Jorge Alessandri, the candidate of a right-wing coalition. The selection of the new president was decided by a joint vote of the Chilean Senate and Chamber of Deputies because no candidate received an absolute majority. Despite attempts by the Conservatives to prevent Allende from gaining enough votes, he was confirmed as president on October 24, 1970, when the Christian Democrats cast their votes for the front-runner. A national state of emergency was in effect due to the assassination of General Rene Schneider on October 22, 1970. After Allende's inauguration on November 3, 1970, he proceeded with his program to nationalize Chile's industries and banks. He also reestablished diplomatic relations with Cuba and established closer economic and political ties with Communist China and Eastern Europe. Allende's rule was beset by numerous difficulties in its early years. In 1972 he narrowly averted a strike by truck owners and shopkeepers, who were opposed to nationalization, by bringing members of the armed forces into his cabinet. This brought about a temporary stability to the country and allowed Allende to visit Mexico, Cuba, the United Nations, and the Soviet Union, where he was awarded the Lenin Peace Prize. The Socialist party made gains in parliamentary elections later in the year, but the country was soon beset by another round of difficulties. Truck owners and others went through with a strike, and members of the armed forces staged an abortive coup. The Chilean inflation rate rose to become one of the highest in the world, and domestic unrest flared into street demonstrations against the government. As Allende's regime became more beleaguered, the armed forces, reportedly with the urging of United States interests, joined with the conservative opposition and deposed Allende in a violent coup on September 11, 1973. After several days of street fighting and Allende's insistence that he would not resign, the armed forces captured the presidential palace. Allende was found dead in his office, reportedly from a self-inflicted gunshot wound, though speculation exists that he was killed by the occupying soldiers. His death effectively ended democratic Marxism in South America and began the long reign of harsh military rule under General Augusto Pinochet.

AUGUSTO PINOCHET UGARTE

(President, September 11, 1973–March 11, 1990). Augusto Pinochet Ugarte was born in Valparaiso on November 25, 1915. After attending local schools, he entered the Chilean military academy in Santiago. After graduation he taught at the military academy. He rose through the ranks and in 1947 was assigned to the northern region of Chile. Two years later he returned to Santiago to attend the War College. He graduated in 1952, and the following year he was promoted to major. Pinochet spent most of the fifties and early sixties either teaching or serving as military attaché at various embassies, including the United States. By 1968 Pinochet had been promoted to brigadier general. Shortly after Socialist leader Salvador Allende was elected president in 1970, Pinochet was given command of the army garrison in Santiago. In that position he enforced a curfew in December of 1971 when rioting between pro- and anti-Allende factions took place. The following year Pinochet temporarily replaced General Carlos Prats Gonzaléz as commander in chief of the army when Prats was appointed Minister of the Interior in the Allende government. Pinochet was appointed to the position permanently on August 24, 1973, when Prats was forced to resign his posts. Allende's political situation had become desperate by this point, with the economy in shambles and strikes and demonstrations occurring regularly. In early September Pinochet met with General Gustavo Leigh of the air force, Admiral Jose Toribio Merino of the navy, and General Cesar Mendoza of the national police to plot the ouster of Allende. On the morning of September 11, 1973, the armed forces moved against the government. Pinochet called for Allende to resign and when he refused the general ordered an attack on the presidential palace. When the palace was seized by the army, Allende was found dead inside and the military junta was in control of the country. Two days later Pinochet was named president of the junta. The government then began a widespread purge of leftists and Allende supporters, who were either arrested or executed. The new government also imposed severe restrictions on the general population by suspending civil rights, banning political parties and labor unions, and imposing strict censorship on the press. The government also moved to desocialize the economy and restored many nationalized companies to their original owners. Under the original plan the leadership of the junta was supposed to rotate between the members, but on June 26, 1974, Pinochet announced that he had taken sole control of the government. He was proclaimed president on December 17, 1974, and his regime often operated under a state of siege. His government was responsible for wide-spread human rights abuses. A prominent critic of the Pinochet regime, Orlando Letelier, was assassinated in Washington, D.C., in September of 1976. Allegations that Chilean secret police officers were involved in the attack damaged relations between Chile and the United States. Pinochet promoted a new constitution in September of 1980 which allowed for a gradual restoration of democratic institutions. Pinochet survived an assassination attempt in September of 1986. He was denied an additional eight years in office in a plebiscite in October of 1988. He allowed elections to be held in December of 1989 and relinquished office to Patricio Aylwin Azócar on March 11, 1990. Pinochet remained commander in chief of the army in the Aylwin government.

PATRICIO AYLWIN AZÓCAR (President, March 11, 1990-). Patricio Aylwin Azócar was born in Vina del Mar on November 26, 1918. He was educated at the University of Chile, where he received a degree in law in 1943. He subsequently taught at the university and became active in politics. In 1945 he joined the Falange Nacional party, and served as the party's president in 1950 and 1951. Aylwin was a founder of the Christian Democratic party in 1957 and was elected to the Chilean Senate in the mid-1960s. He remained a senator until the military coup in 1973. Aylwin continued to be active with the Christian Democrats and advocated the restoration of democratic rule. He was selected as leader of the Christian Democrats in 1987. President Augusto Pinochet was denied an extension on his term of office in a plebiscite in October of 1988. Aylwin was the presidential nominee for a centrist coalition in elections in December of 1989. Aylwin was victorious and assumed office on March 11, 1990. His party was also successful in winning the majority of seats in municipal elections in June of 1992.

China, People's Republic of

(Zhonghua Renmin Gongheguo)

China is a country in eastern Asia.

HEADS OF STATE

MAO TSE-TUNG (Head of State, October 1, 1949–April 27, 1959). Mao Tse-tung (Mao Zedong) was born in Hunan Province on December 26, 1893. He left his family's small farm at an early age to attend various schools in China and studied different political philosophies before graduating in 1918. He took a library position at Peking University, where he met Marxist social critics Li Ta-chao and Ch'en Tu-hsiu. In 1919 Mao returned to his home province to take a teaching position for a short period. The following year he dedicated himself to revolutionary activities. He helped found the Chinese Communist party in 1921 and became the party's leader in Hunan. His success in forming a trade-union movement there brought him to a leadership position in the national party two years later. Mao worked in the party's organizations in Shanghai and Canton. He returned to Hunan and initiated the incorporation of peasants and workers into the Communist party in 1925. Mao also worked in the Kuomintang, the nationalist movement that governed China, serving as chief propagandist. He returned to Hunan shortly before the break between the Communist party and the Kuomintang under Chiang Kai-shek. When Mao led peasant rebellions against the government in 1927, the rebels were crushed and Mao was forced into hiding in the mountains. He formed a Communist government in southeastern China with the assistance of Soviet-trained party leaders who distrusted Mao's dependence on peasant troops and guerrilla tactics. Kuomintang troops forced the Communists to abandon the area in 1934, when the other leaders insisted on traditional military tactics. Mao led his surviving followers to northwest China on the Long March from 1935 until 1936. He became the predominant party leader during this period. China's war with Japan forced the Communists and the Kuomintang into a temporary alliance, but the civil war between the two factions continued after Japan's surrender. The Communists defeated the Nationalists and forced Chiang's supporters to retreat to the island of Taiwan. Mao declared mainland China a people's republic and became president on October 1, 1949. He sought to transform Chinese society by instituting a collective farm system. He negotiated an alliance with the Soviet

Union that gained China necessary financial aid in early 1950. The following year Chinese troops, in support of the Communist regime in North Korea, entered into battle with the United States during the Korean conflict. An armistice agreement was reached in July of 1953 that maintained a divided Korea. Mao stepped down as president on April 27, 1959, and allowed his presumed successor, Liu Shao-ch'i, to assume the office. Mao retained the leadership of the Communist party, and thus the country, however. Relations between China and the Soviet Union deteriorated in the late 1950s, with the party leadership of both countries engaged in a rivalry for domination of international Communism. Soviet technicians were withdrawn from China in July of 1960, and financial assistance was halted. Mao began a process of reforming the Chinese system, which he feared had become too Westernized, during the Cultural Revolution which began in 1965. Mao pitted young Red Guard revolutionaries against the party hierarchy and purged numerous officials in the party and the government. Mao was assisted by his fourth wife, Jiang Qing (Chiang Ch'ing), whom he had married in 1939, and Lin Piao, the minister of national defense from 1959. These two individuals gained great influence in the government during the Cultural Revolution. Lin was selected as Mao's heir apparent, replacing Liu Shao-Ch'i, who had been among those purged. China's internal politics began to stabilize in 1968. Chinese and Soviet troops clashed on the banks of the Ussuri River in the winter of 1969. The Soviets subsequently built up its troop strength on the Chinese border, which further damaged relations between the two Communist countries. Lin Piao attempted to seize power from Mao in September of 1971. When his attempt failed, he and some of his supporters were killed in a plane crash while heading for the Chinese-Soviet border. Mao agreed to the opening of relations with the United States in 1971, which resulted in a visit to China by President Richard Nixon in February of 1972. Mao suffered from poor health during the early 1970s, though he still maintained strong control of the government. His long-time associate Premier Chou En-lai died in January of 1976, and his duties were assumed by Deng Xiaoping (Teng Hsiao-ping). Mao distrusted Deng and purged him from power in April of 1976. Mao died in Peking at the age of 82 on September 9, 1976.

LIU SHAO-CH'I (Head of State, April 27, 1959–October 15, 1968). Liu Shao-ch'i was born in Ning-hsiang in Hunan Province to a prosperous peasant family in 1898. He was educated at the University for Toilers of the East in Moscow and subsequently joined the Chinese Communist party in 1921. He worked as a labor organizer and was elected vice-chairman of the All-China Federation of Labor in 1925. Two years later Liu was elected to the Communist party Central Committee, and he became a member of the Politburo in 1934. He remained in Nationalist controlled areas of China during the Long March to Yenan. Japan invaded China in 1937, and two years later Liu was appointed to lead the Central China Bureau of the Communist party. Following the victory of the Communist party in China, Liu was named one of the six vice-chairmen of the central government of the People's Republic of China on October 1, 1949. When Mao Tse-tung stepped down as head of state on April 27, 1959, Liu was selected to replace him in that position by the National People's Congress. Liu and Mao disagreed on several major policies, including the Sino-Soviet dispute. Liu opposed Mao's anti–Soviet stance, and Mao thought Liu was tainted by capitalistic notions. When Mao announced his Great Proletarian Cultural Revolution in August of 1966, Liu quickly became a leading target of the campaign.

He dropped from sight later in the year, but it was not until October 15, 1968, that it was announced that he had been removed from his positions in the government and the party. Liu was put under house arrest in Peking and remained out of the public eye until October of 1974, when his death was reported in the Chinese Communist newspaper. Liu was rehabilitated by the Communist party Central Committee in February of 1980.

LI XIANNIAN (President, June 18, 1983–April 8, 1988). Li Xiannian (Li Shien-nien) was born in Huangan, Hubei Province, on June 23, 1909. He joined the Communist party in 1927 and participated in the Long March in 1934 and 1935. He held various positions in the party and was selected as governor of Hubei and mayor of Wuhan when the Communists came to power in 1949. Li was appointed vice-premier and minister of finance in 1954. He was largely responsible for China's economic policy in the government of Chou En-lai until Chou's death in 1976. The National People's Congress restored the position of president in 1983, and Li was chosen for the largely ceremonial post on June 18, 1983. He was replaced by Yang Shungkun on April 8, 1988. Li remained a high-ranking official in the Communist party.

YANG SHUNGKUN (President, April 8, 1988–March 27, 1993). Yang Shungkun (Yang Shang-k'un) was born in Tongnan, Sichuan Province, in 1907. He joined the Communist party in 1926 and worked in the party organization. He served in the political department of the Red Army from 1931 and participated in the Long March from 1934 to 1935. Yang served as director of the staff office of the Communist party Central Committee from 1945 until 1966, when he was removed from office during the Cultural Revolution. Yang was rehabilitated in 1979 and was subsequently appointed secretary-general of the Communist Military Command. Yang was a close ally of Deng Xiaopeng and was named to the largely ceremonial position of president of China on April 8, 1988. Yang remained president, though he was removed from his seat on the Politburo in 1992. He did not seek reelection in 1993 and was replaced as president by Communist party leader Jiang Zemin on March 27, 1993.

DENG XIAOPING (Paramount Leader, 1980–). Deng Xiaoping (Teng Hsiao-ping) was born in Kuang-an, Szechwan Province, in 1904. He was educated in Chungking before he went to France to participate in a work-study program in the early 1920s. He met Chou En-lai while in Paris and joined the Communist party. Deng returned to China in 1926 and became active in the Communist movement. He took part in the Long March in the mid-1930s and from 1937 served as a political commissar in the Communist army during the Sino-Japanese War. He was named secretary of the Politburo and the Central Committee of the party in 1945. Deng participated in the military actions that forced Chiang Kai-shek's Nationalist forces from mainland China in 1949. Deng was named to serve as one of the party's six regional leaders after the People's Republic of China was established in October of 1949. He represented the party in the southwest region of China. Deng served as minister of finance in 1953 and was also named secretary-general of the Communist party Central Committee. He rose to vice-premier the following year and served as vice-chairman of the National Defense Council. He was selected to the Politburo of the Communist party in 1955. Deng became closely allied with President Liu Shaoch'i and continued to serve in party and government positions until 1967, when he was removed from office during the Cultural Revolution. Deng reemerged in April of 1973 as deputy premier to Chou En-lai. He returned to the Central Committee and the Politburo later in the year. Deng took over many of the duties of the premier while Chou was suffering from poor health. Deng was widely expected to succeed Chou as premier, but was again forced from power in April of 1976 by "radical" supporters of Mao Tse-tung's wife, Jiang Qing, and the "Gang of Four." Jiang Qing and her close associates were arrested in October of 1976, and Deng began the climb to rehabilitation in the party. He was restored to his positions in the Communist party and named vice premier of the State Council and chief of staff of the armed forces in August of 1977. Deng consolidated his power by replacing members of the Politburo with his supporters in December of 1977. He eclipsed Hua Guofeng, the premier and party chairman, who was dismissed from power in the early 1980s. Deng installed his supporters in the top offices in the party and the government, but chose to remain in secondary positions himself. The Chinese government underwent a period of reform during which it moved towards a market-based economy and the further opening of China to Western influences. The liberalization of domestic policy resulted in a number of student demonstrations calling for democratization of the government in 1986. This resulted in a backlash from the conservatives who remained in power and forced the resignation of the party chairman, Hu Yaobang. More student demonstrations followed the death of Hu in April of 1989. A large number of students occupied Tiananmen Square in May of 1989. Hard-line Communists took control of the government, with Deng's consent, and ordered the military into Tiananmen Square to remove the demonstrators on June 4, 1989. A number of liberal reformers, including Communist party chairman Zhao Ziyang, were removed from power, though Deng remained firmly in control. The government actions and subsequent repression met with widespread international criticism. Despite the setback for domestic reform, Deng remained committed to moving China in the direction of a free-market economy. Deng remained the most powerful figure in the party and government, although he only held the position of chairman of the Central Military Commission.

HEADS OF GOVERNMENT

CHOU EN-LAI (Premier, October 3, 1949–January 8, 1976). Chou En-lai was born in Huaian, Kiangsu Province, in 1898. His family moved to Tientsin in 1911, where he attended a missionary school. He also studied in Japan at Nankai University and went to Paris in 1920. Chou worked there and continued his studies for a year. Traveling throughout Europe, he spent much of his time organizing overseas branches of the Chinese Communist party. He returned to China in 1924 and organized for the Communist party in Shanghai. He also participated in the unsuccessful uprising in Nanchang in 1927. Chou was elected to the Communist party Politburo in 1928 and became the principal advisor on urban revolutionary affairs to Mao Tse-tung in 1931. He took part in the Long March to Shensi Province from 1934 until 1935 and served as the Red Army's political commissar. Chou served as the principal negotiator in the kidnapping of Chiang Kai-shek in Sian in 1936. He secured his release and attempted to persuade Chiang to join the Communists in an anti-Japanese coalition. Chou served as liaison officer in Chungking during most of World War II. He served as the Communists' representative in talks with the United States mission to mediate in the civil war from 1945 until January of 1947. The talks failed to produce a coalition of the Communists and Nationalists. Chou was named premier following the establishment of the People's Republic of China on October 3, 1949. He was also named foreign minister and was China's leading international spokesman.

Chou served as the chief negotiator of a treaty of friendship with the Soviet Union in 1950. He also was instrumental in negotiating the truce that ended the Korean conflict in July of 1953. He attended the Geneva conference of 1954 that ended France's rule in Indochina. Chou also attended the Bandung Conference in early 1955, where he met with the leaders of African and Asian nations. He stepped down from the foreign ministry in 1958, though he continued to represent China's interests in international forums. His position as premier was reaffirmed in 1965. Chou was attacked by extremists during the Chinese Cultural Revolution from 1966 until 1969, but retained his power and position. He was instrumental in improving China's diplomatic relations with the West, which gained China's admission to the United Nations in October of 1971. He also encouraged détente with the United States, which resulted in a visit by President Richard Nixon to China in February of 1972. Chou became ill with cancer in 1972 and spent much of the next few years hospitalized, though he continued to receive foreign dignitaries during this period. He died of cancer in Peking at the age of 78 on January 8, 1976.

HUA GUOFENG (Premier, February 8, 1976–September 10, 1980). Hua Guofeng (Hua Kuo-feng) was born in Shansi Province in 1920. He joined the Communist party while in his teens and participated in the Long March in the mid-1930s. He served in China's Red Army during World War II and the subsequent civil war against the Nationalist forces. Hua served in various regional positions in the Communist party after the establishment of the People's Republic of China in 1949. He was named vice-governor of Hunan Province in 1958, where he was a supporter of Mao Tse-tung. Despite some attacks on Hua during the Cultural Revolution, he avoided being purged and was named vice-chairman of the Hunan Provisional Revolutionary Committee in 1968. Hua was elected to the Communist party Central Committee two years later and also became leader of the civilian government in Hunan. Hua was called to Peking in November of 1971 to investigate the attempted coup led by Defense Minister Lin Piao. He remained in administrative positions in the government and became deputy premier in charge of public security in 1975. When Chou En-lai died in February of 1976, Deng Xiaoping was expected to succeed him as premier. Deng's selection was blocked by Mao Tse-tung's faction, however, and Hua was named acting premier on February 8, 1976. Mao died in September of 1976, and Hua succeeded him as chairman of the Communist party on October 7, 1976. Mao's widow, Jiang Qing, and her supporters, known as the "Gang of Four," were purged from the government and arrested shortly before Hua took control of the party. Hua was reconfirmed as premier in February of 1978. Deng Xiaoping returned to prominence in the government and began to supplant Hua in power. Hua was replaced as premier by Zhao Ziyang on September 10, 1980. Hua was also forced to resign as Communist party chairman on June 29, 1981. He was demoted to vice-chairman and vacated that position the following year. Hua continued to serve on the Communist party Central Committee and opposed many of the economic reforms proposed by Deng.

ZHAO ZIYANG (Premier, September 10, 1980–April 9, 1988). Zhao Ziyang (Chao Tsu-yang) was born in Huaxian County, Henan Province, in 1919. He joined the Communist Youth League in 1932 and took part in the party's land reform programs during the civil war. Zhao worked in the party's organization in Guangdong (Kwangtung) Province after the establishment of the People's Republic of China in 1949. He rose through the ranks to become first secretary of the Communist party in Guangdong in 1965. Zhao was purged during the Cultural Revolution in 1967, but reemerged in 1971 as a party official in Inner Mongolia. In 1975 he was appointed a secretary of the party in Szechwan. He introduced reforms in the agricultural and industrial systems in the province. Zhao was successful in increasing production and was called to Peking to serve on the Politburo in 1979. He was named to replace Hua Guofeng as premier on September 10, 1980. He was a supporter of Deng Xiaoping's reform programs. Zhao was named acting chairman of the Communist party on January 16, 1987, following student demonstrations that resulted in the ouster of Hu Yaobang. Zhao was confirmed as party chairman on April 9, 1988, and relinquished the position of premier to Li Peng. Zhao's initial support of student demonstrators in Tiananmen Square in the spring of 1989 resulted in his dismissal on June 24, 1989, after the Chinese army was called in to disperse the demonstrators. Zhao was purged and placed under house arrest until November of 1989.

LI PENG (Premier, April 9, 1988–   ). Li Peng (Li P'eng) was born in Chengdu, Sichuan Province, in October of 1928. His father, Li Shouxun, was executed by the Nationalists in 1930, and Li was adopted by future Chinese premier Chou En-lai and his wife, Teng Ying-ch'ao (Deng Yingchao). He was educated at the Communist guerrilla headquarters in Shensi Province and the Yan'an Institute of

Natural Sciences. Li joined the Communist party in 1945. He continued his education at the Moscow Power Institute in the Soviet Union in 1948 and returned to China in 1955 to serve as chief engineer at power plants in northeast China. He was named acting party secretary of the Municipal Power Supply Bureau in 1966. Li remained in power during the Cultural Revolution of the late 1960s. He rose to the position of vice-minister of China's power industry in 1979. Li was elected to the Communist party Central Committee in 1982 and became vice-premier in charge of education, energy, transportation, and economic development the following year. He was elevated to the ruling Politburo in 1985. Li succeeded Zhao Ziyang as premier on April 9, 1988, when Zhao became chairman of the Communist party. Li was considered more cautious in regard to China's economic reforms than his predecessor. Li and the more conservative members of the government ousted Zhao in June of 1989, following student demonstrations in the capital. Li remained a moderate supporter of centralization of the economy in opposition to the economic reforms initiated by Deng Xiaoping.

OTHER LEADERS

MAO TSE-TUNG (Chairman, Communist Party, October 1, 1949–September 9, 1976). *See entry under Heads of State.*

HUA GUOFENG (Chairman, Communist Party, October 7, 1976–June 29, 1981). *See entry under Heads of Government.*

HU YAOBANG (Chairman, Communist Party, June 29, 1981–January 16, 1987). Hu Yaobang (Hu Yao-pang) was born in Liuyang City, Hunan Province, in 1915. He joined the Chinese Red Army in the 1930s and took part in the Long March from 1934 until 1935. Hu served as a political officer in the Red Army in the war against Japan. After World War II Hu was active in military campaigns against the Nationalists during the civil war. Hu became a protégé of Deng Xiaoping and was named political commissar of the North Sichuan military district in 1950. Hu accompanied Deng to Peking in 1952 and was named secretary of the Communist Youth League. He rose in rank in the party and the government until the Cultural Revolution, when he was purged from his positions in 1968.

Hu returned to prominence when Deng was rehabilitated in 1973 and served as his aide. The two men were again purged in April of 1976. When Deng returned to power in December of 1977, Hu was appointed director of the Communist party's Organization Department. Hu was appointed to the Politburo in January of 1979. He replaced Hua Guofeng as chairman of the Communist party on June 29, 1981, and was widely regarded as a likely successor to Deng, who had emerged as China's paramount leader. Hu was a leading supporter of Deng's reform programs. When domestic liberalization resulted in student demonstrations demanding greater democratization of the government, Hu was forced to resign in disgrace by hard-liners in the government on January 16, 1987. Hu remained on the Standing Committee of the Politburo, though he was largely inactive in governmental affairs. He died of a heart attack in Peking (Beijing) on April 15, 1989. Hu was eulogized by students as a symbol of democracy and liberalization. His death sparked another round of demonstrations against the government which resulted in the Chinese army being called out against student demonstrators in Tiananmen Square in June of 1989.

ZHAO ZIYANG (Chairman, Communist Party, January 16, 1987–June 24, 1989). *See entry under Heads of Government.*

JIANG ZEMIN (Chairman, Communist Party, June 24, 1989–). Jiang Zemin (Chiang Tse-min) was born in Yangzhou City, Jiangsu (Kiangsu) Province, in 1926. He joined the Communist party in 1946 and graduated from Jiaotang University in Shanghai the following year. He held various party positions and served as a commercial counselor at the Chinese Embassy in the Soviet Union from 1950 until 1956. Jiang was then named assistant to the minister of machine building, where he remained until 1959. Jiang reemerged

in the early 1980s to serve as vice-minister of import and export until 1982. He subsequently served as vice-minister of the electronics industry until 1983, when he became minister. He was selected as mayor of Shanghai in 1985 and served until 1987. Jiang served as first secretary of the party committee in Shanghai from 1987 until 1989. He was a leading supporter of Deng Xiaoping's economic reforms and also supported the government's crackdown on student demonstrators in Tiananmen Square in June of 1989. Jiang was selected by Deng to replace disgraced Zhao Ziyang as chairman of the Communist party on June 24, 1989. Jiang remained a leading supporter of Deng's policies in the party and the government. He was also selected to replace Yang Shunkun as China's president on March 27, 1993.

China, Republic of

(Taiwan)

Taiwan is an island country off the southeast coast of mainland China. The government of the Republic of China fled there following the Communist takeover of mainland China in December of 1949.

HEADS OF STATE

CHIANG KAI-SHEK (President, October 10, 1928–January 21, 1949). Chiang Kai-shek was born in Chikow on October 31, 1886. He left home while in his teens to enter the newly formed Chinese National Military Academy in Paoting. He was sent for further training in Tokyo in 1907, where he attended the Imperial Military Staff College. Chiang also joined the Teng-men-hui, a revolutionary secret society, in 1907. He deserted the Japanese army and returned to China following the overthrow of the Manchu

dynasty in 1911. Chiang served as a military leader in Dr. Sun Yat-sen's republican government. He broke with Sun's successor, Yuan Shi-kai, and led an unsuccessful rebellion against him in 1913. Chiang then fled the country to Japan. He remained out of public life until 1918, when he rejoined Sun Yat-sen in Canton. China was divided into areas controlled by warlords, who feuded among themselves. Sun wished to reunify China and formed the Nationalist Kuomintang for this purpose. Chiang served as a major general in the southern armies from 1921. He went to the Soviet Union for several months in 1923 to study the Red Army. He returned to China to establish a military academy near Canton. Chinese Communists joined with the Kuomintang, and the Soviet Union supplied military advisors and financial assistance. Chiang became leader of the Kuomintang and commander in chief of the revolutionary army following Sun Yat-sen's death in 1925. In 1927 Chiang married Soong Mei-ling, the daughter of the powerful Soong financial family. He withstood attempts by the Communists to force him from power, but was forced into temporary retirement by the Kwangsi generals, Li Tsung-jen and Pai Tsung-hsi, in August of 1927. Chiang returned to power in January of 1928 and launched an attack against the warlords, whom he defeated or neutralized. He captured Peking in 1928 and established a Nationalist government in Nanking with himself as president on October 10, 1928. Chiang retained the support of the Soviets until 1929, when he led a bloody assault against the Communists. The Communists withdrew to the north and established a rival government and army. Japan seized Manchuria in 1931, but Chiang continued his efforts to subdue the Communists before challenging Japan. Chiang also revived the Confucius cult by launching the New Life Movement in 1934 to give moral authority to his government. In December of 1936 Chiang was captured in Sian by Chang Hseuh-liang, the former warlord of Manchuria. He was held hostage for several weeks until his release was negotiated by Communist leader Chou En-lai. Chiang set aside the civil war with the Communists and entered into war with Japan in 1937. China fought alone until the Japanese bombed Pearl Harbor in December of 1941. China then gained the assistance of the Allied powers during World War II. Chiang attended the Cairo Conference in 1943, meeting with President Franklin Roosevelt of the United States and Prime Minister Winston Churchill of Great Britain. The Nationalists and the Communists fought their mutual enemy, the Japanese, until the surrender of Japan in 1945. The United States attempted to negotiate a compromise between the two rival parties, but Chiang was unwilling to form a coalition government with the Communists. The civil war resumed in 1946, and the Communists moved toward Chiang's stronghold in the south. Chiang's popularity had decreased in China due to rising inflation and an absence of promised reforms. His government was also rampant with corruption. The Communists captured Peking, and Chiang resigned as president on January 21, 1949. Chiang and the Nationalists fled from mainland China to the island of Taiwan, or Formosa, later in the year. He reestablished his government on Taiwan and resumed the presidency on March 1, 1950. Chiang continued to receive financial and military assistance from the United States. He instituted land reforms and industrialized the island nation, transforming it into a prosperous exporting country. He excluded Taiwanese from the government and rejected Taiwanese self-rule. Chiang's government continued to be recognized by the West as the legitimate government of China until 1971, when the People's Republic of China was admitted to the United Nations and claimed the seat held by China. The republican government suffered another blow in 1972 when President Richard Nixon of the United States visited the People's Republic of China. Chiang suffered from pneumonia in July of 1972. His health continued to fail until his death at the age of 87 from a heart attack in Taipei on April 5, 1975.

LI TSUNG-JEN (President, January 21, 1949–March 1, 1950). Li Tsung-jen was born in Kweilin, Kwangsi Province, in 1890. He attended the Kweilin

Military Academy before joining the provisional army. He supported Sun Yat-sen in the revolution against the Manchu regime in 1911. Li jointly ruled Kwangsi Province with Pai Tsung-Hsi in support of Chiang Kai-shek's Kuomintang from 1926. Li and Pai forced Chiang into temporary retirement in August of 1927. Chiang resumed power in January of 1928. Li fought with the Nationalists during the capture of Peking in 1928 and supported the purge of the Communists from the Kuomintang. Li controlled one of the six military regions in China and declared the area autonomous in 1929 when Chiang forced his expulsion from the Kuomintang. Li was reinstated in the Kuomintang several years later. He supported a policy of war against Japan following that country's invasion of Manchuria in 1931. He pressured Chiang, who resisted a Sino-Japanese war until the summer of 1937. Li placed his troops under Chiang's command and led the armies at the northern front, where he scored several victories over the Japanese forces before suffering a defeat at Suchow. Li remained a powerful leader after the conclusion of World War II and was a reform candidate for vice president of the Chinese Republic in 1948. He was elected despite the opposition of Chiang. Li became acting president of the Republic of China on January 21, 1949, when Chiang departed Nanking for Taiwan in the hopes that the government could negotiate a settlement with the Communist leaders. Li attempted to reach an agreement with the Communists, who were in control of the majority of mainland China. He went to Hong Kong for reasons of health in December of 1949. He then went to the United States for abdominal surgery. Chiang reformed the Nationalist government on Taiwan and reclaimed power on March 1, 1950. Li refused to go to Taiwan following his recovery. The Nationalist Assembly voted his ouster as vice president in 1954. Li remained in

exile in the United States until July of 1965, when he returned to Peking. He gave his support to the People's Republic of China as the legitimate government of China, though he refused to join the Communist party. He was in poor health at the time of his return, and he died in Peking at the age of 78 on January 30, 1969.

CHIANG KAI-SHEK (President, March 1, 1950–April 5, 1975). *See earlier entry under Heads of State.*

YEN CHIA-KAN (President, April 5, 1975–May 20, 1978). Yen Chia-kan was born on November 23, 1905. He was educated at St. John's University in Shanghai. In 1938 he was appointed commissioner of reconstruction in the Fujian provisional government. The following year he was named finance commissioner in the Fujian government and was appointed chairman of the Fujian Provisional Bank. Yen Chia-kan remained in that position until 1945, when he was appointed communications commissioner in the Taiwan provisional government, a post he kept until 1956. In 1946 he was also named finance commissioner and chairman of the Bank of Taiwan, positions he held until 1949. In 1950 Yen Chia-kan was named minister of economic affairs for the Republic of China. Later in the year he was appointed minister of finance. He held this position until his election as governor of Taiwan in 1954. In 1957 he returned to the cabinet as minister without portfolio. He again served as minister of finance from 1958 until 1963. Yen Chia-kan was appointed to succeed Chen Cheng as premier of the Republic of China on December 16, 1963. He was also named vice president of the government in 1966. He stepped down as premier on March 21, 1972. Yen Chia-kan succeeded Chiang Kai-shek as president of Taiwan on April 5, 1975 and served until his retirement on May 20, 1978. Yen died of heart failure at a New York hospital at the age of 90 on December 24, 1993.

CHIANG CHING-KUO (President, May 20, 1978–January 13, 1988). Chiang Ching-Kuo was born in Fenghua, Chekiang Province, on March 18, 1910. He was the son of Chiang Kai-shek. He was educated in Shanghai and Peking before being sent to the Soviet Union to continue his education in 1925. Chiang Ching-Kuo's father became China's leader in 1926 and turned against his Communist allies the following year. The younger Chiang was forced to remain in the Soviet Union as a political hostage. He was allowed to return to China following the Soviet-Chinese nonaggression pact in August of 1937. Chiang Ching-Kuo was subsequently appointed by his father to serve as regional commissioner in Kiangsi. After World War II he served the Nationalist government in conferences concerning the future of Manchuria. He was sent to Shanghai to serve as an economic coordinator in August of 1948, but resigned the following October when his policies proved unsuccessful. Chiang Ching-Kuo was placed in charge of the Taiwan Provincial Kuomintang Headquarters after the Nationalist government was forced from the mainland in December of 1949. He was appointed to the ministry of national defense as director of the political department the following year. Chiang later served as leader of the Chinese Youth Corps. He was appointed minister of national defense in 1965 and served until 1969, when he was named deputy premier. Chiang was uninjured during an assassination attempt while on a visit to New York City on April 24, 1970. He was appointed premier on June 1, 1972, and succeeded his father as chairman of the Kuomintang Central Committee following the elder Chiang's death on April 5, 1975. Chiang relinquished the premiership when he was elected president of the government of the Republic of China on May 20, 1978. The United States broke diplomatic relations with Chiang's government in order to recognize the Communist government of the People's Republic in 1979. Chiang promoted political reforms in the government and encouraged rapid economic development in Taiwan. He remained president until his death of a heart attack at the age of 77 in Taipei on January 13, 1988.

LEE TENG-HUI (President, January 13, 1988–). Lee Teng-hui was born in Tamsui, Taiwan, on January 15, 1923. He was educated in China, Japan, and the United States, where he studied agricultural economics. In 1948 he returned to Taiwan to teach at the National Taiwan University. He served in the cabinet as minister without portfolio from 1972 until 1978. Lee was elected mayor of Taipei in 1978, and in 1981 he became governor of Taiwan Province. He was elected vice president of Taiwan in 1984 and became the first native Taiwanese to serve as president of the Republic of China when he succeeded Chiang Ching-Kuo on January 13, 1988. Lee was reelected president in March of 1990. He made an effort towards reconciliation between the Nationalist government and the People's Republic of China and also initiated a number of liberal reforms to democratize the government.

HEADS OF GOVERNMENT

T. V. SOONG (Premier, December 4, 1944–March 1, 1947). T. V. Soong was born Sung Tzu-wen in Shanghai in 1894. He was educated locally and in the United States. He received a degree in economics from Harvard University in

1915 and worked in the banking industry in the United States before returning to China in 1917. After his return, he served the nationalist government in Canton, and he was named commissioner of finance in Kwangtung in 1926. Soong's three sisters had married China's most respected leaders: Sun Yat-sen, the father of the Chinese Republic; Chiang Kai-shek, the leader of the Nationalists; and H. H. Kung, a leading Chinese financier. Soong became minister of finance in Chiang's Nationalist government in Nanking in 1928. He gained the support of leading Shanghai bankers for Chiang's Kuomintang. Soong resigned in 1931, but returned to public office as chairman of the Bank of China in 1935. He was sent to the United States as China's special envoy to gain Western financial support for China during the Sino-Japanese war. Soong was appointed foreign minister in 1942, and he represented China at the United Nations organizing session in San Francisco in 1945. Soong also became acting president of the Legislative Yuan, or premier, on December 4, 1944. He resigned on March 1, 1947, after civil war had resumed between the Nationalists and the Communists. He subsequently served as governor of Kwangtung Province. In March of 1949 he resigned and fled to Hong Kong. Soong refused to join the Nationalist government in Taiwan later in the year and went into exile in the United States, where he remained in New York until his death. Soong choked to death on April 25, 1971, when food lodged in his windpipe while he was attending a dinner party in San Francisco.

CHIANG KAI-SHEK (Premier, March 1, 1947–April 18, 1947). *See entry under Heads of State.*

CHANG CHUN (Premier, April 18, 1947–April 18, 1948). Chang Chun was born in 1897. He joined with Sun Yat-sen in the Nationalist party and fought in the revolution to overthrow the Manchu regime in 1911. He attended the Imperial Military Staff College in Japan with Chiang Kai-shek and became a leading advisor to Chiang's Kuomintang regime. He rose to the rank of general in the Nationalist army. Chang served as premier of the Republic of China from April 18, 1947, until April 18, 1948. He accompanied Chiang's government to Taiwan following the victory of the Communists in 1949. Chang remained a leading advisor to the president on matters of foreign policy. Chang Chun died in Taipei of heart and kidney failure at the age of 101 on December 14, 1990.

WONG WEN-HAO (Premier, April 18, 1948–November 26, 1948). Wong Wen-hao was born in Chinhsien in July of 1889. He was educated locally and at Louvain University in Belgium. He received a degree in science in 1913 and returned to China as a teacher. In 1919 he was named director of the National Geological Survey of China. Wong resisted several attempts by Chiang Kai-shek to involve him in the Nationalist government and preferred instead to devote his energies to scientific pursuits. He agreed to become secretary-general of Chiang's cabinet in 1935 and remained in that position for two years. He subsequently served as National Defense Planning Commission director and oversaw China's war production during the Sino-Japanese war. Wong also served as minister of economic affairs during World War II. He was named vice-premier in May of 1945 and was appointed minister of agriculture in May of 1946. He served on the State Council before the approval of the new Chinese constitution in 1947 and subsequently served in the cabinet as minister of economic affairs. Wong was appointed premier of the Republic of China by Chiang on April 18, 1948. He was considered a reformist and moved against corrupt elements in the government. He was unable to provide a workable financial program to balance the budget and offered his resignation on several occasions in October of 1948. Chiang refused to accept his resignation until November 26, 1948, when he was replaced as premier by Sun Fo. Wong remained in the government as minister without portfolio. He accompanied Chiang's Nationalist government to Taiwan in 1949.

SUN FO (Premier, November 26, 1948–March 12, 1949). Sun Fo was born in Choy Hen, Kwangtung Province, in October of 1891. He was the only son of Sun Yat-sen, the leader of the Chinese Revolution. Sun Fo was attending school in Hawaii at the time of the overthrow of the Manchu regime. He briefly returned to China when his father became president of the Republic of China in January of 1912. He then went to the United States to continue his education. In August of 1917 he returned to China and assisted his father in the establishment of a provisional revolutionary government in Canton. Sun Fo became mayor of Canton in 1921 and served until the following year when the republican government was forced to abandon the city. Sun Fo returned to Canton as mayor in 1923, after his father allowed the Communists to join the Kuomintang government. Sun Yat-sen died in March of 1925, and Sun Fo was named to the Kuomintang's Central Executive Committee. He was appointed minister of communication in Chiang Kai-shek's Nationalist government in 1926. Sun Fo opposed Chiang's attack on the Communists later in the year, and Chiang resigned as head of the government in August of 1927. Sun Fo again joined the government as minister of finance. He resigned when Chiang returned to power in January of 1928. He returned to the cabinet shortly thereafter to serve as minister of reconstruction. From 1928 until May of 1931 he served as minister of railways. He

again broke with Chiang and joined with rebel forces in Canton. He attempted to negotiate a settlement between the rebels and Chiang's government in Nanking. Chiang again stepped down briefly, and Sun Fo became president of the Legislative Yuan on December 28, 1931. He continued to serve as premier until January 28, 1932. Sun Fo was instrumental in arranging a truce between the Nationalists and the Communists in 1937 so that both factions could fight the common enemy of Japan. He remained in the Nationalist government during the civil war that resumed after World War II. Sun Fo was appointed premier on November 26, 1948, but resigned on March 12, 1949, as the Communists continued their advance through China. He went into exile in France when the Nationalist government fled mainland China in 1949. Sun Fo later lived in the United States until October of 1964, when he joined the Nationalist government in Taiwan. He subsequently served as a senior advisor in the office of the president. Sun Fo died of a heart attack in Taipei at the age of 81 on September 13, 1973.

HO YING-CHIN (Premier, March 12, 1949–June 6, 1949). Ho Ying-chin was born in Kweichow Province in 1889. He was educated at the Imperial Military Staff College in Tokyo. He graduated in 1916 and became director of the Kweichow Military Institute. He commanded the First Brigade of the Nationalist army in Kwangtung in 1925 and helped to stop insurrections against the government led by provincial warlords in southern China. Ho was elected a member of the Kuomintang Central Executive Committee and appointed chief of staff of the Nationalist army in 1929. He was named minister of war the following year and directed Nationalist troops against the Communists and the Japanese. He was removed from his position by Chiang Kai-shek in November of 1944 because of his difficulties with Maj. Gen. Joseph Stillwell, the commander of United States forces in China. Ho was subsequently appointed commander in chief of the Chinese army and accepted the surrender of Japanese troops in Nanking in September of 1945. He represented China at several military missions to the United States after the war. He returned to the cabinet as minister of defense during the civil war with the Communists in 1948. Ho was appointed premier of the Nationalist government on March 12, 1949. He resigned on June 6, 1949, shortly before the retreat of the Nationalist government to Taiwan. He accompanied Chiang and the Nationalists to Taiwan and continued to serve as minister of defense until his retirement in 1958. Ho also served as president of the Taiwan Red Cross Society. Ho died of heart and lung failure in Taipei at the age of 97 on October 21, 1987.

YEN HSI-SHAN (Premier, June 6, 1949–March 12, 1950). Yen Hsi-shan was born in Shansi in 1883. He graduated from the Imperial Military Staff College in Tokyo in 1911 and became a supporter of Sun Yat-sen's revolution against the Manchu regime. Yen was named military governor of Shansi in 1912. He supported the Kuomintang military efforts against the other warlords and the Communists. Yen broke with the Nationalist government in 1930, but reunited his forces under Chiang during the Sino-Japanese War. He was a leading Chinese military figure during World War II and the subsequent civil war with the Communists. He withstood a Communist siege at Shansi's capital, Taiyuan, until April of 1949. Yen retired to Canton and was named premier of Nationalist China on June 6, 1949. He headed the last republican government on mainland China and accompanied Chiang's supporters to Taiwan later in the year. On March 12, 1950, he resigned as premier and retired from public life. He con-

tinued to serve as a leading military advisor to Chiang until his death in Taipei on May 23, 1960.

CHEN CHENG (Premier, March 12, 1950–June 1, 1954). Chen Cheng was born in Chingtien, Chekiang Province, on January 4, 1898. He attended the Paoting Military Academy and joined the republican forces upon graduation in 1922. He became a protégé of General Chiang Kai-shek in the 1920s and rose to the rank of general in 1930. Chen commanded Chiang's forces against the Communists in northwest China during the 1930s. He served as a leading military figure in the Sino-Japanese war and commanded Chinese troops in Burma in 1943. He was named minister of war in Chiang's government in 1944 and became chief of the general staff two years later. Chen was sent to battle the Communist forces in Manchuria, but was unable to achieve a victory. In 1949 he accompanied Chiang and the republican government to Taiwan. He was named governor of Taiwan and instituted a land reform program on the island. Chen was appointed premier of the Nationalist government on March 12, 1950. He retained office until June 1, 1954, when he declined renomination and was elected as Chiang's vice president. He again was appointed premier following the resignation of O. K. Yui on June 30, 1958. Chen retained his position until December 16, 1963, when he stepped down from office. He remained vice president and was considered Chiang's likely successor until his death. Chen Cheng died of cancer at the age of 67 in Taipei on March 5, 1965.

O. K. YUI (Premier, June 1, 1954–June 30, 1958). O. K. Yui was born Yu Hung-chun in Sunwui in 1896. He was educated in Shanghai and entered the local municipal government in the 1920s. In March of 1937 he became mayor of Shanghai, and he resisted the subsequent Japanese invasion. Yui led the evacuation of Shanghai in November of 1937 and became director of the Central Trust in Nanking. He was appointed vice-minister of finance in 1941, and replaced H. H. Kung as finance minister in November of 1944. He also became governor of the Central Bank of China in July of 1945. Yui accompanied the Nationalist government to Taiwan in 1949. He resumed his duties as governor of the Central Bank of Taiwan. He was named governor of Taiwan in April of 1953 and was appointed to succeed Chen Cheng as premier on June 1, 1954. Yui's government became involved in a disagreement over the powers of the legislative and control branches of the government. Yui was impeached by the Control Yuan on charges of abuse of power in December of 1957. He was reprimanded and offered his resignation to Chiang in February of 1958. Chiang declined to accept his resignation, and Yui continued to serve as premier until June 30, 1958, when he was replaced by Chen Cheng in a governmental shake-up. Yui died in Taipei of complications from asthma at the age of 62 on June 1, 1960.

CHEN CHENG (Premier, July 4, 1958–December 16, 1963). *See earlier entry under Heads of Government.*

YEN CHIA-KAN (Premier, December 16, 1963–March 21, 1972). *See entry under Heads of State.*

CHIANG CHING-KUO (Premier, June 1, 1972–May 20, 1978). *See entry under Heads of State.*

SUN YUN-SUAN (Premier, May 20, 1978–May 20, 1984). Sun Yun-suan was born in Penglai, Shantung, on November 11, 1913. He was educated at the Harbin Polytechnic Institute and trained to be an engineer. He worked with the Taiwan Power Company from 1946 and became its president in 1962. Sun Yun-suan was appointed minister of

communications in 1967 and served until 1969, when he was named minister of economic affairs. He retained that position until 1978. On May 20, 1978, he was named premier, and he served until May 20, 1984. He served as a senior advisor to the president from 1984.

YU KUO-HWA (Premier, May 20, 1984–May 21, 1989). Yü Kuo-Hwa was born in Chekiang on January 10, 1914. He was educated at Tsinghua University and attended Harvard Graduate School. He served as secretary to the president of the National Military Council of China from 1936 until 1944. Yü joined the International Bank for Reconstruction and Development in 1947, where he remained until 1950. The following year he began work with the International Monetary Fund and continued there until 1955. In 1961 he was named chairman of the board of directors of the Bank of China. He retained that position until 1967, when he was appointed minister of finance. Two years later he was named minister of state and governor of the Central Bank of China. Yü retained both positions until May 20, 1984, when he formed a government as premier. He introduced sweeping democratic reforms in the government and liberalized the nation's economic policies. He retained the office of premier until May 21, 1989. He subsequently became a senior advisor to the president of Taiwan.

LEE HUAN (Premier, May 21, 1989–May 30, 1990). Lee Huan was born in Hankow, Hupeh Province, on February 8, 1917. He was educated in China and the United States. He returned to China to work as a journalist before becoming active with the China Youth Corps in 1952. Lee was placed in charge of the Nationalist party's organization and training committee. He attempted a reform program to promote the political power of native-born Taiwanese. He was forced to resign in 1977 following major riots in the city of Chungli. Lee had been a teacher at the National Chengchi University, and he founded the National Sun Yat-sen University in 1978. He served as minister of education from 1984 until 1987, when he was named secretary-general of the ruling Nationalist party. Lee was appointed premier on May 21, 1989. He was replaced by Hau Pei-tsun on May 30, 1990.

HAU PEI-TSUN (Premier, May 30, 1990–February 1993). Hau Pei-tsun was born in 1919. He served in the Nationalist army and rose to the rank of general. Hau retired from the military and served in the cabinet as minister of defense during the 1980s. He was appointed premier by President Lee Teng-hui on May 30, 1990, in the hopes of placating conservatives who were concerned about the government's liberal reforms. Hau's appointment was met with demonstrations by citizens who feared that he would stall proposed reforms. He succeeded in winning over some of his critics, but was forced to resign by liberal members of the ruling party in February of 1993. He was replaced by native Taiwanese Lien Chan.

Ciskei, Republic of

(Iriphabliki Yeciskei)

Ciskei is a country located in South Africa. It was granted independence from South Africa on December 4, 1981.

HEADS OF STATE

LENNOX SEBE (President, December 4, 1981–March 4, 1990). Lennox L. W. Sebe was selected as chief minister to succeed J. T. Mabandla on May 21, 1973, after Ciskei was granted internal self-government by South Africa. He was elected president by the National Assembly when Ciskei was granted independence from South Africa on December 4, 1981. Sebe survived a coup plot organized by his brother, Lt. Gen. Charles Sebe, the head of Ciskei's intelligence service in 1983. General Sebe was arrested, but escaped to Transkei in 1986. President Sebe's son was kidnapped and held hostage in Transkei in October of 1987. He was released several months later after Sebe agreed to the release of political prisoners. Sebe was ousted in a bloodless coup on March 4, 1990, and his regime was charged with corruption and violation of human rights. Sebe's brother was killed in another coup attempt in February of 1991.

JOSHUA OUPA GQOZO (President, March 4, 1990–). Joshua Oupa Gqozo served in the Ciskei army, where he rose to the rank of brigadier. He was chief of military intelligence under President Lennox Sebe. Gqozo succeeded Sebe as head of state following a military coup on March 4, 1990. He survived a coup attempt in February of 1991. Gqozo agreed to a plan to eventually terminate Ciskei's independence and reincorporate it into a democratic South Africa.

Colombia, Republic of

(República de Colombia)

Colombia is a country on the northwestern coast of South America. It was granted independence from Spain on July 20, 1810.

HEADS OF STATE

ALFONSO LÓPEZ PUMAREJO (President, August 7, 1942–August 7, 1945). Alfonso López Pumarejo was born in San Bartolome de las Palmas (now Hondas) on January 31, 1886. He came from a wealthy family and was educated in private schools and then in England and the United States. He returned to Colombia in 1904, where he managed his father's businesses. López became active in the "republicanism" movement and founded the *El Liberal* newspaper in 1910. In 1915 he was elected to the Assembly on the Liberal party ticket. He also remained active in business affairs and became the Colombian head of the American Mercantile Bank in 1919. When Dr. Enrique Olaya Herrera, the Liberal party candidate, was elected president of Colombia with López's support in 1930, López was named minister to London. In 1933 he was appointed to the cabinet as foreign minister. In this position he was instrumental in settling a border dispute and preventing a war with Peru. The following year López announced his candidacy for president and was elected in February of 1934 by an overwhelming majority. He took office on August 7, 1934, and embarked on a campaign to improve the living conditions of the working class by raising the taxes on businesses and the wealthy. He sponsored a new constitution in 1936 which included provisions for workmen's compensation, trade union recognition, and legalized strikes. His policies brought about a backlash from the

right wing, which gained control of Congress and began to stall his legislation. López offered his resignation on May 25, 1937, but the threat of a general strike resulted in Congress's decision not to accept the resignation and to cooperate more closely with his government. López was constitutionally barred from seeking reelection in 1938, and Eduardo Santos, a rightist member of the Liberal party, was nominated and elected. López relinquished the presidency to Santos on August 7, 1938. López made plans to seek the presidency again, but a division between the factions of the Liberal party forced López and his supporters to form a separate party. López was again elected president in May of 1942 and took office on August 7, 1942. As president, López joined Colombia with the Allied cause during World War II. Lopez's popularity was seriously diminished due to major inflation brought on by the wartime economy and several scandals in his administration. He offered his resignation on several occasions, and it was finally accepted in July of 1945. López left office on August 7, 1945, and subsequently represented Colombia at the United Nations. In 1947 he was elected president of the United Nations Security Council. He remained a leading member of the Liberal party and was the victim of right-wing extremism when his house was set on fire in 1952. López subsequently went into exile in Mexico during the presidency of Gustavo Rojas

Pinilla. López returned to Colombia in 1958 following the ouster of Rojas Pinilla and was appointed ambassador to Great Britain in June of 1959. He died of a kidney ailment in London on November 20, 1959.

ALBERTO LLERAS CAMARGO (President, August 7, 1945–August 7, 1946). Alberto Lleras Camargo was born in Bogota on July 3, 1906. He attended the National University in Bogota but left without receiving a degree. He then went to work as a journalist at various liberal newspapers. Lleras entered politics in the late 1920s and was named secretary general of the Liberal party by Alfonso López in 1929. The following year Lleras was elected to the Chamber of Deputies, where he served as speaker in 1931 and 1933. He remained a close associate of López and was appointed general secretary to the president when López won the presidency in 1934. Lleras joined the cabinet as minister of the interior the following year and remained in that position until 1938, when he also served as minister of education. When López left office in 1938, Lleras returned to journalism. He was reelected to the Chamber of Deputies in 1941, where he again served as speaker. In 1943 he was elected to the Senate. When López was reelected president in 1942, Lleras was appointed ambassador to the United States. He returned to Colombia in October of 1943 to rejoin the cabinet as secretary of the interior and the following year was appointed foreign minister. In this capacity he signed the United Nations charter on behalf of Colombia in 1945. When López resigned the presidency in July of 1945, Lleras was selected president-designate by the Colombian Congress. He took office on August 7, 1945, and formed a coalition cabinet with the Conservative party. Lleras was constitutionally barred from succeeding himself and relinquished the presidency to Mariano Ospina Pérez on August 7, 1946. After leaving office, he returned to journalism briefly before being elected director-general of the Pan American Union in Washington, D.C., the following year. Lleras returned to Colombia in 1948 and was selected as the first secretary-general of the Organization of American States. He remained in that position until August of 1954, when he accepted the post of president of the University of Los Andes. In 1956 he served briefly as editor of the *El Independiente* newspaper before being sent to Hungary to investigate the revolt there on behalf of the United Nations. Lleras was also elected director of the Liberal party in 1956, and he reached an agreement with the Conservative party that forced the ouster of President Gustavo Rojas Pinilla in May of 1957. The two major parties formed the National Front, which called for a division of power between the Liberals and Conservatives. Lleras was chosen as the candidate for the Front in the elections scheduled for 1958. Lleras and other government officials were kidnapped on May 2, 1958, by a group of military officers that opposed the election, but Lleras was freed later the same day by troops loyal to the government. Two days later he was again elected president of Colombia, and he took office on August 7, 1958. Lleras began his term of office by restoring civil liberties that had been denied during the rule of Rojas Pinella. He also established an agrarian reform program and began a number of public works projects. In 1961 he was instrumental in the creation of the Latin American Free Trade Association to help reduce tariffs in the region. Lleras left office on August 7, 1962, and became editor of the news magazine *Vision*. He died in Bogota at the age of 83 after a long illness on January 4, 1990.

MARIANO OSPINA PÉREZ (President, August 7, 1946–August 7, 1950). Mariano Ospina Pérez was born in Medellin on November 24, 1891. He received a degree in engineering from the University of Antioquia in 1911 and continued his education in the United States and Belgium before returning to Columbia in 1914. He entered politics and was elected to the Medellin Municipal Council the following year. Ospina Pérez was subsequently elected to the National Assembly. He was elected to the Colombian Senate in 1923. His uncle, General Pedro Nel Ospina, served as Colombia's president from 1922 until 1926. Ospina Pérez was named to the cabinet as minister of public works in the government of Miguel Abadia Mendez in 1926. Ospina Pérez was the Conservative party nominee for president in 1946. His campaign benefited from a division in the Liberal party. He defeated Gabriel Torbay and Jorge Eliecer Gaitan in May of 1946 and was sworn into office on August 7, 1946. Ospina Pérez formed a coalition cabinet and attempted to improve Colombia's economic conditions. Gaitan, a leftist, took control of the Liberal party in March of 1948 and withdrew Liberal members from the coalition government. Ospina Pérez appointed a Conservative cabinet, and his government was beset with riots and demonstrations throughout the country. Conditions deteriorated when Gaitan was assassinated on April 9, 1948. Gaitan's murder led to widespread violence, and Ospina Pérez declared a state of siege to restore order. Presidential elections were advanced from June of 1950 until November of 1949, and violence again resulted when Laureano Gómez was selected as the Conservative party's presidential nominee. On November 9, 1949, Ospina Pérez again declared a state of siege and suspended constitutional rights. The Liberals boycotted the subsequent election, and Gómez was elected president. Ospina Pérez relinquished office to Gómez on August 7, 1950. Ospina Pérez resumed political activity in July of 1952, when he led a rival conservative faction. He remained active in the

moderate faction of the Conservative party until his retirement in 1962. He died in Bogota at the age of 84 on April 14, 1976.

LAUREANO GÓMEZ (President, August 7, 1950–June 13, 1953). Laureano Gómez Castro was born in Bogota on February 20, 1889. He received a degree in engineering from the National University in 1909. He was elected to the National Assembly as a member of the Conservative party in 1911 and served until 1918. Gómez was again a member of the Assembly from 1921 until 1923. He was named Colombia's minister to Argentina in 1923 and served until 1925. He served in the cabinet as minister of public works from 1925 until 1926. In 1930 he was named minister to Germany. Gómez returned to Colombia in 1931 and was elected to the Senate. The following year he became leader of the Conservative party. Gómez was briefly imprisoned in 1944 for his opposition to President Alfonso López Pumarejo. He went into exile in July of 1944 after an unsuccessful revolt against the government, but he returned to Colombia in December of 1944. Conservative candidate Mariano Ospina Pérez was elected president in 1946. Gómez was named to the cabinet as foreign minister in March of 1948 but he resigned following the assassination of Liberal party leader Jorge Eliecer Gaitan in 1948. He went to live in Spain during the subsequent civil violence. In October of 1949 he returned to Colombia to become the Conservative party's nominee for president. Ospina Pérez declared martial law prior to the election in November of 1949, and the Liberals boycotted the election. Gómez was elected unopposed and took office on August 7, 1950. He continued to rule under a state of siege and to wage a ruthless war against the leftist rebels. Gómez became seriously ill in November of 1951, and Roberto Urdaneta Arbeláez served as acting president in his stead. Gómez dismissed Urdaneta on June 13, 1953, and resumed his duties. Gómez was ousted by a coup led by Gustavo Rojas Pinilla later in the day. Gómez was banished to Spain, where he remained until Rojas was ousted in 1957. Gómez again became leader of the rightist faction of the Conservative party, although he suffered from a heart ailment. He agreed to form a National Front government with President Alberto Lleras Camargo in 1960, but was opposed by former president Ospina Pérez and other leading Conservatives. Gómez's health continued to fail, and he died in Bogota at the age of 76 on July 13, 1965.

ROBERTO URDANETA ARBELÁEZ (Acting President, November 1951– June 13, 1953). Roberto Urdaneta Arbeláez was born in 1890. He served as minister of government in the cabinet of President Laureano Gómez. Urdaneta assumed Gómez's duties as acting president in November of 1951 when Gómez was unable to govern due to poor health. Urdaneta was dismissed from office on June 13, 1953, shortly before the Gómez regime was overthrown in a military coup led by Gustavo Rojas Pinilla. Urdaneta gave his support to the subsequent government of Rojas Pinilla.

GUSTAVO ROJAS PINILLA (President, June 13, 1953–May 10, 1957). Gustavo Rojas Pinilla was born in Tinja on March 12, 1900. He was educated locally and entered the Bogota Military Academy in 1917. He graduated three years later and served in the Colombian army. Rojas retired from active service in 1924 and went to the United States to study civil engineering. In 1927 he returned to Colombia and worked as a construction engineer for the Ministry of Public Works. He reentered the army in 1932 and rose through the ranks to become lieutenant general in 1948. The following year he was named minister of communications

in the government of Mariano Ospina Pérez. Rojas commanded Colombia's troops in Korea during the conflict there in 1951. He returned to Colombia in 1953 to find the country still in a state of civil disorder. When Rojas learned that President Laureano Gómez planned to dismiss him from the army in June of 1953, he led a coup against Gómez and ousted him from office on June 13, 1953. Rojas was installed as president and formed a coalition cabinet. He granted amnesty to most political prisoners and fighting in the guerrilla war began to decrease. Rojas installed a Constituent Assembly that confirmed him as president, and he was officially inaugurated on August 7, 1954. Rojas ruled in a dictatorial fashion and greatly increased his personal wealth. On May 8, 1957, he pushed through legislation in the Constituent Assembly that would revise the constitution and extend his presidency for another four years. Dissatisfaction with the brutality and corruption in his regime increased, however, and he was ousted in a coup supported by a coalition of the Liberal and Conservative parties on May 10, 1957. Rojas went into exile in Spain, but returned to Colombia in October of 1958. He was briefly arrested later in the year and charged with illegally profiting from his position. He was stripped of his political rights, but formed the National Popular Alliance in 1960. He illegally ran for the presidency in 1962 and was arrested for conspiring against the government the following year. His party grew in strength, and Rojas was again a candidate for president in 1970. He was narrowly defeated by Misael Pastraña Borrero in April of 1970. Rojas was arrested for several weeks after his defeat resulted in civil disorders throughout the country. Rojas's daughter, Maria Eugenia Rojas de Moreno Diaz, was the Alliance's candidate for president in 1974, but she too was defeated. Rojas died of a heart attack at his home in Bogota at the age of 75 on January 17, 1975.

GABRIEL PARIS (President, May 10, 1957–August 7, 1958). Gabriel Paris was a major general in the Colombia army. He supported President Gustavo Rojas Pinilla's reelection as president on May 8, 1957, but two days later Paris led a five-man military junta to replace Rojas. Paris's provisional government presided over democratic elections in December of 1957. Paris and other members of the junta were kidnapped by members of the military police loyal to Rojas on May 2, 1958. The kidnappers planned to prevent the inauguration of Alberto Lleras Camargo, the winner of the election, as president. Loyal troops quashed the rebellion, and Paris was freed later in the day. The junta stepped down on August 7, 1958, and relinquished office to Lleras Camargo.

ALBERTO LLERAS CAMARGO (President, August 7, 1958–August 7, 1962). *See earlier entry under Heads of State.*

GUILLERMO LEÓN VALENCIA (President, August 7, 1962–August 7, 1966). Guillermo León Valencia was born in Popayan in 1909. He was educated locally and entered politics in 1935. He served in the State Assembly in the Cauca District and was elected to the National Senate in 1939. León Valencia remained in the Senate as a member of the Conservative party until Congress was closed in 1949. He was appointed Ambassador to Spain in 1952 and returned to Colombia the following year. He also served as Colombia's representative to the United Nations. León Valencia was a leading opponent of President Gustavo Rojas Pinilla in the 1950s. He supported Rojas Pinilla's ouster in 1957 and took part in the subsequent National Front coalition. León Valencia was elected president of Colombia in 1962 and took office on August 7, 1962. León Valencia's government was faced with continued guerrilla activity. He declared a state of siege

in May of 1965 after violent student riots erupted in protest of the United States intervention in the Dominican Republic. Colombia's economic conditions also suffered with the decline in the price of coffee. León Valencia completed his term of office on August 7, 1966. He again served as Colombia's ambassador to Spain from 1967 until 1971. On November 4, 1971, León Valencia died of a heart attack at the age of 62 while visiting in New York City.

CARLOS LLERAS RESTREPO (President, August 7, 1966–August 7, 1970). Carlos Lleras Restrepo was born in Bogota on April 12, 1908. He attended the National University, where he received a degree in law. He entered politics and became involved with the radical wing of the Liberal party. In 1934 he was elected to the National Assembly and he became president of the lower chamber in 1935. Lleras Restrepo served as controller general from 1936 until 1937. He was named to the cabinet as minister of finance in the government of Eduardo Santos in 1938. Lleras Restrepo was elected president of the Liberal party in 1941 and also served as editor of the Liberal newspaper *El Tiempo*. In 1942 he was elected to the Senate, and in 1943 he was renamed minister of finance in the government of Alfonso López Pumarejo. He was leader of the Liberal Opposition in the Senate during the administration of President Mariano Ospina Pérez. Lleras Restrepo was again selected as leader of the Liberal party following the assassination of Jorge Eliecer Gaitan in 1948. In 1952 Lleras Restrepo and his family fled to Mexico when his home was burned by a mob. He returned to Colombia in 1954, following the coup led by Gustavo Rojas Pinilla. Lleras Restrepo supported the ouster of Rojas Pinilla in 1957 and was instrumental in negotiating the National Front coalition between the Liberals and Conservatives. He was again elected to the Senate in 1958, but retired briefly from politics in 1959 to study in Europe. The following year he returned to Colombia, and he was reelected to the Senate in 1962. Lleras Restrepo was chosen as the National Front's presidential candidate in 1966. He was elected president and took office on August 7, 1966. Lleras Restrepo threatened to resign in June of 1968 when the Senate failed to pass legislation granting him greater powers to deal with Colombia's economy. He was given a vote of confidence, however, and remained in office. Colombia's economic and political stability improved under Lleras Restrepo. He completed his term of office on August 7, 1970. He again served as Liberal party leader from 1972 until 1973. Lleras Restrepo broke with the Liberal party in 1981 to form the rival New Liberalism party. He remerged his splinter party with the Liberals after failing to make an impact in 1986 parliamentary elections.

MISAEL PASTRAÑA BORRERO

(President, August 7, 1970–August 7, 1974). Misael Pastraña Borrero was born in Neiva on November 14, 1923. He was educated in Bogota, where he received a degree in law. In 1947 he was sent to Rome to serve as a secretary at the Colombian Embassy at the Vatican. He returned to Colombia in 1948 to serve as secretary to President Mariano Ospina Pérez. Pastraña resumed his law practice after Ospina Pérez left office in 1950. He reentered politics in 1957 as part of the coalition National Front formed after the ouster of President Gustavo Rojas Pinilla. In 1960 he represented the Conservative party in the Liberal government of President Alberto Lleras Camargo, where he served in the cabinet as minister of development, public works, and finance until 1961. He then returned to his law practice until 1966, when he was defeated in an election to the Senate. Pastraña was subsequently named to the cabinet of Carlos Lleras Restrepo as minister of the interior. He remained

in that position until 1968, when he was appointed Colombia's ambassador to the United States. He returned to Colombia in 1969 to campaign for the Conservative party's nomination for the presidency. Pastraña was selected as the party's nominee in December of 1969 and defeated former president Gustavo Rojas Pinilla by a narrow margin in the election in April of 1970. Pastraña dedicated himself to reducing unemployment and improving Colombia's social conditions, and he presided over continued economic growth in the country. He completed his term of office on August 7, 1974. Pastraña remained active in the Conservative party and served on the National Committee on Foreign Affairs.

ALFONSO LÓPEZ MICHELSON

(President, August 7, 1974–August 7, 1978). Alfonso López Michelson was born in Bogota on June 30, 1913. He was the son of former Colombian president Alfonso López Pumarejo. He was educated in France, Chile, and the United States. After receiving a degree in law, he became a teacher at Bogota National University. He accompanied his family into exile in Mexico during the regime of President Gustavo Rojas Pinilla from 1952 until 1957. López returned to Colombia in 1958 and was elected to the Chamber of Deputies in 1960. He made an unsuccessful attempt to win the Liberal party's nomination for the presidency in 1962. He was subsequently elected to the Senate and opposed the National Front coalition of the Liberal and Conservative parties. López was selected as governor of the state of Cesar in 1967. He was named to the cabinet as minister of foreign affairs in 1968 and served until 1970. López received the Liberal party's nomination for the presidency in 1974. His election was the first in 16 years that was not governed by the National Front coalition agreement. López defeated Conservative candidate Alvaro Gomez Hurtado and Maria

Eugenia Rojas de Moreno Diaz, the daughter of former President Gustavo Rojas Pinilla, and took office on August 7, 1974. His government was faced with rising inflation and continued guerrilla activity from leftist terrorist groups. He declared a state of siege in June of 1975, but the violence continued. López was also faced with a financial scandal involving his family in 1977. He completed his term of office on August 7, 1978. He was again the Liberal party's nominee for president in 1982, but was defeated by Belisario Betancur Cuartas. López remained an influential leader of the Liberal party and supported Virgilio Barco Vargas in the presidential election in 1986.

JULIO CÉSAR TURBAY AYALA (President, August 7, 1978–August 7, 1982). Julio César Turbay Ayala was born in Bogota on June 18, 1916. He was educated locally and entered politics in 1938. He was elected to the Legislative Assembly in Cundnamarca. Turbay Ayala was elected to the National Assembly as a member of the Liberal party in 1943 and served until 1953. He was minister of mines and energy in the cabinet of the provisional government that ousted President Gustavo Rojas Pinilla in 1957. He was named foreign minister in the cabinet of President Alberto Lleras Camargo in 1958. Turbay Ayala retained that position until 1961 and was elected to the Senate the following year. He also served as Colombia's ambassador to the United Nations from 1967 until 1969. He was named ambassador to Great Britain in 1970. Turbay Ayala returned to Colombia in 1973 and was selected as chairman of the Liberal party. He was elected vice president to Alfonso López Michelsen in September of 1974 and was named ambassador to the United States in April of 1975. In August of 1976 he returned to Colombia to begin plans for a presidential campaign. Turbay Ayala was chosen as the Liberal party's candidate for presi-

dent in 1978. He narrowly defeated conservative candidate Belisario Betancur Cuartas and took office on August 7, 1978. Turbay Ayala was faced with continued violence from guerrilla groups and an increase in drug trafficking in the country. After presidential elections were held in 1982, he lifted the state of siege that had been in effect since 1976. Turbay Ayala completed his term of office on August 7, 1982. He remained a leader in the Liberal party.

BELISARIO BETANCUR CUARTAS (President, August 7, 1982–August 7, 1986). Belisario Betancur Cuartas was born to a poor family in Amaga in 1923. He was educated in Medellin, where he received a degree in law. In the 1940s he became active in politics and joined the Conservative party. He was appointed to the Constituent Assembly by President Laureano Gómez in 1950. Betancur was imprisoned during the subsequent regime of Gustav Rojas Pinilla. Betancur supported the National Front coalition that came into power in 1958. He was elected to the Colombian Senate in the early 1960s and was an unsuccessful candidate for the Conservative party's presidential nomination in 1962. He served as minister of labor in the cabinet of Guillermo Léon Valencia in 1963. Betancur was again defeated for the Conservative presidential nomination in 1970. He was appointed ambassador to Spain in 1974. He returned to Colombia to campaign for president as the Conservative party nominee in 1978, but he was defeated by Liberal party candidate Julio César Turbay Ayala. Betancur was again the Conservative party candidate in the presidential elections in 1982. He defeated former President Alfonso López Michelsen, the Liberal nominee, and Luis Carlos Galan Sarmiento, the New Liberal party candidate. He took office on August 7, 1982. Betancur attempted to curb guerrilla violence in the country. He initiated a peace commission which offered an amnesty to members of guerrilla organizations. Betancur engaged in a confrontation with the Colombian armed forces over the army's role in political affairs in 1984. Betancur's minister of defense, General Fernando Landazabal Reyez and numerous high-ranking officers resigned as a result. Rodrigo Lara Bonilla, Colombia's minister of justice, was assassinated on April 30, 1984, by members of Colombia's drug cartel. Colombia experienced more violence in November of 1985 when radical M-19 guerrillas seized the Palace of Justice in Bogota and took numerous hostages. Betancur refused to negotiate with the terrorists, and government troops stormed the building. Over 100 people were killed in the subsequent fighting, including Supreme Court President Alfonso Reyes Echandia and ten other Supreme Court justices. Betancur completed his term of office on August 7, 1986. He remained active in the leadership of the Conservative party.

VIRGILIO BARCO VARGAS (President, August 7, 1986–August 7, 1990). Virgilio Barco Vargas was born to a wealthy family in Cucuta on September 17, 1921. He attended the National University of Bogota and the Massachusetts Institute of Technology, where he studied civil engineering. He returned to Colombia in 1943 to enter government service. From 1945 until 1946 he served as acting minister of communications. Barco was elected to the House of Representatives as a member of the Liberal party in 1949. He served until later in the year, when the National Assembly was dissolved by President Mariano Ospina Pérez. Barco continued his education in the 1950s and received a doctorate in economics from the Massachusetts Institute of Technology. He was elected to the Colombian Senate in 1958. He also served as minister of public works until 1961. Barco was named ambassador to Great Britain in 1961, but

returned to Colombia the following year. He again served in the cabinet as minister of agriculture from 1963 until 1964, when he briefly served as minister of finance. Barco was selected as mayor of Bogota in 1966. He retained office until 1969, when he became Latin American director of the World Bank. He served in this position until 1974. Barco was subsequently named Colombia's ambassador to the United States. In 1981 he returned to Colombia to receive the Liberal party's nomination for president, but withdrew from the elections shortly thereafter. Barco again campaigned for the presidency as the Liberal nominee in the election of 1986. He defeated Conservative party candidate Alvaro Gomez Hurtado and took office on August 7, 1986. The Liberal party was also victorious in Congressional elections, and Barco was able to name a Liberal cabinet. The country was still facing violence from extremists on the left and the right and from members of Colombia's drug cartels. Political assassinations continued with the murder of Patriotic Union leader Jaime Pardo Leal in October of 1987 and of Attorney General Carlos Mauro Hoyos in January of 1988. Defeated presidential candidate Alvaro Gomez Hurtado was kidnapped by guerrillas in May of 1988, but was released unharmed the following July. The government initiated a crackdown on drug traffickers, who responded by assassinating Liberal party presidential nominee Luis Carlos Galan Sarmiento in August of 1989. The drug cartel was also believed to have been responsible for the crash of a Colombian jet aircraft in November of 1989. Two other presidential candidates, Carlos Pizarro Leon-Gómez of the Democratic Alliance April 19 Movement and Bernardo Jaramillo Ossa of the Patriotic Union, were murdered shortly before elections in May of 1990. Barco completed his term of office on August 7, 1990. He was subsequently appointed ambassador to Great Britain.

CÉSAR GAVIRIA TRUJILLO (President, August 7, 1990–). César Gaviria Trujillo was born in Pereira on March 31, 1947. He was educated at the University of the Andes, where he studied economics. He entered politics in 1970 and was elected mayor of Pereira in 1974. Gaviria was also elected to the House of Representatives as a member of the Liberal party in 1974. He was appointed vice minister of development in the government of President Julio César Turbay Ayala in 1978. He subsequently wrote a column on economics for Bogota's largest newspaper. Gaviria was active in the presidential campaign of Virgilio Barco Vargas in 1986 and was named minister of finance in the subsequent Barco government. He was appointed minister of the interior the following year

and retained his position until February of 1989. He then served as campaign manager for Liberal party presidential nominee Luis Carlos Galan Sarmiento. When Galan was assassinated in August of 1989, Gaviria was selected to succeed him as the Liberal's nominee. He was victorious in the election and took office on August 7, 1990. Gaviria attempted to bring an end to drug-related terrorism. He offered leniency to cartel members who surrendered to authorities and agreed to a policy of nonextradition to the United States. Pablo Escobar Gaviria, the Ochoa brothers, and other Medellin cartel leaders surrendered during 1991, though Escobar escaped from prison the following year. President Gaviria also presided over the formation of a new constitution in 1991.

Comoros, Federal Islamic Republic of the

(République Fédérale Islamique des Comores)

The Comoros are a group of islands in the Mozambique Channel near southeast Africa. They were granted independence from France on July 6, 1975.

HEADS OF STATE

AHMED ABDALLAH (President, July 7, 1975–August 3, 1975). Ahmed Abdallah Abderrahman was born in 1919. He was a leading Comoro businessman and served as a representative of the Comoros in the French Senate from 1959 until 1972. He led the proindependence Democratic Union of the Comoros party and became president of the Comoro Government Council in December of 1972. Abdallah unilaterally declared the Comoro Islands independent on July 7, 1975. He became president and prime minister in the independent government. On August 3, 1975, he was ousted in a coup led

by Ali Soilih. Abdallah remained on his home island of Anjouan until September 22, 1975, when Ali Soilih led an invasion force to capture the deposed president, who was arrested and sent into exile in France. Abdallah was returned to power on May 21, 1978, following a coup led by French mercenary Col. Bob Denard. Abdallah established the Islamic Republic of the Comoros and served as copresident of the ruling Political-Military Directorate with Mohammed Ahmed until Ahmed's resignation on October 3, 1978. Abdallah was elected president in a referendum later in the month. He was reelected unopposed in September of 1984. Abdallah survived a coup attempt in March of 1985 and instituted a crackdown on dissidents. He survived another coup attempt in November of 1987. Abdallah was granted permission to run for another term by a national referendum to amend the constitution in November of 1989. Abdallah was shot to death during an attack by rebels on the presidential palace on November 26, 1989.

ALI SOILIH (President, August 3, 1975–August 5, 1975). Ali Soilih was born on Grande Comoro Island in 1937. He was educated in Madagascar and France, where he studied agriculture. In 1964 he returned to the Comoros to serve as president of the Economic Development Society. He was elected to the Territorial Assembly in 1968. Soilih served in the cabinet of Prince Said Ibrahim as minister of public works from 1970 until 1972. He was the leader of the People's party and was an advocate of a gradual process of independence. He opposed Ahmed Abdallah's unilateral declaration of independence from France on July 7, 1975. Soilih led a coup to oust Abdallah on August 3, 1975. He installed Prince Sa'id Muhammad Jaffar as president and prime minister on August 5, 1975. Soilih was chosen to be president of the Comoros by the National Council of the Revolution on January 3, 1976. Soilih attempted to establish a leftist people's republic and abolish the feudal institutions in the Comoros. He banned political activity in the country and survived several coup attempts. He was ousted on May 13, 1978, in a coup led by French mercenary Col. Bob Denard. Denard's coup returned Ahmed Abdallah to power, and Soilih was placed under house arrest. On May 29, 1978, he was shot and killed, reportedly while trying to escape.

PRINCE SA'ID MUHAMMAD JAFFAR (President, August 5, 1975–December 1975). Sa'id Muhammad Jaffar was born in Mutsamudu on April 14, 1918. He had served as premier of the Comoros during the French colonial period. He was the leader of the pro-independence Democratic Rally of the Comoran People. Sa'id Muhammad Jaffar was named president and prime minister on August 5, 1975, following the coup that ousted Ahmed Abdallah. He retained office until his death while on a pilgrimage to Mecca in December of 1975.

ALI SOILIH (President, January 3, 1976–May 13, 1978). *See earlier entry under Heads of State.*

SAID ATTOURMANI (President, May 13, 1978–May 21, 1978). Said Attourmani served in the first cabinet of the independent Comoros in 1975. He was a devout Muslim who opposed Ali Soilih's suppression of religious observations. He supported the coup that ousted Soilih on May 13, 1978, and served as interim president. Said Attourmani retained office until May 21, 1978, when Ahmed Abdallah returned from exile to assume the presidency.

AHMED ABDALLAH (President, May 21, 1978–November 26, 1989). *See earlier entry under Heads of State.*

MOHAMMED AHMED (Copresident, May 24, 1978–October 3, 1978). Mohammed Ahmed was born in 1914. He served as a deputy to Comoro president Ahmed Abdallah. He returned from exile in France with Abdallah following the coup that ousted President Ali Soilih. Mohammed Ahmed served as copresident of the ruling Political-Military Directorate from May 24, 1978, until he retired from politics on October 3, 1978. Mohammed Ahmed returned to private business in the Comoros. He died on January 27, 1984.

SAID MOHAMMED DJOHAR (President, November 26, 1989–). Saïd Mohamed Djohar became acting president of the Comoros on November 26, 1989, following the assassination of President Ahmed Abdallah. Djohar was sworn in as president on March 20, 1990, following elections earlier in the month. Djohar survived a coup attempt in August of 1991. The president allowed the formation of a coalition government in January of 1992, but dismissed the cabinet in July of 1992 following conflicts between Djohar and Prime Minister Mohamed Taki Abdoulkarim. Djohar survived another coup attempt in September of 1992. The following November legislative elections were conducted, though considerable violence marred the balloting.

HEADS OF GOVERNMENT

AHMAD ABDALLAH (Prime Minister, December 26, 1972–July 6, 1975). *See entry under Heads of State.*

PRINCE SA'ID MUHAMMAD JAFFAR (Prime Minister, August 5, 1975–December 1975). *See entry under Heads of State.*

ABDALLAH MOHAMMAD (Prime Minister, January 6, 1976–December 22, 1978). Abdallah Mohammad was appointed prime minister by President Ali Soilih on January 6, 1976, following the separation of the office from the presidency. Abdallah Mohammad was reappointed to the position by Ahmed Abdallah following the ouster of Ali Soilih in May of 1978. He held office until December 22, 1978, when he stepped down following legislative elections.

SALIM BEN ALI (Prime Minister, December 22, 1978–January 25, 1982). Salim Ben Ali was selected as prime minister of the Comoros on December 22, 1978. He was reappointed prime minister when President Ahmed Abdallah dissolved the government in July of 1980. Salim Ben Ali retained office until January 25, 1982, when he was dismissed by the president.

ALI MROUDJAE (Prime Minister, February 8, 1982–December 31, 1984).

Ali Mroudjae served as minister of foreign affairs in the Comoro government from 1979 until 1982. He was appointed prime minister by President Ahmad Abdallah on February 8, 1982, and remained in office until December 31, 1984, when the position of prime minister was abolished. He subsequently served as minister of state for internal affairs from January until September of 1985. Ali Mroudjae served in various other cabinet positions under Abdallah and was named minister of production and industry in the government of Said Mohamed Djohar in 1989. He was the leader of the Comoran Party for Democracy and Progress (PCDP). He joined his party with the Comoran Union for Progress to form the Opposition to President Djohar in November of 1991.

MOHAMED TAKI ABDULKARIM (Prime Minister, May 10, 1992–July 10, 1992). Mohamed Taki Abdulkarim was defeated by Said Mohamed Djohar in presidential elections in March of 1990. He was involved in a coup attempt against Djohar later in the month and went into exile in Paris, where he formed the National Union for Democracy in the Comoros. Taki was invited to return to the Comoros in November of 1991 after meeting with Djohar. He was appointed to serve as "coordinator of the government action" on January 6, 1992. Taki formed a cabinet as prime minister of a coalition government on May 10, 1992. His transitional government was dissolved by the president on July 10, 1992, following conflicts between the government and the president.

Congo People's Republic
(*République Populaire du Congo*)

Congo People's Republic is a country on the western coast of equatorial Africa. It was granted independence from France on August 15, 1960.

HEADS OF STATE

FULBERT YOULOU (President, August 15, 1960–August 15, 1963). Fulbert Youlou was born in Moumboulo, near Brazzaville, on June 9, 1917. He was educated at Catholic missionary schools and entered the seminary in 1929. He subsequently taught at mission schools in the Middle Congo. Youlou was ordained a priest in 1946. He soon became involved in politics and was suspended from the priesthood for campaigning for public office in 1956. Youlou continued to use the title *abbé* and often wore the white cassock of priesthood. In November of 1956 he was elected mayor of Brazzaville. He founded the Democratic Union for the Defence of African Interests (UDDIA) and was elected to the Territorial Assembly in March of 1957. Youlou served in the government of Premier Jacques Opangault as minister of agriculture, livestock, water, and forests. He was named premier on December 8, 1958, and was faced with demonstrations and rioting by supporters of Opangault. Order was restored with the assistance of French troops, and Opangault was imprisoned. Youlou's party was successful in the elections in 1959, and Youlou was reelected premier in June of 1959. He formed a coalition Cabinet that included Opangault, who was released from prison. Youlou also served in the government as foreign minister and minister of justice. He was elected president in November of 1959 and took office on August 15, 1960, when the independent Republic of the Congo was established. When France cut off financial assistance to the Congo in 1963, Youlou was forced to raise taxes. The country was also faced with inflation and unemployment. Youlou made plans to transform the government of the Congo into a one-party system, but his plans were threatened in August of 1963 by a massive demonstration of leftists and trade unionists. On August 16, 1963, he was ousted in a coup and was imprisoned by the revolutionary regime. He escaped to the former Belgian Congo in March of 1965, where he was granted asylum by Premier Moise Tshombe. Youlou was sentenced to death in absentia by a people's tribunal. He went into exile in Spain in 1966 after he was refused permission to settle in France. Youlou died in Madrid at the age of 55 on May 5, 1972.

ALPHONSE MASSAMBA-DÉBAT (President, August 16, 1963–September 4, 1968). Alphonse Massamba-Débat was born to the southern Lari tribe in Nkolo in 1921. He was educated locally before attending civil service training school in Brazzaville. He worked as a teacher in Fort Lamy from

1940 and joined the Chad Progressive party. In 1947 he returned to the Congo, where he continued to work as a teacher. He also remained involved in politics and joined Fulbert Youlou's Democratic Union for the Defense of African Interests (UDDIA) in 1956. Following the elections in 1957, he served as a secretary to the minister of education. Massamba-Débat was elected to the National Assembly in 1959 and served as president of the Assembly. He was named minister of state in 1961 and was appointed minister of planning and equipment in Youlou's cabinet shortly thereafter. He became a critic of Youlou's policies and resigned from the government in May of 1963. Youlou was ousted on August 15, 1963, and Massamba-Débat was named president of the provisional government the following day. He was elected president in December of 1963. Massamba-Débat's government was pressured by leftist agitation. The Congolese government strengthened its ties with the Soviet Union and the People's Republic of China, and diplomatic relations with the United States were severed in 1965. Three leading Congolese political figures, Supreme Court president Joseph Pouabou, Attorney General Lazare Matsokota, and Congolese Information Agency director Anselme Massouemi, were assassinated under mysterious conditions in 1965. Massamba-Débat survived a mutiny of the military in June of 1966. The political situation in the Congo deteriorated in 1968, and Massamba-Débat was forced to resign on September 4, 1968, following a military coup. He retired to live in seclusion in his native village of Boko. On March 18, 1977, Massamba-Débat was arrested following the assassination of President Marien Ngouabi, who had been a leader in the coup that deposed him. Massamba-Débat was tried and convicted of complicity in the assassination and was executed in Brazzaville on March 25, 1977.

ALFRED RAOUL (President, September 4, 1968–January 1, 1969). Alfred Raoul was born in the Pointe Noire region on December 13, 1938. He was educated in the Congo and France, where he attended the St. Cyr military academy in 1960. He entered the Congolese army and served as adjutant to the armed forces commander in chief. Raoul was named premier by the National Council of the Revolution on August 21, 1968, in a move to reduce the powers of President Alphonse Massamba-Débat. Raoul also assumed the office of interim president following Massamba-Débat's ouster on September 4, 1968. Raoul was replaced by Marien Ngouabi on January 1, 1969, but remained premier until the position was abolished on December 31, 1969. Raoul remained in the government as vice president until he was dismissed in a purge in December of 1971. He was arrested in February of 1972 and charged with conspiring against the government of President Ngouabi. He was convicted and sentenced to ten years imprisonment, but was released in April of 1972. Raoul served as the Congo's ambassador to the European Economic Community in Belgium from 1976 until 1977. He was subsequently appointed ambassador to Egypt.

MARIEN NGOUABI (President, January 1, 1969–March 18, 1977). Marien Ngouabi was born in the northern Koyoyu tribe in Ombele in 1938. He was educated locally and at military academies in France. He returned to the Congo in 1962 and helped to form a paratroop corps in Brazzaville. Ngouabi had risen to the rank of captain when he led a mutiny in 1966 against the plans of Massamba-Débat's government to incorporate the army into the national militia. Ngouabi was demoted, but the government's plan was scrapped. He was subsequently posted to the general staff headquarters. In July of 1968 he was arrested, but he was freed by his supporters in the military. Massamba-Débat was forced to name Ngouabi as chief of staff. Ngouabi also served as president of the National Revolutionary Council. Massamba-Débat was forced from office on September 4, 1968, and Captain Alfred Raoul was named leader of the provisional government. Ngouabi remained leader of the Revolutionary Council and replaced Raoul as president on January 1, 1969. Ngouabi formed the Congolese Worker's party (PCT) in January of 1970. His government survived a right-wing coup attempt two months later. Ngouabi was also challenged by an abortive coup attempt from the left in February of 1972. He established the Congo as a people's republic and maintained close relations with the Soviet Union and Cuba. He retained power until he was shot and killed in his living quarters at his general staff headquarters in Brazzaville on March 18, 1977. His assassination took place during an unsuccessful coup attempt led by Captain Barthelemy Kikadidi that reportedly involved Massamba-Débat.

JOACHIM YHOMBI-OPANGO (President, March 18, 1977–February 5, 1979). Joachim Yhombi-Opango was born in the Fort Rousset region in 1939. He entered the French army in 1957 and was transferred to the Congolese army in 1962. He rose to the rank of captain in 1967 and subsequently served as military attaché at the Congolese Embassy in Moscow. Yhombi-Opango succeeded Marien Ngouabi as commander of the paratroop corps in September of 1968. The following year he was appointed director of the police. He was named leader of the armed forces general staff in 1970. Yhombi-Opango was instrumental in putting down the left-wing coup against Ngouabi in February of 1972. Yhombi-Opango was promoted to colonel in 1973 and was named to the ruling Politburo, but he was dismissed from his positions later in the year. He returned

to the government as director of public works in 1975 and was named president of the Congolese Labor party's military committee in March of 1977. He succeeded as head of state following Ngouabi's assassination on March 18, 1977. Yhombi-Opango's criticism of the Congolese Labor party's economic policies resulted in his ouster on February 5, 1979. The following month he was arrested and expelled from the party. He was detained until November of 1984. Yhombi-Opango was rearrested in September of 1987. He formed the opposition Rally for Democracy and Development after his release. He was an unsuccessful candidate for president in 1992.

DENIS SASSOU-NGUESSO (President, February 8, 1979–August 20, 1992). Denis Sassou-Nguesso was born in Edou in 1943. He was educated locally and attended military schools in France. He was active in the ruling Congolese Labor party. In 1975 Sassou-Nguesso was appointed minister of defense. He rose to first vice president of the ruling military committee in 1977 and succeeded Joachim Yhombi-Opango as interim president on February 8, 1979. He was confirmed as president by the Congress in March of 1979 and was elected to a second term in July of 1984. Sassou-Nguesso survived a coup plot in July of 1987 and a military revolt in July of 1988. He was elected to a third term in July of 1989, but was faced with civil unrest favoring democratization of the Congo. He agreed to convene a multiparty national conference in February of 1991. The constitution was rewritten to diminish the powers of the president. Presidential elections were held in August of 1992, and Sassou-Nguesso relinquished the presidency to the victor, Pascal Lissouba, on August 20, 1992.

PASCAL LISSOUBA (President, August 20, 1992–). Pascal Lissouba was born in Mossendjo on November 29,

1931. He was educated in the Congo, France, and Tunisia. He received a degree in agronomy from the University of Paris before returning to the Congo to work in the ministry of agriculture. Lissouba was named minister of agriculture in Alphonse Massamba-Débat's provisional government in 1963. He was also named premier on August 16, 1963. His government was faced with growing economic difficulties, and he resigned on May 6, 1966. In August of 1968 he returned to the government to serve in Marien Ngouabi's cabinet. Lissouba was dismissed in June of 1969 and taught economics in Brazzaville. In January of 1973 he was appointed to the ruling Congolese Labor party's planning commission. Lissouba was accused of conspiring to overthrow the government of President Ngouabi the following month. He was subsequently acquitted of the charges, and in 1974 he resigned his position. In March of 1976 he was again accused of plotting against the government and was charged with complicity in Ngouabi's assassination in March of 1977. Lissouba was sentenced to life imprisonment, but was released in April of 1979 for reasons of health. In 1981 he was named director of the African Bureau for Science and Technology in Nairobi, Kenya. He became the leader of the opposition Pan-African Union for Social Democracy party and was the party's presidential candidate in 1992. Lissouba defeated Bernard Kolelas of the Congolese Movement for Democracy and Integral Development in a runoff election and took office on August 20, 1992. He dissolved the legislature and called for new legislative elections in October of 1992.

HEADS OF GOVERNMENT

JACQUES OPANGAULT (Premier, November 28, 1958–December 8, 1958). Jacques Opangault was born in Ikagna on December 13, 1907. He was educated in Catholic mission schools and joined the judicial service as a clerk in 1938. He entered politics following World War II and formed the Congolese branch of the French Socialist party. Opangault was elected to the Territorial Assembly in 1946, but was unable to win election to the French National Assembly. In May of 1957 he was elected vice president of the Congo's government council. He became premier of the provisional government on November 28, 1958, but was replaced by Fulbert Youlou on December 8, 1958. Opangault was arrested in February of 1959 following riots of his supporters in Brazzaville. He was released the following August and was appointed minister of state in Youlou's government in 1960. He served as Youlou's vice president in 1961 and was demoted to minister of public works in 1962. Opangault was again arrested following Youlou's ouster in August of 1963. He retired from politics after his release. He died in Brazzaville on August 20, 1978.

FULBERT YOULOU (Premier, December 8, 1958–August 15, 1960). *See entry under Heads of State.*

PASCAL LISSOUBA (Premier, August 16, 1963–May 6, 1966). *See entry under Heads of State.*

AMBROISE NOUMAZALAY (Premier, May 6, 1966–January 12, 1968). Ambroise Noumazalay was born in Brazzaville on September 23, 1933. He was educated in France, where he received a degree in mathematics. He served in the Congo government as director of economic affairs from 1964 until 1966. Noumazalay was an exponent of Marxism and advocated close relations with the Soviet Union and the People's Republic of China. He was appointed premier by President Alphonse Massamba-Débat on May 6, 1966. When Massamba-Débat eliminated the position of premier on January 12, 1968, Noumazalay was dropped from the government. He returned to the government after the ouster of Massamba-Débat and served as minister of planning from August until December of 1968. He was then named minister of agriculture, water, and forests and served in this office until 1969. Noumazalay remained in the government until February of 1972, when he was accused of participating in a coup attempt against President Marien Ngouabi. The following month he was convicted and sentenced to life imprisonment. Noumazalay was released in an amnesty in October of 1973 and returned to the government in 1984 to serve as minister of industry. He remained in the cabinet and was appointed minister of forestry in 1988. He was dropped from the government in 1989.

ALFRED RAOUL (Premier, August 21, 1968–December 31, 1969). *See entry under Heads of State.*

MARIEN NGOUABI (Premier, December 31, 1968–August 27, 1973). *See entry under Heads of State.*

HENRI LOPES (Premier, August 25, 1973–December 13, 1975). Henri Lopes was born in Leopoldville on September 12, 1937. He was educated locally and in France and entered the Congolese government as minister of national education in 1968. He was named minister of foreign affairs in 1973 and retained that position until August 25, 1973, when President Marien Ngouabi appointed him premier. Lopes also served in the government as minister of planning. He was replaced by Louis Sylvain Ngoma on December 13, 1975.

Lopes returned to the government as minister of finance in 1977 and served until 1980. He subsequently worked with the United Nations Educational, Scientific, and Cultural Organization (UNESCO). Lopes was also a prominent Congolese novelist and was the author of the Congolese national anthem.

LOUIS SYLVAIN NGOMA (Premier, December 13, 1975–August 7, 1984). Louis Sylvain Ngoma was born in Pointe Noire on June 28, 1941. He was educated in military academies in France and entered the army engineer corps in 1966. He joined the Congolese army and served as chief of staff from 1968. From 1970 until 1974 he served in the cabinet as minister of public works and transport. Ngoma was appointed premier by President Marien Ngouabi on December 13, 1975, and retained his position following Ngouabi's assassination in March of 1977. He was also named second vice president in the government of Joachim Yhombi-Opango and served until 1979. Ngoma was replaced as premier by Ange-Edouard Poungui on August 7, 1984. He was again named premier in a transitional government on January 9, 1991, but was replaced by Andre Milongo on June 8, 1991.

ANGE-EDOUARD POUNGUI (Premier, August 11, 1984–August 7, 1989). Ange-Edouard Poungui was born in 1942. He served as a member of the National Council for the Revolution in 1968 and served as minister of finance from 1971 until August of 1973. He was appointed vice president of the Council of State and minister for planning in 1973 and served until 1976. Poungui served as director of the Central African Bank from 1976 until 1979. He was appointed premier on August 11, 1984, and retained office until August 7, 1989.

ALPHONSE POATY-SOUCHALATY (Premier, August 7, 1989–December 3,

1990). Alphonse Mouissou Poaty-Souchalaty served in the cabinet as minister of trade. He was named premier by President Denis Sassou-Nguesso on August 7, 1989. Poaty-Souchalaty resigned on December 3, 1990, in opposition to the president's plans to introduce a multiparty system of government.

PIERRE MOUSSA (Premier, December 3, 1990–January 8, 1991). Pierre Moussa served as interim premier following the resignation of Alphonse Poaty-Souchalaty on December 3, 1990. He was replaced by Louis Sylvain Ngoma on January 9, 1991.

LOUIS SYLVAIN NGOMA (Premier, January 9, 1991–June 8, 1991). *See earlier entry under Heads of Government.*

ANDRÉ MILONGO (Premier, June 8, 1991–September 2, 1992). André Milongo was selected as interim premier by a multiparty national conference on June 8, 1991. Milongo clashed with

President Denis Sassou-Nguesso over the premier's establishment of diplomatic relations with Israel in November of 1991. His government survived a coup attempt in early January of 1992, and he retained office until September 2, 1992.

STÉPHANE MAURICE BONGHO-NOUARRA (Premier, September 2, 1992–December 6, 1992). Stéphane Maurice Bongho-Nouarre was asked to form a government on September 2, 1992. The new government was defeated in a vote of no confidence on October 31, 1992, and Bongho-Nouarra was replaced by Antoine Dacosta on December 6, 1992.

ANTOINE DACOSTA (Premier, December 6, 1992–   ). Antoine Dacosta was an agronomist who was named premier in a National Union government on December 6, 1992. Dacosta's government was charged with organizing new legislative elections for the following year.

Costa Rica, Republic of

(República de Costa Rica)

Costa Rica is a country in Central America. It was granted independence from Spain on September 15, 1821.

HEADS OF STATE

TEODORO PICADO MICHALSKI (President, May 8, 1944–April 20, 1948). Teodoro Picado Michalski was born in San Jose on January 10, 1900. He was educated as a lawyer and worked for the United Fruit Company until 1932, when he entered government service. He served as secretary of public education and in 1938 was elected to the

Costa Rican National Assembly. Picado subsequently served as president of the Assembly. He was the candidate of the ruling National Republican party in the presidential elections in 1944. He won by a large margin and was sworn into office on May 8, 1944. Picado allowed Communists to serve in his government and established diplomatic relations with the Soviet Union. In July of 1947 his government was threatened by a general strike organized by the political opposition. Picado was prevented by the constitution from succeeding himself and supported former president Rafael Calderon Guardia in the presidential elections in February of 1948. When Calderon was defeated by Otilio Ulate Blanco, Picado's government nullified the election. Supporters of Ulate went into rebellion against the government, and in March of 1948 José Figueres Ferrer joined forces with the rebels. Picado was forced from office on April 20, 1948, and went into exile in Guatemala. He subsequently went to Nicaragua, where he served as secretary to President Anastasio Somoza. He died in Managua, Nicaragua, on June 1, 1960.

SANTOS LEÓN HERRERA (President, April 20, 1948–May 8, 1948). Santos León Herrera was born in 1874. He served as third vice president in the government of Teodoro Picado Michalski. He was chosen to serve as provisional president following the coup that ousted Picado Michalski on April 20, 1948. He stepped down on May 8, 1948, to allow a ruling junta under José Figueres Ferrer to take power. León Herrera retired from politics and died in 1950.

JOSÉ FIGUERES FERRER (President, May 8, 1948–November 8, 1949). José Figueres Ferrer was born in San Ramon on September 25, 1906. He attended the Massachusetts Institute of Technology, where he studied economics and engineering. Figueres, known as "Don Pepe," returned to Costa Rica in 1926 and became a prosperous coffee planter. He was an opponent of the regime of President Rafael Angel Calderon Guardia, and his criticisms of the government in 1942 resulted in his exile to Mexico in 1942. He returned to Costa Rica in 1944, following Teodoro Picado Michalski's election to the presidency.

When Calderon Guardia was defeated in the 1948 presidential election by Otilio Ulate Blanco, President Picado pressured the National Assembly into nullifying the elections in order to allow Calderon Guardia's return to power. Figueres gathered together a citizens' militia to challenge the government. The rebels defeated the Costa Rican army and a Communist militia and forced Picado and Calderon into exile. Figueres installed a provisional government under Santos León Herrera. Figueres served in the cabinet as minister of justice, foreign affairs, and public security. He became provisional president as leader of an eleven-man junta on May 8, 1948. His government survived an invasion by Calderon Guardia's supporters from Nicaragua in December of 1948 and a coup attempt by his defense minister Edgar Cardona in April of 1949. Figueres abolished the army to prevent future military revolts. He also nationalized the banks and initiated a social security system. Figueres called for new elections to the National Assembly, and Ulate Blanco was confirmed as president by the new Assembly. Figueres was ruled ineligible to be a candidate for vice president in Ulate Blanco's government. Figueres relinquished office to Ulate Blanco on November 8, 1949. Figueres was the target of an abortive assassination plot in 1951. He founded the National Liberation party in March of 1952 and announced his candidacy for president. He won the election in July of 1953 by a landslide and took office as president on November 8, 1953. Figueres maintained close relations with the United States and was an outspoken opponent of dictatorships throughout Latin America. His opposition to Nicaragua's president Anastasio Somoza Debayle resulted in a brief border war between their two countries in 1954. He also supported the rebellion against Fulgencio Batista's government in Cuba, but later broke with rebel leader Fidel

Castro over his Communist leanings. Figueres completed his term of office and stepped down on May 8, 1958. He returned to private business after leaving office, though he continued to serve as leader of the National Liberation party. Figueres served as a visiting professor at Harvard University from 1963 until 1964. He reentered politics in 1970 as the candidate of the National Liberation party. He defeated former president Mario Echandi Jiménez to succeed José Joaquín Trejos Fernández as president on May 8, 1970. Figueres allowed his friend and financial supporter Robert Vesco to remain in Costa Rica to avoid extradition to the United States. Figueres completed his term of office on May 8, 1974. He died of a heart attack at the age of 83 in San Jose on June 8, 1990.

OTILLIO ULATE BLANCO (President, November 8, 1949–November 8, 1953). Otillio Ulate Blanco was born in 1892. He served as a deputy in the Legislative Assembly from 1930 until 1938. He was also the founder and publisher of the newspaper *Diario de Costa Rica*. Ulate was the candidate of the opposition in the presidential elections in February of 1948. He was victorious over former president Rafael Angel Calderon Guardia. The results of the election were annulled by the National Assembly after protests of fraud from Calderon supporters. Ulate was briefly arrested by the government of President Teodoro Picado Michalski. The government's actions prompted a rebellion by José Figueres Ferrer. Figueres ousted the government, and Ulate was reinstated as president-elect. He succeeded Figueres's ruling junta on November 8, 1949. Ulate led a conservative government and was considered a competent administrator. He completed his term of office on November 8, 1953. He was subsequently involved in the creation of the Central American Development Bank and also remained active with the National Union party.

Ulate was appointed minister to Spain in 1971 when Figueres again served as President. Ulate suffered a stroke in October of 1973 and died in a hospital in San Jose at the age of 82 on October 27, 1973.

JOSÉ FIGUERES FERRER (President, November 8, 1953–May 8, 1958). *See earlier entry under Heads of State.*

MARIO ECHANDI JIMÉNÉZ (President, May 8, 1958–May 8, 1962). Mario Echandi Jiménez was born in 1915. He was educated at the University of Costa Rica, where he received a degree in law. In 1938 he opened a successful law practice. He entered politics and served as secretary-general of the National Union party in 1947. Echandi was named Costa Rica's minister to the United States in 1950. The following year he was appointed foreign minister in the government of Otillio Ulate Blanco. Echandi served as a leader of the opposition in the National Assembly during the presidency of José Figueres Ferrer from 1953. Echandi was the conservative National Union party's presidential candidate in the elections of 1958. He was victorious and took office on May 8, 1958. Echandi left in place Figueres's social reform legislation. He also encouraged industry and trade, though he was hampered by the opposition's control of the National Assembly. On May 8, 1962, he completed his term of office and resumed his legal career. Echandi was again the National Union candidate for president in the elections of 1970, but was defeated by José Figueres Ferrer. Echandi subsequently founded the conservative National Movement. He again campaigned for the presidency in 1978, but badly trailed the major party nominees.

FRANCISCO J. ORLICH BOLMARICH (President, May 8, 1962–May 8, 1966). Francisco José Orlich Bolmarich was born in San Ramon on March 10, 1907.

He was a successful manager of his family's farming interests. In 1940 he was elected to the Costa Rican National Assembly. He took part in the revolt in 1948 against the attempt by the government of Teodoro Picado Michalski to thwart the results of the presidential election of that year. Orlich became closely associated with José Figueres Ferrer, a leader of the revolt. Orlich was defeated by Mario Echandi Jiménéz in the election to succeed Figueres as president in 1958. Orlich was again the candidate of the National Liberation party in the presidential election of 1962. He was victorious and assumed office on May 8, 1962. He worked to improve his country's standard of living by taking advantage of financial assistance from the United States under the Alliance for Progress program. He completed his term of office on May 8, 1966. Orlich died of cancer in San Jose at the age of 62 on October 29, 1969.

JOSÉ JOAQUÍN TREJOS FERNÁNDEZ (President, May 8, 1966–May 8, 1970). José Joaquín Trejos Fernández was born in San Jose on April 18, 1916. He was educated at the University of Chicago in the United States, where he received a degree in economics. He returned to Costa Rica to teach at the University of Costa Rica in 1952. Trejos was chosen by a coalition of opposition parties to be the presidential candidate of the National Unification Coalition party in 1966. He narrowly defeated the National Liberation party candidate, Daniel Oduber Quiros, and was sworn into office on May 8, 1966. Trejos met with some success in his effort to stabilize Costa Rica's economy and completed his term of office on May 8, 1970. He retired from politics and returned to his teaching career.

JOSÉ FIGUERES FERRER (President, May 8, 1970–May 8, 1974). *See earlier entry under Heads of State.*

DANIEL ODUBER QUIROS (President, May 8, 1974–May 8, 1978). Daniel Oduber Quiros was born in San Jose on August 25, 1921. After attending the University of Costa Rica, where he received a degree in law, he opened a legal practice in 1945. Oduber supported the rebellion against the government led by José Figueres Ferrer in 1948. Oduber joined the National Liberation party in 1951 and became secretary-general of the party in 1956. He gave up his law career and was elected to the National Assembly in 1958. Oduber was defeated for his party's presidential nomination in 1961. He served in the government of Francisco Orlich Bolmarich as foreign minister from 1962 until 1964. Oduber was his party's candidate for president in 1966, but was narrowly defeated by José Joaquín Trejos Fernández. Oduber was selected as president of the National Liberation party and supported Figueres for President in 1970. He returned to serve in the National Assembly later in the year. He was subsequently elected president of the National Assembly and served until March of 1973. Oduber was again nominated for the presidency in 1974. He won the election in February of 1974 and took office on May 8, 1974. Oduber's government granted legal status to the Communist party in 1975, and Costa Rica restored diplomatic relations with Cuba in 1977. The Costa Rican economy prospered under Oduber's administration. He completed his term of office on May 8, 1978.

RODRIGO CARAZO ODIO (President, May 8, 1978–May 8, 1982). Rodrigo Carazo Odio was born in Cartago on December 27, 1926. He was educated locally and was employed by the Central Bank of Costa Rica. In the 1950s he entered politics as a member of the National Liberation party (PLN). Carazo resigned from the PLN to join the opposition in 1969. He was the candidate of a coalition of opposition parties in the presidential elections in 1978. Carazo attacked the PLN for allowing fugitive financier Robert Vesco to remain in the country. Carazo defeated PLN candidate Luis Alberto Monge Alvarez and took office on May 8, 1978. Vesco left Costa Rica shortly after Carazo's victory. Costa Rica's relationship with Nicaragua deteriorated, and diplomatic relations were severed in November of 1978. Severe economic problems resulted in a loss of support for Carazo's government. The PLN was returned to power in the elections in 1982, and Carazo relinquished office on May 8, 1982. Carazo remained active in politics and was instrumental in the formation of the opposition Social Christian Unity party in 1983.

LUIS ALBERTO MONGE ALVAREZ (President, May 8, 1982–May 8, 1986). Luis Alberto Monge Alvarez was born in Palmares on December 28, 1925. He was educated at San Jose University. He became active with the labor movement and served with the International Labor Organization as a consultant on Latin American affairs from 1950 until 1952. Monge became secretary-general of the Inter-American Labor Organization in Mexico the following year and served until 1957. He was also active in the National Liberation party and was elected to the National Assembly in 1958. Monge served as president of the National Assembly from 1970 until 1974. He was the party's nominee in the presidential election in 1978 and was defeated by Rodrigo Carazo Odio. Monge defeated United party candidate Rafael Angel Calderon Fournier in the election in 1982 and was sworn in as president on May 8, 1982. Monge instituted a program of economic austerity to improve Costa Rica's economy. Costa Rica's relationship with the Sandinista government of Nicaragua deteriorated in 1984 and several border skirmishes occurred. Monge was a popular leader and completed his term of office on May 8, 1986.

OSCAR ARIAS SÁNCHEZ (President, May 8, 1986–May 8, 1990). Oscar Arias Sánchez was born to a wealthy family in Heredia on September 13, 1941. He was educated at Harvard University and the University of Costa Rica, where he studied law and political science. Arias became active in the National Liberation party and supported Daniel Oduber Quiros in his unsuccessful presidential campaign in 1966. Arias then continued his education in England. He returned to Costa Rica in 1969 to teach at the University of Costa Rica until 1972. Arias was appointed minister of national planning in the cabinet of José Figueres Ferrer in August of 1972 and remained in the cabinet in the subsequent government of Daniel Oduber. Arias left the cabinet in July of 1977. He was elected to the National Assembly in February of the following year. He was a leading critic of conservative President Rodrigo Carazo Odio. Arias was elected secretary-general of the National Liberation party in July of 1979. He left the National Assembly to assist Luis Alberto Monge in his campaign for the presidency in 1981. Arias stepped down as party leader to seek the presidential nomination in January of 1984. He led his party to victory against Rafael Angel Calderon Fournier and took office on May 8, 1986. Arias refused to allow United States–backed Nicaraguan Contra rebels to operate in Costa Rica and initiated a Latin American conference to discuss a peace settlement for the region. The meeting took place in February of 1987 and resulted in the formulation of the "Arias Plan." The regional peace proposal was supported by the governments of Costa Rica, Nicaragua, El Salvador, Honduras, and Guatemala. Arias received the 1987 Nobel Peace Prize for his efforts to bring peace to the region. Arias promoted privatization and foreign trade to reduce the trade deficit as part of his domestic policy. Arias completed his term of office on May 8, 1990, and relinquished the presidency to Rafael Angel Calderon Fournier.

RAFAEL ANGEL CALDERON FOUR-NIER (President, May 8, 1990–). Rafael Angel Calderon Fournier was born in Nicaragua in 1949. His father was Rafael Calderon Guardia, who served as Costa Rica's president from 1940 until 1944. Calderon was educated as a lawyer. He was active in the Social Christian Unity party and served in the cabinet of Rodrigo Carazo Odio as minister of foreign affairs. Calderon was his party's unsuccessful candidate for president in 1982 and 1986. He defeated National Liberation party nominee Carlos Manuel Castillo in the presidential election in February of 1990. Calderon took office on May 8, 1990, and instituted austerity measures to reduce the public deficit. Costa Rica's troubled economy contributed to growing public unrest during Calderon's term of office.

Croatia, Republic of
(Republika Hrvatska)

Croatia is a country in southeastern Europe. It declared its independence from Yugoslavia on June 25, 1991.

HEAD OF STATE

FRANJO TUDJMAN (President, May 30, 1990–). Franjo Tudjman was born in 1922. A member of the Croat Democratic Union, he was elected president by the parliament on May 30, 1990, and succeeded Ivo Latin. In December of 1990 a new constitution was adopted to proclaim Croatia's right to secede from federal Yugoslavia and form an independent nation. In a referendum on May 19, 1991, a large majority of the voters supported Croatia becoming an independent country. Fighting broke out in Serbian areas of Croatia, however, where the residents desired a union with Serbia. Croatian and Serbian forces fought throughout 1991, and the unrest ended only with the arrival of a United Nations peacekeeping force in early 1992.

HEADS OF GOVERNMENT

FRANJO GREGURIĆ (Premier, July 18, 1991–September 8, 1992). Franjo Gregurić, a member of the Croatian Democratic Union, was elected premier by the Croatian Assembly on July 18, 1991, succeeding Josip Manolic. Gregurić was replaced by Hrvoje Sarinic on September 8, 1992.

HRVOJE SARINIC (Premier, September 8, 1992–). Hrvoje Sarinic was selected as premier of Croatia following the victory of the Croatian Democratic Union in parliamentary elections in August of 1992. Sarinic took office on September 8, 1992.

Cuba, Republic of
(República de Cuba)

Cuba is an island in the Caribbean Sea. It was granted indepen-dence from Spain on May 20, 1902.

HEADS OF STATE

RAMÓN GRAU SAN MARTIN (President, October 10, 1944–October 10, 1948). Ramón Grau San Martin was born in Pinar del Rio on September 13, 1882. He attended the University of Havana, where he received a medical degree in 1908. He subsequently continued his studies throughout Europe before returning to the University of Havana to serve on the faculty. Grau became involved in politics during a campus demonstration against General Gerardo Machado, the dictator of Cuba. He resigned his position in solidarity with the students. He was arrested by the Machado government in 1929. When he was released shortly thereafter, he went to the United States. Machado was ousted in August of 1933, and his successor, Carlos Manuel de Cespedes, was overthrown the following month. Grau was offered the presidency by the ruling military junta and took office on September 10, 1933. During his brief term of office, he instituted a progressive labor policy, granted voting rights for women, and attacked the Platt Amendment, which granted the United States the right to intervene in Cuban affairs. He also demanded that businesses operating in Cuba must have a fifty percent Cuban work force. The United States refused to recognize Grau's government, and he was ousted by his chief of staff, Fulgencio Batista y Zaldivar, on January 15, 1934. Grau was a critic of Batista and the succession of puppet-presidents he installed. Grau challenged Batista in the presidential election of 1940 and

was defeated, though allegations of election fraud were made. Batista chose not to run for reelection in 1944, and Grau was again the candidate of the opposition. He defeated Batista's designated successor, Carlos Saladrigas Zayas, and took office on October 10, 1944. Grau implemented an economic policy that increased workers' wages and nationalized some businesses. His term of office was also marked by graft and corruption. Grau was ineligible to succeed himself under the Cuban constitution, and he relinquished office to his elected successor, Carlos Prío Socarrás, on October 10, 1948. When Prío Socarrás was ousted by Batista four years later, Grau was again a leading critic of the regime. Batista was ousted by Fidel Castro in January of 1959, and Grau was virtually ignored by the new revolutionary regime. He lived in seclusion in Havana until his death from cancer at the age of 86 on July 28, 1969.

CARLOS PRÍO SOCARRÁS (President, October 10, 1948–March 10, 1952). Carlos Prío Socarrás was born in Bahia Honda on July 14, 1903. He graduated from the University of Havana in 1927. He became active in the opposition to Cuban dictator Gerardo Machado while a student. Prío was arrested by the Machado government on several occasions and was imprisoned for two years. He went to the United States after his release to continue his revolutionary activities against Machado. He returned to Cuba following Machado's overthrow in 1933 and served in the government of Ramón Grau San Martin later in the year. Grau was overthrown in 1944, and Prío organized the Cuban Revolutionary party in opposition to the government of Carlos Mendieta. Prío went into exile in Mexico and the United States. He returned to Cuba in 1939 after some political liberties were restored in the country. He was elected to the National Assembly in 1939 and was elected to the Senate the following year. Prío was named prime minister in 1945 in the government of Grau, who had been elected president the previous year. Prío's cabinet resigned on May 1, 1947, and he was named minister of labor in the new cabinet. Prío was a candidate to succeed Grau in 1948. He defeated Ricardo Nunez Portuonodo and several others to become president on October 10, 1948. He strongly respected the civil liberties of the Cuban people, but his administration was criticized for widespread corruption. Prío was ousted in a military coup led by Fulgencio Batista on March 10, 1952. Prío went into exile in the United States. He met with revolutionary leader Fidel Castro in 1956 and agreed to give financial support to his rebellion. Prío returned to Cuba following Batista's ouster in 1959, but later broke with Castro over the issue of Communism. Prío again went into exile in the United States, where he became a leader of the anti–Castro Cuban community in Miami. He remained an outspoken critic of the Castro regime. Prío died at his home in Miami of a self-inflicted gunshot wound to his chest on April 6, 1977. He was reportedly despondent over personal and financial difficulties.

FULGENCIO BATISTA Y ZALDIVAR (President, March 10, 1952–January 1, 1959). Fulgencio Batista y Zaldívar was born in Banes, Oriente Province, on January 16, 1901. He attended a missionary school and worked in a variety of jobs before entering the Cuban National Army in 1921. He attended night school and was promoted to sergeant first class. In 1928 he was assigned as a stenographer at army headquarters. Batista served as chief clerk at the military trials of political opponents of Cuban dictator General Gerardo Machado. He soon became involved in a conspiracy of military men plotting Machado's ouster. Machado fled Cuba after a general strike spurred a coup against the dictator in 1933. Manuel de Cespedes became provisional president, but he was unable to settle the rampant disorder in the country. Batista led a group of army sergeants in a coup to oust the provisional government on September 4, 1933. The military junta installed Ramón Grau San Martin as president, and Batista was made chief of staff of the army with the rank of colonel. When the Grau regime was refused recognition by the United States, Batista removed Grau from office. Carlos Hevia and Manuel Marquez Sterling served as presidents for periods of several days each before Batista installed Carlos Mendieta as president on January 18, 1934. Batista remained largely in control of the government. Mendieta was replaced by Jose A. Barnet in December of 1935, who was followed by Miguel Mariano Gomez in May of 1936. Gomez gave way to Federico Laredo Bru in December of 1936. Batista sponsored a new constitution in 1940 that liberalized Cuba's political process. He allowed the formation of opposition parties and declared himself a candidate in the presidential election to be held that year. Batista defeated Ramón Grau San Martin and took office as president on October 10, 1940. He supported the Allies during World War II and initiated some social reforms. Since he was barred by the constitution from seeking a second term, he supported the candidacy of Carlos Saladrigas Zayas in the election of 1944. Saladrigas was defeated by

Grau, and Batista stepped down from office on October 10, 1944. He left Cuba and eventually settled in Florida. He returned to Cuba in 1948 to win an election to the Senate. Batista announced his candidacy for president in the 1952 election and accused the government of President Carlos Prío Socarrás of corruption. He staged a military coup on March 10, 1952, and ousted Prío from office. Batista was again sworn into office as president. He clamped down on political dissidents, canceled elections, and banned strikes. Cuba became a tourist resort and gambling center, but Batista's government was charged with corruption and abuse of power. Batista was faced with growing discontent among the populace throughout the 1950s. Fidel Castro launched a guerrilla revolt against the government in December of 1956. The rebellion eventually reached Havana, and Batista fled the country on January 1, 1959. He went into exile and settled in Estoril, Portugal. He died of a heart attack at the age of 72 in Guadalmina, Spain, on August 6, 1973.

MANUEL URRUTÍA LLEO (President, January 2, 1959–July 17, 1959). Manuel Urrutía Lleo was born in Yaguajay, Las Villas Province, on December 8, 1901. He received a law degree from the University of Havana in 1923. In 1928 he was appointed a municipal judge, and he rose through the ranks of the Cuban judiciary. Urrutía retained his position during the years Fulgencio Batista ruled Cuba, despite his opposition to the dictator. He attacked Batista's seizure of power in 1952 and ruled that the takeover was illegal. Urrutía was forced to resign his office in 1957 and went into exile in Mexico and the United States. He supported the ouster of Batista by the rebellion led by Fidel Castro in January of 1959 and returned to Cuba to become provisional president on January 2, 1959. Shortly after taking office, Urrutía condemned Communist influ-

ences in the new government. He was dismissed by Castro and charged with treason on July 17, 1959. He spent several years under house arrest before seeking political asylum at the Venezuelan and Mexican embassies. In 1963 he was allowed to leave the country, and he went into exile in the United States. Urrutía became a vocal critic of the Castro regime and formed the Democratic Revolutionary Alliance in 1964. He was distrusted by other members of the Cuban exile community, however, because of the high position he had held in the Castro government. He withdrew from active politics and accepted several teaching positions. He died in New York City at the age of 79 on July 4, 1981.

OSVALDO DÓRTICOS TORRADO (President, July 17, 1959–December 2, 1976). Osvaldo Dórticos Torrado was born in Cienfuegos, Las Villas Province, on April 17, 1919. He graduated from the University of Havana in 1937. He became active in the revolutionary movement in 1939, when he organized a student strike in Cienfuegos. In 1941 Dórticos received a law degree from the University of Havana and opened a practice. He became a supporter of Fidel Castro's rebellion against President Fulgencio Batista in the 1950s. Dórticos was imprisoned by the Batista government on several occasions. He led the revolutionary underground in Cienfuegos from 1957 until his arrest in December of 1958. He escaped from prison and went to Mexico, where he remained until Batista was overthrown by the rebellion. Dórticos returned to Cuba in January of 1959 to serve as minister of laws of the revolution in the provisional government. He was selected by Castro to succeed Manuel Urrutía Lleo as president on July 17, 1959. The position of president was largely a figurehead one, but Dórticos exercised considerable influence on Cuban economic policies. He took control of the Ministry of the Economy and the

Central Planning Board in 1963. He was named to the Secretariat of the Central Committee of the Cuban Communist party in 1965. Dórticos resigned as president on December 2, 1976, when Castro merged the offices of president and prime minister. He remained a leading advisor to Castro until his death. He shot and killed himself in Havana, Cuba, on June 23, 1983. He was reportedly suffering from a painful spinal ailment and was depressed over the recent death of a close friend.

FIDEL CASTRO RUZ (President, December 3, 1976–). Fidel Castro Ruz was born near Biran, Oriente Province, on August 13, 1927. He worked on his family's sugar cane plantation when he was boy. He was educated at several Jesuit institutions before entering the University of Havana in 1945. Castro became involved in revolutionary politics before he received his doctorate in law in 1950. He opened a law practice in Havana and planned his candidacy for the Cuban Parliament in 1952. The elections of that year were canceled following the coup led by Fulgencio Batista that ousted the elected president, Carlos Prío Socarrás. Castro became an organizer of a group of rebels opposed to Batista's illegal usurpation of power. Castro led a group of approximately 160 men against an army barracks in Santiago de Cuba on July 26, 1953, in the hopes of sparking a general rebellion. The revolutionary group was crushed, and Castro was captured. He was imprisoned until May of 1955, when he was released during a general amnesty. He left the country for Mexico City, where he tried to organize Cuban exiles into a military force against Batista's government. Castro returned to Cuba aboard a yacht with a small invasion force in December of 1956 and landed in Oriente Province. His group was badly defeated by the Cuban military, and Castro and the survivors took to the Sierra Maestra mountains. They con-

ducted guerrilla raids against the government throughout 1957. The rebellion rapidly grew and began achieving victories against the forces of Batista. Castro declared total war against the regime in April of 1958, and the rebels received much support from resistance movements within the major cities. Batista fled the capital on January 1, 1959, and Castro triumphantly entered Havana the following day. Castro installed a civilian provisional government and became commander in chief of the armed forces. The government arrested numerous supporters of the ousted dictator and legalized the Cuban Communist party. Castro became prime minister in the government on February 16, 1959. The relationship between Cuba and the United States deteriorated under Castro's leadership. Castro requested, and received, financial support from the Soviet Union and seized most American-owned properties in Cuba. The United States severed diplomatic relations with Cuba in January of 1961. The following April the United States Central Intelligence Agency supported a group of Cuban exiles seeking to oust the Castro regime. The invasion force landed on Cuba's southern coast, and its members were soundly defeated by Castro's army. The incident became known as the "Bay of Pigs." The following month Castro declared Cuba a Socialist country and proclaimed his allegiance to Marxist-Leninist ideals later in the year. Cuba again clashed with the United States in October of 1962 when Soviet long-range missiles were detected on Cuban soil. The United States government of President John F. Kennedy demanded the removal of the Soviet missiles and established a blockade of Cuba. An agreement was reached between the Soviet Union and the United States that resulted in the removal of the weapons, though Castro criticized Nikita Khrushchev, the Soviet leader, for not gaining more concessions for Cuba during the negotiations. Castro also supported revolutionary groups in other Latin American countries. The Organization of American States (OAS) imposed diplomatic and commercial sanctions on Cuba in 1964. Castro's longtime associate, Che Guevara, was killed in Bolivia in October of 1967 while leading a rebellion there. Castro subsequently decreased his sponsorship of Latin revolutionary groups, and the OAS lifted sanctions in 1974 to allow its member countries to normalize relations with Cuba if they chose. Castro sent Cuban troops to Angola in 1975 to support the Popular Liberation Movement of Angola (MPLA), the Soviet-supported combatant in the Angolan Civil War. Castro restructured the Cuban government in 1976 and created the Council of State. He merged the duties of the prime minister with the president and became president of the Council of State on December 3, 1976. In 1981 Castro organized an exodus of Cuban nationals wishing to leave the country that resulted in over 100,000 Cubans heading for Florida by boat. Cuba's relations with the United States again suffered when the Communist-led government of Grenada was overthrown by a U.S.-led military force in October of 1983. The withdrawal of Cuban troops from Angola was initiated in December of 1988, and Cuban troops fighting in Ethiopia also returned home. The Cuban economy faced a major blow following the withdrawal of Soviet financial support in the early 1990s. Despite the fall of Communist regimes throughout Europe, Castro continued to defend Marxist-Lenininst policies and remained in undisputed control of Cuba.

HEADS OF GOVERNMENT

MANUEL DE VARONA (Prime Minister, October 10, 1948–October 6, 1950). Manuel Antonio de Varona was born in Camaguey on November 25, 1908. He became politically active as an outspoken opponent of the dictatorship of Gerardo Machado. He was arrested and exiled on several occasions before Machado's ouster in 1933. De Varona subsequently opposed the first government of Fulgencio Batista and again was arrested and exiled. He returned to Cuba following Batista's fall and attended the University of Havana, where he received a degree in law. He was elected to Congress in 1940 and became Senate majority leader in 1944. De Varona was selected by President Carlos Prío Socarrás to serve as prime minister on October 10, 1948. He retained the position until October 6, 1950, when he returned to the Senate as president. Batista returned to power in 1952, and de Varona again opposed his government. He was sent into exile again and joined with the forces that sought to overthrow the dictator. When Batista was overthrown by Fidel Castro, de Varona returned to Cuba. He was soon disillusioned with the Castro regime and returned to exile in the United States. He became a leading exile voice against Castro's government and formed the Cuban Democratic Revolutionary Force in 1960. De Varona was a planner of the unsuccessful Bay of Pigs invasion of Cuba in 1961. He was scheduled to lead a provisional government in Cuba had the United States–backed coup ousted Castro. Instead de Varona remained in exile until his death by cancer in Miami on October 29, 1992.

FELIX LANCIS (Prime Minister, October 6, 1950–October 1, 1951). Felix Lancis represented Havana in the Cuban Senate. He was selected as prime minister on October 6, 1950. President Prío Socarrás shifted him to the Education Ministry on October 1, 1951.

OSCAR GANS Y LOPEZ MARTINEZ (Prime Minister, October 1, 1951– March 7, 1952). Oscar Gans y Lopez Martinez was born in Havana on May 12, 1903. He was educated at Havana University, where he received a doctorate of law. He joined the diplomatic corps and served as ambassador to Mexico in 1943. Gans y Lopez Martinez was then named to the cabinet as minister of labor. He served as Cuba's delegate to the United Nations Charter Committee in San Francisco in 1945. He was named ambassador to Italy in 1946 and was subsequently appointed ambassador to Argentina. Gans y Lopez Martinez also held several cabinet positions, including minister of justice and foreign affairs. He served as ambassador to the United States from 1949 until 1950. The following year he was named prime minister under President Carlos Prío Socarrás on October 1, 1951. Gans y Lopez Martinez relinquished his position on March 7, 1952, shortly before the coup led by Fulgencio Batista ousted the Prío government. He went into exile in Mexico in 1962 and died in Mexico City on December 4, 1965.

JOSÉ MIRÓ CARDONA (Prime Minister, January 6, 1959–February 13, 1959). José Miró Cardona was born in Havana in 1902. He received a law degree from the University of Havana and opened a practice in Havana in 1938. He gained a reputation as a leading expert on penal law and served on the faculty at the University of Havana. Miró Cardona kept his distance from partisan politics until the mid-1950s, when he went into opposition against the regime of Fulgencio Batista. He called upon Batista to resign in March of 1958 and was ordered arrested. He escaped to Miami, Florida, in May of 1958 and joined forces with the rebellion led by Fidel Castro. Miró Cardona returned to Cuba following the ouster of Batista and was appointed prime minister in the provisional government on January 6, 1959. He attempted to reform the Cuban judicial system, but found that he was powerless without the approval of Castro. He resigned as prime minister on February 13, 1959. Miró Cardona declined Castro's nomination to become president of Cuba in July of 1959. He accepted the position of ambassador to Spain, but was recalled in January of 1960. He was appointed ambassador to the United States the following May. Miró Cardona resigned his position before assuming the post and took refuge in the Argentine Embassy. He was allowed to go into exile in the United States in October of 1960, and he settled in Miami, Florida. He became a leader of the anti–Castro Cuban exiles and was selected president of the Cuban Revolutionary Council. This organization helped to plan the strategy for the unsuccessful Bay of Pigs invasion of Cuba in 1961. Miró Cardona resigned from the Council in 1963 and accused the United States of betraying its promise to the Cuban people, after his demands were ignored for more assistance to overthrow Castro. He later moved to Puerto Rico, where he served on the faculty of the University of Puerto Rico School of Law. He died of a heart attack in San Juan, Puerto Rico, at the age of 71 on April 10, 1974.

FIDEL CASTRO RUZ (Prime Minister, February 16, 1959–December 3, 1976). *See entry under Heads of State.*

Cyprus, Republic of

(Dimokratia Kyprou)

Cyprus is an island in the eastern Mediterranean Sea. It was granted independence from Great Britain on August 16, 1960.

HEADS OF STATE

MAKARIOS III (President, August 16, 1960–July 15, 1974). Makarios III was born Michael Khristodolou Mouskos in Ano Panayia on August 13, 1913. He was educated locally and at Kykkos Abbey. In 1938 he was ordained a deacon and was sent to the University of Athens Theological College in Greece. Makarios returned to Kykkos Abbey upon graduation in 1943 and was ordained a priest in the Greek Orthodox church three years later. He continued his studies at Boston University in the United States before returning to Cyprus to become bishop of Kition in April of 1948. In October of 1950 he was selected as archbishop and ethnarch of Cyprus, and assumed the name Makarios III. The archbishop became involved in the campaign for Cypriot independence from Great Britain in the early 1950s. Makarios advocated enosis, or union, with Greece, despite a large Turkish minority that opposed the idea. He attended numerous international conferences to promote Cypriot self-determination. A Cypriot guerrilla organization known as EOKA was formed by General George Grivas in 1955. The British authorities suspected Makarios of being involved with the terrorist organization and deported him to the Seychelles Islands in March of 1956. Makarios was released from exile the following year and went to Athens, where he negotiated Cypriot independence from Great Britain. He returned to Cyprus in March of 1959 and was elected president the following December. He took office following the proclamation of independence on August 16, 1960. The independence agreement forbad union between Cyprus and Greece and provided for political representation for the Turkish minority. Fighting between Greek and Turkish Cypriots broke out on Christmas in 1963. United Nations troops were sent to the island to main-

tain order and prevent an invasion by Turkey. Makarios invited General Grivas, who had been in exile in Greece since independence, to return to Cyprus to organize the Cypriot national guard. The Greek and Turkish Cypriots again clashed in 1967, and an invasion by Turkey was halted on the condition that Grivas again leave the country. Makarios had abandoned the idea of union with Greece following the military coup in Greece in 1967. Makarios was reelected president in 1968 and improved Cypriot relations with the Eastern bloc. The right-wing Greek junta began plotting the archbishop's ouster. General Grivas returned to Cyprus in late 1971 to lead EOKA-B, a guerrilla organization dedicated to the removal of Makarios. Makarios survived several assassination attempts planned by EOKA-B and was reelected to the presidency in 1973. When Grivas died in 1974, Makarios moved against the guerrillas. He demanded the removal of Greek officers from the island. The Greek military junta responded by organizing a coup against the archbishop. Makarios escaped an assassination attempt and fled to a British military base on July 15, 1974. The Greek-installed government was ousted on July 23, 1974, following an invasion by Turkey. The military junta in Greece also collapsed as a result of the war. Makarios returned to Cyprus to resume the presidency on December 7, 1974. Turkish forces remained in control of the northern area of Cyprus, and negotiations between Makarios and Turkish Cypriot leader Rauf Denktaş did little to settle the situation. The archbishop suffered a minor heart attack in April of 1977 and suffered a second attack in August. Makarios died at the age of 63 at the archbishop's palace in Nicosia on August 3, 1977.

NIKOS SAMPSON (President, July 15, 1974–July 23, 1974). Nikos Giorgades Sampson was born in Cyprus on December 16, 1935. He fought with General George Grivas in EOKA, the Cypriot nationalist guerrilla organization. Sampson led a terrorist assassination squad against the British during the 1950s. He was captured by the colonial authorities and sentenced to death, but he was released following an amnesty granted shortly before independence. He became a wealthy businessman after Cypriot independence in 1960 and was elected to the Parliament. Sampson also served as publisher of several right-wing pro-Greek Cypriot newspapers. He was chosen to serve as president of a provisional government following a Greek-supported coup that ousted Archbishop Makarios on July 15, 1974. Sampson's government resigned a week later on July 23, 1974, after Turkish troops invaded Cyprus. Sampson was arrested in March of 1976 on charges of using armed forces against the Makarios government during the coup. He remained the publisher of right-wing newspapers.

GLAFKOS CLERIDES (President, July 23, 1974–December 7, 1974). Glafkos John Clerides was born in Nicosia on April 24, 1919. He was educated in London and served in the British Royal Air Force during World War II. In 1942 he was captured by the Germans and remained a prisoner of war until the conclusion of World War II. In 1951 he established a successful law practice in Cyprus and represented many captured EOKA guerrillas during the battle for Cypriot independence in the 1950s. Clerides represented the Greek Cypriots at meetings of the Constitutional Commission from 1959 and served in the pre-independence government as minister of justice from 1959 until 1960. He was elected president of the House of Representatives following independence in August of 1960. He was an opponent of enosis, or union,

with Greece, and instead favored complete independence for Cyprus. Clerides formed the United National party in 1969. He became interim president of Cyprus on July 23, 1974, following the resignation of the pro-Greek government that had been established following a coup against Archbishop Makarios III the previous week. Clerides relinquished office following the return of Makarios on December 7, 1974. He represented the interests of Greek Cypriots at United Nations–sponsored talks with the Turkish Cypriot leader Rauf Denktas from 1975 until 1976. Clerides founded the pro-Western Democratic Rally party in May of 1976, serving as the party's leader. He withdrew as a candidate for president in January of 1978, following the kidnaping of President Spyros Kyprianou's son by right-wing terrorists. He was an unsuccessful candidate in presidential elections in 1983 and 1988.

MAKARIOS III (President, December 7, 1974–August 3, 1977). *See earlier entry under Heads of State.*

SPYROS KYPRIANOU (President, August 3, 1977–February 28, 1988). Spyros Kyprianou was born in Limassol on October 18, 1932. He was educated in Great Britain, where he received a degree in law. In the early 1950s he returned to Cyprus to serve as a public relations officer for Archbishop Makarios III. Kyprianou was named foreign minister by Makarios in the government of independent Cyprus in 1960. He retained his position until 1972, when he resigned at the insistence of the government of Greece. Kyprianou was elected to the House of Representatives in September of 1976 as a member of the Democratic Front. He was subsequently elected president of the House. He became acting president of Cyprus following the death of Makarios on August 3, 1977. Kyprianou was confirmed as president by the

House of Representatives on August 31, 1977. Kyprianou's 21-year-old son was kidnapped by right-wing EOKA-B terrorists in December of 1977. His son was released despite Kyprianou's refusal to negotiate with the terrorists. Kyprianou also rejected suggestions of a permanent division between the Greek and Turkish areas of Cyprus. He was reelected president unopposed in elections in January of 1978 and again won reelection in February of 1983. The Turkish-controlled area of Cyprus declared its independence as the Turkish Republic of Northern Cyprus in November of 1983. Kyprianou was blamed for the breakdown in negotiations between the Greek and Turkish Cypriots and was defeated in presidential elections in February of 1988. He relinquished office to George Vassiliou on February 28, 1988.

GEORGE VASSILIOU (President, February 28, 1988–). George Vassos

Vassiliou was born in Famagusta on May 21, 1931. He accompanied his family to Hungary after World War II and later attended medical school at the University of Geneva. He also attended the University of Vienna and the University of London, where he studied economics and marketing. Vassiliou returned to Cyprus in 1962 to found a successful marketing research business. He became a millionaire and became involved with the Progressive Party of the Working Class (AKEL). Vassiliou was a candidate for president of Cyprus with the support of AKEL and the Liberal party. He defeated Glafcos Clerides in a runoff in February of 1988. Vassiliou took office as president on February 28, 1988 and pledged to seek the reunification of the Greek and Turkish areas of Cyprus. Subsequent negotiations with Turkish Cypriot leader Rauf Denktas were inconclusive.

Cyprus, Turkish Republic of Northern

(Kuzey Kibris Turk Cumhuriyeti)

HEAD OF STATE

RAUF DENKTAŞ (President, November 15, 1983–). Rauf R. Denktaş was born in Ktima on January 27, 1924. He studied law in Great Britain and opened a legal practice in Nicosia in 1947. He served as acting solicitor general in the colonial government from 1956 until 1958. Denktaş then became president of the Turkish Cypriot Associations and served until 1960. He was elected president of the Turkish Communal Chamber in 1960. Denktaş was expelled from Cyprus and went into exile in Turkey in 1964. He returned to Cyprus in 1967, but was arrested and

deported. In April of 1968 he was allowed to return to Cyprus, and he became vice president of the Turkish Cypriot Transitional Administration. The Turkish-dominated northern area of Cyprus was captured by Turkish troops in July of 1974, following a Greek-led coup in Cyprus. The Turkish Federated State of Cyprus was established on February 13, 1975, and Denktaş was elected president by the Executive Council and Legislative Assembly. When the area proclaimed its secession from Cyprus on November 15, 1983, Denktaş remained president. He conducted negotiations with Cypriot president Spyros Kyprianou, but the two leaders were unable to reach an accord on reunification of Cyprus. Denktaş was reelected president in April of 1990.

Czechoslovakia

(Czech and Slovak Federative Republic)

Czechoslovakia is a country in central Europe. It received independence from the Austro-Hungarian Empire on October 28, 1918. Czechoslovakia divided into the Czech Republic and Slovakia on January 1, 1993.

HEADS OF STATE

EDUARD BENEŠ (President, July 23, 1940–June 7, 1948). Eduard Beneš was born in Kozlany on May 28, 1884. He attended the Royal Czech College at Vinohrady and Charles University, where he received a degree in philosophy. He continued his education in Paris, where he received a doctorate in sociology at the Sorbonne. In 1909 He returned to Czechoslovakia and joined the Progressive party led by Thomas Masaryk. He joined with Masaryk after the start of World War I in 1914 to campaign for the liberation of Czechoslovakia from Austrian rule. Beneš became secretary-general of the Czechoslovak National Council in January of 1916. This council served as the forerunner of the Czech provisional government established on October 14, 1918. Beneš served as foreign minister and led the Czech delegation to the Paris peace conference the following year. He remained foreign minister in the Czech republic government. He also served as premier from September 27, 1921, until October 7, 1922. Beneš led the Czech delegation to the League of Nations, and in 1929 he entered his government into an alliance with Romania and Yugoslavia known as the Little Entente. He became president of Czechoslovakia on December 18, 1935, and succeeded the retiring Masaryk. Beneš was faced with the threat of German aggression in 1938, when Adolf Hitler demanded that the German-speaking districts of Czechoslovakia be ceded to Germany. The Munich Agreement between Hitler and Great Britain's prime minister Neville Chamberlain offered little recourse for Beneš but to grant Hitler's demands. He resigned as president on October 5, 1938, and went into exile in France. Following the fall of France, Beneš established a Czech government-in-exile in Great Britain and served as its president from July 23, 1940. He signed a treaty with the Soviet Union in 1943 and attempted to serve as an arbitrator on issues of dispute between Moscow and the West. Beneš became president of the Czech provisional government established in Kosice on March 17, 1945. His health failed when he suffered several strokes in 1947. The Communists in the Czech government, led by Premier Klement Gottwald, demanded that a Communist-dominated government be established in February of 1948. Beneš refused to sign the new Czech constitution and resigned office on June 7, 1948. Three months later, on September 3, 1948, he died of a stroke at the age of 64 at his home in Sezimovo Usti.

KLEMENT GOTTWALD (President, June 7, 1948–March 14, 1953). Klement Gottwald was born in Dedidocz, Moravia, on November 23, 1896. He worked as a farm laborer as a child and was sent to Vienna to learn carpentry at the age of 12. A few years later he joined the Czechoslovak Social Democratic Youth organization. Gottwald was drafted into the Austrian army, where he served in an artillery regiment during World War I. He was wounded in action in Italy and deserted while on leave. In October of 1918 he joined the new Czech army and became active in the Social Democratic party. Gottwald was a founding member of the Czechoslovak Communist party in 1921 and served as editor of the party newspaper. He was elected to the party's central committee in 1925. The following year he went to Prague to serve on the party Politburo. Gottwald also served as director of the party's agitation and propaganda department. He was elected general secretary of the party in 1927. The following year he was elected to the Czech Parliament. Gottwald encouraged civil disturbances among miners and peasants during the early 1930s. He also organized international brigades to fight in the Spanish Civil War in 1936. Gottwald went to Moscow following the Munich Agreement in October of 1938 that gave Nazi Germany a free hand in Czechoslovakia. He remained there throughout the war. Gottwald served as vice-premier in the coalition provisional government formed in Kosice after the liberation of Czechoslovakia in 1945. He was selected as premier in elections held the following year and took office on July 3, 1946. The possibility of a defeat for the Communist party in the elections of 1948 prompted Gottwald to use action committees composed of workers and peasants to take control of the government in February of 1948. He established Czechoslovakia as a one-party state and succeeded Eduard Beneš as president on June 7, 1948. Gottwald was a follower of Josef Stalin and allowed the Soviet economy to dictate the direction of Czech industrial development. Gottwald purged his leading rival, Vice-Premier Rudolf Slansky, in January of 1951. Slansky, former foreign minister Vladimir Clementis, and other leading party figures were charged with treason and executed after a show trial. Gottwald continued to govern Czechoslovakia with a firm hand until March of 1953. He developed a chill while attending Stalin's funeral and died of pneumonia five days later in Prague at the age of 56 on March 14, 1953.

ANTONÍN ZÁPOTOCKÝ (President, March 21, 1953–November 13, 1957). Antonín Zápotocký was born in Zakolany on December 19, 1884. He trained as a stone-mason apprentice and moved to Prague in 1908. He became active in Socialist politics at an early age and was imprisoned on several occasions for his activities. Zápotocký also worked in the trade union movement, and he was elected to the Kladno Town Council in 1911. He served in the Austro-Hungarian army as a private during World War I. He was elected secretary of the Kladno Socialist Democrats after the war. In 1920 he was again arrested for his role in organizing a general strike. Zápotocký joined with Klement Gottwald in founding the Czech Communist party in 1921. He was selected general secretary of the party two years later. Zápotocký was elected to the Czechoslovak Parliament in 1925 and retained his seat until the German occupation in 1939, when he was captured by the Nazis and imprisoned in Prague. He was sent to the Oranienburg concentration camp in 1940 and remained imprisoned until he was released by the Red Army in April of 1945. He returned to Prague to serve as chairman of the Czechoslovak Revolutionary Trade Union. In 1946 he was elected to the National Assembly, and on June 7,

1948, he succeeded Gottwald as premier. He attempted to increase Czechoslovakia's industrial production and negotiated a new trade agreement with the Soviet Union. Zápotocký was elected to succeed Gottwald as president on March 21, 1953. He died of a heart attack in Prague at the age of 72 on November 13, 1957.

ANTONÍN NOVOTNÝ (President, November 19, 1957–March 22, 1968). Antonín Novotný was born in Letnany in Bohemia on December 10, 1904. He was a leader of the Czech underground during the German occupation in World War II. He was arrested in 1941 and spent the remainder of the war in the Mauthausen concentration camp in Austria. Following the liberation of Prague, Novotný was released, and he was elected to the Central Committee of the Communist Party in 1946. A supporter of Josef Stalin, he was instrumental in the Stalinist takeover of the Czechoslovak government in February of 1948. He was elected to the Politburo in 1951 and succeeded Klement Gottwald as general secretary of the Communist party in 1953. Novotný became president of Czechoslovakia on November 19, 1957, following the death of Antonín Zápotocký. In 1964 he was reelected to the position. Novotný's close association with Moscow led to criticism from more liberal and nationalistic members of the Czech Communist party. On January 5, 1968, he was forced to resign as party leader and turn the party over to reformist Alexander Dubček. Novotný was removed as president on March 22, 1968, and stripped of party membership later in the year, but was reinstated in the party in 1971. He died in Prague of a heart ailment at the age of 70 on January 28, 1975.

LUDVÓK SVOBODA (President, March 30, 1968–May 29, 1975). Ludvók Svoboda was born in Hroznatin, Moravia, on November 25, 1895. He served in the Austro-Hungarian army during World War I. He was captured by the Russians and joined the Czechoslovak Legion to fight for Czech independence. Svoboda served in the Czech army following his country's independence. After the German occupation in 1939, he fled the country. He organized a military unit of refugees in Poland and fought with the Soviet Red Army during World War II. Svoboda was named minister of defense in the postwar government and kept the military from resisting the Communists' seizure of power in 1948. He joined the Communist party in 1948 and was subsequently named deputy premier. Svoboda was purged and imprisoned in 1951. He was sent to a collective farm, where he remained until 1955. He returned to Prague to serve as head of the Czechoslovak Military Academy, where he remained until his retirement from the military in 1958. Svoboda was nominated by Czech Communist leader Alexander Dubček to become president of Czechoslovakia, and he took office on March 30, 1968. Czechoslovakia was going through a period of reforms under Dubček, and Soviet-led Warsaw Pact forces invaded the country in August of 1968 to restore Soviet control over the Czech Communist party. Dubček and other reformers were arrested and taken to Moscow. When Svoboda refused to sign the ratification of the new Soviet-installed government until Dubček and his supporters were released, the Soviets allowed the reformers to return to Czechoslovakia. Though he had little power, Svoboda remained as president of Czechoslovakia until he resigned for reasons of health on May 29, 1975. He died in Prague of a heart attack at the age of 83 on September 20, 1979.

GUSTÁV HUSÁK (President, May 29, 1975–December 10, 1989). Gustáv Husák was born in Bratislava, Slovakia, on January 10, 1913. He joined the Slovakian Communist party while a law student at the University of Bratislava in 1933. He received his law degree in 1937 and worked in Vladimir Clementis's law firm. In 1940 he was arrested by the German-controlled Slovakian government for his Communist activities. Husák was released from prison in 1943 and was elected to the party's Central Committee. He also participated in the Slovak National Council, formed in opposition to the government. In 1944 he played a leading role in the national uprising against the government. Husák was elected a delegate to the National Assembly following the defeat of the Germans and the reunification of Czechoslovakia in 1945. He also served as a member of the Slovakian regional Board of Commissioners and became its chairman in 1946. He resigned from the board in October of 1947 in an abortive attempt by the Communist members to take over the Slovak government. Husák returned as chairman when the Communists took control of Czechoslovakia in February of 1948. He was removed from the Slovak Board of Commissioners in 1950 because of his close association with Vladimir Clementis, who was purged and executed in the early 1950s. Husák was expelled from the party and arrested for treason and sabotage in February of 1951. He was convicted in 1954 and sentenced to life imprisonment. Husák was released in May of 1960, and his conviction was declared illegal in June of 1963. He was restored to the Communist party and worked for the Slovak Academy of Sciences as a researcher. Husák became a leading critic of Communist party leader Antonin Novotný, and he became a deputy premier under Oldřich Cerník in April of 1968, following Novotný's replacement by Alexander Dubček. He was reluctant to embrace the reforms sponsored by Dubček and accepted the elimination of Dubček's liberal policies after the Soviet-led invasion in August of 1968. Husák replaced Dubček as

general secretary of the Czechoslovakian Communist party on April 17, 1969, and normalized relations with the Soviet Union. He approved harsh measures that included economic repression and the expulsion of numerous party members from the government. He was also elected president of Czechoslovakia on May 29, 1975. Husák stepped down as party leader on December 17, 1987, when his opposition to liberal reforms promoted by Soviet leader Mikhail Gorbachev forced his replacement. He remained president until December 17, 1987, when he turned over the office to Václav Havel in Czechoslovakia's first non–Communist government. Husák was expelled from the Communist party in 1990. He died in Bratislava on November 18, 1991.

VÁCLAV HAVEL (President, December 29, 1989–July 20, 1992). Václav Havel was born to a wealthy family in Prague on October 5, 1936. His family's wealth and property was seized by the state following the Communist takeover of Czechoslovakia in 1948. Havel was ineligible for an education beyond grammar school because of his family's position. He educated himself primarily at night while working for a chemical company in Prague. Havel began working as a stage hand with a local theater group in 1956 and also began writing essays and then plays. His first play, *The Garden Party*, was performed to wide acclaim in 1963. Havel was named chief literary director at the Balustrade theater in Prague two years later. He wrote *The Memorandum* in 1965, which was honored as the best foreign play of the year when it opened in New York in 1968. Havel supported the reforms initiated by Alexander Dubček in the spring of 1968. He was a leading critic of the Soviet-led invasion and subsequent repression the following August. Though he continued writing to international acclaim, his plays were not allowed to be legally performed in Czechoslovakia. Havel was a leader and spokesman for the human rights movement, Chapter 77. He was arrested shortly after the organization was formed in 1977 and remained under house arrest until 1979. He was then tried for sedition and remained imprisoned until March of 1983. Havel remained under the scrutiny of the state throughout the decade. His arrest in February of 1989 prompted widespread protests against the government, and he was released in May of 1989. Havel was a founder of Civic Forum, the leading opposition group to the government, in November of 1989. The Communist government collapsed the following month, and Havel was chosen by Parliament to serve as interim president on December 29, 1989. His government was faced with a growing separatist movement in Slovakia, and Havel's reelection bid failed in June of 1992 when Slovak deputies withheld their support. Havel resigned two weeks later on June 20, 1992. The presidency remained vacant for the remainder of the year. On January 1, 1993, Czechoslovakia divided into the Czech Republic and Slovakia, and Havel returned to office as president of the Czech Republic.

HEADS OF GOVERNMENT

ZDENĚK FIERLINGER (Premier, April 4, 1945–July 3, 1946). Zdeněk Fierlinger was born in Olomouc, Moravia, on July 1, 1891. He joined Thomas Masaryk to fight for Czechoslovak independence during World War I. Following his country's independence, he served in the Czech foreign service. Fierlinger held diplomatic positions in various countries, including the Netherlands, Switzerland, Austria, and the United States. He represented the Czech government in Moscow before World War II and retained that position under the Czech government-in-exile during the war. Fierlinger was leader of the Social Democratic party and became premier in the first postwar government under President Eduard Beneš on April 4, 1945. Fierlinger stepped down on July 3, 1946, when Communist leader Klement Gottwald was elected to the office. He remained in the National Assembly and merged his Social Democratic party with the Communists when Czechoslovakia became a one-party state in 1948. Fierlinger served as president of the National Assembly from 1953 until 1964. He also served as chairman of the Committee for Czechoslovak-Soviet Friendship. He resigned his chairmanship in 1968 following the Soviet-led invasion of his country. Fierlinger died in Prague at the age of 85 on May 2, 1976.

KLEMENT GOTTWALD (Premier, July 3, 1946–June 7, 1948). *See entry under Heads of State.*

ANTONÍN ZÁPOTOCKÝ (Premier, June 7, 1948–March 21, 1953). *See entry under Heads of State.*

VILIAM SIROKÝ (Premier, March 21, 1953–September 21, 1963). Viliam Siroký was born in Slovakia on May 31, 1902. He worked on the railroad from his early teens. He became active in the Communist trade union movement and organized the Bratislava Communist party in 1921. Siroký was named a member of the Slovak Communist party Central Committee in 1930 and was elected to the Czechoslovakian Parliament in 1935. He escaped to France following the German division of Czechoslovakia in 1938. He went to the Soviet Union in 1940 and returned to Slovakia when the Germans invaded the Soviet Union. Siroký joined the underground to oppose the German-controlled fascist government in Slovakia. He was arrested by the Gestapo during the National Uprising in the spring of 1944 and was imprisoned in Spielberg. He escaped to the Soviet Union the following year. Siroký was named deputy premier in the provisional government established in Kosice after the liberation of Czechoslovakia in 1945. He was elected chairman of the Slovak Communist party in 1947 and served as vice-premier in the Communist-dominated government established in February of 1948. He replaced Vladimir Clementis as foreign minister in March of 1950 and brought Czech foreign policy into closer alignment with the Soviet Union. Siroký succeeded Antonín Zápotocký as premier on March 21, 1953, when Zápotocký assumed the presidency. He played an important part in carrying out the purges through 1954. He implemented plans for the industrialization of Slovakia and later emphasized agriculture and the production of consumer goods. Siroký was reported to be seriously ill in the mid-1950s, but recovered sufficiently to maintain his position. When the Czech economy suffered a serious decline in the early 1960s, Siroký was held responsible. During a resurgence of Slovak nationalism in 1963, he also faced criticism for his role in the purges of the early 1950s. He was dismissed from office on September 21, 1963. His membership in the Communist party was suspended during the reforms of Alexander Dubček in 1968, but was reinstated in early 1971. Siroký died in Prague at the age of 69 on October 6, 1971, after a long illness.

JOZEF LENÁRT (Premier, September 21, 1963–April 4, 1968). Jozef Lenárt was born in Liptovska Porubka on April 3, 1923. He was a leader of the Resistance during World War II and a member of the Communist party from 1943. He was appointed a member of the Central Committee in 1958 and served as secretary of the Slovak Communist party Central Committee. Lenárt was chairman of the Slovak National Council from 1962. He was named premier of Czechoslovakia on September 21, 1963, and assumed the duties of president following the ouster of Antonín Novotný on March 22, 1968. He relinquished presidential powers following the selection of Ludvók Svoboda on March 30, 1968. Lenárt resigned as premier on April 4, 1968, though he retained his position as an alternate member of the Presidium. He was appointed to head the Central Committee's Department of the Economy in May of 1969. He was named first secretary of the Slovak Communist party and was appointed to the Presidium in January of 1970. Lenárt opposed the ouster of Alexander Dubček from the Communist party in February of 1970. He served as secretary for economic development from 1988 until 1989. He relinquished his seat in the Federal Assembly following the institution of democratic reforms in Czechoslovakia. Lenárt was expelled from the Communist party in January of 1990.

OLDŘICH CERNÍK (Premier, April 4, 1968–January 28, 1970). Oldřich Cerník was born in Ostrava on October 27, 1921. He was employed as a factory worker from his early teens until 1949. During the 1950s he joined the Communist party and served on various party committees. Cerník was named secretary of the Czechoslovakian Communist party Central Committee in 1956 and served until 1960. He was minister of fuel and power from 1960 until 1963. Cerník was then named deputy premier and appointed to the Central Committee's Economic Commission. He was considered a liberal and was appointed premier on April 4, 1968, during Alexander Dubček's period of political reforms. He was arrested during the Soviet-led invasion of Czechoslovakia in August of 1968 and participated in the negotiations in Moscow that revoked most of Dubček's reforms. Cerník accompanied the new party leader Gustáv Husák and President Ludvók Svoboda to Moscow in October of 1969 to negotiate a trade agreement. Cerník remained premier until his dismissal on January 28, 1970. He was expelled from the Communist party the following December and spent the next two decades in obscurity until democratic reforms were instituted in Czechoslovakia. He then emerged to serve as Chairman of the council of Urban and Rural Municipalities in January of 1990.

LUBOMÍR STROUGAL (Premier, January 28, 1970–October 11, 1988). Lubomír Strougal was born in Veseli nad Luznief on October 19, 1924. He was educated in Prague and joined the Communist party in 1945. He became a member of the Communist Party's Central Committee in 1958. Strougal served as minister of agriculture from 1959 until 1961, when he was named minister of the interior. He retained that postion until 1965. He served as secretary of the central committee from 1965 until 1968 and then served as deputy premier. Strougal was selected to replace Oldřich Cerník as premier on January 28, 1970. He was an advocate of political reforms in Czechoslovakia. He was ousted by Communist leader Miloš Jakeš on October 11, 1988, and was expelled from the Communist party in February of 1990.

LADISLAV ADAMEC (Premier, October 11, 1988–December 7, 1989). Ladislav Adamec was born in Frenstat pod Radhostem in Moravia on September 10, 1926. He joined the Czecho-

slovak Communist party in 1946. He graduated from the Political College in Prague in 1961. Adamec became a department head in the Communist party Central Committee in 1963 and succeeded Lubomir Strougal as premier on October 11, 1988. He was less supportive of political reforms than his predecessor. The government was faced with massive prodemocracy demonstrations, and Adamec stepped down as premier on December 7, 1989. He briefly replaced Karel Urbanek as general secretary of the Communist party on December 20, 1989. Communist control of Czechoslovakia ended with the selection of Václav Havel as president on December 29, 1989.

MARIÁN CALFA (Premier, December 10, 1989–July 1, 1992). Marián Calfa was born in Trebisov, Slovakia, in 1946. He was educated in Prague, where he received a degree in law. He was employed in the legal department of the Czech press agency. In 1988 he was named to the cabinet as minister without portfolio. Calfa resigned from the Communist party in 1989 and succeeded Ladislav Adamec as premier on December 10, 1989, at the head of a non–Communist government. He also became chairman of the State Defense Council in February of 1990. Calfa stepped down as premier on July 1, 1992, following elections to the Federal Assembly.

JAN STRASKY (Premier, July 1, 1992–January 1, 1993). Jan Strasky was a member of the Czech Civic Democratic party. He was selected as Czechoslovakia's premier on July 1, 1992. Strasky presided over the last Czechoslovakian government and left office when the nation divided into the Czech Republic and Slovakia on January 1, 1993.

OTHER LEADERS

KLEMENT GOTTWALD (General Secretary, March, 1946–March 14, 1953). *See entry under Heads of State.*

ANTONÍN NOVOTNÝ (General Secretary, 1953–January 5, 1968). *See entry under Heads of State.*

ALEXANDER DUBČEK (General Secretary, January 5, 1968–April 17, 1969). Alexander Dubček was born in Uhrovec on November 27, 1921. His father was a member of the Czechoslovak Communist party, and young Dubček was educated in the Soviet Union. He returned to Czechoslovakia in 1938 and joined the Communist party. He was active in the anti–Nazi underground during World War II and was wounded in the Slovak National Uprising against the Germans in the winter of 1944. Dubček remained active in the Communist party after the war and became the leader of the Trencin district party in 1949. He was elected to the Slovak Communist party Central Committee in 1951 and also became a member of the National Assembly that year. Dubček went to Moscow to study at the political college in 1955. He returned to Czechoslovakia in 1958, after receiving a doctorate in political science. He was elected to the Central Committee in Bratislava and then moved to Prague to serve on the national party's Central Committee in 1960. Dubček became first secretary of the Slovakian Central Committee in 1963. He soon became a leading voice in support of liberal reforms. He was a critic of party leader Antonín Novotný and forced his resignation on January 5, 1968. Dubček was elected to succeed him as first secretary of the Czechoslovakian Communist party the same day. He instituted numerous changes in the party and the government. He relaxed censorship restrictions, allowed greater freedom to travel abroad, and made plans for economic reforms. The Soviet Union and other Warsaw Pact nations denounced Dubček's policies, however, and compromises were forced upon him. The Soviets feared that the Czech reformers would try to withdraw Czechoslovakia from the Warsaw Pact, and Soviet-led troops invaded the country on August 20, 1968. Dubček was arrested by the occupation forces and taken to Moscow. He was forced to renounce most of his reforms and grant legitimacy to the invasion. He was allowed to remain as party leader until April 17, 1969, when he was replaced by Gustáv Husák. Dubček was sent to Turkey to serve as ambassador in January of 1970. He was recalled to Czechoslovakia in June of 1970 and expelled from the Communist party. He was then sent to Slovakia to work as a forestry official. Dubček returned to prominence in 1988 when democratic reforms began sweeping Czechoslovakia and the rest of Eastern Europe. He was elected chairman of the Federal Assembly in June of 1992. Dubček was seriously injured in a car crash on September 1, 1992, and died from his injuries at the age of 70 in Prague on November 7, 1992.

GUSTÁV HUSÁK (General Secretary, April 17, 1969–December 17, 1987). *See entry under Heads of State.*

MILOŠ JAKEŠ (General Secretary, December 17, 1987–November 24, 1989). Miloš Jakeš was born in Ceske Krumlov on August 12, 1922. He studied to become an apprentice electrical engineer. In 1945 he joined the Czechoslovak Communist party and served in various local party positions. Jakeš worked for the party's Central Committee from 1958 until 1963, when he became chairman of the Central Administration for the Development of a

Communal Economy. He was named deputy minister of the interior in 1966 and served until 1968. Jakeš gained prominence in the party after the Soviet invasion of Czechoslovakia in 1968 and was named chairman of the Central Control and Auditing Commission. His commission reviewed the membership of the party, and thousands were purged. He retained this position until 1977, when he was named Central Committee secretary for agriculture and food. Jakeš was then named as the Central Committee secretary in charge of economic affairs. He was selected to succeed Gustáv Husák as general secretary of the party on December 17, 1987. Jakeš continued Husák's hardline policies against reforms and succeeded in ousting Premier Lubomír Strougal in October of 1988, but he was faced with calls urging democratic reforms in the country. Jakeš and the party leadership attempted to ignore the demands, but major demonstrations erupted in Prague and other major cities. Jakeš resigned as leader of the party on November 24, 1989, and was replaced by Karel Urbánek.

KAREL URBÁNEK (General Secretary, November 24, 1989–December 10, 1989.). Karel Urbánek was born in Bojkovice Uherske on March 22, 1941. He was a railway worker before he joined the Communist party in Czechoslovakia in 1962. He served in various party positions and became a member of the Presidium of the Central Committee in October of 1988. Urbánek was selected to replace Miloš Jakeš as general secretary of the Czechoslovak Communist party on November 24, 1989. He presided over the installation of a non–Communist government in Czechoslovakia a few days later. He was replaced by Ladislav Adamec on December 20, 1989.

LADISLAV ADAMEC (General Secretary, December 20, 1989–December 29, 1989). *See entry under Heads of Government.*

Denmark, Kingdom of

(Kongeriget Danmark)

Denmark is a country in northern Europe.

HEADS OF STATE

CHRISTIAN X (King, May 14, 1912–April 20, 1947). Carl Frederick Albert Alexander William was born in Charlottenlund Castle near Copenhagen on September 26, 1870. He was the eldest son of Crown Prince Frederik and Princess Louise of Sweden. He entered the Royal Guards in 1889 and became chief of the Guards in 1898. His father ascended the throne as King Frederik VIII following the death of King Christian IX in 1906. Christian became crown prince and was promoted to major general in the Royal Guards. He served as Denmark's ruler while his father was out of the country. He ascended to the throne as King Christian X upon the death of his father on May 14, 1912. Christian maintained Danish neutrality during World War I. He granted Iceland the status of an independent kingdom in November of 1918, and he also ruled as king of Iceland. Christian remained on the throne during the German occupation of Denmark in 1940. He refused to be intimidated by the Germans or to form a government favoring them, a course that gained him much respect from the Danish people. The king became seriously ill following a fall from his horse in 1942. He was placed under palace arrest by the Nazis in August of 1943, following a rebellion against the occupation forces. He remained imprisoned until the defeat of the Germans. Iceland severed its ties with Denmark in May of 1944. Christian suffered a heart attack in early April of 1947 and died at Amalienborg Palace at the age of 76 on April 20, 1947.

FREDERIK IX (King, April 20, 1947– January 14, 1972). Christian Frederik Frantz Michael Carl Valdemar Georg was born in Sorgenfri Castle near Copenhagen on March 11, 1899. He was the eldest son of Prince Christian and Princess Alexandrine Augustine. His father became King Christian X in May of 1912, and Frederik became crown prince. Frederik entered the Danish Naval Academy in 1917 and was commissioned in the Danish navy in 1921. He was elevated through the ranks and became commander in 1935. He married Princess Ingrid, the daughter of King Gustaf Adolf of Sweden, in 1935. Frederik was a close advisor to his father during the Nazi occupation of Denmark during World War II. He served as regent during Christian's illness in 1942 and was placed under palace arrest with the royal family in 1943. Frederik again served as regent after his father suffered a heart attack in April of 1947. He was crowned King Frederik IX at the time of Christian's

death on April 20, 1947. Frederik was very popular among the Danish people. His arms and chest were covered with tattoos of birds and dragons that he had gotten while serving in the navy. He visited the United States in 1960 and called for international disarmament in an address to the United Nations. Frederik became ill in early January of 1972. He suffered a heart attack and died at the age of 72 at Amalienborg Palace on January 14, 1972.

MARGRETHE II (Queen, January 14, 1972–). Margrethe Alexandrine Thorhildur Ingrid was born in Copenhagen on April 16, 1940. She was the eldest daughter of Prince Frederik of Denmark and Princess Ingrid. Her father succeeded to the throne as King Frederik IX in April of 1947. The Danish constitution was changed by a referendum in 1953 to allow female succession to the throne. Margrethe was educated at Copenhagen University. She later attended Cambridge University in Great Britain, where she studied archaeology. She then attended the University of Paris before completing her formal education at the London School of Economics in 1965. Margrethe continued her interest in archaeology and took part in several expeditions. She married Count Henri de Laborde de Monpezat in June of 1967. Margrethe succeeded to the throne upon the death of her father on January 14, 1972. Crowned Margrethe II, she became the second female ruling monarch in Danish history. She was a popular monarch who traveled widely throughout Europe, the Far East, and the Americas.

HEADS OF GOVERNMENT

VILHELM BUHL (Prime Minister, May 5, 1945–November 7, 1945). Vilhelm Buhl was born in Fredericia on

October 16, 1881. He attended Copenhagen University, where he received a degree in law. He joined the finance department in Copenhagen in 1908 and rose to the position of director of taxes in 1924. Buhl was elected to the Folketing, or Parliament, as a member of the Social Democratic party in 1932. He was named minister of finance in the cabinet of Prime Minister Thorvald Stauning in 1937 and initiated a series of tax reforms. Buhl was selected as prime minister on May 3, 1942, during the German occupation of Denmark. He stepped down from office on November 9, 1942, but again became prime minister on May 5, 1945. He guided Denmark's return to democracy in the postwar period. Buhl presided over parliamentary elections and relinquished office on November 7, 1945. He subsequently served as chairman of the Social Democratic party's parliamentary group. He was appointed minister of economic coordination in November of 1947 and retained that position until March of 1950, when he was appointed minister of justice. Buhl left the cabinet in September of 1950. He died in Copenhagen on December 18, 1954.

KNUD KRISTENSEN (Prime Minister, November 5, 1945–November 13, 1947). Knud Kristensen was born on July 13, 1880. He entered politics and became active in the Agrarian party. In 1920 he was elected to the Danish Parliament. He served on the Parliament's Finance Committee from 1927 until he left Parliament in 1929. Kristensen returned to the Parliament in 1932 and was appointed to the cabinet as minister of the interior in 1940. He resigned from the government two years later in protest of the German occupation forces' demands that Erik Scavenius be named prime minister. Kristensen returned to the cabinet following Denmark's liberation and became head of a Liberal-Agrarian coalition government on November 5, 1945. He promoted the incorporation of the German province of South Schleswig into Denmark. His support

for a plebiscite on this issue brought down his government on November 13, 1947. Kristensen left the Agrarian party in 1953 in opposition to plans to revise the Danish constitution to eliminate the upper house of Parliament. Kristensen formed the Independent party, but failed to win any seats in the Parliament. He subsequently retired from politics. Kristensen died in Copenhagen at the age of 81 on September 29, 1962.

HANS HEDTOFT (Prime Minister, November 13, 1947–October 30, 1950). Hans Christian Hedtoft was born in Aarhus on April 21, 1903. He trained as a printer in his early teens and became active with the Danish labor movement. He joined the Social Democratic party and was elected to the Parliament in 1935. Hedtoft became chairman of the Social Democrats in 1939. He was forced to resign his positions by the German occupation forces in 1941 because of his opposition to the Nazis. He worked with the Danish Resistance during the war. After the liberation of Denmark in 1945, he returned to active politics. Hedtoft resumed his leadership position with the Social Democrats and was named to the cabinet as minister of labor and social affairs. He was called upon to form a coalition government as prime minister on November 13, 1947. He supported Denmark's admission into the North Atlantic Treaty Organization and advocated a strong defense for his country. His government was replaced by Erik Eriksen's Liberal-Agrarian-Conservative coalition on October 30, 1950. Hedtoft was instrumental in the formation of the Nordic Council with Norway, Sweden, and Iceland in 1952. He again became prime minister as head of a minority government on September 30, 1953. Hedtoft remained prime minister until his death from a heart attack at the age of 51 at a hotel in Stockholm, Sweden, on January 29, 1955.

ERIK ERIKSEN (Prime Minister, October 30, 1950–September 30, 1953). Erik Eriksen was born in Brangstrup, Ringe, on November 10, 1902. He was educated at the Dalum Agricultural College. He became active in politics and served as chairman of the Liberal party's youth organization from 1929 until 1932. Eriksen was elected to the Parliament in 1935. He was named to the postwar cabinet as minister of agriculture in 1945 and served until 1947. He was elected chairman of the Liberal party in 1950 and became prime minister as head of a Liberal-Agrarian-Conservative coalition on October 30, 1950. Eriksen promoted the creation of a new Danish Constitution, which he signed in June of 1953. The reforms abolished the upper house of the Danish Parliament, made Greenland a part of Denmark, and allowed for female succession to the throne. Eriksen retained office until September 30, 1953, but failed in an attempt to form another coalition government in 1954. He was elected chairman of the Scandinavian Council later in 1954. He died in an Espjerg hospital at the age of 70 on October 7, 1972.

HANS HEDTOFT (Prime Minister, September 30, 1953–January 29, 1955). *See earlier entry under Heads of Government.*

HANS CHRISTIAN HANSEN (Prime Minister, January 29, 1955–February 19, 1960). Hans Christian Svane Hansen was born in Aarhus on November 8, 1906. He joined the Social Democratic party and was elected to the Danish Parliament, or Folketing, in 1936. Hansen was a leading member of the Danish Resistance to the Germans during World War II. He served as finance minister in the postwar government of Vilhelm Buhl from May to November of 1945. He again served in that position from 1947 to 1950 and was instrumental in the stabilization of Denmark's postwar economy. Hansen also served as minister of commerce in 1950 and minister of foreign affairs from 1953 to 1955. He was named prime minister on January 29, 1955. He was a leading proponent of Denmark's continued support of the Western alliance against Soviet imperialism. Hansen underwent surgery for cancer in October of 1958. He resumed his duties until December of 1959, when he was again hospitalized. He remained head of the government until his death from cancer in Copenhagen at the age of 53 on February 19, 1960.

VIGGO KAMPMANN (Prime Minister, February 19, 1960–September 3, 1962). Olfert Viggo Fischer Kampmann was born in Copenhagen on July 21, 1910. He graduated from Copenhagen University in 1934. He worked as an economist and statistician in the government and private industry and served as secretary to the Danish Tax Commission from 1938 until 1948. He was appointed chief assistant to the Social Democratic party's Economics Department in 1947. He briefly served in the cabinet as minister of finance from September until October of 1950. Kampmann was elected to the Parliament as a Social Democrat member in April of 1953. He was again named to the cabinet as minister of finance in the governments of Hans Hedtoft and Hans Hansen. Kampmann became acting prime minister when Hansen became ill in October of 1958. He again served as acting prime minister in January of 1960. He was elected to succeed Hansen as prime minister following Hansen's death on February 19, 1960. Kampmann suffered several heart attacks in 1962 and resigned from office for health reasons on September 3, 1962. He retired from politics and died in Copenhagen at the age of 65 on June 3, 1976.

JENS OTTO KRAG (Prime Minister, September 3, 1962–February 2, 1968). Jens Otto Krag was born in Randers on

September 15, 1914. He graduated from the University of Copenhagen in 1940 and became active in the Social Democratic party. He worked with the Danish Board of Supply during World War II and became director of the labor movement's economic council in 1945. Krag was elected to the Parliament in 1947 and was named to the cabinet of Hans Hedtoft as minister of commerce, industry, and shipping. He left the cabinet in 1950 and was sent to the Danish Embassy in Washington, D.C., to serve as an economic advisor. After his return to Denmark in 1952, he was named minister of economy and labor in Hedtoft's second government. He remained in the cabinet after Hedtoft's death in 1955 and was appointed minister of foreign economic relations in 1957. Krag was named foreign minister in October of 1958 and advocated Denmark's entry into the European Common Market. He retained his position in the government of Viggo Kampmann. Krag became prime minister when Kampmann resigned on September 3, 1962, after suffering a heart attack. Krag remained as head of a minority government until February 2, 1968, when the issue of freezing wage increases brought down the government. He again became prime minister as head of a minority Social Democratic government on October 11, 1971. He achieved his goal of gaining Denmark's entry into the European Common Market and retired from politics the following day, on October 3, 1972. Krag died of a heart attack in Jutland at the age of 63 on June 22, 1978.

HILMAR BAUNSGAARD (Prime Minister, February 2, 1968–October 11, 1971). Hilmar Tormod Ingolf Baunsgaard was born in Slagelse on February 26, 1920. He attended business school and became a store clerk in the early 1940s. He became active in the Radical Liberal party and served as chairman of the party's national youth

organization from 1948 until 1951. Baunsgaard was elected to the Parliament in 1957 and was named to the cabinet as minister of trade in 1961. He retained this office until 1964, when he took a position in private business. He was a leading spokesman in opposition to the Socialist government and formed a Conservative-Liberal coalition government on February 2, 1968. Baunsgaard supported Denmark's entry into the European Common Market and the repeal of Denmark's pornography laws. His government was forced to increase taxes following economic problems in the country, and Baunsgaard was replaced by a Socialist-led government on October 11, 1971. He remained leader of the Radical Liberals until his retirement in 1977. Baunsgaard died at his home in Slagelse at the age of 69 on June 30, 1989.

JENS OTTO KRAG (Prime Minister, October 11, 1971–October 3, 1972). *See earlier entry under Heads of Government.*

ANKER H. JØRGENSEN (Prime Minister, October 3, 1972–December 5, 1973). Anker Henrik Jørgensen was born in Copenhagen on July 13, 1923. He was orphaned at an early age and worked his way through night school to receive a high school diploma. He joined the labor union movement in the early 1950s and became president of the Warehouse Workers Union in 1958. Jørgensen was elected to the Copenhagen City Council in 1961 and became general manager of the General Workers Union in 1962. He was elected to the Danish Parliament in 1964 as a member of the Social Democratic party. He supported Jens Otto Krag's sponsorship of Denmark's entry into the European Common Market, despite a rift among the Social Democrats over the issue. Krag proposed Jørgensen as his successor when he resigned on October 3, 1972. Jørgensen became prime minister, although he had never held a cabinet position. He was faced with a split in the party, when dissident members formed the Centre Democratic party in November of 1973. Jørgensen's government lost a vote in the Parliament over a tax issue, and new elections were called. Jørgensen resigned as prime minister on December 5, 1973. He remained parliamentary leader of the Social Democratic group until February 13, 1975, when he formed another coalition cabinet as prime minister. He broadened the coalition after parliamentary elections in October of 1978. Jørgensen's government faced economic problems in 1982, and his inability to reach a consensus over how to handle the growing budget deficit led to his resignation on September 10, 1982. Jørgensen remained leader of the Social Democrats until September of 1987, when he resigned following the party's loss of seats in the elections. He retained his seat in Parliament into the 1990s.

POUL HARTLING (Prime Minister, December 19, 1973–January 29, 1975). Poul Hartling was born in Copenhagen on August 14, 1914. He received a master's degree in divinity and became curate of Frederiksberg Church in 1941. He became chaplain at the St. Luke Foundation in 1945, where he remained until becoming principal of the Zahle Teachers Training College in 1950. Hartling was elected to the Danish Parliament, or Folketing, as a member of the Liberal party in 1957. He left the Parliament in 1960, but was reelected in 1964. He became chairman of the Liberal party's Parliamentary group the following year. Hartling was appointed to the cabinet of Hilmar Baunsgaard as foreign minister in 1968 and served until 1971. He was elected Liberal party leader in 1973 and formed a government as prime minister on December 19, 1973. His government was beset by economic problems and a rise

in unemployment. Hartling called for new elections in January of 1975 and relinquished office on January 29, 1975. He remained chairman of the Liberal party until he left Parliament in 1977. The following year he was named United Nations high commissioner for refugees, a position he retained until 1985.

ANKER H. JØRGENSEN (Prime Minister, February 13, 1975–September 10, 1982). *See earlier entry under Heads of Government.*

POUL SCHLÜTER (Prime Minister, September 10, 1982–). Poul Holmskov Schlüter was born in Tonder, Jutland, on April 3, 1929. He attended the University of Copenhagen and the University of Aarhus, where he received a degree in law. He became active in the Conservative party and served as chairman of the Young Conservatives from 1952 until 1955. Schlüter was elected to the Parliament in 1964 and was a member of the Council of Europe from 1971 until 1974. He rose through the party ranks to become chairman of the Conservative parliamentary group in 1974 and became party chairman in 1980. Schlüter was selected to serve as Denmark's prime minister on September 19, 1982, following the resignation of Anker Jørgensen. Schlüter's minority government survived parliamentary elections in January of 1984. His Conservative party lost seats in the elections in September of 1987, however. He offered his resignation, but was asked to form a new Conservative-Liberal coalition government. Denmark rejected the Maastricht Treaty to strengthen the European political union in a referendum in June of 1992. Schlüter's government then entered into a series of negotiations to determine Denmark's future status in the European Community.

Djibouti, Republic of

(République de Djibouti)

Djibouti is a country in northeastern Africa. It was granted independence from France on June 27, 1977.

HEAD OF STATE

HASSAN GOULED APTIDON (President, June 24, 1977–   ). Hassan Gouled Aptidon was born to the Issa tribe in 1916. He worked as a trucking contractor before entering politics in 1950. He served as a representative of French Somaliland to the French government from 1952 until 1958. Gouled was elected vice president of the Territorial Assembly in 1958 and was elected a senator in the French National Assembly the following year. He served as minister of education in French Somaliland from 1963 until 1967. He was a founder of the African People's League for Independence party in 1967. The results of a referendum held in March of 1967 indicated the majority of the voters wished to remain associated with France, though many members of the Issa tribe were not registered to vote. French Somaliland's name was subsequently changed to the Territory of the Afars and the Issas. Gouled's organization continued to press for independence for the territory. When another referendum was held in May of 1977, pro-independence forces won by a large margin. Gouled was selected as president by the Chamber of Deputies on June 24, 1977. Three days later the territory became the independent Republic of Djibouti. Gouled formed the Popular Rally for Progress party in 1979 and was reelected president in June of 1981. He attempted to rule fairly, though allegations were made that the Issa tribe dominated the government. Gouled was again reelected without opposition in April of 1987. Tribal conflict flared in 1990 when the government supported a rebellion in neighboring Somalia.

HEADS OF GOVERNMENT

AHMED DINI AHMED (Prime Minister, July 12, 1977–December 17, 1977). Ahmed Dini Ahmed was born to the Afar tribe in Obock in 1932. He served as vice president of the Territorial Assembly in French Somaliland from 1959 until 1960. He served in the cabinet as minister of production from 1963 until 1964 and minister of the interior from 1967 until 1972. Dini was president of the National Assembly in 1977 prior to the territory being granted independence. He was selected as the independent nation's first prime minister on July 12, 1977. Dini and the other Afar members of the government resigned on December 17, 1977, in protest of tribal repression by the ruling Issa tribe. Dini joined the Front for the Restoration of Unity and Democracy (FRUD) in August of 1991. The organization called for the ouster of President Gouled's government.

ABDALLAH MOHAMED KAMIL (Prime Minister, February 5, 1978–

September 21, 1978). Abdallah Mohamed Kamil was born in 1936. He was a member of the Afar tribe. He was selected by President Hassan Gouled Aptidon to form a government as prime minister on February 5, 1978. Gouled dismissed Kamil's government on September 21, 1978, and appointed Barkat Gourad Hamadou to head a new government.

BARKAT GOURAD HAMADOU (Prime Minister, September 30, 1978–   ). Barkat Gourad Hamadou was a member of the Afar tribe. He served in the French Senate and was Minister of Health in the pre-independence government. On September 30, 1978, he was selected by President Hassan Gouled Aptidon to serve as prime minister. He was an advocate of detribalization of the Afar and Issa tribes. Gourad served as first deputy chairman of the ruling Popular Rally for Progress party from March of 1979. He formed a new government in July of 1981 and retained his position following legislative elections in May of 1982. He again reorganized the government following elections in November of 1987. Gourad also served in the government as minister of planning and land development from 1987.

Dominica, Commonwealth of

Dominica is an island in the eastern Caribbean Sea. It was granted independence from Great Britain on November 3, 1978.

HEADS OF STATE

SIR LOUIS COOLS-LARTIQUE (Interim President, November 3, 1978–December 22, 1978). Sir Louis Cools-Lartique was born on January 18, 1905. He entered the civil service in 1924 as a clerk in the Dominican Administrator's Office and was named chief clerk in 1932. He was appointed Dominica's treasurer in 1940 and served in that capacity from 1945 until 1949. He was then appointed assistant administrator of St. Lucia. He became chief secretary of the Windward Islands in 1951, often serving as deputy governor. He was elected speaker of the Dominican Legislative Council in 1961 and was appointed the first native born governor of Dominica in 1967. Cools-Lartique was knighted the following year. He remained Dominica's governor until the nation was granted independence on November 3, 1978. He served as interim president until December 22, 1978, when he was replaced by Federick DeGazon. Cools-Lartique was named to succeed DeGazon as president on June 14, 1979, but was forced to resign from office the following day. Cools-Lartique died at his home in Dominica after a long illness at the age of 88 on August 21, 1993.

FREDERICK DEGAZON (President, December 22, 1978–June 14, 1979). Frederick E. DeGazon served as Speaker of the House of Assembly until he was selected to serve as president of Dominica on December 22, 1978. A general strike and demonstrations against his government forced DeGazon's resignation on June 14, 1979. He subsequently retired to Great Britain.

SIR LOUIS COOLS-LARTIQUE (Interim President, June 15, 1979–June 16,

1979). *See earlier entry under Heads of State.*

JENNER ARMOUR (Interim President, June 21, 1979–February 25, 1980). Jenner Armour was selected to replace Sir Louis Cools-Lartique as interim president of Dominica on June 21, 1979. He retained the largely ceremonial office until February 25, 1980, when Aurelius Marie was chosen as president.

AURELIUS MARIE (President, February 25, 1980–December 19, 1983). Aurelius John Baptiste Lamothe Marie was born in Portsmouth on December 23, 1904. He served as a magistrate before his selection as president of Dominica on February 25, 1980. Marie remained in office until December 19, 1983, when he was replaced by Clarence Seignoret.

SIR CLARENCE AUGUSTUS SEIGNORET (President, December 19, 1983–   ). Clarence Henry Augustus Seignoret was born in Roseau on February 25, 1919. He was educated in Dominica and at Balliol College, Oxford, in Great Britain. He returned to Dominica to serve in administrative positions in the colonial government. Seignoret served as deputy governor from 1966 until Dominica was granted independence in 1978. He subsequently served as deputy president and was acting president on several occasions during the administration of Aurelius Marie. Seignoret was elected president by the House of Assembly on December 19, 1983. He was reelected to a second term on December 20, 1988.

HEADS OF GOVERNMENT

PATRICK ROLAND JOHN (Prime Minister, 1974–June 21, 1979). Patrick Roland John was born on January 7, 1937. He was educated at St. Mary's Academy in Dominica and worked as a teacher there after his graduation. He later worked as a clerk and became active in the trade union movement in 1960. In the early 1960s he founded the Dominica Waterfront and Allied Worker Union. John was elected mayor of Roseau, Dominica's capital, in 1965. He was a member of the ruling Dominica Labor party and was elected to succeed E. O. LeBlanc as prime minister of the British colony in 1974. Following Dominica's independence on November 3, 1978, he remained as head of the government. John's government was challenged by demonstrations in 1979 following revelations that he was involved in business dealings with the Republic of South Africa. The demonstrators were dealt with harshly by the island's defense force. This action resulted in numerous members of John's ruling Labor party going into opposition. John was forced to step down on June 21, 1979, and was denied reelection to the House of Assembly in elections in July of 1980. John's supporters attempted to overthrow the government in 1981, and he was arrested. He was acquitted and released in May of 1982. John was reelected to the House of Assembly in July of 1985. He was again arrested in October of 1985 and retried for conspiracy. He was convicted and sentenced to twelve years in prison, but was released in May of 1990. He was named general secretary of the National Workers' Union the following year.

J. OLIVER SERAPHINE (Prime Minister, June 21, 1979–July 21, 1980). J. Oliver Seraphine was born on August 2, 1943. He was a member of the ruling Dominica Labor party and served as minister of agriculture in the government of Patrick Roland John. Seraphine left the party to form the

Democratic Labor party and was selected to succeed John as prime minister on June 21, 1979. He also served in the government as minister of foreign affairs. The Labor party was defeated by the opposition Dominica Freedom party in elections in July of 1980, and Seraphine was denied reelection to his seat in the National Assembly. He was replaced as prime minister by Eugenia Charles on July 21, 1980. Seraphine remained leader of the Democratic Labor party and merged his party with the Dominica Labor party to form the Labor party of Dominica in 1983. Seraphine was defeated for leadership of the party by Michael A. Douglas in 1985.

EUGENIA CHARLES (Prime Minister, July 21, 1980–). Mary Eugenia Charles was born in Pointe Michel on May 15, 1919. She was educated on Dominica, Grenada, and at the University of Toronto in Canada. She then attended law school at the London School of Economics and Political Science. Charles graduated in 1947, and two years later she returned to Dominica to become the island's first female attorney. She became interested in political and social affairs in the 1950s. Charles was a founder of the Dominica Freedom party in opposition to the government of E. O. LeBlanc in

1968. She was appointed to the legislature two years later and was elected to the House of Assembly in 1975. Dominica was granted independence in November of 1978, and Charles remained leader of the Opposition to Prime Minister Roland Patrick John. The Dominica Freedom party was victorious in legislative elections in July of 1980, and Charles formed a government as prime minister on July 21, 1980. Her government survived a coup attempt by supporters of former prime minister John in early 1981. The government also faced an abortive invasion by right-wing mercenaries from the United States in April of 1981 and a military revolt intending to free the imprisoned John the following December. Charles managed to withstand the threats against her government and retained the strong support of the Dominican populace. She maintained close relations with the United States and was a leading supporter of President Ronald Reagan's decision to send an invasion force to the island of Grenada to oust a Communist revolutionary government in October of 1983. Charles was returned to office following legislative elections in July of 1985 and was again returned to office in May of 1990, though the Dominica Freedom party kept a bare majority in the House of Assembly.

Dominican Republic

(Républica Dominicana)

The Dominican Republic is a country on the eastern portion of the island of Hispaniola, in the Caribbean Sea. It was granted independence from Haiti on February 27, 1844.

HEADS OF STATE

RAFAEL L. TRUJILLO (President, May 18, 1942–May 16, 1952). Rafael Leónidas Trujillo y Molina was born in

San Cristobal on October 24, 1891. He joined the Dominican National Guard in 1918, following the United States occupation. He rose to the rank of major in 1924 and became chief of staff in 1928. President Horacio Vasquez was ousted in a revolt in February of 1930, and Trujillo seized power in the country. He was a candidate of the Confederation of Parties in the subsequent elections. The opposition candidate withdrew from the election under duress, and Trujillo was elected president. He took office on August 16, 1930, and ruled the country in a ruthless fashion, eliminating civil and political rights. Numerous political opponents were arrested or murdered during his regime. Trujillo ordered the slaughter of over 15,000 Haitian immigrant workers in 1937. He stepped down as president on August 16, 1938, and allowed his hand-picked candidate, Jacinto Peynado, to take office. Trujillo remained firmly in control of the country as commander of the army during the presidency of Peynado and Manuel de Jesus Troncoso, who took office in February of 1940. Trujillo again became president on May 18, 1942. He was a competent administrator who brought prosperity to the Dominican Republic despite the corruption and brutality of his government. His administration built hospitals, schools, and roads throughout the country. He again stepped down as president on May 16, 1952, and allowed his younger brother, Hector Trujillo, to take office. Rafael Trujillo retained power in the country despite growing opposition to his regime. Trujillo was implicated in the kidnapping of Dr. Jesus de Galindez, a prominent Dominican exile and opponent of the regime. Galindez disappeared from New York in March of 1956 and was presumed to have been taken to the Dominican Republic and executed. The Organization of American States imposed economic sanctions and severed diplomatic relations with the Dominican Republic in August of 1960 after Trujillo was implicated in an assassination attempt against Venezuelan president Rómulo Betancourt.

Trujillo retained absolute control of the country until he was assassinated by machine-gun fire while driving outside the capital on May 30, 1961. Several of the alleged assassins, including General J. T. Diaz, were captured and executed, but some involved in the conspiracy remained active in Dominican politics.

HECTOR B. TRUJILLO (President, May 16, 1952–August 3, 1960). Hector Bienvenido Trujillo y Molina was born in San Cristobal on April 6, 1908. He was the younger brother of Rafael Trujillo. After attending the University of Santo Domingo, he entered the army. He served as military attaché in various Dominican embassies and became chief of staff of the army in 1936. Trujillo served as head of the National Police from 1938 until 1943. The following year he was promoted to the rank of general. He served in his brother's government as secretary of state for war and the navy from 1942 until his election as president in 1952. He succeeded his brother as head of state on May 16, 1952, though Rafael Trujillo remained the leading political figure in the country. Hector Trujillo remained president until August 3, 1960, when he resigned for reasons of ill health shortly before an Organization of American States fact-finding mission was due to arrive in the country. The OAS conducted an investigation to investigate allegations that the Dominican government had been involved in an attempt to assassinate President Rómulo Betancourt of Venezuela. Hector Trujillo was succeeded by his vice president, Joaquín Balaguer. Hector Trujillo and another brother, Jose, attempted to take control of the government following the assassination of Rafael Trujillo in May of 1961. The brothers were forced into exile by the Balaguer government with the support of the United States. Hector Trujillo went into exile in Bermuda and later settled in Spain.

JOAQUÍN BALAGUER (President, August 3, 1960–January 17, 1962). Joaquín Balaguer y Ricardo was born in Villa Bisono, Santiago Province, on September 1, 1907. He was educated locally and received a degree in law from the University of Santo Domingo in 1929. He worked as a teacher and an attorney until joining the foreign service in 1932. Balaguer served in Paris and Madrid before returning to the Dominican Republic to become undersecretary of state for the presidency in 1936. He was appointed ambassador to Colombia and Venezuela in 1940. He returned to the Dominican Republic in 1944 to serve in the foreign ministry. In 1947 he was named ambassador to Mexico and Honduras. Balaguer was appointed to the cabinet as secretary of education and culture in 1949. He was named secretary of foreign affairs in 1954 and became secretary of state for the presidency two years later. Balaguer was selected as vice president under Rafael Trujillo's brother, Hector, in May of 1957. When Hector Trujillo resigned for reasons of health on August 3, 1960, Balaguer succeeded as president. The Dominican Republic remained firmly under the control of Rafael Trujillo, the leader of the army, however. Trujillo was assassinated in May of 1961, and Balaguer took steps to liberalize the despotic regime and restore the nation's standing in the international community. The United States restored diplomatic relations, and the Organization of American States lifted economic sanctions in 1962. Balaguer was forced to resign as president on January 17, 1962, and was replaced by a military junta following riots in Santo Domingo. He went into exile in Puerto Rico and New York. He was nominated as a candidate for president in the elections in December of 1962, but was prevented from running by the ruling junta. Balaguer remained in New York until he was allowed to return to the Dominican Republic in June of 1965, shortly after the United

States Marines had entered the country to restore order. Balaguer was allowed to contest the presidential election in June of 1966 and defeated Juan Bosch by a wide margin. He took office on July 1, 1966, and was successful in restoring order in the country and improving the sagging economy. He was reelected in a plebiscite in 1970. Balaguer survived an attempted right-wing coup led by retired Air Force Gen. Elias Wessin y Wessin in June of 1971. A band of leftist guerrillas led by Francisco Caamaño Deño landed in the Dominican Republic in February of 1973. Caamaño Deño, who had led a rebel government in 1965, was killed with many of his followers by government troops, and the rebellion was crushed. Balaguer was again reelected in May of 1974. He faced protests from the opposition to his continuation in office. He pledged that he would not be a candidate in the next presidential election, but reneged on his promise in 1978. He was defeated by Antonio Guzmán Fernández and left office on July 1, 1978. Balaguer again ran for the presidency in 1982, but was defeated by Salvador Jorge Blanco. Balaguer resumed office on August 16, 1986, when he defeated Jacobo Majluta Azar. Though elderly and nearly blind, Balaguer defeated former President Juan Bosch and was returned to office in the elections of 1990.

HUBERTO BOGAERT (President, January 17, 1962–January 19, 1962). Huberto Bogaert served as an officer in the Dominican army during the regime of Rafael Trujillo. He was named president of the ruling junta after Maj. Gen. Pedro Rafael Rodriguez Echavarria seized power from the Council of State on January 17, 1962, because of rioting in Santo Domingo. Bogaert was ousted, and the junta was replaced by a Council of State on January 19, 1962.

RAFAEL F. BONNELLY (President, January 19, 1962–February 27, 1963).

Rafael Filberto Bonnelly was born in Santigao on August 22, 1904. He was educated at the University of Santa Domingo, where he received a degree in law. In 1930 he was elected to the Chamber of Deputies. Bonnelly served in the government in various positions, including ambassador to Spain and Venezuela. He also served in the Dominican Senate and was detained in January of 1960 when his son was charged with plotting against the government of Rafael Trujillo. He remained under house arrest until Trujillo was assassinated in May of 1961. Bonnelly was chosen to be vice president of the Council of State under Joaquín Balaguer in December of 1961. A military coup forced the ouster of the Council of State on January 17, 1962. Bonnelly was briefly arrested before the junta was overthrown. He succeeded to the presidency of the Council of State on January 19, 1962. He presided over the transitional government and organized democratic elections in December of 1962. Bonnelly was a candidate for the presidency, but was defeated by Juan Bosch. He relinquished office to Bosch on February 27, 1963. Bonnelly was a candidate for the far-right in elections in June of 1966 and ran third behind Balaguer and Bosch. He died of cancer in Santo Domingo at the age of 75 on December 28, 1979.

JUAN BOSCH (President, February 27, 1963–September 25, 1963). Juan Bosch Gaviño was born in La Vega on June 30, 1909. He was educated in Santo Domingo and became an active opponent of the government of Rafael Trujillo. He went into exile in Cuba in 1937 and traveled throughout Latin America. Bosch became a successful author and essayist. He founded the Dominican Revolutionary party in opposition to Trujillo while in exile in 1939 and led an unsuccessful attack on the Trujillo regime in 1947. Bosch left Cuba for Costa Rica after Fulgencio Batista took power in 1952 and threat-ened his arrest and deportation. Bosch returned to Cuba after Batista's ouster in 1959. He ended his exile and returned to the Dominican Republic after Trujillo's assassination in May of 1961. Bosch announced his candidacy for the presidency later in the year. He won by a wide margin in December of 1962 and was sworn into office as president on February 27, 1963. Bosch attempted to improve the economic and social conditions of the country, but had difficulty enacting specific legislation. When he began a policy of land reform, he was accused of being pro-Communist by right-wing elements in the military. He was ousted in a coup led by Col. Elias Wessin y Wessin on September 25, 1963. He went into exile in Puerto Rico, where he made plans for a countercoup to restore his government. Bosch's supporters went into revolt in April of 1965. The United States, fearing the possibility of the formation of a Communist government, sent troops to put down the rebellion and establish order. Bosch denounced the actions of the United States. He returned to the Dominican Republic later in 1965 and was defeated by Joaquin Balaguer in the presidential election in 1966. He again went into voluntary exile, where he continued to write and travel. In the late 1960s Bosch again returned to the Dominican Republic. He briefly went into hiding in February of 1973 when he was accused of complicity in an unsuccessful guerrilla invasion of the Dominican Republic from Cuba. Bosch organized the Dominican Liberation party in 1974 and was an unsuccessful candidate for president in 1978. He again ran poorly in the presidential elections in 1982. He ran third behind Balaguer and Jacobo Majluta Azar in 1986 and was narrowly defeated by Balaguer in elections in 1990. Bosch's supporters accused the government of electoral fraud when results of the election were withheld for nearly a month.

EMILIO DE LOS SANTOS (President, September 26, 1963–December 22, 1963). Emilio de los Santos served as president of the Electoral College during the elections of 1963. He was selected to serve as President of a three-man civilian junta on September 26, 1963, following the ouster of President Juan Bosch by the military. He resigned on December 22, 1963, in protest of the army's harsh tactics against leftist rebels in the country.

DONALD REID CABRAL (President, December 22, 1963–April 25, 1965). Donald J. Reid Cabral was born in Santiago de los Caballeros on June 9, 1923. He was educated at the University of Santo Domingo and worked in the family's automobile business after graduation. He was elected president of the Automobile Dealers' Association in 1949. Reid Cabral was appointed vice president of the Council of State under Rafael Bonnelly in January of 1962. He also served as the Dominican Republic's ambassador to the United Nations and Israel in 1963. He was named minister of foreign affairs in the junta government of Emilio de los Santos from September until December of 1963. Reid Cabral became leader of a civilian three-man presidency that took power in the Dominican Republic on December 22, 1963. He instituted a policy of economic austerity and a campaign to eliminate corruption. His policies alienated business, labor, and the military. Reid Cabral resigned on April 25, 1965, in the face of a military coup.

JOSE RAFAEL MOLINA URENA (President, April 25, 1965–April 27, 1965). Jose Rafael Molina Urena was a member of Juan Bosch's Domincan Revoltuionary party. He served as president of the Chamber of Deputies during the Bosch presidency in 1963. Molina was installed as provisional president on April 25, 1965. His selection contributed to the growing tensions between the military and the pro-Bosch forces. Molina's supporters realized they could not resist a full military assault and distributed weapons to pro-Bosch civilians. Civil war erupted in the streets of the capital. General Elias Wessin y Wessin, a right-wing military leader, advanced on the capital to prevent pro-Bosch forces from maintaining power. Molina was forced from office on April 27, 1965, and sought refuge in the Colombian Embassy in the capital.

PEDRO BARTOLOME BENOIT (President, April 27, 1965–May 7, 1965). Pedro Bartolome Benoit was a colonel in the Dominican air force. He was chosen to lead a three-man military junta after the ouster of a provisional pro-Bosch government on April 27, 1965. United States marines entered the Domincan Republic in early May of 1965 to establish order in the country. Bartolome's junta stepped down on May 7, 1965, and was replaced with a five-man junta supported by the United States.

ANTONIO IMBERT BERRERAS (President, May 7, 1965–August 30, 1965). Antonio Imbert Berreras was born on December 3, 1920. He entered the Dominican army and served as governor of Puerto Plata Province. He was an opponent of Dominican dictator Rafael Trujillo and participated in the assassination of Trujillo in May of 1961. Imbert became a popular hero after the ouster of Trujillo's supporters from the government later in the year. He was promoted to the rank of brigadier general and served as a member of the Council of State under President Joaquín Balaguer from December 17, 1961. He was a member of the subsequent military junta from January 17, 1962. Imbert resigned shortly after the junta came to power and took asylum in the Brazilian Embassy. He rejoined the government as a member of the Council of State under

Rafael Bonnelly later in the month. He was an opponent of the presidency of Juan Bosch in 1963 and was active in the military coup that ousted Bosch. Imbert remained in the armed forces and opposed the establishment of a pro-Bosch government in April of 1965. He was chosen to lead a five-man military junta on May 7, 1965. His government of National Reconstruction included military and civilian members and was supported by the United States. Imbert's government waged a major offensive against leftist rebels who were supporting the return of former President Juan Bosch. The rebel government was led by Colonel Francisco Caamaño Deño. The Organization of American States sent a peace commission to the Dominican Republic in early June of 1965. The commission proposed a coalition government to restore order to the country, but Imbert's junta opposed the plan and resigned from power on August 30, 1965. He survived an assassination attempt, presumably instigated by supporters of Trujillo, in 1967. Imbert's wife, daughter, and sister were killed in an airline crash in February of 1970. He remained in the military, but avoided political activity. Imbert was appointed inspector general of the army in 1974.

HÉCTOR GARCÍA GODOY (President, September 3, 1965–July 1, 1966). Héctor García Godoy Cáceres was born in Mocca on July 11, 1921. He was educated at the University of Santo Domingo, where he received a degree in law. He subsequently joined the foreign service in the 1950s. García Godoy served as foreign minister in the government of Juan Bosch until the military ousted Bosch in September of 1963. García Godoy refused a request by the military junta to remain in the cabinet. He was called upon to serve as provisional president on September 3, 1965, following a civil war and the intervention of the United States mili-

tary. García Godoy was considered a moderate and was viewed with distrust by both the rebels and the military. He was able to serve as a conciliator, however, and managed to hold the government together until elections could be held. He stepped down on July 1, 1966, following the selection of Joaquín Balaguer as president. García Godoy formed the National Conciliation Movement and was a candidate for President in the elections in 1970. He died in Santo Domingo of a heart attack on April 20, 1970, a month before elections were scheduled to take place.

JOAQUIN BALAGUER (President, July 1, 1966–July 1, 1978). *See earlier entry under Heads of State.*

ANTONIO GUZMÁN FERNÁNDEZ (President, July 1, 1978–July 4, 1982). Silvestre Antonio Guzmán Fernández was born in La Vega on February 12, 1911. He was employed as a store manager while in his teens and later became involved in the agricultural export business, where he experienced great success. Guzmán entered politics following the assassination of Rafael Trujillo and joined the Dominican Revolutionary Party (PRD) in 1963. Guzmán supported Juan Bosch for president in the election of 1963 and served as secretary of agriculture in Bosch's subsequent government. He remained in office until Bosch's ouster in a military coup in September of 1963. Guzmán was promoted as provisional president by Bosch and the United States during the civil war in 1965, but his nomination was rejected by rightist military leaders. Bosch selected Guzmán as his running mate in the elections in June of 1966, but Bosch was defeated by Joaquín Balaguer. Guzmán became the leader of the PRD in 1973 and was nominated as the party's presidential nominee the following year. He withdrew from the race, however, and the PRD boycotted the election. Guzmán challenged Balaguer in 1978 and was elected president, despite an interruption in the vote count by the army. He took office on July 1, 1978, but his economic policies failed to improve the Dominican economy. His choice of his vice president, Jacobo Majluta Azar, to succeed him to the presidency was rejected by the PRD, and Salvador Jorge Blanco was nominated and elected. Guzmán subsequently learned that members of his staff were involved in corrupt financial practices while serving in his government. Guzmán died of a self-inflicted gunshot wound when he shot himself in the head at his office in Santo Domingo on July 4, 1982.

JACOBO MAJLUTA AZAR (Acting President, July 4, 1982–August 16, 1982). Jacobo Majluta Azar was born in 1934. He was a member of the Dominican Revolutionary party (PRD) and served as vice president under Antonio Guzmán Fernández from July of 1978. Majluta was denied the PRD's presidential nomination in 1978, despite the support of Guzmán. Majluta became acting president when Guzmán committed suicide on July 4, 1982. He relinquished office to Salvador Jorge Blanco, the president-elect, on August 16, 1982. Majluta was the PRD's presidential nominee in May of 1986 and was narrowly defeated by Joaquín Balaguer. Majluta subsequently formed the Independent Revolutionary party after losing control of the PRD to Jose Pena Gomez. Majluta was again defeated for the presidency in the election of 1990.

SALVADOR JORGE BLANCO (President, August 16, 1982–August 16, 1986). Salvador Jorge Blanco was born in Santiago on July 5, 1926. He received a degree in law from the University of Santo Domingo in 1950 and continued his education at the University of Madrid. Jorge Blanco returned to the Dominican Republic to teach law. He entered politics following the assassination of Rafael Trujillo in May of 1961. Jorge Blanco joined the Dominican Revolutionary party (PRD) in 1964 and served as attorney general in 1965. He also assisted in negotiations that ended the Dominican civil war later in the year. Jorge Blanco was defeated by Antonio Guzmán for the PRD's presidential nomination in 1977. He subsequently became president of the party and was elected to the Senate. Jorge Blanco received the PRD's nomination for the Presidency in 1982. He defeated Joaquín Balaguer in the subsequent election and took office on August 16, 1982. His government faced widespread protests and rioting following the removal of food subsidies in 1984. Protests resumed the following year when fuel prices were increased. The PRD was unsuccessful in elections in 1986, and Jorge Blanco relinquished office to Joaquín Balaguer on August 16, 1986. Jorge Blanco remained a leader of the PRD. In the early 1990s he was indicted on charges of misappropriation of public funds. He was convicted and sentenced to twenty years imprisonment in August of 1991.

JOAQUIN BALAGUER (President, August 16, 1986–). *See earlier entry under Heads of State.*

OTHER LEADERS

RAFAEL L. TRUJILLO (Commander-in-Chief of the Armed Forces, 1930–May 30, 1961). *See entry under Heads of State.*

RAFAEL "RAMFIS" TRUJILLO, JR. (Commander-in-Chief of the Armed Forces, May 30, 1961–November 14, 1961). Rafael L. "Ramfis" Trujillo, Jr., was born in 1929. He was the son of Dominican dictator Rafael Trujillo. The young Trujillo was named an army major at the age of three and was promoted to brigadier general at age of nine. He rose to the rank of lieutenant general and served as chief of the Dominican air force by the mid-1950s. He attended the Army Command and General Staff College at Ford Leavenworth, Kansas. While in the United States, he gained a reputation as a playboy and was often seen in the company of movie stars such as Zsa Zsa Gabor and Kim Novak. Ramfis was in Paris when his father was assassinated on May 30, 1961. He returned to the Dominican Republic to take his father's place as commander of the armed forces. Ramfis and the Trujillo family struggled for control of the government with President Joaquín Balaguer. Ramfis led a bloody purge against enemies of his father's regime.

The government faced growing opposition in the country and pressure from the United States to institute democratic reforms. Ramfis resigned as leader of the armed forces and the police on November 14, 1961. His uncles launched an abortive coup attempt to gain control of the country for the Trujillo family several days later. Ramfis went into exile in Spain on November 17, 1961. He was convicted in absentia of nine murders in 1965 and sentenced to thirty years in prison. Ramfis remained in exile in Madrid. He was seriously injured in an automobile accident near Madrid when he ran head-on into a car driven by the Duchess of Albuquerque. The duchess was killed, and Ramfis was hospitalized in Madrid. He began to make a recovery from his injuries, but developed pneumonia and died at the age of 40 on December 28, 1969.

Ecuador, Republic of

(República de Ecuador)

Ecuador is a country in northwestern South America. It was granted independence from Spain on May 24, 1822.

HEADS OF STATE

JOSÉ MARÍA VELASCO IBARRA (President, June 1, 1944–August 23, 1947). José María Velasco Ibarra was born in Quito on March 19, 1893. He was educated at the University of Quito and the University of Paris, where he received a degree in law. He returned to Ecuador to serve in the Public Welfare Society. Velasco subsequently became attorney general of Quito. He was also elected to the Chamber of Deputies and became its president. Velasco was a leader of the opposition to President Juan de Dio Martinez Mera. Impeach-

ment charges were brought against Martinez, and he was removed from office in December of 1933. Velasco was a candidate in the subsequent elections and received the support of the Conservative party. He was victorious and took office on September 1, 1934. He was unable to win the support of Congress for his economic legislation, however, and offered his resignation later in the year. When Congress refused to accept his resignation, he remained in office. Velasco became increasingly dictatorial in his rule. He imposed censorship restrictions on the newspapers and had opposition leaders arrested. On August 20, 1935, he was ousted by a military coup. He was briefly imprisoned before going into exile in Colombia. Velasco was again arrested in 1938 when he tried to reenter Ecuador. He led an unsuccessful revolt against the government of Carlos Arroyo del Rio in January of 1940, before returning to exile in Colombia. He was refused permission to reenter Ecuador in late 1943 to campaign in the presidential elections in June of 1944 and thus carried out a presidential campaign from exile. Velasco's supporters initiated a revolt in May of 1944, and President Arroyo del Rio's government resigned. Velasco returned to Quito on May 31, 1944, to take control of the government. His inability to cope with Ecuador's declining economy cost him the popularity of many of his former supporters, however. He resigned the presidency when threatened by a military coup on August 23, 1947, and went into exile in Argentina, where he remained until 1952. Velasco entered the presidential campaign that year and was again elected president. He took office on September 1, 1952. Velasco completed his term of office on August 21, 1956, and returned to Argentina. He came back to Ecuador to run again for president in 1960. He won the election and took office on September 1, 1960. Velasco was faced with general strikes and violent demonstrations against the government. He was ousted by the military on November 9, 1961, and sought asylum in the Mexican embassy before going into exile in Argentina. He returned to Ecuador after the military junta was ousted in March of 1966. Despite attempts by the opposition to prevent Velasco from again becoming president, he was victorious in the election of 1968 and took office on September 1, 1968. He faced growing opposition, however, and claimed dictatorial powers in mid-1970. Velasco was again ousted by a military coup on

February 15, 1972, shortly before his term was scheduled to come to an end. The army's fear of the election of Assad Bucaram as Velasco's successor prompted this ouster of the government. Velasco again went to Argentina, where he remained until February of 1979. He returned to Quito to bury his wife, who had been killed in an automobile accident. Velasco's health deteriorated, and he was hospitalized with a heart ailment. He died of a heart attack in Quito at the age of 86 on March 30, 1979.

CARLOS MANCHENO CAJAS (President, August 23, 1947–September 2, 1947). Carlos Mancheno Cajas was born in 1902. He served in the Ecuadorean military, where he rose to the rank of colonel. He was a member of the Liberal party and served as minister of defense in the government of Jose Velasco Ibarra. Mancheno was threatened with dismissal from the government and forced Velasco from office in a bloodless coup. Mancheno proclaimed himself president on August 23, 1947. He abolished the constitution on August 28, 1947, and declared his intention to rule by decree. He was ousted several days later in a military revolt led by Col. Angel Baquero Davila on September 2, 1947. He fled the country and went into exile in Argentina.

MARIANO SUÁREZ VIENTIMILLA (Acting President, September 2, 1947–September 17, 1947). Mariano Suárez Vientimilla was born in 1897. He was a member of the Conservative party and was selected to be vice president under José Velasco Ibarra in January of 1947. He was ousted with Velasco in a military coup led by Carlos Mancheno in August of 1947. Suárez was called upon to serve as acting president following Mancheno's ouster on September 2, 1947. He remained in office until a successor could be selected. Suárez relinquished office to Carlos

Julio Arosemena on September 17, 1947.

CARLOS JULIO AROSEMENA TOLA

(Acting President, September 17, 1947–August 21, 1948). Carlos Julio Arosemena Tola was born in 1894. He was educated at Cornell University in the United States, where he received a degree in economics. He returned to Ecuador to work in his father's banking business. Arosemena was elected vice president by a special vote of the National Assembly on September 17, 1947. He assumed the duties of president to complete the unexpired term of José Velasco Ibarra and took office on September 17, 1947. Arosemena conducted elections that resulted in Galo Plaza Lasso's selection as president. Arosemena stepped down from office on August 21, 1948. He left politics and returned to the banking business. He died at his home in Guayaquil on February 20, 1952.

GALO PLAZA LASSO (President, September 1, 1948–August 31, 1952). Galo Plaza Lasso was born in New York City on February 17, 1906. His father was General Leonidas Plaza Gutierrez, who twice served as Ecuador's president. The elder Plaza was serving as the Ecuadorean minister to the United States at the time of his son's birth. Plaza was educated in Ecuador until 1925, when he accompanied his family into exile in the United States following a revolution. He attended the University of Maryland until 1929. He returned to Ecuador in 1933 to take over management of his family's farming interests. Plaza entered politics and was elected to the Quito Municipal Council as a member of the Liberal party in 1937. He was elected mayor of Quito the following year and served until 1939. He was subsequently named minister of national defense in the government of President Aurelio Mosquera Narvaez. Plaza left the government when Mosquera left office in 1940.

Plaza was arrested in 1942 for his opposition to the regime of Carlos Arroyo del Rio and again went into exile in the United States, where he remained until later in the year. He was appointed ambassador to the United States in July of 1944. He resigned his position two years later in protest of President José Velasco Ibarra's seizure of dictatorial powers. Plaza was elected to the Senate in 1947 and was the candidate of the Civic Demonstration National Movement for the presidency after Velasco was deposed in 1948. Plaza narrowly defeated Conservative candidate Manuel Elicio Flor and took office on September 1, 1948. He led his country to economic and political stability and became the first president in Ecuador's history to complete a full term of office. He was ineligible to seek reelection under the constitution, however, and relinquished office to his elected successor, José Velasco Ibarra, on September 1, 1952. Plaza returned to manage his farms and also served on several missions for the United Nations. He led an observation mission to Lebanon in 1958 and chaired a committee on the Belgian Congo in 1960. Plaza was defeated by José Velasco Ibarra in the presidential election in 1960. He served as a United Nation's mediator following hostilities in Cyprus in 1964. Plaza was elected secretary-general of the Organization of American States in February of 1968 and completed his term in 1975. He returned to Ecuador to serve as an elder statesman in political affairs of the country. He died of a heart attack in Quito at the age of 80 on January 28, 1987.

JOSÉ MARÍA VELASCO IBARRA

(President, September 1, 1952–August 21, 1956). *See earlier entry under Heads of State.*

CAMILO PONCE ENRÍQUEZ (President, August 21, 1956–September 1, 1960). Camilo Ponce Enríquez was born in 1912. He was educated at the

University of Quito and the University of Santiago in Chile. He entered politics and was elected deputy mayor of Quito in 1943. Ponce was named minister of foreign relations in 1944 and led the Ecuadorean delegation to the conference in San Francisco to establish the United Nations. He was elected to the Congress in 1946 and served as minister of government and justice in the government of José Velasco Ibarra from 1953 until 1956. Ponce was the Conservative party candidate for president in 1956. He was elected by a small margin and took office on August 21, 1956. He was successful in stabilizing the nation's economy and combatting the rampant inflation in Ecuador. Ponce completed his term of office on September 1, 1960. He died of a heart attack in Quito on September 14, 1976.

JOSÉ MARÍA VELASCO IBARRA (President, September 1, 1960–November 9, 1961). *See earlier entry under Heads of State.*

CARLOS JULIO AROSEMENA MONROY (President, November 9, 1961–July 11, 1963). Carlos Julio Arosemena Monroy was born in 1919. He was a counselor at the Ecuadorean Embassy in Washington, D.C., from 1946 until 1952. He was then elected to the Chamber of Deputies and served in the cabinet as minister of defense until 1953. Arosemena served as vice president under José Velasco Ibarra from September of 1960. Arosemena and Velasco clashed over the government's economic policies and relationship with the United States. Arosemena took control of the Congress in November of 1961. He was dismissed and arrested by Velasco, but Velasco was ousted on November 9, 1961, and Arosemena was installed as his successor. Arosemena's decision to maintain diplomatic relations with Fidel Castro's Cuba resulted in anti–Communist demonstrations against the government

in 1962. Arosemena was ousted in a military coup led by Rear Admiral Ramón Castro Jijón on July 11, 1963. He was sent into exile in Panama. In the mid-1960s he returned to Ecuador and was reelected to the Chamber of Deputies. Arosemena remained active in politics and formed the Nationalist Revolutionary Party (PNR). He was declared ineligible to be a candidate in the presidential election in 1978. The party made little impact on the political scene and lost its sole legislative seat in 1988.

RAMÓN CASTRO JIJÓN (President, July 11, 1963–March 29, 1966). Ramón Castro Jijón was born in Esmeraldes in November of 1915. He was educated in the United States, where he studied naval engineering. He returned to Ecuador to serve in the navy. In the 1950s he was military attaché at the Ecuadorean Embassy in London. Castro Jijón subsequently served as commander in chief of the navy. He was the leader of the ruling military junta that ousted President Carlos Julio Arosemena Monroy on July 11, 1963. The junta was challenged by anti-government demonstrations following a decision to raise import taxes in March of 1966. Castro Jijón and the junta resigned on March 29, 1966, and turned over powers to the army high command. Castro Jijón was forced into retirement and went into exile in Brazil.

CLEMENTE YEROVI INDABURÚ (President, March 29, 1966–November 16, 1966). Clemente Yerovi Indaburú was born in Guayaquil in August of 1904. He worked as a businessman in Guayaquil until 1949, when he was appointed minister of the treasury and minister of economy. He remained in the cabinet until 1952. Yerovi subsequently served as minister of agriculture and Ecuador's ambassador to UNESCO. He was considered a political moderate and was selected by the army high command to serve as president of a civilian junta on March 29, 1966. He presided over elections in Ecuador and relinquished office to Otto Arosemena Gómez on November 16, 1966.

OTTO AROSEMENA GÓMEZ (President, November 16, 1966–September 1, 1968). Otto Arosemena Gómez was born in Guayaquil on July 19, 1925. He was educated locally and received a degree in law. He entered politics and was elected to the Chamber of Deputies in 1955. Arosemena served as president of the Chamber from 1955 until 1960, when he was elected to the Senate. He was elected interim president by the Constituent Assembly on November 16, 1966. He was a critic of United States economic policies in Latin America. When Wymberley Coerr, the United States ambassador to Ecuador, criticized the president in October of 1967, Arosemena ordered him out of the country. Arosemena completed his term of office on September 1, 1968. He returned to the Congress where, in October of 1980, he shot a fellow legislator in the thigh during a heated debate. Arosemena served several months in prison following the incident and then returned to the Congress. He died of a heart attack in Quito on April 20, 1984.

JOSÉ MARÍA VELASCO IBARRA (President, September 1, 1968–February 15, 1972). *See earlier entry under Heads of State.*

GUILLERMO RODRIGUEZ LARA (President, February 16, 1972–January 11, 1976). Guillermo Rodriguez Lara was born in Pujili, Cotopaxi Province, on November 4, 1923. He was educated at the Quito Military Academy and joined the Ecuadorean army. He served in various staff assignments and rose through the ranks to become brigadier general. He was named commander in chief of the army in 1971. The following year he led a

coup against President José María Velasco Ibarra shortly before a presidential election was to be held. The military feared the election of leftist candidate Assad Bucaram. Rodriguez became president of the military regime on February 16, 1972. The nation experienced an economic boost in the 1970s and became an oil exporting country. The Rodriguez government instituted some social reforms, including land distribution, in late 1973. The limited scope of the government's reform programs brought increased criticism of the military regime. Rodriguez survived a coup attempt in September of 1975 and was removed from power in a bloodless military coup on January 11, 1976.

ALFREDO POVEDA BURBANO (President, January 11, 1976–August 10, 1979). Alfredo Poveda Burbano was born in Ambato in 1926. He attended military academies in the United States, Argentina, and Brazil. He served in the Ecuadorean navy and was naval attaché at Ecuador's embassies in several Western European countries. Poveda rose to the rank of admiral. He served in the cabinet as minister of the interior from 1973 until 1975. He was then named commander in chief of the navy. He led the military junta that replaced President Guillermo Rodriguez Lara on January 11, 1976. The junta supervised civilian elections in April of 1979, and Poveda relinquished office to the victor, Jaime Roldos Aguilera, on August 10, 1979. Poveda went to Miami, Florida, for treatment for a heart ailment in 1990. He died there of a heart attack at the age of 64 on June 7, 1990.

JAIME ROLDOS AGUILERA (President, August 10, 1979–May 24, 1981). Jaime Roldos Aguilera was born in Guayaquil on November 5, 1940. He received a degree in law from the University of Guayaquil and entered politics. He was elected to Congress in the 1960s. Roldos was chosen to serve as the presidential candidate of the leftist Concentration of Popular Forces (CFP) in the elections in 1979. Assad Bucaram, Roldos' political mentor, had originally been the party's candidate, but was refused permission to run by the ruling military junta because his father was Lebanese. Roldos ran in his stead and won an overwhelming victory in the presidential runoff in April of 1979. Roldos's administration was more moderate than critics had expected, and the president's policies came into conflict with Bucaram, who was leader of the Congress. Much of Roldos's legislation was defeated by Bucaram's supporters in Congress. Roldos broke with Bucaram's party to form the moderate People, Change, and Democracy party in 1980. Roldos and his wife were killed in an airplane crash near the village of Guachanama on the Peruvian border on May 24, 1981.

OSWALDO HURTADO LARREA (President, May 24, 1981–August 10, 1984). Oswaldo Hurtado Larrea was born in 1940. He was a founder of the Ecuadorian Christian Democratic party in 1964. Hurtado was elected to the Congress and served as its president in 1966. He served as under-secretary of labor in 1969. Hurtado was a teacher at the Catholic University in Quito during the 1970s. He joined the leftist Popular Democracy coalition in the 1978 elections and was chosen as the vice presidential nominee to Jaime Roldos Aguilera. The ticket was victorious, and Hurtado became vice president in August of 1979. He succeeded to the presidency when Roldos was killed in an airplane crash on May 24, 1981. Hurtado's coalition government began to unravel, and several of Roldos's supporters on the cabinet resigned in 1982. Hurtado was challenged by labor strikes over the deterioration of Ecuador's economic stability in 1983. He completed his term of office on August 10, 1984, and remained active in the Popular Democracy party.

LEÓN FEBRES CORDERO RIVADENEIRA (President, August 10, 1984–August 10, 1988). León Febres Cordero Rivadeneira was born in Guayaquil on March 9, 1931. He was educated in the United States, where he received a degree in engineering. He returned to Ecuador to embark on a career in business. In 1965 he served as president of the Industrial Association of Ecuador and the Association of Latin American Industrialists. Febres Cordero was elected to the Ecuadorean Senate in 1966 and served until 1970. He joined the Social Christian party in the 1970s and was elected to Congress following the restoration of democratic institutions in 1979. He was a critic of the regimes of Jaime Roldos Aguilera and his successor, Oswaldo Hurtado Larrea. Febres Cordero was a candidate in the presidential election in 1984. He formed the National Reconstruction Front, a coalition of conservative parties that carried him to a victory in a runoff against Rodrigo Borja Cevallos. Febres Cordero took office on August 10, 1984. He gained a working majority in the Congress in June of 1985 when several independent members joined his coalition. The government survived a brief military revolt in March of 1986 when Lt. Gen. Frank Vargas Pazos was dismissed as chief of staff of the armed forces. Febres Cordero was kidnapped by members of the air force at Taura air base in January of 1987. The kidnappers demanded an amnesty for General Vargas, which Febres Cordero agreed to before his release. Febres Cordero completed his term of office on August 10, 1988 and was subsequently elected mayor of Guayaquil.

RODRIGO BORJA CEVALLOS (President, August 10, 1988–August 10, 1992). Rodrigo Borja Cevallos was born in Quito on June 19, 1935. He received a doctorate in law from the Central University of Ecuador in 1960. He entered politics and was elected to the Chamber of Deputies in 1962. Borja also taught political science at the Central University from 1963. He was a founder of the Democratic Left (ID) in 1968. The ruling Ecuadorean military junta allowed presidential elections to be held in 1978. Borja was defeated in the first round of balloting and endorsed Jaime Roldos Aguilera in the runoff. Borja was again a presidential candidate in the election in 1984. He was narrowly defeated in a runoff by León Febres Cordero. Borja defeated Abdala Bucaram in elections in May of 1988 and took office on August 10, 1988. He instituted a policy of economic austerity, which proved unpopular despite its success in stabilizing the economy. The opposition controlled the Chamber of Deputies during most of Borja's term of office, and six of the president's ministers were impeached by the Chamber. Borja completed his term of office on August 10, 1992.

SIXTO DURAN BALLÉN (President, August 10, 1992–). Sixto Duran Ballén was born to a prominent Ecuadorean family in Boston, Massachusetts, in 1922. He was educated in the United States and returned to Ecuador to enter politics in 1951. He served as minister of public works in the government of President Galo Plaza Lasso. Duran worked for the Inter-American Development Bank during the 1960s. He was elected mayor of Quito in the early 1970s and successfully managed the development of Ecuador's capital. Duran was the conservative party's candidate for president in elections in 1978. He was defeated by Jaime Roldos Aguilera and was again unsuccessful in presidential elections in 1988. Duran formed the Republican United party (PUD) in 1991 and was again a candidate for president in elections in 1992. He was victorious this time and took office on August 10, 1992. He initiated a program of economic reform to combat rising inflation and the national debt.

Egypt, Arab Republic of
(Jumhuriyat Misr al-'Arabiyah)

Egypt is located in northeastern Africa. It was granted independence from Great Britain on February 28, 1922.

HEADS OF STATE

FAROUK (King, April 28, 1936–July 22, 1952). Farouk was born in Cairo on February 11, 1920. He was the son of Fuad I and Queen Nazli. His father was sultan of Egypt at the time of Farouk's birth. Fuad became king following Egypt's independence from Great Britain on March 16, 1922. Farouk was raised by an English governess amd was educated by tutors before attending Kenry House and the

Sandhurst Royal Military Academy in England. Farouk returned to Egypt following the death of his father on April 28, 1936. He ruled under a regency until he reached his majority on July 29, 1937. Soon after his coronation, he engaged in a bitter dispute with the Wafd party under Mustafa el-Nahas. He encouraged the formation of anti-Wafd parties. Egypt attempted to remain neutral during World War II, though

Great Britain was allowed to maintain military bases in the country. Farouk appointed Hussein Sirry as prime minister in November of 1940, and the British viewed the government with suspicion. British troops invaded Farouk's palace in February of 1942 and demanded that he appoint a Wafdist government more favorable to the British war effort. Farouk dismissed the Wafd government in October of 1944 after the British no longer felt the need to intervene in Egyptian politics. He was instrumental in the decision to involve the Egyptian army in the war in Palestine in May of 1948. Egypt's defeat in that action contributed to Farouk's unpopularity with the army. His regime was also viewed as corrupt, and the king's self-indulgent playboy life-style did little to endear him to the Egyptian people. Farouk was forced to abdicate the throne in favor of his infant son, Ahmed Fuad, on July 22, 1952, following a military coup led by General Mohammed Naguib and Colonel Gamal Abdel Nasser. Farouk went into exile in Italy, where the ex-king became well known for his frequent visits to night clubs and gambling houses. Farouk suffered a massive heart attack while dining at a restaurant near Rome. He died at a Rome hospital at the age of 45 on March 18, 1965.

FUAD II (King, July 26, 1952–June 18, 1953). Ahmed Fuad was born on January 16, 1952, to King Farouk and Narriman Sadek. He was an infant when he was proclaimed king of Egypt on July 26, 1952, following the military coup that ousted his father, King Farouk. Fuad accompanied his family into exile in Italy, though he remained king under a regency until a republic was declared on June 18, 1953. Fuad's parents were divorced shortly after Farouk's abdication. Fuad settled in Lausanne, Switzerland.

MOHAMMED NAGUIB (President, June 18, 1953–November 14, 1954).

Mohammed Naguib was born in Khartoum in the Sudan on February 20, 1901. He attended the Royal Military Academy in Cairo. He served in the military and also continued his education, studying law, political economy, and languages. He served with distinction as a brigade commander in the Arab-Israeli war in Palestine in 1948. Naguib was promoted to colonel in 1948 and to major general in 1950. He was a critic of the corruption in the palace and took part in the Free Officers Group that ousted King Farouk in July of 1952. Naguib was named commander in chief of the armed forces following the coup. He also became prime minister and minister of war following the resignation of Ali Maher on September 7, 1952. Naguib engaged in a power struggle with Gamal Abdel Nasser, the leader of the Free Officers Group. Naguib felt that the army should remove itself from political affairs and that Egypt should be returned to a democratic civilian government. He became president of Egypt following the establishment of the Egyptian Republic on June 18, 1953. He resigned his positions on February 25, 1954, when Nasser banned the right-wing Muslim Brotherhood without consulting him. Naguib was briefly replaced by Nasser as prime minister, but was reinstated on February 27, 1954. He again resigned as prime minister on April 17, 1954, when pro-Nasser rallies took place throughout the country. He was allowed to remain as president, but was deprived of most of his powers. Naguib was ousted as president on November 14, 1954, following an assassination attempt against Nasser by the Muslim Brotherhood the previous month. Because of Naguib's connections with the organization, he was placed under house arrest at his home outside of Cairo. He was released by President Anwar Sadat in 1971, the year after Nasser's death. Naguib remained out of public life and died of cirrhosis of the liver at a Cairo military hospital at the age of 83 on August 28, 1984.

GAMAL ABDEL NASSER (President, November 17, 1954–September 28, 1970). Gamal Abdel Nasser was born in Beni Mor, Asyut Province, on January 15, 1918. He was educated in Cairo and entered the Royal Military Academy in 1937. He graduated the following year and was posted to the Sudan in 1939. Nasser returned to Cairo in 1941 and served as an instructor at the military academy. He organized and participated in the Free Officers Group, which plotted the overthrow of the monarchy. He was sent to Palestine to lead a battalion in the Arab-Israeli war in 1948. After the armistice agreement in 1949, he returned to Cairo and was promoted to the rank of colonel two years later. Growing discontent in the army spurred Nasser and his fellow conspirators in the Free Officers Group to stage a coup against King Farouk on July 22, 1953. Farouk abdicated the throne, and Nasser and the other junior officers supported Maj. Gen. Mohammed Naguib as head of the government. Friction soon developed between Nasser and Naguib, however. Naguib wanted the regime to revert to a parliamentary system and to allow the reestablishment of political parties. Nasser opposed these plans and formed the National Union in January of 1953 as Egypt's only legal political party. When Egypt was proclaimed a republic in June of 1953, Nasser served as deputy secretary-general of the ruling Revolutionary Council, deputy prime minister, and minister of the interior. His relationship with Naguib continued to deteriorate, and Nasser replaced him as prime minister on February 25, 1954. Naguib returned and dismissed Nasser the following day. When pro-Nasser demonstrations took place throughout Egypt, Naguib was forced to reinstate Nasser as prime minister on April 18, 1954. Naguib was stripped of most of his political power but remained

president until Nasser assumed that office as well on November 17, 1954. Nasser was the target of an assassination attempt in October of 1954. He initiated the suppression of the Muslim Brotherhood in response to the attack. Nasser opposed the Bagdad Pact of 1955 and began to look for financial and military support from the Soviet Union. He instituted a doctrine of Arab Socialism, and while initiating close relations with the Soviet Union, he suppressed the Communist party in Egypt. Nasser proclaimed a new constitution in January of 1956 and was elected president. Nasser planned the construction of the Aswan High Dam to bring water and electric power to the Nile Valley. He was counting on assistance from the United States and Great Britain for the financing of this project. When the assistance was withdrawn, Nasser nationalized the Suez Canal in July of 1956 in retaliation. Great Britain and France planned a military response to Nasser's action, and in October of 1956 Israel invaded the Sinai Peninsula. The Soviet Union and the United States objected to the military actions against Egypt and supported a United Nations resolution to force the cessation of hostilities and the withdrawal of Israel from the Sinai. Egypt joined with Syria to form the United Arab Republic in February of 1958, and Nasser supported the coup that ousted the Hashemite monarchy in Iraq the following July. He also supported an abortive coup against King Hussein of Jordan. Construction began on the Aswan Dam project with financial assistance from the Soviet Union in 1960. The United Arab Republic was dissolved in September of 1961 when Syria withdrew following a coup. Nasser relinquished the position of prime minister to Aly Sabry on September 24, 1962. Nasser supported the republican revolutionists in the civil war in Yemen and intervened militarily in October of 1962. This action brought Egypt into conflict with Saudi Arabia.

Nasser was also involved in subversive activities in numerous other Middle Eastern countries, including Jordan, Lebanon, Libya, and Morocco. A series of Arab summit conferences in 1964 helped to ease tension in the Arab world, and Nasser stopped fomenting subversion. He called for the withdrawal of United Nations forces from Egyptian territory and threatened to close the Gulf of Aqaba to Israeli shipping in 1967. These actions prompted Israel to launch a surprise attack in June of 1967. Nasser was embarrassed militarily when Egypt was soundly defeated in the Six Day War. He blamed the United States and the West for their support of Israel and offered his resignation, but demonstrations in his support convinced him to remain in office. He also reclaimed the position of prime minister on June 19, 1967. Nasser's health deteriorated following the Six Day War. He agreed to a cease-fire along the Suez Canal in 1970 in the hopes of reaching a political settlement for the Middle Eastern conflict. Nasser died in Cairo of a massive heart attack at the age of 52 on September 28, 1970.

ANWAR AL-SADAT (President, September 28, 1970–October 6, 1981). Anwar al-Sadat was born in Talah Monufiya on December 25, 1918. He was educated in Cairo and entered the Royal Military Academy in 1936. He met Gamal Abdel Nasser at the Academy and, after his graduation in 1938, participated in the formation of the Free Officers Group dedicated to the ousting of the Egyptian monarchy. Sadat's hatred of the British resulted in his collaboration with the Germans during World War II. He was arrested and court-martialed for his activities in October of 1942. He was dismissed from the army and imprisoned in a detention camp, but he escaped in November of 1944 and went into hiding. Sadat engaged in revolutionary activities and was again arrested on charges of terrorism in 1946. In 1949 he

was released and he was allowed to resume his career in the army the following year. Sadat was involved in Nasser's conspiracy to overthrow King Farouk on July 22, 1952. Sadat announced the success of the coup to the Egyptian people over the radio the following day. He served as a member of the ruling Revolutionary Command Council and served as Nasser's minister of state from 1954 until 1956. The following year he became secretary-general of the National Union, Egypt's only legal political party. He was elected president of the National Assembly in 1961 and also served as one of Nasser's four vice presidents from 1964 until Nasser restructured the government after the Six Day War in 1967. Nasser named Sadat his vice president in December of 1969, and Sadat succeeded to the presidency when Nasser died of a heart attack on September 28, 1970. The National Assembly confirmed his succession in October of 1970. Sadat vowed to continue Nasser's policies and extended the truce agreement with Israel that Nasser had negotiated. He also dedicated the Aswan Dam in January of 1971, a project that had been initiated by Nasser in 1960. Sadat also negotiated the creation of the Federation of Arab Republics with Libya and Syria in 1971. He expelled Soviet military personnel from Egypt in July of 1972 when he was denied an increase in military assistance. Sadat also took the post of prime minister on March 27, 1973. He abrogated the 1967 cease-fire agreement with Israel on October 6, 1973, and launched an attack across the Suez Canal. Egyptian forces gained ground in the Sinai Peninsula before agreeing to another cease-fire. Egypt also reestablished diplomatic relation with the United States in November of 1973. Sadat stepped down as prime minister on September 25, 1974. The slow process of peace negotiations in the Middle East led Sadat to begin an independent initiative in 1977. In a daring attempt to break the stalemate, Sadat offered to go to Israel to present his views to the Israeli government. Israeli prime minister Menachem Begin issued an invitation, and Sadat visited Jerusalem on November 19, 1977. Negotiations between Egypt and Israel continued with the support of the United States at Camp David, Maryland. This led to the signing of an Israeli-Egyptian peace treaty in March of 1979. Though Sadat and Begin were awarded the Nobel Peace Prize in 1978, Sadat was vilified throughout most of the Arab world for what was considered his betrayal of the long-standing goal to destroy Israel. Sadat initially remained popular in Egypt, but was threatened with domestic unrest when the Egyptian economy failed to improve. Sadat again became prime minister on May 12, 1980, in an attempt to streamline his government. He gained the antipathy of Iran when he offered asylum to the exiled shah in July of 1980. Sadat also initiated a crackdown on Muslim fundamentalists who were involved in civil unrest against the government. On October 6, 1981, Sadat was assassinated during a military parade in Nasr City, near Cairo, by a group of commandos who charged the reviewing stand with grenades and machine guns.

HOSNI MUBARAK (President, October 14, 1981–   ). Mohamed Hosni Mubarak was born in Kafr-El Meselha in northern Egypt on May 4, 1929. He graduated from the Royal Military Academy in 1949 and subsequently attended the Air Force Academy, where he served as a flight instructor from 1952 until 1959. He also attended pilot training courses in the Soviet Union. Mubarak was named commander of the Air Force Academy in 1967 and rose to air force chief of staff in 1969. President Anwar Sadat appointed him deputy minister of war and air force commander in chief in 1972. Mubarak was given much of the credit for the success of Egypt's attack on Israeli positions in the Sinai Peninsula in the early stages of the war in October of 1973. Sadat appointed Mubarak as his vice president in April of 1975. Mubarak was sitting several seats away from Sadat when militant Islamic fundamentalists opened fire on the presidential reviewing stand during a parade on October 6, 1971. The president and other members of his party were killed, but Mubarak escaped with minor injuries. He took over the reins of government as prime minister on October 7, 1981. He was approved as Sadat's successor as president by the Parliament, and he was confirmed by a national election. Mubarak took office on October 14, 1981, and pledged to continue the policies of his predecessor. He appointed Ahmad Fuad Mohieddin as prime minister on January 2, 1982. Mubarak was faced with a seriously declining economy, which he sought to improve with little success. He tried to serve as a mediator between Israel and the Palestinians to find a solution to the ongoing hostilities in the Middle East. He was a leading opponent of the Iraqi invasion of Kuwait in August of 1990. He tried to seek a diplomatic solution to the situation, but when that failed, he committed Egyptian troops to the United States-led multinational forces that forced Iraq to leave Kuwait. Mubarak's government continued to be threatened by terrorist actions by Islamic fundamentalists.

HEADS OF GOVERNMENT

MAHMOUD FAHMY EL-NOKRACHY (Prime Minister, March 7, 1945–February 15, 1946). Mahmoud Fahmy el-Nokrachy was born in Alexandria in 1882. A former teacher, he joined the Egyptian government in 1920 and served in various posts during the 1920s and 1930s. He was Egyptian minister of the interior, education, and finance from 1938 to 1940. Nokrachy served as foreign minister from 1944 until 1945. In 1945 he was elected president of the Sa'adist party, and he became prime minister of Egypt on February 25, 1945, following the assassination of Ahmed Maher Pasha. He resigned on February 15, 1946, following riots in Cairo and Alexandria, but was again appointed prime minister on December 9, 1946. Nokrachy was named Egypt's military governor following Egypt's invasion of Palestine on May 14, 1948. He was a supporter of Egypt's policy advocating the elimination of the state of Israel and was a proponent of the withdrawal of English forces from the Anglo-Egyptian Sudan. Nokrachy outlawed the Muslim Brotherhood in 1948 after that organization had been involved in violent confrontations with the government. Nokrachy was shot to death in the Ministry of the Interior in Cairo by a member of the Muslim Brotherhood on December 28, 1948.

ISMAIL SIDKY (Prime Minister, February 15, 1946–December 8, 1946). Ismail Sidky was born in 1875. He was educated in Cairo and attended the Cairo Law School. In 1899 he served on the Municipal Council of Alexandria. He later worked in the Ministry of the Interior before being named minister of muslim religious institutions. Sidky was a leader in the Egyptian nationalist movement and was a founder of the Wafd party. He was deported to Malta by the British in 1917 after anti-British riots. He returned to Egypt to establish the Liberal Constitution party in 1922 and served as deputy minister of the interior from 1924 until 1926. Sidky became prime minister on June 20, 1930. He survived several assassination attempts over the next year. He implemented a conservative constitution to provide for greater power for the mon-

archy and instituted harsh measures against dissidents to the government. Sidky resigned as prime minister on March 21, 1933. He subsequently served as the Egyptian delegate to meetings that resulted in the Anglo-Egyptian alliance. He served as minister of finance from 1937 until 1939 and then retired from politics. He was recalled to again serve as prime minister on February 15, 1946, following the resignation of Mahmoud Fahmy el-Nokrachy after student riots in Cairo. Sidky settled the disturbances by demanding the removal of the British military from Egypt and using dictatorial methods to crush demonstrations. He went to London to negotiate an agreement with the British over the Sudan. Conflicting interpretations of what the agreement stated forced Sidky to resign as prime minister on December 8, 1946. He remained in the Senate, where he opposed Egypt's invasion of Palestine in 1948. Sidky died of a stroke in a Paris hospital on July 9, 1950.

MAHMOUD FAHMY EL-NOKRACHY (Prime Minister, December 9, 1946– December 28, 1948). *See earlier entry under Heads of Government.*

IBRAHIM ABDUL HADI (Prime Minister, December 28, 1948–July 26, 1949). Ibrahim Abdul Hadi was born in 1901. He was a member of the Sa'adist party and was named to the cabinet as minister of finance in 1946. He was appointed chief of the royal cabinet in 1947 and returned to the finance ministry the following year. Abdul Hadi became prime minister on December 28, 1948, following the assassination of Mahmoud Fahmy el-Nokrachy. The Egyptian government concluded a cease-fire with Israel, while denouncing the recognition of Israel by the West. Abdul Hadi resigned as prime minister on July 26, 1949, following a dispute between the Sa'adist and Liberal party members of his cabinet. Abdul Hadi was arrested after the ouster of King

Farouk in July of 1952 and was brought to trial on charges of having forced the Egyptian army into the disastrous Palestinian War in 1948. He was sentenced to death by a revolutionary court in 1953. His sentence was commuted to life imprisonment, and he was released for reasons of health in 1954. Abdul Hadi's political rights were restored in 1960, though he remained out of politics.

HUSSEIN SIRRY (Prime Minister, July 26, 1949–January 12, 1950). Hussein Sirry was born in Cairo in 1892. He was educated in Egypt and France and received a degree in engineering. He was considered a leading authority on irrigation and an expert on the flow of the Nile River, because he had traveled to its source in the 1920s. Sirry was also responsible for planning the transformation of the Qattara depression near Cairo into a lake. He entered the Egyptian cabinet as minister of public works in 1938. He was elected to the Senate in 1939 and served as minister of war. Later in the year he was named minister of finance and communications and served until 1940. Sirry was appointed prime minister on November 14, 1940, and attempted to maintain Egypt's neutrality during World War II. He was dismissed on February 8, 1942, when the British military forced King Farouk to name a prime minister from the Wafd party. Sirry was named to head a caretaker coalition cabinet on July 26, 1949. He stepped down on January 12, 1950. He also served as foreign minister in 1950. He was again named prime minister on July 2, 1952. Sirry resigned on July 20, 1952, several days before a military coup ousted King Farouk. He retired from politics and died in Cairo at the age of 68 on January 6, 1961.

MUSTAFA EL-NAHAS (Prime Minister, January 12, 1950–January 27, 1952). Mustafa el-Nahas was born in Cairo on June 15, 1876. He attended the Cairo School of Law, where he graduated in 1900. He became a judge in 1914 but was dismissed from government service in 1919 for his political activities. Nahas was deported to Malta in 1921 and released from exile in 1923, following Egyptian independence. He was elected to the National Assembly in 1924 and served as minister of communications in the subsequent cabinet of Said Zaghlul. He was elected vice president of the chamber of deputies in 1927 and succeeded Zaghlul as leader of the Wafd party later in the year. Nahas led opposition to the Anglo-Egyptian treaty of 1928 and demanded that British troops leave Egypt. On March 16, 1928, he was named prime minister, but he was forced to resign by the palace on June 25, 1928. New elections were held in 1929, and the Wafdists were victorious. Nahas returned as prime minister on January 1, 1930. He stepped down on June 20, 1930, when negotiations with the British concerning the status of the Sudan collapsed. He was again named prime minister on May 10, 1936, and negotiated the Anglo-Egyptian Treaty of Alliance in 1936. Nahas also presided over Egypt's entry into the League of Nations. Friction developed between the prime minister and King Farouk, and Nahas was dismissed on December 30, 1937. The Wafd party was badly defeated in the elections of 1938. Nahas claimed electoral fraud and refused to serve in subsequent governments. He was again named prime minister on February 8, 1942, when the British pressured King Farouk for his appointment. Nahas cooperated with the British during World War II and laid the foundation for the formation of the Arab League in October of 1944. He was dismissed by King Farouk on October 8, 1944. The Wafd party boycotted the elections in January of 1945 and went into opposition. Nahas demanded the withdrawal of all British troops from Egypt. He was the target of an unsuccessful assassination attempt in

April of 1946. Nahas and the Wafds refused to participate in negotiations with Great Britain the following month. The Wafds returned to power in elections in January of 1950, and Nahas again became prime minister on January 12, 1950. He proposed social reforms, including the establishment of a social security system. He also abrogated the Anglo-Egyptian treaty of 1936, which caused tense relations with Great Britain in 1951. Rioting broke out in Cairo in 1952, and King Farouk dismissed Nahas for his failure to maintain security on January 27, 1952. Nahas was placed under house arrest following the coup that deposed Farouk in July of 1952. He was deprived of his political rights in 1954. His rights were restored in 1960, but he continued to live in obscurity in Alexandria. Nahas died in Cairo after a long illness at the age of 86 on August 23, 1965.

ALI MAHER (Prime Minister, January 27, 1952–March 1, 1952). Ali Maher was born in Cairo in 1883. He received a degree in law from the Khedive school of law and became a judge in 1907. He served on the Egyptian delegation to London that negotiated the independence of Egypt in 1922. Maher was elected to the Egyptian Parliament in 1924 and served as under-secretary of state for education. He was named minister of education in 1925 and served until the following year. In 1928 he returned to the cabinet as minister of finance. Maher was elected to the Senate in 1930 and was named minister of justice. He retained that position until 1932. He was appointed chief of the royal cabinet in 1935, during the illness of King Fuad. Maher was also named prime minister, minister of the interior, and minister of foreign affairs on January 30, 1936. He stepped down on May 10, 1936, after elections were held. He was again named chief of the royal cabinet after King Farouk, who had succeeded his father to the throne in April of 1936, came of age in July of

1937. Maher represented Egypt in London at the Palestine conference in 1939. He also returned to the Senate in 1939 and formed a cabinet as prime minister after the resignation of Mohammed Tawfiq Nessim on August 18, 1939. He also served as military governor of Egypt after the start of World War II. Maher tried to maintain his country's neutrality during the war, despite Italy's declaration of war on Egypt. He sought a diplomatic solution to the conflict with Italy and was forced to resign on June 22, 1940. Maher was placed under house arrest during the administration of Mustafa el-Nahas because the British believed that Maher had turned over Egyptian defense plans to the Italians. He was released when his brother, Ahmed Maher, became prime minister in October of 1944. His brother was assassinated in February of the following year. Ali Maher opposed the Anglo-Egyptian treaty drafted in 1946. He remained out of the government until January 27, 1952, when he was again called upon to form a cabinet following anti-British riots in Cairo. Maher also became military governor, foreign minister, and minister of the army and navy. He ruled under martial law and demanded that British military forces withdraw from the Suez Canal zone. Maher also supported Egypt's claim for a union with the Sudan. He was replaced on March 1, 1952, but was again appointed prime minister on July 24, 1952, following the coup that ousted King Farouk. Maher's opposition to the ruling junta's agrarian reform program and revolutionary policies led to his resignation on September 7, 1952. He died of a heart attack at the age of 77 on August 23, 1960, while vacationing in Geneva.

AHMED NAGUIB HILALY (Prime Minister, March 1, 1952–June 29, 1952). Ahmed Naguib Hilaly was born in Assiut, Upper Egypt, in 1891. He graduated from the Cairo School of Law and entered government service.

In 1934 he was named minister of education in the cabinet of Mohammed Tawfiq Nessim. He joined the Wafd party and was elected to the Parliament. In 1937 Hilaly was again named minister of education and he served in that position during the war cabinet of Mustafa el-Nahas from 1942 until 1944. He returned to private life to practice law after Nahas's fall. He opposed the Wafd party's hard-line anti-British policies and was expelled from the party in 1951. Hilaly was recalled to government to form an independent cabinet as prime minister on March 1, 1952. He attempted to eliminate corruption in the government and suspended the Parliament for thirty days. He also postponed elections and closed Fuad University after student demonstrations. Hilaly was replaced as prime minister on June 29, 1952. He was asked to form a new government on July 22, 1952. The following day King Farouk was ousted in a military coup, and Hilaly was dismissed by the ruling junta. He was detained by the new government until his release in December of 1952. He was deprived of his political rights in 1954. Hilaly died in Cairo at the age of 67 on December 11, 1958.

HUSSEIN SIRRY (Prime Minister, July 2, 1952–July 20, 1952). *See earlier entry under Heads of Government.*

ALI MAHER (Prime Minister, July 24, 1952–September 7, 1952). *See earlier entry under Heads of Government.*

MOHAMMED NAGUIB (Prime Minister, September 7, 1952–February 25, 1954). *See entry under Heads of State.*

GAMAL ABDEL NASSER (Prime Minister, February 25, 1954–February 26, 1954). *See entry under Heads of State.*

MOHAMMED NAGUIB (Prime Minister, February 27, 1954–April 17, 1954). *See entry under Heads of State.*

GAMAL ABDEL NASSER (Prime Minister, April 18, 1954–September 24, 1962). *See entry under Heads of State.*

ALY SABRY (Prime Minister, September 24, 1962–September 29, 1965). Aly Sabry was born in 1920. He attended the Royal Military Academy and served in the Egyptian air force. He participated in the coup that ousted King Farouk in 1952 and served as the junta's liaison officer with the United States Embassy. A close associate of President Gamal Abdel Nasser, he was appointed foreign minister in 1958. Sabry became minister for presidential affairs in 1960 and was appointed prime minister on September 24, 1962, when Nasser relinquished that position. Sabry promoted closer ties between Egypt and the Soviet Union. He was replaced by Zakaria Mohieddin as prime minister on September 29, 1965, as part of Nasser's restructuring of the Egyptian government. Sabry subsequently became vice president and chairman of the Arab Socialist Union, Egypt's only legal political party. He was considered a leading candidate to succeed Nasser following the president's death in 1970. Anwar Sadat was elected as Nasser's successor, however, and Sabry was named to the new government as one of two vice presidents. Sabry was dismissed by President Sadat in May of 1971. He was arrested and charged with plotting against the government. Sabry was tried and convicted by a military tribunal and sentenced to death. His sentence was commuted to life imprisonment, however, and he was released in 1981 for reasons of health. Sabry remained politically inactive and was hospitalized in Cairo after suffering a blood clot in his lung in 1991. He died from internal bleeding at the age of 71 on August 3, 1991.

ZAKARIA MOHIEDDIN (Prime Minister, September 29, 1965–September 10, 1966). Zakaria Mohieddin was born in the Dakhaliyya region on May 7, 1918. He attended the Royal Military Academy with Gamal Abdel Nasser in 1938. He joined with the Free Officers Group in the ouster of King Farouk in July of 1952. Mohieddin served on the ruling Revolutionary Council and was minister of the interior from 1953 until 1962. He was also named vice president in 1961. Mohieddin served on the Presidency Council from 1962 until 1964, when he was appointed deputy prime minister. He was named prime minister and minister of the interior by Nasser on September 29, 1965. He was replaced by Sidky Soliman on September 10, 1966. Mohieddin was again named as vice president in September of 1966 and was selected to replace Nasser as president when Nasser resigned following the Six Day War on June 9, 1967. Nasser was encouraged to remain in office, and the resignation was rescinded without Mohieddin taking office. Mohieddin again served as deputy prime minister under Nasser from 1967 until 1968. He was considered a possible presidential candidate following Nasser's death in September of 1970. Anwar Sadat was elected president, and Mohieddin held no further positions in the national government.

MOHAMMAD SIDKY SOLIMAN (Prime Minister, September 10, 1966–June 19, 1967). Mohammad Sidky Soliman was born in 1919. He was educated at Fuad University and joined the Egyptian army, where he rose to the rank of colonel. He was named to the cabinet as minister for the Aswan Dam in September of 1962 and retained that position until September 10, 1966, when he was selected by President Gamal Abdel Nasser to form a government as prime minister. Soliman tried to raise productivity and cut government spending to improve the economy. His government resigned on June 19, 1967, following the Arab-Israeli war. President Nasser formed his own government, and Soliman served as deputy prime minister and minister of industry and power until Nasser's death in June of 1970.

GAMAL ABDEL NASSER (Prime Minister, June 19, 1967–June 20, 1970). *See entry under Heads of State.*

MAHMOUD FAWZI (Prime Minister, June 20, 1970–January 17, 1972). Mamhoud Fawzi was born in Cairo in 1900. He studied law at the University of Cairo and the University of Rome, where he received a doctorate degree. He continued his studies in Great Britain and the United States. Fawzi subsequently joined the Egyptian diplomatic corps and served as a vice-consul in the United States from 1926 until 1929. He was then stationed as a consul in Kobe, Japan, where he remained until 1936. He served in the Egyptian embassies in Athens, Greece, and Liverpool, England, before returning to Cairo in 1940. Fawzi served in the ministry of foreign affairs until 1941, when he was appointed consul-general in Jerusalem. He was again posted to the United States in 1944 and became a delegate to the United Nations the following year. He returned to Egypt in 1947 and was appointed foreign minister following the overthrow of King Farouk in 1952. Fawzi retained that position under President Gamal Abdel Nasser until 1964, when he was appointed deputy prime minister for foreign affairs. He was named special presidential advisor on foreign affairs in 1967. Fawzi was appointed prime minister following Nasser's death on June 20, 1970. He was replaced on January 17, 1972, but remained in the government as one of two vice presidents under Anwar Sadat. Fawzi retired from politics in 1974 and died in a Cairo hospital from a brain clot at the age of 81 on June 12, 1981.

AZIZ SIDKY (Prime Minister, January 17, 1972–March 27, 1973). Aziz Sidky was born in Cairo on July 1, 1920. He attended the University of Cairo, where he received a degree in engineering. He continued his studies at Oregon University and Harvard University in the United States. Sidky returned to Egypt in 1951 to serve on the engineering faculty at Alexandria University. He was appointed to Gamal Abdel Nasser's cabinet as minister of industry in 1956. He was named minister of presidential affairs the following year. From 1958 until 1964 he again served as minister of industry. Sidky subsequently served as deputy prime minister in charge of industry until August of 1965, when he resigned following a dispute with Prime Minister Aly Sabry. He returned to the cabinet in October of 1967, where he again served as minister of industry. Sidky was named secretary-general of the Arab Socialist Union in 1971. He was also named deputy prime minister in September of 1971. Sidky was appointed prime minister by Anwar Sadat on January 17, 1972. He instituted financial austerity measures to improve the Egyptian economy. Sadat reorganized the government and took the position of prime minister for himself on March 27, 1973. Sidky remained in government, serving as an advisor to President Sadat. He remained in that position until 1975, when he was dismissed from the government.

ANWAR AL-SADAT (Prime Minister, March 27, 1973–September 25, 1974). *See entry under Heads of State.*

ABDUL AZIZ HEGAZY (Prime Minister, September 25, 1974–April 16,

1975). Abdul Aziz Muhammad Hegazy was born on January 3, 1923. He was educated at Fuad University. He became an educator and served as the dean of Ain Shams University from 1966 until 1968. Hegazy was named to the cabinet as minister of the treasury in 1968. He was elevated to deputy prime minister and minister of finance, economics, and foreign trade in 1973. He became first deputy prime minister to Anwar Sadat in April of the following year. Sadat relinquished the government to Hegazy on September 25, 1974. Hegazy advocated a program of economic liberalization. Workers and students rioted in the streets of Cairo in January of 1975 over inflation and food shortages. Hegazy resigned from office on April 16, 1975. He subsequently left government and worked as a management consultant in the private sector.

MAMDOUH SALEM (Prime Minister, April 16, 1975–October 2, 1978). Mamdouh Salem was born in Alexandria in 1918. He graduated from the Police Academy in 1940 and began a career in the Customs Office in Alexandria. He rose to become chief of the investigations branch. Salem was named governor of Asyut in August of 1967. He was appointed governor of Gharbia in August of 1970 and was named governor of Alexandria the following November. Salem was named to the cabinet in May of 1971 and served as minister of the interior. He rose to become deputy prime minister to Aziz Sidky in January of 1972. He remained in that position under Anwar Sadat in March of 1973 and also served as deputy military governor-general. Salem was appointed prime minister on April 13, 1975, when the previous government could not control violent demonstrations over food shortages and escalating inflation. He reorganized his cabinet in 1978 and merged his Arab Socialist party with the National Democratic party of Anwar Sadat. Salem resigned on October 2, 1978, when his foreign minister, Ibrahim Kamel, resigned in protest over the signing of the Egypt-Israeli peace accords. Salem remained an advisor to Sadat and also advised his successor Hosni Mubarak. Salem went to London for medical treatment in early 1988 and died there at the age of 70 on February 25, 1988.

MUSTAFA KHALIL (Prime Minister, October 2, 1978–May 12, 1980). Mustafa Khalil was born in El Kalyoubieh on November 18, 1920. He was educated at the University of Cairo. He was employed by the Egyptian State Railways from 1941. Khalil attended the University of Illinois in the United States in 1947, where he received a degree in transport engineering. He returned to Egypt and his work with the State Railways. Khalil was named to Gamal Abdel Nasser's government as minister of communications and transport in 1956 and served until his appointment as deputy prime minister in 1964. The following year Khalil was named minister of industry, mineral resources, and electricity. Khalil was dismissed from the cabinet in 1966 over his insistence that Egypt's industrial growth be influenced by economic reality, rather than ideology. He subsequently became head of the State Broadcasting Corporation. He advocated fewer government restrictions on the media and was forced to resign in 1970. Khalil returned to private industry, but often served as a consultant to the government. He returned to the government when he was named prime minister by Anwar Sadat on October 2, 1978. He also served as foreign minister from 1979. Sadat reorganized the government on May 12, 1980, dismissing Khalil and assuming the prime ministership himself. Khalil subsequently became chairman of the Arab International Bank in Cairo.

ANWAR AL-SADAT (Prime Minister, May 12, 1980–October 6, 1981). *See entry under Heads of State.*

HOSNI MUBARAK (Prime Minister, October 7, 1981–January 2, 1982). *See entry under Heads of State.*

AHMAD FUAD MOHIEDDIN (Prime Minister, January 2, 1982–June 5, 1984). Ahmad Fuad Mohieddin was born in 1926. He was educated at Cairo University Medical School, where he received a doctorate in radiology. In 1957 he was elected to the National Assembly. He served as governor of Alexandria from 1968 until 1974, when he was named minister of local government. Later in the year he was appointed minister of health. Mohieddin was named deputy prime minister under Anwar Sadat in May of 1980. He was appointed prime minister by Hosni Mubarak on January 2, 1982. He also served as secretary-general of the National Democratic party, which was victorious in parliamentary elections in May of 1984. Mohieddin died suddenly of a heart attack at his office in Cairo at the age of 58 on June 5, 1984.

KAMAL HASSAN ALI (Prime Minister, June 5, 1984–September 4, 1985). Kamal Hassan Ali was born in Cairo on September 18, 1921. He attended the military academy and entered the army in 1942. He rose through the ranks and participated in four wars between Egypt and Israel. Ali served as head of the Egyptian Intelligence Service from 1975 until 1978. He was subsequently promoted to lieutenant general and named minister of defense by President Anwar Sadat in 1978. He also served as Egypt's representative to the negotiations that led to the 1979 Egyptian-Israeli peace treaty. Ali was appointed foreign minister and deputy prime minister in 1980 and was named Prime Minister by President Hosni Mubarak on June 5, 1984. His government was faced with growing economic difficulties and increased agitation by Muslim fundamentalist extremists. Ali resigned his position on September 4, 1985. He became chairman of the Egyptian Gulf Bank in 1987. Ali died in Cairo at the age of 72 on March 27, 1993.

ALI LUTFI (Prime Minister, September 4, 1985–November 12, 1986). Ali Lutfi Mahmud Lutfi was born in Cairo on October 6, 1935. He was educated in Egypt and served on the faculty of Ain Shams University from 1957. Lutfi was named to the government as minister of finance in 1978. He left the cabinet in 1980 to serve on the board of directors of the Cairo Bank of Commerce and Development. Lutfi became a leading economic advisor to President Hosni Mubarak and was appointed prime minister by Mubarak on September 4, 1985. Egypt's growing economic difficulties forced Lutfi's replacement on November 12, 1986. He was selected as Speaker of the Shoura Council after leaving office and remained an advisor to the government.

ATEF SEDKI (Prime Minister, November 12, 1986–   ). Atef Muhammad Najib Sedki was born in 1930. He attended law school at the University of Paris. In 1958 he returned to Egypt and became a professor of economics at Cairo University. Sedki retained his teaching position until 1973, when he was appointed cultural attaché to the Egyptian Embassy in Paris. He returned to Egypt again in 1980 to serve on the Advisory Council for Economic and Financial Affairs. He was appointed director of the Government Audit Office in 1985. Sedki was named prime minister on November 12, 1986, in order to deal with Egypt's deteriorating economic conditions. He initiated austerity and reform measures to bring Egypt's economy into compliance with recommendations by the World Bank and the International Monetary Fund.

El Salvador, Republic of

(República de El Salvador)

El Salvador is a country on the Pacific coast of Central America. It was granted independence from Spain on September 15, 1821.

HEADS OF STATE

OSMIN AGUIRRE Y SALINAS (President, October 21, 1944–February 28, 1945). Osmin Aguirre y Salinas was born in 1889. He served in the Salvadorean military, where he rose to the rank of colonel. Aguirre was a leader of the coup that forced the resignation of Salvadorean leader Maximiliano Hernández Martinez in May of 1944. Aguirre led another coup against Hernández's vice president and successor Andres Ignacio Menendez on October 21, 1944. Aguirre served as president of the subsequent military regime. He presided over new elections and relinquished office to the victor, Salvador Castañeda Castro, on February 28, 1945. Aguirre subsequently retired from politics. He was shot to death near his home in San Salvador at the age of 88 on July 12, 1977. His assassins were presumed to be members of a leftist terrorist organization.

SALVADOR CASTAÑEDA CASTRO (President, February 28, 1945–December 14, 1948). Salvador Castañeda Castro was born in Cojutedeque on August 6, 1888. He became president of El Salvador on February 28, 1945. His government suspended constitutional liberties in September of 1946. Castañeda Castro survived several plots to overthrow his government in 1947. He scheduled elections for the Constituent Assembly to gain an extension on his term of office that was scheduled to end in 1949. He was deposed in a military coup on December 14, 1948. Castañeda Castro was imprisoned until September 16, 1949, when he was released without standing trial. He died in San Salvador on March 5, 1965.

MANUEL DE JESÚS CÓRDOVA (President, December 17, 1948–January 4, 1949). Manuel de Jesús Córdova served in the Salvadorean army, where he rose to the rank of lieutenant colonel. He was selected to serve as president of the ruling military junta on December 17, 1948, following the ouster of President Salvador Castañeda Castro. Córdova resigned from the junta on January 4, 1949, and was replaced by Major Oscar Osorio.

OSCAR OSORIO (President, January 4, 1949–October 22, 1949). Oscar Osorio was born in 1910. He served in the Salvadorean army and rose to the rank of major. He was appointed to the ruling military junta on December 17, 1948, following the ouster of President Salvador Castañeda Castro. Major Osorio became president of the junta when Lt. Col. Manuel J. Córdova resigned on January 4, 1949. Osorio stepped down on October 22, 1949, to campaign for the presidency. He was the nominee of the Democratic Unity party in elections in 1950. He was elected president and took office on September 14, 1950. Osorio instituted a series of labor and economic reforms. He also led El Salvador into member ship in the Organization of Central American States in 1951. He completed his term of office on September 14, 1956. Osorio was hospitalized in Houston, Texas, in February of 1969. He died after undergoing surgery at the age of 58 on March 6, 1969.

OSCAR BOLANOS (President, October 22, 1949–September 14, 1950). Oscar Bolanos served in the Salvadorean army, where he rose to the rank of major. He was appointed to the ruling military junta on December 17, 1948, following the ouster of President Salvador Castañeda Castro. Bolanos became president of the junta following the resignation of Major Oscar Osorio on October 22, 1949. Bolanos continued to lead the government during elections the following year. He relinquished his duties to Osorio, the election victor, on September 14, 1950.

OSCAR OSORIO (President, September 14, 1950–September 14, 1956). *See earlier entry under Heads of State.*

JOSÉ MARÍA LEMUS (President, September 14, 1956–October 26, 1960). José María Lemus was born in 1911. He received military training in El Salvador and the United States. He was active in the military coup that ousted President Salvador Castañeda Castro in 1948 and was named undersecretary of defense in the subsequent military government. Lemus was promoted to the rank of lieutenant colonel and appointed minister of the interior in 1949. He served in that position until 1955, when he became the presidential candidate for the ruling Revolutionary Party of Democratic Unification. He was elected unopposed and took office on September 14, 1956. Growing opposition to El Salvador's military regime resulted in labor strikes and student demonstrations, however. Lemus was ousted by a coup on October 26, 1960, and replaced by a military-civilian coalition. The deposed president was forced to leave the country. He subsequently went to Guatemala before settling in Costa Rica. Lemus lived in seclusion until September of 1992, when his two pit bull terriers attacked and killed an elderly man in San Jose. Lemus was found guilty of negligence and fined on March 22, 1993. He entered a San Jose hospital on the day of the sentencing and died of Hodgkin's disease at the age of 72 on March 31, 1993.

MIGUEL CASTILLO (President, October 26, 1960–January 25, 1961). Miguel Angel Castillo served in the Salvadorean military, where he rose to the rank of colonel. He was active in the coup that ousted President José María Lemus in October of 1960. Colonel Castillo was chosen to lead the subsequent leftist military-civilian junta on October 26, 1960. The junta was ousted by another coup on January 25, 1961.

ANÍBAS PORTILLO (President, January 25, 1961–January 25, 1962). Aníbas Portillo served in the Salvadorean military and rose to the rank of colonel. He supported the military coup that ousted the ruling leftist civilian-military junta on January 25, 1961. Portillo was named president of the ruling Civil-Military Directorate on January 25, 1961. The directorate stepped down on January 25, 1962, following the selection of Eusebio Rodolfo Cordon Cea as provisional president.

EUSEBIO RODOLFO CORDON CEA (President, January 25, 1962– July 1, 1962). Eusebio Rodolfo Cordon Cea was born in 1899. He was a lawyer and journalist and became president of the Salvadorean Supreme Court. Cordon Cea was chosen by the National Assembly to serve as provisional president on January 25, 1962. He presided over elections in April of 1962 and stepped down when Julio Adalber

to Rivera was sworn in as president on July 1, 1962.

JULIO ADALBERTO RIVERA (President, July 1, 1962–July 1, 1967). Julio Adalberto Rivera Carballo was born in 1922. He served in the Salvadorean army, where he rose to the rank of lieutenant colonel. He served as military attaché in the Salvadorean Embassy in Washington, D.C. Rivera was the leader of the coup that ousted the ruling leftist military-civilian junta in January of 1961. He served on the ruling Civil-Military Directorate for several months before resigning to lead the National Conciliation party (PCN). He was the party's nominee in presidential elections in 1962 and was unopposed in the election. Rivera took office on July 1, 1962. He improved El Salvador's economic condition and instituted social reforms. He governed in a constitutional fashion and completed his term of office on July 1, 1967. Rivera was later appointed El Salvador's ambassador to the United States. He retained that position until his death of a heart attack at his home in San Jose Guayabal, a suburb of San Salvador, at the age of 52 on July 29, 1973.

FIDEL SÁNCHEZ HERNÁNDEZ (President, July 1, 1967–July 1, 1972). Fidel Sánchez Hernández was born on July 7, 1917. He served in the Salvadorean military and was stationed in the Salvadorean Embassy in Washington, D.C., as a military attaché from 1960 until 1962. He rose to the rank of colonel and was named minister of the interior in the government of Julio Adalberto Rivera in 1962. Sánchez was the presidential candidate of the National Conciliation party in 1967. He was elected and took office on July 1, 1967. El Salvador engaged in a border war with Honduras on June 26, 1969. The two countries had had a long-standing border dispute that broke into violence following El Salvador's victory in a soccer match. A cease-fire was arranged by the Organization of American States a week after the fighting began. Relations between the two countries remained tense, and the border between El Salvador and Honduras was closed. El Salvador's economy suffered as a result of the hostilities. Sánchez was constitutionally ineligible to succeed himself in office, and a presidential election was held in February of 1972. Ruling party candidate Arturo Armando Molina Barraza was declared the victor over José Napoleón Duarte. Duarte's supporters claimed the election was fraudulent, and rebel troops seized parts of the capital. Sánchez and his daughter were taken into custody by the rebels. Military units loyal to the government defeated the rebels and gained Sánchez's safe release. Sánchez declared martial law, which remained in effect until June of 1972. He completed his term of office and relinquished the presidency to Molina on July 1, 1972.

ARTURO ARMANDO MOLINA BARRAZA (President, July 1, 1972– July 1, 1977). Arturo Armando Molina Barraza was born in San Salvador on June 18, 1927. He served as an artillery officer in the Salvadorean army after having attended the military academy. He rose to the rank of colonel and was named private secretary to President Fidel Sánchez Hernández in 1969. Molina was the candidate of the ruling National Conciliation party in the presidential elections of 1972. He won a narrow victory over José Napoleón Duarte. Duarte's supporters attempted to overthrow the government and install him as president in February of 1972. Troops loyal to the government put down the rebellion, however, and Molina was sworn in as president on July 1, 1972. Molina attempted to negotiate a settlement to the longstanding border crisis with Honduras. The ruling party was successful in congressional elections in 1976 and in

presidential elections the following year. Demonstrations and riots followed the balloting in February of 1977, and President Molina declared a state of siege. The country was troubled by leftist terrorists and right-wing death squads. Foreign Minister Mauricio Borgonovo Pohl was kidnapped and murdered in April of 1977, and rightists killed two Jesuit priests. Molina completed his term of office on July 1, 1977, and relinquished the presidency to Carlos Humberto Romero Mena.

CARLOS HUMBERTO ROMERO MENA (President, July 1, 1977–October 15, 1979). Carlos Humberto Romero Mena was born in Chalatenango in 1924. He was educated at military schools and entered the Salvadorean army. He served in various administrative positions and rose to the rank of general. Romero served as president of the Central American Defense Council from 1973 until 1977. He also served as minister of war in the cabinet of President Arturo Armando Molina from 1976. Romero was the candidate of the ruling National Conciliation party in the presidential elections of 1977. He defeated Col. Ernest Claramount in February of 1977. Claramount's supporters claimed the balloting was fraudulent, and widespread rioting followed Romero's victory. Romero was sworn into office on July 1, 1977. Civil unrest continued in the country, and opponents of the government were murdered by paramilitary death squads. Romero attempted to appease the opponents of his regime by proposing reforms to democratize the electoral process. Romero was ousted in a military coup led by Col. Adolfo Arnoldo Majano and Col. Jaime Abdul Gutierrez on October 15, 1979. Romero was sent into exile in Guatemala by the new military regime.

ADOLFO MAJANO RAMOS (Co-president, October 15, 1979–December 7, 1980). Adolfo Arnoldo Majano

Ramos was born in 1938. He was educated at Lackland Air Force Base in Texas and the Fort Benning, Georgia, Infantry School. He entered the Salvadorean army and served as administrator of the military college. Majano rose to the rank of colonel. Majano and Col. Jaime Abdul Gutierrez led a military coup against the government of President Carlos Humberto Romero on October 15, 1979. They served as copresidents of the subsequent ruling civilian-military junta. The Christian Democratic party joined the junta in January of 1980. Civil violence continued throughout the country and culminated in the assassination of Archbishop Oscar Romero by right-wing terrorists in March of 1980. The United States cut off financial aid to the country when three American nuns and a lay worker were murdered in early December of 1980. Majano was considered the most liberal member of the ruling junta, and he was ousted from the government on December 7, 1980. The junta established José Napoleón Duarte as president several days later. Majano refused a diplomatic position in Spain and went underground. He was arrested in Guatemala in February of 1981 and was returned to El Salvador. He was briefly imprisoned by the Duarte junta before being sent into exile.

JAIME ABDUL GUTIERREZ (Copresident, October 15, 1979–December 13, 1980). Jaime Abdul Gutierrez was born in 1936. He was educated at the University of Mexico. He served in the Salvadorean military as an engineer and rose to the rank of colonel. Gutierrez and Col. Adolfo Majano Ramos led a military coup against the government of President Carlos Humberto Romero on October 15, 1979. They served as copresidents of the subsequent ruling civilian-military junta. The Christian Democratic party joined the junta in January of 1979. Civil violence continued throughout the country and

culminated in the assassination of Archbishop Oscar Romero by right-wing terrorists in March of 1980. The United States cut off financial aid to the country when three American nuns and a lay worker were murdered in early December of 1980. Gutierrez was considered the most conservative member of the junta. He ousted Majano from the government on December 7, 1980. The junta established José Napoleón Duarte as president several days later, and Gutierrez served as vice president and commander in chief of the armed forces.

JOSÉ NAPOLEÓN DUARTE (President, December 13, 1980–May 2, 1982). José Napoleón Duarte Fuentes was born in San Salvador in 1926. He became active in the student movement that helped to force the ouster of President Maximiliano Hernández Martinez in 1944. A military junta led by Colonel Osmin Aguirre y Salinas took power later in the year, and Duarte tried to join the rebel government of Arturo Romero in exile in Guatemala. Duarte was stopped at the border and was returned to his family. He was sent to complete his education at Notre Dame University in the United States. He received a degree in civil engineering and returned to El Salvador to join a construction firm in 1948. Duarte again became involved in politics in 1960 when he helped form the Christian Democratic party (PDC). He became secretary-general of the party the following year and was elected mayor of San Salvador in 1964. He was reelected in 1966 and 1968. Duarte was successful in administering the city and modernizing and improving its services. He stepped down as mayor in 1970 to prepare for a bid for the presidency in 1972. He received the PDC's nomination and was involved in a bitter campaign against the ruling party's candidate, Arturo Armando Molina. Amidst allegations of electoral fraud, Molina was declared the victor in February of 1972, although Duarte received a plurality of the votes. Duarte's supporters in the army staged a coup attempt on March 25, 1972. The government repressed the revolt, and Duarte was arrested and charged with treason. When international pressure was placed on the military regime, Duarte was released and sent into exile in Guatemala. He subsequently settled in Venezuela, where he resumed his work as an engineer. El Salvador soon became embroiled in a violent civil war. The military government was deposed in October of 1979, and Duarte returned to the country. He survived several assassination attempts and remained out of politics until March of 1980, when he became a member of the ruling junta. Duarte became president of the junta on December 13, 1980. He initiated land reforms and nationalized some industries. He denounced human rights abuses and attempted to reach a reconciliation with the rebels. Duarte was forced to resign from the presidency on May 2, 1982. He was the Christian Democrats' nominee for president in 1984. He defeated Roberto d'Aubuisson, the nominee of the right-wing National Republican Alliance (ARENA), and took office on June 1, 1984. Duarte continued the struggle against the leftist guerrillas with the support of the United States. His government's failure to introduce significant economic and social reforms strengthened support for the rebels. Duarte's daughter, Ines Duarte Duran, was kidnapped by rebels in September of 1985. The president ordered the release of over 100 captured guerrillas to gain the release of his daughter and other hostages several months later. Duarte was diagnosed with cancer in May of 1988. He was constitutionally ineligible to seek a second term of office and was succeeded by rightist candidate Alfredo Cristiani on June 1, 1989. Duarte died of cancer at his home in San Salvador on February 23, 1990.

ALVARO ALFREDO MAGAÑA BORJO (President, May 2, 1982–June 1, 1984). Alvaro Alfredo Magaña Borjo was born in Ahuachapan on October 8, 1925. He attended the University of El Salvador, where he received a degree in law. He continued his education at the University of Chicago and the University of Rome. In 1956 he returned to El Salvador and was employed by the Ministry of Finance. Magaña also taught at the University of El Salvador. He subsequently became the director of the state mortgage bank in 1965. He retained that position until May 2, 1982, when he was called upon to serve as provisional president of El Salvador. The country was still plagued by civil unrest, and Magaña attempted to improve the condition of human rights in El Salvador. He presided over presidential elections in May of 1984 and relinquished office to the victor, José Napoleón Duarte, on June 1, 1984.

JOSÉ NAPOLEÓN DUARTE (President, June 1, 1984–June 1, 1989). *See earlier entry under Heads of State.*

ALFREDO CRISTIANI (President, June 1, 1989–   ). Alfredo Félix Cristiani Buckard was born in San Salvador on November 22, 1947. He was educated at the American University in San Salvador, where he studied business administration. He continued his education at Georgetown University, in Washington, D.C. After returning to El Salvador, he became a lobbyist for agricultural businesses. Cristiani was among a group of hostages seized at the Ministry of Economics in 1980 by leftist guerrillas. He was held for several weeks before his release was negotiated. Cristiani entered politics in 1984 and joined the right-wing National Republican Alliance (ARENA). He was active in the unsuccessful presidential campaign of Roberto d'Aubuisson in 1984. Cristiani replaced d'Aubuisson as leader of ARENA later in September of 1985. He was ARENA's presidential candidate in the election in 1988 and defeated the Christian Democratic party nominee, Fidel Chavez Mena. Cristiani tried to moderate ARENA's image, though d'Aubuisson remained a leading advisor to the government until his death in February of 1992. Cristiani's government successfully negotiated a cease-fire agreement with the leftist guerrillas in January of 1992. The government agreed to a series of provisions that included a general amnesty, land reform, and the elimination of right-wing paramilitary organizations.

Equatorial Guinea, Republic of
(República de Guinea Ecuatorial)

Equatorial Guinea is a country in western Africa that includes five islands off the coast. It was granted independence from Spain on October 12, 1968.

HEADS OF STATE

FRANCISCO MACÍAS NGUEMA (President, October 12, 1968–August 3, 1979). Francisco Macías Nguema Biyogo Negue Ndong was born in Nfenga on January 1, 1924. He was a member of the Fang tribe and was educated at local mission schools. He began work in the Spanish colonial government as a clerk in 1944. After serving in various administrative positions, he was appointed mayor of Mongomo in the late 1950s. Macías Nguema entered the pre-independence government of Bonifacio Ondu Edu as vice president of the Government Council in 1964. Macías Nguema challenged Ondu Edu for Equatorial Guinea's presidency in elections held in September of 1968. When Equatorial Guinea was granted independence from Spain on October 12, 1968, Macías Nguema established a government with himself as minister of defense. He began a campaign to force Spanish troops from the country in 1969. Spanish residents were threatened and attacked by supporters of the government. Foreign Minister Atanasio Ndongo and Saturnino Ibongo, Equatorial Guinea's representative to the United Nations, attempted to negotiate a political settlement with the Spanish government. Macías Nguema charged that Ndongo and Ibongo were part of a Spanish plot to oust the government and had the two men arrested and murdered in prison. Macías Nguema instituted a reign of terror that was considered to be one of the most brutal in the world. Numerous real or supposed opponents of the regime were arrested and summarily executed by the government. Examples of Nguema's exploits include reports that he had several hundred political prisoners executed in a stadium on Christmas Eve while loudspeakers blared the song "Those Were the Days, My Friend." Macías Nguema became president for life in 1972. He also introduced a new constitution the following year and Africanized Spanish names within the country, including his own. Leading a brutal campaign against intellectuals in the country, he killed or drove thousands into exile. Macías Nguema's government reportedly killed in excess of 50,000 people during his reign. The economy of Equatorial Guinea also suffered under Macías Nguema, and the country was bankrupt by the late 1970s. He was widely considered mentally unbalanced, but survived numerous plots to oust his government during his rule. He uncovered an army plot against him in June of 1979 and had the organizers summarily executed. Another military coup, led by Macías Nguema's nephew, Teodoro Obiang Nguema Mbasongo, succeeded in ousting the president on August 3, 1979. Macías Nguema went into hiding in his home village, where he was captured by government troops on August 18, 1979. He was sent to Bata prison to await trial. Macías Nguema was convicted on charges of murder and corruption and was executed on September 29, 1979.

TEODORO OBIANG NGUEMA MBASONGO (President, August 3, 1979–). Teodoro Obiang Nguema Mbasongo was born in the Mongomo District in 1942. He was the nephew of Francisco Macías Nguema and was educated locally. He entered the Saragossa Military Academy in Spain in 1963 and returned to Equatorial Guinea with the rank of lieutenant in 1965. Obiang Nguema served in the territorial guard and was named military governor of the island of Fernando Po by his uncle in the late 1960s. He also served as director of the Playa Negra prison. In 1975 he was promoted to lieutenant colonel and served as a leading aide to the president. He served as

military advisor to the president and was acting head of the armed forces. Obiang Nguema's brother was among the conspirators against Macías Nguema who were executed in the spring of 1979. Obiang Nguema led the coup that ousted his uncle on August 3, 1979. He served as provisional head of state and was inaugurated as president on October 11, 1979. He invited Equatorial Guinean exiles to return to the country, released political prisoners, and attempted to improve the tarnished reputation the nation had gained under Macías Nguema's brutal reign. Obiang Nguema restored Equatorial Guinea's independence constitution in April of 1980 and promoted a new constitution in August of 1982. His term as president was also extended an additional seven years. Obiang Nguema made steps towards democratic reforms and allowed parliamentary elections to be held in August of 1983. His government was still viewed with distrust by exiles, who formed several groups in opposition to his rule. Obiang Nguema survived several coup attempts, including one led by his former minister of defense, Fructoso Mba Onana, in July of 1986. Mba Onana and other conspirators were captured and imprisoned. Obiang Nguema was unopposed in his reelection to the presidency in June of 1989. Equatorial Guinea continued to suffer severe economic difficulties, however, and he was forced to proceed with democratic reforms in 1992 in order to gain foreign assistance.

HEADS OF GOVERNMENT

BONIFACIO ONDU EDO (Premier, December 15, 1963–October 12, 1968). Bonifacio Ondu Edo was born in Evinayong. He was a member of the Fang tribe and was educated at local mission schools. He became active in the Equatorial Guinean independence

movement in the 1950s and went into exile in Gabon in 1959. Ondu Edo returned to Equatorial Guinea in 1960 to serve as mayor of Evinayong. He was a founder of the Movement for the National Unity of Equatorial Guinea (MUNGE) in 1963. Ondu Edo served as premier of the pre-independence government from December 15, 1963. He was a proponent of a gradual process of independence from Spain. He was promoted by the colonial government to serve as president of an independent Equatorial Guinea. Ondu Edo was defeated by Francisco Macías Nguema in a runoff election in September of 1968. When Equatorial Guinea was granted independence on October 12, 1968, Ondu Edu went into exile in Gabon. He was extradited to Equatorial Guinea in November of 1968 and detained by the Macías Nguema government. Ondu Edu was charged with conspiracy and was murdered with members of his family in January of 1969.

CRISTINO SERICHE BIOKO (Premier, August 15, 1982–January 23, 1992). Cristino Seriche Bioko Malabo served in the Equatorial Guinean armed forces after receiving military training in Spain. He was named to the Supreme Military Council that governed Equatorial Guinea following the coup that ousted President Francisco Macías Nguema in 1979. He was appointed military commissioner for public works, housing, and transport in the government of President Teodoro Obiang Nguema Mbasongo in January of 1980. He was named second vice president in the government in December of 1981. President Obiang Nguema appointed him premier on August 15, 1982, following the adoption of a new constitution. He retained office until January 23, 1992, when he was replaced by a transitional government led by Silvestre Siale Bileka.

SILVESTRE SIALE BILEKA (Premier, January 23, 1992–). Silvestre Siale Bileka was appointed premier of Equatorial Guinea by President Obiang as the leader of a transitional government designed to pave the way for the introduction of multiparty politics in the country.

Estonia, Republic of

(Eesti Vabariik)

Estonia is a country in northern Europe on the Baltic Sea. It declared itself independent from the Soviet Union on August 20, 1991.

HEADS OF STATE

ARNOLD RÜÜTEL (President, August 20, 1991–October 5, 1992). Arnold Rüütel was born in 1928. He was educated at the Estonian Agricultural Academy, where he studied agronomy. He was employed at the Estonian Institute of Veterinary Science from 1955 until 1963. Rüütel joined the Communist party the following year. He served as director of the Tartu State Collective Farm from 1963 until 1969 and then headed the Estonian Agriculture Institute until 1972. Rüütel was elected first deputy president of the Council of Ministers in 1979 and became president of the Presidium in 1983. He was elected chairman of the Supreme Soviet in 1989. In March of 1991 a referendum was held, and the vote was overwhelmingly in support of Estonian independence. Parliament declared independence for the Republic of Estonia on August 20, 1991. The following month the Soviet Union conceded Estonia's independent status with Rüütel as president. Free elections were held in Estonia on September 20, 1992, and Rüütel led in the balloting. He did not receive an absolute majority of the votes, however, and the Estonian Parliament, or Riigikogu, elected Lennart Meri as president. Rüütel relinquished office on October 5, 1992.

LENNART MERI (President, October 5, 1992–). Lennart Meri was the candidate for president of the Fatherland coalition. He was selected by the Estonian Parliament as president following the failure of any candidate to receive an absolute majority. Meri took office on October 5, 1992.

HEADS OF GOVERNMENT

EDGAR SAVISAAR (Prime Minister, April 3, 1990–January 23, 1992). Edgar Savisaar was chairman of the Estonian Popular Front, a pro-independence group. His party won a majority of seats in the legislature on March 18, 1990, and Savisaar became prime minister on April 3, 1990. He resigned on January 23, 1992, following the failure of his government to win enough votes in the legislature to support a state of emergency that had been proposed to cope with food and energy shortages.

TIIT VÄHI (Prime Minister, January 30, 1992–October 8, 1992). Tiit Vähi was born in Valgamaa on January 10, 1947. He was educated at the Tallinn Polytechnic Institute. He was employed at the Valga Motor Depot and later was appointed minister of transportation. Vähi became prime minister of a caretaker government on January 30, 1992. He retained office through parliamentary elections held in September of 1992 and stepped down on October 8, 1992.

MART LAAR (Prime Minister, October 8, 1992–). Mart Laar was a member of the right-wing Fatherland coalition. The coalition won over half of the seats in Parliament during Estonia's first multiparty election. Laar was selected by the Parliament to serve as prime minister of Estonia on October 8, 1992.

Ethiopia

(Itiopia)

Ethiopia is a country in northeastern Africa.

HEADS OF STATE

HAILE SELASSIE (Emperor, April 3, 1930–September 12, 1974). Haile Selassie was born Lij Tafari Makonnen on July 23, 1892, at Ejarsa Gora in Harar. He was the son of Ras Makonnen, the cousin and leading advisor of Emperor Menelik II. Tafari was educated by clerical tutors and Roman Catholic missionaries in Harar. His father died in 1906, and two years later Tafari was summoned to the capital of Addis Ababa by the emperor. He was appointed governor of the Sidamo province in southern Ethiopia. His effectiveness in this position resulted in his appointment as governor of Harar, a position formerly held by his father. Emperor Menelik died in 1913 and was succeeded by his grandson Lej Iyasu. Iyasu proved an unpopular leader, and he was deposed in 1916. When Menelik's daughter, Princess Zauditu, assumed the throne as empress, Tafari was named regent and heir apparent. Tafari was a powerful influence during the reign of Zauditu. He actively sought international recognition for Ethiopia and led the country into the League of Nations in 1923. He also sought to expand educational opportunites in the country and bring an end to slavery. Despite efforts to remove Tafari, he assumed the throne as Emperor Haile Selassie upon the death of Zauditu on November 2, 1930. His efforts for further reform in the country were interrupted by the Italian invasion in October of 1934. Haile Selassie led the army against the Italians, but was forced to flee the country when the invaders seized the capital in May of 1936. He went to Geneva, where he addressed the League of Nations and unsuccessfully called for sanctions against Italy. He then settled in Bath, England, where he worked for foreign intervention to reclaim his country. Following the liberation of Ethiopia by British troops in May of 1941, Haile Selassie returned to Addis Ababa. His immediate problem was to maintain Ethiopian independence from Britain, which continued to administer several provinces well into the 1950s. He was also faced with several internal insurrections which were successfully put down. Haile Selassie continued his efforts to modernize the political structure of Ethiopia and presented a new constitution in 1955. Two years later elections were held for the first time, though most of the real power in the country was retained by the emperor. Haile Selassie also became a leading figure in African affairs amd hosted the Economic Commission for Africa in 1958. In December of 1960, while the emperor was out of the country, members of the Imperial Guard staged a coup d'état and attempted to install Haile Selassie's son Asfa Wossen as emperor. Troops loyal to Haile Selassie defeated the revolutionaries, and after four days the Emperor returned to Addis Ababa. He attempted to institute further liberalization in the country to quell liberal sentiments. In November of 1962 Haile Selassie succeeded in reunifying Eritrea with Ethiopia. In May of 1963 he hosted the first meeting of the Organization for African Unity, which established its headquarters in Addis Ababa. He had little success in resolving the conflict with Somalia over the Ogaden region and was faced with continued unrest in Eritrea by factions wanting independence for the region. Haile Selassie continued with political reforms and in 1966 allowed the prime minister to choose his own cabinet for the first time. Discontent worsened in the country in 1973, following a severe drought and the resultant exhibition of corruption and inefficiency in the government's handling of relief efforts. The military in Eritrea revolted in February of 1973, and Haile Selassie was forced to proceed with even more reforms in the government. He appointed Endalkatchew Makonnen, a young progressive, as prime minister and oversaw the drafting of a new, more democratic, constitution. The reforms were unable to curb the unrest in the country, and on September 13, 1974, Haile Selassie was deposed by a coup led by junior military officers. Two months later over 60 of his closest aides and advisors were executed. Haile Selassie was placed under house arrest, and the harsh conditions of his imprisonment led to his death on August 27, 1975, at the age of 80.

AMAN MICHAEL ANDOM (Head of State, September 12, 1974–November 23, 1974). Aman Michael Andom was born in Eritrea in 1924. Andom served with the Resistance in fighting the Italian occupation forces in the 1930s. After the liberation of Ethiopia, Andom joined the regular army. He was stationed in Korea as part of the United Nations troops serving there. Soon afterwards he was named commandant of the Harer Military College. He was active in the border dispute with Somalia and earned the nickname "the Desert Lion." Andom became a leading proponent of political reforms in Ethiopia and earned the displeasure of the emperor. He was moved from the army and served in the Ethiopian Senate. When young army officers took over the government in 1974, Andom was named chief of staff and defense minister. Following the ouster of the emperor in September of 1974, Andom served as chairman of the Provisional Military Administrative Committee. Two months later, on November 23, 1974, he was ousted by more revolutionary members of the government. He was killed in a gun battle with soldiers sent to arrest him on November 24, 1974.

TEFERI BANTI (Head of State, November 28, 1974–February 3, 1977). Teferi Banti was born in 1921. He entered the Ethiopian army and rose through the ranks. He served as military attaché at the Ethopian Embassy in Washington, D.C. Banti was promoted to the rank of brigadier general and served as commander of the army's second division in Eritrea until 1974. He was chosen to succeed Aman Michael Andom, the murdered leader of the ruling Provisional Military Administrative Committee, on November 28, 1974. Banti served as head of state, though most of the real power in the country was held by Mengistu Haile Marriam. Banti attempted to challenge Mengistu's rule by limiting

his political power. Mengistu responded by initiating a gun battle with Banti's supporters at the headquarters of the Coordinating Committee of the Armed Forces, or Dergue. Banti and several of his supporters were killed in the fighting on February 3, 1977.

MENGISTU HAILE MARRIAM (Head of State, February 11, 1977–May 21, 1991). Mengistu Haile Marriam was born in southwestern Ethiopia about 1937. He was educated locally and entered the Ethiopian military. He was trained at the Holeta Military College and Fort Leavenworth, Kansas. While stationed near the Somalian border, he rose to the rank of major. Mengistu was active in the military coup that dethroned Haile Selassie in September of 1974. He was named first vice-chairman of the ruling Provisional Military Administrative Committee and the Coordinating Committee of the Armed Forces, or Dergue. He was instrumental in the ouster of Dergue leader Aman Michael Andom, who was killed in a gun battle with Mengistu's supporters. Mengistu became the leading figure in the revolutionary regime, though Teferi Banti was named leader of the Dergue. Ethiopia was threatened by a growing separatist movement in Eritrea, and Mengistu refused to negotiate autonomy for the region. He survived an assassination attempt in September of 1976 and retaliated by instituting a reign of terror against critics of the regime and potential rivals. The Dergue attempted to limit Mengistu's powers by naming him chairman of the Council of Ministers and granting more authority to Teferi Banti on January 7, 1977. Mengistu orchestrated the murder of Banti and many of his supporters on the Dergue on February 3, 1977. Mengistu was named chairman of the Dergue by surviving members of the government on February 11, 1977. He continued a brutal campaign against dissidents. When the United States withdrew financial and military assistance to Ethiopia in April of 1977, Mengistu turned to the Soviet Union for military aid. Ethiopia became engaged in a war with neighboring Somalia in mid-1977. Somalia supported a separatist movement in Ethiopia's Ogaden region. A peace settlement was reached the following year when Soviet weapons and Cuban troops helped turn the tide of battle for Ethiopia. Mengistu formed a Marxist ruling party in 1984 and tried to transform Ethiopia into a Communist state. The civil war in Eritrea continued to drain Ethiopia's military resources, and the country was beset by periods of drought and famine during the 1980s. A new constitution was drafted in February of 1987, and the country became known as the People's Democratic Republic of Ethiopia. Mengistu was selected president of Ethiopia by the new national legislature on September 10, 1987. His regime continued to be opposed by the Ethiopian People's Liberation Front (EPLF), the leading Eritrean separatist group. The Tigre People's Liberation Front (TPLF) also made gains against Mengistu's forces. Mengistu survived a military coup in May of 1989 and subsequently purged many senior military officers. The TPLF and other opposition groups merged as the Ethiopian People's Revolutionary Democratic Front (EPRDF) in 1989 and made a major offensive against the government. Mengistu renounced his commitment to Marxism in March of 1990 and attempted to institute reforms to gain the survival of his government. The EPLF seized control of most of Eritrea, and the EPRDF marched toward Addis Ababa in early 1991. Mengistu resigned from office and went into exile in Zimbabwe on May 21, 1991, shortly before the EPRDF captured the capital.

TESFAYE GEBRE KIDAN (Acting President, May 21, 1991–May 27, 1991). Tesfaye Gebre Kidan was a lieutenant general in the Ethiopian armed forces. He was appointed vice president and minister of defense by President Mengistu Haile Marriam on April 26, 1991. When Mengistu resigned as president on May 21, 1991, Tesfaye succeeded him as acting president. Tesfaye surrendered the government to the rebel Ethiopian People's Revolutionary Democratic Front on May 27, 1991.

MELES ZENAWI (President, May 27, 1991–). Meles Zenawi was born in 1955. He was the founder and leader of the Tigre People's Liberation Front in the mid-1970s. He merged his organization with other opposition groups to form the Ethiopian People's Revolutionary Democratic Front in January of 1989. Zenawi's rebels defeated the Ethiopian military and captured the capital of Addis Ababa. Zenawi assumed powers as head of state following the surrender of the government of Tesfaye Gebre Kidan on May 27, 1991. He was confirmed as president and appointed chairman of the Council of Representatives on July 21, 1991.

HEADS OF GOVERNMENT

MAKONNEN ENDALKATCHEW (Prime Minister, 1943–April 3, 1958). Makonnen Endalkatchew was born in Tagulat, Shawa, on February 16, 1890. His family was influential in the court of Emperor Menelik II, and Endalkatchew became one of the first students to be educated at the first modern school in Addis Adaba. He served in the court of Empress Zauditu and was named a district governor in 1920. From 1926 until 1931 he served in the cabinet as minister of commerce. Following the ascension of Haile Selassie to the throne, Endalkatchew was appointed ambassador to the League of Nations and Great Britain and served from 1931 until 1933. He then returned to Ethiopia as mayor of Addis Ababa until 1934. The following year he was selected as governor of the Ilubabor province. Endalkatchew served as general in the Ethiopian army during the Italian invasion in 1935 and accompanied Haile Selassie into exile in 1936 following the Italian occupation. Endalkatchew and the emperor returned to Ethiopia in 1940, and Endalkatchew was named minister of the interior the following year. He served until 1943, when he became prime minister. In this position he represented Ethiopia at the opening session of the United Nations in 1946. Endalkatchew served in this position until April 3, 1958. He then became president of the Senate, where he served until his resignation in 1961 for reasons of poor health. He died in Addis Ababa on February 27, 1963.

ABEBE ARAGAI (Prime Minister, April 3, 1958–December, 1960). Abebe Aragai was born to a noble family in Salale on August 18, 1903. He served as a bodyguard for Emperor Haile Selassie until the early 1930s, when he was appointed chief of police in Addis Ababa. Following the occupation of Ethiopia by the Italians in 1936, Abebe returned to his hometown, where he led the guerrilla warfare resistance to the occupying forces. Following the liberation of Ethiopia and the return of the emperor in 1941, Abebe was appointed governor of Addis Ababa. From 1941 until 1942 he served as governor of Sidamo, and from 1943 until 1947 he was governor of Tegre. He was appointed minister of the interior in 1949 and served until April 3, 1958, when he was made prime minister and minister of defense. During the abortive coup d'état in December of 1960, Abebe, along with other influential government leaders, was detained in the palace by the coup leaders. When the Ethiopian military began a countercoup on December 15, 1960, coup leader Germame

Germame Neway and other coup members opened fire on the detainees, killing Abebe and many others.

AKILU HABTE-WOLD (Prime Minister, March 29, 1961–February 28, 1974). Akilu Habte-Wold was born in Addis Ababa in 1908. He was educated in Alexandria, Egypt, and at the University of Paris. He completed his education in 1936, but remained in Europe during the Italian occupation. Akilu returned to Ethiopia in 1941 and was appointed vice minister of foreign affairs in October of 1943. He was Ethiopia's representative to the United Nations Charter session in San Francisco in 1945. He became minister of foreign affairs in 1949 and was also appointed deputy prime minister in 1957. The following year he stepped down as foreign minister. Akilu returned to the Foreign Ministry in 1960, while remaining deputy prime minister. He was abroad with Emperor Haile Selassie when a coup attempt took place in the capital. Akilu's brother, Makonnen Habte-Wold, and other government leaders were killed by the insurgents. The coup was crushed, and Akilu was appointed prime minister on March 29, 1961. He remained head of the government and a leading advisor to the emperor throughout the 1960s. He was granted the right to appoint his own cabinet members in a reorganization of the government in March of 1966. Akilu supported the emperor's land taxation and reform policies and halted a revolt against the land tax in Gojam Province in 1969. Ethiopia experienced a famine in the early 1970s, and the government's inability to cope with the crisis caused widespread dissent. The Ethiopian military mutinied for higher pay in February of 1974. The emperor dismissed Akilu on February 28, 1974, in the hopes of appeasing critics of the government. Akilu was arrested shortly after his ouster. The emperor was dethroned in September of 1974, and Akilu was executed with many other members of Haile Selassie's government on November 24, 1974.

ENDALKATCHEW MAKONNEN
(Prime Minister, February 28, 1974–July 22, 1974). Endalkatchew Makonnen was born in Addis Ababa in 1926. He was the son of Prime Minister Makonnen Endalkatchew. He was educated at Oxford University in Great Britain. Makonnen was subsequently appointed Ethiopia's ambassador to Great Britain, where he remained until 1961. He returned to Ethiopia to serve in the government as minister of commerce and industry. He was appointed Ethiopia's representative to the United Nations in 1966, where he served until 1969. Makonnen returned to the cabinet as minister of communications until his appointment as prime minister on February 28, 1974. He tried to restore order in the country, but could not stop the growing tide of discontent against the regime of Haile Selassie. Makonnen was forced to resign on July 22, 1974, and was arrested shortly thereafter. A military regime forced the ouster of Haile Selassie in September of 1974. Makonnen was executed with many other members of the former government on November 24, 1974.

MICHAEL IMRU
(Prime Minister, July 22, 1974–September 12, 1974). Michael Imru Haile Selassie was born in 1930. He was the son of Prince Imru Haile Selassie, a second cousin to Emperor Haile Selassie. He was educated at Oxford University in Great Britain and returned to Ethiopia to enter government service. Imru worked in the Ministry of Defense and the Ministry of Agriculture before being named Ethiopia's ambassador to the United States. He subsequently served as ambassador to the Soviet Union. He was then sent to lead the Ethiopian delegation to the United Nations in Geneva. In March of 1974 Imru returned to Ethiopia to serve as minister of commerce and industry in the government

of Endalkatchew Makonnen. He was named minister of economic and social affairs the following month. Imru was chosen by the military to replace Endalkatchew as prime minister on July 22, 1974. He retained office until the military deposed Emperor Haile Selassie on September 12, 1974. Imru remained in the military government as minister of information until 1975. He subsequently served as a political advisor to the leader of the Dergue until 1976.

FIKRE-SELASSIE WOGDERESS
(Prime Minister, September 10, 1987–November 8, 1989). Fikre-Selassie Wogderess was the former deputy chairman of the Council of Ministers. He was designated prime minister on September 10, 1987, and retained this position until November 8, 1989, when he resigned for reasons of health.

HAILU YEMENU
(Prime Minister, November 8, 1989–April 26, 1991). Hailu Yemenu served as deputy prime minister under Fikre Selassie Wogderess. He became acting prime minister on November 8, 1989, following Fikre Selassie's resignation. He retained office until April 26, 1991, when Tesfaye Dinka was chosen as prime minister.

TESFAYE DINKA
(Prime Minister, April 26, 1991–May 27, 1991). Tesfaye Dinka was a former foreign minister of Ethiopia. He had close ties to the West and was appointed prime minister by President Mengistu Haile Marriam on April 26, 1991. He retained office until the government collapsed and surrendered to rebel leaders on May 27, 1991.

TAMIRAT LAYNIE
(Prime Minister, June 6, 1991–). Tamirat Laynie was a member of the Ethiopian People's Revolutionary Democratic Front. He was named acting prime minister of Ethiopia on June 6, 1991, and was approved as prime minister by the Council of Representatives on July 29, 1991.

Fiji, Republic of

(Ka-Vakarairai ni Fiji)

Fiji is a large group of islands in the South Pacific Ocean. It was granted independence from Great Britain on October 10, 1970.

HEADS OF STATE

SIR ROBERT FOSTER (Governor-General, October 10, 1970–January 13, 1973). Sir Robert Foster was born in London, England, on August 11, 1913. He served in the Northern Rhodesia Administrative Service office from 1936 and served in the British military from 1940 until 1943. He was a district officer in Northern Rhodesia from 1943 until 1953. Foster then served as senior district officer until 1957 and provisional commissioner until 1960. He was secretary of native affairs from 1960 until 1961 and chief secretary of Nyasaland from 1961 until 1963. He subsequently served as deputy governor of Nyasaland until 1964. Foster was then appointed high commissioner of the West Pacific and served until 1968. He was named governor of Fiji in 1968 and became governor-general of Fiji following independence on October 10, 1970. He retired to England on January 13, 1973.

SIR GEORGE CAKOBAU (Governor-General, January 13, 1973–February 12, 1983). George Kadavulevu Cakobau was born in Suva on November 6, 1912. He was the great-grandson of King Cakobau, who was Fiji's last king in 1874. On January 13, 1973, George Cakobau was the first ethnic Fijian to be named governor-general of the country. He retired from his position on February 12, 1983. Cakobau died on November 25, 1989.

SIR PENAIA GANILAU (Governor-General, February 12, 1983–October 15, 1987). Penaia Kanatabatu Ganilau was born in Fiji on July 28, 1918. He was educated in Fiji and Great Britain. He served with the colonial service and in the Fiji military force. Ganilau became deputy secretary for Fijian affairs in 1961 and served as minister for Fijian affairs and local government from 1965 until 1970. He subsequently served in the independent cabinet as minister of home affairs, lands, and mineral resources. In 1972 he was named minister for communications, works, and tourism. He also served as deputy prime minister from 1973 until 1983. Ganilau then became governor-general on February 12, 1983. He declared a state of emergency following the coup led by Lt. Col. Sitiveni Rabuka in May of 1987. He formed an advisory council to negotiate a settlement of the government crisis that followed the coup. Negotiations broke down in September of 1987, and Rabuka declared Fiji a republic on October 7, 1987. Ganilau resigned as governor-general on October 15, 1987. He was subsequently named president of Fiji on December 5, 1987. Ganilau flew to the United States in November of 1993 to receive medical treatment for leukemia at Walter Reed Medical Center in Washington, D.C. He died there of his illness on December 15, 1993.

SITIVENI RABUKA (Head of State, May 14, 1987–December 5, 1987). Sitiveni Ligamamada Rabuka was born in Nakobo on September 13, 1948. He was educated in New Zealand and

Australia and joined the Fiji military. He served with the United Nations peacekeeping forces in Lebanon. Rabuka led a coup following the election of Timoci Bavadra as prime minister of Fiji. Bavadra's election had resulted in street demonstrations by native Fijians who feared that the new Indian-dominated government would jeopardize their rights. Rabuka participated in a series of negotiations led by Governor-General Ganilau, but failed to reach an agreement. Rabuka led a second coup on September 25, 1987, and imposed martial law and a series of restrictive measures to control the country. He declared Fiji a republic on October 7, 1987. He relinquished control of the government on December 5, 1987, but retained the position of minister of home affairs in charge of security and the armed forces until his resignation from the cabinet in 1990. Rabuka served as deputy prime minister and minister of home affairs in 1991. He organized and led the Fijian Political party, which won an overwhelming victory in legislative elections in May of 1992. Rabuka was selected to lead a coalition cabinet as prime minister on June 2, 1992.

SIR PENAIA GANILAU (President, December 5, 1987–December 15, 1993). *See earlier entry under Heads of State.*

HEADS OF GOVERNMENT

RATU SIR KAMISESE MARA (Prime Minister, October 10, 1970–April 13, 1987). Ratu Sir Kamisese Kapaiwai Tuimacilai Mara was born on May 13, 1920. He was educated locally and at Oxford University and London School of Economics in Great Britain. In 1950 he joined the British colonial service and served in various administrative positions. He was elected to the Fiji Legislative Council in 1953 and became a member of the Executive Council in 1959. Mara founded the Alliance party in 1960 and served as leader of the Fiji delegation to the Constitutional Conference in London in 1965. He was elected chief minister in the pre-independence government on September 20, 1966. Mara became prime minister of Fiji following independence on October 10, 1970. He also served in the government as minister of foreign affairs from 1977. The Alliance party lost its parliamentary majority in elections in April of 1987, and Mara was replaced by Timoci Bavadra on April 13, 1987. Bavadra was ousted by a military coup led by Lt. Col. Sitiveni Rabuka the following month. Rabuka proclaimed the establishment of Fiji as a republic in October of 1987. President Penaia Ganilau reappointed Mara as prime minister on December 5, 1987. Mara retained office until June 2, 1992, when Rabuka was selected as prime minister.

TIMOCI BAVADRA (Prime Minister, April 13, 1987–May 14, 1987). Timoci Bavadra was born in 1934. He was an ethnic Fijian and the leader of the Fiji Labour party (FLP). The FLP was primarily supported by the Indian community in Fiji. Bavadra was named to head a coalition cabinet as prime minister on April 13, 1987, following the FLP's electoral victory. His election resulted in demonstrations against the government by Fijians who feared that ethnic Indians would dominate the government. Bavadra was ousted in a military coup led by Lt. Col. Sitiveni Rabuka on May 14, 1987. He was briefly held under house arrest while Rabuka established a military government. Bavadra died of spinal cancer at the age of 55 in Suva on November 3, 1989.

RATU SIR KAMISESE MARA (Prime Minister, December 5, 1987–June 2, 1992). *See earlier entry under Heads of Government.*

SITIVENI RABUKA (Prime Minister, June 2, 1992–). *See entry under Heads of State.*

Finland, Republic of

(Suomen Tasavalta)

Finland is a country in northern Europe. It received independence from the Soviet Union on December 6, 1917.

HEADS OF STATE

CARL GUSTAV MANNERHEIM (President, August 4, 1944–March 4, 1946). Carl Gustav Emil Mannerheim was born in Villnas on June 4, 1867. He was educated at the Nikolaev Cavalry School and joined the Russian cavalry as a second lieutenant in 1889. He rose through the ranks and served with distinction in the Russo-Japanese War and World War I. After the Russian Revolution he returned to Finland with the rank of lieutenant general in December of 1917. Mannerheim assumed command of the Finnish Civil Guard and defeated an attempt by Bolshevik forces to take control of Finland. He became Finland's regent on December 12, 1918. He was defeated by Kaarlo J. Stahlberg in the election for Finland's first president. Mannerheim retired from his position following the establishment of the Finnish republic on July 25, 1919. He wrote several books on military strategy during his retirement. In 1931 he returned to active duty as president of the Council of Defense. He was promoted to the rank of marshal two years later and led the Finnish forces against an attack by the Soviet Union in November of 1939. A peace settlement was reached the following March. Finland again clashed with the Soviets following a new attack in June of 1941. Finland also partici-

pated in Germany's attack on Leningrad during World War II. Mannerheim became president of Finland on August 4, 1944, following the resignation of pro-German President Risto Ryti. He negotiated a peace settlement with the Soviet Union and later declared war on Germany. Mannerheim remained president following Soviet-controlled elections in March of 1945. He became ill in September of 1945 and went to Lisbon, Portugal, for medical treatment. He returned to Finland in January of 1946 and resigned from office for reasons of health on March 4, 1946. Mannerheim retired to Sweden and Switzerland to write his memoirs. He died following abdominal surgery in Lausanne, Switzerland, at the age of 83 on January 27, 1951.

JUHU K. PAASIKIVI (President, March 9, 1946–March 1, 1956). Juhu Kusti Paasikivi was born in Tampere on November 27, 1870. He was educated in Finland, Sweden, Germany, and Russia. He received a doctorate in law in 1901 and worked in the banking industry. Paasikivi entered politics and was elected to the Finnish Parliament in 1907. He served in the cabinet as minister of finance from 1908 until 1909. Finland declared its independence in July of 1917, following the Russian

Revolution. Paasikivi served as the first prime minister of the independent government from May 27, 1918, until November 27, 1918. Finland engaged in a war with Bolshevik forces intent on establishing a Socialist government. Finland was declared a republic in June of 1919, and Paasikivi headed the Finnish delegation that negotiated a peace treaty with the Soviet Union in October of 1920. He subsequently retired from political activities and served in the Finnish Chamber of Commerce. He was appointed Finland's minister to Sweden in 1936. Paasikivi headed a Finnish delegation to the Soviet Union in 1939 in the hopes of preempting a conflict between the two countries. The negotiations were unsuccessful, and the Soviet Union attacked Finland in November of 1939. Paasikivi was named minister to Moscow in March of 1940 and negotiated a peace settlement. He remained in Moscow until his resignation in May of 1941. He opposed Finland's alliance with Germany during World War II, and he negotiated an armistice with the Soviets and his country's exit from the conflict in 1944. Paasikivi again became prime minister on November 17, 1944, and pledged a peaceful cooperation with the Soviets. He formed a new government in April of 1945 that included Communists in the cabinet and remained prime minister until March 9, 1946, when he succeeded retiring president Carl Gustav Mannerheim. Paasikivi supported a mutual defense pact with the Soviet Union in 1948. He defeated the Communist opposition by a wide margin and was reelected president in 1950. Paasikivi renegotiated the defense pact with the Soviets in 1955 and gained Finland's admittance into the United Nations later in the year. He retired from office after completing his term on March 1, 1956. He died in Helsinki after a long illness at the age of 86 on December 14, 1956.

URHO K. KEKKONEN (President, March 1, 1956–September 11, 1981).

Urho Kaleva Kekkonen was born in Pielavesi on September 3, 1900. He received a degree in law from the University of Helsinki and became an attorney in 1928. He became involved with the Agrarian party and served as its counselor. In 1934 he was elected to the party's executive committee. Kekkonen was elected to the Parliament in 1936 and was named to the cabinet as minister of justice. He was appointed minister of the interior the following year and served until 1939. He led the government department for war refugees from Finland's war with the Soviet Union from 1939 until 1940. Kekkonen withdrew from politics in 1940 in opposition to Soviet peace terms. He advocated neutrality during World War II and urged Finland's withdrawal from the second Russo-Finnish War in 1943. Kekkonen was instrumental in forcing the collapse of the pro–Nazi government of Risto Ryti in 1944. Kekkonen was appointed minister of justice in the cabinet of Juho Paasikivi in November of 1944 and served in this position until March of 1946. He became leader of the Agrarian party and was elected Speaker of the Parliament in 1948. Kekkonen was defeated by Paasikivi in the presidential elections in January of 1950. Kekkonen was subsequently elected prime minister to head a coalition government and took office on March 17, 1950. He also served as foreign minister in the government. He resigned on November 17, 1953, due to Finland's economic problems and conflicts in his cabinet. Kekkonen was again called upon to form a government on October 20, 1954, and retained his position until March 1, 1956, when he was elected by a narrow margin to succeed Paasikivi as Finland's president. Kekkonen sought to reach an accord with the Soviet Union. He tried to convince Moscow that Finland did not threaten Soviet security and agreed to conditions that no foreign power would station troops on Finnish soil. Kekkonen was reelected with only token opposition in 1962 and 1968. He approved a trade agreement with the European Economic Community in 1973, despite Soviet opposition. Kekkonen's term was extended for an additional four years by Parliament in 1974, and he was again reelected in 1978. He suffered from poor health and resigned from office on September 11, 1981. He retired to his home in Tamminiemi, where he died from a circulatory disorder in his brain at the age of 85 on August 31, 1986.

MAUNO KOIVISTO (President, September 11, 1981–). Mauno Henrik Koivisto was born in Turku on November 25, 1923. He attended Turku University, where he received a doctorate in sociology in 1956. He was subsequently employed in the banking industry and joined the International Bank for Reconstruction and Development as governor for Finland in 1966. Koivisto was named minister of finance in the government of Rafael Paasio in May of 1966. He was appointed governor of the Bank of Finland in 1968 and was asked to form a government as

prime minister on March 22, 1968. He instituted austerity measures that improved Finland's economic stability, but were unpopular with Finnish voters. Koivisto's Social Democratic party lost support in subsequent elections, and he stepped down as prime minister on February 19, 1972. He returned to the government to serve as deputy prime minister and minister of finance in Rafael Paasio's cabinet from February until September of 1972. Koivisto resumed his position at the Bank of Finland until May 26, 1979, when he again formed a government as prime minister. President Urho Kekkonen tried to force Koivisto's resignation in April of 1981, but the prime minister refused to step down. Koivisto became acting president when Kekkonen took a medical leave on September 11, 1981. Kekkonen resigned the following month, and Koivisto was nominated as the Social Democrats' candidate for president. He was elected by a wide margin and became President on January 26, 1982. He advocated stable relations with the Soviet Union and was reelected without difficulty in presidential elections in 1988.

HEADS OF GOVERNMENT

JUHO K. PAASIKIVI (Prime Minister, November 17, 1944–March 9, 1946). *See entry under Heads of State.*

MAUNO PEKKALA (Prime Minister, March 24, 1946–July 22, 1948). Mauno Pekkala was born in Sysma, Finland, on January 27, 1890. He studied at the University of Helsinki and joined the forest administration board after receiving a degree. He became involved in political activities and was elected to Parliament in 1926. Pekkala was also elected to head the political union of the small farmers. He was appointed to the cabinet as minister of agriculture

and served in four cabinets during the 1930s. He was selected as prime minister on March 24, 1946. Pekkala signed the Soviet-Finnish treaty of mutual aid in Moscow in April of 1948. He retained office until July 22, 1948. Pekkala ran for the presidency as a candidate of the leftist Finnish People's Democratic League. He was defeated by Juho K. Paasikivi on February 15, 1950. He died in Helsinki at the age of 61 on June 30, 1952.

KARL AUGUST FAGERHOLM (Prime Minister, July 29, 1948–March 17, 1950). Karl August Fagerholm was born in Turku on December 31, 1901.

He was educated locally and became active in the trade union movement in his late teens. He also joined the Social Democratic Youth Movement in 1920. Fagerholm became editor of the party newspaper *Arbetarbladet* in 1923 and was elected to Parliament in 1930. He joined the cabinet as minister of social affairs in the government of A. K. Cajander in 1937, but was forced to resign in December of 1942 when he refused to deport Jewish emigrants in Finland to Germany. He returned to the cabinet shortly thereafter and remained until late 1943. Fagerholm was elected Speaker of the Parliament in 1945. He retained that position until July 29, 1948, when he was asked to form a government as prime minister. He was opposed by the Communists, who accused him of attempting to undermine Finnish-Soviet relations. Fagerholm stepped down on March 17, 1950, and returned to the post of Speaker of Parliament. He was also placed in charge of the state's alcohol monopoly in 1952. In the presidential election in 1956, he was narrowly defeated by Urho Kekkonen. Fagerholm was again called upon to form a government on March 3, 1956. He stepped down on April 24, 1957, when he was defeated for the leadership of the Social Democratic party by Vaino Tanner. Fagerholm formed a coalition cabinet that included members of the anti-Communist Conservative party on August 29, 1958. The Soviet Union put economic and political pressure on the government, and Fagerholm was forced to resign on January 13, 1959, following the Soviet Union's recall of its ambassador to Finland. He was again elected Speaker of the Parliament in 1959 and served until 1961 and again from 1965 until 1966. Fagerholm then retired from politics. He died in Helsinki at the age of 82 on May 22, 1984, following a long illness.

URHO K. KEKKONEN (Prime Minister, March 17, 1950–November-

ber 17, 1953). *See entry under Heads of State.*

SAKARI TUOMIOJA (Prime Minister, November 17, 1953–May 5, 1954). Sakari Tuomioja was born in Tampere on August 29, 1911. He was educated at the University of Helsinki, where he received a degree in law in 1937. He was employed by the Finnish Ministry of Finance until 1944. Tuomioja was named to the cabinet to head the Ministry of Finance in 1945. He also became governor of the Bank of Finland in 1945. He served as minister of trade and industry in 1950 and was foreign minister from 1951 until 1952. Tuomioja was named Finland's prime minister in a caretaker cabinet on November 17, 1953. He retained the office until May 5, 1954. He was an unsuccessful candidate for the Finnish presidency in 1956. Tuomioja was named ambassador to Great Britain the following year and served until 1957. He subsequently became secretary of the United Nations Economic Commission for Europe. In 1959 he was sent to Laos on a fact-finding mission for the United Nations. Tuomioja was appointed ambassador to Sweden in 1961, where he served until 1964. In March of 1964 he was appointed United Nations mediator in the Cyprus dispute. Tuomioja's poor health prevented him from pursuing his duties, and he suffered a stroke in Geneva on August 16, 1964. He died in a Helsinki hospital at the age of 53 on September 9, 1964.

RALF TÖERNGREN (Prime Minister, May 5, 1954–October 20, 1954). Ralf Töerngren was born in Oulu on March 1, 1899. He was educated locally and became active in the Swedish People's party. He was elected to Parliament in 1936 and served in the cabinet as minister of social affairs in 1944. Töerngren became minister of finance in 1946 and served until 1949. He returned to the Ministry of Social Affairs in 1950 and again in 1952. He was named minister of foreign affairs in the government of Urho Kekkonen in 1953. Töerngren was called upon to form a government on May 5, 1954. He was replaced by Kekkonen on October 20, 1954. He returned to the cabinet as minister of foreign affairs in 1956 and served until the following year. He remained active in the government and served as a foreign trade advisor to Prime Minister V. J. Sukselainen. Töerngren died of a heart attack in Turku at the age of 62 on May 15, 1961.

URHO K. KEKKONEN (Prime Minister, October 20, 1954–March 1, 1956). *See entry under Heads of State.*

KARL AUGUST FAGERHOLM (Prime Minister, March 3, 1956–April 24, 1957). *See earlier entry under Heads of Government.*

VAINO J. SUKSELAINEN (Prime Minister, May 27, 1957–October 18, 1957). Vaino Johannes Sukselainen was born in Paimio on October 12, 1906. He was educated in Helsinki and served as secretary to the prime minister from 1941 until 1945. He subsequently taught economics at the University of Turku and then at the University of Tampere. In 1948 he was elected to the Parliament as a member of the Agrarian Union. Sukselainen was named minister of finance in 1950 and served until the following year. He was minister of interior from 1951 until 1953 and served as finance minister again in 1954. He was elected Speaker of the Parliament in 1956 and served until 1957. Sukselainen was named prime minister on May 27, 1957, and served until October 18, 1957, when his government lost a vote of confidence in the Parliament. He was again elected Speaker of the Parliament the following year and served until 1959. Sukselainen was again selected as prime minister on January 13, 1959. He left office on July 14, 1961, after having

been found guilty of mismanagement of the National Pension Fund. He again served as Parliament president from 1968 until 1970 and from 1972 until 1975. Sukselainen retained his position as chancellor of the University of Tampere until his retirement in 1978.

RAINER VON FIEANDT (Prime Minister, November 29, 1957–April 26, 1958). Rainer von Fieandt was born in Turku on December 26, 1890. He was educated in Finland and entered the banking industry in 1924. He served as a delegate to the World Economic Conference in London in 1933. Von Fieandt was named to the cabinet as minister of supply from 1939 until 1940. He served as governor of the Bank of Finland from 1955 until 1957. He was chosen to lead a coalition government of Social Democrats and Agrarians as prime minister on November 29, 1957. His government was defeated on a vote of confidence over the price of grain, and he was replaced by Reino Kuuskojki on April 26, 1958. Von Fieandt subsequently served as governor of Finland at the International Bank for Reconstruction and Development until 1965. He died on April 28, 1972.

REINO KUUSKOJKI (Prime Minister, April 26, 1958–August 29, 1958). Reino Iisakki Kuuskojki was born in Loimijoki on January 18, 1907. He was educated at Helsinki University and served as secretary of the Supreme Administrative Court from 1937 until 1944. He was secretary-general in the Ministry of Justice in 1945 and served as solicitor-general to Parliament from 1946 until 1947. Kuuskojki served as a member of the Supreme Administrative Court from 1947 until 1955. He also served as minister of justice from 1953 until 1954. He was director of the National Pension Institute from 1953 until 1958. Kuuskojki was chosen to lead a caretaker government as prime minister on April 26, 1958. He stepped down on August 29, 1958, following parliamentary elections. Kuuskojki became president of the Supreme Administrative Court later in 1958. He died in Helsinki at the age of 58 on January 27, 1965.

KARL AUGUST FAGERHOLM (Prime Minsiter, August 29, 1958–January 13, 1959). *See earlier entry under Heads of Government.*

VAINO J. SUKSELAINEN (Prime Minister, January 13, 1959–July 14, 1961). *See earlier entry under Heads of Government.*

MARTTI MIETTUNEN (Prime Minister, July 14, 1961–April 13, 1962). Martti Johannes Miettunen was born in Simo on April 17, 1907. He entered politics and was elected to the Parliament in 1945. He served as minister of commerce from 1950 until 1951 and was then named minister of agriculture until 1952. Miettunen returned to lead the Commerce Ministry in 1954 and served until 1956. He was then reappointed minister of agriculture until 1957 and was again reappointed in 1958. Miettunen was also selected as provincial governor of Lapland in 1958. He was called upon to lead an Agrarian party–dominated cabinet on July 14, 1961. His government resigned after President Urho Kekkonen was sworn into office for a second term. Miettunen was replaced as prime minister by Ahti Karjalainen on April 13, 1962. Miettunen returned to the cabinet as minister of agriculture in 1968 and served until 1970. He remained governor of Lapland until 1972 and also served as an executive with the Bank of Finland from 1971 until 1975. He was again named to lead a coalition government on November 30, 1975. Miettunen reformed his government in September of 1976 and led a minority Centre party cabinet until he was replaced by Kalevi Sorsa on May 15, 1977.

AHTI KARJALAINEN (Prime Minister, April 13, 1962–December 18, 1963).

Ahti Kalle Samuli Karjalainen was born in Hirvensalmi on February 10, 1923. He was educated at the University of Helsinki, where he received a degree in political science in 1946. He entered politics as a member of the Agrarian party and was appointed secretary to Prime Minister Urho Kekkonen in 1950. Karjalainen was appointed minister of finance in 1957 and served in the cabinet as minister of trade and industry from 1959 until 1961. He was then named foreign minister and served until 1962. Karjalainen was asked by President Kekkonen to form a government as prime minister on April 13, 1962. His cabinet resigned over the issue of a tax increase on December 18, 1963. He returned to the cabinet as foreign minister in 1964 and served until 1970. He was again named prime minister on July 15, 1970. Karjalainen stepped down on October 29, 1971, when his government could not resolve a dispute over agricultural prices. He returned to the cabinet as foreign minister the following year and retained his position until 1975. He served as minister of economics from 1976 until 1977 and was appointed deputy governor of the Bank of Finland in 1979. Karjalainen was named governor of the Bank of Finland in 1982, but was fired the following year, reportedly due to a problem with alcohol. He retired from politics and wrote his memoirs, which were published as *The President's Man* in 1989. Karjalainen died in Helsinki at the age of 67 on September 7, 1990.

REINO LEHTO (Prime Minister, December 18, 1963–September 12, 1964). Reino Ragnar Lehto was born in Turku on May 2, 1898. He was educated in Finland and received a degree in law. He worked as an attorney in his hometown from 1922 until 1932. Lehto served in the Finnish civil service, where he rose to become chief of the Finnish Office of the Ministry of Trade and Industry. He also served as chief secretary of the Finnish delegation for

War Reparation Industries from 1944 until 1948. Lehto was chosen to lead a nonpolitical cabinet as prime minister on December 18, 1963. Lehto's caretaker government passed legislation that increased pensions and secured price stabilization. Lehto stepped down as prime minister on September 12, 1964. He died in Helsinki at the age of 68 on July 13, 1966.

JOHANNES VIROLAINEN (Prime Minister, September 12, 1964–May 27, 1966). Johannes Virolainen was born in Viipuri on January 31, 1914. He was educated at Helsinki University and was elected to the Parliament in 1945. Virolainen was elected vice chairman of the Agrarian party in 1946. He was appointed minister of education in 1953. The following year he was named minister of foreign affairs, a position he held on several occasions during the 1950s. Virolainen also served as minister of agriculture from 1961 until 1963. He served as deputy prime minister from 1962 until 1963 and was selected as prime minister of Finland on September 12, 1964. The following year he was elected chairman of the Centre party, formerly the Agrarian party. Virolainen left the office of prime minister on May 27, 1966, and became Speaker of Parliament until 1969. He also served again as deputy prime minister from 1968 to 1970. He was first minister of finance from 1972 until 1975 and was again deputy prime minister from 1977 until 1979. Virolainen returned to office as Speaker of the Parliament in 1979 and remained in that position until 1983. He was the unsuccessful candidate of the Centre party for president of Finland in 1982.

RAFAEL PAASIO (Prime Minister, May 27, 1966–March 22, 1968). Rafael Paasio was born in Uskela on June 6, 1903. He was educated in Finland and worked as a journalist. He served as editor of the Social Democratic news-paper, *Turun Paivalehti*, from 1942. Paasio entered politics and was elected to the Turku Municipal Council in 1945. He was also elected to Parliament in 1948 as a member of the Social Democratic party. He served as chairman of the Parliamentary Foreign Affairs Committee from 1949. Paasio was selected to replace Vaino Tanner as chairman of the Social Democratic party in 1963. He was selected to lead a coalition government as prime minister on May 27, 1966. He attempted to stabilize the nation's economy and to convince the Soviet Union of Finland's neutrality. Paasio remained in office until March 22, 1968. He was again called upon to form a minority government on February 23, 1972. His government resigned in July of 1972, though Paasio remained caretaker prime minister until a government was formed by Kalevi Sursa on September 4, 1972. Paasio remained in the Parliament as leader of the Social Democrats until his retirement in 1975. On March 17, 1980, he died in Turku at the age of 76 after a long illness.

MAUNO KOIVISTO (Prime Minister, March 22, 1968–May 14, 1970). *See entry under Heads of State.*

TEUVO AURA (Prime Minister, May 14, 1970–July 14, 1970). Teuvo Ensio Aura was born in Ruskeala on December 28, 1912. He was educated in Finland and went to work for the Bank of Finland in the early 1940s. He became director general of the bank in 1943. Aura was a member of the Liberal party and was appointed to the Cabinet in 1950 as minister of commerce and industry. He served until 1951 and again from 1953 until 1954. He served as minister of the interior in 1957. Aura was also elected to the Helsinki City Council in 1957 and became its chairman. In 1968 he was elected mayor of Helsinki. He was called upon to form a caretaker government on May 14, 1970. Aura relinquished office to Ahti Karjalainen on

July 14, 1970. Aura again became caretaker prime minister on October 29, 1971, in order to prepare for new parliamentary elections. He stepped down on February 23, 1972. Aura remained mayor of Helsinki until 1979.

AHTI KARJALAINEN (Prime Minister, July 15, 1970–October 29, 1971). *See earlier entry under Heads of Government.*

TEUVO AURA (Prime Minister, October 29, 1971–February 23, 1972). *See earlier entry under Heads of Government.*

RAFAEL PAASIO (Prime Minister, February 23, 1972–September 4, 1972). *See earlier entry under Heads of Government.*

KALEVI SURSA (Prime Minister, September 4, 1972–June 13, 1975). Kalevi Sursa was born in Keuruu on December 21, 1930. He was educated in Finland and was subsequently employed by a publishing house. He worked for UNESCO from 1959 and became secretary general of the Finnish UNESCO Committee from 1965. Sursa became secretary general of the Social Democratic party in 1969 and president the following year. He served as minister of foreign affairs from February of 1972 until his selection as prime minister on September 4, 1972. He retained the office until June 13, 1975, and subsequently resumed his position as foreign minister until 1976. Sursa again served as prime minister from May 15, 1977, until May 26, 1979. He once again served as foreign minister until February 19, 1982, when he again became prime minister. His government lasted until April 30, 1987. He remained in the government as deputy prime minister and minister of foreign affairs from 1987 until 1989. Sursa was subsequently elected Speaker of Parliament. He retired from Parliament in 1991.

KEIJO LIINAMAA (Prime Minister, June 13, 1975–November 30, 1975). Keijo Liinamaa was born in 1929. He was a member of the Social Democratic party and served as state labor arbitrator, the senior civil servant in the Ministry of Labor. He was named minister of justice in Teuvo Aura's caretaker cabinet from May until July of 1970. Liinamaa was called upon to form a caretaker government composed of civil servants on June 13, 1975. He retained office until Martti Miettunen was able to form a five-party coalition government on November 30, 1975.

MARTTI MIETTUNEN (Prime Minister, November 30, 1975–May 15, 1977). *See earlier entry under Heads of Government.*

KALEVI SURSA (Prime Minister, May 15, 1977–May 26, 1979). *See earlier entry under Heads of Government.*

MAUNO KOIVISTO (Prime Minister, May 26, 1979–February 19, 1982). *See entry under Heads of State.*

KALEVI SURSA (Prime Minister, February 19, 1982–April 30, 1987). *See earlier entry under Heads of Government.*

HARRI HOLKERI (Prime Minister, April 30, 1987–April 26, 1991). Harri Hermanni Holkeri was born in Oripaa on January 6, 1937. He was educated in Finland and became active in the National Coalition party Youth League. He was elected to the Helsinki City Council in 1969 and was elected to Parliament the following year. Holkeri was elected chairman of the National Coalition party in 1971. He became chairman of the Helsinki City Council in 1981 and served until 1987. Holkeri was defeated by Mauno Koivisto in the presidential election in 1982. He was selected prime minister of Finland on

April 30, 1987. Holkeri's government was unable to combat rising unemployment and interest rates, and he was again defeated by Koivisto in the presidential election in 1988. The National Coalition party lost support in the election in 1991, and Holkeri stepped down as prime minister on April 26, 1991.

ESKO AHO (Prime Minister, April 26, 1991-   ). Esko Aho was born in Veteli in 1949. He was elected to the Parliament in 1982 as a member of the Centre party and was selected as leader of the Center party in 1990. Aho formed a center-right coalition as prime minister of Finland on April 26, 1991. Finland experienced economic difficulties following the collapse of the Soviet Union, and Aho applied for Finland's entry into the European Economic Community in March of 1992.

France

(République Française)

France is a country in western Europe.

HEADS OF STATE

CHARLES DE GAULLE (President, September 10, 1944–June 19, 1946). Charles André Joseph Marie de Gaulle was born in Lille on November 22, 1890. He graduated from Saint-Cyr, the French military school, in 1911 and was commissioned a second lieutenant. During World War I he served under Col. Philippe Pétain. He was wounded in 1916 and was taken prisoner by the Germans. Following his repatriation de Gaulle served as a commandant with the French Army in Poland. He subsequently attended the War College in Paris, and in 1927 he was named to the general staff of the Army of the Rhine. He headed the French military missions to Egypt, Syria, Iraq, and Persia from 1929 until 1932. Upon his return to France, he was promoted to lieutenant colonel and became secretary-general of the High Council of National Defense. De Gaulle advocated a mobile mechanized force for the French armed forces and questioned the French strategy of warfare based on the impregnability of the Maginot Line. He wrote a book, *The Army of the Future*, in 1934 to voice his opinions. De Gaulle's theories were proved correct when the German army overran the French forces in May of 1940. De Gaulle was promoted to brigadier general and named undersecretary of national defense and war in June of 1940. He refused to accept the truce negotiated by Premier Philippe Pétain with the Germans. Following the German occupation, de Gaulle went to London, where he became president of the French government in exile and commander of the Free French Army. Following the Allied victory in North Africa in 1943, de Gaulle served as copresident of the French Committee of National Liberation with Henri Giraud. Giraud resigned following a power struggle with de Gaulle, and following the liberation of France in 1944, de Gaulle became president and premier of the provisional government on September 10, 1944. He relinquished his position as premier on January 27, 1946. When de Gaulle's proposal for a strong executive presidency was rejected, he resigned from office on

June 19, 1946. The following year he founded the Rally of the French People party. When he suffered electoral defeat in 1953, he retired from politics. De Gaulle resumed power as premier on June 1, 1958, following a revolt by the French army in Algeria. The French National Assembly granted de Gaulle broad powers to deal with the threat of civil war. He was inaugurated as president of the French Fifth Republic on January 8, 1959. De Gaulle disappointed right-wing elements in the army by granting independence to Algeria in 1962 and was the target of several assassination attempts by the Secret Army Organization in the early 1960s. De Gaulle governed in an authoritarian manner and sought to assure France's position as the leading power in European affairs. He vetoed the admission of Great Britain to the European Community on several occasions. Though forced into a runoff, he was reelected to the presidency in 1965. In 1966 de Gaulle removed French military forces from the North Atlantic Treaty Organization and ordered that NATO's headquarters leave France. He was also a frequent critic of United States policy in Southeast Asia. In July of 1967 he created a furor when he shouted "Long live free Quebec" while on a visit to Canada. The incident outraged the Canadian government, and de Gaulle was forced to cut his trip short. De Gaulle's government was faced with a crisis in May and June of 1968 when a strike by students and workers resulted in violent street rioting. De Gaulle dissolved the National Assembly and called for new elections, which resulted in an overwhelming victory for de Gaulle. He promised reforms in France's educational policies and labor relations to help settle the crisis. In April of 1969 de Gaulle supported a referendum to centralize the government and reorganize the French Senate. He said that he would resign from office if the referendum failed, and following the defeat of

the referendum, he stepped down as president on April 27, 1969. He returned to his home in Colomby-les-deux Eglises, to write his memoirs. He died of a heart attack at his home on November 9, 1970.

VINCENT AURIOL (President, January 18, 1947–January 18, 1954). Vincent Auriol was born in Revel on August 25, 1884. He received a doctorate of law and a doctorate of economics from the University of Toulouse. In 1905 he joined the Socialist party, and he became editor of the newspaper *Le Midi Socialiste* four years later. He was elected to the Chamber of Deputies in 1914 and became general secretary of the Socialists in the Chamber in 1919. Auriol served on the Chamber's finance committee and gained a reputation as an expert on economic matters. He was named minister of finance in the government of Léon Blum in 1936 and was shifted to the Justice Ministry in Georges Bonnet's government later in the year. Auriol opposed the granting of power to Marshal Philippe Pétain following the fall of France to German troops in June of 1940. Auriol was subsequently arrested by the Vichy government and remained imprisoned until his release for reasons of health in 1943. He escaped to London in October of that year and joined the Free French government in exile. After the liberation of France, Auriol became head of the Foreign Affairs Committee of the provisional government in November of 1944. He was elected to the Constituent Assembly in October of 1945 and was appointed minister of state the following month. He was elected Speaker of the Constituent Assembly in January of 1946 and helped insure the passage of a new constitution. De Gaulle had opposed the constitution because it provided for little power for the president of the Republic, and he subsequently resigned from office. Auriol was elected president of the Fourth Republic and took office on

January 18, 1947. He presided over the formation of fifteen governments during his term of office. He completed his term on January 18, 1954, and relinquished his position to René Coty. Auriol emerged from retirement in 1958 to enlist the support of the Socialists for Charles de Gaulle's return to power. He became a critic of de Gaulle in 1960, when he charged the president had violated his own constitution. Auriol's health failed in 1963, and he retired to his home in Cap Benat. His last political act was to endorse François Mitterrand in his unsuccessful campaign for president against de Gaulle in 1965. Auriol broke his hip in November of 1965 and was taken to a Paris hospital. He died there at the age of 81 on January 1, 1966.

RENÉ COTY (President, January 18, 1954–January 8, 1959). René Coty was born in Le Havre on March 20, 1882. He was educated at the University of Caen where he received a degree in law. He opened a law practice in 1902 and served in the French Army during World War I. Coty entered politics in 1923 and was elected to the National Assembly. He was appointed undersecretary of state for the interior in 1931 and was elected to the Senate in 1935. He retired from politics during World War II, after casting a vote supporting Marshal Philippe Petain's ascension to power. Coty returned to the National Assembly after the German occupation and served as minister of reconstruction and urbanism from 1947 until September of 1948. He returned to the Senate in 1948 and was reelected in 1952. When President Vincent Auriol refused a second term of office, the National Assembly deadlocked for nearly a week before settling on Coty as a compromise candidate. He was sworn in as president of the Fourth Republic on January 18, 1954. His administration was beset with difficulty in regard to the question of Algerian independence. When a group of French army

officers threatened a civil war in May of 1958, Coty called on the National Assembly to bring General Charles de Gaulle to power. Coty threatened to resign his office if the Assembly refused to confirm de Gaulle in office. Coty stepped down as president on January 8, 1959, in favor of de Gaulle and went into retirement. He died in Le Havre of a heart condition at the age of 80 on November 22, 1962.

CHARLES DE GAULLE (President, January 8, 1959–April 27, 1969). *See earlier entry under Heads of State.*

ALAIN POHER (President, April 27, 1969–June 20, 1969). Alain Emile Louis Marie Poher was born in Ablon-sur-Seine on April 17, 1909. He received a degree in law from the University of Paris and worked in the ministry of finance from 1935 until 1946. He was also elected mayor of Ablon-sur-Seine in 1945. Poher was elected to the Senate in 1946 and served until 1948, when he was named commissioner for German and Austrian affairs. He served as the French delegate to the International Ruhr Authority from 1950 and was reelected to the Senate in 1952. He was a dedicated advocate of European unity and served as president of the Common Market Commission from 1955 until 1957. Poher was also a delegate to the European Parliament from 1958. He was elected president of the Senate in 1968 and opposed President Charles de Gaulle's referendum that would have curtailed the powers of the Senate. When the referendum failed, de Gaulle resigned his office. Poher became acting president of France following de Gaulle's resignation on April 27, 1969. He was an unsuccessful candidate to succeed de Gaulle in the subsequent election and relinquished office to Georges Pompidou on June 20, 1969. When Pompidou died in office on April 2, 1974, Poher again became acting president and served until Valéry

Giscard d'Estaing took office on May 27, 1974. Poher stepped down as Ablon-sur-Seine's mayor in 1977, but remained president of the Senate.

GEORGES POMPIDOU (President, June 20, 1969–April 2, 1974). Georges Jean Raymond Pompidou was born in Montboudif on July 15, 1911. He was educated at the École Normale Superieure and the École Libre des Sciences Politiques and began teaching in Marseilles in 1935. He served briefly in the French army in 1939, but returned to teaching in Paris following the fall of France and the German occupation. After the liberation of France, Pompidou joined the staff of General Charles de Gaulle. He became a close associate of de Gaulle and remained his aide following the general's resignation as president of the provisional government in January of 1946. Pompidou was hired by the Rothschild bank in 1954 and became director-general of the bank in 1956. He remained close to de Gaulle and was named chief of cabinet when de Gaulle became premier in June of 1958. He returned to his position at the bank when de Gaulle became president of the Fifth Republic in January of 1959. Pompidou was also named to the Constitutional Council and served as de Gaulle's representative to a secret meeting with Algerian nationalists in Switzerland in 1961. His meetings led to an agreement to grant Algeria independence from France in April of 1962. Pompidou was appointed premier of France shortly thereafter and took office on April 14, 1962. His connections with the banking industry led to criticism by members of the left-wing. Pompidou usually remained behind the scenes in French politics, with most major issues being handled by de Gaulle. Pompidou's administrative abilities earned him considerable prestige, and he became a leader of the Gaullist party. France was beset by strikes by students and workers in May of 1968. Pompidou was left to negotiate an end to the crisis. He was able to reach a settlement that granted workers a sizeable increase in their annual income. Pompidou then persuaded de Gaulle to hold new elections. Pompidou led the Gaullists to a major victory, but then, in an effort to reassert his authority, de Gaulle dismissed Pompidou as premier on July 11, 1968. The following year de Gaulle conducted a referendum on a political reform bill he supported. The referendum failed and de Gaulle resigned as president. Pompidou announced his candidacy for the presidency. He was elected with the support of the Gaullists in a runoff election and took office on June 20, 1969. Pompidou embarked on an effort to improve France's relations with the United States and other countries. He also dropped de Gaulle's demands that Great Britain be refused entry to the European Common Market. He undertook an effort to modernize French industry and improve economic conditions in the country. Pompidou succeeded in keeping France's economy in good shape until 1973, when the country, and most of the West, was hit by rampant inflation. Pompidou's health began to fail, and it was rumored that he suffered from cancer of the bone marrow. He died in Paris at the age of 62 on April 2, 1974.

ALAIN POHER (President, April 2, 1974–May 27, 1974). *See earlier entry under Heads of State.*

VALÉRY GISCARD D'ESTAING (President, May 27, 1974–May 21, 1981). Valéry Giscard d'Estaing was born on February 2, 1926, in Coblenz, Germany, where his father was serving as a financial director for the French Occupation Administration. He served in the French army in North Africa in 1944 before returning to the École Polytechnique to earn a degree. Giscard then attended the École Nationale d'Administration before entering the civil service in 1952. He worked in the Ministry of Finance, where he became an aide to Finance Minister Edgar Faure. He was elected to the National Assembly in 1956 as a member of the National Center of Independents and Peasants. When Charles de Gaulle returned to power in January of 1959, Giscard was appointed secretary of state for finance. He rose to the position of minister of finance in January of 1962 and instituted an austerity program that resulted in the first balanced budget in over three decades. His policies succeeded in lowering the rate of inflation, though a temporary recession resulted. Giscard was dismissed from the cabinet in January of 1966 following criticism from labor and business interests. He continued to lead the Independent Republican party in the National Assembly and went into opposition against de Gaulle. He opposed the president's referendum to reorganize political power in the country, and when the measure failed in a referendum, de Gaulle resigned from office. Giscard returned to the cabinet as minister of finance and economic affairs following the election of Georges Pompidou as president. He attempted to restore the French economy that had suffered as a result of the student and worker strikes the previous year. Giscard devalued the franc in August of 1969 and instituted other measures to restore economic stability to the country. He announced his candidacy for president following the death of Pompidou in April of 1974. He waged an American-style political campaign and defeated Socialist candidate François Mitterrand by a narrow margin in a runoff election in May of 1974. Giscard's majority coalition was successful in the election in March of 1978. Widespread unemployment and rising inflation caused the French economy to continue to deteriorate during Giscard's term of office, however. Giscard was defeated in his campaign for reelection by François Mitterrand and

left office on May 21, 1981. Giscard was returned to the National Assembly in 1984, where he remained until his election to the European Parliament in 1989.

FRANÇOIS MITTERRAND (President, May 21, 1981–). François Maurice Adrien Marie Mitterrand was born in Jarnac, in western France, on October 26, 1916. He attended the University of Paris, where he received a degree in law. In 1939 he joined the French army, and he was wounded and captured by the Germans in June of the following year. In December of 1941 he escaped from a German prison camp and returned to France, where he worked with the Resistance during the occupation. Mitterrand served in Charles de Gaulle's provisional government after the liberation in 1944. He was elected to the National Assembly in November of 1946 as a member of the Democratic and Socialist Resistance Union (UDSR). He was appointed to the cabinet as minister of war veterans in 1947. In the years that followed he served in various other cabinet positions, including minister of overseas territories from 1950 until 1951 and minister of state from 1952 until 1953. Mitterrand served as minister of the interior from 1954 until 1955 and was minister of state for justice from 1956 until 1957. He opposed the new constitution that created the French Fifth Republic and granted Charles de Gaulle greater power as president in 1958. Mitterrand was elected to the Senate in 1959, but returned to the National Assembly in 1962. He ran against de Gaulle in the presidential election of 1965 as a candidate supported by a united coalition of the left. Mitterrand forced the president into a runoff election, which was won by de Gaulle. Mitterrand continued to lead the leftist coalition to electoral successes until 1968, when the Gaullists swept elections following student and worker strikes. Mitterrand became leader of the new Socialist party in June of 1971. The Socialists entered into a coalition with the Communists in the election to succeed the late president Georges Pompidou in May of 1974, and Mitterrand was defeated by Valéry Giscard d'Estaing by a narrow margin. The Socialist-Communist alliance separated in 1977, and the leftist parties lost power in elections the following year. Mitterrand survived a challenge to his leadership of the Socialists in 1979 and again ran for the presidency in the election of 1981. Mitterrand forced incumbent President Giscard d'Estaing into a runoff and was elected president in May of 1981. He took office on May 21, 1981, and the Socialists won a majority in the National Assembly the following month. Mitterrand instituted a number of economic and political reforms,

including the nationalization of the French banking industry. He also increased government spending for social programs. The French economy declined as a result of his policies, and the government was forced to institute austerity measures in 1984. A rightist coalition gained a majority in the National Assembly in March of 1986, and Mitterrand was forced to name his rival, Jacques Chirac, as premier. Mitterrand was reelected president in May of 1988 by defeating Chirac in a runoff. The Socialists also regained control of the Assembly. In the early 1990s the government was buffeted by a series of financial scandals. Mitterrand and his government's popularity dropped substantially, and the president also suffered from poor health.

HEADS OF GOVERNMENT

CHARLES DE GAULLE (Premier, September 10, 1944–January 27, 1946). *See entry under Heads of State.*

FÉLIX GOUIN (Premier, January 27, 1946–June 24, 1946). Félix Gouin was born in Peypin, Bouches-du-Rhone, on October 4, 1884. He received a degree in law in 1907 and worked as an attorney. During World War I he served as a private, and he was elected mayor of Istres in 1923. He was a member of the Socialist party and was elected to the National Assembly in 1924. Gouin won reelection throughout the 1920s and 1930s. He opposed the granting of power to Marshal Philippe Pétain during the German occupation of France in 1940 and subsequently joined the Free French administration under General Charles de Gaulle. He was elected president of the Consultative Assembly in Algiers following the Allied landings in North Africa and remained in that position after the government moved to Paris. In

October of 1945 he was elected to the Constituent Assembly and he became president of the Assembly the following month. Gouin was selected as leader of the provisional government on January 27, 1946, following the resignation of General de Gaulle. He retained that position until June 24, 1946. He served as deputy premier in the subsequent government of Georges Bidault and was also minister of state under Premier Paul Ramadier in 1947. Gouin remained in the Assembly until his retirement in 1958. He died in Nice at the age of 93 on October 25, 1977.

GEORGES BIDAULT (Premier, June 24, 1946–December 16, 1946). Georges Augustin Bidault was born in Moulins on October 5, 1899. He served briefly in the French army near the end of World War I. He then completed his studies at the Sorbonne and began a teaching career. From 1932 until 1939 he also worked as a writer for *l'Aube*, a Catholic daily. Bidault was defeated in an election to the Chamber of Deputies in 1935. He again served in the French Army in World War II. He was captured by the Germans in 1940 and was released the following year. During the German occupation he returned to Paris. Bidault became the leader of the French Resistance following the death of Jean Moulin in 1943. After the liberation of France in 1944, Bidault was named foreign minister in the government of General Charles de Gaulle. He attended the founding meeting of the United Nations in San Francisco as head of the French delegation the following year. He helped to organize the Mouvement Républicain Populaire (MRP) and was also elected to the National Assembly in 1945. Bidault succeeded Félix Gouin as premier of France on June 24, 1946. He stepped down as foreign minister in November of 1946 and resigned as premier on December 16, 1946. He was reappointed foreign minister in January of the following year and retained the position until July of 1947. Bidault was again selected by the National Assembly to serve as premier on October 27, 1949, and remained in office until June 30, 1950. He remained in the cabinet and again served as foreign minister from 1953 until 1954. He worked to improve his country's relations with Germany and negotiated France's entrance into the European Coal and Steel Community. Bidault also became a leading supporter of France's interests in Algeria and opposed any movement toward independence for the colony. He left the MRP and founded the Democratie Chrétienne en France, a right-wing political party in 1958. He was subsequently elected to the first National Assembly of the Fifth Republic. Bidault strongly opposed de Gaulle's plans to grant independence to Algeria and allied himself with the Secret Army Organization (OAS), a group that used terrorist tactics to maintain French control of Algeria. The following year

Bidault founded the National Council of Resistance and went underground. He was accused of participating in insurrectional activities and went into exile. He traveled to various European countries before he was allowed to settle in Brazil in 1963. Bidault returned to France in 1968 after de Gaulle granted an amnesty to those charged with political crimes during the Algerian conflict. Bidault remained generally inactive in political affairs after his return, but formed the Movement of Justice and Peace, a far-right political party in the late 1970s. When the party failed to make an impact in French politics, Bidault went into seclusion. He suffered a stroke in December of 1982 and died the following month in a hospital at Cambo-les-Bains at the age of 83 on January 26, 1983.

LÉON BLUM (Premier, December 16, 1946–January 22, 1947). Léon Blum was born in Paris to an Alsatian Jewish family on April 9, 1872. He received a degree in law from the Sorbonne in 1894. He subsequently worked as a drama critic. Blum joined the Socialist party in 1899 and was a supporter of the republicans during the Dreyfus affair. He was elected to the Chamber of Deputies in 1919 and served as chairman of the Socialist party executive board. He broke with the Socialists in 1921, when the Communists took control of the party. Blum founded the Moderate Socialist party and created the journal *Le Populaire*. He was defeated for reelection to the Chamber of Deputies in 1928, but was returned the following year. In 1936 he formed the Popular Front, a coalition of leftist parties opposed to Fascism, and led the coalition to victory. He became premier on June 3, 1936. His government carried out a number of social reforms, including nationalizing the leading French armament industries and the Bank of France and instituting a forty-hour work week. His reforms were bitterly opposed by the business community and the right-wing. By trying to maintain France's neutrality during the Spanish Civil War, he alienated many of his leftist supporters. Blum resigned on June 23, 1937, when the French Senate refused to grant him special powers to deal with the French economic crisis. He served as vice premier in the subsequent government of Camille Chautemps and returned as premier on March 12, 1938. He was again forced to resign on April 10, 1938, and refused to participate in the government of Radical leader Edouard Daladier. Following the defeat of France by the Germans in October of 1940, Blum was charged with betrayal of his office by the Vichy authorities. He was brought to trial in February of 1942, but the trial was suspended after several months because of the spirited defense offered by Blum and his codefendants. He was returned to prison in a German concentration camp, where he remained until he was freed by United States troops in May of 1945. Blum returned to France and again became premier of an interim Socialist government on December 16, 1946. He stepped down on January 22, 1947, following the election of a president for the new French Fourth Republic. He was narrowly defeated for another term as premier in November of 1947 and joined the government of André Marie as vice premier in August of 1948. Despite ill health, Blum remained a leading political figure in France. He died of a heart attack at his country cottage in Jouy-en-Josas at the age of 77 on March 30, 1950.

PAUL RAMADIER (Premier, January 22, 1947–November 22, 1947). Paul Ramadier was born in La Rochelle, France, on March 17, 1888. He studied law at the University of Toulouse and the University of Paris. He became an advocate at the Court of Appeals in 1909 and was elected mayor of Decaseville in 1919. Ramadier was elected to the National Assembly in

1928 and served in the cabinet of Camille Chautemps as minister of labor from 1937 until 1938. He refused to support Marshal Pétain's ascension to power following the German conquest of France in 1940 and worked with the Resistance during the German occupation. After the liberation of France, Ramadier reentered politics. He served as minister of supplies in the provisional government of Charles de Gaulle from November of 1944 until March of 1945. He was named minister of justice by Premier Léon Blum in December of 1946 and was appointed premier by President Vincent Auriol on January 22, 1947. The Ramadier government faced a crisis when the premier opposed his Communist vice-premier, Maurice Thorez, on the question of wage increases. Ramadier dismissed the Communists in his cabinet after they voted against the government. His cabinet barely survived a vote of confidence in May of 1947. Ramadier was unable to settle the labor strikes that were sweeping the country, and he resigned on November 22, 1947. He remained in the National Assembly until 1951 and served as minister of national defense from 1948 until 1949. He was reelected to the National Assembly in 1956 and served as minister of finance in the cabinet of Guy Mollet until 1957. Ramadier retired from politics the following year. He died at a clinic in Rodez on October 14, 1961, at the age of 73.

ROBERT SCHUMAN (Premier, November 22, 1947–July 24, 1948). Robert Schuman was born to a Lorraine family in Luxembourg on June 29, 1886. He was educated in Germany and received a doctorate in law from the University of Strasbourg. He practiced law in Metz before World War I. Though of draft age during the war, he claimed he never entered the German army. After the war, Alsace-Lorraine was restored to French rule. Schuman joined the Popular Democratic party in

1919 and was elected to the Chamber of Deputies. He served as a member of the Chamber's Finance Commission. Schuman was appointed undersecretary of state for refugees by Premier Paul Reynaud in 1940, shortly before the fall of France to the Germans. He was arrested by the Gestapo after the surrender of France and was imprisoned in Metz. He was later placed under house arrest in Neustadt, where he worked with the French Resistance. Schuman returned to the Constituent Assembly in November of 1945, following the liberation of France. He helped form the Popular Republican party and was named minister of finance in the government of George Bidault from June until December of 1946. He returned to the cabinet in Paul Ramadier's government from January until November of 1947. Schuman was asked to form a government as premier on November 22, 1947. He resigned on July 24, 1948, and served as foreign minister in the subsequent government of André Marie. He was again named premier on August 31, 1948, but his government was defeated in the Assembly and he resigned on September 10, 1948. Schuman was then again named to the cabinet as foreign minister and became a champion of European unity and Franco-German reconciliation. In May of 1950 Schuman introduced a proposal to pool European coal and steel that evolved into the European Coal and Steel Community. He also proposed the formation of a unified European army. The Gaullists and others in the National Assembly opposed this plan, and Schuman stepped down as foreign minister in January of 1952. He subsequently served in the cabinet as minister without portfolio and was named minister of justice in February of 1955. He retained that position until January of 1956. Schuman was elected president of the European Parliamentary Assembly in March of 1958. He stepped down in March of 1960 and was named honorary president of the

assembly. He suffered an accident in January of 1961 when he collapsed on a county road near his home and lay all night in the cold rain before being rescued. His health remained poor after this incident, and he died at his home in Scy-Chazelles, near Metz, at the age of 77 on September 5, 1963.

ANDRÉ MARIE (Premier, July 24, 1948–August 31, 1948). André Désiré Paul Marie was born in Honfleur, Normandy, on December 3, 1897. He received a law degree from the University of Caen and then joined the Court of Appeals in Rouen. He served with distinction in the army during World War I. After the war he entered politics, and he was elected to the Rouen city council in 1925. Marie was elected to the Chamber of Deputies in 1928 as a member of the Radical Socialist party. He was named to the cabinet as undersecretary of state for Alsace-Lorraine in 1933. The following year he was named undersecretary of state for foreign affairs. Marie rejoined the French army at the start of World War II and was captured by the Germans early in 1940. He was released after the fall of France and became active in the Resistance to the German occupation. Marie was arrested by the Nazis in September of 1943 and was imprisoned in concentration camps before being liberated by the United States army in April of 1945. He reentered politics in postwar France and was elected mayor of Barentin. He also served in the Constituent Assembly and was elected to the National Assembly in November of 1946. Marie was named to the cabinet as minister of justice in the government of Robert Schuman in November of 1947. Marie was asked to form a government following Schuman's resignation, and he formed a cabinet on July 24, 1948, that represented a wide range of political philosophies. The cabinet's divergencies could not be reconciled, however, and the Marie government collapsed on August 31,

1948. He remained in the cabinet as minister of justice and vice-premier. He was named minister of education in July of 1950 and retained that position until June of 1954. In 1956 Marie broke with the Radical party and formed a splinter party dedicated to maintaining French control of Algeria. This position brought him into conflict with President Charles de Gaulle, and Marie lost his seat in the National Assembly in 1962, the same year Algeria was granted independence. He retired from national politics and returned to Barentin, where he remained mayor. Marie had suffered from poor health brought on by a lung ailment since the war. He died in Barentin at the age of 76 on June 12, 1974.

ROBERT SCHUMAN (Premier, August 31, 1948–September 10, 1948). *See earlier entry under Heads of Government.*

HENRI QUEUILLE (Premier, September 10, 1948–October 27, 1949). Henri Queuille was born in Neuvic d'Ussel on March 31, 1884. He studied medicine in Paris and entered practice in his home town. He was elected mayor of Neuvic in 1912 and was elected to the Chamber of Deputies two years later. He served in the army as a medical officer during World War I. After the war he resumed his seat in the Chamber, and he was appointed undersecretary for agriculture in 1920. Queuille subsequently held various ministry positions and was appointed to the cabinet as minister of telegraphs and telephones in June of 1932. The following December he was named minister of agriculture. He retained that position until 1934, when he became minister of health. Queuille returned to the cabinet in June of 1937 as minister of public works and remained there until March of 1938. The following month he was again named minister of agriculture. He was shifted to the Ministry of Food Supplies in March of

1940. He resigned from the government after the surrender of France and the establishment of the Vichy regime. Queuille worked with the French Resistance until April of 1943, when he escaped to London. He joined the Free French government of General Charles de Gaulle and served as acting president of the French Commission of National Liberation in Algeria from November of 1943. After the liberation of France, he returned to the National Assembly and became chairman of the Radical Socialist party. He was named to the cabinet as minister of state in July of 1948. Queuille was asked to form a government as premier on September 10, 1948. His premiership became the longest government in the French Fourth Republic, lasting until October 27, 1949. Queuille again served briefly as premier from July 1, 1950, until July 4, 1950, and from March 9, 1951, until July 10, 1951. He continued to serve in various cabinets until June of 1954, when he resigned as vice-premier and retired from national politics. Queuille died in Paris after a long illness at the age of 86 on June 15, 1970.

GEORGES BIDAULT (Premier, October 27, 1949–June 30, 1950). *See earlier entry under Heads of Government.*

HENRI QUEUILLE (Premier, June 30, 1950–July 11, 1950). *See earlier entry under Heads of Government.*

RENÉ PLEVEN (Premier, July 11, 1950–March 9, 1951). René Pleven was born in Rennes on April 15, 1901. He attended the University of Paris, where he graduated with a degree in law. He left France to go to Canada after failing to pass an examination for the French civil service and became an executive with the telephone company in Canada and Great Britain. Pleven became active with the French Resistance movement during World War II. He was named national commissioner for the economy, finance, the colonies, and foreign affairs by Charles de Gaulle's French National Committee in 1941. Following the liberation of France, Pleven became minister of the economy and finance. He subsequently broke with de Gaulle and founded the Democratic and Socialist Union of the Resistance in 1946. Pleven served in several cabinets and was minister of defense from 1949 until 1950. He was selected as premier of France on July 11, 1950, and retained the office until March 9, 1951, following a movement to the right by the National Assembly. Pleven was again named premier on August 8, 1951. He resigned on January 17, 1952, over a dispute concerning budget deficits. Pleven remained in the National Assembly, where he was a leading supporter of European unity. He again served as defense minister in 1954 and presided over the fall of France's colonial power in Indochina. Pleven was defeated for reelection to the Assembly in 1973 and subsequently became president of the regional development council in Brittany. He died in Paris of heart failure on January 13, 1993.

HENRI QUEUILLE (Premier, March 9, 1951–August 8, 1951). *See earlier entry under Heads of Government.*

RENÉ PLEVEN (Premier, August 8, 1951–January 17, 1952). *See earlier entry under Heads of Government.*

EDGAR FAURE (Premier, January 17, 1952–March 6, 1952). Edgar Faure was born in Herault on August 18, 1908. He received a doctorate of law from the University of Paris and practiced law in Paris before the Court of Appeal. He supported the Resistance during World War II and escaped to Algiers in 1942. Faure served on the French Committee of National Liberation from 1943 until 1944. After the war he was France's assistant delegate to the International Military Tribunal in Nuremberg, which prosecuted war criminals. He was elected to the National Assembly as a member of the Radical-Socialist party in November of 1946. Faure was appointed secretary of state for finance in the cabinet of Henri Queuille in February of 1949. He was named minister of the budget in July of 1950 and became minister of justice in August of 1951. When René Pleven's government collapsed in January of 1952, Faure was named premier. He formed a centrist cabinet on January 17, 1952, but resigned on March 6, 1952, when his government failed to win a vote of confidence in the National Assembly. He was again named minister of finance in 1953 and served in the cabinet until 1954. Faure again served as premier from February 23, 1955, until January 31, 1956, during which time the French government passed legislation providing for West German rearmament. He returned to the cabinet as minister of finance in 1958 and served until he was defeated for reelection to the National Assembly after the selection of Charles de Gaulle as president. Faure was elected to the Senate the following year. He conducted several diplomatic missions for President de Gaulle, including negotiating the recognition of the People's Republic of China. He remained in the Senate until 1966, when he was appointed minister of agriculture. Faure retained that position until 1968, when de Gaulle appointed him minister of education following student strikes in May of 1968. He initiated reforms in the French educational system that included giving universities more autonomy. He left the cabinet in 1969 and stepped down from the National Assembly in 1978. Faure was also a novelist who wrote detective stories under the pseudonym of Edgar Sanday. He was elected to the French Academy in June of 1978. He served in the European Parliament from 1979 until 1981 and helped to organize the celebration of the 200th anniversary of the French Revolution shortly before his death. Faure was hospitalized in February of 1988 and underwent surgery for intestinal disorders. He died in Paris at the age of 79 on March 30, 1988.

ANTOINE PINAY (Premier, March 6, 1952–January 7, 1953). Antoine Pinay was born in Saint-Symphorien-sur Coise on December 30, 1891. He was educated in Saint-Chamond, where he entered a tannery business upon graduation. He served as an artillery officer during World War I and was wounded in action. After the war he became director of the Tanneries Fouletier. Pinay entered politics and was elected mayor of Saint-Chamond in 1929. He was elected to the National Assembly as a member of the Independent Radical party in 1936. He was elected to the Senate in 1938 and supported turning over the French government to Marshal Philippe Pétain after the collapse of France in 1940. Pinay remained mayor of Saint-Chamond during the war and occupation, but avoided charges of collaboration because he stood up to the Nazis to protect his city. He was again elected to the National Assembly in 1946 and was named secretary of state for economic affairs in September of 1948. He retained that position until October of 1949. Pinay returned to the cabinet as minister of public works, transportation, and tourism in July of 1950 and served until February of 1952. He was asked to form a government as premier on March 6, 1952, and also served as minister of finance in the cabinet. He made efforts to improve France's economic stability and simplified the French tax code. Pinay resigned from office on December 23, 1952. He returned to the cabinet to serve as foreign minister from 1955 until 1956. He was appointed minister of finance and economic affairs by Charles de Gaulle in 1958 and remained in the

cabinet until 1960. Pinay subsequently served on various industrial boards and retired as mayor of Saint-Chamond in 1977.

RENÉ MAYER (Premier, January 7, 1953–May 21, 1953). René Joël Simon Mayer was born in Paris on May 4, 1895. He received a degree in law from the University of Paris in 1914. He served in the French army during World War I and entered the civil service after the war. In 1923 he was named deputy attorney general in the Council of State. Mayer served in several ministries until 1928, when he became a director of the Railroad Company of Northern France. He advocated the nationalization of French railways and was instrumental in the creation of the S.N.C.F., the national railway company, in 1937. He also was involved in the merger of France's private airlines into Air-France. Mayer escaped from France during the German occupation in 1943 and served on the French Committee of National Liberation in Algiers. He served as minister of transport and public works in the provisional government after the liberation of France. He was elected to the Constituent Assembly in June of 1946 and was elected to the National Assembly the following December. Mayer entered the cabinet as minister of finance and economic affairs in November of 1947 and instituted programs to halt inflation and balance the budget. He remained finance minister until July of 1948 and was reappointed to that position in the cabinet of René Pleven in 1951. His austerity programs proved unpopular and brought down the Pleven government in March of 1951. Mayer formed a government as premier on January 7, 1953. He supported France's continued involvement in the war in Indochina and continued to seek a solution to the country's rising inflation. He retained office until May 21, 1953, when he resigned after the National Assembly refused to grant the government special powers to deal with the economy. Mayer succeeded Jean Monnet as president of the High Authority of the Coal and Steel Community in 1955. He resigned from his position in 1957 and subsequently retired from politics. Mayer died in Paris at the age of 77 on December 13, 1972.

JOSEPH LANIEL (Premier, June 26, 1953–June 18, 1954). Joseph Laniel was born in Vimoutiers, Normandy, on October 12, 1889. He attended the Lycée Janson-de-Sailly and entered his family's textile business upon graduation. He served with distinction in the French cavalry during World War I. Laniel returned to the family business after the war and entered politics in 1919, when he was elected Mayor of Notre-Dame-de-Courson. In 1932 he was elected to succeed his father in the National Assembly. He was named undersecretary of state for finance in 1940. Laniel refused to support the Assembly's granting of extraordinary powers to Marshal Philippe Pétain after the fall of France in 1940. Laniel served as a leader of the French Resistance during World War II and served in the provisional government after the war. He was elected to the Constituent Assembly in October of 1945 and to the National Assembly in November of 1946. He served briefly as secretary of state for finance and the economy in 1948 and was named minister of posts, telegraphs, and telephones in 1951. Laniel was appointed minister of state later in the year and served until February of 1952. He was named premier of France on June 26, 1953. He was faced with the continued French military action in Indochina and a wave of nationalist activity in French North Africa. His government was forced to resign on June 18, 1954, after the French military defeat at Dien Bien Phu in Indochina. Laniel subsequently retired from national politics to write his memoirs, which were published in 1971. He died in Paris at the age of 85 after a long illness on April 9, 1975.

PIERRE MENDÈS-FRANCE (Premier, June 18, 1954–February 23, 1955). Pierre Mendès-France was born in Paris on January 11, 1907. He received a degree in law from the École des Sciences Politique in 1925. He was active in politics, having joined the Radical Socialist party while in college. When he was elected to the Chamber of Deputies in 1932, he became the nation's youngest deputy. Mendès-France was appointed undersecretary of state to the treasury in the government of Léon Blum in 1938 and served for four weeks until the cabinet fell. He joined the French air force in 1939 and was stationed in Syria. He traveled to North Africa after the fall of France in 1940 and was arrested by the Vichy authorities on charges of desertion. Mendès-France escaped from prison and joined the Free French forces in London under Charles de Gaulle. He participated in several bombing raids against the Germans. In November of 1943 Mendès-France joined the Committee for National Liberation as commissioner of finance, and he led the French delegation to the Bretton Woods monetary conference the following year. In September of 1944 he was named minister of national economy in the provisional government after the liberation of France. Mendès-France resigned in early 1945 when his anti-inflationary policies were rejected by the government. He subsequently refused to accept cabinet appointments, but promoted his economic policies from the National Assembly. He also served on several international economic commissions. In June of 1953 Mendès-France attempted to form a government, but failed to secure approval from the National Assembly. He was again called upon to serve as premier in June of 1954, following the resignation of Joseph Laniel. Mendès-France took office on June 18, 1954, and vowed to withdraw France from the conflict in Indochina, where France had suffered a military defeat at Diem Bien Phu. He successfully negotiated a cease-fire treaty with the Vietminh rebels in July of 1954. Mendès-France won National Assembly approval for West German rearmament and granted autonomy to Tunisia. The latter action cost his government the support of the right-wing and precipitated nationalist activity in Algeria. He was forced to resign on February 23, 1955. Mendès-France was briefly named minister of state in the government of Guy Mollet in 1956. He opposed the formation of the French Fifth Republic under de Gaulle and was defeated for his seat in the National Assembly in 1958. He remained out of office in the national government until 1967, when he was returned to the Assembly. He was narrowly defeated by the Gaullists the following year. He subsequently retired from national politics, but emerged to attend the inauguration of Socialist leader François Mitterrand as president in May of 1981. Mendès-France died of a heart attack at his home in Paris at the age of 75 on October 18, 1982.

EDGAR FAURE (Premier, February 23, 1955–January 31, 1956). *See earlier entry under Heads of Government.*

GUY MOLLET (Premier, January 31, 1956–June 13, 1957). Guy Mollet was born in Flers in Normandy on December 31, 1905. He was educated at the University of Le Havre, where he received a degree in English. He joined the Socialist party in 1923 and began a career as a teacher. In 1932 he was dismissed from his position after campaigning against the Conservative premier, André Tardieu. Mollet joined the army medical corps in 1939 and was captured by the invading Germans in 1940. He was released after the fall of France and joined the French Resistance. Mollet was elected to the Con-

stituent Assembly following France's liberation, and he helped draft the new French constitution. He was elected secretary-general of the Socialist party in September of 1946 and served briefly as minister of state in the government of Léon Blum later in the year. He was a supporter of European Unity and served as France's representative to several European commissions. Mollet was selected as premier on January 31, 1955, after joining forces with the Radical party. His government was faced with a crisis in North Africa, and Mollet was badly received by French Algerines when he visited Algiers. He instituted a draft to supply men for the army in Algeria to protect French interests there. Mollet faced another crisis in the Middle East when President Gamal Abdel Nasser of Egypt nationalized the Suez Canal in July of 1956. The French government joined with Great Britain to send troops in support of Israel in the Arab-Israeli conflict when Israel attempted to seize the canal. The action failed when the United States refused to support the move. Despite the fiasco, Mollet's government remained in office until June 13, 1957, when it was voted down on a tax-increase bill. Mollet remained in the National Assembly and supported the formation of the French Fifth Republic under Charles de Gaulle. He led the Socialists in opposition in the National Assembly, but supported de Gaulle's policies on Algeria. He continued to lead the Socialists in their coalition with the Communists and other leftist parties in the presidential elections of 1965. Mollet stepped down as Socialist leader in 1968, but remained a member of the National Assembly and mayor of Arras. He died of a heart attack at his home in Paris at the age of 69 on October 3, 1975.

MAURICE BOURGÈS-MAUNOURY (Premier, June 13, 1957–November 5, 1957). Maurice Jean-Marie Bourgès-Maunoury was born in Luisant on August 19, 1914. He received a degree in law from the University of Paris. In 1939 he joined the French army as an artillery lieutenant. He was captured by the Germans during the invasion of France in 1940, but was released the following year. Bourgès-Maunoury joined the French Resistance and escaped to London in 1943. He joined the Free French forces and fought for the liberation of France. He was discharged from the army after the conclusion of World War II and entered politics. Bourgès-Maunoury joined the Radical Socialist party and was elected to the National Assembly in 1946. He was named secretary of state for the budget in November of 1947 and was elected mayor of Bessières in 1949. He was appointed to the cabinet as minister of public works in July of 1950. Bourgès-Maunoury served in various government positions in the early 1950s and was appointed minister of finance in January of 1953. He served as minister of industry and commerce in the government of Pierre Mendès-France from June of 1954 until his resignation on September 3, 1954, over the National Assembly's rejection of the European Defense Community. In January of 1955 he returned to the cabinet as minister of the armed forces, and he was named minister of the interior by Premier Edgar Faure the following month. Bourgès-Maunoury was given responsibility for the colonial administration of Algeria in this position. He attempted to grant greater autonomy to the Muslim areas of Algeria in the hopes of quelling disturbances in the colony. He resigned from the Faure cabinet in January of 1956 and was named minister of defense in the subsequent government of Guy Mollet. Bourgès-Maunoury was asked to form a government as premier on June 13, 1957. The major issue during his term of office was the growing civil war in Algeria. Bourgès-Maunoury was unable to negotiate a settlement of the conflict and stepped down as premier on November 5, 1957, when his Algerian home-rule bill did not receive a vote of confidence in the National Assembly. He remained in the cabinet of Premier Félix Gaillard as minister of the interior until May of 1958. He retired from national politics following the formation of the French Fifth Republic and entered private business, though he remained mayor of Bessières until 1971. Bourgès-Maunoury died in Paris at the age of 78 on February 10, 1993.

FÉLIX GAILLARD (Premier, November 5, 1957–May 13, 1958). Félix Gaillard was born in Paris on November 5, 1919. He graduated from the Ecoles Libre des Sciences Politiques with a doctorate in law in 1943. He served in the French Resistance and used his expertise in economics to harass German occupation forces in France during World War II. After the liberation of France, he joined the Radical Socialist party, and he was elected to the National Assembly in 1946. Gaillard was appointed undersecretary of state for economic affairs in the cabinet in November of 1947 and served until July of 1948. He held various other government positions in the late 1940s and early 1950s. Gaillard was named minister of financial and economic affairs in the government of Maurice Bourgès-Maunoury in June of 1957. He was asked to form a government after a prolonged cabinet crisis and took office as premier on November 5, 1957. His government received a vote of no confidence in the National Assembly over the issue of granting concessions to Tunisia to negotiate a settlement for the Algerian conflict. Gaillard was forced to step down on May 13, 1958. He served as president of the Radical Socialist party from 1958 until 1961, though his political influence was limited under the presidency of Charles de Gaulle. He remained out of national politics during the 1960s. Gaillard died in a yachting accident in July of 1970. His body was found near the island of Jersey in the English Channel on July 11, 1970.

PIERRE PFLIMLIN (Premier, May 13, 1958–June 1, 1958). Pierre Eugene Jean Pflimlin was born in Roubaix on February 5, 1907. He attended the Catholic Institute of Paris and Strasbourg University and received a doctorate in law. He practiced law in Strasbourg from 1933 until he joined the French army in 1939. Pflimlin saw active duty in Belgium and France until the fall of France in 1940. He spent the German occupation in Thonon-les-Bains. After the conclusion of the war, he entered politics, and he was elected to the Strasbourg Municipal Council in May of 1945. Pflimlin was elected to the National Assembly in 1946 and was named undersecretary of state for public health and population. He served in several governments before being named minister of agriculture by Premier Henri Queuille in June of 1950. He was named minister of commerce in the government of René Pleven in August of 1951 and also served in the cabinets of Edgar Faure and Antoine Pinay. Pflimlin was defeated for the presidency of the National Assembly in January of 1954. He was asked to form a government in February of 1955, but was unable to receive approval from the National Assembly. He was named minister of finance and economic affairs in the subsequent cabinet of Edgar Faure. Pflimlin remained in the cabinet until 1956 and again served as minister of finance from 1957 until 1958. He formed a government as premier on May 13, 1958, as the crisis in Algeria continued to grow. Riots broke out among European Algerians who demanded that Charles de Gaulle take control of the French government. Pflimlin was granted emergency powers to deal with the crisis, but was unable to halt the growing tide towards de Gaulle. Pflimlin tried to retain power, but was forced to resign in favor of de Gaulle on June 1, 1958. He served in de Gaulle's cabinet as minister of state until 1959. He was elected mayor of Strasbourg in 1959 and served as president of the Council of Europe from 1963 until 1966. Pflimlin was elected a member of the European Parliament in 1979 and served as its president from 1984 until 1987. He stepped down from the European Parliament in 1989 and retired to Strasbourg.

CHARLES DE GAULLE (Premier, June 1, 1958–January 8, 1959). *See entry under Heads of State.*

MICHEL J. P. DEBRÉ (Premier, January 8, 1959–April 14, 1962). Michel Jean Pierre Debré was born in Paris on January 15, 1912. He attended the Saumur Cavalry School, where he attained the rank of major in 1932. He also graduated from the École Libres des Sciences Politique, where he received a doctorate in law. In 1934 he became a magistrate in the Council of State, and he served in several other government positions before France entered World War II in 1939. Debré rejoined the cavalry and was captured in May of 1940. He escaped to Morocco, where he worked with the French Resistance. He was named special commissioner of the republic for the Angers region in August of 1944. Debré went to Paris in 1945 to assist in public administration reforms. He was defeated in his campaign for the National Assembly in 1946, but was elected to the French Senate as a Gaullist in 1948. He served on the party's Foreign Affairs Committee during much of the 1950s. Debré was named minister of justice when Charles de Gaulle became premier in June of 1958. He drafted a new French constitution that established the Fifth Republic and granted greater powers to the president. Debré succeeded de Gaulle as premier on January 8, 1959, when de Gaulle assumed the presidency. Debré resigned as premier on April 14, 1962, when de Gaulle reorganized the government and appointed Georges Pompidou to the premiership. Debré was elected to the National Assembly in 1963 and was named minister of finance and economic affairs in 1966. He was appointed foreign minister in 1968 and served until 1969. He was then named minister of defense and retained that position until 1973. Debré was also elected to the European Parliament in 1979. He retired from politics in the late 1980s.

GEORGES POMPIDOU (Premier, April 14, 1962–July 11, 1968). *See entry under Heads of State.*

MAURICE COUVE DE MURVILLE (Premier, July 11, 1968–June 20, 1969). Jacques Maurice Couve de Murville was born in Reims on January 24, 1907. He received a doctorate in law from the Sorbonne and a degree in history from the École des Sciences Politiques. He became an inspector of finance in 1930. Couve de Murville remained in the ministry of finance through the early years of World War II. He continued to serve in the Finance Ministry under the Vichy government until he was dismissed in 1943. He subsequently left France and went to North Africa, where he joined the Free French government. Couve de Murville was named ambassador to Italy by the provisional government following the conclusion of World War II in 1945. He was named deputy foreign minister later in the year and attended several international conferences. He was appointed ambassador to Egypt in 1950 and retained that position during the ouster of the Egyptian monarchy in 1952. In September of 1954 he returned to Paris to serve as France's representative to the North Atlantic Treaty Organization (NATO). Couve de Murville was appointed ambassador to the United States several months later and was named ambassador to West Germany in 1956. He returned to Paris after Charles de Gaulle became premier in June of 1958 and was named foreign minister in the de Gaulle government. He retained that position

until May of 1968, when he briefly served as minister of finance. Couve de Murville was named to succeed Georges Pompidou as premier on July 11, 1968. He retained office until June 20, 1969, when Pompidou replaced de Gaulle as president of France. Couve de Murville lost his seat in the National Assembly in the elections of 1969. He returned to Assembly in 1973 and served as president of the Foreign Affairs Committee until 1981. He was elected to the French Senate in 1986.

JACQUES CHABAN-DELMAS (Premier, June 10, 1969–July 5, 1972). Jacques Michel Pierre Delmas was born in Paris on March 7, 1915. He was educated at the École Libre des Sciences Politiques and received a degree in law. He served in the French Reserve Officers Training Corps in 1939 and worked with the French Resistance during the German occupation. Delmas was given command of all military operations in occupied France in 1943 and rose to the rank of brigadier general. He used the name Chaban while working with the Resistance and added it to his family name after the war. He worked in the Ministry of Information in the postwar provisional government and was elected to the National Assembly in November of 1946. Chaban-Delmas was also elected mayor of Bordeaux the following year. He joined the Gaullist organization, the Rally of the French People, in 1947. He was selected as chairman of the Social Republican party in July of 1953. Chaban-Delmas joined the cabinet of Pierre Mendès-France as minister of public works in June of 1954. He served as minister of state from 1956 until 1957 and was named minister of national defense in November of 1957. He defended the government's policies concerning the Algerian civil war, but supported the establishment of the Fifth Republic under Charles de Gaulle. Chaban-Delmas was elected president of the

National Assembly when de Gaulle took power in 1958. He was appointed premier by President George Pompidou on June 10, 1969, but was replaced on July 5, 1972, following his involvement in a tax scandal. Chaban-Delmas was an unsuccessful candidate in the French presidential elections of 1974 to replace Pompidou. He was reelected to the National Assembly in 1978 and served until 1981. He again returned to the Assembly from 1986 until 1988. Chaban-Delmas remained mayor of Bordeaux into the 1990s.

PIERRE MESSMER (Premier, July 5, 1972–May 27, 1974). Pierre August Joseph Messmer was born in Vincennes on March 20, 1916. He received a degree in law from the University of Paris in 1934. He continued his studies and entered the French colonial service in 1938. At the start of World War II, he joined the French army, and he continued to fight with the Free French forces following the fall of France in 1940. Messmer served as a paratroop officer in the Foreign Legion and saw action throughout Europe. He was sent on a mission to Calcutta in 1944 and to Indochina in 1945, where he was captured by the Viet-Minh nationalist forces who were opposed to both the Japanese and the French. He returned to France after a period of imprisonment and rejoined the colonial office in 1946. Messmer was stationed in French Indochina until January of 1951, when he became chief administrator in the Ministry of Overseas Departments and Territories. He became acting governor of Mauritania in April of 1952 and was sent to the Ivory Coast as governor in 1954, where he remained until February of 1956. He was appointed high commissioner of the French Cameroons in April of 1956 and high commissioner to French Equatorial Africa in January of 1958. Messmer was named high commissioner to French West Africa later in the year, where he remained until the position was abolished in December of 1959. He briefly joined the military in Algeria before he was recalled to Paris by Charles de Gaulle in February of 1960 to become minister of defense. Messmer was the target of an assassination attempt in March of 1962 because of his role in crushing the attempted coup led by military officers in Algeria the previous year. He remained minister of defense until 1969, when he joined de Gaulle in retirement. He returned to the cabinet as minister of overseas departments and territories in February of 1971. Messmer was appointed by President Georges Pompidou to succeed Jacques Chaban-Delmas as premier on July 5, 1972. He stepped down on May 27, 1974, following the death of Pompidou and the election of Valéry Giscard d'Estaing as president. He was returned to the National Assembly in the elections of 1978. Messmer also served in the European Parliament from 1979 until 1984. He was reelected to the National Assembly in 1986 and served as parliamentary leader of the Rally for the Republic party until his retirement in 1988.

JACQUES CHIRAC (Premier, May 27, 1974–August 25, 1976). Jacques René Chirac was born in Paris on November 29, 1932. He was educated in Paris and attended the Institut d'Etudes Politiques. After his graduation in 1954, he continued his education at Harvard University in the United States. He returned to France to join the French cavalry and served with distinction during the Algerian revolution. Chirac entered the École Nationale d'Administration on his return to France in 1957. He graduated two years later and joined the government auditing office. He became a protégé of Georges Pompidou and worked in the premier's office. Chirac was elected to the National Assembly in 1967 and was named secretary of state for social affairs. He held several other government positions before being appointed to the cabinet as minister of agriculture and rural development in 1972. He was appointed minister of the interior in 1974. Chirac supported Valéry Giscard d'Estaing's candidacy for the presidency following the death of Pompidou in 1974. Chirac was appointed premier on May 27, 1974, following Giscard's election. Giscard and Chirac often clashed over government policy. Chirac pressed Giscard to dissolve the Parliament and hold new elections in 1976. Giscard refused and Chirac resigned on August 26, 1976. He subsequently formed the conservative Rally for the Republic (RPR). Chirac was elected mayor of Paris in March of 1977. He challenged Giscard and Socialist leader François Mitterrand in the presidential elections in 1981. He ran third in the election and became a leader of the right-wing opposition when Mitterrand was elected president. The conservatives won a victory over the Socialists and their allies in parliamentary elections in March of 1986, and Mitterrand was forced to accept Chirac as premier on March 20, 1986. Chirac challenged Mitterrand in the presidential elections in 1988 and was decisively defeated in a runoff in May. Chirac resigned as premier on May 10, 1988, but remained mayor of Paris and a leading opponent of the Socialist government.

RAYMOND BARRE (Premier, August 25, 1976–May 21, 1981). Raymond Barre was born on the French island of Réunion, in the Indian Ocean, on April 12, 1924. He was educated on Réunion and then attended the University of Paris to study law and economics. He also studied political science at the Institut d'Etudes Politiques and joined the faculty in 1950. Barre subsequently taught at the University of Tunis in Tunisia until 1954. He then joined the faculty of the University of Caen in Normandy, where he remained until 1963. He also served as a professor of economics at the University of Paris from 1962. Barre was appointed to represent France at the European Economic Community in Brussels in July of 1967. He returned to France in 1972 and was appointed to the board of directors of the Bank of France the following year. Barre was named to Jacques Chirac's cabinet as minister of foreign trade in January of 1976. He was named by President Valéry Giscard d'Estaing to replace Chirac as premier on August 25, 1976. Barre also served as minister of economy and finance in the cabinet. He remained premier following Parliamentary elections in 1978 in which the conservatives retained their majority. Giscard was defeated by Socialist leader François Mitterrand in presidential elections in 1981, and Barre was replaced as premier in the new government on May 21, 1981. He remained in the National Assembly. In 1988 he was the candidate of the Union for French Democracy party (UDF) in the presidential elections. He finished behind Mitterrand and Chirac in the balloting. Barre was also an unsuccessful candidate for mayor of Lyon in 1989.

PIERRE MAUROY (Premier, May 21, 1981–July 17, 1984). Pierre Mauroy was born in Cartignies on July 5, 1928. He was educated at the Lycée de Cambrai and became a teacher in Colombes in 1952. He became active in Socialist politics in the early 1950s and served on the national executive bureau of the Socialist party from 1963. Mauroy supported François Mitterrand in his bid to claim the leadership of the Socialists in 1971. He subsequently served as Mitterrand's deputy and was elected to the Parliament in 1973. He was also elected mayor of Lille. Mauroy was a member of the European Parliament from 1979 until 1981. He was a spokesman for Mitterrand in the presidential campaign in 1981. Mauroy was named premier after Mitterrand was elected president and took office on May 21, 1981. Mauroy was dismissed on July 17, 1984, when Mitterrand reorganized the government. He was reelected to the National Assembly in 1986.

LAURENT FABIUS (Premier, July 17, 1984–March 20, 1986). Laurent Fabius was born in Paris on August 20, 1946. He attended the École Nationale d'Administration and the École Normale Supérieure and became an auditor for the Council of State in 1973. He entered politics in 1977 and was elected first deputy mayor of Grand-Quevilly. Fabius was elected to the National Assembly as a member of the Socialist party in 1978. He became a leading economic advisor to President François Mitterrand. He managed Mitterrand's campaign for president in 1981 and was named to the cabinet as minister for the budget following Mitterrand's victory. Fabius was appointed minister of industry and research in March of 1983. Mitterrand appointed Fabius premier on July 17, 1984. He resigned on March 20, 1986, following the victory of the rightist parties in elections to the National Assembly. Fabius remained in the National Assembly and served as its president from 1988 until 1991.

JACQUES CHIRAC (Premier, March 20, 1986–May 10, 1988). *See earlier entry under Heads of Government.*

MICHEL ROCARD (Premier, May 10, 1988–May 15, 1991). Michel Louis Leon Rocard was born in Paris on August 23, 1930. He was the son of Yves Rocard, a leading physicist who helped develop the French atomic bomb. Michel Rocard attended the Institut d'Études Politiques and the École National d'Administration. He also became active in the Socialist party. He was employed in the French Ministry of Finance as an economic official. Rocard left the Socialist party in 1958 to form the Autonomous Socialist party (PSA). Two years later the PSA merged with other small Socialist parties to become the Unified Socialist party (PSU). Rocard became national secretary of the party in 1967. He was a candidate for president of France in 1969, but received a small percentage of the vote. He was elected to the National Assembly the following year. Rocard supported François Mitterrand for the presidency in a coalition of leftist parties in 1974. Rocard rejoined the Socialist party following Mitterrand's defeat and served on the party's executive committee. He attempted to unseat Mitterrand as the Socialists' leader in 1979, but was unsuccessful. He again supported Mitterrand's presidential candidacy in 1981. Rocard was appointed minister of economics following Mitterrand's election. He was named minister of agriculture in 1983 and served until his resignation in 1985. He again sought to challenge Mitterrand for leadership of the Socialists and declared his candidacy for president in 1988. Rocard withdrew from the race after Mitterrand announced his plans to seek reelection. Rocard's support for Mitterrand was rewarded on May 10, 1988, when he was appointed premier of France. In 1990 Rocard's government was faced with massive demonstrations by nurses and farmers seeking better working conditions. When Rocard was unable to settle the disputes, Mitterrand replaced him as premier with his rival, Edith Cresson, on May 15, 1991.

EDITH CRESSON (Premier, May 15, 1991–April 2, 1992). Edith Campion was born in Boulogne-sur-Seine on January 27, 1934. She attended the School of Higher Commercial Studies and received a doctorate in demography. In 1959 she married automobile executive Jacques Cresson. She joined the Socialist party as a youth organizer in 1965 and was active in François Mitterrand's unsuccessful presidential campaign. Cresson was defeated in an election to the French Parliament in 1974. She was elected mayor of Thure in 1977 and was elected a member of the European Parliament two years later. She served in the cabinet as minister of agriculture from 1981 until 1983 and was minister of foreign trade and tourism from 1983 until 1984. Cresson was appointed minister of industrial redeployment and foreign trade in 1984 and served until 1988, when she became minister of european affairs. She resigned from the cabinet in 1990 to enter private industry. The following year Mitterrand appointed her as France's first female premier, and she took office on May 15, 1991. Her blunt remarks sparked much criticism, and she was unsuccessful in her attempts to improve the popularity of the Socialist party. The Socialists lost support in parliamentary elections in March of 1992, and Cresson resigned from office on April 2, 1992.

PIERRE BÉRÉGOVOY (Premier, April 2, 1992–March 29, 1993). Pierre Eugene Bérégovoy was born in Deville-les-Rouen on December 23, 1925. He worked in a factory from his early teens and was employed by the national gas utility, Gaz de France, from 1950. He worked his way up to the post of direc-

tor of the company in 1978. Bérégovoy served as a campaign manager for Socialist candidate François Mitterrand in the presidential elections in 1981. He was named secretary-general to the presidency following Mitterrand's election. Bérégovoy was appointed to the cabinet as minister of social affairs and national solidarity in 1982. He was elected mayor of Nievre in 1983 and served as minister of economy, finance, and the budget from 1984 until 1986. He was then appointed minister of state for the economy, finance, and budget. Bérégovoy retained this position until April 2, 1992, when he was named premier of France. The Socialist party suffered a major defeat in parliamentary elections in March of 1993, and Bérégovoy was replaced by Edouard Balldur on March 29, 1993. Bérégovoy was implicated in a financial scandal concerning the personal use of campaign funds. He shot himself in his hometown of Neivre, where he remained mayor, and died en route to a Paris hospital on May 1, 1993.

Gabon (Gabonese Republic)

(République Gabonaise)

Gabon is a country on the western coast of Africa. It was granted independence from France on August 17, 1960.

HEADS OF STATE

LÉON MBA (President, August 17, 1960–February 17, 1964). Léon Mba was born into the Fang tribe in Libreville in 1902. He was educated in Roman Catholic schools there and took a job as an accountant with the French administration. He also worked as a journalist for the French newspaper in Libreville. In 1924 he became canton chief of the Fang tribe in Libreville. Mba engaged in nationalist activi-

ties in the 1930s and was accused of ritual killings and cannibalism by the French authorities. He was tried and exiled to Ubangi-Chari (now Central African Republic) in 1933. He returned to Gabon in 1946 and reinvolved himself in political activities. Mba became a leader of the Gabon Democratic Bloc and was elected to the Territorial Assembly in 1952. Four years later he was elected mayor of Libreville. In 1957

Mba was selected as vice president of the first Government Council of Gabon, and in July of 1958 he became president of the council. He was a leading opponent of the planned federation of French West Africa because he preferred independence for Gabon. He also favored maintaining close ties with France. On February 19, 1959, Mba became Gabon's first prime minister under a new parliamentary constitution. He remained prime minister following Gabon's independence on November 3, 1960. The following year Mba sponsored a new constitution that called for a presidential form of government, and he became Gabon's first president. He initially tried to govern in a conciliatory fashion by bringing members of the opposition into his cabinet. In 1963 Mba tried to transform Gabon into a single party state, but met with much resistance. In January of 1964 Mba dissolved Parliament, further antagonizing dissident forces. On February 17, 1964, rebellious political and military forces under the leadership of Jean-Hilaire Aubaume ousted Mba and seized control. The coup's success was short-lived due to the arrival of French troops that answered Mba's call for aid. A French paratrooper detachment quickly crushed the rebels and restored Mba to office on February 20, 1964. When new parliamentary elections were held later in the year, Mba's party received a majority of the seats. His regime became increasingly authoritarian in nature in the face of widespread opposition to his rule. In August of 1966 Mba went to Paris for medical treatment. While still hospitalized, he called for new elections in March of 1967 and was reelected as president with Albert Bongo, his handpicked successor who had been governing the country in his absence, confirmed as vice president. Mba died of cancer in Paris on November 28, 1967.

JEAN HILAIRE AUBAUME (President, February 17, 1964–February 19,

1964). Jean Hilaire Aubaume was born into the Fang tribe in Libreville on November 10, 1912. He was educated locally and became a clerk in the French colonial administration. He supported the Free French movement during World War II. In 1944 he became an advisor to Governor-General Andre Bayardelle. Two years later he was elected to the French National Assembly. Aubaume also organized the Gabonese Democratic and Social Union in 1946. He was reelected to the French National Assembly in 1951 and the following year he was also elected to the Gabon Territorial Assembly. In 1956 he was again reelected to the French National Assembly, and he served until the fall of the Fourth French Republic in September of 1958. Aubaume was narrowly defeated by Léon Mba as vice president of the first Government Council in Gabon. Following independence, Aubaume was elected to the National Assembly and served as minister of foreign affairs in a coalition government. In May of 1962 Aubaume was demoted to minister of state for foreign affairs following a disagreement with President Mba. The following year he was dropped from the cabinet after he refused to support Mba's call for a single-party government. Mba appointed Aubaume president of the Supreme Court in early 1963, but he resigned on January 10, 1964, rather than forfeit his parliamentary immunity. When dissident elements of the military ousted Mba on February 17, 1964, Aubaume was called in to head the revolutionary government. The coup was crushed several days later, and Aubaume was arrested by the restored Mba government. He was tried in August of 1964 and sentenced to imprisonment and banishment. He was released from prison by President Omar Bongo in 1972. Aubaume retired from politics and went into exile in Paris.

LÉON MBA (President, February 20, 1964–November 28, 1967).

See earlier entry under Heads of State.

OMAR BONGO (President, November 28, 1967–). Albert Bernard Bongo was born in Lewai, Haut-Ogooue Province, on December 30, 1935. He was educated in Brazzaville, the Congo, and received a degree in commerce. He entered the French air force in 1958 and served as a lieutenant. From October of 1960 he served in the Ministry of Foreign Affairs. Bongo became a chief aide to President Léon Mba in 1962. He was also placed in charge of the government's information and tourism department from 1963 until 1964. Bongo was placed in charge of national defense following an abortive coup against Mba in February of 1964. He was named to the cabinet as minister of defense the following September. Bongo was appointed Mba's vice president in November of 1966. He was confirmed in that position in an election in March of 1967. Bongo succeeded to the presidency when Mba died on November 28, 1967, and he also served in the government as prime minister, and minister of defense, interior, and planning. He founded the Gabonese Democratic party in March of 1968 and transformed Gabon into a single-party state. Bongo was unopposed in his reelection to the presidency in February of 1973. He converted to Islam in September of 1973 and took the name El Hadj Omar Bongo. He ruled Gabon in an authoritarian manner and was again reelected in December of 1979. He relinquished some governmental responsibilities to his premier, Léon Mebiame, in August of 1981. Bongo survived a military plot to oust his government in May of 1985. He was again reelected president in November of 1986. Gabon suffered from a declining economy in the late 1980s, and Bongo was faced with increasing demands to democratize his government. He agreed to allow the formation of opposition political parties in April of 1990 and multiparty parliamentary elections were held the following September.

HEADS OF GOVERNMENT

LÉON MBA (Premier, November 28, 1958–August 17, 1960). *See entry under Heads of State.*

LÉON MEBIAME (Premier, April 16, 1975–May 3, 1990). Léon Mebiame was born in Libreville on September 1, 1934. He was educated in Gabon, the Congo, and France. He joined the police and was stationed in Chad from 1957 until 1959. Mebiame served in the Gabonese national police from 1962. He was appointed to the cabinet in January of 1967 and was selected as mayor of Libreville two years later. Mebiame was subsequently appointed vice president of Gabon and was named premier by President Omar Bongo on April 16, 1975. He retained the post until May 3, 1990, when he resigned following the implementation of a multiparty political system in Gabon.

CASIMIR OYE-MBA (Premier, May 3, 1990–). Casimir Oye-Mba was born in Libreville on April 20, 1942. He was educated in France and returned to Gabon to work in the Central Bank. He served as acting governor of the International Monetary Fund for Gabon from 1969 until 1976 and held other major banking positions until his appointment as premier on May 3, 1990. Oye-Mba resigned on June 7, 1991, following a call by President Omar Bongo to establish a consensus government. Opposition parties rejected the idea, and Oye-Mba was reappointed premier on June 15, 1991, as head of a cabinet containing representatives of the opposition.

Gambia, Republic of the

The Gambia is a country on the northwestern coast of Africa. It was granted independence from Great Britain on February 18, 1965.

HEADS OF STATE

SIR JOHN W. PAUL (Governor-General, February 18, 1965–February 9, 1966). John Warburton Paul was born in Weymouth on March 29, 1916. He was educated at Selwyn College at Cambridge University. During World War II he served with the Royal Tank Regiment. Paul entered the Colonial Service in 1947 and served in the colonial government in Sierra Leone until 1962. He was then named governor of the Gambia. Paul assisted Chief Minister Pierre N'Jie and his successor, Dawda Jawara, in drafting a constitution for an independent Gambia. Paul served as governor-general of the Gambia following independence on February 18, 1965. He resigned his position on February 9, 1966, and relinquished office to native-born Gambian Alhaji Sir Farimang Singhateh. Paul was subsequently appointed governor of British Honduras, where he served from 1966 until 1972. He was then named governor of the Bahamas until 1973. He served as lieutenant governor of the Isle of Man from 1973 until his retirement in 1980.

ALHAJI SIR FARIMANG SINGHATEH (Governor-General, February 9, 1966–April 24, 1970). Alhaji Farimang Mamadi Singhateh was born in Georgetown on November 30, 1912. He was a Muslim and a member of the Mandingo tribe. He was educated in mission schools and was employed at the Gambia Medical Department. Singhateh was a member of the ruling People's Progressive party when he was named governor-general of the Gambia on February 9, 1966. He retained the position until the Gambia was declared a republic on April 24, 1970.

SIR DAWDA JAWARA (President, April 24, 1970–). Dawda Kairaba Jawara was born in Barajally on McCarthy Island on May 11, 1924. He was educated at local mission schools and continued his education in Ghana, where he received a veterinary science degree at Achimota College. He then attended the University of Glasgow in Scotland on a scholarship and qualified as a veterinary surgeon. Jawara returned to the Gambia in 1954 and was employed as a veterinary officer. He entered politics in 1959 and helped to form the People's Progressive party (PPP). He led the party in legislative elections the following year and served in the government as minister of education. Jawara resigned from the government following the selection of United party leader Pierre S. N'Jie as chief minister in 1961. Jawara led the PPP to a narrow victory in legislative elections in May of 1962 and became chief minister. He remained leader of the government when the Gambia was granted self-government on October 4, 1963. He continued to serve as prime minister in the first independent government of the Gambia on February 18, 1965. Jawara sponsored a referendum to declare the Gambia a republic in November of 1965, but the referendum failed to obtain the two-thirds majority necessary for passage. The Gambia was declared a republic following another referendum vote in 1970, and Jawara became president on April 24, 1970. He was reelected in 1972. He led a democratic government and was committed to human rights. In 1977 he was again reelected by a large margin. Jawara's government was threatened by a rebellion in July of 1981. The Marxist Socialist and Revolutionary Labor party led by Kukoi Samba Sanyang took over the capital. Troops loyal to the government were assisted by forces from neighboring Senegal in putting down the rebellion. Jawara and Senegalese president Abdul Diouf agreed to the partial merger of Senegal and the Gambia as the Senegambian Confederation on February 1, 1982. Jawara was again reelected to the presidency in May of 1982. The confederation became a political issue, with the opposition claiming that the Gambia was relinquishing its autonomy to Senegal. Jawara's margin of victory decreased in presidential elections in March of 1987. The Senegambian Confederation was dissolved in September of 1989 with the agreement of both governments. Jawara was returned to office for a fifth term in elections in April of 1992.

HEAD OF GOVERNMENT

SIR DAWDA JAWARA (Prime Minister, February 18, 1965–April 24, 1970). *See entry under Heads of State.*

Georgia, Republic of
(Sakartvelos Respublika)

Georgia is a country in western Asia on the Black Sea. It became independent following the breakup of the Soviet Union on December 25, 1991.

HEADS OF STATE

ZVIAD GAMSAKHURDIA (President, May 1991–January 6, 1992). Zviad Konstantinovich Gamsakhurdia was born in Tbilisi, Georgia, on March 31, 1939. He was a leading supporter of democratic reform and human rights during the 1970s. He was arrested in 1977 and detained until 1979. Gamsakhurdia became the leader of the Popular Georgian Front in 1989 and was elected to the Georgia Supreme Soviet the following year. He also served as Chairman of the Supreme Soviet from 1990. Georgia was declared an independent republic following a referendum in April of 1991. Gamsakhurdia was elected president of Georgia in May of 1991. After a period of civil unrest, he was deposed by a military council led by Tengiz Sigua on January 6, 1992. Followers of Gamsakhurdia attempted a coup on June 24, 1992, but they were crushed by the Georgian security forces. Gamsakhurdia led rebel forces in an offensive on Tbilisi in September of 1993, but after several weeks of fighting he was forced to retreat. He reportedly shot himself to death on December 31, 1993, when he was surrounded in Western Georgia by troops loyal to President Eduard Shevardnadze.

EDUARD SHEVARDNADZE (Chairman of the State Council, January 1992–). Eduard Amvrosiyevich Shevardnadze was born in Georgia on January 25, 1928. He attended school locally and joined the Communist party in 1948. He served in various party and government positions. Shevardnadze served as a member of the Georgian Communist party Central Committee from 1958 and became a member of the Politburo in 1972. He served as first secretary from 1972 until 1985. He also served as a deputy to the Supreme Soviet from 1978 and was elected to the Politburo of the Soviet Union in 1985. Shevardnadze served as foreign minister in the Soviet government from 1985 until his resignation in 1990. He briefly held the post again in November of 1991 and served until the dissolution of the Soviet Union the following month. He returned to Georgia where he was selected as chairman of the State Council in January of 1992. In the first post-Soviet parliamentary elections, held on October 11, 1992, Shevardnadze was elected Georgia's head of state as Speaker of the Parliament.

HEAD OF GOVERNMENT

TENGIZ SIGUA (Premier, March 10, 1992–). Tengiz Ippolitovich Sigua was born in Georgia on November 9, 1939. He was educated locally as an engineer and was active in the democratic reform movement in Georgia. On November 14, 1990, he was named premier by Zviad Gamsakhurdia. He resigned on August 18, 1991, and became a leader of the opposition to Gamsakhurdia. Sigua was a leader of the coup that ousted the president in January of 1992. He was the leader of the subsequent military council that took control of Georgia on March 10, 1992. He was confirmed as premier in the elections on October 11, 1992.

German Democratic Republic

(East Germany)

The German Democratic Republic was a country in northeastern Europe. It reunited with the German Federal Republic on October 1, 1990.

HEADS OF STATE

WILHELM PIECK (President, October 11, 1949–September 7, 1960). Wilhelm Pieck was born in Guben on January 3, 1876. He joined the Socialist party as a young man and was elected to the Reichstag in 1905. He was expelled from the party in 1915 because of his radical views. Following World War I he was a founder of the German Communist party and served on the Executive Committee of the Comintern. Pieck fled to the Soviet Union after Adolf Hitler's rise to power in 1933. While in exile he directed the

Communist propaganda apparatus directed at German prisoners of war during World War II. He returned to Germany after the Soviet capture of Berlin and became chairman of the German Communist party's Executive Committee in 1945. Pieck soon became the first chairman of the Communist-dominated Socialist Unity party when the Communists merged with the Social Democratic party. He was selected as the first president of the German Democratic Republic on October 11, 1949, and was reelected in 1953 and 1957. His position was largely ceremonial, with most of the political power in East Germany held by Walter Ulbricht, the secretary-general of the Socialist Unity party. Pieck retained the presidency until his death from a heart attack in Berlin at the age of 84 on September 7, 1960.

WALTER ULBRICHT (President, September 12, 1960–August 1, 1973). Walter Ulbricht was born in Leipzig on June 30, 1893. He was active in the trade union movement in his youth and joined the Socialist party in 1912. He served in the German army during World War I and saw action in Macedonia. In 1918 he deserted and served several months in prison. Ulbricht became a member of the Spartacus Society and helped to found the German Communist party in 1919. He worked as a Communist party organizer in the 1920s and was elected to the party's Central Committee in 1927. The following year he was elected to the German Reichstag. He remained in the Reichstag until the rise of Hitler in 1933. Ulbricht then went underground and escaped to Paris in late 1933. He made his way to Moscow in 1935 and survived the Stalinist purges of the late 1930s. He served in the political administration of the Red Army fighting against Nazi Germany during World War II. Ulbricht returned to the Soviet-occupied section of Germany in April of 1945. He organized the merger of the Communists and Social Democrats to

form the Socialist Unity party in 1946 and served as vice-chairman of the new party. He became deputy premier following the formation of the German Democratic Republic in October of 1949. Ulbricht was named secretary-general of the Socialist Unity party in July of 1950 and became the most powerful figure in East Germany. He survived a challenge to his leadership in June of 1953 when food shortages and increased work quotas resulted in massive demonstrations against the government. The dissension was crushed with the assistance of the Soviet military. Ulbricht was responsible for improving East Germany's economic stability and ordered the production of more consumer goods. He also forced the collectivization of German farms, which resulted in the exodus of millions of Germans to the West. Ulbricht also assumed the position of president of East Germany on September 12, 1960, following the death of Wilhelm Pieck. Ulbricht sought to put a stop to the flight of East Germans to West Berlin and ordered the construction of the Berlin Wall in August of 1961. Ulbricht was also a leading proponent of the Soviet-led invasion of Czechoslovakia in 1968 that resulted in the removal of democratic reforms in that country. Ulbricht's relationship with the Soviet Union deteriorated in the late 1960s. The Soviet leadership was interested in pursuing closer relations with Western Europe and the United States, and Ulbricht resisted any moves to improve relations with West Germany. The decline of the East German economy in the early 1970s also caused dissension in the German Communist party. Ulbricht's policies were held responsible, and he was replaced as party leader by Erich Honecker on May 3, 1971. Ulbricht was granted the honorary chairmanship of the Socialist Unity party and retained the ceremonial position of president. He suffered a stroke in July of 1973 and died of heart failure in Berlin on August 1, 1973.

WILLI STOPH (President, October 3, 1973–October 29, 1976). Willi Stoph was born in Berlin on July 8, 1914. He worked in the construction industry in his youth and joined the Communist party in the early 1930s. He worked in the Communist underground following Hitler's rise to power in 1933. After the start of World War II, he was drafted into the German army. He was captured by Soviet troops on the Eastern front and served as an advisor to the Soviet Red Army when Germany was occupied in 1945. Stoph worked with the Communist-dominated Socialist Unity party and served on the party's executive committee from 1947. He was elected to the Parliament of the German Democratic Republic in 1950. He also worked in the economics section of the secretariat of the Central Committee of the Socialist Unity party. Stoph was instrumental in the creation of the East German army in the early 1950s. He was appointed minister of justice in May of 1952 and became Otto Grotewohl's second deputy premier in November of 1954. He resigned from the Interior Ministry in June of 1955 and was appointed East Germany's first minister of defense in January of 1956. Stoph left the Defense Ministry in 1960 to serve as deputy chairman of the Council of Ministers. He was de facto premier during Otto Grotewohl's illness from 1960 and succeeded Grotewohl to the position on September 24, 1964. Stoph remained premier until October 3, 1973, when he was chosen to replace Walter Ulbricht as East Germany's president, or chairman of the Council of State. Stoph was replaced as president by Erich Honecker on October 29, 1976, and returned to the premiership. Stoph remained as premier until the Communist leadership in East Germany was threatened by growing demands for democratic reforms. He was forced from office on November 13, 1989. Stoph was arrested by East Germany's first non-Communist government in December of 1989, but

was released the following February due to ill health. He was again arrested in May of 1991, following the reunification of Germany. He was charged with responsibility for ordering border guards to shoot to kill East Germans fleeing to the West during the 1970s.

ERICH HONECKER (President, October 29, 1976–October 24, 1989). Erich Honecker was born in Wiebelskirchen on August 25, 1912. He joined the Communist Youth League in his early teens and became a member of the Communist party in 1929. He worked in the Communist underground following Hitler's rise to power in 1933. In December of 1935 he was arrested by the Gestapo and convicted of treason. Honecker was imprisoned at Brandenburg prison, where he remained until he was freed by Soviet troops after the fall of Germany in April of 1945. Honecker joined the newly formed Communist-dominated Socialist Unity party and was named to the party's Central Committee in 1946. He also helped to form the Free German Youth organization and served as its chairman. He was elected to the German Democratic Republic's Parliament in 1949. Honecker was named to the Politburo as a candidate member in 1950 and was a staunch supporter of Communist party leader Walter Ulbricht. Honecker left the Free German Youth movement in 1955 to attend the Communist party's training school in Moscow for two years. He returned to East Germany and was promoted to full membership in the Politburo in 1958. He was also placed in charge of state security and the People's Army. Honecker served as supervisor during the construction of the Berlin Wall in 1961. He remained a hard-line supporter of the Soviet Union and was chosen to replace Walter Ulbricht as secretary-general of the Socialist Unity party on May 3, 1971. He was more willing than his predecessor to pursue a policy of peaceful coexistence with the

West. Honecker also assumed the duties of president when he became chairman of the Council of State on October 29, 1976. East Germany's economy improved under Honecker, and East Germany became the most economically successful country in the Eastern bloc. Honecker rejected Soviet leader Mikhail Gorbachev's policies of glasnost and perestroika in regard to East Germany and tried to resist the democratic reforms that were sweeping other Eastern European countries. Demonstrations demanding reforms took place throughout East Germany in October of 1989, and Honecker was forced to resign as Communist party leader on October 18, 1989. He also stepped down as chairman of the Council of State and was replaced by Egon Krenz on October 24, 1989. He was admitted to a Soviet military hospital in April of 1990. The non–Communist government of East Germany attempted to arrest Honecker in December of 1990, but Soviet authorities claimed that Honecker was too ill to leave the hospital and refused to turn him over to the German authorities. Honecker went to Moscow following the reunification of the East and West Germany. On May 15, 1992, he was charged with ordering border guards to kill East Germans fleeing to the West. Honecker took refuge in the Chilean Embassy in Moscow to avoid extradition. He was returned to Germany to stand trial, but was released by Berlin's Constitutional Court on January 12, 1993, on the grounds of poor health. Honecker subsequently went into exile with his family in Chile.

EGON KRENZ (President, October 24, 1989–December 6, 1989). Egon Krenz was born in Kolberg on March 19, 1937. He was a member of the Socialist Unity party from 1955 and attended the Communist party university in Moscow. He was elected to the East German Parliament in 1971. Krenz was also a candidate member of the Communist party Central Committee from 1971 and became a full member in 1973. He was a candidate member of the Politburo from 1976 and a full member from 1983. Krenz became a member of the Council of State in 1981 and rose to deputy chairman in 1984. He replaced Erich Honecker as secretary-general of the Communist party on October 18, 1989, following widespread protests against the Communist regime. He also replaced Honecker as chairman of the Council of State, or president, on October 24, 1989. Demonstrations continued against the Communist government, and protesters demanded democratic reforms. Krenz resigned as Communist party leader on December 3, 1989, and stepped down as Chairman of the Council of State three days later. He was expelled from the Communist party in 1990 and retired from politics. Krenz became a real estate developer following the reunification of East and West Germany in October of 1990.

MANFRED GERLACH (President, December 6, 1989–April 5, 1990). Manfred Gerlach was born in Leipzig on May 8, 1928. He studied law and was active in politics. He joined the Liberal-Democratic party in 1945 and was mayor of Leipzig from 1950 until 1953. Gerlach was deputy chairman of the State Council from 1960 until 1989. He also served as chairman of the Liberal-Democratic party from 1967 until 1989. Gerlach became acting president on December 6, 1989 and served as East Germany's first non–Communist head of state until April 5, 1990.

SABINE BERGMANN-POHL (Interim President, April 5, 1990–October 3, 1990). Sabine Bergmann-Pohl was a physician and member of the Christian Democratic party. She was elected to Parliament in 1990 and was chosen as Speaker. She became acting president of East Germany on April 5, 1990, and served until the reunification of East and West Germany took place on October 3, 1990.

HEADS OF GOVERNMENT

OTTO GROTEWOHL (Premier, October 11, 1949–September 21, 1964). Otto Grotewohl was born in Braunschweig on March 11, 1894. He was educated in Hanover and Berlin and worked as an insurance official. He joined the Social Democratic party after World War I and became chairman of the party in Brunswick. Grotewohl was also elected to the City Council and the State Parliament in 1920. He served as minister of the interior and popular education in the state government from 1921 until 1922. He subsequently served as state minister of justice from 1923 until 1924. Grotewohl was elected as a deputy to the German Reichstag in 1925. He served until 1933, when he was forced to retire by the Nazi government. Grotewohl was imprisoned on several occasions during World War II for conspiring with the Socialist underground. He returned to prominence after the war as treasurer of a West Berlin district. He was selected as chairman of the reunified Social Democratic party Central Committee. Grotewohl supported the merger of the Social Democratic party and the Communist party in April of 1946. He served as cochairman of the newly formed Socialist Unity party from 1946 and helped establish the German Democratic Republic, or East Germany, in 1949. He served as the German Democratic Republic's first premier from October 11, 1949. Communist party leader Walter Ulbricht was considered the most powerful figure in the East German government, and Grotewohl was viewed as his chief lieutenant. During the 1950s Grotewohl lost influence in the government. He reportedly suffered from leukemia from 1960 and relinquished most of his duties to Deputy Premier Willi Stoph. Grotewohl retained the premiership until his death in East Berlin at the age of 70 on September 21, 1964.

WILLI STOPH (Premier, September 24, 1964–October 3, 1973). *See entry under Heads of State.*

HORST SINDERMANN (Premier, October 3, 1973–October 29, 1976). Horst Sindermann was born in Dresden on September 5, 1915. He joined the Communist Youth League in the 1930s and was imprisoned by the Nazi government from 1935 until the conclusion of World War II in 1945. Sindermann became editor of the Communist party newspaper in the German Democratic Republic following the division of Germany. He was transferred to East Berlin in 1954 and was named director of the Communist party Central Committee's propaganda section. He was elected to the Central Committee in 1963 and became a member of the Politburo in 1967. Sindermann was appointed first deputy premier in May of 1971. He replaced Willi Stoph as premier on October 3, 1973, following the death of East German leader Walter Ulbricht. Stoph was again named premier on October 29, 1976, and Sindermann was elected president of the Parliament. He retained that position until November of 1989, when the Communist-dominated government was ousted by a prodemocracy revolt. Sindermann died of a heart attack in East Berlin at the age of 74 on April 21, 1990.

WILLI STOPH (Premier, October 29, 1976–November 13, 1989). *See entry under Heads of State.*

HANS MODROW (Premier, November 13, 1989–April 12, 1990). Hans Modrow was born in Jasenitz on January 27, 1928. He served in the German army during World War II and was a prisoner of war until 1949. He joined the Communist party and served as first secretary of the East Berlin Committee from 1953 until 1961. Modrow also served on the East Berlin City Council from 1953 until 1971. He held other party and government posts before his selection as premier on November 13, 1989. He resigned his position on April 12, 1990, when revelations were made about corruption of the Communist leadership and democratic reforms were instituted. He subsequently served in the German Bundestag.

LOTHAR DE MAIZIERE (Premier, April 12, 1990–October 3, 1990). Lothar de Maiziere was born in Nordhausen on March 2, 1940. He was a member of the Christian Democratic Union and served as party leader from 1989. He also served as deputy prime minister of the German Democratic Republic from 1989. De Maiziere became East Germany's first democratically elected premier on April 12, 1990. He supported the reunification of the German Democratic Republic with the Federal Republic of Germany. He remained premier until unification was effected on October 3, 1990. De Maiziere had been offered a ministerial position in the unified government of Helmut Kohl. He was forced to resign following allegations that he had been an agent of the Stasi, East Germany's secret police. He served as a Christian Democratic Union member of the Bundestag until 1991.

OTHER LEADERS

WALTER ULBRICHT (Secretary General, July, 1950–May 3, 1971). *See entry under Heads of State.*

ERICH HONECKER (Secretary General, May 3, 1971–October, 18, 1989). *See entry under Heads of State.*

EGON KRENZ (Secretary General, October 18, 1989–December 3, 1989). *See entry under Heads of State.*

GREGOR GYSI (Secretary General, December 9, 1989–October 3, 1990). Gregor Gysi was born in East Berlin on January 16, 1948. He was educated at Humboldt University, where he studied law until 1970. He became a prominent East German lawyer who gained a reputation for defending political dissidents. Gysi was a leading proponent of reform in the East German Communist party. He was chosen to succeed Egon Krenz as chairman of the Communist party on December 9, 1989. The party changed its name to the party of Democratic Socialism. Gysi opposed the reunification of East and West Germany because he feared that East Germany would be absorbed by the West. He continued to lead the party following reunification on October 3, 1990, though the party had little success in parliamentary elections in December of 1990.

Germany, Federal Republic of

(Bundesrepublik Deutschland)

Germany is located in north central Europe.

HEADS OF STATE

THEODOR HEUSS (President, September 12, 1949–September 12, 1959). Theodor Heuss was born in Brackenheim, Wurttemberg, on January 31, 1884. He attended the University of Munich and the University of Berlin. He studied economics and political science and received a doctorate in 1905. Heuss became a student of Protestant theologian Friedrich Naumann and served as editor of the weekly journal *Die Hilfe* from 1905 until 1912. He subsequently worked on the liberal daily newspaper *Neckarzeitung* until 1918. Heuss also worked as a trade union organizer and was elected to the Schoenberg District Council in 1919. He was elected to the Weimar Republic Reichstag in 1924 and served as the leader of the liberal German Democratic party. He was replaced as party leader in 1933, when he opposed the party caucus's decision to grant dictatorial powers to Adolf Hitler. Heuss was ousted from the Reichstag by the Nazis in 1933. He again became editor of *Die Hilfe* in 1933 and used the publication as a forum to appeal for justice for German Jews. Heuss was forced into retirement by the Nazis in 1936. He wrote several biographies in the period of seclusion that followed until the fall of the Nazi government in 1945. Heuss was named minister of education in the state government of Wurttemberg-Baden by the United States occupation forces. He also served as editor of the Heidelberg newspaper *Rhein-Neckar Zeitung*. He was a professor of politics and economics at Stuttgart University in 1948. Heuss subsequently founded the Free Democratic party and assisted in the drafting of a constitution for the German Federal Republic. He was elected to serve as West Germany's first president on September 12, 1949. He was a well-respected figure and helped to rebuild Germany's reputation internationally.

Heuss was reelected in 1954 and completed his second term on September 12, 1959. He retired from politics, but continued with his writings. He also traveled widely until his health began to fail in the summer of 1963. His left leg was amputated following a circulatory disease. Heuss returned to his home in Stuttgart, where he died at the age of 79 on December 12, 1963.

HEINRICH LUEBKE (President, September 12, 1959–September 12, 1969). Heinrich Luebke was born in Enkhausen on October 14, 1894. He was educated in Bonn, Berlin, and Munster and studied agronomy and engineering. He served in the German army during World War I and rose the rank of lieutenant. Luebke became active in independent farm organizations after the war. He joined the Catholic Center party and was elected to the Prussian Legislative Assembly in 1931. He was removed from his positions following the Nazis' rise to power in 1933. Luebke was imprisoned for several years and banned from political activities. He was employed as a construction worker from 1935 until the conclusion of World War II. He joined the Christian Democratic party after the war and served as minister of agriculture in the state of North Rhine-Westphalia. Luebke was elected to the Bundestag in 1949 and was appointed minister of food, agriculture, and forestry in the federal government in October of 1953. He was instrumental in the modernization of German agriculture. Luebke remained in the cabinet until 1959, when he became the Christian Democratic candidate for federal president. He was victorious and assumed office on September 12, 1959. Luebke made numerous state visits during his term of office. He was reelected in 1964, despite allegations that he was involved in the construction of concentration camps during

World War II. An inquiry declared that the allegations were without foundation. Luebke tried, without much success, to increase the largely ceremonial powers of the presidency. He completed his second term of office on September 12, 1969. Luebke died in Bonn at the age of 77 on April 6, 1972, from complications from surgery for intestinal bleeding.

GUSTAV HEINEMANN (President, September 12, 1969–June 1, 1974). Gustav Walter Heinemann was born in Schwelm, Westphalia, on July 23, 1899. He served as an artillery officer during World War I. He left the army after the war and studied at universities throughout Germany. Heinemann was active in the democratic student movement and joined the liberal German Democratic party in the early 1920s. He received a doctorate in political science from the University of Marburg in 1922 and a doctorate in law from the University of Munster in 1929. He worked as a lawyer for several corporations during the 1920s and 1930s. Heinemann also served on the faculty of the University of Cologne from 1933 until 1939. He opposed the Nazi party and was allowed to reenter politics after the defeat of Germany in 1945. Heinemann was a founder of the Christian Democratic party in 1946. He was elected to the Legislative Assembly of North Rhine-Westphalia in 1947 and served in the state government as minister of justice from 1947 until 1948. He was elected president of the German Evangelical church in 1949. Heinemann was also appointed to Konrad Adenauer's federal government as minister of the interior in September of 1949. He resigned in 1950 following a dispute with Adenauer over the rearmament of West Germany. Heinemann returned to his law practice and founded the All-German People's party in 1952. His stand against rearmament resulted in his defeat for the Evangelical church's presidency in 1955. Heinemann merged his political party with the Social Democratic party in 1957. He was also elected to the German Federal Parliament in 1957, where he remained an outspoken critic of the Adenauer government. Heinemann was appointed to Kurt Kiesinger's coalition cabinet as minister of justice in December of 1966. He was the Social Democratic party's candidate for president in 1969 and was narrowly elected by the German Parliament. He took office on September 12, 1969. Heinemann completed his term in the largely ceremonial office on June 1, 1974, and refused to run for a second term due to his advanced age. He retired to his home in Essen and died from a circulatory ailment at the age of 76 on July 7, 1976.

WILLY SCHEEL (President, June 1, 1974–July 1, 1979). Willy Scheel was born in Solinger on July 8, 1919. He was educated locally and was employed by a mercantile bank in 1938. He was drafted into the German Luftwaffe at the start of World War II in 1939. Scheel rose to the rank of first lieutenant before his discharge at the conclusion of the war in 1945. He worked in private industry after the war and joined the Free Democratic party in 1946. He was elected to the state Legislative Assembly in North Rhine-Westphalia in 1950. Scheel was elected to the German Federal Parliament in 1953 and served as his party's economic affairs committee chairman. He also served as West Germany's representative to the European Parliament from 1955. Scheel was named to Konrad Adenauer's coalition cabinet as minister for economic cooperation in 1961. He retained that position until 1966, when the Free Democrats left the cabinet. He returned to the cabinet in 1969 in a coalition government with the Social Democratic party and served as foreign minister and vice-chancellor to Willy Brandt. Scheel served as interim chancellor following Brandt's resignation on May 7, 1974, and relinquished office to Helmut

Schmidt on May 16, 1974. Scheel was elected president of the German Federal Republic and took office on June 1, 1974. He completed his term of office on July 1, 1979. He served as chairman of the German Council of European Movement from 1980 until 1985.

KARL CARSTENS (President, July 1, 1979–July 1, 1984). Karl Carstens was born in Bremen on December 14, 1914. He was educated in Germany and France and received a degree in law from the University of Hamburg in 1936. He served in the German army during World War II as a member of the Nazi party. Following the war, he opened a law practice in Bremen. Carstens was elected to the West German Parliament as a member of the Christian Democratic party in 1949 and served as West Germany's representative to the Council of Europe in 1954. He was instrumental in the drafting of the Treaty of Rome, which formed the European Common Market. Carstens was appointed deputy defense minister in 1966 and served as head of the chancellor's office under Kurt Georg Kiesinger in 1968. Carstens left the government following the Christian Democrats' defeat by Willy Brandt's Socialist party in 1969. He returned to the Bundestag, or Parliament, in 1972, and served as leader of the opposition until 1975. The following year he was elected president of the Bundestag. Carstens retained that position until his election to the ceremonial office of president in 1979. He took office on July 1, 1979, and completed his term on July 1, 1984. He declined to seek a second term and retired to his home in Meckenheim. Carstens suffered a stroke in May of 1992 and died several weeks later on May 30, 1992, at the age of 77.

RICHARD VON WEIZSÄCKER (President, July 1, 1984–). Richard von Weizsäcker was born in Stuttgart on April 15, 1920. He served in the infantry during World War II. He later attended the University of Oxford and the University of Grenoble. Weizsäcker received a degree in law and opened a practice in 1955. He entered politics and was elected to the Bundestag as a member of the Christian Democratic party in 1969. He served on various parliamentary committees and was elected deputy speaker in 1979. Weizsäcker was elected mayor of West Berlin in 1981. He was regarded as a competent administrator and was nominated by the Christian Democratic party as a candidate for president in 1984. He was elected by a large margin and took office on July 1, 1984. Weizsäcker was reelected to a second term in May of 1989 and remained president following the reunification of East and West Germany in October of 1990.

HEADS OF GOVERNMENT

KONRAD ADENAUER (Chancellor, September 20, 1949–October 15, 1963). Konrad Adenauer was born in Cologne in 1876. He attended the Universities of Freiburg, Munich, and Bonn and received a degree in law. He returned to Cologne to practice law and served as Cologne's chief burgomaster from 1917 until 1933. Adenauer joined the Centre party and was also president of the Prussian State Council from 1920 until 1933. He was dismissed from office by the Nazis in 1933. He was imprisoned briefly the following year and was politically inactive during Hitler's rule. Adenauer was again arrested in 1944 and was released following the collapse of the Nazi government. He was renamed burgomaster of Cologne in 1945, but was dismissed on the grounds of inefficiency by the British military administration. Adenauer was instrumental in the formation of the Christian Democratic party, and following the establishment of the German Federal Republic, or West Germany, Adenauer was elected chancellor on September 20, 1949. He helped to rebuild his country and to establish West Germany as an integral part of Europe. He also served as foreign minister from 1951 until 1955. The German Federal Republic was allowed admittance into the North Atlantic Treaty Organization (NATO) during Adenauer's administration. He went to Moscow in 1955 to establish diplomatic relations with the Soviet Union and was instrumental in improving Franco-German relations. Adenauer was reelected to office in 1957. He considered retiring from the chancellor's office to accept the largely ceremonial position of president in 1960, but decided to continue as chancellor. He retired from office on October 15, 1963. He fell ill with bronchitis and influenza and died at his home in Rhondorf at the age of 91 on April 19, 1967.

LUDWIG ERHARD (Chancellor, October 16, 1963–December 1, 1966). Ludwig Erhard was born in Furth, in Upper Bavaria, on February 4, 1897. He attended schools locally before he was drafted into the army during World War I. He served in an artillery regiment and was seriously injured in battle in 1917. After leaving the army in 1919, he continued with his education. Erhard entered the University of Frankfurt in 1923 and received his doctorate in economics three years later. He joined the Nuremberg Commercial Institute, a government-sponsored market-research organization, in 1928 and rose to become the institute's director. He was dismissed from his position in 1942, however, because of his refusal to support the Nazi party. Erhard was appointed Bavaria's minister of economics after the collapse of the Nazi regime in 1945. He became director of the economic council of the United States and the British occupation zones

in Germany in 1947. He was elected to the Bundestag of the Germany Federal Republic as a member of the Christian Democratic party in 1949. Erhard was subsequently appointed minister of economics in the government of Konrad Adenauer. He was widely credited with revitalizing the West German economy. He revalued the Deutschemark, ended rationing, and encouraged industrial growth and a free enterprise economy. Erhard also became vice chancellor in 1957. He was expected to become chancellor in 1959 when Adenauer made plans to step down to become president. Adenauer decided, however, to continue as chancellor rather than allow Erhard to be his successor. Erhard did succeed as chancellor on October 16, 1963, following Adenauer's retirement. He continued West Germany's close relationship with the United States and was an avid supporter of NATO. His government was faced with numerous economic problems in 1966. West Germany was in the midst of a recession and a growing budget deficit. The Christian Democratic party lost ground in parliamentary elections that year, and Erhard stepped down on December 1, 1966, to allow the formation of a coalition cabinet between the Christian Democrats and the Social Democrats. Erhard subsequently retired from politics. He suffered from poor health in the mid-1970s and was injured in an automobile accident in March of 1977. Erhard died in a Bonn hospital of heart failure at the age of 80 on May 5, 1977.

KURT GEORG KIESINGER (Chancellor, December 1, 1966–October 20, 1969). Kurt Georg Kiesinger was born in Ebingen on April 6, 1904. He was educated at the University of Tubingen and the University of Berlin, where he received a degree in law. He joined the Nazi party in 1933, but was soon disillusioned with the movement. Kiesinger opened a law practice in 1934 and moved to Berlin the following year. He worked in the radio propaganda division of the German Foreign Ministry during World War II. He was interned after Germany's surrender, but was released in 1947 and subsequently cleared in a German denazification court. Kiesinger resumed his law practice and entered politics as a member of the Christian Democratic party. He was elected to the Bundestag of the German Federal Republic in 1949. He served on the parliamentary committee on foreign relations and became its chairman in the 1950s. He also accompanied Chancellor Konrad Adenauer on a diplomatic mission to Moscow in 1955 that resulted in diplomatic relations being established between West Germany and the Soviet Union. Kiesinger relinquished his seat in the Bundestag when he failed to receive a cabinet-level or ambassadorial appointment in the Adenauer government. He was subsequently elected premier of the state of Baden-Wurttemberg. Kiesinger was instrumental in gaining greater powers for the German states. He was called back to national politics in 1966 when the Christian Democrats chose him to succeed Ludwig Erhard as chancellor in a coalition government. Kiesinger took office on December 1, 1966. The government was successful in restoring West Germany's economic prosperity and improving relations with Eastern Europe. Kiesinger was able to hold the coalition together for three years. When the Christian Democrats were unable to form a government following parliamentary elections in 1969, Kiesinger was replaced as chancellor by Social Democratic leader Willy Brandt. Kiesinger remained leader of the Christian Democratic party until 1971. He left the Bundestag in 1980 to retire to his home in Tubingen, where he died of heart failure at the age of 83 on March 9, 1988.

WILLY BRANDT (Chancellor, October 21, 1969–May 7, 1974). Willy Brandt was born Herbert Frahm in Lubeck on December 18, 1913. He attended local schools and became active in the Social Democratic party. He was an opponent of the Nazis in the early 1930s and joined the Socialist Workers party in 1931. Frahm adopted the name of Willy Brandt when he fled Germany to Oslo, Norway, in April of 1933 because he feared arrest by the Gestapo following Hitler's rise to power. He attended Oslo University and returned to Berlin briefly in 1936 to help establish the anti–Nazi underground. Brandt worked for the *Arbeiterbladet*, the Labor party newspaper, during much of his exile in Oslo. He entered the Norwegian army during the German invasion of Norway and was captured in 1940. He was interned for a month before his release. Brandt then went to Stockholm, Sweden, where he continued his journalistic career during the war. He returned to Germany in October of 1945 following the conclusion of World War II. Brandt resumed his German citizenship in 1947 and accepted a position with the Social Democratic party. He served as an aide to Berlin mayor Ernst Reuter during the Soviet blockade of Berlin from 1948 until 1949. He was elected to represent Berlin in the newly created German Federal Republic's Bundestag in 1949. Brandt was also elected a member of the Berlin House of Representatives in 1950 and served as its chairman from 1955 until 1957. He was selected as Mayor of West Berlin in October of 1957. He also became chairman of the Social Democratic party in Berlin in 1958. Brandt refused the demand of the Soviet Union that West Berlin break ties with the German Federal Republic and join with the Communist-dominated German Democratic Republic. He also criticized the construction of the Berlin Wall in August of 1961. The following month he was the candidate for chancellor of the Social Democratic party, but he was unable to unseat Konrad Adenauer. Brandt was elected chairman of the national Social Democratic party in February of 1964. He was again a candidate for chancellor in September of 1965. The Social Democrats made some gains, but Christian Democrat Ludwig Erhard was victorious. The Social Democrats formed a coalition government with the Christian Democrats in October of 1966, with Kurt Kiesinger as chancellor. Brandt was selected as vice-chancellor and foreign minister. He sought to improve ties with France, and he established diplomatic relations with Romania and Yugoslavia. The Social Democrats withdrew from the coalition after the elections in September of 1969, and Brandt formed a government as chancellor on October 21, 1969. He instituted a policy of reconciliation with the German Democratic Republic and Eastern Europe. Brandt's policies of Ostpolitik helped to ease tensions throughout Europe and earned him a Nobel Peace Prize in 1971. The Social Democrats were again successful in parliamentary elections in the fall of 1972. Brandt was forced to step down as chancellor on May 7, 1974, after Gunter Guillaume, a close aide, was arrested as an East German spy. Brandt remained chairman of the Social Democrats and was also elected chairman of the Socialist International in 1976. He resigned from the leadership of the Social Democrats in 1987. Two years later he was warmly welcomed by huge crowds in East Germany following the collapse of Communism and the fall of the Berlin Wall. Brandt fell ill with intestinal cancer in 1991. He died at his home in Unkel, near Bonn, at the age of 78 on October 8, 1992.

HELMUT SCHMIDT (Chancellor, May 16, 1974–October 1, 1982). Helmut Heinrich Waldemar Schmidt was born in Barmbek on December 23, 1918. He served in the Hitler Youth in the 1930s and entered the Wehrmacht in 1937. He served with distinction during World War II and rose to the rank of first lieutenant. Schmidt was captured by the British during the Battle of the Bulge and joined the Social Democrats while a prisoner of war. He returned to Germany after the war and entered the University of Hamburg. Schmidt received a degree in political economy in 1949 and served in the Hamburg city administration. He was elected to the Bundestag in 1953 and served on various parliamentary committees. He remained in the Bundestag until 1961, when he returned to Hamburg to serve in the state government as minister of the interior. In 1965 he was reelected to the Bundestag, where he served as the Social Democrats' spokesman for the opposition on foreign affairs. Schmidt was elected vice-chairman of the party under Willy Brandt in March of 1968. In October of 1969 he was appointed minister of defense in the government led by Brandt's Social Democrats. He was named minister of economics and finance in July of 1972 and remained finance minister in the Brandt government formed after elections in November of 1972. When Brandt resigned as chancellor on May 6, 1974, Schmidt was elected to succeed him. He took office as head of a coalition government of Social Democrats and Free Democrats on May 16, 1974. The Social Democrats lost support in elections to the Bundestag in October of 1976, but Schmidt remained head of the government. The party made narrow gains in elections in October of 1980. Schmidt's coalition cabinet collapsed when Free Democrat ministers resigned in September of 1982. Schmidt was replaced as chancellor by Christian Democratic leader Helmut Kohl on October 1, 1982. Schmidt remained vice chairman of the Social Democrats until 1984 and retired from the Bundestag in 1987.

HELMUT KOHL (Chancellor, October 1, 1982–　). Helmut Michael Kohl was born in Ludwigshafen on April 3, 1930. He attended the University of Frankfurt and received a doctorate of philosophy from Heidelburg University in 1958. He was active in the Christian Democratic Union and was elected to the state legislature of Rhineland-Palatinate in April of 1959. In 1966 he was elected chairman of the Christian Democrats' state organization, and in May of 1969 he became minister-president of the Rhineland-Palatinate. Kohl unsuccessfully challenged Rainer Barzel for the chairmanship of the Christian Democrats following the resignation of Kurt Georg Kiesinger in 1971. Kohl was a critic of the government of Willy Brandt in the early 1970s and defeated Barzel for the party chairmanship in June of 1973. He was elected to the Bundestag, or Federal Parliament, in 1976. The Christian Democrats were unsuccessful in their attempt to unseat Chancellor Helmut Schmidt in elections in 1976, and Kohl remained leader of the opposition. Franz-Josef Strauss, the leader of the Christian Democrats' coalition part-

ner, the Bavarian Christian Social Union, was the coalition's candidate for chancellor in 1980. Schmidt's Social Democrats defeated the conservative alliance. Kohl was selected as chancellor on October 1, 1982, following the resignation of the Social Democrats' coalition partners, the Free Democrats, from the government. He was confirmed as chancellor in parliamentary elections in March of 1983. He continued to lead a coalition government following elections in January of 1987. Kohl presided over the reunification of East and West Germany on October 1, 1990. Kohl's Christian Democrats were the overwhelming victors in elections held in the former East Germany on October 14, 1990. Kohl's government was faced with the task of transforming East Germany to a free-market economy and was forced to raise taxes to subsidize the East. Germany was also faced with an increase of right-wing violence against immigrants.

Ghana, Republic of

Ghana is a country in western Africa. It received independence from Great Britain on March 6, 1957.

HEADS OF STATE

SIR CHARLES ARDEN-CLARKE (Governor-General, March 6, 1957–May 14, 1957). Charles Noble Arden-Clarke was born in Bournemouth in 1898. He served in the British army during World War I and joined the Colonial Service in 1920. He was posted to Nigeria, where he remained until 1936. Arden-Clarke was then sent to Bechuanaland, where he became resident commissioner in 1942. He was appointed governor of Sarawak in 1946 and served until 1949. Arden-Clarke was subsequently named governor of the Gold Coast. He attempted to work with

nationalist leader Kwame Nkrumah, though he briefly had him arrested following violent strikes in 1950. Arden-Clarke became the first governor-general of Ghana when the Gold Coast received independence on March 6, 1957. He retired from his position on May 14, 1957. Arden-Clarke subsequently served as an advisor to Swaziland's constitutional committee. He died at the age of 64 on December 16, 1962.

KOBRINA ARKU KOSAH (Acting Governor-General, May 14, 1957–November 13, 1957). Kobrina Arku Kosah served as acting governor-general of Ghana following the resignation of Sir Charles Arden-Clarke on May 14, 1957. He stepped down on November 13, 1957, when the Earl of Listowel was sworn into office.

WILLIAM FRANCIS HARE, EARL OF LISTOWEL (Governor-General, November 13, 1957–March 6, 1960). William Francis Hare was born on September 28, 1906. He was educated at Oxford and London University. He joined the Labor party and served as deputy leader of the party in the House of Lords from the late 1930s. Hare served as Great Britain's secretary of state for India until independence was granted in 1947 and for Burma until 1948. He subsequently served as minister of state for colonial affairs until 1950. He was appointed governor-general of Ghana in June of 1957 and took office on November 13, 1957. Hare retained his position until March 6, 1960, when Ghana was declared a republic. He returned to Great Britain to serve as a committee chairman in the House of Lords until his retirement in 1976.

KWAME NKRUMAH (President, July 1, 1960–February 24, 1966). Kwame Nkrumah was born Francis Nwia Kofi in Nkroful, Nzimaland, on September 21, 1909. He attended mission schools and became a teacher in 1931. In 1935 he went to the United States to continue his education. He remained there for ten years and then went to England, where he received a law degree. Nkrumah became involved in the nationalist movement while overseas and returned to the Gold Coast in 1947 to serve as general secretary of the United Gold Coast Convention political organization. Two years later he broke with the party and formed his own organization, the Convention People's party. Nkrumah was detained by the authorites for his nationalist activities in 1950. The following year he was elected to the legislative assembly,

and two days later he was released from prison. He became leader of the government, and on March 22, 1952, he became the first prime minister of the Gold Coast. He remained in office despite the emergence of a strong opposition party and presided over the Gold Coast's independence as Ghana on March 6, 1957. Nkrumah remained prime minister in the new government. On July 1, 1960, he sponsored a plebiscite that resulted in Ghana becoming a republic, with Nkrumah as the nation's president. On May 1, 1961, he assumed complete control of Ghana, eliminated the opposition, and jailed many of its leaders. He also embarked on a career as a leading international spokesman on Third World matters and traveled to the Soviet Union, China, Egypt, the United States, and other countries. He was awarded the Lenin Peace Prize by the Soviet Union in July of 1962. The following month he survived a bombing attempt on his life, and he survived a second assassination attempt several weeks later. In December of 1963 Nkrumah dismissed the Supreme Court over a political issue. Early in 1964 he was again the target of an unsuccessful assassination attempt. Nkrumah's financial excesses contributed to Ghana's economic decline and, coupled with his political megalomania, led to greater dissatisfaction with his rule. On February 24, 1966, while Nkrumah was on a visit to Peking, China, the army moved against his regime and ousted his government. Nkrumah returned to Africa and settled in Conakry, Guinea, where President Sekou Toure named him copresident of Guinea. On April 27, 1972, Nkrumah died of cancer while in exile in Conakry.

JOSEPH A. ANKRAH (President, February 24, 1966–April 3, 1969). Joseph Arthur Ankrah was born to the Ga tribe in Accra on August 18, 1915. He was educated at a mission school, where he later became a teacher. He served in the army during World War II and later served with the Ghanian peacekeeping force in the Congo, now Zaire. Ankrah served as deputy chief of the Defense Staff of Ghana from 1961 until we was ousted by President Kwame Nkrumah in July of 1965. When Nkrumah was ousted by the military on February 24, 1966, Ankrah was named chairman of the National Liberation Council and commander of the armed forces. Following a financial scandal involving Ankrah's acceptance of money from foreign interests, he resigned all offices on April 3, 1969, and retired from the military and the government.

AKWASI AFRIFA (President, April 3, 1969–August 7, 1970). Akwasi Amankwa Afrifa was born to an Ashanti family in Mampong on April 24, 1936. He attended mission schools locally and received a scholarship to Cape Coast's Adisadel College. He was expelled from college and entered the army. Afrifa attended officers training school and graduated from Sandhurst in 1960. He saw duty as part of the United Nations Peacekeeping Forces in the Congo, now Zaire, in the early 1960s. On his return to Ghana, he began making plans for a coup against the Nkrumah regime, which he took part in on February 24, 1966. Following the ouster of Nkrumah, he served on the National Liberation Council, as minister of finance and economic affairs. When J. A. Ankrah was forced to resign on April 2, 1969, Afrifa replaced him as chairman. He supervised a return to civilian rule by allowing an election in August of 1969. He remained a member of the supervisory Presidential Commission until the following year. From December of 1970 he served as a member of the Council of State under President Akufo-Addo. When another military coup ousted the civilian government, Afrifa's resistance to the coup leaders resulted in his arrest and detention until July 3, 1973. He remained in political retirement until 1978, when he became an active member of the People's Movement for Freedom and Justice. He was elected to Parliament in June of 1979. Afrifa was arrested following the coup led by Flight Lieutenant Jerry Rawlings in June of 1979. He was charged with abuse of power and misuse of state funds and executed near Accra on June 26, 1979.

NII AMAA OLLENNU (President, August 7, 1970–August 31, 1970). Nii Amaa Ollennu was born to the Ga tribe in Labadi in 1906. He was educated in Ghana and Great Britain, where he studied law. He returned to Ghana as a teacher at the Accra High School in 1929 and served on the Accra City Council from 1944 until 1950. Ollennu was also a member of the Legislative Council from 1946 until 1950. He was appointed a high court judge in 1956 and was appointed to the Supreme Court in 1969. Ollennu was elected Speaker of the National Assembly in 1969. He served as acting president of Ghana from August 7 until August 31, 1970, prior to the inauguration of President-Elect Edward Akufo-Addo. Ollennu returned to the National Assembly, where he remained until the military coup in January of 1972. He retired from politics and died on December 19, 1986.

EDWARD AKUFO-ADDO (President, August 31, 1970–January 13, 1972). Edward Akufo-Addo was born in Akwapiin on June 26, 1906. He attended local schools until 1932, when he entered St. Peter's Hall, Oxford, on scholarship. He received a law degree in 1940 and returned to Ghana to practice. Akufo-Addo was instrumental in founding the United Gold Coast Convention and served on the Legislative Council from 1949 until 1950. He was appointed to the Supreme Court of Ghana in 1962, but was removed from office by President Kwame Nkrumah two years later for his failure to convict the president's political opponents. Following Nkrumah's ouster, Akufo-Addo was appointed chief justice on September 26, 1966. He served as chairman of the Constitutional Convention which helped prepare Ghana to return to democracy. Following the return to civilian rule, Akufo-Addo was elected president and took office on August 31, 1970. He remained in the primarily ceremonial position until the military coup of January 13, 1972. Akufo-Addo went into political retirement following his ouster. He died on July 1, 1979.

IGNATIUS K. ACHEAMPONG (President, January 13, 1972–July 5, 1978). Ignatius Kuti Acheampong was born in Kumasi on September 23, 1931. He was educated at local mission schools and at the Central College of Commerce in Agona Swedru. He worked as a teacher until the early 1950s, when he joined the army. Acheampong was commissioned as an officer in 1959 and attended military training schools in Great Britain and the United States. He continued to serve in the army following Ghanaian independence and served in the United Nations peacekeeping force in the former Belgian Congo in 1962. Acheampong was promoted to the rank of colonel and was named commander of the 1st Infantry Brigade in Accra in November of 1971. He led the military coup that ousted the elected government on January 13, 1972. Acheampong served as head of state and chairman of the National Redemption Council. His military government suspended the constitution and dissolved the National Assembly. He continued to serve as head of the ruling Supreme Military Council until he was ousted by other members of the council on July 5, 1978. He was detained by the new government and was dismissed from the army following his release. Acheampong was again arrested following the coup led by Jerry Rawlings in June of 1979. He was tried on charges

of corruption and was executed in Accra on June 16, 1979.

FRED W. K. AKUFFO (President, July 5, 1978–June 4, 1979). Fred W. K. Akuffo was born in Akuropon on March 21, 1937. He was educated at local missionary schools and entered the army in 1957. He was sent to the British Royal Military Academy at Sandhurst for training and was commissioned in 1960. Akuffo served on the United Nations peacekeeping force in the former Belgian Congo in the early 1960s. He was given command of the Ghana Parachute Battalion and rose to the rank of colonel. He became a member of the ruling Supreme Military Council under Ignatius Acheampong in 1975 and served as chief of the defense staff. Akuffo joined with other members of the council to oust Acheampong on July 5, 1978, and he became Ghana's head of state. He vowed to restore Ghana to a parliamentary democracy and freed many political prisoners. He instituted austerity measures to improve Ghana's sinking economy. Akuffo's insistence on an amnesty for himself and other members of the military government before he would allow a return to civilian rule sparked a coup by junior officers. He was ousted by Flight Lieutenant Jerry Rawlings on June 5, 1979. He was arrested and charged with abuse of power and misuse of state funds and was executed near Accra on June 26, 1979.

JERRY RAWLINGS (President, June 5, 1979–September 24, 1979). Jerry John Rawlings was born in Accra on June 22, 1947. He was educated at Achimoto College in Accra and entered the military. He was commissioned as a second lieutenant in 1969. Rawlings distinguished himself as a jet fighter pilot and rose to the rank of flight lieutenant in 1978. He was a critic of the corruption and mismanagement of the military regime that ruled Ghana from 1972 and led a coup of junior officers against the

Supreme Military Council on May 15, 1979. The coup failed and Rawlings was arrested. He became a popular figure in Ghana during his public court-martial hearing and was freed from prison by other junior officers in early June of 1979. He ousted President Fred Akuffo on June 5, 1979, and became head of the ruling Armed Forces Revolutionary Council. The junta tried and executed Akuffo and two other former heads of state as well as other members of the ousted military government. Rawlings also continued with plans to restore Ghana to civilian rule. Elections took place on June 18, 1979, followed by a runoff the following month. Hilal Limann was elected president, and Rawlings and the military junta relinquished the government on September 24, 1979. Rawlings soon became a critic of the Limann government, and he was retired from the air force in November of 1979. He entered politics on a full time basis and was briefly arrested in November of 1980 on charges of plotting against the government. Rawlings led a coup against Limann's government on December 31, 1981, and he again became head of state as chairman of the Provisional National Defense Council. Rawlings succeeded in reorganizing the judicial and administrative branches of the government. He survived several coup attempts during the 1980s and made plans to restore Ghana to a multiparty democracy. Elections were held for district assemblies in December of 1988, and a new constitution providing for free elections was promoted in 1992.

HILAL LIMANN (President, September 24, 1979–December 31, 1981). Hilal Limann was born in Gwollu on December 12, 1934. He was educated locally and at a teacher training college in Tamale. He began a career as a teacher in 1952. Limann also entered politics in the early 1950s and was elected to the Tumu district council. He served as chairman of the council from 1953 until 1955. Limann went to Great Britain in 1956 to continue his education. He received a degree in economics from the London School of Economics and Political Science in 1960 and subsequently studied constitutional law at the University of Paris. He returned to Ghana in 1965 and worked as a foreign service officer at the Foreign Ministry. Limann was instrumental in drafting a constitution for Ghana following the military coup that ousted President Kwame Nkrumah in 1966. He served in the Ghana Embassy in Togo from 1969 until 1971 and was then named counselor to Ghana's permanent mission to the United Nations in Geneva. He returned to Ghana in 1975 to continue work at the Foreign Ministry. He left the government in January of 1979 when the military government allowed the formation of political parties to prepare for a return to civilian rule. Limann joined the People's National party and was nominated as the party's candidate for president in April of 1979. Elections were allowed to proceed despite a military coup led by Jerry Rawlings in June of 1979. Limann defeated Victor Owusu in a runoff election in July of 1979 and was sworn into office as president on September 24, 1979. He attempted to solve Ghana's economic problems with a series of austerity programs, but met with little success. His government was ousted on December 31, 1981, by another military coup led by Jerry Rawlings. Limann was arrested by the new government and held in protective custody until September of 1983.

JERRY RAWLINGS (President, December 31, 1981–). *See earlier entry under Heads of State.*

HEADS OF GOVERNMENT

KWAME NKRUMAH (Prime Minister, March 6, 1957–July 1, 1960). *See entry under Heads of State.*

KOFI A. BUSIA (Prime Minister, September 3, 1969–January 13, 1972). Kofi Abrefa Busia was born in 1913 to the Royal house of Wenchi in Ashanti. He attended local missionary schools and the Methodist Secondary School in Cape Coast. Following graduation, he taught at Wesley College in Ashanti. Busia obtained a bachelor's degree in London in 1939 and received a scholarship to Oxford University. He returned to the Gold Coast in 1942. He was appointed assistant district commissioner in 1943, but returned to Oxford in 1946. The following year he obtained a doctorate in philosophy and again returned to the Gold Coast. In 1951 he was elected to the Gold Coast legislature. The following year Busia was elected leader of the Ghana Congress party in opposition to Kwame Nkrumah. The party merged with other opposition parties to form the United party in October of 1957, and Busia remained leader. When Nkrumah began a campaign to crack down on the opposition, Busia fled the country shortly before he was scheduled to be arrested in 1959. He went into exile in The Hague, where he taught sociology. He remained a vocal opponent of the Nkrumah regime during his years in exile. Busia was in Oxford when Nkrumah was overthrown in February of 1966, and he subsequently returned to Ghana. He served on the National Liberation Council and served in the Constituent Assembly which drafted a new constitution. He also founded the Progress party which won the elections in August of 1969. Busia was sworn in as prime minister on September 3, 1969. He immediately faced many difficulties in trying to lead the country. In 1970 he purged the civil service of supporters of Nkrumah who had refused to cooperate with his leadership. His austerity program to stabilize the economy provoked widespread dissent when inflation hit basic commodities. Busia went to England to receive medical treatment and was ousted by the army in a coup on January 13, 1972. He remained in exile in England and returned to Oxford University, where he died of a heart attack on August 28, 1978.

Greece (Hellenic Republic)

(Elleniki Demokratia)

Greece is a country in southeastern Europe. It received independence from the Ottoman Empire on March 25, 1827.

HEADS OF STATE

GEORGE II (King, November 3, 1935–April 1, 1947). George was born at Totoi, near Athens, on July 20, 1890. He was the eldest son of King Constantine of Greece and Princess Sophia of Prussia. He succeeded his father to the throne as King George II when King Constantine was forced to abdicate in

September of 1922. His rule was marred by uprisings and republican sentiments. George left Greece on December 19, 1923, and traveled to Bucharest. He was officially deposed, and Greece was declared a republic on March 25, 1924. He spent the next decade in exile in various European capitals. In Greece, George Kondylis staged a military coup in October of 1935. Kondylis abolished the republican constitution and revived the monarchy. George was recalled to Greece and restored to the throne in November of 1935. He assumed command of the Greek army following the Italian invasion of Greece in 1940. He fled with his government to Crete in April of 1941, shortly before the German army reached Athens. George eventually landed in London, where he established a government in exile. Following the expulsion of the Germans from Greece, some elements in the country were unwilling to accept the return of George to the throne. He accepted Archbishop Damaskinos as regent in his stead in December of 1944. Following a plebiscite in September of 1946, George II was invited to return to the throne. He arrived in Greece later that month. He had been back on the throne for less than a year when he died suddenly of a heart attack in Athens on April 1, 1947.

DAMASKINOS (Regent, January 1945–September 4, 1946). Archbishop Damaskinos was born George Papandreou in Dorvitsa on March 3, 1891. He was educated in Karditsa and at the University of Athens. He was ordained into the priesthood in 1917 and was elected bishop of Corinth in 1922. Damaskinos was a leading opponent of the regime of Prime Minister Ioannis Metaxas, and when he was elected archbishop of Athens and primate of Greece in 1938, the prime minister annulled his election. Damaskinos was exiled to a monastery in the Greek mountains until the German-Italian occupation of Greece in 1942. He was

then asked to assume his office and became the primary spiritual leader of Greece. Following the liberation of Greece in 1944, the country broke into civil war between royalist and Communist elements. Archbishop Damaskinos was asked to serve as regent while King George II remained in exile. He also served as prime minister from October 17, 1945, until November 3, 1945. Following a plebiscite on September 1, 1946, the king was invited to return to the throne. King George II returned to Greece on September 27, 1946, and Archbishop Damaskinos retired from political activities. He died in Psychiko, near Athens on May 20, 1949.

PAUL I (King, April 1, 1947–March 6, 1964). Paul was born in Athens on December 14, 1901. He was the son of King Constantine of Greece and Princess Sophia of Prussia. Paul accompanied his family into exile in 1916 when Constantine was deposed for having pro-German sentiments during World War I. Paul's brother, Alexander, was proclaimed king of Greece. When Alexander died from an infection caused by a monkey bite in 1920, Paul was offered the throne by a plebiscite, but was unable to take the throne because his father and older brother were unwilling to renounce their claims. King Constantine was restored to the throne in December of 1920, and Paul returned to Greece with his family. In September of 1922 King Constantine was again forced to relinquish the throne. He was succeeded by his oldest son, who was crowned King George II. The following year George was also asked to leave Greece. Paul accompanied his brother into exile, and the monarchy was abolished in Greece. The royal family was invited to return to Greece in 1935, and Paul accompanied his brother as crown prince. Paul served in the army General Staff following the attack by the Italians and Albanians in 1940. The royal family was again forced to flee Greece following the German invasion in April of 1941. Paul remained in exile during the war years and assisted the war effort by broadcasting radio messages to the Greek people during the occupation. Paul's brother was restored to the throne in September of 1946. King George II died suddenly on April 1, 1947, and Paul was sworn in as monarch. He was active in trying to restore unity in the country. A long-running Communist insurrection was defeated in 1949, and Paul was instrumental in organizing the relief effort for the areas that had suffered the most during the fighting. In the early 1950s Paul engaged in a political struggle with Field Marshal Alexandros Papagos, who had led the government forces against the Communist insurgents. The two leaders reconciled their differences shortly before Papagos's death in 1955. The king suffered from ill health during much of 1963. His condition deteriorated in December of 1963, but he kept his illness secret until after the elections in February of 1964. He collapsed shortly after the swearing-in ceremonies of the new government and was rushed to surgery. He died in Athens of postoperative complications on March 6, 1964.

CONSTANTINE II (King, March 6, 1964–June 1, 1973). Constantine was born at Psychico, near Athens, on June 2, 1941. He was the son of King Paul I and Queen Helen. He attended Athens University and received military training. Following the death of his father on March 6, 1964, he succeeded to the throne as King Constantine II. He also married Princess Anne-Marie of Denmark that year. Constantine's turbulent relationship with leftist Prime Minister Georgios Papandreou resulted in the prime minister's dismissal in 1965. The subsequent civil disorders and governmental confusion led to a military coup on April 21, 1967. Constantine reluctantly accepted the subsequent dictatorship. He urged a return to democratic rule and was forced to flee with his family to Rome in December of 1967 following an unsuccessful attempt to oust the ruling military junta. Constantine was formally deposed on June 1, 1973, and the Greek monarchy was abolished by a national referendum in December of 1974. Constantine remained in exile in London.

GEORGE PAPADOPOULOS (President, June 1, 1973–November 25, 1973). George Papadopoulos was born in Eleochorion on May 5, 1919. He attended military school in Greece and joined the army. He fought in the Greek Italian war in 1940 and served in the Resistance during the German occupation. Papadopoulos rose through the ranks to lieutenant colonel in 1956 and colonel in 1960. He held various military commands, and in April of 1967 he led the military coup that overthrew the government. He subsequently served as minister to the prime minister's office. He took over the office of prime minister on December 13, 1967, and also served as minister of defense. Papadopoulos was also foreign minister from 1970 until 1973. He served as regent from 1972 and became president of the Greek Republic on June 1, 1973, following the abolition of the monarchy. He resigned as prime minister on October 1, 1973, and announced plans to hold democratic elections. His efforts were too late to save his faltering regime, and his government was ousted in a coup on November 25, 1973. Papadopoulos was arrested in October of 1974 and tried for high treason and insurrection. He was sentenced to death but his sentence was later commuted to life imprisonment in Kordallous Prison.

PHAIDON GIZIKIS (President, November 25, 1973–December 15, 1974). Phaidon Gizikis was born in Arta on June 16, 1917. He attended military school and joined the army. In the early years of World War II, he fought on the Albanian front, and he was active in the government's battles against Communist insurgents during the late 1940s. Gizikis had risen to the rank of colonel by the time of the military coup of 1967. He was promoted rapidly by the junta and rose to lieutenant general. He was also placed in command of the military in the Athens District and was in charge of the enforcement of martial law in the capital. In 1970 he was given command of the First Army. President George Papadopoulos attempted to oust Gizikis from his command in October of 1973. Instead, Papadopoulos was himself ousted in a coup led by military police chief Brig. Gen. Demetrios Ioannidis, and he was replaced as president by Gizikis on November 25, 1973. In July of 1974 the Greek government sponsored an attempted coup against the government of Cyprus. Greece's involvement there prompted a counterinvasion by Turkey and the threat of war between the two countries. Gizikis and the military leaders relinquished power to civilian politicians in order to avoid war with Turkey. Konstantine Karamanlis was named prime minister and a cease-fire was arranged with Turkey. Gizikis remained president under the civilian government until a referendum creating a new democratic constitution could be enacted. He resigned as president on December 15, 1974.

MICHAEL STASSINOPOULOS (President, December 18, 1974–June 20, 1975). Michael Stassinopoulos was born in Calamata on July 27, 1905. He was educated in Athens and received a degree in law. He served as a law professor at Athens University from 1937 and became dean in 1951. Stassinopoulos served in the cabinet as minister of the press and then as minister of labor in 1952. He again served as minister of the press in 1958 and was named vice president of the State Council in 1963. He served as president of the State Council from 1966 until 1969. Stas-

sinopoulos was elected to Parliament in November of 1974 and was selected as interim president on December 18, 1974. He retained the office until the election of Konstantinos Tsatsas on June 20, 1975. He subsequently served as an ad hoc judge on the International Court of Justice in The Hague until 1978.

KONSTANTINOS TSATSAS (President, June 20, 1975–May 15, 1980). Konstantinos Tsatsas was born in Athens on July 1, 1899. He was educated at the Universities of Athens and Heidelberg, where he studied law and philosophy. He taught philosophy at the University of Athens during the 1930s. During the Italian-German occupation of Greece during World War II, he went into exile and was an advisor to the government-in-exile. Following the war, Tsatsas served in the cabinet as minister of the interior. He subsequently served as minister of the press and air. He was appointed minister of education in 1949. Tsatsas was an ally of Prime Minister Konstantine Karamanlis in the 1950s and early 1960s. He was serving as minister of justice at the time of the military coup in 1967. Tsatsas was an opponent of the military junta that ruled Greece until 1974. He was instrumental in the drafting of a new constitution following Greece's return to democratic rule. Tsatsas was nominated as president of the new republic by Karamanlis and took office on June 20, 1975. He completed his term of office on May 15, 1980, and retired from politics. He remained active as a writer and scholar until his death from a heart ailment on October 8, 1987, in Athens, at the age of 88.

KONSTANTINE KARAMANLIS (President, May 15, 1980–March 10, 1985). Konstantine Karamanlis (Caramanlis) was born in Prote, in Macedonia, on February 23, 1907. He attended the University of Athens, where he received a law degree in 1932. He entered politics and was elected to Parliament in 1935. Karamanlis declined a position in the government of Ioannis Metaxas in 1936 after the dictator had closed Parliament. Karamanlis was politically inactive during World War II. He was again elected to Parliament in March of 1946. He was named minister of labor in the subsequent government of Constantine Tsaldaris. Karamanlis served as minister of transport in 1947, minister of social welfare from 1948 until 1950, and minister of national defense from 1950 until 1952. He achieved much popularity for his efforts as minister of public works from 1952 until 1954. He was serving as minister of communications and public works when he was named by King Paul to be prime minister on October 6, 1955, following the death of Alexandros Papagos. Karamanlis subsequently formed the National Radical Union party and was victorious in the elections held the following February. He was forced to resign as prime minister following the defection of members of his party to the opposition on March 3, 1958, but regained the position following general elections on May 17, 1958. Karamanlis was instrumental in negotiating an agreement with Turkey that allowed the establishment of an independent republic of Cyprus in 1960. He again stepped down as prime minister on September 20, 1961. His party was again successful in the subsequent elections, despite criticism by the opposition that there was electoral fraud. Karamanlis again headed the government from November 4, 1961. He remained in office until June 11, 1963, when he resigned following a dispute with King Paul concerning the powers of the monarchy and the prime minister. Karamanlis left Greece for exile in Paris the following month. He spent the next decade in relative political retirement, but following the military takeover in 1967, he occasionally issued statements calling for the reestablishment of democracy. Following the crisis between Greece and Turkey over Cyprus, Karamanlis was asked to return to Greece and form a civilian government on July 24, 1974. He negotiated a settlement to the war in Cyprus and instituted democratic reform measures in Greece. He lifted the junta's ban on freedom of speech and the press and eliminated most martial law measures. Karamanlis also founded the New Democracy party, which ruled as a majority party under his leadership. Karamanlis stepped down as prime minister on May 9, 1980, following his election as president of Greece. He was sworn in as president on May 15, 1980. He planned to seek a second term as president but Prime Minister Andreas Papandreou withdrew his support, and Karamanlis resigned on March 10, 1985. Karamanlis was again elected president of Greece at the age of 83 and took office on May 5, 1990.

CHRISTOS SARTZETAKIS (President, March 30, 1985–May 5, 1990). Christos A. Sartzetakis was born in Salonika on April 6, 1929. He was educated in Greece and France, where he received a degree in law. He served as a judge from 1956. Sartzetakis was appointed magistrate to investigate the assassination of Grigoris Lambrakis in 1963. During the course of the investigation, he disproved the official police version of the incident, which had reported Lambrakis had been killed in a traffic mishap. He also exposed the relationship between police officials and the right-wing thugs who had murdered Lambrakis. His investigations were the subject of Vasilis Vasilikos's novel *Z*, and the subsequent Costa-Gavras film. Sartzetakis went to France in 1965 for postgraduate studies. He returned to Greece in 1967 to serve on the Court of Misdemeanors. He was removed from office and arrested by the ruling military junta in 1969. Sartzetakis was detained until his release in an amnesty in 1971. He was reinstated to the judiciary and promoted to appeal court judge in 1974, following the ouster of the military junta. He was named to the Greek Supreme Court in 1982. Sartzetakis was nominated for president to succeed Konstantine Karamanlis in March of 1985. He was elected with the support of Prime Minister Andreas Papandreou's Panhellenic Socialist Movement and took office on March 30, 1985. Sartzetakis completed his term and left office on May 5, 1990.

KONSTANTINE KARAMANLIS (President, May 5, 1990–). *See earlier entry under Heads of State.*

HEADS OF GOVERNMENT

GEORGIOS PAPANDREOU (Prime Minister, May 26, 1944–December 31, 1944). Georgios Papandreou was born in Kalentzi on February 13, 1888. He was educated at the University of Athens, where he received a degree in law. He entered politics in 1915 and became prefect of Chios. Papandreou served as governor general of the Aegean Islands from 1917 until 1920. He was elected to the Greek Parliament in 1923 and was named minister of the interior in the government of General Nikolas Plastiras. He served as minister of education from 1929 until 1933. Two years later he founded the Democratic Socialist party. Papandreou was sent into exile during the dictatorship of Ioannis Metaxas. He was an opponent of the Italian-German occupation of Greece during World War II. He was arrested by the Italians, but escaped to Egypt, where he joined the government in exile. Papandreou was named prime minister in King George II's exile government on May 26, 1944. The government moved to Naples on September 7 and returned to Athens on October 18, 1944. Papandreou was asked by the king to remain as prime minister, but declined because of his opposition to the monarchy and resigned on December 31, 1944. He remained active in government, however, and served as minister of the interior in 1947 and deputy prime minister from 1950 until 1951. He spent the remainder of the 1950s in opposition to the government. Papandreou formed the Center Union party in September of 1961 and led the party to victory in the elections in November of 1963. He became prime minister on November 7, 1963, but resigned on December 24, 1963, in order to call for new elections to increase his majority. Papandreou's party was given an absolute majority in the subsequent elections, and he again became prime minister on February 19, 1964. He resigned from office on July 15, 1965, following a dispute with King Constantine over the question of control of the armed forces. Papandreou's party was again expected to win the elections of 1967, but the government was taken over by the military in April of 1967. Papandreou was arrested by the junta leaders and imprisoned. He was in poor health at the time and was sent to a military hospital for treatment. He was released and placed under house arrest until he was granted amnesty in December of 1967. Papandreou died in Athens following surgery for a bleeding ulcer on November 1, 1968. His funeral served as an occasion for his supporters to express their opposition to the leaders of the ruling junta.

NIKOLAS PLASTIRAS (Prime Minister, January 2, 1945–April 9, 1945). Nikolas Plastiras was born in Kardhitsa, Thessaly, in 1883. He served in the Greek army and fought in the Balkan War. He was promoted to colonel in

1920. In the early 1920s he led a Greek expedition against the Turks in Anatolis and distinguished himself by successfully leading the Greek evacuation after the Turkish victory. Plastiras returned to Greece to lead a coup that forced the abdication of King Constantine on September 2, 1922. He organized the ruling Revolutionary Committee and served as acting prime minister. He stepped down in November of 1923 in favor of General Stylianos Gonatos, a fellow coup leader, but returned as prime minister shortly thereafter. Plastiras again resigned following the elections in January of 1924. His political mentor, Eleutherios Venizelos, became prime minister, and Plastiras went into political retirement. The following year Venizelos was ousted, and Plastiras was arrested and sent into exile by the government of General Theodoros Pangalos. Plastiras made several attempts to overthrow the Pangalos government and was sentenced to death in absentia. He was allowed to return to Greece following the ouster of Pangalos in August of 1926. Venizelos returned as prime minister in 1928, and Plastiras helped to reorganize the army. The royalist opposition was successful in the elections of 1933, and Plastiras, with the approval of Venizelos, staged a coup on March 7, 1933. His government lasted less than a day before he was ousted by General Georgios Kondylis. Plastiras fled to Bulgaria and eventually to Egypt. He led an unsuccessful uprising when the monarchy was reestablished in 1935. He was a leading opponent of the subsequent dictatorship of General Ioannis Metaxas and led several unsuccessful attempts against the government. Plastiras was politically inactive during the German occupation during World War II. He returned to Greece following the liberation of the country from occupation forces and the defeat of Communist insurgents. On January 2, 1945, he became prime minister. He stepped down three months later on April 9, 1945,

following general elections. Plastiras reentered politics and again became prime minister as head of a coalition government on April 15, 1950. He was forced to resign on August 18, 1950, following the resignation of the liberal members of his government. Plastiras was again named prime minister on November 1, 1951, when Alexandros Papagos, leader of the majority party, refused to form a coalition government. Plastiras was able to establish a coalition government, but his health deteriorated during his term of office and forced his resignation on October 11, 1952. He recovered sufficiently to run in the election of November of 1952, but his party was defeated and he lost his seat in Parliament. Plastiras suffered a series of heart attacks in July of 1953. He died in Psychico, near Athens, on July 26, 1953.

PETROS VOULGARIS (Prime Minister, April 9, 1945–October 9, 1945). Petros Voulgaris was born on the island of Hydra in 1884. He attended the Naval Cadet School and served as chief of the naval air force during World War I. Voulgaris was stationed in Ankara, Turkey, as a naval attaché when he was dismissed on charges that he supported a coup against the Greek government. He went into exile in Egypt following the German occupation of Greece during World War II. He served as air minister in the government-in-exile. He successfully led a group of naval officers on a mission to seize all Greek warships in Alexandria harbor from Communist sympathizers who had control of the ships. Following the liberation of Greece, Admiral Voulgaris was asked to become prime minister on April 9, 1945, as leader of an interim government in anticipation of democratic elections. Voulgaris faced the opposition of the various political parties in Greece and resigned on October 9, 1945. He died of a heart ailment at the Athens Naval Hospital on November 26, 1957.

DAMASKINOS (Prime Minister, October 17, 1945–November 1, 1945). *See entry under Heads of State.*

PANAYOTIS KANELLOPOULOS (Prime Minister, November 1, 1945–November 20, 1945). Panayotis Kanellopoulos (Canellopoulos) was born in Patras on December 13, 1902. He was educated in Greece and Germany, where he studied law and sociology. In the late 1920s he taught sociology at Athens University. He left the university to enter politics in 1935 and founded the National Unionist party in opposition to the restoration of the monarchy. Kanellopoulos was an opponent of the dictatorship of Ioannis Metaxas and spent most of the period between 1936 and 1940 in exile. He joined the Greek military service in 1940 following the Italian invasion of Greece. He was a leader of the Resistance following the German occupation of Greece and left the country for the Middle East in 1942. There he joined the Greek government-in-exile as minister of war. He returned to Greece in 1944 to supervise the German withdrawal. Kanellopoulos was named prime minister on November 1, 1945, but his government could not survive the fighting between the various political factions. He stepped down on November 20, 1945. He was elected to Parliament the following year and served in various cabinet positions over the next two decades. Kanellopoulos was minister of air in 1947 and minister of war from 1949 until 1950. He joined with Alexandros Papagos's Greek Rally party in 1952 and served as deputy prime minister and minister of national defense until Papagos's death in 1955. He was a leading contender to succeed Papagos, but was bypassed in favor of Konstantine Karamanlis. Kanellopoulos served as deputy prime minister under Karamanlis from 1959 until 1963. When Karamanlis withdrew from politics in 1963, Kanellopoulos was elected leader of the National Radical Union party. He again served as prime minister when his party withdrew its support from Ioannis Paraskevopoulos's caretaker government. Kanellopoulos was selected to succeed him as prime minister on April 3, 1967. His interim government was given the mandate to hold elections the following May. Instead, a military junta toppled the government on April 21, 1967, and Kanellopoulos and many members of his cabinet were arrested. Following his release, he remained an outspoken critic of the military regime. Kanellopoulos was again elected to Parliament after the collapse of the junta in 1974. He was the unsuccessful nominee of the Centre party for the Greek presidency the following year. He subsequently retired from politics. He died of a heart attack in Athens at the age of 83 on September 11, 1986.

THEMISTOCLES SOPHOULIS (Prime Minister, November 21, 1945–April 1, 1946). Themistocles Sophoulis was born in Vathy, on the island of Samos, on November 25, 1861. He was an archaeologist and writer and served as a leader of the opposition to Turkish rule on the island of Samos. When Samos was granted its liberty from Turkey, Sophoulis became the leader of the island's government. He led the island into union with Greece later that year. In 1914 he was appointed governor-general of Macedonia, and the following year he was elected to the Greek Parliament as the representative from Samos. Sophoulis was an ally of Liberal leader Eleutheries Venizelos, and in 1916 he joined with him in the revolutionary pro-Allied government at Salonika. He returned to Athens in 1917 after King Constantine was deposed. He was elected president of the Chamber of Deputies that same year and retained that office until 1920. Sophoulis was elected prime minister of the new Greek Republic on July 24, 1924, and served until October 1, 1924. He succeeded Venizelos as leader of the

Liberal party upon the latter's death in 1936. During the dictatorship of Ioannis Metaxas from 1936 until 1941, Sophoulis held no public office. He was arrested in 1944 following the German occupation of Greece and remained in the Haidari concentration camp until the liberation. He became prime minister of the postwar government on November 21, 1945, and remained in office until April 1, 1946, following the election victory of the Populist party. He again formed a government on September 7, 1947, and presided over a coalition cabinet of Liberals and Populists. He retained the office of prime minister until his death in Kifissia, Greece, on June 24, 1949.

PANAGHIOTIS POULITSAS (Prime Minister, April 7, 1946–April 21, 1946). Panaghiotis Poulitsas (Politzas) was born near Sparta in 1881. He was educated in Athens, Munich, and Berlin. He received a degree in law and entered the judiciary in 1907. Poulitsas was appointed an appeals judge in 1922. He served as president of the council of state from 1943 until 1951. During that period he was chosen as interim prime minister from April 7 until April 21 of 1946. He was elected to Parliament in 1951 as a member of Field Marshal Papagos's Greek Rally party. Poulitsas died in Athens at the age of 86 on January 16, 1968.

CONSTANTINE TSALDARIS (Prime Minister, April 21, 1946–January 22, 1947). Constantine Tsaldaris was born to a prominent Greek family in Alexandria, Egypt, in 1884. He received a degree in law from the University of Athens and continued his studies in Great Britain, France, and Germany. He returned to Greece in 1910 and subsequently entered politics. From 1916 until 1917 he served as prefect of Corfu. Tsaldaris was named governor of Crete in 1920 and served until 1922. He was briefly imprisoned in 1926 because of his activities in opposition

to the Greek Republic. He was elected to the Parliament in 1932 and served as undersecretary of communications in the government of his uncle, Panagis Tsaldaris, in 1934. Tsaldaris also served as undersecretary of state in the subsequent government of Ioannis Metaxas. He was arrested by the Italians during the occupation of Greece in the early 1940s, but escaped and went to Egypt. He returned to Greece to lead the Populist party after the country's liberation. Tsaldaris became prime minister following the party's victory in the elections of 1946 and was sworn into office on April 21, 1946. He was a staunch royalist and supported the referendum to return the monarchy to the throne. Tsaldaris stepped down as prime minister on January 22, 1947, to allow the formation of a coalition government to deal with the Communist insurrection. He remained as deputy prime minister and foreign minister in the subsequent government of Demetrios Maximos. He again served briefly as interim prime minister from August 30 until September 5, 1947, when Maximos resigned. Tsaldaris remained foreign minister in the subsequent governments of Themistocles Sophoulis and Alexandros Diomedes. Tsaldaris was instrumental in persuading the United Nations to send a team to Greece to investigate the Communist insurgency. The reports of the team led to military and economic assistance from the United States to end the revolt in 1949. Tsaldaris's political fortunes dwindled following his party's loss in the 1950 elections. He again served briefly in Parliament in 1956 and retired from politics following his defeat in 1958. He died in Athens of cirrhosis of the liver at the age of 88 on November 15, 1970.

DEMETRIOS MAXIMOS (Prime Minister, January 24, 1947–August 25, 1947). Demetrios Maximos was born in Patras on July 6, 1873. He was educated in Greece and France and subsequently was employed by the National Bank of Greece. He rose to become the bank's governor in 1914. Maximos was a friend of the Greek royal family and voluntarily shared their exile in 1922. He retired from politics following the abdication of King George II in 1924. He returned to the government when the Populist party gained power in 1933 and accepted the post of foreign minister in the government of Panayotis Tsaldaris. He again retired in 1934 and remained out of political life until after World War II. Maximos was persuaded by King George II, who had recently returned to the throne, to become prime minister on January 24, 1947. He attempted to arrange a settlement of the guerrilla fighting in northern Greece and pushed for foreign financial assistance in the rebuilding of his war-torn country. His government was challenged by moderates, who questioned his ability to unite the country and stop the fighting. Maximos resigned on August 25, 1947, and retired from politics. He died in Athens on October 16, 1955.

CONSTANTINE TSALDARIS (Prime Minister, August 30, 1947–September 5, 1947). *See earlier entry under Heads of Government.*

THEMISTOCLES SOPHOULIS (Prime Minister, September 8, 1947–June 24, 1949). *See earlier entry under Heads of Government.*

ALEXANDROS DIOMEDES (Prime Minister, June 30, 1949–January 5, 1950). Alexandros Diomedes was born in 1875. He was educated in Greece and received a degree in economics. He served as minister of finance from 1912 until 1914 in the Liberal government of Eleutherios Venizelos. Diomedes retired from politics after the end of World War I and worked with the Greek National Bank. He became governor of the bank in 1923 and was instrumental in the creation of the

Bank of Greece in 1928. He retired from public life in 1930 to study and write. Diomedes was named president of the Supreme Reconstruction Board after the German occupation of Greece. He joined the government of Themistocles Sophoulis as deputy prime minister in January of 1949. He became prime minister on June 30, 1949, following Sophoulis's death. Diomedes served as leader of a Populist-Liberal coalition cabinet. The Communist insurrection that had plagued Greece since the German occupation was finally settled during Diomedes' term. He resigned on January 5, 1950, following the collapse of his coalition government over the issue of when to conduct parliamentary elections. Diomedes died in Athens shortly thereafter on November 11, 1950, of a kidney ailment.

IOANNIS THEOTOKIS (Prime Minister, January 7, 1950–March 5, 1950). Ioannis Theotokis was born in Corfu in 1880. He attended the University of Vienna and received a degree in agriculture. He entered politics as a member of the Populist party in the 1920s. Theotokis served as minister of agriculture in 1932 and again in 1935. He was deputy prime minister and foreign minister in the government of General Georgios Kondylis from 1935 and supported the restoration of the monarchy. He was exiled from Athens during the Metaxas dictatorship from 1936 until 1941. Theotokis returned to Greece and remained there during World War II. He served as minister of the interior in the 1946 postwar government and was elected Speaker of the Parliament later that year. He retired from politics in 1949, but was recalled by King Paul to serve as caretaker prime minister on January 7, 1950. His government was given the special mandate to hold elections. Theotokis stepped down as prime minister on March 5, 1950, following the results of the general elections. He lived in retirement on Corfu Island from 1951 until his death on June 6, 1961.

SOPHOCLES VENIZELOS (Prime Minister, March 23, 1950–April 14, 1950). Sophocles Venizelos was born in Canea, Crete, on November 17, 1894. He was the son of Eleutherio Venizelos, the founder of the Greek Liberal party. Venizelos was educated at the Athens Military Academy and served in the Greek army during World War I. He subsequently entered politics and was elected a deputy from Canea in 1920. He accompanied his father into exile in France in 1923, but was soon recalled to active military service. He was stationed at the Greek Legation in Paris as a military attaché until 1930. Venizelos returned to private life in the early 1930s, but again went into exile following the establishment of the dictatorship of Ioannis Metaxas in 1936. Venizelos's father also died in 1936, and the younger Venizelos became a member of the Liberal party's executive committee. He remained in exile in France and the United States until 1943, when he joined the Greek government-in-exile in Egypt. He served as minister of the navy until April of 1944, when he was appointed prime minister. He relinquished the position to Georgios Papandreou the following month. Venizelos served until the following September as vice president of the Council of Ministers. He served in various coalition governments in postwar Greece. During this period he sought to gain the leadership of his father's Liberal party. He quit the party to form the Venizelosist Liberal party in 1946, but returned as deputy leader under Themistocles Sophoulis. Venizelos succeeded to the leadership of the Liberal party following Sophoulis's death in June of 1949. He became prime minister on March 23, 1950. He stepped down on April 14, 1950, to serve as deputy prime minister in the government of Nikolas Plastiras. Venizelos was again named prime minister on August 21, 1950, and served until October 27, 1951. He remained in government again as Plastiras's deputy prime minister and foreign minister. As foreign minister he helped restore Greek-Yugoslav and Greek-Italian relations and negotiated Greece's membership in the North Atlantic Treaty Organization (NATO). He also served as acting prime minister while Plastiras suffered from poor health in 1952. Venizelos was elected to the Chamber of Deputies in 1953, but resigned his government and party positions the following year to retire from politics. His retirement was short-lived, however, as he reentered politics in 1955 to found the Democratic Liberal party. He remerged his party with the Liberals under Georgios Papandreou in 1957. Venizelos again served as foreign minister in the Papandreou cabinet from November until December of 1963. He died of a lung tumor at sea on February 6, 1964, while traveling from Crete.

NIKOLAS PLASTIRAS (Prime Minister, April 15, 1950–August 18, 1950). *See earlier entry under Heads of Government.*

SOPHOCLES VENIZELOS (Prime Minister, August 21, 1950–October 27, 1951). *See earlier entry under Heads of Government.*

NIKOLAS PLASTIRAS (Prime Minister, November 1, 1951–October 11, 1952). *See earlier entry under Heads of Government.*

DEMETRIOS KIOUSSOPOULOS (Prime Minister, October 11, 1952–November 19, 1952). Demetrios Kioussopoulos was born in Andritsaina in 1892. He was appointed prime minister by King Paul on October 11, 1952, to lead an interim government while awaiting new elections. He stepped down on November 19, 1952, following the victory of Alexandros Papagos's Greek Rally party.

ALEXANDROS PAPAGOS (Prime Minister, November 19, 1952–October 4, 1955). Alexandros Papagos was born in Athens on December 9, 1883. He was educated in military schools in Belgium and Greece. He fought in the Balkan War in 1912 and was promoted to major during World War I. Papagos participated in the unsuccessful Greek war against Turkey in the early 1920s and rose to the rank of lieutenant general. He was named deputy chief of staff of the Greek Army in 1932. In 1935 he was given command of the Third Army Corps and later was given command of the First Army Corps. He became chief of the Greek army general staff the following year under the dictatorship of General Ioannis Metaxas. Papagos commanded the Greek forces when his country was invaded by Italian and Albanian troops in the winter of 1940. The Greek army had some initial success, but the following year Greece was occupied by German troops. Papagos retired in April of 1941 and was arrested the following month by the occupation forces for his activities in the Resistance. He was interned in a concentration camp for the remainder of the war until his liberation by American troops in 1945. He subsequently served as military advisor to King George. He was placed in charge of Greek troops during the Communist insurrection in northern Greece in 1947. Papagos was successful in defeating the rebels and was promoted to field marshal in 1949. He resigned as chief of the Greek armed forces in May of 1951 following a dispute with King Paul. Papagos entered politics in September of 1951 as the leader of the newly formed Greek Rally party. Though his party won the most seats of any party in Parliament in the November elections, it did not receive an absolute majority. Papagos refused to form a coalition cabinet and went into opposition. New elections were held in November of 1952 and the Greek Rally party won the vast majority of seats in Parliament. Papagos became prime minister on November 19, 1952. His victory gave Greece its first stable government in the postwar period. Papagos initiated a policy of economic austerity to ease the country's growing economic difficulties. Papagos suffered from health problems and was confined to bed in January of 1955. He died suddenly at his home outside of Athens after suffering a lung hemorrhage and heart failure on October 4, 1955.

STEPHEN C. STEPHANOPOULOS (Prime Minister, October 4, 1955–October 6, 1955). Stephen C. Stephanopoulos was born in Pyrgos in 1898. He was educated in Athens and Paris and received a degree in law. He returned to Greece in 1930 and entered politics. Stephanopoulos joined the Populist party and was elected to Parliament. He served as minister of the national economy prior to the German occupation of Greece during World War II. He remained in Greece during the war and was active in the Resistance. Following the liberation in October of 1944, he was named minister of transport. Stephanopoulos served as minister of economic coordination in the Populist-led government from 1946. He left the government following the Liberal party victory in 1950. Later in the year Stephanopoulos broke with the Populists and led a conservative splinter party. He joined forces with Alexandros Papagos's Greek Rally party in 1951. When Papagos took office as prime minister the following year, Stephanopoulos was named foreign minister. He briefly succeeded to the office of prime minister on October 4, 1955, following Papagos's death. He relinquished the office to Konstantine Karamanlis two days later on October 6, 1955. Stephanopoulos helped form the Centre Union party with Georgios Papandreou in 1961. He served as deputy prime minister in the government of Papandreou, but broke with him to lead a coalition government as prime minister on November 17, 1965. Stephanopoulos formed the new Liberal Democratic Centre party the following month. His government was unstable and collapsed on December 22, 1966. He was politically inactive while the military junta ruled Greece from 1967 until 1974. Stephanopoulos formed the National Rally, a right-wing party, following Greece's return to democracy, but he failed to win reelection in 1977. He died of heart and respiratory problems in Athens on October 4, 1982.

KONSTANTINE KARAMANLIS (Prime Minister, October 6, 1955–March 3, 1958). *See entry under Heads of State.*

KONSTANTINE GEORGACAPOULOS (Prime Minister, March 3, 1958–May 17, 1958). Konstantine Georgacapoulos was born in Tripolis in 1890. He studied law in Athens and became a military judge in 1913. He was discharged from the army as a colonel in 1923 and went into private practice. Georgacapoulos became president of the Greek Red Cross in 1948 and was asked to form a caretaker government on March 3, 1958, following the collapse of Prime Minister Konstantine Karamanlis's government. Georgacapoulos's government was given the mandate to hold general elections. Karamanlis's party was successful in the elections, and he again became prime minister on May 17, 1958. Georgacapoulos subsequently returned to his duties as president of the Greek Red Cross. He died in Athens on July 25, 1973.

KONSTANTINE KARAMANLIS (Prime Minister, May 17, 1958–September 20, 1961). *See entry under Heads of State.*

KONSTANTINE DOVAS (Prime Minister, September 30, 1961–November 4, 1961). Konstantine Dovas was born in Konitsa on December 20, 1898.

He attended military school in Athens and Paris and served in the Greek army. He served with distinction in the Greek army's battles against Communist insurgents in the late 1940s. Dovas succeeded in defending his hometown from the rebels in 1947 and was seriously injured in the battle. He rose to the rank of lieutenant general in 1951 and served as coordinator between the Greek military and NATO until 1953. The following year he was named chief of the national defense general staff. He was discharged from the army in 1958 and was chosen to serve as chief of King Paul's military household in 1960. Dovas was briefly chosen as caretaker prime minister from September 30 until November 4 of 1961. He remained in the largely ceremonial position as head of the royal military household following the death of King Paul and the succession of his son Constantine. He accompanied King Constantine into exile in Rome following the military coup of 1967. He was allowed to return to Greece in 1968 and lived in seclusion in Athens, where he died after a long illness on July 24, 1973.

KONSTANTINE KARAMANLIS (Prime Minister, November 4, 1961–June 11, 1963). *See entry under Heads of State.*

PANAYIOTIS PIPINELIS (Prime Minister, June 19, 1963–September 26, 1963). Panayiotis Pipinelis was born in Piraeus on March 21, 1899. He was educated in Switzerland and received a degree in law. He entered the Greek diplomatic service in 1922 and served in various European capitals. At the time of the German invasion of Greece in 1941, he was serving as minister in Budapest. Pipinelis accompanied the Greek government-in-exile and was named ambassador to Moscow in 1941. He subsequently represented the Greek government as ambassador to the Polish and Belgian governments-in-exile in London in 1943. He was a staunch monarchist and served as an advisor to King George prior to the referendum that reestablished the monarchy. Pipinelis served as undersecretary for foreign affairs from 1947 until 1950, when he was named foreign minister in a caretaker cabinet. He was appointed Greece's permanent representative to NATO in 1952 and resigned from the diplomatic service the following year. He then entered politics and joined the National Radical Union party. He was twice defeated for a seat in Parliament before being named extra-parliamentary minister of trade in 1961. He was appointed prime minister on June 17, 1963, following the resignation of Konstantine Karamanlis in a dispute with King Paul. Pipinelis served until September 26, 1963, when King Paul gave in to Liberal party pressure to name a nonpolitical prime minister to organize new general elections. Pipinelis was subsequently elected to Parliament. He served as minister of economic coordination in the cabinet of Panayotis Kanellopoulos until the government was ousted by the military coup in April of 1967. Pipinelis accepted a cabinet position in the subsequent military government and served again as minister of economic coordination. He was named foreign minister a few months later, and also served as the Greek government's liaison with the exiled King Constantine. As a representative of the repressive junta's government in foreign capitals, he served as an apologist for the regime and was considered a traitor by many of his former colleagues. He remained foreign minister until he died of a heart attack in Athens on July 19, 1970.

STYLIANOS MAVROMIHALIS (Prime Minister, September 28, 1963– November 7, 1963). Stylianos Mavromihalis was born in 1900. He was educated in Greece, Germany, and Switzerland and received a degree in law. He became a judge in 1923. He was the leader of the small Progressive party

and was chosen as interim prime minister on September 28, 1963. He remained in office until November 7, 1963. Mavromihalis subsequently became president of the Greek Supreme Court and served until 1968.

GEORGIOS PAPANDREOU (Prime Minister, November 7, 1963–December 24, 1963). *See earlier entry under Heads of Government.*

IOANNIS PARASKEVOPOULOS (Prime Minister, December 30, 1963– February 19, 1964). Ioannis Paraskevopoulos was born in Olympia on December 25, 1900. He was educated in Greece and Germany and subsequently worked as a banker in Germany and Great Britain. He returned to Greece in 1930 and worked with the National Bank of Greece. Paraskevopoulos held various cabinet positions, including minister of supply and minister of national economy. He was chosen on December 30, 1963, to serve as caretaker prime minister following the resignation of Georgios Papandreou. He retained office until February 19, 1964, when Papandreou, after winning a majority in the election, reclaimed the prime ministership. Paraskevopoulos again formed a government on December 22, 1966, but he was forced to resign when the National Radical Union party withdrew its support from his caretaker government on March 30, 1967.

GEORGIOS PAPANDREOU (Prime Minister, February 19, 1964–July 15, 1965). *See earlier entry under Heads of Government.*

GEORGE ATHANASIADIS-NOVAS (Prime Minister, July 15, 1965–August 5, 1965). George Athanasiadis-Novas was born in Nafpatkos on February 9, 1893. He was educated at Athens University, where he received a degree in law. He worked as a lawyer and journalist and published his first collection of poems under the name George Athanas in 1920. Athanasiadis-Novas was elected to Parliament in 1926 and retained his seat and joined the Progressive party in 1928. He was reelected in 1932 and 1936. He lived in Italy during the dictatorship of Ioannis Metaxas. Athanasiadis-Novas returned to Greece and lived on his family estate during the German occupation. His home was destroyed by Communist insurgents following World War II, and Athanasiadis-Novas, suffering from shock, returned to Italy in 1945. He returned to Greece in 1949 and joined the Liberal party. He was reelected to Parliament the following year and was named minister of education, a post he held until 1951. Athanasiadis-Novas served in several other cabinets in the 1950s. His party merged with the Centre Union party in 1961, and he was selected as president of the Chamber of Deputies when Georgios Papandreou became prime minister in 1964. He was selected as interim prime minister on July 15, 1965, following King Constantine's clash with Papandreou. Athanasiadis-Novas's government was initially faced with the problem of protests and rioting by supporters of the deposed prime minister, Papandreou. He was able to restore order, but failed to receive a vote of confidence from the Parliament. He resigned his position on August 5, 1965. He was named deputy prime minister the following month and served until 1966. Athanasiadis-Novas retired from politics following the military takeover in 1967. He lived in retirement until his death in Athens at the age of 94 on August 10, 1987.

ELIAS TSIRIMOKOS (Prime Minister, August 19, 1965–August 29, 1965). Elias Tsirimokos was born in Lamia on August 2, 1907. He received a degree in law from Athens University in 1926. He continued his studies in Paris before returning to Athens to practice criminal law in 1931. Tsirimokos was elected

to Parliament as a Liberal deputy in 1936, shortly before that body was suspended by the dictatorship of Ioannis Metaxas. Tsirimokos was a leading figure in the Resistance during the German occupation. He served as secretary of justice in the Political Committee of National Liberation, a Communist-dominated Resistance organization, shortly before the country's liberation by the Allies. He served as minister of national economy in the government of Georgios Papandreou in May of 1944. Tsirimokos resigned from the cabinet shortly thereafter and founded the Union of Popular Democracy party. He was elected to Parliament in 1950, but was defeated in 1951, 1952, and 1956. He returned to Parliament in 1958 and disassociated himself with the extreme left-wing soon after. He was elected president of Parliament in 1963, but his reelection was prevented the following year by Papandreou. Tsirimokos led a brief revolt in Papandreou's Centre Union party, but the two men soon settled their dispute. Tsirimokos was appointed minister of the interior in the subsequent cabinet. Breaking with the Centre Union party, Tsirimokos was selected by King Constantine to form a cabinet on August 19, 1965. As prime minister he helped to put down the pro-Papandreou rioting that resulted from Papandreou's ouster. Tsirimokos's government was defeated in a vote of confidence on August 29, 1965. He was replaced by Stephanos Stephanopoulos and served as deputy prime minister in the government. He resigned from the cabinet in April of 1966 over his support for Archbishop Makarios, the president of Cyprus. He returned to Parliament, where he remained until his death at the age of 60 in Athens on July 13, 1968.

STEPHANOS STEPHANOPOULOS (Prime Minister, November 17, 1965–December 22, 1966). *See earlier entry under Heads of Government.*

IOANNIS PARASKEVOPOULOS (Prime Minister, December 22, 1966–March 30, 1967). *See earlier entry under Heads of Government.*

PANAYOTIS KANELLOPOULOS (Prime Minister, April 3, 1967–April 21, 1967). *See earlier entry under Heads of Government.*

CONSTANTINE KOLLIAS (Prime Minister, April 21, 1967–December 13, 1967). Constantine V. Kollias was born in Stylia in 1901. He was educated at Athens University, where he received a degree in law. He served as a prosecutor on the Greek Court of Appeals from 1945 until 1946. Kollias was vice-prosecutor on the Supreme Court from 1946 and Supreme Court prosecutor from 1962. He was named prime minister on April 21, 1967, following the military coup that ousted the civilian government. He was replaced by George Papadopoulos, the junta leader, on December 13, 1967.

GEORGE PAPADOPOULOS (Prime Minister, December 13, 1967–October 1, 1973). *See entry under Heads of State.*

SPYRIDON MARKEZINIS (Prime Minister, October 1, 1973–November 25, 1973). Spyridon Markezinis was born in Athens in 1909. He was educated at the University of Athens and served as legal advisor to King George II from 1936. He was active in the Greek Resistance during World War II and was elected to the Parliament in 1946. Markezinis served in the cabinet from 1949 until 1954. He founded the Progressive party in 1955. He was a leading Greek historian, having written the eight-volume *Political History of Modern Greece.* Markezinis was selected by President George Papadopoulos to serve as prime minister in a demilitarized government on October 1, 1973. Markezinis initiated moves to end price controls and

revalue the drachma. The government was beset by student and labor unrest that resulted in the ouster of President Papadopoulos on November 25, 1973. Markezinis was replaced as prime minister by Adamantios Androutsopoulos, but he remained active in politics and reformed the Progressive party in 1977. He also wrote the four-volume *Political History of Greece in the Last Fifty Years.*

ADAMANTIOS ANDROUTSOPOULOS (Prime Minister, November 25, 1973–July 24, 1974). Adamantios Androutsopoulos was born in Psari in 1919. He was educated in Greece and the United States and received a degree in law. He taught in the United States before his return to Greece to become minister of finance in 1967. Androutsopoulos became minister of the interior in 1971 and was selected as prime minister on November 25, 1973. He was replaced by Konstantine Karamanlis on July 24, 1974.

KONSTANTINE KARAMANLIS (Prime Minister, July 24, 1974–May 9, 1980). *See entry under Heads of State.*

GEORGE J. RALLIS (Prime Minister, May 9, 1980–October 21, 1981). George J. Rallis was born in Athens on December 26, 1918. His father had served as prime minister in a Nazi-backed government of Greece under the German occupation during World War II. He was educated at Athens University and served in the Greek army from 1940 until 1941. Rallis also served in the Greek Tank Corps from 1945 until 1948. He was elected to the House of Deputies in 1950 and served as minister of public works and communications from 1956 until 1958. He resigned from the government over a disagreement concerning reform of electoral law. Rallis returned to the House of Deputies in 1961 and was named minister of the interior until

1963. He was serving as minister of public order at the time of the military coup in April of 1967. He was arrested and placed under house arrest until the following month. Rallis was again arrested in May of 1968 and was sent into exile until September of 1968. He was again elected to the House of Deputies as a member of the New Democratic party following the restoration of democracy in 1974. He was named minister of education until 1977 and served as minister of coordination and planning from 1977 until 1978. Rallis was subsequently named minister of foreign affairs and served until 1980. When Prime Minister Konstantine Karamanlis was elected president, Rallis was chosen to succeed him as prime minister on May 9, 1980. The New Democratic party was defeated by Andreas Papandreou's Panhellenic Socialist Movement in October of 1981, and Rallis left office on October 21, 1981. He was replaced by the rightist former defense minister Evangelos Averoff as party leader two months later. Rallis remained active in the New Democratic party until 1987.

ANDREAS PAPANDREOU (Prime Minister, October 21, 1981–July 2, 1989). Andreas George Papandreou was born on the island of Chios on February 5, 1919. He was the son of former prime minister Georgios Papandreou. He attended the University of Athens law school and became a Trotskyist critic of the dictatorship of Ioannis Metaxas. Papandreou was arrested in 1939 and was tortured into giving a confession. He went to the United States the following year. He attended Columbia University and Harvard, where he received his doctorate in 1943. Papandreou became a United States citizen the following year and served two years in the United States navy. He subsequently taught economics at various universities, including Harvard, the University of Minnesota, and the University of California at Berkeley.

He returned to Greece in 1959 and, at the behest of his father, remained to become the director of the Center of Economic Research. Papandreou renounced his American citizenship in January of 1964 and was elected to Parliament as a member of his father's Centre Union party. The party was victorious in the election, and Georgios Papandreou became prime minister. Andreas was appointed his father's chief advisor in the post of minister to the prime minister. He was a vocal critic of the king and the military and was forced to resign his positions in November of 1964 after allegations of corruption. He was reinstated the following spring, but his father was dismissed in July of 1965. Andreas Papandreou was considered a dangerous leftist by the parties of the right. In April of 1967, shortly before national elections were to be held, the Greek military staged a coup and took over the government. Both Papandreous were arrested, and Andreas was charged with high treason. He was kept in solitary confinement for eight months before his release in an amnesty in December of 1967. The following month he went into exile, where he became a vocal critic of the junta. He founded the anti-junta Panhellenic Liberation Movement in 1968, the year of his father's death. During his period of exile, he also taught at the University of Stockholm and York University in Toronto. He also wrote several books on Greek politics and economics. Papandreou returned to Greece in August of 1974 following the ouster of the military government. He refused the leadership of his father's Centre Union party and founded the Panhellenic Socialist Movement. The party was unsuccessful in subsequent parliamentary elections, but Papandreou spent the following years attacking the government of Konstantine Karamanlis. His party made gains in the elections of 1977. Karamanlis stepped down as prime minister to become president in 1980 and was succeeded by George Rallis. Papandreou's party was victorious over Rallis's New Democratic party in 1981. Papandreou became prime minister on October 21, 1981, and instituted a series of Socialist reforms. His party remained in power following parliamentary elections in June of 1985. His government's popularity plummeted in 1988 and Papandreou was accused of corruption and misuse of power. His party was defeated in elections in June of 1989 and he stepped down as prime minister on July 2, 1989. Papandreou was indicted in September of 1989 after his parliamentary immunity was lifted, but he was acquitted of corruption charges in January of 1992.

TZANNIS TZANNETAKIS (Prime Minister, July 2, 1989–October 11, 1989). Tzannis Tzannetakis was born in 1927. He served in the Greek navy as a submarine commander. He was an opponent of the military junta that ruled Greece from 1967 until 1974 and was jailed and exiled during that period. Tzannetakis was a member of the conservative New Democracy party and was chosen on July 2, 1989, to form a government. He was able to put together a coalition between the conservatives and the Communists. He also served as foreign minister in the government. His government's primary purpose was to bring corruption charges against the previous government of Prime Minister Andreas Papandreou. Tzannetakis resigned from office on October 11, 1989. He was subsequently named minister of national defense on November 23, 1989.

YIANNIS GRIVAS (Prime Minister, October 11, 1989–November 23, 1989). Yiannis Grivas was born in 1923. He served as president of the Greek Supreme Court. On October 11, 1989, he was chosen to serve as caretaker prime minister. He retained the position until elections could be

held and stepped down on November 23, 1989.

XENOPHON ZOLOTAS (Prime Minister, November 23, 1989–April 10, 1990). Xenophon Zolotas was born in Athens on March 26, 1904. He attended the University of Athens, the University of Leipzig, and the University of Paris. He returned to Greece to teach economics at the University of Athens in 1931 and remained on the faculty until 1968. In 1952 Zolotas served as vice-chairman of the Economic Commission for Europe. He was named governor of the Bank of Greece in 1955 and remained in that position until the military coup in 1967. He served as minister of finance in the government of Konstantine Karamanalis from July to November of 1974. He then returned to the position of governor of the Bank of Greece, where he remained until 1981. On November 28, 1989, Zolotas was asked to form a coalition government as prime minister to deal with Greece's economic crisis. He was unable to insure the support of his cabinet for the harsh austerity measures called for, however, and he left office on April 10, 1990, when the coalition fell apart.

CONSTANTINE MITSOTAKIS (Prime Minister, April 11, 1990–   ). Constantine Mitsotakis was born in Chania, Crete, in 1918. He was educated at the University of Athens and joined the army in 1940. He fought against the Nazi occupation in Crete during World War II. Mitsotakis was arrested on several occasions by the Nazis and survived a death sentence. Following the war, he was elected to Parliament in 1946. He was named acting minister for communications and public works in 1951 and became minister of finance in 1963. Mitsotakis was arrested by the military junta in 1967 and was subsequently placed under house arrest. He escaped and went into exile. Following the restoration of democratic rule in 1974, he returned to Greece. He joined the New Democracy party in 1978 and was named minister for economic coordination in 1978. Mitsotakis became foreign minister in 1980 and served until 1981. He became leader of the New

Democracy party following the resignation of Evangelos Averoff in September of 1984. He was elected prime minister of Greece by a narrow margin on April 11, 1990.

Grenada, State of

Grenada is an island nation in the southeastern Caribbean Sea. It was granted independence from Great Britain on February 7, 1974.

HEADS OF STATE

LEO V. DE GALE (Governor-General, February 7, 1974–December 1978). Leo Victor de Gale was born in St. Andrews on December 28, 1921. He was educated in Grenada and Canada and worked as a teacher. He served as a member of the Public Service Commission from 1960. De Gale was named acting governor of Grenada on January 24, 1974. He became governor-general of Grenada following independence on February 7, 1974. He retired from office in December of 1978. De Gale died on March 23, 1986.

SIR PAUL SCOON (Governor-General, December 1978–June 8, 1992). Paul Scoon was born on July 4, 1935. He was educated in Canada and subsequently taught school in Grenada. He served in the civil service and held several government positions before being named governor-general of

Grenada in December of 1978. Scoon requested the intervention of the United States following the ouster and execution of Prime Minister Maurice Bishop in October of 1983. The United States deposed the revolutionary government on October 25, 1993, and Scoon retained executive power. He appointed an advisory council in November of 1983 and delegated power to the council under Nicholas Brathwaite on December 9, 1983. Scoon remained governor-general until his retirement on June 8, 1992

REGINALD PALMER (Governor-General, June 8, 1992–). Reginald Oswald Palmer was the senior civil servant in the Grenadan government. He was appointed to succeed Sir Paul Scoon as governor-general of Grenada on June 8, 1992.

HEADS OF GOVERNMENT

ERIC GAIRY (Prime Minister, February 7, 1974–March 13, 1979). Eric Matthew Gairy was born in St. Andrews on February 18, 1922. He was educated locally and was employed as a teacher in the late 1930s. He later worked in

Aruba for a Dutch oil refinery. Gairy became active in the trade union movement and worked as a union organizer following his return to Grenada in 1951. He organized the United Labor party and was elected to the Grenadan

Legislative Council in 1951. He was briefly exiled by the British colonial government in 1951 after organizing a general strike. Gairy was named to the cabinet as minister of trade and production in 1956 and replaced Herbert Blaize as chief minister and minister of finance in the government in 1961. He was removed from office by the British colonial government in 1962 on charges of malfeasance. Gairy was restored to office as prime minister in 1967 when Grenada became a member of the West Indies Associated States. Gairy was a corrupt and flamboyant leader who used a parapolice squad of thugs known as the Mongoose Gang to intimidate opponents of his regime. Gairy remained prime minister when Grenada was granted independence on February 7, 1974, despite a general strike against his government. He reportedly was a practitioner of voodoo-like rituals and had an interest in unidentified flying objects. He proposed on several occasions that the United Nations begin a study of UFOs, which he believed were extraterrestrial visitors. Gairy's party maintained a majority in parliamentary elections in December of 1976. The opposition claimed that widespread fraud and corruption tainted the elections. Gairy was ousted from office by the leftist New Jewel Movement while he was on a visit to the United States on March 13, 1979. He remained in exile until the revolutionary government was ousted by the United States military in October of 1983. Gairy returned to Grenada to lead the Grenada United Labour party. The party was defeated by the National Democratic Congress in parliamentary elections in 1984. Gairy was defeated for a legislative seat in elections in March of 1990 and faced the defection of many members of his party.

MAURICE BISHOP (Prime Minister, March 13, 1979–October 13, 1983). Maurice Bishop was born to a wealthy family in Grenada on May 29, 1944. He was educated locally and at London University, where he received a degree in law in 1969. He returned to Grenada to establish a legal practice with Bernard Coard in 1970. Bishop was an opponent of the government of Eric Gairy and founded the New Jewel Movement in opposition to Gairy in 1972. Bishop was badly beaten by Gairy's parapolice force in 1973, and his father, Rupert Bishop, was murdered by the police during an antigovernment demonstration several months later. Bishop organized labor strikes against the Gairy government prior to Grenadan independence in February of 1974. He was elected to Parliament in 1976 and led a coup to oust Gairy on March 13, 1979. Bishop served as chairman of the ruling Revolutionary Council. He established a Marxist government and depended on economic aid from the Soviet Union and Cuba. Relations between Grenada and the United States deteriorated during his rule. Bishop attempted to thaw relations with the United States in the spring of 1983. His more moderate positions led to a left-wing coup on October 13, 1983, which was led by his deputy prime minister, Bernard Coard. Bishop was placed under house arrest, but was freed by a crowd of supporters six days later. Bishop and his supporters marched to the army headquarters at Fort Rupert and engaged in a brief battle with government troops. The crowd was dispersed, and Bishop and several members of his ousted government were summarily executed on October 19, 1983.

BERNARD COARD (Prime Minister, October 13, 1983–October 19, 1983). Bernard Coard was born in 1944. He was educated as a lawyer and opened a law practice in Georgetown with Maurice Bishop in 1970. He was an opponent of Eric Gairy's government and worked with Bishop in the New Jewel Movement from 1972. Coard became deputy prime minister under Bishop following the ouster of Gairy in March of 1979. Coard broke with Bishop in 1983 over the government's attempts to establish more moderate policies. Coard denounced Bishop's hesitancy to implement Socialist policies and supported his ouster on October 13, 1983. Coard served as head of the government until a ruling Revolutionary Military Council was established on October 19, 1983. He was arrested following the ouster of the revolutionary government by United States troops on October 25, 1983. He was imprisoned and tried for conspiracy to murder Bishop. Coard was convicted and sentenced to death in July of 1991. His sentence was commuted to life imprisonment the following month.

HUDSON AUSTIN (Head of Government, October 19, 1983–October 25, 1983). Hudson Austin served in the Grenadan army. He rose to the rank of general and commanded the People's Revolutionary Army during the administration of Maurice Bishop. Austin supported the coup that ousted Bishop in October of 1983 and seized power as head of the Revolutionary Military Council following Bishop's execution on October 19, 1983. The United States invaded Grenada at the request of Governor-General Sir Paul Scoon on October 25, 1983. Austin was arrested following the ouster of his revolutionary government by the United States troops. He was imprisoned and tried for conspiracy to murder Bishop. He was convicted and sentenced to death in July of 1991. Austin's sentence was commuted to life imprisonment the following month.

NICHOLAS BRATHWAITE (Head of Government, December 9, 1983–December 4, 1984). Nicholas A. Brathwaite was an educator and civil servant in the Commonwealth government. He was living abroad when he was requested by Governor-General Paul Scoon to return to Grenada to serve as chairman of the advisory council in November of 1983. The council became the provisional governing body of Grenada on December 9, 1983, following the withdrawal of United States troops. He relinquished his position following the selection of a new Parliament on December 4, 1984. Brathwaite remained involved in political affairs and joined the National Democratic Congress party. He was elected leader of the party in January of 1989. The party was victorious in the subsequent parliamentary elections, and Brathwaite became prime minister of Grenada on March 16, 1990. In August of 1991 Brathwaite commuted the death sentences of Bernard Coard, Hudson Austin, and twelve others convicted of complicity in the 1988 murder of Maurice Bishop to life imprisonment.

HERBERT A. BLAIZE (Prime Minister, December 4, 1984–December 19, 1989). Herbert Augustus Blaize was born in Carriacou on February 26, 1918. He was educated locally and worked for the Department of the Treasury from 1937. He left Grenada to work as an oil refinery clerk in 1944. Blaize returned to Grenada in 1952 and formed the Grenada National party the following year. He was elected to Parliament in 1957 and served in the government as minister of trade and production. Blaize became chief minister of Grenada in 1960, but his party was defeated by Eric Gairy's United Labour party the following year. He returned to office when Gairy was removed from power on charges of corruption in 1962. Blaize remained chief minister until Gairy regained power in 1967. Blaize remained an opponent of the government until Gairy was ousted by a coup led by Maurice Bishop in 1979. Blaize subsequently retired from politics during the revolutionary regime. He came out of retirement following the invasion of Grenada by the United States and the subsequent ouster of the revolutionary government in October of 1983. Blaize formed the New National party to participate in elections when democracy was restored in 1984. His party was victorious, and he became prime minister of a coalition centrist government on December 4, 1984. Blaize suffered from poor health, including prostate cancer and degenerative arthritis, and was confined to a wheelchair during his term of office. He died at his home in St. Georges after a long illness at the age of 71 on December 19, 1989.

BEN JONES (Prime Minister, December 20, 1989–March 16, 1990). Ben Joseph Jones was born in St. Andrews on August 5, 1924. He was educated locally and at the University of London, where he received a degree in law in 1962. He returned to Grenada to open a legal practice in 1964. Jones served as a magistrate from 1965 until 1966. He was elected to the Grenadan Senate as a member of the opposition to the government of Eric Gairy. He retired from politics following the ouster of Gairy in 1979 and remained

out of politics until the subsequent revolutionary government was forced from office in 1983. Jones was reelected to the National Assembly as a member of the New National party. He served in the government of Prime Minister Herbert Blaize as minister of external affairs and legal affairs. He was also deputy prime minister and held other cabinet positions in the Blaize government. Jones was selected as prime minister on December 20, 1989, following Blaize's death. He called for new parliamentary elections, and the New National party lost support in the Parliament. Jones supported the selection of Nicholas Brathwaite as prime minister on March 16, 1990. He returned to the cabinet as minister of foreign affairs and served until January 5, 1991, when he resigned when the New National party returned to the Opposition over a budgetary disagreement.

NICHOLAS BRATHWAITE (Prime Minister, March 16, 1990–). *See earlier entry under Heads of Government.*

Guatemala, Republic of

(República de Guatemala)

Guatemala is a country in the northern part of Central America. It was granted independence from Spain on September 15, 1821.

HEADS OF STATE

JACOBO ARBENZ GUZMÁN (President, October 20, 1944–March 15, 1945). Jacobo Arbenz Guzmán was born in Quetzaltenango on September 14, 1913. He was educated at the military academy in Guatemala City and served in the Guatemalan army. He was involved in the military uprising that forced the ouster of President Jorge Ubico Castenada in July of 1944.

Arbenz went into exile in El Salvador in opposition to the subsequent government of General Federico Ponce. Arbenz led another coup against Ponce's government on October 20, 1944, and served as leader of the junta until March 15, 1945, when Juan José Arévalo was inaugurated as president. Arbenz served as minister of defense in the Arévalo government and succeeded in putting down numerous attempts to oust the government. His leading rival in the government, Colonel Francisco Javier Araña, was assassinated in July of 1949. Arbenz resigned from the government in June of 1950 to become a candidate for the presidency. He was elected in November of 1950 and took office on March 1, 1951. Arbenz continued the land reform measures of his predecessor. He also established relations with Communist nations and expropriated United States–owned businesses, including the United Fruit Company. His actions drew the criticism of the United States and rightists in the military, who accused his government of being controlled by the Communists. Arbenz survived a coup attempt in 1953 and instituted repressive measures against his opponents. He was ousted following an invasion and right-wing military coup supported by the United States Central Intelligence Agency on June 27, 1954. Arbenz went into exile in France. He subsequently lived in Switzerland, Czechoslovakia, and Cuba before settling in Mexico City. Arbenz was found dead in the bathroom of his home on January 27, 1971. He supposedly slipped and fell into the tub, drowning in the scalding water.

JUAN JOSÉ ARÉVALO (President, March 15, 1945–March 1, 1951). Juan José Arévalo Barmejo was born in Taxisco on September 10, 1904. He was educated at the University of La Plata in Argentina, where he received a doctorate in education in 1934. He returned to Guatemala and worked in the Education Ministry briefly before returning to Argentina, where he served on the faculty of the University of Tucuman. He again returned to Guatemala following the ouster of President Jorge Ubico Castenada in 1944. Arévalo was the presidential candidate of the revolutionaries and was the overwhelming victor in the subsequent election. He took office on March 15, 1945.

He lifted restrictions on the press and the labor unions and initiated a program of agrarian reform. Arévalo also launched a social security program and began reforms in education, health, and sanitation facilities. He survived numerous attempts to oust his government. Arévalo's likely successor, Colonel Francisco Javier Araña, was assassinated in July of 1949. Arévalo completed his term of office on March 1, 1951. He served as ambassador-at-large in the government of his successor, Jacobo Arbenz Guzmán. Arbenz was ousted by a right-wing military coup in 1954, and Arévalo went into exile in Argentina. In 1961 he wrote a book critical of United States policy in Latin America entitled *The Shark and the Sardines*. Arévalo returned to Guatemala to run for the presidency in 1963, but Colonel Enrique Peralta Azurdia staged a coup to prevent the election. Arévalo again returned to Guatemala following the restoration of a civilian government in 1986. He died in Guatemala City at the age of 86 on October 6, 1990.

JACOBO ARBENZ GUZMÁN (President, March 1, 1951–June 27, 1954). *See earlier entry under Heads of State.*

CARLOS ENRIQUE DÍAZ (President, June 27, 1954–June 29, 1954). Carlos Enrique Díaz served in the Guatemalan army, where he rose to the rank of colonel. He served as the chief of the armed services in the government of Jacobo Arbenz Guzmán. Díaz became head of state when Arbenz resigned in the wake of a right-wing revolt against the government on June 27, 1954. The rebels refused to accept Díaz's government and continued the revolt. Díaz was ousted at gunpoint by Colonel Elfego Monzón on June 29, 1954.

ELFEGO J. MONZÓN (President, June 29, 1954–July 8, 1954). Elfego J. Monzón served in the Guatemalan army, where he rose to the rank of colonel. He became head of a three-man junta following the ouster of President Jacobo Arbenz Guzmán and his successor, Colonel Carlos Enrique Díaz, on June 29, 1954. Monzón met with rebel leader Carlos Castillo Armas in July of 1954 and negotiated a settlement that included Castillo Armas as a member of a five-man ruling junta. Monzón was replaced as leader of the junta on July 8, 1954. He remained in the junta until giving his resignation on September 1, 1954. He remained in the Castillo Armas government.

CARLOS CASTILLO ARMAS (President, July 8, 1954–July 26, 1957). Carlos Castillo Armas was born in Santa Lucia Cotzumalguapa on November 4, 1914. He graduated from the military academy in Guatemala City in 1936. He participated in the revolt that ousted President Jorge Ubico in July of 1944 and supported the ouster of Ubico's successor, General Federico Ponce, in October of 1944. Castillo Armas was a supporter of Colonel Francisco Araña, the armed forces chief of staff who was assassinated in July of 1949. Castillo Armas led a revolt against the government shortly before the election of Jacobo Arbenz Guzmán as president in November of 1950. The revolt was unsuccessful, and Castillo Armas was wounded and arrested. He escaped to the Colombian Embassy in the summer of 1951 and was allowed to leave the country. He went into exile in Honduras, where he remained an opponent of the Arbenz regime. In June of 1954 he led an invasion of Guatemala that was supported by the United States Central Intelligence Agency. Arbenz was forced to resign, and Castillo continued the revolt against his successor, Colonel Carlos Enrique Díaz. Díaz was ousted by a military junta led by Colonel Elfego Monzón, and Castillo Armas agreed to join the junta on July 2, 1954. He replaced Monzón as provisional president on July 8, 1954. The remaining junta members resigned on September 1, 1954, and Castillo Armas was formally installed as president. He was a vehement anti-Communist and purged the government and unions of those suspected of leftist sympathies. He also redesigned the agrarian reform programs of his predecessor and returned much of the land to the original owners. The government promoted a new constitution in 1956, and Castillo Armas was installed as president for a four-year term. Castillo Armas was shot to death by a leftist sympathizer in the presidential palace in Guatemala City on July 26, 1957.

LUIS A. GONZÁLEZ LÓPEZ (President, July 26, 1957–October 24, 1957). Luis Arthur González López was born in Zacapa on December 12, 1900. He worked as a lawyer and was named to the Supreme Court in 1945. He was a critic of the regime of Jacobo Arbenz Guzmán and was dismissed from the court in 1952 when he rendered a verdict that displeased the Communists. González was named counselor to the president following Carlos Castillo Armas's seizure of power in 1954. He was also appointed to the Council of State in 1954 and served as acting president for several weeks in 1956 while Castillo Armas was on a state visit in the United States. González became president of the National Constituent Assembly later in 1956 and drafted a new Guatemalan constitution. He became the first president of the National Congress under the new constitution. González succeeded to the presidency following Castillo Armas's assassination on July 26, 1957. His government held elections in October of 1957, and riots and strikes resulted after allegations of electoral fraud. González was ousted by a military coup on October 24, 1957. He died of cancer at the age of 65 in Guatemala City on November 11, 1965.

GUILLERMO FLORES AVENDAÑO (President, October 26, 1957–March 2,

1958). Guillermo Flores Avendaño was born in 1898. He served in the Guatemalan military, where he rose to the rank of colonel. He retired from the military and served as second vice president in the government of Carlos Castillo Armas. Luis González López became acting president following the assassination of Castillo Armas in July of 1957, and his party was successful in the elections of October of 1957. Following allegations that there had been fraud in the election, a military coup ousted González on October 24, 1957. Flores Avendaño was named leader of the junta two days later. The junta supported claims by Miguel Ydígoras Fuentes that a new presidential election should be held. Ydígoras was victorious in the election in January of 1958, and Flores Avendaño's junta stepped down on March 2, 1958.

MIGUEL YDÍGORAS FUENTES (President, March 2, 1958–March 31, 1963). Miguel Ydígoras Fuentes was born in Pueblo Nuevo, Ratalhuleu, on October 17, 1895. He attended the military academy in Guatemala City and was commissioned into the infantry in 1915. He served as military attaché at the Guatemalan Embassy in Washington, D.C., in 1918. Ydígoras was subsequently posted at the embassy in Paris before returning to Guatemala in 1919. He represented Guatemala at the Versailles Peace Conference following World War I. He served on the staff of the military academy until 1920 and then served as governor of several provinces. Ydígoras became governor of San Marcos in 1922 and was promoted to general in 1937. He remained in San Marcos until 1939, when he was named director of roads in the government of Jorge Ubico Castenada. He remained in the government until Ubico's ouster in 1944. Ydígoras was then sent into diplomatic exile and served in various diplomatic positions in the government of Juan José Arévalo. He returned to Guatemala in 1950 to campaign for

the presidency. He was defeated by Jacobo Arbenz Guzmán and went into exile in El Salvador. Ydígoras led a Guatemalan exile group in opposition to Arbenz's government and supported Carlos Castillo Armas's rebellion in June of 1954. Ydígoras was named ambassador to Colombia after Castillo Armas seized power. He returned to Guatemala in August of 1957 following the assassination of Castillo Armas. He was again a candidate for the presidency in October of 1957. Ydígoras was narrowly defeated by Miguel Ortiz Passarelli, the government-supported candidate. Ydígoras's supporters claimed fraud, and the election was voided following strikes and demonstrations. A military junta took control of the country, and new elections were held in January of 1958. Ydígoras was the victor and took office on March 2, 1958. He was a strong supporter of the United States and allowed the Central Intelligence Agency to train Cuban rebels in Guatemala in preparation for the abortive Bay of Pigs invasion of Cuba in 1961. Ydígoras survived a coup attempt by the air force in 1962. He was ousted in a military coup led by his defense minister, General Enrique Peralta Azurdia, on April 1, 1963. Ydígoras died of a cerebral hemorrhage in a military hospital in Guatemala City at the age of 86 on October 6, 1982.

ENRIQUE PERALTA AZURDIA (President, April 1, 1963–July 1, 1966). Enrique Peralta Azurdia was born in Guatemala la Nuevo on June 17, 1908. He entered the Guatemalan army in 1926 and rose to the rank of colonel. He held various administrative positions and also served as Guatemala's ambassador to Cuba, El Salvador, and Costa Rica during the 1940s and 1950s. Azurdia served in the government of Miguel Ydígoras Fuentes as minister of agriculture from 1959 until 1960. He was appointed minister of defense in 1961. He led a military coup to oust Ydígoras on April 1, 1963, to prevent former president Juan José Arévalo from returning to power. Peralta presided over democratic elections in 1966. His military government relinquished power to the victor, Julio Méndez Montenegro, on July 1, 1966. Peralta Azurdia was the presidential candidate of the right-wing National Liberation Movement in 1978. He was narrowly defeated by Maj. Gen. Fernando Romeo Lucas García.

JULIO CÉSAR MÉNDEZ MONTE-NEGRO (President, July 1, 1966–July 1, 1970). Julio César Méndez Montenegro was born in Guatemala la Nuevo on November 23, 1915. He was educated in Guatemala and received a degree in law. He served on the faculty of the University of San Carlos from 1950 and became director of the law school. Méndez Montenegro was the candidate of the Revolutionary party following the reestablishment of democratic institutions in Guatemala in 1966. He was elected and took office on July 1, 1966. His government faced the threat of leftist guerrillas and right-wing militarists. He completed his term of office on July 1, 1970, and relinquished the presidency to Carlos Araña Osorio. Méndez Montenegro subsequently served as Guatemala's ambassador to Mexico.

CARLOS ARAÑA OSORIO (President, July 1, 1970–July 1, 1974). Carlos Manuel Araña Osorio was born in Barbarena, Santa Rosa, on July 17, 1918. He attended the military academy in Guatemala City. He served in the Guatemalan army, where he rose to the rank of colonel. In 1966 he was appointed military governor of Zacapa and launched a bloody campaign against the leftist guerrillas in the province. Araña was relieved of duty and sent to Nicaragua as Guatemala's ambassador in 1968. He returned to Guatemala in 1970 to accept the presidential nomination of the rightist National Liberation Movement. He was elected and took

office on July 1, 1970. Araña declared a state of siege to combat guerrilla activity in Guatemala. He initiated stringent censorship and curfew requirements, and right-wing death squads murdered many leftist-sympathizers and leaders of the democratic opposition. Araña completed his term of office on July 1, 1974, and handed over the government to his hand-picked successor, Kjell Eugenio Laugerud García.

KJELL E. LAUGERUD GARCÍA (President, July 1, 1974–July 1, 1978). Kjell Eugenio Laugerud García was born in Guatemala City on January 24, 1930. He graduated from the military academy in 1949 and served as superintendent of the military academy from 1965. In the late 1960s he served as military attaché in the Guatemalan Embassy in Washington, D.C. He rose to the rank of general and was appointed minister of defense in the government of Carlos Araña Osorio in 1970. Laugerud García resigned from the government in 1973 to become the presidential candidate of the National Liberation Movement. He finished second in the balloting to Efraín Ríos Montt, but was selected as president by the government-controlled Electoral Commission. He succeeded Araña Osorio as president on July 1, 1974. Laugerud García's government was more moderate than expected and lost support of some of his rightist backers. Guatemala was devastated by a major earthquake in February of 1976. Despite these difficulties and continued violence by leftist guerrillas, Guatemala experienced a period of economic growth under Laugerud García. He completed his term of office on July 1, 1978.

FERNANDO ROMEO LUCAS GAR-CÍA (President, July 1, 1978–March 23, 1982). Fernando Romeo Lucas García was born in Chamelco on July 4, 1924. He entered the military in 1947 and graduated from the Polytechnic Institute in 1949. He served in the Guatemalan

Congress from 1958 until 1963. Lucas
García remained in the military and
rose to the rank of brigadier general in
1973. He served as minister of defense
in the government of Kjell Laugerud
García from 1975 until 1976. He resigned
from the government to campaign for
the presidency in 1978. Lucas García
narrowly defeated Colonel Enrique
Peralta Azurdia. Political violence
continued in Guatemala, and several
high-ranking figures, including former
foreign minister Alberto Fuentes
Mohr, former Guatemala City mayor
Manuel Colom Argueta, and army
chief of staff General David Cancinos
Barrios, were assassinated in 1979. Vice
President Francisco Villagran Kramer
resigned in September of 1980 in opposition to human rights abuses carried
out by the government. Lucas García
supported his former defense minister
Gen. Angel Aníbal Guevara in presidential elections in March of 1982. The
government was accused of electoral
fraud, and junior officers led a coup
that ousted Lucas García on March 23,
1982. Lucas García and Aníbal Guevara
were put under house arrest, and results of the election were declared void.

EFRAÍN RÍOS MONTT (President,
March 23, 1982–August 8, 1983).
Efraín Ríos Montt was born in Hue-
huetenango on June 16, 1926. He joined
the army in 1943 and received military
training in Guatemala, the United
States, and Italy. He rose through the
ranks to become a brigadier general.
Ríos Montt served as director of the
military academy in Guatemala City
and became army chief of staff in the
early 1970s. He was considered a moderate and opposed the administration
of President Carlos Araña Osorio.
Ríos Montt was posted to Washington,
D.C., in July of 1973. He returned to
Guatemala early in 1974 to accept the
presidential nomination of the Christian Democratic party. Ríos Montt was
opposed by the government-backed
candidate Kjell Eugenio Laugerud

García. Laugerud García was declared
president by the government-controlled
Electoral Commission following a bitter campaign. Ríos Montt's supporters
accused the government of electoral
fraud and initiated strikes and demonstrations against the government. Ríos
Montt was sent into diplomatic exile in
Madrid, Spain, where he served as
military attaché. He returned to Guatemala in 1978 and became a lay evan-
gelist in the Pentecostal El Verbo
church. Ríos Montt was asked to serve
as president of a three-man junta when
the government of President Romeo
Lucas García was ousted on March 23,
1982. Ríos Montt ousted the other junta
members and took the title of president
on June 9, 1982. He attempted to end
the violence plaguing Guatemala and
offered an amnesty to guerrillas in June
of 1982. After the amnesty expired, he
declared a state of siege and launched a
military campaign to destroy the leftist
rebels. Ríos Montt also began a
crackdown on corruption and made
plans to institute agrarian reforms.
Ríos Montt was ousted and placed
under house arrest following another
military coup led by his defense minister, General Oscar Mejía Víctores, on
August 8, 1983. Ríos Montt attempted
a political comeback in 1990 as a
presidential nominee of a right-wing
coalition, but his candidacy was declared invalid because of his involvement in the coup in 1982. Ríos Montt
backed the subsequent candidacy of
Jorge Serrano Elías, who won a runoff
in January of 1991.

**OSCAR HUMBERTO MEJÍA VÍC-
TORES** (President, August 8, 1983–
January 14, 1986). Oscar Humberto
Mejía Víctores was born in 1930. He
joined the Guatelaman army in 1948
and was educated at military schools.
He rose through the ranks to become
brigadier general in 1980. Mejía was appointed inspector general of the army
in the early 1980s. He served as minister
of defense in the military government

of Efraín Ríos Montt. He ousted Ríos Montt on August 8, 1983, and became president of the ruling junta. Mejía proceeded with his predecessor's plans to hold free elections. Parliamentary elections where held in 1984, and a presidential election took place in November of 1985. Mejía relinquished office to the victor, Marco Vinicio Cerezo Arévalo, on January 14, 1986.

MARCO VINICIO CEREZO ARÉVALO (President, January 14, 1986–January 14, 1991). Marco Vinicio Cerezo Arévalo was born on December 26, 1942. He was educated at the University of San Carlos and received a degree in law. He became active in politics and joined the Christian Democratic party. Cerezo was elected to the Guatemalan Congress in 1974. He was an unsuccessful candidate for mayor of Guatemala City in 1978. He was a leading critic of the military regimes that ruled Guatemala and survived several attempts on his life in the early 1980s. Cerezo was the candidate of the Christian Democrats when presidential elections were allowed by the ruling military junta in November of 1985. He defeated rightist candidate Jorge Carpio Nicolle and took office on January 14, 1986. Cerezo refused to cooperate with the United States in opposing the Sandinista government in Nicaragua. He supported the regional peace proposal of Costa Rican president Oscar Arias Sánchez in 1987. Cerezo initiated negotiations with Guatemalan guerrilla organizations and attempted to control right-wing paramilitary groups operating in the country. Cerezo's government was faced with a rising rate of inflation in 1988. His government survived a military coup attempt in May of 1988, but opposition groups stymied his plans for social and economic reform. Cerezo completed his term of office on January 14, 1991, and was succeeded by Jorge Serrano Elías.

JORGE SERRANO ELÍAS (President, January 14, 1991–June 1, 1993). Jorge Serrano Elías was born in Guatemala City on April 26, 1945. He attended the University of San Carlos and Stanford University in the United States. Serrano was a fundamentalist Christian and a leading advisor to General Efraín Ríos Montt. He served as a member of the Presidential Advisory Council of State during Ríos Montt's dictatorship from 1982 until 1983. Serrano was an unsuccessful candidate for president in the elections of 1985. He was a founder of the Solidarity Action Movement in 1990 and became the party's presidential candidate when Ríos Montt's candidacy was disqualified. Serrano led a coalition of right-wing parties to victory and took office on January 14, 1991. His government was faced with continued violence from leftist guerrillas, right-wing death squads, and drug traffickers. The government carried on negotiations with the leading guerrilla organization, the Guatemala National Revolutionary Unity, but no agreement was reached. Serrano faced demonstrations by workers and students over the government economic policies. He dissolved the Parliament and instituted dictatorial rule in May of 1993. Widespread opposition to his actions and threats of economic sanctions by the international community prompted a military coup. Serrano was ousted by the army on June 1, 1993. The Guatemalan Congress selected human-rights-activist Ramiro de Leon Carpio to succeed Serrano as president on June 6, 1993.

Guinea, Republic of

(Républic de Guinee)

Guinea is a country in western Africa. It was granted independence from France on October 2, 1958.

HEADS OF STATE

SÉKOU TOURÉ (President, October 2, 1958–March 26, 1984). Ahmed Sékou Touré was born in Faranah on January 9, 1922. He attended the Georges Poiret Teachers College in Conakry, but was expelled in 1937 for leading a strike. He began work as a postal worker in 1941 and began organizing for the Post Office Workers' Union. Touré later became a full-time trade union organizer. He was a founder of the Democratic party of Guinea in 1947. He was elected to the Guinean Territorial Assembly in 1953, and in March of 1957 he was elected vice president of the Government Council of Guinea. Touré became mayor of Conakry the following year. On September 27, 1958, he supported a referendum granting Guinea complete independence from France, and on October 2, 1958, Touré became the first president of the new independent nation. Guinea's relationship with France deteriorated in 1960 when France was implicated in a planned coup against Touré's government. It was the first in a series of real or imagined plots against his government. Touré used these conspiracies as an excuse to crush his opponents, many of whom were arrested or executed. Following the ouster of Ghana's president Kwame Nkrumah in February of 1966, Touré welcomed him to Guinea, where he named him copresident until his death in 1972. Touré survived an assassination attempt in June of 1969, and his regime withstood an invasion by exiles and mercenaries in November of 1970. Touré, who received a Lenin Peace Prize from the Soviet Union in 1960, remained a leading spokesman for Third World matters, despite the repressive nature of his regime. In March of 1984 Touré traveled to the United States for medical treatment. He died on March 26, 1984, of a heart attack during surgery at a Cleveland hospital.

LOUIS LANSANA BEAVOGUI (President, March 27, 1984–April 3, 1984). Louis Lansana Beavogui was born in Macenta in 1923. He was educated as a doctor and served as a medical officer in Guekedou and Kissidoujou. In 1953 he was elected to the Kissidoujou Town Council, and the following year he became mayor. Beavogui was elected to the French National Assembly in January of 1956 and became minister of economic affairs in the first Guinean independent government in October of 1958. He was appointed foreign minister in 1961 and served until 1969, when he again became minister of economic affairs. Beavogui was appointed to the new position of prime minister by President Sékou Touré on April 26, 1972. He also held various other ministries in the government, including the army, foreign affairs, and financial control. Beavogui succeeded Sékou Touré as president after his death on March 26, 1984. He was ousted by a military coup several days later on April 3, 1974. Beavogui was arrested by the new government and remained imprisoned until he became ill in mid–August of 1984. He died of complications from diabetes in a Conkary hospital on August 26, 1984.

LANSANA CONTÉ (President, April 3, 1984–). Lansana Conté was born in Coyah in 1935. He attended military school and joined the French army in 1955. He joined the Guinean army after independence and was involved in the suppression of several attempts to overthrow President Sékou Touré. In 1973 he fought against the Portuguese with nationalists in Guinea-Bissau. Conté was appointed deputy chief of staff for land forces in 1975 and was elected a deputy in 1980. Following the death of President Touré, Conté led a military overthrow of the government on April 3, 1984. He was named head of the ruling Military Committee for National Redress and served as Guinea's head of state. Conté also took over the duties of prime minister in December of 1984. He survived a coup attempt led by his former prime minister Diara Traore on July 4, 1985.

Conté's rule was challenged by violent demonstrations in the early 1990s calling for the democratization of Guinea. Conté agreed to a constitutional rule in April of 1992, though he resisted the scheduling of elections.

HEADS OF GOVERNMENT

LOUIS LANSANA BEAVOGUI (Premier, April 26, 1972–April 3, 1984). *See entry under Heads of State.*

DIARA TRAORÉ (Premier, April 5, 1984–December 18, 1984). Diarra Traoré was born in 1934. He joined the French army and later served in the Guinean army. He was a colonel in the Guinean army when he took part in the military coup that overthrew the Guinean government in April of 1984. Traoré became prime minister in the new government under President Lansana Conté on April 5, 1984. In December of 1984 he was demoted to minister of education. He led an unsuccessful coup attempt against the Conté government in July of 1985. Following the failure of the coup, Traoré went into hiding, but he was arrested on July 7, 1985, and sentenced to death for his part in the coup attempt. His sentence was commuted to life imprisonment, and he was released in December of 1988.

LANSANA CONTÉ (Premier, December 18, 1984–). *See entry under Heads of State.*

Guinea-Bissau, Republic of

(República da Guine-Bissau)

Guinea-Bissau is an island country off the northwestern coast of Africa. It was granted independence from Portugal on September 24, 1973.

HEADS OF STATE

LUIS DE ALMEDA CABRAL (President, September 26, 1973–November 14, 1980). Luis de Almeda Cabral was born in Bafata in September of 1929. He worked as a clerk in a Portuguese shipping business and became active in the union movement and the movement to liberate Guinea-Bissau from the Portuguese colonial government. He was a founder of the African Party for the Independence of Guinea-Bissau and Cape Verde (PAIGC) with his brother, Amilcar Cabral, in 1956. Luis Cabral went into exile in 1960 to escape arrest from the colonial authorities. He served on PAIGC's Council of War from 1965. He was placed in charge of the reconstruction of liberated areas in Guinea-Bissau in 1970. Luis Cabral succeeded his brother as PAIGC's leader following Amilcar Cabral's assassination on January 20, 1973. He served as president of the State Council of Guinea-Bissau's self-proclaimed independent government from September 26, 1973. Portugal acknowledged Guinea-Bissau's independence the following year. Luis Cabral was deposed in a coup led by João Bernardo Vieira on November 14, 1980. He was imprisoned until January 1, 1982, when he was released and went into exile in Cape Verde. He subsequently went to Cuba and to Portugal.

JOAO BERNARDO VIEIRA (President, November 14, 1980–). João Bernardo Vieira was born in Bissau in 1939. He was educated locally and was an early member of the African Party for the Independence of Guinea-Bissau and Cape Verde (PAIGC). He fought against the Portuguese colonial authorities during the 1960s, using the name Commander Nino. Vieira received military training in the Soviet Union, Algeria, and Cuba. He was named state commissioner for the armed forces following Guinea-Bissau's independence in September of 1973. He also served as president of the National Assembly. Vieira was chosen as premier on September 28, 1978. A new constitution was introduced in November of 1980 that eliminated most of the premier's powers. Vieira responded by ousting President Luis Cabral on November 14, 1980. Vieira became head of state as leader of a Revolutionary Council. The coup ended plans to unify Guinea-Bissau with the Cape Verde Islands. Vieira promoted a new constitution in March of 1984 and was elected president of the Council of State by a newly elected National People's Assembly in May of 1984. Vieira survived a coup attempt led by Vice President Paulo Correia in November of 1985. Correia and other plotters were put to death the following year. Vieira was reelected president of the Council of State in June of 1989. In December of 1991 he restored the position of prime minister, which had been eliminated in 1984.

HEADS OF GOVERNMENT

FRANCISCO MENDES (Premier, March 13, 1973–July 7, 1978). Francisco Mendes was born in Enxude in 1939. He was a founding member of the African Party for the Independence of Guinea-Bissau and Cape Verde (PAIGC). He was a major in the revolutionary army and became premier following independence on March 13, 1973. Mendes retained his position until he was killed in a car accident on July 7, 1978.

CONSTANTINO TEIXEIRA (Acting Premier, July 7, 1978–September 28, 1978). Constantino Teixeira became acting premier of Guinea-Bissau following the death of Francisco Mendes on July 7, 1978. He was replaced by João Bernardo Vieira on September 28, 1978.

JOÃO BERNARDO VIEIRA (Premier, September 28, 1978–November 14, 1980). *See entry under Heads of State.*

VÍCTOR SAUDE MARIA (Premier, May 14, 1982–March 8, 1984). Víctor Saude Maria served as foreign minister in the government of João Vieira. He was appointed premier by Vieira on May 14, 1982. He was distrusted by the leadership of the ruling party because of his right-wing tendencies. Maria opposed Vieira's plans to decrease the powers of the premier. Maria was accused of plotting a coup against President Vieira and was dismissed on March 8, 1984. Fearing arrest, he took refuge in the Portuguese Embassy. He subsequently went into exile and remained an opponent of the Vieira regime.

CARLOS CORREIA (Premier, December 27, 1991–). Carlos Correia was a former minister of rural development and agriculture. He was appointed to the revived position of premier by President João Vieira on December 27, 1991.

Guyana, Cooperative Republic of

Guyana is a country in northeastern South America. It was granted independence from Great Britain on May 26, 1966.

HEADS OF STATE

SIR RICHARD E. LUYT (Governor-General, May 26, 1966–July 30, 1966). Richard Edmunds Luyt was born in Cape Town, South Africa, on November 18, 1915. He was educated at the University of Cape Town and Trinity College at Oxford University. He served in the army during World War II and entered the British Colonial Service after the war. Luyt served in Northern Rhodesia from 1946 until 1953. He was then posted to Kenya, where he remained until 1961. He returned to Northern Rhodesia as chief secretary of the government from 1962 until 1964. Luyt was appointed governor of British Guiana in 1964. He retained his position until the colony was granted independence as Guyana on May 26, 1966. He served as Guyana's first governor-general until July 30, 1966. Luyt then returned to South Africa, where he served as vice-chancellor of the University of Cape Town until his retirement in 1980. Luyt died in Cape Town on February 12, 1994, at the age of 78.

SIR DAVID J. E. ROSE (Governor-General, July 30, 1966–November 10, 1969). David J. E. Rose was born in British Guiana on April 10, 1923. He served in the British colonial government in the Caribbean and was named superintendent of police in British Guiana in 1948. He rose to the post of senior superintendent in 1955. Rose also served in the colonial administrations of Antigua and Saint Lucia. British Guiana was granted independence as Guyana in May of 1966. Rose became the first native-born governor-general of Guyana when he succeeded Sir Richard Luyt to the position on July 30, 1966. Rose went to London in November of 1969 in anticipation of relinquishing his position when Guyana became a republic in early 1970. He was killed when scaffolding, erected for cleaning a building near the British Parliament, collapsed on his parked limousine on November 10, 1969.

ARTHUR CHUNG (President, March 17, 1970–October 6, 1980). Arthur Chung was born in Windsor Forest on January 10, 1918. He was educated in Guyana and Great Britain, where he received a law degree. He resided in England until 1948, when he returned to Guyana. In 1954 he became a magistrate. Chung served as a judge on the Guyana Supreme Court from 1962 until 1970. He became president when Guyana became a republic on March 17, 1970. He retired from politics on October 6, 1980.

LINDEN FORBES S. BURNHAM (President, October 6, 1980–August 6, 1985). Linden Forbes Sampson Burnham was born in Kitty, East Demarara, on February 20, 1923. He was educated locally and at the University of London, where he received a degree in law in 1947. He returned to British Guiana in 1949 and set up a law practice in Georgetown. Burnham was a founder of the pro-independence People's Progressive party with Cheddi Jagan the following year. He was elected to the newly created National Assembly in April of 1953 and served as minister of education in the government. The British government feared the radical nature of the government under Chief Minister Cheddi Jagan and expelled the government. Burnham broke with Jagan over the Marxist drift of the People's Progressive party and formed the People's National Congress in 1955. Burnham was reelected to the National Assembly when elections were resumed in 1957. Jagan's party received a majority of seats in the assembly, and he became prime minister. The British introduced a new constitution in September of 1964 designed to make Jagan's reelection more difficult by requiring a system of proportional representation. The People's National Congress was victorious in elections in December of 1964, and Burnham formed a coalition government. He became prime minister on December 14, 1964, and remained head of the government when British Guiana was granted independence as Guyana on May 25, 1966. Burnham was returned to office in elections in 1968, though allegations of electoral fraud tainted the victory. Guyana was declared a republic on March 17, 1970. Burnham was again reelected as head of the government in 1973. His government was socialist in nature and supported the nationalization of foreign businesses and a cooperative economy. Guyana became the headquarters of various religious sects during the 1970s, including the People's Temple commune.

It was alleged that the People's Temple and other cults gave financial support to the ruling party in return for being allowed to settle in Guyana. Jim Jones, the leader of the People's Temple, led his followers in a mass suicide-murder ritual that claimed nearly 1000 lives in November of 1978. Burnham promoted a new constitution in October of 1980 that provided for an executive presidency. He stepped down as prime minister to assume the office of president on October 6, 1980. A new election was held the following December, and amidst widespread claims of fraud and corruption, the Burnham government retained power. Opposition to Burnham's rule increased during the 1980s as the Guyanan economy deteriorated. He survived a plot against his life in late 1983. Burnham retained power until his death during surgery at a Georgetown hospital on April 6, 1985.

DESMOND HOYTE (President, August 6, 1985–October 9, 1992). Hugh Desmond Hoyte was born in Georgetown on March 9, 1929. He was educated in Great Britain. He subsequently worked as a teacher and a lawyer. Hoyte entered politics as a member of the People's National Congress. He was elected to Parliament in 1968 and served as minister of home affairs from 1969 until 1970. He was named minister of finance in 1970 and minister of works and communications in 1972. Hoyte served as minister of economic development in 1974. He subsequently served in various party positions until his election as prime minister on August 16, 1984. He succeeded to the presidency following the death of Linden Burnham on August 6, 1985. Hoyte was defeated in the presidential election on October 5, 1992, by Cheddi Jagan. He left office on October 9, 1992.

CHEDDI JAGAN (President, October 9, 1992–). Cheddi Berret Jagan was born in Port Mourant on March 22,

1918. He was educated in Georgetown before entering Howard University in Washington, D.C., in 1936. He entered dental school in Chicago, Illinois, in 1938 and received a degree in dental surgery in 1942. Jagan returned to British Guiana in 1943 and set up a practice in Georgetown. He became involved in the trade union movement and was elected to the British Guianan legislature in 1947. He was a founder of the pro-independence People's Progressive party (PPP) in January of 1950. Jagan served as leader of the party and was elected chief minister of the government when a new constitution provided for home rule in April of 1953. He also served as minister of agriculture, lands, and mines. The British colonial authorities opposed the leftward tilt of the Jagan government, however. The British government of Winston Churchill suspended the British Guianan constitution and sent troops to restore order when strikes and demonstrations supporting Jagan took place in October of 1953. Jagan was dismissed from office. He was unable to convince the British government to rescind its decision on a visit to London later in the year. He returned to British Guiana and instituted a campaign of civil disobedience against the colonial government. He was restricted to Georgetown and was arrested in April of 1954 when he violated the order. Jagan was released the following September and continued to lead the PPP. A new constitution was approved for British Guiana in April of 1956, and the PPP won a majority in legislative elections in August of 1957. Jagan served

as minister of trade and industry in the new government led by Governor Patrick Renison. British Guiana was granted internal self-government in August of 1961. Elections were held amid charges that the PPP supported communism. Jagan's party won a majority, and he was sworn into office as prime minister on September 5, 1961. He introduced an austerity budget to improve the economy the following year, generating a wave of strikes and demonstrations against his government. The British introduced a new constitution in September of 1964 that required the ruling party to gain a majority rather than a plurality of seats in the National Assembly. Linden Burnham's People's National Congress formed a coalition government without the PPP, and Jagan was replaced as prime minister on December 14, 1964. Jagan served as leader of the opposition to Burnham's government. Jagan and other members of the opposition refused to claim their seats in the National Assembly following elections in 1973. He led a sugar workers' strike in February of 1975 to gain the government's recognition of the Guyana Agricultural Workers' Union. The PPP participated in Assembly elections in 1980 and 1985, though they failed to gain a majority in the Assembly. Jagan was the candidate of the PPP in presidential elections in October of 1992. Despite a lengthy association with Marxist theory, he campaigned in support of a free-market economy. He defeated incumbent President Desmond Hoyte and was sworn into office on October 9, 1992.

HEADS OF GOVERNMENT

CHEDDI JAGAN (Prime Minister, September 5, 1961–December 14, 1964). *See entry under Heads of State.*

LINDEN FORBES S. BURNHAM (Prime Minister, December 14, 1964–

October 6, 1980). *See entry under Heads of State.*

PTOLEMY REID (Prime Minister, October 6, 1980–August 16, 1984). Ptolemy A. Reid was chosen as Guyana's prime minister on October 6, 1980, following the establishment of a new constitution and Forbes Burnham's assumption of the office of executive president. Guyana's economic situation deteriorated and Reid stepped down as prime minister on August 16, 1984, for reasons of health.

DESMOND HOYTE (Prime Minister, August 16, 1984–August 6, 1985). *See entry under Heads of State.*

HAMILTON GREEN (Prime Minister, August 6, 1985–October 9, 1992). Hamilton Green was born in Georgetown on November 9, 1934. He was educated in Guyana and became active in politics. He served as general secretary of the People's National Congress. Green served in several cabinet positions before becoming vice president and prime minister of Guyana on August 6, 1985. When the ruling People's National Congress party was defeated in the elections in October of 1992, Green was replaced as prime minister on October 9, 1992.

SAM HINDS (Prime Minister, October 9, 1992–). Sam Hinds was the vice presidential candidate in Cheddi Jagan's People's Progressive party (PPP) in the elections held on October 5, 1992. The PPP was victorious in the balloting, and Hinds was selected as prime minister on October 9, 1992.

Haiti, Republic of
(République d'Haïti)

Haiti is a country that occupies the western part of the island of Hispaniola in the northern Caribbean Sea. It was granted independence from France on January 1, 1804.

HEADS OF STATE

ELIE LESCOT (President, May 15, 1941–January 11, 1946). Elie Lescot was born in Saint-Louis du Nord on December 9, 1883. He was active in politics and served as secretary of public education and agriculture in the cabinet of President Louis Borno from 1922 until 1930. He was subsequently named secretary of justice and the interior under President Stenio Vincent. Lescot served as Haiti's ambassador to the United States from 1937. When President Vincent declined to run for a third term, Lescot was elected president of Haiti and took office on May 15, 1941. He was initially a popular leader, but soon lost favor in the country. He was accused of using his position to allow his sons to acquire government property in an unfair manner. The economy also suffered under his administration, with the cost of living tripling. Lescot ruled by martial law and kept a tight rein on the press and the opposition. His unpopular regime was ousted by the military on January 11, 1946. He subsequently remained inactive in political affairs. Lescot died in La Boule, Haiti, at the age of 90 on October 22, 1974.

FRANK LAVAUD (President, January 11, 1946–August 16, 1946). Frank Lavaud was a colonel in the Haitian army. He headed the three-man military junta that ousted President Elie Lescot on January 11, 1946. The junta remained in power until the election of Dumarsais Estimé on August 16, 1946. Lavaud again led Haiti when the military ousted President Estimé on May 10,

1950 and served until the election of Paul Magloire on December 6, 1950.

DUMARSAIS ESTIMÉ (President, August 16, 1946–May 10, 1950). Dumarsais Estimé was born in Verelleses on April 21, 1900. He worked as a teacher and a lawyer before his election to the National Assembly. He later served as Speaker of the Assembly and was named secretary of education in the cabinet of President Stenio Vincent in the 1930s. Estimé was elected president of Haiti following the ouster of President Elie Lescot. He took office on August 16, 1946, and was credited with improving education and tourism. His political opponents charged that Estimé granted special favors to political allies. Estimé's agricultural reform programs also failed to produce results. He attempted to seek reelection in 1950, but the National Assembly refused to allow his reelection. Estimé was forced to resign on May 10, 1950. He subsequently went into exile in New York, where he died of uremia at the age of 53 on July 20, 1953.

FRANK LAVAUD (President, May 10, 1950–December 6, 1950). *See earlier entry under Heads of State.*

PAUL E. MAGLOIRE (President, December 6, 1950–December 12, 1956). Paul Eugène Magloire was born in Cap-Haitien on July 19, 1907. He attended the military academy and joined the Haitian army. He rose through the ranks of the military and also earned a law degree in 1939. In the 1940s he was posted to the capital, where he served as chief of the police force in 1944. Magloire was promoted to colonel in 1946. He was active in the military coup that ousted President Elie Lescot in January of 1946 and served under Frank Lavaud in the subsequent ruling military junta. The junta stepped down upon the election of Dumarsais Estimé in August of 1946. The junta again assumed power in May of 1950 and forced the resignation of President Estimé. Magloire was a candidate for president and was elected in October of 1950. He took office on December 6, 1950. He planned to complete his term and step down in favor of his finance minister, Clement Jumelle, in 1956. Magloire was faced with opposition in the military as his term neared an end, however. When he seized complete power on December 6, 1956, general strikes occurred throughout the country. The military reacted, and Magloire was forced to resign on December 12, 1956. He went into exile in Jamaica and then the United States.

JOSEPH N. PIERRE-LOUIS (President, December 12, 1956–February 7, 1957). Joseph Nemours Pierre-Louis was born in 1900. He served as chief justice of the Haitian Supreme Court and succeeded to the presidency of Haiti following the resignation of President Paul Magloire on December 12, 1956. He was criticized for being slow in preparing for new elections and was forced to resign on February 7, 1957.

FRANK SYLVAIN (President, February 7, 1957–April 2, 1957). François Sylvain was an authority on Haitian constitutional law. He was chosen as interim president of Haiti on February 7, 1957. Sylvain was accused of favoring the interests of François Duvalier in the planned general election. Haiti was beset by another general strike in March of 1957. Sylvain was placed under house arrest and forced to resign the presidency on April 2, 1957. He was replaced by a short-lived Executive Council.

LÉON CANTAVE (President, May 20, 1957–May 26, 1957). Léon Cantave was born in Mirebalais on July 4, 1910. He served in the Haitian military and was an opponent of President Paul Magloire's government in 1954. He was imprisoned during Magloire's administration, but returned to his army posts following Magloire's ouster in 1956.

Cantave was named army chief of staff and served during the Haitian disorders of 1957. In May of 1957, Cantave was accused of failing to maintain order in the country, and his removal was ordered by the ruling Executive Council. With the backing of the army, Cantave instead ousted the council and took executive power on May 20, 1957. Five days later Cantave was faced with an attempted coup led by Colonel Pierre Armand, the chief of the National Police. Various political and military leaders in the country quelled the volatile situation by naming a new coalition government under Daniel Fignole on May 26, 1957. Cantave was an opponent of François Duvalier and fled the country following Duvalier's election as president in 1957. He remained a leading opponent of Duvalier both in and out of exile. He led a rebellion against Duvalier's regime in September of 1963. It was unsuccessful and he was forced to leave the country again. He died in Paris after a brief illness on February 16, 1968.

DANIEL FIGNOLE (President, May 26, 1957–June 14, 1957). Daniel Fignole was born in Pestel on November 12, 1914. He was a professor of mathematics before becoming involved in the labor union movement. He was popular with the poorer classes and announced his candidacy for the presidency following the ouster of President Paul Magloire in 1956. Fignole was chosen as provisional president on May 26, 1957, following a period of political instability in the country. He announced that elections would be held the following month, with himself as a candidate. He was opposed by supporters of Louis Dejoie, another presidential contender, who orchestrated his ouster by the military on June 14, 1957. Fignole was then forced into exile in the United States. His supporters were persecuted under the subsequent rule of President François Duvalier. Fignole remained in exile until the

ouster of Duvalier's son, Jean-Claude, in February of 1986. He returned to Port-au-Prince, where he died of prostate cancer on August 27, 1986.

ANTOINE T. KEBREAU (President, June 14, 1957–October 22, 1957). Antoine T. Kebreau was born in Port-au-Prince on November 11, 1909. He graduated from the military academy in 1930 and served in the Haitian military. He was named to replace Léon Cantave as army chief of staff in May of 1957. Kebreau led a military coup that ousted Provisional President Daniel Fignole on June 14, 1957. Kebreau assumed power in Haiti and presided over elections in September of 1957 which resulted in the selection of François Duvalier as president. Kebreau relinquished his executive powers to Duvalier on October 22, 1957. He remained army chief of staff in the early days of the Duvalier regime, but he was considered a threat to Duvalier's rule. Duvalier removed him from his military post and appointed him ambassador to Italy and the Vatican. Kebreau died, possibly having been poisoned, in Port-au-Prince on January 13, 1963.

FRANÇOIS DUVALIER (President, October 22, 1957–April 21, 1971). François Duvalier was born in Port-au-Prince on April 14, 1907. He received a degree in medicine from the Faculty of Medicine of Haiti in 1934. He worked in several local hospitals and assisted the United States Army Medical Corps in combatting yaws and malaria. Duvalier also wrote a book in 1944 on the evolution of voodoo. He became known as "Papa Doc" and was named director of the National Public Health Service in 1946. He was appointed secretary of labor in the government of Dumaraise Estimé in 1950. Duvalier left the government following the coup that installed Paul Magloire as president in December of 1950. He opposed Magloire's regime and was forced to go underground in 1954. He reemerged following a general amnesty in 1956 and announced his candidacy for the presidency. Magloire resigned in December of 1956, and Haiti was ruled by a succession of provisional governments. Duvalier won the presidential election in September of 1957 with the support of the military. He was sworn into office on October 22, 1957. Duvalier soon embarked on a reign of terror against opponents of his regime. He formed a gang of brutal thugs known as the Tonton Macoutes, which means "bogeymen" in Creole. They tortured and murdered Duvalier's political enemies and collected protection money from Haitian businesses. Duvalier survived a serious heart attack in 1959, and Tonton Macoutes leader Clement Barbot assumed executive powers in his absence. Following his recovery, Duvalier accused Barbot of trying to supplant him as president and imprisoned his former aide. Duvalier's government was rampant with corruption, and the United States cut off most economic assistance to the country in 1961. Duvalier also declared himself reelected to the presidency in 1961, two years before elections were scheduled. Clement Barbot was released from prison in April of 1963 and embarked on a plot to oust Duvalier by kidnapping his children. The plot failed, and Duvalier ordered a massive search for Barbot and his supporters. During the search, word reached Duvalier that Barbot had transformed himself into a black dog. Duvalier then ordered that all black dogs in Haiti be put to death. Barbot was captured and shot to death by the Tonton Macoutes in July of 1963. Duvalier survived several other invasions and coup attempts. He once ordered the head of an executed rebel packed in ice and brought to the presidential palace so he could commune with his spirit. Duvalier had himself declared president for life in June of 1964. His bloody repression continued throughout the 1960s, and Haiti remained the poorest nation in the western hemisphere. Duvalier suffered another heart attack in November of 1970. He subsequently named his son, Jean-Claude, as his heir apparent. Duvalier died in Port-au-Prince after a long illness at the age of 64 on April 21, 1971.

JEAN-CLAUDE DUVALIER (President, April 22, 1971–February 7, 1986). Jean-Claude Duvalier was born in Port-au-Prince on July 3, 1951. He was the only son of François Duvalier, who became Haiti's president in 1957. Jean-Claude was raised in luxury in the presidential palace. He narrowly escaped an abortive kidnap plot in 1963. He was educated in Port-au-Prince and entered the University of Haiti in 1970. François Duvalier began making plans for Jean-Claude to succeed him as president. He amended the constitution to lower the legal age to become president from forty to twenty. A plebiscite confirmed Jean-Claude as heir apparent in February of 1971. François Duvalier died after a long illness on April 21, 1971, and Jean-Claude was sworn into office as president for life. Jean-Claude, who became known as "Baby Doc," initially maintained the government composed of his father's advisors. He gradually improved his country's record on human rights and instituted budgetary reforms in the hopes of securing increased financial aid from the United States. He allowed the formation of opposition political parties in the early 1980s, and multiparty elections where held for the National Assembly in 1984. Many of these reforms were cosmetic in nature to appease international pressure on the regime, however. Demonstrations and riots against the government took place in November of 1985, and all of Haiti's schools were closed in January of 1986 following a student boycott. Anti-government sentiment escalated, and Duvalier fled the country with his family on February 7, 1986. He went into exile in Mougins, France.

HENRI NAMPHY (President, February 7, 1986–February 7, 1988). Henri Namphy was born on November 2, 1932. He served in the Haitian military where he rose to the rank of lieutenant general. Namphy led troops in quashing an armed rebellion against the Duvalier government in 1982 and was subsequently named army chief of staff. He led the military coup that forced the resignation of President Jean-Claude Duvalier on February 7, 1986. He subsequently served as head of state and president of the National Governing Council. Namphy stepped down as president on February 7, 1988, following the election of Leslie Manigat as president. Namphy again led a military coup and ousted Manigat on June 20, 1988. He served as head of state until September 17, 1988, when he was ousted by General Prosper Avril. Namphy went into exile in Dominica.

LESLIE MANIGAT (President, February 7, 1988–June 20, 1988). Leslie Manigat was born in Port-au-Prince on August 16, 1930. He was educated at the University of Haiti. He was an opponent of the regime of President François Duvalier and was forced into exile in 1963. Manigat subsequently served on the faculties of universities in the United States, France, Trinidad and Tobago, and Venezuela. He returned to Haiti in 1986 and was the candidate of the Rally of Progressive National Democrats in the elections of 1987. He was elected to the presidency and was sworn into office on February 7, 1988. Manigat was ousted on June 20, 1988, by a military coup and went into exile. He returned from exile in 1990, but was stripped of political rights.

HENRI NAMPHY (President, June 20, 1988–September 17, 1988). *See earlier entry under Heads of State.*

PROSPER AVRIL (President, September 17, 1988–March 10, 1990).

Prosper Avril was born in 1938. He attended military school in Haiti and served as an advisor to President Jean-Claude Duvalier. He subsequently advised the ruling military junta led by General Henri Namphy in 1986. Avril served as commander of the Presidential Guard in 1988 and was a leader of the military coup that ousted President Leslie Manigat in June of 1988. Avril subsequently led the coup that removed General Namphy, and he replaced him as president of Haiti on September 17, 1988. Avril survived two coup attempts in April of 1989. He was faced with massive antigovernment demonstrations and resigned from office on March 10, 1990. Avril subsequently went into exile in the United States, where he settled in Florida.

HERARD ABRAHAM (President, March 10, 1990–March 13, 1990). General Herard Abraham served as army chief of staff under President Prosper Avril. He became interim president of Haiti following Avril's resignation on March 10, 1990. He stepped down on March 13, 1990, to allow Ertha Pascal-Troillot to assume the presidency.

ERTHA PASCAL-TROILLOT (President, March 13, 1990–February 7, 1991). Ertha Pascal-Troillot was born in Petionville on August 13, 1943. She attended law school and became a lower court judge in 1980. She was named to the Supreme Court in 1986. Pascal-Troillot was appointed acting president of Haiti on March 13, 1990. She served until elections were held the following year and relinquished office to Jean-Bertrand Aristide on February 7, 1991. She was arrested in April of 1991 on charges of being involved in a coup attempt against President Aristide the previous January.

JEAN-BERTRAND ARISTIDE (President, February 7, 1991–October 8, 1991). Jean-Bertrand Aristide was born in

Douyon on July 15, 1953. He received a religious education from the Salesian order and was ordained a priest in 1982. He was an active opponent of President Jean-Claude Duvalier and an important figure in the popular movement that forced Duvalier's ouster by the military in February of 1986. Aristide survived an attack on his congregation in 1988 by members of Duvalier's Tonton Macoutes. He was subsequently expelled from the Salesian order because of his political activities. Aristide continued to work as a priest, primarily in the poorer sections of the country. He announced his candidacy for the presidency of Haiti in 1990 and was overwhelmingly elected. His inauguration was threatened by an unsuccessful coup attempt in January of 1991. The attempt was thwarted, and Aristide took office on February 7, 1991. His administration was short-lived, as he was ousted in a military coup led by Brig. Gen. Raoul Cedras on October 8, 1991. Aristide subsequently went into exile, where he advocated that international pressure be placed on Haiti to restore his government and democratic rule.

JOSEPH NERETTE (President, October 8, 1991–June 19, 1992). Joseph Nerette served as a member of the Haitian Supreme Court. He was named president of Haiti after the ouster of President Jean-Bertrand Aristide on October 8, 1991. He stepped down on June 19, 1992, following the selection of Marc Bazin as prime minister.

HEADS OF GOVERNMENT

RÉNE PREVAL (Prime Minister, February 13, 1991–October 11, 1991). Réne Preval was born in Port-au-Prince on January 17, 1943. He was an opponent of President Jean-Claude Duvalier and spent much of the 1980s in exile in the United States. He returned to Haiti following Duvalier's ouster and served as a member of the Group for Defense of the Constitution. Preval served as prime minister in the government of President Jean-Bertrand Aristide from February 13, 1991. He left office following the ouster of Aristide by the military on October 11, 1991.

JEAN-JACQUES HONORAT (Prime Minister, October 11, 1991–June 19, 1992). Jean-Jacques Honorat was a former diplomat and government official who had been sent into exile by Jean-Claude Duvalier in 1981. Honorat was named interim prime minister on October 11, 1991, following the coup that ousted President Jean-Bertrand Aristide. He resigned his office prior to the inauguration of Marc Bazin as prime minister on June 19, 1992.

MARC BAZIN (Prime Minister, June 19, 1992–June 8, 1993). Marc Louis Bazin was born in Saint-Marc on March 6, 1932. He was educated in Haiti, France, Belgium, and the United States and received a degree in law. He served as a financial advisor for the Haitian government and was employed by the World Bank International Board of Reconstruction and Development in West Africa. Bazin was appointed minister of economics in 1982 by President Jean-Claude Duvalier. He was ousted from that position five months later when he began an investigation of corruption in the government. Bazin subsequently broke with the Duvalier family and founded the Movement for the Installation of Democracy in Haiti in 1986. He was an unsuccessful candidate for president in 1987 and in 1990, when he was defeated by Jean-Bertrand Aristide. Bazin supported the coup that ousted Aristide in

October of 1991. Bazin was appointed prime minister by the interim government and was confirmed by the Haitian legislature. He was sworn into office on June 19, 1992. Bazin's government attempted to end the trade embargo against Haiti that the Organization of American States had initiated following the coup against Aristide. Bazin stepped down as prime minister on June 8, 1993, after failing to retain the support of the army.

Honduras, Republic of
(Républica de Honduras)

Honduras is a country in Central America. It was granted independence from Spain on September 15, 1821.

HEADS OF STATE

TIBURCIO CARÍAS ANDINO (President, February 1, 1933–January 1, 1949). Tiburcio Carías Andino was born in Tegucigalpa on March 15, 1876. He received a law degree from Central University in 1898. He joined the Honduran army and served as commandant and governor of Honduras's Northern Zone from 1903 until 1907. Carías subsequently entered politics and was elected a delegate to the Federal Convention of Central America in 1921. He was the founder of the Nationalist party and was a candidate for president of Honduras in October of 1925. He received a majority of the popular vote, but the Honduran Congress refused to confirm his election. Carías was again the Nationalist party's candidate for president in 1928, but he was defeated in a close election. In 1932 Carías defeated Angel Zuñiga Huete for the presidency and took office on February 1, 1933. Carías was a popular leader, and the economy of Honduras improved during his administration. A new constitution was introduced in 1936 that allowed for Carías to remain in office until 1943. Several years later his term of office was extended until 1949. Carías relinquished the presidency to his protégé, Juan Manuel Gálvez, on January 1, 1949. He again sought election to the presidency in 1954, but received less than a third of the vote. He boycotted the subsequent Congress, and a military coup took place. Carías went into retirement to his home in Tegucigalpa, where he died at the age of 94 on December 23, 1969.

JUAN MANUEL GÁLVEZ (President, January 1, 1949–January 15, 1954). Juan Manuel Gálvez was born in 1887. He worked for the United Fruit Company as a lawyer before joining the government of Miguel Paz Barahona as minister of the interior in the 1920s. He later served as minister of defense in the administration of General Tiburcio Carías Andino. Gálvez was the only presidential candidate in the elections held in October of 1948 to succeed Carías Andino. He was elected and took office on January 1, 1949. Gálvez continued many of the policies of his predecessor, though he modernized the nation's tax system and allowed more civil liberties in the country. He suffered from poor health during the final year of his term, and his vice president, Julio Lozano Díaz, served as acting president from January 15, 1954. Gálvez left Honduras for medical treatment on

December 6, 1954, and Lozano Díaz was sworn in as president. Gálvez subsequently made little impact on the political process in Honduras. He died in Tegucigalpa of a cerebral hemorrhage at the age of 85 on August 19, 1972.

JULIO LOZANO DÍAZ (President, January 15, 1954–October 21, 1956). Julio Lozano Díaz was born in Tegucigalpa in 1885. He was educated at the National Institute, where he majored in business administration. He was subsequently employed by the government's general revenue division. Lozano was then employed by a mining company for twelve years. He joined the government as minister of the treasury in 1924, but returned to private industry five years later. He served in several government positions, including minister of finance, foreign minister, minister of agriculture and labor, and Honduran ambassador to the United States during the 1930s. Lozano was elected vice president under President Juan Manuel Gálvez in 1949. Lozano became acting head of state on January 15, 1954, and became president on December 6, 1954, when the Honduran Congress dissolved without declaring a winner in the presidential election from the previous October. Lozano refused to call new elections because he claimed the expense of holding two elections in one year was too great. He was faced with widespread dissension during his term of office. He survived a general strike in July of 1956 and a military revolt the following month. Lozano went to Miami, Florida, in September of 1956 for treatment for hypertension. He was ousted by a military coup on October 21, 1956. He remained in exile in Miami, where he died on August 20, 1957.

ROQUE I. RODRÍGUEZ (President, October 21, 1956–December 21, 1957). Roque I. Rodríguez was born in 1901. He served in the Honduran army, where he rose to the rank of general. Rodríguez was commandant of the military academy when he led the coup that ousted Julio Lozano Díaz on October 21, 1956. He served as leader of the military junta that included Colonel Hector Caraccioli of the air force and Major Roberto Galvez Barnes, the former minister of development. Elections to the Constituent Assembly were allowed to take place in September of 1957. The assembly selected José Ramón Villeda Morales to serve as president, and the junta relinquished power on December 21, 1957.

JOSÉ RAMÓN VILLEDA MORALES (President, December 21, 1957–October 3, 1963). José Ramón Villeda Morales was born in Ocotepeque on November 26, 1909. He attended the University of Guatemala, where he received a medical degree in 1933. He opened a pediatric clinic in Santa Rosa de Copan. Villeda Morales went to Munich, Germany, to further his studies in 1938. He returned to Honduras to open a clinic in Tegucigalpa two years later. He was active in Liberal party politics and became known as a persuasive orator. In 1949 he was elected chairman of the Honduran Liberal party, and he was the founder of *El Pueblo*, the party's newspaper. Villeda Morales ran for the presidency in 1954 and led in the balloting. He did not receive an absolute majority of the votes, however, and the election was sent to the Congress to be decided. When a stalemate developed, Julio Lozano Díaz, the acting president, emerged as the country's leader. Villeda Morales led a general strike against the regime of Lozano Díaz in July of 1956. He was exiled to Costa Rica for his opposition to the government. He returned to Honduras following Lozano Díaz's ouster in a military coup in October of 1956 and was named Honduran ambassador to the United States. Villeda Morales was elected president of the Constituent

Assembly the following year. He was chosen by the Assembly to become president of the republic and took office on December 21, 1957. He ruled as a progressive leader and sponsored numerous programs to modernize the country's transportation systems. He also sought to improve the educational and public health facilities in the country. Two months before Villeda Morales was scheduled to complete his term of office, he was ousted in a military coup led by Osvaldo López Arellano on October 3, 1963. He again went into exile in Costa Rica. He subsequently returned to Honduras, and following the election of Ramón Ernesto Cruz as president in 1971, he was appointed head of the Honduran delegation to the United Nations. He died in New York of a heart attack shortly afterwards on October 8, 1971.

OSVALDO LÓPEZ ARELLANO (President, October 3, 1963–June 6, 1971). Osvaldo López Arellano was born in Danli on June 30, 1921. He attended the Military Aviation and Flight Training School in the United States and joined the Honduran air force in 1939. He rose through the ranks to lieutenant in 1947. López Arellano was named chief of the armed forces in 1956 and was promoted to colonel two years later. He was a leader of the military coup that ousted President Ramón Villeda Morales on October 3, 1963. The coup was carried out to prevent leftist Modeste Rodas Alvarado, the leading candidate, from becoming president of Honduras. López Arellano became provisional president in the military government. He reversed a number of social reform programs instituted by the Villeda Morales government. Elections for the Constituent Assembly were held in 1965, and a new constitution was drafted later in the year. López Arellano became constitutional president on June 6, 1965. He briefly declared martial law in 1968 following a general strike. Honduras was involved in a

border dispute with El Salvador that escalated into a war in June of 1969, following El Salvador's victory in the World Cup soccer contest. Honduras broke off diplomatic relations with El Salvador, and El Salvador responded by sending an invasion force into Honduras. The Organization of American States negotiated a peace treaty between the two countries the following month. López Arellano declined to seek reelection to the presidency in 1971 and relinquished the position to Ramón Ernesto Cruz on June 6, 1971. López Arellano remained chief of the armed forces. When Cruz was ousted by the military on December 4, 1972, López Arellano again took the reins of government. Amid allegations of corruption in the government, López Arellano was ousted in a bloodless military coup led by Colonel Juan Alberto Melgar Castro on April 22, 1975. López Arellano was allowed to remain in the country and subsequently became president of an air transportation service in Honduras.

RAMÓN ERNESTO CRUZ (President, June 6, 1971–December 4, 1972). Ramón Ernesto Cruz Uclés was born in San Juan de Flores on January 4, 1903. He was educated at the Central University of Honduras, where he received a degree in law. He was appointed to the Honduran Supreme Court in 1949. Cruz served as Honduras's chief counsel at the International Court of Justice from 1958 until 1960 and defended Honduran interests in a border dispute with Nicaragua. He was the presidential candidate for the National party in 1963, but a military coup canceled the elections. Cruz was elected president in 1971 and replaced the military government of General Osvaldo López Arellano on June 6, 1971. Cruz's term was cut short when López Arellano reclaimed the presidency in a bloodless coup on December 4, 1972. Cruz was briefly placed under house arrest, but was released shortly thereafter. He died of a heart attack at the age of 82 in Tegucigalpa on August 6, 1985.

OSVALDO LÓPEZ ARELLANO
(President, December 4, 1972–April 22, 1975). *See earlier entry under Heads of State.*

JUAN ALBERTO MELGAR CASTRO
(President, April 22, 1975–August 7, 1978). Juan Alberto Melgar Castro was born in 1938. He served in the Honduran military, where he rose to the rank of colonel. He served as minister of the interior in the government of Osvaldo López Arellano from 1972. Melgar replaced López as commander in chief of the armed forces on March 31, 1975. He then led the bloodless coup that ousted López as president on April 22, 1975. Melgar was removed from office by the joint chiefs of staff on August 7, 1978. He remained active in political affairs and sought the presidency of the National party in 1982. He died of a heart attack in San Pedro Sula at the age of 52 on December 2, 1987.

POLICARPIO PAZ GARCÍA
(President, August 7, 1978–January 27, 1982). Policarpio Paz García was born in 1931. He served in the Honduran military, where he rose to the rank of brigadier general. He was chosen by the joint chiefs of staff to serve as leader of a three-man junta following the ouster of Juan Alberto Melgar Castro on August 7, 1978. Paz García was named provisional president by the Constituent Assembly on July 25, 1980. His government allowed presidential elections to take place in November of 1981. He relinquished the presidency to Roberto Suazo Córdova on January 27, 1982.

ROBERTO SUAZO CÓRDOVA
(President, January 27, 1982–January 27, 1986). Roberto Suazo Córdova was born in 1928. He attended the University of San Carlos, where he studied medicine, and then opened a private practice in La Paz. Suazo Córdova became active in the Liberal party in 1979. He was elected to the Constituent Assembly in 1981 and became president. He received the presidential nomination of the Liberal party in 1981. Suazo Córdova defeated Ricardo Zuñiga Augustinus, the Nationalist party nominee, and took office on January 27, 1982. The Honduran economy continued to deteriorate under Suazo Córdova's government. A constitutional crisis developed in 1985 when he tried to control the candidate selection process of the major parties in the upcoming presidential election. The National Assembly dismissed five justices on the Supreme Court who were supporters of Suazo Córdova, and the president retaliated by arresting the chief justice and charging him with treason. A compromise was negotiated that resulted in the release of the chief justice and the implementation of reforms in the Supreme Court and the electoral system. Suazo Córdova completed his term on January 27, 1986, and relinquished the presidency to José Simeón Azcona Hoyo.

JOSÉ SIMEÓN AZCONA HOYO
(President, January 27, 1986–January 27, 1990). José Simeón Azcona Hoyo was born in La Ceiba on January 26, 1927. He was educated in Honduras and Mexico and subsequently worked as a civil engineer. He became active in politics in the early 1960s as a member of the Liberal party. Azcona was a member of the party's Central Executive Committee from 1978 and served as secretary-general from 1981. He managed the presidential campaign of Roberto Suazo Córdova in November of 1981. Suazo Córdova was elected, and Azcona was named minister of communications, public works, and transport in the cabinet the following year. He resigned in 1983 in opposition to Suazo Córdova's attempts to centralize the Liberal party. Azcona

was the Liberal party's candidate for president in the elections in November of 1985. Azcona ran behind National party candidate Rafael Leonardo Callejas in the popular vote, but changes in the electoral system resulted in Azcona's election as president. He took office on January 27, 1986. His party controlled a minority of seats in the National Assembly, and he negotiated an arrangement with the Nationalists that allowed them a presence in the government. He also eliminated most Nicaraguan rebel contra bases in Honduras and supported a regional peace plan. Azcona completed his term of office on January 27, 1990.

RAFAEL LEONARDO CALLEJAS (President, January 27, 1990–). Rafael Leonardo Callejas was educated in the United States as an agronomist. He served as minister for agriculture and natural resources from 1978 until 1981. He was the Nationalist party candidate for president in 1985. Though he gained the majority of the popular vote, he was denied office due to changes in the electoral system. He again ran for the presidency in 1989 and was elected. He took office on January 27, 1990, and continued his predecessor's policy of including members of the opposition in the government.

Hungary (Hungarian Republic)

(Magyar Köztársaság)

Hungary is a country in eastern Europe.

HEADS OF STATE

ZOLTÁN TILDY (President, February 1, 1946–July 30, 1948). Zoltán Tildy was born in 1889. He was educated in Budapest and became a minister with the Hungarian Reformed Evangelical Church. He entered politics and was elected to Parliament as a member of the Smallholders party. Tildy later became leader of the party. During World War II he was active in the underground Resistance to the Germans. He was selected as president of the Budapest National Committee following the Soviet occupation of Hungary at the conclusion of the war. The Smallholders party was victorious in the elections in November of 1945, and Tildy became prime minister of Hungary on April 4, 1945. He relinquished the office to become president of the new Hungarian Republic on February 1, 1946. Mátyás Rákosi, the leader of the

Hungarian Communist party, forced Tildy to resign on July 30, 1948. He was put under house arrest and remained politically inactive until October of 1956, when he joined the government of Imre Nagy as minister of state. When Nagy's rebellion was crushed by the Soviet Union in November of 1956, Tildy was arrested and sentenced to six years in prison. He was released in April of 1959, due to poor health. He died in Budapest on August 3, 1961.

ARPÁD SZAKASITS (President, August 3, 1948–May 8, 1950). Arpád Szakasits was born in Budapest on December 8, 1888. He became active in the labor movement as a young man and became secretary of the Construction Workers Union. He was active in the rebellion led by Bela Kun in 1919 and was arrested and imprisoned following

Kun's defeat. Szakasits continued his work on the Social Democratic newspaper *Nepszava* after his release. He became a member of the Social Democrat party's central committee and became editor of *Nepszava* in 1939. He was a critic of the pro-Fascist government during World War II and became secretary-general of the Social Democrats following Hungary's collapse in 1945. He served in the postwar government and founded the Hungarian Working People's party in June of 1948. Szakasits became chairman of the Presidium of the People's Republic following the resignation of Zoltán Tildy on July 30, 1948. He remained president until May 8, 1950, when he was ousted and imprisoned with other leading Social Democrats. Szakasits was released from prison in 1954 and was officially pardoned two years later. He was elected to the Central Committee in 1959. He died at the age of 77 in Budapest on May 3, 1965.

SÁNDOR RÓNAI (President, May 8, 1950–August 14, 1952). Sándor Rónai was born on October 6, 1892. He was a member of the Social Democratic party. He was the only member of the party not purged from the Communist-dominated government in 1950. Rónai was selected to replace Arpád Szakasits as Hungary's head of state on May 8, 1950, but was demoted to chairman of the National Assembly on August 14, 1952. He was appointed as an alternate member of the Politburo in July of 1956. He remained a member of the Politburo until his death in Budapest at the age of 73 on September 27, 1965.

ISTVÁN DOBI (President, August 14, 1952–August 14, 1967). István Dobi was born on December 31, 1898. He joined the Social Democratic party at an early age. He later helped form the Smallholders party. Dobi served in the Hungarian army as a labor battalion guard during World War II. He returned to politics after the war and was elected

to the National Assembly. He served in the government as minister of agriculture until his dismissal by Prime Minister Ferenc Nagy in 1946. Dobi became leader of the Smallholders party following the arrest of Bela Kovacs in February of 1947. He returned to the cabinet in May of 1947 as minister without portfolio. Dobi was selected as Hungary's prime minister in December of 1948 and retained that position until August 14, 1952, when he was selected to replace Sándor Rónai as Hungary's head of state. His position was largely ceremonial, and he had little impact on the Hungarian revolution of 1956. Dobi joined the Hungarian Socialist Workers, or Communist, party in 1959 and was elected to the Central Committee. He remained chairman of the Presidium of the People's Republic until his retirement for reasons of health on August 14, 1967. He died in Budapest at the age of 70 on November 24, 1968.

PÁL LOSONCZY (President, August 14, 1967–June 25, 1987). Pál Losonczy was born on September 18, 1919. He was active in the Communist party and became a member of the Central Committee of the Hungarian Socialist Workers party following World War II. He was elected to parliament in 1953 and served in the government as minister of agriculture from 1960 until 1967. Losonczy was named to the largely ceremonial position of chairman of the Presidential Council on August 14, 1967. He retired due to poor health on June 25, 1987, and was replaced by Károly Németh.

KÁROLY NÉMETH (President, June 25, 1987–June 19, 1988). Károly Németh was born in Paka on December 14, 1922. He joined the Communist party in 1945 and was elected to Parliament in 1958. Németh rose through the party ranks to become first secretary of the Budapest Central Committee in 1965. He served on various party committees and was named to the newly created post of deputy general secretary in March of 1985. He was selected to succeed Pál Losonczy as chairman of the Presidential Council on June 25, 1987. Németh was replaced by Bruno Ferenc Straub on June 19, 1988.

BRUNO FERENC STRAUB (President, June 19, 1988–October 18, 1989). Bruno Ferenc Straub was born on January 5, 1914. He was educated in Hungary and received a degree in biological sciences. He served as director of the Biology Center of the Hungarian Academy of Sciences from 1970 until 1978 and was director of the Institute of Enzymology from 1979. He became the first non-Communist chairman of the Hungarian Presidential Council on June 19, 1988 and served until the Presidential Council was abolished on October 18, 1989, and Mátyás Szürös was chosen as acting president of the Hungarian Republic.

MÁTYÁS SZÜRÖS (President, October 18, 1989–May 2, 1990). Mátyás Szürös was born in Puspokladany on September 11, 1933. He was educated in Moscow and worked with the Foreign Ministry from 1959. He was active in

the Communist party and served as Hungary's ambassador to East Germany from 1975 until 1978. Szürös was then named ambassador to the Soviet Union, where he served until 1982. He became secretary of the Communist party's Central Committee in 1982. He resigned from the Communist party and was elected president of Parliament in 1988. Szürös was named acting president of the Hungarian Republic on October 18, 1989. He was replaced by Arpád Göncz on May 2, 1990.

ARPÁD GÖNCZ (President, May 2, 1990–   ). Arpád Göncz was born in 1921. He was educated in Budapest and worked as a bank clerk. He was active with the Smallholders party and was arrested following the Soviet occupation of Hungary in 1956. Göncz was tried and sentenced to life imprisonment in 1958. He was released in an amnesty in 1963 and subsequently worked as a writer and translator. He was active in the prodemocratic movement in Hungary and was selected by Parliament to serve as acting president on May 2, 1990. Göncz was elected to a five-year term of office by the Parliament in August of 1990.

HEADS OF GOVERNMENT

ZOLTÁN TILDY (Prime Minister, April 4, 1945–February 1, 1946). *See entry under Heads of State.*

FERENC NAGY (Prime Minister, February 2, 1946–May 31, 1947). Ferenc Nagy was born to a peasant family in Hungary in 1903. He worked as a laborer and was largely self-educated. He joined the Smallholders party in 1932 and served as national secretary of the party. In 1939 he was elected to Parliament. Nagy was jailed by the German Gestapo in 1944. He subsequently escaped and worked in

the anti-Fascist underground. He served as minister of reconstruction in the first postwar government. The Smallholders party was the winner in the first postwar election, and Nagy became prime minister on February 2, 1946. He was forced to resign on May 31, 1947, while vacationing in Switzerland. The Communists took control of the government and held Nagy's 4-year-old son as a hostage until he agreed to step down. He remained in exile and went to the United States. Nagy attempted to return to Hungary during the uprising in 1956, but Soviet troops crushed the revolt before he could enter the country. Nagy returned to the United States, where he worked as a writer and dairy farmer. He died of a heart attack in Herndon, Virginia, at the age of 75 on June 12, 1979.

LAJOS DINNYÉS (Prime Minister, May 31, 1947–December 1948). Lajos Dinnyés was born in 1901. He was educated at the Keszthely Agriculture Academy. He was a member of the Smallholders party and served in Parliament before World War II. Dinnyés served as minister of defense in the government of Prime Minister Ferenc Nagy from early 1947. He was selected to succeed Nagy as head of government on May 31, 1947. He led the government during elections that granted the Communist party control of the country. Dinnyés remained prime minister until December of 1948, when he was accused of having neglected his own political party. He subsequently joined the Communist party and served as vice president of the Hungarian Parliament. He died in Budapest at the age of 60 on May 4, 1961.

ISTVÁN DOBI (Prime Minister, December 1948–August 14, 1952). *See entry under Heads of State.*

MÁTYÁS RÁKOSI (Prime Minister, August 14, 1952–July 4, 1953). Mátyás Rákosi was born in Ada on March 14, 1892. He attended the Eastern Academy in Budapest and won a scholarship to the Bankers' Association language school in London. He remained in England to work at a bank. At the start of World War I in 1914, he returned to Hungary. Rákosi entered the Hungarian army and was taken prisoner by the Russians in 1915. He became active in the Bolshevik movement after meeting Lenin during the Russian Revolution. He returned to Hungary in 1918 and joined the Hungarian Communist party. Rákosi supported the revolution led by Bela Kun in February of 1919 and

briefly served as a minister in the Kun government. Rákosi accompanied the Communists into exile. He returned to Hungary in 1924 and was arrested by the government of Miklos Horthy. He was sentenced to be executed, but his life was saved by international pressure on the Horthy regime. He was imprisoned until 1940, when his release was ransomed by Joseph Stalin. Rákosi was banished to the Soviet Union, where he remained until the liberation of Hungary in January of 1945. He accompanied the Red Army to Budapest and served in the postwar government as vice premier. He also served as secretary-general of the Hungarian Workers party. The Communists took complete control of the government in 1947, and Rákosi led a purge of the party in 1949. Foreign Minister Laszlo Rajk and other leading political figures were tried and executed for treason. Rákosi became Hungary's prime minister on April 14, 1952. He relinquished the office of prime minister to Imre Nagy on July 4, 1953. Rákosi still remained the dominant political force in the country as secretary-general of the Communist party. He was forced from power in July of 1956 and went into exile in the Soviet Union. He was in poor health during the 1960s, and his death was erroneously reported in 1963. Rákosi remained in the Soviet Union until his death in Gorky at the age of 78 on February 5, 1971.

IMRE NAGY (Prime Minister, July 4, 1953–April 18, 1955). Imre Nagy was born in Kaposvar in 1895. He served in the Austro-Hungarian army during World War I. He was captured by the Russians and joined the Communist party during his imprisonment. After his release he returned home and became instrumental in the development of the Hungarian Communist party. Nagy was a supporter of the pro–Communist revolution led by Bela Kun in 1919. He was forced to go into exile in France following Kun's ouster. He returned to Hungary in 1923 to help organize the underground Communist party. Nagy was arrested in 1927 by the government of Miklos Horthy, but escaped from prison and returned to the Soviet Union in 1930. He remained there until the end of World War II. Nagy returned to Hungary to serve as minister of agriculture in the first provisional government from 1945 to 1946. He briefly served as minister of the interior and was appointed deputy premier under Mátyás Rákosi in 1951. He succeeded Rákosi as prime minister on July 4, 1953. Nagy was a protégé of Georgi M. Malenkov, prime minister of the Soviet Union, and when Malenkov was forced out of office in February of 1955, Nagy soon followed. He was removed as prime minister on April 18, 1955. At the start of the Hungarian national uprising in October of 1956, Nagy was again named prime minister and took office on October 24, 1956. One of the first acts of his new government was to announce the withdrawal of Hungary from the Warsaw Pact and the establishment of Hungary as a neutral nation. The Soviet Union responded by sending in the Soviet army and forcing Nagy's removal from office on November 4, 1956. Nagy fled to the Yugoslav Embassy in November of 1956, but was captured two weeks later when he emerged after being promised safe conduct by the Soviets. He was secretly taken to Romania by Soviet security officers. He was returned to Budapest in 1957 and was secretly put on trial for treason. Nagy and other liberal reformers were executed in Budapest on June 17, 1958.

ANDRÁS HEGEDÜS (Prime Minister, April 18, 1955–October 24, 1956). András Hegedüs was born in 1922. He was an agricultural expert and served as minister of state farms and forests from March of 1952 until July of 1953, when he was named minister of agriculture. He also served as deputy prime

minister from July of 1953. Hegedüs was selected to replace Imre Nagy as prime minister of Hungary on April 18, 1955. He sponsored some reforms in Hungary, including opening the borders to Yugoslavia. In October of 1956 the government was faced with a massive demonstration in Budapest calling for democratic reforms. Hegedüs stepped down on October 24, 1956, and Nagy was again installed as prime minister. Hegedüs fled to the Soviet Union, but was allowed to return to Hungary in 1958. Hegedüs subsequently became a leading party revisionist. He was reprimanded in 1968 for criticizing Hungary's role in the Czech invasion.

IMRE NAGY (Prime Minister, October 24, 1956–November 4, 1956). *See earlier entry under Heads of Government.*

JÁNOS KÁDÁR (Prime Minister, November 4, 1956–January 27, 1958). János Kádár was born János Czermanik in the village of Fiume on May 26, 1912. He was active in the trade union movement while in his teens and joined the outlawed Hungarian Communist party in 1931. He worked in the Communist underground and was a leader of the Hungarian Resistance during World War II. He took the name János Kádár during this period. He was arrested by the Gestapo near the end of the war. Kádár escaped from prison prior to the occupation of Hungary by the Soviet Red Army. He was named to the Communist party Central Committee after the war and was elected to the National Assembly in the provisional government in 1945. Kádár was appointed minister of the interior in 1949 and also served as head of the Hungarian secret police. He was arrested in April of 1951 by the order of Communist party leader Mátyás Rákosi. Kádár remained imprisoned until November of 1953, when he was released during an amnesty spurred by the death of Joseph Stalin.

Kádár resumed his work in the Communist party and held various minor positions. He joined with party reformers to force Rákosi's ouster as party leader in July of 1956. Kádár supported the liberal rebellion that returned Imre Nagy to power as prime minister in October of 1956. Kádár replaced Erno Gero as first secretary of the Communist party on October 25, 1956. Kádár opposed Nagy's move to withdraw Hungary from the Warsaw Pact, and he deserted the Nagy government when the Soviet Union invaded Hungary on November 4, 1956. Kádár was installed to replace Nagy as head of the Soviet-supported government. He instituted repressive measures against the Hungarian rebels that culminated in the execution of Nagy and other reformist leaders in June of 1958. Kádár had relinquished the post of prime minister to Ferenc Münnich on January 27, 1958. He continued to control the country as party leader and again became prime minister on September 13, 1961. Kádár sought a policy of national reconciliation in the early 1960s and purged many hard-line Stalinists from the party. He again stepped down as prime minister on June 28, 1965. He also instituted numerous economic reforms that allowed for a measure of free enterprise. Hungary's economy prospered under Kádár, who also instituted other liberal reforms in the country. The Hungarian economy stagnated in the 1980s, and Kádár was replaced as party leader by Károly Grósz on May 22, 1988. He was given the ceremonial position of party president, which he held until his resignation in early 1989 due to poor health. Kádár died in Budapest of pneumonia and circulatory problems at the age of 77 on July 6, 1989.

FERENC MÜNNICH (Prime Minister, January 27, 1958–September 13, 1961). Ferenc Münnich was born in Seregelyes in 1886. He was educated at Cluj University and received a degree in law. He served in the Austro-Hungarian army during World War I and was captured by the Russians. Münnich joined the Communists while in prison and fought with the Bolsheviks during the Russian Revolution. In 1918 he returned to Hungary to lead the Hungarian army. He served in the Communist government of Bela Kun in 1919. Münnich fled to the Soviet Union following the collapse of the Kun regime later in the year. He worked in the Comintern and fought with the Loyalists during the Spanish Civil War. Münnich was deported to France after the Loyalists' defeat and was briefly detained before returning to the Soviet Union. He fought in the Soviet Red Army during World War II and returned to Hungary after the war. He served as chief of police in Budapest before entering the diplomatic service. Münnich served as Hungary's ambassador to Finland, Bulgaria, the Soviet Union, and Yugoslavia during the 1950s. He returned to Hungary to serve as minister of the interior in the government of Imre Nagy in October of 1956. He supported János Kádár's ouster of Nagy's anti-Soviet government and served as minister of the interior and minister of defense in the subsequent Kádár government. Münnich was named first deputy premier in February of 1957 and succeeded Kádár as prime minister on January 27, 1958. Münnich led the government under the direction of party leader Kádár until September 13, 1961. Münnich subsequently served as minister of state. He remained on the party's Central Committee until his retirement in 1966. He died of a stroke in Budapest at the age of 81 on November 29, 1967.

JÁNOS KÁDÁR (Prime Minister, September 13, 1961–June 28, 1965). *See earlier entry under Heads of Government.*

GYULA KÁLLAI (Prime Minister, June 28, 1965–April 14, 1967). Gyula

Kállai was born in Berettyoujfalu on June 1, 1910. He joined the Hungarian Communist party in 1931 and worked as a party organizer in Budapest during the 1930s. He was arrested in 1939. Kállai worked for the party newspaper *Nepszava* after his release. He became a member of the Communist party Central Committee following World War II and served as undersecretary of state from 1945 until 1949. He was then named minister of foreign affairs. Kállai served until April of 1951, when he was arrested by the order of Communist party leader Mátyás Rákosi. He remained imprisoned until November of 1953, when he was released during an amnesty following the death of Joseph Stalin. He returned to the government as deputy minister of culture in 1955 and rose to minister the following year. Kállai was appointed minister of state in 1958. He was a close associate of Communist party leader János Kádár and served as deputy premier from 1960. He replaced Kádár as prime minister on June 28, 1965. Kállai was replaced by Jenö Fock on April 14, 1967. He subsequently served as Speaker of the Parliament until 1971 and retired from the Politburo in 1975.

JENÖ FOCK (Prime Minister, April 14, 1967–May 15, 1975). Jenö Fock was born in Budapest on May 17, 1916. He worked as a mechanic and became active in the Communist party in 1937. He served as deputy minister of metallurgy and energy from 1951 until 1954. Fock subsequently served as secretary of the National Council of Trade Unions until 1957. He was selected secretary of the Central Committee of the Hungarian Socialist Workers party in 1957 and served until 1961. He was deputy chairman of the Council of Ministers from 1961 and became prime minister on April 14, 1967. Fock resigned his position for reasons of health on May 15, 1975, and retired from politics in 1980.

GYÖRGY LÁZÁR (Prime Minister, May 15, 1975–June 25, 1987). György Lázár was born in Isaszeg on September 15, 1924. He joined the Hungarian Socialist Workers party in 1945. He attended technical school in Budapest and worked as a draftsman until 1948. Lázár was subsequently employed by the National Planning Office, where he rose to become a department head in 1953. Lázár remained with the National Planning Office and served as deputy president from 1958. He was appointed to the cabinet as minister of labor in January of 1970 and was appointed to the Communist party Central Committee later in the year. Lázár was named deputy premier in June of 1973 and also became president of the National Planning Office. He replaced Jenö Fock as prime minister of Hungary on May 15, 1975. Lázár sponsored economic reforms in the country and attempted to make Hungarian products more competitive in the world market. Hungary's economy took a downturn in the 1980s, however, and Lázár was replaced as prime minister by Károly Grósz on June 25, 1987. Lázár subsequently served as deputy general secretary of the Communist party until 1988.

KÁROLY GRÓSZ (Prime Minister, June 25, 1987–November 23, 1988). Károly Grósz was born in Miskolc on August 1, 1930. He was educated in Budapest and became a teacher. He subsequently attended the Communist party school and began work in the party organization. Grósz served as editor of the newspaper *North Hungary* from 1958 and was named party secretary for the Hungarian Radio and Television Committee in 1961. He served in the party's propaganda department as deputy leader from 1968 and as leader from 1974. Grósz was appointed first secretary of the Borsod County Party Committee in 1979 and became first secretary of the Party Committee in Budapest in 1984. He was elected to the Politburo the following year. Grósz was appointed to replace György Lázár as prime minister on June 25, 1987. He instituted an austerity program to stabilize Hungary's economy. He was successful in gaining the support of the party leadership and ousted János Kádár as first secretary of the Communist party on May 22, 1988. Grósz instituted liberal reforms in the party and the country and stepped down as prime minister on November 23, 1988. The Hungarian people were granted freedom of assembly in early 1989, and demonstrators demanded free elections and the removal of Soviet troops. The Hungarian Socialist Workers, or Communist, party renounced Marxism on October 7, 1989, and became the Hungarian Socialist party. Rezso Nyers became leader of the new party, and Grósz joined with other hard-line Communists to launch the János Kádár Society. The new party made little impact in elections in 1990.

MIKLÓS NÉMETH (Prime Minister, November 23, 1988–May 3, 1990). Miklós Németh was born in Monok on January 24, 1948. He was educated at Karl Marx University in Budapest and Harvard University in the United States. He became active in the Communist party and worked in the party's economic department from 1981. Németh was named to the Central Committee in June of 1987 and served as secretary in charge of economic policy. He was elected to the Politburo in May of 1988 and was selected to suc-

ceed Károly Grósz as prime minister on November 23, 1988. He continued the austerity measures and market-oriented economic policies of his predecessor. Németh was replaced as prime minister on May 3, 1988, following the collapse of the Communist government and democratic parliamentary elections. He subsequently served as vice president of the European Bank for Reconstruction and Development from 1991.

JÓZSEF ANTALL (Prime Minister, May 3, 1990–December 12, 1993). József Antall was born in Budapest on April 8, 1932. He was educated at the University of Budapest and later worked as a history teacher and librarian. He was active in the Smallholders party and was arrested following the Soviet occupation of Hungary in 1956. Antall was banned from teaching and political activities until 1963. He worked with the Semmelweis Museum, Library and Archives of Medical History, from 1964. He became active in the Hungarian democratic movement and served as president of the Hungarian Democratic Forum in 1989. Antall was elected to parliament the following year and became prime minister of Hungary on May 3, 1990. He suffered from lymphoma and underwent an operation in 1990. Concern over his health grew in 1992, when he canceled two trips abroad in the spring of that year. Antall remained president of Hungary until his death in Budapest from lymphatic cancer on December 12, 1993.

OTHER LEADERS

MÁTYÁS RÁKOSI (First Secretary, January 1945–July 1956). *See entry under Heads of Government.*

ERNO GERO (First Secretary, July 18, 1956–October 25, 1956). Erno Gero was born in 1898. He was active in the

Hungarian Communist party after the conclusion of World War II and served as a deputy to Communist leader Mátyás Rákosi. Gero replaced Rákosi as leader of the party on July 18, 1956, and attempted to stop the rising tide of anti-Soviet feelings in Hungary without success. He was forced to resign as party leader on October 25, 1956, and was replaced by János Kádár. Gero left Hungary for the Soviet Union during the 1950s. He returned the following decade but remained largely out of political activities. He died of a heart attack in Budapest at the age of 81 on March 12, 1980.

JÁNOS KÁDÁR (First Secretary, October 25, 1956–May 22, 1988). *See entry under Heads of Government.*

KÁROLY GRÓSZ (First Secretary, May 22, 1988–October 7, 1989). *See entry under Heads of Government.*

Iceland, Republic of

(Lýthveldith Ísland)

Iceland is an island nation in the North Atlantic Ocean near the Arctic Circle. It was granted independence from Denmark on June 7, 1944.

HEADS OF STATE

SVEINN BJÖRNSSON (President, August 1, 1945–January 25, 1952). Sveinn Björnsson was born in Copenhagen, Denmark, on February 27, 1881. After his graduation from the University of Copenhagen in 1907, he went to Reykjavík to practice law. He entered politics and was elected to the Reykjavík Town Council in 1912. He joined the Independence party and was elected to Iceland's Parliament, or Althing, in 1914. Iceland became a sovereign state united under the Danish crown on December 1, 1918. Björnsson served as minister to Denmark from 1920 until 1924 and again from 1926 until 1941. Following the German invasion of Denmark, Björnsson returned to Iceland, where he was elected regent by the Parliament on June 17, 1941. Björnsson was elected the first president of the new Icelandic republic on June 17, 1944 and took office on August 1, 1945. He was returned to office in 1949. Björnsson fell seriously ill with a heart ailment in 1950, but remained president until his death in Reykjavík on January 25, 1952.

ASGEIR ASGEIRSSON (President, August 1, 1952–July 30, 1968). Asgeir Asgeirsson was born in Koranesi on May 13, 1894. He was educated in Iceland and served on the faculty of the Teachers College of Iceland. He entered politics and was elected to the Icelandic Parliament in 1923. Asgeirsson served on various parliamentary committees and was elected Speaker in 1930. He was named minister of finance in 1931 and formed a government as prime minister on June 2, 1932. He retained office until March 29, 1934, when he was replaced by Hermann Jónasson. Asgeirsson chaired the government's Bureau of Education from 1934 until 1938 and then became director of the Fisheries Bank of Iceland. He served as Iceland's representative to the Bretton Woods Economic and Monetary Conference in 1944. He was also elected president of the Parliament in 1944. Asgeirsson was named governor of the International Monetary Fund in 1946. He also served in the Icelandic delegation to the United Nations in 1947 and 1948. Asgeirsson was elected president of Iceland in June of 1952 and took office on August 1, 1952. He was reelected without opposition to the largely ceremonial position in 1956, 1960, and 1964. He retired after completing his fourth term of office on July 30, 1968. Asgeirsson died in Reykjavík at the age of 78 on September 15, 1972.

KRISTJÁN ELDJÁRN (President, July 30, 1968–August 1, 1980). Kristján Eldjárn was born in Tjorn on December 6, 1916. He was educated at the University of Iceland and the University of Copenhagen in Denmark. He was a leading authority on Icelandic literature and history and also wrote several books on archaeology. Eldjárn was named curator of the National Museum in Reykjavík in 1947. He also served as editor of the *Icelandic Archaeological Society Journal.* He remained at the National Museum until 1968, when he was elected president of Iceland. He took office on July 30, 1968. Eldjárn was unopposed for reelection in 1972

and 1976. He completed his third term and retired on August 1, 1980. Eldjárn went to Cleveland, Ohio, for treatment of a heart ailment in 1982 and died there at the age of 65 on September 13, 1982.

VIGDÍS FINNBOGADÓTTIR (President, August 1, 1980–). Vigdís Finnbogadóttir was born in Reykjavík on April 15, 1930. She was educated in Switzerland, France, Denmark, and Iceland. She later taught drama at the University of Iceland and became director of the Reykjavík Theatre Company in 1972. Finnbogadóttir served on the Cultural Affairs Committee in Nordic Countries from 1976 and became chairwoman in 1978. She was elected to the largely ceremonial position of president of Iceland on August 1, 1980, and thus became the first democratically elected female head of state. She was unopposed for reelection in 1984 and faced only token challenges in 1988 and 1992.

HEADS OF GOVERNMENT

OLAFUR THORS (Prime Minister, October 21, 1944–February 3, 1947). Olafur Tryggvason Thors was born in Bogarnes on January 19, 1892. He was educated at the University of Copenhagen in Denmark, where he received a degree in philosophy in 1913. He subsequently served as director of an industrial business in Reykjavík. Thors became active in politics in 1924 and served on the central committee of the Conservative party. He was elected to the Icelandic Parliament and was a founding member of the Independence party in 1928. He served as chairman of the party, and in 1939 he was named to the cabinet as minister of industries. Thors was selected to replace Hermann Jónasson as prime minister on May 18, 1942 and served until December 18, 1942. Thors again formed a government

as prime minister on October 21, 1944. His government resigned in October of 1946, but Thors remained head of an interim government until February 3, 1947. He was again returned to office on December 6, 1949 and served until March 14, 1950. Thors again formed a coalition government on September 13, 1953. His government resigned on July 21, 1956, following the Progressive party's withdrawal from the coalition. Thors formed another government on November 20, 1959. He retained office until November 12, 1963, when he resigned for reasons of health. He died at the age of 72 after suffering a stroke in Reykjavík on December 31, 1964.

STEFÁN JÓHANN STEFFÁNSSON (Prime Minister, February 3, 1947– December 6, 1949). Stefán Jóhann

Steffánsson was born on July 20, 1894. He was elected president of the Social Democratic party in 1937. He formed a coalition government as prime minister on February 3, 1947. Steffánsson also served in the cabinet as minister of social welfare. He remained head of the government until December 6, 1949. He was defeated for leadership of the Social Democrats by Hannibal Valdimarsson in December of 1952.

OLAFUR THORS (Prime Minister, December 6, 1949–March 14, 1950). *See earlier entry under Heads of Government.*

STEINGRÍMUR STEINTHÓRSSON (Prime Minister, March 14, 1950–September 13, 1953). Steingrímur Steinthórsson was born in Alftagardur on February 12, 1893. He was educated at the Copenhagen Agricultural College and returned to Iceland to teach at the Hvanneyri Agricultural School in 1924. He became headmaster of the Holar Agricultural School in 1928. Steinthórsson was elected to the Parliament in 1931. He left the school in 1935 to serve as minister of agriculture. He was a member of the Progressive party and was asked to form a government as prime minister on March 14, 1950. Steinthórsson retained office until September 13, 1953. He died on November 14, 1966.

OLAFUR THORS (Prime Minister, September 13, 1953–July 21, 1956). *See earlier entry under Heads of Government.*

HERMANN JÓNASSON (Prime Minister, July 21, 1956–December 4, 1958). Hermann Jónasson was born in northern Iceland on December 25, 1896. He was educated at the University of Iceland, where he received a degree in law. He served as a judicial assistant in Reykjavík until 1928 and then became police commissioner of the city. Jónasson left the police in 1934 to enter politics. He was elected to the Parliament as a member of the Progressive party and became prime minister on March 29, 1934. He remained prime minister of a coalition government in 1937. Iceland had been granted independence from Denmark in 1918, but recognized the king of Denmark as its monarch. The Parliament granted executive powers to the prime minister in April of 1940 following the German occupation of Denmark. Jónasson continued to serve as prime minister when Iceland was declared an independent republic in May of 1941, but he offered his resignation in October of 1941 after Iceland experienced increased inflation. His resignation was not accepted until the following month. He remained as head of the government until a new government under Olafur Thors took office on May 18, 1942. Jónasson returned to serve as prime minister of a leftist coalition government that included Communist Ludvig Josepsson on July 21, 1956. Jónasson remained in office until December 4, 1958. He died on November 2, 1976.

EMIL JÓNSSON (Prime Minister, December 23, 1958–November 20, 1959). Emil Jónsson was born in Hafnarfjordur on October 27, 1902. He was educated at the University of Copenhagen, where he received a degree in engineering in 1925. Jónsson was elected mayor of Hafnarfjordur in 1930. He was a member of the Social Democratic party and was elected to Parliament in 1934. He also remained Hafnarfjordur's mayor until 1937, when he was appointed state director of lighthouses and harbors. Jónsson served in that position until 1944, when he was appointed minister of commerce and communications. He returned to the Lighthouse and Harbors Ministry in 1949 and served until 1957. He was also elected Speaker of the Parliament in 1956 and served as chairman of the Social Democratic party in 1957. Jónsson formed an interim government as prime minister on December 23, 1958 and served until November 20, 1959. He remained in the government as minister of social affairs and fisheries until 1965. He was then named foreign minister. Jónsson retained that position until his retirement in 1971. He died in Reykjavík at the age of 84 on November 30, 1986.

OLAFUR THORS (Prime Minister, November 20, 1959–November 12, 1963). *See earlier entry under Heads of Government.*

BJARNI BENEDIKTSSON (Prime Minister, November 14, 1963–July 10, 1970). Bjarni Benediktsson was born in Reykjavík on April 30, 1908. He was educated at the University of Iceland and continued his education in Berlin and Copenhagen. He returned home to become a professor at the University of Iceland in 1932. Benediktsson remained in that position until he entered politics in 1940. He joined the Independence party and was elected mayor of Reykjavík in 1940. He was elected to the Parliament in 1942 and was named Iceland's representative to the United Nations in 1946. Benediktsson served as foreign minister from 1947 until 1953. Following the electoral defeat of the Independence party in 1956, he became editor of the daily newspaper *Morgunbladid* and remained in this post until 1959. He was elected prime minister as head of a coalition government including the Independence party and the Social Democrats on November 14, 1963. Benediktsson sponsored legislation designed to improve social welfare in the country and was also successful in improving Iceland's economic conditions. His government also maintained a close relationship with the United States. Benediktsson, his wife, and grandson were killed in a fire at the prime minister's official summer residence in Thingvellir, near Reykjavík, on July 10, 1970.

JOHANN HAFSTEIN (Prime Minister, July 10, 1970–July 14, 1971). Johann Hafstein was born on September 19, 1915. He was educated at the University of Iceland. He went to Great Britain in 1938 to study law. Hafstein returned to Iceland in 1939 to serve as manager of the Independence party. He was elected to the Reykjavík City Council in 1946. He was also elected to Parliament in 1946. Hafstein served as general manager of the Fisheries Bank of Iceland from 1952 until 1963. He was then appointed to the cabinet as minister of justice and industry. Hafstein succeeded Bjarni Benediktsson as prime minister on July 10, 1970. He relinquished the office to Olafur Jóhannesson on July 14, 1971, following parliamentary elections. He remained the leader of the Independence party until 1973. Hafstein died on May 15, 1981.

OLAFUR JÓHANNESSON (Prime Minister, July 14, 1971–August 28, 1974). Olafur Jóhannesson was born in Skagafjordur on March 1, 1913. He was educated at the University of Iceland, where he received a degree in law. He entered politics in 1946 and served on the Progressive party Central Committee. Jóhannesson also served as a law professor at the university from 1947. He was elected to Parliament in 1959. He was elected vice president of the Progressive party in 1960 and became president in 1968. Jóhannesson formed a government as prime minister on July 14, 1971. He led the coalition government until August 28, 1974, and continued to serve in the government as minister of justice and trade. Jóhannesson was again named prime minister on August 31, 1978. He retained office until October 15, 1979, when his coalition government collapsed. He was named minister of foreign affairs in February of 1980 and served until 1983. Jóhannesson remained active in the Progressive party.

GEIR HALLGRÍMSSON (Prime Minister, August 28, 1974–August 31, 1978). Geir Hallgrímsson was born in Reykjavík on December 16, 1925. He was educated in Iceland and the United States and received a degree in law. He was elected to the Reykjavík City Council in 1954 and became mayor in 1959. Hallgrímsson was also elected to the Parliament in 1959. He became chairman of the Independence party in 1973 and was selected as prime minister on August 28, 1974. He retained office until August 31, 1978. Hallgrímsson resigned as Independence party chairman in 1983 and was subsequently named foreign minister. He served in that position until 1986, when he became governor of the Central Bank of Iceland.

OLAFUR JÓHANNESSON (Prime Minister, August 31, 1978–October 15, 1979). *See earlier entry under Heads of Government.*

BENEDIKT GRÖNDAL (Prime Minister, October 15, 1979–February 8, 1980). Benedikt Gröndal was born in Onundarfjordur on July 7, 1924. He was educated in Iceland, the United States, and Great Britain. He worked as a journalist and was elected to Parliament in 1956. Gröndal became chairman of the Social Democratic party in 1974 and served in the cabinet as foreign minister from 1978. He was selected as prime minister of a caretaker coalition government on October 15, 1979. He served until February 8, 1980. Gröndal served as ambassador to Sweden from 1982 until 1987. He was ambassador to the Asia Pacific area in 1987 and served as Iceland's ambassador to the United Nations from 1989 until 1991.

GUNNAR THORODDSEN (Prime Minister, February 8, 1980–May 26, 1983). Gunnar Thoroddsen was born in Reykjavík on December 29, 1910. He was educated at the University of Iceland and received a degree in law.

He entered politics in 1934 and was elected to the Parliament as a member of the Independence party. Thoroddsen also became a law professor at the University of Iceland in 1940. He was named minister of finance in 1959 and served as Iceland's ambassador to Denmark from 1965 until 1969. He was a justice on Iceland's Supreme Court in 1970. Thoroddsen returned to the cabinet as minister of industry, energy, and social affairs in 1974 and served until 1978. He led the Conservative Independents, a splinter group of the Independence party, and formed a coalition government as prime minister on February 8, 1980. His government was unable to gain a working majority on economic issues, however. Thoroddsen called for new elections in April of 1983 and retired from office on May 26, 1983. He died in Reykjavík at the age of 72 on September 25, 1983.

STEINGRÍMUR HERMANNSSON (Prime Minister, May 26, 1983–July 8, 1987). Steingrímur Hermannsson was born on June 22, 1928. He was the son of Hermann Jónasson, who later served as Iceland's prime minister. He was educated in Iceland and the United States. Hermannsson worked as an engineer in the 1950s and became director of Iceland's National Research Council in 1957. He later entered politics and became secretary of the Progressive party in 1971. He became chairman in 1979. The following year he was named minister of fisheries and communications. Hermannsson remained in the cabinet until his selection as prime minister in a coalition government on May 26, 1983. His party lost seats in the elections in the spring of 1987, and he left office on July 8, 1987. He served as foreign minister and minister of foreign trade in the subsequent cabinet. Hermannsson was again asked to form a government on September 28, 1988. He served until April 30, 1991, and subsequently resigned the chairmanship of the Progressive party.

THORSTEINN PÁLSSON (Prime Minister, July 8, 1987–September 28, 1988). Thorsteinn Pálsson was born on October 29, 1947. He received a degree in law from the University of Iceland in 1974. He worked as editor of *Visir*, the Conservative afternoon newspaper, from 1975 until 1979. Pálsson then served as director of Iceland's Employer's Federation until his election to Parliament in April of 1983. He was chairman of the Independence party and served in the cabinet as minister of finance from 1985 until 1987. He was elected prime minister of Iceland on July 8, 1987, serving until his coalition government collapsed over differences in economic policy on September 28, 1988. Pálsson remained chairman of the Independence party until the following year.

STEINGRÍMUR HERMANNSSON (Prime Minister, September 28, 1988– April 30, 1991). *See earlier entry under Heads of Government.*

DAVID ODDSSON (Prime Minister, April 30, 1991–). David Oddsson was born in Reykjavík on January 17, 1948. He was educated in Iceland and served on the Reykjavík City Council from 1974. He was elected mayor of Reykjavík in 1982 and served until 1991. Oddsson became vice-chairman of the Independence party in 1989 and was elected chairman in 1991. He was also elected to the Parliament that year. He became prime minister of Iceland on April 30, 1991.

India, Republic of

(Bharat)

India is a country on the Indian subcontinent in South Asia. It was granted independence from Great Britain on August 15, 1947.

HEADS OF STATE

LOUIS MOUNTBATTEN (Governor-General, August 15, 1947–June 21, 1948). Prince Louis Francis Albert Victor Nicholas of Battenberg was born in Windsor, England, on June 25, 1900. He was the son of Prince Louis of Battenberg and Princess Victoria. He served in the Royal Navy during World War I. The family name of Battenberg was changed to Mountbatten in 1917 as a result of anti-German feelings. Mountbatten rose to the rank of captain prior to World War II. He commanded a destroyer flotilla in the early months of the war. He was made chief of combined operations in 1941 and planned the invasion of Europe. Mount-batten was named supreme allied commander for Southeast Asia in 1943. He led the recapture of Burma from Japanese control in 1945. Mountbatten was created a viscount in 1946 and became earl of Burma in 1947. He was named the last British viceroy of India on February 20, 1947. He presided over the end of British rule in India and served as India's first governor-general after independence on August 15, 1947. Mountbatten relinquished his position on June 21, 1948, and returned to Great Britain. He returned to the Royal Navy as a rear admiral and became commander in chief of the Mediterranean fleet in 1952. He served as first sea lord from 1955 until 1959. Mountbatten was as the first chief of the British Defense Staff from 1959 until his retirement in 1965. He was killed in a bomb blast aboard his fishing boat off the coast of County Sligo, Ireland, on August 27, 1978. His assassination was attributed to the Irish Republican Army.

CHAKRAVARTI RAJAGOPALA-CHARI (Governor-General, June 21, 1948–January 26, 1950). Chakravarti Rajagopalachari was born to a Brahmin family in the Salem District of Madras State on December 8, 1878. He was educated at Bangalore Central College and Madras University. He received a degree in law while in his late teens and began a successful practice in Salem. Rajagopalachari became involved in the Indian nationalist movement and joined Mohandas Gandhi's noncooperation movement in 1919. He abandoned his law practice to become one of Gandhi's closest advisors. Rajagopalachari was briefly imprisoned by the British colonial authorities for his activities in 1929. He served as acting president of the Indian Congress party while Gandhi was incarcerated during the 1930s. Rajagopalachari's daughter married Gandhi's son, Devi Das Gandhi, in 1932. Rajagopalachari was elected to the Madras Legislative Assembly in 1935 and served as chief minister of Madras from 1937 until 1939. He supported Gandhi's policy of neutrality in the early years of World War II and was arrested for antiwar statements. He broke with Gandhi and the Congress party in 1942 when he changed his position to support the Allied war effort against Japan. Rajagopalachari also gave his support to the British plan for Muslim autonomy in Pakistan as part of India's independence agreement. His differences with the Congress party and Gandhi were largely resolved by 1944. Rajagopalachari served in the interim government in New Delhi from 1946 until 1947. He subsequently served as governor of West Bengal before he succeeded Louis Mountbatten as governor-general of India on June 21, 1948. He retained office until January 26, 1950, when the position was abolished and India was declared a republic. Rajagopalachari served in the cabinet as minister for home affairs from 1950 until 1952. He then returned to Madras to serve as chief minister until he was forced to resign in March of 1954. Rajagopalachari gradually went into opposition to the Congress party government in the 1950s and formed the right-wing Swatantra, or Freedom, party in 1959. He was also a leading advocate of a nuclear test ban treaty. He remained politically active until his death in Madras at the age of 94 on December 25, 1972.

RAJENDRA PRASAD (President, January 26, 1950–May 13, 1962). Rajendra Prasad was born in the Saran District of Bihar Province on December 3, 1884. He was educated at Presidency College in Calcutta and Allahabad University, where he received a degree in law in 1911. He opened a legal practice and also served as a law professor at the University Law College in Calcutta from 1914 until 1916. Prasad joined Mohandas Gandhi's movement of noncooperation with the British colonial government in 1917 and abandoned his law practice to campaign for Indian independence three years later. He served as secretary and president of the Bihar Province Congress Committee in 1920 and was secretary of the Indian National Congress party in 1922. He was arrested by the colonial authorities for nationalist activities on several occasions in the early 1930s. Prasad was elected to succeed Gandhi as president of the National Congress party in 1934. He was again elected president of the party in 1939. Prasad was imprisoned during World War II for his opposition to the British war effort. He was released in June of 1945 and joined the interim government as minister of food and agriculture in September of

1946. He was elected president of the Indian Constituent Assembly later in the year. Prasad retained his position in the cabinet when India was granted independence in August of 1947, and he was elected president of the Indian National Congress in November of 1947. Prasad was nominated by Prime Minister Jawaharlal Nehru to become India's first president. He was unanimously elected and took office when India was declared a republic on January 26, 1950. He was reelected following parliamentary elections in the spring of 1952. Prasad was a candidate for another term in 1957 and was again victorious. He made numerous state visits overseas during the late 1950s. He retired from office on May 13, 1952, and died of pneumonia in Patna at the age of 79 on February 28, 1963.

SARVEPALLI RADHAKRISHNAN

(President, May 13, 1962–May 13, 1967). Sarvepalli Radhakrishnan was born in Tiruttani on September 5, 1888. He was educated at the Madras Christian College. In 1921 he began teaching philosophy at Calcutta University, and he wrote *Indian Philosophy* during the mid-1920s. He left Calcutta University in 1931. He became the first Indian to hold a chair at Oxford in 1936. Radhakrishnan returned to India in 1939 to serve as a member of the Constituent Assembly. He became chairman of the United Nations Educational, Scientific, and Cultural Organization (UNESCO) in 1949 and later in the year was named India's ambassador to the Soviet Union. He returned to India in 1952 to become vice president. Radhakrishnan retained this position until May 13, 1962, when he was elected to the largely ceremonial position of president of India. He completed his term of office on May 13, 1967. He also published *Religion in a Changing World* that year. Radhakrishnan died in Madras at the age of 86 on April 16, 1975.

ZAKIR HUSAIN (President, May 13, 1967–May 3, 1969). Zakir Husain was born in Hyderabad on February 8, 1897. He attended Aligarh Muslim University, where he received a degree in economics. He supported Mohandas K. Gandhi's movement to gain independence for a united India. Husain helped to found the Islamic college, Jamia Millia, in New Delhi in 1927. He served as vice-chancellor after receiving a doctorate from Berlin University. He became vice-chancellor of Aligarh University in 1948, following the partition of India and Pakistan. Husain remained at the university until 1956, when he became a member of the upper house of Parliament. He was appointed governor of Bihar State in 1957. He became the first Muslim vice president of India in 1962. Husain was the Congress party's nominee for president in 1967. He was victorious after a bitter campaign that made an issue of his religion. Husain took office on May 13, 1967. He retained the largely ceremonial position until his death from a heart attack in New Delhi at the age of 72 on May 3, 1969.

V. V. GIRI (President, May 3, 1969–August 24, 1974). Varahagiri Venkata Giri was born in Berhampur on August 10, 1894. He attended the local Kallikota College and received a degree in law from the National University of Ireland. Giri became involved with the Sinn Fein while in Ireland and took part in anti-British demonstrations. He became friendly with Irish nationalists Eamon De Valera and Michael Collins. He took part in the Easter Rebellion in 1916 and was subsequently deported to India. Giri practiced law in Berhampur and joined the Indian National Congress. He supported Mohandas K. Gandhi's independence movement and took part in various demonstrations. He was arrested in 1921 and led a hunger strike while in prison the following year. Giri became involved in the trade union movement after his release. He was a founder of the All-India Railway Union and served as general secretary from 1929 until 1936. Giri was elected to the legislative assembly in Madras in 1937. He also served in the Madras government as minister of labor, industry, and commerce from 1937. He retained his position until India was granted dominion status in August of 1947. Giri then served as India's ambassador to Ceylon until 1951. He was elected to the lower house of Parliament as a member of the Congress party in 1952. He was named to Jawaharlal Nehru's cabinet as minister of labor and served until September of 1954, when he resigned in opposition to a government wage recommendation. Giri was appointed governor of Uttar Pradesh State in June of 1957. He became governor of Kerala State in 1961 and of Mysore State in 1965. He was elected vice president of India in May of 1967. Giri became acting president following the death of Zakir Husain on May 3, 1969. He resigned from office on July 20, 1969, to enter the campaign for president. He was denied the nomination of the Congress party and ran as an independent with the support of Prime Minister Indira Gandhi. He narrowly defeated Congress party candidate Neelam Sanjiva Reddy and was sworn into office on August 24, 1969. Giri supported the Gandhi government while serving in his largely ceremonial office. He completed his term on August 24, 1974, and was denied a nomination for a second term. He retired to Madras to write his memoirs. Giri founded the Labor party of India in 1979. He died of a heart attack at his home in Madras at the age of 85 on June 24, 1980.

FAKHRUDDIN ALI AHMED (President, August 24, 1974–February 11, 1977). Fakhruddin Ali Ahmed was born in Delhi on May 13, 1905. He graduated from St. Catharine's College, Cambridge, in 1927, where he received a degree in law. He returned to India and joined the Congress party in 1931. Ahmed was elected to the state legislature in Assam in 1935 and served as minister of finance from 1938 until 1939. He served in the Assam local government following Indian independence in 1947. He served in Indira Gandhi's national government from 1966 and remained loyal to her following the split in the Congress party in 1969. Ahmed succeeded V. V. Giri as India's president on August 24, 1974. He retained the office until his death in New Delhi on February 11, 1977.

BASAPPA D. JATTI (President, February 11, 1977–July 25, 1977). Basappa Danappa Jatti was born in Savalgi, Bijapur District, on September 10, 1912. He attended Sykes Law College and opened a practice in Jamkhandi after receiving his degree. He entered politics in Jamkhandi and rose to the position of chief minister. Jatti served in the Bombay Legislative Assembly and was named deputy minister of health and labor in the Bombay government in 1952. He later served in the Mysore Legislative Assembly and was chief minister from 1958 until 1962. He remained in the Mysore government as minister of finance until 1965 and subsequently served as minister of food until 1967. Jatti served as governor of Orissa from 1972 until 1974, when he was elected vice president of India. He served as acting president of India following the death of Fakhruddin Ali Ahmed on February 11, 1977. Jatti swore in Moraji Desai as prime minister to replace Indira Gandhi the following month. Jatti remained acting president until Neelam Sanjiva Reddy was sworn into office on July 25, 1977. He returned to the position of vice president and also served as chairman of the upper house of the Indian Parliament, the Rajya Sabha, until 1979.

NEELAM SANJIVA REDDY (President, July 25, 1977–July 25, 1982). Neelam Sanjiva Reddy was born in

Illuru, Andhra Pradesh, on May 19, 1913. He attended the University of Madras and joined Mohandas Gandhi's movement of noncooperation with the British in 1931. He was active in the Congress party and served as secretary of the Andhra Pradesh Congress Committee from 1936. Reddy was imprisoned by the British during most of World War II. He was a member of the independent Indian Constituent Assembly in 1947 and served as a member of the Madras government from 1949 until 1951. He was elected to the Andhra Pradesh Legislative Assembly in 1953 and served as deputy chief minister. Reddy rose to the position of chief minister of Andhra Pradesh in 1956 and served until 1959. He was president of the Indian National Congress from 1960 until 1962. He then returned to serve as Andhra Pradesh's chief minister until 1964. He joined the national government of Lal Bahadur Shastri as minister of steel and mines in 1964 and served until 1965. Reddy served in the cabinet as minister of transportation from 1966 until 1967. He subsequently served as Speaker of the Lok Sabha, the lower house of the Indian Parliament. He resigned from his position to campaign for the presidency in 1969. Reddy received the nomination of the Congress party, but was defeated in the election by V. V. Giri, who campaigned with the support of prime minister Indira Gandhi. Reddy withdrew from politics following a subsequent defeat in a parliamentary election. He worked in farming in Anantapur District until 1977, when he returned to the Parliament as a member of the Janata party. He was again elected Speaker of the Lok Sabha in March of 1977. Reddy was unanimously selected to complete the late Fakhruddin Ali Ahmed's term as India's president on July 25, 1977. He completed his term of office and was succeeded by Zail Singh on July 25, 1982.

ZAIL SINGH (President, July 25, 1982–July 25, 1987). Zail Singh was born

Jarnail Singh in Sandhwan, Faridkot District, Punjab, on May 5, 1916. At an early age he joined the Akali Dal, the Sikh nationalist organization that opposed British rule in the Punjab. He founded the nationalist party Praja Mandal in 1938 and was arrested by the local government. Singh was imprisoned for nearly five years. He remained active in the local government following India's independence in 1947. He was elected to the upper house of the Indian Parliament, the Rajya Sabha, in 1956. Singh returned to the Punjab in 1962 to serve in the state assembly. He was Punjab's minister of state from 1966. Singh was chosen as chief minister of the Punjab in 1972 and retained office until 1977. He was a loyal supporter of Prime Minister Indira Gandhi and returned to the national government as minister of home affairs in her cabinet in 1980. Gandhi nominated Singh for the largely ceremonial position of president of India. He became India's first Sikh president on July 25, 1982. The Indian government was faced with a growing Sikh autonomy movement in the Punjab. The Gandhi government ordered the army to attack the Golden Temple in Amritsar, the Sikh's holiest shrine, in June of 1984. Hundreds of Sikh militants were killed in the fighting. The priests of the Golden Temple declared Zail Singh a renegade to his faith and barred him from worshiping at the shrine. His banning was rescinded following the Gandhi government's removal of military troops from the Golden Temple in September of 1984. Gandhi was assassinated the following month by her Sikh bodyguards in retaliation for the attack on the Golden Temple. Zail Singh completed his term of office on July 25, 1987.

RAMASWAMY VENKATARAMAN (President, July 25, 1987–July 25, 1992). Ramaswamy Venkataraman was born in Rajamadam in Madras State on December 4, 1910. He attended Madras University, where he received a degree in law. He served as an advocate of the Madras High Court from 1935 and was a founding member of the Congress Socialist party. Venkataraman was also active as a counsel for Indian trade unionists. He was arrested by the British colonial authorities for his nationalist activities in 1942 and remained imprisoned for the remainder of World War II. He was elected to the Provisional Parliament in 1950 and served as a member of the Lok Sabha, or lower house of Parliament, from 1952. Venkataraman entered the local Madras government as minister for industry and labor in 1957 and served until 1967. He then served on the Planning Commission until 1971. He subsequently retired from politics to serve as editor of the English weekly *Swarajaya*. Venkataraman returned to the Lok Sabha in 1977 and was appointed minister of finance and industry in the cabinet of Prime Minister Indira Gandhi in 1980. He was named minister of defense in 1982 and was elected vice president of India under Zail Singh in August of 1984. Venkataraman was the Congress-I candidate for the presidency in 1987. He was elected by a wide margin and succeeded Zail Singh on July 25, 1987. Venkataraman completed his term and relinquished office to Shankar Dayal Sharma on July 25, 1992.

SHANKAR DAYAL SHARMA (President, July 25, 1992–   ). Shankar Dayal Sharma was born in Bhopal, Madhya Pradesh State, on August 19, 1918. He was educated in India and at Cambridge University in Great Britain, where he received a degree in law. He returned to India to begin a legal practice in Lucknow in 1940. Sharma also became active in the Indian nationalist movement in Bhopal and was arrested by the British colonial authorities. He joined the All-India Congress Committee in 1950 and served as chief minister of Bhopal from 1952 until 1956. He was subsequently elected to the Madhya Pradesh legislative assembly and served in the cabinet of the state government. Sharma was elected to the national Parliament in 1971 as a member of the Congress party. He served in Parliament until 1977 and again from 1980. He served as governor of Andhra Pradesh from 1984 until 1985 and was governor of Punjab from 1985 until 1986. Sharma was selected as governor of Maharashtra in 1986 and served until his election as vice president in August of 1987. He was selected to succeed Ramaswamy Venkataraman to the largely ceremonial position of president of India on July 25, 1992.

HEADS OF GOVERNMENT

JAWAHARLAL NEHRU (Prime Minister, August 15, 1947–May 27, 1964). Jawaharlal Nehru was born in Allahabad on November 14, 1889. He accompanied his family to England in 1905, where he was educated at Trinity College, Cambridge. He received a law degree and returned to India to practice law in 1912. Nehru also entered politics and joined the Indian National Congress. He became part of the nationalist movement led by Mohandas Gandhi following the massacre at Amritsar in 1919. He was imprisoned by the British for his activities in 1921. Nehru succeeded his father, Motilal Nehru, as president of the Congress party in 1929 and was again president from 1936 until 1937. He was again arrested in 1942 and remained in prison until Britain agreed in 1945 to grant India independence. He became vice president of the pre-independence interim government in 1946, and following independence on August 15, 1947, he served as India's first prime minister. Mohandas Gandhi was assassinated in Delhi on January 30, 1948. Nehru remained prime minister following India's declaration as a republic in January of 1950, and his party was successful in general elections in 1952 and 1957. He led India as a nonaligned nation and sent Indian troops on various United Nations peacekeeping missions during the 1950s and 1960s. Kashimir was incorporated into India in 1957, and India annexed Portuguese Goa in 1961. India engaged in a border war with the People's Republic of China in 1962. Nehru remained India's prime minister until his death in New Delhi at the age of 74 on May 27, 1964.

GULZARILAL NANDA (Acting Prime Minister, May 27, 1964–June 9, 1964). Gulzarilal Nanda was born in Sialkot in the Punjab State on July 4, 1898. He was educated in India and became involved in the Indian independence movement. He was secretary of a textile labor association from 1922 until 1936. Nanda was arrested by the British on five occasions prior to Indian independence in 1947. He was appointed to the cabinet by Jawaharlal Nehru in 1951 and served as minister of planning. He was appointed home minister in 1963 and used his position to eliminate corruption in the Indian government. Nanda served as acting prime minister following the death of Nehru on May 27, 1964. He was a leading candidate to succeed Nehru, but his association with the leftist labor unions cost him support. Lal Bahadur Shastri was selected as prime minister instead and took office on June 9, 1964. Nanda remained in the cabinet as home minister and was again interim prime minister following Shastri's death on January 11, 1966. He retained the position until Indira Gandhi was selected as head of government on January 24, 1966. Nanda served in Gandhi's cabinet as home minister until he was forced to resign on November 9, 1966.

LAL BAHADUR SHASTRI (Prime Minister, June 9, 1964–January 11, 1966). Lal Bahadur was born in the village of Maghalsarai in Uttar Pradesh on October 2, 1904. Shastri became involved in the Indian independence movement while a student in Varanasi. He was arrested by the colonial authorities for his participation in Gandhi's noncooperation movement in 1921. Following his release, he continued his education and received his degree in modern philosophy. He then adopted the name Shastri. He became active in the Indian National Congress and was again imprisoned in 1930 because of his support for Gandhi's protest movement against British salt laws. He was released in 1933 and in 1935 was selected to serve as general secretary of the United Provinces Provincial Congress Committee. He was elected to the United Provinces Legislative Assembly in 1937. Shastri became a leading figure in the United Provinces government and in 1946 became chief minister of the area. Following India's independence in 1947, Shastri was appointed minister for police and transport in the United Provinces, now known as Uttar Pradesh. He worked with the Indian National Congress in the general elections in 1951 and was instrumental in the party's victory that year. Shastri was elected to Parliament the following year and was named to the cabinet as minister for transport and rails. He resigned this office in November of 1956, following a major railway accident. He was reelected to Parliament in 1957 and served in Nehru's government as minister for transportation and communications. Shastri was named minister of commerce in March of 1958 and was appointed home minister in April of 1961. He again worked as the Congress party's chief political organizer in the elections of 1962. Nehru dismissed Shastri from the government in August of 1963 following a cabinet reshuffle. Shastri returned to Nehru's government as minister without portfolio in January of 1964, and he was selected to become prime minister following Nehru's death in May of 1964. He took office on June 9, 1964. Shortly afterwards Shastri suffered a heart attack which prevented him from attending a conference of Commonwealth prime ministers. Following his recovery, he attempted to improve India's relations with neighboring countries. India's increasing economic problems caused a loss of support for his government, but his stature was restored following his firmness in standing up to Pakistan after the outbreak of armed conflict in 1965. Shastri attended a peace conference in Tashkent in the Soviet Union and signed a treaty with Pakistan's president Mohammed Ayub Khan. Shastri died of a heart attack before the conference adjourned on January 11, 1966.

GULZARILAL NANDA (Acting Prime Minister, January 11, 1966–January 24, 1966). *See earlier entry under Heads of Government.*

INDIRA GANDHI (Prime Minister, January 24, 1966–March 22, 1977). Indira Gandhi was born Indira Priyadarshini Nehru in Allahabad on November 19, 1917. She was the only child of Jawaharlal Nehru. She became involved at an early age in the work of her father and Mohandas Gandhi to free India of British rule. She was educated in India and Switzerland before entering Somerville College at Oxford University in 1936. She returned to India two years later before completing her studies. She joined the Indian Congress party in 1938 and married Feroze Gandhi against the wishes of her family in February of 1942. She and her husband were arrested by the British colonial authorities later in the year and were imprisoned for over a year. Her father became head of the provisional government of India in 1946, and Indira Gandhi served as his official hostess. She accompanied Nehru on numerous state visits following Indian independence in August of 1947. She soon separated from her husband, who later served in

the Indian Parliament and died in 1960. Indira Gandhi became an important member of the Congress party in her own right. She was elected president of the Congress party in February of 1959, but stepped down as the party's leader the following year. Nehru died of a stroke in May of 1964 and Gandhi accepted a cabinet position in the subsequent government of Lal Bahadur Shastri. She served as minister of information until Shastri's death in January of 1966. Gandhi was a candidate to succeed Shastri and defeated Moraji Desai by a large margin. She took office as prime minister on January 24, 1966. The Congress party was returned to power by a narrow margin in elections in 1967. Gandhi broke with the Congress party in opposing the nomination of Neelam Sanjiva Reddy to the Indian presidency. Gandhi supported V. V. Giri, who was elected in August of 1969. The Congress party expelled Gandhi later in the year, but she received a vote of confidence from Congress party members in the Parliament. She called for new elections in 1971, and her supporters increased their margin of victory. Gandhi supported the Bengalis in East Pakistan in the civil war against West Pakistan that resulted in the formation of Bangladesh in late 1971. Gandhi lost much of her popularity as India experienced severe economic difficulties several years later. She was convicted on a charge of electoral corruption by an Allahabad court in 1975. Her opponents increased their criticism of her rule and tried to force her resignation. Gandhi declared a state of emergency instead. She jailed her leading political opponents and imposed censorship restrictions on the press. She ruled by decree and instituted a number of controversial policies, including the use of compulsory sterilization as a birth control measure. Gandhi called new elections in March of 1977, and her party was defeated by a wide margin. She and her son Sanjay were both defeated for their seats in the Parliament, and she was replaced as prime minister by Moraji Desai on March 22, 1977. Gandhi was arrested on charges of corruption in October of 1977, but she was released for lack of evidence several days later. She formed the splinter Congress-I (for Indira) party in early 1978 and was returned to Parliament in a by-election in November of 1978. She was again briefly arrested the following month. Gandhi helped to encourage discord in the ruling Janata party, and the Janata government collapsed in early 1980. When new elections were held in January of 1980, Gandhi was returned to power. She again became prime minister on January 14, 1980. Gandhi's younger son and potential successor, Sanjay Gandhi, died in an aircraft accident later in the year. Her government continued to face serious problems, including a growing autonomy movement by the Sikhs in Punjab State. The unrest culminated in an attack by the Indian army on the Golden Temple, the Sikhs' holiest shrine, in Amritsar in June of 1984, an attack that killed hundreds of Sikh militants. Gandhi was assassinated on October 31, 1984, by her two Sikh bodyguards while she was walking to her office in New Delhi.

MORAJI DESAI (Prime Minister, March 24, 1977–June 15, 1979). Moraji Ranchhodji Desai was born in In Bhadeli, Gujarat, on February 29, 1896. He was educated at Bombay University and worked in the Bombay Civil Service from 1918 until 1930. He then joined Mahatma Gandhi's civil disobedience movement. Desai was arrested twice during the 1930s. He was active in the All-India Congress Committee and served as minister for revenue, cooperation, agriculture, and forests from 1937 until 1939. He was arrested by the British authorities in 1940 and was detained until 1945. Desai served as home and revenue minister of Bombay from 1946 and became chief

minister of Bombay in 1952. He retained that position until 1956. He served in the national government as minister for commerce and industry from 1956 until 1958 and was minister of finance from 1958 until 1963. He returned to the cabinet as minister of finance in 1967 and also served as deputy prime minister until 1969. Desai went into opposition against Prime Minister Indira Gandhi in 1969, following her support of V. V. Giri for president of India. He was arrested in 1975 when Gandhi declared a state of emergency, and was detained until 1977. He served as the chairman of the opposition Janata party from 1977 and became prime minister when his coalition defeated Indira Gandhi's Congress-I party. He was sworn into office on March 24, 1977. Desai retained the position until June 15, 1979, when he resigned after the Janata party was reduced to minority status in the government. He subsequently retired from active politics.

CHAUDHURY CHARAN SINGH (Prime Minister, July 28, 1979–January 14, 1980). Chaudhury Charan Singh was born in Noorpur, Meerut District, on December 23, 1902. He was educated at Agra University and received a degree in law. He joined the Indian National Congress party in 1929. Singh was arrested on several occasions by the British colonial authorities for his nationalist activities. He was elected to the state assembly of his home state of Uttar Pradesh in northern India in 1937. He held various ministerial positions in the state government following Indian independence in 1947. Singh served as chief minister of Uttar Pradesh from 1967 until 1968. He broke with the Congress party in 1969 and formed various rural parties. He was arrested with other opposition leaders during the state of emergency called by Prime Minister Indira Gandhi in 1975. Singh joined the Janata party in opposition to Gandhi in 1977 and served in the cabinet of Moraji Desai as home minister from 1977 until 1978. He broke with Desai in 1978, but returned to the government the following January to serve as deputy prime minister. He again broke with the government in July of 1979 and formed the Lok Dal, or People's party. Desai was elected prime minister with the support of the Congress party and took office on July 28, 1979. The Congress party withdrew its support the following month, however, and forced new elections. Singh remained as caretaker prime minister until January 14, 1980, when Gandhi returned to power. He continued to lead the Lok Dal in opposition to the Gandhi government until November of 1985, when he suffered a stroke and retired from politics. He died of cardiac arrest at his home in New Delhi at the age of 84 on May 29, 1987.

INDIRA GANDHI (Prime Minister, January 14, 1980–October 31, 1984). *See earlier entry under Heads of Government.*

RAJIV GANDHI (Prime Minister, October 31, 1984–December 2, 1989). Rajiv Gandhi was born in Bombay on August 20, 1944. He was the son of Indira Gandhi and the grandson of Jawaharlal Nehru. His grandfather became prime minister in 1947, and Rajiv was raised in the prime minister's residence. He was educated in India and at Cambridge University in Great Britain, where he studied engineering. He trained as an airline pilot while in Great Britain and became a pilot with Indian Airlines. Rajiv remained aloof from politics until his younger brother, Sanjay, was killed in an airplane crash on June 23, 1980. Sanjay had been widely viewed as a likely successor to his mother, Prime Minister Indira Gandhi. Gandhi and the Congress-I party convinced Rajiv to enter politics, and he was elected to Parliament to fill Sanjay's seat in June of 1981. He became a

leading advisor to his mother and was appointed secretary of the Congress-I party in February of 1983. Rajiv Gandhi was selected to succeed his mother as party leader and prime minister when Indira Gandhi was assassinated on October 31, 1984. He was confirmed in office by a general election two months later. He was considered to have great integrity and was initially a popular leader. Rajiv Gandhi strengthened India's relationship with the United States and the West and attempted to liberalize his nation's economic system. He lost much public support, however, for his decision to send Indian troops to maintain order in Sri Lanka in 1987. His government also faced continuing violence from militant Sikh nationalists, who were responsible for numerous terrorist acts. Gandhi continued to lose support in the Parliament, and the Congress party was defeated by a coalition of antigovernment parties in elections in November of 1989. He stepped down as prime minister on December 2, 1989, and became leader of the Opposition. Gandhi forced the collapse of the government of his successor, Vishwanath Pratap Singh, in November of 1990. New elections were scheduled for May of 1991. Gandhi was assassinated by a terrorist bomb hidden in a flower basket while campaigning for the Congress party in Sriperumbudur on May 21, 1991. His assassins were believed to be members of a Tamil separatist organization.

VISHWANATH PRATAP SINGH (Prime Minister, December 2, 1989–November 10, 1990). Vishwanath Pratap Singh was born in Allahabad on June 25, 1931. He was educated in India and was elected to the Legislative Assembly in 1969. He was a member of the Congress-I party and served as the deputy minister for commerce from 1974 until 1976. Singh was state minister for commerce from 1976 until 1977. He served as chief minister of Uttar Pradesh from 1980 until 1982. He was named minister of finance in 1984 and served until 1986, when he was named minister of defense. Singh was expelled from the Congress-I party and the cabinet in 1987 due to his enthusiastic anticorruption campaign. He returned to the Parliament as an independent in June of 1987 and organized the opposition Jan Morcha party. Rajiv Gandhi's Congress party lost support in parliamentary elections in November of 1989, and Singh was selected as prime minister on December 2, 1989. Singh's government lost the support of the right-wing Bharatiya Janata party as part of his ruling coalition in October of 1990. Singh lost a vote of confidence in the Parliament and was forced to resign on November 10, 1990.

CHANDRA SHEKHAR (Prime Minister, November 10, 1990–June 21, 1991). Chandra Shekhar Singh was born in Ballia District, Uttar Pradesh State, on April 17, 1927. He attended the Benares Hindu University in Varanasi, where he received a degree in 1956. He became active in politics and joined the Congress party. Shekhar was a critic of Prime Minister Indira Gandhi in the early 1970s and was imprisoned when she called a state of emergency in 1975. Shekhar subsequently joined the opposition Janata party. The Janata party merged with the Janata Dal in 1989 and defeated Rajiv Gandhi's Congress party in parliamentary elections. Shekhar and other members of the Janata Dal left the party to form the Janata Dal-Socialist party. When the government of Vishwanath Pratap Singh lost a vote of confidence, Shekhar was selected to become prime minister with the support of Rajiv Gandhi's Congress party and took office on November 10, 1990. Shekhar and Gandhi broke their alliance in March of 1991, and new parliamentary elections were held. Elections were postponed due to the assassination of Gandhi in May of 1991. Shekhar remained prime minister until June 21, 1991, when he was replaced by P. V. Narasimha Rao.

P. V. NARASIMHA RAO (Prime Minister, June 21, 1991–). Pamulaparti Venkata Narasimha Rao was born in Karimnagar, Andhra Pradesh, on June 28, 1921. He was educated at Bombay University and Nagpur University, where he received degrees in science and law. He was active in the Indian nationalist movement prior to independence and joined the Indian Congress party. Rao was elected to the Legislative Assembly in Andhra Pradesh in 1957. He became chairman of Telugu Academy in Andhra Pradesh in 1968. He joined Indira Gandhi's Congress-I party in 1969 and was elected chief minister of Andhra Pradesh in 1971. Rao was elected to the national Parliament in 1972. He returned to the Andhra Pradesh government the following year. He was again elected to the Parliament in 1977 and in 1980. Rao was appointed to Indira Gandhi's cabinet as foreign minister in 1980. He retained that position until 1984, when he was named minister of home affairs. He served as minister of defense in Rajiv Gandhi's government in 1985. Rao was subsequently named minister of human resource development until 1988. He again served as foreign minister from 1988 until 1989. Rao was chosen to be leader of the Congress-I party following the assassination of Rajiv Gandhi in May of 1991. He led the party to victory in elections in May and June of 1991 and was sworn in as prime minister on June 21, 1991.

Indonesia, Republic of

(Republik Indonesia)

Indonesia is a country that consists of an archipelago of islands southeast of Asia near the equator. An independent republic was established on August 17, 1945, and independence was recognized by the Netherlands on December 27, 1949.

HEADS OF STATE

HUBERTUS J. VAN MOOK (Acting Governor-General, January 1948–October 11, 1948). Hubertus J. Van Mook was born in Indonesia in 1895. He served as a member of the Dutch civil service in Indonesia in the 1920s and 1930s. He was also a member of the editorial board of *De Stuw* (*The Dam*), a liberal Dutch publication. Van Mook served as minister of colonies in the previous Dutch government-in-exile in London during World War II. Following the war, Van Mook returned to Indonesia, where he served as lieutenant governor-general of the Dutch East Indies. During the postwar period, the colonial government was beset with demands for independence from such leading Indonesian nationalists as Sukarno and Mohammed Hatta. Van Mook met with Sukarno in October of 1945 in an attempt to negotiate a settlement with the nationalists, though they were unable to come to terms. For several years there were numerous armed conflicts between the Dutch forces and the nationalists. Van Mook was a strong proponent of a negotiated settlement of the fighting. In January of 1948 Van Mook was instrumental in the negotiation of an agreement that established a truce between the Dutch colonial government and the new Indonesian republic. Van Mook resigned his position in the colonial government on October 11, 1948. He was succeeded by former Dutch prime minister Louis J. M. Beel. Van Mook came to the United States in

1950, where he wrote *The Stakes of Democracy in Southeast Asia* and served as a visiting lecturer at the University of California. The following year he was named as chief of the United Nations Technical Administration's public administration division. Two years later Van Mook taught at Cornell University as a visiting professor. In 1957 he was named to lead a program cosponsored by the United Nations and New York University designed to train administrators of underdeveloped countries. He died of lung disease near Avignon, France, on May 10, 1965, at the age of 70.

LOUIS J. M. BEEL (Acting Governor-General, October 11, 1948–May 14, 1949). Louis Joseph Maria Beel was born in Roermond on April 12, 1902. He attended the Catholic University of Nijmegen, where he received a degree in law. He subsequently entered politics as a member of the Catholic People's party. Beel was selected as prime minister on July 2, 1946, and served until August 5, 1948, when he was unable to form a coalition government. He was then named the high commissioner in the Dutch East Indies. He served as acting governor-general of the colony from October 11, 1948. Beel administered the area during the period of time when the Netherlands negotiated recognition of Indonesia's independence. Beel relinquished his position on May 14, 1949. He returned to the

Netherlands and was again named prime minister, as head of a caretaker cabinet, on December 22, 1958. He stepped down on May 19, 1959, after general elections were held and a new government was formed by Jan de Quay. Beel subsequently served as vice president of the Council of State from 1959 until 1972. He died in Utrecht at the age of 74 on February 11, 1977, following a long illness.

SUKARNO (President, December 27, 1949–March 27, 1968). Sukarno was born in Surabaja, Java, on June 6, 1901. He was educated at a Dutch technical college in Bandung and received an engineering degree. He became involved in the nationalist movement in the late 1920s and founded the National party in 1927. Sukarno was arrested by the Dutch colonial authorities in 1929. He was released in 1931 and continued with his political activities. He was again arrested in 1937 and was sent into exile in South Sumatra. Sukarno returned to Indonesia in 1942 and collaborated with the Japanese occupation forces in the country. He proclaimed Indonesia a republic on August 17, 1945. When the Dutch tried to reestablish their authority in Indonesia, Sukarno formed a nationalist army to continue the revolt. He was captured by Dutch paratroopers at the nationalists' headquarters in Jogjakarta in 1948. He was exiled to Prapat until July of 1949, when the Dutch were forced by world opinion to release him and grant Indonesia independence. The Dutch relinquished control over the country on December 27, 1949, and Sukarno became the first president of the Republic of Indonesia. He received financial aid from the United States and the Soviet Union and sought to balance his country between the two world powers. He hosted the first Afro-Asian conference in Bandung in 1955 and became a leading spokesman for the Third World. Sukarno ruled in an increasingly authoritarian manner and

was faced with a military rebellion in Sumatra in 1958. The Indonesian army was able to put down the revolt. Sukarno allowed the Communists to become increasingly influential in the government the following year. He embarked on a confrontational policy with Malaysia in 1963, and fighting between the two countries seriously damaged Indonesia's economic stability. Indonesia's relationship with the United States also became estranged in the mid-1960s. Sukarno removed Indonesia from the United Nations in 1965 and turned to the People's Republic of China for financial support. The Communists attempted a coup in September of 1965, with the alleged support of Sukarno. The army crushed the revolt and Sukarno's powers were greatly diminished. General Suharto claimed most of Sukarno's executive power on March 12, 1966, though Sukarno was allowed to retain the title of president until March 27, 1968. Sukarno remained under house arrest at his home near Jakarta until June of 1970, when he was admitted to a Jakarta military hospital for high blood pressure and kidney disease. He died at the age of 69 on June 21, 1970.

SUHARTO (President, March 27, 1968–   ). Suharto was born in Sedaju-Godean, Java, on February 20, 1921. He served in the Dutch colonial army and was educated at the military academy in Java. He joined the Japanese-sponsored Indonesian defense corps following the Japanese occupation of Indonesia in the early 1940s. Suharto served as an officer in the rebel nationalist army and fought against the Dutch colonial army, which was trying to reestablish Dutch authority in the colony. Indonesia was granted independence in December of 1949, and Suharto served as a lieutenant colonel in the Indonesian army. He served on the faculty of the National Military Academy from 1957 and was promoted to brigadier general in 1960. He was named commander in chief of Indonesia's defense forces in 1961 and led the campaign to incorporate West Irian into the Republic of Indonesia the following year. Suharto also was involved in Indonesia's policy of military confrontation with Malaysia in 1963. He assumed control of the Indonesian army during the Communist coup attempt in September of 1965 and led a bloody purge of leftist insurgents after the coup was crushed. He subsequently served on the ruling military junta and became head of the government on March 12, 1966. Suharto was officially elected by the People's Consultative Assembly to replace Sukarno as president of Indonesia on March 27, 1968. He eliminated many of the excesses of his predecessor and was reelected in 1973. His government faced widespread student demonstrations in 1978 over the increasing rate of inflation. Suharto was reelected president later in the year and again in 1983. He was elected to his fifth term by the People's Consultative Assembly in March of 1988.

HEADS OF GOVERNMENT

SUTAN SJAHRIR (Prime Minister, November 1945–June 27, 1947). Sutan Sjahrir was born in the village of Kota Gedang, Sumatra, on March 5, 1910. He attended school in Bandung, West Java, and studied law at the University of Amsterdam from 1929 to 1931. During this period Sjahrir became involved in the Indonesian nationalist student movement. In 1931 he returned to Indonesia, where he continued his work with the independence movement. He was arrested by the Dutch authorities in 1934 and remained imprisoned in New Guinea and the Moluccas until the Japanese occupation of Indonesia in 1942. During World War II Sjahrir served as leader of the youth resistance movement to the Japanese forces. Following the war, Sjahrir wrote several works in support of the end of Dutch colonial rule in Indonesia. Sjahrir was considered a moderate by the Dutch, and he became the first prime minister of Indonesia recognized by the Dutch government. Sjahrir, who also served as foreign minister in the new government, was perceived by his critics as being a pawn of the Dutch. He survived a Communist coup in July of 1946 and went on to negotiate an agreement with the Dutch government in November of that year. The agreement gave the Indonesian government authority over Java and Sumatra and led to a sovereign Indonesia by 1949. Sjahrir resigned the premiership on June 27, 1947, but remained an advisor to the Sukarno government for the following year. He also served as Indonesia's representative to the United Nations. In 1948 Sjahrir left the Socialist party after a disagreement with the pro–Communist members of the party. He founded the Partai Sosialist Indonesia (PSI) the same year. The PSI was an influential force in Indonesian politics until 1953, when the party was removed from all cabinet positions. Sjahrir's influence in the Sukarno administration continued to diminish as Sukarno established closer ties with the Communist party. In 1960 Sukarno outlawed the PSI, and in January of 1962 he imprisoned Sjahrir. He remained jailed until 1965, when he was released in order to travel to Switzerland for medical treatment. Sjahrir suffered a stroke in early April and died on April 9, 1966, in Zurich, Switzerland, at the age of 56.

AMIR SJARIFUDDIN (Prime Minister, July 3, 1947–January 29, 1948). Amir Sjarifuddin was born in 1912 in North Sumatra. In 1937 he was a founder and leader of the Gerindo, or

Indonesian Movement, a political party dedicated to the independence of Indonesia. He was a leader of the anti-Japanese resistance during World War II and had been captured and tortured by the Japanese. Sjarifuddin was also active in the struggle for Indonesian independence from Dutch colonial rule and served as minister of information in President Sukarno's first nationalist government. In 1945 he was named deputy chairman of the Working Committee in the new Parliament of the Indonesian Republic. He served as minister of defense in the government of Sutan Sjahrir and succeeded him as prime minister on July 3, 1947. Sjarifuddin, though more of a leftist than his predecessor, found it necessary to appease the Dutch colonial government on most major issues. He negotiated the Renville Agreement, which left nearly two-thirds of Indonesia in the hands of the colonial government. This proved unpopular with the majority of the nationalists. Sjarifuddin was also closely linked with the Communist elements in Indonesia and was forced to resign on January 29, 1948. Following his resignation, he denounced the Renville Agreement and joined with the Communists in opposition to the new government of Mohammed Hatta. On September 18, 1948, the Communists went into open rebellion against the government. The revolt was short-lived and its leader, Communist party chief Musso, was killed on October 31, 1948. Sjarifuddin and several of his aides were captured on December 1, 1948. The Hatta government made plans to try Sjarifuddin publicly, but the former prime minister was executed by the military in the field.

MOHAMMED HATTA (Prime Minister, January 29, 1948–September 5, 1950). Mohammed Hatta was born in Sumatra on August 12, 1902. Hatta was a member of the Sumatra Young Men's League while a student and later became that organization's president.

In 1922 Hatta went to the University of Rotterdam to study economics. He received two doctoral degrees from the university. Hatta also became involved in the Indonesian nationalist movement while a student. He returned to Indonesia in the early 1930s and continued his efforts against the Dutch colonial rule. He served as chairman of the Pendikan Nasional Indonesia and edited a nationalist periodical. In 1935 Hatta was imprisoned by the colonial authorities and was interned in New Guinea and the Moluccas. He remained in custody until the Japanese occupation of Indonesia. Hatta, along with Sukarno, collaborated with the Japanese occupation forces and served as Sukarno's leading advisor in the Poetera, or Central People's party. The Japanese recognized the independent Indonesian government under Sukarno on August 17, 1945, and Hatta was named vice president. Following the end of World War II, the Dutch tried to resume authority over Indonesia, but met with widespread resistance. Sukarno and Hatta refused to accept any agreement that would result in a resumption of colonial rule. An agreement was reached in November of 1946 which recognized the authority of the Indonesian Republic over the territory that Sukarno and Hatta occupied. The treaty did little to halt the continued fighting throughout the Indonesian territory, however. Hatta was named deputy commander in chief of the republican army in August of 1947. Hostilities were finally settled in January of 1948 under a United Nations-sponsored agreement. Hatta became prime minister in the new government and retained the position of vice president. Hatta's government was considered moderate, and extremist elements attempted to stage a coup. He survived a Communist revolt in October of 1948. The Dutch feared that the Indonesian Republic would not be able to survive and sought to insure that the Communists would not gain control of Indonesia. The Dutch organized a "police action" in December of 1948 and occupied the capital. Hatta and other leading political figures were arrested. In May of 1949 the Dutch troops were forced to evacuate as a result of United Nations intervention. Hatta resumed his duties as prime minister until September 5, 1950. He was reelected Sukarno's vice president on October 14, 1950, and remained in that position until he resigned on December 2, 1956, in a dispute with Prime Minister Ali Sastroamidjojo. Hatta remained a popular figure with the Masjumi party, which advocated his reappointment as prime minister during the crisis in Sumatra during the mid-1950s, but Sukarno refused to bring Hatta back into the government. Hatta made little impact on political affairs following General Suharto's military coup in 1965. Hatta died in Jakarta on March 14, 1980, at the age of 78.

MOHAMMED NATSIR (Prime Minister, September 5, 1950–April 20, 1951). Mohammed Natsir was born in Alahan Pandjang on July 17, 1908. He began his career in government in 1946 when he was named to the cabinet as information minister. He served as leader of the Masjumi party and was selected to succeed Mohammed Hatta as prime minister on September 5, 1950. Natsir was forced to resign on April 20, 1951, when his government was boycotted by members of the Nationalist party. The Masjumi party was outlawed following an Islamic rebellion against the Sukarno government. In 1958 Natsir joined with the rebels in Sumatra in opposing the leftist tilt of the Sukarno government. The rebellion was defeated by the Indonesian army in the early 1960s. Natsir was politically inactive after the military coup led by General Suharto in 1965. He died of a heart attack at the age of 84 in Jakarta on February 6, 1993.

SUKIMAN WIRJOSANDJOJO (Prime Minister, April 26, 1951–February 23, 1952). Sukiman Wirjosandjojo was born in 1896. He was a member of the Masjumi party and was named prime minister on April 26, 1951. The army forced the resignation of several members of his cabinet, including the minister of justice. He resigned on February 23, 1952, when it was learned that his foreign minister, Achmed Subardjo, had secretly accepted aid from the United States under a mutual security agreement. Sukiman was a leading opponent of the Sukarno government in the late fifties and was imprisoned by the government in January of 1962.

WILOPO (Prime Minister, April 1, 1952–June 2, 1953). Wilopo was born in 1910. He was an attorney and former school teacher. He joined the center-left Nationalist party in the early 1950s. Wilopo became prime minister on April 1, 1952, following the fall of the Sukiman government. He opposed Indonesia accepting aid from the United States and favored trade with Eastern bloc nations. He also acted to lift the state of siege that Indonesia had been under since the days of the colonial government and freed numerous political prisoners. The Wilopo government survived a crisis on October 17, 1952, when the army attempted a coup against the government. Following the coup attempt, President Sukarno emerged with broader powers. Wilopo resigned on June 3, 1953, when his government fell under pressure from Nationalists and Communists who opposed the government's agrarian reform program in East Sumatra.

ALI SASTROAMIDJOJO (Prime Minister, July 30, 1953–July 23, 1955). Ali Sastroamidjojo was born in Grabag-Merbabu in Central Java on May 21, 1903. He attended school in Jakarta and Batavia until 1923, when he went to the Netherlands to study law. He received a doctor of laws degree in 1927 from the University of Leyden. While in the Netherlands, Sastroamidjojo became involved in the Perhimpunan Indonesia, or Indonesian Association, a nationalist organization working towards Indonesian independence. He was arrested by the Dutch authorities in September of 1927 and returned to Java to practice law in 1928. He joined with Sukarno's National party of Indonesia (PNI) and continued his efforts toward Indonesian independence. In 1937 Sastroamidjojo joined the new Gerindo, or Indonesia Movement, party. Following the Japanese occupation of Indonesia, Sastroamidjojo was named deputy minister of information in the first republican cabinet of Sukarno. In July of 1947 Sastroamidjojo was appointed minister of education and culture in the cabinet of Prime Minister Amir Sjarifuddin. He remained in that position in the government of Sjarifuddin's successor, Mohammed Hatta. In February of 1948 Sastroamidjojo addressed the United Nations Security Council as spokesman for Indonesia in its dispute with the Netherlands. Following the Dutch "police action" in December of 1948, Sastroamidjojo was arrested. He was released in early 1949 and continued as a member of the Indonesian delegation to negotiate a settlement with the Dutch colonial government. He resigned his cabinet positions in July of 1949 to concentrate on the negotiations. A settlement was reached, and on December 27, 1949, Indonesia was recognized as an independent nation. Sastroamidjojo was subsequently appointed as Indonesia's first ambassador to the United States. He served in that position until 1953, when he was named ambassador to Mexico and Canada. He returned to Indonesia in July of 1953 to succeed Wilopo as prime minister on July 30, 1953. Sastroamidjojo served as the leader of a neutralist government, and, while not appointing any Communists to his cabinet, he did have a measure of Communist support. His government survived a cabinet crisis in November of 1954 when three members of the Greater Indonesia party resigned in protest of the government's economic policies. Sastroamidjojo remained as prime minister until July 23, 1955, when he was forced to relinquish the position following a conflict with the military over the appointment of the army chief of staff. The following year he was again selected as prime minister and took office on March 20, 1956. During his second term he was beset with a military crisis in Sumatra when the army rebelled. The army insisted that Sastroamidjojo be replaced by Mohammed Hatta as head of the government. Ali survived another government crisis in December of 1956, but continued attacks against the government forced his resignation as prime minister on March 14, 1957. That same year he was appointed Indonesia's representative to the United Nations. He held that position until 1960, when he was named deputy chairman of the advisory parliament. In 1967, following the ouster of President Sukarno, Sastroamidjojo was briefly arrested by the army. He was released shortly afterward without being brought to trial. Sastroamidjojo's political career was brought to an end by the army takeover, and he died in Jakarta on March 13, 1975, at the age of 72.

BURHANUDDIN HARAHAP (Prime Minister, August 12, 1955–March 20, 1956). Burhanuddin Harahap was born in 1917. He was a member of the Masjumi party and was selected as prime minister on August 12, 1955. His government, which excluded members of the Nationalist and Communist parties, was known for its moderate policies. Harahap was replaced by his predecessor, Ali Sastroamidjojo, on March 20, 1956. In December of 1957 Harahap joined with the rebel insurgents in Sumatra.

ALI SASTROAMIDJOJO (Prime Minister, March 20, 1956–March 14, 1957). *See earlier entry under Heads of Government.*

KARTAWIDJAJA DJUANDA (Prime Minister, April 9, 1957–July 8, 1959). Kartawidjaja Djuanda was born in the town of Tasikmalaja in West Java on January 14, 1911. He attended the Dutch schools in Tjirebon and Bandung and received a degree in civil engineering from the Bandung Technical College in 1933. He was employed as a secondary school principal from 1935 to 1937 and then worked as a civil engineer until the Japanese occupation in 1942. In the first government of the Indonesian Republic under Prime Minister Sutan Sjahrir, Djuanda served as vice-minister of transport. He was later named minister of transport and public works and minister of communications. He remained in the latter position in the government of Prime Minister Sjarifuddin from 1947 until 1948. He also served in the cabinet of the Hatta administration and was a representative to the independence treaty talks with the Dutch government in The Hague in November of 1949. Following the recognition of Indonesian independence, Djuanda served as minister of economic affairs in the government of Mohammed Hatta. He continued serving as the leader of various ministries in three succeeding cabinets. In 1953 he was named by prime minister Sastroamidjojo to the directorship of the State Planning Board. When the Masjumi, or Muslim, party withdrew from the government in January of 1957, Djuanda replaced the Masjumi minister of finance. Prime Minister Sastroamidjojo resigned in March of 1957 after army revolts broke out in parts of Indonesia. The following month Djuanda, who was not a member of any political party, was selected to serve as prime minister and minister of defense. He took office on April 9, 1957. In February of 1958 dissident elements in the country formed a revolutionary government calling for the ouster of Djuanda and the return of Mohammed Hatta as prime minister. The rebellion was short-lived, but President Sukarno took steps to consolidate his power. In 1959 Sukarno reinstated Indonesia's constitution of 1945, which gave him the combined power of president and prime minister. Djuanda resigned as prime minister on July 8, 1959, though he remained in the new government as first minister and minister of finance. He continued to hold these positions until his death from a heart attack in Jakarta on November 7, 1963, at the age of 52.

SJAFRUDDIN PRAWIRANEGARA (Prime Minister, Revolutionary Government, February 15, 1958–September 1961). Sjafruddin Prawiranegara was born in 1912. He was a leader of the Masjumi party and served as governor of the Bank of Indonesia in the 1950s. Sjafruddin was a leading anti-Communist and was endangered by the Communist uprisings in December of 1957. He felt that President Sukarno was unwilling or unable to protect the country from Communist insurgents and fled to rebel territory in Sumatra. In February of 1958 he was named the leader of a revolutionary government to oppose Sukarno's rule. After three years of revolt, the rebels surrendered to the Indonesian army. Sjafruddin accepted a general amnesty issued by Sukarno in mid-September of 1961 and retired from politics to become an Islamic preacher. He died in Jakarta on February 15, 1989, at the age of 76.

SUKARNO (Prime Minister, November 3, 1963–March 12, 1966). *See entry under Heads of State.*

SUHARTO (Prime Minister, March 12, 1966–   ). *See entry under Heads of State.*

Iran, Islamic Republic of
(Jomhori-e-Islami-e-Irân)

Iran is a country in western Asia.

HEADS OF STATE

MOHAMMED REZA PAHLAVI (Shah, September 16, 1941–January 16, 1979). Mohammed Reza Pahlavi was born in Teheran on October 26, 1919. He was the son of Reza Shah Pahlavi, who was chosen as shah of Iran by the National Assembly in 1925. The crown prince was educated in Rolle, Switzerland, from 1931 until 1936, when he returned to Iran to attend the Officers Training Academy. He was subsequently made an officer in the Iranian army and became more involved in matters of state. Iran was invaded by British and Soviet troops in 1941 following Reza Shah Pahlavi's refusal to force Axis nationals to leave Iran during World War II. Reza Shah Pahlavi was forced to abdicate the throne on September 16, 1941. Mohammed Reza Pahlavi succeeded to the Peacock Throne and soon thereafter granted greater political power to the Iranian Parliament, or Majlis. Early the following year he signed a treaty with Great Britain and the Soviet Union, and in 1943 he extracted a promise that Iranian sovereignty would be preserved after the end of the war. Iran declared war on the Axis powers in September of 1943. Following the war, Iran became involved in a dispute with the Soviet Union over control of the Azerbaijan province in northwestern Iran. The shah was faced with a revolt led by the Soviet-oriented Tudeh party, but the rebellion was crushed in December of 1946. The shah also rejected an oil pact with the Soviet Union in 1947, and this caused further deterioration in relations between the two countries.

The shah was shot during an assassination attempt on February 4, 1949, but recovered from his injuries. In 1950 a financial scandal developed when it was learned that the Anglo-Iranian Oil Company was underpaying the Iranian government on oil royalties. The company was nationalized in April of the following year. Nationalism in Iran escalated during this period, and the shah named Mohammed Mossadegh prime minister in April of 1951. The Iranian government broke diplomatic relations with Great Britain in October of 1952. Mossadegh threatened the shah's rule with a proclamation of martial law, and the shah fled Iran, going to Baghdad on August 16, 1953. A brief period of civil war followed, with the shah's troops, led by General Fazlollah Zahedi and aided by the United States Central Intelligence Agency, defeating the rebel mobs. The shah returned to Teheran on August 22, 1953. The shah then began the process of reform in Iran, which was called the White Revolution. He announced a policy of land reform, women's rights, profit-sharing for workers, national health reform, and other programs. The shah survived another assassination attempt on April 10, 1965. He also pushed for further concessions from the oil companies that were developing Iran's oil resources. In December of 1973 Iran, along with other Persian Gulf oil states, raised its oil prices by a large margin. The shah's modernization plans met with opposition from Muslim fundamentalists within the country. In the face of rising conflict, the shah's regime became increasingly oppressive. He banned all political parties in March of 1975 to end dissent to his rule. The vast increase of oil wealth in the country contributed to widespread inflation and corruption in the government. The shah's regime faced ever greater opposition during the late 1970s. Student protests, strikes, and riots resulted in a declaration of martial law, which only served to increase the opposition to the government. The shah was forced to leave Iran on January 16, 1979. His exit also marked the return of the Ayatollah Ruhollah Khomeini to Iran. The Muslim fundamentalist emerged as the leading figure in the country. The shah went first to Egypt, then on to Morocco and the Bahamas. The new government in Iran demanded his extradition and the return of his vast financial holdings. The shah's health deteriorated during his exile. He went to New York for gall bladder surgery in October of 1979, a move that prompted Iranian militants to take over the United States Embassy in Teheran. He subsequently continued his exile in Panama and then in Egypt, the only country that would allow him entry. He was again hospitalized there for the removal of his enlarged spleen. He died of a hemorrhage in a Cairo hospital on July 27, 1980.

ABOLHASSAN BANI-SADR (President, February 4, 1980–June 21, 1981). Abolhassan Bani-Sadr was born in the village of Hamaden on March 22, 1933. He was educated at the University of Teheran, where he studied theology and economics. He subsequently worked with the Institute of Social Research and became active in the opposition movement to the shah. Bani-Sadr was arrested on several occasions in the early 1960s because of his antigovernment activities. He went to France in 1963 after having been wounded during a student revolt. He attended the Sorbonne, where he also taught. Bani-Sadr remained active in the Islamic nationalist movement and became associated

with the Ayatollah Khomeini when the Ayatollah began his exile in France. Bani-Sadr returned with Khomeini to Iran on February 1, 1979, following the overthrow of the shah. He was named to the Revolutionary Council and served as deputy minister of the economy in the government of Mehdi Bazargan from July of 1979. He was named acting foreign minister the following November. On January 25, 1980, Bani-Sadr was elected by a large majority to become the first president of the Islamic Republic of Iran. He was sworn into office on February 4, 1981. Bani-Sadr was faced with the opposition of the hard-line Islamic Republican party. He was forced to name Mohammed Ali Raja'i as prime minister and engaged in a power struggle with Raja'i. He tried to prevent Raja'i from appointing political opponents to the Cabinet, but was overruled by the Majlis, or Parliament. Relations between the president and the Parliament continued to deteriorate, and on June 10, 1981, he was dismissed as commander in chief of the armed forces. He was ousted as president by a vote of the Parliament on June 21, 1981, and a warrant was issued for his arrest. He escaped to Paris, where he founded the National Council of Resistance in opposition to the Iranian government.

MOHAMMED ALI RAJA'I (President, June 24, 1981–August 30, 1981). Mohammed Ali Raja'i was born in Kazvin in 1933. He was educated at the Graduate Teachers College in Teheran, where he received a degree in 1960. became involved in antigovernment activities in the 1960s and was arrested and tortured on several occasions. Following the overthrow of the shah in January of 1979, he became a leader of the Association of Islamic Teachers. He was subsequently named to the cabinet as minister of education. Raja'i was nominated under duress by President Abolhassan Bani-Sadr to succeed Medhi Bazargan as prime minister on

August 12, 1980. When Bani-Sadr was forced out of the presidency the following year, Raja'i was elected to succeed him on June 24, 1981. His term of office was cut short when he was killed along with numerous other Iranian politicians in a bomb blast in the prime minister's office on August 30, 1981.

SAYYED ALI KHAMENEI (President, October 12, 1981–June 4, 1989). Sayyed Ali Khamenei was born in Mashhad in 1940. He studied at the theological school in Qom from 1958 and became active in the opposition movement against the shah. He was arrested on several occasions during the 1960s. Khamenei was a follower of the exiled Ayatollah Khomeini and became a close associate of the Ayatollah following his return from exile in February of 1979. Khamenei served as the spiritual leader of Teheran. He was named to the Revolutionary Council and subsequently served as deputy minister of defense. He was seriously injured in an assassination attempt in June of 1981, when a bomb exploded during a press conference. Khamenei subsequently recovered from his injuries. He became secretary-general of the Islamic Republican party following the assassinations of Ayatollah Mohammad Beheshti and Mohammad Javad Bahonar in separate bomb blasts. He announced his intention to seek the presidency following the death of President Mohammed Ali Raja'i in the explosion that also killed Bahonar. He was victorious in the election and took office as president on October 12, 1981, though the ultimate power in the country remained with the Ayatollah Khomeini. Khamenei suffered a political setback when the Islamic Republic party was dissolved in June of 1987. He was selected to succeed the Ayatollah Khomeini as Iran's spiritual leader following Khomeini's death in June of 1989. Khamenei stepped down as president to accept this position on June 4, 1989.

HASHEMI RAFSANJANI (President, August 3, 1989–). Ali Akbar Hashemi Rafsanjani was born in Rafsanjan, in the province of Kerman, in 1934. He was educated at the theological seminary in Qom, where he studied under the Ayatollah Khomeini. He graduated in the late 1950s with the Shi'ite clerical rank of Hojatolislam. Rafsanjani was an opponent of the shah's regime and was active in establishing an underground revolutionary movement following the exile of Khomeini in 1964. Rafsanjani was arrested on several occasions for his antigovernment activities. In 1975 he was accused of collaborating with the Muhajidin al-Khlaq, a leftist revolutionary group. He was convicted and sentenced to six years in prison, but was released in 1978. Following the ouster of the shah in January of 1979, Rafsanjani was instrumental in organizing the Islamic Republican party. He also served on the Revolutionary Council, which transformed Iran into a theocracy under the Ayatollah Khomeini. Rafsanjani was shot and seriously wounded in an assassination attempt in May of 1979, but he recovered from his injuries. He was elected to the Iranian Parliament, or Majlis, in 1980. In July of that year, he was selected as Speaker of the Parliament. He was instrumental in the removal of Abolhassan Bani-Sadr as president in June of 1981 and established himself as a leading political figure in Iran. Rafsanjani was appointed to the Council of Guardians in June of 1987 and was named commander in chief of the Iranian armed forces by Khomeini in June of 1988. Rafsanjani was largely responsible for convincing Khomeini to accept a cease-fire treaty with Iraq in August of 1988. Following the death of Khomeini, Sayyed Ali Khamenei stepped down as president to become Grand Ayatollah. Khamenei was succeeded by Rafsanjani, who took office on August 3, 1988. Rafsanjani was granted greater powers than his predecessor had enjoyed as president and was viewed as the leading voice in the Iranian government. He was reelected president in June of 1993, despite his failure to improve Iran's declining economic condition.

HEADS OF GOVERNMENT

IBRAHIM HAKIMI (Prime Minister, May 11, 1945–June 4, 1945). Ibrahim Hakimi was born in 1870. He studied medicine in Teheran and Paris and returned to Iran as a physician. He served as the head of the Council of Physicians in the war ministry from 1907 until 1912. Hakimi served in various pre-World War II cabinets and held the portfolios of finance, foreign affairs, and justice. He also served in the Iranian Senate as Speaker. He first served as prime minister from May 11, 1945, until June 4, 1945, when he resigned over differences with the cabinet. He was again asked to form a government on November 4, 1945. During this term of office, Hakimi's government was faced with the threat of Soviet military involvement in the Iranian province of Azerbaijan. When he was unable to reach a settlement on the issue with the Soviet government, he sent the matter to the United Nations and resigned on January 21, 1946. Hakimi was again appointed prime minister on December 23, 1947. His third term of office also resulted in a confrontation with the Soviet Union, which protested Iran's military assistance from the United States. Hakimi accused the Soviets of violating the Russo-Iranian Friendship Treaty of 1921. Hakimi received a vote of no confidence from the Iranian Parliament and resigned on June 12, 1948. He subsequently served on the Royal Council formed in 1949 to rule during the shah's absence from Iran while on a visit to the United States. Hakimi retired from active politics and died in Teheran at the age of 89 on October 20, 1959.

MOHSEN SADR (Prime Minister, June 12, 1945–October 22, 1945). Mohsen Sadr was born in 1865. He served as a judge during the rule of Reza Shah Pahlavi. He was an extreme conservative and had presided over the execution of liberal intellectuals during the Constitutional Revolution in the early part of the century. He was chosen as prime minister on June 12, 1945, with the backing of the National Union party, the royalists, and other conservative elements in the Parliament. His selection outraged liberal members, who boycotted Parliament for three months. Sadr also took the position of minister of the interior in a cabinet composed primarily of pro-British ministers. His government was faced with a secessionist movement in the Azerbaijan region. Sadr postponed elections to the Parliament and greatly increased the military budget before stepping down on October 22, 1945.

IBRAHIM HAKIMI (Prime Minister, November 4, 1945–January 21, 1946). *See earlier entry under Heads of Government.*

AHMAD QAVAM ES-SALTANEH (Prime Minister, January 26, 1946–December 10, 1947). Ahmad Qavam es-Saltaneh was born in Azerbaijan in 1882. He entered government service as a scribe in the shah's court in 1898. He received his first cabinet appointment in 1909 when he was named minister of justice. He was subsequently appointed minister of the interior. Qavam served as governor-general of the Korasan Province from 1913. He was arrested by order of Prime Minister Seyyid Zia Tabatabay in 1921. He was released and installed as prime minister following the coup led by Reza Shah Pahlavi later in the year. In 1923 he was removed from office and charged with plotting against Reza Shah Pahlavi. Qavam subsequently went into exile in Europe, where he remained until he was allowed to return to Iran in 1929. He reentered politics, and following the abdication of the shah, he again became prime minister on August 3, 1942. His term of office was a turbulent one, and though he managed to restore order during antigovernment riots in 1942, he was forced to resign on February 15, 1943, after being charged with nepotism. Qavam remained in the Iranian Parliament as a leading spokesman of the minority parties. He again emerged as prime minister on January 26, 1946. He appointed a moderate cabinet, but retained the positions of foreign minister and minister of the interior for himself. He was able to negotiate the withdrawal of Russian troops from Iran. He also reached a settlement with pro-independence supporters in the Azerbaijan region, which resulted in Azerbaijan returning as a province of Iran. In 1947 he sponsored a Soviet-Iranian oil treaty that was rejected by the Iranian Parliament. After a vote of no confidence, he was forced from office on December 10, 1947. Following a period of illness that saw him hospitalized in France, Qavam returned to Iran, where in May of 1948 he was cleared of charges of misconduct in office. Qavam was again appointed prime minister on July 17, 1952, following the resignation of Mohammed Mossadegh. Qavam resigned four days later following a general strike and rioting demanding Mossadegh's return. Qavam was briefly arrested, but charges against him were dismissed. He subsequently went into political retirement and died in Teheran after a lengthy illness on July 23, 1955.

IBRAHIM HAKIMI (Prime Minister, December 23, 1947–June 12, 1948).

See earlier entry under Heads of Government.

ABDUL HUSSEIN HAJIR (Prime Minister, June 13, 1948–November 8, 1948). Abdul Hussein Hajir was born in 1897. Hajir served in various cabinets until his appointment as finance minister in the government of Prime Minister Ahmad Qavam es-Saltaneh in 1946. He remained in the government until the following year. He served as minister without portfolio in the government of Ibrahim Hakimi, and on June 13, 1948, he succeeded Hakimi as prime minister. Hajir was a devoted Muslim and enforced the strict observance of Ramadan. His government received little support from the Majlis, and his proposals were blocked. His inability to govern forced his resignation on November 8, 1948. He was subsequently named minister of the imperial court. Hajir was shot and mortally wounded at the Sapah Salar mosque in Teheran while attending a religious ceremony. He died the following day on November 5, 1949.

MOHAMMED SAID MARAGHEI (Prime Minister, November 9, 1948–March 23, 1950). Mohammed Said Maraghei was born in 1881. He entered the Iranian diplomatic service as a clerk at the Iranian consulate in Istanbul, Turkey. He subsequently held positions in Batum and Baku. Said was named Iran's ambassador to the Soviet Union prior to World War II. He was serving in this position when Soviet and British troops invaded Iran in 1941. He was subsequently named minister of foreign affairs, and on February 21, 1944, he was named prime minister. During his term of office, he rejected a Soviet proposal to exploit Iran's oil deposits. On November 9, 1944, he was forced to step down as prime minister, due to some extent to pressure from Moscow. Said returned as prime minister on November 9, 1948. The following year he also served on the ruling

Royal Council during the shah's visit to the United States. He resigned on March 23, 1950. Said subsequently retired from active politics. He died in Teheran at the age of 92 on November 1, 1973, after a long illness.

ALI MANSOUR (Prime Minister, March 23, 1950–June 26, 1950). Ali Khan Mansour was born in 1895. He served as minister of roads and railways prior to World War II and was instrumental in the construction of the Trans-Iranian Railway. He was appointed prime minister on June 27, 1940, and was serving in that position when British and Soviet troops invaded Iran in August of 1941. Mansour resigned shortly afterwards on August 27, 1941. Following World War II, Mansour was appointed to a council to establish Iran's policy in Azerbaijan regarding Soviet troops that remained in the province. Following the withdrawal of Soviet troops, Mansour was named governor-general of Azerbaijan in late 1946. In 1948 he headed a royal commission designed to draw up a seven-year plan for the devlopment of Iran. Mansour was again named prime minister on March 23, 1950 and served briefly until June 26, 1950. He was appointed Iran's ambassador to Turkey in 1953. He was the father of Hassan Ali Mansour, who served as Iran's prime minister from 1964 until his assassination in early 1965. Ali Mansour died in Teheran at the age of 79 on December 8, 1974.

HAJI ALI RAZMARA (Prime Minister, June 27, 1950–March 7, 1951). Haji Ali Razmara was born in Teheran in 1901. He graduated from the French military academy of Saint-Cyr in 1925. He became director of the Teheran Military Cadet College in 1938, where he wrote a history of the Persian military. Razmara was promoted to general by the shah during the Allied occupation of Iran in 1944 and was ordered to reorganize the military. He led government troops during the ouster of the Soviet-sponsored Communist Tudeh government in Azerbaijan in December of 1946. Razmara was promoted to chief of staff in 1948, and on June 26, 1950, he was appointed prime minister by the shah. Razmara, a moderate with little political following, was a strong supporter of the shah. He opposed the nationalization of the oil industry, as he felt that the Iranians would be unable to run the industry without foreign technicians. He also attempted to institute land reform measures, but was blocked by the powerful landowners in the Parliament. Razmara was shot to death by Abdullah Rastigar, a member of the radical Fadayian Islam organization, outside the Maschede Soltaneh mosque in Iran on March 7, 1951.

HUSSEIN ALA (Prime Minister, March 7, 1951–April 29, 1951). Hussein Ala was born in Teheran in December of 1882. He was the son of Prince Mohammed Ali Khan Ala-os-Saltaneh, a former prime minister of Persia. Ala was educated in Great Britain and received a law degree from the University of London. He entered the Persian diplomatic corps and served under his father at the Persian Embassy in London. Ala subsequently returned to Iran, where he served as chief of the cabinet in the Foreign Ministry from 1906 until 1917. He was named to the cabinet as minister of agriculture, commerce, and public works in 1918. Ala served as a member of the Persian delegation to the peace conference at Versailles from 1919 until 1920. He subsequently represented Persia as the minister to Spain. He was named chief envoy to the United States in 1921 and remained there until 1924. Ala returned to Iran and was elected to the Parliament in 1924. He again served in the cabinet as minister of agriculture, trade, and public works in 1927. Later in the year he was appointed Persia's minister to France and also served as a delegate to the League of Nations. He returned to Persia in 1932 as president of Iran's National Bank. In 1934 Ala was appointed Iran's ambassador to Great Britain. He again returned to Iran in 1936 and became minister of commerce from 1937 until 1938. He was governor of Iran's National Bank from 1941 until 1942 and subsequently served as minister of the imperial court. Ala was named ambassador to the United States in 1945. The following year he presented his country's case against the Soviet Union's presence in the Azerbaijan region to the United Nations. He returned to Iran in 1950 and was appointed prime minister on March 7, 1951, following the assassination of Ali Razmara. His term was brief, and he relinquished the position to Mohammed Mossadegh on April 29, 1951. He remained a close advisor to the shah and was again named prime minister on April 7, 1955. During his second term, Iran joined the Baghdad Pact. On April 3, 1957, Ala stepped down as prime minister and exchanged positions with Manouchehr Eghbal, the minister of the imperial court. He retained that position until 1963, when he was elected to the Iranian Senate. Ala died of pneumonia at his home near Teheran at the age of 81 on July 13, 1964.

MOHAMMED MOSSADEGH (Prime Minister, April 29, 1951–July 17, 1952). Mohammed Mossadegh was born to an affluent family in Teheran in 1879. He was educated in Iran and abroad. He entered the Ministry of Finance in 1896 as a tax collector for Khorasam. Mossadegh left the ministry in 1906 and went to Europe to continue his education. He received a law degree from the University of Neuchâtel in Switzerland in 1914. The following year he returned to Iran, and in 1917 he was named undersecretary for finance. Mossadegh was appointed minister of justice following the coup led by Reza Shah Pahlavi in 1921. Shortly thereafter he was named governor-general of the southern province of Farsistan. Mossadegh returned to Teheran as finance minister in 1921. He subsequently served briefly as governor of Tabriz before being named foreign minister. He served as a member of the Majlis, or Parliament, from 1923 until 1927 and then left the government following a disagreement with the shah. Mossadegh was arrested and imprisoned in Teheran before being banished to an agricultural area. He remained there until he was released by the military governor in 1941 following the ouster of Reza Shah Pahlavi. Mossadegh reentered politics in 1944 and was again elected to the Parliament. He gained a reputation as an outspoken nationalist as leader of the National Front. He was a leading critic of the Anglo-Iranian oil treaty in 1949. Mossadegh became prime minister on April 29, 1951, with the support of the anti–Western parties. He proceeded to nationalize the Iranian oil industry in 1951, which brought the nation to the verge of financial bankruptcy. Mossadegh's demands for increased powers were refused by the shah, and he resigned as prime minister on July 17, 1952. His removal resulted in widespread rioting, and he was reinstated four days later. In August of 1953 the shah again dismissed Mossadegh, but the prime minister refused to leave office. The shah fled the country in the face of antiroyalist rioting. The proroyalist elements of the army under General Fazlollah Zahedi were able to gain control of the country, and the shah returned to Teheran. Mossadegh was forced from office on August 19, 1953, and was arrested and charged with treason. He was convicted and sentenced to three years imprisonment. He was released from prison later in the year, though he remained under house arrest at his estate near Teheran. Mossadegh spent his remaining years in seclusion before he died at the age of 86 of intestinal bleeding at a Teheran hospital on March 5, 1967.

AHMED QAVAM ES-SALTANEH (Prime Minister, July 17, 1952–July 21, 1952). *See earlier entry under Heads of Government.*

MOHAMMED MOSSADEGH (Prime Minister, July 22, 1952–August 19, 1953). *See earlier entry under Heads of Government.*

FAZLOLLAH ZAHEDI (Prime Minister, August 19, 1953–April 5, 1955). Fazlollah Zahedi was born in Hamadan in 1897. He attended the Teheran Military Academy and served in the Persian army from 1916. He was named military governor of Khuzistan in 1926 and subsequently served as military governor of Gorgon. Zahedi returned to Teheran in 1929 to serve as the commanding officer of the gendarmerie. He was named Teheran's chief of police in 1932 and in 1935 was appointed inspector general of the army. He retained that position until 1941. The following year he was arrested and charged with pro-German activities by the British army that had occupied Iran. Zahedi was incarcerated in Palestine until the end of World War II. He then returned to Iran and was promoted to major general. He retired from the army in 1949 and again served as chief of police. The following year Zahedi was appointed to the Iranian Senate by the shah. He served in the cabinet of Prime Minister Mohammed Mossadegh in 1950. He resigned from the government the following year over a dispute with Mossadegh's nationalization of the oil industry. Zahedi became a prominent opponent of Mossadegh, and in 1952 he was charged with conspiracy to subvert the government. Zahedi was appointed prime minister to succeed Mossadegh on August 15, 1953, but riots and demonstrations followed his appointment. The shah was forced to flee Iran, and Zahedi went into hiding, where he led a pro-Royalist countercoup against Mossadegh. Zahedi, now a full general, took control of the government on August 19, 1953, and arrested Mossadegh and his followers. Zahedi was pro-Western in his policies and worked to maintain close relations with the United States. He also attempted to restore Iran's oil industry and crushed the outlawed Communist-dominated Tudeh party. He resigned as prime minister on April 5, 1955, for reasons of health and went to Switzerland. He was named Iran's permanent representative to the United Nations European headquarters in Geneva in 1960. He retained this position until he died of a heart attack at the age of 66 in Geneva on September 2, 1963.

HUSSEIN ALA (Prime Minister, April 7, 1955–April 3, 1957). *See earlier entry under Heads of Government.*

MANOUCHEHR EGHBAL (Prime Minister, April 3, 1957–August 29, 1960). Manouchehr Eghbal was born in the village of Meshed in northeastern Iran in September of 1909. He was educated in Iran and France, where he received a doctorate in medicine at the University of Paris in 1933. He then returned to Iran, where he practiced medicine. Eghbal accepted the position of head of the department of infectious diseases at Pahlavi Hospital in Teheran in 1939. He also served as a professor of medicine at the University of Teheran. Eghbal was appointed undersecretary for public health in 1942 and was named minister of posts and telegraphs in 1947. The following year he served as minister of education and was minister of roads and commerce and minister of the interior in 1949. He served as governor-general of Azerbaijan from 1950 until 1951, during which period he gained a reputation as an anti-Communist. Eghbal was elected to the Iranian Senate in 1953, and in 1955 became dean of the University of Teheran's School of Medicine. He was named by the shah to serve as minister of the imperial court in 1956. The following year Eghbal replaced Hussein Ala as prime minister on April 3, 1957. As prime minister, Eghbal lifted martial law, which had been in effect for most of the period of time since World War II. His government allowed for the formation of political parties, and Eghbal became the leader of the ruling government party, the Nation, in February of 1958. He was a close advisor and supporter of the shah during his term of office. He was forced to resign as prime minister on August 29, 1960, following allegations that general elections held that year were rigged in favor of the ruling party. Eghbal was subsequently appointed Iran's permanent representative to the United Nations Educational, Scientific, and Cultural Organization (UNESCO). He stepped down in 1963 to become president of the National Iranian Oil Company. He retained that position until his death from a heart attack in Teheran at the age of 68 on November 25, 1977.

JAFFAR SHARIF IMAMI (Prime Minister, August 29, 1960–May 5, 1961). Jaffar Sharif Imami (Emami) was born in Teheran in 1910. He was educated at the German Central Railway School and the Boras Technical School in Sweden. He entered the Persian civil service in 1930 and worked on the Iranian railway as a technical assistant from 1943 until 1946. Sharif Imami served as director of the Irrigation Authority from 1946 until 1950 and was named to the cabinet as minister of roads in 1950. He retained that position until the following year. He was elected to the Iranian Senate in 1955. Sharif Imami served as minister of mines and industries in the government of Manouchehr Eghbal from 1957 and replaced Eghbal as prime minister on August 29, 1960. He resigned on May 5, 1961, following demonstrations against the government by students and teachers demanding higher salaries. He served as president of the Parliament in 1963. Sharif Imami was again appointed prime minister on August 27, 1978, as

head of a government of reconciliation. He tried to appease Muslim leaders opposed to the monarchy, but was unable to stop the growing civil disorder. He resigned on November 5, 1978. Sharif Imami escaped the country following the overthrow of the shah in early 1979. He was sentenced to death in absentia by the Islamic Revolutionary Court.

ALI AMINI (Prime Minister, May 5, 1961–July 17, 1962). Ali Amini was born in Teheran in June of 1907. He was educated in Iran and France, where he received a doctorate of law at the Sorbonne in Paris in 1931. He subsequently returned to Iran, where he was appointed to the Iranian judiciary. Amini joined the Ministry of Finance in 1933 and was appointed economic director to the ministry in 1938. He was elected to the Iranian Parliament in 1940. He served as deputy prime minister in the early 1940s and was named undersecretary to Prime Minister Ahmad Qavam es-Saltaneh in 1943. Amini led several Iranian delegations to international conferences in the late 1940s. He returned to the cabinet in June of 1950 as minister of national economy in the government of General Ali Razmara. He served in this capacity until Razmara's assassination in March of 1951. Amini was appointed minister of finance in the government of General Fazlollah Zahedi in August of 1953. He was instrumental in negotiating a settlement with international oil companies regarding Iran's nationalization of the oil industry during the government of Mohammed Mossadegh. Amini was well regarded by the shah and was named minister of justice in May of 1955 to help reorganize the ministry. He was appointed Iran's ambassador to the United States in November of 1955. He was recalled in 1958 and remained politically inactive until 1960, when he was again elected to the Parliament. Amini was selected by the shah to serve as prime minister on

May 5, 1961. He began the shah's controversial agrarian reform project, which was opposed by wealthy landowners and the Shi'ite Muslim clergy. Amini resigned as prime minister on July 17, 1962, blaming the lack of financial aid from the United States for the failure of his government to achieve financial stability. Amini was accused of plotting to overthrow the government of Prime Minister Emir Abbas Hoveida in 1968. He subsequently went into political retirement until 1979, when the shah was overthrown by Muslim fundamentalists. Amini escaped Iran and went into exile in Paris. He became the leader of the Front for the Liberation of Iran, an exile group whose goals were the ouster of the Khomeini regime and the restoration of the monarchy. The Front received little support and further deteriorated as Amini's health failed. He died in Paris at the age of 87 on December 12, 1992.

ASSADOLLAH ALAM (Prime Minister, July 19, 1962–March 7, 1964). Assadollah Alam was born in 1919 in Birjand. He was educated in Teheran and subsequently entered government service in the ministry of agriculture. He later served in several Iranian cabinets as minister of health, minister of the interior, and minister of labor. He was a close friend and advisor of the shah of Iran and was removed from the government during the tenure of Prime Minister Mohammed Mossadegh in 1953. Alam returned to the government following Mossadegh's fall from power. Alam was closely identified with the shah's White Revolution to modernize Iran. He was appointed prime minister on July 19, 1962. In June of the following year, Alam's firm handling of demonstrators against the government helped to salvage the shah's plans. Alam stepped down as prime minister on March 7, 1964, to become minister of the imperial court. He retained that position until ill health forced his resignation. He died in a New York

hospital at the age of 59 on April 14, 1978.

HASSAN ALI MANSOUR (Prime Minister, March 7, 1964–January 27, 1965). Hassan Ali Mansour was born in Teheran in 1923. He was the son of Ali Mansour, who served as Iran's prime minister in 1950. Hassan Ali Mansour was educated in Teheran and Paris and received a degree in political science. He returned to Iran to join the diplomatic corps and served in posts in Paris, Stuttgart, and the Vatican. He was appointed deputy prime minister in 1959 and became minister of labor the following year. He was named minister of commerce in 1961, and that year he also formed the Progressive Center, a political advisory group. He was a leader of the group during the elections in 1963 and subsequently became leader of the newly formed New Iran party. He was selected to become Iran's prime minister on March 7, 1964. Mansour was an advocate of the shah's modernization plans and ran afoul of conservative Muslim leaders while carrying out his reforms. Mansour was shot twice by Mohammad Bakarii, an Iranian student, while entering the Iranian Parliament on January 21, 1965. He died at the age of 41 in a Teheran hospital five days later on January 26, 1965.

EMIR ABBAS HOVEIDA (Prime Minister, January 27, 1965–August 6, 1977). Emir Abbas Hoveida was born in Teheran on February 18, 1919. He was educated in Belgium and France and then returned to Teheran to join the Iranian Foreign Office. He was stationed in various overseas embassies, including Paris and Bonn, and also served at the United Nations in New York. Hoveida returned to Teheran to serve on the board of the National Iranian Oil Company in 1958. He was named minister of finance in the government of Hassan Ali Mansour and was appointed to replace Mansour as prime minister when he was assassinated on January 26, 1965. He also became leader of the New Iran party and led the party to victory in the elections of 1971. Iran's economic prosperity secured Hoveida's position during the early 1970s, though the nation continued to be plagued by Islamic fundamentalists who opposed the shah's rule. Hoveida was replaced as prime minister following criticism of his government's handling of public services. He remained in the government as minister of the royal court until September of 1978. He was briefly detained by the military government installed by the shah in November of 1978. Hoveida was arrested following the ouster of the shah in February of 1979. He was charged with crimes against the nation and sentenced to death. He was executed by a firing squad in Teheran on April 7, 1979.

JAMSHID AMOUZEGAR (Prime Minister, August 7, 1977–August 27, 1978). Jamshid Amouzegar was born in Teheran in 1922. He received degrees in law and engineering from the University of Teheran. He subsequently attended Cornell University in the United States, where he received a doctorate. In the early 1950s he returned to Iran and worked with the ministry of health. Amouzegar was named minister of labor in the cabinet in 1958. He subsequently served as minister of agriculture and was named minister of health in 1964. He was named finance minister in the cabinet of Prime Minister Emir Abbas Hoveida in 1965. Amouzegar retained that position until May of 1974, when he was appointed minister of the interior. He was elected general secretary of the National Resurgence, or Rastakhiz, party in September of 1976. He was selected to replace Hoveida as prime minister on August 7, 1977. Amouzegar's attempts to negotiate with elements opposed to the shah's government met with little success, and he was criticized for his lack of communication with Muslim religious leaders and students. Divisions within his own party led to Amouzegar's resignation on August 27, 1978.

JAFFAR SHARIF IMAMI (Prime Minister, August 27, 1978–November 5, 1978). *See earlier entry under Heads of Government.*

GHOLAM REZA AZHARI (Prime Minister, November 5, 1978–January 4, 1979). Gholam Reza Azhari was born in 1917. He served the shah as chief of staff of the armed forces during the uprising against the monarchy in 1978. He was placed at the head of a military government on November 5, 1978, and declared martial law the following day. Azhari was unable to quell the growing opposition to the shah's rule and was replaced as prime minister and chief of staff on January 4, 1979. He escaped the country following the overthrow of the monarchy. He was sentenced to death in absentia by the Islamic Revolutionary Court later in 1979.

SHAHPUR BAKHTIAR (Prime Minister, January 4, 1979–February 5, 1979). Shahpur Bakhtiar was born in Teheran in 1916. He was educated in Lebanon and France, where he studied political science and law at the Sorbonne. He served in the French army during World War II. Bakhtiar returned to Iran in 1946 and entered the Ministry of Labor. He served as deputy labor minister in the government of Mohammed Mossadegh in 1953. Following the ouster of Mossadegh, Bakhtiar remained active in the National Front, an anti-shah political organization. His opposition to the shah resulted in his arrest on several occasions. On January 4, 1979, the shah selected Bakhtiar to form a government as prime minister in the hopes of preserving the monarchy. As a condition to accepting the appointment, Bakhtiar insisted that the shah leave the country, and he did so on January 16, 1979. Bakhtiar, in the hopes of stabilizing the government, tried to delay the return of the Ayatollah Khomeini to Iran. He was forced, however, to allow Khomeini to enter Teheran on February 1, 1979. Bakhtiar was unable to gain the support of the leading anti-shah organization, the National Front. The Islamic fundamentalists forced him to leave office on February 5, 1979. He went into hiding before going into exile in Paris. There he formed the National Movement of the Iranian Resistance in opposition to the rule of the Ayatollah Khomeini. He was the target of several assassination attempts before he was found stabbed to death outside of his Paris home on August 6, 1991.

MEDHI BAZARGAN (Prime Minister, February 5, 1979–November 6, 1979). Medhi Bazargan was born in Teheran in September of 1905. He was educated in France and returned to Iran to become an engineering professor at the University of Teheran in 1936. He was a supporter of Prime Minister Mohammed Mossadegh in the 1950s and served as undersecretary of state for education in Mossadegh's government. Bazargan was also chairman of the National Iranian Oil Corporation until 1953, when Mossadegh was forced from office. Bazargan left the government and joined the National Resistance Movement. He was active in the formation of the Iranian Liberation Movement in 1961. Bazargan's opposition to the shah led to his arrest on several occasions. He joined the Ayatollah Khomeini's Iranian Committee for Defense of Liberty and Human Rights in 1963. The following year he was convicted of treason and sentenced to ten years imprisonment. Bazargan was pardoned in 1967 and left politics to become director of the Yad Construction Company. He was again arrested in 1978 for antigovernment activities. On February 5, 1979, Bazargan was named prime minister by the Ayatollah following the ouster of the shah

and the Ayatollah's return from exile. He resigned on November 6, 1979, two days after Iranian militants seized the United States Embassy in Teheran. His resignation followed accusations that he was engaged in negotiations with the United States. He subsequently served as a member of Parliament from 1981 until 1984.

MOHAMMED ALI RAJA'I (Prime Minister, August 12, 1980–August 4, 1981). *See entry under Heads of State.*

MOHAMMED JAVAD BAHONAR (Prime Minister, August 4, 1981–August 30, 1981). Mohammed Javad Bahonar was born in Kerman in 1934. He studied theology under the Ayatollah Khomeini in Qom and was active in the opposition movement to the shah's regime. He was arrested in the early 1960s for his activities, and in 1962 he was a founder of an underground political organization with Mohammed Ali Raja'i. He was a follower of the Khomeini while the Ayatollah was in exile and was instrumental in organizing strikes and demonstrations against the shah. Following the ouster of the shah in January of 1979, Bahonar served as a member of the Revolutionary Council. He was also involved in the drafting of the new Iranian constitution. He was named to Raja'i's cabinet as minister of education in March of 1981. He was also elected leader of the Islamic Republic party following the death of Ayatollah Mohammed Beheshti in an bomb explosion on June 28, 1971. When Prime Minister Raja'i was elected to replace Abolhassan Bani-Sadr as president, Bahonar was named prime minister. He took office on August 4, 1981. His term of office was brief, as he was killed along with Raja'i and other government leaders in a bomb blast in the prime minister's office on August 30, 1981.

MOHAMMED REZA MAHDAVI-KANI (Prime Minister, September 1, 1981–October 15, 1981). Mohammed Reza Mahdavi-Kani was a leading Islamic clergyman and key supporter of the Ayatollah Khomeini. He served as leader of the revolutionary neighborhood committees in the early days of the shah's ouster in 1979. He was the leader of the Association of Combatant Clerics of Teheran, a rival political organization to the Islamic Republican party. Mahdavi-Kani served as minister of the interior in the government of Mohammed Javad Bahonar. He was selected to succeed Bahonar as provisional prime minister on September 1, 1981, after Bahonar's death in a bomb explosion. Mahdavi-Kani announced his candidacy for the presidential elections in October of 1981, but Sayyed Ali Khamenei was elected president. Mahdavi-Kani resigned as prime minister on October 15, 1981, in order to allow the new president to select his own candidate. He remained in the cabinet as minister of the interior until he was dismissed in August of 1982.

MIR HOSSEIN MOUSSAVI (Prime Minister, October 29, 1981–August 3, 1989). Mir Hossein Moussavi was born in 1937. He was educated at the National University in Teheran, where he became active in the Islamic Society. He was a critic of the government of the shah and was imprisoned in 1973. Moussavi was a founder of the Islamic Republic party in 1979 and served as editor of the Islamic newspaper. He was named foreign minister in August of 1981 and was selected as prime minister on October 29, 1981. He retained that position until it was abolished on August 3, 1989. He subsequently served as an advisor to President Hashemi Rafsanjani.

OTHER LEADERS

AYATOLLAH RUHOLLAH KHOMEINI (Grand Ayatollah, February 1, 1979–June 3, 1989). Ayatollah Ruhollah Khomeini was born Ruhollah Musawi in Khomein, a village southwest of Teheran, on May 17, 1900 (some sources indicate September 23, 1902). He was the son of a local religious leader who was murdered shortly after Khomeini's birth. He attended local Islamic schools, and when he was in his teens, he studied with the Ayatollah Abdul Karim Haeri, a leading Islamic scholar. Khomeini accompanied Haeri to the city of Qom in 1922 and assisted in the foundation of the Islamic school, the Madresseh Faizieh. Khomeini continued his education and became a teacher in Qom. He became a leader in the Shi'ite Muslim community and wrote a book critical of Reza Shah Pahlavi in 1941. He was later a critic of his son and successor, Shah Mohammed Reza Pahlavi.

He became a fervent nationalist during the 1950s and by the 1960s was recognized as the leading figure in the Shi'ite community. His criticisms of the shah's modernization of Iran resulted in a military action by government troops in 1963 that caused the deaths of nearly 20 of his followers at the Madresseh Faizieh. As a result, the government of the shah was faced with widespread strikes and demonstrations. The following year Khomeini was arrested. He spent a year either in prison or under house arrest. In November of 1964 he refused to recant his criticisms and was sent into exile, first in Turkey and then in Iraq the following year. He headed a theological school there in An Najaf and remained an outspoken critic of the shah. Khomeini was forced to leave Iraq in October of 1978 and went to France. There, by means of tape-recorded speeches and writings, he was instrumental in orchestrating the demonstrations that brought down the shah's regime in January of 1979. The shah fled the country, and on February 1, 1979, Khomeini returned to Iran. He forced the resignation of the government of Prime Minister Shapour Bakhtiar on February 11, 1979, and installed Mehdi Bazargan as head of the provisional government. Khomeini returned to Qom and declared Iran an Islamic Republic with himself as the "interpreter of divine will" and the leading political and spiritual figure in the country. His followers ruthlessly crushed any opposition, imprisoning or executing thousands of opponents. Khomeini also remained an implacable foe of the United States and supported the fundamentalist students who cap-

tured the U.S. Embassy in Teheran on November 4, 1979, and took the embassy staff hostage. The Ayatollah also oversaw Iran's war with Iraq, following the latter's invasion of Iran in 1980. Fighting continued until a cease-fire was accepted by Khomeini in 1988. One of Khomeini's final acts was to condemn British novelist Salman Rushdie for writing *The Satanic Verses*, which Khomeini considered blasphemous to the Islamic faith. He sentenced Rushdie to death and placed a bounty on his head. Khomeini died in Qom following surgery for intestinal bleeding on June 3, 1989.

SAYYED ALI KHAMENEI (Grand Ayatollah, June 4, 1989–). *See entry under Heads of State.*

Iraq, Republic of

(al-Jumhuriyah al-'Iraqiyah)

Iraq is a country in western Asia. It was granted independence under a League of Nations mandate administered by Great Britain on October 3, 1932.

HEADS OF STATE

FEISAL II (King, April 4, 1939–July 14, 1958). Feisal was born in Baghdad on May 2, 1935. He was the son of King Ghazi, who ruled Iraq from September of 1933. Feisal succeeded his father as king of Iraq when Ghazi was killed in an automobile accident on April 4, 1939. Feisal ruled through the regency of his uncle, Abdul-Ilah, during which time he was educated at Harrow in Great Britain. His classmates included his cousin, Hussein, who was to become king of Jordan. Feisal returned to Iraq in 1952 and assumed his royal duties on May 2, 1953, after having come of age. He remained close friends with his cousin,

King Hussein, and planned to federate their nations in response to the militant nationalist policies of Gamal Nasser's newly formed United Arab Republic. Feisal and Hussein reached an agreement in February of 1958 to unify Iraq and Jordan the following July, with Feisal as head of the federation. The proposed federation was aborted when Feisal was ousted in a nationalist coup led by Brigadier Abdul Karim Kassem. The king surrendered to the coup leaders on July 14, 1958, when he was given a promise of safe conduct. Instead he and much of the royal family were slaughtered and their butchered bodies dragged through the streets of Baghdad.

ABDUL-ILAH (Regent, April 4, 1939–May 2, 1953). Abdul-Ilah was born in Taif on November 14, 1913. He was the son of Ali ibn Husain, who had ruled as king of the Hejaz from 1924 until his defeat and ouster by King Saud of Saudi Arabia in 1925. On the death of King Ghazi in 1939, Abdul-Ilah was named regent of Iraq for Feisal II, his nephew. The regency was briefly deposed by pro-German Rashid Ali Gailani, following Abdul-Ilah's declared support for the Allies in 1941. Abdul-llah returned to Baghdad following Gailani's ouster and proceeded to declare war on the Axis powers. He was made crown prince in 1943, and following the assassination of Jordan's King Abdullah, he was recognized as the head of the Hashemite royal family. Abdul-Ilah's moderate pro-Western policies brought him into conflict with some of the more militant Arab nationalists in the region. After Feisal came of age, Abdul-Ilah continued to serve as the king's close advisor. He was murdered on July 14, 1958, with Feisal and other members of the royal family, following a nationalist coup.

NAJIB AL-RUBAI (President, July 14, 1958–February 8, 1963). Najib al-Rubai was born in Baghdad in 1904. He served in the Iraqi military, where he rose to the rank of general. He was selected to head the three-man Sovereignty Council following the coup that overthrew the monarchy on July 14, 1958. He was reportedly involved in the plot to assassinate Prime Minister Abdul Karim Kassem in October of 1959.

ABDUL SALAM MOHAMMED ARIF (President, February 8, 1963–April 13, 1966). Abdul Salam Mohammed Arif was born in Baghdad on March 21, 1921. He served in the Iraqi military and was a commander in the Arab-Israeli war of 1948. He was a prominent part of the coup that ousted the Hashemite monarchy in July of 1958. Arif served as deputy prime minister, minister of the interior, and commander in chief of the armed forces in the subsequent government of Abdul Karim Kassem. Arif was relieved of his duties and sent to Bonn as ambassador to West Germany following a disagreement with Kassem later in 1958. He returned to Baghdad several months later and was arrested on charges of conspiring against the Kassem government. He was condemned to death, but was pardoned by Kassem in November of 1961. When Kassem was ousted by another military coup on February 8, 1963, Arif was called upon to assume the presidency. Arif reorganized the government, ousting the Ba'ath party, in a countercoup in November of 1963. The Arif government improved relations with President Gamal Abdel Nasser of Egypt, though he was less successful in other endeavors. The proposed unification of Iraq with Egypt was scuttled, the Kurdish rebellion continued, and an agreement with the Iraq Petroleum Company was abrogated due to nationalist pressure. Arif retained the presidency until he was killed in an air crash near Al Qurnah on April 13, 1966.

ABDUL RAHMAN ARIF (President, April 17, 1966–July 17, 1968). Abdul Rahman Arif was born in 1916. He was educated at the Baghdad Military Academy and served in the Iraqi army. He assisted his brother, Abdul Salam Mohammed Arif, in the military coup that ousted Prime Minister Abdul Karim Kassem in February of 1963. Arif was appointed chief of staff of the Iraqi armed forces the following year. He succeeded his brother as president on April 17, 1966, following Abdul Salam Mohammed Arif's death. He also served as Iraq's prime minister from May 10 until July 10 of 1967. Arif remained president until July 17, 1968, when he was ousted in a Ba'athist coup led by Ahmed Hassan al-Bakr. He subsequently went into exile.

AHMED HASSAN AL-BAKR (President, July 17, 1968–July 16, 1979). Ahmed Hassan al-Bakr was born in Takrit in 1912. He was educated as a teacher, but joined the Iraqi army in 1938. He was dismissed from the army following his participation in the short-lived revolt led by Rashid Ali Gailani in 1941. Bakr was reinstated in the armed forces in the 1950s and was involved in Abdul Karim Kassem's overthrow of the Hashemite monarchy in July of 1958. He subsequently broke with the Kassem regime and joined the Ba'ath party. He was active in the coup that ousted Kassem in February of 1963. Bakr was subsequently named vice president, but was dismissed from office following an anti-Ba'athist countercoup led by President Abdul Salam Mohammed Arif in November of 1963. Arif was killed in a plane crash in April of 1966 and was succeeded by his brother, Abdul Rahman Arif. Bakr led a coup against Arif, ousting him as president on July 17, 1968. Bakr became president of Iraq and earned a reputation for ruthlessness in his purges of political opponents. During his term of office, he crushed the Kurdish rebellion in northern Iraq. He also sent Iraqi troops to fight with the Syrians in the war against Israel in October of 1973. Bakr resigned as president for health reasons on July 16, 1979, and was succeeded by Saddam Hussein. Bakr died in Baghdad after a lengthy illness at the age of 68 on October 4, 1982.

SADDAM HUSSEIN (President, July 16, 1979–). Saddam Hussein al-Takriti was born near the town of Takrit on April 28, 1937. He was educated in Baghdad during the 1950s and became involved in the Ba'ath Socialist party. He supported the overthrow of the Hashemite monarchy in July of 1958, but the succeeding regime of Abdul Karim Kassem also proved inhospitable for the Ba'ath party. Hussein participated in an assassination attempt against Kassem in October of 1959. Kassem and Hussein were both wounded in the attack. Hussein escaped from Iraq to Syria and was sentenced to death in absentia. He later went to Egypt, where he became a protégé of President Gamal Abdel Nasser. He entered law school at the University of Cairo in 1962 and returned to Iraq the following year after the ouster of Kassem. Hussein was again forced to go underground following the purge of Ba'athists in the government in November of 1963. He was arrested in November of 1964 and was imprisoned for two years. In 1966 he escaped and established himself as a leader of the Ba'athist militia. He was active in the coup that installed a Ba'athist government in July of 1968. Hussein served as second in command to President Ahmed Hassan al-Bakr and was considered the power behind the Bakr regime. Hussein succeeded to the presidency when Bakr resigned for reasons of health on July 16, 1979. Hussein also became chairman of the Revolutionary Command Council, prime minister, commander of the armed forces, and secretary-general of the Ba'ath party. He immediately launched a bloody purge of rival Ba'athists. The following year he started a war against Iran, which continued until a cease-fire was signed in 1988. Hussein also became involved in a conflict over oil prices with Kuwait and Saudi Arabia. Hussein launched an attack against Kuwait and conquered the small country on August 2, 1990. This unprovoked act of aggression brought the condemnation of the world community. The United Nations issued an ultimatum demanding Iraq's withdrawal from Kuwait. When Iraq refused to comply, the United States led a multinational attack against the Iraqi forces in early 1991. The Iraqis were firmly defeated, though Hussein retained power. He was beset with rebellions by the Kurds in northern Iraq and Shi'ite Muslims in the south, both of which he tried to ruthlessly suppress. He also continued to plague the world community by stalling United Nations attempts to learn the status of Iraq's nuclear weapons program.

HEADS OF GOVERNMENT

HAMDI AL-PACHACHI (Prime Minister, June 4, 1944–January 31, 1946). Hamdi al-Pachachi was born to a wealthy family in Baghdad in 1891. He served as minister of social welfare from 1941 until 1944. He subsequently became president of the Chamber of Deputies. Pachachi was asked to form a cabinet as prime minister on June 4, 1944. He was forced to resign on January 31, 1946. He was named foreign minister in January of 1948 and retained that position until his death in Baghdad from a heart attack on March 27, 1948.

TAUFIQ AL-SUWAIDI (Prime Minister, February 23, 1946–May 31, 1946). Taufiq al-Suwaidi was born in 1891. He was educated as a lawyer and served as a legal advisor to the Iraqi government from 1921 until 1927. He was named to the cabinet as minister of education in 1927 and served until the following year. Suwaidi served as prime minister and foreign minister from April 28 until August 25, 1929, and again from November 18, 1929, until March 9, 1930. He served as foreign minister from 1937 until 1938. He again held that position in 1941 following the ouster of the pro–German regime of Rashid Ali Gailani. Suwaidi was selected as prime minister on February 23, 1946, and held the position until May 31, 1946. He again headed the government from February 5, 1950, until September 4, 1950. He served as foreign minister again in 1950 and in 1953. Suwaidi was named deputy prime minister in 1958 and was foreign minister of the Iraqi-Jordanian federation from May until July of 1958. He was arrested following the overthrow of the Hashemite monarchy in July of 1958. He was sentenced to life imprisonment, but was released in July of 1961. He went into exile in Lebanon, where he remained until his death in 1968.

ARSHAD AL-UMARI (Prime Minister, June 1, 1946–November 14, 1946). Arshad al-Umari was born in 1888. He was educated in Istanbul, Turkey, as an engineer. He subsequently entered politics and was elected to the first Iraqi Parliament. Umari served as director-general of posts and telegraphs in 1931 and was director-general of irrigation from 1931 until 1932. He also served as mayor of Baghdad from 1931 until 1933. He was named to the cabinet as minister of works in 1935. Umari again served as Baghdad's mayor from 1936 until 1944. He was appointed foreign minister in 1944 and was chairman of the Iraqi delegation that ratified the Arab League Pact. He formed an interim government as prime minister on June 1, 1946 and served until November 14, 1946. Umari was appointed minister of defense in January of 1948 and subsequently served in the Iraqi Senate. Umari was again named prime minister as head of a caretaker government on April 29, 1954. His government conducted parliamentary elections in June, and Umari resigned on August 4, 1954.

NURI AL-SAID (Prime Minister, November 21, 1946–March 30, 1947). Nuri al-Said was born in Baghdad in 1888. He attended the Military Academy in Istanbul in 1903 and joined the Iraqi army as an officer in 1908. He was an early Arab nationalist and joined the

Arab Revolt during World War I. He was a close advisor to King Feisal II's grandfather, Emir Feisal, and served as his chief of staff during the Arab Revolt led by Lawrence of Arabia. Nuri remained with Emir Feisal during his rule in Syria in 1920 and accompanied him the following year when Feisal was named the first king of Iraq. He was named to the cabinet as minister of defense in November of 1922 and again served in that position during three cabinets between 1923 and 1928. During the next twenty-five years, he remained a major political figure in Iraq and served as prime minister from March 23, 1930, until October 27, 1932, during which time he signed the Anglo-Iraqi Treaty of 1930. Nuri served as foreign minister in several cabinets during the early 1930s. He was forced to flee the country following the coup led by General Bakr Sidqi Al-'Askari in October of 1936. He returned to Iraq following Sidqi's assassination in August of 1937. Nuri served in several diplomatic positions abroad before again serving as prime minister from December 26, 1938, until March 31, 1940. He again fled Iraq following the pro-German coup led by Rashid Ali Gailani. He returned to Iraq following Gailani's ouster and was again named prime minister on October 19, 1941. Nuri led the Iraqi government in declaring war on the Axis powers during World War II. He retained office until June 4, 1944. He was a leading proponent of Arab unity and a founder of the Arab League. Nuri again formed a government on November 21, 1946, and served until March 30, 1947. He was again prime minister from January 6 until November 7 of 1949 and founded the Constitutional Union party. He served as head of government again from September 16, 1950, until July 9, 1952, when he was forced to resign following student rioting. Nuri remained in the government as minister of defense. He was again named prime minister on August 4,

1954. During this term of office, Iraq broke off diplomatic relations with the Soviet Union and signed the Baghdad Pact with Turkey, Pakistan, Iran, and Great Britain. His opposition to Egypt's President Gamal Abdel Nasser, along with his moderate pro-Western policies, met with opposition from the militant nationalists. He stepped down on June 16, 1957, for reasons of health. Nuri's last term as prime minister was from March 3 until May 13 of 1958, when he resigned in preparation to become prime minister of the newly formed federation between Iraq and Jordan. Following the ouster of Feisal II, Nuri was captured and brutally killed on July 14, 1958, when he tried to escape from Baghdad dressed as a woman. His body was reportedly dismembered by an angry mob.

SALEH JABUR (Prime Minister, March 30, 1947–January 29, 1948). Saleh Jabur was born in al-Nasseriyya in 1896. He attended the Baghdad Law School and served as a judge from 1926 until 1930. He was elected to Parliament in 1930 and was named to the cabinet as minister of education in 1933. Jabur was appointed governor of Karbala in 1935 and returned to Baghdad to serve as minister of justice the following year. He was named director-general of customs in 1937 and was appointed minister of education in 1938. He served as governor of Basra from 1940 until 1941 and was acting foreign minister from 1941 until 1942. Jabur then served for a year as minister of finance. He became the first Shi'ite Muslim to hold the position of prime minister on March 30, 1947. In January of 1948 he negotiated a treaty to replace the Anglo-Iraqi treaty of 1930. This treaty proved unpopular with nationalist elements in Iraq, and widespread demonstrations and rioting occurred. Jabur was forced to resign on January 29, 1948, and the treaty was overruled by his successor. Jabur returned to the cabinet as minister of the interior for a brief period in 1950. The following year he founded the People's Socialist party, but met with little success in the elections. He died of a heart attack on June 6, 1957, while addressing the Iraqi Senate.

MOHAMMED EL-SADR (Prime Minister, January 29, 1948–June 22, 1948). Mohammed el-Sadr was born in Kazimija in 1882. He was named prime minister on January 29, 1948, following the resignation of Saleh Jabur. Sadr announced that the Iraqi government repudiated the Anglo-Iraqi treaty negotiated by his predecessor. Sadr's government presided over new elections, and he stepped down as prime minister on June 22, 1948, following the election of a new government.

MUZAHIM AL-PACHACHI (Prime Minister, June 26, 1948–January 6, 1949). Muzahim al-Pachachi was born in 1891. He was educated at the Istanbul Law School and became active in the Arab nationalist movement prior to World War I. He served as a member of the committee which drafted Iraq's constitution in 1924. Pachachi was also appointed to the cabinet as minister of communications and public works that year. He was elected to Parliament in 1925, and in 1927 he was sent to London as Iraq's representative. He returned to Iraq in 1928 and was an opponent of the Anglo-Iraqi Treaty of 1930. Pachachi returned to the cabinet as minister of economics in 1931 and was appointed minister of the interior later in the year. He was sent to Geneva in 1933 to serve as Iraq's representative to the League of Nations. He was named minister to Italy in 1935 and was appointed minister to France in 1939. Pachachi left France for Switzerland following the German occupation in 1942. He returned to Iraq after the conclusion of World War II. He served on the committee for the defense of Palestine from 1946 until 1947. Pachachi was selected as prime minister on June 26,

1948. His government rejected the United Nation's imposed truce in Palestine and recognized the Palestinian government in Gaza. He stepped down as prime minister on January 6, 1949, and was succeeded by Nuri al-Said. Pachachi was appointed foreign minister and deputy prime minister in December of 1949 and served until February of 1950. He left Iraq in 1951 following his failure to establish a pro-Egyptian political party. Pachachi returned to Iraq in 1958 after the coup that deposed King Feisal II, though he remained inactive in political affairs. He died in 1982.

NURI AL-SAID (Prime Minister, January 6, 1949–November 7, 1949). *See earlier entry under Heads of Government.*

ALI JAWDAT AL-AYUBI (Prime Minister, December 10, 1949–February 1, 1950). Ali Jawdat al-Ayubi was born in Mosul in 1887. He was educated at the Military College in Istanbul and subsequently served in the Ottoman army. He deserted the Ottomans and joined Sharif Hussein's Arab rebellion in 1916. Ayubi served as governor of Aleppo under Feisal's reign in Syria from 1920 until 1921. The following year Ayubi returned to Iraq and became a leader of the right-wing nationalist Al-Ikha party. He was named minister of the interior in 1923 and served until 1924. He returned to the cabinet as minister of finance in 1930 and was an opponent of the Anglo-Iraqi Treaty of that year. Ayubi became chief of the royal household in 1933. He was first named prime minister on August 26, 1934 and served until February 24, 1935. He subsequently served as Speaker of the Parliament before being named Iraq's minister to London later in 1935. Ayubi was sent to Paris as Iraq's representative in 1937 and then returned to Iraq to serve as foreign minister in 1939. He left Iraq during the pro–German rule of Rashid

Ali Gailani in 1941. He returned following the restoration of the pro-British regime under Nuri al-Said. Ayubi was appointed minister to Washington, D.C., in 1944. He returned to Iraq to serve as foreign minister in 1948. He was again named prime minister on December 10, 1949, and retained the position until February 1, 1950. Ayubi was deputy prime minister from 1953 until 1957 and served another brief term as prime minister from June 17, 1957, until December 10, 1957. He fled to Lebanon following the military coup that deposed King Feisal in 1959. Ayubi died in Beirut of a heart attack at the age of 82 on March 3, 1969.

TAUFIQ AL-SUWAIDI (Prime Minister, February 5, 1950–September 4, 1950). *See earlier entry under Heads of Government.*

NURI AL-SAID (Prime Minister, September 16, 1950–July 9, 1952). *See earlier entry under Heads of Government.*

MUSTAFA EL-UMARI (Prime Minister, July 12, 1952–November 23, 1952). Mustafa el-Umari was born in 1894. He attended the Baghdad Law College and worked as a teacher from 1919. He was employed by the ministry of the interior from 1921 until 1922. Umari was a district governor from 1922 until 1930, when he became a provincial governor. He served as inspector general of finance from 1935 until 1936 and was elected to the Iraqi Senate the following year. He served in the cabinet as minister of the interior from 1937 until 1938 and served as minister of justice in 1938. Umari was minister of the interior from 1941 until 1944 and again in 1948. He also served as minister of economics in 1948. He was named on July 12, 1952, to lead a nonparty cabinet to prepare for elections. Umari was forced to resign on November 23, 1952, following antigovernment riots.

NUR AL-DIN MAHMUD (Prime Minister, November 23, 1952–January 29, 1953). Nur al-din Mahmud was born in 1889. He was educated in Turkey and attended the staff college in Camberly. He joined the Iraqi army in 1921 and served as military attaché in London. Mahmud commanded Iraqi forces in Palestine and served as acting chief of staff in May of 1941. He negotiated a treaty with Great Britain at that time to end the pro-German coup led by Rashid Ali Gailani. He was named chief of staff of the armed forces in 1951. Mahmud was named to head a military government as prime minister, minister of defense, and minister of the interior on November 12, 1952. He ruled under martial law to halt strikes and demonstrations that had broken out throughout the country. His government also held new elections, and Mahmud stepped down on January 29, 1953. He was subsequently appointed to the Iraqi Senate by the king. Mahmud died in 1958.

JAMIL AL-MIDFAI (Prime Minister, January 29, 1953–September 1, 1953). Jamil al-Midfai was born in Mosul in 1890. He attended the Istanbul School of Engineering and served with the Ottoman army during World War I. He deserted the Ottomans to join with the Arab Revolt in 1916. Midfai served as an advisor to Feisal in Damascus, Syria, from 1918 until 1919. He returned to Iraq in 1920, where he was active in the anti-British nationalist movement. He was forced to leave Iraq later in the year because of his activities. Midfai remained in exile in Transjordan until 1923. He returned to Iraq and served as governor of several provinces. He was named to the cabinet as minister of the interior in 1930. Midfai served as prime minister from November 9, 1933, until August 25, 1934, and again from March 1 until March 16, 1935. He again formed a government on August 17, 1937, serving until December 26, 1938. He was again prime minister from

June 2 until October 10 of 1941. Midfai again fled to Transjordan in 1941 following the pro-German coup led by Rashid Ali Gailani. He returned to Iraq following Gailani's ouster and the restoration of the Hashemite monarchy. Midfai served as president of the Senate from 1944 until 1945 and was named minister of the interior in 1948. He served another term as prime minister from January 29, 1953, until his resignation on September 1, 1953. He was elected president of the Senate again in 1955 and retained the position until his death in 1958.

MOHAMMED FADIL AL-JAMALI (Prime Minister, September 16, 1953–April 29, 1954). Mohammed Fadil al-Jamali was born to a prominent Shi'ite family in Kadhaimain in 1902. He graduated from the local Teachers Training College in 1920 and received a scholarship to the American University of Beirut in Lebanon. He graduated with a degree in education in 1927. Jamali continued his studies and taught during the late 1920s. Following Iraqi independence in October of 1932, Jamali worked with the department of education. He joined the foreign ministry in 1942 and was a delegate to the first United Nations General Assembly in 1946. He was a founder and president of the Arab League and was named foreign minister in June of 1946. Jamali was an opponent of Zionism and represented Iraq before several international commissions on Palestine. He remained foreign minister until late 1948 and again held the position from April until September of 1949. He was elected president of the Chamber of Deputies in October of 1950 and retained the position until he was again appointed foreign minister in August of 1952. Jamali was replaced in January of 1953, and on September 16, 1953, he formed a cabinet as prime minister. He resigned on April 29, 1954, following criticism of his government's handling of the flooding of the Tigris River

the previous month. He subsequently returned to serve as Iraq's chief delegate to the United Nations. Jamali supported the Egyptian position during the Suez crisis in 1956, but was an opponent of Egypt's attempts to influence the Iraqi government. It was reported that he had been killed in Baghdad following the coup that overthrew King Feisal II on July 14, 1958, but he was later revealed to have survived the coup. He was tried and sentenced to death by the military government. His sentence was reduced to ten years in prison in March of 1960, and he was released under an amnesty in July of 1961. In the late 1960s Jamali was involved in the Arab attempt to secure the return of Palestine from Israel. He was a frequent critic of United States support for the Israeli position.

ARSHAD EL-UMARI (Prime Minister, April 29, 1954–August 4, 1954). *See earlier entry under Heads of Government.*

NURI AL-SAID (Prime Minister, August 4, 1954–June 17, 1957). *See earlier entry under Heads of Government.*

ALI JAWDAT AL-AYUBI (Prime Minister, June 17, 1957–December 10, 1957). *See earlier entry under Heads of Government.*

ABDUL WAHAB MARJAN (Prime Minister, December 5, 1957–March 3, 1958). Abdul Wahab Marjan was named to the cabinet as minister of communications in June of 1957. He formed a government as prime minister on December 5, 1957. Marjan resigned on March 3, 1958, to allow Nuri al-Said to form a strong government to implement Iraq's federation with Jordan. Marjan died on March 16, 1964.

NURI AL-SAID (Prime Minister, March 3, 1958–May 13, 1958). *See earlier entry under Heads of Government.*

AHMED MUKHTAR BABAN (Prime Minister, May 19, 1958–July 14, 1958). Ahmed Mukhtar Baban was born in 1900. He was an Arab Kurd and served as a member of the law faculty of the University of Baghdad. He was a close associate of Nuri al-Said and served in various cabinet positions in Said governments, including social affairs, justice, and education. Baban was appointed minister of defense in 1957. He was named prime minister on May 19, 1958, when Nuri al-Said stepped down to become head of the government of the Iraqi-Jordanian Federation. Baban retained office until July 14, 1958, when the monarchy was overthrown by a military coup led by Abdul Karim Kassem. Baban was arrested by the new regime and tried for crimes against the state. He was sentenced to death, but his sentence was reduced to ten years imprisonment in March of 1960. Baban was released under an amnesty in July of 1961.

ABDUL KARIM KASSEM (Prime Minister, July 14, 1958–February 8, 1963). Abdul Karim Kassem was born in Baghdad on November 21, 1914. He attended the Iraq Military Academy before joining the Iraqi army in 1934. He rose through the ranks and served as a commander during the Palestine campaign. In 1955 he was promoted to brigadier. Kassem was an Arab nationalist and, with Abdul Salam Arif, led an army uprising against the government of King Feisal II in July of 1958. Following the overthrow and murder of Feisal, Kassem became prime minister on July 14, 1958. He instituted a series of agrarian reform measures later in the year. He broke with Abdul Salam Arif over his support of Egyptian president Gamal Abdel Nasser and imprisoned Arif. Kassem was wounded in an assassination attempt in October of 1959, but recovered after several months of hospitilization. In June of 1961 Kassem declared that Kuwait was an integral part of Iraq. The British

army mobilized to protect the sheikdom. Though Iraq made no military move toward Kuwait, Kassem continued to insist that the countries should be unified. The Kassem regime was also faced with a rebellion by the Kurds in northeast Iraq. Abdul Salam Arif organized a military uprising against Kassem on February 8, 1963, and ousted him as leader of the government. Kassem was tried and convicted by the revolutionary court and was executed on February 9, 1963.

AHMED HASSAN AL-BAKR (Prime Minister, February 8, 1963–November 18, 1963). *See entry under Heads of State.*

TAHIR YAHIA (Prime Minister, November 20, 1963–September 2, 1965). Tahir Yahia was born in Takrit in 1913. He served in the army before his dismissal on charges of subversion in the 1950s. He was active in organizing the coup that ousted King Feisal in July of 1958. Yahia subsequently served as director-general of the police under President Abdul Karim Kassem. He sided with Colonel Shawwaf's unsuccessful pro–Nasser mutiny in March of 1959 and was dismissed from his position. He was again active in the coup that ousted Kassem in February of 1963. Yahia was named prime minister on November 20, 1963. He resigned the position on September 2, 1965. He was again appointed prime minister on July 10, 1967. Yahia attempted to negotiate a settlement of border disputes with neighboring Iran during his term of office. He resigned on July 15, 1968, two days before the coup that ousted President Arif. He was arrested by the new government, but was never brought to trial. Yahia was released from custody in late 1970. He died in May of 1986.

ARIF ABDEL RAZZAK (Prime Minister, September 6, 1965–September 16, 1965). Arif Abdel Razzak was born in

1924. He was a commander in the Iraqi air force and was named prime minister by President Abdul Salam Mohammed Arif on September 6, 1965. He formed a cabinet composed primarily of Arab nationalists wanting closer ties with Egypt. Razzak led a coup attempt against President Arif on September 16, 1965, when the president was attending a meeting in Casablanca. The plot was foiled by the president's brother, Maj. Gen. Abdul Rahman Arif. Razzak fled the country with his family and settled in Egypt.

ABDUL RAHMAN AL-BAZZAZ (Prime Minister, September 16, 1965– August 6, 1966). Abdul Rahman al-Bazzaz was born on February 20, 1913, to a Sunni Muslim family in Baghdad. He attended the University of London, where he received a doctorate in law. He became active in the nationalist movement and was arrested for his anti-British sympathies in 1941. Bazzaz was named dean of the Baghdad Law School in 1955, though he was dismissed the following year for criticizing the monarchy. After the ouster of the monarchy in July of 1959, Bazzaz was named president of the Court of Cassation by General Abdul Karim Kassem. The following year he was removed from office and arrested after a disagreement with Kassem. He went into exile in Cairo, Egypt, after his release. Bazzaz returned to Iraq after Kassem's ouster in February of 1963. He was named Iraq's ambassador to Egypt by the new government and was instrumental in negotiating an agreement that would unite the governments of Egypt, Syria, and Iraq. The agreement was later discarded. Bazzaz was named ambassador to Great Britain in 1964. He also served as secretary-general of the Organization of Petroleum-Exporting Countries (OPEC) in 1964. He returned to Iraq in September of 1965 to serve as foreign minister and deputy prime minister. Bazzaz was asked to form a government as prime minister

following the ouster of Arif Abdel Razzak on September 16, 1965. Bazzaz was a moderate Socialist and was regarded as a competent administrator. He was successful in improving Iraq's economic and political stability. His attempts to restore a civilian government made him unpopular with elements of the military, however. He briefly served as acting president following the death of President Abdul Salam Mohammed Arif in an air crash on April 13, 1966. Bazzaz was forced to resign as prime minister on August 6, 1966, after a treaty he negotiated with Kurdish rebels met with opposition in Baghdad. He went into exile in London. He returned to Iraq in 1968 and was arrested by the authorities. Bazzaz was threatened with trial and execution over the next several years before he was released to his home. His health had reportedly suffered during his imprisonment, and he died at the age of 60 in Baghdad on June 28, 1973.

NAJI TALIB (Prime Minister, August 9, 1966–May 10, 1967). Naji Talib was born in Nasiriya in 1917. He was educated at military schools in Iraq and Great Britain and served as Iraq's military attaché to London from 1954 until 1955. He commanded the Basra Garrison from 1957 until 1958 and was director of military training at the time of the military coup that overthrew the monarchy in July of 1958. In that position he was able to supply the coup leaders with ammunition needed for the revolt. Talib was appointed minister of social affairs in the subsequent revolutionary government of Abdul Karim Kassem. He resigned from the cabinet in February of 1959 and left the country soon after. He returned to Iraq in 1962. Talib was named minister of industry in 1963, following the ouster of Kassem. He was appointed foreign minister in 1964 and served until 1965. He was chosen as a compromise candidate for prime minister on August 9, 1966. Talib was unable to settle the factionalism rampant in the government and resigned on May 10, 1967.

ABDUL RAHMAN ARIF (Prime Minister, May 10, 1967–July 10, 1967). *See entry under Heads of State.*

TAHIR YAHIA (Prime Minister, July 10, 1967–July 17, 1968). *See earlier entry under Heads of Government.*

ABDUL RAZAK AL-NAIF (Prime Minister, July 17, 1968–July 30, 1968). Abdul Razak al-Naif was born in 1933. He served in the Iraqi military, where he rose to the rank of colonel. He served as deputy director of the Iraqi military intelligence system and masterminded the bloodless coup that ousted President Abdul Rahman Arif on July 17, 1968. Naif was named prime minister in the new government. He was in turn ousted several weeks later on July 30, 1968, by President Ahmed Hassan al-Bakr. Naif subsequently fled Iraq and was sentenced to death in absentia. He went into exile in London, where he survived an assassination attempt at his home in 1972. He was again the target of an assassination attempt on July 9, 1978, when he was shot twice in the head in front of the Inter-Continental Hotel in London. He died of his wounds at the age of 44 on July 10, 1978.

AHMED HASSAN AL-BAKR (Prime Minister, July 30, 1968–July 16, 1979). *See entry under Heads of State.*

SADDAM HUSSEIN (Prime Minis-ter, July 16, 1979–March 23, 1991). *See entry under Heads of State.*

SA'DUN HAMMADI (Prime Minister, March 23, 1991–September 13, 1991). Sa'dun Hammadi was born in Karbala on June 22, 1930. He was educated in Lebanon and the United States. In 1957 he returned to Iraq to teach economics at the University of Baghdad. Hammadi was employed by the National Bank of Libya from 1961 until 1962, when he returned to Iraq to serve in the cabinet as minister of agrarian reform. The following year he served as an economic advisor to the Syrian government. He became president of the Iraq National Oil Company in 1968 and was named minister of oil and minerals the following year. Hammadi served until 1974, when he was appointed minister of foreign affairs. He left the cabinet in 1983 and returned as deputy prime minister in early 1991. President Saddam Hussein relinquished his position as prime minister to Hammadi on March 23, 1991. Hammadi retained the position until September 13, 1991, when he was dismissed by the president for the government's failure to solve the economic problems in Iraq.

MOHAMMED HAMZAH AL-ZUBEIDI (Prime Minister, September 13, 1991–). Mohammed Hamzah al-Zubeidi served as deputy prime minister and minister of transport and communications in the government of Sa'dun Hammadi from March until September of 1991. He was then chosen to replace Hammadi as prime minister on September 13, 1991.

Ireland, Republic of

(Éire)

Ireland is an island country in the North Atlantic west of Great Britain.

HEADS OF STATE

DOUGLAS HYDE (President, December 29, 1937–June 25, 1945). Douglas Hyde was born in Frenchpark, County Roscommon, on January 17, 1860. He attended Trinity College in Dublin and joined the Society for the Preservation of the Irish Language in 1878. He later organized the Gaelic Union in order to publish periodicals in the Irish language. Hyde served as founder and president of the Gaelic League from 1893 until 1915. He wrote numerous books, including *Story of Early Gaelic Literature* (1895), *A Literary History of Ireland* (1899), and *Mediaeval Tales from the Irish* (1899). He also wrote poems and plays and recounted old Irish legends, sometimes under the pseudonym An Craoibhin Aoibhinn, meaning "the delightful little branch." Hyde became a professor of modern Irish at University College in Dublin in 1909 and remained in that position until 1932. He was also elected to the Irish Senate in 1925, and when the Irish constitution was created in 1937, he was selected to be the first president of Eire. He took office on December 29, 1937, and remained in office until his retirement on June 24, 1945. He died in Dublin at the age of 89 on July 12, 1949.

SEAN T. O'KELLY (President, June 25, 1945–June 25, 1959). Sean Thomas O'Kelly was born in Dublin on August 25, 1882. He was educated in Ireland and was employed at the Dublin National Library after graduation. He joined the Irish Republican Brotherhood as a young man and was a founder of the Sinn Fein party in 1902. O'Kelly was elected an alderman in Dublin in 1906. He remained involved in nationalist activities and took part in the Easter Rebellion in 1916. He was arrested and interned by the British until June of 1917. O'Kelly was elected to the Parliament from North Dublin in

December of 1918, but refused to take his seat. He instead entered the illegal Parliament of Ireland, or Dail Eireann, and served as its Speaker. He subsequently represented the Irish nationalists in Paris and Rome. O'Kelly supported Eamon De Valera's opposition to the treaty creating the Irish Free State in 1921. He was dismissed from the government the following year and was imprisoned from 1922 until 1923. He was then reelected to the Dail and represented De Valera in the United States from 1924 until 1926. O'Kelly was a founder of the Fianna Fail and served as the party's vice president from 1927. He became vice president of the Executive Council and minister of local government and public health in the government of De Valera in March of 1932. The Irish Free State became Eire in 1937, and O'Kelly was named minister of education two years later. He subsequently served as minister of finance and successfully reduced Eire's national debt. He was elected to succeed Douglas Hyde as Eire's president and took office on June 25, 1945. O'Kelly presided over the country when Eire withdrew from the British Commonwealth and was proclaimed the Irish Republic in 1949. He was unopposed in his bid for reelection in 1952. He remained president until his retirement on June 25, 1959. O'Kelly withdrew from politics to write his memoirs at his home in County Wicklow. He died in Dublin after a long illness at the age of 84 on November 23, 1966.

EAMON DE VALERA (President, June 25, 1959–June 25, 1973). Eamon De Valera was born in New York City on October 14, 1882. His father was a Spanish musician, and his mother was Irish. De Valera was brought to live with his maternal grandmother in County Limerick, Ireland, following his father's death in 1884. He was educated in Ireland and received a degree in mathematics. He embarked on a career as a teacher and soon became interested in Gaelic studies. De Valera joined the Gaelic League, and in 1913 he became associated with the Irish Volunteers, a group dedicated to Ireland's independence from Great Britain. He was arrested during the Easter Rebellion in 1916 and was spared from the death sentence handed to many of the other leaders of the Rebellion because of his American birth. He was sentenced to life imprisonment but was released in June of 1917 following a general amnesty. De Valera subsequently was elected president of the Sinn Fein nationalist organization and was also elected to the British Parliament, though he never took office because of his refusal to swear allegiance to the British crown. He was again arrested in 1918 following his opposition to Ireland's involvement in World War I. He escaped from Lincoln Prison in February of 1919 and returned to Ireland. De Valera soon went to America on a mission to seek United States aid in Ireland's independence movement. Upon his return to Ireland, he entered into peace negotiations with the British government led by Prime Minister David Lloyd George. De Valera did not personally take part in the meetings which resulted in a treaty granting the 26 counties of southern Ireland limited independence. De Valera and other nationalist leaders repudiated the treaty, and in June of 1922 a bloody civil war resulted. De Valera was instrumental in calling an end to the battle in May of 1923 because he felt the Irish Republicans could not defeat the British army through warfare. In 1925 De Valera attempted to get the Sinn Fein to accept election to the Irish Parliament regardless of the oath to the crown. His position was rejected by the Sinn Fein, and De Valera formed the Fianna Fail, or "Soldiers of Destiny," as his own political party. Two years later De Valera took his seat in Parliament. De

Valera's party was successful in subsequent elections, and he took office as Ireland's prime minister on March 9, 1932. He also served as foreign minister during his term of office. He was active in the League of Nations, where he served as president of the Council in 1932 and president of the Assembly of the League in 1938. De Valera's government drafted a new constitution in December of 1937 and established the independent state of Eire the following year. Ireland under De Valera remained neutral during World War II, and the Fianna Fail was again successful in the elections of 1944. Four years later De Valera's party lost its absolute majority, and John Costello replaced De Valera as prime minister on February 18, 1948. After a new election was called in May of 1951, De Valera was narrowly returned as prime minister and took office on June 13, 1951. He was again defeated by Costello's Fine Gael party and was replaced on June 2, 1954. Costello's ruling coalition collapsed in January of 1957, and De Valera was returned as prime minister on March 20, 1957. De Valera, suffering from failing eyesight, retired from parliamentary politics on June 23, 1959, to take office as the president of the Republic of Ireland on June 25, 1959. He won reelection to the largely ceremonial office in 1966. He retired to a Dublin nursing home on June 25, 1973. De Valera died there of pneumonia at the age of 92 on August 29, 1975.

ERSKINE CHILDERS (President, June 25, 1973–November 17, 1974). Erskine Childers was born in London, England, on December 11, 1905. His father, Erskine Childers, the distinguished author of *The Riddle of the Sands*, was executed by the Irish Free State during the civil war in 1922. The younger Childers became active in the Fianna Fail party led by Eamon De Valera. Childers served as secretary of the Federation of Irish Manufacturers until 1944, when he joined the Fianna Fail government. He served as minister of public health from 1951 until 1954. He held a succession of cabinet positions, including land, transport, and power and in 1969 was named deputy prime minister. Childers was a strong voice in opposition to the violence in Northern Ireland. He was elected president of Ireland, defeating the favored candidate, Tom O'Higgins, and took office on June 25, 1973. He hoped to use his office to make noncontroversial pronouncements and encourage intellectual debate, but his term was cut short when he died of a heart attack in Dublin on November 17, 1974.

CEARBHALL O'DALAIGH (President, December 19, 1974–October 22, 1976). Cearbhall O'Dalaigh (Carroll O'Daly) was born in County Wicklow on February 12, 1911. He became active in politics in the early 1930s and joined Eamon De Valera's Fianna Fail party. He was a great admirer of De Valera and was named attorney general in 1946. O'Dalaigh served in that position until 1948 and again from 1951 until 1953. He was then named to Ireland's Supreme Court. O'Dalaigh became chief justice of the court in 1961 and served until 1973. He was subsequently appointed to the Court of Justice of European Communities in Luxembourg. He returned to Ireland the following year after an agreement by the major political parties that he should succeed Erskine Childers as Ireland's president following Childers's death. O'Dalaigh took office on December 19, 1974. As president, O'Dalaigh attempted to delay the implementation of legislation that would have given the police greater powers in detaining suspected terrorists. O'Dalaigh's actions were criticized by the minister of defense, and the law was upheld by the Irish Supreme Court. O'Dalaigh resigned the presidency on October 22, 1976. He retired to Sneem, in County

Kerry, where he died of a heart attack on March 21, 1978.

PATRICK J. HILLARY (President, December 3, 1976–December 3, 1990). Patrick John Hillary was born in County Clare on May 2, 1923. He received a doctorate in medicine from University College in Dublin. He was a practicing physician before his election to the Parliament in 1951. Hillary was a member of the Fianna Fail party and served as minister of education from 1959 until 1965. He was then named minister of industry and commerce and served until 1966, when he was appointed minister of labor. He retained that position until 1969, when he became Ireland's foreign minister. In January of 1973 Hillary was named Ireland's first representative to the Commission of the European Economic Community in Brussels, Belgium. He returned to Ireland to accept the presidency of the Republic on December 3, 1976, following the resignation of Cearbhall O'Dalaigh. Hillary was reelected without opposition in 1983. He completed his second term and retired from public office on December 3, 1990.

MARY ROBINSON (President, December 3, 1990–). Mary Robinson was born Mary Bourke in Ballina, County Mayo, on May 21, 1944. She was educated in Ireland and the United States, where she received a degree in law. She served on the law faculty at Trinity College in Dublin from 1969. Though a Roman Catholic, she married a protestant, Nicholas Robinson, in 1970. She became politically active in the 1970s and served on the Dublin City Council and worked with various political and social organizations. Robinson was elected to the Irish Senate in 1970 as a member of the Labour party. She was an advocate of legal divorce and birth control, which often put her at odds with the Catholic leadership. She was nominated to run as the leftist Labour party's candidate for president in 1990. Robinson narrowly defeated Fianna Fail nominee Brian Lenihan and became the Irish Republic's first female president on December 3, 1990.

HEADS OF GOVERNMENT

EAMON DE VALERA (Prime Minister, March 9, 1932–February 18, 1948). *See entry under Heads of State.*

JOHN A. COSTELLO (Prime Minister, February 18, 1948–June 13, 1951). John Aloysius Costello was born near Dublin on June 20, 1891. He received a law degree at King's Inns in London in 1914. He represented many of the arrested rebels following Ireland's Easter Rebellion in 1916. Costello joined the Irish Free State Government in 1922 and was named attorney general in 1926. He served in that position until 1932, when the government of William T. Cosgrave was defeated. He resumed his law practice, but remained active in politics. Costello continued to serve in the Irish Parliament as a member of the Fine Gael party and was the chief parliamentary opposition to the government of Prime Minister Eamon De Valera. When De Valera's Fianna Fail party failed to achieve an absolute majority in the parliamentary elections in 1948, Costello became prime minister as head of a coalition government on February 18, 1948. During his first term as prime minister, Costello withdrew Ireland from the British Commonwealth. The Fianna Fail party was victorious in the elections of 1951, and Costello was replaced by De Valera as prime minister on June 13, 1951. Costello again returned to the prime minister's office on June 2, 1954, following Fianna Fail's defeat at the polls. His government was charged with failing to create a cohesive economic policy for Ireland, and he was again replaced by De Valera on March 20, 1957. Costello remained in Parliament as leader of the

opposition until his retirement in 1959. He spent his later years at his home in Dublin, where he died of cancer at the age of 84 on January 5, 1976.

EAMON DE VALERA (Prime Minister, June 13, 1951–June 2, 1954). *See entry under Heads of State.*

JOHN A. COSTELLO (Prime Minister, June 2, 1954–March 20, 1957). *See earlier entry under Heads of Government.*

EAMON DE VALERA (Prime Minister, March 20, 1957–June 23, 1959). *See entry under Heads of State.*

SEAN F. LEMASS (Prime Minister, June 23, 1959–November 10, 1966). Sean Francis Lemass was born in Dublin on July 15, 1899. He was educated locally and was active in the Irish independence movement that culminated in the Easter Week Rebellion in 1916. He was arrested by the British forces following the collapse of the rebellion and was spared the fate of execution or imprisonment due to his youth. Lemass joined the Irish Republican Army and was again captured during revolutionary activities. He remained interned until July of 1921, when a truce was declared. Lemass fought with the Irish Republican Army during the civil war that broke out in July of 1922. He was captured, but escaped soon afterwards. He was again captured in December of 1922 and remained imprisoned until the Republicans were defeated in the spring of 1923. Lemass resigned from the Sinn Fein party with Eamon De Valera and joined De Valera's new Fianna Fail party. He was elected to the Irish Parliament in 1924. When De Valera became prime minister in 1932, Lemass was named to the cabinet as minister of industry and commerce. He was appointed minister of supplies in 1939 and retained that position until 1945. He was also named deputy prime minister following the conclusion of World War II and remained in that position until the Fianna Fail was defeated in the 1948 elections. Lemass served as managing editor of the Fianna Fail's party newspaper, the *Irish Press*, until his party was again returned to power in 1951. Lemass returned as De Valera's deputy prime minister and minister for industry and commerce. The Fianna Fail party was again out of power from 1954 until 1957, at which time Lemass returned to the cabinet. When De Valera resigned as prime minister to become Ireland's president, Lemass was chosen as his successor. He took office on June 23, 1959. As prime minister, he undertook negotiations with Northern Ireland with the hopes of reuniting the country. Lemass also negotiated a free trade pact with Great Britain in 1965. He resigned as prime minister on November 10, 1966, though he remained in the Parliament until his retirement from politics in 1969. He subsequently served as director of several business interests. Lemass died of lung cancer in Dublin at the age of 71 on May 11, 1971.

JOHN LYNCH (Prime Minister, November 10, 1966–March 14, 1973). John Mary Lynch was born in Blackpool on August 15, 1917. He was educated at an Irish Christian Brothers' school and received a degree in law from King's Inns in 1945. He was also a leading Irish athlete and recipient of six All-Ireland medals in sports. Lynch entered politics in 1948 and was elected to the Parliament as a member of Eamon De Valera's Fianna Fail party. Three years later he was appointed to the cabinet as minister of lands and served until the Fianna Fail defeat in 1954. He returned to the cabinet following De Valera's resumption of the post of prime minister in 1957. Lynch was named minister of education in June of 1957. He was appointed minister of industry and commerce in the subsequent government of Sean Lemass. Lynch was a leading advocate of Ireland's participation in the European Common Market. He was appointed minister of finance in April of 1965. Following Lemass's retirement in 1966, Lynch was selected as leader of the Fianna Fail party and took office as prime minister on November 19, 1966. The Fianna Fail party lost its majority in the elections of 1973, and Lynch stepped down as prime minister on March 14, 1973. He remained leader of the Fianna Fail party and again became prime minister on July 5, 1977. He retained office until he retired from politics on December 11, 1979. He subsequently served as a director of various Irish business firms, including the Irish Distillers Group and Galway Irish Crystal.

LIAM COSGRAVE (Prime Minister, March 14, 1973–July 5, 1977). Liam Cosgrave was born in Dublin on April 30, 1920. He was the son of William T. Cosgrave, who served as prime minister of the Irish Free State from 1922 until 1932. He was educated in Dublin and received a degree in law from King's Inns. Cosgrave entered politics and was elected to the Parliament as a member of the Fine Gael in 1943. Cosgrave was named foreign minister in 1954 in the government of John A. Costello. He served until 1957, during which time he also led the Irish delegation to the United Nations General Assembly. Cosgrave was elected leader of the Fine Gael party in 1965. Following the victory of the National Coalition of the Fine Gael and Labor parties in the elections of 1973, Cosgrave became prime minister of Ireland on March 14, 1973. He was a moderate leader who attempted to ease tensions concerning the Republic of Ireland's intentions toward Northern Ireland. The National Coalition government was defeated by the Fianna Fail party in an upset victory in the elections in June of 1977, and Cosgrave stepped down as prime minister on July 5, 1977. He also resigned the leadership of the Fine Gael party. He remained in Parliament until 1981, when he retired from politics.

JOHN LYNCH (Prime Minister, July 5, 1977–December 11, 1979). *See earlier entry under Heads of Government.*

CHARLES J. HAUGHEY (Prime Minister, December 11, 1979–June 30, 1981). Charles James Haughey was born in Castlebar, County Mayo, on September 16, 1925. He was educated at the University College and King's Inns in Dublin. Haughey married Maureen Lemass, the daughter of former prime minister Sean Lemass, in 1951. He was elected to the Dublin City Council in 1953 and served until 1955. He was elected to Parliament in 1957 as a member of the Fianna Fail party. Haughey was named to the cabinet as minister for justice in 1961 and was named minister of agriculture in 1964. He served as minister of finance from 1966 until May of 1970, when he was forced to resign after accusations that he was involved in gunrunning for the Irish Republican Army. He was tried and acquitted, though his political career was badly damaged. Haughey returned to the cabinet as minister of health and social welfare in 1977. When John Lynch retired from politics in 1979, Haughey was selected to succeed him as president of the Fianna Fail party. Haughey took office as prime minister on December 11, 1979. He was replaced by a coalition government led by Garret FitzGerald on June 30, 1981. Haughey was returned to office as leader of a coalition government on

March 9, 1982, but was again forced from office on December 14, 1982, after losing a vote of confidence. The Fianna Fail party was again successful in the elections of 1987, and Haughey returned as prime minister on March 10, 1987. After a series of political scandals, Haughey was challenged for the leadership of the Fianna Fail party. He was replaced as party leader and prime minister by Albert Reynolds on February 11, 1992.

GARRET FITZGERALD (Prime Minister, June 30, 1981–March 9, 1982). Garret FitzGerald was born in Dublin on February 9, 1926. He was educated at Belveder College and the University College in Dublin. He received a degree in law in 1946, though he never practiced. FitzGerald entered politics and was elected to the Parliament as a member of the Fine Gael party in 1969. He was named to the cabinet as minister of foreign affairs in 1973 and served until 1977. FitzGerald was selected as leader of the Fine Gael in 1977. He became prime minister of a coalition government with the Irish Labour party on June 30, 1981. His government's budget was defeated by a narrow margin in Parliament in January of 1982, and new elections were called the following month. The Fianna Fail party was victorious, and FitzGerald relinquished office to Charles Haughey on March 9, 1982. FitzGerald again formed a government as prime minister on December 14, 1982. He met with little success in reducing government spending or halting the rate of unemployment. He narrowly survived a no-confidence motion in October of 1986. His government collapsed over a budget matter in January of 1987, and FitzGerald was again replaced by Haughey on March 10, 1987, following parliamentary elections. FitzGerald resigned as leader of the Fine Gael the following day. He remained a member of the Parliament and served on various public and private commissions.

CHARLES J. HAUGHEY (Prime Minister, March 9, 1982–December 14, 1982). *See earlier entry under Heads of Government.*

GARRET FITZGERALD (Prime Minister, December 14, 1982–March 10, 1987). *See earlier entry under Heads of Government.*

CHARLES J. HAUGHEY (Prime Minister, March 10, 1987–February 11, 1992). *See earlier entry under Heads of Government.*

ALBERT REYNOLDS (Prime Minister, February 11, 1992–   ). Albert Reynolds was born in Rooskey, County Roscommon, on November 3, 1935. He was educated in Ireland and worked in the private sector. He was elected to the Longford County Council in 1974 and was elected to the Dail in 1977. Reynolds served as minister for posts, telegraphs, and transport from 1979 until 1981. He subsequently served as minister for industry and energy from March until December of 1982. He was returned to that position in 1987 and served until his appointment as minister of finance and public service in 1988. He remained minister of finance from 1989 until 1991. Reynolds defeated Charles Haughey for the leadership of the Fianna Fail party in 1992 and took office as prime minister on February 11, 1992.

Israel, State of

(Medinat Yisr'el)

Israel is a country in western Asia, on the eastern shore of the Mediterranean Sea. It was granted independence from a League of Nations mandate administered by Great Britain on May 14, 1948.

HEADS OF STATE

CHAIM WEIZMANN (President, May 16, 1948–November 9, 1952). Chaim Weizmann was born in the village of Motol in Russia on November 27, 1874. He was educated in Pinsk and later attended universities in Germany and Switzerland. He received a doctorate of science at the University of Fribourg in Switzerland in 1900. The following year he took a teaching position at the University of Geneva. Soon afterwards he joined the Zionist movement and became a leading spokesman for Zionism. He later joined the faculty of the organic chemistry department of the University of Manchester in England and became a British citizen in 1910. He remained active in the Zionist movement and became the leader of the Democratic Zionist Faction. During World War I Weizmann headed the Admiralty Laboratories, where he developed a method of synthesizing acetone. His contributions to the war efforts led to the Balfour Declaration in 1917 that provided for the eventual establishment of a Jewish homeland in Palestine. In March of 1918 Weizmann chaired the first Zionist Commission. During the 1920s and 1930s, he conducted many negotiations with the British and the Arabs in regard to the creation of a Jewish homeland. He moved to Palestine in 1934, where he accepted the directorship of the Daniel Sieff Research Institute in Rehovot. During World War II Weizmann came to the United States, where he assisted the Office of War Production's synthetic rubber program. Following the conclusion of the war, Weizmann was again a leader in negotiations that led to the creation of the state of Israel. Though he was not reelected president of the Zionist Congress in 1946, he remained a leading voice for the Zionist cause. He participated in the presentation of the Jewish position to the United Nations Special Commission in Jerusalem in 1947. Following the establishment of the nation of Israel, Weizmann accepted the position of president of the provisional government and took office on May 16, 1948. He was reelected to the primarily ceremonial position in November of 1951. He remained president, despite poor health, until his death from a respiratory inflammation at his home in Rehovot on November 9, 1952.

ISAAC BEN-ZVI (President, December 10, 1952–April 23, 1963). Isaac Ben-Zvi was born in Poltava, Ukraine, on November 24, 1884. He was educated at the University of Kiev. He went to Palestine in 1907, which was then part of the Ottoman Empire. Ben-Zvi attended the University of Constantinople in 1912, where he met David Ben-Gurion. He studied Turkish law and, with Ben-Gurion, founded the Hashomer. Ben-Zvi was exiled during World War I and spent some time in the United States. He returned to Palestine after the war and joined the Jewish Legion designed to assist the British in removing the Turks from Palestine. He organized the Histadrut, the Jewish labor federation, in 1920. In 1929 he founded the Vaad Leumi, or National Council, and he served as chairman from 1931 until 1944. Ben-Zvi was a signer of Israel's declaration of independence in 1948 and was elected to the Israel Knesset, or Parliament,

later in the year. He was nominated for president by the Mapai party in 1952. He was victorious in the elections and took office on December 10, 1952. Ben-Zvi was reelected in 1957 and in 1962. He died of cancer at his home in Jerusalem at the age of 78 on April 23, 1963.

ZALMAN SHAZAR (President, May 21, 1963–May 23, 1973). Zalman Shazar was born Shneor Zalman Rubashev in Mir, Russia, on October 6, 1889. He became active in the Zionist movement while in his teens and served as a translator for a Zionist newspaper in Vilna. He was arrested in June of 1907 and attended the Academy of Jewish Learning in St. Petersburg after his release. Shazar went to Palestine for several months in 1911. He returned to Russia to serve in the army and subsequently continued his studies in Germany. He returned to Palestine in 1924 and was a founder of *Davar*, the daily newspaper of the Histadrut, or General Federation of Jewish Labor. Shazar became editor of the newspaper in 1944. He was active in the Zionist Labor party and participated in several international conferences. He was instrumental in drafting the Israeli proclamation of independence in 1948. Shazar was named minister of education in the first Israeli cabinet the following year. He was removed from the cabinet in 1950 and served as an executive of the World Zionist Organization, where he headed the department for education and culture. He was elected to succeed Isaac Ben-Zvi as president of Israel on May 21, 1963. Shazar remained committed to Jewish cultural and historical matters. He served as host to numerous Bible researchers during his term of office. He was reelected president in 1968 and retired after completing his second term on May 23, 1973. Shazar's health failed, and he was hospitalized in Jerusalem on several occasions in 1974. He died in Jerusalem at the age of 84 on October 5, 1974, after a long illness.

EPHRAIM KATZIR (President, May 23, 1973–May 29, 1978). Ephraim Katzir was born Ephraim Katchalski in Kiev, the Ukraine, on May 16, 1916. He immigrated to Palestine in 1925 and attended the Hebrew University in Jerusalem. He studied chemistry and bacteriology and received his degree in 1937. Katzir received his doctorate in 1941 and remained at the university as an assistant in the chemistry department. He was also active in the Haganah, the Jewish pro-independence army. Katzir was named head of the department of biophysics at the newly founded Weizmann Institute of Science in Rehovot in 1949. He became internationally known for his research on proteins and synthetic polypeptides. He was elected to the United States National Academy of Sciences in 1966 and served as chief scientist at the Israeli Ministry of Defense until 1968. Katzir often worked with his brother, Aharon Katchalski, who was killed in May of 1972 by Palestinian terrorists at Tel Aviv's Lod Airport. Ephraim Katchalski was elected president of Israel in 1973. He Hebraized his name to Ephraim Katzir upon taking office on May 29, 1973. He declined to seek a second term to the largely ceremonial office and stepped down on May 29, 1978. Katzir returned to the Weizmann Institute as a professor and also served on the faculty of Tel Aviv University. He also continued his scientific research on the function of living cells.

YITZHAK NAVON (President, May 29, 1978–May 5, 1983). Yitzhak Navon was born in Jerusalem on April 19, 1921. He was educated at the Hebrew University in Jerusalem and worked as a teacher after graduation. He joined the Haganah, the Zionist militia, in 1946 and served as the director of the Arabic Department. Navon retained this position until Israel's independence in 1948. He subsequently served with the Israeli legation in Uruguay and Argentina until 1951. He was

appointed political secretary to Foreign Minister Moshe Sharett in 1951. The following year he became chief political secretary to Prime Minister David Ben-Gurion. Navon remained in the prime minister's office until Ben-Gurion's resignation in 1963. He headed the Department of Culture at the Ministry of Education until 1965, when he was elected to the Knesset as a member of Ben-Gurion's Rafi party. He served as Deputy Speaker of the Knesset until the early 1970s and subsequently served as chairman of the Defense and Foreign Affairs Committee. Navon was elected to the largely ceremonial position of president of Israel and took office on May 29, 1978. Navon declined to seek reelection to a second term and stepped down from office on May 5, 1983. He was named deputy prime minister and minister of education and culture in 1984 and served until his retirement in 1990.

CHAIM HERZOG (President, May 5, 1983–May 13, 1993). Chaim Herzog was born in Belfast, Northern Ireland, on September 17, 1918. He was the son of the chief rabbi of Ireland and immigrated with his family to Palestine in 1935. He was educated in Palestine and Dublin and at Cambridge University, where he received a degree in law. Herzog enlisted in the British army during World War II and attended the Royal Military College at Sandhurst. He was discharged from the British army with the rank of lieutenant colonel in 1947. He returned to Palestine and was named director of military intelligence in 1948. Herzog served with the Israeli army during the country's war for independence in May of 1948. He served as Israel's defense attaché in Washington, D.C., from 1950 until 1953. He subsequently served in the Israeli Embassy in Ottawa, Canada. Herzog returned to Israel in 1954 to serve as military commander of the Jerusalem district. He was reappointed director of military intelligence in 1959. He left active military service in 1962 to work in private in-dustry. Herzog served as a military commentator during the Six-Day War in June of 1967 and became Israel's military governor of the West Bank following the capture of Jerusalem. He opened a law firm in Tel Aviv in 1972 and was appointed Israel's ambassador to the United Nations in August of 1975. He defended Israel's position against attacks from the Arab world and the Soviet bloc. Herzog returned to Israel in 1978 and resumed his law prac-tice. He was elected to the Knesset in 1981 as a member of the Labor party. He was elected to succeed Yitzhak Navon as president of Israel and took office on May 5, 1983. Herzog made a state visit to the United States in 1987. He was reelected to a second term the following year. He served as a leading defender of Israel's policy in occupied Palestinian territory. Herzog completed his term of office and retired as presi-dent on May 13, 1993. He was replaced by Ezer Weizman, the nephew of former President Chaim Weizmann.

HEADS OF GOVERNMENT

DAVID BEN-GURION (Prime Min-ister, May 14, 1948–December 8, 1953). David Ben-Gurion was born David Green in Plonsk, Poland, on Octo-ber 16, 1886. He became involved in Zionism and socialism at an early age. He migrated to Palestine in 1906 and helped to establish the Palestine Labor party. He became editor of the party newspaper, *Achdut*, or *Unity*, and adopted the last name of Ben-Gurion, or "son of the lion." Ben-Gurion also continued his education in Turkey until the outbreak of World War I in 1915. He returned to Palestine, but was exiled by the Turkish government because of his support for the Allies. He went to the United States, where he helped to establish the American Jewish Congress. Ben-Gurion also organized the Jewish Legion in 1917 and fought with the British Empire forces during the war. He returned to Palestine after the liberation from Turkish rule and founded the His-tradut, or General Federation of Jewish Labor. He served as general secretary of the organization from 1921. Ben-Gurion resigned in 1933 to join the Jewish Agency for Palestine and became chairman two years later. He continued to campaign for a Jewish homeland and opposed the British White Paper limiting Jewish immigra-tion to Palestine in 1939. He supported the British during World War II and was instrumental in formulating Israel's declaration of independence. Ben-Gurion became Israel's first prime minister on May 14, 1948. He also served as minister of defense and led the na-tion through the Arab-Israeli war later in 1948. He established the Israeli Defense Force and continued to en-courage Jewish immigration to Israel. Ben-Gurion retired from office on December 8, 1953, and was succeeded by Moshe Sharett. He spent several years at the Negev kibbutz at Sde Boker. He returned to the government in February of 1955 to replace Pinhas Lavon as minister of defense. Ben-Gurion was again selected as prime minister on November 3, 1955. He helped to negotiate the Franco-Israeli Pact and granted diplomatic recogni-tion to West Germany. He cooperated with Great Britain and France in a war against Egypt over President Gamal Abdel Nasser's seizure of the Suez Canal in 1956. The Israeli army cap-tured the Sinai Peninsula, but was forced to withdraw under pressure from the United States and the Soviet Union. Ben-Gurion was faced with a governmental crisis in September of

1961. Pinhas Lavon, who had resigned as minister of defense in 1955 under accusations that he had plotted a terrorist action to engage the United States in a conflict with Egypt, accused members of the government of having framed him. Ben-Gurion rejected a new inquiry into the incident and resigned from office on June 16, 1963. He was succeeded by Levi Eshkol. Ben-Gurion broke with the Eshkol government in June of 1965 and founded the opposition Israel Workers List, or Rafi, party. The party won few seats in the Israeli Knesset, or Parliament, and Ben-Gurion retired from politics in June of 1970. He returned to his home in Sde Boker to write his memoirs. He suffered a brain hemorrhage in November of 1973 and died at a Tel Aviv hospital at the age of 87 on December 1, 1973.

MOSHE SHARETT (Prime Minister, December 8, 1953–November 3, 1955). Moshe Sharett was born Moshe Tchertok in Kherson, the Ukraine, on October 15, 1894. He accompanied his family to Turkish-ruled Palestine in 1906. He later went to Istanbul to study law. His studies were interrupted by World War I, and he served in the Turkish army during the conflict. Sharett entered the London School of Economics and Political Science after the war and was active in the Zionist movement. He returned to Tel Aviv in 1925 and joined the staff of the daily Labor party newspaper, *Davar.* He became editor of the paper's English-language supplement in 1929. Sharett joined the staff of the Political Department of the Jewish Agency in 1931 and became director of the department following the murder of Haim Arlosoroff in 1933. He became the leading Zionist spokesman to the British and the Arabs. Sharett formed the Jewish Brigade Group to oppose the Nazis in 1944 and assisted in the relocation of survivors of the Holocaust to Palestine. He was briefly arrested by the British in 1946 for his Zionist activities.

He negotiated the passage of the United Nations' Partition Resolution in 1947 that established a Jewish state. Sharett signed the Israeli proclamation of independence in 1948 and served as foreign minister in the government of David Ben-Gurion. Sharett succeeded to the prime minister's office when Ben-Gurion resigned on December 8, 1953. Ben-Gurion resumed office as prime minister on November 3, 1955, and Sharett remained in the government as foreign minister. He resigned from the cabinet in 1956 in a dispute over Ben-Gurion's confrontational policies with the Arabs. Sharett became chairman of the World Zionist Executive in 1959 and traveled widely espousing the Zionist cause. He retained this position until his death of cancer at the age of 70 in the Israeli sector of Jerusalem on July 7, 1965.

DAVID BEN-GURION (Prime Minister, November 3, 1955–June 16, 1963). *See earlier entry under Heads of Government.*

LEVI ESHKOL (Prime Minister, June 19, 1963–February 26, 1969). Levi Eshkol was born Levi Shkolnik in Oratova, the Ukraine, on October 25, 1895. He was educated in Lithuania, where he became involved in the Zionist movement. He went to Palestine in 1914 and worked as an agricultural laborer. Eshkol joined the Jewish Legion in 1918 and fought with the British against Turkey in the later stages of World War I. He returned to Palestine in 1920 and became active in the Zionist labor party, Hapoel Hazair. The party merged with the Mapai in 1929, and Eshkol served on the party's central committee. He was sent to Berlin following the rise of the Nazis to power in Germany in 1933. He helped to arrange the transfer of people and property to Palestine. Eshkol became director of the settlement department of the Jewish Agency for Palestine in 1942 and assisted in the foundation of the Haganah, the Jewish defense organization. He served in the Ministry of Defense as director-general following the establishment of the independent state of Israel in May of 1948. He was named to David Ben-Gurion's cabinet as minister of agriculture in 1951 and was appointed minister of finance the following year. Eshkol remained a popular figure in Israel despite economic difficulties and rising taxes. He was chosen to succeed Ben-Gurion as prime minister on June 19, 1963. He later engaged in a bitter feud with Ben-Gurion which split the Mapai party. Eshkol led his party to victory in elections in 1965 and retained the post of prime minister. He brought leaders of the opposition into the cabinet in May of 1967 in anticipation of a conflict with Egypt and Syria. Eshkol led Israel through the successful Six-Day War in June of 1967. He remained prime minister until his death of a heart attack at his home in Jerusalem on February 26, 1969.

YIGAL ALLON (Prime Minister, February 26, 1969–March 17, 1969). Yigal Allon was born Yigal Paicovitch in the village of Kefar Tavor in Galilea on October 10, 1918. He attended the Agriculture College in Kadoorie and Jerusalem's Hebrew University. He was a founder of the Kibbutz Ginossar in 1937 and joined the Haganah, an underground Jewish militia. Allon was a founder of the Haganah's commando unit, the Palmah, and served as its commander from 1945 until 1948. He served as a commanding officer on Israel's southern front during the Arab-Israeli War in 1948. He retired from the armed services as a major general in 1950 and became secretary-general of the Labor Unity party. Allon was elected to the Knesset, Israel's Parliament, in 1955. He was appointed to the cabinet as minister of labor in 1961 and served in that position until 1968. He was instrumental in the creation of the Israel Labor party and was named

deputy prime minister to Levi Eshkol in 1968. When Eshkol died of a heart attack on February 26, 1969, Allon served as acting prime minister until Golda Meir took office on March 17, 1969. Allon served as minister of education and culture in Meir's cabinet. He was named foreign minister in June of 1974 by Prime Minister Yitzhak Rabin. He was the architect of Israel's policy for peace in the occupied West Bank of the Jordan River, which was rejected by the Jordanian government. Allon was also instrumental in negotiating an interim agreement with Egypt that eventually led to the Israel-Egyptian peace treaty. He remained foreign minister until the Labor party was voted out of office in June of 1977. He was subsequently unsuccessful in attempting to secure the leadership of the Labor party. Allon died suddenly of a heart attack at the age of 61 in Asulla on February 29, 1980.

GOLDA MEIR (Prime Minister, March 17, 1969–June 3, 1974). Golda Meir was born Goldie Mabovit in Kiev, the Ukraine, on May 3, 1898. She came with her family to the United States in 1906 and settled in Milwaukee, Wisconsin. She attended the Teachers Training College there and was subsequently employed as a librarian and part-time teacher. Meir also became interested in the Zionist movement and joined the Poale Zion. She married Morris Meyerson in 1917, and following a meeting with David Ben-Gurion, they moved to Palestine in 1921. She later adopted Hebraized name of Meir. The couple relocated in Tel Aviv in 1923 and subsequently moved to Jerusalem. Meir joined the World Zionist Congress in 1928 and traveled extensively in Europe and the United States in support of Zionist causes during the 1930s. She served on the British War Economic Advisory Council during World War II and was active in the struggle for a Jewish homeland following the war. She worked with David Ben-Gurion's faction and became acting head of the Jewish Agency's political department following the arrest of many of the agency's members in June of 1946. Meir was one of the signers of Israel's independence proclamation on May 14, 1948, and subsequently served as the only female member of the provisional legislature. She was appointed Israel's minister to the Soviet Union in September of 1948. She was elected to the Israeli Parliament, or Knesset, the following January as a member of the Mapai party Meir was subsequently named minister of labor and social insurance in the cabinet of David Ben-Gurion. In this position she was instrumental in the creation of Israel's national insurance plan. She was appointed minister of foreign affairs in June of 1956 and was a supporter of Ben-Gurion's strong stance against Arab aggression. Meir also represented Israel at the United Nations General Assembly during the Suez crisis in 1957. She left the cabinet in early 1966 and became secretary-general of the Mapai party, which became the Israel Labor party in 1968. She resigned her party position in July of 1968. Prime Minister Levi Eshkol died of a heart attack in February of 1969, and Meir was chosen to succeed him as head of an interim government on March 17, 1969. She remained prime minister following general elections in October of 1969. When the Arab nations attacked Israel in October of 1973, Meir was criticized for not having been prepared for the situation. She announced her retirement as prime minister and left office on June 3, 1974. She briefly emerged from retirement in 1977 to meet with Egyptian president Anwar al-Sadat during his visit to Jerusalem. Meir was hospitalized in Jerusalem in August of 1978. She died on December 8, 1978, of complications from leukemia, a condition that she had had for 12 years but was only revealed after her death.

YITZHAK RABIN (Prime Minister, June 3, 1974–April 8, 1977). Yitzhak Rabin was born in Jerusalem on March 1, 1922. He was educated in Palestine and joined the Palmach, the commando unit of the Zionist army, the Haganah, in 1941. He fought with the British army during World War II and rose to the rank of deputy commander. Rabin went underground after the war and fought against the British authorities who were preventing Jewish immigration to Palestine. Rabin was arrested in 1946 for blowing up a British police station in Jenin and was imprisoned for six months. Israel was granted independence in 1948, and Rabin served as commander of the Palmach Har-El brigade in the subsequent war against the Arabs. He was promoted to colonel and served as Israel's military representative to armistice negotiations with the Egyptians in 1949. He remained in the army and served as chief of operations in the early 1950s. Rabin was promoted to brigadier general in 1954 and was named commander of the northern sector two years later. He served as deputy chief of staff from 1960 and became chief of staff of the Israel Defense Forces in January of 1964. He led the Israeli army to victory during the Six-Day War against the Arabs in June of 1967. Rabin retired from the army in January of 1968 and was appointed Israel's ambassador to the United States. He successfully presented his nation's policies to the United States government. Rabin caused a stir in 1972 when he seemed to endorse the reelection candidacy of United States president Richard Nixon. Rabin returned to Israel in March of 1973 to enter politics. He was elected to the Knesset as a member of the Labor party in December of 1973 and was named to Golda Meir's cabinet as minister of labor. When Meir resigned in April of 1974, Rabin was selected to replace her as prime minister. He took office on June 3, 1974. He announced his resignation in December of 1976 following his government's defeat in a vote of confidence in Parliament. Rabin remained as head of a caretaker government until April 8, 1977, when he resigned from leadership of the Labor party for having violated an Israeli law concerning deposits in foreign banks. Shimon Peres succeeded him as party leader and became acting prime minister. The Labor party was defeated by Menachem Begin's Likud coalition in elections the following month. Rabin remained a member of the Knesset and returned to the government as minister of defense in 1984. He remained in the National Unity government until 1990. Rabin defeated Peres for leadership of the Labor party in February of 1992. The Labor party returned to power in elections in July of 1992, and Rabin again became prime minister on July 12, 1992.

SHIMON PERES (Acting Prime Minister, April 8, 1977–June 21, 1977). Shimon Peres was born Shimon Persky in Volozhin, Poland, on August 1, 1923. His family emigrated to Palestine in 1934, and he was educated in Tel Aviv. He joined the Zionist military organization, the Haganah, in 1947. Peres served in the Ministry of Defense as head of the Navy Department following Israel's independence in 1948. He went to the United States to continue his education in 1950 and was named director-general of the Defense Ministry in November of 1952. He was named deputy defense minister in the government of David Ben-Gurion in December of 1959. Peres remained in the government of Ben-Gurion's successor, Levi Eshkol, until May of 1965. He then joined Ben-Gurion's Rafi party in opposition to the government. Peres served as secretary-general of the new party and was elected to the Knesset in November of 1965. He negotiated the merger of the Rafi and Mapai parties into the Israel Labor party in January of 1968. He served in Golda Meir's government and was named minister of transport and communications in August of 1970. Peres was unsuccessful

in his bid to succeed Meir as prime minister in June of 1974. He served in Yitzhak Rabin's subsequent government as minister of defense. He succeeded Rabin as leader of the Labor party in 1977 and became acting prime minister on April 8, 1977. The Labor party was defeated by Menachem Begin's right-wing Likud coalition in parliamentary elections in May of 1977, and Peres relinquished office to Begin on June 21, 1977. Peres remained leader of the opposition until August of 1984, when a national unity coalition government was formed with the Likud and Labor parties. Peres replaced Yitzhak Shamir as prime minister on September 14, 1984, and Shamir served as Peres's deputy prime minister. In accordance with the coalition agreement, Peres relinquished office to Shamir on October 20, 1986. He continued to serve in the government as deputy prime minister and minister of foreign affairs. The coalition remained in effect following inconclusive parliamentary elections in November of 1988. Peres remained in the government as minister of finance. His opposition to Shamir's handling of peace talks with the Palestinians resulted in his dismissal in March of 1990. The Labor party withdrew from the coalition, and Peres became leader of the opposition. Peres was defeated for the leadership of the Labor party by Yitzhak Rabin in February of 1992. When the Labor party returned to power in July of 1992, Peres returned to the government as minister of foreign affairs.

MENACHEM BEGIN (Prime Minister, June 21, 1977–October 10, 1983). Menachem Begin was born in Brest-Litovsk, Poland, on August 16, 1913. He joined the militant Zionist youth organization Betar while in his teens. He attended the University of Warsaw, where he received a degree in law in 1935. Begin continued his Zionist activities and became the leader of the Betar in 1939. He was arrested by Soviet authorities the following year and was deported to Siberia. He was released to join the Polish army in exile following the German invasion of the Soviet Union in 1941. Begin went to Palestine, where he founded the Irgun Zva'i Leumi terrorist army in 1943. He served as leader of the Irgun and was responsible for the bombing of the King David Hotel in Jerusalem that killed over 90 civilians in July of 1946. The Irgun also tortured and killed two British soldiers in 1947 in reprisal for the execution of Irgun terrorists. Begin left the Irgun following the establishment of an independent Israel in May of 1948. He was the leader of the Herut, or Freedom, party and was elected to the Knesset, or Parliament, in 1949. He was suspended from his seat in Parliament in 1952 after leading riots against Prime Minister David Ben-Gurion's decision to accept reparations from West Germany for the actions of the Nazis during World War II. The Herut became the leading party of the opposition in 1955, and Begin entered into an opposition coalition with the Liberal party in 1965. He became minister without portfolio in a coalition government under Levi Eshkol after the Six-Day War in June of 1967. He resigned the following August in opposition to a peace settlement promoted by the United States. Begin formed the rightist Likud, or Unity, party in September of 1973. The Likud defeated the ruling Labor party in parliamentary elections in May of 1977, and Begin formed a coalition government with several Orthodox religious parties. He took office as prime minister on June 21, 1977. Begin accepted Egyptian president Anwar Sadat's offer to come to Israel to negotiate a peace settlement later in 1977. Sadat's visit and subsequent negotiations between Sadat, Begin, and United States president Jimmy Carter resulted in the Camp David peace accords. Begin and Sadat were awarded the 1978 Nobel Prize for Peace. Israel relinquished control of the Sinai Peninsula to Egypt

in 1979 as part of the peace arrangement. Begin's Likud coalition won a narrow victory in parliamentary elections in June of 1981. Relations between Israel and Egypt cooled following the assassination of Sadat in October of 1981. Relations between the two nations further deteriorated when Begin authorized Israel's invasion of Lebanon in 1982. His government was held responsible for the massacre of numerous Palestinian refugees in West Beirut. Begin's wife and longtime confidant, Aliza, died in November of 1982. Protests against Israel's military involvement in Lebanon and the prime minister's failing health led Begin to announce his intention to resign in August of 1983. He was replaced as prime minister by Yitzhak Shamir on October 10, 1983. Begin spent his retirement in virtual seclusion in a Jerusalem apartment. He died of a heart attack at a Jerusalem hospital at the age of 78 on March 9, 1992.

YITZHAK SHAMIR (Prime Minister, October 10, 1983–September 14, 1984). Yitzhak Shamir was born Yitzhak Jazernicki in Bialystok, Poland, on November 3, 1914. He attended the University of Warsaw, where he studied law. He emigrated to Palestine in 1935 and chose the Hebraized last name Shamir, meaning "sharp thorn." He continued his education at the Hebrew University and received a degree in law. Shamir joined the Zionist guerrilla organization, the Irgun Zva'i Leumi, in 1937. He fought with the Irgun against the British and Arabs. He rejected the Irgun's support of the British war effort against the Germans during World War II and joined with Abraham Stern's Freedom Fighters for Israel, known as the Stern Gang. Shamir was arrested by the British in 1941, but escaped from detention the following year. He became a leader of the Stern Gang after Stern was shot to death by British police in February of 1942. Shamir's organization was responsible for the assassination of Lord Moyne, the British resident minister in the Middle East, in November of 1944. Shamir was again arrested by the British following the bombing of the King David Hotel in July of 1946. He was deported to a prison camp in Eritrea, but escaped in January of 1947. Shamir was granted asylum by the French. He returned to Israel after independence was granted in May of 1948. He remained underground and was sought by the Israel police following the assassination of United Nations mediator Count Folke Bernadotte later in 1948. The Stern Gang was banned by the Israeli government, and Shamir emerged from hiding to form the Lohamim, or Fighter, party. The party disbanded in the late 1940s, and Shamir abandoned politics. He joined the Israeli intelligence service, the Mossad, in 1955, and was stationed in France until May of 1965. He subsequently entered private industry until 1970, when he returned to politics as a member of Menachem Begin's Herut party. Shamir was elected to the Knesset in 1973 and served on several parliamentary committees. He became Speaker of the Knesset when the right-wing Likud bloc took power in June of 1977. Shamir was appointed to Begin's cabinet as foreign minister in March of 1980, despite the opposition of moderate members of the government. He opposed the return of the Sinai Peninsula to Egypt as part of the Camp David peace accords. Shamir was elected to succeed Begin as leader of the Herut party and became prime minister

on October 10, 1983. Shamir's government was forced to form a coalition with the opposition Labor party in September of 1984. He relinquished office to Labor party leader Shimon Peres on September 14, 1984, and served as Peres's deputy prime minister. In accordance with the agreement made by the two parties, Shamir resumed the office of prime minister on October 20, 1986. The coalition remained in effect following parliamentary elections in November of 1988. The Labor party withdrew from the government in March of 1990 in opposition to Shamir's failure to proceed with peace negotiations with the Palestinians. Shamir formed a right-wing government the following June. The Likud bloc was defeated by the Labor party in elections in July of 1992, and Yitzhak Rabin replaced Shamir as prime minister on July 12, 1992. Shamir remained leader of the Opposition until March of 1993, when he was replaced by Benjamin Netanyahu as leader of the Likud.

SHIMON PERES (Prime Minister, September 14, 1984–October 20, 1986). *See earlier entry under Heads of Government.*

YITZHAK SHAMIR (Prime Minister, October 20, 1986–July 12, 1992). *See earlier entry under Heads of Government.*

YITZHAK RABIN (Prime Minister, July 12, 1992–). *See earlier entry under Heads of Government.*

Italy (Italian Republic)
(Repubblica Italiana)

Italy is a country on a peninsula jutting into the Mediterranean Sea from southern Europe.

HEADS OF STATE

VICTOR EMMANUEL III (King, July 29, 1900–May 9, 1946). Victor Emmanuel was born at Capodimonte Palace in Naples on November 11, 1869. He was the only son of King Umberto I and Margherita of Savoy-Genoa. Victor Emmanuel became prince of Naples and heir apparent as a child. He received a military education and was given command of the Naples Army Corps in 1896. Later in the year he married Princess Helena of Montenegro. He succeeded to the throne of Italy as King Victor Emmanuel III following the assassination of his father by an anarchist on July 29, 1900. Victor Emmanuel was a popular monarch who traveled extensively throughout his kingdom. He survived an assassination attempt by an anarchist in March of 1912. The king abrogated Italy's alliance with Germany and Austria at the start of World War I in 1914. Italy joined the Allies and declared war on Austria in May of 1915. The Italians were victorious and an armistice was signed in November of 1917. The country experienced a growing antimonarchist movement in the years following the war. Victor Emmanuel allowed Benito Mussolini's National Fascist party to march on Rome and seize political power in October of 1922. The king's powers were limited under the subsequent fascist dictatorship. Victor Emmanuel concentrated on his interest in numismatics by writing books on the subject and acquiring one of the world's most valuable collections of coins. The king opposed Italy's alliance with Germany, but was unable to convince Mussolini to remain neutral during World War II. Italy declared war on Great Britain and France in June of 1940. Italy suffered military reversals during the war, and Mussolini was dismissed in July of 1943. The king named Marshal Pietro Badoglio as premier, and Italy remained allied with

Germany. The new government agreed to a surrender to the Allies in September of 1943, and Rome was then occupied by the Germans. The royal family and the government escaped the city. Rome was captured by the Allies on June 5, 1944, and Victor Emmanuel relinquished power to his son, Crown Prince Umberto. Victor Emmanuel retained the title of king until his abdication on May 9, 1946. He went into exile in Alexandria, Egypt, where he died of lung congestion at the age of 78 on December 28, 1947.

UMBERTO II (King, May 9, 1946–June 3, 1946). Umberto was born at Racconigi Palace in Piedmont on September 15, 1904. He was the only son of King Victor Emmanuel III and Queen Helena. He was educated at the Royal Military Academy in Turin and served as a lieutenant in the Italian army. Umberto was promoted to general and given command of a division after Benito Mussolini became dictator of Italy in 1922. The crown prince married Princess Marie Jose of Belgium in January of 1930. Umberto was given command of Italy's northern army after the start of World War II. He was promoted to the rank of marshal of the Italian army in October of 1942. Mussolini was ousted in 1943, and the Allies captured Rome on June 5, 1944. King Victor Emmanuel III relinquished power to Umberto, who was given the title of lieutenant of the king. Victor Emmanuel abdicated the throne on May 9, 1946, and Umberto II was installed as king of Italy. A referendum was passed the following month that declared Italy a republic. The monarchy was abolished on June 3, 1946, and Umberto was sent into exile. He and the royal family were barred from re-entering Italy by the republican constitution. Umberto settled in exile in Portugal, never to return to Italy. He died in Geneva at the age of 78 after a long illness on March 18, 1983.

ENRICO DE NICOLA (President, June 28, 1946–May 11, 1948). Enrico de Nicola was born in Naples on November 9, 1877. He attended the University of Naples and became a prominent lawyer and political figure in Naples. He was elected to the Parliament in 1909. De Nicola served in several cabinets and refused the premiership on four occasions. He was a foe of the Fascists and retired from Parliament in 1924 instead of accepting reelection on the fascist ticket. He remained out of political affairs during Mussolini's regime. De Nicola again became active in governmental affairs following Mussolini's ouster. He was elected provisional president after the removal of the monarchy and took office on June 28, 1946. He was confirmed as president of the new Italian Republic on January 1, 1948, following the institution of a new constitution. He resigned the office on May 11, 1948, and accepted an honorary lifetime membership in the Italian Senate. He died in Naples from complications from pneumonia at the age of 82 on October 1, 1959.

LUIGI EINAUDI (President, May 11, 1948–April 29, 1955). Luigi Einaudi was born in Carru on March 24, 1874. He received his doctorate in economics from the University of Turin in 1895 and served as professor there from 1900 to 1949. Einaudi was the author of numerous books and articles on economics during this period. He was also elected to the Italian Senate in 1919 and was a leading opponent of Benito Mussolini. Einaudi left Italy for Switzerland in 1943 and returned to Italy following the conclusion of World War II. In 1945 he became the governor of the Bank of Italy and was elected to the Constituent Assembly the following year. He was appointed minister of the budget and vice-premier under Alcide De Gasperi in 1947. In 1948 Einaudi

was elected under the new constitution as president of the Republic of Italy and took office on May 11, 1948. He served his full seven-year term, but was rejected when he offered himself for reelection. He left office on April 29, 1955. After his term of office, he returned to teaching at the University of Turin. He died of a heart disorder in Rome on October 30, 1961, at the age of 87.

GIOVANNI GRONCHI (President, April 29, 1955–May 6, 1962). Giovanni Gronchi was born in Pontedera on September 10, 1887. He attended the University of Pisa, where he earned a degree in law and letters. He served in the Italian army during World War I and was elected to Parliament in 1919. Gronchi was a founder of the People's party and a leading Catholic political figure. He was named undersecretary for industry and commerce in Benito Mussolini's government in 1922. He resigned from the cabinet the following year in opposition to Mussolini and was ousted from Parliament. Gronchi returned to private enterprises in Milan but emerged during World War II as a leading figure in the underground. He served as a representative of the Christian Democratic party on the National Liberation Front. He was minister for industry, commerce, and labor in the postwar governments in Italy. Gronchi was elected Speaker of the Chamber of Deputies in May of 1948. He was a leader of the policy of attempting to ally Socialists and other leftist parties with the Christian Democratic party. He sought the premiership several times in the early 1950s but was rejected by his own party on the grounds that he was overly lenient to Communist members of the Chamber of Deputies. Gronchi was elected president of Italy and took office on April 29, 1955. He made numerous state visits during his term of office, including a trip to Moscow in 1959 that received some criticism. He completed his term of office and stepped down on May 6, 1962. He died on October 17, 1978, at the age of 91 following a lengthy illness in Rome.

ANTONIO SEGNI (President, May 6, 1961–December 6, 1964). Antonio Segni was born in Sassari on the island of Sardinia on February 2, 1891. He was educated at Sassari University and received a degree in law. He began a career as an educator and taught at various universities. Segni became active in the Popular party and was an opponent of Benito Mussolini. He was active in the Sardinian underground during World War II and served on the First Regional Council of Sardinia following Italy's surrender in 1943. He was also an early leader of the Christian Democratic party. Segni was named undersecretary of state for agriculture and forestry in the government of Ivanoe Bonomi in December of 1944. He retained that position in the succeeding government and was elected to the Constituent Assembly in June of 1946. He continued to serve as minister of agriculture and forestry until 1951. During this period he initiated a program of land reform which earned him the animosity of the right-wing. Segni subsequently served as minister of education and was elected premier in a coalition government on July 6, 1955. The government collapsed following the resignation of the Social Democrats, and Segni stepped down as premier on May 6, 1957. He subsequently served as vice-premier and minister of defense. He was again chosen as premier on February 15, 1959, following the ouster of Amintore Fanfani. His minority government collapsed when the Liberal party withdrew their support, and Segni resigned on February 24, 1960. He served in the succeeding government as foreign minister until 1961, when he defeated Giuseppe Saragat for the presidency. He took office on May 6, 1961. Segni suffered a serious stroke that partially paralyzed him in August of 1964. He was unable to continue his duties as president and resigned on December 6, 1964. Segni spent his remaining years in political retirement and died at his home in Rome on December 1, 1972.

GIUSEPPE SARRAGAT (President, December 29, 1964–December 29, 1971). Giuseppe Sarragat was born in Turin on September 19, 1898. He attended the University of Turin and received a degree in economics. He joined the Italian Socialist party in 1922 and became a member of its executive committee in 1925. In 1926, following the outlawing of opposition parties by Benito Mussolini's government, Sarragat went into exile and settled in Vienna, Austria. He went to Paris in 1935 and was active in anti-Fascist organizations. He avoided capture during the German occupation of France and returned to Italy in September of 1943 to assist in the anti-Fascist underground. Sarragat was arrested by the Germans but was able to escape. He went into hiding and joined the Italian People's Socialist Unity party. Following the liberation of Rome in June of 1944, Sarragat joined the provisional government. He served as ambassador to France from 1945 until 1946. He was elected to the Constituent Assembly in June of 1946 and became president of the Assembly. Sarragat broke with the Socialist party in 1947 and founded the Socialist Party of Italian Labor. He resigned as assembly president to serve as the new party's secretary. He served as deputy premier from 1947 until 1948, when he was elected to the Chamber of Deputies. Sarragat remained deputy premier and became minister of the merchant marine in 1948, a post he held until October of 1949. He subsequently worked in party affairs and reformed his party as the Democratic Socialist party. He was again appointed deputy premier in 1954, but resigned in May of 1957, bringing down the government. Sarragat was defeated by Antonio Segni for the Italian presidency in May of 1962. He was appointed foreign minister in 1963. The following year he was elected president of Italy when Segni resigned because of poor health. Sarragat took office on December 29, 1964. He completed his term in the largely ceremonial position and left office on December 29, 1971. He again became secretary of the Democratic Socialist party in 1975 and served until 1983, when he was elected president of the party for life. He died of heart disease in Rome on June 11, 1988, at the age of 89.

GIOVANNI LEONE (President, December 29, 1971–June 15, 1978). Giovanni Leone was born in Pomigliano Darco, near Naples, on November 3, 1908. He was educated at the University of Naples, where he received a degree in law. He began a teaching career at various universities in Italy. Leone served in the Italian army during World War II and joined the Christian Democratic party in 1944. He was elected to the postwar Constituent Assembly in 1946 and was instrumental in drafting a new Italian constitution. He was elected to the Chamber of Deputies in the subsequent national elections of 1948. Leone was elected vice president of the Chamber in 1950 and became Speaker in 1955. He gained a reputation as a conciliator who was admired by most political factions. Leone was called upon to serve as premier on June 21, 1963, following a month-long stalemate in which no one had been able to form a government. He retained the office long enough for a suitable replacement to be found and resigned on December 5, 1963, to return to the Chamber of Deputies. Leone was a candidate for the Italian presidency in 1964, but withdrew from the race when his election seemed unlikely. He was named senator for life by President Giuseppe Sarragat in August of 1967. Leone was once again called upon to serve as premier during a governmental crisis on June 25, 1968. He retained the position until December 12, 1968, when

the Christian Democratic party and Socialist party were able to agree on a new government. Leone returned to the Senate, where he remained until his election as president of the Republic. He took office on December 29, 1971. Leone dissolved Parliament in February of 1972 and called for early elections to help settle another governmental crisis. In early 1978 Leone and members of his family were accused of tax evasion and misuse of his office. He resigned on June 15, 1978, following calls for his removal.

SANDRO PERTINI (President, July 9, 1978–July 9, 1985). Alessandro Pertini was born in Stella on September 25, 1896. He served in the Italian army during World War I and joined the Socialist party in 1918. He received a law degree from Genoa University after the war. Pertini was an early opponent of Benito Mussolini's Fascist dictatorship, and he was arrested in 1925 for anti-Fascist activities. He was sentenced to eight months in prison, but escaped the following year and fled to France. He returned to Italy in 1929 and continued his anti-Fascist activities. Shortly afterwards he was again arrested in connection with a plot to assassinate Mussolini. Pertini served ten years in prison before his release. He was again arrested in 1943 and sentenced to death by the German forces that occupied Italy at the time. He escaped from prison in 1944 and joined the anti-Nazi underground. Following the war, Pertini was elected to the Constituent Assembly. He won election to the Chamber of Deputies in 1946 and served as secretary of the Socialist party. He was elected president of the Chamber of Deputies in 1968 and served until 1975. Pertini was unsuccessful in a bid for the Italian presidency in 1971. He emerged as a compromise candidate for president in 1978, following the resignation of Giovanni Leone. Pertini took office on July 9, 1978. He completed his term of office and stepped down on July 9, 1985. He died at the age of 93 at his home in Rome after a lengthy illness on February 24, 1990.

FRANCESCO COSSIGA (President, July 9, 1985–April 28, 1992). Francesco Cossiga was born in Sassari on July 26, 1928. Cossiga became a member of the Christian Democratic party in 1945. He previously received a law degree at Sassari University in 1948. He embarked on a political career and was elected to the Chamber of Deputies in 1958. Cossiga served as undersecretary of defense from 1966 until 1970 and was named to the cabinet as minister without portfolio in 1974. He was named minister of the interior in the cabinet of Aldo Moro in 1976. He was faced with the daunting task of dealing with an epidemic of urban violence and political terrorism. His office at the Interior Ministry was bombed by radicals in April of 1977. Cossiga was put in charge of the investigation of the kidnapping of former premier Aldo Moro in March of 1978. He refused to negotiate with the terrorists, and when Moro was murdered in May of 1978, Cossiga resigned his office. He was called upon to lead a coalition government in 1979 and became premier on August 5, 1979. He immediately proposed legislation that would assist in the fight against terrorism. Cossiga resigned the premiership rather than face a vote of no confidence on March 19, 1980. He

was immediately asked to form another government. He did so by putting together a coalition of Christian Democrats and Socialists. Cossiga resigned from office on October 18, 1980, after his economic plan to support the value of the lira was narrowly defeated in Parliament. He subsequently served as president of the Senate from July of 1983 until 1985. He was elected president of the Republic by an absolute majority in a joint session of the Chamber of Deputies and the Senate and took office on July 9, 1985. He resigned from office on April 28, 1992.

OSCAR LUIGI SCALFARO (President, May 28, 1992–). Oscar Luigi Scalfaro was born in Novara on September 9, 1918. He was educated in Milan and became active in the Christian Democratic party following World War II. He was elected to the Chamber of Deputies in 1948. Scalfaro served as undersecretary in various ministries during the 1950s and was named undersecretary of the interior from 1959 until 1962. He subsequently served as minister of transport and civil aviation and minister of education. He was appointed minister of the interior in 1983 and served until 1987. He was unsuccessful in an attempt to form a government as premier in April of 1987. Scalfaro was chosen as president of Italy on May 25, 1992, and sworn in three days later.

HEADS OF GOVERNMENT

FERRUCCIO PARRI (Premier, June 20, 1945–November 24, 1945). Ferruccio Parri was born in Turin on June 19, 1890. He worked as a high school teacher before joining the Italian army during World War I. He served with distinction and received four decorations for valor. After the war he became involved in anti-Fascist activities. Parri was arrested in 1926 for

his part in aiding the escape from Italy of Socialist party leader Filippo Turati. He gave a spirited defense and was sentenced to a minimal prison sentence. Parri remained an opponent of Benito Mussolini and was often arrested during the next decade. During World War II Parri led a partisan brigade which conducted a guerrilla war in northern Italy against German occupation troops. He became known by the code names "General Maurizio" and "The Uncle" and became the leader of the anti-Nazi Resistance following the ouster of Mussolini. He was captured by the Germans in 1945, but was released after a short time in a prisoner exchange. Parri founded the Action party after the war. He was selected to lead a government as premier on June 20, 1945. He was forced to resign on November 24, 1945, when the rightist parties withdrew from the cabinet in protest of his plans to dismantle several large corporations. Parri later founded the Republican party. He was appointed to the Italian Senate for life as an independent leftist in 1963. He died in a military hospital in Rome after a long illness at the age of 91 on December 8, 1981.

ALICIDE DE GASPERI (Premier, December 10, 1945–August 17, 1953). Alicide de Gasperi was born in Pieve Tesino, Trentino, on April 3, 1881. He was educated at the University of Vienna. He worked as the editor of the *Il Nuovo Trentino* newspaper. De Gasperi entered politics and was elected to the Austrian Parliament in 1911, where he served as an Italian Irredentist representative. He was elected to the Italian Parliament in 1921, following the union of his province with Italy. His opposition to the dictatorship of Benito Mussolini resulted in the shutting down of his newspaper and his arrest in 1926. De Gasperi was released from prison after serving 16 months of a four-year sentence. He subsequently worked in the Vatican library, where he rose to the position of secretary-general. De Gasperi was active in the Italian Resistance during World War II. Following the ouster of Mussolini, de Gasperi was named minister without portfolio in the cabinet of Premier Ivanhoe Bonomi in June of 1944. He was appointed foreign minister in December of 1944. He subsequently was elected leader of the Christian Democratic party. De Gasperi replaced Ferruccio Parri as

Italy's premier on December 10, 1945. During his term of office, Italy's economy improved and the country regained international prestige. The Christian Democratic party was unable to capture an absolute majority in the elections in June of 1953, however, and de Gasperi's government lost a vote of confidence the following month. De Gasperi stepped down as premier on August 17, 1953. He remained leader of the Christian Democrats until his resignation in June of 1954. He died of a heart attack in Sella di Valsugana, Trentino, on August 19, 1954.

GIUSEPPE PELLA (Premier, August 17, 1953–January 5, 1954). Giuseppe Pella was born in Valdengo on April 18, 1902. He attended Turin University, where he received a doctorate in economics. He subsequently achieved great financial success as a tax consultant. Pella was elected deputy mayor of Biella as a member of the Fascist party shortly before World War II. During the war he became actively involved with the Catholic Action movement. In 1946 he was elected to the Constituent Assembly as a member of the Christian Democratic party. He was subsequently named undersecretary of finance in the government of Alcide de Gasperi. Pella was appointed minister of finance in June of 1947. In June of the following year, Pella was named minister of the budget. He dedicated himself to a conservative economic policy and attempted to protect the value of the lira in the postwar European economic confusion. Pella was selected to succeed de Gasperi as premier on August 17, 1953, following a period of political disarray. During his term of office, Italy became involved in a dispute with Yugoslavia concerning the occupation of Trieste. Pella's caretaker government resigned on January 5, 1954. Pella was again named to the cabinet by Premier Adone Zoli and served as foreign minister from 1957 until 1958 and again from 1959 until 1960. He was appointed minister of the budget in 1960 and retained that position until 1962. Pella subsequently retired from politics. He died in Rome at the age of 79 after a short illness on May 31, 1981.

AMINTORE FANFANI (Premier, January 18, 1954–January 30, 1954). Anintore Fanfani was born in Pieve Santo Stefano in Tuscany on February 6, 1908. He attended the Catholic University of the Sacred Heart in Milan. He received a doctorate in political economics in 1932. Fanfani subsequently taught at the university and wrote several books. He went into exile in Switzerland in 1943 to avoid service in the Fascist Italian army during World War II. He returned to Italy after the war and became active in the Christian Democratic party. Fanfani was elected to the Constituent Assembly in June of 1946. He was named to Alcide de Gasperi's cabinet in May of 1947 and served as minister of labor and social welfare. He resigned from the government in January of 1950 following a dispute over de Gasperi's refusal to grant him more power to carry out his economic programs. Fanfani returned to the cabinet as minister of agriculture and forests in July of 1951. In July of 1953 he was appointed minister of the interior. Following the resignation of the government of Giuseppe Pella, Fanfani briefly served as premier from January 18, 1954, until January 30, 1954. In June of 1954 he was elected president of the Christian Democratic party. He was again called upon to form a government on July 1, 1958. Fanfani's government was faced with opposition from rival parties as well as members of his own Christian Democratic party. He was forced to resign as premier on February 15, 1959, and resigned as secretary of the party shortly thereafter. Fanfani again attempted to form a left-of-center government following the resignation of Antonio Segni in February of 1960. He was unable to gain the necessary sup-

port, but he was again chosen as premier following the resignation of Fernando Tambroni on July 27, 1960. He retained the position until June 21, 1963. He was named as Italy's foreign minister in 1965. Fanfani was subsequently elected president of the United Nations General Assembly and served until 1966. He returned to the cabinet as foreign minister and held that office until 1968. Fanfani was then elected president of the Senate. He served in that position until 1973, when he was again chosen as secretary of the Christian Democratic party. He stepped down in 1975, though he again served as the Christian Democratic party's chairman from April until October of 1976. He was again elected president of the Senate and served until 1982. When the Christian Democratic party regained the premiership on November 30, 1982, Fanfani again served as premier. His coalition government collapsed in April of 1983, and Fanfani was replaced as premier by Bettino Craxi on August 4, 1983. Fanfani again briefly served as premier from April 18, 1987. His government was charged with holding new elections, and he stepped down on July 29, 1987. He subsequently served as minister of the interior until 1988, when he was appointed minister of the budget. He retained that position until 1989.

MARIO SCELBA (Premier, February 10, 1954–June 22, 1955). Mario Scelba was born in Caltagirone, Sicily, on September 5, 1901. He attended the University of Rome, where he received a doctorate in law. He entered politics in 1919 and joined the Popular party. When the party was suppressed by the Fascists in 1923, Scelba retired from political activities. He joined the Catholic party in 1941 and was briefly arrested during the Nazi occupation for his publication of an underground newspaper. Scelba was elected to the Constituent Assembly following the war and served as minister of posts and communications in the cabinet. In 1947 he was named minister of the interior. He was a leading opponent of Communism and took harsh measures against a Communist uprising in early 1950. Scelba became Italy's premier as head of a center-right coalition government on February 10, 1954. His government proposed an economic and social policy that included a more equitable tax system and was designed to benefit a large segment of the Italian people. He also negotiated the return of Trieste to Italian control from Yugoslavia. Scelba was forced to resign on June 22, 1955, when his governing coalition dissolved. He returned to the cabinet as minister of the interior in 1960 and served until 1962. He was elected to the Chamber of Deputies the following year and served as leader of the Christian Democratic party in 1966. Scelba was elected to the Senate in 1968 and was president of the European Parliament from 1969 until 1971. He retired from politics in 1983 and died in Rome on October 29, 1991.

ANTONIO SEGNI (Premier, July 6, 1955–May 6, 1957). *See entry under Heads of State.*

ADONE ZOLI (Premier, May 19, 1957–July 1, 1958). Adone Zoli was born in Cesena on December 16, 1887. Zoli was a prominent lawyer and a member of the anti-Fascist movement. He helped to organize the Christian Democratic party following World War II and was elected president of the party in 1954. He served in the Italian Senate from 1948 and was minister of justice from 1951 to 1953. In 1954 he was named minister of finance, and from 1956 to 1957 he served as minister of the budget. Zoli became premier of Italy on May 19, 1957, and served until July 1, 1958. He remained in the Senate until his death in Rome on February 20, 1960, at the age of 72.

AMINTORE FANFANI (Premier, July 1, 1958–February 15, 1959). *See*

earlier entry under *Heads of Government.*

ANTONIO SEGNI (Premier, February 15, 1959–February 24, 1960). *See entry under Heads of State.*

FERNANDO TAMBRONI (Premier, March 26, 1960–July 19, 1960). Fernando Tambroni was born in Ascoli Piceno in 1901. He entered politics at an early age and was arrested for his opposition to the Fascists in 1926. Following his release, he remained out of politics until 1943, when he was one of the founders of the Christian Democratic party. He was elected to the Chamber of Deputies after World War II and served in various cabinet positions. Tambroni was appointed minister for merchant marine in 1953 and served again from 1954 until 1955. He was named minister of the interior in 1955 and again held that position in 1957 and 1958. He served as minister of the budget in the cabinet of Antonio Segni from 1959. Tambroni became premier of a caretaker Christian Democratic government on March 26, 1960. The government depended on support from the neo–Fascist Italian Socialist movements. Riots took place in Genoa and Central Italy against Fascist participation in the government. Tambroni was forced to resign on July 19, 1960. He remained active in politics until his death of a heart attack in Rome at the age of 61 on February 18, 1963.

AMINTORE FANFANI (Premier, July 27, 1960–June 21, 1963). *See earlier entry under Heads of Government.*

GIOVANNI LEONE (Premier, June 21, 1963–December 5, 1963). *See entry under Heads of State.*

ALDO MORO (Premier, December 5, 1963–June 5, 1968). Aldo Moro was born in Maglie, in southern Italy, on September 23, 1916. He was educated at the University of Bari, where he became involved in a Catholic student organization. He graduated from the university with a doctorate in law in 1940. Moro joined the Christian Democratic party after World War II and was elected to the Constituent Assembly in 1946. He served on the committee that drafted the constitution that created the Republic of Italy in June of 1946. He was elected to the Chamber of Deputies in April of 1948 and became an influential member of the Christian Democratic parliamentary group. Moro was appointed undersecretary of state in the government of Alcide de Gasperi in May of 1948. He was named to the cabinet as minister of justice in July of 1955 and was instrumental in reforming the Italian prison system. He was shifted to the Ministry of Education in May of 1957 and became the leader of the Christian Democrats in March of 1959. Moro supported a coalition between the Christian Democrats and the Socialists and became premier of a center-left government on December 5, 1963. He reorganized the government in July of 1964 and February of 1966. He remained premier until June 5, 1968, when the Socialists refused to participate in a new government. Moro subsequently served as foreign minister until November 23, 1974, when he formed a coalition government with the Republican party. He remained premier of a minority government from February of 1976 until July 30, 1976. Moro was then elected president of the Christian Democrats. He was expected to be a candidate for president of Italy when he was kidnapped by Red Brigade terrorists while en route to the Parliament on March 16, 1978. The Italian government refused to negotiate with the kidnappers, and Moro was tried and executed by the terrorists. His body was found in Rome on May 9, 1978.

GIOVANNI LEONE (Premier, June 25, 1968–December 12, 1968). *See entry under Heads of State.*

MARIANO RUMOR (Premier, December 12, 1968–July 6, 1970). Mariano Rumor was born in Vicenza on June 16, 1915. He attended the University of Padua and received a doctorate in literature in 1939. He worked as a teacher in Vicenza before entering politics as a member of the Catholic Action party. Rumor served in the Italian cavalry during World War II. Rumor joined the Resistance movement against the Germans following the ouster of Benito Mussolini in 1943. He was a founding member of the Christian Democratic party and worked as a party organizer in his home district after the war. He was elected to the Chamber of Deputies in 1948 and served as his party's spokesman on labor issues. Rumor was named undersecretary of agriculture in July of 1951 and was appointed undersecretary to the premier in the government of Amintore Fanfani in January of 1954. He was appointed minister of agriculture in the cabinet of Antonio Segni in February of 1959. He retained that position until June of 1963, when he served as minister of internal affairs until the following December. Rumor subsequently was selected to succeed Aldo Moro as the Christian Democrats' political secretary. He formed a coalition government as premier on December 12, 1968, but his coalition collapsed on July 6, 1970, following widespread labor unrest. Rumor served as minister of home affairs from 1972 until he again became premier of a center-left coalition government on July 8, 1973. His government was faced with a deteriorating economy, student demonstrations, and terrorist violence. The Christian Democrats lost a referendum vote to repeal the Italian divorce law. Rumor offered his resignation in June of 1974, but President Giovanni Leone rejected it. Rumor remained as leader of the government until October 3, 1974, when the Social Democrats left the coalition. He subsequently served as foreign minister until 1976. He was implicated in a financial corruption scandal involving bribes from Lockheed Aircraft in 1976. Rumor was cleared of charges by Parliament in 1978 and was elected to the Italian Senate the following year. He was also elected to the European Parliament in 1979 and served until 1984. Rumor continued to serve in the Italian Senate until his death of a heart attack at his home in Vicenza at the age of 74 on January 22, 1990.

EMILIO COLOMBO (Premier, August 6, 1970–January 15, 1972). Emilio Colombo was born in Potenza on April 11, 1920. He was educated at the University of Rome, where he received a degree in law. He was a member of the Catholic Action organization and was elected to Italy's provisional Constituent Assembly in 1946. Colombo was elected to the newly formed Italian Parliament in 1948. He served in the Ministry of Agriculture as an undersecretary until 1953, when he was shifted to the Ministry of Public Works. He was appointed to the cabinet as minister of agriculture in 1955. Colombo was named minister of foreign trade in 1958 and minister of industry and commerce the following year. He was appointed minister of the treasury in 1963. He retained that position until he was asked to form a government as premier on July 25, 1970. Colombo introduced austerity measures to ease Italy's economic difficulties and allowed the passage of legislation legalizing divorce. He also succeeded in reforming Italy's income tax structure. Colombo was forced to resign on January 15, 1972, when the Republican party withdrew from the coalition government. He remained in the government as minister without portfolio in charge of United Nations affairs. He was appointed minister of finance in 1973 and served as minister of the treasury from 1974 until 1976. Colombo was elected to the European

Parliament in 1976 and was selected as president the following year. He left the European Parliament in 1980 and was appointed foreign minister, a post he held until 1983. He returned to the government as minister of the budget and economic planning in 1987. Colombo was appointed minister of finance the following year and served until 1989.

GIULIO ANDREOTTI (Premier, February 17, 1972–June 12, 1973). Giulio Andreotti was born in Rome on January 15, 1919. He attended the University of Rome, where he received a degree in law. He served as president of the Federation of Catholic Universities from 1942 until 1945. Andreotti was elected to the Constituent Assembly as a member of the Christian Democratic party in 1945 and entered the Chamber of Deputies in 1947. He was an advisor to Premier Alcide de Gasperi and served as an undersecretary in his government from 1947 until 1953. He was appointed minister of the interior in the cabinet of Amintore Fanfani in 1954. Andreotti served as minister of finance from 1955 until 1958 and was minister of the treasury from 1958 until 1959. He then served as minister of defense until 1966. He remained in the government as minister of industry and commerce until 1968. Andreotti was chosen to lead a single-party interim government on February 17, 1972. He formed a center coalition government after elections the following May. Andreotti resigned on June 12, 1973. He was again appointed minister of defense in 1974 and was named minister of the budget later in the year. He was asked to form a government as premier on July 30, 1976. Andreotti led a single-party Christian Democratic government with the support of the Communist party until August 5, 1979, when the Communists withdrew their support for the government. Andreotti was named to the government as minister of foreign affairs in 1983. He was unsuccessful in an attempt to form a government in 1986. He remained foreign minister until July 23, 1989, when he again became premier. Andreotti led a five-party coalition until the Socialists withdrew their support in March of 1991. He reformed his government and remained premier until April 24, 1992, when he stepped down following general elections. Andreotti was under investigation in April of 1993 on charges of financial corruption and alleged links to the Mafia.

MARIANO RUMOR (Premier, July 8, 1973–October 3, 1974). *See earlier entry under Heads of Government.*

ALDO MORO (Premier, November 23, 1974–July 30, 1976). *See earlier entry under Heads of Government.*

GIULIO ANDREOTTI (Premier, July 30, 1976–August 5, 1979). *See earlier entry under Heads of Government.*

FRANCESCO COSSIGA (Premier, August 5, 1979–October 18, 1980). *See entry under Heads of State.*

ARNALDO FORLANI (Premier, October 18, 1980–May 26, 1981). Arnaldo Forlani was born in Pesaro on December 8, 1925. He was educated at the University of Urbino, where he received a degree in law. He became active in the Christian Democratic party and was elected to the Chamber of Deputies in 1958. Forlani served as deputy leader of the Christian Democrats from 1962 until 1969, when he became leader of the party. He also served in the cabinet as minister of state enterprise from 1969 until 1970. He retained the leadership of the Christian Democrats until 1973. Forlani was appointed minister of defense in the government of Aldo Moro in

1974. He was named foreign minister in 1976 and served until 1979. Forlani formed a government as premier on October 18, 1980. Italy was challenged by a new round of terrorism from the leftist Red Brigade. The organization carried out a number of terrorist acts, including the kidnapping of Brig. Gen. James Dozier of the United States, who was a senior NATO officer. Forlani's government was also faced with a scandal when it was revealed that a number of leading officials were members of a secret Masonic lodge that had been implicated in an oil tax evasion scheme. Forlani resigned from office on May 26, 1981. He returned to the government as deputy premier in 1983 and served until 1987. He again became leader of the Christian Democrats in February of 1989. Forlani stepped down following the party's reversal in parliamentary elections in April of 1992. He was investigated in April of 1993 on charges of corruption involving a state road-building contract.

GIOVANNI SPADOLINI (Premier, June 28, 1981–November 30, 1982). Giovanni Spadolini was born in Florence on June 21, 1925. He attended the University of Florence and served as a history professor there following graduation. He also embarked on a career as a journalist. Spadolini wrote political columns for several newspapers and became editor of the Bologna newspaper *Il Resto del Carlino* in 1955. He left the paper in 1968 to serve as editor of the Milan newspaper *Corriere della Sera*. He entered politics in 1972 and was elected to the Italian Senate as a member of the Republican party. Spadolini served as minister of the environment from 1974 until 1976. He also served in the cabinet as minister of education for several months in 1979. He became leader of the Republican party in 1979. Spadolini was selected to lead a government as premier on June 28, 1981, and became the first person outside the Christian Democratic party to hold that position in the postwar period. Spadolini sought to clean up the political scandal that had plagued the previous government. The Socialists withdrew from the coalition government in August of 1982, but Spadolini was able to reform the government. He was forced to step down on November 30, 1982, following conflict over the government's economic policies. He returned to the government as minister of defense in 1983 and served until 1987, when he was elected president of the Senate.

AMINTORE FANFANI (Premier, November 30, 1982–August 4, 1983). *See earlier entry under Heads of Government.*

BETTINO CRAXI (Premier, August 4, 1983–April 18, 1987). Benedetto "Bettino" Craxi was born in Milan on February 24, 1934. He joined the Socialist Youth Movement in the early 1950s and was active in the Socialist party. He was elected to the Milan Community Council in 1960. Craxi was elected to the Chamber of Deputies in 1968 and became deputy secretary of the Socialist party two years later. He became general secretary of the Socialist party in July of 1976 and succeeded in unifying the various elements of the party. He was reelected party leader in 1981 and became the first Socialist Italian premier on August 4, 1983. The government instituted an austerity budget to improve the economy and was faced with a series of labor strikes. The *Achille Lauro*, an Italian cruise ship, was hijacked by Palestinian terrorists in October of 1985. The government's negotiations with the terrorists through the Palestinian Liberation Organization and the release of the suspected organizer of the hijacking led to a governmental crisis. The Republican party withdrew from the coalition, but rejoined the government later in the month. Craxi again offered his resigna-

tion in June of 1986 when the government was defeated on a revenue bill. He was able to form a new government in August that survived until April 18, 1987. Craxi remained leader of the Socialists and maintained enough power in the Italian government to force the resignation of several subsequent governments. Craxi resigned as leader of the Socialist party on February 11, 1993, following allegations of political corruption.

AMINTORE FANFANI (Premier, April 18, 1987–July 29, 1987). *See earlier entry under Heads of Government.*

GIOVANNI GORIA (Premier, July 29, 1987–April 13, 1988). Giovanni Goria was born in Asti on July 30, 1943. He was educated at Turin University, where he became active in the Christian Democratic party. He was elected to the Chamber of Deputies in 1976. Goria served in the government as undersecretary for the budget from 1981 until 1983. He was appointed minister of the treasury in the government of Amintore Fanfani in 1983. He retained that post until July 29, 1987, when he was asked to form a government as premier. Goria offered his resignation in February of 1988 when he was unable to secure passage of his budget bill. His resignation was refused, and his bill was subsequently passed. Goria's coalition government collapsed over a nuclear-power bill, and he relinquished office to Ciriaco De Mita on April 13, 1988. Goria returned to the government as minister of agriculture in April of 1991.

CIRIACO DE MITA (Premier, April 13, 1988–July 12, 1989). Luigi Ciriaco De Mita was born in Fusco, on February 2, 1928. He was educated at the Catholic University in Milan and received a degree in law. He joined the Christian Democratic party in the mid-1950s and served as a party councillor.

De Mita was elected to the Parliament for one year in 1963. He returned to the Chamber of Deputies in 1972 and was named to the cabinet as minister of industry and commerce the following year. He was appointed minister of foreign trade in 1974 and served until 1976. De Mita remained in the government as minister without portfolio for Mezzogiorno until 1979. He became secretary-general of the Christian Democrats in 1982. He was reelected party chairman in 1986 and replaced Giovanni Goria as premier on April 13, 1988. De Mita remained party leader until February of 1989 and was forced to step down as premier on July 12, 1989, under pressure from the Socialists. He remained active in the leadership of the Christian Democrats.

GIULIO ANDREOTTI (Premier, July 23, 1989–April 24, 1992). *See*

earlier entry under Heads of Government.

GIULIANO AMATO (Premier, June 28, 1992–April 22, 1993). Giuliano Amato was born in Turin on May 13, 1938. He was a professor of constitutional law and a member of the Italian Socialist party from 1958. He served on the party's Central Committee from 1978. Amato was elected to the Chamber of Deputies in 1983 and was reelected in 1987. He subsequently served as minister of the treasury from 1987 until 1989. He was sent to lead the Milan branch of the Socialist party in early 1992. Amato was chosen to succeed Giulio Andreotti as premier on June 28, 1992. Amato resigned from office on April 22, 1993, but remained as head of a caretaker government until Carlos Azeglio Ciampi was named to succeed him.

Ivory Coast

(République de Côte d'Ivoire)

The Ivory Coast is a country on the western coast of Africa. It was granted independence from France on August 7, 1960.

HEADS OF STATE

FÉLIX HOUPHOUËT-BOIGNY (President, August 7, 1960–December 7, 1993). (Félix Boigny was born in Yamoussoukio on October 18, 1905. His father was the chief of the Akwe tribe. Boigny was educated locally and at the Dakar School of Medicine, where he received a degree in 1925. He worked as a public health official before entering politics in 1944. He founded the Ivory Coast Democratic party to campaign for the rights of Africans in the French colony in 1945. Boigny was elected to the French

National Assembly later in the year and added Houphouët, meaning "battering ram," to his name. He was a founder of the African Democratic Rally in 1946 and was active in the Pan-African movement in the French colonial empire in Africa. He joined with the Communists in a violent campaign to drive the French from the Ivory Coast in the late 1940s. Houphouët-Boigny broke with the Communists in 1950 and allied his party with the French Socialists. His party lost support in territorial elections in 1951, but again achieved victory in 1956. Houphouët-Boigny was named minister delegate in the cabinet of French premier Guy Mollet in January of 1956. He remained in the French cabinet until May of 1959 and was instrumental in negotiating independence for the Ivory Coast. A referendum granting the Ivory Coast autonomy within the French community was passed in September of 1958. Houphouët-Boigny was elected prime minister of the Ivory Coast in April of 1959 and took office on May 2, 1959. He led the Ivory Coast to full independence on August 7, 1960, and became president. He also served as minister of defense and held various other ministerial positions. His government survived several coup attempts in the early 1960s. Houphouët-Boigny was reelected in 1965 and was unopposed in subsequent reelection bids. The Ivory Coast remained relatively stable under Houphouët-Boigny, despite major student demonstrations in 1968 and a minor revolt in the Bete region in 1973. The constitution was changed to enlarge the National Assembly in November of 1980, and the ruling Democratic party of the Ivory Coast remained the only party represented in the election. The country's economy deteriorated in the early 1980s, and the government was faced with labor unrest. The government closed the university in 1982 in response to continuing student demonstrations. The government allowed the formation of opposition parties in May of 1990, and Houphouët-Boigny was elected to his seventh term of office the following October. The president's ruling party remained firmly in control of the government, despite a coup attempt in July of 1991 and rioting in February of 1992. Houphouët-Boigny retained power until his death on December 7, 1993, following surgery for prostate cancer.

HEADS OF GOVERNMENT

FÉLIX HOUPHOUËT-BOIGNY (Prime Minister, May 2, 1959–August 7, 1960). *See entry under Heads of State.*

ALASSANE OUATTARA (Premier, November 7, 1990 -Alassane D. Ouattara was born in Dimbokro on January 1, 1942. He was educated in the United States, where he received a degree in economics. He worked as an economist with the International Monetary Fund (IMF) from 1968. Ouattara worked with the African Department of the IMF and became its director in 1984. He served as advisor to the director-general from 1987 until 1990. Ouattara was chosen to be prime minister of the Ivory Coast following the creation of the position on November 7, 1990.

Jamaica

Jamaica is an island country in the northern Caribbean Sea. It was granted independence from Great Britain on August 6, 1962.

HEADS OF STATE

SIR CLIFFORD CAMPBELL (Governor-General, August 6, 1962–February 28, 1973). Clifford Clarence Campbell was born in Petersfield, Westmoreland, on June 28, 1892. He was educated locally and became a teacher in 1944. Campbell entered politics in 1944 and was elected to the House of Representatives as a member of the Jamaica Labor party. He served as chairman of the Education Committee from 1944 until 1949 and was Speaker of the House in 1950. Campbell remained in the House until 1952. He was president of the Senate in 1962 when he was chosen to be the first governor-general of independent Jamaica on August 6, 1962. Campbell retained office until his retirement on February 28, 1973.

SIR HERBERT DUFFUS (Acting Governor-General, February 28, 1973–June 27, 1973). Herbert Duffus served as chief justice of the Jamaican Supreme Court. He became acting governor-general of Jamaica following the retirement of Sir Clifford Campbell on February 28, 1973. He was replaced by Sir Florizel Glasspole on June 27, 1973.

SIR FLORIZEL A. GLASSPOLE (Governor-General, June 27, 1973–March 31, 1991). Florizel Augustus Glasspole was born in Kingston on September 25, 1909. He was educated at Oxford in Great Britain and worked as an accountant from 1932. He was active in the Jamaican trade unions and served as general secretary of the Jamaican United Clerks Association from 1937 until 1948. Glasspole was also active with various other unions

and was elected to the House of Representatives in 1944 as a member of the People's National party (PNP). He was named to the cabinet as minister of labor in 1955. He was appointed minister of education in 1957 and served until 1962. Glasspole again served as minister of education from 1972 until 1973. He was selected as governor-general of Jamaica on June 27, 1973, and served in this capacity until his retirement on March 31, 1991.

EDWARD ZACCA (Acting Governor-General, March 31, 1991–August 14, 1991). Edward Zacca served as acting governor-general of Jamaica following the retirement of Sir Florizel Glasspole on March 31, 1991. He was replaced by Sir Howard Cooke on August 14, 1991.

SIR HOWARD COOKE (Governor-General, August 14, 1991–). Howard Cooke was born in Goodwill on November 13, 1915. He was educated locally and at the University of London. He returned to Jamaica to work as a teacher and was later employed as an insurance executive. Cooke entered politics in 1958 and was elected to the West Indies Federal Parliament as a member of the People's National party. He remained in the Parliament until the West Indies Federation was dissolved in 1962. Cooke served as minister of government in the cabinet of Michael Manley from 1972 until 1980. He was elected president of the Senate in 1989 and was chosen to serve as governor-general of Jamaica on August 14, 1991.

HEADS OF GOVERNMENT

NORMAN MANLEY (Prime Minister, August 14, 1959–April 10, 1962). Norman Washington Manley was born in Roxburg on July 4, 1893. He was educated at Jamaica College and received a Rhodes scholarship to Oxford University. His education was inter-

rupted by World War I, and he served with distinction in the Royal Field Artillery. He returned to Oxford and received a degree in law in 1921. Manley subsequently returned to Jamaica and began a successful legal practice. He entered politics in 1938 and served as a negotiator between the government and striking sugar workers. He subsequently formed the People's National party. His party was defeated by the conservative Jamaica Labor party led by his cousin, Alexander Bustamante, in general elections in 1944. Manley was elected to the Jamaican Assembly in 1949, and his party gained a majority in 1955. He replaced Bustamante as chief minister in 1955. He was a leader in the formation of the West Indies Federation in 1958 and became Jamaica's first prime minister on August 14, 1959. A referendum permitting Jamaica's entry into the West Indies Federation failed in 1961, and the federation collapsed in May of 1962. Manley's party was defeated in elections in April of 1962, and he was replaced as prime minister by Bustamante on April 10, 1962. Jamaica was granted independence in August of 1962, and Manley served as leader of the Opposition. He retired from politics in February of 1969 and relinquished the leadership of the People's National party to his son, Michael Manley. Norman Manley died of a heart attack at his home in Kingston at the age of 76 on September 2, 1969.

SIR ALEXANDER BUSTAMANTE (Prime Minister, April 10, 1962–February 22, 1967). William Alexander Bustamante was born to a poor family in Blenheim on February 24, 1884. He was adopted by a Spanish army officer and taken to Spain when he was fifteen years old. He was educated in Spain and entered the Spanish army. Bustamante fought the Riffs in Spanish Morocco before leaving the military and going to Cuba. He went to New York in the 1920s, where he prospered during the stock market crash in 1929. He returned to Jamaica in 1932 and became active in political affairs. Bustamante was interned by the British colonial government in 1940. He founded the Jamaica Labor party in 1943 and won a majority in the House of Representatives the following year. His party

remained in power, and Bustamante was chosen as chief minister in May of 1953. The People's National party led by Norman Manley defeated Bustamante's party in elections in 1955, and Bustamante stepped down as chief minister. He served as leader of the Opposition and was firmly against Jamaica's entry into the West Indies Federation. He was instrumental in drafting Jamaica's independent constitution, and the Jamaica Labor party returned to power in elections on April 10, 1962. Jamaica was granted independence on August 6, 1962, and Bustamante continued to serve as the independent nation's first prime minister. He instituted many social programs during his administration and was a leading opponent of Cuba's premier, Fidel Castro. Bustamante suffered a major stroke in the spring of 1965 and relinquished most of his duties to Donald Sangster. Bustamante retired from office on February 22, 1967, and died in Irish Town after a long illness at the age of 93 on August 6, 1977.

SIR DONALD SANGSTER (Prime Minister, February 22, 1967–April 11, 1967). Sir Donald Burns Sangster was born in Kingston on October 26, 1911. He was educated at Munroe College, where he received a degree in law. He opened a law practice and became involved in politics. Sangster was defeated for election to the House of Representatives in 1944. He was elected to the House in 1949 as a member of the Jamaica Labor party. He served in the government of Alexander Bustamante as minister of social welfare from 1950 until 1953. Sangster was named minister of finance and served as party leader in the House of Representatives from 1953 until 1955. He went into opposition following the victory of the People's National party in elections in 1955. He was reappointed to the cabinet as finance minister when Bustamante reclaimed office in April of 1962. Sangster also served as foreign minister and minister of defense when Bustamante fell ill in 1964. He served as acting prime minister after Bustamante suffered a stroke the following spring. Bustamante retired in February of 1967, and Sangster was elected leader of the Jamaica Labor party. He took office as prime minister on February 22, 1967, and led the party to victory in parliamentary elections. Sangster suffered a brain hemorrhage in March of 1967. He was taken to Montreal, Canada, for treatment and went into a coma on April 1, 1967. He was knighted by Queen Elizabeth II while he was still in a coma. Sangster died in Montreal at the age of 55 on April 11, 1967.

HUGH L. SHEARER (Prime Minister, April 11, 1967–March 2, 1972). Hugh Lawson Shearer was born in Martha Brae on May 18, 1923. He was educated at St. Simon's College and worked as a journalist after graduation. He joined the Jamaica Labor party and became active in politics. Shearer was elected to the House of Representatives in 1955 and served until 1959. He was a member of the Legislative Council from 1961. He served as minister without portfolio and as Jamaica's delegate to the United Nations in the government of Sir Alexander Bustamante from 1962 until 1967. Bustamante retired in February of 1967 and was replaced by Donald Sangster. Shearer was elected leader of the Jamaica Labor party following the death of Sangster on April 11, 1967. He also succeeded Sangster as Jamaica's prime minister. Shearer also served as minister of defense and foreign minister until the Jamaica Labor party was defeated by the People's National party led by Michael Manley. Shearer relinquished the office of prime minister to Manley on March 2, 1972. He served as leader of the Opposition until 1974, when he was replaced by Edward Seaga. He was reelected to the House of Representatives in 1976 and served

as deputy prime minister and foreign minister in Seaga's government from 1980 until 1989. Shearer returned to the Opposition following the defeat of the Jamaica Labor party in February of 1989.

MICHAEL MANLEY (Prime Minister, March 2, 1972–November 1, 1980). Michael Norman Manley was born in Kingston on December 10, 1924. He was the son of Norman Manley. He was educated at Jamaica College and served in the Royal Canadian Air Force during World War II. Manley entered the London School of Economics after the war in 1945. He worked as a journalist after graduating in 1949 and returned to Jamaica to work as an editor and political columnist for the newspaper, *Public Opinion*. He also became active in the trade union movement, where he served as a negotiator for the National Workers' Union. Manley joined the union as a full-time official in August of 1953. His father was elected chief minister of Jamaica in 1955, and Michael Manley at first resisted entering politics because he did not want to capitalize on his family name. He relented, however, and accepted an appointment to the Senate in 1962. Manley was narrowly elected to the Jamaican House of Representatives in 1967 and succeeded his father as leader of the People's National party (PNP) in February of 1969. He served as leader of the Opposition and led the party to victory in general elections in February of 1972. He was sworn in as prime minister of Jamaica on March 2, 1972. Manley introduced social and economic reforms in an attempt to improve the standard of living of the lower classes, but his programs brought Jamaica's economy to the point of bankruptcy by the mid-1970s. Manley declared a state of emergency following sporadic violence in June of 1976. His party won a major victory in parliamentary elections the following December. Jamaica's economy continued to deteriorate, and Manley was forced to call early elections in October of 1980. The PNP was defeated in a bitter, and sometimes violent, campaign by the Jamaica Labor party, and Manley was replaced as prime minister by Edward Seaga on November 1, 1980. Manley led a boycott of parliamentary elections in December of 1983 that resulted in the PNP holding no seats in the House of Representatives. The party served as an extraparliamentary opposition until elections were held in February of 1989. The PNP defeated the Jamaica Labor party, and Manley returned to power as prime minister on February 10, 1989. The government continued to face a deteriorating economy and widespread inflation. Manley resigned as prime minister and party leader on March 23, 1992, for reasons of health.

EDWARD SEAGA (Prime Minister, November 1, 1980–February 10, 1989). Edward Phillip George Seaga was born in Boston, Massachusetts, on May 28, 1930. His Jamaican parents were vacationing in the United States at the time of his birth. He attended Harvard University and received a degree in sociology in 1952. Seaga subsequently returned to Jamaica to spend several years studying revivalist cults and the supernatural. He also visited Haiti to study voodoo rituals. He entered Jamaican politics in 1959, when he joined the Jamaica Labor party. Seaga entered the upper house of the Legislature on the recommendation of party leader Alexander Bustamante. He was instrumental in drafting the constitution for an independent Jamaica in 1962 and was elected to the House of Representatives in April of 1962. He was named to the Bustamante government as minister of development and welfare. Seaga was reelected to the House of Representatives and was appointed minister of finance and planning. He remained in the government until the Jamaica Labor party was

defeated by the People's National party led by Norman Manley in March of 1972. He remained in the Parliament as a member of the Opposition and was elected to succeed Hugh Shearer as leader of the Jamaica Labor party in 1974. Seaga accused the government of Michael Manley of attempting to transform Jamaica into a Communist state. The Jamaica Labor party was defeated by a wide margin in general elections in December of 1976. Seaga remained leader of the Opposition and led his party to victory in October of 1980. He took office as prime minister on November 1, 1980. He attempted to improve Jamaica's economic condition and eliminated some of the social programs of his predecessor. Seaga supported the United States invasion of Grenada in October of 1983, sending Jamaican troops to participate in the military action. He called an early general election in December of 1983, and the People's National party boycotted the balloting. The Jamaica Labor party held all the seats in the House of Representatives because of the boycott. His government continued to face criticism from the Opposition in the form of public rallies and demonstrations. When Jamaica was devastated by Hurricane Gilbert in September of 1988, Seaga declared a state of emergency. He extended parliamentary terms beyond their five-year mandate. He was forced to hold general elections in February of 1989, and the People's National party returned to power. Seaga relinquished office to Michael Manley on February 10, 1989, but remained the leader of the Opposition in Parliament.

MICHAEL MANLEY (Prime Minister, February 10, 1989–March 23, 1992). *See earlier entry under Heads of Government.*

P. J. PATTERSON (Prime Minister, March 23, 1992–   ). Percival J. Patterson was born in 1935. He was named deputy prime minister and finance minister in the cabinet of Michael Manley in 1989. He was forced to resign in January of 1992 because of a scandal over the waiver of import duties for Shell Oil Company. Pat-terson was selected to succeed Manley as prime minister and leader of the People's National party on March 23, 1992, when Manley resigned due to ill health.

Japan

(Nippon)

Japan is a country that inhabits a chain of islands off the east coast of Asia.

HEADS OF STATE

HIROHITO (Emperor, December 25, 1926–January 7, 1989). Hirohito was born in the Aoyama Palace in Tokyo on April 29, 1901. He was the son of Crown Prince Yoshihito. He was educated by tutors and at the Peers' School and developed an interest in natural history and marine biology. Hirohito was proclaimed heir apparent on September 9, 1912, when his grand-father, Emperor Meiji, died and his father was crowned Emperor Tashio. Hirohito became the first Japanese prince to travel abroad in 1921, when he visited Europe. He was appointed prince regent in November of 1921 due to his father's mental illness. Hirohito married Princess Nagako Kuni in January of 1924. He succeeded to the throne upon his father's death on De-cember 25, 1926. He designated his reign as Showa, or "Enlightened Peace." Hirohito initially supported a policy of moderation in regard to Japan's military activities. He report-edly opposed the army's actions in Manchuria in the late 1920s that culminated in the annexation of Man-churia in 1931. Hirohito ordered the suppression of a rightist revolt in Feb-ruary of 1936. He also opposed the en-try of Japan into war against the United States because he feared the risks involved in such a confrontation. He was unable to convince his ministers of his points of view, however, and ultimately supported his government's actions. Japan was on the verge of defeat in the summer of 1945 after atomic bombs devastated the cities of Hiroshima and Nagasaki. While the nation's leaders debated whether to surrender to the Allies or resist an inva-sion of the home islands, Hirohito made the decision for peace. He declared Japan's surrender in a radio address on August 15, 1945. The Allies declined to try Hirohito as a war criminal and retained him as emperor. He was forced to renounce his divinity, however, and the Japanese Constitu-tion was changed to reflect the em-peror's role as "the symbol of the state and of the unity of the people." The oc-cupation forces pressed Hirohito to be-come more accessible to the Japanese people. The emperor's popularity soared under the newly established constitutional monarchy in 1952. Hiro-hito attended the opening of the Tokyo Olympic Games in 1964. When he traveled to Europe in 1971, he be-came Japan's first sitting monarch to travel abroad. He visited the United States in 1975 and was received at the White House by President Gerald Ford.

Hirohito's health deteriorated in September of 1988. He relinquished his duties to the Crown Prince Akihito. Hirohito died at the Imperial Palace of intestinal cancer at the age of 87 on January 7, 1989.

AKIHITO (Emperor, January 7, 1989–). Akihito Tsugunomiya was born in Tokyo on December 23, 1933. He was the son of Emperor Hirohito and the Empress Nagako. He was educated by tutors and at the Peers' School. Akihito subsequently attended school with commoners following Japan's defeat in World War II. He at-tended Gakushuin University in 1952 and, like his father, developed a keen interest in marine biology. He traveled abroad to attend the coronation of Elizabeth II in Great Britain in 1953. Akihito married Michiko Shoda, a commoner, on April 10, 1959. He traveled extensively on state visits during his father's reign. Akihito assumed the duties of emperor when Hirohito became seriously ill on September 18, 1988. He ascended to the throne upon his father's death on January 7, 1989. He designated his reign as Heisei, or "Achieving Peace."

HEADS OF GOVERNMENT

NARUHIKO HIGASHIKUNI (Prime Minister, August 17, 1945–October 9, 1945). Naruhiko Higashikuni was born in 1887. He was a member of the Japanese royal family and the uncle of Emperor Hirohito. He attended the Tokyo Military Academy and was stationed as a military attaché in Paris in 1920. His playboy reputation resulted in his recall to Japan in 1927. Higashikuni remained in the military and in 1937 was named chief of military aviation. Two years later he was promoted to general, and following the Japanese attack on Pearl Harbor in December of 1941, he was named to head the home defense headquarters. Following the defeat of Japan at the conclusion of World War II, Higashikuni was named by the emperor to form the first postwar cabinet on August 17, 1945. His government was unable to restore order to the country, and he resigned on October 9, 1945. Higashikuni was stripped of his royal title during the Allied occupation of Japan and became a Buddhist monk. He spent the remainder of his days away from political affairs and died at the age of 102 on January 20, 1990.

KIJURO SHIDEHARA (Prime Minister, October 9, 1945–May 22, 1946). Kijuro Shidehara was born in Osaka on August 11, 1872. He received a law degree from Tokyo Imperial University's Law College in 1895. He worked in the Departments of Agriculture and Commerce before entering the diplomatic corps in 1899. Shidehara served as counselor in the Japanese Embassy in Washington in 1912 and was appointed to the same position in London in 1914. He was named Japan's minister to the Netherlands later that year, serving until 1915. He returned to Japan in late 1915, where he became vice-minister of foreign affairs. In 1919 he was appointed Japanese ambassador to the United States, where he remained until 1922. Shidehara was made a baron in 1920. He returned to the cabinet as minister of foreign affairs in 1924 and served in that capacity in six cabinets until 1931. Shidehara briefly served as acting prime minister following an assassination attempt against Prime Minister Yuko Hamaguchi in November of 1930. Shidehara continued to serve as foreign minister until December of 1931, when the government of Baron Reijiro Wakatsuki collapsed.

Shidehara's opposition to right-wing militarist policies resulted in his exclusion from subsequent governments. Shidehara's political career was not reestablished until after World War II. He was asked to form a postwar government by Emperor Hirohito on October 6, 1945. He administered the reconstruction programs ordered by General Douglas MacArthur under the occupation. Shidehara promoted a democratic reform package, and on April 10, 1946, Japan held its first postwar election. The election resulted in no party receiving a majority. Shidehara was unable to form a coalition cabinet and stepped down on April 22, 1946. He remained acting prime minister until Shigeru Yoshida took over the reins of government on May 22, 1946. Shidehara became vice-premier in the Yoshida cabinet. He was subsequently elected Speaker of the House of Representatives and remained in that position until his death of a heart attack in Tokyo on March 10, 1951.

SHIGERU YOSHIDA (Prime Minister, May 22, 1946–May 24, 1947). Shigeru Yoshida was born in Tokyo on September 22, 1878. He was adopted by Kenzo Yoshida, a friend of his father, who wanted an heir to carry on the Yoshida name. He attended Tokyo Imperial University and received a law degree in 1906. Yoshida joined the diplomatic corps and served as a viceconsul in China, Manchuria, and London. In 1909 he was assigned to the Japanese Embassy in Rome as third secretary. In 1912 he was stationed in Manchuria as a consul and remained there until 1916. He was then assigned to the United States in 1917, China in 1918, and Great Britain from 1920 until 1922. Yoshida returned to China as consul general of Tientsin from 1922 until 1925 and served in the same capacity in Mukden, Manchuria, from 1925 until 1928. In Manchuria he was an active proponent of Japan's designs on the territory. Following a brief stay

in Sweden, Yoshida returned to Japan as vice-minister of foreign affairs, a position he held from 1928 until 1930. He then served as ambassador to Italy until 1932. Yoshida was viewed as an opponent of right-wing militarist policies, and his appointment as foreign minister was vetoed by the army in 1936. Instead he was appointed ambassador to Great Britain, where he remained until 1939. Yoshida went into political retirement during World War II. He was arrested in June of 1945 on charges of negotiating a peace proposal with the British. He remained imprisoned until Japan's surrender in August of 1945. Yoshida was then appointed foreign minister in the first postwar cabinet. Following the first postwar elections, Yoshida, as leader of the Liberal party, was asked to form a government on May 22, 1946. Yoshida's government quickly became a target of leftist elements, who called for his resignation. He remained in office and carried out the policies of the occupation authorities. His party suffered reversals in the elections in April of 1947, and Yoshida resigned as prime minister on May 24, 1947. On October 19, 1948, following two short-lived governments, Yoshida returned to the post of prime minister. Japan remained under an occupation force until 1951, when Yoshida went to San Francisco to sign the peace treaty and security treaty with the United States. His Liberal party remained in power in the election of 1952, but he was faced with factionalism in the party. Japan was also forced to adopt a strict deflationary policy, which caused financial hardship for most small businessmen. Nevertheless, Yoshida followed a policy which successfully led Japan toward the status of a modern industrial state. Following the merger of the Liberal and Progressive parties, Yoshida resigned as prime minister on December 7, 1954. He remained active in political affairs and served in the Diet until 1962. He traveled abroad as an elder statesman to represent Japan at several ceremonial occasions, including the funeral of General Douglas MacArthur in 1964. Yoshida died in Oisi following complications from a gallbladder infection on October 20, 1967, at the age of 89.

TETSU KATAYAMA (Prime Minister, May 24, 1947–March 10, 1948). Tetsu Katayama was born to a prosperous family in Wakayama-ken on July 28, 1887. He graduated from the Tokyo Imperial University Law College in 1912. He became involved with Socialist politics and helped Isoo Abe found the Social Democratic party in 1926. Katayama was subsequently elected to the lower house of the Diet. He was an opponent of militarist policies and was forced from politics when the Socialists were purged by the imperial government in 1940. Following the defeat of Japan in World War II, Katayama began another Socialist party and served as its secretary-general. After the elections of 1946, in which Katayama was returned to the Diet, he failed in an attempt to form a coalition government. The following year the Socialist party increased its vote totals and received a plurality. Katayama formed a coalition government on May 24, 1947, despite the Liberal party's refusal to join the cabinet. Katayama was able to win support in the Diet for his controversial proposal to nationalize the coal industry. This was one of the few major pieces of legislation that the Katayama government was able to enact. Economic conditions forced the government to enact unpopular postage and railway rate hikes, and he was beset by problems from the labor unions. Katayama was forced to resign and was succeeded by Hitoshi Ashida on March 10, 1948. He refused an appointment as foreign minister in the Ashida cabinet and instead returned to the Diet as the Socialist party chairman. He later retired from politics and died in

Fujisawa City at the age of 90 on May 30, 1978.

HITOSHI ASHIDA (Prime Minister, March 10, 1948–September 14, 1948). Hitoshi Ashida was born in Nakamutobe, in Kyoto-fu, on November 15, 1887. He received a law degree from Tokyo Imperial University's Law College in 1912 and joined the diplomatic corps. He was stationed at the embassy in Russia in 1917 and from 1918 to 1920 served at the Japanese Embassy in Paris. He served in the Japanese delegation to the League of Nations in 1920 and 1921. He continued to serve in various diplomatic posts in Switzerland, Turkey, and Belgium until he resigned from the diplomatic corps following his election to the Diet in 1932. While serving in the Diet, he was an opponent of Japan's military action in Manchuria. Ashida also became president of the *Japan Times*, an English-language newspaper owned by the Foreign Ministry. Ashida remained in the Diet until 1940. He was inactive politically during World War II. Following Japan's defeat in the war, Ashida was instrumental in the formation of the Liberal party and served in the cabinet of Prime Minister Kijuro Shidehara as minister of welfare. He was also instrumental in drafting a new constitution for Japan. Ashida left the Liberal party to form the Democratic party in 1947 and subsequently became its leader. Following the resignation of Tetsu Katayama as prime minister on March 10, 1948, Ashida was narrowly elected prime minister with the support of the Socialists. Ashida's coalition government was soon beset by scandals when a leading chemical company received favored treatment from the Reconstruction Finance Bank by bribing high-ranking officials. Ashida was forced to resign on September 14, 1948, when two members of his cabinet were arrested for complicity in the scandal. Ashida was himself arrested on December 8, 1948, in connection with the affair. He was reelected to the Diet in January of 1949, despite criminal charges against him. The remainder of his political career remained under a cloud, as he was not cleared of suspicion until 1958. Ashida died of cancer in Tokyo on June 20, 1959.

SHIGERU YOSHIDA (Prime Minister, October 19, 1948–December 7, 1954). *See earlier entry under Heads of Government.*

ICHIRO HATOYAMA (Prime Minister, December 9, 1954–December 20, 1956). Ichiro Hatoyama was born in Tokyo on January 1, 1883. He received a law degree from Tokyo Imperial University in 1907 and practiced law briefly before his election to the Tokyo Municipal Assembly. He was elected to the lower chamber of the Diet as a member of the Seiyukai party in 1915. Hatoyama served as cabinet secretary in the government of Baron Gi-ichi Tanaka from 1927 until 1929. From 1931 he served in several governments as minister of education. In 1938 he wrote the best-selling book *Sekai no Kawo* (*The Face of the World*). Hatoyama was prevented from becoming the leader of the Seiyukai party because of the military's distrust of his Westernized style and ideals. Despite opposition from the government, he was reelected to the Diet in 1942, though he retired to a mountain village during most of the war. Following the surrender of Japan, Hatoyama formed the Liberal party and became its leader. He was reelected to the Diet in April of 1946 and was expected to form a government as prime minister. His selection was vetoed by the occupation forces, however, which also refused to allow him to take his seat in the Diet. They alleged that he had been involved in militarist and nondemocratic activities during his years of government service. Hatoyama appealed the ruling, but he was not cleared of suspicion until mid-1951. Meanwhile, Shigeru Yoshida had become Liberal party

leader and prime minister, and Hatoyama had suffered a stroke which had left him partially paralyzed. Yoshida refused to step aside as prime minister in favor of Hatoyama, who was reelected to the Diet in 1952. In December of 1954 Hatoyama and his supporters left the Liberal party and joined with the Progressives to form the Democratic party, which forced Yoshida's resignation on December 7, 1954. Hatoyama was named prime minister two days later, and in February of the following year, he was reelected to the position. In October of 1956 Hatoyama went to Moscow to negotiate the Soviet-Japanese pact, which formally established peace between the two nations. It also resulted in Japan's admission to the United Nations with the support of the Soviet Union. Hatoyama's failing health contributed to his resignation as prime minister and party leader on December 20, 1956. He died in Tokyo of a heart attack on March 7, 1959, at the age of 76.

TANZAN ISHIBASHI (Prime Minister, December 23, 1956–February 23, 1957). Tanzan Ishibashi was born in Tokyo on September 25, 1884. He graduated from Tokyo's Waseda University in 1908. He became a reporter and joined the staff of the *Oriental Economist* in 1911. By 1924 he had risen to managing editor of the financial publication. During the 1920s and 1930s, he also wrote numerous books on economics. Ishibashi also served on several government commissions during the 1930s. His antimilitarist policies jeopardized his magazine's publication during World War II. After Japan's surrender Ishibashi joined the Liberal party and served as minister of finance in the cabinet of Prime Minister Shigeru Yoshida. In 1947 he was elected to the Diet, but later in the year he was purged by the occupation authorities for having promoted economic imperialism in the pages of his magazine. The ban on his political activities was lifted in June of 1951. The following year he was elected to the House of Representatives. He was expelled from the Liberal party for his criticisms of Prime Minister Yoshida and joined with a dissident group of Liberals led by Ichiro Hatoyama to form the Democratic party in 1954. Ishibashi was appointed minister of international trade and industry in the subsequent government of Prime Minister Hatoyama. Following the merger of the Liberal and Democratic parties and the resignation of Hatoyama as party chairman, Ishibashi defeated Nobusuke Kishi for the chairman's post. He was subsequently elected prime minister and took office on December 23, 1956. He tried to enact bold legislation in the areas of public works, social welfare, and industrial investment, but was forced to compromise on most issues. Ishibashi was also an early advocate of normalizing relations between Japan and the People's Republic of China. He retired as prime minister for reasons of health on February 23, 1957. Ishibashi died in Tokyo at the age of 88 on April 24, 1973.

NOBUSUKE KISHI (Prime Minister, February 25, 1957–July 18, 1960). Nobusuke Kishi was born to the Sato family in the Yamaguchi prefecture on November 13, 1896. He was adopted by a member of his father's family. He graduated from the Law College at Tokyo Imperial University in 1920. Kishi worked in the Ministry of Agriculture and Commerce and in 1935 became director of the industrial bureau at the Ministry of Commerce and Industry. The following year he went to Manchuria to help reorganize industry in the areas seized by Japan. He returned to Japan to serve as vice-minister of commerce and industry in 1939 and was appointed minister in 1941. During World War II Kishi served as state minister and vice-minister of munitions in the wartime government of General Hideki Tojo. Kishi was forced to resign

in July of 1944 following a dispute with Tojo. Following Japan's surrender, Kishi was arrested by the occupation authorities as a war criminal and was detained in Sugamo Prison. He was never brought to trial and was released in 1948. He was allowed to reenter politics in 1952, and the following year he was elected to the Diet as a member of the Liberal party. Kishi was among the Liberal party leaders who opposed Prime Minister Shigeru Yoshida and formed the Democratic party in 1954. Kishi served as secretary general of the new party. He was narrowly defeated for the presidency of the Liberal-Democratic party by Tanzan Ishibashi following the resignation of Ichiro Hatoyama in December of 1956. Kishi was named foreign minister in the subsequent Ishibashi government. When Ishibashi resigned in February of 1957, Kishi was elected to succeed him as party leader and prime minister and took office on February 25, 1957. Kishi was a leading proponent of close relations with the United States. He also sought to improve Japan's education system and helped to establish Japan as a dominant economic force in Southeast Asia. Kishi sponsored a new security treaty between Japan and the United States in 1960. Massive antigovernment demonstrations opposing the treaty followed. On July 14, 1960, Kishi was stabbed in the leg by an ultranationalist. Kishi recovered from his wounds, but resigned his office four days later on July 18, 1960. He retired to the role of elder statesman and served as an unofficial advisor when his brother Eisaku Sato served as prime minister from 1964 to 1972. Kishi died in a Tokyo hospital after a long illness on August 7, 1987, at the age of 90.

HAYATO IKEDA (Prime Minister, July 18, 1960–October 25, 1964). Hayato Ikeda was born in Yoshina in the Hiroshima Prefecture on December 3, 1899. He graduated from the Kyoto Imperial University in 1925. Two years later he began working for the Ministry of Finance. In the early 1930s Ikeda was afflicted by a rare skin disorder which confined him to bed for five years. Following his recovery, he returned to the Finance Ministry, where he worked in the tax bureau. He had risen to become director of the tax bureau by the end of World War II. His experience in financial matters was instrumental in stabilizing the inflation rate during the occupation of Japan. Ikeda served as vice-minister of finance in Prime Minister Shigeru Yoshida's government from 1947 until 1948. The following year he was elected to the House of Representatives and was subsequently appointed minister of finance in Yoshida's government in February of 1949. Ikeda served as a member of the delegation that negotiated the Japanese–United States peace and security treaties. In October of 1952 Yoshida appointed Ikeda as minister of international trade and industry. He was forced to resign his position the following month after a vote of no confidence in the House of Representatives. He remained an influential leader in the Liberal party and was elected secretary-general of the party. Ikeda returned to the government as minister of finance in the cabinet of Tanzan Ishibashi in 1956. He retained his position in the subsequent government of Nobusuke Kishi and later served as minister of state and minister of international trade and industry. Kishi resigned from office in July of 1960, and Ikeda was elected party president and prime minister on July 18, 1960. Ikeda was successful in improving Japan's economic position by removing overseas trade barriers against Japan. He also continued to support the pro–American policies of his predecessors. In September of 1964 Ikeda was hospitalized with a throat ailment. His health prevented him from continuing as prime minister, and he resigned on October 25, 1964, and turned over the government to Eisaku Sato. Ikeda died of throat cancer in Tokyo on August 13, 1965.

EISAKU SATO (Prime Minister, November 9, 1964–July 5, 1972). Eisaku Sato was born in Tabuse in the Yamaguchi Prefecture on March 27, 1901. He graduated with a law degree from Tokyo Imperial University in 1924. He then entered government service by joining the Ministry of Railways. Sato became a transportation specialist and was in charge of Japan's railway system by the end of World War II. He was appointed vice-minister of transportation in the government of Prime Minister Tetsu Katayama in 1947. The following year he resigned from the Ministry of Transportation and entered politics as a member of the Democratic-Liberal party. Sato was appointed chief cabinet secretary in the government of Shigeru Yoshida in October of 1948. In January of 1949 Sato won a seat in the House of Representatives. He remained in the cabinet and served as a leading advisor to Prime Minister Yoshida. He subsequently served as minister of posts and telecommunications and minister of construction. He resigned from the cabinet to take the position of secretary-general of the Democratic-Liberal party in 1953. In 1954 Sato was accused of accepting a bribe from a shipbuilding association. He was eventually acquitted during a general amnesty following Japan's admittance to the United Nations, but his political career was badly damaged. He resigned his offices and remained out of politics until June of 1958, when he was appointed finance minister in the cabinet of his older brother, Nobusuke Kishi. He remained in that position until Kishi's resignation in July of 1960. The following year Sato was appointed minister of international trade and industry in the government of Hayato Ikeda. He resigned after a year, citing his dissatisfaction with Ikeda's slowness in implementing his policies. In July of 1963 Ikeda reappointed Sato to his cabinet as state minister. He also served as director of the committee that organized the Tokyo Olympics held in the fall of

1964. Sato resigned from the cabinet again in July of 1964 and announced his plans to challenge Ikeda for the office of prime minister. Ikeda was suffering from poor health and when he resigned in October of 1964, he chose Sato as his successor. Sato took office on November 9, 1964. As prime minister he encouraged Japan's growth as an industrial power and assisted in fostering the economic development of Southeast Asia. He also improved Japan's relations with South Korea and negotiated the return of Japanese sovereignty over the island of Okinawa from the United States. Sato had supported the United States position in regard to Communist China, and his government was caught off guard by President Richard Nixon's visit to China in 1972. Many Japanese felt that Japan should pursue its own course in normalizing relations with Communist China, but Sato was heavily influenced by pro-Taiwan elements in his party. Sato was defeated as leader of the Liberal-Democratic party by Kakuei Tanaka and resigned as prime minister on July 5, 1972. Two years after his resignation Sato was awarded the Nobel Prize for Peace for having been "the main exponent of a reconciliation policy that contributed to a stabilization of conditions in the Pacific area." He was also praised for having led Japan's refusal to develop nuclear weapons. On May 19, 1975, Sato suffered a major stroke in a Tokyo restaurant. He went into a coma, and his condition was so critical that physicians were forced to treat him in the restaurant for a week before he was able to be moved. He died in a Tokyo hospital on June 3, 1975, at the age of 74.

KAKUEI TANAKA (Prime Minister, July 6, 1972–December 9, 1974). Kakuei Tanaka was born in Nishiyama in the Niigata Prefecture on May 4, 1918. He came from a poor family, and after receiving a primary education at local schools, he went to Tokyo, where he worked as a laborer while in his teens. He was drafted in 1939 and spent two years in Manchuria before being discharged for health reasons in 1941. Tanaka returned to construction and founded the Tanaka Civil Engineering Company in 1943. The war years brought prosperity to his business, and he became a leader in the construction industry. Tanaka entered politics in 1945, when he joined the Liberal party. He was defeated for a seat in the House of Representatives in the first postwar election, but was elected the following year. Tanaka was appointed vice-minister of justice in Prime Minister Shigeru Yoshida's cabinet in 1948, but was forced to resign following accusations that he accepted bribes from the coal industry. He was indicted, but was reelected to his House seat while imprisoned. Tanaka was acquitted of the charges several years later. His business interests continued to be successful, and he became president of the Nagaoka Railway Company in 1950. Tanaka joined the newly formed Liberal-Democratic party in 1955. He was appointed minister of posts and telecommunications in the cabinet of Prime Minister Nobusuke Kishi and served from July of 1957 until June of 1958. In 1962 he was appointed minister of finance in the cabinet of Hayato Ikeda, and he retained the position in Eisaku Sato's government until 1965. Tanaka also remained an important leader in party affairs. He made plans to challenge Sato for leadership of the party prior to Sato's resignation in July of 1972. Tanaka was elected party leader on the second ballot, defeating Takeo Fukuda, and subsequently became prime minister on July 6, 1972. Tanaka began a campaign to improve trade relations with the United States and Europe. He also made a state visit to the People's Republic of China and established diplomatic relations between Japan and China. Tanaka was initially a popular leader, but his standing with the public suffered a major setback when he was accused of the improper use of public funds. Financial scandals continued to shake his government, and he was forced to resign on December 9, 1974. Tanaka was arrested on charges of accepting $1.6 million in bribes to arrange the purchase of Lockheed aircraft for Japan's airlines. Tanaka continued to be a major figure in Japanese politics and led a powerful wing of the Liberal-Democratic party. He was instrumental in the selection of Japan's next four prime ministers. Tanaka's legal troubles continued, and after a lengthy trial, he was convicted on bribery charges in 1983. He was sentenced to four years in prison and given a substantial fine. He appealed his conviction and remained a powerful leader in Japanese politics until he suffered a serious stroke in 1985. Tanaka died in a Tokyo hopsital after a long illness on December 16, 1993.

TAKEO MIKI (Prime Minister, December 9, 1974–December 24, 1976). Takeo Miki was born in the Tokushima Prefecture on March 17, 1907. He graduated from Meiji University in Tokyo in 1929. He studied abroad in Europe and the United States before returning to Japan and receiving a law degree in 1936. Shortly after his graduation he was elected to the House of Representatives. Miki advocated a peaceful relationship between Japan and the United States and thus earned the animosity of the military government during World War II. Miki continued in politics when the war ended and formed the People's Cooperative party in 1947. He served as minister of commerce in the cabinet of Prime Minister Tetsu Katayama from 1947 until 1948. In December of 1954 Miki joined the cabinet of Ichiro Hatayama as minister of transportation. The following year he was instrumental in the negotiations that created the Liberal-Democratic party. Miki was a powerful leader in the new party and served in cabinet posts in the governments of Nobusuki Kishi and Hayato

Ikeda. In 1965 he was named minister of international trade and industry in the government of Eisaku Sato. The following year Sato appointed him foreign minister. He remained in Sato's cabinet until October of 1968, when he resigned to challenge Sato unsuccessfully for the post of prime minister. He remained out of government, but again challenged Sato in 1970 without success. When Sato resigned in June of 1972, Miki again sought the leadership of the party. He ran fourth in the first balloting before throwing his support to the eventual victor, Kakuei Tanaka. Miki was rewarded with another cabinet position and became deputy prime minister in August of 1972. Miki supported better relations between Japan and the Arab nations when Japan was economically threatened by the oil embargo following the Yom Kippur War in 1973. Miki's tour of Arab nations the following year resulted in the relaxation of the embargo on Japan. Miki resigned from Tanaka's cabinet in July of 1974 after financial scandals had rocked the Tanaka government. When Tanaka was forced to resign on December 9, 1974, Miki was chosen to succeed him as a compromise candidate between the two major factions. Miki tried to regain the people's trust in the scandal-ridden Liberal Democratic party. Powerful factions in the party began calling for Miki's resignation in August of 1976. When the party lost support in the general elections in December of 1976, Miki took responsibility for the poor showing and resigned on December 24, 1976. Miki remained the leader of a faction of the Liberal Democratic party and supported a vote of no confidence against the government of Masayoshi Ohira in 1979. In June of 1988 he suffered a cerebral hemorrhage. He died in a Tokyo hospital on November 13, 1988, at the age of 81.

TAKEO FUKUDA (Prime Minister, December 24, 1976–December 7, 1978).

Takeo Fukuda was born in the Gamma Prefecture on January 14, 1905. He graduated from Tokyo Imperial University with a degree in law in 1929. He joined the Ministry of Finance, where he rose through the bureaucratic ranks. From 1941 until 1943 he served as financial advisor to the Japanese puppet government in China. Fukuda remained in the Finance Ministry, where he rose to the post of director of the budget in 1947. He resigned from the ministry in 1950 when he was accused of accepting bribes. He was acquitted of the charges two years later. Fukuda was elected to the House of Representatives later that year. He became a leader of the Liberal Democratic party and was appointed minister of agriculture and forestry in the cabinet of Nobusuke Kishi in 1959. He was named minister of finance in Eisaku Sato's government in 1965. Fukuda retained that position until July of 1971, when he was appointed foreign minister by Sato. Fukuda was widely viewed as a likely successor to Sato, but when Sato's popularity crumbled in 1972, Fukuda was also politically damaged. When Sato was forced to resign on July 5, 1972, Fukuda lost the party leadership, and thus the office of prime minister, to Kakuei Tanaka. The following year Fukuda was appointed finance minister in the Tanaka government. He implemented policies designed to ease Japan's inflation rate. He resigned in July of 1974, complaining of increasing disunity within the party. When Tanaka was forced to resign on December 9, 1974, following allegations he had accepted bribes, Fukuda and Masayoshi Ohira were viewed as the strongest candidates to succeed him. Since neither candidate would step aside, they agreed on Takeo Miki as a compromise choice to keep from splintering the party. Fukuda was named deputy prime minister in the Miki government. When the Liberal Democratic party was nearly defeated in the elections of 1976, Miki resigned as leader and was succeeded by Fukuda.

He took office as prime minister on December 24, 1976. His temporary alliance with Ohira came to an end in 1978. Ohira, a leading opponent of Japan's rearmament, felt Fukuda was being influenced by people who wanted Japan to become a nuclear power. Fukuda was defeated in the ensuing power struggle and relinquished the office of prime minister to Ohira on December 7, 1978. Fukuda remained a powerful force in the Liberal Democratic party and was instrumental in the passage of a no confidence vote against Ohira's government in 1979.

MASAYOSHI OHIRA (Prime Minister, December 7, 1978–June 12, 1980). Masayoshi Ohira was born in the Kagawa Prefecture on March 12, 1910. He majored in economics at the Tokyo Commercial College and was employed at the Ministry of Finance upon his graduation in 1936. He remained in the ministry, where he became private secretary to the minister of finance in 1949. Ohira retained this position until his election to the House of Representatives in 1952. He was named chief cabinet secretary in the government of Hayato Ikeda in 1960. Two years later Ikeda appointed him foreign minister. Ohira left the cabinet in 1964 to become deputy secretary-general of the Liberal Democratic party. He returned to the cabinet as minister of international trade and industry in the government of Eisaku Sato. He was instrumental in establishing diplomatic relations between Japan and the People's Republic of China. Ohira served as foreign minister in the government of Kakuei Tanaka from 1972 until 1974. He was then appointed finance minister, a position he held for two years before he resigned to become secretary-general of the Liberal Democratic party. In 1978 he challenged the leadership of Prime Minister Takeo Fukuda. Ohira, with the support of the party faction led by former Premier Tanaka, defeated Fukuda as party leader. He was sworn in as prime minister on December 7, 1978. Ohira called for early elections for the Diet in 1979, but the Liberal Democrats, still suffering from allegations of financial corruption in previous governments, were nearly defeated at the polls. Ohira refused to resign from office. In October of 1979 the Socialist party introduced a motion of no confidence against the government. In a surprising move the motion passed with the support of Liberal-Democratic factions led by Miki and Fukuda. The House was dissolved, and Ohira called for new general elections to be held in June of 1980. Ohira died of a heart attack in Tokyo on June 12, 1980, ten days before the scheduled elections.

MASAYOSHI ITO (Acting Prime Minister, June 12, 1980–July 17, 1980). Masayoshi Ito was born in Fukushima Prefecture on December 15, 1913. He was educated at Tokyo University and entered the Japanese civil service. He served in the Ministry of Agriculture from 1936. Ito rose through the ranks of the ministry and was named vice minister of agriculture and forestry in 1962. He was elected to the Diet the following year as a member of the Liberal Democratic party. Ito served as minister of state and chief cabinet secretary in the government of Masayoshi Ohira from 1979. Ito became acting prime minister following Ohira's death on June 12, 1980. He was replaced by Zenko Suzuki on July 17, 1980. He subsequently served as foreign minister in Suzuki's government until 1981. Ito remained active in the Liberal Democratic party and was elected to the executive committee in 1987.

ZENKO SUZUKI (Prime Minister, July 17, 1980–November 26, 1982). Zenko Suzuki was born in Yamada, in the Iwate Prefecture, on January 11, 1911. He graduated from the Imperial Fisheries Institute in 1935 and returned to his home distict, where he worked for the government fishery agency. He remained in this capacity throughout most of World War II. After the war he was active as a national fisheries labor leader and joined the Socialist party. Suzuki was elected to the House of Representaives in April of 1947. Two years later he joined the Liberal party, and in 1955 he was an early member of the Liberal Democratic party following the merger of the two parties. Suzuki became closely associated with the party faction led by Masayoshi Ohira. He was appointed minister of posts and telecommunications in the cabinet of Hayato Ikeda in 1960 and held this office until July of 1961. In 1964 Ikeda appointed him chief cabinet secretary. When Ikeda resigned in November of 1964, Suzuki was appointed minister of health and welfare in the subsequent government of Eisaku Sato. He left Sato's cabinet in December of 1966. Suzuki became increasingly active in party affairs and served as chairman of the Liberal Democratic executive committee from December of 1968. He was appointed minister of agriculture, forestry, and fisheries by Takeo Fukuda in December of 1976 and served in this office until November of the following year. Suzuki remained a close aide of Masayoshi Ohira, who became prime minister on December 7, 1978. When Ohira died on June 12, 1980, Suzuki received the support of the Ohira faction to succeed him as party leader. He was sworn in as prime minister on July 17, 1980, to replace Masayoshi Ito, Ohira's chief cabinet secretary, who had served as caretaker prime minister in the interval following Ohira's death. Though Suzuki was considered a compromise choice, he rapidly gained popularity as a competent and honest leader. In October of 1982 Suzuki announced his intention not to stand for reelection. He supported Yasuhiro Nakasone as his successor and left office on November 26, 1982. Two years later Suzuki led an unsuccessful attempt to unseat Nakasone as party leader.

YASUHIRO NAKASONE (Prime Minister, November 26, 1982–November 6, 1987). Yasuhiro Nakasone was born in Takasaki, in the Gamma Prefecture, on May 27, 1918. He majored in political science at the University of Tokyo and joined the Ministry of Home Affairs upon his graduation. During World War II he served in the navy and rose to the rank of lieutenant colonel. Near the end of the war, Nakasone viewed at a distance the first atomic bomb blast at Hiroshima. For several years following the Japanese surrender, Nakasone wore a black tie in mourning for Japan's defeat. He entered politics in December of 1946 and was viewed by the occupation authorities as a right-wing nationalist. He was elected to the House of Representatives in April of the following year. Nakasone traveled extensively over the next two decades. He adopted a Western style of campaigning from Robert Kennedy and used the un-Japanese gesture of shaking hands with people he met. He served as minister of state and director-general of science and technology in the government of Nobusuke Kishi from 1959 until 1960. He supported Eisaku Sato to be prime minister and served in the Sato cabinet as minister of transport from 1967 until 1968. Nakasone served as minister of state and director-general of defense from 1970 until 1971. In 1972 he was named minister of international trade and industry in the cabinet of Kakuei Tanaka and he remained in the cabinet until Tanaka's government fell in December of 1974. Nakasone earned the nickname "Weathervane" for his shifting of political allegiance whenever the political winds blew. In 1980 he was appointed director-general of administrative management and he attempted to streamline the government. Nakasone created a stir when he threatened to commit suicide when his plan to cut waste from the national budget was jeopardized. Following Suzuki's resignation in October of 1982, Nakasone received the backing of three of the four major factions in the Liberal Democratic party to succeed him. He was sworn in as prime minister on November 26, 1982. Nakasone sought to strengthen Japan's ties with the United States and improve the economic conditions of the country. He was re-elected party leader in 1984, despite opposition from his predecessor, Zenko Suzuki. Japan was faced with economic recession, and Nakasone's sales tax proposal cost him much support. He stepped down as leader of the Liberal party in October of 1987 and was replaced as prime minister by Noboru Takeshita on November 6, 1987. Nakasone was implicated in an insider trading scandal involving the Recruit business services organization in late 1988. He resigned from the Liberal party, but rejoined it in April of 1991 following the resignation of Secretary-General Ichiro Ozawa.

NOBORU TAKESHITA (Prime Minister, November 6, 1987–June 2, 1989). Noboru Takeshita was born in Shimane on February 26, 1924. He was educated at Waseda University and worked as a teacher. He entered politics in 1951 and was elected to the local Prefecture Council. Takeshita was elected to Parliament in 1958. He served in the Ministry of International Trade and Industry as vice-minister from 1963 until 1964. He was named chief cabinet secretary in 1971. Takeshita served until 1972 and again in 1974. He was appointed minister of construction in 1976. Takeshita served as minister of finance from 1979 until 1980. He was reappointed to the Finance Ministry in the government of Yasuhiro Nakasone in 1982 and served until 1986. Takeshita was selected to replace Nakasone as leader of the Liberal Democratic party in October of 1987. He took office as prime minister on November 6, 1987. The Takeshita government was faced with a major scandal involving insider trading with the Recruit business services organization. Takeshita was implicated in having received financial gain from confidential information provided by the business. He was forced to step down as party leader and prime minister and was replaced by Sousuke Uno on June 2, 1989.

SOUSUKE UNO (Prime Minister, June 2, 1989–August 9, 1989). Sousuke Uno was born in Shiga on August 27, 1922. He was educated at the Kobe University of Commerce. He entered politics in the 1950s and was elected to the Japanese Parliament as a member of the Liberal Democratic party. Uno served in the Ministry of International Trade and Industry as parliamentary vice-minister from 1966 until 1969. He served in various government agencies during the 1970s and was chairman of the Atomic Energy Commission from 1976 until 1977. He served in the cabinet as minister of state from 1979 until 1980 and was minister of international trade and industry in 1983. Uno was appointed foreign minister in 1987. He retained that position until he replaced Noboru Takeshita as prime minister on June 2, 1989. Uno was forced to resign on August 9, 1989, following a sex scandal involving a part-time geisha.

TOSHIKI KAIFU (Prime Minister, August 9, 1989–November 6, 1991). Toshiki Kaifu was born in Nagoya on January 2, 1931. He attended Waseda University and received a degree in law in 1954. He entered politics and worked as secretary to a Liberal party member of the Diet. Kaifu was elected to the lower house of the Diet in 1960. He served in several government and party positions during the government of Takeo Miki from 1974 until 1976. He was named minister of education in 1976 and served until the following year. In 1985 he returned to the cabinet as minister of education in the govern-

ment of Yasuhiro Nakasone. Kaifu was selected as leader of the Liberal party in August of 1989 following a series of scandals involving the top leadership of the party. He replaced Sousuke Uno as prime minister on August 9, 1989. The Liberal party retained power after elections in February of 1990. Kaifu's popularity diminished as a result of the Persian Gulf crisis in 1991, and a government proposal to send members of the Japanese Self-Defense Force to fight in the Gulf was withdrawn due to widespread opposition. Kaifu completed his term of office on November 6, 1991, and was replaced by Kiichi Miyazawa.

KIICHI MIYAZAWA (Prime Minister, November 6, 1991–). Kiichi Miyazawa was born in Tokyo on October 8, 1919. He was educated at the Tokyo Imperial University. Miyazawa worked in the Finance Ministry from 1942. He served in the House of Councillors from 1953 and was named parliamentary vice-minister of education in 1959. He served until 1960. Miyazawa served as minister of state for economic planning from 1962 until 1964 and again from 1966 until 1968. He was elected to the House of Representatives in 1967 and served in the cabinet as minister of international trade and industry from 1970 until 1971. Miyazawa served as foreign minister from 1974 until 1976. He returned to serve as minister of state for economic planning from 1977 until 1978. He was named minister of finance in 1986 and also served as deputy prime minister until 1988. Miyazawa was forced to resign from the cabinet following revelations of an insider trading scandal in the government. He was elected to succeed Toshiki Kaifu as leader of the Liberal Democratic party and became prime minister on November 6, 1991.

Jordan, Hashemite Kingdom of
(al-Mamlakah al-Urduniyah al-Hashimiyah)

Jordan is a country in western Asia. It was granted independence from a League of Nations mandate administered by Great Britain on May 25, 1946.

HEADS OF STATE

ABDULLAH IBN AL-HUSSEIN (King, 1921–July 20, 1951). Abdullah ibn Al-Hussein was born in Mecca in 1882. He was the second son of Emir Hussein, the king of the Hejaz from 1916 until 1924. In 1893 Abdullah accompanied his father into exile in Turkey. He served in the Ottoman Parliament in 1907. Abdullah was vice president of the Turkish Parliament in 1914, when he and his father participated in the Arab revolt against the Turks during World War I. He assumed the title of king of the Arab countries. Ibn Sa'ud, the king of Nejd, resented the title, and a territorial dispute developed on the Nejd and Hejaz border. Ibn Sa'ud's army defeated the Hejaz army led by Abdullah in May of 1919. Two years later, after the separation of Trans-Jordan from Palestine, Britain offered Abdullah the territory to rule as an emir under a British mandate. Abdullah was crowned king of the Hashemite Kingdom of Trans-Jordan on May 25, 1946. Trans-Jordan declared war against Israel in May of 1948, but was forced to sign a peace treaty the following year. In 1949 Trans-Jordan's name was changed to Jordan. Abdullah annexed Arab Palestine to Jordan in April of 1950. He was also a leading proponent of a union between Jordan, Syria, and Iraq. He was assassinated by a Palestinian extremist while entering the El Aqsa Mosque in Jerusalem on July 20, 1951.

NAIF IBN ABDULLAH EL-HASHIM (Regent, July 20, 1951–September 6, 1951). Naif ibn Abdullah el-Hashim was the youngest son of King Abdullah. He attended Victoria College in Cairo. Naif became regent of Jordan following the death of King Abdullah, because his brother, Crown Prince Talal, was in poor health. Naif ruled in his brother's stead until September 6, 1951, when Talal was judged fit to assume the throne and returned to Jordan. Naif died in 1983.

TALAL IBN ABDULLAH EL-HASHIM (King, September 6, 1951–August 11, 1952). Talal ibn Abdullah was born in Mecca in 1909. He was the eldest son of King Abdullah. He was educated in Amman and joined the Arab Legion in 1927. He soon went to the Sandhurst Royal Military Academy in Britain, where he graduated in 1929 with the rank of lieutenant. Talal returned to the Middle East to serve as an aide to his grandfather, King Hussein, who was in exile in Cyprus at the time. He subsequently joined his father in Amman, the capital of Trans-Jordan. Talal advanced through the ranks in the Arab Legion to become general in 1948. When his father, King Abdullah, was assassinated on July 20, 1951, Talal was in a clinic in Switzerland being treated for mental illness. His younger brother, Emir Naif, had been named regent in his absence. Talal was judged fit to assume the throne, and he returned to Jordan on September 6, 1951. He initially seemed competent to rule, but he was afflicted by violent mood swings and periods of depression. He was removed from the throne by Parliament as mentally unfit on August 11, 1952, and was succeeded by his young son, Hussein. Talal went to Egypt and later to an island in the Bosporus, where he received medical care and lived in seclusion. He died in a sanatorium in Istanbul, Turkey, on July 8, 1972.

HUSSEIN IBN TALAL EL-HASHIM (King, August 11, 1952–). Hussein ibn Talal was born in Amman on November 14, 1935. He was the oldest child of Crown Prince Talal. His grandfather, King Abdullah, took an interest in Hussein and oversaw his education in Arabic and English. Hussein often accompanied his grandfather on state business. He was with Abdullah when the king was assassinated in Jerusalem. Hussein narrowly escaped being killed himself when he tried to capture the assassin and was fired upon. Hussein's father, Talal, succeeded to the throne, and Hussein was sent to complete his education at Harrow, in Great Britain. His father, who suffered from mental illness, was forced to abdicate on August 11, 1952, and Hussein was recalled to Jordan. Following the rule of a Regency Council, Hussein was crowned when he came of age on May 2, 1953. He quickly became the target of Arab nationalists, who accused him of being controlled by Britain and the United States. In an attempt to appease nationalist sentiment, he dismissed Sir John Bagot Glubb, the British commander of the Arab Legion, in March of 1956. Hussein narrowly survived a coup attempt in April of 1957 when army officers who supported Egypt's President Gamal Abdel Nasser made an unsuccessful attempt to overthrow the monarchy. To offset Nasser's growing influence and power in the Arab world, Hussein and his cousin, King Feisal of Iraq, agreed to a federation between the countries of Iraq and Jordan. Before final arrangements could take place, however, Feisal was ousted

and murdered by leftist army officers. Shortly afterwards Hussein again narrowly escaped being overthrown by elements of the Jordanian military. Britian and the United States sent military assistance to support Hussein against the plotters. While Jordan's political problems continued, economic conditions improved in the country during Hussein's reign. During the 1960s the increase of Palestinian refugees in Jordan became a serious problem. Palestinian guerrilla groups operated against Israel from Jordanian bases and also called for the overthrow of Hussein. In June of 1967 Hussein was pressured to join with other Arab nations in the Six-Day War against Israel. The Jordanian army was defeated, and Israel took control of the West Bank and East Jerusalem. Hussein's government was again threatened by Palestinians in 1970. The Palestinian Liberation Organization (PLO) had established military bases in Jordan and were ignoring the Jordanian government. In September of 1970 Hussein ordered the military to strike back at the guerrillas. Jordan narrowly averted being thrown into a state of civil war, with neighboring countries also prepared to join the fray. The military was able force the PLO out of Jordan by August of the following year. Hussein, who was widely viewed as one of the most moderate and pro-Western Arab leaders, broke with the United States when he denounced the Camp David Peace accords between Egypt and Israel. Hussein's comments were welcomed by the other Arab nations who had also condemned the peace initiatives. Hussein subsequently sought to negotiate a settlement with Israel that would gain the return of Jordanian lands and satisfy the desires of the Palestinians, but he received little cooperation from PLO leader Yasir Arafat. Hussein ultimately accepted the loss of the West Bank in 1988, when he renounced Jordanian claims to the area. Hussein again found himself in a difficult position when Iraq, under Saddam Hussein, invaded Kuwait in August of 1990. King Hussein criticized the Iraqi attack, but refused to join with the United States and other Arab nations in a coalition against Iraq. Hussein's position cost him much financial aid from Saudi Arabia and other anti-Iraq countries. Following the liberation of Kuwait, Hussein tried to reestablish himself as an Arab leader and continued to seek a peaceful settlement for the Middle East.

HEADS OF GOVERNMENT

IBRAHIM HASHEM (Prime Minister, May 25, 1946–February 1947). Ibrahim Hashem was born in Nablus, Palestine, in 1878. He graduated from the Istanbul Law School in 1906 and joined the Ottoman civil service. He became active in the Arab nationalist movement and in 1922 was appointed minister of justice in Trans-Jordan by Emir Abdullah. In November of 1933 he accepted the post of chief minister in Abdullah's government. Hashem's disagreement with the British Consul led to his resignation in September of 1938. He returned to the position in May of 1945, and following independence from Britain, he became prime minister on May 25, 1946. He resigned the office in February of 1947 over a disagreement concerning the Jordan-Turkey Friendship Pact. Hashem returned briefly as prime minister on December 21, 1955, after the resignation of Said el-Mufti, and served until January 1, 1956. He was again appointed prime minister on April 25, 1957, following the attempted overthrow of King Hussein. He remained in that position until May 19, 1958. Hashem was subsequently named deputy prime minister of the Arab Union of Jordan and Iraq. The 80-year-old Hashem was in Baghdad attending talks concerning the union at the time of the revolt that overthrew King Feisal of Iraq. Hashem was murdered in the streets of Baghdad on July 14, 1958, during the unrest that followed.

SAMIR EL-RIFAI (Prime Minister, February 1947–May 3, 1949). Samir el-Rifai was born in Safad, Northern Palestine, on January 3, 1901. He was educated locally, and in 1922 he entered the civil service in Palestine. He later joined the civil service in Trans-Jordan in 1925. Rifai was considered a competent and loyal official, and in 1944 he was appointed Trans-Jordan's minister of the interior by King Abdullah. He subsequently was named chief minister. He served as prime minister from February of 1947 until May 3, 1949, and again from December 4, 1950, until July 25, 1951, shortly after the assassination of King Abdullah. Rifai returned to the government as prime minister under King Hussein on January 9, 1956, and became a leading advisor to Hussein. He was a proponent of the union between Jordan and Iraq to counterbalance Gamal Abdel Nasser's United Arab Republic. He remained as prime minister until May 20, 1956, and served again from May 19, 1958, until May 5, 1959, when he resigned for reasons of health. Rifai was again named prime minister on March 28, 1963, but was forced to resign after a vote of no confidence in the Jordanian Chamber of Deputies on April 21, 1963, following demonstrations calling for Jordan to join the United Arab Republic. Rifai subsequently became chairman of the Jordanian University's board of trustees. He died of a heart attack in Amman on October 12, 1965.

TEWFIK ABUL-HUDA (Prime Minister, May 3, 1949–April 13, 1950). Tewfik Abul-Huda was born in Acre, Palestine, in 1895. He served in the

Ottoman army, then joined Emir Feisal in his brief government in Damascus in 1919. In 1922 he went to Trans-Jordan, where he worked in the civil service. He was appointed director of the Agricultural Bank in 1932 and served until 1937. Abdul-Huda was chief minister from 1939 until 1944. He was foreign minister in 1945 and again in 1947, before being named prime minister on May 3, 1949. He resigned on April 13, 1950, over opposition with Jordan's peace settlement with Israel. He was elected president of the Senate in 1950, but again became prime minister on July 25, 1951, following the assassination of King Abdullah. As prime minister he forced the ouster of Abdullah's son, Talal, as king of Jordan because of his mental health. Abul-Huda served as prime minister until May 5, 1953. He was again appointed prime minister on May 2, 1954, and served until May 30, 1955. Abul-Huda's health declined in 1956, and he committed suicide by hanging himself in his home in Amman on July 1, 1956.

SAID EL-MUFTI (Prime Minister, April 13, 1950–December 3, 1950). Said el-Mufti was born in Amman in 1898. He joined the civil service in Amman in 1924, where he became a leading Jordanian nationalist opposed to British rule. He became a leader of the non-Arab Circassian community in Jordan. Mufti was appointed minister of communications in 1944. He also served as interior minister from 1944 until 1945 and again from 1948 until 1950. He was appointed prime minister on April 13, 1950, and opposed King Abdullah's negotiations with Israel. Mufti resigned on December 3, 1950. He again served as interior minister from 1951 until 1953 and served on the Regency Council that governed Jordan during the period of time between King Talal's abdication on August 11, 1952, and King Hussein's accession on May 2, 1953. Mufti again served as prime minister from May 30 until Decem-

ber 14, 1955, and from May 22, 1956, until October 29, 1956. During this period he helped to ease tension over Jordan's possible inclusion in the Baghdad Pact, a security plan supported by the United States. Mufti was named interior minister again in 1957 and remained in most cabinets until 1963. He then became Speaker of the Senate until he retired from politics in 1974. In 1985 one of his sons, Azmi al-Mufti, was assassinated while serving as Jordan's ambassador to Greece. Mufti died of natural causes in Jordan on March 25, 1989.

SAMIR EL-RIFAI (Prime Minister, December 4, 1950–July 25, 1951). *See earlier entry under Heads of Government.*

TEWFIK ABUL-HUDA (Prime Minister, July 25, 1951–May 5, 1953). *See earlier entry under Heads of Government.*

FAWZI EL-MULKI (Prime Minister, May 5, 1953–May 2, 1954). Fawzi el-Mulki was born in Irbid in 1910. He studied at the American University of Beirut and at Edinburgh and Cambridge Universities in Great Britain. He went to work at the Department of Education in Jordan in 1934. Mulki was appointed as an economic advisor to the government in 1940 and was named consul general in Cairo two years later. In 1947 Mulki was appointed ambassador to Egypt. He later served as minister of foreign affairs and minister of defense. In the early 1950s he was named ambassador to Great Britain and later was named ambassador to France. On May 5, 1953, he was appointed King Hussein's first prime minister and served until his resignation on May 2, 1954. The following year he again served as ambassador to Egypt and in 1956 was renamed foreign minister. He served as minister of public works in 1957 and was appointed to represent Jordan as chief delegate to the United Nations in

1961. He retained that position until his death in New York City on January 10, 1962, following a long illness.

TEWFIK ABUL-HUDA (Prime Minister, May 2, 1954–May 30, 1955). *See earlier entry under Heads of Government.*

SAID EL-MUFTI (Prime Minister, May 30, 1955–December 14, 1955). *See earlier entry under Heads of Government.*

HAZZAA MAJALI (Prime Minister, December 14, 1955–December 19, 1955). Hazzaa Majali was born in the village of Kerak in 1916. He received a degree in law from Damascus University and practiced law until 1947. He then entered royal service as chief of protocol to the Royal Palace. Majali subsequently was elected mayor of Amman in 1948 and served until the following year. In 1950 he was appointed minister of agriculture, and he served briefly as minister of justice and defense. He was an ardent supporter of King Hussein and was pro–Western in his outlook. Majali was appointed prime minister on December 14, 1955, but was forced to resign five days later following widespread strikes and riots opposing his support for Jordan joining the Baghdad Pact. He was subsequently appointed chairman of Jordan's Development Board, where he remained until his appointment as minister of the Royal Court. He was again named prime minister on May 5, 1959. In March of 1960 Jordanian authorities uncovered a conspiracy to assassinate Majali that implicated Egyptian interests. The prime minister was killed on August 29, 1960, when two time bombs exploded in the government building that housed the prime minister's office and buried him under the rubble.

IBRAHIM HASHEM (Prime Minister, December 21, 1955–January 7, 1956). *See earlier entry under Heads of Government.*

SAMIR EL-RIFAI (Prime Minister, January 9, 1956–May 20, 1956). *See earlier entry under Heads of Government.*

SAID EL-MUFTI (Prime Minister, May 22, 1956–October 29, 1956). *See earlier entry under Heads of Government.*

SULEIMAN NABULSI (Prime Minister, October 29, 1956–April 10, 1957). Suleiman Nabulsi was born in Salt, Palestine, in 1910. He graduated from the American University of Beirut in 1933. He returned to Trans-Jordan where he became involved in the Arab nationalist movement. Nabulsi was arrested by the British in 1936 and was imprisoned for a year. Upon his release he went to work at the Agricultural Bank of Trans-Jordan and became its director. He remained in that position until 1946, when he was appointed minister of finance and economy. He left the cabinet the following year and was briefly arrested on the order of King Abdullah because of his anti–British sentiments. Nabulsi returned to the cabinet as minister of finance in 1950 and served until 1951. He was appointed ambassador to Great Britain in 1953, but resigned the following year in opposition to the proposed Baghdad Pact. He returned to Jordan, where he helped found the National Socialist party, a leftist, pro–Egyptian organization that favored Arab unity. The party was largely responsible for the dismissal of Britain's Lt. Gen. John Bagot Glubb as commander of the Arab Legion in 1956. In the elections of 1956, Nabulsi was defeated for a seat in the Parliament, but the National Socialists won a majority. King Hussein called on Nabulsi to form a government, and he took office as prime minister and foreign minister on October 29, 1956. He supported an alliance between Jordan and Egypt and favored the termination of the Anglo-Jordanian Treaty. Nabulsi was dismissed by King Hussein on April 10, 1957, following an attempt by Palestinian politicians and members of the army to overthrow the king and eliminate the monarchy. Nabulsi was briefly placed under house arrest during the period of martial law that followed the crisis. He remained active politically and led the opposition with an agenda that supported Egypt and Palestinian guerrilla operations against Israel. Nabulsi retired from politics in 1972 and died in Amman at the age of 68 on October 14, 1976.

HUSSEIN KHALIDI (Prime Minister, April 15, 1957–April 24, 1957). Hussein Fakhri Khalidi was born to a prominent Palestinian family in Jerusalem in 1895. He graduated from the American University of Beirut, where he received a medical degree in 1915. He entered the Turkish army and was seriously wounded during World War I. Khalidi deserted from the Turks to join Emir Feisal and Col. T. E. Lawrence in the Arab army that captured Damascus. After the war he served as a senior medical officer with the British Palestine Government Health Department. He resigned to run for the Jerusalem Municipal Council in 1934 and was elected mayor the following year. Khalidi founded the Reform party in 1936 and served as a member of the Arab High Committee. His nationalist activities resulted in his expulsion as mayor in 1937 and his exile by the British to the Seychelles, where he remained until 1938. He settled in Beirut for several years before returning to Palestine in 1943. Khalidi again involved himself in Arab political affairs, and when the west bank of the Jordan River was annexed by Jordan following the Arab-Israeli War of 1948, he became a Jordanian citizen. He was appointed to the Jordanian Senate, and from 1953 until 1954 he served as foreign minister. He also headed the Ministry of Health and Social Affairs and again served as foreign minister from 1955 until 1956. He served as prime minister from April 15 until April 24 of 1957, during the crisis that resulted from an attempt to overthrow King Hussein. Dr. Khalidi remained active in political affairs, though he was not appointed again to a cabinet position. He died of complications from a stomach ulcer in Amman on February 6, 1962.

IBRAHIM HASHEM (Prime Minister, April 25, 1957–May 19, 1958). *See earlier entry under Heads of Government.*

SULEIMAN TOUKAN (Military Governor, April 26, 1957–July 1957). Suleiman Toukan was born in 1890. He was educated in Istanbul, where he studied law. In 1925 he was elected mayor of Nablus and served until 1948. He was a founder of the National Defense party in 1934 and was a leading supporter of Emir Abdullah. Toukan was elected to the Jordanian Senate in 1950. He was appointed minister of defense the following year. He served as minister of the Royal Court from 1953 until 1957 and was again appointed minister of defense in 1957. Following the abortive coup against King Hussein in April of 1957, Toukan served as military governor of Jordan and he remained in that position until July of 1957. He was then named minister of the Royal Court again. Toukan was appointed minister of defense in the federation of Jordan and Iraq. He was in Iraq to help administer the union between the two countries when King Feisal of Iraq was ousted. Toukan was killed in Baghdad during the revolution on July 14, 1958.

SAMIR EL-RIFAI (Prime Minister, May 19, 1958–May 5, 1959). *See earlier entry under Heads of Government.*

HAZZAA MAJALI (Prime Minister, May 5, 1959–August 29, 1960). *See* *earlier entry under Heads of Government.*

BAHJAT AL-TALHOUNI (Prime Minister, August 29, 1960–January 27, 1962). Bahjat al-Talhouni was born in 1913. He graduated with a law degree from Damascus University and worked in the court system. He was appointed minister of the interior in 1953 and served as chief of the Royal Court from 1954 until 1960. Talhouni was appointed prime minister on August 29, 1960, and served until January 27, 1962. He also was foreign minister from 1961 until 1962. From 1963 until 1964 Talhouni again served as chief of the Royal Court. He was a supporter of Egypt's Gamal Abdel Nasser and was often called upon to lessen tension between Jordan and Egypt. He was named prime minister again on July 6, 1964, and served until February 13, 1965. Talhouni was recalled again as prime minister on October 7, 1967, and served until March 24, 1969. He again led the government from August 12, 1969, until June 27, 1970. He was out of government following the violent clashes between the Jordanian army and Palestinian guerrillas in the fall of 1970. Talhouni was appointed to the Senate in May of 1973, where he remained until his death in Amman at the age of 82 on January 29, 1994.

WASFI AL-TAL (Prime Minister, January 28, 1962–March 28, 1963). Wasfi al-Tal was born in Irbid in 1920. He was educated at the American University in Beirut and became a teacher upon graduation. He joined the British army in 1942 and served as a liaison officer in London. Tal worked in the Arab information office in London from 1945 until 1948. He then returned to Palestine to fight in the Arab-Israeli war in 1948. He subsequently worked in various administrative offices in the Jordanian government before being appointed director of the Jordan Government's Press Bureau. Tal's strong support for Jordan's involvement in the Baghdad Pact resulted in his being sent to the West German Embassy as a counselor when demonstrations against the pact brought down the government. He returned to Jordan in 1957, where he again held several positions before being appointed ambassador to Iran in 1961. Tal was recalled to Jordan, and on January 28, 1962, he was named prime minister. His support for the royalist cause during the Yemini civil war brought Jordan into direct conflict with the interests of Gamal Abdel Nasser's Egypt. On March 28, 1963, Tal resigned as prime minister because of widespread criticism of his pro-Western views. He was once again named prime minister on February 13, 1965, and his government generated a climate of improved economic activity. He remained in office until March 4, 1967. In September of 1970 the Jordanian army engaged in an armed conflict with Palestinian guerrilla groups in Jordan. Tal, who had encouraged the army's crackdown on the guerrillas, was appointed prime minister on October 28, 1970. His activities gained him the enmity of the Palestinians. In November of 1971 he attended a meeting of the Arab League's Joint Defense Council in Cairo, Egypt. On November 28, 1971, he was shot to death in the lobby of his hotel by three gunmen, who were members of the Palestinian Black September organization.

SAMIR EL-RIFAI (Prime Minister, March 28, 1963–April 21, 1963). *See earlier entry under Heads of Government.*

SHERIF HUSAIN IBN NASSER (Prime Minister, April 21, 1963–July 6, 1964). Husain ibn Nasser was born in 1906. He was the great uncle of King Hussein. He had formerly served as minister of the Royal Court before his appointment as prime minister on April 21, 1963. His appointment indicated a period of direct rule from the palace. He left office on July 6, 1964.

BAHJAT AL-TALHOUN (Prime Minister, July 6, 1964–February 13, 1965). *See earlier entry under Heads of Government.*

WASFI AL-TAL (Prime Minister, February 13, 1965–March 4, 1967). *See earlier entry under Heads of Government.*

SAAD JUMAA (Prime Minister, March 4, 1967–October 7, 1967). Saad Jumaa was born in 1916. He was educated at the Syrian University in Damascus. He worked in several civil service positions before joining the diplomatic corps. Jumaa was appointed ambassador to Iran and Syria in the early 1960s and served as ambassador to the United States from 1962 until 1965. He was appointed prime minister on March 4, 1967, but resigned on October 7, 1967. Jumaa returned to the diplomatic corps and served as ambassador to Great Britain from 1969 until 1970. He died of heart disease while vacationing in London on August 19, 1979.

BAHJAT AL-TALHOUNI (Prime Minister, October 7, 1967–March 24, 1969). *See earlier entry under Heads of Government.*

ABDEL MONEM RIFAI (Prime Minister, March 24, 1969–August 12, 1969). Abdel Monem Rifai was born in Tyre, Lebanon, in 1917. He was educated at the University of Beirut and worked in the Jordanian civil service from 1938. He was appointed minister to Teheran in 1951 and minister to Washington in 1953. Rifai remained there until he was named ambassador to Lebanon in 1957, where he served until the following year, when he was apppointed ambassador to Great Britain. He served as Jordan's chief delegate to the United Nations from 1962 until 1965 and represented Jordan in the Arab League in 1966. He was appointed foreign minister in 1968. King Hussein named Rifai as prime minister on March 24, 1969, in the hopes that he could be instrumental in achieving a peaceful settlement in the Middle East. He was replaced on August 12, 1969, when no settlement appeared forthcoming. Rifai was again named prime minister on June 27, 1970, with the task of reaching a compromise between the Jordanian army and the Palestinian guerrillas. He negotiated a truce which would have turned over several of Jordan's major cities to the guerrillas. King Hussein refused to accept the truce agreement and when fighting broke out between the two camps, Rifai was dismissed and replaced by a military government on September 15, 1970. Rifai died of a heart attack in Amman on October 17, 1985.

BAHJAT AL-TALHOUNI (Prime Minister, August 12, 1969–June 27, 1970). *See earlier entry under Heads of Government.*

ABDEL MONEM RIFAI (Prime Minister, June 27, 1970–September 15, 1970). *See earlier entry under Heads of Government.*

MOHAMMED DAOUD (Prime Minister, September 15, 1970–September 24, 1970). Mohammed Daoud served as a career military officer in the Jordanian army. He was a brigadier when he was named to lead a military cabinet as prime minister and foreign minister on September 15, 1970, during the Palestinian crisis. A few days after forming a government, he went to Cairo, Egypt, to attend an Arab summit. Daoud was reported missing during the conference and shortly thereafter he sought asylum in Egypt. He later went to Libya, where he fell ill. He returned to Cairo for treatment and then went to Paris, where he had an operation. He asked King Hussein to allow his return to

Jordan in late 1971. He entered a military hospital in Amman and died there on January 19, 1972.

AHMED TOUKAN (Prime Minister, September 26, 1970–October 28, 1970). Ahmed Toukan was born on August 15, 1903. He served in the Jordanian government and was appointed prime minister of an interim government on September 26, 1970. He held office during the fighting that drove the Palestinian guerrillas from Jordan and was replaced by Wasfi al-Tal on October 28, 1970. Toukan died in Amman after a long illness on January 4, 1982.

WASFI AL-TAL (Prime Minister, October 28, 1970–November 28, 1971). *See earlier entry under Heads of Government.*

AHMED AL-LAWZI (Prime Minister, November 29, 1971–May 26, 1973). Ahmed al-Lawzi was born in Jubeiha, near Amman, in 1925. He became a teacher in the early 1950s and later joined the civil service. He was employed by the Royal Court and the Ministry of Foreign Affairs until 1961, when he was elected to Parliament. Lawzi was appointed minister without portfolio in 1964, and in 1967 he served as minister of municipal affairs. He was appointed minister of finance in 1970. He was named prime minister on November 29, 1971, following the assassination of Wasfi al-Tal. Lawzi became ill in May of 1973 and resigned as prime minister on May 26, 1973. He served as president of the National Consultative Council from 1978 until 1979.

ZAID AL-RIFAI (Prime Minister, May 26, 1973–July 13, 1976). Zaid al-Rifai was born in Amman on November 27, 1936. He was the nephew of former prime minister Abdel Monem Rifai. He was educated at Victoria College in Alexandria and entered the Foreign Service in 1957. Rifai moved to the Royal Court in 1965 and became minister of the Royal Court in 1970. In 1971 he was appointed ambassador to Great Britain. He was appointed prime minister on May 26, 1973, and served also as foreign minister and minister of defense. Rifai resigned on July 13, 1976. He was again appointed prime minister and minister of defense on April 4, 1985, and remained in office until April 24, 1989.

MUDAR BADRAN (Prime Minister, July 13, 1976–December 19, 1979). Mudar Badran was born in Jerash in 1934. He was educated at the University of Damascus in Syria and joined the Jordanian army in 1957. He worked in the intelligence department and rose to become its chief in 1968. Badran also served as the king's special advisor on the occupied territories. He retired from the military in 1970 to become King Hussein's national security advisor. He served as minister of the Royal Court in 1972 and was minister of education from 1973 until 1974. Badran was again named minister of the Royal Court in 1974. He was appointed prime minister on July 13, 1976, and also became minister of defense and foreign affairs. He was replaced on December 19, 1979. Badran again served as prime minister from July 28, 1980, until January 10, 1984, and from December 4, 1989, until June 19, 1991.

SHARIF ABDUL HAMID SHARAF (Prime Minister, December 19, 1979–July 3, 1980). Sharif Abdul Hamid Sharaf was born in Baghdad in 1939. He was educated at the American University in Beirut and joined the Arab Nationalist Movement while a student there. He joined the Foreign Ministry in Jordan in 1962. Following the 1967 Arab-Israeli war, Sharaf was appointed ambassador to the United States, a position he held for five years. He also served as Jordan's chief delegate to the United Nations. He was appointed chief of the Royal Cabinet in 1976 and assisted King Hussein in reconciling differences with the Palestinian leaders. Sharaf was appointed prime minister on December 19, 1979. He also served as foreign minister and defense minister in the government. He died suddenly of a heart attack at his home in Amman at the age of 41 on July 3, 1980.

QASSIM EL-RIWAI (Prime Minister, July 3, 1980–August 28, 1980). Qassim el-Riwai was born in Palestine in 1918. Riwai, a former deputy prime minister, served as minister of agriculture in the cabinet of Abdul Sharaf. When Sharaf died on July 3, 1980, Riwai was named prime minister. He presided over a caretaker government until August 28, 1980. He died in 1982.

MUDAR BADRAN (Prime Minister, July 28, 1980–January 10, 1984). *See earlier entry under Heads of Government.*

AHMED ABDEL OBEIDAT (Prime Minister, January 10, 1984–April 4, 1985). Ahmed Abdel Obeidat was born in Hartha, Irbid, in 1938. He was educated at the University of Baghdad and later became a teacher. In 1957 he was named to the Jordanian cabinet as minister of education. Obeidat entered the intelligence service in 1964 and served as director from 1974 until 1982. He was named minister of the interior in 1982 and served until his appointment as prime minister and minister of defense on January 10, 1984. He was replaced by Ziad al-Rifai on April 4, 1985. He subsequently worked with the Law and Arbitration Center in Amman.

ZIAD AL-RIFAI (Prime Minister, April 4, 1985–April 24, 1989). *See earlier entry under Heads of Government.*

SHARIF ZEID IBN SHAKER (Prime Minister, April 27, 1989–December 4, 1989). Sharif Zeid ibn Shaker was born in Amman on September 4, 1934. He

was educated at Victoria College in Alexandria and Sandhurst Royal Military College in Great Britain. He joined the army and rose through the ranks to become chief of staff for operations in 1972. Shaker served as commander in chief of the Jordanian armed forces from 1976 until 1988. He was then named minister of state and military advisor to his cousin, King Hussein. He was appointed prime minister on April 27, 1989 and served until December 4, 1989, when he returned to his previous position. Shaker was reappointed prime minister on November 16, 1991.

MUDAR BADRAN (Prime Minister, December 4, 1989–June 19, 1991). *See earlier entry under Heads of Government.*

TAHER AL-MASRI (Prime Minister, June 19, 1991–November 16, 1991). Taher Nashat al-Masri was born in Nablus on March 5, 1942. He attended North Texas State University and then returned to Jordan in 1965 to work at the Central Bank of Jordan. He was elected to Parliament in 1973 and served as minister of state for the occupied territories from 1973 until 1974. Masri was appointed ambassador to Spain in 1975, to France in 1978, and to Great Britain in 1983. He also served as the Jordanian delegate to the United Nations Educational, Scientific, and Cultural Organization (UNESCO) from 1978 until 1983. He was appointed minister of foreign affairs in 1984 and served until 1988. Masri was named deputy prime minister in April of the following year and served until August. He was renamed minister of foreign affairs in January of 1991. He was appointed prime minister and minister of defense on June 19, 1991, and served until November 16, 1991.

SHARIF ZEID IBN SHAKER (Prime Minister, November 16, 1991–). *See earlier entry under Heads of Government.*

Kazakhstan, Republic of

(Kazakhstan Respublikasy)

Kazakhstan is a country in central Asia. It became independent following the breakup of the Soviet Union on December 25, 1991.

HEAD OF STATE

NURSULTAN NAZARBAEV (President, December 10, 1991–). Nursultan Abishevich Nazarbaev was born in Chemolgran on July 6, 1940. He attended local technical schools and joined the Communist party in 1962. He worked as an engineer during the 1960s before his election to the Communist party local committee in 1969. Nazarbaev rose thorugh the ranks of the party hierarchy and became chairman of the Council of Ministers of Kazakh in 1984. He was elected first secretary of the Central Committee of the Kazakh Communist party in 1989. He resigned from the Communist party to lead the Socialist party in 1991. Nazarbaev was elected chairman of the Supreme Soviet of the Kazakh S.S.R. on February 22, 1990, succeeding K. U. Medeubekov. He became the first president of independent Kazakhstan on December 10, 1991.

HEAD OF GOVERNMENT

SERGEI A. TERESHCHENKO (Prime Minister, December 10, 1991–). Sergei A. Tereshchenko was born in the Chimkent Region on March 30, 1961. He worked in government and was elected first deputy chairman of the Council of Ministers of the Kazakh Soviet Republic in 1989. He served as vice president of Kazakhstan from April to May of 1991. Tereshchenko succeeded K. Karamanov as chairman of the Council of Ministers of independent Kazakhstan following the installation of President Nursultan Nazarbaev on December 10, 1991.

Kenya, Republic of

(Djumhuri ya Kenya)

Kenya is a country in eastern Africa. It was granted independence from Great Britain on December 12, 1963.

HEADS OF STATE

MALCOLM MacDONALD (Governor-General, December 12, 1963– December 12, 1964). Malcolm John MacDonald was born in Lossiemouth,

Scotland, in August of 1901. He was the son of James Ramsay MacDonald, who served as prime minister of Great Britain in 1924 and again from 1929 until 1935. The younger MacDonald attended Oxford University and entered politics in 1923. He was defeated for a seat in Parliament that year and again in 1924. MacDonald was elected to Parliament in 1929 and served in his father's cabinet as undersecretary. He was named colonial secretary in November of 1935 and became secretary of state for dominion affairs in May of 1938. He was appointed to Winston Churchill's cabinet as minister of health in May of 1940 and served until February of 1941. MacDonald subsequently served as Britain's high commissioner in Canada. He was named the first governor-general of the Malayan Union and Singapore in April of 1946 and was named commissioner-general in Southeast Asia in 1948. He remained in that position until 1955, when he was appointed Britain's high commissioner to India, where he remained until 1960. MacDonald was appointed governor-general of Kenya on December 12, 1963. He helped insure the country's stability during its first year of independence. MacDonald retained office until December 12, 1964, when Kenya became a republic. He remained as Britain's high commissioner until 1965. MacDonald continued to represent Great Britain in Africa as a special representative to Commonwealth countries. He retired in 1969 and was awarded the Order of Merit. MacDonald died at his home in Kent at the age of 79 on January 11, 1981.

JOMO KENYATTA (Prime Minister, June 1, 1963–December 12, 1964; President, December 12, 1964–August 22, 1978). Jomo Kenyatta was born at Gatundu in Kiambu District on October 20, 1891 (sources vary, ranging from 1889 to 1897). He was a member of the Kikuyu tribe and attended the Church of Scotland mission school in Kikuyu, near Nairobi. He entered school under the name Kamau wa Ngengi and took the name Johnstone Kamau after he was baptized in 1914. He later was given the name Kenyatta from the beaded belt he always wore. Kenyatta worked in the public works division of the Nairobi municipality as a clerk from 1921. He joined the Young Kikuyu Association the following year. He became general secretary of the Kikuyu Central Association in 1928 and served as editor of the party's newspaper. Kenyatta represented his tribe in London over a land dispute in 1929. He traveled extensively throughout Europe before returning to Kenya. Upon his return his support for the establishment of government schools brought him into conflict with church authorities. Kenyatta returned to Great Britain to study in 1931. He attended Quaker College in Woodbroke until 1933, when he took an assistant's position at the School of African and Oriental Studies in London. He also appeared briefly as an African chief in the 1934 film *Sanders of the River* with actor Paul Robeson. Kenyatta remained in Great Britain during World War II. He married an English girl, Edna Clarke, in 1942. He joined with Kwame Nkrumah and other African nationalists to form the Pan African Federation in 1945. He returned to Kenya in September of 1946 as the leader of the Kenyan nationalist movement. He was elected president of the Kenya African Union (KAU) in 1947, and colonial authorities feared his growing power. A violent nationalist organization known as the Mau Mau was formed in 1948. The activities of that terrorist group prompted colonial officials to declare a state of emergency in October of 1952. Kenyatta and his top aides in the KAU were arrested. Despite evidence that Kenyatta was not associated with the Mau Mau, he was tried and convicted of supporting terrorist activities. He was sentenced to seven years imprisonment and taken to Lokitaung

Prison. The violence in Kenya continued after Kenyatta's imprisonment until the Mau Mau movement was crushed in the mid-1950s. Kenyatta was released from prison in April of 1959, but remained detained in the frontier district of Lodwar. Kenyan nationalists had continued to press the British government for Kenyatta's release, as well as for Kenyan independence. Kenyatta was elected president in absentia of the newly formed Kenya African National Union (KANU) in March of 1960. KANU was victorious in elections to the Kenyan Legislative Council in February of 1961, but refused to form a government while Kenyatta remained detained. The British colonial authorities released Kenyatta on August 21, 1961, and he was elected to the Legislative Assembly in January of 1962. He subsequently served as a minister in the coalition government. Kenyatta was elected prime minister of Kenya on June 1, 1963, and retained that position when Kenya received its independence on December 12, 1963. He became Kenya's president when his country became a republic on December 12, 1964. Kenya was a one-party state until 1967, when Oginga Odinga, who had been dismissed as vice president the previous year, formed the Kenya People's Union (KPU). Tribal violence flared after the assassination of Tom Mboya, a cabinet minister and leading contender to succeed Kenyatta, in July of 1969. Mboya was a member of the Luo tribe, and his death sparked demonstrations and riots. Kenyatta blamed the opposition KPU for the unrest. He banned the party and arrested its leadership. The next threat to Kenyatta's leadership came from J. M. Kariuki, who led a group of radicals in the early 1970s. Kariuki was murdered in 1975 after beginning a campaign of unrest against the government. The government was implicated in Kariuki's death, but no action was taken. Kenyatta's government continued to silence dissent with the arrest of prominent

government critics throughout the 1970s. Kenyatta remained firmly in power until he died peacefully in his sleep at the State House in Mombassa on August 22, 1978.

DANIEL ARAP MOI (President, August 22, 1978–). Torotich arap Moi was born in Sacho, Baringo District, in 1924. He was a member of the small Kalenjin tribe. He attended local mission schools and took the name Daniel when he was baptized. Moi became a schoolteacher in 1945 and became active in politics in 1950. He supported the nationalist movement and was appointed to the Kenyan Legislative Council in 1955. Moi joined the Kenya African National Union (KANU) in 1960 and was elected treasurer of the party. He withdrew from the Luo- and Kikuyu-dominated KANU in 1961 and formed the Kenya African Democratic Union (KADU) to protect the interests of the Kalenjin tribe. He served as chairman of KADU and was named minister of education in the Legislative Council in December of 1961. Moi was appointed minister of local government in the coalition government formed in 1962. KADU was badly defeated in National Assembly elections in 1963, and Moi rejoined KANU the following year. He was appointed minister of home affairs in the Kenyatta government after independence in December of 1964. He was appointed vice president of Kenya in 1967 in order to avoid a power struggle between the Kikuyu and Luo tribes. Moi was a close advisor and trusted aide to Kenyatta, who died on August 22, 1978. Moi succeeded him to the presidency and was confirmed in the position by an election in October of 1978. He continued many of the programs of his predecessor. Moi survived an attempted military coup in August of 1982 and dissolved the Kenyan air force in response. He also detained numerous political opponents who were implicated in the coup attempt. Moi was unopposed for reelection in

August of 1983. He dismissed his powerful minister of constitutional affairs, Charles Njono, whom he considered a potential rival. Njonjo was arrested and tried for conspiracy against the government and other charges. He was convicted, but was later pardoned by the president. Moi's government was faced with student demonstrations and strikes in 1985 and 1986. Moi was again reelected in 1988 and released all political prisoners in an amnesty in June of 1989. Members of the Moi government were implicated in the murder of Foreign Minister Robert Ouko in 1990, and Moi suspended a public investigation into the case. He resisted calls for the democratization of Kenya, though rival parties were established in 1992. Moi's government was also charged by international organizations with human rights abuses. Moi was reelected president, and his ruling government party remained in control of Parliament in elections in December of 1992.

Kiribati, Republic of

(I Kiribati)

Kiribati is a country that consists of numerous atolls in the mid-Pacific Ocean. It was granted independence from Great Britain on July 12, 1979.

HEADS OF STATE

IEREMIA TABAI (President, July 12, 1979–July 3, 1991). Ieremia T. Tabai was born in Nonouti in 1950. He was educated in New Zealand and was elected to the Gilbert Islands House of Assembly in 1974. The Gilbert Islands received limited self-government on November 1, 1976, and Tabai was leader of the opposition party until his election as chief minister in 1978. He became president following full independence of the Gilbert Islands as the Republic of Kiribati on July 12, 1979. He retired as president on July 3, 1991, after having served the full twelve years allowed by law. Tabai subsequently became secretary-general of the South Pacific Forum.

TEATAO TEANNAKI (President, July 3, 1991–). Teatao Teannaki represented Abiang as a member of Kiribati's Parliament. He served as vice president under Ieremia Tabai from 1979. Teannaki also served in the government as minister of home affairs in 1987. He was minister of finance from 1987 until 1991. He was narrowly elected to succeed Tabai as president and took office on July 3, 1991. Teannaki also served in the government as foreign minister from 1992.

Korea, Democratic People's Republic of

(North Korea) (Chosŏn Minchu-chui Inmin Konghwa-guk)

The Democratic People's Republic of Korea is a country in the northern portion of the Korean peninsula in eastern Asia. It was granted independence on September 10, 1948.

HEADS OF STATE

CHOI YONG KUN (Head of State, May 1, 1948–December 28, 1972). Choi Yong Kun was born in Sossok on June 21, 1900. He attended the Yunan Military Academy in the 1920s and joined the Chinese Communist party. He moved to the Soviet Union in 1940 and served in the Soviet Red Army during World War II. Choi returned to the Soviet-occupied area of Korea after the war and served as chief of state security. He served as chairman of the Presidium of the Supreme People's Assembly from May 1, 1948. He also served as minister of defense during the Korean War. Choi remained head of state of the Democratic People's Republic of Korea until December 28, 1972, when Kim Il Sung assumed the presidency of North Korea. Choi remained in the government as first vice president until his death after a long illness at the age of 76 on September 19, 1976.

KIM IL SUNG (Head of State, December 28, 1972–   ). Kim Il Sung was born Kim Song Ju near Pyongyang on April 15, 1912. He accompanied his family to Manchuria as a child. He joined the Communist Youth League and received military training. Kim fought the Japanese following the invasion of Manchuria in 1931. He became the leader of the guerrilla army against the Japanese in Manchuria and Korea. He received further military training in the Soviet Union and served in the Soviet Red Army at Stalingrad in 1942. Kim rose to the rank of general and returned to Korea following the Soviet occupation of the northern sections of Korea above the 38th parallel in August of 1945. He was elected chairman of the Provisional People's Committee of North Korea on February 9, 1946. Kim served as the first secretary-general of the Korean Communist party and became leader of the newly formed North Korean Labor party in July of 1946. The Soviets refused to allow the United Nations Temporary Commission on Korea to enter the north to facilitate the reunification and independence of Korea. A constitution was created to establish the Democratic People's Republic of Korea in February of 1948, and a Supreme National Assembly was elected the following August. Kim was elected premier on September 9, 1948, and North Korea was granted independence the following day. The Republic of Korea in the south had received independence under President Syngman Rhee the previous month. North Korean troops crossed the 38th parallel and invaded the south on June 25, 1950. Kim served as supreme commander of the Korean People's army during the Korean War. The United States and other member nations of the United Nations sent troops in support of the Republic of Korea. The Chinese army entered the fighting on the side of North Korea in October of 1950. The fighting reached a stalemate, and peace talks began in Kaesong in July of 1951. The fighting continued for two years until an armistice was reached on July 27, 1953. After the war Kim sought to consolidate his power in North Korea by eliminating potential rivals. Kim's government initially supported the Chinese in the Sino-Soviet rift, and the Soviet Union cut off aid in 1964. Kim subsequently purged pro-Chinese elements from the party. He relinquished the position of premier on December 28, 1972, to assume the newly created post of president of the Democratic People's Republic of Korea. Kim began to groom his son, Kim Jong Il, as his successor, allowing the young Kim to take a leading role in the government. Kim was erroneously reported to have been assassinated in November of 1986. He subsequently made public appearances to dispel the rumor and was reelected president by the National Assembly in December of 1986. North Korea maintained cordial relations with most other Communist nations. The government also attempted to restore relations with Japan in 1990. North Korea's reluctance to allow inspection of its nuclear facilities damaged the country's relations with the West in the early 1990s.

HEADS OF GOVERNMENT

KIM IL SUNG (Premier, September 9, 1948–December 28, 1972). *See entry under Heads of State.*

KIM IL (Premier, December 28, 1972– April 30, 1976). Kim Il was born in 1911. He joined the Communist party in 1932 and fought the Japanese during Korea's colonial occupation. He served on the Politburo following the independence of the Democratic People's Republic of Korea in 1948. He was named vice-premier in 1956 and served as first vice-premier from 1957. Kim Il was named premier on December 28, 1972, when Kim Il Sung relinquished the position to become president. He retained office until April 30, 1976, when he resigned due to ill health. Kim Il subsequently served as first vice president of the Supreme People's Assembly. He died at the age of 73 on March 9, 1984.

PAK SUNG CHUL (Premier, April 30, 1976–December 15, 1977). Pak Sung Chul was born in 1912. He served on the North Korean Communist party Politburo and was chosen to replace ailing Premier Kim Il on April 30, 1976. Pak was replaced by Li Jong Ok on December 15, 1977.

LI JONG OK (Premier, December 15, 1977–January 27, 1984). Li Jong Ok was a member of the North Korean Communist party. He served in the cabinet as minister of light industry from 1951. He was stripped of his positions in the government and the party in 1970 for failing to meet economic goals in the late 1960s. Li was rehabili-

tated the following year and was named minister of industry in 1972. He subsequently served as chairman of the heavy industry commission and was chosen as deputy premier in November of 1976. Li was chosen to lead a government of technocrats on December 15, 1977. He retained office until January 27, 1984, when he was replaced by Kang Song San. Li was subsequently named vice president of North Korea.

KANG SONG SAN (Premier, January 27, 1984–December 29, 1986). Kang Song San studied economics in Moscow. He was named premier by Marshal Kim Il Sung on January 27, 1984, and served until December 29, 1986. He was again named head of government when he was selected to replace Premier Yong Hyong Muk on December 11, 1992.

LI GUN MO (Premier, December 29, 1986–December 12, 1988). Li Gun Mo served in the North Korean government as minister of machine industry and vice-premier. He was chosen to replace Kang Song San as premier on December 29, 1986, following Kim Il Sung's reelection as president. Li stepped down as premier for reasons of health on December 12, 1988.

YON HYONG MUK (Premier, December 12, 1988–December 11, 1992). Yon Hyong Muk was born on November 3, 1931. He was educated locally and employed as a farm worker. In 1967 Yon was selected as a deputy to the Supreme People's Assembly. He

rose through the ranks to become director of the Central Commmittee of the
Workers Party of Korea. He became a
member of the Central Committee in
November of 1970. Yon served as vice-
premier in the 1980s, and on December 12, 1988, he was selected as premier
of North Korea. He was dismissed by
Kim Il Sung on December 11, 1992, because of North Korea's worsening economic condition.

KANG SONG SAN (Premier, December 11, 1992–   ). *See earlier entry
under Heads of Government.*

Korea, Republic of
(South Korea) (Taehan-min'guk)

*The Republic of Korea is a country in the southern part of the
Korean peninsula in eastern Asia. It was formed in May of 1948.*

HEADS OF STATE

SYNGMAN RHEE (President, July 20,
1948–April 27, 1960). Syngman Rhee
was born to a prominent family in
Whanghae Province on April 26, 1875.
He received a classical education and
became involved in the Korean nationalist movement. He joined the Independence Club in 1894 and campaigned
against government corruption and the
influence of the Japanese. Rhee also
founded the first Korean daily newspaper, *Independence.* He became
leader of the reform movement the following year. He led a student demonstration against the government and
was arrested. Rhee was sentenced to
life imprisonment and was subjected to
six months of torture. He remained imprisoned until 1904, when he was released in a general amnesty. He then
traveled to the United States, where he
continued his education. Korea was annexed by Japan in 1910, and Rhee
returned to Seoul as a representative of
the Young Men's Christian Association
the following year. He coupled his missionary work with a campaign against
the Japanese occupiers. He was again
forced to flee Korea when the Japanese
learned of his activities. Rhee went to
Hawaii, where he established the
Korean Methodist Church. He remained
a leading opponent of the Japanese occupation of Korea and helped to organize the Mansei Revolution in 1919. The
revolution failed, and a Korean provisional government-in-exile was formed
with Rhee as president later in the year.
He joined with other exile leaders in
Shanghai, China, and organized guerrilla activity against the Japanese. He
also worked with the Chinese when the
Japanese invaded Manchuria in the
early 1930s. Rhee remained leader of
the exile group until 1941, when he relinquished his position to rightist leader
Kim Koo. Rhee returned to Korea in
1945, following the defeat of Japan in
World War II. Korea was divided into
United States- and Soviet-controlled
sectors, with the 38th parallel serving as
the dividing line. Rhee campaigned for
an independent, unified Korea. The
sector of Korea occupied by the United
States held elections to the National
Assembly in 1948, and Rhee's supporters received an overwhelming majority.
Rhee was selected by the Assembly to
serve as the independent Republic of
Korea's first president and took office

on July 20, 1948. He supported South Korea's reunification with the Communist-dominated North Korea. Kim Koo, Rhee's leading political rival, was assassinated by an army officer in June of 1949. North Korea invaded South Korea in June of 1950. The Soviet-backed army of North Korea captured Seoul, and Rhee's government was forced to flee to Chinhae. The United Nations condemned the invasion, and the United States and other member nations sent troops to support South Korea. United States troops under General Douglas MacArthur recaptured Seoul, but Rhee's government was again forced to flee in January of 1951, following the intervention of the Chinese Communist army. The South Korean government resettled in Pusan. Rhee was reelected to the presidency in August of 1952. The war continued for the next two years and reached a stalemate. Rhee opposed armistice negotiations in Kaesong and Panmunjom that did not include the reunification of Korea. He jeopardized negotiations by releasing North Korean prisoners of war who wished to remain in South Korea. The peace talks proceeded, and an armistice was reached on July 27, 1953. Rhee continued to serve as president and leader of the conservative Liberal party. His rule became increasingly authoritarian, and he faced opposition from the public and members of the National Assembly. Rhee's Democratic party opponent, P. H. Shinicky, died during the presidential campaign in 1956. Rhee's other opponent, Cho Bong Am, withdrew from the campaign under threats of assassination. Rhee was returned to office unopposed, though Shinicky's running mate, John Myun Chang, was elected vice president. The government arrested Progressive party leader Cho Bong Am and executed him on charges of plotting with North Korea in July of 1959. Chough Pyonk Ok was chosen as the Democratic party nominee to oppose Rhee in the 1960 presidential election.

Rhee chose to call the election after Chough was hospitalized in the United States. Chough died following surgery, and the deadline for naming a new candidate had passed. Chough's vice presidential nominee, John Myun Chang, challenged Rhee's nominee, Lee Ki Poong. Lee was elected in obviously fraudulent balloting, and student rioting took place throughout South Korea. The government declared martial law on April 19, 1960, and the Rhee cabinet resigned two days later. Rhee resigned as leader of the Liberal party later in the month, but demonstrations continued against the government. The police killed over one hundred demonstrators, and Rhee called upon the army to restore order. The army refused to support Rhee's regime, and the president resigned on April 27, 1960. Lee Ki Poong committed suicide with his family the following day. Rhee went into exile in Hawaii. He was refused permission to return to Korea in 1962. He suffered a stroke in March of 1962, and his health prevented his return to Korea the following year when the government relented to allow his reentry. Rhee remained hospitalized in Honolulu, where his health continued to deteriorate. He died of a stroke at the age of 90 on July 19, 1965.

HO CHONG (President, April 27, 1960–August 12, 1960). Ho Chong was born in 1896. He was active in the Korean nationalist movement during the Japanese occupation. He served in various government positions after the establishment of the Republic of Korea in 1948. Ho Chong was named foreign minister in the government of Syngman Rhee in April of 1960. He succeeded to the presidency in the absence of a vice president when Rhee was forced to resign on April 27, 1960. He remained acting president until the election of Yun Po Sun by the National Assembly on August 12, 1960. Ho Chong was nominated for the presidency by the Party of the People in

1963, but withdrew from the campaign before the election was held. He was a critic of the subsequent military regime and was banned from political activities by the government of Chung Hee Park. He died after a long illness at his home in Seoul at the age of 92 on September 18, 1988.

YUN PO SUN (President, August 12, 1960–March 22, 1962). Yun Po Sun was born in Asan, Chungchongnam, in 1897. He was educated at the University of Edinburgh in Scotland. He returned to Korea and was elected mayor of Seoul following the establishment of the Republic of Korea in 1948. Yun joined the Democratic party in opposition to the government of Syngman Rhee and was elected to the National Assembly in 1954. He was selected as president of South Korea on August 12, 1960, following student demonstrations that forced the ouster of Rhee. Yun's government was ousted by a military coup led by Maj. Gen. Chung Hee Park in May of 1961. Yun remained as a figurehead president during the subsequent military government. He resigned from office in protest of Park's authoritarian rule on March 22, 1962. Yun challenged Park in presidential elections in 1963 and was narrowly defeated. He was again defeated by Park for the presidency in 1967. He remained a leading critic of the Park government and was arrested on several occasions for antigovernment activity. Park was assassinated in October of 1979, and Yun was tried for organizing a protest against the subsequent military government. He was given a two-year suspended sentence and retired from political affairs. He died at his home in Seoul from complications from diabetes at the age of 92 on July 18, 1990.

CHUNG HEE PARK (President, March 24, 1962–October 26, 1979). Chung Hee Park (Pak) was born in Sangmo-ri, Kyongsang-pukdo Province, on September 30, 1917. He was educated in Korea and worked as a teacher after his graduation in 1937. Park entered the Manchukuo Military Academy under the Japanese administration of Korea in 1940. He entered the Japanese Imperial Military Academy two years later and graduated in 1944. Park served in the Japanese army as a lieutenant in Manchuria during World War II. He returned to Korea following Japan's defeat in August of 1945. He entered the Korean Military Academy and was commissioned as a captain in the Korean army in December of 1946. Park was arrested and court-martialed on charges of conspiring against the government in 1948. He was spared from prosecution by serving as a witness against the other conspirators. Park returned to the army and rose to the rank of brigadier general during the Korean War. He served in various military positions during the 1950s and was promoted to major general in 1958. He was also given command of the First Army in 1958. President Syngman Rhee was forced to resign from office in April of 1960. Park led a military coup to overthrow the subsequent government of Premier John Myun Chang in May of 1961. Park served as vicechairman of the ruling Supreme Council for National Reconstruction. He replaced Chang Do Young as chairman of the ruling military junta in July of 1961. Park became acting president of the Republic of Korea on March 24, 1962. He also served briefly as premier from June 18 until July 9 of 1962. Park retired from the army as a full general in August of 1963 to be the governmentsponsored Democratic Republican party candidate in presidential elections the following October. He narrowly defeated Yun Po Sun and was sworn into office in December of 1963. He led the government in establishing diplomatic and trade relations with Japan in August of 1965, despite demonstrations against his policy. He was also successful in leading Korea to economic prosperity. Park again defeated Yun

Po Sun in presidential elections in May of 1967. Park was a supporter of the United States policy in Vietnam and committed Korean troops to the military action there. He was the target of an unsuccessful North Korean assassination plot in January of 1968. A referendum was passed in October of 1969 to allow Park to run for a third term in office. He defeated Kim Dae Jung in a close contest in 1971. Park declared martial law in October of 1972 and amended the constitution to grant himself near dictatorial powers. Park jailed opposition political leaders as dissent to his rule continued to grow. Park's wife, Yook Young Soo, was killed in an unsuccessful assassination attempt against the president on August 15, 1974. He was also faced with international criticism for human rights abuses in the country. Park was assassinated by South Korean intelligence chief Kim Jae Kyu while at a dinner party in Seoul on October 26, 1979.

CHOI KYU HAH (President, October 26, 1979–August 16, 1980). Choi Kyu Hah was born in Wonju City on July 16, 1919. He was educated in Japan and Manchuria. He returned to Korea to teach at the Seoul National University in 1945. He worked in the Ministry of Foreign Affairs as director of the Economic Affairs Bureau from 1951 until 1952. Choi was then named consul general to Japan, where he served until 1957. He served as vice-minister of foreign affairs from 1959 until 1960. He was appointed ambassador to Malaysia in 1964 and served until his appointment as minister of foreign affairs in 1967. Choi retained that position until 1971, when he was named special presidential assistant for foreign affairs. He became acting premier on December 19, 1975, and remained premier until December 19, 1979. He became acting president following the assassination of Chung Hee Park on October 26, 1979. Choi resigned his position on August 16, 1980.

PARK CHOONG HOON (Acting President, August 16, 1980–August 27, 1980). Park Choong Hoon was born in Cheju-Do Province on January 19, 1919. He was educated in Japan and returned to Korea in 1947 to work with the Ministry of Commerce and Industry. He subsequently served in the Korean air force and retired as a major general in 1961. Park served as vice-minister of commerce and industry in 1961 and was named minister in 1963. He was deputy premier and minister of economic planning from 1967 until 1969. He served on the Korea–United States Economic Council from 1974 until 1980. Park served as premier from May 21, 1980, until September 2, 1980. He was also acting president from August 16 until August 27, 1980. He subsequently was active in the Korea Industrial Development Research Institute.

CHUN DOO HWAN (President, August 27, 1980–February 25, 1988). Chun Doo Hwan was born in Kyongsangnamdo Province on January 18, 1931. He attended the Korean Military Academy and was commissioned into the army in 1955. He rose through the ranks and served in various capacities in the Korean military. Chun was named senior aide to the chief of staff in 1969 and commanded a regiment in Vietnam the following year. He became commander of the Defense Security Command in 1979 and was acting director of the Korean CIA from April until June of 1980. He was promoted to general shortly before his retirement from the army in 1980. He was elected president of Korea and took office on August 27, 1980. He also served as president of the Democratic Justice party from 1981. A Korean Air Lines passenger plane was shot down by a Soviet jet fighter in September of 1983 when the plane strayed into Soviet air space. Chun narrowly survived a bomb blast in Rangoon, Burma, on October 9, 1983, while on a state visit. The blast killed economic advisor Kim Jae Ik, Deputy Premier Suh Suk Joon, Foreign Minister Lee Bum Suk, and other members of the government. Chun accused North Korea of complicity in the attack. Chun's government faced increasing criticism from leaders of the opposition. He stepped down as leader of the Democratic Justice party in 1987. Roh Tae Woo was elected president in December of 1987, and Chun relinquished office on February 25, 1988. Chun Doo Hwan was accused of corruption and abuse of power after leaving office. He made a public apology on November 23, 1988, for human rights abuses that occurred during his term of office. He then went into internal exile at a Buddhist temple in the Sorak mountains. Chun Doo Hwan returned from exile in December of 1990.

ROH TAE WOO (President, February 25, 1988–February 25, 1993). Roh Tae Woo was born in Taegu on December 4, 1932. He was educated at military schools and served in the South Korean army during the Korean War in 1950. He rose through the ranks and retired as a four-star general in 1981. Roh subsequently served as minister of

state for national security and foreign affairs until 1982. He held several other cabinet positions and was chairman of the Democratic Justice party from 1985 until 1987. He succeeded Chun Doo Hwan as president of the party in July of 1987. Roh was the Democratic Justice party's candidate for president in elections in December of 1987. The opposition was divided between Kim Dae Jung and Kim Young Sam, and Roh received a plurality of the votes. He took office on February 25, 1988, and presided over the Olympic Games that were held in Seoul in September of 1988. Roh reorganized the cabinet in December of 1988 to eliminate the remaining holdovers from the previous administration. He also negotiated the merger of the ruling Democratic Justice party with two opposition parties in January of 1990 to form the Democratic Liberal party. His government continued to be faced with demonstrations against its domestic policies. Roh remained as president until his term expired on February 25, 1993. He was replaced by Kim Young Sam, his former political rival, who was elected as the candidate of Roh's ruling Democratic Liberal party.

HEADS OF GOVERNMENT

LEE BUM SUK (Premier, August 2, 1948–April 22, 1950). Lee Bum Suk (Yi Bom Sok) was born in Seoul on December 12, 1900. He received military training in China and Manchuria. He formed a nationalist Korean army to fight against the Japanese occupation forces in Korea. Lee's troops scored a major victory against the Japanese on the Manchurian plains in 1919, but he was forced to withdraw to Russia. He soon returned to China and fought with the Manchurian army against the Japanese invasion in the early 1930s. Lee served as chief of the general staff of the Chinese 51st Army during the

Sino-Japanese War. He established the Korean Restoration Army during World War II and was the wartime commander of the anti-Japanese Korean forces in China. The Japanese surrendered to the Allies in August of 1945. The Japanese occupying forces north of the 38th parallel surrendered to the Soviet Union, and the remainder surrendered to the United States. Lee returned to the United States–occupied area of Korea later in the year. He formed the paramilitary Korean National Youth Organization. The Republic of Korea, or South Korea, was formed on May 10, 1948, and Lee was selected by the National Assembly to serve as the nation's first premier. His selection was confirmed on August 2, 1948. He also served as minister of defense until March of 1949. Lee remained premier until April 22, 1950, when he resigned from office following the government's abolition of his youth corps as an official organization. He remained a leading military figure in South Korea and was placed in command of the police as minister of home affairs in May of 1952. He was the Liberal party nominee for vice president of the republic the following July. President Syngman Rhee considered Lee a potential rival and engineered his defeat. Lee's supporters were subsequently purged from the party and the government. Lee remained largely inactive in political affairs after his defeat and died in 1972.

SHIN SUNG MO (Premier, April 22, 1950–November 23, 1950). Shin Sung Mo was born in 1891. He served as minister of defense in the government of Lee Bum Suk. Following the resignation of Lee on April 22, 1950, Shin was appointed acting premier, despite massive opposition from the National Assembly. He remained head of the government until the appointment of John Myun Chang as premier on November 23, 1950. Shin remained in the government as minister of defense until April 25, 1951, when he resigned following a public outcry against the summary executions of several hundred alleged Communist collaborators. Shin died in 1960.

JOHN MYUN CHANG (Premier, November 23, 1950–April 20, 1952). John Myun Chang was born in Seoul on August 28, 1899. He was educated in Korea and the United States and received a degree from Manhattan College in New York. He returned to Korea in 1926 to work as a teacher at Catholic missionary schools. Chang later served as a principal at a Seoul

high school. He was elected to the provisional Representative Democratic Council in the United States–occupied area of Korea following the defeat of Japan in 1945. South Korea was granted independence as the Republic of Korea in May of 1948, and Chang was elected to the National Assembly. He was named South Korea's representative to the United Nations later in the year and attempted to negotiate South Korea's entry into the United Nations. Chang was appointed Korea's ambassador to the United States in January of 1949. He was nominated premier on November 23, 1950, and returned to Seoul to take office on January 28, 1951. He resigned on April 20, 1952, for reasons of health. Chang broke with the Rhee government and went into opposition over the government autocratic rule. He was a founder and leader of the Democratic party and was the party's candidate for vice president in 1956. He received minor injuries in an assassination attempt in 1956, but went on to defeat Rhee's nominee, Lee Ki Poong. Chang served as vice president under Rhee and remained a leader of the opposition to president. He was defeated by Lee Ki Poong for reelection in 1960 in fraudulent balloting. Rhee was forced to resign in April of 1960, and Chang was elected premier by the National Assembly on August 12, 1960. Chang's government was forced from office in a military coup led by Maj. Gen. Chung Hee Park on May 18, 1961. Chang was prevented from engaging in political activities by the subsequent military government. Chang was hospitalized in January of 1966 and died at his home in Seoul of cirrhosis of the liver at the age of 67 on June 4, 1966.

LEE YUN YUNG (Acting Premier, April 24, 1952–May 1952). Lee Yun Yung was born in 1871. He served as minister without portfolio in the government of John Myun Chang. He was named acting premier on April 24,

1942, following the resignation of Chang. He was replaced by Chang Taek-Sang in May of 1952.

CHANG TAEK-SANG (Premier, May 1952–October 5, 1952). Chang Taek-sang (T. S. Chang) was born in 1893. He served as chief of police in Seoul before being appointed foreign minister in the first government of the Republic of Korea under Lee Bum Suk in 1948. He was elected vice-speaker of the National Assembly in 1950. Chang was appointed premier in May of 1952. He resigned on October 5, 1952, following accusations that he allowed the former Japanese mayor of occupied Seoul to enter the country without a permit. He died in Seoul of lung cancer on August 1, 1969.

PAIK TOO CHIN (Premier, April 24, 1953–June 24, 1954). Paik Too Chin was born on October 31, 1908. He graduated from the Tokyo Community College in 1934. He served in the cabinet as minister of finance in 1951. Paik Too Chin served as acting premier from September of 1952 and was appointed premier on April 24, 1953. He resigned from office on June 18, 1954. Paik Too Chin was again named premier by President Chung Hee Park on December 19, 1970. He presided over the government during the elections of 1971 that returned Park to office as president. Paik Too Chin was replaced by Kim Jong Pil on June 3, 1971.

PYUN YUNG TAI (Premier, June 28, 1954–July 31, 1955). Pyun Yung Tai (Y. T. Pyun) was born in Seoul in 1893. He was educated in Korea and Manchuria. He returned to Korea in 1916 to teach high school English. Pyun became an English professor at Korea University following the ouster of the Japanese occupation government in 1945. He entered government service in 1949 when he was sent by President Syngman Rhee on a diplomatic mission to the Philippines. Pyun was named to the cabinet as foreign minister in 1951. He negotiated the mutual defense treaty between South Korea and the United States after the Korean War ended in 1953. Pyun was also named premier on June 28, 1954. He resigned from the government on July 31, 1955, and returned to his position at Korea University. Pyun reentered politics in 1963, when he was an unsuccessful candidate for the presidency against Chung Hee Park. He lost his home and was nearly bankrupted during the course of the campaign. Pyun took a position as an English teacher at a private school. His health failed in December of 1968, and he died of a cerebral thrombosis at his home in Seoul at the age of 76 on March 10, 1969.

JOHN MYUN CHANG (Premier, August 12, 1960–May 18, 1961). *See earlier entry under Heads of Government.*

CHANG DO YONG (Premier, May 18, 1961–July 3, 1961). Chang Do Yong was born in 1923. He was educated in Japan and served in the Japanese army during World War II. He was named deputy commander in chief of the South Korean army in 1956 and subsequently became army chief of staff. Chang participated in the military coup that ousted Premier John Myun Chang in May of 1961. He served as chairman of the Supreme Council of National Reconstruction from May 18, 1961, until his ouster by Gen. Chung Hee Park on July 3, 1961. Chang was arrested after his ouster, and he was sentenced to death in January of the following year. His sentence was commuted, however, and he was released later in the year.

CHUNG HEE PARK (Premier, July 3, 1961–January 2, 1962). *See entry under Heads of State.*

SONG YO CHAN (Premier, January 2, 1962–June 16, 1962). Song Yo Chan was born in 1919. He served in the Korean army, where he rose to the rank of lieutenant general. He participated in the military coup that ousted the government of John Myun Chang in May of 1961 and served in the subsequent military junta as foreign minister. He was named chairman of the Economic Planning Board in 1962. Song was named premier in the military government of Chung Hee Park on January 2, 1962. He resigned on June 16, 1962, following the government's currency reform policy. He was nominated for the presidency by the Liberal Democratic party in 1963, but withdrew from the campaign before the election was held.

CHUNG HEE PARK (Premier, June 18, 1962–July 9, 1962). *See entry under Heads of State.*

KIM HYUN CHUL (Premier, July 10, 1962–December 12, 1963). Kim Hyun Chul was born in 1901. He served in the government as director of the Economic Planning Board before being named premier on July 10, 1962, after the resignation of Song Yo Chan. He was replaced on December 12, 1963, following elections to the National Assembly. He died in 1989.

CHOI DOO SUN (Premier, December 12, 1963–May 9, 1964). Choi Doo Sun was born in 1894. He was the publisher of *Dong-A Ilbo*, South Korea's largest newspaper, from 1947. Choi was chosen by Chung Hee Park to be South Korea's premier on December 12, 1963, after Park's election to the presidency. Choi resigned from office on May 9, 1964, following protests against the government's plans to restore diplomatic relations with Japan. Choi later served as president of the Korean Red Cross from 1971 until 1973. He died in Seoul at the age of 80 on September 9, 1974.

CHUNG IL KWON (Premier, May 11, 1964–December 19, 1970). Chung Il Kwon was born on November 21, 1917. He attended military schools in Japan, the United States, and Great Britain. He served in the Korean military and became army chief of staff and then chairman of the Joint Chiefs of Staff. Following his retirement from the military, he served in various diplomatic posts, including ambassador to the United States. He served as minister of foreign affairs in 1963, and on May 11, 1964, he was named premier. He retained that position until December 19, 1970. Chung was elected to the National Assembly in 1971 and became chairman of the Democratic Republican party the following year. He served as Speaker of the National Assembly from 1973 until 1979. Chung died of cancer at a hospital in Hawaii at the age of 76 on January 17, 1994.

PAIK TOO CHIN (Premier, December 19, 1970–June 3, 1971). *See earlier entry under Heads of Government.*

KIM JONG PIL (Premier, June 3, 1971–December 19, 1975). Kim Jong Pil was born in Puyo on January 7, 1926. He was educated at the Seoul National University and the Korean Military Academy. He served in the Korean army and saw action during the Korean War in the early 1950s. Kim served as director of the Korean Central Intelligence Agency from 1961 until 1963. He was elected to the National Assembly in 1963 as a member of the Democratic Republican party and also served as leader of the party from 1963 until 1968. Kim served as an advisor to the president in 1970. He was named premier on June 3, 1971, and retained office until December 19, 1975.

CHOI KYU HAH (Premier, December 19, 1975–December 10, 1979). *See entry under Heads of State.*

SHIN HYON HWAK (Premier, December 10, 1979–May 20, 1980). Shin Hyon Hwak was born in 1920. He served in the government of Choi Kyu Hah as deputy premier and director of the Economic Planning Board. He was named to succeed Choi as premier on December 10, 1979, following the assassination of President Chung Hee Park and Choi's assumption of that position. Shin resigned from office on May 20, 1980, after a military takeover of the government.

PARK CHOONG HOON (Acting Premier, May 21, 1980–September 2, 1980). *See entry under Heads of State.*

NAM DUCK WOO (Premier, September 2, 1980–January 3, 1982). Nam Duck Woo was born on October 10, 1924. He was educated in South Korea and the United States. He was employed by the Bank of Korea from 1952 until 1954. Nam then accepted a position in the economics department at Kook Min College, where he remained until 1964. He was appointed minister of finance in 1969 and subsequently worked with the International Monetary Fund and World Bank. He was named deputy premier and minister of economic planning in 1974 and served until 1978. Nam was a special assistant to the president for economic affairs in 1979 and was appointed premier on September 2, 1980. He was the architect of the country's high-growth and high-inflation economic policies. Nam's management of the economy led to his replacement as premier on January 3, 1982.

YOO CHANG SOON (Premier, January 3, 1982–June 24, 1982). Yoo Chang Soon was born in Anju, Pyongan Namdo, on August 6, 1918. He was educated at Hastings College in the United States and was employed by the Bank of Korea on his return to the country. He served as governor of the Bank of Korea from 1961 until 1962, when he was appointed minister of commerce and industry. In February of 1963 he was named chairman of the Economic Planning Board. He returned to private life in December of 1963. On January 3, 1982, Yoo Chang Soon was asked to form a government as premier. He was given a mandate to help settle South Korea's economic problems. A financial scandal implicated many members of the government in May of 1982, and Yoo Chang Soon resigned on June 24, 1982. He was subsequently named president of the Republic of Korea's National Red Cross.

KIM SANG HYUP (Premier, June 24, 1982–October 14, 1983). Kim Sang Hyup was born on April 20, 1920. He attended Tokyo University and served as a professor at Korea University from 1946 until 1962. He was then appointed minister of education. Kim returned to Korea University as president in 1970 and served until 1975 and again from 1977 until 1982. He was appointed premier on June 24, 1982. Kim retained the position until October 14, 1983, shortly after four members of his cabinet were killed in a terrorist bombing in Rangoon, Burma.

CHIN IEE CHONG (Premier, October 14, 1983–February 18, 1985). Chin Iee Chong was born in Kochang on December 13, 1921. He was educated in Seoul and worked in the Ministry of Commerce and Industry from 1943. He was director of the Bureau of Mines from 1948 until 1952 and subsequently practiced law. Chin was elected to the National Assembly in 1971. He served as minister of health and social affairs from 1979 until 1981. He was elected chairman of the ruling Democratic Justice party in 1983 and was appointed premier on October 14, 1983. Chin was replaced on February 18, 1985, following disappointing election results for the Democratic Justice party.

LHO SHIN YONG (Premier, February 18, 1985–May 26, 1987). Lho Shin Yong was born in the South Pyongyang Province on February 28, 1930. He was educated in Korea and the United States. He joined the diplomatic corps in 1966 and worked in the Ministry of Foreign Affairs from 1967. Lho was appointed consul-general in Los Angeles in 1969 and served until 1972. He was named ambassador to India in 1973 and to Switzerland in 1976. He was named foreign minister in 1980 and served until 1982, when he became director of the Agency of National Security Planning. Lho was appointed premier on February 18, 1985. He resigned on May 26, 1987, following revelations of a police cover-up of the torture and murder of a student dissident.

LEE HAN KEY (Premier, May 26, 1987–July 13, 1987). Lee Han Key was born in 1910. He was a law professor at Seoul National University before he was appointed premier by President Chun Doo Hwan on May 26, 1987. He was replaced by Kim Chung Yul on July 13, 1987.

KIM CHUNG YUL (Premier, July 13, 1987–February 25, 1988). Kim Chung Yul was born in Seoul in 1917. He served in the South Korean air force following World War II and was chief of staff of the air force in the late 1940s. During the Korean War he served as chief of the Korean armed forces. He was minister of national defense from 1957 until 1962. Kim served as ambassador to the United States from 1963 until 1966. He was subsequently elected to the National Assembly. He was named premier on July 13, 1987, by President Chun Doo Hwan, and he was instrumental in arranging general elections for the country. He remained premier until February 25, 1988, when he was replaced by the newly elected president, Roh Tae Woo. Kim died after a long illness on September 7, 1992.

LEE HYUN JAE (Premier, February 25, 1988–December 5, 1988). Lee Hyun Jae was a leading Korean economist and a former professor at Seoul National University. He was a moderate who had opposed the government's crackdown on students in 1985. Lee was named premier by newly elected President Roh Tae Woo on February 25, 1988. President Roh replaced the cabinet and dismissed Lee as premier on December 5, 1988.

KANG YOUNG HOON (Premier, December 5, 1988–December 27, 1990). Kang Young Hoon was born on May 30, 1922. He was educated in Manchuria and the United States. He served in the South Korean army and was a military attaché to the Korean Embassy in Washington, D.C., from 1952 until 1953. Kang served as assistant minister of defense from 1955 until 1956 and retired from the army in 1961. He subsequently lectured and taught at various universities in Korea and the United States. Kang was appointed ambassador to Great Britain in 1981 and served until 1984. He served as ambassador to the Vatican from 1985 until 1988. He returned to Korea to serve as premier on December 5, 1988. Public support for the government dwindled during the late 1980s, and Kang was replaced as premier on December 27, 1990.

RO JAI BONG (Premier, December 27, 1990–May 24, 1991). Ro Jai Bong was born in Masan in South Kyongsang Province. He served as chief presidential secretary from March of 1990 until his appointment as premier on December 27, 1990. Ro was replaced as premier on May 24, 1991, following a series of street demonstrations against the government.

CHUNG WON SHIK (Premier, May 24, 1991–October 7, 1992). Chung Won Shik was born in 1929. He served as minister of education from 1988 until 1990. He subsequently served as South Korea's envoy to Africa. Chung was appointed to replace Ro Jai Bong as premier on May 24, 1991. He resigned the position on October 7, 1992, following a poor showing by the Democratic Liberal party in elections to the National Assembly.

HYUN SOONG JONG (Premier, October 7, 1992–February 22, 1993).

Hyun Soong Jong was a leading South Korean law professor and university president. He was a political independent and was selected as premier of a caretaker government on October 7, 1992. His government was charged to supervise elections in December of 1992. He retained office until February 22, 1993, when newly elected President Kim Young Sam appointed Hwang In Sung to form a government.

Kuwait, State of
(Dawlat al-Kuwayt)

Kuwait is a country in the northeastern section of the Arabian peninsula. It was granted independence from Great Britain on June 19, 1961.

HEADS OF STATE

ABDULLAH AS-SALIM AS-SABAH (Emir, February 25, 1950–November 24, 1965). Abdullah as-Salim as-Sabah was born in Kuwait in 1895. He was the eldest son of Sheikh Salim al-Mubarak. Sheikh Salim ruled Kuwait from 1917 until 1921. Abdullah served as chancellor of the Exchequer in the government during World War II. He succeeded his cousin Sheikh Ahmad al-Jabir al-Sabah as sultan of Kuwait on February 25, 1950. Kuwait became a leading oil-producing nation, and Sheikh Abdullah used much of the country's wealth for the welfare of the Kuwaiti people. Kuwait was granted independence from Great Britain on June 19, 1961, and Sheikh Abdullah was formally designated emir. The country was threatened by Iraqi president Abdul Karim Kassem, who claimed that Kuwait was a legitimate district of Iraq. The British sent military units to the region to protect the sovereignty of Kuwait. Kuwait was admitted to the United Nations in 1963. Sheikh

Abdullah's government continued to provide free medical care for his people. He also improved the educational facilities in the country. He remained Kuwait's leader until his death from a heart attack at the age of 70 on November 24, 1965.

SABAH AS-SALIM AS-SABAH (Emir, November 24, 1965–December 31, 1977). Sabah as-Salim as-Sabah was born in 1913. He served in the government of his brother, Sheikh Abdullah, as foreign minister following Kuwait's independence in June of 1961. He was named prime minister on February 2, 1963. Sheikh Sabah succeeded his brother as emir of Kuwait on November 24, 1965. He continued his brother's policies of providing public welfare to the Kuwaiti people. He decreased oil production in the country to preserve Kuwait's oil reserves and was a leader of the oil embargo following the Middle East war in 1973. The sheikdom maintained the highest per capita gross national product in the world under Sheikh Sabah. He suffered several heart attacks in 1976 and turned over many of his duties to the crown prince, Sheikh Jabir al Ahmed al-Jabir as-Sabah. Sheikh Sabah died of a heart attack at the age of 65 on December 31, 1977.

JABIR AL-AHMED AL-JABIR AS-SABAH (Emir, December 31, 1977–). Jabir al-Ahmed al-Jabir as-Sabah was born on June 29, 1926. He was the son of Sheikh Ahmad al-Jabir al-Sabah, who served as Kuwait's sultan from 1921 until 1950. He was educated locally and served as governor of Ahmadi from 1949 until 1959. Sheikh Jabir led the Kuwait Department of Finance and Economy from 1959 and served in the cabinet as minister of finance from 1962 until 1965. Sheikh Jabir was named prime minister on December 4, 1965, following the death of Sheikh Abdullah and the succession of Sheikh Sabah to the throne. Sheikh Jabir was named crown prince to Sheikh Sabah on May 31, 1966. Sheikh Sabah suffered from poor health later in his reign and turned over many of the duties of state to Sheikh Jabir. Sheikh Jabir succeeded as emir upon the death of Sheikh Sabah on December 31, 1977. Sheikh Jabir's government was threatened by a growing Islamic fundamentalist movement by Shi'ite Muslims in Kuwait following the ouster of the shah of Iran in 1979. Sheikh Jabir supported Iraq financially in its war against Iran during the 1980s. The sheikh survived an assassination attempt in the early 1980s, and Kuwaiti airplanes were hijacked by pro–Iranian militants. Kuwait cut off financial support to Iraq following the conclusion of the war in 1988. Iraq's president, Saddam Hussein, launched an invasion of Kuwait on August 2, 1990. Sheikh Jabir and most of the royal family escaped from the country and went into exile in Saudi Arabia. The United States led a multinational force to liberate Kuwait from its Iraqi occupiers. Iraq was forced to withdraw, and Sheikh Jabir returned to take control of the country in March of 1991. The sheikh was faced with demands for democratic reforms in the country. He was also criticized for his government's harsh treatment of alleged Iraqi collaborators and antigovernment critics.

HEADS OF GOVERNMENT

SABAH AS-SALIM AS-SABAH (Prime Minister, February 2, 1963–November 24, 1965). *See entry under Heads of State.*

JABIR AL-AHMED AL-JABIR AS-SABAH (Prime Minister, December 4, 1965–December 31, 1977). *See entry under Heads of State.*

SAAD ABDULLA AL-SALIM AS-SABAH (Prime Minister, February 8, 1978–). Saad Abdulla al-Salim as-Sabah was born in 1930. He was the son of Sheikh Abdullah as-Salim as-Sabah, who ruled Kuwait from 1950 until 1965. Sheikh Saad was named crown prince upon the ascension of Sheikh Jabir as emir of Kuwait on December 31, 1977. He was named prime minister on February 8, 1978. He was reappointed to the position in March of 1985. Saad's cabinet resigned in March of 1991, following the ouster of the Iraqi occupation army and the restoration of the Kuwaiti government. Sheikh Saad formed a new government the following month. The opposition party won a majority in the National Assembly on October 5, 1992, but Saad was reappointed prime minister on October 12, 1992. He formed a government that included several members of the Opposition.

Kyrgyzstan, Republic of
(Kyrgyzstan Respublikasy)

Kyrgyszstan is a country in central Asia. It received independence following the breakup of the Soviet Union on December 25, 1991.

HEAD OF STATE

ASKAR AKAYEV (President, October 28, 1990–). Askar Akayev was elected president of Kirghizia on October 28, 1990. Kirghizia declared itself an independent state in September of 1991, and Akayev was reelected president on October 12, 1991. Kirghizia became a member of the Commonwealth of Independent States as the Republic of Kyrgyzstan in December of 1991.

HEADS OF GOVERNMENT

NASIRIDIN ISANOV (Prime Minister, January 22, 1991–November 29, 1991). Nasiridin Isanov served as vice president of Kirghizia prior to being named head of the cabinet on January 22, 1991. He retained the position until he was killed in an automobile accident on November 29, 1991.

TURSUNBEK CHYNGYSHEV (Prime Minister, November 29, 1991–). Tursunbek Chyngyshev was selected to succeed Nasiridin Isanov as prime minister of Kirghizia. He was confirmed to office by the Supreme Council on November 29, 1991.

Laos (Lao People's Democratic Republic)
(Sathalanalat Paxathipatai Paxaxôn Lao)

Laos is a country in central Southeast Asia. It was granted independence from the French on October 23, 1953.

HEADS OF STATE

SISAVANG VONG (King, March 24, 1904–August 21, 1959). Sisavang Vong was born in Luang Prabang on July 14, 1885. He was the son of King Zakarine and Queen Tiao Thongsi. Laos became a semi-independent kingdom under the protection of France in 1893. Sisavang Vong was educated in Saigon and Paris. He succeeded to the throne of Luang Prabang on March 24, 1904, following the death of his father. He had 13 wives and over 50 children, though he lost 14 sons as a result of a canoe accident. He ruled peacefully under the French administration until World War II. The Vichy government of France allowed the Japanese to use Laos as a base of military operations during World War II. The Japanese declared Laos independent of France in March of 1945. Japan surrendered to the Allies the following August, and France began to reassert its authority over its empire. The Lao-Issara, or Free Laos, party forced Sisavang Vong's abdication in September of 1945 and declared Laos an independent state. French troops arrived in Indochina in early 1946 and forced the Lao-Issara government into retreat. Sisavang Vong was reestablished as king of Luang Prabang and the two other Lao-speaking provinces, Champassac and Vientiane, and thus became monarch of a unified Laos in the summer of 1946. Sisavang Vong sponsored a constitution that made Laos a parliamentary monarchy in May of 1947. Laos signed a treaty with France in June of 1949 that granted the kingdom limited self-government as an associated state within the French Union. Pro-Communist Pathet Laos rebels were assisted by Viet-Minh troops in an invasion of Laos in 1953. The king refused to leave the capital as the rebels advanced. The rebels withdrew to northern Laos before reaching the capital. Sisavang Vong's son, Crown Prince Savang Vatthana, visited France in October of 1953 to sign a treaty establishing Laos as an independent nation. The king suffered from arthritis and became increasingly infirm during the 1950s. He relinquished many of his duties to the crown prince. Sisavang Vong died of cancer at the age of 74 at the Royal Palace in Luang Prabang on October 29, 1959.

SAVANG VATTHANA (King, August 21, 1959–December 2, 1975). Savang Vatthana was born in Luang Prabang on November 13, 1907. He was the son of King Sisavang Vong. He studied law and political science in Hanoi and Paris. Savang Vatthana was

appointed secretary-general of the Laotian Kingdom in 1930 and was recognized as crown prince in 1941. He was named by his father as prime minister in April of 1946 and retained that position until March of 1947. He was proclaimed regent on August 21, 1959, when his father suffered from a serious illness. Savang Vatthana succeeded his father as king when Sisavang Vong died on October 29, 1959. He attempted to mediate during the period of civil war in the late 1950s and early 1960s. He was forced to abdicate when the monarchy was abolished on December 2, 1975, following the Communist takeover of Laos. Savang Vatthana was named advisor to the new government, but instead retired from public life. He was sent to a reeducation center in northeast Laos in 1977 and reportedly died of natural causes in 1981.

PRINCE SOUPHANOUVANG (President, December 2, 1975–October 31, 1986). Souphanouvang was born in 1912. He was the son of Prince Boun Khong and was the half-brother of Prince Souvanna Phouma. He was educated in Paris and received a degree in engineering. Souphanouvang returned to Laos in 1938 to work in the civil service in the colonial government of French Indochina. He was posted to Vietnam, where he met Vietnamese nationalist leader Ho Chi Minh. Souphanouvang became a leader of the Laotian nationalist movement. He became active in the Lao Issara, or Free Laos, movement and helped establish a provisional independent government in Laos in 1945. The French returned to claim power the following year, and Souphanouvang was forced to flee to Thailand. He left the Lao Issara to form the more radical Pathet Lao. He participated in an invasion of Laos by Viet-Minh and Pathet Lao forces that captured two provinces in northern Laos in the early 1950s. The Pathet Lao reached an agreement with the royal government of Souvanna Phouma in

1956, and Souphanouvang joined the government as minister of planning, reconstruction, and urbanism in 1958. The Souvanna Phouma government collapsed, and a rightist government was established the following year. Souphanouvang was arrested by the new government and placed under house arrest. He escaped in May of 1960 and rejoined the Pathet Lao as its leader. Souphanouvong returned to the government in 1962 following negotiations in Geneva, Switzerland, to end the civil war in Laos. He served as vice-premier and minister of economic planning in the government of Souvanna Phouma. The government collapsed the following year, and Souphanouvang was again arrested. He escaped from prison and set up a rebel government in Sam Neua Province in northern Laos. He returned to the capital in 1974 to serve as chief of the Joint National Political Council in a government dominated by the Pathet Lao. The Pathet Lao took full control of the country in December of 1975. The monarchy was abolished on December 2, 1975, and Souphanouvang became president of the Lao People's Democratic Republic. He reportedly suffered a stroke in September of 1986 and stepped down as president on October 31, 1986. He remained a member of the Politburo until 1991.

PHOUMI VONGVICHIT (President, October 31, 1986–August 15, 1991). Phoumi Vongvichit was a leading figure in the Pathet Lao and a close aide to Prince Souphanouvang. He was given the post of minister of religious affairs in the coalition government of Souvanna Phouma in November of 1957. Phoumi Vongvichit was ousted from the government of Souvanna Phouma's successor, Phoui Sananikone, and was jailed in July of 1959. He returned to the Laotian government following the Geneva conference that ended the Laotian civil war in 1962. Phoumi Vongvichit served as minister of information

until the coalition government collapsed and he resumed hostilities with the Pathet Lao. He joined Souphanouvang's rebel government in Sam Neua Province in northern Laos. Phoumi Vongvichit returned to the capital in 1974 and was named deputy chairman of the Council of Ministers in the Communist-dominated government the following year. Phoumi Vongvichit succeeded Souphanouvang as Laos's head of state on October 31, 1986. He retained office until he was replaced by Kayson Phomvihan on August 15, 1991. Phoumi died of heart disease on January 7, 1994, at the age of 84.

KAYSONE PHOMVIHAN (President, August 15, 1991–November 21, 1992). Kaysone Phomvihan was born in Na Seng, Savannakhet Province, on December 13, 1920. He was educated in Hanoi and fought against the French in Vietnam in the mid-1940s. He joined the Laos nationalist movement in 1945 and served as minister of defense in the Free Lao Front resistance government in 1950. Kaysone Phomvihan was commander in chief of the Pathet Lao forces from 1954 until 1957. He was an unsuccessful candidate for a seat in the Laotian Supreme People's Assembly in 1958. He remained a ranking member of the Lao Patriotic Front and resumed the fight against the Laotian government following the purge of leftists in 1964. Kaysone Phomvihan was instrumental in the removal of the monarchy in 1975. He was named prime minister of the Lao People's Democratic Republic on December 2, 1975. Laos maintained close ties with neighboring Vietnam throughout the 1980s. Kaysone Phomvihan made attempts to normalize relations with France and Japan in the early 1990s. He promoted a new constitution in 1991 and stepped down as prime minister to become president on August 15, 1991. He retained office until his death in Vientiane on November 21, 1992.

NOUHAK PHOUNSAVANH (President, November 25, 1992–). Nouhak Phounsavanh was an early member of the Laotian nationalist movement. He served as foreign minister in the Free Lao Front resistance government and was a founding member of the Laos Revolutionary People's party in 1955. Nouhak Phounsavanh was elected to the Laotian National Assembly in 1957. He was arrested in 1959, but escaped the following year. He served as a member of the peace delegation in 1961. Nouhak Phounsavanh served as vice-chairman of the Council of Ministers and minister of finance following the Communist takeover in 1975. He remained minister of finance until 1982 and was vice-chairman of the Council of Ministers until 1990. Nouhak Phounsavanh was considered an ally of the Vietnamese. He was selected to replace Kaysone Phomvihan as president on November 25, 1992.

HEADS OF GOVERNMENT

PRINCE PETSARATH (Prime Minister, 1941–October 10, 1945). Petsarath was born in 1890. He was the son of Prince Boun Khong. Petsarath was educated in Paris and returned to Laos in 1913. He joined the staff of the French chief resident the following year. Petsarath became director of the Laotian Civil Service in 1919 and served on the Government Council for Indochina. He became prime minister and viceroy following changes in the constitution in 1941. The Vichy French government allowed the Japanese the use of Laos during World War II, and Japan declared that Laos was no longer a colonial province of France in March of 1945. Prince Petsarath confirmed independence in August of 1945 and formed the Lao Issara, or Free Lao, to fight the resumption of French colonial rule. Following the defeat of Japan and the conclusion of World War II, the French renewed their claim on Laos. King Sisavang Vong stripped Prince Petsarath of his office on October 10, 1945. The king underestimated the strength of Petsarath's support and was himself deposed when he refused to accept a new independent constitution and government. Sisavang Vong finally accepted the Lao Issara demands and returned to the throne. Prince Petsarath remained the leading force behind Lao Issara, but did not again become prime minister. When France began military action to restore its colonial rule, Petsarath went into exile in Thailand and called himself regent in the government-in-exile. He remained an outspoken foe of any compromise with the French and demanded instead a completely independent Laotian state. The Lao Issara movement was disbanded in 1949 following French acceptance of many of its demands. Many of the movement's leaders returned to Laos, but Prince Petsarath remained in exile in Thailand until 1957. He then returned to Laos and was granted the honorary title of viceroy of Luang Prabang. He died of a stroke in Luang Prabang on October 14, 1959.

PRINCE PHAYO KHAMMAO VILAY (Prime Minister, October 20, 1945–April 29, 1946). Phayo Khammao Vilay was born in Luang Prabang on September 23, 1891. He was serving as governor of the Vientiane Province when, in October of 1945, he was proclaimed prime minister of Laos by a provisional people's assembly in defiance of France. Khammao's government fell on April 29, 1946, when French troops entered the capital. He fled to Thailand with other members of the Lao Issara government. Phayo Khammao was allowed to return to Laos in 1949. He died in Vientiane on July 23, 1965.

PRINCE SAVANG VATTHANA (Prime Minister, April 1946–March 1947). *See entry under Heads of State.*

PRINCE SOUVANNARATH (Prime Minister, March 1947–March 1948). Souvannarath was the son of the former viceroy, Prince Boun Khong. He served as minister of economy in the government of his half-brother Prince Petsarath in the early 1940s. Souvannarath was chosen as prime minister in March of 1947. A constitution was promulgated two months later. Souvannarath was replaced as prime minister by Prince Boun Oum in March of 1948. He died in 1960.

PRINCE BOUN OUM (Prime Minister, March 1948–February 1950). Boun Oum na Champassac was born in Bassac in southern Laos on December 12, 1912. He was the son of Prince Ratsadanay, head of the former royal family of Champassac. He was educated at French schools in Laos, Vietnam, and Paris. Boun Oum was active in the anti-Japanese underground during World War II and supported the return of the French after the war. Prince Boun Oum was named prime minister in March of 1948. He assisted in the negotiations with France that granted Laos limited self-government in June of 1949. He was replaced as prime minister by Phoui Sananikone in February of 1950. Boun Oum remained a leading rightist spokesman and opposed the neutralist policies of Souvanna Phouma. Boun Oum was renamed prime minister on December 13, 1960, after a right-wing military coup. His pro–Western government was challenged by the pro–Communist Pathet Lao and forces loyal to neutralist Souvanna Phouma. A conference was held in Geneva, Switzerland, that included representatives of the three major factions. A truce agreement was negotiated that named Souvanna Phouma as prime minister–designate in

October of 1961. Boun Oum remained prime minister until Souvanna Phouma was able to form a government on June 22, 1962. Boun Oum rejoined the government in 1966 to serve as minister of religion and remained in Souvanna Phouma's cabinet until 1972. Boun Oum left Laos for Thailand in 1974 as the Pathet Lao became more dominant in the government. When the Pathet Lao abolished the monarchy in December of 1975, Boun Oum went into exile in Paris. He was tried in absentia by the government of the People's Democratic Republic of Laos and sentenced to death. Boun Oum died in Paris after a long illness at the age of 68 on March 17, 1980.

PHOUI SANANIKONE (Prime Minister, February 1950–November 1951). Phoui Sananikone was born in Vientiane on September 6, 1903. He was educated in Laos and entered the civil service during the French administration. He served as governor of Upper Mekong Province from 1941. Phoui Sananikone fought with the Resistance against the Japanese during World War II and supported the return of the French in 1945. He entered politics in 1947 and was elected to the National Assembly. He was named to the cabinet as minister of education, health, and social welfare in March of 1947 and was also elected president of the Assembly later in the year. Phoui Sananikone was named to form a government as prime minister in February of 1950. He remained prime minister until he was replaced by Prince Souvanna Phouma in November of 1951. He remained in the government as deputy prime minister and also served as minister of the interior and defense until 1954. Phoui Sananikone was named foreign minister in March of 1954 and served until August of 1958. He was named to head a non–Communist government as prime minister on August 15, 1958. He resumed the government's conflict with leftist rebels and placed

Pathet Lao leader Prince Souphanouvang under house arrest. Phoui Sananikone was dismissed by the king on December 31, 1959, when he could not resolve the conflicts in the government. He returned to the National Assembly as leader of the conservative nationalist party, Rassemblement du Peuple Lao. He also served as president of the Assembly from 1960 until 1974. Phoui Sananikone went to Thailand following the Communist takeover of Laos in May of 1975. He then went into exile in France. He was tried and sentenced to death in absentia by the Communist government in September of 1975. Phoui Sananikone served as prime minister in the Lao government-in-exile from October of 1978. He died in Paris at the age of 80 on December 4, 1983.

PRINCE SOUVANNA PHOUMA (Prime Minister, November 1951–November 25, 1954). Souvanna Phouma was born in Luang Prabang on October 7, 1901. He was the son of Prince Ouphat Boun Khong and the nephew of King Sisavang Vong. He was educated at the University of Paris and the University of Grenoble and received degrees in engineering. Souvanna Phouma returned to Laos in 1931 to work in the Public Works Service in French Indochina. He served with the Bureau of Architecture in Vientiane until 1940 and held various positions in the Public Works Service during World War II. He joined with his half-brothers, Prince Souphanouvang and Prince Petsarath, to establish an independent Lao Issara, or Free Laos, government after the war. Souvanna Phouma served as prime minister of the provisional government before he was forced into exile in Thailand by the return of the French. Laos was established as a constitutional monarchy in 1946, and Souvanna Phouma returned from exile to serve in the government in late 1949. He was appointed to the cabinet as minister of public works, telecommu-

nications, and planning in February of 1950. He became the leader of the National Progressive party and was named prime minister in November of 1951. Shortly afterwards Laos was invaded by Communist Viet-Minh forces acting in concert with the Pathet Lao, led by Prince Souphanouvang. The rebels took control of several provinces in northern Laos. Defense Minister Kou Voravong was assassinated in September of 1954, and Souvanna Phouma was replaced as prime minister by Katay Sasorith on November 25, 1954. He remained in the government as deputy prime minister and minister of defense. He was reappointed prime minister on March 21, 1956, and also served as foreign minister and minister of defense. Souvanna Phouma negotiated a truce with Souphanouvang's Pathet Lao in August of 1956. He established a government of national unity the following year that included Souphanouvang in the cabinet. Souvanna Phouma was again forced to resign on July 22, 1958. He was unable to form a new government and was replaced by Phoui Sananikone as leader of an anti–Communist government the following month. Souvanna Phouma was subsequently sent to France to serve as Laos's ambassador. He also served as ambassador to Italy before returning to Laos to serve as president of the National Assembly in May of 1960. He returned to office as prime minister on August 15, 1960, after a military coup led by Captain Kong Le. Souvanna Phouma was again forced from office on December 10, 1960, and went into exile following a rightist countercoup led by General Phoumi Nosavan. Souvanna Phouma participated in negotiations to end the conflict between the leftists and the rightists and returned to Laos to lead a coalition cabinet on June 24, 1962. The coalition collapsed the following year, and the Pathet Lao resumed military hostilities with the government. Souvanna Phouma initiated peace talks with the Pathet Lao in 1972, and a proposal was accepted the following February. A new coalition government was established in April of 1974 that retained Souvanna Phouma as prime minister. The Pathet Lao became increasingly powerful in the government following the fall of Cambodia and South Vietnam to the Communists in 1975. The monarchy was abolished, and Souvanna Phouma was eliminated from the government on December 2, 1975. Souvanna Phouma served as an advisor to the new government. He died in Vientiane at the age of 82 after a long illness on January 10, 1984.

KATAY D. SASORITH (Prime Minister, November 25, 1954–December 29, 1955). Katay Don Sasorith was born in 1904. He was educated locally and entered the civil service in French Indochina in 1926. Katay was a founder of the Lao Issara, or Free Laos, movement during World War II. He served as minister of finance in the short-lived Lao Issara government from 1945 until the reestablishment of French rule in 1946. He went into exile in Thailand until he was allowed to return to Laos in 1949. Katay was elected to the National Assembly as a member of the National Progressive party in 1951. He was elected president of the Assembly and served in the government as minister of finance. He was selected to succeed Prince Souvanna Phouma as prime minister of Laos on November 25, 1954. Katay supported negotiations with the Pathet Lao to reunify the country. He stepped down on December 29, 1955, to allow Souvanna Phouma to again become prime minister. Katay remained in the government as deputy prime minister and also served as minister of the interior and justice. He died in Vientiane at the age of 55 on December 29, 1959.

PRINCE SOUVANNA PHOUMA (Prime Minister, March 21, 1956–

July 22, 1958). *See earlier entry under Heads of Government.*

PHUI SANANIKONE (Prime Minister, August 15, 1958–December 31, 1959). *See earlier entry under Heads of Government.*

PHOUMI NOSAVAN (Head of Government, December 31, 1959–January 7, 1960). Phoumi Nosavan was born in Savannakhet in southern Laos on January 7, 1920. He was a cousin of Marshal Sarit Thanarat, who served as prime minister of Thailand. Phoumi joined the Lao Issara in 1945 and fought with the revolutionary group to expel the French colonial administration. He rose to chief of staff, but abandoned the organization when Prince Souphanouvang, the leader of the Lao Issara, became closely involved with Vietnamese Communists. Phoumi joined the Royal Laotian army and advanced to chief of staff in 1955. He received further military training at the French War College in Paris. He was a founder of the conservative Committee for the Defense of the National Interests in 1958 and joined the government of Phoui Sananikone as secretary of state for national defense in 1959. Phoumi seized power in a right-wing military coup on December 31, 1959. He allowed the formation of a civilian government under Kou Abhay Og Long on January 8, 1960. He served in the government as minister of national defense. Phoumi remained a powerful figure in the government until Captain Kong Le led a neutralist military coup in August of 1960. Phoumi briefly served in the coalition government of Souvanna Phouma before withdrawing to Savannakhet. He led another coup in December of 1960 that installed Prince Boun Oum as head of the government. Phoumi remained in the government as deputy prime minister following the return of Souvanna Phouma as prime minister in June of 1962 as a result of negotiations between the major combatants in Laos's civil war. When Souvanna Phouma initiated an attempt to curtail Phoumi's power in the military in February of 1965, Phoumi led a coup attempt in response. The coup was unsuccessful, and Phoumi went into exile in Thailand. He remained active in exile politics and was an opponent of the Communist seizure of the government in 1975. Phoumi died in Bangkok on November 3, 1985.

KOU ABHAY OG LONG (Prime Minister, January 7, 1960–May 31, 1960). Kou Abhay Og Long was born in 1892. He served in the French colonial administration of Indochina. He later served as president of the King's Council. Kou was selected by former prime minister Phoui Sananikone and General Phoumi Nosavan as a compromise candidate for prime minister on January 7, 1960. His government was charged with returning Laos to civilian rule and holding elections to the National Assembly. Kou's caretaker cabinet resigned on May 31, 1960.

PRINCE SOMSANITH (Prime Minister, May 31, 1960–August 9, 1960). Somsanith was a nephew of Prince Souvanna Phouma. He served as minister of the interior in the caretaker cabinet of Kou Abhay Og Long. He was a member of General Phoumi Nosavan's Democratic party for Social Progress and opposed negotiations with the Laos Communist party. He replaced Kou as prime minister on May 31, 1960. A coup by rebellious army officers led by Captain Kong Le forced Somsanith's resignation on August 9, 1960, and installed a neutralist government led by Prince Souvanna Phouma.

KONG LE (Head of Government, August 9, 1960–August 15, 1960). Kong Le was born in Muon Phalane in Savannakhet Province in 1934. He joined the military in the late 1940s and fought with the French against the Viet

Minh. He was promoted to the rank of captain in the territorial army in 1952. He received further military training in the United States and the Philippines in 1957 and returned to Laos in January of the following year to command the Second Paratroop Battalion. Kong Le led a military coup against the government on August 9, 1960, ousting the conservative administration of Prince Somsanith that was dominated by General Phoumi Nosavan. Kong Le supported a neutralist position for Laos and called upon Prince Souvanna Phouma to serve as prime minister on August 15, 1960. A rightist revolt led by General Phoumi Nosavan forced Kong Le and his troops to retreat to the Plain of Jars. Kong Le continued to lead the neutralist forces of Souvanna Phouma in the subsequent civil war. The assassination of Colonel Ketsana Vongsouvan, Kong Le's chief of staff, on February 12, 1963, led to a schism in the neutralist forces, and Kong Le was forced into exile in Paris the following year. He remained in France and was a critic of the Pathet Lao government following its takeover of Laos in 1975.

PRINCE SOUVANNA PHOUMA (Prime Minister, August 15, 1960–December 10, 1960). *See earlier entry under Heads of Government.*

SUNTHONE PATTAMAVONG (Head of Government, December 10, 1960–December 11, 1960). Sunthone Pattamavong served in the Laotian army. He rose to the rank of general and served as army chief of staff. He led the Military High Committee that ruled Laos following the military coup on December 10, 1960. A rival leftist government was formed by Quinim Pholsena the following day.

QUINIM PHOLSENA (Head of Government, December 11, 1960–December 13, 1960). Quinim Pholsena was born in 1915. He was raised as a ward in the family of Prince Souvanna

Phouma. He was educated in Vietnam, where he studied law. Quinim Pholsena joined the civil service and became governor of Sam Neua Province in northern Laos in 1945. He retained that position until 1955. Quinim Pholsena also served as a leftist member of the National Assembly until his defeat in 1960. He supported Captain Kong Le's military revolt against the pro-Western government of Laos in December of 1960. He served as Kong Le's leading political advisor and was briefly head of the government from December 11 until December 13, 1960. Quinim Pholsena continued to support the leftist revolt until a truce was negotiated in Geneva among the major combatants. He was named to Souvanna Phouma's coalition government as foreign minister in June of 1962. He maintained his association with the pro-Communist Pathet Lao forces. Quinim Pholsena was shot and killed by a soldier guarding his home in Vientiane on April 1, 1963.

PRINCE BOUN OUM (Prime Minister, December 13, 1960–June 22, 1962). *See earlier entry under Heads of Government.*

PRINCE SOUVANNA PHOUMA (Prime Minister, June 24, 1962–December 2, 1975). *See earlier entry under Heads of Government.*

KAYSONE PHOMVIHAN (Prime Minister, December 2, 1975–August 15, 1991). *See entry under Heads of State.*

KHAMTAI SIPHANDON (Prime Minister, August 15, 1991–). Khamtai Siphandon served in the Laotian army and was a member of the Lao People's Revolutionary party. He served as deputy prime minister and minister of national defense in the government of Kaysone Phomvihan. He succeeded Kaysone Phomvihan as prime minister on August 15, 1991.

Latvia, Republic of
(Latvijas Republika)

Latvia is a country in northern Europe on the Baltic Sea. It declared itself independent from the Soviet Union on August 21, 1991.

HEAD OF STATE

ANATOLIJS GORBUNOVS (President, August 21, 1991–). Anatolijs V. Gorbunovs was born in the Ludza District in 1942. He was educated in Moscow and served in the Red Army from 1962 until 1965. He was active in the Latvian Communist party from 1974 and became chairman of the Supreme Council of Latvia in 1988. The Latvian Supreme Soviet overwhelmingly passed a resolution calling for independence from the Soviet Union on May 3, 1990, and Gorbunovs became chairman of the Latvian Supreme Soviet Presidium. A referendum in March of 1991 supported the independence movement, and full independence was granted on August 21, 1991, with Gorbunovs serving as president of the Republic.

HEAD OF GOVERNMENT

IVARS GODMANIS (Prime Minister, May 3, 1990–). Ivars Godmanis was born in Riga on November 27, 1951. He was educated locally and received a degree in science. He worked with the Latvian Academy of Sciences from 1973 until he became a teacher at the Latvian University in 1986. He was active in the Latvian independence movement and succeeded Vilnis Edvins Bresis as prime minister on May 3, 1990. He retained the position following independence on August 21, 1991.

Lebanon, Republic of

(al-Jumhuriyah al-Lubnaniyah)

Lebanon is a country in western Asia. It was granted independence from a League of Nations mandate administered by the French on November 22, 1943.

HEADS OF STATE

BISHARA KHALIL EL-KHOURY (President, September 21, 1943–September 18, 1952). Bishara Khalil el-Khoury was born in Beirut on August 10, 1890. A Maronite Christian, he graduated from the Jesuit St. Joseph University in 1909. He subsequently went to Paris to study law and received a degree in 1912. He returned to Lebanon to practice law and also entered politics. El-Khoury fled to Egypt during World War I when the Ottoman Empire reestablished control over the country. He returned following the conclusion of World War I and presided over Lebanon's Court of Appeal under the French mandate. He served as prime minister of the government from 1926 until 1928 and also served as minister of the interior. El-Khoury was elected president of the Senate the following year. When the constitution was abolished in 1932, el-Khoury founded the Destour, or Constitutional, party and became its leader. He fought to restore the Lebanese Constitution and to gain independence from France for the country. He was defeated in the 1936 election for the presidency by Emile Edde, the pro-French candidate. El-Khoury was elected president on September 21, 1943, but was arrested shortly after taking power for trying to eliminate Vichy French influences in the country. British troops entered the country and enforced Lebanon's independence under an agreement with the Free French. El-Khoury succeeded in forcing all foreign troops from Lebanon in 1946. He also amended the constitution to allow for a second term of office when his term came to an end in 1948. He was widely criticized for this action and was accused of allowing his family to profiteer from his position. El-Khoury was forced to resign from office on September 18, 1952, and was succeeded by Camille Chamoun. He joined critics of Chamoun's government in 1957 in the hopes that he would again be chosen as president. He was unsuccessful in that endeavor and retired from politics. He died in Beirut at the age of 73 on January 11, 1964.

CAMILLE CHAMOUN (President, September 23, 1952–September 23, 1958). Camille Nimer Chamoun was born to a Maronite Christian family in Deir al-Kamar in 1900. He graduated from the University of Beirut Law School in 1924. He was elected to the Chamber of Deputies in 1934. Chamoun served in the cabinet as minister of finance in 1938 and was minister of public works from 1938 until 1941. He was named minister of the interior in the first postindependence cabinet of Riad es-Solh in 1943. He was sent to London as Lebanon's ambassador to Great Britain in 1944. Chamoun also served as Lebanon's first representative to the United Nations General Assembly in 1946. He returned to Lebanon in 1948 to serve as foreign minister. He resigned from the cabinet later in the year in opposition to President Bishara el-Khoury's amendment of the constitution to allow him to serve a second term in office. Chamoun supported the Kamal Jumblatt's Socialist National Front party in opposition to el-Khoury. When El-Khoury was forced to resign in 1952, Chamoun was elected to succeed him as president. He took office on September 23, 1952. He closely aligned the government of Lebanon with the United States and distrusted the pan–Arab policies of Egypt's Gamal Abdel Nasser. Chamoun's government was threatened in 1957 by an uprising of Muslim nationalists and leftists backed by Syria and Egypt. He petitioned the United States for assistance, and President Dwight Eisenhower sent American troops to protect Beirut in July of 1958. Chamoun stepped down as president on September 23, 1958, and founded the National Liberation party. He subsequently withdrew from politics, but reemerged in the mid-1960s to form an alliance with Maronite Christian leaders Pierre Gemayel and Raymond Edde. In July of 1968 Chamoun survived one of many assassination attempts. The alliance dissolved following the presidential election in

1970. After the outbreak of the civil war in 1975, Chamoun was again named to the cabinet as minister of the interior. He also led a Maronite militia army, known as the Tigers, that controlled Juniyah in northern Lebanon. His militia was crushed by the Christian Phalangist army of Bashir Gemayel in 1979, when Gemayel was trying to unify the Christian forces. Chamoun was nominated to run for the presidency in 1982 following president-elect Bashir Gemayel's assassination. He withdrew in a gesture of national unity several days before the election and thus assured the presidency for Gemayel's brother, Amin. Chamoun took part in several conferences of national reconciliation held in Switzerland in 1983 and 1984. He stepped down as leader of the National Liberation party in 1986 and turned over control to his youngest son, Dany (who was assassinated in October of 1990). Camille Chamoun was serving as minister of finance in the cabinet of Selim al-Hoss when he suffered a heart attack. He died in Christian East Beirut at the age of 87 on August 7, 1987.

FUAD CHEHAB (President, September 23, 1958–September 23, 1964). Fuad Chehab (Shihab) was born in Jounieh on March 9, 1902. He was a Maronite Christian and attended the French military academy at St. Cyr. He served in the Lebanese army during World War II and rose to the rank of general in 1943. Chehab was named commander of the army following Lebanon's independence. He refused to support President Bishara el-Khoury when the government was charged with corruption in September of 1952. Chehab briefly served as prime minister and minister of defense from September 18, 1952, when President el-Khoury resigned, until September 25, 1952. Chehab disagreed with the policy of President Camille Chamoun that brought United States troops into Lebanon in 1958 to assist in settling civil disorder. Chehab, who was considered politically neutral, was chosen as a compromise candidate to replace Chamoun as president on September 23, 1958. He negotiated a settlement with President Gamal Abdel Nasser of Egypt that ended the crisis in Lebanon. He restored economic and social stability to the country by launching a series of reforms aimed at assisting the Muslim population. Chehab refused an offer by a majority of the Parliament to remain president for a second term and stepped down on September 23, 1964. He remained a powerful figure in Lebanese politics and had the support of the army and the intelligence services. He again refused to become a candidate for president in the elections of 1970. Chehab died of a heart attack at his home near Beirut at the age of 70 on April 25, 1973.

CHARLES HÉLOU (President, September 23, 1964–September 23, 1970). Charles Hélou was born in Beirut on September 24, 1912. He was educated in Lebanon and received a degree in law. He practiced law in Lebanon and also founded newspapers in Syria and Lebanon. Hélou served on the Political Directorate until 1947, when he was named minister to the Vatican. He returned to Lebanon to serve as minister of justice in the cabinet of Prime Minister Riad es-Solh. He was elected to the Lebanese Parliament in 1951. Hélou served as minister of justice and health from 1954 until 1955 and then joined the political opposition in 1957. He did not run for reelection to the Parliament in 1960 and retired from active politics. He returned to the cabinet as minister of education in February of 1964 and retained that position until taking office as president on September 23, 1964. Hélou continued the policies of his predecessor, General Fuad Chehab. He completed his term as president and relinquished office to Suleiman Franjieh on September 23, 1970. He remained the leader of the Catholic Action party.

Hélou again served in the government as minister of state from July until August of 1979.

SULEIMAN FRANJIEH (President, September 23, 1970–September 23, 1976). Suleiman Franjieh was born in Zegharta in northern Lebanon on June 14, 1910. He was from a leading Maronite Christian family and was educated in Beirut. He worked in the family business before entering politics in 1960, following the retirement of his brother Hamid Franjieh. He was elected to the Parliament that year and served in the cabinet as minister of posts, telegraphs, and telephones and minister of agriculture until 1961. Franjieh was named minister of the interior in 1968 and served as minister of justice, economy, and public works from 1969 until 1970. He was a candidate for the Centre party in the presidential elections of 1970. He received the support of the alliance of Camille Chamoun, Pierre Gemayel, and Raymond Edde, as well as the leftist faction of Kamal Jumblat. He narrowly defeated Elias Sarkis and took office as president on September 23, 1970. Lebanon erupted into civil war in 1975 when fighting broke out between leftwing Palestinian guerrillas and rightwing Christian Phalangists. The fighting spread to Beirut, and Franjieh named a military cabinet in May of 1975. The cabinet received little political support and was forced to resign. Franjieh then appointed Rashid Karami as prime minister in the hopes of forming a government to bring an end to the fighting. The Syrian government was called upon to help formulate a peace settlement and established a cease-fire in January of 1976. Franjieh was called upon to resign by the military commander of Beirut in March of 1976. He refused and remained at the presidential palace in Baabda. He moved to the coastal town of Juniyah later in the month. Elias Sarkis was elected president in May of 1976, but

Franjieh refused to step down until the end of his term. He relinquished his office to Sarkis on September 23, 1976. Franjieh participated in national reconciliation talks in Geneva in October of 1983 and made an unsuccessful attempt to succeed President Amin Gemayel in 1988. Franjieh was hospitalized for heart and stomach ailments in July of 1992. He died of acute pneumonia at the American University Hospital in Beirut at the age of 82 on July 23, 1992.

ELIAS SARKIS (President, September 23, 1976–September 23, 1982). Elias Sarkis was born in the village of Shabaniyah on July 20, 1924. He attended the Jesuit University of St. Joseph in Beirut and received a law degree in 1948. He was appointed to the government's Audit Office as a magistrate in 1953. When General Fuad Chehab became Lebanon's president in 1958, Sarkis was appointed Chehab's legal advisor. He rose to become chief of staff in 1962 and organized the Deuxième Bureau to monitor the country's various factions. He remained chief of staff in the government of President Charles Helou until 1967, when he was appointed governor of the Central Bank of Lebanon. Sarkis helped restore Lebanon's economic stability and was a candidate for president in 1970. He was defeated by Suleiman Franjieh. He again announced his candidacy for president in the election of 1976. Lebanon was in a state of civil war at this time and Sarkis, who was considered a moderate, had the support of the Syrian government. He defeated Raymond Edde in the elections and took office on September 23, 1976. Sarkis tried to negotiate a settlement to the war that continued to ravage the country. He called upon the Arab League to send peacekeeping forces, and Syrian troops entered the country to try and stop the fighting. The war continued to rage on, and in 1982 Israeli forces invaded the stronghold of the Palestine Liberation Organization

(PLO) in Lebanon. This action forced the withdrawal of the PLO from Beirut. Sarkis suffered from ill health as his term of office came to an end. He stepped down from office on September 23, 1982. Sarkis retired to Paris, where he died at the age of 60 after a long illness on June 27, 1985.

AMIN GEMAYEL (President, September 23, 1982–September 23, 1988). Amin Gemayel was born in Bikfayya in 1942. He was the son of Pierre Gemayel, the founder of the Phalangist party. He graduated from the Jesuit St. Joseph University in 1966 with a degree in law. Gemayel practiced law and served as business manager for the many companies owned by the Phalangist party. He was elected to Parliament in 1970 as a representative of the Maronite Christian district of Metn. He was overshadowed by his brother, Bashir, when civil war broke out in Lebanon in 1975. Bashir led the Lebanese Forces Christian militia, and when the Israeli army intervened in Lebanon to drive out the Palestinian Liberation Army, Bashir Gemayel emerged as the dominant political leader in the country. Bashir was elected president of Lebanon on August 23, 1982. He was assassinated in a bomb blast shortly before taking office on September 14, 1982. Amin Gemayel was elected to take his brother's place the following week and took office as president on September 23, 1982. He was considered a more moderate leader than his brother and had the support of the Islamic coalition in the Parliament. Gemayel sponsored national reconciliation talks in Geneva in October of 1983. The talks were overshadowed by separate car bomb attacks on the military barracks that housed United States and French peacekeeping forces on October 23, 1983. These attacks killed nearly three hundred soldiers. A peace treaty was signed in Syria by leaders of the three most powerful militia forces in December of 1985, but the agreement collapsed a few weeks later. The assassination of Prime Minister Rashid Karami in June of 1987 further damaged hopes for a lasting peace. As Gemayel's term of office came to a close, no successor had been elected to replace him. Gemayel appointed Michel Aoun, the commander of the army, to serve as the head of a military government before he stepped down on September 23, 1988.

RENÉ MOAWAD (President, November 5, 1989–November 22, 1989). René Anis Moawad was born in Zgharta in 1925. He attended the Jesuit University of St. Joseph in Beirut and received a law degree in 1947. He became active in politics and was elected to the Parliament in 1957. Moawad served as chairman of the Administration of Justice Parliamentary Commission from 1959 until 1961 and subsequently served as minister of post, telephone, and telegraph until 1964. He was named minister of public works in 1969. He returned to the cabinet in 1980 to serve as minister of education until 1982. Moawad was elected president in a

special session of Parliament and took office on November 5, 1989. He was a moderate Maronite Christian who had the support of the Syrian government. Moawad's term of office was cut short when he was killed in an explosion on November 22, 1989, while riding in a motorcade returning from Muslim West Beirut.

ELIAS HRAWI (President, November 24, 1989–   ). Elias Hrawi was born in Zahle in 1930. He was a prominent Lebanese businessman and a Maronite Christian Deputy. He was elected president of Lebanon in 1989 to succeed René Moawad. Hrawi was sworn into office on November 24, 1989, and attempted to form a balanced government between Christian and Muslims. The Lebanese army assisted the Syrians in driving General Michel Aoun's rebel militia from East Beirut. The government approved a plan to disarm most of the remaining militias in March of 1991. Lebanon continued to face serious economic problems despite a decrease in civil disorders.

HEADS OF GOVERNMENT

RIAD ES-SOLH (Prime Minister, July 3, 1944–January 10, 1945). Riad es-Solh was born in Saida in 1894. He was active in the Arab nationalist movement and was arrested by the Turkish authorities during World War I. He was sentenced to death, but the sentence was commuted to deportation. Following World War I, he returned to Lebanon where he fought against the French mandate. Solh was again sentenced to death by a French court-martial, but was pardoned in 1924. He continued his opposition to French rule and opposed the Franco-Lebanese treaty of November 13, 1936. He was exiled by the French government, but again returned to Lebanon to form a government as prime minister on Sep-

tember 25, 1943. His government amended the constitution to remove the legal right of the French to administer Lebanon under a League of Nations mandate. Solh and his cabinet were arrested by French forces in Lebanon. When widespread demonstrations against the French occurred, the British stepped in to demand that Lebanon be granted independence. Solh remained as the first prime minister of independent Lebanon until November 14, 1943. He was again named prime minister on July 3, 1944, and served until January 10, 1945. He was again asked to form a government on December 14, 1946. An attempt was made by the Syrian National Socialist party to overthrow the Lebanese government in 1948. The leader of the attempt, Anton Sa'adeh, was sentenced to death and executed in 1949. His supporters vowed to seek revenge against Solh, whom they held responsible for Sa'adeh's death. An attempt was made to assassinate Solh in March of 1950. He stepped down as prime minister on February 13, 1951, and paid a state visit to King Abdullah of Jordan in July of 1951. He was shot to death by members of the Syrian National Socialist party on July 16, 1951, while en route to the Amman airport.

ABDUL HAMID KARAMI (Prime Minister, January 10, 1945–August 10, 1945). Abdul Hamid Karami was the Grand Mufti, or Muslim religious leader, of Lebanon. He was named prime minister of Lebanon on January 10, 1945. He announced the formation of the Lebanese National Army in May of 1945. Karami resigned on August 10, 1945, after demanding that constitutional reforms be made to prevent corruption in the government. Karami's son, Rashid Karami, later served as Lebanon's prime minister on numerous occasions. Karami died on November 23, 1950.

SAMI ES-SOLH (Prime Minister, August 22, 1945–May 18, 1946). Sami es-Solh was born in Acca in 1890. He was educated in Beirut, Istanbul, and Paris, where he studied law. He became active in the Arab nationalist movement and was involved in an attempted revolt against the Ottomans in 1916. After World War I he traveled to Syria and Egypt to meet with other Arab leaders. Solh returned to Lebanon in 1920, where he served as attorney general. He was subsequently appointed a criminal court judge under the French mandate. He remained in the judiciary until he entered politics in 1942 and was elected to the Parliament. Solh was appointed prime minister on July 29, 1942, and served until March 19, 1943. He again formed a government as prime minister on August 22, 1945, and

remained in office until May 18, 1946. He returned to power on February 11, 1952, but was forced to resign on September 9, 1952, when political opponents charged his government with corruption. Solh was again named prime minister on September 19, 1954, and remained in office until he was forced to resign on September 19, 1955. He was again asked to form a government on November 18, 1956. He won a victory in parliamentary elections in June of 1957 and retained office until September 20, 1958, when he resigned with President Camille Chamoun. Lebanon was in a state of civil disorder, and Solh was criticized for supporting Chamoun's calling of United States forces into the country to put down the Arab rebellion. Fearful for his life, Solh left the country aboard a United States military plane in 1958. He remained in Turkey for two years before he returned to Lebanon. He was defeated for reelection to the Parliament in 1960, but was victorious in 1964. Four years later he was again denied reelection. He died in Beirut at the age of 79 on November 6, 1968.

SAADI MUNLA (Prime Minister, May 22, 1946–December 14, 1946). Saadi Munla was appointed prime minister and minister for national economy on May 22, 1946. He resigned on December 14, 1946, when opposition parties attacked his government's economic plans. Munla was again called upon to head the government in September of 1952, but he was unable to form a cabinet.

RIAD ES-SOLH (Prime Minister, December 14, 1946–February 13, 1951). *See earlier entry under Heads of Government.*

HUSSEIN EL-OWEINI (Prime Minister, February 14, 1951–April 7, 1951). Hussein el-Oweini was born in Beirut in 1898. He served in the cabinet as finance minister before being named prime minister as head of a caretaker government on February 14, 1951. He was replaced by Abdullah Aref al-Yafi on April 7, 1951. Oweini served in Rashid Karami's cabinet as foreign minister from 1959 until 1960. He retired from politics and worked in the private sector until he was again asked to form a caretaker government on February 20, 1964. He remained in office after winning a vote of confidence from the Parliament following elections in May of 1964. Oweini resigned on July 20, 1965, over the question of a purge of members of the government. He died of a heart attack in Beirut at the age of 72 on January 11, 1971.

ABDULLAH AREF AL-YAFI (Prime Minister, April 7, 1951–February 9, 1952). Abdullah Aref al-Yafi was born in Beirut in 1901. He graduated from the Jesuit St. Joseph University in 1922. He subsequently attended the Sorbonne in Paris, where he received a doctorate in law in 1926. Yafi returned to Lebanon to practice law. He also entered politics and was elected to the Lebanese Parliament in 1932. He was elected to the Chamber of Deputies in 1938 to represent Beirut. On November 1, 1938, he became prime minister, and he served until September 21, 1939. During the 1940s Yafi became involved in the quest for Arab unity. He served on the Lebanese delegation to the conference founding the Arab League in 1944. He was appointed to the cabinet as minister of justice in December of 1946 and served until April of 1947. Yafi was asked to form a government as prime minister on April 7, 1951. He resigned from the government on February 9, 1952, and allied himself with Camille Chamoun. Their opposition brought down the presidency of Bishara el-Khoury. Yafi was again named prime minister on August 16, 1953, after Chamoun had become president. He resigned on September 17, 1954, after being attacked in Parliament for failing to follow through with domestic re-

forms that he had promised. Chamoun asked him to form another government on March 20, 1956. Yafi resigned on November 16, 1956, because he opposed Chamoun's pro–Western stance and his failure to sever diplomatic ties with Great Britain and France during the Suez Crisis. Yafi became a leading spokesman for the opposition in the Parliament, but was defeated in parliamentary elections in 1958. He became a supporter of Egyptian president Gamal Abdel Nasser and called for a unification of Lebanon into the United Arab Republic under Nasser. Yafi was a leader of the abortive revolt in the spring of 1958. He subsequently became a rival of Muslim leader Saab Salaam and was defeated in parliamentary elections in 1960 and 1964. He again served as prime minister from April 10, 1966, until December 2, 1966. Yafi was named to replace Rashid Karami as prime minister on February 8, 1968. He offered his resignation in November of 1968, following student demonstrations supporting the Palestinian Liberation Organization, but was persuaded to remain in office. He resigned on January 8, 1969, after the Lebanese army failed to prevent an Israeli raid in Beirut.

SAMI ES-SOLH (Prime Minister, February 11, 1952–September 9, 1952). *See earlier entry under Heads of Government.*

NAZIM AKKARI (Prime Minister, September 9, 1952–September 12, 1952). Nazim Akkari (Accari) was born in Beirut in 1902. He was named by President Bishara el-Khoury as head of a three-man emergency cabinet on September 9, 1952, when the el-Khoury regime was under attack by members of the opposition in Parliament. Akkari's caretaker government was replaced on September 12, 1952.

SAAB SALAAM (Prime Minister, September 12, 1952–September 17, 1952).

Saab Salaam was born in Beirut in 1905. He attended the American University of Beirut. He was elected to Parliament in 1943 and served as deputy prime minister from 1943 until 1947. He also served as minister of the interior and minister of foreign affairs in 1946. Salaam served briefly as prime minister from September 12, 1952, until September 17, 1952, when the cabinet resigned with President Bishara el-Khoury. Salaam was again named prime minister by President Camille Chamoun on April 30, 1953. He also served in the cabinet as minister of defense and the interior until parliamentary elections were held. He stepped down on August 10, 1953. Salaam served as minister of state in the government of Abdullah Aref al-Yafi from March of 1956. He resigned with al-Yafi in opposition to President Chamoun's pro-Western policies. He subsequently became a leader of the pro-Nasser opposition and was defeated in parliamentary elections the following year. He was a leader of the rebels who threatened civil war in Lebanon in 1958. Salaam returned to Parliament in the elections of 1960 and formed a government on August 2, 1960. His government faced several crises during the following year and was accused of corruption by the opposition. He stepped down on October 23, 1961. During the 1960s Salaam was a leader of the Muslim representatives from Beirut in opposition to Rashid Karami's political base in Tripoli. Salaam's bloc supported Suleiman Franjieh in the presidential election. When Franjieh was victorious, he called upon Salaam to again form a government on October 13, 1970. In April of 1973 Israeli commandos killed three Palestinian leaders in a raid on Beirut. The government accused the military of offering little resistance to the Israeli raid, and Salaam resigned when President Franjieh refused to dismiss the army commander in chief. Salaam remained a leading spokesman for Muslim interests and participated in the

Lebanese Reconciliation Conference in Geneva in 1983.

FUAD CHEHAB (Prime Minister, September 18, 1952–September 25, 1952). *See entry under Heads of State.*

KHALED CHEHAB (Prime Minister, September 30, 1952–April 28, 1953). Khaled Chehab was born in Hasbaya in 1892. He served as prime minister and minister of justice from March 21, 1938, until October 24, 1938. He was called upon to form a government composed primarily of neutral civil servants on September 30, 1952. Chehab also served in the cabinet as minister of the interior and justice. He was given dictatorial decree-making powers to carry out election reforms, grant political rights to women, and decentralize the government. He resigned on April 28, 1953, over criticism of civil service reforms that had resulted in the dismissal of numerous government employees.

SAAB SALAAM (Prime Minister, April 30, 1953–August 10, 1953). *See earlier entry under Heads of Government.*

ABDULLAH YAFI (Prime Minister, August 16, 1953–September 17, 1954). *See earlier entry under Heads of Government.*

SAMI ES-SOLH (Prime Minister, September 19, 1954–September 19, 1955). *See earlier entry under Heads of Government.*

RASHID KARAMI (Prime Minister, September 19, 1955–March 15, 1956). Rashid Abdul Hamid Karami was born in Miriata on December 30, 1921. His father was Abdel Hamid Karami, the Grand Mufti of Lebanon who served as prime minister in 1945. Rashid Karami was educated in Cairo, Egypt, and received a degree in law in 1947. He returned to Beirut to practice law and became the political leader of Tripoli following the death of his father in 1950. He was elected to the Parliament in 1951 and served in the cabinet as minister of justice. Karami served as minister of national economy and social affairs from 1953. He was appointed prime minister by President Camille Chamoun on September 19, 1955, following the resignation of Sami es-Solh. The government resigned on March 15, 1956. Karami subsequently broke with the Chamoun presidency and became a leading spokesman of the pro-Egyptian faction of Lebanon. He was a leader of the civil insurrection that threatened Chamoun's presidency. Following the election of General Fuad Chehab as president, Karami was again named prime minister on September 24, 1958. He resigned on May 14, 1960, but again formed a government on October 31, 1961. Karami remained prime minister until February 19, 1964, and was reappointed on July 26, 1965. He stepped down again on March 30, 1966, and was again renamed to the position on December 6, 1966. His government lasted until February 5, 1968. He returned to office on January 16, 1969, and his government was threatened with the presence of Palestinian guerrillas in Lebanon. Karami threatened to resign on several occasions during 1969, but was persuaded to remain in office by President Charles Hélou until September 30, 1970. He went into opposition against President Suleiman Franjieh in 1974. President Franjieh reluctantly agreed to accept Karami as prime minister on May 29, 1975, in the hopes that his support from the Islamic leftist opposition would help settle the civil war that developed in the country. Karami was unsuccessful in his attempts to reach a settlement and resigned on December 9, 1976. He supported the election of Elias Sarkis as president in 1976 and announced his retirement from politics the following year. He reemerged in 1977 and recon-

ciled his differences with former president Franjieh. Karami was again named prime minister by President Amin Gemayel on April 30, 1984, as head of a government of national unity. Karami announced his resignation in May of 1987, but Gemayel refused to act upon it. Karami was killed in a bomb explosion on board the helicopter that was carrying him from Tripoli to Beirut on June 1, 1987.

ABDULLAH YAFI (Prime Minister, March 20, 1956–November 16, 1956). *See earlier entry under Heads of Government.*

SAMI ES-SOLH (Prime Minister, November 18, 1956–September 20, 1958). *See earlier entry under Heads of Government.*

RASHID KARAMI (Prime Minister, September 24, 1958–May 14, 1960). *See earlier entry under Heads of Government.*

AHMED DAOUK (Prime Minister, May 14, 1960–July 20, 1960). Ahmed Daouk was born in Beirut in 1892. He served as prime minister from December 1, 1941, until July 24, 1942. He later served as Lebanon's ambassador to France. Daouk was called upon to form a caretaker government on May 14, 1960. He stepped down on July 20, 1960, following parliamentary elections.

SAAB SALAAM (Prime Minister, August 2, 1960–October 23, 1961). *See earlier entry under Heads of Government.*

RASHID KARAMI (Prime Minister, October 31, 1961–February 19, 1964). *See earlier entry under Heads of Government.*

HUSSEIN EL-OWEINI (Prime Minister, February 20, 1964–July 20, 1965). *See earlier entry under Heads of Government.*

RASHID KARAMI (Prime Minister, July 26, 1965–March 30, 1966). *See earlier entry under Heads of Government.*

ABDULLAH YAFI (Prime Minister, April 10, 1966–December 2, 1966). *See earlier entry under Heads of Government.*

RASHID KARAMI (Prime Minister, December 6, 1966–February 5, 1968). *See earlier entry under Heads of Government.*

ABDULLAH YAFI (Prime Minister, February 8, 1968–January 8, 1969). *See earlier entry under Heads of Government.*

RASHID KARAMI (Prime Minister, January 16, 1969–September 30, 1970). *See earlier entry under Heads of Government.*

SAAB SALAAM (Prime Minister, October 13, 1970–April 23, 1973). *See earlier entry under Heads of Government.*

AMIN HAFEZ (Prime Minister, April 23, 1973–June 14, 1973). Amin Hafez was born in 1911. He was a former Palestinian with strong ties to the guerrilla movement. He served in the Lebanese Parliament and was chairman of the foreign relations committee. Hafez was called upon to form a government on April 23, 1973, in the hopes that he would be able to negotiate with the Palestinians. He was forced to resign on June 14, 1973, following the resignation of several cabinet ministers and criticism from Sunni Muslims who claimed that Hafez did not represent their sect.

TAKIEDDIN ES-SOLH (Prime Minister, July 8, 1973–September 25, 1974). Takieddin es-Solh was born in 1909. He was educated at the American University and the Jesuit St. Joseph University in Beirut. He was elected to Parliament in 1957 and served as minister of the interior from 1964 until 1965. Solh was the leader of the Nidal al-Qawmi party and was appointed prime minister by President Suleiman Franjieh on July 8, 1973. He resigned on September 25, 1974, and was succeeded by his cousin, Rashid es-Solh. He died of a heart attack at the age of 80 at a Paris clinic on November 27, 1988.

RASHID ES-SOLH (Prime Minister, October 31, 1974–May 15, 1975). Rashid es-Solh was born in Beirut in 1926. He received a degree in law and served in the Lebanese judiciary. He served in the Chamber of Deputies in 1964 and 1972. Solh served as prime minister from October 31, 1974, until May 15, 1975. He was again appointed prime minister on May 13, 1992, and retained the office until October 22, 1992.

RASHID KARAMI (Prime Minister, May 29, 1975–December 9, 1976). *See earlier entry under Heads of Government.*

SELIM AL-HOSS (Prime Minister, December 9, 1976–October 25, 1980). Selim al-Hoss was born in 1919. He served as chairman of the Banking Control Commission from 1967 until 1973 and was chairman of the National Bank for Industrial and Tourist Development from 1973 until 1976. He was then chosen to be prime minister of Lebanon on December 9, 1976. Hoss also served as minister of the economy and trade until 1979. He resigned as prime minister in July of 1980, but remained in a caretaker capacity until his replacement was selected on October 25, 1980. He returned to the government as minister of labor, fine arts, and education in 1984 and resigned the following year. Hoss was named acting prime minister following the assassination of Rashid Karami on June 1, 1987. He served until December 24, 1990.

SHAFIQ AL-WAZZAN (Prime Minister, October 25, 1980–April 30, 1984). Shafiq al-Wazzan was born in Beirut in 1925. He was educated at St. Joseph University in Beirut and began a law practice in 1947. Wazzan served in the Lebanese Muslim Congress from 1963. He was elected a deputy to the National Assembly in 1968. From January to October of 1969, Wazzan served in the cabinet as minister of justice. He became prime minister on October 25, 1980. He remained in office during the assassination of President-Elect Bashir Gemayel and the subsequent selection of Amin Gemayel as president. Wazzan's government resigned in February of 1984, but Wazzan remained as prime minister until a new government was formed by Rashid Karami on April 30, 1984.

RASHID KARAMI (Prime Minister, April 30, 1984–June 1, 1987). *See earlier entry under Heads of Government.*

SELIM AL-HOSS (Prime Minister, June 1, 1987–December 24, 1990). *See earlier entry under Heads of Government.*

OMAR KARAMI (Prime Minister, December 24, 1990–May 6, 1992). Omar Karami was the brother of former prime minister Rashid Karami, who was assassinated in 1987. He served as minister of education and the arts until 1990, when he was chosen prime minister of Lebanon. He took office on December 23, 1990. Karami resigned on May 6, 1992, following an economic crisis and the threat of a general strike.

RASHID ES-SOLH (Prime Minister, May 13, 1992–October 22, 1992). *See earlier entry under Heads of Government.*

RAFIK AL-HARARI (Prime Minister, October 22, 1992–). Rafik al-Harari was born in 1944. He was educated in Beirut and was subsequently employed as an accountant to a prominent Saudi family. He became a successful businessman and was made a Saudi citizen by King Fahd. His fortune increased and he engaged in various philanthropic endeavors, including the founding of the Harari Foundation, which supplies funds for educational assistance and scholarships. Harari served as a special envoy of King Fahd to the conference to bring peace to the warring Lebanese Muslim and Christian factions in 1989. He was chosen as prime minister on October 22, 1992, to help solve Lebanon's escalating financial crisis.

Lesotho, Kingdom of

Lesotho is a country in central southern Africa. It was granted independence from Great Britain on October 4, 1966.

HEADS OF STATE

MOTLOTHEHI MOSHOESHOE II (Paramount Chief, March 12, 1960–October 4, 1966. King, October 4, 1966–November 12, 1990). Motlothehi Moshoeshoe II was born Constantine Bereng Seeiso in Thabang in the Mok-hotlong district on May 2, 1938. He was the son of Seeiso Griffith, the paramount chief of Basutoland. He was educated locally and in England. Moshoeshoe succeeded as paramount chief of Basutoland on March 12, 1960.

When Basutoland was granted independence from Great Britain on October 4, 1966, he became King Moshoeshoe II of the kingdom of Lesotho. He was prohibited by the constitution from involving himself in party politics and was forced to abdicate on April 3, 1970, when he backed the opposition to prime minister Leabua Jonathan. Moshoeshoe went into exile in the Netherlands, and Queen Mamohato Seeiso ruled as regent. Moshoeshoe was allowed to resume the throne on December 4, 1970, following his promise to abstain from political activities. He was stripped of his executive powers on February 21, 1990, by Justin Metsino Lekhanya, the chairman of the ruling military council. Moshoeshoe was sent into exile in Britain the following month and dethroned in favor of his son, Prince Letsie, on November 12, 1990. Moshoeshoe was allowed to return to Lesotho in July of 1992.

LETSIE III (King, November 12, 1990–   ). Letsie David Seeiso was born on July 17, 1963. He was the son of King Moshoeshoe II. He succeeded to the throne as King Letsie III following the ouster of his father on November 12, 1990. He held little power in the country, which was governed by the Military Council.

HEADS OF GOVERNMENT

CHIEF SEKHONYANA MASERIBANE (Prime Minister, May 1, 1965–July 5, 1965). Chief Sekhonyana Maseribane was born to the Lesotho royal family in Mount Moorosi on May 4, 1918. He was educated locally at Roman Catholic mission schools. He later went to South Africa, where he served as a medical assistant. Maseribane became the first prime minister of Lesotho when Chief Leabua Jonathan was defeated in the general election in April of 1965. Maseribane served in an interim capacity from May 1, 1965, until Chief Jonathan was elected to the Parliament on July 5, 1965. He was subsequently named deputy prime minister in Chief Jonathan's government. Maseribane later served in the cabinet as minister of home affairs. He died on November 3, 1986.

CHIEF JOSEPH LEABUA JONATHAN (Prime Minister, July 5, 1965–January 20, 1986). Joseph Leabua Jonathan was born in Leribe on October 30, 1914. He was the son of Chief Molapo and the great-grandson of King Moshoeshoe I. He was educated at local mission schools before working in the Rand mines in South Africa. Jonathan was appointed to the local government in Basutoland by Chief Jonathan Mathealira in 1937. He was elected to the Basutoland National Council in 1956 and was a member of the Basutoland delegations to London to discuss self-government for the area. Jonathan formed the Basutoland National party in 1959. His party was defeated by the Congress party in elections in 1959. The National party won a narrow victory in elections in May of 1965, though Jonathan was defeated for a seat in the National Assembly. He entered the assembly in a by-election the following July and became Lesotho's prime minister on July 5, 1965. He remained head of government following Lesotho's independence on October 4, 1966. Jonathan placed King Moshoeshoe II under house arrest the following December because of the king's involvement in politics. Jonathan suspended the constitution when the Congress party appeared likely to win general elections in January of 1970. He forced the abdication of the king the following April, though Moshoeshoe II was allowed to resume the throne in December of 1970.

Jonathan initiated close ties with South Africa, but relations deteriorated as Jonathan allowed the African National Congress to seek asylum in Lesotho. He further angered the South African government in 1982 by allowing Communist nations to establish embassies in Lesotho. The African National Congress established guerrilla bases for attacks on South Africa in Lesotho, and the South African government retaliated by imposing a blockade in December of 1985. Jonathan was ousted in a military coup on January 20, 1986. He died of stomach cancer in a South African hospital in Pretoria at the age of 72 on April 5, 1987.

JUSTIN LEKHANYA (President, January 24, 1986–May 2, 1991). Justin Lekhanya was born in 1938. He served as a commander in the Lesotho army and was leader of the Military Council and

Council of Ministers following the ouster of Leabua Jonathan in January of 1986. He also served as minister of defense and internal security until his ouster by Elias Tutsoane Ramaema on May 22, 1991. Lekhanya was placed under house arrest in August of 1991 for conspiring to overthrow the Ramaema government.

ELIAS TUTSOANE RAMAEMA (President, May 2, 1991–). Elias Tutsoane Ramaema was born in Mapoteng on November 10, 1933. He served in the police force from 1959 and was a lieutenant colonel in charge of welfare in the 1970s. He served as a member of the ruling Military Council following the military coup against the government of Leabua Jonathan in 1986. Ramaema ousted Justin Lekhanya as leader of the ruling Military Council on May 2, 1991.

Liberia, Republic of

Liberia is a country in western Africa. It declared its independence on July 26, 1847.

HEADS OF STATE

WILLIAM V. S. TUBMAN (President, January 1, 1944–July 23, 1971). William Vacanararat Shadrach Tubman was born in Harper on November 29, 1895. He was educated locally and received a degree in law. He began a legal practice in 1917 and served as an official of the court. Tubman entered politics in 1923 and was elected to the Senate. He stepped down from the Senate in 1931, following a government slavery scandal. Tubman returned to the Senate in 1934 and was appointed to the Liberian Supreme Court in 1937. Tubman was the candidate of the True Whig party in presidential elections in 1943 and was elected on May 4, 1943.

He took office on January 1, 1944. Tubman, who was known in the country as "Brother Shad," encouraged foreign investment in Liberia and received financial assistance from the United States. Tubman sponsored a constitutional amendment to allow him another term in office. He was challenged by Didwe Twe in the presidential campaign in 1951. Twe was disqualified as a candidate, and Tubman was reelected unopposed in May of 1951. He received little opposition in future elections. His opponent in the 1955 elections, William Bright, received 16 votes to Tubman's nearly 260,000. Liberia prospered under Tubman, and he

became recognized as an elder statesman in Africa during the 1960s. Tubman remained president until his death
at the age of 75 from complications
from prostate surgery at a hospital in
London on July 23, 1971.

WILLIAM R. TOLBERT, JR. (President, July 23, 1971–April 12, 1980).
William Richard Tolbert, Jr., was born
in Bensonville on May 13, 1913. He was
educated locally and received a degree
from Liberia College in 1934. He was
employed in the Liberian civil service
the following year. Tolbert entered
politics and was elected to the House of
Representatives as a member of the
True Whig party in 1943. He was elected
vice president under William V. S.
Tubman in 1955. Tolbert exercised
little power during Tubman's administration, though he continued to serve as
Tubman's running mate in subsequent
elections. Tolbert succeeded to the
presidency when Tubman died in office
on July 23, 1971. Tolbert sponsored
some liberal reforms in the country and
allowed the formation of the opposition Progressive Alliance of Liberia in
1973. He was reelected with little opposition in 1975. His government faced
increasing criticism for the economic
disparity in the country, however. The
army fired upon a large group of
demonstrators protesting the increase
in the price of rice in April of 1979 and
killed over 70 of the protestors. This
action set off a wave of antigovernment
rioting throughout the country. Tolbert
ordered the arrest of leaders of the opposition in March of 1980. A military
coup led by Master Sergeant Samuel
Doe ousted the Tolbert government on
April 12, 1980. Tolbert was shot and
killed during the coup, and many
members of his government were captured and executed.

SAMUEL K. DOE (President, April 12,
1980–September 9, 1990). Samuel Kan-
yon Doe was born in Tuzon on May 6,
1951. He was educated locally and

entered the Liberian military in 1969.
He was promoted to corporal in 1975
and subsequently received further military training from United States Special
Forces troops. Doe became involved
with the People's Progressive party, the
leading group opposing the regime of
President William Tolbert. Doe led a
military coup against Tolbert in April
of 1980. Tolbert was killed during the
coup, and Doe served as chairman of
the People's Redemption Council from
April 12, 1980. His regime tried and
executed many members of Tolbert's
government. He also ordered the release of opposition leaders, many of
whom served in Doe's subsequent government. The government promoted a
new constitution in April of 1981. Elections where held in October of 1985,
though opposition parties were placed
under restrictions. Doe was elected
president and survived a coup attempt
the following month. The coup was led
by Brig. Gen. Thomas Quiwonkpa,
who was later captured and executed.
Doe's regime was threatened by several
other coup attempts in the late 1980s.
Charles Taylor led a revolt in northeastern Liberia in 1989 that developed
into a major tribal conflict. The Liberian army was unable to prevent the
rebels' advance through the country. A
second rebel group under Prince
Johnson broke with Taylor's National
Patriotic Forces of Liberia, and fighting continued among the rival groups.
The Economic Community of West
African States sent a peacekeeping force
into Liberia in August of 1990. Johnson's rebels took control of much of the
capital. Doe was wounded in a gunfight
with the rebels when he emerged from
the executive mansion on September 9,
1990. He was taken prisoner and killed
by the rebels.

AMOS SAWYER (President, November 22, 1990–). Amos Sawyer was
born in Greenville on June 15, 1945. He
was educated locally and received a
degree from the University of Liberia

in 1966. He continued his education and joined the university as a teacher in 1971. Sawyer was an independent candidate for mayor of Monrovia in 1979. The government of President William Tolbert canceled the elections when Sawyer's victory seemed likely. This action spurred widespread demonstrations against the government and led to the ouster of Tolbert in April of 1980. Sawyer served as chairman of the commission that drafted a new constitution during the administration of Samuel Doe. Sawyer subsequently served as dean at the University of Liberia. He was arrested in August of 1984 on charges of conspiring against the government. He was released the following

October and served as president of the Liberian People's party. Sawyer was prevented from challenging Doe in presidential elections in October of 1985. Sawyer was selected as leader of an interim government of National Unity in August of 1990 by guerrilla groups that were involved in armed conflict against the government of Samuel Doe. Doe was ousted and killed in September of 1990, and Sawyer was recognized as president on November 22, 1990, by the Economic Community of West African States peacekeeping force in Liberia. The fighting continued, and rebels led by Charles Taylor controlled most of the country outside of the capital.

Libya (Socialist People's Libyan Arab Jamahiriya)

(al-Jamahiriyah al-'Arabiyah al-Libiyah al-Sha'biyah al-Ishtirakiyah)

Libya is a country in North Africa along the coast of the Mediterranean Sea. It was granted independence from Italy on December 24, 1951.

HEADS OF STATE

IDRIS I (King, December 24, 1951– September 1, 1969). Sidi Mohammed Idris el-Mahdi es-Senussi was born in the Yaghbub Oasis on March 12, 1890. He was the grandson of Mohammed ben Ali el-Senussi, the founder of the Senussi Muslim sect. He was acknowledged as leader of the Senussi sect in 1917 and was recognized by the Italians as emir of Cyrenaica, now Libya. Idris attempted to negotiate independence for his country from Italy, but met with little success. He went into exile in Egypt in 1922 and led the Cyrenaican nationalist movement in a guerrilla war against the Italian colonial authorities.

He also accepted the title of emir of Tripolitania in 1922. Idris and his followers reached an agreement with the British government in World War II, and the Cyrenaican nationalists fought with the Allies against the Italians. The Italians were driven from Cyrenaica after the war, and Idris returned to Benghazi. He negotiated an independence agreement with the British, who now controlled the territory. Cyrenaica was granted self-governing status, with Idris as head of the government in 1949. Full independence was granted to the Libyan provinces on December 24, 1951, and Idris was crowned king of

Libya. Libya under Idris was pro-Western in its foreign relations and received much financial aid from Great Britain and the United States for allowing air bases to be established in the country. Idris was criticized by other Arab nationalist leaders for his continued support of the Western powers, particularly after the Suez Crisis in 1956. Idris had married his third wife, Fatima, in 1933. The king had produced no heirs, despite two previous marriages. A crisis developed in the royal household in 1954 when Ibrahim el-Shali, the minister of palace affairs and Idris's closest advisor, offered the king his daughter for his fourth wife. El-Shalhi was assassinated by Queen Fatima's nephew, who was then executed. Idris did take a fourth wife the following year, yet still produced no sons. In the late 1950s Libyan oil fields were developed, bringing vast wealth to the country. Idris's rule became increasingly threatened by Arab nationalism during the 1960s. The king was suffering from poor health and went to Turkey for medical treatment. He was ousted by a military coup led by Muammar al-Qaddafi on September 1, 1969. Idris went into exile in Cairo, Egypt, where he died at the age of 93 on May 25, 1983.

MUAMMAR AL-QADDAFI (President, September 1, 1969–   ). Muammar al-Qaddafi was born to a Bedouin family in Misurata in 1942. He attended Islamic schools in Sirte and Sebha and became a supporter of Egyptian president Gamal Abdel Nasser's Arab nationalism. He became involved in conspiracies against the Libyan government in 1959. Qaddafi received a degree from the University of Libya in 1963 and graduated from the Libyan military academy in Benghazi two years later. He entered the Libyan army and became the organizer of the Free Officers Movement. He rose through the ranks to become a captain by August of 1969. Qaddafi and his supporters had long

planned the overthrow of the Libyan monarchy, and on September 1, 1969, he led the military coup that ousted King Idris. He dissolved the Parliament and became chairman of the Revolutionary Command Council. Qaddafi moved Libya away from its previous status as an ally of the United States and the West. He closed down British and United States air force bases in the country and took control of the banks and oil industry. He also formed closer relations with the Soviet Union and other Arab nations. Qaddafi became Libya's prime minister on January 16, 1970. He participated in a plan to unite the governments of Libya, Egypt, and Syria, but later broke with Egyptian president Anwar Sadat. Qaddafi supported a coup attempt against Sadat in 1974. He relinquished his administrative positions on April 2, 1974, in order to concentrate on ideological matters. He promoted a philosophy of Islamic socialism, which he explained in his "Green Book," in 1976. Libya became known as a center for international terrorism, and it was believed that Qaddafi gave assistance to various organizations, including the Black Panthers, the Red Army Faction, the Red Brigade, and the Irish Republican Army. He formed the General People's Congress in March of 1979 to take over duties previously held by the Revolutionary Command Council. Libya became involved in the civil war in Chad in the late 1970s. The Libyan economy began to suffer in the early 1980s, and Qaddafi sought to improve Libya's relationship with other Arab nations. In April of 1986 United States president Ronald Reagan ordered an air strike against Libya in response to Qaddafi's support for international terrorism. Qaddafi narrowly escaped the bombings with his life. The Libyan government subsequently took a less confrontational approach, and Qaddafi decreased his posturing on international events. Libya did oppose the United States–led coalition against

Iraq in 1991, but offered no military support to Iraq during the Gulf War. Libya's economy improved some dur-

ing the early 1990s, and Qaddafi remained in power.

HEADS OF GOVERNMENT

MAHMOUD MUNTASSER (Prime Minister, December 24, 1951–February 15, 1954). Mahmoud Muntasser was born to a prominent Tripolitanian family in 1913. He was educated in Italy and was a proponent of close Libyan relations with Great Britain. He was appointed prime minister by King Idris in Libya's first provisional government in March of 1951 and became the leader of the first national government on December 24, 1951. Muntasser remained in office until February 15, 1954, when he resigned following a dispute between the provincial governors and the national government. He was then appointed ambassador to Great Britain. Muntasser was again appointed prime minister on January 24, 1964. During this term of office, he was instrumental in not renewing military agreements with Great Britain and the United States. In October of 1964 parliamentary elections were held, but King Idris dissolved the Parliament following disputes over the validity of the election. Muntasser remained in office until March 21, 1965, when he resigned for reasons of health. He subsequently served as head of the Royal Diwan. He died on October 3, 1970.

MOHAMMED AL-SAKIZLY (Prime Minister, February 19, 1954–April 11, 1954). Mohammed al-Sakizly was a former governor of Cyrenaica. He also served as head of the Royal Diwan, or council. He was appointed to succeed Mahmoud Muntasser as prime minister on February 18, 1954. Sakizly became involved in a power struggle between the cabinet and the royal household. He attempted to dissolve the Parliament, but when this action was

declared unconstitutional, he resigned on April 11, 1954.

MUSTAFA BIN HALIM (Prime Minister, April 12, 1954–May 23, 1957). Mustafa Bin Halim was born in 1922. He was educated at Alexandria University in Egypt and worked in an engineering company. He returned to Libya to serve as minister of communications in the Sakizly government. Bin Halim was appointed prime minister on April 12, 1954. He helped negotiate the American-Libyan Agreement, which allowed the United States government to maintain military bases on Libyan soil. This action met with disapproval from Arab nationalists in Libya and throughout the Arab world. Bin Halim was also instrumental in negotiating diplomatic relations with the Soviet Union and helped secure Libya's admission to the United Nations. Following the Suez Crisis in July of 1956, Bin Halim's government was successful in maintaining ties to both Great Britain and Egypt. Bin Halim's government resigned on May 23, 1957, over regional conflicts and power struggles in the royal household.

ABDUL MAJID KUBAR (Prime Minister, May 26, 1956–October 16, 1960). Abdul Majid Kubar was born in 1909. He was appointed prime minister on May 26, 1956, and was active in attempting to balance the federal budget and ensuring the continuation of foreign aid. He was instrumental in passing an election reform package in 1959 which led to a fairer general election in January of the following year. In 1960 Kubar came under criticism concerning the cost of a road being built between Fezzqan and Sebha. The cost of the road contract had tripled, and Kubar resigned from office on October 16, 1960, rather than face a vote of no confidence over the issue.

MOHAMMED BIN OTHMAN ES-SAID (Prime Minister, October 16, 1960–March 21, 1963). Mohammed bin Othman es-Said was born in 1910. Othman, a Fezzanese, was named prime minister on October 16, 1960, and was faced with the problem of maintaining a strong central government in the face of provincial disputes. After failing to restore confidence between the government and monarchy, Othman resigned on March 21, 1963, for reasons of health.

MOHIEDDINE AL-FEKINI (Prime Minister, March 21, 1963–January 24, 1964). Mohieddine al-Fekini was appointed prime minister on March 21, 1963. His government gave Libyan women the right to participate in elections and changed the government from a federal to a unitary system. Fekini's administration was faced with riots supporting Palestinian causes in January of 1964. A number of students were killed and injured when the Cyrenaica Defense Force was called in to restore order. Fekini demanded that King Idris force the resignation of Mahmud Bukuwaytin, the commander of the Cyrenaica Defense Force. The king refused the request and asked for Fekini's resignation instead. Fekini left office on January 24, 1964.

MAHMOUD MUNTASSER (Prime Minister, January 24, 1964–March 21, 1965). *See earlier entry under Heads of Government.*

HUSSAIN MAZIK (Prime Minister, March 21, 1965–June 28, 1967). Hussain Mazik was born in 1910. A leading member of the Barassa tribe, he had served as wali, or governor, of Cyrenaica during the 1950s. He was appointed prime minister on March 21, 1965. Libya experienced a period of economic and political stability during the early years of Mazik's government. This was to end following the Arab-Israeli war in June of 1967. Arab nationalists took to the streets and caused widespread disorder. The government was also beset by a strike by oil industry workers. Mazik was unable to restore order and resigned on June 28, 1967. He went into exile following the overthrow of the king in October of 1969. He was reportedly involved in a coup attempt against the revolutionary government in July of 1970.

ABDEL KADER EL-BADRY (Prime Minister, June 29, 1967–October 25, 1967). Abdel Kader al-Badry was named prime minister on June 29, 1967. He used strong measures to put down demonstrations against the government by Palestinian sympathizers, and he ordered the arrest and prosecution of the leaders of the oil workers strike. His harsh policies resulted in his resignation on October 25, 1967.

ABDUL HAMID BAKKUSH (Prime Minister, October 25, 1967–September 4, 1969). Abdul Hamid Bakkush was born in 1932. He succeeded Abdel Kader al-Badry as prime minister on October 25, 1967. He was considered a progressive and made attempts to modernize the Libyan armed forces and bureaucracy. Bakkush also attempted to involve Libya in a positive fashion in international and regional affairs. Bakkush was forced to resign on September 4, 1969, following a conflict with the more conservative members of the cabinet and Parliament. Following the coup in September of 1969, Bakkush went into exile in Egypt and became a leader of the Libyan Liberation Organization, a group organized to overthrow the rule of Muammar al-Qaddafi. Bakkush was the target of an assassination attempt in November of 1984. Egyptian authorities learned of the plot and arrested the conspirators. They then used fake photographs of a bleeding Bakkush to trick the Libyan government into announcing his assassination.

WANIS AL-QADDAFI (Prime Minister, September 4, 1968–September 1, 1969). Wanis al-Qaddafi was born in Benghazi on November 22, 1922. Qaddafi was named prime minister on September 4, 1968. He was responsible for negotiating an arms agreement with Great Britain in April of 1969. His term of office was cut short when he was ousted in the coup that dissolved the monarchy on September 1, 1969.

MAHMOUD SOLIMAN AL-MAGHREBY (Prime Minister, September 3, 1969–December 1969). Mahmoud Soliman al-Maghreby was born in Palestine in 1934 and was educated in the United States. He served as a lawyer for the oil industry in the 1960s and was arrested in 1967 for his role in the oil workers' strike. Following the coup that overthrew the monarchy on September 1, 1969, Maghreby was appointed prime minister by the ruling Revolutionary Command Council. Maghreby found it difficult to govern, as he had to receive approval from the Revolutionary Council for all cabinet decisions. He was forced to resign in December of 1969 after several of his military advisors were accused of plotting to overthrow the government.

MUAMMAR AL-QADDAFI (Prime Minister, January 16, 1970–July 16, 1972). *See earlier entry under Heads of Government.*

ABDUL SALAM JALLOUD (Prime Minister, July 16, 1972–March 2, 1977). Abdul Salam Jalloud was born in Mizda on December 15, 1944. He attended the Sebha Preparatory School, where he became friends with Muammar al-Qaddafi. He was an original member of the Revolutionary Command Council, and when Qaddafi became prime minister in January of 1970, Jalloud was named deputy prime minister and minister of the interior and local government. When Qaddafi relinquished his role as head of government in April of 1974, Jalloud became prime minister. He retained the position until it was abolished on March 2, 1977.

Liechtenstein, Principality of
(Fürstentum Liechtenstein)

Liechtenstein is a country in central Europe.

HEADS OF STATE

FRANZ JOSEF II (Prince, August 25, 1938–November 13, 1989). Franz Josef was born in Frauenthal Castle in Austria on August 16, 1906. He was a nephew of Archduke Franz Ferdinand of Austria. Franz Josef was educated in Austria and Switzerland. He succeeded his uncle, Prince Franz, to the Liechtenstein throne as sovereign prince on August 25, 1938. He succeeded in keeping Liechtenstein neutral during World War II and was able to avoid occupation by the Germans. After the war, Franz Josef refused Soviet demands to extradite Russians who had sought refuge in Liechtenstein during the war.

Liechtenstein became one of the world's most prosperous nations under Franz Josef. He was also an advocate of women's suffrage and succeeded in passing a referendum on the issue in 1984. Franz Josef relinquished most of his executive power to his son, Hans Adam, in August of 1984. He died at the age of 83 after a long illness in Grabs, Switzerland, on November 13, 1989.

HANS ADAM II (Prince, November 13, 1989-   ). Hans Adam was born on February 14, 1945. He was the son of Prince Franz Josef II and Princess Gina. He was educated in Austria and Switzerland and received a degree in economics in 1965. Hans Adam served as chief executive of the Prince of Liechtenstein Foundation from 1970 and acted as financial manager of the princely estate. He served as regent from August 26, 1984, when his father turned over executive power to him. Hans Adam succeeded his father as sovereign prince upon his death on November 13, 1989.

HEADS OF GOVERNMENT

FRANZ JOSEF HOOP (Prime Minister, August 4, 1928–July 20, 1945). Franz Josef Hoop was born in Essen on December 14, 1895. He replaced Gustav Schaedler as prime minister of Liechtenstein on August 4, 1928, and retained office until July 20, 1945. Hoop subsequently served as president of the Landtag, or Parliament. He became president of the National Court of Justice in 1953. Hoop died in Chur, Switzerland, following complications from surgery on October 19, 1959.

ALEXANDER FRICK (Prime Minister, September 3, 1945–June 23, 1962). Alexander Frick was born in Schaan on February 18, 1910. He attended the Training College for Teachers in Liechtenstein and worked as a teacher from 1929. Frick served as an official in the State Tax Department from 1930 until 1936. He served as chief of the Tax Department in 1936. Frick was chosen to replace Franz Josef Hoop as prime minister of Liechtenstein on September 3, 1945, and retained office until June 23, 1962. Frick served as president of the Diet in 1969.

GERARD BATLINER (Prime Minister, July 16, 1962–March 18, 1970). Gérard Batliner was born in Eschen on December 9, 1928. He was educated in Switzerland and France and received a degree in law. He returned to Liechtenstein in 1954 to set up a practice. Batliner joined the Progressive Citizen's party and was elected vice-mayor of Eschen in 1960. He became prime minister on July 16, 1962. The Progressive Citizen's party lost support in parliamentary elections in 1970, and Batliner was replaced as prime minister by Alfred Hilbe on March 18, 1970. He was elected president of the Parliament in 1974 and became vice president in 1978. Batliner also served on the Liechtenstein delegation to the Council of Europe from 1978 until 1982. He subsequently served as a member of the European Commission on Human Rights until 1990.

ALFRED J. HILBE (Prime Minister, March 18, 1970–March 27, 1974). Alfred J. Hilbe was born in Gmunden, Austria, on July 22, 1928. He was educated in Switzerland, France, and Austria, and joined the Liechtenstein Foreign Service in 1954. He served as a counselor at the embassy in Switzerland until 1965, when he returned to Liechtenstein to serve as leader of the Fatherland Union party. Hilbe served as deputy prime minister in the government of Gerard Batliner. The Fatherland Union received a plurality in parliamentary elections in 1970, and Hilbe was selected to serve as prime minister on March 18, 1970. The Progressive Citizen's party returned to victory in elections in 1974, and Hilbe was replaced by Walter Kieber on March 27, 1974. He subsequently went into the private sector as a financial consultant.

WALTER KIEBER (Prime Minister, March 27, 1974–February 3, 1978). Walter Kieber was born in Feldkirch, Austria, on February 20, 1931. He received a degree in law from the University of Innsbruck in 1955. He set up a legal practice in Vaduz later in the year. Kieber became head of the Government Legal Office in 1959 and was named to head the presidential Office in 1965. He became the leader of the Progressive Citizens' party and served as deputy prime minister from 1970. He led the party to victory in parliamentary elections in 1974 and succeeded Alfred Hilbe as prime minister on March 27, 1974. When the Progressive Citizens' party lost its plurality in 1978,

Kieber relinquished office to Hans Brunhart. A constitutional crisis ensued when Kieber refused to give up the post of foreign minister. Prince Franz Josef II intervened and divided the responsibilities of the office between Kieber and prime minister Brunhart. Kieber remained in the government as deputy prime minister until July of 1980. He subsequently left government service to continue his law practice.

HANS BRUNHART (Prime Minister, February 3, 1978–   ). Hans Brunhart was born in Balzers on March 28, 1945. He was educated in Liechtenstein and Switzerland. He served as deputy prime minister from 1974. Brunhart led the Fatherland Union party to victory in 1978 and replaced Walter Kieber as prime minister on February 3, 1978. He was reappointed following Fatherland Union victories in 1982 and 1986. Brunhart called an early election in March of 1989 following a parliamentary dispute over the construction of an art gallery. The Fatherland Union retained its plurality, and Brunhart remained prime minister.

Lithuania, Republic of
(Lietuvos Respublika)

Lithuania is a country in northern Europe on the Baltic Sea. It declared itself independent from the Soviet Union on March 11, 1990.

HEADS OF STATE

VYTAUTAS LANDSBERGIS (President, March 11, 1990–November 25, 1992). Vytautas Landsbergis was born in Kaunas on October 12, 1932. He was educated in Lithuania and received a degree in musicology. He taught at the Vilnius Conservatoire. Landsbergis was a leading member of the Lithuanian

nationalist movement. He was selected as president of the Lithuanian Assembly in November of 1988. He was elected president of the Supreme Council on March 11, 1990, to succeed Algirdas Brazauskas. Lithuania proclaimed its independence on March 11, 1990, and was recognized as a fully independent nation on September 6, 1991. Landsbergis's Lithuania Reform Movement party was defeated in the elections in November of 1992, and Landsbergis was replaced as head of state on November 25, 1992.

ALGIRDAS BRAZAUSKAS (President, November 25, 1992–   ). Algirdas Mykolas Brazauskas was the leader of the Lithuanian Communist party. He served as chairman of the Supreme Soviet Presidium until March 11, 1990. Brazauskas resigned from the Communist party and formed the Lithuanian Democratic Labor party. His party defeated the ruling party of Vytautus Landsbergis in November of 1992, and Brazauskas became chairman of the Supreme Council on November 25, 1992.

HEADS OF GOVERNMENT

KAZIMIERA PRUNSKIENĖ (Prime Minister, March 11, 1990–January 8, 1991). Kazimiera Danutė Prunskienė was born in the Shvenchene Region on February 26, 1943. She was educated at the Vilnius State University and subsequently served on the faculty there until 1985. She became deputy chairperson of the Council of Ministers in 1989. The following year, on March 11, 1990, Prunskienė became chairperson, succeeding Vytautas Sakalauskas. She resigned on January 8, 1991, after massive demonstrations by ethnic Russians following a period of economic hardship and inflation.

GEDIMINAS VAGNORIUS (Prime Minister, January 8, 1991–May 28, 1992). Gediminas Vagnorius was born in Zhemaitiya on June 10, 1957. He was educated in Vilnius as an engineer and economist. He served in the Lithuanian Academy of Sciences from 1980 and was elected to the Presidium of the Lithuanian Supreme Soviet in 1990. Vagnorius became prime minister of independent Lithuania on January 8, 1991. He resigned on May 28, 1992.

ALEKSANDRAS ABIŠALA (Prime Minister, July 23, 1992–December 2, 1992). Aleksandras Abišala was a member of the Lithuanian Reform Movement. He formed a government on July 23, 1992. He stepped down on December 2, 1992, following elections in which his party was defeated at the polls.

BRONISLOVAS LUBYS (Prime Minister, December 2, 1992–   ). Bronislovas Lubys was born in 1938. He served as an independent member of the Lithuanian Parliament and was deputy prime minister under Alexsandras Abisala. He was chosen to succeed Abisala as prime minister and formed a government on December 2, 1992.

Luxembourg, Grand Duchy of
(Grand-Duché de Luxembourg)

Luxembourg is a country in central western Europe.

HEADS OF STATE

CHARLOTTE (Grand Duchess, January 15, 1919–November 12, 1964). Charlotte Aldegonde Elise Marie Wilhelmine was born in Colmar Berg Castle on

January 23, 1896. She was the daughter of Grand Duke William IV of Luxembourg and Princess Marie-Anne of Braganza. Grand Duke William was succeeded by Charlotte's older sister, Marie Adelaide, on February 26, 1912. Luxembourg was occupied by Germany during World War I. Grand Duchess Marie Adelaide was charged with supporting the Germans following the conclusion of World War I. She abdicated the throne on January 15, 1919, and went into a convent in Italy, where she died five years later. Charlotte ascended to the throne and remained grand duchess following a referendum that confirmed the continuation of the monarchy in September of 1919. She married Prince Felix of Bourbon-Parma several months later. She ruled as a popular monarch until she was forced into exile in Paris following the German occupation of Luxembourg in May of 1940. Charlotte subsequently went to Lisbon, Portugal, and remained in exile during the war. She helped to maintain the morale of her subjects through daily radio broadcasts. She was greeted by widespread rejoicing upon her return to Luxembourg in April of 1945. Charlotte continued her reign over the grand duchy until November 12, 1969, when she abdicated in favor of her son, Jean. She continued to appear at state functions during her retirement. She became ill in June of 1985 and died at Fischbach Castle at the age of 89 on July 9, 1985.

JEAN (Grand Duke, November 12, 1964–   ). Jean Benoit Guillaume Marie Robert Louis Antoine Adolphe Marc D'Aviano was born in the castle of Colmar Berg on January 5, 1921. He was the son of Grand Duchess Charlotte and Prince Felix of Bourbon-Parma. He married Princess Josephine-Charlotte of Belgium in 1953. Jean served as his mother's representative from 1961 and succeeded to the throne upon her abdication on November 12, 1964. The grand duke was a popular figure in Luxembourg and made numerous appearances at state functions.

HEADS OF GOVERNMENT

PIERRE DUPONG (Prime Minister, November 5, 1937–December 22, 1953). Pierre Dupong was born in Luxembourg on November 1, 1885. He was educated at universities in Germany, Switzerland, and France. He received a degree in law and began a legal practice in Luxembourg in 1911. Dupong was elected to the Parliament as a member of the Social Christian party in 1915. He was named to the government as director-general of finances and social welfare in 1926. He subsequently joined the cabinet of Prime Minister Joseph Bech as minister of labor. Dupong succeeded Bech as prime minister on November 5, 1937, when the Socialist party refused to join Bech's coalition cabinet. Dupong escaped from Luxembourg with the royal family following the German invasion in May of 1940. He led a government-in-exile first in Paris and then in London until the country was liberated in September of 1944. He continued to lead a national coalition government and initiated reconstruction plans for the war-damaged areas of the country. Dupong was hospitalized in December of 1953 after breaking his left leg in a fall in the prime minister's office. He died of a heart attack in a Luxembourg hospital at the age of 68 on December 22, 1953.

JOSEPH BECH (Prime Minister, December 29, 1953–March 26, 1958). Joseph Bech was born in Diekirch, Luxembourg, on February 17, 1887. He was educated at the University of Paris and received a degree in law in 1912. He returned to Luxembourg and was elected to the Parliament as a member of the Social Christian party in 1914. Bech retained office throughout the German occupation of Luxembourg during World War II. He was named to the cabinet of Prime Minister Emile Reuter in 1921 and served as minister of justice and home affairs. He was selected as prime minister of Luxembourg on July 16, 1926. Bech also served in the government as foreign minister and represented the country at the League of Nations from 1925. He retained office until October 19, 1937, when he resigned as prime minister, but he remained in the government of Pierre Dupong as foreign minister. Bech joined the government-in-exile in Paris following the German occupation of Luxembourg in May of 1940. He subsequently accompanied the government to London. He returned to Luxembourg following the liberation in September of 1944 and remained in the cabinet as foreign minister. Bech was instrumental in the negotiations that led to the Benelux economic agreement with Belgium, the Netherlands, and Luxembourg in 1946. He was a chief architect of the Council of Europe in 1949 and signed the North Atlantic Treaty in Washington later in the year. Bech returned to office as prime minister on December 29, 1953, following the death of Dupong. He signed the Treaty of Rome, which established the European Common Market, in 1957. Bech again stepped down as prime minister on March 26, 1958. He remained foreign minister in the subsequent government of Pierre Frieden. Bech retired from politics in 1959. He died in Luxembourg at the age of 88 on March 8, 1975.

PIERRE FRIEDEN (Prime Minister, March 31, 1958–February 23, 1959). Pierre Frieden was born in Mertert on October 28, 1892. He served as minister of education and the interior in the government of Joseph Bech. He succeeded Bech as prime minister of a Catholic-Socialist coalition on March 31, 1958. Frieden's government resigned in December of 1958 following allegations of attempted bribery in the ministry of transportation. New elections were held on February 1, 1959, and Frieden's Social-Christian party lost seats in the Parliament. He remained as prime minister in a caretaker government until his death in Zurich, Switzerland, at the age of 66 on February 23, 1959.

PIERRE WERNER (Prime Minister, March 7, 1959–May 27, 1974). Christian Pierre Werner was born in Saint Andre, Lille, France on December 29, 1913. He was educated at the University of Paris and the University of Luxembourg. He received a law degree and began the practice of law in 1938. Werner worked in the banking industry from 1939 until 1944, when he returned to his law practice for a year. In 1946 Werner was named commissioner of bank control. He remained in this position until 1953, when he was appointed minister of finance and armed forces in the cabinet. On March 7, 1959, Werner was named prime minister of Luxembourg. During the 1960s he also served in other cabinet positions, including minister of finance, minister of foreign affairs, minister of the treasury, and minister of justice. When Werner's Christian Social party was defeated in the elections of 1974, Werner stepped down as prime minister on May 27, 1974. He remained chairman of the Christian Social party, and on July 19, 1979, he again was selected as prime minister. Werner retired from office on July 20, 1984.

GASTON THORN (Prime Minister, June 15, 1974–July 19, 1979). Gaston Thorn was born on September 3, 1928. He was educated in France, where he received a degree in law. He was elected to the Legislature in 1959 and also served as a member of the European Parliament. He became President of the Democratic party in 1961 and served as minister of foreign affairs from 1969. Thorn was elected prime minister on June 15, 1974. He also served as president of the United Nations General Assembly from 1975 until 1976. He resigned as prime minister on July 19, 1979, following his party's defeat in the elections. He subsequently served as minister of justice and deputy prime minister until 1980. The following year he served as president of the Commission of the European Communities until 1984. In 1985 Thorn became president of the Bank of Luxembourg.

PIERRE WERNER (Prime Minister, July 19, 1979–July 20, 1984). *See earlier entry under Heads of Government.*

JACQUES SANTER (Prime Minister, July 20, 1984–). Jacques Santer was born in Wasserbillig on May 18, 1937. He was educated in France and returned to Luxembourg to work in the government. He served as Parliament secretary for the Christian Socialist party from 1966. Santer became secretary-general of the party in 1972 and president in 1974. He also served as secretary of state for cultural and social affairs from 1972 until 1974. He was elected to the Chamber of Deputies in 1974 and served until 1979. Santer also served as a member of the European Parliament from 1975 until 1979. He was appointed minister of finance, labor, and social security in 1979. Santer was appointed prime minister on July 20, 1984. The Christian Social party maintained its plurality in parliamentary elections in 1989, and Santer remained prime minister. The government approved the European Community's Maastricht Treaty in July of 1992 that provided for Luxembourg's inclusion in the further unification of Europe.

Macedonia, Republic of

(Republika Makedonija)

Macedonia is a country is southeastern Europe. It declared its independence from Yugoslavia on September 8, 1991.

HEAD OF STATE

KIRO GLIGOROV (President, December 20, 1990–). Kiro Gligorov was born in Stip on May 3, 1917. He was active in the Yugoslavian Resistance during World War II and served as deputy secretary-general to the government of Yugoslavia following the war. He served as assistant minister of finance from 1947 until 1952 and remained a leading economic advisor in the Yugoslavian government. Gligorov was selected as a member of the presidency of the Federal Republic of Yugoslavia in 1972 and was elected president of Parliament in 1974. He retained that position until 1978. Gligorov was named president of the Macedonian Assembly on December 9, 1990, to succeed Vladimir Mitkov. Macedonia supported a referendum on September 8, 1991, which favored Macedonian sovereignty. Gligorov continued to serve as president of the independent Macedonian government. The European Community refused to recognize Macedonia until 1993 because of a conflict with Greece over the use of the name.

HEAD OF GOVERNMENT

NIKOLA KLJUSEV (Prime Minister, December 9, 1990–   ). Nikola Kljušev was a member of the Social-Democratic League of Macedonia. He was ap-pointed prime minister of Macedonia on December 9, 1990. He remained head of a reformed government on August 23, 1992.

Madagascar, Democratic Republic of

(Republique Democratique de Madagascar)

Madagascar is an island country in the western Indian Ocean off the southeast coast of Africa. It was granted independence from France on June 26, 1960.

HEADS OF STATE

PHILIBERT TSIRANANA (President, April 27, 1959–October 8, 1972). Philibert Tsiranana was born in Anahidrano on October 18, 1910. He was educated in France and then returned to Madagascar to teach in a Tananarive technical school. He was elected to the Madagascan Assembly in 1952 and served as a deputy in the French National Assembly from 1956. Tsiranana also founded the Social Democratic party in 1956, and two years later he was named leader of the provisional government. Tsiranana took office as president of Madagascar on April 27, 1959, and continued to lead the government following full independence from France on June 26, 1960. Tsiranana was a pro–Western leader who tried to keep Communism from gaining a foothold in Madagascar. He was reelected president in 1965 and in January of 1972. In May of 1972 his government was faced with a crisis when riots and demonstrations broke out throughout the country. He turned power over to a military government under General Gabriel Ramanantsoa, and Tsiranana was forced to resign as president on October 8, 1972. He was arrested for complicity in the assassination of President Richard Ratsimandrava in February of 1975. Tsiranana was acquitted of all charges. He died in Tananarive on April 16, 1978.

GABRIEL RAMANANTSOA (President, October 12, 1972–February 5, 1975). Gabriel Ramanantsoa was born in Tananarive on April 13, 1906. He was educated locally and in France, where he attended the French Military College at St. Cyr. He served in the French army during World War II and in Vietnam. Ramanantsoa was promoted to the rank of colonel in 1959. He was involved in the negotiations for Madagascar's independence from France. Ramanantsoa was named chief of the general staff of the armed forces when independence was granted, and Madagascar became known as the Malagasy Republic in 1960. Major General Ramanantsoa was named to head the government following three days of rioting in May of 1972. He succeeded Philibert Tsiranana as president on October 12, 1972. Dissension in the military and conflicts with followers of former president Tsiranana caused

Ramanantsoa's removal from office several years later on February 5, 1975. Ramanantsoa went into retirement, and in May of 1979 he went to Paris for medical treatment. He died in a Paris military hospital on May 9, 1979, at the age of 73.

RICHARD RATSIMANDRAVA (President, February 5, 1975-February 11, 1975). Richard Ratsimandrava was born on March 21, 1931. He attended the French Military College in St. Cyr and served in the French gendarmerie. He was stationed in France, Morocco, and Algeria until he returned to Madagascar following independence in 1960. Ratsimandrava became a leader in the Madagascan army, where he rose to lieutenant colonel in 1968. He was appointed minister of the interior in the military government under President Gabriel Ramanantsoa. He orchestrated the ouster of Ramanantsoa and became president on February 5, 1975. He was assassinated six days later on February 11, 1975, while driving to his residence in Tananarive from the presidential palace.

GILLES ANDRIAMAHAZO (President, February 11, 1975-June 15, 1975). Gilles Andriamahazo was born at Fort Dauphin on May 5, 1919. He joined the French colonial army and served in Europe near the end of World War II. He later served in Algeria and France before returning to Madagascar after independence. Andriamahazo joined the Madagascan army and rose to the rank of brigadier general in 1971. He served as inspector general of the armed forces before being named to the military cabinet as minister of works and communications. He also served as military governor of Tananarive. Andriamahazo served as chairman of the ruling military junta following the assassination of President Richard Ratsimandrava on February 11, 1975. He was successful in preventing a civil war following the assassination. He served as head of state until June 15, 1975, when he resigned in favor of Admiral Didier Ratsiraka. Andriamahazo resigned from the military in 1976. He died of a heart attack in Tananarive on September 14, 1989.

DIDIER RATSIRAKA (President, June 15, 1975–). Didier Ratsiraka was born in Vatomandry on November 4, 1936. He was educated in Tananarive and was admitted to the French Naval Officer's School. He served in the French navy and returned to Madagascar following independence. Ratsiraka served as a military attaché in the Madagascan Embassy in Paris. He was appointed to the military cabinet as minister of foreign affairs in May of 1972. On June 15, 1975, he suceeded Gilles Andriamahazo as president of the Supreme Council of Revolution. Ratsiraka served as prime minister and minister of defense from June until December of 1975. He was selected as president of Madagascar in January of 1976. Ratsiraka's government survived several coup attempts. In the 1990s the government allowed the formation of opposition parties. Presidential elections were held on November 25, 1992, and Ratsiraka ran a distant second to Albert Zafy. Zafy did not receive a majority of the votes, however, and a runoff election was postponed until February of 1993.

HEADS OF GOVERMENT

GABRIEL RAMANANTSOA (Prime Minister, May 18, 1972-January 25, 1975). *See entry under Heads of State.*

JOEL RAKOTOMALALA (Prime Minister, January 11, 1976-July 30, 1976). Joël Rakotomalala was born in 1929.

He served in the Madagascan military, where he rose to the rank of lieutenant colonel. He was named as prime minister of a national unity government composed of military and civilian members on January 11, 1976. He retained office until his death in a helicopter crash near the capital of Tananarive on July 30, 1976.

JUSTIN RAKATONIAINA (Prime Minister, August 12, 1976–August 14, 1977). Justin Rakatoniaina was born in 1933. He taught law at the University of Madagascar before being named ambassador to Algeria in 1973. He served in the cabinet as minister of national education from 1975 until 1976. Rakatoniaina was named prime minister on August 12, 1976, and served until August 14, 1977.

DÉSIRÉ RAKOTOARIJOANA (Prime Minister, August 14, 1977–February 12, 1988). Désiré Rakotoarijoana was born in 1934. He served in the Madagascan military, where he rose to the rank of colonel. Rakotoarijoana served on the ruling Supreme Revolutionary Council from 1975. He was appointed minister of finance in February of 1975 and served until the

following June. Rakotoarijoana was named prime minister on August 14, 1977. He resigned from office on February 12, 1988.

VICTOR RAMAHATRA (Prime Minister, February 12, 1988–August 8, 1991). Victor Ramahatra was born in Antananarivo on September 6, 1945. He served as a lieutenant colonel in the Corps of Engineers. He was minister of public works in the cabinet of Prime Minister Désiré Rakotoarijoana. Ramahatra was appointed to replace Rakotoarijoana as prime minister on February 12, 1988. He was replaced by Guy Razanamasy on August 8, 1991.

GUY RAZANAMASY (Prime Minister, August 8, 1991–   ). Guy Willy Razanamasy served as mayor of Antananarivo. He was appointed prime minister of Madagascar on August 8, 1991. Razanamasy was granted increased executive powers following widespread protests against the government. He formed a national consensus cabinet in November of 1991 and leading opposition figure Albert Zafy served as president of the transitional High State Authority.

Malawi, Republic of

Malawi is a country in southern central Africa. It was granted independence from Great Britain on July 6, 1964.

HEADS OF STATE

SIR GLYN JONES (Governor General, July 6, 1964–July 6, 1966). Glyn Smallwood Jones was born in Chester, England, on January 9, 1908. He entered the British Colonial Service in 1931 and served in Northern Rhodesia. He was promoted to district commissioner in 1938 and provincial commis-

sioner in 1956. Jones served as minister of native affairs in 1960 and served as chief secretary of Nyasaland from 1960 until 1961. He was then named governor of Malawi. Jones became governor-general of Malawi when the country was granted independence from Great Britain on July 6, 1964. He retained his position until Malawi became a republic on July 6, 1966. Jones subsequently retired from the colonial service to enter private business.

HASTINGS K. BANDA (President, July 6, 1966–). Hastings Kamuzu Banda was born to the Chewa tribe in the Kasunga district of northern Nyasaland on May 14, 1906. He received an education at the Church of Scotland mission in Livingstonia and then left home on foot to go to South Africa. He worked as an orderly at a Southern Rhodesian hospital en route and was employed as a clerk in the gold fields in Johannesburg after reaching South Africa. Banda earned passage to the United States in 1923 and attended the Wilberforce Institute in Xenia, Ohio. He graduated in 1928 and attended Indiana University. He subsequently attended the University of Chicago and earned a bachelor's degree in 1931. Banda then entered Meharry Medical College in Nashville, Tennessee, and earned a medical degree in 1937. He studied medicine in Scotland and worked as a physician in Liverpool during World War II. In 1945 he opened a practice in London, where he remained until 1953. Banda became involved with various African nationalist leaders and founded the Nyasaland African Congress in 1950. He opposed the federation of Nyasaland with Rhodesia and returned to Africa in 1953. He practiced medicine in the Gold Coast (now Ghana) and remained active in Nyasaland nationalist politics. Banda returned to Nyasaland in July of 1958 to lead the Nyasaland African Congress. Follow-

ing civil disturbances, the congress was outlawed in March of 1959 by the governor, Sir Robert Armitage, and a state of emergency was declared. The colonial government arrested Banda and imprisoned him in Southern Rhodesia. Banda's followers organized the Malawi Congress party in September of 1959 and demanded his release. He was set free on April 1, 1960, and attended conferences in London to decide the future of Nyasaland. A new constitution was introduced, and elections were scheduled for the Legislative Council. He also succeeded in preventing the federation of Nyasaland with Rhodesia. Banda was victorious in elections held in September of 1961 and served as minister of natural resources and local government. He became prime minister on February 1, 1963, when Malawi was granted internal self-government. Malawi achieved complete independence on July 6, 1964. Banda became president of Malawi when the nation was declared a republic on July 6, 1966. The Malawi Constitution was amended in 1970, and Banda was named president-for-life on July 6, 1971. Later in the month he became the first black African leader to visit South Africa. Banda survived criticism to his rule from within his nation and from neighboring African countries. A long succession of presumed heirs apparent fell from favor and were dismissed from their government positions. Banda maintained his rule by developing a cult of personality. He kept a tight rein on dissidents, but violent antigovernment demonstrations took place in early May of 1992.

HEAD OF GOVERNMENT

HASTINGS K. BANDA (Prime Minister, February 1, 1963–July 6, 1966). *See entry under Heads of State.*

Malaysia

Malaysia is a country in Southeast Asia. It was granted independence from Great Britain on August 31, 1957.

HEADS OF STATE

TUANKU ABDUL RAHMAN (Paramount Ruler, August 31, 1957–April 1, 1960). Abdul Rahman Ibini al-Marhum Tuanku Muhammad was born in Malaya on August 24, 1895. He became head of state of Negri Sembilan in 1933. He was active in the Malaya independence movement and served as minister of home affairs in the British colonial government of Malaya. He was elected yang di-pertuan agong, or paramount ruler, of the independent nation of the Federation of Malaya upon independence on August 31, 1957. He died in Kuala Lumpur on April 1, 1960.

TUANKU HISAMUDDIN ALAM SHAH (Paramount Ruler, April 14, 1960–September 1, 1960). Hisamuddin Alam Shah al-Haj Ibini al-Marhum Sultan Alaiddun Sulaiman Shah was born in Bandar in Selangor on May 13, 1898. He was the son of the sultan of Selangor and succeeded to the sultanate following the death of his father in 1938. He was deposed by the Japanese during the occupation of Malaya in 1942. He was reinstated by the British colonial administration following the conclusion of World War II. He served as deputy head of state of Malaya after independence in August of 1957. He was selected as paramount ruler of Malaya on April 14, 1960, following the death of Tuanku Abdul Rahman. His rule was brief, as he died in Kuala Lumpur on September 1, 1960.

TUANKU SYED PUTRA IBINI AL-MARHUM SYED HASSAN JAMALUL-LAIL (Paramount Ruler, September 21, 1960–September 21, 1965). Tuanku Syed Putra ibini al-Marhum Syed Hassan Jamalullail was born in 1920. He was appointed heir presumptive to the throne of Perlis in April of 1938. He ascended to the throne as rajah of Perlis in 1945 and was officially installed four years later. He was selected by the Conference of Rulers to succeed Tuanku Hisamuddin Alam Shah as yang di-pertuan agong on September 21, 1960. He remained paramount ruler of Malaysia until September 21, 1965, and continued to rule as rajah of Perlis.

TUANKU ISMAIL NASIRUDDIN SHAH (Paramount Ruler, September 21, 1965–September 21, 1970). Tuanku Ismail Nasiruddin Shah was born on January 24, 1907. He entered Trengganu civil service in 1929 and rose to the position of chief magistrate. He ascended to the throne of Trengganu in 1945 and was officially installed four years later. He was selected to become paramount ruler of Malaysia on September 21, 1965. He completed his term on September 21, 1970. He remained on the throne of Trengganu until his death in September of 1979.

TUANKU ABDUL HALIM MU'AZ-ZAM SHAH (Paramount Ruler, September 21, 1970–September 21, 1975). Tuanku Abdul Halim Mu'azzam Shah was born on November 28, 1927. He succeeded his father as sultan of Kedah in July of 1958. He was selected by the Conference of Rulers to serve as paramount ruler of Malaysia on September 21, 1970. He completed his five-year term on September 21, 1975.

TUANKU YAHYA PUTRA IBINI AL-HARHUM SULTAN IBRAHIM (Paramount Ruler, September 21, 1975–March 29, 1979). Tuanku Yahya Putra ibini al-Harhum Sultan Ibrahim was born on December 10, 1917. He served as president of the Council of Religion and Malay Customs from 1948 until 1953. He also served as regent of Kelantan on several occasions during the 1950s. He ascended to the throne as sultan of Kelantan in 1960. He was chosen paramount ruler of Malaysia on September 21, 1975, and retained his position until his death on March 29, 1979.

TUANKU SULTAN HAJI AHMAD SHAH AL-MUSTA'IN BILAH IBNI AL-MARHUM SULTAN ABU BAKAR RI'AYATUDDIN AL-MU'ADZAM SHAH (Paramount Ruler, March 29, 1979–April 26, 1984). Tuanku Sultan Haji Ahmad Shah al-Musta'in Bilah ibni al-Marhum Sultan abu Bakar Ri'Ayatuddin al-Mu'adzam Shah was born in 1930. He was the sultan of Penang when he was elected to succeed Tuanku Yahya Putra on March 29, 1979, as paramount ruler of Malaysia. He completed his term on April 26, 1984.

TUANKU MAHMOOD ISKANDER IBNI AL-MARHUM SULTAN ISMAIL (Paramount Ruler, April 26, 1984–April 26, 1989). Tuanku Mahmood Iskander ibni al-Marhum Sultan Ismail was born in Johore Bahru on April 8, 1932. He was educated in Malaysia and Australia. He became crown prince of Johore in 1959 and succeeded as the sultan of Johore on May 11, 1981. He was selected as paramount ruler of Malaysia on April 26, 1984, and served until April 26, 1989.

AZLAN MOHIBBUDDIN SHAH IBNI SULTAN YUSOF IZZUDIN (Paramount Ruler, April 26, 1989–). Azlan Mohibbuddin Shah Ibni Sultan Yusof Izzudin was born in Batu Gajah on April 19, 1928. He was educated in Malaysia and Great Britain and received a degree in law. He returned to Malaysia, where he worked in the justice department. He was named a judge in the Federal Court in 1973 and became chief justice of Malaysia in 1979. He became the sultan of Perak in January of 1984 and became paramount ruler of Malaysia on April 26, 1989.

HEADS OF GOVERNMENT

TUANKU ABDUL RAHMAN (Prime Minister, August 31, 1957–April 15, 1959). Abdul Rahman ibni al-Marhum Sultan Abdul Hamid Halim Shah was born in Alor Star, Kedah, on February 8, 1903. He was a son of the sultan of Kedah. He was educated in Malaya and Great Britain, where he received a degree from Cambridge University. Abdul Rahman returned to Malaya to work in the civil service in the legal department in Kedah. He went to Great Britain in 1938 to study law, but returned to Malaya at the outbreak of World War II. He served in the civil defense for Kedah and remained in Malaya during the Japanese occupation. After

the war he joined the United Malay National Organization (UMNO) and served as a leader in northern Malaya. Abdul Rahman was sent to Great Britain in 1947 to continue his studies and received a degree in law in 1949. He returned to Malaya to work in the public prosecutor's office. He became president of UMNO in 1951 and led the party to victory in municipal elections the following year. Abdul Rahman subsequently entered UMNO into a coalition with Chinese and Indian groups and formed the Alliance party. He became chief minister of the Executive Council following legislative elections in July of 1955. He also served as minister of home affairs in the government. Abdul Rahman negotiated for Malaya's independence and became prime minister of the Independent Federation of Malaya on August 31, 1957. He stepped down as prime minister on April 15, 1959, to lead the Alliance party in state elections. He resumed office on August 21, 1959, following the Alliance party victory. Abdul Rahman remained head of the government when Sarawak, Sabah, and Singapore entered the federation on September 16, 1963, and the country became known as Malaysia. Singapore withdrew from Malaysia in August of 1965, and Malaysia engaged in an armed dispute with Indonesia over the status of Sabah until 1966. When Malaysia was faced with civil disorders between Chinese and Malayan ethnic groups in Kuala Lumpur, Abdul Rahman declared a state of emergency and suspended Parliament. He stepped down as prime minister on September 22, 1970, but he remained interested in political affairs and wrote a weekly newspaper column until 1987. Abdul Rahman emerged from retirement to campaign against Prime Minister Datuk Ser Mahathir bin Mohamad in elections in 1988. Mahathir was reelected despite Abdul Rahman's efforts. Abdul Rahman suffered from heart and kidney problems and died in a Kuala Lumpur hospital at the age of 87 on December 6, 1990.

TUN ABDUL RAZAK (Prime Minister, April 15, 1959–August 21, 1959). Abdul Razak bin Hussein was born in Pekan, Pahang State, on March 11, 1922. He was educated in Malaya and Singapore. He fought in the Resistance during the Japanese occupation in World War II. After the war he went to London and received a degree in law. Abdul Razak returned to Malaya and joined the civil service in Pahang in 1950. He entered the United Malay National Organization with Tuanku Abdul Rahman. The party was victorious in legislative elections in 1956, and

Abdul Razak served as minister of education in Abdul Rahman's government. He participated in the constitutional negotiations with Great Britain that resulted in Malaya's independence in 1957. Abdul Razak was named deputy prime minister in the independent government. He briefly served as prime minister from April 15, 1959, until August 21, 1959, when Abdul Rahman stepped down to lead the party in elections. Abdul Razak continued to serve as deputy prime minister and negotiated the peace settlement that ended the fighting between Malaysia and Indonesia in 1966. He was named director of operations in 1969 and led the government's efforts to halt race riots between ethnic Chinese and Malays. Abdul Razak became prime minister on September 22, 1970, when Abdul Rahman retired from office. He led Malaysia from its previous pro–Western policies to a position of nonalignment. He opened diplomatic relations with the People's Republic of China in 1975. Abdul Razak dealt harshly with Communist insurgents within Malaysia and received emergency powers to deal with a rebellion in mid-1975. Abdul Razak was hospitalized in London in December of 1975 for acute leukemia. He died in London at the age of 53 on January 14, 1976.

TUANKU ABDUL RAHMAN (Prime Minister, August 21, 1959–September 22, 1970). *See earlier entry under Heads of Government.*

TUN ABDUL RAZAK (Prime Minister, September 22, 1970–January 14, 1976). *See earlier entry under Heads of Government.*

DATUK HUSSEIN BIN ONN (Prime Minister, January 14, 1976–July 16, 1981). Hussein bin Onn was born in Bharu, in Johore, on February 22, 1922. He was the son of Onn bin Jaafar. He was educated locally and at the Indian Military Academy at Dehra

Dun. Hussein's father founded the United Malay National Organization in 1946, and Hussein worked in the party's youth league. Hussein and his father withdrew from the party over a disagreement with the leadership in 1953. Hussein then went to London to study law. He returned to Malaya to establish a law practice. He was persuaded by Tuanku Abdul Rahman to reenter politics in 1968. The following year he was elected to Parliament. Hussein was named deputy prime minister and minister of finance in the government of Abdul Razak in 1973. Hussein suffered a heart attack in March of 1974, but recovered and returned to office. He became prime minister on January 14, 1976, after the death of Abdul Razak. He resigned from office on July 16, 1981, following a coronary bypass operation. Hussein broke with his successor Mahathir bin Mohamad in 1988 and supported a rival faction of the United Malay National Organization opposing the government. Hussein suffered a heart attack in April of 1990 and was hospitalized in California. He died in Daly City, California, from a second heart attack at the age of 68 on May 28, 1990.

DATUK SER MAHATHIR BIN MOHAMAD (Prime Minister, July 16, 1981–). Datuk Ser Mahathir bin Mohamad was born in Alur Setar, in Kedah, on December 20, 1925. He attended the University of Malaya in Singapore, becoming a medical officer. He was elected to the Umno Baru Supreme Council in 1965 and served until 1969 and again from 1972. Mahathir served as president of the Council from 1981. He was named to the cabinet as minister of education in 1974 and served until 1977 when he was named minister of trade and industry. He also served as deputy prime minister from 1976. Mahathir was selected as prime minister on July 16, 1981, and also served as minister of defense. Mahathir called early elections in April of 1982 and was returned to office by a large margin. His party was again victorious in elections in August of 1986. Mahathir was challenged for leadership of the United Malay National Organization in April of 1987. He defeated Razaleigh Hamzah by a narrow margin, and the party divided into two factions. Mahathir ousted the president of the Malaysian Supreme Court in August of 1988 when he ruled against Mahathir's faction of the party. Mahathir's government also faced increased tension from the hereditary rulers of Malaysia's nine states.

Maldives, Republic of

(Dhivehi Jumhuriyah)

The Maldives is a country on a chain of islands in the Indian Ocean. It received its independence from Great Britain on July 26, 1965.

HEADS OF STATE

AMIN DIDI (President, January 1, 1953–September 3, 1953). Amin Didi was born in 1912. He became the first president of the Maldive Islands when the country instituted a republican form of government on January 1, 1953. The

Maldives went into turmoil on August 21, 1953, when a food crisis resulted in massive demonstrations against the government. Amin Didi was ousted on September 3, 1953, and charged with food offenses. Didi went into exile on Male Atoll. He died on January 19, 1954, from injuries he received when he was beaten by a crowd of angry demonstrators.

IBRAHIM MOHAMED DIDI (Co-president, September 3, 1953–March 7, 1954). Ibrahim Mohamed Didi was the cousin of Amin Didi and served as deputy president in his government. He was named to succeed Amin Didi as part of a joint president–prime minister system with Ibrahim Ali Didi on September 3, 1953. The two remained in power until March 7, 1954, when the sultanate was restored. He retained office until December of 1957.

IBRAHIM ALI DIDI (Copresident, September 3, 1953–March 7, 1954). Ibrahim Ali Didi served in the government of Amin Didi as minister without portfolio. He served with Ibrahim Mohamed Didi as joint president-prime minister from September 3, 1953. The two remained in power until March 7, 1954, when the sultanate was restored. Ibrahim Ali Didi was subsequently named to head a new government as prime minister on March 12, 1954.

MOHAMMAD FARID DIDI (Sultan, March 8, 1954–November 1, 1968). Mohammad Farid Didi was born in 1901. He was the son of Abdulmajid Didi, a former sultan-designate. Mohammad Farid Didi served as prime minister of the Maldives prior to independence. On February 22, 1954, the National Assembly voted to restore the sultanate, and Mohammad Farid Didi was selected to be the ninety-third

sultan. He assumed office on March 8, 1954. The Maldives became a republic on November 1, 1968, and Ibrahim Nasir was selected to become head of state of the new government.

IBRAHIM NASIR (President, November 1, 1968–November 11, 1978). Ibrahim Nasir was born in Male on September 2, 1926. He was educated in Sri Lanka and returned to the Maldvies to work in government. He served as minister of public safety in 1956 and was minister of home affairs in 1957. Nasir was elected prime minister in December of 1957 and also held other ministries. He was reelected in 1959 and 1964. He retained the office following Maldivian independence on July 26, 1965. When Maldive became a republic on November 1, 1968, Nasir became the first president of the republic. He retired from the office on November 11, 1978. He subsequently went to Singapore, and in 1980 he was charged with embezzlement of public funds. Nasir was convicted in absentia and banished for 25 years. He was granted a pardon in July of 1990 by President Maumoon Abdul Gayoom.

MAUMOON ABDUL GAYOOM (President, November 11, 1978–   ). Maumoon Abdul Gayoom was born on December 29, 1937. He was educated in Egypt and became a teacher. After teaching in Nigeria, he returned to the Maldives in 1971. He worked in various government bureaus and was appointed deputy ambassador to Sri Lanka in 1975. The following year Gayoom was appointed ambassador to the United Nations. He was subsequently named minister of transport in 1977. He was selected to succeed Ibrahim Nasir as president on November 11, 1978. Gayoom also served as minister of defense and national security from 1982 and minister of finance from 1989.

HEADS OF GOVERNMENT

IBRAHIM ALI DIDI (Prime Minister, March 12, 1954–December 1957). *See entry under Heads of State.*

AHMED ZAKI (Prime Minister, August 1972–March 6, 1975). Ahmed Zaki was born in 1932. He was named prime minister of the Maldives in August of 1972. He was reappointed prime minister in February of 1975. Zaki was accused of plotting a leftist coup against President Ibrahim Nasir in March of 1975. He was ousted from office on March 6, 1975, and banished to a remote atoll. Zaki was pardoned by President Nasir in November of 1978.

Mali, Republic of

(*République du Mali*)

Mali is a country in northwestern Africa. It received its independence from France on September 22, 1960.

HEADS OF STATE

MODIBO KEITA (President, April 4, 1959–November 19, 1968). Modibo Keita was born in Bamako on June 4, 1915. He was educated in Dakar, Senegal, and became a teacher in the French Sudan. He was a founder of the Bloc Soudanais in 1945. The party affiliated with the Rassemblement Démocratique Africain (RDA) the following year. Keita was arrested by French colonial authorities for his nationalist activities later in the year. He was released in 1947 and became secretary-general of the Union Soudanaise-RDA. He was elected to the French Sudan's Territorial Assembly in July of 1948 and became vice president in 1952. Keita was also elected to the French National Assembly for the French Sudan in January of 1956. He was named secretary of state for overseas territories in June of 1956 and remained in the cabinet as secretary of state to the presidency until May of 1958. The French Sudan became the Sudanese Republic on November 24, 1958, following a referendum approving autonomy within the French community. Keita served as prime minister of the Sudanese Republic and was instrumental in forming the Mali Federation with other newly independent countries in French West Africa on January 17, 1959. He became president of the Mali Federation on April 4, 1959. The Mali Federation was granted full independence on June 20, 1960. Senegal withdrew from the federation the following August, and the Sudanese Republic formally changed its name to the Republic of Mali. Keita transformed Mali into a Socialist state, and after visiting the People's Republic in China in 1964, he became a disciple of Chinese Communist party chairman Mao Tse-tung. Keita adopted Chinese-style Marxism in the country, and Mali's economy deteriorated. Discontent against Keita's government led him to dissolve the National Assembly in 1968. He was ousted in a military coup led by junior officers on November 19, 1968. Keita was placed under house arrest by the subsequent military government. He died at a hospital in Bamako at the age of 61 on May 16, 1977.

MOUSSA TRAORÉ (President, November 19, 1968–March 26, 1991). Moussa Traoré was born in Kayes on September 15, 1936. He served in the French army and returned to Mali in 1960. He subsequently joined the Malian army where he rose to the rank of lieutenant in 1964. Traoré was an instructor at the Kati Military School when he participated in the coup that deposed President Modibo Keita on November 19, 1968. He subsequently served as president of the Military Committee for National Liberation and commander in chief of the armed forces. His former commanding officer, Captain Yoro Diakite, served as head of the military government. Traoré centralized the military government in 1972 and imprisoned Diakite for plotting to overthrow the government. Traoré survived subsequent coup attempts in 1976 and February of 1978. Traoré began Mali's transition to civilian rule on June 19, 1979, and was unopposed in his election to the presidency. He also served in the government as minister of defense and security. His government faced widespread discontent in the early 1990s. He was ousted in a military coup led by Lt. Col. Amadou Toumani Touré on March 26, 1991, and was placed under arrest.

AMADOU TOUMANI TOURÉ (President, March 26, 1991–June 6, 1992). Amadou Toumani Touré served as a paratroop commander when he led the coup that ousted President Moussa Traoré. He served as the leader of the National Reconciliation Council from March 26, 1991. The new government allowed the formation of political parties and scheduled multiparty elections for the following year. Touré stepped down from office on June 6, 1992, following the election of Alpha Oumar Konaré.

ALPHA OUMAR KONARÉ (President, June 6, 1991–). Alpha Oumar Konaré was elected to the presidency of Mali under the Alliance for Democracy in Mali party banner in April of 1992. He was sworn into office on June 6, 1992.

HEADS OF GOVERNMENT

YORO DIAKITE (Head of Military Government, November 19, 1968–September 19, 1969). Yoro Diakite was born in Bangassi-Arabala on October 17, 1932. He attended military school and joined the French army in 1951. He joined the Malian army in 1960 with the rank of lieutenant and served in the United Nations peacekeeping forces in the Congo in the early 1960s. Diakite rose to the rank of captain and served as director of the Kati Military School. He was a leader of the military coup that ousted President Modibo Keita on November 19, 1968. The Military Committee of National Liberation was formed with Lieutenant Moussa Traoré as president and Diakite as first vice president. Diakite also served as head of the provisional military government. He was removed as head of government on September 19, 1969, though he remained in the government as minister of transport, telecommunications, and tourism. He was named minister of the interior, security, and defense in September of 1970. Diakite was dismissed from the government and was arrested in April of 1971 for plotting against Traoré's regime. He was sentenced to life imprisonment with hard labor in July of 1972. Diakite died in jail at the age of 40 on July 30, 1973.

MAMADOU DEMBELÉ (Prime Minister, June 6, 1986–June 6, 1988). Mamadou Dembelé was named to the newly created post of prime minister during a cabinet reshuffle on June 6, 1986. He retained office until the position was abolished on June 6, 1988.

SOUMANA SACKO (Prime Minister, March 2, 1991–June 8, 1992).

Soumana Sacko served as Mali's minister of finance from March until June of 1987. He was appointed prime minister on March 2, 1991. He was replaced by Yohoussi Touré on June 8, 1992.

YOHOUSSI TOURÉ (Prime Minister, June 8, 1992–). Yohoussi Touré was a former president of the Central Bank of Mali. He was selected as Mali's prime minister on June 8, 1992.

Malta, Republic of
(Repubblika ta' Malta)

Malta is a country located on several islands in the central Mediterranean Sea. It was granted independence from Great Britain on September 21, 1964.

HEADS OF STATE

SIR MAURICE HENRY DORMAN (Governor-General, September 21, 1964–June 21, 1971). Maurice Henry Dorman was born in Stafford, England, on August 7, 1912. He was educated at Magdalene College, Cambridge. He worked in the British colonial department and served in Tanganyika Territory, Malta, and Palestine during the 1930s and 1940s. Dorman was named acting governor of Trinidad in 1954. He was appointed governor of Sierra Leone in 1956. He became the first governor-general of independent Sierra Leone on April 27, 1961, and retained that position until July 7, 1962. He was subsequently named governor of Malta and became that country's first governor-general following independence on September 21, 1964. Dorman retained that post until June 21, 1971. He served as deputy chairman of the Pearce Committee on Rhodesia in 1972. He subsequently returned to Great Britain and

retired from the government, but continued to serve on various public and private commissions until his death at the age of 81 on October 26, 1993.

SIR ANTHONY MAMO (Governor-General, June 21, 1971–December 13, 1974; President, December 13, 1974–December 27, 1976). Anthony Joseph Mamo was born in Birkirkara on January 9, 1909. He was educated at the Royal University of Malta, where he received a degree in law. He served on the Statute Law Revision Commission from 1936 until 1942. Mamo subsequently served as crown counsel until 1951. He also served as a law professor at the Royal University. He was named deputy attorney general in 1952 and served as attorney general in 1955. Mamo was appointed chief justice of the Court of Appeals in 1957. He was appointed governor-general on June 21, 1971. When Malta was declared a republic on December 13, 1974, Mamo became the nation's first president. He retained office until his retirement on December 27, 1976.

ANTON BUTTIGIEG (President, December 27, 1976–February 26, 1982). Anton Buttigieg was born in Gozo on February 19, 1912. He served as a police inspector during World War II. Buttigieg became a journalist in 1944 and served as a law reporter for the *Times of Malta* until 1948. He was also a respected poet whose collections include *From the Balcony of My Youth* (1945). Buttigieg was elected to Parliament in 1956. He served as president of the Malta Labor party from 1959 until 1961 and subsequently served as deputy leader. He was a delegate to the Maltese Constitutional Conferences in London in the early 1960s. Buttigieg served as deputy prime minister to Dominic Mintoff from 1971 until 1974. He also served in the cabinet as minister of justice from 1971 until 1976. Buttigieg was selected as president of Malta and took office on December 27, 1976. He completed his term and relinquished office to Agatha Barbara on February 16, 1982. Buttigieg died at the age of 71 on May 5, 1983.

AGATHA BARBARA (President, February 16, 1982–February 15, 1987). Agatha Barbara was born in Zabbar on March 11, 1923. She was educated locally and entered politics in 1946. Barbara joined the Labor party and was elected Malta's first female member of Parliament in 1947. She was named minister of education in the government of Dominic Mintoff in 1955 and served until the cabinet resigned in 1958. She remained in the opposition until 1971, when Mintoff returned to power. Barbara resumed her position as minister of education until 1974, when she was named minister of labor, culture, and welfare. She left the cabinet in 1981 and was elected president of Malta. She took office on February 16, 1982, and served until February 15, 1987.

PAUL XUEREB (President, February 15, 1987–April 4, 1989). Paul Xuereb was born in Rabat, Morocco, on July 21, 1923. He was educated in Malta and London. He was elected to the Maltese Parliament in 1962 and subsequently served as parliamentary secretary in the office of the prime minister. Xuereb served in the cabinet as minister of trade and industry from 1971 until 1976. He was elected Speaker of the House of Representatives in 1986. On February 15, 1987, Xuereb became acting president of Malta, and he remained in that position until April 4, 1989.

VINCENT TABONE (President, April 4, 1989–). Vincent (Censu) Tabone was born in Victoria on March 30, 1913. He attended the University of Malta and Oxford University, where he received a degree in ophthalmology. He served in the Royal Malta Artillery during World War II. He returned to Malta to serve as an ophthalmic specialist at various hospitals. Tabone also entered politics and joined the Nationalist party. He served as secretary-general of the party from 1962. He was elected to Parliament in 1966 and served in the government as minister of labor, employment, and welfare. Tabone became first deputy leader of the party in 1972 and was elected president of the party in 1978. He served as foreign minister in the government of Eddie Fenech Adami from 1987 until 1989. Tabone was elected president of Malta by the House of Representatives and took office on April 4, 1989.

HEADS OF GOVERNMENT

GEORGE BORG OLIVIER (Prime Minister, March 3, 1962–June 17, 1971). George Borg Olivier was born in Valletta on July 5, 1911. He was educated at the Royal University of Malta, where he received a degree in law in 1937. He entered politics and was elected to Malta's council of Government in 1939. He remained on the council during World War II and was elected to the Legislative Assembly in 1947. Borg Olivier served in the government of Enrico Mizzi as minister of works and education in 1950. He succeeded Mizzi as leader of the Nationalist party in 1950 and took office as prime minister on December 20, 1950. His coalition government collapsed in 1955, and he was replaced by Labor party leader Dominic Mintoff on March 11, 1955. Borg Olivier remained leader of the Opposition. Great Britain revoked Maltese self-government in 1959, and Borg Olivier led the Nationalist party to victory in elections in 1962. He again became prime minister when self-government was restored on March 3, 1962. Borg Olivier led his country to independence from Great Britain on September 21, 1964. He maintained close economic ties with Great Britain, as Malta's revenue was largely dependent on British military bases on the island. British defense cuts damaged Malta's economy, and Borg Olivier attempted to increase manufacturing and tourism. The Nationalist party was defeated by the Labor party in elections in 1971, and Borg Olivier was again replaced as prime minister by Mintoff on June 17, 1971. He remained leader of the Opposition until his retirement in 1977. Borg Olivier died at his home in Sliema at the age of 69 on October 29, 1980.

DOMINIC MINTOFF (Prime Minister, June 17, 1971–December 22, 1984). Dominic Mintoff was born in Cospicua on August 6, 1916. He was educated at the University of Malta and attended Oxford University as a Rhodes scholar. He worked in Great Britain before returning to Malta in 1943 to become an architect. Mintoff entered politics and joined the Maltese Labor party the following year. He was elected to the Council of Government in 1945 and was named deputy leader and minister of works and reconstruction in 1947. Mintoff was involved in a dispute with the leadership of the Labor party concerning an ultimatum issued by Mintoff to Great Britain stating that the government would seek financial aid from the United States should the British refuse to provide it. The Labor party divided over the issue, and Mintoff replaced Paul Boffa as leader of the party in 1950. He served as leader of the Opposition to the subsequent Nationalist party government of George Borg Olivier. Mintoff formed a government as prime minister on March 11, 1955. He petitioned Great Britain for Malta's admission to the United Kingdom and threatened to succeed from the British Empire if his demands were not met. The Mintoff government resigned on April 24, 1958, and the Nationalist party was unable to form a government. Great Britain suspended Malta's self-rule, and the colonial governor, Sir Robert Laycock, assumed direct control of the government. Mintoff remained leader of the Opposition following the restoration of self-rule in 1962 and the election of Borg Olivier as prime minister. Mintoff led the Labor party to victory in elections in June of 1971 and returned to office as prime minister on June 17, 1971. He forced the removal of British military bases on Malta. He also sought closer economic ties with Libya. The Labor party remained in power following elections in September of 1976 and December of 1981. The opposition Nationalist party led a boycott of the Parliament the following year to demand reforms in the electoral system. The government was faced with demonstrations and strikes, and Mintoff stepped down as prime minister on December 22, 1984. He remained as an advisor to Prime Minister Carmelo Mifsud Bonnici. Mintoff was elected to the Maltese House of Representatives following the election of a Nationalist party government in May of 1987.

CARMELO MIFSUD BONNICI (Prime Minister, December 22, 1984–May 12, 1987). Carmelo Mifsud Bonnici was born in Cospicua, on July 17, 1933. He attended the Royal University of Malta, where he received a degree in law. He served as legal consultant for the General Workers' Union from 1969. Mifsud Bonnici entered politics in 1980 and became deputy leader of the Labor party. Two years later he was elected to Parliament. He served as minister of labor and social services in the government of Dominic Mintoff from 1982 until 1983. Mifsud Bonnici was then named deputy prime minister and minister of education. He was selected to succeed Mintoff as Labor party leader in 1984 and became prime minister on December 22, 1984. The Labor party was defeated in general elections in 1987, and Mifsud Bonnici was replaced as prime minister by Nationalist party leader Eddie Fenech Adami on May 12, 1987. Mifsud Bon-

nici remained leader of the Opposition.

EDDIE FENECH ADAMI (Prime Minister, May 12, 1987–). Eddie Fenech Adami was born in Birkirkara on February 7, 1934. He was educated at the Royal University of Malta, where he received a degree in law. He opened a legal practice in 1959. Fenech Adami joined the Nationalist party and was unsuccessful in campaigns for the Parliament in 1962 and 1966. He was elected to the Parliament in a by-election in 1969. He served as spokesman for the Opposition on labor and social services. Fenech Adami succeeded George Borg Olivier as leader of the Nationalist party in April of 1977. The Nationalist party received a majority of votes in parliamentary elections in 1981, though they received a minority of parliamentary seats. Fenech Adami led a boycott of Parliament to demand reforms in the electoral system. He led a campaign of civil disobedience against the government of Dominic Mintoff until March of 1983, when the Nationalists resumed their seats in the Parliament. The Nationalists captured a majority in Parliament in elections in May of 1987, and Fenech Adami formed a government as prime minister on May 12, 1987. The Nationalists increased their majority in elections in February of 1992, and Fenech Adami remained as head of the government.

Marshall Islands, Republic of the

The Marshall Islands are two island chains in the western Pacific. They were granted independence from a United Nations trustee-ship administered by the United States on October 21, 1986.

HEAD OF STATE

AMATA KABUA (President, May 1, 1979–). Amata Kabua became the

first president of the Republic of the Marshall Islands on May 1, 1979. He was reelected in 1983 and retained his position following the Marshall Islands' independence on October 21, 1986.

Kabua was again reelected in 1987. He was elected to his fourth term of office in November of 1991.

Mauritania, Islamic Republic of

(al-Jumhuriyah al-Islamiyah al-Muritaniyah)

Mauritania is a country in northwestern Africa. It was granted independence from France on November 28, 1960.

HEADS OF STATE

MOKHTAR OULD DADDAH (President, November 28, 1960–July 10, 1978). Mokhtar Ould Daddah was born in Boutilimit on December 25, 1924. He was educated locally and in Senegal. He worked as an interpreter before going to France, where he entered the Paris Law School. Daddah returned to Mauritania to practice law in 1955. He entered politics and joined the Mauritanian Progressive Union. He was elected to the Territorial Assembly in March of 1957 and served as minister of youth, sports, and education. Later in the year he was elected president of the Executive Council. Daddah supported Mauritania's autonomy within the French Community in a referendum in November of 1958 and proposed a new constitution declaring Mauritania an Islamic republic the following March. Daddah became prime minister and minister of the interior on June 23, 1959. He remained leader of the government and became Mauritania's president upon independence on November 28, 1960. He was reelected to the presidency in August of 1961. Daddah formed the Mauritanian People's party and abolished all other political parties later in the year. He attempted to maintain the unity of the country, which was divided between Moors in the north and black Africans in the south. Daddah launched a national currency in

1973 and nationalized the mining industry in 1974. He supported Morocco's plan to partition the Western Sahara in 1975, withdrawing Mauritania's claims to the northern section of the area. He signed an agreement with Morocco in November of 1975, and Mauritania entered into a war with the Polisario Front guerrillas, who were fighting for the independence of the Western Sahara. The Polisario Front defeated the Mauritanian army in several encounters, and Daddah lost the support of much of the army. He signed a defense pact with Morocco in May of 1977 which resulted in Moroccan troops being stationed in Mauritania. The army moved against Daddah's government on July 10, 1978, and replaced the president with a military junta. He was held under house arrest until 1979, when he went into exile. He was tried in absentia in November of 1980 and sentenced to life imprisonment.

MUSTAPHA OULD MOHAMED SALEK (President, July 10, 1978–June 3, 1979). Mustapha Ould Mohamed Salek was born in 1935. He was educated at the Saumur Military Academy in France and joined the Mauritanian army. He was named armed forces chief of staff in 1968 and commanded the Third Military Region in 1977.

Salek led the military coup that ousted President Mokhtar Ould Daddah on July 10, 1978, and served as president of the ruling Military Committee for National Recovery. The new government announced its intention to withdraw Mauritania from the conflict in the Western Sahara. When Salek was removed from power on April 6, 1979, Ahmed Ould Bouceif was named prime minister. Salek remained the figurehead head of state until he was forced to resign on June 3, 1979. He was arrested in March of 1982 for conspiring against the government of Mohamed Khouna Ould Haidalla and was sentenced to ten years imprisonment.

MOHAMED MAHMOUD OULD AHMED LOULY (President, June 3, 1979–January 4, 1980). Mohamed Mahmoud Ould Ahmed Louly served in the Mauritanian military, where he rose to the rank of lieutenant colonel. He was a supporter of the military coup that ousted President Mokhtar Ould Daddah in July of 1978. He served as minister for control and investigation in the military government until January of 1979. Louly held several other high-ranking positions in the ruling Military Committee for National Salvation before being chosen to replace Mustapha Ould Mohamed Salek as president of Mauritania on June 3, 1979. Louly negotiated a peace settlement with Polisario rebels in the Mauritanian sector of the Western Sahara and withdrew troops from the area. He was ousted by Mohamed Khouna Ould Haidalla on January 4, 1980.

MOHAMED KHOUNA OULD HAIDALLA (President, January 4, 1980–December 12, 1984). Mohamed Khouna Ould Haidalla was born in the Western Sahara in 1940. He joined the Mauritanian army in 1962 and received military training in France. He rose to the rank of lieutenant colonel and was active in the military coup that ousted Mokhtar Ould Daddah in July of 1978.

Haidalla was named chief of the general staff in the military government. He was appointed to succeed Ahmed Ould Bouceif as prime minister of Mauritania on May 31, 1979, following Bouceif's death in a plane crash. Haidalla supported improving relations with Algeria, which had been damaged by Mauritania's policy concerning the Western Sahara. Haidalla also became head of state of Mauritania when he ousted Mohamed Mahmoud Ould Ahmed Louly as head of the Military Committee for National Salvation on January 4, 1980. He relinquished the office of prime minister to allow the formation of a civilian cabinet on December 12, 1980. Haidalla survived coup attempts in March of 1981 and February of 1982. He resumed the position of prime minister on March 8, 1984, and retained power until December 1, 1984, when he was ousted in a bloodless coup led by Colonel Maaouya Ould Sid'Ahmed Taya, the army chief of staff.

MAAOUYA OULD SID'AHMED TAYA (President, December 12, 1984–). Maaouya Ould Sid'Ahmed Taya was born in 1943. He served in the Mauritanian army and fought in the Saharan War from 1976 until 1978. Taya was named minister of defense in 1978 and became commander of the national gendarmerie in 1979. He was promoted to the rank of colonel and served as army chief of staff from 1980 until his selection as prime minister on April 26, 1981. He also served as minister of defense until he was replaced in a cabinet shuffle on March 8, 1984. Taya again became army chief of staff and in this position ousted President Mohamed Khouna Ould Haidalla on December 12, 1984. Taya became president and prime minister in the new government. He survived an alleged coup attempt in October of 1987. Taya was reelected president in January of 1992. He relinquished the office of prime minister on April 20, 1992.

HEADS OF GOVERNMENT

MOKHTAR OULD DADDAH (Prime Minister, June 23, 1959–July 10, 1978). *See entry under Heads of State.*

MUSTAPHA OULD MOHAMED SALEK (President, July 10, 1978–April 6, 1979). *See entry under Heads of State.*

AHMED OULD BOUCEIF (Prime Minister, April 6, 1979–May 27, 1979). Ahmed Ould Bouceif was born in 1933. He served in the Mauritanian army, where he rose to the rank of lieutenant colonel. He was active in the military coup that ousted President Mokhtar Ould Daddah in July of 1978. Bouceif served in the military government as chief of staff and minister of industry and fishing. The ruling Military Committee for National Recovery stripped Mustapha Ould Mohamed Salek of power in April of 1979. Bouceif was named prime minister in the new government on April 6, 1979. Salek remained head of state, though Bouceif held most of the power in the government. Bouceif was killed on May 27, 1979, when his plane crashed into the Atlantic Ocean off the coast of Senegal during a sandstorm. Boucief and an economic delegation were en route to Senegal to attend a summit meeting of the Economic Community of West African States.

AHMED SALEM OULD SIDI (Interim Prime Minister, May 27, 1979–May 31, 1979). Ahmed Salem Ould Sidi was born in 1934. He served in the Mauritanian army, where he rose to the rank of lieutenant colonel. He was active in the Military Committee for National Recovery that took over the government in July of 1978. Sidi served in the government as minister of development. He was chosen to serve as interim prime minister on May 27, 1979, following the death of Ahmed Ould Bouceif. He was replaced by Mohamed Khouna Ould Haidalla on May 31, 1979.

MOHAMED KHOUNA OULD HAIDALLA (Prime Minister, May 31, 1979–December 12, 1980). *See entry under Heads of State.*

SID AHMED OULD BENEIJARA (Prime Minister, December 12, 1980–April 25, 1981). Sid Ahmed Ould Beneijara was named to head a civilian government in Mauritania on December 12, 1980, when President Mohamed Khouna Ould Haidalla relinquished the position of prime minister. His appointment was to have been the first step toward the return of democratic rule to Mauritania, but this policy was reversed following a military coup attempt in March of 1981. Beneijara was replaced by a military government led by Maaouya Ould Sid'Ahmed Taya on April 26, 1981. Beneijara was accused of plotting the ouster of President Haidalla in February of 1982. He was arrested and sentenced to ten years in prison the following month.

MAAOUYA OULD SID'AHMED TAYA (Prime Minister, April 26, 1981–March 8, 1984). *See entry under Heads of State.*

MOHAMED KHOUNA OULD HAIDALLA (Prime Minister, March 8, 1984–December 1, 1984). *See entry under Heads of State.*

MAAOUYA OULD SID'AHMED TAYA (Prime Minister, December 12, 1984–April 20, 1992). *See entry under Heads of State.*

SIDI MOHAMED OULD BOUBAKER (Prime Minister, April 20, 1992–).

Sidi Mohamed Ould Boubaker was named prime minister of a civilian government following legislative elec- tions in March of 1992. He took office on April 20, 1992.

Mauritius, Republic of

Mauritius is an island country in the southwestern Indian Ocean. It was granted independence from Great Britain on March 12, 1968.

HEADS OF STATE

SIR JOHN RENNIE (Governor-General, March 12, 1968–September 3, 1968). John Shaw Rennie was born in Glasgow, Scotland, on January 12, 1917. He was educated at Oxford University and served in the British Overseas Civil Service from 1940. He was posted to Tanganyika and then to Mauritius. Rennie became governor of Mauritius on September 17, 1962. When Mauritius was granted independence from Great Britain on March 12, 1968, Rennie remained as governor-general. He was replaced by Sir Leonard Williams on September 3, 1968. Rennie subsequently worked with the United Nations Relief Agency for Palestine Refugees, and served as commissioner general of the agency from 1971 until 1977.

SIR LEONARD WILLIAMS (Governor-General, September 3, 1968– December 27, 1972). Arthur Leonard Williams was born in Birkenhead, England, on January 22, 1904. He worked as a railway porter as a young man and joined the National Union of Railwaymen. He joined the Independent Labor party in the early 1920s and worked as a trade union organizer. Williams was an unsuccessful candidate for Parliament in 1929 and 1935. He was named secretary of the Labor party in Leeds in 1936 and edited the *Leeds Weekly Citizen.* He remained a leading party organizer and became a national agent in 1951. Williams served as general secretary of the Labor party from 1962 until 1968. Williams was named to serve as governor-general of Mauritius and assumed his post on September 3, 1968. He remained the queen's representative in Mauritius until his death there at the age of 68 on December 27, 1972.

SIR ABDOOL RAMAN MUHAMMAD OSMAN (Governor-General, December 27, 1972–April 26, 1979). Sir Abdool Raman Muhammad Osman was born in Mauritius on August 29, 1902. He was educated in London, where he received a degree in law. He returned to Mauritius to practice law in 1925. Osman was named attorney general in 1939 and was appointed to the Mauritius Supreme Court in 1950. He retired from the Supreme Court in 1961. He subsequently served as chairman of the National Wages Council. Osman served as acting governor-general while Sir Leonard Williams was ill from August until October of 1970 and again from December of 1971 until February of 1972. Osman was named the first Mauritian-born governor-general following Williams's death on December 27, 1972. He retained the position until his retirement on April 26, 1979.

DAYENDRANATH BURRENCHO-BAY (Governor-General, April 26, 1979–December 1983). Dayendranath Burrenchobay was born in Plaine Magnien on March 24, 1919. He attended the Imperial College in London and subsequently worked with the British Electricity Authority. He returned to Mauritius, where he worked with the Department of Education. Burrenchobay was a leading advisor to Prime Minister Seewoosagur Ramgoolam and worked in the prime minister's office from 1968 until 1976. He subsequently served as head of the civil service. Burrenchobay was appointed to succeed Sir Abdool Raman Osman as governor-general on April 26, 1979, and served until December of 1983. He subsequently returned to private enterprise as chairman of Burrenchobay Ltd.

SIR SEEWOOSAGUR RAMGOOLAM (Governor-General, December 1983–December 15, 1985). Seewoosagur Ramgoolam was born in Belle Rive on September 18, 1900. He was educated at the Royal College in Mauritius and University College in London. He remained in Great Britain until the early 1930s, when he returned to Mauritius to work to organize the Hindu majority in the colony. Ramgoolam was elected to the Municipal Council in Port Louis in 1940. He also served on the Legislative Council and was elected to the Legislative Assembly in 1948. Ramgoolam joined the Labor party and was reelected to the Assembly in 1953. He served as liaison officer with the Department of Education. He became leader of the Labor party in 1958 and was elected chief minister of Mauritius. He took office on September 26, 1961, and also served in the government as minister of finance. Ramgoolam became prime minister on March 12, 1964, when the government was reorganized. He was knighted the following year. Mauritius was granted independence on March 12, 1968, and Ramgoolam continued to lead the government

as the nation's first independent prime minister. He also served as minister of defense and internal security following independence. Ramgoolam remained in power as leader of a coalition government despite the emergence of the leftist Mauritian Militant Movement (MMM) as the largest party in the Parliament in 1976. A declining economy and widespread unemployment led to a sweep of the parliamentary elections by the MMM in 1982. Ramgoolam was replaced as prime minister by Aneerood Jugnauth on June 16, 1982. He was appointed to the post of governor-general in December of 1983. He retained that position until his death in Le Reduit on December 15, 1985, at the age of 85 after a long illness.

SIR VEERASAMY RINGADOO (Governor-General, January 17, 1986–March 12, 1992. President, March 12, 1992–June 30, 1992). Sir Veerasamy Ringadoo was born in Port Louis in 1920. He was educated in Port Louis and London and became a lawyer in 1949. He returned to Mauritius and was elected to the Legislative Council in 1951. Ringadoo served as minister of labor and social security from 1959 until 1964 and was minister for education from 1964 until 1967. He was subsequently named minister of agriculture and natural resources and served until 1968. He was minister of finance in the government of Sir Seewoosagur Ramgoolam from 1968 until the defeat of Ramgoolam's government in June of 1982. Ringadoo was named to succeed Ramgoolam as governor-general on January 17, 1986. He became interim president of the country following the establishment of Mauritius as a republic on March 12, 1992. He stepped down on June 30, 1992.

CASSAM UTEEM (President, June 30, 1992–). Cassam Uteem was born on March 22, 1941. He was educated locally and at the University of Paris. He entered politics and was elected to the Legislative Assembly in 1976. Uteem served as a municipal councillor for Port Louis from 1977 until 1982. He served in the cabinet as minister of social security and national solidarity from 1982 until 1983. Uteem was selected as lord mayor of Port Louis in 1986 and remained on the municipal council until 1988. He returned to the cabinet as minister of industry in 1990. He was appointed president of the Republic of Mauritius by the Legislative Assembly on June 30, 1992.

HEADS OF GOVERNMENT

SIR SEEWOOSAGUR RAMGOOLAM (Chief Minister, September 26, 1961– March 12, 1964. Prime Minister, March 12, 1964–June 16, 1982). *See entry under Heads of State.*

ANEEROOD JUGNAUTH (Prime Minister, June 16, 1982–   ). Aneerood Jugnauth was born in Palma on March 29, 1930. He was educated locally and in Great Britain, where he received a degree in law. He returned to Mauritius and was elected to the Legislative Assembly in 1963 as a member of the Independent Forward Block. Jugnauth served as minister of state and development from 1965 until 1967, when he was named minister of labor. He became a district magistrate later that year. He was a founder of the Mauritius Militant Movement in 1971 and served as leader of the Opposition from 1976. In the elections in June of 1982, Jugnauth's party defeated the ruling coalition led by Sir Seewoosagur Ramgoolam. Jugnauth became prime minister on June 16, 1982. The MMM split in March of 1983 following a government crisis that resulted in the resignation of twelve members of the cabinet. Jugnauth formed the Mauritian Socialist Movement (MSM) and joined forces with Ramgoolam's Mauritius Labor party. The coalition retained power following legislative elections in August of 1987. Jugnauth reformed the cabinet the following month, and the MMM joined the government. A government-sponsored movement to transform Mauritius into a republic was approved in December of 1991.

Mexico (United Mexican States)
(Estados Unidos Mexicanos)

Mexico is a country in the southernmost section of North America. It was granted independence from Spain on September 16, 1910.

HEADS OF STATE

MANUEL AVILA CAMACHO (President, December 1, 1940–December 1, 1946). Manuel Avila Camacho was born in Teziutlan, Puebla, on April 24, 1897. He studied accounting to become a bookkeeper before he joined the Mexican Revolution in 1914 to fight in the successful revolt against Victoriano

Huerta. He fought against the Cristero Rebellion in 1923 and served under Lázaro Cárdenas. Camacho gained recognition for his ability to arbitrate military disputes. He continued to serve in the military and was named First undersecretary of war in 1933. He was promoted to secretary of war in 1938 and was given the rank of general of a division later in the year. Comacho was nominated for the presidency in November of 1939 and was elected the following July. He succeeded Cardenas to office on December 1, 1940. Avila Camacho moved the government away from the leftist positions of his predecessor to a more moderate level. He also advocated close ties to the United States and pushed through a declaration of war against the Axis powers during World War II. He completed his term of office on December 1, 1946, and retired from the political scene. He died of a heart ailment at his ranch near Mexico City on October 13, 1955.

MIGUEL ALEMÁN VÁLDES (President, December 1, 1946–December 1, 1952). Miguel Alemán Váldes was born in Sayula, Vera Cruz, on September 29, 1903. He attended the National Law School and opened his own law office in 1928. Alemán was named consulting attorney for the Department of Agriculture in 1930. He was appointed a magistrate of the Supreme Court of Justice of the Federal District in 1935 and was elected to the National Congress as a Senator the same year. The next year he was elected governor for the state of Vera Cruz, and in 1939 he was again elected to the Senate. He resigned as governor to run the presidential campaign of Manuel Avila Camacho in 1940 and was appointed secretary of the interior after Avila Camacho was elected. In 1946 Aleman was the Institutional Revolutionary party (PRI) candidate for the presidency. He was elected to succeed Camacho as president of Mexico and took office on December 1, 1946. As the first Mexican

president without a military background, Alemán was a leading proponent of economic and social reform. He also modernized agriculture and expanded the country's industry by his favorable economic policies. During his administration Alemán was also active in international affairs. He proposed a settlement to the Korean conflict and was nominated for the 1952 Nobel Peace Prize for his efforts. He stepped down as president on December 1, 1952. After he left office, there were allegations of corruption during his presidency, but formal charges were never made. He was appointed president of the National Tourist Council in the early 1960s. He retained that position until his death at the age of 82 from a heart attack at his home in Mexico City on May 14, 1983.

ADOLFO RUIZ CORTINES (President, December 1, 1952–December 1, 1958). Adolfo Ruiz Cortines was born in Vera Cruz on December 30, 1890. He was educated locally and worked as an accountant as a young man. He became active in politics during the Mexican Revolution and served in the army as a paymaster in 1914. He rose to the rank of major before leaving military service. Ruiz Cortines was named to the Secretariat of National Economy as chief of the Bureau of Statistics in 1932. He served in the federal district government as a chief clerk from 1935 until his election to the Congress in 1937. He became governor of the state of Vera Cruz in 1944, and remained in that position until he was appointed minister of the interior in the cabinet of President Miguel Aleman in 1947. He was a leading advisor to President Alemán and was chosen by the Institutional Revolutionary party (PRI) as their candidate to succeed Alemán in 1952. He was elected president of Mexico and took office on December 1, 1952. He sought to reform the government and eliminate political corruption. After taking office, he published a list of his own financial assets and ordered other members of his administration to do the same. He restored confidence in the government and granted women the right to vote. He completed his term on December 1, 1958. He returned to Vera Cruz, where he died of a heart attack at the age of 82 on December 3, 1973.

ADOLFO LÓPEZ MATEOS (President, December 1, 1958–December 1, 1964). Adolfo López Mateos was born in Atizapan de Zaragoza on May 26, 1910. He was educated in Toluca and at the National Autonomous University of Mexico in Mexico City, where he received a degree in 1929. He gained a reputation as an orator and became the private secretary of Carlos Riva Palacio, the leader of the National Revolutionary party. López Mateos received a degree in law in 1934. He was employed at the Workers' National Development Bank as an auditor and served in several government agencies. He was a supporter of Miguel Alemán in the presidential elections in 1946. López Mateos was also elected to the Senate in 1946. Alemán appointed him to lead the Mexican delegation to the United Nations Economic and Social Council in Geneva. He returned to Mexico following the election of Adolfo Ruiz Cortines in 1952 and was appointed secretary-general of the Institutional Revolutionary party (PRI). He served as minister of labor and social welfare in the Ruiz Cortines government. López Mateos was nominated for the presidency by the PRI in November of 1957. He was elected president of Mexico and took office on December 1, 1958. López Mateos was a popular leader in his country. He nationalized the electric industry and brought foreign investment into Mexico. He was also recognized as a leader in Latin America and served as host to numerous international leaders. He completed his term of office on December 1, 1964, and was named head of the Olympic Organizing Committee, which selected Mexico City to host the Summer Olympics in 1968. López Mateos was hospitalized for a cranial aneurysm in November of 1965. Two years later he suffered a crippling stroke and was in a coma for several weeks. He died in Mexico City at the age of 59 on September 22, 1969, as a result of a heart attack.

GUSTAVO DÍAZ ORDAZ (President, December 1, 1964–December 1, 1970). Gustavo Díaz Ordaz was born in Ciudad Serdan, Puebla, on March 12, 1911. He received a degree in law from Puebla University. He subsequently served as a judge and rose to become president of the Puebla State Supreme Court of Justice. Días Ordaz also served as a teacher of labor law at the University of Puebla. He served as the assistant to the governor of Puebla from 1941 until 1945. He was elected to the Legislative Assembly in 1946 and to the Senate in 1952. Díaz Ordaz was named by President Adolfo Ruiz Cortines to serve as director-general of judicial affairs in the Ministry of the Interior in 1952. He was appointed to the cabinet as interior minister under President Adolfo López Mateos in 1958. He was a hard-line anti–Communist and ordered the arrest of labor leaders and pro–Castro demonstrators he considered a threat to the country. Díaz Ordaz succeeded López Mateos as president of Mexico on December 1, 1964. His term of office was marred by student unrest in Mexico City in 1968. The president called out the troops to disperse the demonstrators in October of 1968, shortly before the Olympics were scheduled for Mexico City. The students and soldiers clashed, and numerous students were killed in the capital's Tlatelolco Square. Díaz Ordaz was faced with widespread criticism for the massacre at home and abroad. He completed his term of office on December 1, 1970. He was appointed ambassador to Spain in 1977, but resigned after four months due to eye trouble. He returned to Mexico City, where he died of a heart attack at the age of 68 on July 15, 1979.

LUIS ECHEVERRÍA ALVÁREZ (President, December 1, 1970–December 1, 1976). Luis Echeverría Alvárez was born in Mexico City on January 17, 1922. He attended the University of Mexico and received a degree in law in 1945. He returned to the university in 1947 to join the law faculty. Echeverría also became active in politics and joined the Institutional Revolutionary party (PRI). He served in several party positions until November of 1952, when he was named to the Ministry of the Navy as administration and accounting director. He returned to work with the PRI in 1957 and was active in the campaign of Adolfo López Mateos for the presidency. Following López Mateos's election, Echeverría was appointed to the Ministry of the Interior. He became acting secretary of the interior following Gustavo Díaz Ordaz's resignation in 1963. He remained secretary of the interior after Díaz Ordaz was elected president the following year. He was held partially responsible for the death of student demonstrators in Tlatelolco who were killed by riot police in October of 1968. Echeverría was nominated by the PRI in October of 1969 to run for the presidency. He stepped down from the cabinet to conduct his campaign and was elected the following year. He was sworn into office on December 1, 1970. Echeverría promoted liberal reforms in Mexico's universities and released nearly all political prisoners arrested during the riots of 1968. In international affairs his government established diplomatic relations with the People's Republic of China and sponsored that country's admission to the United Nations. Echeverría completed his term of office on December 1, 1976. He was appointed Mexico's ambassador at large from 1977 until 1978 and was ambassador to Australia from

1979 until 1980. He also served as general director of the Center for Economic and Social Studies in the Third World from 1976 until 1987.

JOSE LÓPEZ PORTILLO (President, December 1, 1976–December 1, 1982). José López Portillo y Pachecho was born in Mexico City on June 16, 1920. He received a degree in law from the University of Mexico in 1946 and joined the university's law faculty in the early 1950s. He entered the government in 1959, when he was named to the Ministry of National Patrimony. López Portillo was moved to the Ministry of the Presidency in 1965 and became undersecretary in charge of planning three years later. Following the election of his former classmate Luis Echeverría Alvárez as Mexico's president in 1970, López Portillo was named director of the Federal Electricity Commission. He was appointed minister of finance and public credit the following year. He was selected as the ruling Institutional Revolutionary party's candidate for the presidency in 1975. López Portillo was successful in the election the following year and was sworn into office on December 1, 1976. He instituted election reforms to give greater representation to minority parties. He also increased Mexico's development of its oil resources and nationalized the nation's banking industry. López Portillo completed his term of office on December 1, 1982.

MIGUEL DE LA MADRID HURTADO (President, December 1, 1982–December 1, 1988). Miguel de la Madrid Hurtado was born in Colima on December 12, 1934. He was raised in Mexico City after his father, a lawyer who was defending peasant land rights, was murdered in 1936. He attended the National University of Mexico and graduated with a degree in law in 1957. De la Madrid was subsequently employed by the National Bank of Foreign Commerce and moved to the

Bank of Mexico in 1960. He received a scholarship to attend Harvard University, where he obtained a master's degree in public administration in 1965. He returned to Mexico to work in the Finance Ministry until 1970, when he became director of finances at the national oil monopoly, Pemex. De la Madrid returned to the Finance Ministry in 1972 to serve as director of public sector credit. He was appointed deputy minister of finance in 1976 and retained this position until May of 1979. He was then appointed to the cabinet as minister of planning and budget. In this position he was largely responsible for Mexico's first Global Development Plan. De la Madrid was selected as the Institutional Revolutionary party's candidate for president in September of 1981. He was elected the following July and took office on December 1, 1982. Upon taking office he introduced an austerity program to help deal with Mexico's economic crisis. De la Madrid's ruling political party was also accused of fraud in the municipal elections of 1985. The opposition National Action party (PAN) protested results of mayoral elections. Mexico City was also devastated by a major earthquake in September of 1985, and the government was accused of mishandling the rescue operation. De la Madrid completed his term of office on December 1, 1988.

CARLOS SALINAS DE GORTARI (President, December 1, 1988–   ). Carlos Salinas de Gortari was born in Mexico City on April 3, 1948. He graduated from the National University of Mexico in 1969 with a degree in economics. He worked at the Ministry of Finance and then went on to earn a master's degree in public administration from Harvard University in 1973. Salinas also received a degree in political economy in 1976 and was awarded a doctorate in political economy and government two years later. He returned to Mexico to serve as director of economic and social policy to Miguel de la Madrid, the minister of budget and planning. He succeeded de la Madrid to the position of minister when de la Madrid was nominated for president in 1981. Salinas was instrumental in developing President de la Madrid's economic austerity program after taking office. Salinas was nominated by the ruling Institutional Revolutionary party as its candidate for president in 1987. The party's nomination had usually been tantamount to election, but in 1988 Salinas was challenged by Cuauthtémoc Cárdenas, leader of the leftist Authentic party of the Mexican Revolution, and Manuel Clouthier, nominee of the rightist National Action party. In the balloting in June of 1988, Salinas received a narrow majority in an election that was clouded by allegations of fraud. When Salinas took office on December 1, 1988, he vowed to modernize Mexican politics and eliminate election malpractices. He began the process of reprivatizing Mexico's banks, which had been nationalized by President José López Portillo in 1982. Mexico's economic situation continued to improve under Salinas, and his party increased its popular majority in gubernatorial elections in 1992.

Micronesia, Federated States of

Micronesia is a group of islands in the western Pacific Ocean. It was granted independence from a United Nations trusteeship administered by the United States on November 3, 1986. Micronesia gained full independence on December 22, 1990.

HEADS OF STATE

TOSIWO NAKAYAMA (President, November 3, 1986–May 15, 1987). Tosiwo Nakayama was elected president of Micronesia on November 3, 1986. He retained office until May 15, 1987, when he was replaced by John R. Haglelgam.

JOHN R. HAGLELGAM (President, May 15, 1987–May 15, 1991). John R. Haglelgam was born on Yap. He was elected president of the Federated States of Micronesia on May 15, 1987. He remained president when the former Caroline Islands were granted full independence following the termination of the Trusteeship Agreement administered by the United States on December 22, 1990. He was forced to resign the office on May 15, 1991, after he was defeated in a state senatorial election the previous March.

BAILEY OLTER (President, May 15, 1991–). Bailey Olter was born on Pohnpei in 1932. He served as vice president in the administration of President Tosiwo Nakayama. He was a member of the Senate when he was selected to become president on May 11, 1991. He was sworn into office four days later.

Moldova, Republic of
(Republica Moldoveneasča)

Moldova (formerly Moldavia) is a country in eastern Europe. It became independent following the breakup of the Soviet Union on December 25, 1991.

HEAD OF STATE

MIRCEA SNEGUR (President, September 3, 1991–). Mircea Ivanovitch Snegur was born on January 17, 1940. He joined the Communist party in 1964 and served on the Central Committee from 1985 until 1989. He served as chairman of the Presidium of the Supreme Soviet of Moldavia from 1989. Snegur was named chairman of the Supreme Soviet on April 27, 1990. Moldova declared itself independent in August of 1991, and Snegur was named president on September 3, 1991. He remained president following a popular election on December 8, 1991.

HEADS OF GOVERNMENT

VALERIU MURAVSCHI (Prime Minister, May 1991–June 30, 1992). Valeriu Muravschi was a member of the Moldovan Popular Front. He served as minister of finance from 1990 until March of 1991, when he became deputy premier. He was selected to replace Mircea Druk as prime minister of Moldavia in May of 1991. His government resigned on June 30, 1992.

ANDREI SANGHELI (Prime Minister, July 1, 1992–). Andrei Sangheli was educated in agronomy. He became active in Moldovan politics and served as a mediator in the government's peace negotiations with Slav and Gagauz secessionists. Sangheli was chosen to serve as prime minister on July 1, 1992.

Monaco, Principality of

(Principauté de Monaco)

Monaco is a small enclave in southeastern France. It was restored to independence by France in 1861.

HEADS OF STATE

LOUIS II (Prince, June 26, 1922– May 9, 1949). Louis Honore Charles Antoine de Grimaldi was born in Baden-Baden, Germany, on July 12, 1870. He was the only son of Prince Albert, the ruler of Monaco. Louis attended the St. Cyr Military Academy in France and joined the French army in 1883. He served in the French Foreign Legion in Africa, and during World War I he was a cavalry commander in the French army. He distinguished himself in action and rose to the rank of brigadier general. Louis succeeded his father as head of state of Monaco on June 26, 1922. Louis preferred to live in France and spent relatively little time in the nation that he ruled. He fell ill in May of 1949 and relinquished his duties to his grandson and successor, Prince Rainier, on May 4, 1949. He died in Monaco on May 9, 1949.

RAINIER III (Prince, May 9, 1949–). Rainier Louis Henri Maxence Bertrand de Grimaldi was born in Monaco on May 31, 1923. He was the only son of Pierre de Polignac and Princess Charlotte of Monaco. He was educated in Great Britain, Switzerland, and France. Rainier served in the French army during World War II as Lieutenant Grimaldi. He served with distinction in the Alsatian campaign. Rainier completed his education at the University of Paris after the war. He succeeded his seriously ill grandfather, Prince Louis II, to become ruling Prince Rainier III of Monaco on May 4, 1949. Louis died several days later. Rainier married American film actress Grace Kelly in 1956, and the couple gave birth to a daughter, Princess Caroline, the following year. Rainier remained a popular figure in Monaco. He improved educational facilities in the country and provided a stable economy. A new constitution was instituted in December of 1962 that granted the prince executive power in the country. Princess Grace was killed in an automobile accident on September 14, 1982. The country's economy suffered in the late 1980s as tourism and gambling declined. Monaco attempted to diversify its economic base through a land reclamation program.

Mongolia

(Mongol Uls)

Mongolia is a country in central Asia. It gained independence from China on March 13, 1921, and was recognized as an independent nation by China on January 5, 1946.

HEADS OF STATE

GONCHIGHIYIN BUMATSENDA (Head of State, January 5, 1946–September 12, 1953). Gonchighiyin Bumatsenda was born on September 11, 1881. He was active in the revolution that established the Mongolian People's Republic in March of 1921. He was selected as chairman of the Presidium of the Small Hural, the lower house of Mongolia's National Assembly, in 1940. Bumatsenda was a member of the Mongolian People's Revolutionary party and became a member of the Politburo of the party's Central Committee in 1943. He became Mongolia's head of state as chairman of the Presidium of the People's Great Hural in July of 1951. He retained his postion until his death in Ulan Bator at the age of 72 on September 23, 1953.

ZHAMSARANGHIN SAMBU (Head of State, April 1954–May 21, 1972). Zhamsaranghin Sambu was born in Buren Somon District on June 23, 1895. He joined the Mongolian People's Revolutionary party in 1922 and served in the Ministry of Finance until 1930. He held other government positions until 1937, when he was appointed Mongolia's ambassador to the Soviet Union. Sambu served in that position during World War II and returned to Mongolia in 1946. He then worked as a department director at the Foreign Ministry until 1950, when he was appointed envoy to North Korea. He returned to Mongolia in 1952 to serve as deputy foreign minister. He was selected to succeed Gonchighiyin Bumatsenda as chairman of the Presidium of the Great Hural in April of 1954. He also became a member of the Central Committee and Politburo of the Mongolian People's Revolutionary party. He remained Mongolia's head of state until his death in Ulan Bator at the age of 76 on May 21, 1972, after a long illness.

SONOMYN LUVSAN (Acting Head of State, May 21, 1972–June 11, 1974). Sonomyn Luvsan was born in 1924. He was a member of the Politburo of the Mongolian People's Revolutionary party. He served as first deputy chairman of the Council of Ministers and was named deputy chairman of the Presidium in May of 1972. He became acting chairman following the death of Zhamsaranghin Sambu on May 21, 1972. He was replaced by Yumzhaghiyun Tsedenbal on June 11, 1974.

YUMZHAGHIYUN TSEDENBAL (Head of State, June 11, 1974–August 23, 1984). Yumzhaghiyun Tsedenbal was born in Ubsunum Aimak in Uvs Province on September 17, 1916. He was educated in the Soviet Union at the Irkutsk Institute of Finance and Economics. He returned to Mongolia as a teacher and joined the Mongolian People's Revolutionary party in 1939. Tsedenbal was subsequently named to the government as minister of finance. He became first secretary of the party's Central Committee in 1940. He was named deputy premier in December of 1948 and succeeded Khorloghiyin Choibalsan as premier on May 28, 1952. Tsedenbal was replaced by Dashiyin Damba as first secretary in April of 1954. Tsedenbal remained premier and resumed the party leadership in November of 1958. Damba was dismissed from the party in March of the following year. Tsedenbal was a hard-line pro–Soviet leader. He allowed Soviet troops to be stationed on the Mongolia-China border and followed an economic policy of central planning. He stepped down as premier on June 11, 1974, to assume the position of chairman of the Presidium of the People's Great Hural and thus became Mongolia's head of state. Tsedenbal continued to rule Mongolia until August 23, 1984, when he was removed from his party and government positions while on vacation in the Soviet Union. He remained in exile in the Soviet Union and was accused of excesses during his rule. He was denounced by the Mongolian government in 1988, but was ruled unfit to stand trial due to his failing health. In March of 1990 he was formally expelled from the Communist party. Tsedenbal died in Moscow at the age of 74 on April 20, 1991, after a long illness.

ZHAMBYN BATMUNKH (Head of State, December 12, 1984–March 21, 1990). Zhambyn Batmunkh was born in Khyargas, in the Ubsa-Nur region, on March 10, 1926. He was educated in Mongolia and the Soviet Union and returned to Mongolia to work as a teacher. In 1948 he joined the Mongolian People's Revolutionary party. Batmunkh continued to teach and joined the faculty of the State University in 1967. He was named director of the

party's science and education departments in 1973 and became deputy chairman of the Council of Ministers in May of the following year. He replaced Yumzhaghiyun Tsedenbal as chairman of the Council of Ministers on June 11, 1974. Batmunkh was named first secretary of the Mongolian People's Revolutionary party on August 23, 1984, following the ouster of Tsedenbal by the Central Committee. Batmunkh also replaced Tsedenbal as chairman of the presidium of the Great People's Hural on December 12, 1984. He relinquished the office of premier to Dumaagiyn Sodnom in December of 1984. He was reconfirmed to his positions in July of 1986. The liberal reforms that were sweeping Communist nations in Eastern Europe also affected Mongolia. The party Central Committee dismissed the Politburo on March 14, 1990, and Batmunkh was succeeded by Gombojavyn Ochirbat as party leader. Batmunkh was replaced by Punsalmaagiyn Ochirbat as chairman of the Presidium on March 21, 1990.

PUNSALMAAGIYN OCHIRBAT (Head of State, March 21, 1990–). Punsalmaagiyn Ochirbat was born in the Tudevtei District in 1942. He was educated at the Soviet Mining Institute and worked with the Ministry of Industry from 1966. He was appointed deputy minister for fuel, power, industry, and geology in 1972 and became minister in 1976. Ochirbat was a member of the Mongolian People's Revolutionary party until his resignation in 1989. He served in the People's Assembly and became chairman of the Presidium on March 21, 1990. Ochirbat was elected president of the republic in September of 1990.

HEADS OF GOVERNMENT

KHORLOGHIYIN CHOIBALSAN (Premier, 1939–January 26, 1952).

Khorloghiyin Choibalsan was born in Tsetsenkhan Aimak on February 8,

1895. He was educated locally and in Irkutsk. He became a leader of a pro-Communist revolutionary group that opposed the Chinese occupation of Mongolia in October of 1919. The Chinese were forced from the capital by a White Russian force in October of 1920, and Choibalsan continued to fight for independence. He merged his organization with Suhe Baator's nationalist force later in 1920 and formed the Mongolian People's party. The nationalists were assisted by Soviet troops in defeating the White Russians, and a nationalist government was formed in July of 1921. Lama Bodo headed the new government, and Choibalsan remained a leader of the Mongolian military. The Living Buddha, Mongolia's religious leader, died in May of 1924, and the government allowed for no further incarnation. Choibalsan served as commander in chief of the Mongolian army from 1924 until 1928. He served as chairman of the Presidium of the Lesser People's Hural from 1928 until 1930, when he was named minister of foreign affairs following the Japanese invasion of Manchuria. He and Premier Gendung negotiated a military alliance between Mongolia and the Soviet Union in November of 1934. Gendung was executed as a Japanese spy the following month, and Choibalsan became first deputy premier. He was given the rank of marshal in 1936 and became Mongolia's premier in 1939. He signed a Soviet-Mongolian mutual assistance treaty in 1939, and Soviet troops assisted Mongolia's fight against the Japanese during World War II. The Allies acknowledged Mongolia as part of the Soviet sphere of influence in a secret agreement at Yalta in February of 1945. A plebiscite was held the following October confirming independence, and China recognized the Mongolian People's Republic on January 5, 1946. Choibalsan remained premier and commander in chief until his death in Moscow at the age of 56 on January 26, 1952, following surgery for kidney cancer.

YUMZHAGHIYUN TSEDENBAL (Premier, May 28, 1952–June 11, 1974). *See entry under Heads of State.*

ZHAMBYN BATMUNKH (Premier, June 11, 1974–December 12, 1984). *See entry under Heads of State.*

DUMAAGIYN SODNOM (Premier, December 12, 1984–March 21, 1990). Dumaagiyn Sodnom was born in 1933. He studied economics in the Soviet Union and subsequently worked with the Ministry of Finance from 1950. He was appointed minister of finance in 1963 and served until 1969. Sodnom then worked with the State Planning Commission and became chairman in 1972. He was named deputy chairman of the Council of Ministers in 1974. When Zhambyn Batmunkh was named chairman of the Presidium on December 12, 1984, Sodnom replaced him as chairman of the Council of Ministers. He was dismissed from his position on March 21, 1990. He was subsequently named director of the State Oil Company.

SHARAVYM GUNGAADORJ (Premier, March 21, 1990–September 10, 1990). Sharavym Gungaadorj was born in 1935. He was educated at the Soviet Academy of Agriculture and worked as an agronomist at the Department of State Farms from 1959 until 1967. He subsequently served in the Ministry of Agriculture before being named first deputy minister for state farms in 1980. The following year Gungaadorj was named an alternate member to the Communist party Central Committee. He served as minister of agriculture from 1986 until 1990. He was named premier of Mongolia on March 21, 1990, and served until September 10, 1990. The following year he was named Mongolia's ambassador to the People's Republic of Korea.

DASHLYN BYAMBASUREN (Premier, September 10, 1990–July 21, 1992). Dashlyn Byambasuren was born in the Binder Somon District in 1942. He studied economics in Moscow and subsequently served on the State Committee for Prices and Standardization from 1970 until 1976. Byambasuren was named to the Council of Ministers in 1989 and became premier on September 10, 1990. He was replaced as premier on July 21, 1992, following general elections.

PUNTSAGIYN JASRAY (Premier, July 21, 1992–). Puntsagiyn Jasray was a member of the Mongolian People's Revolutionary party. He was approved as premier by the Great Hural on July 21, 1992, following general elections.

Morocco, Kingdom of
(al-Mamlakah al-Maghribiyah)

Morocco is a country in northwestern Africa. It was granted independence from France on March 2, 1956.

HEADS OF STATE

MOHAMMED V (Sultan, November 17, 1927–August 14, 1953). Sidi Mohammed ben Youssef was born in Fez on August 10, 1909. He was the youngest of three sons of Sultan Moulay Youssef of Morocco. His father died on November 17, 1927, and Mohammed was chosen by the Council of Ulemas, or Muslim wise men, to succeed to the throne. Mohammed was considered by the French to be more controllable than his older brothers. He ruled under the regency of the grand vizier until 1930. He continued to cooperate with the French colonial authorities. Mohammed suffered from poor health and underwent major surgery in December of 1937. He initially gave his support to the Vichy regime during World War II, but later sided with the Allies after the United States landed in Casablanca in November of 1942. Mohammed became involved in the Moroccan independence movement after the war. He demanded that the French end the protectorate status of Morocco. Mohammed was deposed by the pro-French pasha of Marrakech, Hadj Thami el Mezouari el Glaoui, on August 20, 1953. He was sent into exile by the French and was replaced on the throne by his uncle, Sidi Mohammed ben Moulay Arafa. Mohammed was sent to Corsica, where he remained until being removed to Madagascar in April of 1954. The exiled sultan became a rallying point for the independence movement. Riots and demonstrations took place throughout Morocco, and the French were forced to restore Mohammed to the throne on November 6, 1955. The French also agreed to grant independence to Morocco on March 2, 1956. The sultan adopted the title of King Mohammed V on August 11, 1957. Mohammed dismissed the cabinet of leftist Prime Minister Abdullah Ibrahim and led his own cabinet from May 20, 1960. Mohammed died suddenly in Rabat on February 26, 1961, following a minor operation to remove a growth in his throat.

SIDI MOHAMMED BEN MOULAY ARAFA (Sultan, August 14, 1953–October 30, 1955). Sidi Mohammed ben Moulay Arafa was born in 1889. He was the son of Moulay Arafa and an uncle of Sultan Mohammed ben Youssef. Sidi Mohammed was selected by the French to serve as sultan following the exile of Mohammed ben Youssef. Moroccan nationalists went into rebellion under the new government, and Sidi Mohammed survived several assassination attempts. He stepped down from the throne on October 30, 1955, and Mohammed ben Youssef was reinstalled as sultan. Sidi Mohammed went into exile in Tangier. He later went to Nice, France, where he died at his home at the age of 87 on July 18, 1976.

MOHAMMED V (Sultan, November 6, 1955–August 11, 1957; King, August 11, 1957–February 26, 1961). *See earlier entry under Heads of State.*

HASSAN II (King, February 26, 1961–). Moulay Hassan was born into the Alawite dynasty in Rabat on July 9, 1929. He was the oldest son of Sultan Mohammed V. He was educated privately at the royal palace in Rabat. Hassan continued his education at the University of Bordeaux in France. He accompanied his family to Corsica when the French exiled his father for nationalist activities in August of 1953. The royal family was allowed to return in November of 1955 when the French agreed to negotiate Morocco's independence. Hassan assisted in the negotiations that led to Morocco's independence on March 2, 1956. Hassan was named crown prince and heir to the throne by his father in July of 1957. He also served as commander-in-chief of the Royal Moroccan Army. Hassan was named minister of defense and deputy prime minister in May of 1960. He succeeded to the throne on February 26, 1961, following

the death of his father. He also served as Morocco's prime minister until May 3, 1961. Hassan attempted to improve the educational system of his country and to provide employment for his subjects. He served as foreign minister in the government until 1963. Hassan formed his own government as prime minister on June 7, 1965, and declared a state of emergency the following month. Exiled opposition leader Mehdi Ben Barka was assassinated in Paris in October of 1965. Hassan's interior minister, General Muhammad Oufkir, was implicated in the murder. Hassan relinquished the prime minister's office to Mohamed Benhima on July 7, 1967. Hassan survived a military coup during his birthday party at Skhirat Palace on July 10, 1971. He was captured by rebel troops, but was freed when forces loyal to the government crushed the coup attempt. Hassan instituted a purge of the military, and many senior officers were executed for complicity in the rebellion. He promoted a new constitution in March of 1972. Hassan survived another assassination attempt in August of 1972. General Oufkir was the presumed leader of the plot, and he committed suicide following the coup's failure. Hassan attempted to annex the Western Sahara in 1974. His policies led his country into a war against the Popular Front for the Liberation of Saguia el Hamra and Rio de Oro (Polisario), which was supported by Algeria. Municipal elections were held in November of 1976, and elections to the new House of Representatives took place in June of 1977. Elections were postponed in 1980 when a constitutional amendment extended the terms of members of the House of Representatives. Hassan again postponed elections in 1983 and appointed a unity cabinet with Mohamed Karim Lamrani as prime minister in November of 1983. Legislative elections were held in October of 1984, and Lamrani continued as head of government. The king engaged in talks with the leaders of the Polisario in early 1989. Hassan sponsored a national referendum in December of 1989 to postpone legislative elections and to allow participation of residents of Western Sahara in the elections if the area supported unification with Morocco. Hassan also supported the United States–led coalition against Iraq following the invasion of Kuwait in August of 1990 and committed Moroccan troops to the military effort against Iraq.

HEADS OF GOVERNMENT

MUHAMMAD EL-MUQRI (Grand Vizier, August 19, 1917–1955). Muhammad el-Muqri was born in Fez in 1841. He entered the service of Sultan Hassan I in the 1880s. He remained in the government of Hassan's successor, Sultan Abdul Aziz. El-Muqri served as Morocco's representative at the Conference of Algeciras in 1906. He was subsequently appointed minister of finance. He was appointed grand vizier in the court of Sultan Abdul Aziz in 1908. El-Muqri was named minister of finance in 1909 following the succession of Sultan Abdul Hafid. El-Muqri was again named grand vizier in 1911. He stepped down from office in 1913, but was recalled as grand vizier by Sultan Yusef in 1917. He retained office throughout the reign of Sultan Yusef and continued during the reign of Sultan Mohammed V from 1927. El-Muqri served as a mediator between the sultanate and the French resident-general. He was retained by the French after the ouster of Sultan Mohammed in August of 1953. He served on the Regency Council following the abdication of Sultan Moulay Arafa in October of 1955. Mohammed returned to the throne the following month, and El-Muqri withdrew from politics prior to Morocco's independence. He died in Rabat at the age of 116 on September 9, 1957.

M'BAREK BEN MUSTAFA EL-BEKKAI (Prime Minister, December 7, 1955–April 15, 1958). M'Barek ben Mustafa el-Bekkai was born to the Berber Beni Snassen tribe in 1907. He attended military school and joined the French army. He served with distinction during World War II and rose to the rank of lieutenant colonel. Bekkai was badly wounded during the war and lost a leg in action in France. He was named pasha of Sefrov after the war. He resigned in protest over the French government's ouster of Sultan Mohammed V in 1953. He was instrumental in the negotiations with the French that gained Mohammed's return in November of 1955. Bekkai was named the first prime minister of Morocco on December 7, 1955. He continued negotiations with France that led to Morocco's independence on March 2, 1956. He retained office until the Istiqlal, or Independence party, formed a government on April 15, 1958. He was recalled to the government in May of 1960 when King Mohammed served as prime minister. Bekkai served as minister of the interior until his death of a heart attack in Rabat at the age of 54 on April 12, 1961.

AHMED BALAFREJ (Prime Minister, May 12, 1958–December 3, 1958). Ahmed Balafrej was born in Rabat in 1908. He was educated in Cairo, Egypt, and at the Sorbonne in Paris. He returned to Morocco to join the nationalist movement in opposition to the French colonial government. Balafrej was a founder of the Istiqlal, or Independence party, in 1944. He was imprisoned by the French from 1944 until 1946. He was subsequently sent into exile, but returned to Morocco in 1955. When Morocco was granted independence the following year, Balafrej was named minister of foreign affairs, and he served in this office until 1958. He was appointed to lead an Istiqlal-dominated government as prime minister on May 12, 1958. Balafrej was forced to resign on December 3, 1958, following a conflict with the leftist president of the Constitutional Assembly, Mehdi Ben Barka. He served as ambassador at large from 1960 until 1961 and was deputy prime minister in June of 1961. Balafrej was named minister of foreign affairs in 1961 and served until his appointment as personal representative of King Hassan in 1963. He held that position until 1977, when he resigned in protest over the continued imprisonment of his son on charges of leftist subversion.

MULAY ABDULLAH IBRAHIM (Prime Minister, December 16, 1958– May 20, 1960). Mulay Abdullah Ibrahim was born in Marrakesh in 1918. He was a member of the Istiqlal, or Independence party, and was active in the Resistance movement during French colonial rule. He was named to head a government of technicians on December 16, 1958, following the resignation of Ahmed Balafrej. Ibrahim also served in the government as minister of foreign affairs. He was expelled from the Istiqlal by right-wing leader Allal el Fassi in April of 1959. Ibrahim became a leader of the leftist National Union of Political Forces. King Mohammed V dismissed Ibrahim on May 20, 1960. The king claimed the office of prime minister for himself to settle the cabinet crisis Ibrahim's dismissal initiated.

MOHAMMED V (Prime Minister, May 20, 1960–February 26, 1961). *See entry under Heads of State.*

HASSAN II (Prime Minister, February 26, 1961–May 3, 1961). *See entry under Heads of State.*

AHMAD REDA GUEDIRA (Prime Minister, May 3, 1961–November 13, 1963). Ahmad Reda Guedira was born in 1922. He was educated in Morocco and at the Sorbonne in Paris, where he received a degree in law in 1947. He returned to Morocco and served as an advisor to Sultan Mohammed. Guedira was named to the cabinet as minister of defense following Morocco's independence in 1956 and retained that position until 1959. He was instrumental in the drafting of the Moroccan Constitution in 1961. Guedira served as director of the royal cabinet and was given the powers of prime minister by King Hassan II on May 3, 1961. He also served as minister of agriculture and the interior. Ahmed Bahmini was selected as prime minister on November 13, 1963, and Guedira remained in the cabinet as foreign minister until 1964. He subsequently returned to his private law practice. Guedira again returned to the government in 1969 to serve as minister of higher education. He resigned the following year. In 1977 he was named personal counselor to King Hassan.

AHMED BAHMINI (Prime Minister, November 13, 1963–June 7, 1965). Ahmed Bahmini was born in 1914. He was appointed president of the Supreme Court following Morocco's independence in 1956. Bahmini was named to the cabinet as minister of justice in 1963. He was appointed prime minister by King Hassan II on November 13, 1963. His government was threatened by major riots in Casablanca in March of 1965. Bahmini was dismissed on June 7, 1965, when King Hassan declared a state of emergency and became his own prime minister. Bahmini was renamed president of the Supreme Court and retained that position until he was killed by rebel army troops during an unsuccessful coup attempt against the king. Bahmini was a guest at Hassan's birthday reception at

Skhirat Palace when the rebellion occurred. He was among the numerous guests that were killed when the rebels seized the palace on July 10, 1971.

HASSAN II (Prime Minister, June 7, 1965–July 7, 1967). *See entry under Heads of State.*

MOHAMED BENHIMA (Prime Minister, July 7, 1967–October 6, 1969). Mohamed Benhima was born in Safi on June 25, 1927. He studied medicine in France and then returned to Morocco to work in the Ministry of Public Health. He was appointed governor of the Agadir and Tarfaya provinces in 1960 and served until 1961. Benhima was appointed minister of education in 1965 and served until his appointment as prime minister on July 7, 1967. He was replaced by Ahmed Laraki on October 6, 1969. He was then named minister of state for agriculture and served until 1970. Benhima was appointed minister of internal affairs in 1972 and was named minister of state for cooperation and training the following year, a position he held until 1977. He also served as minister of the interior from 1977 until his retirement for reasons of health in March of 1979.

AHMED LARAKI (Prime Minister, October 6, 1969–August 6, 1971). Moulay Ahmed Laraki was born in Casablanca on October 15, 1931. He was educated in Paris and joined the Ministry of Foreign Affairs in 1956. He was named Morocco's representative to the United Nations in 1957 and served until 1959. Laraki was appointed ambassador to Spain in 1962 and served until 1965, when he was posted to Switzerland. He was named ambassador to the United States in 1967 and retained this office until his appointment as prime minister on October 6, 1969. He was replaced by Mohammed Karim Lamrani on August 6, 1971. Laraki subsequently served as minister of

medical affairs from 1971 until 1974. He was named foreign minister in 1974 and served until 1977.

MOHAMMED KARIM LAMRANI (Prime Minister, August 6, 1971–November 2, 1972). Mohammed Karim Lamrani was born in Fez on May 1, 1919. He served as an economic advisor to King Hassan II from 1966. He was minister of finance in 1971 and was appointed prime minister on August 6, 1971, a position he held until November 2, 1972. Lamrani was again named prime minister on November 30, 1983, and served until September 30, 1986, when he resigned for reasons of health. He was asked to serve as interim prime minister on August 11, 1992.

AHMED OSMAN (Prime Minister, November 2, 1972–March 22, 1979). Ahmed Osman was born in Oujda on January 3, 1930. He was educated in Morocco and France and worked with the Foreign Affairs Ministry from 1957. He was named secretary-general of the Ministry of National Defense in 1959 and in 1961 was appointed ambassador to West Germany. Osman worked with the Ministry of Industry and Mines from 1963 until 1964 and subsequently became president of the Moroccan Navigation Company. He returned to the diplomatic corps in 1967 when he was appointed ambassador to the United States. He retained that position until 1970, when he returned to Morocco as minister of administrative affairs. Osman was married to King Hassan's sister, Princess Lalla Nezha, and was named director of the royal cabinet in July of 1971, following an assassination attempt against the king. He was named prime minister of Morocco on November 2, 1972, and served until March 22, 1979. Osman continued to serve in Parliament, and in 1980 he became leader of the Independent Liberal party. He was elected president of the Chamber of Representatives in 1984.

MAATI BOUABID (Prime Minister, March 22, 1979–November 19, 1983). Maati Bouabid was born in Casablanca on November 11, 1927. He was educated in Morocco and France and became a lawyer. He was public prosecutor in Tangier from 1956 until 1957 and was named minister of labor and social affairs in 1958. Bouabid held that position until 1960. He was appointed minister of justice in 1977 and served until 1981. He was also named prime minister on March 22, 1979, and served until November 19, 1983. Bouabid founded the Constitutional Union party in 1983 and served in the government of Mohammed Karim Lamrani as a minister without portfolio. His party received a plurality in legislative elections in October of 1984, though Lamrani remained head of the government.

MOHAMMED KARIM LAMRANI (Prime Minister, November 30, 1983–September 30, 1986). *See earlier entry under Heads of Government.*

AZZEDINE LARAKI (Prime Minister, September 30, 1986–August 11, 1992). Azzedine Laraki was born in Fez in 1929. He studied medicine in France and joined the Ministry of Public Health in 1959. He became a director of Avicenne Hospital in 1960. Laraki served as minister of national education from 1977 until 1986. He was named prime minister on September 30, 1986.

MOHAMMED KARIM LAMRANI (Prime Minister, August 11, 1992–) *See earlier entry under Heads of Government.*

Mozambique, Republic of

(República de Moçambique)

Mozambique is a country on the eastern coast of Africa. It was granted independence from Portugal on June 25, 1975.

HEADS OF STATE

SAMORA MACHEL (President, June 25, 1975–October 19, 1986). Samora Möisés Machel was born in Xilembena, in Gaza Province, on September 29, 1933. He was educated in local mission schools and worked as a nurse. He joined the Mozambique Liberation Front (Frelimo) in Tanzania in 1962 and was sent to Algeria for military training. Machel was placed in charge of Frelimo's guerrilla operations in 1964 and became commander in chief of the organization in 1968. He became leader of Frelimo following the assassination of Eduardo Mondlane on February 3, 1969. Mozambique gained its independence from Portugal on June 25, 1975, and Machel served as the nation's first president. He attempted to establish Mozambique as a Socialist state. He maintained relations with the West and South Africa, which provided financial assistance to Mozambique. His government was threatened by the Mozambique National Resistance (Renamo), which fought a guerrilla rebellion against the government. Machel was killed in a plane crash near Nkomati, South Africa, while returning from a state visit to Zambia on October 19, 1986.

JOAQUIN CHISSANO (President, November 6, 1986–). Joaquin Alberto

Chissano was born in Chibuto on October 2, 1939. He was active with the Mozambique Liberation Front (Frelimo) from 1963 and served as secretary to the president from 1966 until 1969. He was Frelimo's chief representative in Dar-es-Salaam from 1969 until 1974. Chissano became premier in Mozambique's first independent government on September 20, 1974, and served until June 25, 1975. He was minister of foreign affairs from 1975 until 1986. Chissano succeeded Samora Machel as president of Mozambique on November 6, 1986. Chissano's government abandoned Marxism in favor of a free-market economy in November of 1990. Chissano also sought to end the ongoing civil war being waged by the Mozambique National Resistance (Renamo) movement. A truce was signed by the warring factions on August 7, 1992.

HEADS OF GOVERNMENT

JOAQUIN CHISSANO (Premier, September 20, 1974–June 25, 1975). *See entry under Heads of State.*

MÁRIO DE GRAÇA MACHUNGO (Premier, July 17, 1986–   ). Mário Fernandes de Graça Machungo served as an economic advisor to the Mozambique government of Samora Machel. He was instrumental in liberalizing the country's economic policies. He was chosen by President Machel to serve in the newly created post of premier on July 17, 1986. He was reappointed to the office on January 11, 1987.

Myanmar, Union of (Burma)
(Pyidaungsu Myanmar Naingngan)

Myanmar is a country in the northwestern section of Southeast Asia. It was granted independence from Great Britain on January 4, 1948.

HEADS OF STATE

SAO SHWE THAIK (President, January 4, 1948–March 12, 1952). Sao Shwe Thaik was born in 1896. He joined the Burma army and was active in the military during World War I and World War II. In 1929 he succeeded as sawbwa, or chieftain, of the Yawnghwe in the Shan State of Burma. In January of 1948 he was named as the first provisional president of the newly independent Burma. Thaik subsequently served as Speaker of the Chamber of Nationalities until 1960. He was arrested by the Burmese Revolutionary Government following the coup in March of 1962. He died of a heart attack in Rangoon on November 21, 1962, while still in custody.

BA U (President, March 12, 1952–March 13, 1957). Agga Maha Thiri Thudhamma Ba U was born in Bassein on May 26, 1887. He was educated in Burma and Great Britain, where he received a degree in law. He returned to Burma and was appointed a district judge in 1921. Ba U was later appointed a judge to the High Court and was named to the Supreme Court during the Japanese occupation in World War II. He became chief justice following the return of the British in 1946 and was instrumental in drafting Burma's independence constitution. He remained chief justice following Burma's independence in 1948. Ba U headed the parliamentary Elections Commission in 1951, which supervised free elections that year. He was elected president of Burma and took office on March 12, 1952. Ba U completed his term on March 13, 1957, and went into political retirement. He died in Rangoon on November 9, 1963.

MAHN WIN MAUNG (President, March 13, 1957–March 2, 1962). Mahn Win Maung was born on April 17, 1916. He attended Rangoon University and was active in the Anti-Fascist People's Freedom League. He served in the cabinet of Prime Minister U Nu following independence and held various ministries. Maung was elected to replace Ba U as president and took office on March 13, 1957. Mahn Win Maung was ousted shortly before the military coup led by General Ne Win on February 16, 1962. He was imprisoned by the new regime for five years. He went into political retirement following his release. Mahn Win Maung died after a long illness in Rangoon on July 4, 1989.

NE WIN (President, March 2, 1962–November 9, 1981). Ne Win was born Shu Maung in Paungdale on May 24, 1911. He attended Rangoon University and became involved with the Burmese nationalist movement. He accompanied U Aung San to Japan in 1941 to receive military training. Shortly thereafter he adopted the name Ne Win. He served with the Burma Independence Army and assisted the Japanese in fighting against the British in Burma. Ne Win became commander in chief of the army in the puppet government

established by the Japanese in August of 1943. The Burma Independence Army turned against the Japanese occupation forces and assisted the British in the recapture of Burma in August of 1945. Burma was granted independence from Great Britain in January of 1948, and General Ne Win served as defense minister in the government of U Nu. Following a period of disorder concerning amnesty for Communist guerrillas, Ne Win succeeded U Nu as caretaker prime minister on October 29, 1958. He was successful in restoring stability to the country. He remained in office until elections were held, and he relinquished the position back to U Nu on April 4, 1960. Burma experienced another period of disorder in 1962, and Ne Win led a military coup that ousted U Nu's government on March 2, 1962. He declared martial law and presided over a military government as prime minister and chairman of the Revolutionary Council. He formed the Burma Socialist Program party in 1973 and allowed elections to a People's Assembly in 1974. Ne Win stepped down as prime minister on March 2, 1974. He maintained a strong rule in Burma, even after he relinquished the presidency on November 9, 1981. During the 1980s Ne Win was faced with a growing pro-democracy movement. He resigned as chairman of the ruling Burma Socialist Program party on July 23, 1988, following rioting earlier in the year. Ne Win's close associate, General Saw Maung, took control of the country in a military coup in September of 1988.

U SAN YU (President, November 9, 1981–July 25, 1988). U San Yu was born in Prome in 1919. He was educated at the University of Rangoon and attended military college in the United States. He joined the army and served during World War II. U San Yu became a leading member of the Burmese military, and in 1963 he was appointed minister of finance and revenue. He became a leader of the Burmese Socialist Program party and served as deputy prime minister from 1971 until 1974. He also served as minister of defense and chief of the general staff from 1972 until 1974. U San Yu became secretary of the Council of State in 1974, and on November 9, 1981, he was named president of Burma. He resigned with General Ne Win on July 25, 1988.

U SEIN LWIN (President, July 25, 1988–August 12, 1988). U Sein Lwin was born in 1924. He served in the Burmese army and commanded a company of troops that killed over twenty student demonstrators at Rangoon University during Ne Win's 1962 coup. He retired from the military as a general and served as head of the Council of State. U Sein Lwin was chosen by General Ne Win to succeed him as chairman of the Burma Socialist Program party on July 25, 1988. He also took the office of president at that time. U Sein Lwin's selection was met with demonstrations against the government, and he resigned on August 12, 1988.

U MAUNG MAUNG (President, August 19, 1988–September 18, 1988). U Maung Maung was born in 1925. He was a Western-educated lawyer who was instrumental in writing Burma's 1974 constitution. He was a member of the Burma Socialist Program party's central committee and served as attorney general in the cabinet of Prime Minister U Tun Tin. U Maung Maung was named to replace U Sein Lwin as president on August 19, 1988. U Maung Maung's selection failed to halt demonstrations against the government, and he was ousted on September 18, 1988, in a military coup led by General Saw Maung.

SAW MAUNG (President, September 18, 1988–April 23, 1992). Saw Maung was born on December 5, 1928. He joined the Burmese army in 1945 and rose through the ranks as an infantryman. He became vice chief of staff of the army in 1983. Maung was a close associate of President Ne Win and was named chief of staff of the defense forces of Burma in 1986. He briefly served as minister of defense in the government of U Sein Lwin from July until August of 1988. The government of Burma was faced with demonstrations and civil disorder during the year, and Saw Maung led a military coup on September 18, 1988, to oust the government and crush a growing prodemocracy movement. He led the government as chairman of the State Law and Order Restoration Council. Saw Maung led an oppressive dictatorship that crushed dissent and imprisoned leaders of the opposition, including Aung San Suu Kyi, the daughter of late Burmese independence leader U Aung San. Saw Maung changed the name of Burma to the Union of Myanmar on June 19, 1989. Saw Maung was reportedly suffering from physical and mental disorders in early 1992 and was replaced as Burma's leader on April 23, 1992.

THAN SHWE (President, April 23, 1992–). Than Shwe served as a general in Burma's armed forces. He was vice-chairman of the ruling State Law and Order Restoration Council. He was chosen to replace Saw Maung as defense chief and head of the army in March of 1992. Than Shwe also assumed the offices of president and prime minister from Saw Maung on April 23, 1992. He released some political prisoners shortly after taking office.

HEADS OF GOVERNMENT

U AUNG SAN (Premier, September 26, 1946–July 19, 1947). U Aung San was born in 1914. He was a student at Rangoon University when he joined the

Burmese nationalist movement. He was arrested for subversive activities while still attending the university. U Aung San escaped to Japan shortly after the start of World War II and received military training there. He met with the British following the Japanese occupation of Burma. In April of 1945 he joined with the Allies against the Japanese, after negotiating for Burmese independence. He founded the Anti-Fascist Peoples' Freedom party shortly before the liberation of Burma. U Aung San joined the interim government as deputy chairman and counselor for defense and foreign affairs on September 26, 1946. He led a delegation to London in January of 1947 to discuss full independence for Burma. His party won a vast majority of the seats in elections for a Constituent Assembly in April of 1947. He and seven other members of the Executive Council were assassinated by gunmen in the council's chamber in Rangoon on July 19, 1947.

U NU (Prime Minister, July 24, 1947–June 12, 1956). U Nu was born Thakin Nu in Wakena on May 25, 1907. He attended Rangoon University, where he graduated in 1929. He later became a teacher and was involved with the Burmese nationalist movement. U Nu led an anti–British student strike in 1936 and was imprisoned for subversive activities near the start of World War II. He was released from prison following the Japanese occupation and served in the wartime puppet government of Dr. Ba Maw. He was foreign minister from 1943 until 1944 and minister of publicity and propaganda from 1944 until 1945. U Nu later joined with U Aung San's Anti-Fascist People's Freedom League in opposition to the Japanese occupation. He became vice president of the Freedom League following the Allied victory in Burma. He was elected Speaker of the Constituent Assembly in 1947. When U Aung San was assas-

sinated on July 19, 1947, U Nu was called upon by the British governor to serve as premier and party leader. Burma was granted full independence on January 4, 1948, and U Nu served as his nation's first prime minister. U Nu's government was threatened by several Communist guerrilla groups. He resigned as prime minister in July of 1948, but consented to remain on as head of government due to the state of emergency existing in the country. He again resigned as prime minister on June 12, 1956, and reorganized the Anti-Fascist People's Freedom League. U Nu returned as prime minister on March 1, 1957, and served until his government coalition collapsed on October 29, 1958. He again served as prime minister from April 4, 1960, until his ouster in a military coup led by General Ne Win on March 2, 1962. U Nu was detained by the new government until 1966, when he was allowed to leave the country for health reasons. He went into exile in Thailand in 1969 to organize the Burmese opposition groups against Ne Win's government. He returned to Burma to lead an unsuccessful revolution against the government in October of 1970. U Nu then returned to exile in Thailand and then in India. He abandoned his struggle against Ne Win in 1974. He was pardoned by the Ne Win government and invited to return to Burma in July of 1980. U Nu attempted to form an alternate government as the Democracy party in Burma following the military coup led by General Saw Maung in 1988, but received little support for his efforts. He was subsequently arrested for his opposition to the government, but was released on April 25, 1992.

U BA SWE (Prime Minister, June 12, 1956–March 1, 1957). U Ba Swe was born in Tavoy on April 19, 1915. He was educated at Rangoon University and was a founder of the People's Revolutionary party in 1939. He was active in the Burmese Resistance movement against the

Japanese during World War II. Ba Swe was arrested by the Japanese, but was released after the liberation of Burma. He subsequently served as secretary-general of the Anti-Fascist People's Freedom League from 1947. He was elected to Parliament and served in U Nu's cabinet as minister of defense. Ba Swe replaced U Nu as prime minister for a short period from June 12, 1956, until March 1, 1957. He remained minister of defense until 1958. He went into opposition to the government in 1958. Ba Swe was detained following the military coup in 1962 led by General Ne Win. He was released in 1966.

U NU (Prime Minister, March 1, 1957–October 29, 1958). *See earlier entry under Heads of Government.*

NE WIN (Prime Minister, October 29, 1958–April 4, 1960). *See entry under Heads of State.*

U NU (Prime Minister, April 4, 1960–March 2, 1962). *See earlier entry under Heads of Government.*

NE WIN (Prime Minister, March 2, 1962–March 2, 1974). *See entry under Heads of State.*

U SEIN WIN (Prime Minister, March 4, 1974–March 29, 1977). U Sein Win was elected prime minister on March 4, 1974, following the first election in Burma after the 1962 coup led by General Ne Win. The country's economic conditions deteriorated over the next few years, and U Sein Win was forced to resign on March 29, 1977.

U MAUNG MAUNG KHA (Prime Minister, March 29, 1977–July 26, 1988). U Maung Maung Kha was born in 1917. He was a member of Ne Win's Burma Socialist Program party and served as minister of industry and labor from 1973 until 1974. He remained Minister of Industry until 1975 and was minister of mines from 1975 until 1977. U Maung Maung Kha was named prime minister of Burma on March 29, 1977. He was dismissed on July 26, 1988, the day after the resignation of General Ne Win.

U TUN TIN (Prime Minister, July 26, 1988–September 18, 1988). U Tun Tin served as finance minister in the cabinet of Prime Minister U Maung Maung Kha. He was named prime minister on July 26, 1988, in the government of President U Sein Lwin. He retained his position when Sein Lwin was replaced as president by U Maung Maung. Tun Tin was ousted with the government by a military coup led by General Saw Maung on September 18, 1988.

SAW MAUNG (Prime Minister, September 21, 1988–April 23, 1992). *See entry under Heads of State.*

THAN SHWE (Prime Minister, April 23, 1992–). *See entry under Heads of State.*

Namibia, Republic of

Namibia is a country in southwest Africa. It was granted independence from South Africa on March 21, 1990.

HEAD OF STATE

SAM NUJOMA (President, March 21, 1990–). Sam Shafilshuna Nujoma was born in Ongandjera on May 12, 1929. He was educated at local missionary schools. He worked with the State Railways until 1957 and then worked as a store clerk. Nujoma was a founder of the South West Africa People's Organization (SWAPO) in April of 1959. He was arrested the following December and subsequently went into exile. He continued to serve as leader of SWAPO and set up headquarters in Tanzania in March of 1961. Nujoma was again arrested when he returned to Windhoek and was exiled in March of 1966. He began an armed uprising against South Africa for the liberation of South West Africa in August of 1966. He returned to South West Africa, now called Namibia, in September of 1989. Nujoma became independent Namibia's first president on March 21, 1990.

HEAD OF GOVERNMENT

HAGE GEINGOB (Prime Minister, March 21, 1990–). Hage Gottfried Geingob was born in Otji Warongo on August 3, 1941. He joined the South West Africa People's Organization (SWAPO) in 1962 and served as SWAPO's representative to the United Nations from 1964. He was instrumental in negotiations that led to South West Africa formally gaining independence from South Africa in March of 1990. Geingob was subsequently installed as independent Namibia's first prime minister on March 21, 1990.

Nauru, Republic of

(Naoero)

Nauru is an island in the central Pacific Ocean. It was granted independence from a United Nations trusteeship administered by Australia, New Zealand, and Great Britain on January 31, 1968.

HEADS OF STATE

HAMMER DE ROBURT (President, January 31, 1968–December 18, 1976). Hammer De Roburt was born in Nauru on September 25, 1922. He was educated in Nauru and Australia and returned to Nauru to teach in 1940. He went into exile during the Japanese occupation, but returned to serve in the Department of Nauruan Affairs as an educational advisor from 1947 until 1951. De Roburt returned to teaching and in 1955 served on the Nauru Government Council. He became chairman of the council in 1965, and following Nauru's independence on January 31, 1968, he became its first president. Nauru's economic prosperity under De Roburt was assured by the government's control of the phosphate industry. De Roburt was returned to office in 1971 and 1973. He was defeated in the elections of 1976 and vacated the presidency to lead the opposition on December 18, 1976. He was returned to office on August 19, 1978, and served until September 17, 1986, when he was forced from office following a defeat of his budget bill. De Roburt's parliamentary opponents reversed their stance, and he was again returned to office on October 1, 1986. He retired from office on August 17, 1989, after losing a vote of confidence in the Parliament. De Roburt died in Nauru on July 15, 1992.

BERNARD DOWIYOGO (President, December 18, 1976–August 19, 1978). Bernard Dowiyogo was born in Nauru on February 14, 1946. He studied law in Nauru and Australia and was elected to Parliament in 1973. He led the Nauru party to victory in 1976 and became president on December 18, 1976. Dowiyogo retained office until August 19, 1978. He served as minister of justice from December of 1983 and was chairman of the Bank of Nauru from 1985. Dowiyogo was again selected as president of Nauru by the Parliament on December 12, 1989, following the resignation of President Kenas Aroi for reasons of health.

LAGUMONT HARRIS (President, April 19, 1978–May 11, 1978). Lagumont Harris was selected as president of Nauru on April 19, 1978, after the resignation of Bernard Dowiyogo. Harris resigned from office on May 11, 1978, following the Parliament's rejection of an appropriation bill.

HAMMER DE ROBURT (President, May 15, 1978–September 17, 1986). *See earlier entry under Heads of State.*

KENNAN ADEANG (President, September 17, 1986–October 1, 1986). Kennan Ranibok Adeang was selected by Parliament to succeed Hammer De Roburt as president on September 17, 1986. He was forced from office on a vote of no-confidence on October 1, 1986, and De Roburt was returned to office.

HAMMER DE ROBURT (President, October 1, 1986–August 17, 1989). *See earlier entry under Heads of State.*

KENOS AROI (President, August 17, 1989–December 12, 1989). Kenos Aroi succeeded Hammer De Roburt as president when De Roburt lost a vote of confidence on August 17, 1989. Aroi retained the presidency until December 12, 1989, when he resigned for reasons of health and went to Australia to seek medical treatment.

BERNARD DOWIYOGO (President, December 12, 1989–). *See earlier entry under Heads of State.*

Nepal, Kingdom of
(Nepál Alhirajya)

Nepal is a country in the Himalayan mountain range in central Asia.

HEADS OF STATE

TRIBHUVAN (King, December 11, 1911–March 13, 1955). Tribhuvan Bir Bikram Shah Dev was born in 1906. He was the only son of King Prithvi. Tribhuvan ascended to the throne on December 11, 1911, at the age of five, following the death of his father, who was allegedly the victim of a slow-acting poison. The Nepal monarch was controlled by the Rana family, the hereditary prime ministers of Nepal. The Rana family wanted Nepal to join forces with the British in World War I, but the queen mother and the army wished to remain neutral. To force the monarchy to accept their position, Prime Minister Chandra Shumshere Rana put a loaded gun to the head of the queen mother and ordered King Tribhuvan to address the military on his behalf. The military's loyalty to the monarch resulted in Nepal's alliance with Britain during the war. The young king was kept a virtual prisoner of the Rana family and was coerced into serving as spokesman for their plans, which included the suppression of all liberal and democratic movements in the country. As King Tribhuvan reached adulthood, he chafed under the restraints the Ranas placed on him. The Praja Panchayat movement, formed in 1936, was one of several movements designed to restore power to the monarchy and end the rule of the Ranas. The movements were brutally suppressed, and many of the members were imprisoned or executed. The king's life was reportedly threatened by the Ranas in 1940. Tribhuvan was saved by the influence of the British, who recognized his importance in controlling the military, which was assisting the Allies during World War II. By 1946 opposition to the Ranas had grown to the extent that the Nepali Congress party was formed. King Tribhuvan was in sympathy with the democratic movements, and in November of 1950 he escaped from the palace with most of his family and took refuge in the Indian Embassy. He was subsequently allowed to gain asylum in India. Prime Minister Mohan Shumshere Rana attempted to install Tribhuvan's young grandson, Jagendra, on the throne, but was thwarted by the refusal of other nations to recognize the new monarch. Early in 1951 the Ranas accepted democratic reforms, and Tribhuvan returned to Nepal and was restored to the throne as a constitutional monarch on February 18, 1951. Tribhuvan suffered from heart disease and went to Zurich, Switzerland, for treatment in 1954. He died in Zurich of a heart attack at the age of 48 on March 13, 1955.

MAHENDRA (King, March 14, 1955–January 31, 1972). Mahendra Bir Bikram Shah Deva was born on June 11, 1920. He was the son of King Tribhuvan. He was educated in the royal palace in Katmandu, where he and his family were virtual prisoners of the ruling hereditary prime ministers, the Rana family. Mahendra accompanied his father to India in 1950 prior to the ouster of the Ranas from power. Mahendra was granted the powers of regent in February of 1955 while his father was suffering from poor health in Europe. He dismissed the cabinet of Matuika Prasada Koirala on March 2, 1955, and took personal control of the government. Mahendra was proclaimed king following the death of his father on March 14, 1955. The new king attempted to democratize Nepal. He appointed a new government on January 27, 1956, and allowed the formation of political parties to participate in a free election in 1959. The king dismissed the government of B. P. Koirala on December 15, 1960, revoked the constitution, and restored the monarchy to full power. Under Mahendra's rule Nepal began to participate to a greater extent in international affairs. He continued to maintain Nepal's status as a nonaligned country in foreign affairs. Mahendra promoted cordial relations with the People's Republic of China, and the two nations reached an agreement on a long-standing border dispute. He appointed a new government with Tulsi Giri as prime minister on April 2, 1963. The king again served as chairman of the Council of Ministers following the resignation of Kirti Nidhi Bista on April 12, 1970. Bista returned as prime minister in April of 1971. Mahendra died of a heart attack in Katmandu at the age of 51 on January 31, 1972.

BIRENDRA (King, January 31, 1972-). Birendra Bir Bikram Shah Dev was born in Katmandu on December 28, 1946. He was the son of King Mahendra and Princess Indra. He was educated in India, Great Britain, Japan, and the United States. Birendra succeeded his father to the throne on January 31, 1972, and continued his father's policies. His rule was threatened by a growing democratic movement in the country, however. A student demonstration in 1979 led to an unsuccessful referendum to mandate multiparty elections the following May. Birendra made a number of constitutional reforms in December of 1980 and allowed direct election to the National Assembly. When Nepal's economy suffered in the late 1980s, Birendra was faced with further demands for democratization. He granted amnesty to all political prisoners and was forced to allow multiparty elections to take place in May of 1991.

HEADS OF GOVERNMENT

JUDDHA SHUMSHERE RANA (Prime Minister, September 1, 1932–November 28, 1945). Juddha Shumshere Jung Bahadur Rana was born in April of 1875. He was the son of General Dhir Shumshere Rana. He succeeded to the hereditary prime ministership of Nepal on September 1, 1932, following the death of his elder brother, Maharaja Bhim Shumshere Jung Rana. Two years later Nepal was devastated by a major earthquake, which setback his efforts to modernize the country. Juddha Shumshere was able to effect numerous social reforms and made advancements in the education and transportation systems of Nepal. During World War II he was a firm ally of Great Britain and increased the number of Gurkha battalions that fought alongside the Allied powers. He also opened Nepal's first foreign embassy in London in 1941 and made efforts to industrialize Nepal. Juddha Shumshere retired from office on November 28, 1945, because he feared the returning Gurkha soldiers would bring home with them democratic ideas that would threaten the rule of the Rana family. He was succeeded by his brother, Padma Shumshere Rana. Juddha Shumshere retired to West Nepal, renouncing worldly life and dedicating the remainder of his life to religious contemplation. He died in Dehra Dun, Nepal, on November 23, 1952.

PADMA SHUMSHERE J. B. RANA (Prime Minister, November 28, 1945–February 9, 1948). Padma Shumshere Jung Bahadur Rana was born in 1882. He served as commander in chief of the Nepal army and succeeded to the hereditary office of prime minister following the retirement of his brother, Juddha Shumshere Rana, on November 28, 1945. Padma Shumshere began an effort to liberalize Nepal and approved a new constitution in 1948 which gave limited rights to the people. The constitution was never implemented, however, and he resigned on

February 9, 1948. He died of a heart attack near Calcutta, India, on April 11, 1961, at the age of 70.

MOHAN SHUMSHERE J. B. RANA (Prime Minister, February 9, 1948–November 16, 1951). Mohan Shumshere Jung Bahadur Rana was born on December 23, 1885. He was the son of former prime minister Chandra Shumshere. His father wished for Mohan to succeed him in office, but because of a pact signed in 1913, he was forced to allow his brother, Juddha, to succeed. Mohan plotted against Juddha and his successor, Padma Shumshere, until the latter's resignation on February 9, 1948. Mohan subsequently became prime minister. He attempted to retain the power of the Rana family, but democratic forces, with the support of the king, conspired against him. In 1950 Mohan engineered a palace coup against King Tribhuvan and forced the monarch into temporary exile in India. When the king returned to the throne the following year, Mohan was forced to approve a constitution that drastically curtailed the power of the prime minister. Mohan was unable to govern as part of a coalition government and resigned on November 16, 1951. He went into exile in Bangalore, South India.

MATUIKA PRASADA KOIRALA (Prime Minister, November 16, 1951–March 2, 1955). Matuika Prasada Koirala was born on January 1, 1912. He was educated in India and served as president of the Nepali Congress party. He served as prime minister of Nepal from November 16, 1951, until March 2, 1955. Koirala was arrested in December of 1960 following King Mahendra's abolition of political parties, but was released the following month. He later served in the upper house of Parliament and was ambassador to the United States from 1962 until 1964. Koirala also served as Nepal's representative to the United Nations during that period. He later went into exile in India because of his prodemocracy leanings.

MAHENDRA (Prime Minister, March 2, 1955–January 27, 1956). *See entry under Heads of State.*

TANKA PRASAD ACHARYA (Prime Minister, January 27, 1956–July 9, 1957). Tanka Prasad Acharya was born in 1912. He was a founder of the Nepal Praja Partishad, Nepal's first political party, in the 1930s. He was a leader of the movement to oust the ruling Rana family. Acharya was arrested in 1940 and was sentenced to death for his political activities. His sentence was commuted to life imprisonment because he was a member of the Brahmin caste, and Hindu law forbade the killing of Brahmins. Acharya was released from prison following a revolution that gave more power to King Tribhuvan in 1951. Acharya was selected as prime minister by King Mahendra on January 27, 1956. During his term of office, Nepal established diplomatic relations with the People's Republic of China. Acharya remained prime minister until July 9, 1957. He was defeated as a candidate for the People's party in general elections in March of 1959. He was arrested in December of 1960 after King Mahendra's royal coup. Acharya was released the following year. He subsequently made little impact in Nepali politics. He died of kidney complications in Katmandu on April 23, 1992.

KUNVAR INDERJIH SINGH (Prime Minister, July 26, 1957–November 14, 1957). Kunvar Inderjih Singh was born in 1906. Singh was a Socialist who earned the nickname "Robin Hood of the Himalayas" when he organized a land reform movement to help peasant farmers during a revolt against the Rana dynasty in 1950. Two years later Singh led a coup and held power for two days before being ousted by the Nepalese army. He fled first to Tibet and then to the People's Republic of

China. King Mahendra granted him amnesty and allowed him to return to Nepal in 1955. Singh led the United Democratic party and was named prime minister on July 26, 1957. He resigned on November 14, 1957, after a disagreement with the king. Singh was defeated in elections in March of 1959. King Mahendra dismissed the government and banned political parties the following year. Singh was again arrested and imprisoned until 1965. He was subsequently forced into exile once more. He remained a supporter of democratic elections in Nepal. He died of throat cancer in Bangkok, Thailand, on October 4, 1982, at the age of 77.

BISHEWAR PRASAD KOIRALA (Prime Minister, May 27, 1959–December 15, 1960). Bishewar Prasad Koirala was born in Biratnagar in 1915. He was educated in India and was active in the Indian National Congress. He formed the Nepali National Congress following India's independence in the late 1940s. Koirala returned to Nepal to advocate democratic reforms in the government. Elections were held in 1959, and Koirala's party was victorious. He took office as prime minister on May 27, 1959. Koirala's government attempted to institute reforms to limit the power of the monarchy and provide for democratic rule. King Mahendra abrogated the constitution on December 15, 1960, and dismissed the government. Koirala was arrested following his ouster and remained imprisoned until 1968. He was then sent into exile in India. He returned to Nepal in 1976 and was arrested for treason. He was subsequently acquitted by a government tribunal. Koirala was briefly placed under house arrest following prodemocracy demonstrations in April of 1979. He remained an advocate of multiparty democracy, though a referendum to restore political parties was defeated in 1980. Koirala died of lung cancer in Katmandu at the age of 67 on July 21, 1982.

MAHENDRA (Prime Minister, December 15, 1960–April 2, 1963). *See entry under Heads of State.*

TULSI GIRI (Prime Minister, April 2, 1963–December 1963). Tulsi Giri was born in September of 1926. He served as deputy minister of foreign affairs in 1959 and was named minister of foreign affairs, the interior, public works, and communications in 1961. He served as chairman of the Council of Ministers from April 2, 1963, until December of 1963 and again from February 27, 1964, until January 26, 1965. Giri also served as foreign minister during this period. He served on the Royal Advisory Committee from 1969 until 1974. He was named prime minister, minister of palace affairs, and minister of defense in December of 1975. Giri disagreed with King Birendra's decision to release B. P. Koirala and other political prisoners and left office on September 12, 1977. He remained a leading advisor to King Birendra.

SURYA BAHADUR THAPA (Prime Minister, December 1963–February 27, 1964). Surya Bahadur Thapa was born in Muga on March 20, 1928. He was educated in India and served as Speaker of the House of Assembly in 1958. He served as minister of forests, agriculture, commerce, and industry in 1960 and was named minister of finance and economic affairs in 1962. Thapa served as chairman of the Council of Ministers from December of 1963 until February 27, 1964, and again from January 26, 1965, until April 7, 1969. He was a member of the Royal Advisory Committee from 1969 until his arrest shortly after the ascension of King Birendra in 1972. Thapa was again arrested in 1975 on charges of conspiring against the monarchy. He was named prime minister of Nepal and minister of palace affairs on May 30, 1979, following student demonstrations demanding political reforms. His government was charged with official corruption, and he was forced to resign on July 12, 1983.

TULSI GIRI (Prime Minister, February 27, 1964–January 26, 1965). *See earlier entry under Heads of Government.*

SURYA BAHADUR THAPA (Prime Minister, January 26, 1965–April 7, 1969). *See earlier entry under Heads of Government.*

KIRTI NIDHI BISTA (Prime Minister, April 7, 1969–April 12, 1970). Kirti Nidhi Bista was born in 1927. He was named minister of education in 1962 and minister of foreign affairs in 1964. He was also named deputy prime minister and minister of education in 1967 and served until 1968. He was then appointed as Nepal's representative to the United Nations until 1969. Bista served as prime minister from April 7, 1969, until April 12, 1970. He remained minister of finance and was again named prime minister in April of 1971. He resigned as head of the government on July 17, 1973. Bista was appointed prime minister for a third time on September 12, 1977, and served until May 30, 1979.

MAHENDRA (Prime Minister, April 12, 1970–April 1971). *See entry under Heads of State.*

KIRTI NIDHI BISTA (Prime Minister, April 1971–July 17, 1973). *See earlier entry under Heads of Government.*

NAGENDRA PRASAD RIJAL (Prime Minister, July 17, 1973–December 1975). Nagendra Prasad Rijal served as chairman of Nepal's National Assembly. He was chosen to replace Kirti Nidhi Bista as prime minister on July 17, 1973. He retained office until December of 1975 and was succeeded by Tulsi Giri. Rijal again served as interim prime minister during parliamentary elections from March 20, 1986, until June 15, 1986.

TULSI GIRI (Prime Minister, December 1975–September 12, 1977).

See earlier entry under Heads of Government.

KIRTI NIDHI BISTA (Prime Minister, September 12, 1977–May 30, 1979). *See earlier entry under Heads of Government.*

SURYA BAHADUR THAPA (Prime Minister, May 30, 1979–July 12, 1983). *See earlier entry under Heads of Government.*

LOKENDRA BAHADUR CHAND (Prime Minister, July 12, 1983–June 15, 1986). Lokendra Bahadur Chand was chosen by King Birendra to serve as prime minister following the resignation of Surya Bahadur Thapa on July 12, 1983. He retained office until March 20, 1986, when he stepped down to participate in parliamentary elections. He was named to replace Marish Man Singh Shrestha as prime minister on April 6, 1990, following demonstrations calling for multiparty elections. Chand was replaced by prodemocracy leader Krishna Prasad Bhattarai on April 19, 1990, when King Birendra bowed to pressure to hold democratic elections.

NAGENDRA PRASAD RIJAL (Prime Minister, March 20, 1986–June 15, 1986). *See earlier entry under Heads of Government.*

MARISH MAN SINGH SHRESTHA (Prime Minister, June 15, 1986–April 6, 1990). Marish Man Singh Shrestha was born in Khalanga in 1942. He served as a member of the National Assembly from 1975. He was appointed minister for water, power, and irrigation in 1979 and assumed the portfolios of law and justice in 1980. Shrestha became minister of education in 1980 and became chairman of the National Assembly the following year. He was elected prime minister on June 15, 1986, following parliamentary elections, and served until April 6, 1990, when he was forced to resign by calls for a more democratic form of government.

LOKENDRA BAHADUR CHAND (Prime Minister, April 6, 1990–April 19, 1990). *See earlier entry under Heads of Government.*

KRISHNA PRASAD BHATTARAI (Prime Minister, April 19, 1990–May 26, 1991). Krishna Prasad Bhattarai was born in 1924. He was acting president of the banned Nepali Congress party and was imprisoned for fourteen years for his opposition to the Nepalese monarchy. Following the restoration of multiparty government, Bhattarai was named prime minister on April 19, 1990. He remained in office until May 26, 1991, following multiparty parliamentary elections. Bhattarai subsequently served as president of the Nepali Congress from 1992.

GINJA PRASAD KOIRALA (Prime Minister, May 26, 1991–). Ginja Prasad Koirala was the brother of former prime minister B. P. Koirala. He served as general secretary of the Nepal Congress party. He was named prime minister on May 26, 1991, after general elections earlier in the month. He also served in the government as foreign minister and minister of defense.

Netherlands, Kingdom of the

(Koninkrijk der Nederlanden)

The Netherlands is a country in western Europe.

HEADS OF STATE

WILHELMINA (Queen, November 23, 1890–September 3, 1948). Wilhelmina Helena Pauline Maria was born in The Hague on August 31, 1880. She was the daughter of William III and Emma of the Netherlands. She succeeded to the throne following the death of her father on November 23, 1890. Wilhelmina ruled under the regency of her mother until September 6, 1898, when she came of age to become queen. She married Prince Hendrik in February of 1901. She supported the neutrality of the Netherlands during World War I. Wilhelmina left the Netherlands following the Nazi invasion of her country in May of 1940. She stayed in London during World War II, where she remained a symbol of opposition to the German occupation. She returned to the Netherlands following the defeat of the Axis powers in 1945. Wilhelmina abdicated the throne in favor of her daughter, Juliana, on September 4, 1948. She spent her retirement involved in gardening and writing her memoirs, which were published in 1959. She died of heart disease in Apeldoorn at the age of 82 on November 28, 1962.

JULIANA (Queen, September 4, 1948–April 30, 1980). Juliana Emma Marie Wilhelmina, Princess of Orange-Nassau, Duchess of Mecklenburg, was born in the royal palace at The Hague, on April 30, 1909. She was the daughter of Queen Wilhelmina of the Netherlands and Prince Henry of Mecklenburg-Schwerin. She married Prince Bernhard of Lippe-Biesterfeld in 1937. Juliana went to Canada following the German occupation of the Netherlands in 1940 and went to England in 1944. She returned to the Netherlands in 1945 and served as princess regent from October of 1947. She succeeded to the throne upon the abdication of her mother, Queen Wilhelmina, on September 4, 1948. In 1949 the royal family consulted Dutch faith healer Greet Hofmans to help cure their daughter Christina of a congenital eye disorder. When Hofmans failed in her attempts, she was ordered from the palace by Prince Bernhard. Juliana continued to consult with Hofmans, who became known as the "Rasputin of the Dutch Court." When the incident, which caused a rift in the royal household, became public in 1956, the queen broke off all relations with Hofmans. In 1976 the royal family faced another scandal when Prince Bernhard was accused of accepting bribes in excess of $1 million from Lockheed Aircraft Corporation in return for granting military procurement contracts. Prince Bernhard was cleared of accepting bribes following an official investigation that ruled that he did exercise poor judgment in his dealings with Lockheed officials. Juliana considered

abdicating following the revelations, but was persuaded to reconsider by Prime Minister Joop Den Uyl. Juliana did abdicate the throne in favor of her eldest daughter, Beatrix, on April 30, 1980.

BEATRIX (Queen, April 30, 1980–). Beatrix Wilhelmina Armgard, Princess of the Netherlands, Princess of Orange-Nassau, Princess of Lippe-Biesterfeld, was born at Soestdijk Palace in Baarn on January 31, 1938. She was the daughter of Queen Juliana of the Netherlands and Prince Bernhard of Lippe-Biesterfeld. She attended the University of Leiden, where she received a doctorate in political science in 1961. Beatrix married Claus George Willem Otto Frederik Geert von Amsberg in 1966. Her marriage caused a brief stir in the Netherlands when it became known that her husband had served in the German army during World War II. She succeeded to the throne of the Netherlands following the abdication of her mother, Queen Juliana, on April 30, 1980. Beatrix remained a popular monarch and handled her ceremonial duties with dignity.

HEADS OF GOVERNMENT

PIETER S. GERBRANDY (Prime Minister, September 4, 1940–June 25, 1945). Pieter Sjoerds Gerbrandy was born in Goengamieden on April 13, 1885. He was educated at the Zetten Gymnasium and the Amsterdam Free University, where he received a degree in law. He subsequently served as a law professor at the University from 1930 until 1939. Gerbrandy was named minister of justice in 1939 and accompanied the Dutch government in exile in London following the German occupation of the Netherlands in 1940. He succeeded Dirk J. de Geer as prime minister of the Dutch government-in-exile on September 4, 1940. He also retained his position as minister of justice and served as

minister of the colonies until 1942. Gerbrandy was minister of coordination and warfare from 1942 until 1945. His government returned to the Netherlands following the liberation of the country. He and his cabinet announced their resignations in February of 1945, and he was replaced as prime minister by Willem Schermerhorn on June 25, 1945. Gerbrandy subsequently served in the Dutch Parliament. He was named an honorary minister of state in 1955. He died in The Hague at the age of 76 on September 7, 1961.

WILLEM SCHERMERHORN (Prime Minister, June 25, 1945–July 2, 1946). Willem Schermerhorn was born in

Akersloot on December 17, 1894. Educated as a civil engineer, he was the founder of the Dutch Institute of Geodesy and served as its director until 1931. He surveyed New Guinea at the request of the Dutch government in 1936 and assisted the Chinese government of Chiang Kai-shek as a cartographical advisor in 1937. Schermerhorn was an advisor to the Dutch Ministry of Public Works and was the leader of the Dutch Anti-Fascist League prior to World War II. He was arrested by the Germans during the occupation of the Netherlands. When he was released in 1943, he became the leader of the Dutch Resistance. Schermerhorn was a founder of the Labor party after the liberation of the Netherlands and was selected to head an interim coalition government as prime minister on June 25, 1945. He retained the position until general elections could be held and stepped down on July 2, 1946. He subsequently served as president of a government commission on the Dutch East Indies from 1946 until 1947. Schermerhorn entered Parliament in 1948 and was elected to the Senate in 1951. He also served as professor of geodesy at the Delft Technical University from 1951. He retired from politics in 1963 and left his teaching position the following year. Schermerhorn died in Akersloot at the age of 82 on March 10, 1977.

LOUIS J. M. BEEL (Prime Minister, July 2, 1946–August 5, 1948). Louis Joseph Maria Beel was born in Roermond on April 12, 1902. He attended the Catholic University of Nijmegen, where he received a degree in law. He subsequently entered politics as a member of the Catholic Peoples' party. Beel was selected as prime minister on July 2, 1946, and served until August 5, 1948, when he was unable to form a coalition government. He then served as the high commissioner in the Dutch East Indies until 1949. Beel administered the area during the period of time when the Netherlands granted independence to Indonesia. He returned to the Netherlands and was again named prime minister, as head of a caretaker cabinet, on December 22, 1958. He stepped down on May 19, 1959, after general elections were held and a new government was formed by Jan de Quay. Beel subsequently served as vice president of the Council of State from 1959 until 1972. He died in Utrecht on February 11, 1977, at the age of 74 following a long illness.

WILLEM DREES (Prime Minister, August 5, 1948–December 22, 1958). Willem Drees was born in Amsterdam on July 5, 1886. He joined Social Democratic Labor party after completing high school in 1903. He worked as a stenographer in the Parliament from 1906 and was elected chairman of the local Social Democratic party in 1911. He was elected to the Municipal Council of The Hague in 1913. Drees was also elected to the Parliament in 1933 and became his party's parliamentary leader in 1939. He was arrested for anti–German activities following the occupation of the Netherlands and was imprisoned at Buchenwald concentration camp from October of 1940 until October of 1941. He became active in the Dutch Resistance movement following his release. After the liberation of the Netherlands, Drees served as minister of social affairs in the coalition cabinets of Willem Schermerhorn and Louis Beel. Drees formed a coalition government as prime minister on August 5, 1948. His government instituted a number of social reforms, including national health care, unemployment compensation, and a pension program. Drees was also faced with a growing independence movement in the Dutch East Indies. He sent troops to the area in 1948 to reestablish Dutch control. The military action met with international condemnation, however, and the Dutch government recognized the sovereignty of the Republic of Indonesia in

1949. The Netherlands also joined the North Atlantic Treaty Organization (NATO) and the European Common Market under Drees's leadership. Drees remained prime minister until December 22, 1958, when he resigned after his coalition government fell apart over the issue of proposed tax increases. He resigned from the Labor party in 1971 after criticizing the left-wing of the party for refusing to allow NATO to deploy cruise missiles on Dutch soil. Drees died in The Hague after a long illness at the age of 101 on May 14, 1988.

LOUIS JOSEPH M. BEEL (Prime Minister, December 22, 1958–May 19, 1959). *See earlier entry under Heads of Government.*

JAN EDUARD DE QUAY (Prime Minister, May 19, 1959–July 24, 1963). Jan Eduard de Quay was born in s'Hertogenbosch on August 26, 1901. He was educated at St. Willibrordus College in Katwijk and received a doctorate in psychology from the State University of Utrecht in 1927. He was a lecturer and then a professor at the Catholic School of Economics in Tilburg from 1928 until 1946. De Quay was also director of the Technical Economic Institute from 1933 until 1946. During the German occupation of the Netherlands, de Quay was a founder of the Dutch Union, which attempted to reach an accommodation with the occupation force. The union was banned in 1941, and de Quay was imprisoned by the German authorities from 1942 until 1943. De Quay was named minister of war in the postoccupation government of Pieter Gerbrandy in April of 1945, and served until the following June. He was appointed governor of the North Brabant province following the Catholic People's party's victory in the election in May of 1946. He also served as chairman of the Council for Emigration Affairs from 1952. De Quay was asked to form a government as prime minister following elections in March

of 1959. He became the head of a coalition government on May 19, 1959, and served until July 24, 1963. He became chairman of the Royal Dutch Airlines in 1964 and was minister of transportation from 1966 until 1967. De Quay retired from politics in 1969 and resigned his position with the Royal Dutch Airlines in 1972. He died at his home in Beers at the age of 83 on July 4, 1985.

VICTOR G. M. MARIJNEN (Prime Minister, July 24, 1963–February 26, 1965). Victor Gérard Marie Marijnen was born in Arnhem on February 21, 1917. He was educated at the Catholic University of Nijmegen. He was employed by the Ministry of Agriculture following the German occupation of the Netherlands in 1940. Marijnen became active in the Catholic People's party and served as secretary of the Federation of Agriculture. He was subsequently named to the Dutch cabinet as minister of agriculture and fisheries in 1959. Marijnen formed a coalition government on July 24, 1963. His government collapsed on February 26, 1965, following the resignation of the cabinet over the issue of a proposed introduction of commercial radio and television into the Netherlands. Marijnen was elected mayor of The Hague in 1968 and retained that position until April 5, 1975, when he died of a heart ailment at the age of 58.

JOSEPH M. L. T. CALS (Prime Minister, April 14, 1965–November 22, 1966). Joseph Maria Laurens Theo Cals was born in Roermond on July 18, 1914. He studied law at Nijmegen University. He began his political career as a member of the Catholic People's party following the liberation of the Netherlands from German occupation in 1945. Cals accepted the position of state secretary at the Ministry of Education in 1950 and was appointed minister of education in 1952. He retained this position until 1963, when he returned to the Parliament. He formed a left-wing coalition cabinet and became prime minister on April 14, 1965. The Netherlands was faced with serious economic problems, but Cals was considered too radical by members of his own party. After a vote of no confidence, his government collapsed on November 22, 1966. Cals subsequently joined with the left-wing in splitting from the Catholic party. He was appointed to chair a royal commission to reform the Dutch Constitution in 1967. He died in The Hague at the age of 57 on December 30, 1971, after a long illness.

JELLE ZIJLSTRA (Prime Minister, November 22, 1966–April 5, 1967). Jelle Zijlstra was born in Barradeel on August 27, 1918. He graduated from the Netherlands School of Economics. In 1948 he became a professor of economics at the Free University of Amsterdam. Zijlstra remained there until 1952, when he was named minister of foreign affairs in the government of Willem Drees. In 1959 he was appointed minister of finance. In 1963 he left the government to return to the faculty of the University of Amsterdam. Zijlstra became prime minister of the Netherlands on November 22, 1966. His government lasted until April 5, 1967. Shortly thereafter Zijlstra became president of the Netherlands Bank and a governor of the International Monetary Fund. He remained in those positions until 1981. The following year he was appointed a member of the supervisory board of the Royal Dutch Petroleum Company.

PIET J. S. DE JONG (Prime Minister, April 5, 1967–July 6, 1971). Piet Josef Sietse de Jong was born in Apeldoorn on April 3, 1915. He was educated at the Royal Naval College and joined the Royal Navy in 1931. He served as a submarine commander during World War II. De Jong was named state secretary for defense in 1959 and was appointed minister of defense in 1963. He

was selected as prime minister of a coalition government led by the Catholic People's party on April 5, 1967. He stepped down on July 6, 1972, following his party's loss of support in parliamentary elections. He continued to serve in Parliament until his retirement 1974.

BAREND W. BIESHEUVEL (Prime Minister, July 6, 1971–May 11, 1973). Barend Willem Biesheuvel was born in Haarlemmerliede on April 5, 1920. He was educated in the Netherlands and worked with the ministry of agriculture from 1945. He became general secretary of the National Protestant Farmers' Union in 1952 and was its president from 1959 until 1963. Biesheuvel also served as a member of Parliament from 1957. He was named minister of agriculture and fisheries, and deputy prime minister in 1963 and served until 1967. He subsequently became leader of the Anti-Revolutionary party in Parliament in 1967 and was selected as prime minister on July 6, 1971. Biesheuvel was unable to solve the Netherland's economic difficulties and resigned on May 11, 1973. He subsequently served on the board of the National Investment Bank until 1991.

JOOP DEN UYL (Prime Minister, May 11, 1973–December 19, 1977). Johannes Marten "Joop" den Uyl was born in Hilversum on August 9, 1919. He was educated at the University of Amsterdam and worked as a journalist. He was active in the Resistance during World War II and joined the Labor party following the liberation of the Netherlands. Den Uyl was selected as the party's Scientific Bureau director in 1949. He was elected to the Amsterdam City Council in 1953 and was elected to Parliament three years later. He was a dedicated Socialist and served in the cabinet as minister of economic affairs from 1965 until 1966. Den Uyl was elected leader of the Opposition in 1967, and on May 11, 1973, he formed a coalition government of left-wing parties. During his term of office, the Netherlands granted independence to the Dutch colony of Suriname in 1975. Den Uyl also convinced Queen Juliana not to abdicate when her husband, Prince Bernhard, was implicated in a financial scandal in 1976. Den Uyl was unable to form a new government in 1977, despite Labor's gains in the election, and stepped down as prime minister on December 19, 1977. He served as minister of social affairs from 1981 until 1982 and was again leader of the Opposition in Parliament from 1982 until 1986. He died of cancer at his home in Amsterdam at the age of 68 on December 24, 1987.

ANDREAS VAN AGT (Prime Minister, December 19, 1977–November 4, 1982). Andreas A. M. van Agt was born in Geldrop on February 2, 1931. He was educated in the Netherlands and was subsequently employed at the Ministry of Agriculture. He worked in the Ministry of Justice from 1958 until 1968 and was appointed minister of justice in 1971. Van Agt was also selected as deputy prime minister in 1973. He refused to support a land expropriation bill sponsored by Prime Minister Joop den Uyl's Socialist government in March of 1977 and thus precipitated the resignation of the Christian Democratic members of the coalition cabinet. Following elections in May of 1977, den Uyl was unable to form a new government, and Van Agt was asked to become prime minister. He took office on December 19, 1977, and retained it until November 4, 1982, when he resigned unexpectedly after his party lost several seats in the Parliament. Van Agt served as governor of the Noord-Brabant Province from 1983 until 1987, when he was named ambassador to Japan for the European Communities.

RUUD LUBBERS (Prime Minister, November 4, 1982–). Rudolph Frans Marie "Ruud" Lubbers was born in Rotterdam on May 7, 1939. He was educated at Erasmus University in Rotterdam, where he studied economics and engineering. He joined the family business, Lubbers Hollandia Engineering Works, and became codirector in 1965. Lubbers was elected to Parliament as a member of the Catholic People's party in November of 1972. His party joined the coalition government of Prime Minister Joop Den Uyl, and Lubbers was named minister of economic affairs in 1973. The coalition dissolved in March of 1977, and Lubbers was reelected to Parliament on the new Christian Democratic Appeal ticket in May of 1977. He was selected as prime minister on November 4, 1982, following the resignation of Andreas Van Agt. Lubbers remained head of a new coalition government after elections in May of 1986. He was forced to resign when his government collapsed on May 2, 1989, but remained as head of a caretaker cabinet. He headed a new center-left coalition government following elections in September of 1989.

New Zealand

New Zealand is an island country in the South Pacific Ocean. It was granted independence from Great Britain on September 26, 1907.

HEADS OF STATE

SIR CYRIL L. N. NEWALL (Governor-General, February 22, 1941–April 19, 1946). Cyril Louis Norton Newall was born in England on February 15, 1886.

He joined the British army and served in India before the start of World War I. He became a pilot in 1911 and served in the Royal Flying Corps in France during the war. Newall became an early member of the Royal Air Force. He was named chief of the air staff in 1937 and was instrumental in preparing Britain's defenses against Germany during World War II. Newall remained leader of the air command until October of 1940, when he was appointed governor-general of New Zealand. He assumed the position on February 22, 1941, and assisted the British war effort. After Newall completed his term on April 19, 1946, he returned to England, where he was given a barony and granted the title of Baron Newall of Clifton-upon-Dunsmoor. He died in London at the age of 77 on November 30, 1963.

SIR BERNARD C. FREYBERG (Governor-General, June 17, 1946– August 15, 1952). Bernard Cyril Freyberg was born in London on March 21, 1889. He attended Welling College in New Zealand and was in the Royal Navy during World War I. He served with distinction at Gallipoli and the Battle of Somme in France. Freyberg was awarded the Victoria Cross and the Croix de Guerre and was wounded nine times. He served in the army after the war and rose to the rank of general in 1934. He retired from the military for health reasons in 1937 while stationed in India. Freyberg returned to active duty at the start of World War II. He was appointed commander in chief of the New Zealand Expeditionary Forces in 1939. His division provided the defense of Crete during the evacuation in 1941. He also led his troops into battle in North Africa and Italy. Freyberg was appointed governor-general of New Zealand after the war and took office on June 17, 1946. He was warmly received by the New Zealand people. He was created Lord Freyberg in 1951. He completed his term of office on August 15, 1952,

and returned to Great Britain. Freyberg was appointed deputy constable and lieutenant governor of Windsor Castle the following year. He died at Windsor, Surrey, at the age of 74 on July 4, 1963, after a long illness.

SIR CHARLES WILLOUGHBY NORRIE (Governor-General, December 2, 1952–July 23, 1957). Charles Willoughby Moke Norrie was born in 1893. He was educated at the Sandhurst Royal Military Academy and entered the British army in 1913. He saw action during World War I and commanded the 10th Royal Hussars from 1931 until 1935. Norrie was promoted to the rank of colonel in 1935 and was given command of the 1st Cavalry Brigade the following year. He was named commander of the 1st Armored Brigade in 1938 and served until 1940. He rose to the rank of major general and served in the Royal Armored Corps in the Middle East during World War II. Norrie was appointed governor of South Australia in 1944. He was subsequently named governor-general of New Zealand and took office on December 2, 1952. He completed his term and retired from government service on July 23, 1957. Norrie was subsequently raised to the peerage and created 1st Baron. He served as chancellor of the Order of St. Michael and St. George from 1960 until his retirement in 1968. Norrie died at the age of 83 on May 25, 1977.

VISCOUNT COBHAM (Governor-General, September 5, 1957–September 13, 1962). Charles John Lyttleton was born on August 8, 1909. He was the only son of the 9th Viscount Cobham. He was educated at Trinity College, Cambridge, where he received a degree in law. Cobham served in the military in France during World War II. He entered politics and was elected to Parliament in 1948. He stepped down from office the following year after the death of his father. In 1949 he succeeded as the 10th Viscount Cobham. He was appointed governor-general of New Zealand and assumed the post on September 5, 1957. Cobham was an extremely popular figure in New Zealand and fulfilled the constitutional and ceremonial duties of the position with distinction. He completed his term on September 13, 1962, and returned to Great Britain. Cobham served on various private and public boards and was president of the Royal National Institute for the Blind from 1964 until 1975. He also served as lord steward of the Queen's Household from 1967 until 1972. Viscount Cobham died at his home in Worchestershire at the age of 67 on March 20, 1977.

SIR BERNARD E. FERGUSSON (Governor-General, November 9, 1962–December 17, 1966). Bernard Edward Fergusson was born in London on May 6, 1911. He was educated at the Sandhurst Royal Military Academy and joined the Black Watch in 1931. He served as a brigade intelligence officer in Palestine in 1937 and was an instructor at Sandhurst prior to World War II. Fergusson was stationed in India until October of 1942 and then served under Orde Wingate in Burma. He directed the Military Combined Operation Headquarters from 1945 until 1946. He was defeated for a seat in Parliament in 1946. Fergusson returned to Palestine later in the year to serve in the Police Mobile Forces against the Zionist terrorist organization, the Stern Gang. Fergusson wrote a history of the Black Watch entitled *The Black Watch and the King's Enemies* in 1950. He was stationed in Germany in 1951 and served in the Suez Expedition in 1956. He retired from the military in 1958. Fergusson was appointed governor-general of New Zealand and took office on November 9, 1962. He retired from office on December 17, 1966. He headed the British delegation on the international observer team for the Nigerian Civil War from 1968 until 1969. He was created a Life Peer as Lord Ballantrae

in 1972 and was named chancellor of the University of St. Andrews the following year. Fergusson died in London at the age of 69 on November 28, 1980.

SIR ARTHUR PORRITT (Governor-General, December 17, 1966–September 1972). Arthur Porritt was born in Wanganui on August 10, 1900. He was educated in New Zealand and Great Britain, where he received a medical degree from St. Mary's Medical School in London. He served on the surgical staff of St. Mary's Hospital from 1936 until 1965. Porritt was surgeon to King George VI of Great Britain from 1946 until 1952 and served as sergeant-surgeon to Queen Elizabeth from 1953 until 1967. He also served as president of the Royal Society of Medicine from 1966 until 1967. He was named governor-general of New Zealand on December 17, 1966, and served until his retirement in September of 1972. Porritt died at his home in London on January 1, 1994.

SIR DENIS BLUNDELL (Governor-General, September 1972–September 27, 1977). Edward Denis Blundell was born in Wellington on May 29, 1907. He attended Cambridge University, where he received a degree in law in 1929. He returned to New Zealand to open a legal practice. Blundell served with distinction in the New Zealand army during World War II and rose to the rank of lieutenant colonel. He continued his legal career after the war and served as president of the New Zealand Law Society from 1962 until 1968. Blundell, who was knighted in 1967, was named New Zealand high commissioner in Great Britain in 1968. He returned to New Zealand to accept an appointment as governor-general in September of 1972. Blundell completed his term of office on September 27, 1977. He died while vacationing in Queensland, Australia, at the age of 77 on September 24, 1984.

SIR KEITH J. HOLYOAKE (Governor-General, September 27, 1977–October 25, 1980). Keith Jacka Holyoake was born on North Island on February 11, 1904. He worked on his family's small farm in his youth. He joined numerous agricultural associations and was made president of the local Farmers' Union branch. Holyoake was narrowly defeated by an incumbent in his first bid for a Parliament seat as a member of the National party in 1931. When the incumbent died in office the following year, Holyoake won the special election and became New Zealand's youngest representative at the age of 28. He remained in Parliament until 1938, when he was defeated for the Motueka seat. In 1940 he was selected as the Farmers' Union executive officer. Holyoake was returned to Parliament in the elections of 1943 to represent Pahiatua. He was elected deputy leader of the Nationalist Opposition in 1947 and became deputy prime minister when the party won a majority in the elections in November of 1949. Holyoake also served as minister of agriculture in the government of Sidney Holland. When Holland resigned as party leader and prime minister on September 20, 1957, Holyoake succeeded him in both positions. He held office for only three months, as the Labor party claimed a slight majority in the elections in November of 1957. He remained leader of the Nationalist party and returned as prime minister when the party received a majority in the elections in November of 1960. Holyoake took office on December 11, 1960, and also claimed the portfolios for external affairs and the ministership in charge of the audit office and the legislative department. He initiated movement toward diversifying New Zealand's agricultural economy. He was also a supporter of the United States position in the war in Southeast Asia. Later in his term Holyoake was forced to face the decline of New Zealand's traditional produce markets when Britain was admitted into the European Common Market. Holyoake, who was knighted in 1970, remained as prime minister until his resignation as party leader on February 2, 1972. He remained in the government until 1976. He was appointed New Zealand's governor-general and assumed office on September 27, 1977. The appointment was criticized by many on the grounds that the position should not be held by a political figure. Holyoake resigned from that position on October 25, 1980, due to failing health. He suffered a stroke in October of 1983 and died in Wellington on December 8, 1983.

SIR DAVID STUART BEATTIE (Governor-General, November 6, 1980–November 22, 1985). David Stuart Beattie was born in Sydney, Australia, on February 29, 1924. He was educated in New Zealand and served in World War II as a naval officer. He was a Supreme Court judge from 1969 until 1980. Beattie was appointed governor-general on November 6, 1980, and served until November 22, 1985. He subsequently served as chairman of the New Zealand International Festival of the Arts from 1987 and was chairman of the Meat Industry Association of New Zealand from 1988 until 1990.

SIR PAUL REEVES (Governor-General, November 22, 1985–November 20, 1990). Paul Alfred Reeves was born on December 6, 1932. He was educated in New Zealand and became a priest in the Anglican Church in 1960. He held various positions in the church before he was named Bishop of Waiapu in 1971. Reeves was made bishop of Auckland in 1979 and served as archbishop of New Zealand from 1980 until 1985. He was appointed governor-general of New Zealand on November 22, 1985, and served until November 20, 1990. He subsequently served as the Anglican church's representative to the United Nations.

DAME CATHERINE TIZARD (Governor-General, November 20, 1990–   ).

Catherine Tizard was born Catherine Anne Maclean on April 4, 1931. She was educated in New Zealand and married Robert James Tizard in 1951. She began teaching at the University of Auckland in 1967 and was elected to the Auckland City Council in 1971. Tizard was elected mayor of Auckland in 1983. She was appointed governor-general of New Zealand and assumed office on November 20, 1990.

HEADS OF GOVERNMENT

PETER FRASER (Prime Minister, April 1, 1940–December 12, 1949). Peter Fraser was born in Fearn, Ross-shire, Scotland, on August 28, 1884. Though his father was a member of the local Liberal party, Fraser joined the Independent Labor party when he moved to London in 1908. Fraser relocated to New Zealand in 1910 and took a job as a longshoreman in Auckland. He became president of the Auckland General Laborers' Union and served as editor of the Maoriland *Worker*, a Socialist national newspaper. He was imprisoned for several months during World World I for his opposition to conscription. Fraser was elected to the House of Representatives in 1918, and the following year he was also elected as a member of the Wellington City Council. He remained on the council until 1923 and served again from 1933 until 1936. He was selected as deputy leader of the Labor party in 1934 and was appointed to the cabinet in the Labor government from 1935 to 1940 as minister of education, health, and marine. In 1939 Fraser advanced to deputy prime minister, and he became acting prime minister in August due to the ill health of his predecessor, Michael Joseph Savage. He became party leader and prime minister after Savage's death the following year on April 1, 1940. He led the New Zealand government throughout World War II and threw the weight of New Zealand's forces solidly behind the Allied cause. He also continued to advocate the social security and welfare legislation enacted by his predecessor. Following the war,

Fraser was an active participant in the formation of the United Nations and served as chairman of the committee which drafted the trusteeship chapter of the United Nations charter. Fraser remained as head of the government until the Labor party's defeat in the elections of 1949, which forced him to step down as prime minister on December 12, 1949. He remained as leader of the Opposition until his death in Wellington from heart failure on December 12, 1950.

SIR SIDNEY G. HOLLAND (Prime Minister, December 13, 1949–September 20, 1957). Sidney George Holland was born in Greendale on October 18, 1893. He joined the army during World War I and served with distinction in France. He was a member of the National party and was elected to the New Zealand Parliament in 1935 to succeed his father, who had declined to run for reelection due to reasons of health. Holland was elected leader of the Opposition in 1940 and served briefly as a member of the war cabinet in June of 1942. He resigned from the cabinet several months later in opposition to the government's handling of a coal miners strike in Waikato. His party made gains in the elections of 1943 and 1946 and received a majority in the 1949 parliamentary elections. Holland formed a new government as prime minister on December 13, 1949. He also served as minister of finance until 1954. He began a policy of increased construction in New Zealand and removed many government controls over private industry. In 1951 his administration was faced with a waterfront strike, which he was credited for settling. Holland remained as prime minister during the 1951 and 1954 general elections. Suffering from failing health, he retired on September 20, 1957, and was subsequently knighted by Queen Elizabeth II. Holland spent his retirement at his sheep and cattle farm in North Canterbury and died in Wellington on August 5, 1961.

SIR KEITH J. HOLYOAKE (Prime Minister, September 20, 1957–December 12, 1957). *See entry under Heads of State.*

SIR WALTER NASH (Prime Minister, December 12, 1957–December 11, 1960). Walter Nash was born in Kidderminster, England, on February 12, 1882. After studying law at St. Johns' Church School in Kidderminster, he began a career as a merchant in Birmingham, England. He moved to New Zealand in 1909, where he took a job as a British publishing and manufacturing house representative. Nash entered politics shortly after his arrival and joined the Labor party. He was elected to the Labor party's national executive committee in 1919 and attended the Second International Labor Conference in Geneva in 1920. He served as secretary of the Labor party from 1922 until 1932. Nash was elected to Parliament in 1929 as a representative of Hutt and was appointed minister of finance and customs in the first Labor government in 1935. He was instrumental in passing much of the social welfare legislation introduced by the government. In 1938 he was also appointed minister of social security. In 1940 Nash was selected as deputy prime minister in the government of Peter Fraser. Two years later he represented the New Zealand government as minister in the United States and served on the Pacific War Council. Following Labor's victory in the elections of 1943, he was recalled by the

Fraser government to serve as minister of finance. Nash also headed the New Zealand delegation to the International Monetary Conference at Bretton Woods in 1944. The Labor party was defeated in the election in November of 1949. The following year, upon the death of Peter Fraser, Nash succeeded as Labor party leader in Opposition. Labor again suffered defeats in the elections of 1951 and 1954, though Nash remained on as leader. Following the resignation of Prime Minister Sydney Holland, the Labor party won a slight majority over the Nationalists headed by Keith Holyoake. Nash took office on December 12, 1957. His policies of increased social welfare reform led to increased taxation and caused a backlash against the government. Nash also supported the admission of Communist China as a member of the United Nations and was an opponent of the United States military action in Southeast Asia. The Labor party was defeated in the elections of 1960, and Nash was replaced by the previous prime minister, Keith Holyoake, on December 11, 1960. Nash remained as leader of the Opposition until 1963, when he resigned and was succeeded by Arnold Nordmeyer. He retained his seat in Parliament and remained active, traveling extensively in his later years. He died in Auckland at the age of 86 on June 4, 1968.

SIR KEITH J. HOLYOAKE (Prime Minister, December 11, 1960–February 2, 1972). *See entry under Heads of State.*

JOHN ROSS MARSHALL (Prime Minister, February 7, 1972–December 8, 1972). John Ross Marshall was born in Wellington, New Zealand, on March 5, 1912. He attended Victoria University in Wellington, where he graduated with a master's degree in law and a degree in political science in 1934. He began practicing law in 1936, and at the start of World War II, he joined the army. Marshall served in the infantry during the war. He was first elected to Parliament in 1945 and was invited to join the National party cabinet in 1949. Marshall headed numerous ministries in succeeding cabinets. He served as minister of health from 1951 to 1954 and minister of justice from 1954 to 1957. He was selected as deputy leader of the National party in 1957 and served as minister of industry and commerce from 1960 to 1969 and minister of labor and immigration from 1969 to 1972. As minister of overseas trade, Marshall was also instrumental in negotiating New Zealand's trade agreement with the European Economic Community when Britain joined the community in 1971. He succeeded Sir Keith Holyoake as party leader and prime minister on February 7, 1972, but his government was short-lived. Marshall was defeated by the Labor party under Norman Kirk in the elections of November and relinquished office on December 8, 1972. He remained as National party leader until his ouster by Robert Muldoon shortly before the elections of 1975. Marshall, who was knighted in 1974, retired from politics and spent the remainder of his life in the private sector. He died on August 30, 1988, at the age of 76, while making a visit to London.

NORMAN E. KIRK (Prime Minister, December 8, 1972–August 31, 1974). Norman Eric Kirk was born in Waimate, on New Zealand's South Island, on January 2, 1923. He worked as a laborer and engineer before entering politics. In 1952 he was elected mayor of Kaiapo, a small town near Christchurch. Kirk was elected to Parliament in 1957 as a member of the Labor party to represent the port district of Lyttleton. He made a rapid rise in the ranks of the party and defeated party leader Arnold Nordmeyer in a caucus vote in 1965. The Labor party was defeated in the elections of 1965 and 1969. In the parliamentary elections of 1972, Labor achieved a majority, and Kirk replaced John Ross Marshall as prime minister

on December 8, 1972. As prime minister, Kirk opposed the French nuclear tests in the Pacific and banned all South African visiting sports teams. He also withdrew New Zealand's troops from the conflict in South Vietnam and recognized the government of the People's Republic of China. Early in 1974 Kirk suffered from health problems after having complications following an operation on his varicose veins. Kirk was planning on taking an extended leave from his duties when he died of a heart seizure in Wellington on August 31, 1974.

WALLACE E. ROWLING (Prime Minister, September 6, 1974–December 12, 1975). Wallace Edward Rowling was born on Motueka, South Island, on November 15, 1927. He was educated in New Zealand and served in the New Zealand army. He was elected to Parliament in 1962 and became president of the Labor party in 1970. Rowling served as minister of finance from 1972 until 1974. He was selected to succeed Norman E. Kirk as prime minister on September 6, 1974, following Kirk's death. The National party defeated the Labor party in the elections in November of 1975. Rowling relinquished the office of prime minister on December 12, 1975. He remained leader of the Opposition until 1983. Rowling became president of the New Zealand Institute of International Affairs in 1990.

ROBERT D. MULDOON (Prime Minister, December 12, 1975–July 26, 1984). Robert David Muldoon was born in Auckland on September 25, 1921. He was educated in New Zealand and received a degree in economics. In 1960 he was elected to Parliament. Muldoon was named minister of tourism and publicity in 1967 and became minister of finance later that year. He served until 1972 and also served as deputy prime minister in 1972. He became leader of the opposition National party in 1973. The party was successful in the elections of 1975, and Muldoon took office as prime minister on December 12, 1975. He remained prime minister until July 26, 1984, following the Labor party victory in parliamentary elections. He stepped down as leader of the National party in November of 1984, but remained in Parliament until 1991. Muldoon died in Auckland at the age of 70 on August 5, 1992.

DAVID R. LANGE (Prime Minister, July 26, 1984–August 8, 1989). David Russell Lange was born in Otahuhu in September of 1942. He was educated in New Zealand and became a lawyer. In 1977 he was elected to Parliament as a member of the Labor party. Lange became deputy leader of the party in 1979 and leader in 1983. He became prime minister following Labor's victory in 1984 and took office on July 26, 1984. He also held the portfolios of foreign affairs from 1984 until 1987 and education from 1987 until 1989. Lange resigned as prime minister on August 8, 1989, following a dispute in the cabinet with Finance Minister Roger Douglas. He remained in the cabinet as attorney general and minister of state until 1990.

GEOFFREY PALMER (Prime Minister, August 8, 1989–September 4, 1990). Geoffrey Winston Russell Palmer was born in Nelson on April 21, 1942. He was educated in New Zealand and the United States and became a lawyer. In 1979 he was elected to Parliament as a member of the Labor party. Palmer became deputy leader of the party in 1983 and also became minister of justice in 1984 and minister of the environment in 1987. He became leader of the Labor party and prime minister upon the resignation of Prime Minister David Lange on August 8, 1989. Palmer resigned from office in the face of a no confidence vote on August 8, 1989.

MIKE MOORE (Prime Minister, September 4, 1990–October 27, 1990). Michael Kenneth Moore was born in Whakatane in 1949. He was elected to Parliament in 1972. He was named to Prime Minister David Lange's cabinet as minister of overseas trade and marketing and minister of tourism in 1984. Moore served as minister of foreign affairs in 1990 and succeeded Geoffrey Palmer as Labor party leader and prime minister on September 4, 1990. He left office the following month on October 27, 1990, after Labor's defeat at the polls. Moore subsequently served as leader of the Opposition.

JIM BOLGER (Prime Minister, October 27, 1990–). James Brendan Bolger was born in Taranaki in 1935. He ran a sheep and cattle farm in Te Kuiti and was elected to Parliament in 1972. He served as minister of fisheries in 1977 and minister of labor from 1978 until 1984. Bolger served as deputy leader of the National party in 1984 and became leader the following year. After the National party's victory over Labor in October of 1990, Bolger was elected prime minister and assumed office on October 27, 1990.

Nicaragua, Republic of

(République du Nicaragua)

Nicaragua is a country in Central America. It was granted independence from Spain on September 28, 1821.

HEADS OF STATE

ANASTASIO SOMOZA GARCÍA

(President, January 1, 1937–May 1, 1947). Anastasio Somoza García was born in San Marcos on February 1, 1896. He was educated in Nicaragua and at Pierce Commercial College in Philadelphia, Pennsylvania. He worked with the Paige Motor Company before returning to Nicaragua. Somoza joined the Liberal party and gained influence by serving as an interpreter during the intervention of United States Marines in Nicaragua from 1927. Liberal party candidate José M. Moncada was elected president in November of 1928, and Somoza was appointed governor of León. He also achieved prominence in the Civil Guard, where he rose to the rank of general. Juan B. Sacasa, the uncle of Somoza's wife, was elected president in 1932, and Somoza was named minister of war. The Nicaraguan army and United States Marines continued to battle insurgents led by Cesar Sandino. Sandino accepted an armistice with the Nicaraguan government and attended a dinner meeting with President Sacasa on February 21, 1934, under a promise of safe conduct. He was arrested by officers of Somoza's National Guard following the meeting, however, and was summarily executed. Somoza became the leading figure in the Nicaraguan government and ousted Sacasa in 1936. He installed Carlos Brenes Jarquin as interim president. Somoza was unopposed for the presidency in elections in December of 1936 and was sworn into office on January 1, 1937. He was reelected president in 1942. He declined to be a candidate in the presidential election in 1947 and relinquished office to his hand-picked successor, Leonardo Arguello, on May 1, 1947. Arguello attempted to govern without consulting Somoza and was ousted by a military coup later in the month. Somoza installed Victor Román y Reyes as president in August of 1947.

Somoza was again elected president by Congress on May 7, 1950, following the death of Román y Reyes. He was reelected in government-controlled elections in May of 1951. During Somoza's reign the economic situation of Nicaragua greatly improved due to the president's rigid control over the country. Somoza's personal wealth and that of his family also greatly increased. Nicaragua engaged in a brief border war with Costa Rica in January of 1955. Somoza challenged Costa Rican president Jose Figueres Ferrer to a duel before the Organization of American States negotiated an end to the fighting. Somoza was shot four times and seriously wounded in León on September 21, 1956. His assailant, Rigoberto Lopez Perez, was immediately killed by Somoza's bodyguards. Somoza was taken to a hospital in the Panama Canal Zone, where he underwent surgery. He died of his wounds on September 29, 1956, was succeeded to the presidency by his son, Luis.

LEONARDO ARGUELLO (President, May 1, 1947–May 26, 1947). Leonardo Arguello was born in León in 1875. He studied medicine in Nicaragua and in Europe. He was active in the revolution of 1912 and was elected a deputy to the National Congress shortly thereafter. Arguello also held several cabinet positions and in particular served a distinquished term as minister of education. In 1936 Arguello was defeated for the presidency. He again ran for the office in 1946, with the support of General Anastasio Somoza, and defeated Enoc Aguado for the presidency in February of 1947. He took office on May 1, 1947, but quickly alienated political leader Somoza by trying to eliminate military influence in the government. Arguello was deposed by Somoza after less than a month in office on May 26, 1947. He took refuge in the Mexican embassy and remained there for the next six months. Arguello was permitted to leave for Mexico City on November 20, 1947. He died there at the age of 72 on December 15, 1947.

BENJAMIN LACAYO SACASA (President, May 26, 1947–August 15, 1947). Benjamin Lacayo Sacasa was born in 1884. He was chosen as provisional president of Nicaragua on May 26, 1947, following the military coup that ousted Leonardo Arguello. Lacayo Sacasa dissolved Congress and called for national elections for a Constituent Assembly. The Constituent Assembly chose Victor Román y Reyes as president on August 15, 1947. Lacayo Sacasa died in Granada at the age of 75 on May 4, 1959.

VICTOR ROMÁN Y REYES (President, August 15, 1947–May 6, 1950). Victor Manuel Román y Reyes was born in Jinotepe on October 3, 1872. He attended the Hahneman Medical College in Philadelphia, Pennsylvania, and returned to Nicaragua to practice medicine in 1897. Román served as Nicaragua's consul general in San Francisco from 1901 until 1902. He was elected mayor of Jinotepe in 1909 and served until the following year. He was elected to the Senate as a member of the Liberal party in 1923. Román also served as vice president and minister of finance in 1923. He was forced from the cabinet in 1925 following his capture by members of the Conservative Republican party. He temporarily sought asylum at the American Legation in Managua. Román subsequently served as director of general health in 1931. He was named governor of Carazo during the administration of Anastasio Somoza in 1938. He retained that position until 1946, when he was appointed secretary of state for foreign affairs. Somoza stepped down from office to allow the election of Leonardo Arguello as president in May of 1947. Somoza subsequently ousted Arguello in a military

coup later in the month. Román was chosen by the Constituent Assembly to serve as president on August 15, 1947. General Somoza remained the most powerful figure in the government during Román's term of office. Román was hospitalized with stomach cancer in March of 1950. He underwent surgery and died of complications at the age of 77 on May 6, 1950.

ANASTASIO SOMOZA GARCÍA (President, May 7, 1950–September 29, 1956). *See earlier entry under Heads of State.*

LUIS SOMOZA DEBAYLE (President, September 29, 1956–May 1, 1963). Luis Anastasio Somoza Debayle was born on November 18, 1922. He was the son of Anastasio Somoza García. Luis Somoza was educated in the United States, where he received a degree in agriculture from the University of California. He returned to Nicaragua to manage the family's business interests. Somoza was elected to the Chamber of Deputies in 1950 and was subsequently elected president of the Chamber. He was selected as president by the Congress following his father's assassination on September 29, 1956. His younger brother, Anastasio Somoza Debayle, succeeded his father as commander of the National Guard. Luis Somoza was elected president in February of 1957. He initiated some political reforms, but was forced to suspend the constitution for six months following a rebel invasion from Costa Rica in June of 1959. Somoza was a leading opponent of Cuba's Communist premier, Fidel Castro, and allowed Nicaragua to be used as a base for opponents of Castro's regime. Nicaragua's economy continued to improve under Somoza. He was not a candidate in elections in 1963 and relinquished office to his hand-picked successor, René Schick Gutiérrez, on May 1, 1963. Somoza entered the Nicaraguan Senate, where he remained until his death from a heart attack at his home in Managua at the age of 44 on April 13, 1967.

RENÉ SCHICK GUTIÉRREZ (President, May 1, 1963–August 3, 1966).

René Schick Gutiérrez was born in Managua in 1909. He studied law before becoming a teacher. In the 1950s he joined the government as minister of education. He served as foreign minister in the government of Luis Somoza. Schick was chosen as the presidential candidate of the Liberal party when Luis Somoza relinquished office in 1963. He was elected with little opposition and took office on May 1, 1963. He continued his predecessor's policy of allowing Cuban rebels to use Nicaragua as a base for anti-Castro activities. Schick was prohibited from seeking reelection and presided over the party convention in July of 1966 that selected Anastasio Somoza Debayle as the presidential nominee. Schick remained president until his death from a heart attack in Managua on August 3, 1966.

LORENZO GUERRERO GUTIÉRREZ (President, August 4, 1966–May 1, 1967).

Lorenzo Guerrero Gutiérrez was born in Granada on November 13, 1900. He attended medical school and worked as a physician. He served in Nicaragua's diplomatic corps under Anastasio Somoza. Guerrero was appointed ambassador to Mexico in 1934 and served again in 1945. He was named ambassador to Costa Rica in 1953. Guerrero was elected to the Senate in 1957. He later served in the cabinet as minister of education. He was named minister of the interior and vice president in the government of René Schick Gutiérrez. Guerrero was chosen to succeed to the presidency on August 4, 1966, following Schick's death. He presided over elections that resulted in a victory for Anastasio Somoza Debayle. Guerrero relinquished office to Somoza on May 1, 1967, but remained in the government as foreign minister until 1972.

ANASTASIO SOMOZA DEBAYLE (President, May 1, 1967–May 1, 1972).

Anastasio Somoza Debayle was born in León, on December 5, 1925. He was the son of Anastasio Somoza García, who ruled Nicaragua from 1937. The younger Somoza was educated at military schools in Nicaragua and the United States, where he graduated from West Point in 1946. He returned to Nicaragua to serve in the National Guard. He had risen to the rank of colonel by the time of his father's assassination in 1956. His brother, Luis Somoza, succeeded to the presidency in 1956, and Anastasio Somoza became commander of the National Guard. Luis Somoza relinquished office to René Schick Gutiérrez in May of 1963, and Anastasio Somoza began making plans for obtaining the presidency for himself. He received the nomination of the Liberal party in August of 1966 and defeated Conservative leader Fernando Agüero Rocha in February of 1967. Somoza was sworn into office on May 1, 1967. He attempted to modernize the country and invoked austerity measures on the economy to provide funds for education and health programs. Somoza reached an agreement with leaders of the Conservative opposition to draft a new constitution and provide free elections. He turned over the presidency to a civilian triumvirate on May 1, 1972, in order to prepare for democratic elections. Somoza was reelected in September of 1974, though critics accused the government of electoral fraud. Somoza again took office on December 1, 1974. His later regime was marked for its corruption and human rights abuses. The Sandinista National Liberation Front launched an attack on the government in October of 1977. A bloody civil war ensued that resulted in Somoza's ouster by the Sandinistas on July 17, 1979. Somoza went into exile in Asuncion, Paraguay. He was assassinated there when his car was hit with bazooka and machine-gun fire on September 17, 1980.

ROBERTO MARTÍNEZ LACAYO

(Copresident, May 1, 1972–December 1, 1974). Roberto Martínez Lacayo was a leader of the Liberal party (PLN). He was chosen on May 1, 1972, to serve as a member of a ruling triumvirate to govern Nicaragua in preparation for elections to be held in September of 1974. The triumvirate stepped down on December 1, 1974, following the reelection of Anastasio Somoza Debayle.

ALFONSO LOVO CORDERO (Copresident, May 1, 1972–December 1, 1974). Alfonso Lovo Cordero was a leader of the Liberal party (PLN). He was chosen on May 1, 1972, to serve as a member of a ruling triumvirate to govern Nicaragua in preparation for elections to be held in September of 1974. The triumvirate stepped down on December 1, 1974, following the reelection of Anastasio Somoza Debayle.

FERNANDO AGÜERO ROCHA (Copresident, May 1, 1972–March 1, 1973). Fernando Agüero Rocha was born in Managua on June 11, 1917. He was the leader of the Conservative party and served as the party's candidate in presidential elections in 1967. He was defeated by Anastasio Somoza. Agüero Rocha was chosen to serve on a ruling triumvirate to govern Nicaragua in preparation for elections. The triumvirate took power on May 1, 1972. Agüero Rocha was dismissed from the government by the National Assembly on March 1, 1973.

EDMUNDO PAGUAGA IRIAS (Copresident, March 1, 1973–December 1, 1974). Edmundo Paguaga Irias, a member of the Conservative party, was chosen to replace Fernando Agüero Rocha on March 1, 1973, as a member of Nicaragua's ruling triumvirate. He was a candidate for president in the election held in September of 1974, but was soundly defeated by Anastasio Somoza Debayle, who returned to the presidency on December 1, 1974.

ANASTASIO SOMOZA DEBAYLE

(President, December 1, 1974–July 17, 1979). *See earlier entry under Heads of State.*

FRANCISCO URCOYO MALEAÑO

(President, July 17, 1979–July 18, 1979). Francisco Urcoyo Maleaño was born in 1925. He was a prominent member of the Liberal party and a close aide to President Anastasio Somoza. Urcoya was president of the Chamber of Deputies at the time of Somoza's resignation on July 17, 1979. He was chosen to serve as provisional president of Nicaragua by the Congress. Urcoyo was expected to transfer power to the Sandinista rebels, but made a last minute bid to retain power. His attempts were thwarted when the National Guard collapsed and surrendered major bases to the Sandinistas. Urcoyo relinquished office on July 18, 1979, and fled to Guatemala.

DANIEL ORTEGA SAAVEDRA (Junta Leader/President, July 18, 1979–April 25, 1990). Daniel Ortega Saavedra was born in La Libertad on November 11, 1945. He attended the Central American University in Managua briefly, but left after several months to join the underground Sandinista National Liberation Front (FSLN). He became a leader of the rebels and was placed in charge of the urban resistance movement in 1967. Ortega was captured by the National Guard and was imprisoned until 1974. He went into exile in Cuba after his release and then returned to Nicaragua to continue the guerrilla war against the regime of Anastasio Somoza. He was a commander of the rebel forces that ousted President Somoza in July of 1979. Ortega led the ruling junta of the Government of National Reconstruction after the Sandinistas took power on July 18, 1979. The other junta members included Violetta Barrios de Chamorro, Moisés Hassan Morales, Sergio Ramirez Mercado, and Alfonso Robelo Callejas.

Chamorro and Robelo resigned in April of 1980 and were replaced by Rafael Cordova Riva and Arturo José Cruz. Hassan and Cruz resigned in March of 1980, and Ortega remained leader of a three-man junta. The Sandinistas were victorious in elections in November of 1984, and Ortega was elected president. He took office on January 19, 1985. The United States continued to pressure the leftist regime and supported insurgent "contra" rebels who continued to fight against the government. The Ortega government agreed to peace arrangements based on proposals by Costa Rican president Oscar Arias Sanchez. Ortega and the Sandinistas were defeated in elections held in February of 1990. He relinquished office to Violetta Barrios de Chamorro on April 25, 1990. He remained a leader of the Sandinistas and was elected to the new position of secretary-general in July of 1991.

VIOLETTA BARRIOS DE CHAMORRO (President, April 25, 1990-). Violetta Barrios de Chamorro was born Violetta Barrios Torres in Rivas in 1929. She was educated at women's colleges in the United States. She returned to Nicaragua in 1949 and met Pedro Joaquin Chamorro Cardenal. She married Chamorro the following year. Her husband was a leading member of the Conservative party and an opponent of the ruling Somoza family. He was also the editor of the *La Prensa* newspaper.

Violetta Chamorro raised her family during the years the Somoza family remained in power, and her husband was frequently imprisoned or exiled for his opposition to the regime. Pedro Chamorro was assassinated in Managua by unknown gunmen on January 10, 1978. Violetta Chamorro became a symbol of the opposition to Anastasio Somoza's government, and she supported the Sandinista rebellion that ousted Somoza in July of 1979. Chamorro served on the five-member revolutionary government that took power on July 18, 1979. She resigned from the government in April of 1980 in opposition to the Sandinista's leftist tilt. She returned to *La Prensa*, where she became a leading spokesperson for the moderate opposition to the government of Daniel Ortega. *La Prensa* was banned in June of 1986, but it was allowed to resume publication in October of 1987 and to operate without prior censorship. Chamorro was selected as the presidential candidate of the coalition National Opposition Union in September of 1989. She defeated Daniel Ortega in the presidential election in February of 1990 and was sworn into office on April 25, 1990. The Chamorro government attempted to disarm Sandinista and Contra forces in the country. She was also successful in improving Nicaragua's economic condition. She was criticized by both the left and the right for her attempts to maintain a delicate balance of power in the government.

Niger, Republic of
(République du Niger)

Niger is a country in central western Africa. It was granted independence from France on August 3, 1960.

HEADS OF STATE

HAMANI DIORI (President, August 3, 1960–April 15, 1974). Hamani

Diori was born in Soudoure on June 6, 1916. He was educated in Dahomey and

Senegal. He returned to Niger in 1936 to work as a teacher. Diori taught at the Institute of Overseas Studies in Paris from 1938 until 1946. He returned to Niger to assist Boubou Hama in founding the Niger Progressive party (PPN), the local division of the Rassemblement Démocratique Africain. Diori was elected to the French National Assembly in November of 1946. He was defeated for reelection in January of 1951 and returned to teaching. He narrowly defeated Djibo Bakary in elections to the French National Assembly in January of 1956. Diori was elected to the Territorial Assembly in May of 1957, though Bakary's Nigerian Democratic Union party gained a majority. Diori was subsequently elected Deputy Speaker of the French National Assembly. He led the campaign for Niger's independence in a referendum in September of 1958. Diori's PPN was victorious in elections to the provisional government the following December, and Diori became prime minister on December 14, 1958. Diori banned opposition parties the following year, forcing Bakary into exile. Niger was granted full independence on August 3, 1960, and Diori became the country's first president. He was confirmed in office the following November. Diori's government was threatened by several unsuccessful coup attempts instigated by Bakary during the 1960s. Diori also survived an assassination attempt in April of 1965, when a bomb exploded near him at a mosque in Niamey. He was reelected president in September of 1965. Diori's reputation as a mediator grew throughout Africa, and he was often called upon to settle regional disputes. He was reelected for a third term in October of 1970. Niger suffered from a major famine brought on by a drought in the early 1970s. The mishandling of international aid to the country further exposed the corruption rampant in Diori's administration. He

was ousted in an army coup led by Lieut. Col. Seyni Kountché on April 15, 1974. His wife, Aissa Diori, was killed during the coup when she attempted to fight off soldiers sent to arrest her. Diori was imprisoned for six years by the military regime. He was put under house arrest in 1980 and was granted his freedom by President Ali Seibou in 1987. He went into exile in Morocco and died in Rabat, Morocco, at the age of 72 on April 23, 1989.

SEYNI KOUNTCHÉ (President, April 17, 1974–November 10, 1987). Seyni Kountché was born in Fandou on July 1, 1931. He was educated in French military schools and joined the French colonial army in 1949. He served in Indochina and Algeria and joined the Niger army following independence in 1960. Kountché served as deputy chief of staff of the armed forces from 1966 and became chief of staff in 1973. He led a coup that ousted President Hamani Diori, and he became head of state and president of the Supreme Military Council on April 17, 1974. Kountché was successful in improving the economy of Niger. He became ill in December of 1986 and made several trips to Paris for treatment. He died in Paris of a brain tumor on November 10, 1987.

ALI SEIBOU (President, November 10, 1987–). Ali Seibou was a colonel in the Niger army. He was a cousin of President Seyni Kountché and succeeded him as chief of state and president of the Supreme Military Council on November 10, 1987. Niger was beset by strikes and demonstrations calling for a return to democracy in 1989 and 1990. Seibou allowed a national conference to meet in July of 1991. The conference declared its sovereignty and suspended the constitution. President Seibou was stripped of most of his executive powers and elections were called for 1993.

HEADS OF GOVERNMENT

MAMANE OUMAROU (Premier, January 24, 1983–November 14, 1983). Mamane Oumarou served in the cabinet as minister of youth, sport, and culture. He was selected as premier following the creation of that position by President Seyni Kountché on January 24, 1983. After a coup attempt against President Kountché in October of 1983, the president removed all military personnel from his cabinet, replacing Oumarou on November 14, 1983. Oumarou subsequently served as president of the National Development Council. Oumarou was again named premier by President Ali Seibou on July 15, 1988. He served until December 10, 1989, when the position of premier was temporarily eliminated.

HAMID ALGABID (Premier, November 14, 1983–July 15, 1988). Hamid Algabid served in the cabinet as minister of state for planning, commerce, and transportation. He was minister of finance before he was appointed by President Seyni Kountché as premier on November 14, 1983. Algabid served in this position until after Kountché's death. He was dismissed by President Ali Seibou on July 15, 1988.

MAMANE OUMAROU (Premier, July 15, 1988–December 10, 1989). *See earlier entry under Heads of Government.*

ALIOU MAHAMIDOU (Premier, March 2, 1990–November 1, 1991). Aliou Mahamidou served in the Niger Ministry of Industry. He was named to the restored position of premier on March 2, 1990. A national conference met in July of 1991 to institute government reforms. President Ali Seibou was stripped of most of his executive powers, though Mahamidou was allowed to retain office until November 1, 1991, when he was replaced by a transitional government led by Amadou Cheiffou.

AMADOU CHEIFFOU (Premier, November 1, 1991–). Amadou Cheiffou was born in 1942. He was elected by a national conference to serve as premier of a transitional government on November 1, 1991. He was mandated to lead the government until multiparty elections could be held in January of 1993. Cheiffou dissolved the transitional government in March of 1992 following an abortive military coup. He formed a new government on March 27, 1992.

Nigeria, Federal Republic of

Nigeria is a country on the western coast of Africa. It was granted independence from Great Britain on October 1, 1960.

HEADS OF STATE

NNAMDI AZIKIWE (Governor-general, December 12, 1959–October 1, 1963; President, October 1, 1963–January 15, 1966). Benjamin Nnamdi Azikiwe was born in Zungeru on November 16, 1904. He was a member of the Ibo tribe and was educated at local missionary schools. He continued his education in the United States, where he studied journalism and anthropology. Azikiwe returned to Africa in 1934 and worked for a newspaper in the Gold Coast. He founded the newspaper *West African Pilot* in Lagos in 1937, and he formed Zik Enterprises, which published a chain of newspapers in Nigeria. Azikiwe became a leader of the Nigerian nationalist movement and became secretary-general of the National Council of Nigeria and the Cameroons in 1946. He was elected to the Legislative Council of Nigeria in 1947. He became leader of the opposition to the government of Chief Obafemi Awolowo in the Western Region's House of Assembly in 1951. Azikiwe moved to the Eastern Region the following year and was elected chief minister in May of 1952. He supported Sir Abubakar Tafawa Balewa's attempt to form a government in December of 1959. Azikiwe became governor-general of Nigeria on December 12, 1959, and Nigeria was granted independence on October 1, 1960. He became president when Nigeria was declared a republic on October 1, 1963. Azikiwe's alliance with Balewa became strained in 1964, and protests and rioting took place following Balewa's victory in elections in December of 1964. Azikiwe went to Great Britain for medical treatment in October of 1965. He returned to Nigeria after the military coup that ousted Balewa's government on January 15, 1966. Azikiwe withdrew from politics to his home in Nuskka. He became an advisor to Biafran secessionist leader Odumgwu Ojukwu following the military coup in July of 1966. Azikiwe became a leading spokesman for Biafra's interests throughout Africa. He supported peace negotiations in 1968 as Biafran forces were being defeated by the federal army. He continued to advocate a peace settlement after returning to Nigeria from Great Britain in February of 1969. Azikiwe was named chancellor of Lagos University in February of 1972. He left the university in 1976 and formed the Nigeria People's party in 1979. He was an unsuccessful candidate for president of Nigeria in August of 1979. Azikiwe was again defeated in 1983, and the military government banned political parties the following year. He retired from politics in 1986.

JOHNSON AGUIYI-IRONSI (President, January 15, 1966–July 29, 1966). Johnson T. U. Aguiyi-Ironsi was born on March 3, 1924. He was a member of the Ibo tribe. He served in the Nigerian army, where he rose to the rank of major general. In the early 1960s he commanded United Nations forces in the former Belgian Congo. He served as head of the Nigerian army following the country's independence. Junior officers led a coup against the government of Sir Abubakar Tafawa Balewa in January of 1966. Balewa and other members of the government were murdered during the coup. Aguiyi-Ironsi escaped assassination by the rebels and rallied the army to put down the coup. Aguiyi-Ironsi became Nigeria's head of state on January 15, 1966. Northern Nigerian leaders distrusted the new government, and riots against Ibo control of the government took place throughout the North. Northern officers led a coup on July 29, 1966, and Aguiyi-Ironsi was seized and executed by the rebels.

YAKUBU GOWON (President, July 29, 1966–July 29, 1975). Yakubu Gowon was born in Garam on October 19, 1934. He attended the Sandhurst Royal Military Academy. He joined the Nigerian army in 1960 and served as part of the United Nations peacekeeping force in the Congo in 1961 and 1963. Gowon rose through the ranks and became a lieutenant colonel in 1963. He was appointed chief of staff in 1966. He became head of the Federal Military Government following the assassination of Johnson Aguiyi-Ironsi on July 29, 1966. Gowon's government was faced with a secessionist movement in Eastern Nigeria, and Odumgwu Ojukwu declared Biafra independent in May of 1967. Civil war raged for three years, with starvation taking a heavy toll on Biafra. A peace settlement was reached in January of 1970 which reunified the country. The federal government grew in power during Gowon's rule. His refusal to restore Nigeria to a civilian government led to another military coup on July 29, 1975. Gowon was ousted while attending an Organization of African Unity summit meeting in Kampala, Uganda. He went into exile in Great Britain. He was accused of complicity in the assassination of President Murtala Ramat Mohammed in February of 1976. Gowon subsequently attended Warwick University until 1983, when he returned to Nigeria. He again went into exile and settled in Togo in January of 1984.

MURTALA RAMAT MOHAMMED (President, July 29, 1975–February 13, 1976). Murtala Ramat Mohammed was born in Kano, in Northern Nigeria, on November 8, 1938. He was educated in Nigeria and at the Royal Military Academy at Sandhurst in Great Britain. He entered the Nigerian army in 1960 and served with the United Nation's peace-keeping troops in the Congo in 1962. Mohammed became commander of the Army Signals in November of 1965. He was promoted to lieutenant colonel in April of 1966. He was a leader of the military coup in July of 1966 that resulted in General Yakubu Gowon becoming Nigeria's head of state. Mohammed was a military leader during the civil war against Biafran secessionists in the late 1960s. He led a military coup against the government of Gowon on July 29, 1975, and assumed the presidency. He attempted to eliminate corruption in the government, but was unsuccessful in halting economic inflation. Mohammed was ambushed during an unsuccessful coup attempt on February 13, 1976. Dissident troops shot and killed him when his limousine was caught in a traffic jam in Lagos. The coup, led by Lieut.

Col. Bukar S. Dimka, was crushed by the army, and Dimka and other rebel leaders were executed in May of 1976.

OLUSEGUN OBASANJO (President, February 13, 1976–October 1, 1979). Olusegun Obasanjo was born in Abeokuta on March 5, 1937. He was educated locally and in Great Britain. He joined the Nigerian army in 1958 and rose through the ranks to captain in 1963, major in 1965, and colonel in 1969. Obasanjo accepted the surrender of the Biafran forces in January of 1970. He served as a member of the Supreme Military Council from 1975 and succeeded Murtala Ramat Mohammed as head of the military government and commander in chief of the armed forces on February 13, 1976. He retired as head of the military government and returned the government to civilian rule on October 1, 1979. Obasanjo subsequently served on several government commissions and retired from government to become a farmer.

ALHAJI SHEHU SHAGARI (President, October 1, 1979–December 31, 1983). Alhaji Shehu Usman Aliu Shagari was born in Shagari in May of 1925. He was educated locally and became a teacher. He was elected to the Federal Parliament in 1954 and served until 1958. Shagari served as parliamentary secretary to the prime minister from 1958 until 1959 and was federal minister of economic development from 1959 until 1960. He continued to serve in the Nigerian cabinet until the military took control of the government in January of 1966. He subsequently served as federal commissioner for economic development and reconstruction from 1970 until 1971 and was federal commissioner for finance from 1971 until 1975. Shagari was elected president of Nigeria as the candidate for the National party of Nigeria (NPN), following the restoration of democratic government. He took office on October 1, 1979, and also served as commander in chief of the armed forces and minister of defense from 1982. He was ousted in a military coup on December 31, 1983, and was placed under house arrest until 1986. Shagari was subsequently banned from political activity and was confined to his home village until 1988.

MOHAMMED BUHARI (President, December 31, 1983–August 27, 1985). Mohammed Buhari was born in Daura, in the Katsina Province, on December 17, 1942. He was educated in military schools in Nigeria and Great Britain and joined the Nigerian army in 1962. He rose through the ranks, and in 1975 he was named military governor of the North Eastern State, where he served until 1976. Buhari subsequently served as federal commissioner for petroleum until 1978. Major General Buhari ousted President Alhaji Shehu Shagari on December 31, 1983. He served as chairman of the Supreme Military Council and commander in chief of the armed forces. When his government proved unable to cope with the economic difficulties in Nigeria, he was overthrown by another military coup on August 27, 1985. He was arrested and detained until 1988.

IBRAHIM BABANGIDA (President, August 30, 1985–). Ibrahim Babangida was born in Minna on August 17, 1941. He received military training in Nigeria and India and joined the Nigerian army in 1963. He served in the Biafran civil war and was promoted to lieutenant colonel in 1974. Babangida took part in the military coup that ousted President Shehu Shagari in 1983. He subsequently served as a member of the Supreme Military Council and as army chief of staff. He led the coup that ousted Mohammed Buhari as head of state and replaced him as president on August 30, 1985. He also served as minister of defense from 1989 until 1990. Babangida allowed democratic elections to be held in June of 1993, but the government opposed the results and ordered the elections voided. Babangida faced international pressure to restore democracy to the country and announced the intention of the military govenment to restore the country to civilian rule later in 1993.

HEADS OF GOVERNMENT

SIR ABUBAKER TAFAWA BALEWA (Prime Minister, October 1, 1960–January 15, 1966). Abubaker Tafawa Balewa was born in Bauchi in northern Nigeria in December of 1912. He was educated locally and became a teacher in 1944. He continued his education at London University's Institute of Education and returned to Nigeria in 1946. Balewa also entered politics in 1946 and was elected to the Northern House of Assembly. He was elected to the Legislative Council the following year. He represented the interests of the north in constitutional talks in the early 1950s. Balewa was a founder of the Northern People's Congress (NPC) with Ajhaji Ahmadu Bello, the sardauna of Sokoto, in 1951. He became minister of works in the government in 1952 and became minister of transport the following year. He was involved in constitutional conferences in London in May of 1957. Balewa was elected chief minister in September of 1957 and formed a coalition government with Nnamdi Azikiwe's National Council of Nigeria and the Cameroons following parliamentary elections in December of 1959. Nigeria was granted independence from Great Britain on October 1, 1960, and Balewa remained prime minister in the independent government. Political unrest and regional factionalism plagued his government. Balewa remained prime minister following general elections in December of 1964. He was kidnapped during a coup led by rebels in the Nigerian army on January 15, 1966. The rebels assassinated Alhaji Sir Ahmadu Bello, the sardauna of Sokoto and premier of Northern Nigeria, Chief Samuel Ladoke Akin-tola, the premier of the Western Region, and Finance Minister Chief Festus Sam Okotie-Eboh. Balewa was also killed during the early hours of the coup, and his body was found on a road near Lago on January 21, 1966.

Norway, Kingdom of
(Kongeriket Norge)

Norway is a country in the western Scandinavian peninsula in northern Europe. It was granted independence from Sweden on October 26, 1905.

HEADS OF STATE

HAAKON VII (King, November 18, 1905–September 21, 1957). Haakon was born Christian Frederick Charles George Waldemar Axel in Charlottenlund, Denmark, on August 3, 1872. He was the second son of the future king Frederick VIII of Denmark. He was known as Prince Carl, and he entered the Danish navy in 1886. Prince Carl married Princess Maud, the daughter of the future king Edward VII of Great Britain in July of 1896. He was asked to become king of the newly independent country of Norway following the dissolution of the Swedish-Norway union in 1905. He agreed to assume the throne provided a referendum was held in which the Norwegian people would approve his selection. They did so by a large majority, and Prince Carl was crowned King Haakon VII of Norway on November 18, 1905. He supported Norway's neutrality during World War I. King Haakon attempted to insure Norway's neutrality and independence during World War II. Germany invaded Norway in April of 1940, and the king fled with the royal family to avoid capture. He went to Great Britain, where he remained in exile during the war. He returned to Oslo in June of 1945, following the liberation of Norway. Haakon celebrated the golden anniversary of his rule in 1955. He died in Oslo from a respiratory ailment at the age of 85 on September 21, 1957.

OLAV V (King, September 21, 1957–January 17, 1991). Olav was born at Appleton House, near Norfolk, England, on July 2, 1903. He was the son of Prince Charles of Denmark, later King Haakon VII of Norway, and Princess Maud, daughter of King Edward VII of Great Britain. He became crown prince of Norway when his father was given the throne of the newly independent country in 1905. Olav was educated at the military academy in Norway and at Balliol College, at Oxford University, in England. He was an avid sportsman and won a gold medal in yachting in the Olympic Games of 1928. The following year he married Princess Martha of Sweden. Olav was active with the Norwegian government-in-exile during World War II. He served as regent while awaiting his father's return to the throne after Norway's liberation in 1945. Olav again served as regent when his father was recuperating from a badly broken leg in 1955. He succeeded to the throne on King Haakon's death on September 21, 1957. Olav was a popular monarch and was beloved by his people. He suffered a stroke in June of 1990 and relinquished many of his duties to his son, Crown Prince Harald. He died in Oslo on January 17, 1991.

HARALD V (King, January 17, 1991–). Harald was born in Skaugum on February 21, 1937. He was the son of King Olav V and Crown Princess Martha of Norway. He lived in Washington, D.C., during the German occupation of Norway in World War II. Harald was educated in Norway and Great Britain and was a sailing enthusiast. He represented Norway at several Olympic Games and, as crown prince, often represented his father abroad. He was also an environmentalist and served as president of the Norwegian branch of the World Wildlife Fund from 1970. Harald succeeded his father as king when Olav died on January 17, 1991.

HEADS OF GOVERNMENT

JOHN NYGAARDSVOLD (Prime Minister, March 16, 1935–November 1, 1945). John Nygaardsvold was born in Hommelvik on September 6, 1879. In the early 1900s Nygaardsvold went to the United States, where he worked on the railroads. He returned to Norway in 1907 and became involved in politics. He joined the Labor party and was elected to the Storting, or Parliament, in 1916. Nygaardsvold rose to the rank of speaker in 1928 and later in the year was appointed minister of agriculture in the Labor cabinet, which lasted eighteen days. He again served as Speaker of the Storting in 1934 and 1935. Nygaardsvold was chosen as prime minister on March 16, 1935. Following the German invasion of Norway in June of 1940, Nygaardsvold escaped to London where he headed the Norwegian government-in-exile. He remained prime minister until after the liberation and retired on June 25, 1945. He died in Trondheim on March 13, 1952.

EINAR GERHARDSEN (Prime Minister, November 1, 1945–November 13, 1951). Einar Henry Gerhardsen was born in Oslo on May 10, 1897. He worked in construction in the Oslo Office of Roads from 1914. Becoming active in the trade union movement, he served as chairman of the Road Repairer's Union in 1919. He became secretary of Oslo's Labor party in 1925 and was elected to the Oslo Town Council in 1932. Gerhardsen became secretary of the Norwegian Labor party in 1935 and was elected mayor of Oslo in 1940. He was dismissed from office following the German invasion in April of 1940. He worked with the Resistance during the German occupation and was arrested by the Gestapo in September of 1941. Gerhardsen was imprisoned in Sachsenhausen concentration camp in Germany until 1944. He was subsequently imprisoned at Gestapo headquarters in Oslo until the liberation of Norway in May of 1945. He was returned to office as mayor of Oslo and became leader of the Labor party. Gerhardsen formed a coalition government as prime minister on June 22, 1945. He presided over the reconstruction of postwar Norway and implemented numerous social welfare programs in the country. He also approved Norway's entry into the North Atlantic Treaty Organization (NATO) in 1949. Gerhardsen resigned from office on November 13, 1951, and was replaced as prime minister by Oscar Torp. He resumed office on January 22, 1955, as head of a Labor government. Gerhardsen was forced to step down on August 28, 1963, following a vote of no confidence over the government's alleged mismanagement of the Spitsbergn mines. He returned to office on September 23, 1963, and replaced a short-lived Conservative coalition government led by John Lyng. The Labor party was defeated in parliamentary elections in September of 1965, and Gerhardsen stepped down from office on October 12, 1965. He remained a leading figure in the Labor party until his retirement from Parliament in 1972. Gerhardsen died from a heart condition at a nursing home in Lilleborg at the age of 90 on September 19, 1987.

OSCAR TORP (Prime Minister, November 13, 1951–January 22, 1955). Oscar Fredrik Torp was born in Skjeberg on June 8, 1893. He worked as a carpenter and electrician and became active in the trade union movement while in his teens. He became chairman of the National Council of Labor in Oslo in 1923. Torp served as chairman of the Oslo Municipal Council from 1934 until 1935. He was then named to the government of Johan Nygaardsvold as deputy minister of defense. He was soon appointed minister of defense and served until 1936, when he was named minister of social affairs. Torp was also elected to the Norwegian Parliament, the Storting, in 1937. He was named finance minister in July of 1939. Torp arranged the transport of Norway's gold reserves to safety in England when Germany invaded Norway in April of 1940, and he joined the government-in-exile in London. Torp's citizenship was revoked by the Nazi puppet government of Vidkun Quisling in 1942. Torp became minister of defense in the government-in-exile in 1942. He returned to Norway following the liberation in 1945 and served in Einar Gerhardsen's government as minister of defense from June of 1945. He was named minister of supply and reconstruction following parliamentary elections in October of 1945. Torp resigned from the cabinet in 1948 to become governor of Vestfold District. He remained in the Parliament and was a leading proponent of Norway's entry into the North Atlantic Treaty Organization (NATO) in 1949. Torp was chosen to succeed Gerhardsen as prime minister on November 13, 1951. He led a Labor government until January 22, 1955, when he was replaced by Gerhardsen. Torp subsequently served as president of the Parliament, a position he retained until his death in Oslo at the age of 64 on May 1, 1958.

EINAR GERHARDSEN (Prime Minister, January 22, 1955–August 28, 1963). *See earlier entry under Heads of Government.*

JOHN LYNG (Prime Minister, August 28, 1963–September 20, 1963). John Lyng was born on August 22, 1905. He was educated at Oslo University, where he received a degree in law in 1932. He subsequently opened a legal practice in Oslo. Lyng served as a legal advisor to the Norwegian government-in-exile in London during World War II. He served as a public prosecutor in the trials of Nazi collaborators following the war. He was also elected to Parliament in 1945 and served until 1953. Lyng returned to Parliament in 1958 and became the leader of the Parliamentary Conservative party. He was named to lead a coalition government as prime minister on August 28, 1963. He retained office until the Labor party returned to power on September 20, 1963. Lyng was replaced by Per Borten as Conservative party leader in 1965. He served as foreign minister in Borten's Conservative government from October of 1965. He remained in the cabinet until his retirement in 1970. Lyng died of lung cancer in Oslo at the age of 72 on January 18, 1978.

EINAR GERHARDSEN (Prime Minister, September 23, 1963–October 12, 1965). *See earlier entry under Heads of Government.*

PER BORTEN (Prime Minister, October 12, 1965–March 4, 1971). Per Borten was born in Fla Gauldal on April 3, 1913. He was educated in Norway and worked with the Provincial Agriculture Administration in Sor-Trondelag from 1946. He was elected to Parliament in 1950 and became chairman of the Center party in 1955. Borten became prime minister of a coalition government on October 12, 1965, following the defeat of the Labor party in elections. He served until March 4, 1971, when the Labor party was returned to power. Borten remained in Parliament until his retirement in 1977.

TRYGVE BRATTELI (Prime Minister, March 10, 1971–October 7, 1972). Trygve Martii Bratteli was born in Notteroy on January 11, 1910. He had little formal education and worked in construction as a young man. He joined the Labor Youth Organization in 1928. Bratteli was selected as secretary of the organization in 1934 and held this office until 1940. He was active in the Resistance to the German occupation of Norway during World War II. He was arrested in 1942 and spent the remainder of the war in concentration camps in Germany. At the time of his liberation in 1945, Bratteli was found near death in a heap of corpses. He was selected as vice-chairman of the Labor party in 1945 and was elected to the Norwegian Parliament, the Storting, in 1950. He served in the government of Einar Gerhardsen as minister of transport and communications from 1960 until 1964. Bratteli succeeded Gerhardsen as leader of the Labor party in 1965 and led the Opposition until March 10, 1971, when he formed a minority Labor government as prime minister. He supported Norway's entry into the European Economic Community and resigned from office on October 7, 1972, following the defeat of a referendum supporting membership. He returned to office as head of a coalition government on October 16, 1973. Bratteli stepped down as prime minister on January 9, 1976, for personal reasons. He remained in the Parliament until his retirement in 1981. Bratteli died in an Oslo hospital at the age of 75 on November 20, 1984, after suffering a brain hemorrhage.

LARS KORVALD (Prime Minister, October 18, 1972–October 16, 1973). Lars Korvald was born in Nedre Eiker on April 29, 1916. He was educated at the College of Agriculture and became a teacher. He was elected to Parliament in 1961 as a member of the Christian People's party. Korvald served as a delegate to the United Nations General Assembly in 1963 and again in 1968. He was elected party chairman in 1967 and was elected president of the upper house of Parliament in 1969. He was asked to form a coalition government on October 18, 1972. The Labor party returned to power in general elections in September of 1973, and Korvald stepped down as prime minister on October 16, 1973. He remained party chairman until 1975 and served in that position again from 1977 until 1979. He was elected governor of the Ostfold District in 1981 and held this office until 1986.

TRYGVE BRATTELI (Prime Minister, October 16, 1973–January 9, 1976). *See earlier entry under Heads of Government.*

ODVAR NORDLI (Prime Minister, January 9, 1976–February 4, 1981). Odvar Nordli was born in Stange on November 3, 1927. He was educated in Norway and received a degree in business administration. He worked in local government prior to his election to the Parliament as a member of the Labor party in 1961. Nordli held various party offices and in 1971 was named minister of labor and municipal affairs, an office he held until 1972. He was elected parliamentary Leader of the Labor party in 1973 and was named chairman of the Committee of Defense in 1974. He became prime minister following the resignation of Trygve Bratteli on January 9, 1976. Nordli resigned office for reasons of health on February 4, 1981.

GRO HARLEM BRUNDTLAND (Prime Minister, February 4, 1981–October 14, 1981). Gro Harlem was born in Oslo on April 20, 1939. She married political scientist Arne Olav Brundtland in 1960. She was educated at the University of Oslo, where she received a degree in medicine in 1963. Brundtland continued her studies at the Harvard University School of Public Health in the United States. After she returned to Norway in 1965, she worked in the ministry of health and social affairs from 1965 until 1967. She was appointed minister of environmental affairs in the government of Trygve Bratteli in 1974 and served until 1979. Brundtland was elected deputy leader of the Labor party in 1975 and became leader of the party's parliamentary group in 1981. She was selected as the first female prime minister of Norway on February 4, 1981, following the resignation of Odvar Nordli. She served until October 14, 1981, when she was replaced with a Conservative government following elections. Brundtland formed a minority government on May 9, 1986, and served as prime minister until October 16, 1989. She was again asked to form a minority Labor government on November 3, 1990.

KARE ISAACHSEN WILLOCH (Prime Minister, October 14, 1981–May 9, 1986). Kare Isaachsen Willoch was born in Oslo on October 3, 1928. He attended the University of Oslo. He was elected to Parliament in 1958 and joined the Conservative party. Willoch was named minister of trade and shipping in 1963 and again served in that position from 1965 until 1970. He served as secretary-general of the party from 1963 until 1965 and was chairman from 1970 until 1974. He was selected prime minister of a minority Conservative government on October 14, 1981. Willoch's government resigned on May 9, 1986, following a parliamentary vote of no confidence on a proposed tax increase on gas. He subsequently headed the Foreign Affairs Committee in Parliament until 1989. He was then named cogovernor of Oslo and Akershus.

GRO HARLEM BRUNDTLAND (Prime Minister, May 9, 1986–October 16, 1989). *See earlier entry under Heads of Government.*

JAN PEDER SYSE (Prime Minister, October 16, 1989–November 3, 1990). Jan Peder Syse was born on November 25, 1930. He was educated at the University of Oslo. He joined the Conservative party and served as deputy director of the Ministry of Trade from 1967 until 1969. Syse was state secretary at the Ministry of Justice from 1970 until 1971 and was elected to the Parliament in 1973. He served as chairman of the Oslo Conservative party from 1974 until 1982. He was minister of industry from 1983 until 1985. Syse was elected chairman of the Conservative party in 1988. He became prime minister on October 16, 1989. The following year the coalition government split over the issue of Norway's involvement with European Communities. Syse was replaced by a minority Labor government on November 3, 1990.

GRO HARLEM BRUNDTLAND (Prime Minister, November 3, 1990–). *See earlier entry under Heads of Government.*

Oman, Sultanate of

(Sultanat 'Uman)

Oman is a country in the southeastern Arabian peninsula. It was recognized as an independent sultanate by Great Britain on December 20, 1951.

HEADS OF STATE

SAID BIN TAIMUR (Sultan, February 28, 1932–July 23, 1970). Said bin Taimur bin Feisal bin Turki was born on April 13, 1910. He was the son of Taimur bin Feisal, the sultan of Muscat. He was educated in Iraq and India. He deposed his father to become sultan of Muscat on February 28, 1932. Said also held sovereignty of the provinces of Oman and Dhofar. He continued to rule Muscat and Oman under a treaty of friendship with Great Britain. The sultanate was recognized as an independent state on December 20, 1951. Sultan Said refused to use his country's income from oil concessions for the benefit of his subjects. He faced a separatist revolt from the iman of Oman in 1955 and crushed the rebellion with the assistance of the British. He survived another rebellion by the iman in July of 1957 that was supported by the Saudi Arabian and Egyptian governments. The western province of Dhofar went into revolt in 1965 and the sultan survived an assassination attempt the following year. The revolt in Dhofar continued with the support of Communist China and leftist Arab nationalists. The sultan's son, Qabus bin Said, ousted his father in a coup on July 23, 1970. Said was slightly injured in the coup and was sent into exile in Great Britain. He lived on a pension at the Dorchester Hotel in London until his death of a heart attack at the age of 62 on October 19, 1972.

QABUS BIN SAID (Sultan, July 23, 1970–). Qabus bin Said was born in Salalah on November 18, 1940. He was the son of Sultan Said bin Taimur. He was educated at the Sandhurst Royal Military Academy in Great Britain. After he returned to Oman in 1965, he remained a virtual prisoner in the palace of his father. Qabus deposed Sultan Said on July 23, 1970, and claimed the throne. He allowed the return of his uncle Tariq bin Taimur, whom he named to head the new government. He continued to face a separatist revolt in the province of Dhofar. His government received assistance from Saudi Arabia, Jordan, and other Arab nations to crush the rebellion, and a cease-fire was announced in March of 1976. Qabus continued to serve as absolute monarch in Oman and also served in the government as foreign minister and minister of defense. He was one of the few Arab leaders to support the Middle Eastern peace initiative of President Anwar Sadat of Egypt in 1977. Oman also served as a base for United States military activities in the Perisan Gulf and supported the multinational military campaign against Iraq following that nation's seizure of Kuwait in August of 1990.

Pakistan, Islamic Republic of

(Islami Jamhuria-e-Pakistan)

Pakistan is a country in southern Asia. It was granted independence from Great Britain on August 15, 1947.

HEADS OF STATE

MOHAMMED ALI JINNAH (Governor-General, August 15, 1947–September 11, 1948). Mohammed Ali Jinnah was born in Karachi, India, on December 25, 1876. He was educated locally and studied law in Great Britain. He returned to Bombay to practice law and was appointed to the Bombay High Court as an advocate in 1897. Jinnah was selected to serve on the Imperial Legislative Council in 1910. He soon became a leader of the Congress party. He also joined the Muslim League in 1913. Jinnah was instrumental in negotiating the Lucknow Pact in 1916, which provided for separate elections for Hindus and Muslims. He became president of the Muslim League later in the year and resigned from the Legislative Council in 1919. His disagreements with Mohandas Gandhi's policies led to his withdrawal from the Congress party in 1920. His growing distrust of Hindu intentions toward the Muslim minority in India led to his withdrawal from politics in 1932. Jinnah returned to lead a restructured Muslim League in 1934 and became a leading proponent of a separate Muslim homeland within India. The Muslim League became the principal opposition party following elections to the provincial legislatures in 1937. Jinnah gave his support to the British war effort during World War II in return for Britain's consideration of his proposals for the partition of India. He ordered his Muslim supporters not to comply with the Congress party's civil disobedience campaign during the war.

Jinnah's followers were victorious in elections in Muslim-dominated areas after the war. He demanded that the provinces of Baluchistan, the Punjab, Bengal, Sind, Assam, and the Northwest Frontier be granted a separate independence as Muslim Pakistan. Attempts by the colonial government and the Congress party to divide several of the provinces between India and Pakistan led to violent riots between Muslims and Hindus in Calcutta. Thousands of people were killed in the fighting and Jinnah subsequently accepted the British proposal. Jinnah became known as the quaid-i-azam, or "great leader." He became the first governor-general of independent Pakistan on August 15, 1947. He was suffering from poor health and stepped down as chairman of the Muslim League in March of 1948. Jinnah remained governor-general until his death in Karachi from heart failure at the age of 72 on September 11, 1948.

KHWAJA NAZIMUDDIN (Governor-General, September 14, 1948–October 17, 1951). Khwaja Nazimuddin was born in Dacca on July 19, 1894. He was educated in England at Cambridge University. He then returned to the Bengal State in India, where he entered politics. Nazimuddin was elected chairman of the Dacca Municipal Council in 1922 and served until 1929. He was a member of the Bengal Executive Council from 1934 until 1937. He was subsequently named home minister and held this post until 1941. Nazimuddin served as chief minister from 1943 until 1945. He became premier of East Pakistan after the partition from India in August of 1947. He succeeded Mohammed Ali Jinnah as governor-general on September 14, 1948. Nazimuddin was selected as prime minister following the assassination of Liaquat Ali Khan on October 16, 1951. He was dismissed by Governor-General Ghulam Mohammed on April 17, 1953, following his government's inability to cope with a severe economic crisis. Nazimuddin remained active in politics until Mohammed Ayub Khan seized power in October of 1958. He emerged from retirement to lead the Councillors' Muslim League in opposition to the government of Ayub Khan in 1962. Nazimuddin died in Dacca of a heart attack at the age of 70 on October 22, 1964.

GHULAM MOHAMMED (Governor-General, October 17, 1951–October 6, 1955). Ghulam Mohammed was born in Lahore, India, on August 29, 1895. He attended the Aligarh Muslim University and received a degree in law. He entered the Indian Audit Service in 1920. His thoroughness led to rapid promotions, and he served as commissioner of development of Bhopol State from 1932 until 1934. Mohammed subsequently served as a financial consultant to the Indian government in New Delhi. He also became secretary to the Supply Department during World War II. Mohammed left government service after the war to enter private industry. He returned to the government following the establishment of an independent Pakistan in August of 1947 and became minister of finance in the cabinet of Prime Minister Liaquat Ali Khan. He was successful in improving the new nation's economic stability. Mohammed was appointed to succeed Khwaja Nazimuddin as governor-general when Nazimuddin replaced the assassinated Liaquat Ali Khan as Prime Minister on October 17, 1951.

Mohammed dismissed Nazimuddin's government in April of 1953 and named Muhammed Ali to form a government. He also dismissed the National Assembly in October of 1954 when the assembly promoted a new constitution designed to limit the power of the governor-general. Mohammed claimed emergency powers and drafted a new constitution. He suffered from poor health and sought medical treatment in Great Britain in July of 1955. He returned to Pakistan the following month and relinquished most of his duties to Iskander Mirza. Mohammed resigned for reasons of health on October 6, 1955. He died in Karachi after a long illness at the age of 61 on August 29, 1956.

ISKANDER MIRZA (Governor-General, October 6, 1955–February 29, 1956). President, February 29, 1956–October 7, 1958). Iskander Mirza was born in Murchidabad on November 13, 1899. He was educated at Elphinstone College in Bombay. He subsequently entered the Royal Military Academy at Sandhurst in Great Britain. Mirza became the first Indian cadet to become an officer in the British army in 1920. In 1926 he entered the political service of the British Raj. He was promoted to political agent in the Khyber in 1938 and became deputy commissioner of Peshawar in 1941. Mirza held several other positions before becoming joint secretary in the Ministry of Defense in New Delhi in 1946. He joined with Pakistan following the partition of India in 1947 and was assigned to organize the Pakistani army. He was named governor of East Pakistan in 1954 and was granted full emergency powers to deal with the disorders in the region. Mirza arranged for a fair distribution of food in the area and used hard measures to restore order. He returned to the capital in November of 1954 to serve as minister of the interior, states, and the frontier. Mirza took over the duties of governor-general when Ghulam Mohammed suffered from poor health in July of 1955. He succeeded to the office when Mohammed resigned on October 6, 1955. When Pakistan was declared a republic on February 29, 1956, Mirza became its first president. His rule became increasingly autocratic in the face of a short food supply, rising inflation, and an economy facing bankruptcy. In October of 1958 he abrogated the constitution and ended parliamentary government. He declared martial law and named General Mohammed Ayub Khan to administer it. Ayub Khan forced Mirza's resignation later in the month and replaced him as president on October 7, 1958. Mirza went into exile in London the following month. He died from a heart attack at his London residence at the age of 70 on November 12, 1969.

MOHAMMED AYUB KHAN (President, October 7, 1958–March 25, 1969). Mohammed Ayub Khan was born in Rihana in the Northwest Frontier Province of British India, now part of Pakistan, on May 14, 1907. He was educated at the Aligarh Muslim University in India and the Royal Military Academy at Sandhurst in England. He entered the Indian army as an officer in 1928 and led a battalion in Burma during World War II. When Pakistan was granted independence in 1937, Ayub was appointed commander in chief of the army. In 1954 he was also named defense minister. He was appointed to administer martial law under President Iskander Mirza in October of 1958. Ayub ousted Mirza on October 7, 1958, and continued to govern the country under martial law. Ayub restructured the political mechanisms of the country and was confirmed as president on October 28, 1958. He tried to improve the economy, encourage industry, and enact agrarian reform, but met with little success in dealing with Pakistan's many problems. Although he was reelected president in 1965, he continued

to meet with widespread discontent in the country. Pakistan engaged in a war with India over the status of Kashmir in 1965. Ayub's administration faced even greater problems in 1968 when massive student demonstrations took place throughout the country. Ayub resigned from office on March 25, 1969, and retired to private life. He died of a heart attack at his home near Islamabad at the age of 66 on April 20, 1974.

MOHAMMED YAHYA KHAN (President, March 31, 1969–December 20, 1971). Agha Mohammed Yahya Khan was born in Chakwal, in Jhelum District, on February 4, 1917. He attended Government College in Lahore and received a degree from Punjab University in 1936. He subsequently entered the Royal Indian Military Academy at Dehra Dun and was commissioned as a lieutenant in 1938. Yahya fought in the British army during World War II and saw action in the Middle East, Cyprus, and Italy. He held several staff positions after the war and entered the Pakistani army when India was partitioned in 1947. He established the Pakistani Staff College and was promoted to lieutenant colonel in October of 1947. Yahya continued to rise through the ranks and became a brigadier in 1951. He was promoted to major general in 1957 and was appointed chief of the army general staff. He supported General Mohammed Ayub Khan's military coup in October of 1958. Yahya was assigned as a commander in East Pakistan from December of 1962 until August of 1964. He served as a division commander in the war between India and Pakistan over Kashmir in 1965. He was appointed deputy commander in chief of the army the following year. Yahya rose to become commander in chief in September of 1966. President Ayub Khan was forced to resign on March 25, 1969, following widespread disorders that centered around a growing separatist movement in East Pakistan. Yahya took control of the country as chief martial law administrator and declared himself president on March 31, 1959. He allowed national elections to take place in 1970, and Sheik Mujibur Rahman's Awami League scored a major victory in East Pakistan. Zulfikar Ali Bhutto's Pakistan People's party received a majority in West Pakistan. An agreement could not be reached on a compromise government, and Yahya used harsh measures to crush the separatist movement in East Pakistan. He ordered the arrest of Mujibur Rahman and banned the Awami League. Civil war broke out in the region, and Bengali Separatists declared East Pakistan's independence as Bangladesh. India entered the war on the side of the Bengalis in November of 1971, and Pakistan was forced to agree to a ceasefire. Yahya resigned from office on December 20, 1971, and turned the government over to Zulfikar Ali Bhutto. Yahya suffered a paralytic stroke shortly after leaving office. He was held under house arrest until 1977. He died from internal bleeding at the age of 63 at a Rawalpindi military hospital on August 9, 1980.

ZULFIKAR ALI BHUTTO (President, December 20, 1971–August 14, 1973). Zulfikar Ali Bhutto was born to a wealthy family near Larkana, in the Sind Province, on January 5, 1928. He attended the University of California at Berkeley, where he graduated with a degree in political science in 1950. He then attended Oxford University in Great Britain, where he received a degree in law. Bhutto returned to Pakistan to practice law in Karachi in 1953. He served as a member of the Pakistani delegation to the United Nations in 1957 and represented Pakistan at a United Nations conference in Geneva, Switzerland, the following year. He was named to the cabinet of Mohammed Ayub Khan as minister of commerce in 1958. Bhutto was shifted to the Ministry of Information and

National Reconstruction in January of 1960. He headed several other ministries in Ayub Khan's government and was elected to the restored National Assembly in June of 1962. He was appointed foreign minister in January of 1963. Bhutto came into disagreement with the Ayub Khan government over Pakistan's relationship with the United States. Bhutto advocated closer ties with the People's Republic of China and condemned United States pressure that led to the peace settlement between Pakistan and India in January of 1966. He was dismissed from the government in July of 1966 and became a leading spokesman of dissent to Ayub Khan's rule. Bhutto founded the Pakistan People's party in December of 1967. He was arrested for antigovernment activities in November of 1968, and he became the central figure in the opposition by the time of his release in February of 1969. Ayub Khan was replaced the following month by General Mohammed Yahya Khan, who allowed a national election to take place in 1970. Bhutto's party won a victory in West Pakistan, and Sheikh Mujibur Rahman's Awami League received a vast majority in East Pakistan. Sheikh Mujibur, who advocated autonomy for East Pakistan, would have become prime minister because East Pakistan had the largest delegation in the National Assembly. Bhutto announced plans to boycott the assembly, and Yahya annulled the election. A civil war developed in East Pakistan when supporters of Sheikh Mujibur proclaimed the region the independent nation of Bangladesh. Yahya Khan appointed Bhutto as deputy prime minister and foreign minister in December of 1971, following India's involvement in the conflict. The government was forced to accept a cease-fire later in the month, and Yahya resigned as president on December 20, 1971. Bhutto was placed in charge of the government. He returned the country to civilian rule and also served in the government as minister of defense, the interior, and foreign affairs. He promoted a new constitution in August of 1973 that reduced the presidency to a ceremonial position. Bhutto stepped down as president on August 14, 1973, but remained head of government as prime minister. He was successful in improving Pakistan's economic stability and helped to restore his nation's self-esteem that had been damaged by the war with Bangladesh and India. The Pakistan People's party won a major victory in elections to the National Assembly in March of 1977. The opposition Pakistan National Alliance claimed electoral fraud and strikes, and demonstrations took place throughout the country. The army staged a coup and ousted Bhutto as prime minister on July 5, 1977. General Mohammed Zia ul-Haq imposed martial law and ordered Bhutto's imprisonment the following September. Bhutto was charged with having ordered the assassination of Ahmed Raza Kasuri, a political opponent, in 1974. Kasuri's father, Nawab Mohammed Ahmed Khan, was killed in the attempted assassination. Bhutto was convicted on March 18, 1978, and sentenced to death by the Lahore High Court. The Pakistan Supreme Court upheld the verdict and sentence, and Bhutto was executed by hanging in Rawalpindi on April 4, 1979.

FAZAL ELAHI CHAUDHRY (President, August 14, 1973–September 14, 1978). Fazal Elahi Chaudhry was born in Gujrat in the Punjab on January 1, 1904. He was educated as a lawyer and entered politics in 1931. He served on the Gujarat District Board in the colonial Indian government. In 1945 Chaudhry was elected to the Punjab Legislative Assembly as a member of the Muslim League. He served as a Pakistani delegate to the United Nations in the early 1950s and was elected to the Punjab Provincial Assembly in 1956. He served as Speaker of the assembly until 1958. Chaudhry was elected to the National Assembly in 1962 and was selected as Speaker in 1971. He became president of Pakistan on August 14, 1973, when Zulfikar Ali Bhutto relinquished the office to serve as prime minister. Chaudhry retained the largely ceremonial office after the military coup that ousted Bhutto in July of 1977. He resigned from office on September 14, 1978, following disagreements with the military government. Chaudhry retired from politics and died of a heart ailment at his home in Lahore at the age of 78 on June 1, 1982.

MOHAMMED ZIA UL-HAQ (President, September 16, 1978–August 17, 1988). Mohammed Zia ul-Haq was born in Jullundur, in East Punjab, on August 12, 1924. He attended St. Stephen's College in Delhi and the Royal Indian Military Academy at Dehra Dun. He was commissioned into the British army in May of 1945 and saw action in Burma and Indonesia near the end of World War II. Zia entered the Pakistani army after the partition of India in 1947. He received further military training in Pakistan and the United States. He was promoted to lieutenant colonel in 1964 and participated in the war between Pakistan and India the following year. Zia rose to the rank of brigadier general in 1969 and commanded an armored brigade. He was sent to Jordan later in the year to serve as a military advisor to the Royal Jordanian Army during its conflict with Palestinian guerrillas. He returned to Pakistan in 1971 and served as a deputy division commander in the civil war that resulted in the formation of Bangladesh. Zia was promoted to general in March of 1976 and was named army chief of staff by President Zulfikar Ali Bhutto. Riots and civil disorders followed allegations of fraud in general elections held in March of 1977. Fearing civil war, Zia led a military coup to oust Bhutto on July 5, 1977. He took control of the government and declared martial law. He ordered Bhutto's arrest in September of 1977 and clamped down on all political activity in the country. Zia made plans to restore Pakistan to civilian rule in 1978 and appointed a civilian cabinet in August of 1978. He assumed the presidency on September 16, 1978, and introduced an Islamization plan for the country. He continued to face widespread discontent against his rule. Protests against the government escalated following the execution of Bhutto in April of 1979, and Zia restored military rule. Bhutto's daughter, Benazir, became the leader of the Pakistan People's party, and she was imprisoned and forced into exile by the Zia government. A referendum approved Zia's Islamization plan in December of 1984. He allowed elections to the National Assembly in February of 1985 and lifted martial law restrictions later in the year. Zia approved a civilian government with Mohammed Khan Junejo as prime minister on March 24, 1985. He dismissed Junejo's government in May of 1988 and called for new elections. He banned political parties in the elections scheduled for later in the year. Zia was killed when the C-130 transport plane he was traveling in with the United States ambassador to Pakistan, Arnold L. Raphel, exploded in midair and crashed near Bahawalpur on August 17, 1988.

GHULAM ISHAQ KHAN (President, August 17, 1988–). Ghulam Ishaq Khan was born in 1915. He was educated locally and joined the civil service. He worked for various government agencies, and became secretary of finance in 1966. He served until 1970 and subsequently became governor of the State Bank of Pakistan from 1971 until 1975. Khan was secretary-general at the Ministry of Defense from 1975 until 1977 and was appointed advisor to the Chief Martial Law Administrator in 1978. He served as minister of finance from 1979 until 1985. He also held several other cabinet positions during this period. Khan served as chairman of the Senate from 1985 until 1988. He became acting president on August 17, 1988, following the death of Mohammed Zia ul-Haq. In December of 1988 he was approved as president. Khan dismissed Prime Minister Benazir Bhutto on charges of corruption in August of 1990. He engaged in a power struggle with Prime Minister Nawaz Sharif and dismissed the government in April of 1993.

HEADS OF GOVERNMENT

LIAQUAT ALI KHAN (Prime Minister, August 15, 1947–October 16, 1951). Liaquat Ali Khan was born in Karnal on October 1, 1895. He received a degree in law from Exeter College at Oxford University and returned to India to practice law. He entered politics in 1923 and joined the All-India Muslim League led by Mohammed Ali Jinnah. Liaquat served in the United Provinces Legislative Council from 1926 until his election in 1940 to the Central Legislative Assembly. In 1936 he was elected secretary-general of the Muslim League, and shortly thereafter he became Jinnah's deputy leader of the party. Following the establishment of independent Pakistan on August 15, 1947, Liaquat was selected as the nation's first prime minister. After Jinnah's death the following year, Liaquat assumed complete responsibility for the governing of Pakistan. The territorial dispute with India over Kashmir was the major issue facing Liaquat's government. His negotiations with Prime Minister Jawaharlal Nehru of India and his refusal to consider a war with India over the issue led to his assassination by a Muslim fanatic on

October 16, 1951, while he was addressing a public meeting in Rawalpindi.

KHWAJA NAZIMUDDIN (Prime Minister, October 17, 1951–April 17, 1953). *See entry under Heads of State.*

MOHAMMED ALI (Prime Minister, April 17, 1953–August 11, 1955). Mohammed Ali was born in Bogra, East Bengal, on October 19, 1909. He graduated from Calcutta University in 1930. He entered government service and was elected deputy mayor of Bogra in 1932. Mohammed Ali served as district chairman of the Muslim League and was elected to the Bengal Legislative Assembly in 1937. He was parliamentary secretary to East Bengal premier Khwaja Nazimuddin from 1944 until 1945 and served in the cabinet as minister of finance from 1946 until 1947. Mohammed Ali was elected to the National Assembly following Pakistan's independence in August of 1947. He also served as Pakistan's ambassador to Burma in 1948. He was named high commissioner to Canada the following year. Mohammed Ali was appointed ambassador to the United States in 1952. He returned to Pakistan following Nazimuddin's dismissal as prime minister and appointed to the office by Governor General Ghulam Mohammed on April 17, 1953. Mohammed Ali also served in the government as minister of defense. He was unable to form a cabinet following elections in 1955 and was replaced by Chaudry Mohammed Ali on August 11, 1955. Mohammed Ali was reappointed ambassador to the United States, where he remained until Mohammed Ayub Khan's military coup in October of 1958. He was named to Ayub Khan's cabinet as minister of foreign affairs in 1962 and retained that position until his death in Dacca after a brief illness at the age of 53 on January 23, 1963.

CHAUDRY MOHAMMED ALI (Prime Minister, August 11, 1955–September 8, 1956). Chaudry Mohammed Ali was born in Jullundur on July 15, 1905. He graduated from Punjab University in Lahor in 1927. He entered government service in 1928 and served in the Indian Audit and Accounting Service. Chaudry Mohammed Ali became private secretary to Finance Minister Sir James Grigg in 1936. He remained in the Finance Ministry, where he became financial advisor of war and supply in 1945. He was named secretary-general of the government when Pakistan was granted independence in August of 1947 and was appointed minister of finance in October of 1951. Chaudry Mohammed Ali replaced Mohammed Ali as president of the Muslim League party in August of 1955, following inconclusive elections the previous month. He was named to head a government as prime minister on August 11, 1955. He also served in the government as minister of defense. Chaudry Mohammed Ali presided over the consolidation of the four provinces of West Pakistan in September of 1955. He resigned from the Muslim League and stepped down as prime minister on September 8, 1956. He returned to Parliament, where he was a vocal opponent of the military government of Mohammed Ayub Khan following the coup in 1958. Chaudry Mohammed Ali retired in 1971. He died after a brief illness in Dacca at the age of 75 on December 1, 1980.

HUSAIN SHAHID SUHRAWARDY (Prime Minister, September 12, 1956–October 11, 1957). Husain Shahid Suhrawardy was born in Midnapore, West Bengal, on September 8, 1893. He graduated from St. Xavier's College in Calcutta in 1913. He continued his education at Oxford University, where he received a degree in law. After Suhrawardy returned to Calcutta, he entered government service. He served as deputy mayor of Calcutta and joined the Muslim League in 1921. He was also elected to the Bengal Legislative Assembly. In 1930 he was named to the provincial cabinet as minister of labor and finance. Suhrawardy headed various other ministries and served as minister of food from 1943 until 1945. He became prime minister of the Bengal government in 1946. He opposed the Congress party's plan to divide Bengal during the partition of India and Pakistan. His proposal to make Bengal an independent state was opposed by Muslim League leader Mohammed Ali Jinnah. Suhrawardy worked with Mohandas Gandhi to put an end to Muslim and Hindu violence in Bengal following the partition of India in 1947. He remained in India until 1949, when he relocated to Pakistan. He was considered a traitor by the Muslim League, which tried to force him out of politics. Suhrawardy founded the Awami League and received much support in East Pakistan after accusing the Muslim League of corruption. He served as the leader of the Opposition in the National Assembly and was asked to form a coalition cabinet as prime minister on September 12, 1956. His government collapsed when the Republican party withdrew from the cabinet, and he stepped down on October 11, 1957. Political parties were banned following the military coup led by General Mohammed Ayub Khan in October of 1958, and Suhrawardy was barred from political activities. He was arrested for antigovernment activities in January of 1962 and sentenced to a year in prison. His arrest sparked riots and demonstrations in East Pakistan. He was released in August of 1962 when political activities were allowed to resume. Suhrawardy became a leader of the National Democratic Front and campaigned to restore parliamentary government in Pakistan. He was forced to seek treatment for a heart condition in Europe in January of 1963. Suhrawardy died of a heart attack at the age of 70 while recuperating in Beirut, Lebanon, on December 5, 1963.

I. I. CHUNDRIGAR (Prime Minister, October 18, 1957–December 11, 1957). Ismail Ibrahim Chundrigar was born in 1897. He was educated at the University of Bombay, where he studied law. He was elected to the Almedabad Municipal Council in 1924 and also became a member of the Bombay Legislative Assembly in 1937. Chundrigar served as minister of commerce in the preindependence Indian government from 1946 and retained that position in Pakistan's government following independence in August of 1947. He subsequently served as Pakistan's ambassador to Afghanistan. He returned to Pakistan to serve as governor of the Northwest Frontier Province and Punjab. Chundrigar returned to the cabinet as minister of law in August of 1955. He was a parliamentary leader of the Muslim League and served as leader of the Opposition following the selection of Awami League leader H. H. Suhrawardy as prime minister in September of 1956. Chundrigar was asked to form a government on October 18, 1957, following the collapse of Suhrawardy's cabinet. He formed a coalition government with the Republican party, but the coalition crumbled and Chundrigar stepped down on December 11, 1957. Chundrigar suffered from poor health in 1960 and went to Great Britain for treatment. He died in a London hospital at the age of 63 on September 25, 1960.

MALIK FIROZ KHAN NOON (Prime Minister, December 16, 1957–October 27, 1958). Malik Firoz Khan Noon was born near Lahore on May 7, 1893. He was educated locally and at Oxford University in England, where he received a degree in law in 1916. He returned to Lahore to practice law. Noon was elected to the Punjab Legislative Assembly in 1920. He served in the provincial government as minister of education, medicine, and public health from 1931 until 1936. He was India's high commissioner to London from June of 1936, until he was recalled to serve on the Viceroy's Council in September of 1941. Noon was named minister of defense shortly after his return. He was again sent to London to represent India on Winston Churchill's war cabinet in 1944. He served as India's delegate to the United Nations Conference in San Francisco the following year. Noon returned to India later in 1945 and was elected to the Punjab Legislative Assembly. He was a member of the Muslim League and served in the first Pakistan National Assembly following independence in August of 1947. He served as governor of East Pakistan from 1950 and was elected chief minister of the Punjab in 1953. Noon was elected to the Pakistan National Parliament in June of 1955 and became the leader of the Republican party. He served as foreign minister in the cabinet of H. H. Suhrawardy from September of 1956 until the government fell in October of 1957. Noon formed a government as prime minister on December 16, 1957. He retained office until Mohammed Ayub Khan imposed a military government on October 27, 1958. He continued to serve as leader of the Republican party. Noon died in Lahore at the age of 77 on December 9, 1970.

MOHAMMED AYUB KHAN (Prime Minister, October 28, 1958–March 31, 1969). *See entry under Heads of State.*

MOHAMMED YAHYA KHAN (Prime Minister, March 31, 1969–December 7, 1971). *See entry under Heads of State.*

NURUL AMIN (Prime Minister, December 7, 1971–December 24, 1971). Nurul Amin was born in East Bengal in 1894. He entered politics and was elected to the Bengal Legislative

Council in 1942. He served on the Bengal Legislative Assembly from 1946, becoming Speaker of the Assembly. He served in Khwaja Nazimuddin's provincial cabinet following Pakistan's independence and replaced Nazimuddin as chief minister of East Pakistan in 1948. Amin's Muslim League was defeated by the opposition United Front in elections in 1954, and Amin was replaced as chief minister by Abdul Kasem Fazlul Haq. Amin remained the leader of the Muslim League in East Pakistan until political parties were banned by Mohammed Ayub Khan in 1958. He was elected to the Pakistan National Assembly in 1965 and was reelected to the National Assembly from East Pakistan in the elections in 1970. Amin was one of two members of the Pakistan Democratic party to survive the political sweep of the Awami League. He opposed the separatist movement in East Pakistan and became acting prime minister of the central government on December 7, 1971. He was replaced by Zulfikar Ali Bhutto on December 24, 1971. Bhutto subsequently appointed Amin as Pakistan's vice president following East Pakistan's separation from Pakistan to become Bangladesh. Amin remained vice president until the position was abolished in 1973. He died of a heart attack at the age of 80 in Rawalpindi on October 2, 1974.

ZULFIKAR ALI BHUTTO (Prime Minister, December 24, 1971–July 5, 1977). *See entry under Heads of State.*

MOHAMMED ZIA UL-HAQ (Prime Minister, July 5, 1977–March 24, 1985). *See entry under Heads of State.*

MOHAMMED KHAN JUNEJO (Prime Minister, March 24, 1985–May 29, 1988). Mohammed Khan Junejo was born in Sindhri on August 18, 1932. He was educated in

Pakistan and Great Britain. In 1962 he was elected to the West Pakistan Provincial Assembly. Junejo served as minister for railways from 1978 until 1979. He was selected as prime minister following elections in 1985. He took office on March 24, 1985. Junejo opposed General Mohammed Zia ul-Haq on several important issues and was dismissed by President Zia for "incompetence, corruption, and lack of attention to the Muslim faith" on May 29, 1988. He was appointed ambassador to Bahrain in 1989 and served until 1991. Junejo suffered from poor health, reportedly leukemia, and entered Johns Hopkins Hospital in Baltimore, Maryland, in early 1993. He died there at the age of 61 on March 17, 1993.

MOHAMMED ZIA UL-HAQ (Prime Minister, June 9, 1988–August 17, 1988). *See entry under Heads of State.*

BENAZIR BHUTTO (Prime Minister, December 2, 1988–August 6, 1990). Benazir Bhutto was born on June 21, 1953. She was the daughter of Pakistani leader Zulfikar Ali Bhutto. She was educated in the United States and Great Britain. Bhutto became a leader of her father's political organization, the Pakistan People's party, following his execution in April of 1979. She was placed under house arrest by the government of Mohammed Zia ul-Haq from 1977 until 1984. Following her release, she went into exile in London, where she founded the Movement for the Restoration of Democracy in Pakistan. Bhutto returned to Pakistan in 1986 and ran in the parliamentary elections in 1988 as leader of the Pakistan People's party. The party was victorious and she was named prime minister on December 2, 1988. Bhutto was charged with corruption, nepotism, and abuse of power, however. She was dismissed by President Ghulam Ishaq Khan on August 6, 1990. Bhutto's husband was arrested in October of 1990 on charges of kidnapping a critic of her government. Bhutto's party was defeated in elections later in the month. She remained a leader of the Opposition.

GHULAM MUSTAFA JATOI (Prime Minister, August 6, 1990–November 6, 1990). Ghulam Mustafa Jatoi was born in Sind Province. He was a founding member of the People's party and an aide to Prime Minister Zulfikar Ali Bhutto. He served as minister of communications in his cabinet. Jatoi was arrested in 1977 following the ouster of Bhutto. Following his release, he was an outspoken opponent of the military government of Mohammed Zia ul-Haq. He was elected to the National Assembly in 1988 and served as leader of the Opposition. He was asked to form a government as caretaker prime minister following the dismissal of Benazir Bhutto on August 6, 1990. He retained office until a successor was chosen by election on November 6, 1990.

NAWAZ SHARIF (Prime Minister, November 6, 1990–April 18, 1993). Mian Mohammad Nawaz Sharif was born in 1949. He served as Punjab's provincial minister of finance in 1981. He was president of the Islamic Democratic Alliance and was chief minister of the Punjab from 1985 until 1990. During this period he became an opponent of Benazir Bhutto over distribution of government funds to the Punjab. He subsequently served as parliamentary leader of the Pakistan Muslim League. Sharif's Islamic Democratic Alliance defeated the ruling party in elections in October of 1990, and he was named prime minister on November 6, 1990. Sharif clashed often with President Ghulam Ishaq Khan and introduced legislation to weaken the powers of the presidency. Khan dissolved the Parliament and fired Sharif on April 18, 1993.

Panama, Republic of

(República de Panamá)

Panama is a country in southern Central America. It was granted independence from Colombia on November 3, 1903.

HEADS OF STATE

RICARDO DE LA GUARDIA (President, October 9, 1941–June 15, 1945). Ricardo Adolfo de la Guardia was born in Panama City on March 14, 1899. He was educated locally and entered government service in 1919. He returned to private business in 1930. De la Guardia was appointed governor of the Province of Panama by President Juan Demóstenes Arosemena in 1936. He again left the government in 1938 to become superintendent of the Santo Tomas Hospital. He returned to the government to serve as minister of justice in the cabinet of President Arnulfo Arias in October of 1940. Arias was ousted from office when he left the country without the permission of the cabinet on October 9, 1941. Vice President Ernest Jaen Guardia served as interim president before de la Guardia was elected president by the new cabinet later in the day. De la Guardia eliminated pro-Nazi members of the government and established closer relations with the United States. He also banned gambling in Panama and established price ceilings on food products. He also instituted other social reforms in the country. De la Guardia suspended the constitution in 1945 to remain in office, despite calls for his resignation. The Panamanian Congress ousted him on June 15, 1945, and replaced him with Enrique Adolfo Jiménez. De la Guardia remained active in Panamanian politics. He was arrested in 1951 following the return to power of Arnulfo Arias on charges of insulting the president. He was beaten and briefly imprisoned, though his sentence was later dismissed. De la Guardia died in Panama City after a long illness at the age of 72 on December 29, 1969.

ENRIQUE ADOLFO JIMÉNEZ (President, June 15, 1945–October 1, 1948). Enrique Adolfo Jiménez was born in 1888. He was a prominent Panamanian politician who had served as president of the National Assembly, minister of finance, ambassador to the United States, and vice president on two occasions. He was elected provisional president by Panama's Constitutional Congress on June 15, 1945, following the ouster of Ricardo de la Guardia. Jiménez presided over elections held in 1948. Domingo Díaz Arosemena was declared the victor over Arnulfo Arias, although Arias received a majority of the votes. Arias's supporters protested against the results, and Jiménez declared a state of siege in July of 1948. The National Assembly voted to dismiss Jiménez on July 12, 1948. He defied the ouster and remained in office with the support of Colonel José Remón, the National Police chief. Jiménez relinquished office to Díaz Arosemena on October 1, 1948.

DOMINGO DÍAZ AROSEMENA (President, October 1, 1948–July 28, 1949). Domingo Díaz Arosemena was born in Panama City on January 25, 1875. He was educated at Seton Hall College in New Jersey in the United States. He returned to Panama and fought with the Liberals in the revolution in 1900. Díaz Arosemena subsequently managed his family's business interests and became one of the nation's wealthiest citizens. He founded the Doctrinal Liberal party in 1931 and was elected president of the National Assembly the following year. He briefly served as acting president in October of 1933 while President Harmodio Arias was out of the country. Díaz Arosemena was an unsuccessful candidate for president in 1936. He remained leader of the Liberal party and was again a candidate for president in 1948. He defeated former president Arnulfo Arias in a bitter campaign and took office on October 1, 1948. Díaz Arosemena maintained close relations with the United States. He suffered a heart attack in July of 1949 and relinquished office to his vice president on July 28, 1949. He died in Panama City several weeks later at the age of 74 on August 23, 1949.

DANIEL CHANIS PINZÓN (President, July 28, 1949–November 20, 1949). Daniel Chanis Pinzón was born in 1892. He was educated at the University of Edinburgh in Scotland, where he received a degree in medicine in 1917. After his return to Panama, he served in the Ministry of Labor and Public Works. Chanis later served as minister of finance and was first vice president in the government of President Domingo Díaz Arosemena. Chanis succeeded to the presidency on July 28, 1949, when Díaz Arosemena stepped down due to ill health. Chanis lifted the state of siege imposed by his predecessor and sought to end the monopolies controlled by the national police. This policy brought him into conflict with Colonel José Antonio Remón, the commander of the National Police. Remón forced Chanis's resignation on November 20, 1949. Chanis rescinded his resignation on November 24, 1949, claiming it had been given under duress. He was ousted by Colonel Remón later in the day.

Chanis subsequently went into exile. He later returned to Panama, but he remained out of politics. He died in Panama City after a long illness at the age of 69 on November 2, 1961.

ROBERTO F. CHIARI (President, November 20, 1949–November 25, 1949). Roberto Francisco Chiari was born in Panama City on March 2, 1905. He was the son of Rodolfo Chiari, who served as Panama's president from 1924 until 1928. The younger Chiari was educated locally and entered politics. He was elected to the National Assembly and served in several governments. He served as second vice president under President Domingo Díaz Arosemena. Daniel Chanis became president when Díaz Arosemena relinquished office in July of 1949. Colonel José Antonio Remón, the commander of the National Police, forced Chanis's resignation on November 20, 1949, and Chiari succeeded to the presidency. He remained president until November 25, 1949, when former President Arnulfo Arias was returned to office. Chiari was the candidate of the National Patriotic Coalition in the presidential elections in 1952. He was defeated by Colonel Remon. Chiari again ran for the presidency in 1960. He defeated Ricardo M. Arias Esponisa and took office on October 1, 1960. He negotiated a new agreement with the United States concerning the Canal Zone that allowed the Panamanian flag to fly in appropriate places in the zone. Riots took place in the Canal Zone in January of 1964 when American students attempted to remove Panama's flag from the area. The subsequent violence resulted in a temporary break in diplomatic relations with the United States. Chiari completed his term of office and relinquished the presidency to his cousin, Marco Robles, on October 1, 1964.

ARNULFO ARIAS (President, November 25, 1949–May 10, 1951). Arnulfo Arias Madrid was born in Penonome on August 15, 1901. He was educated in the United States and received a degree in medicine from Harvard University in 1924. He subsequently worked at Boston City Hospital before returning to Panama in 1925. Arias continued to practice medicine and also became involved in politics. He was a leader of the coup that ousted President Florencio Harmodio Arosemena in January of 1931 and installed Ricardo J. Alfaro as president. Arias was shot in an assassination attempt later in the year, but recovered from his injuries. He was appointed to direct the Department of Health and implemented numerous reforms in Panama's public welfare system. He was instrumental in the election of his brother, Harmodio Arias, to the presidency in 1932. Arnulfo Arias served in his brother's government as secretary of agriculture and public works until August of 1934, when he was sent to Italy as an envoy. He returned to Panama the following year to form the National Revolutionary party. The government banned all opposition parties and secured the election of Juan Demóstenes Arosemena as president in 1936. Arias returned to Italy as ambassador. He also represented Panama in France and Sweden and served as a delegate to the League of Nations. He returned to Panama near the start of World War II in 1939. Arias was a victorious candidate for the presidency in 1940 and took office on October 1, 1940. He instituted Panama's social security system and promoted a new constitution in January of 1941. The constitution granted women the right to vote and extended the term of the president from four to six years. Arias's government was accused of supporting the Axis powers during the war, and Arias was ousted in a coup when he left the country on October 9, 1941. He remained in exile until 1945, but was again a candidate for president in 1948. He received a slight majority of the popular vote, but his opponent was declared the

victor. A military coup the following year resulted in the election results being reversed, and Arias was again installed as president on November 25, 1949. He ruled in a dictatorial fashion, dissolving the National Assembly and ruling by decree. He was ousted in a coup led by the National Guard on May 10, 1951. Arias was stripped of his political rights until 1960. He was an unsuccessful candidate for the presidency in 1964, but was again victorious in 1968. He took office on October 1, 1968, but was ousted by a military coup eleven days later on October 12, 1968. Arias went into exile in Miami, Florida, where he was a vocal critic of the military regime of Brig. Gen. Omar Torrijos. He returned to Panama in June of 1978 and was the candidate for the Authentic Panamanian party in the presidential election in 1984. He was defeated, though his supporters accused the government of electoral fraud. Arias went back into exile in Miami, where he remained a critic of the government of Panamanian strongman General Manuel Noriega. Arias died of a heart attack at his home in Miami at the age of 87 on August 10, 1988.

ALCIBIADES AROSEMENA (President, May 10, 1951–October 1, 1952). Alcibiades Arosemena was born in Los Santos on November 20, 1883. He was educated locally and left school to fight with the Liberals in the Panamanian Civil War in 1900. He went into farming following Panama's independence in 1903. Arosemena became a member of Arnulfo Arias's National Revolutionary party and served in the municipal government in Panama City. He was a candidate for first vice president on a ticket with Arias in elections in 1948. Domingo Díaz Arosemena was declared the winner in the election, but the results were overturned the following year. Arias and Arosemena were sworn into office on November 25, 1949. Arosemena also served in the government as minister of finance. He broke with Arias over the president's economic policies in March of 1951. He was subsequently appointed Panama's minister to Spain, but refused to accept the appointment. Arias was ousted on May 10, 1951, and Arosemena was sworn into office to complete his unexpired term. He remained president until October 1, 1952, when he relinquished office to José Antonio Remón. Arosemena was subsequently appointed ambassador to France. He died of a heart attack in Panama City at the age of 75 on April 8, 1958.

JOSÉ ANTONIO REMÓN CANTERA (President, October 1, 1952–January 2, 1955). José Antonio Remón Cantera was born on July 1, 1908. He was educated at the military academy in Mexico and joined the Panamanian National Police in 1932. He was promoted to deputy chief of police in the early 1940s and rose to first commandant of the police in 1947. Remón led the military coup that ousted interim president Daniel Chanis in 1949 and restored Arnulfo Arias to the presidency. He continued to support Arias until 1951, when he broke with the president over a constitutional question. He joined with the opposition to remove Arias from office in May of 1951. Remón retired as chief of police later in the year to become a candidate for the presidency. He defeated Roberto Chiari in May of 1952 and took office on October 1, 1952. Remón's administration was noted for its seeming lack of corruption and its sound fiscal policies. He also attempted to diversify Panama's economy to eliminate dependence on the Canal Zone for revenue. Remón remained president until January 2, 1955, when he was shot and killed at a Panama City racetrack by assassins wielding machine guns.

JOSÉ RAMÓN GUIZADO (President, January 3, 1955–January 15, 1955). José Ramón Guizado was born

in 1899. He was a successful construction engineer in Panama when he entered politics. He was chosen first vice president and minister of foreign affairs in the government of President José Antonio Remón. Guizado succeeded to the presidency when Remón was assassinated on January 2, 1955. Guizado was removed from office by the National Assembly on January 15, 1955, when he was implicated in the assassination of Remón. On March 29, 1955, Guizado was convicted of being an accomplice in Remón's murder. He served two years of a six-year prison term before being exonerated on all charges. Guizado died of a heart attack at a hotel in Miami Beach, Florida, at the age of 65 on January 22, 1964.

RICARDO M. ARIAS ESPONISA (President, January 15, 1955–October 1, 1956). Ricardo M. Arias Esponisa was born in the Panamanian Embassy in Washington, D.C., in 1912. He was educated in the United States and Chile. He was appointed minister of agriculture, commerce, and industries in 1949 and served until 1951. He was subsequently elected second vice president of Panama in the government of President José A. Remón. He also served as minister of labor and social welfare. Arias became president on January 15, 1955, following the assassination of President Remón and the subsequent resignation of his successor, José Ramón Guizado. Arias retained office until the next election and relinquished the presidency on October 1, 1956. He was defeated for the presidency in the elections of 1960. Arias served as ambassador to the United States from 1964 until 1968. He died in Panama City at the age of 80 on March 15, 1993.

ERNESTO DE LA GUARDIA, JR. (President, October 1, 1956–October 1, 1960). Ernesto de la Guardia, Jr., was born in Panama City on May 30, 1904. He was educated in Panama and at

Dartmouth College in New Hampshire, in the United States. He graduated in 1925. De la Guardia entered the Panamanian diplomatic service and served as consul general in San Francisco from 1925 until 1928. He returned to Panama in 1928 to serve as chief of the diplomat corps. He was named undersecretary for foreign affairs in 1931. De la Guardia left the government in 1939 to enter private business. He was a member of the Popular Front party and briefly served as first vice president in 1945. He became president of the New Reform party the following year. De la Guardia was chairman of the National Electoral Jury in 1952. He was the candidate of the National Patriotic Coalition in the presidential election in 1956. He defeated Victor Florencio Goytia and took office on October 1, 1956. In April of 1959 Roberto Arias and his wife, British ballerina Dame Margot Fonteyn, organized a rebellion with members of the Cuban militia to oust de la Guardia's government. Troops loyal to the government put down the rebellion, however. Relations between Panama and the United States were strained in November of 1959 when anti–American demonstrations and riots took place, protesting the continued presence of the United States in the Canal Zone. De la Guardia completed his term of office on October 1, 1960, and subsequently retired from politics. He died in Panama City at the age of 79 on May 2, 1983.

ROBERTO F. CHIARI (President, October 1, 1960–October 1, 1964). *See earlier entry under Heads of State.*

MARCO A. ROBLES (President, October 1, 1964–October 1, 1968). Marco Aurelio Robles Méndez was born in Aguadulce on November 8, 1905. He attended the University of Panama and the University of Paris. He subsequently served on the

Panamanian Embassy staff in Paris and London during the late 1920s. Robles returned to Panama in 1931 and joined the Liberal party. He was inactive in politics following the coup that installed the Arias family to power in 1932. He supported the ouster of Arnulfo Arias in 1951 and subsequently served as a deputy in the National Assembly. Robles was named minister of government and justice in the cabinet of his cousin, Roberto F. Chiari, in 1960. Robles was the candidate of the government coalition in 1964 and campaigned to renegotiate the Panama Canal Treaty with the United States. He defeated former President Arnulfo Arias and took office on October 1, 1964. He acted to prevent renewed rioting in the Canal Zone by calling out the National Guard to prevent an anti–American mob from entering the area in January of 1965. Robles reached an agreement with United States president Lyndon Johnson in September of 1965, and three treaties granting Panama more control over the Canal Zone were drafted in June of 1967. Robles was unsuccessful in convincing the National Assembly to ratify the treaties, however. He supported the candidacy of David Samudio in the presidential election in 1968. The National Assembly accused him of using his influence as president to affect the outcome and voted for his impeachment on March 15, 1968. Max Delvalle, the first vice president, was proclaimed president, but Robles refused to vacate the office. He was supported by the National Guard, and the Panamanian Supreme Court ruled in early April of 1968 that his impeachment was invalid. Samudio was subsequently defeated by Arnulfo Arias, and Robles stepped down from office on October 1, 1968. He went into voluntary exile in Florida and remained in the United States during the military regimes of Omar Torrijos and Manuel Noriega. He died at his home in Miami at the age of 84 after a long illness on April 14, 1990.

ARNULFO ARIAS (President, October 1, 1968–October 12, 1968). *See earlier entry under Heads of State.*

JOSE M. PINILLA (President, October 12, 1968–December 18, 1969). José María Pinilla Fábrega was born in Ciudad de Panama on March 28, 1919. He joined the National Guard in December of 1941. He rose to the rank of colonel and was second in command to Colonel Omar Torrijos when the military ousted President Arnulfo Arias in October of 1968. Pinilla was named provisional president by the ruling military junta on October 12, 1968. He served primarily as a figurehead in the government, with Torrijos retaining most of the executive power. Pinilla was suspected of involvement in a coup attempt against Torrijos on December 16, 1969. He was deposed as president two days later. He was subsequently inactive in political affairs. Pinilla died of a heart attack at the age of 60 at his home in Panama City on August 10, 1979.

DEMETRIO LAKAS BAHAS (President, December 18, 1969–October 11, 1978). Demetrio Basilio Lakas Bahas was born in Colon on August 29, 1925. He was educated at Texas Technical College in the United States. He returned to Panama and entered the civil service. Lakas Bahas rose to the position of director of the Social Security Department. He was selected as provisional president on December 18, 1969, and was reelected to a six-year term in September of 1972. He completed his term and relinquished the office on October 11, 1978.

ARÍSTIDES ROYO SANCHEZ (President, October 11, 1978–July 31, 1982). Arístides Royo Sanchez was born in La Chorrera on August 14, 1928. He was educated in Panama and received a degree in law. He served as minister of education from 1973 until 1978. He was selected as president of Panama by General Omar Torrijos and took office on October 11, 1978, but resigned under pressure from the National Guard on July 31, 1982. He subsequently was named ambassador to Spain, where he served until 1985.

RICARDO DE LA ESPRIELLA (President, July 31, 1982–February 13, 1984). Ricardo de la Espriella served as vice president under Arístides Royo. He succeeded to the presidency when Royo was forced to resign by the National Guard on July 31, 1982. De la Espriella abruptly resigned from office on February 13, 1984, and was succeeded by vice president Jorge Illueca.

JORGE ILLUECA (President, February 13, 1984–October 11, 1984). Jorge E. Illueca was born in Panama City on December 17, 1918. He was educated in Panama and the United States and received a law degree. He was a member of the Panamanian delegation to the United Nations in 1957 and was permanent representative in 1960. Illueca served as a special ambassador to the United States in charge of negotiating a new Panama Canal treaty in 1964 and led the negotiating team again in 1972. He served as a member of the Permanent Court of Arbitration in The Hague, the Netherlands, from 1974 until 1976. Illueca again served as Panama's permanent representative to the United Nations from 1976 until 1981. He was selected as provisional vice president of Panama in July of 1982. He assumed the presidency following the resignation of Ricardo de la Espriella on February 13, 1984. Illueca retained the office through the elections and then stepped down on October 11, 1984. Illueca also served as president of the United Nations General Assembly from 1984 until 1985.

NICOLÁS ARDITO BARLETTA (President, October 11, 1984–September 28, 1985). Nicolás Ardito Barletta Vallarina was born in Aguadulce on August 21, 1938. He was educated in the United

States at North Carolina State University, where he received a degree in agricultural engineering. He returned to Panama to teach economics and was named director of planning in the government in 1968. Barletta then worked with the Organization of American States as director of economic affairs from 1970 until 1973. He served as minister of planning from 1973 until 1978. He served as a negotiator of the Panama Canal Treaties in 1976 and 1977 and concentrated on their economic impact. In 1978 Barletta was selected as vice president of the World Bank for Latin America. He was the government's candidate for president in the election held in May of 1984 and narrowly defeated former president Arnulfo Arias. Barletta took office on October 11, 1984. He was forced to initiate austerity measures to aid Panama's economic situation, but the measures were not popular with the National Guard. Barletta further antagonized General Manuel Noriega by insisting upon an investigation into the murder of government critic Dr. Hugo Spadafora. Noriega forced Barletta's resignation on September 25, 1985.

ERIC ARTURO DELVALLE (President, September 28, 1985–February 26, 1988). Eric Arturo Delvalle Henríquez was born in Panama on February 2, 1937. He was educated in Panama and the United States and subsequently worked in private enterprises. He was elected to the National Assembly, where he served as vice president in 1968. Delvalle was elected leader of the Republican party and became vice president of Panama in 1984. He assumed the presidency after President Nicolás Ardito Barletta was forced to resign on September 28, 1985. Following the indictment of General Manuel Noriega on charges of drug trafficking and racketeering, Delvalle called for his resignation. When Noriega did not reply, Delvalle dismissed the general on February 25, 1988. The following day the National Assembly, at the direction of General Noriega, ousted Delvalle as president and installed Manuel Solis Palma as his successor. Delvalle was placed under house arrest, but he subsequently escaped and went into hiding. He remained an opponent of Noriega's dictatorship until United States troops forced the general's ouster in December of 1989.

MANUEL SOLIS PALMA (President, February 26, 1988–September 1, 1989). Manuel Solis Palma was minister of education from 1984 until 1988. He subsequently served as first vice president. Solis Palma was selected to succeed Eric Arturo Delvalle as president following Delvalle's ouster on February 26, 1988. Solis Palma retained the office until September 1, 1989.

FRANCISCO RODRIGUEZ (President, September 1, 1989–December 20, 1989). Francisco Rodriguez was born in 1938. He served in the government as comptroller general of the treasury. He was a close associate of General Manuel Noriega and was chosen as president by the Council of State after elections of the previous May were annulled. Rodriguez took office on September 1, 1989. The United States invaded Panama on December 20, 1989, and ousted Noriega's regime. Guillermo Endara, who had previously been declared the winner in the presidential election, was allowed to take office on December 21, 1989.

GUILLERMO ENDARA GALIMANY (President, December 21, 1989–). Guillermo Endara Galimany was a prominent Panamanian labor lawyer. He had served as an aide to former president Arnulfo Arias. Endara was the leader of the Antimilitarist Opposition Democratic Alliance and was the party's candidate for president in May of 1989. He defeated the government's nominee, Carlos Duque Jaén, but the military regime of General Manuel Noriega annulled the elections. Endara was installed as president on December 21, 1989, following the United States invasion of Panama and the ouster of Noreiga's regime.

OTHER LEADERS

OMAR TORRIJOS HERRERA (National Guard Commander, October 12, 1968–July 31, 1981). Omar Torrijos Herrera was born in Santiago on February 13, 1929. He attended military schools and entered the National Guard as a second lieutenant in 1952. He served in various military positions and rose to the rank of lieutenant colonel in 1966. Torrijos and Major Boris Martínez led the military coup that ousted President Arnulfo Arias from office on October 12, 1968. The junta installed Colonel José M. Pinilla as president, and Torrijos became commander of the National Guard. The junta dissolved the National Assembly and banned all political parties. Torrijos consolidated his power and sent his rival, Colonel Martínez, into exile in March of 1969. He also promoted himself to the rank of brigadier general. Torrijos survived a rightist coup attempt in December of 1969. He dismissed President Pinilla, who supported the coup, and installed Demetrio Basilio Lakas as president. Torrijos initiated a series of land reform measures. He also demanded that the Panama Canal Treaty with the United States be renegotiated. He promoted a new constitution in August of 1972 that established the National Guard as an official governing body. He was granted full civil and military powers in a referendum on September 12, 1972, and became chief of government and supreme leader of the Panamanian Revolution. Torrijos succeeded in negotiating a treaty with the United States in 1977 that provided for the restoration of the Canal Zone to Panama's control at the turn of the century. Torrijos installed Arístides Royo as president in October of 1978 and relinquished political authority to the new government. He remained commander in chief of the National Guard. Torrijos was killed when the Panamanian air force plane he was a passenger in crashed over western Panama on July 31, 1981. Allegations surfaced in the late 1980s that the crash was an act of sabotage instigated by Manuel Noriega.

FLORENCIO FLORÉZ AGUILAR (National Guard Commander, July 31, 1981–February 1982). Florencio Floréz Aguilar was born in 1931. He was a colonel in the Panamanian National Guard when he was selected to succeed Omar Torrijos Herrera as commander after his death on July 31, 1981. He was not granted the full powers that were exercised by Torrijos, as his powers were limited by the general staff of the National Guard. Colonel Floréz retired in February of 1982 after a series of conflicts between the National Guard and the president.

RUBÉN DARÍO PAREDES DEL RÍO (National Guard Commander, February 1982–August 1983). Rubén Darío Paredes del Río was born in 1931. He was educated at the military academy in Nicaragua and rose through the ranks to colonel. He served as minister of agricultural development from 1975 until 1978. Paredes became commander of the National Guard in February of 1982 and was promoted to general. He resigned in August of 1983 over a dispute concerning the government's attitude towards United States involvement in Nicaragua. He was an unsuccessful candidate for president of Panama in 1984. Paredes emerged from retirement in July of 1987 to call for the resignation of General Manuel Noriega.

MANUEL A. NORIEGA (National Guard Commander, August 1983– December 20, 1989). Manuel Antonio Noriega Morena was born in Panama City on February 11, 1940. He attended military school in Lima, Peru, and entered the Panamanian National Guard. He rose to the rank of first lieutenant in 1968 and was active in the military coup that ousted President Arnulfo Arias in October of 1968. Noriega supported National Guard commander Omar Torrijos against a right-wing military coup in December of 1969. He was promoted to lieutenant colonel and named chief of military intelligence. Torrijos was killed in a plane crash in 1981, and Noriega became the chief of staff of General Rubén Darío Paredes, who became National Guard Commander in February of 1982. Noriega succeeded Paredes in August of 1983. The National Guard was combined with other branches of the military to form the National Defense Force later in the year. Noriega orchestrated the election of Nicolás Ardito Barletta as president in October of 1984. Dr. Hugo Spadafora, the former minister of health, accused Noriega of being involved in drug trafficking in 1984. Spadafora was kidnapped by intelligence officers. He was tortured and mutilated, and his decapitated body was found crammed in a United States mail bag inside the Costa Rican border in September of 1985. Noriega forced the resignation of President Barletta later in the month when the president insisted on an investigation into Spadafora's murder. The United States government protested the ouster of Barletta and slashed economic aid to the country. Noriega was accused in June of 1987 of having ordered Spadafora's murder and also of having been involved in the plane crash that killed General Torrijos. Noriega declared a state of emergency to put down subsequent demonstrations demanding his resignation. The United States government also called upon Noriega to resign and asked that the charges against him be investigated. Noriega allowed a mob of supporters to attack the United States Embassy in Panama on June 26, 1987. Relations between the United States and Panama deteriorated, and the United States withdrew all military and financial aid to the country. Noriega was indicted on charges of drug trafficking by a United States federal grand jury in February of 1988. President Eric Delvalle attempted to dismiss Noriega from his position, but Noriega orchestrated Delvalle's ouster by the National Assembly. He survived a coup attempt led by Major Moisés Giroldi Vega in October of 1989. Giroldi and a number of his supporters were captured and executed. Noriega was granted executive power on December 15, 1989, and declared that Panama was in a state of war with the United States. President George Bush responded by sending an invasion force to Panama on December 20, 1989. Noriega took refuge in the Vatican Embassy, where he remained until January 3, 1990. He was subsequently seized and taken to the United States. He was held in a high security prison to await trial. Noriega was tried and convicted on drug and racketeering charges on July 10, 1992, and was sentenced to forty years in prison.

Papua New Guinea, Independent State of

(Gau Hedinarai ai Papua-Matamata Guinea)

Papua New Guinea is a country on the eastern portion of the island of New Guinea and numerous other islands southeast of

Asia. *It was granted independence from a United Nations trusteeship administered by Australia on September 16, 1975.*

HEADS OF STATE

SIR JOHN GUISE (Governor-General, September 16, 1975–February 8, 1977). John Guise was born on Papua on August 29, 1914. He served in the Department of Native Affairs during the 1950s and was a member of the East Papua Legislative Council from 1961 until 1963. He was elected to the House of Assembly in 1964 and served as Speaker and minister of the interior. Guise became the first governor-general of Papua New Guinea after it was granted independence from Australia on September 16, 1975. He was the leader of the National Alliance party and resigned as governor-general on February 8, 1977, to run unsuccessfully against Michael Somare for the office of prime minister. Guise died on February 7, 1991.

SIR TORE LOKOLOKO (Governor-General, February 18, 1977–March 1, 1983). Tore Lokoloko was born in Iokea on September 21, 1919. He was the son of Paramount Chief Lokoloko Tore. He served as a member of the House of Assembly from 1968 and also served as minister of health from 1968 until 1972. Lokoloko was selected to replace Sir John Guise as governor-general on February 18, 1977. He retained the position until March 1, 1983. Lokoloko subsequently became chairman of the Indosuez Niugine Bank until 1989.

SIR KINGSFORD DIBELA (Governor-General, March 1, 1983–February 27, 1990). Kingsford Dibela was born on March 16, 1932. He was employed as a primary school teacher from 1949 until his election as president of the Weraura Local Government Council in 1963. He was elected to Parliament in 1975 and served as Speaker from 1977 until 1980.

Dibela was named governor-general on March 1, 1983. He resigned from office on February 27, 1990.

SIR SEREI ERI (Governor-General, February 27, 1990–October 1, 1991). Vincent Serei Eri was born on September 12, 1936. He attended the University of Papua New Guinea. He worked as a school teacher and was later employed in the civil service. Eri was a founder of the People's Action party in 1986. He succeeded Sir Kingsford Dibela as governor-general on February 27, 1990. He was faced with a constitutional crisis when Deputy Prime Minister Ted Diro was found guilty of corruption. According to the constitution, the governor-general was obligated to dismiss him. Eri refused to leave office, and Prime Minister Rabbie Namaliu requested that Queen Elizabeth II replace him. Eri resigned his office on October 4, 1991, before the request was acted upon, however. He died at his home in Port Moresby at the age of 57 on May 25, 1993.

DENNIS YOUNG (Acting Governor-General, October 1, 1991–November 18, 1991). Dennis Young was Speaker of the Assembly when Sir Vincent Serei Eri resigned as governor-general on October 1, 1991. Young served as acting governor-general until the selection of Sir Wiwa Korowi as governor-general on November 18, 1991.

SIR WIWA KOROWI (Governor-General, November 18, 1991–). Wiwa Korowi was born in 1948. He was a member of the National party and was elected by Parliament to replace Sir Serei Eri as governor-general on November 18, 1991.

HEADS OF GOVERNMENT

SIR MICHAEL T. SOMARE (Prime Minister, September 16, 1975–March 11, 1980). Michael Thomas Somare was born on April 9, 1936. He was educated locally and became a teacher. He was elected to the Parliament in 1968 and served as leader of the Pangu party. He served as chief minister of Papua New Guinea from 1972, and following Papua New Guinea's independence, he became prime minister on September 16, 1975. He retained the office until March 11, 1980, when he resigned following a no confidence vote in Parliament. Somare was returned to office on August 2, 1982, when the Pangu party was victorious in parliamentary elections. A dispute over Somare's economic policies led to another vote of no confidence, and he again left office on November 21, 1985. Somare retired from leadership of the Pangu party in 1988 and was named foreign minister in the government of Rabbie Namaliu.

SIR JULIUS CHAN (Prime Minister, March 11, 1980–August 2, 1982). Julius Chan was born in Tanga, on New Ireland, on August 29, 1939. He was educated in Australia and was elected to the House of Assembly in 1968. He became parliamentary leader of the People's Progress party in 1970 and served as minister of finance from 1972 until 1977. Chan served as deputy prime minister and minister for primary industry from 1977 until 1978. He was elected to succeed Michael Somare as prime minister on March 11, 1980. Chan retained the position until August 2, 1982, when Somare was returned to office. He subsequently returned to Parliament and served as deputy prime minister and minister of trade and industry from 1986 until 1988.

SIR MICHAEL T. SOMARE (Prime Minister, August 2, 1982–November 21, 1985). *See earlier entry under Heads of Government.*

PAIAS WINGTI (Prime Minister, November 21, 1985–July 4, 1988). Paias Wingti was born in 1951. He was educated at the University of Port Moresby. He was elected a member of Parliament and served as minister of transport and minister of planning in the government of Michael Somare. Wingti founded the People's Democratic Movement in March of 1985. On November 21, 1985, he was elected prime minister. He remained in office until July 4, 1988, when he resigned after a vote of no confidence in Parliament. Wingti was returned to office on July 17, 1992, following elections the previous month.

RABBIE NAMALIU (Prime Minister, July 4, 1988–July 17, 1992). Rabbie Langanai Namaliu was born in Raluana in the East New Britain Province on April 3, 1947. He was educated in Papua New Guinea, Australia, and the United States. He was subsequently employed by the University of Papua New Guinea. Namaliu was elected to Parliament in 1982 and served as minister of foreign affairs and trade from 1982 until 1984. He then served as minister for primary industry until 1985. He was a close advisor to Michael Somare and succeeded him as leader of the Pangu party in June of 1988. Namaliu became prime minister on July 4, 1988, and served until July 17, 1992.

PAIAS WINGTI (Prime Minister, July 17, 1992–). *See earlier entry under Heads of Government.*

Paraguay, Republic of

(República del Paraguay)

Paraguay is a country in central South America. It was granted independence from Spain on May 14, 1811.

HEADS OF STATE

HIGINIO MORÍÑIGO (President, September 7, 1940–June 3, 1948). Higinio Moríñigo was born in Paraguari on January 11, 1897. He attended military college and entered the army in 1922. He saw action during the Chaco War against Bolivia from 1932 until 1935. Moríñigo was promoted to general and named to the cabinet of General José Félix Estigarribia as minister of war in May of 1940. When President Estigarribia was killed in an airplane crash on September 7, 1940, General Moríñigo was chosen as interim president by the cabinet. Moríñigo proclaimed a dictatorship on November 30, 1940, and dissolved all opposition parties. He was elected to the presidency unopposed in February of 1943. He led Paraguay during World War II and promoted a policy of neutrality. Moríñigo led a primarily military government until June of 1946. He then dismissed Colonel Benitez Vera, the rightist leader of the army. He crushed a brief revolt by Vera's supporters and appointed a civilian cabinet from members of the Colorado and Febrerista parties. The leftist Febrerista party resigned from the government and went into revolt against Moríñigo in January of 1947. The rebellion was led by former president Rafael Franco, who established a rebel government in northern Paraguay. The rebellion was crushed by the loyalist military in August of 1947. Moríñigo proceeded to hold national elections in February of 1948 and supported the candidacy of Juan Natalicio González. González

was elected unopposed, and his supporters, who feared that Moríñigo might retain power, forced the president's resignation on June 3, 1948. He went into exile in Argentina. Moríñigo reentered Paraguay briefly in 1956 and then returned to Argentina. He remained politically inactive and reportedly died in 1985.

JUAN MANUEL FRUTOS (President, June 3, 1948–August 15, 1948). Juan Manuel Frutos was a lawyer and jurist who served as president of the Paraguayan Supreme Court. He was appointed by Congress as interim president following the resignation of President Higinio Moríñigo on June 3, 1948. He stepped down on August 14, 1948, to allow the inauguration of President-Elect Juan Natalicio González and returned to the Supreme Court.

JUAN NATALICIO GONZÁLEZ (President, August 15, 1948–January 30, 1949). Juan Natalicio González was born in Villarrica on September 8, 1897. He joined the Colorado party in 1914 and became the editor of the party newspaper. He was elected to the Chamber of Deputies in 1926. González went into exile in 1931 and became a noted economist and poet. He returned to Paraguay in 1945 and was named minister to Uruguay later in the year. He served in the cabinet of General Higinio Moríñigo as minister of finance from July of 1946. González was the candidate of the Guion faction of the Colorado party in presidential elections in February of 1948. He was elected unopposed in balloting that was largely controlled by the army. President Moríñigo was ousted from office to insure González's inauguration. González took office on August 15, 1948. He declared an amnesty for political refugees and retained the support of the army during a brief revolt in October of 1948. González was ousted by a leftist military coup led by General Raimundo Rolón on January 30, 1949. He returned to the government during the administration of General Alfredo Stroessner and was named Paraguay's ambassador to Mexico in 1956. He retained that position until his retirement in 1965. González remained in Mexico City, where he died of a heart attack at the age of 64 on December 6, 1966.

RAIMUNDO ROLÓN (President, January 30, 1949–February 26, 1949). Raimundo Rolón was born in 1903. He served in the Paraguayan army, where he rose to the rank of general. He was a supporter of leftist former president Rafael Franco and led the military coup that ousted President Juan Natalicio González on January 30, 1949. Rolón was removed from office in a coup led by the Colorado party on February 26, 1949.

FELIPE MOLAS LÓPEZ (President, February 26, 1949–September 10, 1949). Felipe Molas López was born in 1901. He worked as a dentist in the capital and was a member of the Guion faction of the Colorado party. He served as minister of education in the government of Juan Natalicio González. Molas López was installed as provisional president on February 26, 1949, following the ouster of General Raimundo Rolón. He was elected to the presidency unopposed in April of 1949 and was officially inaugurated as president on April 17, 1949. The Democratico faction of the Colorado party forced Molas López's resignation as president on September 10, 1949. He

died of a heart attack in Asuncion at the age of 51 on March 2, 1954.

FEDERICO CHAVEZ (President, September 11, 1949–May 6, 1954). Federico Chavez was born in 1880. He was a leader of the Democratico faction of the Colorado party during the 1940s and had served in the government as foreign minister and as Paraguay's ambassador to France and Spain. He was chosen by the governing board of the Colorado party to replace Felipe Molas López as president on September 11, 1949. Chavez instituted an economic program that included the nationalization of industries and wage and price controls. The conservative wing of the Colorado party objected to the policies of Chavez's government, and he was ousted in a bloody military rebellion led by General Alfredo Stroessner on May 6, 1954. Chavez remained politically inactive during Stroessner's regime. He died in Asuncion on April 24, 1978, at the age of 97 after a long illness.

TOMÁS ROMERO PEREIRA (President, May 6, 1954–July 11, 1954). Tomás Romero Pereira was born in 1886. He was an architect and a leader of the Colorado party. He was chosen as interim president on May 6, 1954, following the military overthrow of President Federico Chavez. Romero relinquished the presidency to the coup leader, General Alfredo Stroessner, on July 11, 1954.

ALFREDO STROESSNER (President, July 11, 1954–February 3, 1989). Alfredo Stroessner Mattiauda was born in Encarnacion on November 3, 1912. He was educated at the military college in Asuncion and subsequently joined the Paraguayan army. He rose through the ranks to general and was named commander in chief of the armed forces in 1951. Stroessner led a military coup that ousted President Federico Chavez. Stroessner subsequently won a special election on July 11, 1954, to fill the remainder of Chavez's term. Stroessner retained the presidency for over three decades. He was again reelected in February of 1988. Stroessner was ousted by General Andrés Rodríguez in a bloodless coup on February 3, 1989. He subsequently went into exile in Brazil.

ANDRÉS RODRÍGUEZ PEDOTTI (President, February 3, 1989–). Andrés Rodríguez Pedotti was born in Borja on June 19, 1924. He joined the Paraguayan Cavalry and served as commander of the Asuncion Division from 1981. He rose to the rank of general and was named leader of the First Army Corps. Rodríguez led a military coup to overthrow the government of President Alfredo Stroessner on February 3, 1989. Rodríguez was elected president in May of 1989 to complete Stroessner's term of office. A new constitution was presented in June of 1992 that included a ban on presidential reelections. Luís Maria Argaña was chosen as the ruling Colorado party's candidate for president in elections to be held in May of 1993.

Peru, Republic of

(República del Perú)

Peru is a country on the western coast of South America. It was granted independence from Spain on July 28, 1821.

HEADS OF STATE

MANUEL PRADO Y UGARTECHE (President, December 3, 1939–July 28, 1945). Manuel Prado y Ugarteche was born in Lima on April 21, 1889. He was the son of General Mariano Ignacio Prado, who served as Peru's president from 1865 until 1868 and from 1876 until 1879. The younger Prado was educated at the University of San Marcos, where he received a degree in engineering. He subsequently entered the Peruvian army and saw action in the cavalry during Peru's brief border conflict with Ecuador in 1910. Prado also continued his studies at the University of San Marcos and served on the faculty in the Department of Mathematics from 1912. He entered politics and was elected to the Chamber of Deputies in 1919. He was a leading opponent of the regime of Agusto B. Leguía and was forced into exile in Europe in 1923. Prado returned to Peru in 1932 following the ouster of Leguia. He became president of the Central Reserve Bank of Peru in 1934. Prado was chosen as the hand-picked successor of President Oscar Benavies in 1939. He was the only candidate in the subsequent election and took office on December 3, 1939. He encouraged close relations with the United States and entered Peru into World War II on the side of the Allies. Prado increased industrialization in the country and successfully negotiated a settlement to the long-standing border dispute with Ecuador in 1942. He completed his term of office on July 28, 1945, and relinquished the presidency to José Luis Bustamente y Rivero. Prado was the candidate of the National Coalition party in the presidential election in 1956 and returned to office with the support of the leftist American Popular Revolutionary Alliance (APRA). He took office on July 28, 1956. He allowed the return of Aprista leader Victor Haya de la Torre from exile in July of 1957. Prado became one of the first South American leaders to break diplomatic relations with Fidel Castro's Cuba. He maintained close relations with the United States and ended censorship restrictions on the Peruvian press. Prado was ousted in a military coup on July 19, 1962, following a presidential election that resulted in a victory for Haya de la Torre. Prado was sent into exile in Paris, where he died of a heart attack at the age of 78 on August 14, 1967.

JOSÉ LUIS BUSTAMENTE Y RIVERO (President, July 28, 1945–October, 28, 1948). José Luis Bustamente y Rivero was born in Arequipa on January 15, 1894. He was educated in Peru and received a degree in law. He was active in the revolt that ousted the dictatorship of Augusto Leguía in 1930. Bustamente served in the government as minister of education in 1931 and subsequently joined the faculty of the University of San Augustin in Arequipa as a professor of civil law. He left the university to enter the Foreign Ministry in 1934. He served as Peru's ambassador to various South American countries, including Bolivia, Paraguay, and Uruguay. Bustamente was elected president in 1945 and took office on July 28, 1945. His government was challenged by the leftist American Popular Revolutionary Alliance (APRA) which controlled a majority in the Peruvian Congress. Bustamente declared a state of emergency in October of 1948 and ruled by decree. The Aprista party attempted a left-wing revolt on October 3, 1948, but the rebellion was crushed by the army the following day. The president was subsequently ousted in a rightist coup led by his minister of war, Manuel Odría, on October 28, 1948. Bustamente returned to private life to practice law. He also became the dean of the Lima

Law College. He was appointed to the International Court of Justice in The Hague in 1961 and served as its president from 1967 until 1970. Bustamente also served as a mediator in the war between El Salvador and Honduras in 1977. He was hospitalized with heart problems in 1988 and died in a Lima hospital at the age of 94 on January 11, 1989.

ZENON NORIEGA (President, October 29, 1948–October 31, 1948). Zenon Noriega served in the Peruvian army, where he rose to the rank of general. He commanded the army in Lima and was instrumental in crushing the leftist revolt in early October of 1948. He served as provisional president following the ouster of President José Luis Bustamente y Rivero on October 29, 1948. Noriega relinquished control of the government to General Manuel Odría two days later. Noriega again became Peru's president on June 1, 1950, when Odría resigned to become a candidate in the elections. Noriega stepped down on July 28, 1950, following Odría's election to the presidency. He remained in the government as minister of war and head of the cabinet. Noriega was accused of leading an unsuccessful revolt against Odría in August of 1954. He was removed from the government and sent into exile.

MANUEL A. ODRÍA (President, October 31, 1948–June 1, 1950). Manuel Apolinario Odría Amoretti was born in Tarma on November 26, 1897. He attended the Peruvian Military School and entered the army as a second lieutenant in 1919. He served as an instructor at the school until 1927, when he continued his education at the War College. Odría graduated in 1930 and subsequently attended the navy school. He rose to the rank of colonel during a brief border war with Ecuador in 1941. Odría was appointed chief of staff of the army with the rank of brigadier general by President José Luis Bustamente y Rivero in 1946. He was also named minister of the interior and chief of police in Bustamente's government in January of 1947, following the assassination of newspaper publisher Francisco Grana Garland. The leftist Popular Revolutionary Alliance for America (APRA) controlled the Congress during Bustamente's administration. The Apristas attempted to overthrow the government in October of 1948. The army crushed the revolt and then ousted Bustamente on October 29, 1948. Odría became head of the ruling military junta several days later. The Aprista party was outlawed and its leader, Victor Raul Haya de la Torre, was forced to seek asylum in the Colombian Embassy. Odría stepped down as provisional president on June 1, 1950, to become a candidate in the presidential election the following month. He was elected unopposed following the disqualification of the candidacy of General Ernesto Montagne. Odría was sworn into office on July 28, 1950. He attempted to improve Peru's economy by encouraging foreign investment in the country. He succeeded in raising wages and instituting social reform programs, but he ruled in an authoritarian fashion and banned most opposition to the government. Aprista leader Haya de la Torre was allowed to leave the country in 1954. Odría permitted democratic elections in 1956, and Manuel Prado was elected with the support of the Apristas. Odría went into voluntary exile in the United States. He returned to Peru in March of 1961 to become a presidential candidate in a campaign that was marked by disorder and violence. In the election in June of 1962, Odría ran third behind Haya de la Torre and moderate Fernando Belaúnde Terry. The army attempted to prevent the selection of Aprista leader Haya de la Torre. Odría negotiated an agreement with Haya de la Torre which would have granted Odría the presidency with the support

of the Apristas. The army ousted the government in July of 1962 to eliminate Aprista involvement in the government. New elections were held in June of 1963, and Odría was again a candidate. He again placed third in the balloting. Odría subsequently entered into an alliance with his old enemy, Haya de la Torre, in opposition to the government of Fernando Belaúnde Terry. He remained politically active until 1968, when the military again took control of the government. Odría died of a heart attack in Lima at the age of 77 on February 18, 1974.

ZENON NORIEGA (June 1, 1950– July 28, 1950). *See earlier entry under Heads of State.*

MANUEL A. ODRÍA (President, July 28, 1950–July 28, 1956). *See earlier entry under Heads of State.*

MANUEL PRADO Y UGARTECHE (President, July 28, 1956–July 19, 1962). *See earlier entry under Heads of State.*

RICARDO PÉREZ GODOY (President, July 19, 1962–March 3, 1963). Ricardo Pérez Godoy was born on June 9, 1905. He attended military school and joined the Peruvian army. He was appointed controller-general of the army in 1958 and became chief of staff of the armed forces in 1960. In June of 1962 a presidential election was held in which Victor Haya de la Torre, the candidate of the American Popular Revolutionary Alliance (APRA) party, narrowly defeated Fernando Belaúnde Terry. Belaúnde charged that fraud had been perpetrated during the election. Though the charges could not be proved, the military, who opposed Haya de la Torre and the Apristas, staged a coup in which President Manuel Prado was overthrown. General Pérez Godoy became president of the ruling military junta on July 19, 1962. He established Peru's Institute of Planning and several government housing agencies during his administration. He was forced out of office by the junta on March 3, 1963.

NICOLÁS LINDLEY LÓPEZ (President, March 3, 1963–July 28, 1963). Nicolás Lindley López served in the Peruvian army. He rose to the rank of general and became a member of the ruling military junta following the coup in July of 1962. When the junta ousted Ricardo Pérez Godoy as president, Lindley assumed the office on March 3, 1963. He retained his position until elections were held, and he relinquished the presidency to the victor, Fernando Belaúnde Terry, on July 28, 1963.

FERNANDO BELAÚNDE TERRY (President, July 28, 1963–October 3, 1968). Fernando Belaúnde Terry was born in Lima on October 7, 1913. He was educated in France and the United States. He was elected to the Chamber of Deputies in 1945 and served until 1948. Belaúnde was trained as an architect and was dean of the Lima School of Architecture from 1948 until 1956. He again entered politics in 1956 as leader of the Popular Action party. He was an unsuccessful candidate for president in 1956. Belaúnde again ran for office in 1962 and was narrowly defeated by Victor Haya de la Torre. The military refused to allow Haya de la Torre to take office and staged a military coup. In a new election held the following year, Belaúnde was victorious and took office on July 28, 1963. He remained president until October 3, 1968, when following a dispute over the exploitation of Peru's national resources by foreign companies, he was ousted by a military coup. He went into exile in the United States, where he lectured at Harvard University. Belaúnde returned to Peru in December of 1970, but was deported near the end of the month. He was allowed to return in January of 1976. Belaúnde again ran for the presidency in 1980. He was elected by a wide margin and took office on July 28, 1980. His first acts as president included the restoration of civil liberties and freedom of the press, which had been suspended during the previous military governments. He served out his term of office and then relinquished the position to his elected successor, Alan García Pérez, on July 28, 1985. He remained a leader of the Popular Action party.

JUAN VELASCO ALVARADO (President, October 3, 1968–August 29, 1975). Juan Velasco Alvarado was born in Piura on June 16, 1910. He entered the army in 1929 and attended military school. He rose through the ranks to become lieutenant colonel in 1949. Velasco was promoted to colonel in 1955 and to brigadier general in 1959. He held various military positions, including teaching assignments at the military academy. He also served as military attaché to France. Velasco was named commander in chief of the army during the administration of Fernando Belaúnde Terry in 1966. General Velasco led a military coup that ousted Belaúnde on October 3, 1968, and he became president of the subsequent military junta. He nationalized the United States–owned International Petroleum Company shortly after taking office. He also instituted a series of land reform measures. His policies strained relations with the United States. Velasco led Peru into a neutralist position internationally and established diplomatic relations with Cuba, the Soviet Union, and China. He suffered from poor health during the later years of his administration. On August 30, 1975, he was ousted in a military coup led by Francisco Morales Bermúdez. Velasco was hospitalized in December of 1977 and underwent surgery for an inflammation of the pancreas. He died in a Lima hospital from blood poisoning at the age of 67 on December 24, 1977.

FRANCISCO MORALES BERMÚDEZ (President, August 30, 1975–July 28, 1980). Francisco Morales Bermúdez was born in Lima on October 4, 1921. He was the grandson of Remiro Morales, who served as Peru's president from 1890 until 1894. He attended military school and joined the army. Morales was named minister of economy and finance in the military government from 1968 until 1974. He served as chief of the Army General Staff from 1974, and on February 1, 1975, he was named prime minister of Peru. Morales ousted President Juan Velasco Alvarado in a bloodless coup on August 30, 1975. He remained leader of the military government until July 28, 1980, when he relinquished the office following a return to democratic rule.

FERNANDO BELAÚNDE TERRY (President, July 28, 1980–July 28, 1985). *See earlier entry under Heads of State.*

ALAN GARCÍA PÉREZ (President, July 28, 1985–July 28, 1990). Alan García Pérez was born in Lima on May 23, 1949. He was educated in Peru, Spain, and France and became a lawyer. He was elected to the Constituent Assembly in 1978. García was a member of the American Popular Revolutionary Alliance (APRA) party and was elected to the Parliament in 1980. He became secretary-general of APRA in 1982 and ran for president in 1984. He was victorious and was sworn into office on July 28, 1985. García served out his term and left office on July 28, 1990. He was subsequently elected to the Senate. García went into hiding after President Alberto Fujimori suspended the constitutional government on April 5, 1992. He was granted asylum in Columbia in June of 1992.

ALBERTO FUJIMORI (President, July 28, 1990–). Alberto Keinya Fujimori was born in Lima in 1938. He was the son of Japanese immigrants and was educated at the National School of Agriculture. He joined the faculty of the National Agrarian University in 1984. He was a founder of the Cambio '90 political party and was a candidate for president in elections in 1990. He defeated novelist Mario Vargas Llosa in the election and took office on July 28, 1990. Fujimori suspended the constitutional government on April 5, 1992, and governed as a dictator from that point. The government launched an assault on the Shining Path Maoist guerrilla movement and its leader, Abimael Guzman Reynoso, was captured in September of 1992. Fujimori survived a coup attempt on November 13, 1992. He subsequently allowed elections to a Constituent Congress. Fujimura's supporters gained an absolute majority in the Congress, though opposition parties boycotted the election.

HEADS OF GOVERNMENT

PEDRO BELTRAN (Prime Minister, July, 1959–November, 1961). Pedro Gerado Beltran was born in Lima on February 17, 1897. He graduated from the London School of Economics in 1918. He returned to Peru to manage his family's business interests. Beltran purchased the Lima newspaper *La Prensa* in 1934. He also assisted the Peruvian government in economic matters and served as president of the Central Reserve Bank on two occasions. He served as Peru's ambassador to the United States from 1944 until 1946. Beltran often clashed with the government of President Manuel Odría during the 1950s. His newspaper was shut down on several occasions, and

Beltran was briefly imprisoned in 1956. Odría left office in July of 1956. Beltran chaired the government commission in charge of land reform in the subsequent government of Manuel Prado. He was appointed to the cabinet as prime minister and minister of finance in July of 1959. He attempted to improve Peru's faltering economy and succeeded in cutting the nation's high inflation rate. Beltran announced his resignation from the government in November of 1961 to stand as the presidential candidate of the newly formed New Independent party. His candidacy received little support, and he endorsed Victor Haya de la Torre in the elections in 1962. He returned to *La Prensa* after leaving the government and was a critic of the military regime of Juan Velasco Alvarado, who seized power in 1968. Velasco's government dismissed Beltran and seized the paper in 1974. Beltran went into exile in the United States, where he remained a critic of the military government. He subsequently returned to Peru and died of a heart attack in Lima at the age of 82 on February 16, 1979.

FERNANDO SCHWALB LÓPEZ ALDANA (Prime Minister, July, 1963– September 13, 1965). Fernando Schwalb López Aldana was born in Lima on August 26, 1916. He was educated in Peru and joined the diplomatic corps in 1939. He began a private law practice in 1949 and entered politics. In 1962 he was elected to the Senate, but he was prevented from assuming office because of a military coup. Schwalb López was named prime minister and foreign minister by President Fernando Belaúnde Terry in July of 1963. He retained office until his cabinet resigned on September 13, 1965. He was president of the Central Reserve Bank of Peru from 1966 until 1968 and was a consultant with the International Monetary Fund from 1969 until 1982. Schwalb López also served as Peru's ambassador to the United States from

1980 until 1982. He was again named prime minister and foreign minister on December 9, 1982 and served until April 10, 1984. He remained a leader of the Popular Action party.

DANIEL BECERRA DE LA FLOR (Prime Minister, September 13, 1965– September 7, 1967). Daniel Becerra de la Flor was born in Moquegua on January 23, 1906. He attended medical school and became a surgeon. He served as professor of surgery at the National University of San Marcos in Lima from 1954 until 1961. Becerra entered politics and was elected to the Senate in 1963. He was chosen by president Fernando Belaúnde Terry to serve as prime minister on September 13, 1965. He also served in the government as minister of public health. Becerra remained prime minister until September 7, 1967, and remained in the Senate until the following year. He then served as president of the Peruvian Academy of Surgery until 1969. Becerra died at the age of 82 on March 1, 1987.

EDGARDO SEOANE CORRALES (Prime Minister, September 7, 1967– November 16, 1967). Edgardo Seoane Corrales was born in Chorrillos on May 15, 1903. He attended the National Agricultural University and entered politics. He was a founder of the Popular Action party in 1956. Seoane was elected vice presdent under Fernando Belaúnde Terry in 1963. He served as Peru's prime minister from September 7, 1967, until November 16, 1967, and served as secretary-general of the Popular Action party from 1967 until 1969. He was an announced candidate for the Peruvian presidency in the elections to be held in 1969, but received little support from President Belaúnde. The lack of political stability in the party resulted in a military coup that ousted Belaúnde in October of 1968 and postponed the elections. Seoane was named president of the Agricultural Development Bank by President

Juan Velasco Alvarado in August of 1973.

RAÚL FERRERO REBAGLIATI (Prime Minister, November 16, 1967–May 29, 1968). Raúl Ferrero Rebagliati was born in Lima in 1911. He was named by President Fernando Belaúnde Terry to serve as prime minister on November 16, 1967. He also served as foreign minister and finance minister from January of 1968. Ferrero resigned from office on May 29, 1968, following a censure motion passed by Congress over his government's failure to solve Peru's economic crisis.

OSVALDO HERCELLES (Prime Minister, May 31, 1968–October 2, 1968). Osvaldo Hercelles was appointed prime minister by President Fernando Belaúnde Terry on May 31, 1968. He was replaced on October 1, 1968, shortly before the coup that ousted Belaúnde. Hercelles was one of Belaúnde's few cabinet ministers who were not arrested by the new military regime.

MIGUEL MUJICA GALLO (Prime Minister, October 2, 1968–October 3, 1968). Miguel Mujica Gallo was appointed by President Fernando Belaúnde Terry to succeed Osvaldo Hercelles as prime minister on October 2, 1968. He was in office for less than a day when the army ousted Belaúnde and his government.

ERNESTO MONTAGNE SÁNCHEZ (Prime Minister, October 3, 1968–February 1, 1973). Ernesto Montagne Sánchez was born in Lima on August 18, 1916. He was educated at the military school in Chorrillos and entered the army. He rose through the ranks to captain in 1944, colonel in 1958, and brigadier general in 1963. Montagne Sánchez served in the government as minister of public works from October of 1964 until July of 1965. He subsequently served as commandant of the War College and inspector general of

the army. He was appointed prime minister on October 3, 1968, following the military coup that ousted President Fernando Belaúnde Terry. Montagne Sánchez also served in the government as minister of war and commanding general of the army. He was replaced as prime minister by Luis Edgardo Mercado Jarrín on February 1, 1973.

LUIS EDGARDO MERCADO JARRÍN (Prime Minister, February 1, 1973–February 1, 1975). Luis Edgardo Mercado Jarrín was born in Lima on September 19, 1919. He attended military school and joined the army in 1940. He was named minister of foreign affairs in October of 1968 and served until January of 1972. Mercado subsequently served as army chief of staff until the following December. He was named prime minister and minister of war on February 1, 1973. Mercado survived an assassination attempt in December of 1974. He remained prime minister until February 1, 1975, and lost much of his political influence following the ouster of President Juan Velasco Alvarado the following August.

FRANCISCO MORALES BERMÚDEZ (Prime Minister, February 1, 1975–August 30, 1975). *See entry under Heads of State.*

OSCAR VARGAS PRIETO (Prime Minister, September 1, 1975–January 31, 1976). Oscar Vargas Prieto served as a general in the Peruvian army. He was named chairman of the Joint Chiefs of Staff on January 2, 1975. Vargas was named prime minister by President Francisco Morales Bermúdez on September 1, 1975, following Morales's ouster of Juan Velasco Alvarado. Vargas was replaced as prime minister on January 31, 1976.

JORGE FERNÁNDEZ MALDONADO SOLARI (Prime Minister, January 31, 1976–July 16, 1976). Jorge Fernández Maldonado Solari was born in Ilo on

May 29, 1922. He attended the military school in Chorillos and worked in the Army Intelligence Service, where he rose to director. He served as minister of energy in the cabinet of President Juan Velasco Alvarado from 1968 until 1975. Fernández served as army chief of staff from 1975 until 1976. He was appointed prime minister on January 31, 1976, and also served as minister of war until his retirement on July 16, 1976. Fernández was elected to the Senate in 1985. He was elected secretary-general of the Intergovernmental Council of Copper Exporting Countries in Paris in 1990.

GUILLERMO ARBULÚ GALLIANI (Prime Minister, July 16, 1976–January 30, 1978). Guillermo Arbulú Galliani was born in Trujillo. He attended military school and joined the army. He rose through the ranks to become a captain in 1949 and a major in 1955. Arbulú Galliani was promoted to colonel in 1964 and to brigadier general in 1971. He was appointed prime minister and minister of defense on July 16, 1976, and served until January 30, 1978. He was named ambassador to Chile in 1978 and was ambassador to Spain from 1979 until 1980.

OSCAR MOLINA PALLOCHIA (Prime Minister, January 30, 1978–February 2, 1979). Oscar Molina Pallochia was a general in the Peruvian army. He was the former chairman of the joint chiefs of staff and was chosen as prime minister on January 30, 1978. He resigned from office and retired from the military on February 2, 1979.

PEDRO RICHTER PRADA (Prime Minister, February 2, 1979–July 28, 1980). Pedro Richter Prada was born in Ayachucho on January 4, 1920. He attended military school and entered the army in 1946. He served in various military positions and was military attaché at the Peruvian Embassy in Bolivia from 1961 until 1962. Richter Prada became a member of the Council of Presidential Advisors in the government of President Juan Velasco Alvarado in 1970. He was appointed director of the National Intelligence Service in January of the following year and was appointed to the cabinet as minister of the interior in May of 1971. He served as chief of staff of the army before being named chairman of the joint chiefs of staff in January of 1978. Richter Prada was named prime minister on February 2, 1979, and also served as minister of war and commander in chief of the armed forces. He retained office until July 28, 1980.

MANUEL ULLOA ELÍAS (Prime Minister, July 28, 1980–December 9, 1982). Manuel Ulloa Elías was born in 1922. He studied law in Lima and came to the United States in the early 1960s. He worked as an investment banker in New York City before returning to Peru in 1963 to serve as finance minister in the cabinet of President Fernando Belaúnde Terry. Ulloa went into exile in Spain and Argentina following the army coup that deposed Belaúnde in 1968. He returned to Peru following Belaúnde's return to power, and on July 28, 1980, he was named prime minister in the cabinet of President Belaúnde. He served until December 9, 1982. Ulloa died of cancer in Madrid, Spain, on August 9, 1992.

FERNANDO SCHWALB LÓPEZ ALDANA (Prime Minister, December 9, 1982–April 10, 1984). *See earlier entry under Heads of Government.*

SANDRO MARIÁTEGUI (Prime Minister, April 10, 1984–October 13, 1984). Sandro Mariátegui Chiappe was born on December 5, 1922. He was elected to the Chamber of Deputies from Lima in 1963 and served as minister of finance and trade from 1965 until 1967. He was a founder and leader of the Popular Action party.

Mariátegui Chiappe was elected to the Senate in 1980 and served as president of the Senate from 1982 until 1983. He was appointed prime minister and foreign minister on April 10, 1984, and served until October 13, 1984.

LUIS PERCOVICH ROCA (Prime Minister, October 13, 1984–July 28, 1985). Luis Percovich Roca was president of the Chamber of Deputies from 1981 until 1983. He was named minister of fisheries in January of 1983 and became minister of the interior in April of 1983. Percovich Roca was appointed prime minister and foreign minister on October 13, 1984, and served until July 28, 1985.

LUIS ALVA CASTRO (Prime Minister, July 28, 1985–June 22, 1987). Luis Alva Castro was born in Trujillo. He was educated locally and became active in politics. He was a member of the American Popular Revolutionary Alliance (APRA) and was named prime minister on July 28, 1985. Alva Castro also served as minister of economy and finance until June 22, 1987. He became general secretary of APRA in December of 1988 and was an unsuccessful candidate for president in the elections in 1990.

GUILLERMO LARCO COX (Prime Minister, June 26, 1987–May 13, 1988). Guillermo Larco Cox was born on February 19, 1932. He was a member of the American Popular Revolutionary Alliance (APRA) and served as mayor of Trujillo from 1964 until 1966 and again from 1967 until 1968. He was a member of Parliament from 1980 and was elected to the Senate in 1985. Larco Cox was appointed prime minister on June 26, 1987, and served until May 13, 1988. He was subsequently named foreign minister, and on September 30, 1989, he was again named prime minister. He served in these positions until July 28, 1990.

ARMANDO VILLANUEVA DEL CAMPO (Prime Minister, May 13, 1988–May 15, 1989). Armando Villanueva del Campo was born in 1915. He became the leader of the American Popular Revolutionary Alliance (APRA) following the death of Victor Haya de la Torre in August of 1979. Villanueva served as president of the Peruvian Senate and was appointed prime minister on May 13, 1988. He resigned office on May 15, 1989, following an increase in violence by leftist guerrillas, but remained a leader of the Apristas.

LUIS ALBERTO SANCHEZ (Prime Minister, May 15, 1989–September 30, 1989). Luis Alberto Sanchez was born in Lima on October 12, 1900. He worked as a journalist and was a member of the Constituent Assembly in 1931. He was elected to Parliament in 1945 and became a teacher the following year. Sanchez was elected to the Senate in 1963 and served again in the Constituent Assembly in 1978. He became chairman of the Assembly the following year. He was again elected to the Senate in 1980 and was appointed first vice president in 1985. Sanchez was named prime minister on May 15, 1989, and served until the following September 30, 1989. He was subsequently renamed first vice president, serving until Alberto Fujimora took power in July of 1990. Sanchez died of a kidney infection in Lima at the age of 93 on February 6, 1994.

GUILLERMO LARCO COX (Prime Minister, September 30, 1989–July 28, 1990). *See earlier entry under Heads of Government.*

JUAN CARLOS HURTADO MILLER (Prime Minister, July 28, 1990–February 15, 1991). Juan Carlos Hurtado Miller was a supporter of Mario Vargas Llosa in his unsuccessful bid for the presidency in 1990. He was appointed prime minister by President Alberto Fujimori on July 28, 1990, and also served in the government as minister of finance. He resigned from office on February 15, 1991.

CARLOS TORRES Y TORRES LARA (Prime Minister, February 15, 1991–November 6, 1991). Carlos Torres y Torres Lara was named prime minister and minister of foreign affairs on February 15, 1991. He resigned from office on November 6, 1992, and was replaced by Alfonso de los Heros Perez Albela.

ALFONSO DE LOS HEROS PEREZ ALBELA (Prime Minister, November 6, 1991–April 5, 1992). Alfonso de los Heros Perez Albela was born in 1940. He was named prime minister and minister of the economy on November 6, 1991. He resigned when President Alberto Fujimori dismissed the constitutional government on April 5, 1992.

OSCAR DE LA PUENTA (Prime Minister, April 5, 1992–). Oscar de la Puenta Raygada served in the government as minister of education. He was appointed prime minister on April 5, 1992, following President Alberto Fujimori's seizure of dictatorial powers.

Philippines, Republic of the

(Republica de Filipinas)

The Philippines is an archipelago off the coast of southeastern Asia. It was granted independence from the United States on July 4, 1946.

HEADS OF STATE

SERGIO OSMEÑA (President, August 1, 1944–May 28, 1946). Sergio Osmeña was born in Cebu on September 9, 1878. He attended the University of the Philippines, where he received a degree in law. He entered politics and was elected governor of Cebu Province. In 1906 he was elected to the House of Representatives. Osmeña was leader of the independence movement and head of the Nationalist party and was elected Speaker of the House in 1907. He was elected to the Senate in 1922. He attended the independence conference in the United States in 1931. Osmeña was elected vice president under Manuel Quezon after the establishment of the Philippine Commonwealth and he took office on November 15, 1935. He went to the United States following the Japanese occupation of the Philippines in 1942. He returned to the Philippines with United States troops in October of 1944. President Quezon died in office on August 1, 1944, and Osmeña succeeded him as president. He ran for reelection in 1946, but was defeated by Manuel Roxas y Acuna. He relinquished office to Roxas on May 28, 1946. Osmeña died at his home in Cebu at the age of 83 from heart and kidney ailments on October 19, 1961.

MANUEL A. ROXAS Y ACUNA (President, May 28, 1946–April 15, 1948). Manuel A. Roxas y Acuna was born in Capiz, on Panay Island, on January 1, 1892. He received a degree in law and entered politics. He was elected to the Philippine House of Representatives in 1921 and rose to the rank of Speaker of the House. Roxas was an associate of President Manuel Quezon and served as a member of the 1934 Constitutional Convention. During World War II, Roxas served as a colonel under General Douglas MacArthur. He refused to leave the islands during the Japanese invasion and was captured by the Japanese. He refused the Japanese offer to lead an occupation government and worked with the resistance to the occupation forces. Following the war, Roxas was nominated by the Liberal party to run for the presidency. He defeated incumbent President Sergio Osmeña for the position and took office as president of the Philippine Commonwealth on May 28, 1946. The Philippines were granted full independence on July 4, 1946, and Roxas remained President of the Philippine Republic. He maintained close relations between the United States and the Philippines during his term of office. He remained in office until his death of a heart attack at Clark Field in Pampagna at the age of 56 on April 15, 1948.

ELPIDIO QUIRINO (President, April 15, 1948–December 30, 1953). Elpidio Quirino was born in Vigan, Ilocus Sur Province, on November 16, 1890. He attended the University of the Philippines, where he received a degree in law in 1915. He worked as a clerk in the Philippine Senate before being elected to the House of Representatives in 1919. Quirino joined Manuel Quezon's Collectivist party and was elected to the Senate in 1925. He became chairman of the Special Joint Committee on Taxation and was appointed secretary of finance in Quezon's cabinet in 1934. He was also named minister of the interior two years later. Quirino refused to join the Japanese puppet government of José P. Laurel during World War II and became a leader of the Resistance. He was imprisoned during the occupation, and his wife and two sons were killed by the Japanese. He was elected vice president on the Liberal party ticket under Manuel Roxas after the war and

took office on May 28, 1946. Quirino also served in the government as secretary of finance. He was named minister of foreign affairs after the establishment of the independent Republic of the Philippines in July of 1946. Quirino succeeded to the presidency on April 15, 1948, following Roxas's death from a heart attack. Quirino completed Roxas's unexpired term and defeated Jose Laurel for reelection the following year. His government was responsible for an increase in industrialization in the Philippines, which contributed to the economic stability of the country. Quirino's government was accused of electoral fraud in the 1949 elections, which led to the Nationalist party achieving gains in parliamentary elections in 1951. Despite poor health, Quirino was a candidate for reelection in 1953. He was unsuccessfully challenged by Carlos P. Romulo for the Liberal party nomination, and faced Nationalist party candidate Ramón Magsaysay and Romulo, who ran as an independent candidate in the presidential elections. Magsaysay defeated Quirino, who relinquished office on December 30, 1953. His health continued to deteriorate, and he died of a heart attack at his home in Novaliches at the age of 65 on February 28, 1956.

RAMÓN MAGSAYSAY (President, December 30, 1953–March 17, 1957). Ramón Magsaysay was born in Iba, Zambales Province, on August 31, 1907. He was educated at the University of the Philippines and at the Jose Rizal College Institute of Commerce, where he graduated in 1932. He subsequently worked as an auto mechanic. Magsaysay joined the United States forces in the Philippines after the Japanese attack on Pearl Harbor in 1941. Magsaysay commanded the Philippine guerrilla resistance forces following the Japanese occupation of the country. He was named military governor of Zambales after the war. He was elected to the House of Representatives in 1946 and joined the government of President Elpidio Quirino as secretary of defense in 1950. Magsaysay was instrumental in reforming the army and led the government's fight against the Communist Hukbalahap rebels. He left the Liberal party to become the presidential candidate of the Nationalist party in the elections in 1953. He defeated incumbent President Quirino and took office on December 30, 1953. Magsaysay was a popular leader and maintained close relations with the United States. He was killed when the C-47 twin-engine transport plane he was a passenger in exploded and crashed on Mt. Bago, near Cebu City, on March 17, 1957.

CARLOS P. GARCÍA (President, March 17, 1957–November 14, 1961). Carlos P. García was born in Talibon, Bohol Province, on November 4, 1896. He was educated in the Philippines and received a degree in law from the Philippine Law School in 1923. He entered politics and was elected to the House of Representatives in 1925. García left the House in 1931 and was elected governor of Bohol two years later. He retained that position until 1941, when he was elected to the Senate as a member of the Nationalist party. He remained in the Philippines during the Japanese occupation in 1941 and became a leader of the underground Resistance movement. García returned to the Senate after the war and served as minority floor leader until 1951. He was nominated for the vice presidency on the Nationalist ticket with Ramon Magsaysay in 1953. He was elected and took office on December 30, 1953. García also served in the government as foreign minister. He succeeded to the presidency when Magsaysay was killed in an airplane crash on March 17, 1957. García defeated Liberal party candidate José Yulo in elections in November of 1957, but his running mate, José P. Laurel, Jr., was defeated by Diosadado Macapagal. García campaigned for honesty in government, but his administration

was plagued with incidents of graft and corruption. He also inaugurated a Filipino First policy which strained relations with the United States, though García was considered staunchly pro-American. The faltering economy of the Philippines led to his defeat by Macapagal in the 1961 presidential election, and García stepped down from office on November 14, 1961. He remained an influential figure in politics and was chosen president of the Constitutional Convention in June of 1971. He died three days later of a heart attack at his home in Quezon City at the age of 74 on June 14, 1971.

DIOSADADO MACAPAGAL (President, November 14, 1961–December 30, 1965). Diosadado Macapagal was born in Luabao on September 28, 1910. He attended Santo Tomas University, where he received a degree in law in 1941. He entered the diplomatic corps in 1946 and was posted to the Philippine Embassy in Washington, D.C. two years later. Macapagal returned to the Philippines in 1949 and was elected to the House of Representatives. He served as chairman of the House Committee on Foreign Affairs from 1950 until 1953 and was reelected in 1953. Macapagal was elected to the vice presidency under Carlos P. García in 1957. He was also chosen as chairman of the Liberal party. He had little influence during García's Nationalist administration, and he was nominated for the presidency by the Liberal party in January of 1961. Macapagal defeated García in his reelection bid and took office as president of the Philippines on November 14, 1961. He was defeated for reelection by Ferdinand Marcos in a bitter campaign and left office on December 30, 1965. Macapagal served as president of the Constitutional Convention in 1971.

FERDINAND E. MARCOS (President, December 30, 1965–February 25, 1986). Ferdinand Edralin Marcos was born in

Sarrat, Illocos Province, on September 11, 1917. He attended the University of the Philippines, where he studied law. Marcos was accused of the assassination of Julio Nalundasan in 1939. Nalundasan, who was murdered in September of 1935, had defeated Marcos's father in a legislative election. Marcos was found guilty in November of 1939, but his conviction was overturned by the Supreme Court. He subsequently became a lawyer and joined his father's law firm. Marcos served in the Philippines armed forces as an officer during World War II. He worked with the Resistance following the Japanese occupation in 1941. Following the war, Marcos served as an assistant to President Manuel Roxas from 1946 until 1947. He was elected to the House of Representatives in 1949. Marcos married former beauty queen Imelda Romanuldez in 1954. He was defeated by Diosadado Macapagal for the Liberal party nomination for vice president in 1957. Marcos was elected to the Senate in 1959 and was defeated by Macapagal for the presidential nomination in 1961. Macapagal reneged on his promise to retire after his first term of office as president, and Marcos left the Liberal party to accept the Nationalist party nomination for the presidency in 1965. He defeated Macapagal in a bitter election and took office on December 30, 1965. Marcos ran for reelection in 1969 and defeated Liberal party candidate Sergio Osmeña, Jr., by a wide margin. The Philippines was faced with a Communist insurgency movement, and Marcos declared a state of siege in August of 1971, following guerrilla attacks in Manilla. He imposed martial law in September of 1972, suspended the constitution, clamped restrictions on the press, and jailed opposition leaders, including Liberal party secretary-general Benigno Aquino, Jr. Marcos introduced a new constitution on January 17, 1973, that provided for a parliamentary system of government. He also assumed the position of

premier in the new government. Marcos's newly formed New Society Movement party won a majority of Assembly seats in elections in April of 1978. He lifted martial law in January of 1981 and named Cesar Virata as premier on April 8, 1981. Benigno Aquino, who had been released from prison to undergo heart surgery in the United States in 1980, returned to the Philippines on August 21, 1983. He was assassinated as he stepped off the plane. Demonstrations and rioting followed Aquino's killing, and international pressure was placed on Marcos's regime to allow democratic elections. Marcos suffered from serious kidney problems in 1984, and his wife became more influential in the government. He called an early presidential election in February of 1986 and was declared the winner over Aquino's widow, Corazon. The opposition accused the government of massive electoral fraud, and Defense Minister Juan Ponce Enrile and General Fidel V. Ramos led a military revolt against Marcos's regime later in the month. Marcos was forced to leave the country on February 25, 1986, and went to Honolulu, Hawaii. The Philippine government filed a law suit against Marcos that claimed he had stolen over $5 billion during his years in office. Criminal charges were also filed against him in New York on charges of embezzlement and racketeering. Marcos was declared too ill to stand trial in October of 1986. His health continued to fail and he was hospitalized in January of 1989 for heart, lung, and kidney ailments. He remained in the Honolulu hospital until his death from heart failure at the age of 72 on September 28, 1989.

CORAZON AQUINO (President, February 25, 1986–June 30, 1992). Corazon Aquino was born Maria Corazon Cojuangco in Tarlac Province on January 25, 1933. She was educated in the United States and graduated from Mount St. Vincent College in the Bronx in 1953. She returned to the Philippines to study law, but left law school to marry Benigno Aquino, Jr., in October of 1954. Her husband became a prominent politician in the Philippines, and she remained in the background. Benigno Aquino was imprisoned in 1972 when President Ferdinand Marcos imposed martial law. Corazon Aquino became her husband's spokesperson to the outside world while he remained imprisoned for the next eight years. She accompanied her husband into exile when he was allowed to go to the United States for heart surgery in 1980. She became the heir to her husband's political legacy when he was assassinated on his return to the Philippines in August of 1983. Aquino became the opposition party candidate for the presidency in December of 1985. She was defeated by President Marcos in February of 1986 in an election that was widely viewed as fraudulent. Marcos was forced from office by a military revolt on February 25, 1986, and Aquino was installed as president. She introduced a new constitution in February of 1987, and her supporters won a large victory in elections to the Parliament in May of 1987. Aquino survived a coup attempt led by Colonel Gregorio Honasan in August of 1987. She faced several other attempts to overthrow her government in the next few years. The Aquino government was unable to secure ratification of a treaty with the United States to extend American use of military installations in the Philip-

pines. The United States began a withdrawal from Clark Air Base and Subic Bay Naval Station in 1991. Aquino declined to seek reelection and supported the candidacy of Fidel Ramos for the presidency in 1992. Ramos was elected, and Aquino stepped down from office on June 30, 1992.

FIDEL V. RAMOS (President, June 30, 1992–). Fidel V. Ramos was born in Lingayen on March 18, 1928. He graduated from the West Point military academy in the United States in 1950. He served in the Philippine army and saw action in Korea and Vietnam. Ramos was appointed chief of the Philippine constabulary and in 1972 helped to enforce Marcos's martial law declaration. He was named deputy chief of staff in 1981, and in February of 1986 he was promoted to chief of staff of the armed forces. Ramos turned against the president shortly afterwards and sided with the revolution that ousted Marcos in favor of Corazon Aquino. He helped President Aquino put down a rightist military coup in November of 1986 and was named secretary of national defense in January of 1988. He was also instrumental in preventing five other coup attempts against the government. Ramos was a candidate to succeed President Aquino in the election held in May of 1992. He was the leading candidate and was declared the victor. Ramos took office as president on June 30, 1992.

HEADS OF GOVERNMENT

FERDINAND E. MARCOS (Premier, January 17, 1973–April 8, 1981). *See entry under Heads of State.*

CESAR E. VIRATA (Premier, April 8, 1981–February 25, 1986). Cesar Enrique Virata was born in Manila on December 12, 1930. He was educated at the

University of Pennsylvania and the University of the Philippines. He served as dean of the College of Business Administration at the University of the Philippines from 1961 until 1969. Virata served as undersecretary of industry from 1967 until 1969 and was minister of finance from 1970. He was named premier by President Ferdinand Marcos on April 8, 1981, and retained office until February 25, 1986, when Marcos was forced from power. Virata left government to work as a management consultant. In February of 1989 he also became an advisor to the Philippines Aid Plan.

SALVADOR H. LAUREL (Premier, February 25, 1986–March 25, 1986). Salvador Hidalgo Laurel was born in Manila on November 18, 1933. He attended the University of the Philippines and Yale University. He was elected to the Senate in 1967 and remained there until martial law was declared in 1973. Laurel was a founder of the Legal Aid Society of the Philippines and worked in opposition politics from 1982. He served as chairman of the United Nationalist Democratic Organization from 1981. Laurel was elected vice president with Corazon Aquino in February of 1986. He also served as premier from February 25, 1986, until March 25, 1986. He subsequently served as minister of foreign affairs until 1987. Laurel served as president of the Nationalist party from 1989.

Poland (Polish Republic)

(Polska Rzeczpospolita)

Poland is a country in eastern Europe.

HEADS OF STATE

BOLESŁAW BIERUT (President, December 31, 1944–November 20, 1952). Bolesław Bierut was born Bolesław Krasnodebski in Laczna on April 18, 1892. He was educated locally and joined the trade union movement as a young man. He became a Communist during World War I and worked as a party organizer after the war. Beirut was imprisoned for six months in 1922 for editing a leftist newspaper. He left Poland in 1928 to work with the Comintern in Vienna. In 1932 he returned to Poland in 1932 and was again arrested. He escaped several years later and fled to the Soviet Union. Bierut accompanied Soviet troops in the invasion of Poland in 1939 and organized the purge of non-Communists throughout the country. He used several aliases during his revolutionary activities, including Bienkowski and Rutkowski, before he adopted the name Bierut. He again fled to Moscow following the German occupation of Poland, but was sent back to Poland in 1942 to establish an underground Communist government. Bierut organized the Polish Worker's party the following year. He became acting president of the provisional government of Poland in Lublin on December 31, 1944. A government of National Unity, including members of the democratic Polish government-in-exile was proclaimed on June 28, 1945. The new government established close relations with the Soviet Union. Parliamentary elections were held in January of 1947 that resulted in a major victory for the Communists. Bierut was elected president of Poland on February 5, 1947. He stepped down as president to become premier of Poland on November 20, 1952. He served as head of the government until March 19, 1954. Bierut remained first secretary of the Communist party and the leading political figure in the country until his death. He suffered a heart attack while attending the 20th Congress of the Soviet Communist party in Moscow in February of 1956. He died in a Moscow hospital of a heart attack at the age of 63 on March 12, 1956.

ALEKSANDER ZAWADSKI (President, November 20, 1952–August 7, 1964). Aleksander Zawadski was born in Dabrowa Gornicza on December 16, 1899. He worked in the coal mines in his youth and joined the Communist Youth Union in 1923. He soon became a party organizer. Zawadski was arrested in 1925 and remained imprisoned for the next six years. He went into exile in the Soviet Union after his release. Zawadski returned to Poland in 1939. He was again arrested, but was liberated during the Soviet invasion. He fought with the Soviets during World War II and became a general in the Polish army formed in the Soviet Union in 1942. He also served on the Central Committee of the Polish Workers' party. He represented the Polish government in Silesia after the war. Zawadski was elected to the Sejm, or Parliament, in 1947. He served as vice-premier in the early 1950s and was chosen as Poland's president of the Council of State to succeed Bolesław Bierut on November 20, 1952. He served in the largely ceremonial position until his death from cancer in Warsaw at the age of 65 on August 7, 1964.

EDWARD OCHAB (President, August 12, 1964–August 11, 1968). Edward Ochab was born in Krakow on April 16, 1906. He joined the Communist party in 1929 and was jailed for his activities during the 1930s. He served in the Communist government after World War II and was elected to the Parliament in 1947. Ochab was named deputy minister of national defense in 1949 and served until the following year. He was appointed to the Central Committee of the Polish Workers' party in 1950 and became first secretary on March 20,

1956, following the death of Bolesław Bierut. He led the party during anti-Soviet demonstrations in the country that resulted in the army killing demonstrators during riots in Poznan. Ochab was replaced by Władysław Gomułka on October 21, 1956. He remained in the Polish government and served as minister of agriculture from 1957 until 1959. He then returned to the Central Committee. Ochab served as vice president of the Council of State from 1961 until August 12, 1964, when he replaced Aleksander Zawadski as president of the Council of State. He resigned on August 11, 1968, in protest of the government anti-Semitic campaign. He retired from politics and died in Warsaw at the age of 83 on May 2, 1989.

MARIAN SPYCHALSKI (President, April 11, 1968–December 23, 1970). Marian Spychalski was born in Lodz on December 6, 1906. He joined the Communist party in 1931 and fought against the Germans in the Resistance during World War II. He was elected mayor of Warsaw after the war and served in the government as deputy minister of national defense from 1945 until 1948. Spychalski was also named to the Politburo in 1948. He was an ally of Communist leader Władysław Gomułka and was purged by Stalinist elements in the party for his criticism of the Soviet policy toward Yugoslavia's Marshal Tito in 1949. He was imprisoned in 1950, but was released after Stalin's death and rehabilitated in 1956. Spychalski was reappointed to the Politburo and named minister of national defense. He became president of the Council of State on April 11, 1968. He remained Poland's ceremonial president until December 23, 1970, when Gomułka fell from power following food riots. Spychalski remained in the Polish Parliament until 1972 and then retired from politics. He died at the age of 73 on June 7, 1980.

JÓZEF CYRANKIEWICZ (President, December 23, 1970–March 28, 1972). Józef Cyrankiewicz was born in Tarnow on July 21, 1911. He was educated at Jagiellonian University in Krakow and became involved with the Polish Socialist party. He served as the party's organizer in Krakow from 1935. Cyrankiewicz fought against the Germans during the occupation of Poland in 1939. He was captured, but soon escaped to join the Resistance. He was arrested in 1941 and spent the remainder of the war imprisoned in a concentration camp. He was liberated by United States troops in 1945. Cyrankiewicz was appointed minister without portfolio in the Polish Government of National Unity after the war. He also became secretary-general of the Socialist party and agreed to the merger of the Socialists and the Communists as the Communist Polish Workers' party in November of 1946. He was elected to the Parliament in 1947 and became premier on February 7, 1947. Cyrankiewicz remained head of the government until November 20, 1952, when he was replaced by Bolesław Bierut. He remained in the government as vice-premier and was restored to the premiership on March 19, 1954. He worked closely with Communist party leader Wladyslaw Gomulka during the next two decades. Cyrankiewicz successfully negotiated the Warsaw Treaty with West Germany in 1970 that formally established Poland's borders with West Germany. He was forced from office following riots over the increase in food prices on December 23, 1970. He was subsequently appointed chairman of the Council of State. Cyrankiewicz remained Poland's ceremonial head of state until his retirement on March 28, 1972. He died in Warsaw at the age of 77 on January 20, 1989.

HENRYK JABŁOŃSKI (President, March 28, 1972–November 6, 1985). Henryk Jabłoński was born in Waliszewo on December 27, 1909. He was educated at the University of Warsaw and subsequently served as a professor there. He served as a member of the National Council from 1945 until 1947, when he was elected to Parliament. Jabłoński served as deputy minister of education from 1947 until 1953. He was a member of the Polish Socialist party until 1948, when he joined the Central Committee of the Polish United Workers', or Communist, party. He served as minister of education from 1965 until 1972. Jabłoński was elected chairman of the Council of State on March 28, 1972. He retained the position until November 6, 1985, when he was replaced as head of state by Wojciech Jaruzelski. He also served as chairman of the Supreme Council of the Association of Fighters for Freedom and Democracy from 1983 until 1990.

WOJCIECH JARUZELSKI (President, November 6, 1985–December 22, 1990). Wojciech Jaruzelski was born in Kurow on July 6, 1923. He attended military school in Warsaw and served with the Polish armed forces during World War II. He rose through the ranks to become brigadier general in 1956. Jaruzelski was elected to the Parliament in 1961 and was named deputy minister of national defense in 1962. He became chief of the general staff in 1965 and was appointed minister of defense in 1968. Jaruzelski was elected to the Politburo in 1971 and was promoted to general of the army in 1973. He was selected as premier of Poland on February 11, 1981. The Central Committee felt that General Jaruzelski was the only member of the Politburo who could restore order to the country, and he was elected first secretary of the Communist party on October 18, 1981. He was unable to reach a settlement with the Solidarity Movement leaders and declared martial law in December of 1981. Jaruzelski stepped down as premier on November 6, 1985, but immediately was named as chairman of the Council of State. He was reelected first secretary of the party the following year. Strikes organized by the Solidarity Movement continued throughout Poland and the government was forced to open negotiations with the still-outlawed union in February of 1989. Jaruzelski agreed to a number of political reforms, and parliamentary elections were held the following June. Solidarity-backed candidates were overwhelmingly elected. Jaruzelski was narrowly reelected president of Poland in July of 1989. A Solidarity-led government was formed in September of 1989, and the nation was transformed from the People's Republic of Poland to the Polish Republic. The Communist party disbanded on January 29, 1990, and Jaruzelski stepped down as president on December 22, 1990, following the election of Lech Wałęsa in democratic balloting.

LECH WAŁĘSA (President, December 22, 1990–). Lech Wałęsa was born in Popowo on September 29, 1943. He was educated locally and studied agricultural mechanics. He was employed at the State Agricultural Depot before going to Gdansk in 1967 to work at the Lenin Shipyard. Wałęsa was involved in the strike by shipyard workers that was crushed by the Polish army in 1970. He continued to work for the establishment of free trade unions in Poland. He became a leader of the striking workers in Gdansk in August of 1980. The government was forced to recognize the Solidarity Movement, and Wałęsa was elected president of Solidarity the following year. He was arrested in December of 1981 following the imposition of martial law and was interned for nearly a year. He remained a leader of the underground trade union movement and was awarded the 1983 Nobel Prize for Peace. He participated in negotiations with the government of Wojciech Jaruzelski that led to free elections being held in June of 1989. Solidarity-supported candidates were the overwhelming victors in parliamentary elections. Wałęsa was a candidate for president in elections in November of 1990. He defeated Stanislaw Tyminski in a runoff the following month. He replaced Jaruzelski as president on December 22, 1990. Wałęsa was faced with a declining economy and conflicts with the Parliament. He broke with the Solidarity movement in June of 1993 after Solidarity was responsible for bringing down the government of Premier Hanna Suchocka the previous month.

HEADS OF GOVERNMENT

EDWARD OSÚBKA-MORAWSKI (Premier, June 28, 1945–February 7, 1947). Edward Osúbka-Morawski was born in Blizyn on October 5, 1909. He was an early member of the Polish Socialist party and was imprisoned for antigovernment activity in 1934. He remained a leading Socialist organizer after his release and edited the underground Socialist newspaper *Robotnik*. Osúbka-Morawski participated in the defense of Warsaw during World War II and was president of the Political Committee for National Liberation during the war. He was named premier of the provisional government on June 28, 1945. He retained office until February 7, 1947, when the Communist party took control of the government. Osúbka-Morawski remained in the government as minister of public administration until January of 1949. He was then named director of the State Holiday Resorts Corporation. Osúbka-Morawski was granted membership in the Communist party in 1956. He was dropped from the ballot in January of the following year and was subsequently inactive in political affairs.

JÓZEF CYRANKIEWICZ (Premier, February 7, 1947–November 20, 1952). *See entry under Heads of State.*

BOLESŁAW BIERUT (Premier, November 20, 1952–March 19, 1954). *See entry under Heads of State.*

JÓZEF CYRANKIEWICZ (Premier, March 19, 1954–December 23, 1970). *See entry under Heads of State.*

PIOTR JAROSZEWICZ (Premier, December 23, 1970–February 15, 1980). Piotr Jaroszewicz was born in Niewiez on October 8, 1909. He worked as a teacher before joining the Polish army during World War II. He also joined the Polish Workers' party in 1944. Jaroszewicz remained in the army following the liberation of Poland and rose to the rank of brigadier general in 1950. He served in various government and party positions and became an alternate member of the Politburo in 1964. He was subsequently appointed deputy premier, and he replaced Józef Cyrankiewicz as premier on December 23, 1970. Jaroszewicz's government promoted economic policies that led to a shortage of goods and increased inflation. Economic hardships led to the formation of the Solidarity Union and forced Jaroszewicz's ouster on February 15, 1980. He was purged from the party the following year. He spent his retirement in seclusion at his luxurious home in the Warsaw suburb of Anin. Jaroszewicz's body and that of his wife were found in his home on September 2, 1992. He had been tortured and hanged, and his wife had been shot.

EDWARD BABIUCH (Premier, February 18, 1980–August 24, 1980). Edward Babiuch was born in Grabocin on December 28, 1927. He was educated at a technical school in Warsaw and joined the Polish United Workers' party in 1948. He worked in party organizations from 1955 and was named to the Central Committee in 1964. Babiuch was elected to the Parliament in 1969 and was named a member of the Politburo the following year. He was a member of the State Council from 1972 and served as deputy chairman from 1976 until 1980. He was named to replace Piotr Jaroszewicz as premier on February 18, 1980. Babiuch was ousted from office on August 24, 1980, following a major strike at the Lenin Shipyard in Gdansk. He was expelled from the party the following year and was imprisoned until 1982.

JÓZEF PINKOWSKI (Premier, August 24, 1980–February 9, 1981). Józef Pinkowski was born in Siedlce on April 17, 1929. He was educated locally and received a degree in economics. He served in the Polish army as an officer from 1952 until 1956. Pinkowski worked in the Ministry of Food Industries as an inspector from 1956 until 1958 and was subsequently named to the Voivodship National Council. He served as vice-chairman from 1960 until 1965 and chairman from 1965 until 1971. He was also elected to the Parliament in 1969 and became a member of the Central Committee in 1971. Pinkowski served on the parliamentary Committee of Economic Planning and Finance from 1974. He replaced Edward Babiuch as premier on August 24, 1980. His government was challenged by the growing power of the independent trade union Solidarity. Pinkowski was dismissed from office on February 9, 1981, and was replaced by General Wojciech Jaruzelski as premier.

WOJCIECH JARUZELSKI (Premier, February 11, 1981–November 6, 1985). *See entry under Heads of State.*

ZBIGNIEW MESSNER (Premier, November 6, 1985–September 27, 1988).

Zbigniew Messner was born in Stryj on March 13, 1929. He attended the Higher School of Economics in Katowice and subsequently became a teacher there. He rose to the position of rector in 1975. Messner was a member of the Polish United Workers' party and served on the Central Committee from 1981. He was named vice-chairman of the Council of Ministers in 1983 and became premier on November 6, 1985. Poland's economic situation worsened during Messner's term, and he resigned on September 27, 1988. He subsequently served as a member of the Council of State until 1989.

MIECZYSŁAW RAKOWSKI (Premier, September 27, 1988–August 2, 1989). Mieczysław Franciszek Rakowski was born in Kowalewko on December 1, 1926. He was educated in Krakow and Warsaw and joined the Communist United Polish Workers' party in 1949. He worked on the party newspaper and became editor in chief in 1958. Rakowski became a deputy member of the Central Committee of the party in 1964 and a member in 1975. He was also elected to the Parliament in 1972. He served as deputy chairman of the Council of Ministers from 1981 until 1985 and was Deputy Speaker of Parliament from 1985 until 1988. Rakowski was considered a leading economic reformist in the party and was named premier on September 27, 1988. He stepped down from office on August 2, 1989, following parliamentary elections. He was elected first secretary of the newly formed Social Democracy of the Polish Republic party after the disbanding of the Communist Polish Workers' party on July 29, 1989. The party was badly defeated in elections to the Parliament in 1991. Rakowski subsequently became editor of a monthly magazine.

CZESŁAW KISZCZAK (Premier, August 2, 1989–August 24, 1989). Czesław Kiszczak was born in Roczyny on October 19, 1925. He fought in the Resistance during World War II and entered the Polish People's Army in 1945. He served in the military counterintelligence department and became chief of military intelligence in 1972. Kiszczak rose to the rank of major general the following year. He was named chief of the Military Police in 1979 with the rank of lieutenant general. Kiszczak became a member of the Central Committee in August of 1981 and served in the government as interior minister. He was promoted to general in 1983 and was elected to the Parliament in 1985. Kiszczak was appointed premier by General Wojciech Jaruzelski on August 2, 1989. He was forced to step down on August 24, 1989, when the Solidarity-supported candidate Tadeusz Mazowiecki was able to form a government. Kiszczak remained in the government as vice-premier until 1990.

TADEUSZ MAZOWIECKI (Premier, August 24, 1989–January 4, 1991). Tadeusz Mazowiecki was born in Plock on April 18, 1927. He attended Warsaw University and was active in Catholic organizations. He was elected to the Polish Parliament in 1961 and served until 1972. Mazowiecki was active in organizations opposing the government and took part in various protests. He joined the Solidarity Movement in 1980 and became chief editor of the Solidarity weekly newspaper. He was imprisoned from 1981 until 1982 and subsequently became an advisor to Polish cardinal Jozef Glemp. Mazowiecki became premier of a Solidarity-supported government on August 24, 1989. Mazowiecki was defeated by Lech Wałęsa in the presidential elections in 1990, with the Solidarity movement splitting between the two candidates. Mazowiecki founded the Democratic Union party in opposition to the government. He refused a reappointment to the premiership in December of 1990 and left office on January 4, 1991. He returned to the Polish Parliament in 1991 as leader of the Democratic Union party.

JAN KRZYSZTOF BIELECKI (Premier, January 4, 1991–December 5, 1991). Jan Krzysztof Bielecki was born in Bydgoszcz on May 3, 1951. He attended Gdansk University. He was on the staff of the Ministry of Trade and Ministry of Machine Industry from 1972 until 1982. He became involved as an economic advisor to the Solidarity Trade Union in August of 1980. Bielecki remained involved in union activities during the period of martial law. He was named premier of Poland on January 4, 1991. His policies of economic reform diminished his popularity during the year, and in the elections held in October, Bielecki's Liberal Democratic Congress won few seats in the Parliament. He remained premier until December 5, 1991, while awaiting the formation of a coalition government.

JAN OLSZEWSKI (Premier, December 6, 1991–June 5, 1992). Jan Olszewski was born in Warsaw on August 20, 1930. He attended Warsaw University and worked in the Polish Academy of Sciences Legal Department from 1951 until 1956. He then worked as a journalist until he was banned in 1957. Olszewski was a trial lawyer from 1962, but was suspended in 1968 following his defense of anti-Communist demonstrators. He was allowed to return to work as a lawyer in 1970. He founded the Polish Independence Alliance and served as its chairman until 1981. Olszewski also served as a legal advisor to the Solidarity National Committee from 1980. He represented Solidarity during discussions of legal and judicial reforms in 1989. He was elected to

Parliament in October of 1991, where he was a critic of free-market reforms. Olszewski was named premier in a coalition government on December 6, 1991. He was ousted by a vote of no confidence in Parliament on June 5, 1992.

WLADEMAR PAWLUK (Premier, June 5, 1992–July 8, 1992). Wlademar Pawluk was born in 1959. He was the chairman of the Polish Peasant party and was nominated by Lech Wałęsa to serve as premier following the ouster of Jan Olszewski. Pawluk's selection was approved by Parliament on June 5, 1992. He resigned on July 2, 1992, when he was unable to put together a workable coalition. President Wałęsa initially refused to accept the resignation, and Pawluk remained premier until July 8, 1992, when Hanna Suchocka was selected as his replacement.

HANNA SUCHOCKA (Premier, July 8, 1992–   ). Hanna Suchocka was born in Pleszew in 1946. She attended the University of Poznan and received a degree in law in 1968. She subsequently served on the faculty of the University of Poznan and the University of Lublin. Suchocka was elected to the Parliament in 1980 as a member of the Democratic party. She was expelled from the party in 1984 when she opposed the government's banning of the Solidarity Union. She joined with Solidarity and was a founder of the Democratic Union. Suchocka was again elected to the Parliament in 1989. She was selected to serve as premier in a coalition government on July 8, 1992. Her government collapsed in June of 1993 due to the opposition of the Solidarity Movement, but she remained premier of a caretaker government.

OTHER LEADERS

WŁADYSŁAW GOMUŁKA (First Secretary, November 23, 1943–September 5, 1948). Władysław Gomułka as

born in Krosno on February 6, 1905. He worked in an oil refinery as a young man and became active in the trade union movement. He became an organizer for the banned Communist party in the 1920s and was arrested on several occasions. Gomułka was arrested for union activities in 1933 and spent four years in prison. He went to the Soviet Union after his release and attended the International Lenin School there. He returned to Poland to work as a party organizer in Lodz and was again arrested. Gomułka remained imprisoned until the German invasion of Poland in 1939 at the start of World War II. He joined the Resistance and fought against the Nazis during the war. He became a member of the Central Committee of the Polish Workers' party in 1942 and became first secretary of the party on November 23, 1943. Gomułka served as deputy premier in the provisional government of Poland formed in December of 1944 and retained that position in the Government of National Unity the following year. He also served in the government as minister of recovered western areas. Gomułka disagreed with the Stalinist position that opposed Yugoslavia's leader, Marshal Tito. He was replaced as first secretary of the United Polish Workers' party by Bolesław Bierut on September 5, 1948. He was ousted from the cabinet in January of 1949 and purged from the party the following November. Gomułka was imprisoned for "nationalist deviations" on orders from Soviet leader Josef Stalin in July of 1951. He was released from prison in 1954, following Stalin's death the previous year. He was rehabilitated in the party in April of 1956 and returned to power as first secretary of the Communist party on October 21, 1956, after riots broke out in several Polish cities in opposition to the influence of the Soviet Union in Poland. Gomułka convinced Soviet leader Nikita Khrushchev not to send Soviet troops to interfere in the dispute. He instituted some liberal reforms in the government and reached an accommodation with the Roman Catholic church by reinstating Cardinal

Stefan Wyszynski. Gomułka remained the most powerful figure in Poland during the 1950s and 1960s. He later abandoned his reform policies, however, and Poland's economy suffered in the late 1960s. Strikes and riots broke out in 1970, and the government sent security forces to put down a strike in the Gdansk shipyards. Dozens of striking workers were killed by the security forces. Gomułka was forced from power on September 6, 1970, and was replaced as party leader by Edward Gierek. He retired from public life to write his memoirs. Gomułka suffered from poor health in the early 1980s and died of cancer in Warsaw at the age of 77 on September 1, 1982.

BOLESŁAW BIERUT (First Secretary, September 5, 1948–March 12, 1956). *See entry under Heads of State.*

EDWARD OCHAB (First Secretary, March 20, 1956–October 21, 1956). *See entry under Heads of State.*

WŁADYSŁAW GOMUŁKA (First Secretary, October 21, 1956–September 6, 1970). *See earlier entry under Other Leaders.*

EDWARD GIEREK (First Secretary, September 6, 1970–September 6, 1980). Edward Gierek was born in Porabka on January 6, 1913. He went to France in 1923 and returned to Poland in 1934 to attended the Krakow Academy of Mining and Metallurgy. He then went to Belgium in 1937, where he was a leader of the Belgian Resistance to the German occupation during World War II. Gierek served as chairman of the National Council of Poles in Belgium before returning to Poland in 1948. He subsequently joined the Polish United Workers' party. He was elected to Parliament in 1952 and became secretary of the party's organization in Katowice in 1957. Gierek became a member of the Politburo

Central Committee in March of 1959. He became first secretary of the Communist party following the ouster of Władysław Gomułka on December 20, 1970. Following a decade of political and economic upheavals in Poland, Gierek relinquished his position on September 6, 1980, reportedly after suffering a heart attack. He was arrested in December of 1981 following the imposition of martial law by General Wojciech Jaruzelski. Gierek remained imprisoned until December of 1982.

STANISŁAW KANIA (First Secretary, September 6, 1980–October 18, 1981). Stanisław Kania was born in Wrocanka on March 8, 1927. He served in the Resistance to the German occupation during World War II. He joined the Communist party in April of 1945 and served as an organizer of the party's youth movement in Rzeszow. Kania graduated from the party school in 1952 and rose through the ranks of the party. He was named an alternate member of the Central Committee in 1964 and was promoted to full membership in 1968. He was also named to the Politburo in December of 1975. Kania was selected as first secretary of the United Polish Workers' party on September 6, 1980, to succeed ailing Edward Gierek. Kania was considered a moderate, and his selection was viewed as a compromise between the liberal and hard-line wings of the party. Lech Wałęsa formed the National Committee of Solidarity in Gdansk to advocate for workers' rights shortly after Kania took office. Kania remained leader of the Communist party following a secret ballot at the party congress in July of 1981. He resigned as first secretary on October 18, 1981, and was replaced by General Wojciech Jaruzelski. Kania subsequently retired from the political scene.

WOJCIECH JARUZELSKI (First Secretary, October 18, 1981–July 29, 1989). *See entry under Heads of State.*

Portugal (Portuguese Republic)
(República Portuguesa)

Portugal is a country on the Iberian Peninsula in southwest Europe.

HEADS OF STATE

ANTÓNIO OSCAR DE FRAGOSO CARMONA (President, November 26, 1926–April 18, 1951). António Oscar de Fragoso Carmona was born in Lisbon on November 24, 1869. He joined the Portuguese military and was a full general when he first became involved in politics. He served as a member of the cabinet from November to December of 1923. Carmona led a coup d'état on May 28, 1926, and led a military junta composed of himself, Gen. Gomes da Costa, and Cmdr. Mendes Cebecadas. Carmona ousted the other two members of the junta, and on July 9 he became premier of Portugal. He also assumed the presidency on November 26, 1926. He was confirmed as president by a plebiscite in March of 1928 and relinquished the post of premier on November 12, 1928. When António de Oliveira Salazar was named premier in 1932,

Carmona remained as head of state, but held little power. He was reelected as president in 1935, 1942, and 1949. He was promoted to the rank of first marshal of Portugal on May 28, 1947. Carmona remained in office until his death in Lisbon from influenza at the age of 81 on April 18, 1951.

FRANCISCO HIGINO CRAVEIRO LOPES (President, July 22, 1951–August 9, 1958). Francisco Higino Craveiro Lopes was born in Lisbon to a prominent military family on April 12, 1894. He entered the Army School in 1911 and was commissioned as an officer in 1915. He fought the Germans in Portuguese East Africa during World War I. Craveiro Lopes joined the Portuguese air force in 1918 and rose to the rank of captain in 1922. He was stationed in Gao in 1929 where he served as an aide to his father, the governor-general of Portuguese India. He returned to Portugal as a lieutenant colonel in 1939. Craveiro Lopes was promoted to colonel in 1941 and negotiated the agreement that allowed Great Britain to use air and naval bases in the Azores during World War II, while maintaining Portuguese neutrality. He entered the Military Staff College in 1943 and was promoted to brigadier general the following year. He was also placed in command of the Portuguese Legion. Craveiro Lopes was elected to the National Assembly in 1945 and was promoted to the rank of full general in 1949. When President Antonio Oscar de Fragoso Carmona died in office on April 18, 1951, Craveiro Lopes was chosen by Premier António Salazar to run as the government party's candidate for the position. He was unopposed in the election and took office on July 22, 1951. He served in the largely ceremonial position of president until his retirement on August 9, 1958. He emerged briefly from his retirement in 1963 to speak out against Portugal's policy regarding its colonial empire. He questioned the practicality

of a military solution to the problem of growing nationalist movements in Portugal's colonies. Craveiro Lopes died of a heart attack at his home in Lisbon on September 3, 1964.

AMÉRICO DEUS RODRIGUES TOMÁS (President, August 9, 1958–April 25, 1974). Américo Deus Rodrigues Tomás was born in Lisbon on November 19, 1894. He graduated from the Lisbon Naval Academy in 1916. He saw action in World War I and was promoted to the rank of second lieutenant in 1918. Tomás was stationed with the Marine Ministry and assigned to survey coastal waters from 1920 until 1936. He was appointed as assistant to the minister of the navy in 1936 and was named president of the Merchant Marine National Board in 1940. He was promoted to captain in 1941 and named minister of the navy in 1944. Tomás advanced to the rank of rear admiral in 1951. He was chosen by Premier António Salazar to be the government's candidate for president in 1958. He defeated Gen. Humberto Delgado in the election and took office on August 9, 1958. Direct presidential elections were subsequently abolished, and Tomás was reelected by an electoral college in 1965. When Salazar suffered a stroke in 1968, Tomás was called upon to appoint Marcello Caetano as his successor. Tomás was again reelected as president in 1972 and retained office until the government was overthrown by a military junta on April 25, 1974. Tomás went into exile in Brazil, but was allowed to return to Portugal in 1978. He died at his home in Cascais at the age of 92 on September 18, 1987.

ANTÓNIO DE SPÍNOLA (President, May 15, 1974–September 30, 1974). António Sebastiaõ Ribeiro de Spínola was born in Estremoz on April 11, 1910. He was educated at military schools and attended the University of Lisbon. He joined the Portuguese army and rose through the ranks. He was promoted to lieutenant colonel in 1961 and commanded a cavalry group in Angola until 1964. Spínola was named governor and commander in chief of the armed forces in Portuguese Guinea in 1968 and was promoted to general the following year. He served in Portuguese Guinea until 1973, when he was named deputy chief of staff of the Portuguese armed forces. He was a leader of the coup that ousted the dictatorship of Marcello Caetano, and he served as leader of the ruling junta. Spínola became president of Portugal on May 15, 1974, and retained that position until September 30, 1974. He retired from the army the following November. Spínola was implicated in an unsuccessful coup in March of 1975 and went into exile in Brazil and Switzerland. When he returned to Portugal, he was arrested. He was released and went back into exile in August of 1976. Spínola was allowed to return to Portugal, and his rank of general was restored in 1978. He was promoted to the rank of marshal in 1981.

FRANCISCO DA COSTA GOMES
(President, September 30, 1974–July 23, 1976). Francisco da Costa Gomes was born in Chaves on June 30, 1914. He was educated at military schools and joined the Portuguese army. He served in Macau from 1949 until 1951 and subsequently served in Europe. Costa Gomes was named undersecretary of the army staff in 1959. He was stationed in Mozambique from 1965 until 1969 and served as commander in chief of military forces there from 1968. He was named commander in chief of the Portuguese forces in Angola in 1970. Costa Gomes returned to Portugal as chief of staff of the armed forces in 1972. He was a leader of the coup that ousted the Caetano regime in April of 1974 and served on the ruling junta. He became president of Portugal on September 30, 1974, and served until July 23, 1976.

ANTÓNIO DOS SANTOS RAMALHO
EANES (President, July 23, 1976–March 9, 1986). António dos Santos Ramalho Eanes was born in Alcains on January 25, 1935. He was educated in Lisbon and joined the army in 1953. He fought in Portugal's colonial wars in Africa during the 1960s and early 1970s. Eanes was an opponent of Portugal's colonial policies and supported the coup in April of 1974. He returned to Portugal from Angola following the coup and served as the Armed Forces Movement's representative to the Portuguese television network. He retained that position until March of 1975, when he was implicated in a countercoup led by supporters of General António de Spínola. Eanes was exonerated after an inquiry. He returned to the military and became an opponent of the nationalization program sponsored by the government of Premier Vasco dos Santos Goncalves. He was instrumental in suppressing a left-wing coup in November of 1975. Eanes was elected president of Portugal and took office on July 23, 1976. He also served as commander in chief of the armed forces until 1981. He retired from the presidency on March 9, 1986, but remained leader of the Portuguese Democratic Renewal party until 1987.

MÁRIO SOARES (President, March 9,
1986–). Mário Alberto Nobre Lopes Soares was born in Lisbon on December 7, 1924. He was the son of Joao Soares, a liberal who had served in the republican government that was overthrown by the military in 1926. Mário Soares became involved with radical politics at an early age. He attended the University of Lisbon, where he founded the United Democratic Youth Movement in 1946. The following year he was arrested, for the first of many times, for antigovernment activities and served four months in prison. Soares was active in the campaign of opposition presidential candidate General José Norton de Mattos in 1949, but

Mattos was forced to withdraw before the election. In the 1950s Soares continued with his education and received an arts degree from the University of Lisbon in 1951 and a doctorate in law from the Sorbonne in Paris in 1956. Soares was again active in the 1958 presidential campaign and backed the unsuccessful opposition candidate General Humberto Delgado. Soares subsequently opened a law practice in Lisbon and became a leading opponent of the Salazar regime. When General Delgado was murdered in Spain in 1965, Soares served as the Delgado family's lawyer and gained international attention by implicating Salazar's secret police in the crime. Soares was again arrested in March of 1968 and exiled to the island of Sao Tome. He was allowed to return to Portugal in November of 1968, after a serious illness forced Salazar from office. The new government of Marcello Caetano initiated some democratic reforms, but Soares's opposition party was unable to win a seat in the National Assembly in elections in October of 1969 because of campaign restrictions. Soares again went into exile and spent the early 1970s traveling and teaching at the Sorbonne in Paris. He remained a leading critic of the Caetano regime and founded the Portuguese Socialist party while in West Germany in April of 1973. Caetano was ousted by a military junta led by General António de Spínola on April 25, 1974, and Soares returned to Portugal several days later. He was appointed foreign minister in the new government in May of 1974. He immediately moved to end the conflicts in Portugal's overseas colonies. Soares met with the various revolutionary committees and negotiated agreements granting independence to Guinea-Bissau, Mozambique, and Angola. Supporters of General Spinola, who had resigned as president the previous year, made an unsuccessful coup attempt in March of 1975. Soares was dismissed as foreign minister in a subsequent cabinet reorganization, but remained in the government as minister without portfolio. The Socialist party won a majority in the Constituent Assembly in elections the following month, but the leftist military rulers threatened to ignore the election results. Soares and the other Socialists resigned from the government in protest in July of 1975. Soares organized demonstrations against the government and forced the resignation of General Vasco Goncalves the following month. In April of 1976 the Socialists again won a majority of the assembly seats. Soares was elected premier and took office on July 23, 1976. He lost a vote of confidence in December of 1977 over the issue of an International Monetary Fund agreement. His government collapsed in June of 1978, and he was forced to step down on August 18, 1978. Soares again became premier as head of a coalition government on June 9, 1983. The coalition unraveled in 1985, and Soares resigned as premier on November 6, 1985. He had already announced his candidacy for the presidency in elections scheduled for the following year. He ran second to Diogo Freitas do Amaral in the election held on January 26, 1986. Soares defeated Freitas do Amaral in a runoff held the following month and took office as president on March 9, 1986.

HEADS OF GOVERNMENT

ANTÓNIO DE OLIVEIRA SALAZAR (Premier, July 5, 1932–September 27, 1968). António de Oliveira Salazar was born to a peasant family in the village of Santa Comba Dao on April 28, 1889. He was educated at the Jesuit seminary in Viseu with the intention of becoming a priest. He decided instead to pursue a career in education and in 1910 entered the University of Coimbra. Salazar graduated in 1914 and joined the teaching staff. He continued his education as well and received a doctorate in law in 1918. He entered politics in 1921 as a founder of the Portuguese Catholic Centre party and was elected to the Cortes, or Parliament. Salazar returned to his teaching career shortly thereafter because he believed that his influence in Parliament was limited. He was called back into government service following the military coup led by General Gomes da Costa and General António Oscar de Fragoso Carmona in May of 1926. He was appointed minister of finance to solve the serious economic difficulties Portugal was facing, but resigned after two days when his demands for autonomy in his position were refused by the government leaders. When General Carmona ousted General Gomes da Costa in November of 1926, Salazar was again named minister of finance with full authority to deal with Portugal's economy. He instituted harsh taxation measures and slashed the government's budget. His austerity measures succeeded in producing a balanced budget for the nation after his first year in office. Salazar was also named colonial minister in 1930 and was appointed premier by President Carmona on July 5, 1932. The following year he drafted a new constitution for the nation which resulted in his being the virtual dictator of Portugal. He also became foreign minister in 1936 and sided with Generalissimo Francisco Franco's rebellion against the Republican government in Spain. Portugal remained neutral during World War II, but Salazar did allow the use of the Azores Islands for Allied air and naval bases. Salazar had relinquished the Finance Ministry in 1940, and he stepped down as foreign minister in 1947. After the conclusion of World War II, Salazar took some

steps to democratize Portugal and permitted opposition candidates to stand for office in the election in November of 1945. When the opposition coalition, the Movimento Unidade Democratica, gained support, Salazar outlawed the party in 1948. He was offered the presidency when Carmona died in office on April 18, 1951, but turned the office down, and remained premier instead. Salazar's party was challenged by Lt. Gen. Humberto Delgado in the presidential elections of 1958. Salazar's candidate, Admiral Americo Tomás, defeated the challenger decisively, but Delgado, who subsequently went into exile, remained a major critic of the regime until his bludgeoned corpse was discovered in Spain in 1965. In the early 1960s Portugal was faced with insurrections in its colonial empire when nationalist movements in Angola, Mozambique, Cape Verde, Portuguese Guinea, Macao, and Timor demanded independence. Salazar's policy in dealing with the insurrections was to meet them with military force. This was successful in the short run, but was financially expensive and cost Portugal much in the way of soldiers and negative world opinion. Salazar's rule faced several abortive revolts during the 1960s, but they scarcely threatened his power. He suffered a major stroke in early September of 1968. As his condition worsened, he was replaced as premier by Marcello Caetano on September 27, 1968, but was not told of his removal because his doctors feared the shock might kill him. Salazar lived for the next twenty months believing that he still controlled the country. He died in Lisbon at the age of 81 on July 27, 1970.

MARCELLO CAETANO (Premier, September 27, 1968–April 25, 1974). Marcello Jose das Neves Alves Caetano was born in Lisbon on August 17, 1906. He received a degree in law from the University of Lisbon in 1927. He went to work under António Salazar in the

Ministry of Finance in 1929. Caetano received his doctorate of law in 1931 and became an assistant law professor at the University of Lisbon in 1933. He also helped to draft the new constitution promoted by Salazar, who was now premier, in 1933. Caetano subsequently served the Salazar regime in a variety of posts. He served on the Council of the Colonial Empire from 1936 and was placed in charge of the Portuguese youth movement in 1940. He served as minister of overseas territories from 1944 until 1947. Caetano served on several commissions in the early 1950s, was appointed minister of state of the presidency, and became Salazar's second in command in 1955. Caetano left government service in 1958 and became rector of the University of Lisbon the following year. He resigned in 1962 in protest of a police ban on student meetings, though he continued to remain on the faculty. Caetano returned to government service in 1968 when Salazar suffered a severe stroke. Salazar was unable to carry out his duties and was removed from office by President Américo Tomás. The president and the Council of State agreed on Caetano as Salazar's successor, and he was sworn into office on September 27, 1968. He pledged to continue Salazar's policies domestically and abroad. Over the next several years, he liberalized Portugal's political process by relaxing censorship restrictions and providing for universal suffrage. He continued with Salazar's harsh policies regarding Portugal's colonial empire, however. Caetano's reforms proved too little to halt a growing tide of liberalism in the country. He was ousted by a military junta led by General António de Spínola on April 25, 1974. Caetano was sent into exile in Brazil, where he was granted political asylum. He took a position as a law professor at Rio University. He died of a heart attack at his home in Rio de Janerio at the age of 74 on October 26, 1980.

ADELINO DE PALMA CARLOS (Premier, May 16, 1974–July 13, 1974). Adelino de Palma Carlos was born in Faro on March 3, 1905. He was educated in Lisbon, where he received a degree in law. He became active in politics as a young man and founded the Republican Youth League in 1923. Palma Carlos was a leading constitutional lawyer when he was chosen by President António de Spínola to serve as premier in the first government following the ouster of the dictatorship of Marcello Caetano on May 16, 1974. Palma Carlos's cabinet consisted of various moderate and leftist elements, and he was unable to bring the opposing factions together. He petitioned the Council of State to grant him more powers, and when they refused, he resigned on July 13, 1974. He subsequently founded the Social Democratic party in opposition to the new government. Palma Carlos was also a leading spokesman against the granting of independence to Portugal's African colonies. He died in Lisbon after a long illness at the age of 87 on October 25, 1992.

VASCO DOS SANTOS GONÇALVES (Premier, July 13, 1974–July 17, 1975). Vasco dos Santos Gonçalves was born in Lisbon on May 3, 1921. He was educated at the Military College and joined the Portuguese army in 1942. He rose through the ranks to become a captain in 1954 and served in Portugal's African colonies in the mid-1950s. Gonçalves was promoted to major in 1963 and lieutenant colonel in 1967. He had become friends with General Francisco da Costa Gomes and organized the coup that ousted the government of Marcello Caetano in April of 1974. Gonçalves served as chairman of the Armed Forces Movement in the first provisional government. He was named premier on July 13, 1974, and retained office until the government was dissolved on July 17, 1975. Gonçalves subsequently served on the Revolutionary

Directorate, which served as the policy-making body of Portugal until September of 1975.

JOSÉ PINHEIRO DE AZEVEDO
(Premier, August 29, 1975–July 23, 1976). José Baptista Pinheiro de Azevedo was born in Luanda, Angola, on June 5, 1917. His father worked for the colonial government in Angola, and Azevedo joined the Naval Academy in Lisbon in 1934. He rose through the ranks and became an instructor at the Naval Academy in 1955. He returned to Angola in 1963 to lead sea defenses against rebel forces. Azevedo became commander of the marine corps in 1972, and following the military coup in April of 1974, he was promoted to admiral. He served as a member of the ruling junta. He was a close friend of President Francisco da Costa Gomes, and following anti–Communist riots against the government, Azevedo was named premier on August 29, 1975. The Socialist party won a majority of the seats in the National Assembly in elections in April of 1976. Azevedo ran for the presidency in June of 1976, but was defeated by António dos Santos Ramalho Eanes. He suffered a heart attack during the campaign and was replaced by Mário Soares as premier on July 23, 1976. He died of a heart attack in Lisbon at the age of 66 on August 10, 1983.

MÁRIO SOARES
(Premier, July 23, 1976–August 28, 1978). *See entry under Heads of State.*

ALFREDO NOBRE DA COSTA
(Premier, August 28, 1978–November 22, 1978). Alfredo Nobre da Costa was born in 1925. Nobre da Costa had served as head of Sacor, the state petroleum corporation. He served as minister of technology in the first provisional government in 1976. He was appointed premier in a caretaker capacity on August 28, 1978. Nobre da Costa

retained the position until a new government was sworn in on November 22, 1978.

CARLOS DA MOTA PINTO
(Premier, November 22, 1978–June 7, 1979). Carlos da Mota Pinto was born in 1936. He was an educator who became a professor of civil law. He earned a doctorate in political science in 1970. Mota Pinto served on the Council of Law at Coimbra University from May of 1974. He was elected to the Legislative Assembly in April of 1975 as a member of the Social Democratic party. He left the party following a disagreement with Francisco Sá Carneiro, the party leader, in December of 1975. Mota Pinto was named minister of commerce and tourism in the government of Mário Soares in July of 1976 and served until December of 1977. He was named premier on November 22, 1978, and began an attempt to control the inflation rate in Portugal. His government survived a vote of no confidence in December of 1978, but his budget plans were defeated by a leftist coalition in the Assembly in March of 1979. Mota Pinto resigned from office on June 7, 1979. He served as deputy premier and minister of defense in the government of Mário Soares from 1983, but resigned from those positions because of factionalism in the Social Democratic party. He died of a heart attack in Lisbon at the age of 48 on May 7, 1985.

MARIA DE LOURDES PINTASILGO
(Premier, August 1, 1979–January 3, 1980). Maria de Lourdes Pintasilgo was born in Abrantes on January 18, 1930. She was educated in Lisbon and was active in Catholic women's organizations. She served as president of Pax Romana from 1956 until 1958 and served as vice president of the Grail from 1965 until 1969. Lourdes Pintasilgo was named chairman of the National Committee on the Status of Women in 1970 and served until 1974. She also served as a member of the Portuguese delegation

to the United Nations from 1971 until 1972. Following the ouster of the Caetano government in 1974, she was named minister of social affairs until 1975. She served as ambassador to the United Nations Educational, Scientific and Cultural Organization (UNESCO) from 1976 until 1979. Lourdes Pintasilgo was appointed premier in a caretaker government on August 1, 1979. She resigned the position on December 27, 1979, following general elections, but remained as caretaker until a new government was formed on January 3, 1980. She subsequently served as an advisor to the president from 1981 until 1985 and remained active in various civic and religious organizations. Lourdes Pintasilgo was an independent candidate for the presidency in elections held in January of 1986, but finished fifth in the balloting.

FRANCISCO SÁ CARNEIRO (Premier, January 3, 1980–December 4, 1980). Francisco Sá Carneiro was born in Oporto on July 19, 1934. He graduated from law school and worked as a lawyer in Oporto. In 1969 he was elected to the National Assembly. He was active in attempting to liberalize the authoritarian regime of Premier Marcello Caetano and resigned from the Assembly in 1973. Following the military coup that ousted the Caetano government in April of 1974, Sá Carneiro founded the Popular Democratic party. He served in the cabinet of Adelino da Palma Carlos as minister without portfolio, but resigned in protest of the government's nationalization policies. In the elections of December of 1979, Sá Carneiro led the Democratic Alliance party to victory. He became premier on January 3, 1980, and began plans for the reduction of nationalization of industry and for seeking Portugal's admission to the European Economic Community. Sá Carneiro remained premier until December 4, 1980, when he was killed in a light-plane crash near Lisbon.

FRANCISCO PINTO BALSEMÃO (Premier, December 22, 1980–June 9, 1983). Francisco Jose Pereira Pinto Balsemão was born in Lisbon on September 1, 1937. He studied law but instead became a journalist, serving as editor of *Mais Alto* from 1961 until 1963. In 1973 he became the publisher of the weekly newspaper *Expresso*. He served in the National Assembly, where he was a vocal critic of the government of Marcello Caetano. Following the military ouster of Caetano in April of 1974, Pinto Balsemão cofounded the Popular Democratic party with Francisco Sá Carneiro. He served as vice president of the Constituent Assembly in 1975 and was the spokesman for the opposition on foreign affairs in 1977. He was elected to the Assembly in December of 1979 and served as deputy premier in Sá Carneiro's government. Pinto Balsemão became premier on December 22, 1980, following Sá Carneiro's death. He resigned as premier on June 9, 1983, following the breakup of the Democratic Alliance coalition government. He left government to accept a position with the Francisco da Carneiro Institute and in 1990 served as president of the European Institute for the Media.

MÁRIO SOARES (Premier, June 9, 1983–November 6, 1985). *See entry under Heads of State.*

ANÍBAL CAVACO SILVA (Premier, November 6, 1985–). Aníbal Cavaco Silva was born in Loule on July 15, 1939. He studied economics in Great Britain and became a professor of economics and financial studies. He served as director of research and statistics at the Bank of Portugal in 1977 and was named to the cabinet as minister of finance and planning in 1980. Cavaco Silva returned to the Bank of Portugal in 1981. He also became president of the Council for National Planning in 1981. He became leader of the Social Democratic party in 1985. Following the general elections of 1985, he became premier of Portugal in a minority government on November 6, 1985. In April of 1987 the government was brought down by a censure vote, and new elections were called.

Cavaco Silva remained as caretaker premier until the elections. His party won a majority of seats in Parliament, and he formed a new cabinet. The Social Democratic party was again victorious in the elections in January of 1991.

Qatar, State of

(Dawlat Qatar)

Qatar is a country on a peninsula on the western coast of the Persian Gulf. It was granted independence by Great Britain on September 3, 1971.

HEADS OF STATE

AHMAD IBN ALI IBN ABDULLAH ATH-THANI (Emir, October 24, 1960–February 22, 1972). Ahmad ibn Ali ibn Abdullah ath-Thani was born in 1917. He was crowned emir of Qatar following the abdication of his father, Sheikh Ali ibn Abdullah ibn Qasim, on October 24, 1960. Sheikh Ahmad attempted to join Qatar in a Federation of Arab Emirates with the Trucial Sheikhdoms and Bahrain following Great Britain's announcement of its intention to withdraw from the Persian Gulf in 1968. The sheikhdoms could not agree on a governmental structure, and Qatar opted for independence. A treaty was signed with Great Britain establishing Qatar's full independence on September 3, 1971. Sheikh Ahmad ruled as emir of Qatar until he was ousted by his cousin the prime minister, Sheikh Khalifah ibn Hamad ath-Thani, on February 22, 1972.

KHALIFAH IBN HAMAD ATH-THANI (Emir, February 22, 1972–). Khalifah ibn Hamad ath-Thani was born in Doha in 1932. He was the son of Sheikh Hamad bin Abdullah bin Jassim al-Thani. He attended the Royal Military College in Great Britain and was named heir apparent of Qatar following the death of his father in 1948. Sheikh Khalifah subsequently served as chief of security forces and in 1960 became deputy ruler. He also served as minister of education from 1960 until 1970. Following Qatar's independence from Great Britain on September 3, 1971, Sheikh Khalifah became prime minister and also served as minister of finance. He deposed his cousin, Emir Ahmad, on February 22, 1972, in a bloodless coup while Ahmad was on a hunting trip. Sheikh Khalifah ruled Qatar as an absolute monarch. Qatar remained a strong supporter of the Palestinian cause and broke relations with Egypt following the signing of the Egyptian-Israeli peace treaty in 1979. Qatar joined with other Gulf states in forming the Gulf Cooperation Council in 1981. Sheikh Khalifah denounced the Iraqi takeover of Kuwait in August of 1990 and participated in the subsequent United States–led war against Iraq. Qatar signed a defense pact with the United States in May of 1992.

HEAD OF GOVERNMENT

KHALIFAH IBN HAMAD ATH-THANI (Prime Minister, September 3, 1971– February 22, 1972). *See entry under Heads of State.*

Romania

Romania is a country in southeastern Europe.

HEADS OF STATE

MICHAEL (King, September 6, 1940– December 30, 1947). Michael was born on October 25, 1921. He was the son of Carol II of Romania and Princess Helene of Greece. Michael was named heir apparent to his grandfather, King Ferdinand of Romania, in 1926 when his father was disinherited. He succeeded to the throne under a Regency Council upon King Ferdinand's death on July 20, 1927. Carol returned from exile in 1930 and was proclaimed king on June 9, 1930. When King Carol was forced to abdicate on September 6, 1940, Michael was reinstated as king. Michael led the coup that ousted Ion Antonescu, the pro-Nazi dictator, in 1944. He was forced to abdicate on December 30, 1947, following the Communist takeover of Romania. He went into exile in Great Britain and subsequently went to Switzerland in 1956, where he worked as a test pilot. Michael later worked as a stockbroker and worked for an electronics company. Following the overthrow of the Communist government of Nicolae Ceauşescu, Michael returned to Romania in December of 1990, but was subsequently deported. Michael was invited by the Eastern Orthodox Primate of Suceava to celebrate Easter in Romania, and he visited the country on April 26, 1992.

CONSTANTINE I. PARHON (President, April 13, 1948–June 2, 1952).

Constantine I. Parhon was born in Cimpulung on October 27, 1874. He graduated from the University of Bucharest in 1898. He was a leading authority in gerontology and a founder of the field of endocrinology. Parhon was the coauthor of *Interna Secretion* in 1909, the first book in the field of endocrinology. He served on the faculty at the University of Iasi, where he headed the department of neurology and psychiatry from 1912. He was named head of the endocrinology department at the University of Bucharest in 1934 and became a member of the Romanian Academy in 1939. Parhon organized the Institute of Endocrinology in 1946. He joined the Communist party in 1944 and was elected to the first Romanian Parliament following World War II. He was selected as president of the Romanian Grand National Assembly on April 13, 1948. Parhon remained Romania's head of state until June 2, 1952. He served as chairman of the Romanian Society for Friendship with the Union of Soviet Socialist Republics until 1967, when he was named honorary chairman. Parhon died in Bucharest at the age of 94 on August 9, 1969.

PETRU GROZA (President, June 2, 1952–January 7, 1958). Petru Groza was born in Bacia, Transylvania, on December 6, 1884. He attended the Universities of Budapest, Berlin, and

Leipzig and received a degree in law. He returned to Deva, where he opened a legal practice. Groza served on the Grand Council of Transylvania from 1918 until 1919, when he was elected to the Romanian Chamber of Deputies as a member of the Progressive Peasants' party. He served in the cabinet of Alexandru Averescu as minister for Transylvania from 1920 until 1921 and as minister of public works and communications from 1926 until 1927. He then retired from politics until 1933, when he founded the Ploughmen's Front. Groza reemerged to prominence on March 6, 1945, when the Soviet Union forced King Michael to name him as prime minister to succeed General Nicolae Radescu. Groza forced King Michael's abdication in December of 1947 and declared Romania a people's republic. Communist party leader Gheorghe Gheorghiu-Dej remained the most powerful political figure in the country and replaced Groza as prime minister on June 2, 1952. Groza was named to the position of chairman of the Presidium of the Grand National Assembly and thus served as Romania's head of state. He was renamed to the chairmanship in March of 1957. Groza suffered from poor health in 1957 and was hospitalized for a stomach operation. He died in Bucharest at the age of 72 on January 7, 1958.

ION GHEORGHE MAURER (President, January 11, 1958–March 21, 1961). Ion Gheorghe Maurer was born in Bucharest on September 23, 1902. He studied international law and was active in the Romanian Communist party from 1936. He was confined at Tirgu Jiu concentration camp for his anti-Fascist activities during World War II. Maurer entered the government following the liberation of Romania in August of 1944 and served as deputy minister of transportation and public works from 1945 until 1946. He subsequently served as deputy minister of the national economy until 1947. He was

elected to the Central Committee of the Romanian Communist party the following year. Maurer served as foreign minister from 1957 until 1958. He was elected president of the Grand National Assembly on January 11, 1958, and served until his appointment as prime minister on March 21, 1961. He also served on the Politburo of the Romanian Workers' party from 1960 until 1965. He then served on the Executive Committee of the Communist party of Romania. He remained prime minister until his retirement on March 26, 1974.

GHEORGHE   GHEORGHIU-DEJ (President, March 21, 1961–March 19, 1965). Gheorghe Gheorghiu-Dej was born in Birlad on November 8, 1901. He was active in the labor movement as a young man and joined the outlawed Romanian Communist party in 1930. He was arrested for his activities as a strike organizer and sentenced to twelve years in prison in 1933. Gheorghiu-Dej was released from prison in 1944, after the Soviet liberation of Romania. He was then named by Josef Stalin as general secretary of the Romanian Workers' party and was instrumental in forcing the abdication of King Michael in December of 1947. He also served in the government as vice-chairman of the Council of Ministers from 1948. Gheorghiu-Dej consolidated his leadership of the party in the early 1950s by purging former foreign minister Anna Pauker and Vassili Luka. He replaced Petru Groza as prime minister on June 2, 1952. Gheorghiu-Dej stepped down as prime minister on October 3, 1955, but retained the party chairmanship. He was also elected president of the State Council on March 21, 1961, and became head of state of Romania. Relations between Romania and the Soviet Union became strained in the early 1960s over Romania's independent policy of encouraging industrial development rather than serving as a food supplier to the Soviet-bloc nations. Gheorghiu-Dej sought an independent

position from the Soviet Union and remained neutral in the growing Sino-
Soviet dispute. He retained his government and party positions until his death
from pneumonia in Bucharest at the
age of 63 on March 19, 1965.

CHIVU STOICA (President, March 22,
1965–December 9, 1967). Chivu Stoica
was born in Smeieni, Buzau District,
on August 8, 1908. He was employed as
a railway worker in his youth and became involved in the trade union movement. He joined the Romanian Communist party in 1930 and was active in
the railway workers' strike in Grivitza
in 1933. Stoica was arrested for his part
in the strike and was sentenced to
fifteen years in prison. He was released
following the Soviet Union's invasion
of Romania in August of 1944. He was
elected to the Communist party's Central Committee and Politburo in 1945
and was elected to the Grand National
Assembly the following year. Stoica
served in the government as minister of
industry from April of 1948 until November of 1949. He remained minister
of metal and chemical industries and
later served as minister of metallurgical
industry. He was also appointed vice-
chairman of the Council of Ministers in
March of 1950. Communist party
leader Gheorghe Gheorghiu-Dej relinquished the position of prime minister
on October 3, 1955, and Stoica was
named to replace him. He was replaced
in a government reorganization on
March 21, 1961, and was named to the
position of secretary of the party's Central
Committee. Stoica succeeded Gheorghiu-
Dej as chairman of the State Council
on March 22, 1965. He retained office
until December 9, 1967, when Communist party leader Nicolae Ceauşescu took
the office of president. Stoica was also
dropped from his position as party secretary in 1969. He was elected to the exe-
cutive-political committee of the party
as a candidate member in November of
1974. Stoica died in Bucharest at the
age of 67 on February 18, 1975.

NICOLAE CEAUŞESCU (President,
December 9, 1967–December 25, 1989).
Nicolae Ceauşescu was born in Scor-
nicesti on January 26, 1918. He worked
in a factory in Bucharest and joined the
workers movement in his early teens.
He became active in the Union of
Communist Youth in 1933 and became
a leading organizer of the outlawed
Romanian Communist party. Ceauşescu was arrested in 1936 and served
several years in prison. He served on
the party's central committee on youth
after his release and was again imprisoned in 1940. He escaped from prison
following the Soviet army's invasion of
Romania in August of 1944. Ceauşescu
again served as a leading figure in the
Union of Communist Youth and was
elected a candidate member of the Communist party's Central Committee in
October of 1945. He was subsequently
appointed to the political directorate of
the Romanian army, with the rank of
brigadier general. He was also elected
to the Grand National Assembly in November of 1946. Ceauşescu was named
to the Central Committee of the Romanian Workers' party in 1952 following
the consolidation of power in the party
by party leader Gheorghe Gheorghiu-
Dej. He was named a full member of
the Politburo in December of 1955. He
became deputy to the party first secretary, Gheorghiu-Dej, in 1957 and was
chosen as Gheorghiu-Dej's successor to
lead the party. Ceauşescu was selected
as first secretary on March 22, 1965,
following Gheorgiu-Dej's death. He
also assumed the post of president of
the State Council on December 9, 1967.
He continued his predecessor's policy
of independence from the Soviet Union
and was a critic of Soviet intervention
in Czechoslovakia in 1968. While his independent policies earned him respect
among the Western powers, Romania's
declining economic conditions in the
1980s led to increased dissent against
his rule. His attempts to pay off Romania's foreign debts by exporting food
and fuel led to widespread shortages

throughout the country. His opposition to liberal reforms during the late 1980s led to increasingly repressive measures. Democratic reforms were sweeping Communist nations in Eastern Europe, and demonstrations against the Ceauşescu regime took place throughout Romania. The government ordered troops to open fire on protesters in Timisoara on December 17, 1989. This action led to a violent revolt against the government. The armed forces turned against Ceauşescu and he and his wife, Elena, were captured. They were tried and summarily executed near Bucharest on December 25, 1989.

ION ILIESCU (President, December 26, 1989-   ). Ion Iliescu was born in Oltenita, in the Ilfov District, on March 3, 1930. He was educated in Bucharest and Moscow and joined the Romanian Communist party in 1953. He was elected to the National Assembly in 1957. Iliescu served in various party positions and was a member of the Central Committee of the Romanian Communist party from 1968 until 1984. He worked as the director of a technical publishing house from 1984 until 1989. Iliescu was named provisional president following the ouster of Nicolae Ceauşescu on December 25, 1989. He served as president of the National Salvation Front and was president of the Provisional Council for National Unity from February until elections were held in May of 1990. Iliescu was elected president of Romania and took office in June of 1990. He was reelected in a presidential runoff on October 11, 1992.

HEADS OF GOVERNMENT

PETRE GROZA (Prime Minister, March 6, 1945-June 2, 1952). *See entry under Heads of State.*

GHEORGHE GHEORGHIU-DEJ (Prime Minister, June 2, 1952-October 3, 1955). *See entry under Heads of State.*

CHIVU STOICA (Prime Minister, October 3, 1955-March 21, 1961). *See entry under Heads of State.*

ION GHEORGHE MAURER (Prime Minister, March 21, 1961-March 26, 1974). *See entry under Heads of State.*

MANEA MĂNESCU (Prime Minister, March 26, 1974-March 29, 1979). Manea Mănescu was born in Braila on August 9, 1916. He joined the Romanian Communist party in 1936 and served in various party and governmental positions. He was named minister of finance in 1955 and served until 1957.

Mănescu was elected to the Central Committee in 1960 and became a member of the Grand National Assembly the following year. He served as vice president of the State Council from 1969 until 1972, when he became vice-chairman of the Council of Ministers. Mănescu was selected as prime minister on March 26, 1974, and retained office until March 29, 1979. He resumed the position of vice president of the State Council in 1982 and became first vice president in 1987. He retained this office until the overthrow of the government of Nicolae Ceauşescu in December of 1989. Mănescu was arrested the following January. He was tried on charges of complicity in genocide and sentenced to life imprisonment.

ILIE VERDET (Prime Minister, March 29, 1978-May 21, 1982). Ilie Verdet was born in Comanesti, in Bacau County, on May 10, 1925. He was educated in Bucharest and joined the Communist party in 1945. He rose through the ranks of the party and was elected to the Grand National Assembly in 1961. Verdet held various party and government positions and served as first deputy chairman of the Council of Ministers from 1966 until 1974. He subsequently served as secretary of the Central Committee until he was named prime minister on March 29, 1978. He retained that position until May 21, 1982, when he returned to the Central Committee as secretary. Verdet served in this post until 1985 and then served as minister of mines from 1985 until 1986.

CONSTANTIN DĂSCĂLESCU (Prime Minister, May 21, 1982–December 25, 1989). Constantin Dăscălescu was born in Breaza in 1923. He was educated in Bucharest and joined the Romanian Communist party in 1945. He was active in the trade union movement and in the Communist party. Dăscălescu was elected to the Grand National Assembly in 1965. He became a member of the State Council in 1973 and was named chairman of the Council of Ministers on May 21, 1982. He retained the office until the ouster of Nicolae Ceauşescu on December 25, 1989. Dăscălescu was arrested by the new government in January of 1990.

PETRE ROMAN (Prime Minister, December 26, 1989–October 1, 1991). Petre Roman was born in Bucharest on July 22, 1946. He was educated in Bucharest and Toulouse. He subsequently served as a professor in the Hydraulics Department at the Bucharest Polytechnic Institute. Roman was a leader of the National Salvation Front and was chosen as prime minister on December 26, 1989, following the ouster of the regime of Nicolae Ceauşescu. He stepped down from office on October 1, 1991, and remained the leader of the National Salvation Front.

THEODOR STOLOJAN (Prime Minister, October 16, 1991–November 4, 1992). Theodor Dumitru Stolojan was born in Tirgoviste on October 23, 1943. He studied economics in Bucharest and was employed by the Ministry of the Alimentary Industry from 1966 until 1972. He worked in the Ministry of Finance from 1972 until 1982. Stolojan worked in the Department of Foreign Currencies and International Financial Relations from 1982 until 1987. He was named first deputy minister of finance in 1989 and became minister in 1990. He retained that office until October 16, 1991, when he was confirmed as prime minister of Romania. Stolojan was replaced on November 4, 1992.

NICOLAE VACAROIU (Prime Minister, November 4, 1992–). Nicolae Vacaroiu was an official in the Ministry of Economy and Finance. He was asked by President Ion Iliescu to form a government on November 3, 1992.

Russia (Russian Federation)

(Rossiiskaya Federatsiya)

Russia is a country that stretches from eastern Europe across northern Asia to the Pacific Ocean.

HEAD OF STATE

BORIS YELTSIN (President, July 10, 1991-). Boris Nikolayevich Yeltsin was born in Sverdlovsk on February 1, 1931. He attended the Urals Polytechnical Institute, where he received a degree in engineering in 1955. He worked as a construction engineer and joined the Communist party in 1961. Yeltsin became active as a party organizer in the Sverdlovsk District in 1968 and rose to become first secretary of the party committee there in 1976. He was brought to Moscow by Mikhail Gorbachev in April of 1985 and became first secretary of the Moscow Communist party. When Yeltsin attempted to eliminate corruption in the party, he came into conflict with powerful party figures. Gorbachev dismissed Yeltsin in November of 1987 to preserve unity in the party following Yeltsin's criticism of his conservative rival, Yegor Ligachev. Yeltsin was subsequently named first deputy chairman of the State Committee for Construction. He became a leading symbol of the democratic movement in the Soviet Union and was elected to the Congress of Peoples' Deputies in March of 1989. He was selected as chairman of the Russian Supreme Soviet on May 29, 1990. Yeltsin defeated former Soviet premier Nikolai Ryzhkov for the presidency of Russia on June 12, 1991, and was sworn in on July 10, 1991. Communist hardliners staged a coup attempt against the reformist government of Soviet president Mikhail Gorbachev on August 19, 1991. Yeltsin avoided being captured by the rebels and went to the White House, the Russian Parliament building in Moscow. He led the resistance to the coup and rallied the support of the people. The coup collapsed within several days, and Gorbachev was returned to power. Yeltsin began acting independently of the Soviet government and banned the Communist party in Russia. He assumed the duties of prime minister on November 6, 1991, as the successor to Ivan Silayev, who had resigned the previous September. He joined with the leaders of other Russian republics to announce the formation of the Commonwealth of Independent States on December 8, 1991. When Gorbachev resigned from office on December 25, 1991, Yeltsin took control of the armed forces in Russia. He also became minister of defense in March of 1992. He stepped down as prime minister on June 15, 1992, and appointed his economic advisor, Yegor Gaidar, to the office. The Russian Congress of People's Deputies challenged Yeltsin's economic policies and refused to confirm Gaidar as prime minister. Yeltsin was forced to reach a compromise with conservative members of the Parliament in December of 1992 that reduced his executive powers.

HEADS OF GOVERNMENT

BORIS YELTSIN (November 6, 1991–June 15, 1992). *See entry under Heads of State.*

YEGOR TIMUROVICH GAIDAR (Prime Minister, June 15, 1992–December 14, 1992). Yegor Timurovich Gaidar was born to a distinguished Soviet family in 1956. He attended Moscow State University, where he received a degree in economics. He became a proponent of Western economic theory and became the economic editor of the Communist party journal, *Kommunist* in 1987. Gaidar later served as economic editor at *Pravda* for six months in 1990. He formed the Institute for Economic Policy to promote his ideas in 1991. He supported Boris Yeltsin's resistance to the right-wing coup in August of 1991 and subsquently worked with Yeltsin to propose economic reforms for Russia. When Yeltsin became prime minister of Russian in November of 1991, Gaidar became minister of finance. Yeltsin stepped down as prime minister on June 15, 1992, and Gaidar was appointed acting chairman of the Council of Ministers by presidential decree. He remained a guiding force behind Boris Yeltsin's economic policies. On December 9, 1992, the Russian Congress refused to confirm Gaidar's appointment as prime minister. In a compromise with the Congress, President Yeltsin replaced Gaidar with Viktor Chernomydrin on December 14, 1992.

VIKTOR CHERNOMYRDIN (Prime Minister, December 14, 1992–). Viktor Stepanovich Chernomyrdin was born in the Orenburg region in 1938. He was educated from a correspondence technical school and worked in an oil refinery. He was employed in the industrial department of the Communist party in Orsk from 1967 until 1973. Chernomyrdin subsequently worked in the gas industry, and he became a deputy minister in 1985. He transformed the gas industry into the Gazprom, a state corporation, and served as chairman from 1989. He was appointed to Yegor Gaidar's government as deputy prime minister for fuel and energy in May of 1992. The Congress of People's Deputies refused to confirm Gaidar as prime minister, and President Boris Yeltsin named Chernomyrdin to the position as a compromise choice. He was confirmed into office on December 14, 1992.

Rwanda, Republic of

(République Rwandaise)

Rwanda is a country in central Africa. It was granted independence from a United Nations trusteeship administered by Belgium on July 1, 1962.

HEADS OF STATE

GRÉGOIRE KAYIBANDA (President, October 26, 1961–July 5, 1973). Grégoire Kayibanda was born at Tare, in Gitarama, on May 1, 1924. He was a member of the Hutu tribe and was educated at local Roman Catholic mission schools. He was employed as a teacher in 1949 and was named inspector of schools in 1953. Kayibanda formed the Muhutu Social Movement in 1957 and was an advocate of Hutu rights in the Tutsi government. Mwami Matari III, the leader of the Tutsis, died under suspicious circumstances on July 25, 1959,

and the new mwami, Kigeri V, attempted to eliminate the Hutu leadership. Kayibanda was given protection by the Belgian colonial authorities, and a violent Hutu uprising forced Kigeri V into exile in 1959. Kayibanda's party won a majority of the seats in assembly elections in June of 1960. The Rwanda monarchy was abolished in September of 1961, and Rwanda was declared a republic. Kayibanda was selected as Rwanda's president, and he retained power when the country was granted independence on July 1, 1962. Tutsi guerrillas launched a civil war against the government in December of 1963, and Kayibanda's harsh reprisals drove thousands of Tutsis into exile the following year. Kayibanda was reelected to the presidency in October of 1965 and October of 1969. There were more outbreaks of Tutsi violence in the early 1970s, and Kayibanda was ousted in a military coup led by General Juvénal Habyarimana on July 5, 1973. He was placed under house arrest following the coup and died on December 22, 1976.

JUVÉNAL HABYARIMANA (President, July 5, 1973–April 6, 1994). Juvénal Habyarimana was born in Gasiza, Gisenyi, on August 3, 1937. He was educated at Lovanium University in Kinshasa and entered the Officers' Training College at Kigali in 1960. He received further military training in Belgium and served as an officer in the Rwandan armed forces. Habyarimana was promoted to commander of the army in June of 1965 and was named to the cabinet as minister of defense the follow-

ing November. Continued fighting between the rival Hutu and Tutsi tribes led Habyarimana to lead a military coup that ousted the government of Grégoire Kayibanda on July 5, 1973. He formed a civilian-military government and organized the National Revolutionary Movement for Development as the only legal party in 1976. Habyarimana promoted a new constitution in December of 1978 and was confirmed for an additional term of office as president. He survived a coup attempt in 1980 and was again unopposed for reelection to the presidency in December of 1988. Habyarimana allowed the formation of rival political parties in 1991 and made plans for multiparty elections. Habyarimana and President Cyprian Ntayamira of Burundi were killed in an air crash on April 6, 1994, near the Rwandan capital when returning from a meeting with other East African leaders in Tanzania. Amidst claims that the leaders' plane had been shot down by rebels, a wave of violence broke out between the ruling Hutus and rebel Tutsis.

HEADS OF GOVERNMENT

SYLVESTRE NSANZIMANA (Prime Minister, October 12, 1991–April 2, 1992). Sylvestre Nsanzimana served as minister of justice in the government of President Juvenal Habyarimana. He was selected to serve in the newly created position of prime minister on October 12, 1991. Nsanzimana stepped down on April 2, 1992, following the

refusal of opposition parties to take part in the government.

DISMAS NSENGIYAREMYE (Prime Minister, April 2, 1992–). Dismas Nsengiyaremye was named prime minister by President Juvenal Habyarimana on April 2, 1992. He formed a transitional coalition government two weeks later.

Saint Kitts and Nevis,
Federation of
(Federation of Saint Christopher and Nevis)

Saint Kitts and Nevis form a country consisting of two islands in the eastern Caribbean Sea. It was granted independence from Great Britain on September 19, 1983.

HEAD OF STATE

SIR CLEMENT ARRINDELL (Governor-General, September 19, 1983–   ). Clement Athelston Arrindell was born in Saint Kitts on April 16, 1932. He studied law in London and returned to Saint Kitts to practice in 1959. He served as a district magistrate from 1966 until 1974. Arrindell was named chief magistrate in 1975 and served until 1977. The following year he was named a puisne judge and served until his appointment as governor in 1981. He became the first governor general of independent Saint Kitts andNevis on September 19, 1983.

HEAD OF GOVERNMENT

KENNEDY A. SIMMONDS (Prime Minister, February 18, 1980–   ). Kennedy Alphonse Simmonds was born on April 12, 1936. He studied medicine at the University of the West Indies and practiced anesthesiology in Jamaica, the Bahamas, and Pittsburgh before returning to Saint Kitts in 1969. After several unsuccessful attempts, he was elected to Parliament in 1979. Simmonds led the People's Action party to victory and became prime minister of a coalition government with the Nevis Reformation party on February 18, 1980. He remained head of the government following the islands' independence on September 19, 1983. He also served in the government as minister of finance, home, and foreign affairs from 1984. Simmonds's coalition government remained in power following legislative elections in June of 1984 and March of 1989.

Saint Lucia

Saint Lucia is an island country in the southeastern Caribbean Sea. It was granted independence from Great Britain on February 22, 1979.

HEADS OF STATE

ALLEN MONTGOMERY LEWIS (Governor-General, February 22, 1979–February 22, 1980). Allen Montgomery Lewis was born in Castries on October 26, 1909. He studied law in Saint Lucia and began practicing in 1931. He was elected to the Castries Town Council in 1942 and served until 1956. During the 1950s he served as a judge on various courts. Lewis served as president of the West Indies Senate from 1958 until 1959. He became chief justice of the West Indies Associated States Supreme Court in 1967 and became governor of Saint Lucia in 1974. Lewis was appointed governor-general when Saint Lucia was granted independence on February 22, 1979, and remained in office until his retirement on February 22, 1980. He was reappointed governor-general in December of 1982 and served until April 30, 1987. He also served as chancellor of the University of the West Indies from 1975 until his retirement in 1989. Lewis died in February of 1993 at the age of 84.

BOSWELL WILLIAMS (Acting Governor-General, February 22, 1980–December 1982). Boswell Williams was appointed acting governor-general following the retirement of Allen Montgomery Lewis on February 22, 1980. He remained acting governor-general until December of 1982, when Lewis was reappointed to the office.

ALLEN MONTGOMERY LEWIS (Governor-General, December 1982–April 30, 1987). *See earlier entry under Heads of State.*

SIR VINCENT FLOISSAC (Governor General, April 30, 1987–October 10, 1988). Sir Vincent Floissac was named to replace Allen Montgomery Lewis as governor-general on April 30, 1987. He served until October 10, 1988, when he was replaced by Sir Stanislaus A. James.

SIR STANISLAUS A. JAMES (Governor-General, October 10, 1988–). Stanislaus Anthony James was born in Castries on November 13, 1919. He was educated locally and in Canada. He returned to Saint Lucia to work in the civil service and served as justice of the peace from 1955. James was named acting governor-general following the resignation of Sir Vincent Floissac on October 10, 1988. He was confirmed to the position on February 22, 1992.

HEADS OF GOVERNMENT

JOHN G. M. COMPTON (Prime Minister, February 22, 1979–July 2, 1979). John George Melvin Compton was born in Canouan on St. Vincent in 1926. He received a degree in law from the London School of Economics and opened a legal practice in Saint Lucia in 1953. He joined the Labor party in 1954 and served in the government as minister of trade and production in 1957. Compton was elected deputy leader of the Labor party in 1957. He resigned from the party to form the United Workers' party in 1961 and served as its leader from 1964. He was also elected chief minister of Saint Lucia in 1964. Saint Lucia was granted statehood by Great Britain in 1967, and Compton remained head of government as premier. He became Saint Lucia's first prime minister following independence on February 22, 1979. The United Workers' party was defeated by the Labor party in elections, and Compton was replaced by Allan Louisy as prime minister on July 2, 1979. The United Workers'

party returned to power in elections in 1982, and Compton was renamed prime minister on May 3, 1982. He barely retained office following a close election in April of 1987. Saint Lucia's economy improved under Compton's leadership, however, and the United Workers' Party increased their victory margin in parliamentary elections in April of 1992.

ALLAN LOUISY (Prime Minister, July 2, 1979–May 4, 1981). Allan Fitzgerald Laurent Louisy was born in 1916. He was educated locally and received a degree in law in 1945. He worked as a registrar of the Supreme Court from 1946 until 1950. Louisy served as senior magistrate in Antigua from 1951 until 1954. He subsequently held legal positions in Montserrat, Dominica, and Jamaica, where he served on the Associated States Appeal Court from 1964. He retired from the judiciary in 1973 and joined the opposition Saint Lucia Labor party. Louisy was elected to the House of Assembly the following year and became leader of the Labor party in 1976. The Labor party defeated John Compton's United Workers' party in July of 1979 in Saint Lucia's first elections following independence the previous February. Louisy took office as prime minister on July 2, 1979. He was challenged for leadership of the Labor party by Deputy Prime Minister George Odlum. Louisy resigned on April 30, 1981, following failure to win approval for his budget proposals. He relinquished office to Winston Cenac on May 4, 1981. Louisy remained in the government as minister without portfolio until January of 1982, when he was named minister of legal affairs. He left the government following the defeat of the Labor party in May of 1982. He continued to remain active in the Labor party.

WINSTON F. CENAC (Prime Minister, May 4, 1981–January 16, 1982). Winston Francis Cenac was born in Saint Lucia on September 14, 1925. He was educated at St. Mary's College in Saint Lucia and worked as a court clerk. He continued his studies and received a law degree from the University of London in 1954. Cenac held various legal positions and was appointed attorney general of Saint Lucia in 1962. He was named attorney general of Saint Vincent in 1964 and of Grenada in 1966. He served as director of public prosecutions in Grenada

from 1967 until 1969, when he returned to Saint Lucia to practice law. Cenac returned to the judiciary as a puisne judge in Saint Vincent in 1971 and puisne judge in Saint Kitts and Nevis and the British Virgin Islands in 1972. He again returned to private practice in 1973. Cenac was elected to the House of Assembly in 1979 as a member of the Labor party. He was selected to serve as prime minister of Saint Lucia on May 4, 1981, following the resignation of Allan Louisy. Cenac's government resigned on January 16, 1982. Cenac served as president of the Saint Lucia Bar Association in 1989.

MICHAEL PILGRIM (Interim Prime Minister, January 17, 1982–May 3, 1982). Michael Pilgrim was appointed interim prime minister on January 17, 1982, following the resignation of the Labor Party government of Winston Cenac. He formed an all-party government and held elections in May of 1982. Pilgrim relinquished office to John Compton on May 3, 1982, following the victory of the United Workers' party in the election. Pilgrim was a member of the United Workers' party and remained active in political affairs.

JOHN G. M. COMPTON (Prime Minister, May 3, 1982–). *See earlier entry under Heads of Government.*

Saint Vincent and the Grenadines

Saint Vincent and the Grenadines is a country consisting of a large island and a group of smaller islands in the southeastern Caribbean Sea. It was granted independence from Great Britain on October 27, 1979.

HEADS OF STATE

SIR SYDNEY GUN-MUNRO (Governor-General, October 27, 1979–February 28, 1985). Sydney Douglas Gun-

Munro was born on November 29, 1916. He was educated at King's College, where he received a degree in medicine.

He worked as a surgeon at the General Hospital in Saint Vincent from 1949 until 1971. Gun-Munro became governor of Saint Vincent in 1977 and was appointed governor-general when the island was granted independence on October 27, 1979. He resigned his position on February 28, 1985.

SIR JOSEPH LAMBERT EUSTACE (Governor General, February 28, 1985–February 29, 1988). Joseph Lambert Eustace was born on February 28, 1908. He was elected to Parliament in 1966 and served until 1971. He was elected Speaker of the House of Assembly and served until 1974. Eustace was appointed governor-general of Saint Vincent and the Grenadines on February 28, 1985. He served until his retirement on February 29, 1988.

HENRY HARVEY WILLIAMS (Acting Governor-General, February 28, 1988–September 20, 1989). Henry Harvey Williams was named acting governor-general of Saint Vincent and the Grenadines following the resignation of Sir Joseph Eustace on February 28, 1988. He remained in that position until Sir David Jack was chosen as governor-general on September 20, 1989.

SIR DAVID JACK (Governor-General, September 20, 1989–   ). David Emmanuel Jack was born in Victoria Village on July 16, 1918. He was educated locally and at LaSalle University in Chicago. He returned to Saint Vincent in 1934 and worked as a teacher. Jack trained to be an accountant and entered private industry in 1943. He entered politics and was elected to the House of Assembly in 1984. He served in the cabinet as minister of house, labor, and community development from 1984 until 1986. Jack was appointed minister of health in 1987 and served until 1989. He retired from the House of Assembly in May of 1989. Jack was appointed to succeed Henry H. Williams as governor-general on September 20, 1989.

HEADS OF GOVERNMENT

MILTON CATO (Prime Minister, October 27, 1979–July 30, 1984). Robert Milton Cato was born on June 3, 1915. He served in the Canadian army during World War II. He served on various public boards in Saint Vincent and was a representative to the West Indies Federal Parliament from 1958 until 1962. Cato was chief minister of Saint Vincent from 1967 until 1969 and subsequently served as premier from 1969 until 1972 and again from 1974. He became the first prime minister of the independent nation of Saint Vincent and the Grenadines on October 27, 1979. Cato's Saint Vincent Labor party was defeated in elections in July of 1984, and he was replaced as prime minister by New Democratic party leader James F. Mitchell on July 30, 1984. He remained leader of the Opposition till his retirement the following year.

JAMES FITZ-ALLEN MITCHELL (Prime Minister, July 30, 1984–   ). James Fitz-Allen "Son" Mitchell was born in the Grenadines on May 15, 1931. He studied agriculture in Trinidad and British Columbia and became chief agricultural officer of Saint Vincent in 1958. He served in the Ministry of Overseas Development in London from 1960 until 1966. Mitchell returned to the Grenadines and was elected to Parliament in 1966. He served in the cabinet as minister of trade, agriculture, labour, and tourism from 1967 until his resignation in 1972. Mitchell was expelled from the Saint Vincent

Labour party in 1972 and subsequently ran for Parliament as an independent. He was reelected and served as a compromise choice as prime minister from 1972 until 1974. Mitchell was defeated for a seat in the House of Assembly in 1979, but was returned to office in June of the following year. Mitchell, leading the New Democratic party, was elected prime minister of Saint Vincent and the Grenadines on July 30, 1984. The New Democratic party won an overwhelming victory in elections in May of 1989 and captured all fifteen seats in the House of Assembly.

San Marino, Most Serene Republic of

(Serenissima Repubblica di San Marino)

San Marino is an independent republic located in north-central Italy.

HEADS OF STATE AND GOVERNMENT

San Marino is ruled by a Grand and General Council. The Council is led by two members who are selected by the Council to serve six-month terms as Captains Regent.

Sao Tome and Principe,
Democratic Republic of

(República Democrática de São Tomé e Príncipe)

Sao Tome and Principe is a country consisting of a group of islands off the west coast of Africa. It received independence from Portugal on July 12, 1975.

HEADS OF STATE

MANUEL PINTO DA COSTA (President, July 12, 1975–April 3, 1991). Manuel Pinto da Costa was born in Agua Grande on August 5, 1937. He was the founder of the Movement for the Liberation of Sao Tome and Principe (MLSTP) in 1972. His organization fought for independence from the Portuguese colonial government. Portugal agreed to grant Sao Tome and Principe independence following a military coup in Portugal in 1974. The MLSTP formed a transitional government in December of 1974. When independence was granted on July 12, 1975, and Costa became the nation's first president. He dismissed Prime Minister Miguel Trovoada in October of 1979 and also took on the duties of head of government. Costa survived several coup attempts and introduced economic reforms in 1987. The government also began a process of political liberalization and eliminated the single-party system of government in January of 1991. Presidential elections were held in March of 1991, but Costa declined to be a candidate. The ruling party was defeated by the Party of Democratic Convergence, and Miguel Trovoada replaced Costa as president on April 3, 1991. Costa subsequently retired from politics.

MIGUEL TROVOADA (President, April 3, 1991–). Miguel Anjos da Cunha Lisboa Trovoada was born in 1946. He worked with the Sao Tome

and Principe Liberation Movement as a director of foreign relations. He became premier of Sao Tome and Principe following independence from Portugal on July 12, 1975. Trovoada was removed from office and arrested in October of 1979. He remained imprisoned until 1981 and then went into exile in Lisbon. Trovoada subsequently returned to Sao Tome and Principe as leader of the Party of Democratic Convergence-Reflection Group. In the first multiparty election in March of 1991, Trovoada won the presidency, and he took office on April 3, 1991.

HEADS OF GOVERNMENT

MIGUEL TROVOADA (Premier, July 12, 1975–October, 1979). *See entry under Heads of State.*

CELESTINO ROCHA DA COSTA (Premier, January 8, 1988–February 7, 1991). Celestino Rocha da Costa served as minister of labor, education and social security. Following the restoration of the position of premier, Costa was named to head the government on January 8, 1988. He retained the position until the ruling party was defeated in multiparty elections in January of 1991. He left office on February 8, 1991.

DANIEL LIMA DOS SANTOS DAIO (Premier, February 7, 1991–

May 16, 1992). Daniel Lima Dos Santos Daio was secretary-general of the Party of Democratic Convergence. He was appointed prime minister on February 7, 1991. His government's austerity program created economic hardship in the country, and Daio was dismissed as prime minister on May 16, 1992.

NORBERTO JOSÉ D'ALVA COSTA ALEGRE (Premier, May 16, 1992–). Norberto José d'Alva Costa Alegre was minister of finance in the government of Daniel Lima dos Santos Daio. He was appointed to succeed Daio as prime minister on May 16, 1992.

Saudi Arabia, Kingdom of
(al-Mamlakah al-'Arabiyah al-Su'udiyah)

Saudi Arabia is a country that occupies most of the Arabian peninsula in southwestern Asia.

HEADS OF STATE

IBN SAUD (King, September 18, 1932–November 9, 1953). Ibn Saud was

born 'Abdul-ul-'Aziz ibn 'Abd-ul-Rahman ibn Feisal al Saud in Riyadh on October 21, 1882. He was the son of Emir Abdur Rahman and the grandson of Emir Feisal, who ruled the Nejd from 1834 until 1867. Ibn Saud accompanied his family into exile in 1891 when Ibn Rashid claimed Riyadh. Abdur Rahman was defeated in an attempt to depose Ibn Rashid in 1900 and relinquished his rights of succession to his son the following year. Ibn Saud recaptured Riyadh in January of 1902 and proclaimed himself king of the Nejd. He withstood an attack from the Turks in 1904. Ibn Saud supported the British against the Turks during World War I and signed a treaty of friendship with Great Britain in 1915. He engaged in a successful military action against Ibn Rashid following the war and added Rashid's territory to his own. He also engaged in a rivalry with Hashemite King Hussein, the grand sherif of Mecca. War broke out between Ibn Saud and Hussein in 1924, and Ibn Saud captured the Hejaz and Mecca. He was recognized as king of the Hejaz, Nejd, and their dependencies by Great Britain in May of 1927. Ibn Saud put down several revolts in the early 1930s and renamed his kingdom Saudi Arabia in September of 1932. He granted oil concessions to a United States oil company in 1933, which eventually brought vast riches to his country. He defeated Yemen in a battle over a territorial dispute in 1934, though he allowed Imam Yahya of Yemen to remain on the throne. Ibn Saud maintained close relations with Great Britain during World War II, but Saudi Arabia remained officially neutral. When Ibn Saud's health and eyesight began to fail in the early 1950s, he relinquished many of his duties to his son Saud. Ibn Saud died in Riyadh after a long illness on November 9, 1953.

SAUD (King, November 9, 1953–November 2, 1964). Saud ibn Abdul Aziz al Faisal al Saud was born on January 15, 1902. He was the third son of Ibn Saud, who had captured the

kingdom of Nejd the previous year. Saud served as a close advisor to his father from his youth. He was appointed viceroy of Nejd in 1926 and became crown prince of the kingdom of Saudi Arabia in 1933. He took on many of his father's duties in the early 1950s due to Ibn Saud's failing health. He served as chairman of the newly formed Council of Ministers from 1953 and succeeded to the throne upon his father's death on November 9, 1953. Saudi Arabia's relationship with Great Britain deteriorated over a territorial dispute in 1955, and Saud broke off diplomatic relations with Great Britain following the British military action at the Suez Canal in 1956. He initially encouraged close relations with Egypt and Syria, but refused to participate in Egyptian president Gamal Abdel Nasser's formation of the United Arab Republic in 1958. He subsequently broke with Egypt and was accused of instigating a plot to assassinate Nasser. Saudi Arabia's economic difficulties led Saud to name his brother, Crown Prince Faisal, as premier in March of 1958 and to grant him control of Saudi Arabia's financial and foreign policies. Saud dismissed Faisal in December of 1960 and assumed direct control of the government himself. Saud suffered from poor health in the early 1960s and underwent ulcer surgery in the United States in November of 1961. He received further treatment at a private clinic in Switzerland from December of 1962. Faisal reemerged as head of the government in 1962, and the Council of Ministers forced Saud's abdication as king on November 2, 1964. Saud went into exile in Europe and then settled briefly in Egypt in December of 1966. Saud returned to Athens the following year. He died of a heart attack at a hotel in Athens at the age of 67 on February 23, 1969.

FAISAL (King, November 2, 1964–March 25, 1975). Faisal ibn Abdul-Aziz al Saud was born in Riyadh in 1905. He was the son of King Ibn Saud and was raised in the home of his maternal grandfather. He commanded Ibn Saud's troops in a battle for the Hejaz against Hashemite King Hussein Ibn-Ali in 1925. Faisal was subsequently appointed viceroy of the Hejaz by his father. Faisal was named foreign minister in his father's government in 1932. He represented Saudi Arabia at numerous international conferences and served as his country's representative to the United Nations Charter Conference in San Francisco in 1945. Faisal's older brother, Saud, succeeded to the throne in November of 1953 following the death of Ibn Saud. Faisal was named crown prince and also served in the government as Saudi Arabia's first prime minister. Faisal attempted to control his brother's extravagant financial habits which had brought Saudi Arabia close to bankruptcy. A dispute between the brothers resulted in Faisal's resignation as prime minister in 1960. He continued to serve as foreign minister, however. Faisal supported the Royal Council's decision to force the abdication of King Saud on November 2, 1964, and he succeeded his brother to the throne. In the fall of 1973, Faisal was the first Arabian monarch to use his oil-rich country's leading export as a weapon against Western countries in an attempt to sway their Middle Eastern policies. Faisal was shot to death by his nephew, Prince Faisal ibn Musad, during an audience with the oil minister of Kuwait on March 25, 1975.

KHALID (King, March 25, 1975– June 13, 1982). Khalid ibn Abdul Aziz al Saud was born in Riyadh in 1913. He was the son of King Ibn Saud of Saudi Arabia. He was a close advisor to his older half-brother, Faisal, from the 1930s and accompanied him on several diplomatic missions. Faisal deposed another brother, King Saud, in November of 1964. Khalid was designated as crown prince in March of 1965. He also served in the government as deputy

prime minister. Although he suffered from poor health in the early 1970s, he succeeded King Faisal to the throne on March 25, 1975, following Faisal's assassination. He named another half-brother, Fahd, as crown prince and delegated many of his administrative duties to him. Saudi Arabia imposed economic sanctions against Egypt in March of 1979 when President Anwar el-Sadat negotiated a peace treaty with Israel. Khalid survived an armed revolt in November of 1979 when rebels seized the Grand Mosque in Mecca. The Saudi army put down the revolt, and over sixty leaders of the rebellion were executed the following year. Khalid's health continued to deteriorate, and he died of a heart attack in Ta'if on June 13, 1982.

FAHD (King, June 13, 1982–). Fahd ibn Abdul Aziz al Saud was born in Riyadh in 1922. He was a son of King Ibn Saud of Saudi Arabia. He was named minister of education in Saudi Arabia's first cabinet in 1953. Fahd resigned from the cabinet in 1960 when his half-brother, Crown Prince Faisal, was dismissed as prime minister by another half-brother, King Saud. He returned to the government as minister of the interior in 1962 when Faisal was reappointed prime minister. Faisal succeeded Saud as king in November of 1964, and Fahd was appointed deputy prime minister to Crown Prince Khalid in 1968. Khalid succeeded to the throne following Faisal's assassination in March of 1975, and Fahd was named crown prince and prime minister. Since Khalid suffered from poor health, Fahd was largely responsible for the administrative duties in the country. He succeeded to the throne on June 13, 1982, following Khalid's death. He designated another half-brother, Abdullah, as crown prince. Fahd's rule was threatened by a growing radical Islamic movement in the Middle East. He was also faced with declining revenue from oil resources. He requested assistance from the United States and other Western powers in August of 1990 following Iraq's invasion of neighboring Kuwait. The Saudi government feared Iraq's intentions, and a multinational force was deployed on the Saudi-Kuwait border. The subsequent Gulf War forced Iraq's withdrawal from Kuwait and further secured Saudi Arabia's sovereignty.

Senegal, Republic of

(République du Sénégal)

Senegal is a country on the northwestern coast of Africa. It was granted independence from France on June 20, 1960.

HEADS OF STATE

LÉOPOLD SÉDAR SENGHOR (President, August 20, 1960–December 31, 1980).Léopold Sédar Senghor was born in Joal on October 9, 1906. He was educated at local mission schools and received a scholarship to study in Paris in 1928. He graduated from the Lycée Louis-le-Grand and continued his studies at the University of Paris. Senghor became the first black African to receive a license to teach in France and served on the faculty in Tours from 1935. Senghor served in the French infantry during World War II and was interned by the Germans following the fall of France. He was released in 1942 and worked with the Resistance. He was elected to the Constituent Assembly after the war and represented Senegal in the French National Assembly from November of 1946. Senghor formed the Senegal Democratic Bloc in 1948, and his supporters were victorious in elections to the Territorial Assembly in 1951. His party was merged with the Socialist party to become the Senegal Progressive Union in 1958. Senghor was a proponent of African autonomy within a federal union. Senegal was granted autonomy within the French Community on November 25, 1958. Senghor united Senegal with the Sudanese Republic to form the Mali Federation in January of 1959. The Mali Federation was granted full independence on June 20, 1960, and Senghor served as president of the Federal Assembly. When Senegal withdrew from the federation on August 20, 1960, Senghor became president of the independent Republic of Senegal. He survived a challenge to his leadership from Premier Mamadou Dia in December of 1962. He subsequently governed under an executive presidency and was reelected in December of 1963. Senghor was again returned to office in elections in 1968. He reinstituted the position of premier in 1970 and appointed Abdul Diouf. Senghor was again reelected president in January of 1973. His government faced violent student protests the following month. He allowed the formation of political parties by a constitutional amendment in 1976 and was again returned to office by a wide margin in February of 1978. Senghor retired from office on January 1, 1981, and was replaced by Premier Abdul Diouf. Senghor was also noted as a leading African scholar and poet. He was the recipient of numerous literary awards and was elected to the French Academy in June of 1983.

ABDUL DIOUF (President, January 1, 1981–   ). Abdul Diouf was born in Louga on September 7, 1935. He was educated locally and in Paris, where he received a degree in law in 1958. He returned to Senegal to enter public service. Diouf served in several ministries and was named governor of the Sine-Saloum Region in December of 1961. He returned to the capital to serve as departmental director of the Foreign Ministry in December of 1962. He became secretary-general of the government in February of 1964 and was named to the cabinet as minister of planning and industry in March of 1968. President Léopold Sédar Senghor reinsti-

tuted the position of premier on February 28, 1970, and appointed Diouf to the office. He remained a loyal supporter of Senghor and succeeded to the presidency when Senghor resigned on January 1, 1981. He was confirmed into office by a wide margin in elections in February of 1983. Diouf was again returned to office in February of 1988 in elections clouded by allegations of fraud. He attempted to appease his critics by forming a coalition government which included members of the opposition in April of 1991.

HEADS OF GOVERNMENT

MAMADOU DIA (Premier, November 25, 1958–December 17, 1962). Mamadou Dia was born in Kombole on July 18, 1910. He attended school in Dakar and served as a councillor in Senegal from 1946 until 1952. He served in the Senegal Senate from 1949 until 1955. Dia was elected to the Grand Council for French West Africa in 1952 and served until 1957. He also served as a deputy to the French National Assembly from 1956 until 1959. He was selected as president of the Council of Ministers on November 25, 1958. Dia remained head of the government following Senegal's independence in August of 1960. He led an unsuccessful coup attempt against President Léopold Sédar Senghor on December 17, 1962. Dia was arrested following the failure of the revolt and was sentenced to life imprisonment in May of 1963. He was released in 1974, and his political rights were restored two years later.

ABDUL DIOUF (Premier, February 28, 1970–December 31, 1980). *See entry under Heads of State.*

HABIB THIAM (Premier, January 1, 1981–April 3, 1983). Habib Thiam was born in Dakar on January 21, 1933.

He served in government from 1963 and became minister of planning and development in 1964. He served until 1967 and was named minister of rural economy the following year. Thiam retained that position until 1973, when he was elected to the National Assembly. He was appointed premier on January 1, 1981. He resigned on April 3, 1983, pending the abolition of the post of premier. Thiam subsequently became president of the National Assembly and served until 1984. He was again appointed premier when the position was reestablished on April 7, 1991. He led a coalition cabinet that included members of the political opposition.

MOUSTAPHA NIASSE (Interim Premier, April 3, 1983–April 29, 1983). Moustapha Niasse was born in Senegal on November 4, 1939. He was educated in Dakar and Paris. He joined government service and worked in the Information Ministry from 1968 until 1969. Niasse served as a presidential advisor from 1970 and became minister of town planning, housing, and the environment in 1978. He was appointed minister of foreign affairs later that year and served until 1984. He also served as interim premier from April 3, 1983, until the abolition of the position of premier on April 29, 1983.

HABIB THIAM (Premier, April 7, 1991–). *See earlier entry under Heads of Government.*

Seychelles, Republic of

The Seychelles are a group of islands in the western Indian Ocean. They received independence from Great Britain on June 29, 1976.

HEADS OF STATE

JAMES R. MANCHAM (President, June 29, 1976–June 5, 1977). James Richard Marie Mancham was born in Victoria, Mahe, on August 11, 1939. After he studied law in Paris and London he returned to the Seychelles in 1961. He was elected to the Legislative Council in 1961 and served on the Government Council in 1967. Mancham served as leader of the Social Democratic party from 1964 and became chief Minister of the seychelles in 1970. He became the first prime minister of the independent Seychelles on October 1, 1975. Mancham became president when the Seychelles became a republic on June 29, 1976. He was deposed by a coup led by his prime minister, France Albert Rene, on June 5, 1977. Mancham subsequently served as an international trade consultant.

FRANCE ALBERT RENE (President, June 5, 1977–). France Albert Rene was born in the Seychelles on November 16, 1935. He was educated in the Seychelles, Switzerland, and Great Britain and became a lawyer in 1957. He founded the leftist Seychelles People's United party in 1964 and was elected to Parliament the following year. Rene served as minister of works and land development from 1975 and became prime minister on June 29, 1976. He served as part of a coalition government with President Mancham until Mancham was deposed by a coup on June 5, 1977. Rene subsequently became president.

HEADS OF GOVERNMENT

JAMES R. MANCHAM (Prime Minister, October 1, 1975–June 29, 1976). *See entry under Heads of State.*

FRANCES ALBERT RENE (Prime Minister, June 29, 1976–). *See entry under Heads of State.*

Sierra Leone, Republic of

Sierra Leone is a country in west central Africa. It was granted independence from Great Britain on April 27, 1961.

HEADS OF STATE

SIR MAURICE DORMAN (Governor-General, April 27, 1961–July 7, 1962). Maurice Henry Dorman was born in Stafford, England, on August 7, 1912. He was educated at Magdalene College, Cambridge. He worked for the British colonial department in Tanganyika Territory, Malta, and Palestine during the 1930s and 1940s. He was named acting governor of Trinidad in 1954. Dorman was appointed governor of Sierra Leone in 1956. He became the first governor-general of independent Sierra Leone on April 27, 1961. He retained that position until July 7, 1962. Dorman was subsequently named governor of Malta and became that country's first governor-general following independence on September 21, 1964. He retained that post until June 21, 1971. He served as deputy chairman of the Pearce Committee on Rhodesia in 1972. Dorman subsequently returned to Great Britain and retired from the government. He continued to serve on various public and private commissions until his death at the age of 81 on October 26, 1993.

SIR HENRY J. LIGHTFOOT BOSTON (Governor General, July 7, 1962–March 21, 1967). Henry J. Lightfoot Boston was born on August 19, 1898. He attended Durham University, where he received a degree in 1919. He worked with the civil service until 1922, when he went to Great Britain to study law at Lincoln's Inn in London. Boston returned to Sierra Leone in 1926 to practice law. He later served as city solicitor for Freetown. Boston was named a police magistrate in 1946. He was elected to the House of Representatives in October of 1957 and served as speaker. He retained that position until July 7, 1962, when he was the first native-born Sierra Leonean to be named governor-general. Boston was relieved of his position when a military junta took over Sierra Leone on March 21, 1967.

He went into exile in Britain. When the junta was ousted in 1968, Boston was invited to return to his post. He was suffering from poor health, however, and declined to return to Sierra Leone. He died at his home in London at the age of 70 on January 11, 1969.

DAVID LANSANA (Head of State, March 21, 1967–March 23, 1967). David Lansana was born on March 27, 1922. He was educated locally and entered the army in 1947. He attended officer training school in Great Britain and was commissioned in 1952. Lansana rose to the rank of captain in 1956 and colonel in 1964. He was appointed commander of the Royal Sierra Leone military forces on January 1, 1965. Lansana declared martial law on March 21, 1967, following Siaka Stevens's victory in general elections. Lansana's action prevented Stevens from taking office as prime minister. Lansana was arrested and detained by other senior officers several days later. He was given a diplomatic position in New York City. He returned to Sierra Leone in 1968 and was sentenced to five years in prison for his illegal seizure of power. Lansana was released in 1973, but was again arrested and charged with treason in July of 1974. He was convicted of the charges and executed at Pademba Road Prison in Freetown in July of 1975.

AMBROSE GENDA (Head of State, March 23, 1967–March 27, 1967). Ambrose P. Genda was born in Gerihun on April 20, 1927. He served as a lieutenant colonel in the Sierra Leone army. He was appointed chairman of the National Reformation Council on March 23, 1967, in the military government that had taken control of the country. Genda was removed from power on March 27, 1967, by Lt. Col. Andrew Juxon-Smith. Genda was subsequently appointed Sierra Leone's ambassador to Liberia. He served as his country's high commissioner to London from 1968 until 1969 and was high commissioner to Moscow from 1969 until 1970. He subsequently went into exile in London.

ANDREW JUXON-SMITH (Head of State, March 27, 1967–April 19, 1968). Andrew T. Juxon-Smith was born in Freetown in 1933. He was educated locally and attended the Sandhurst Royal Military Academy in Great Britain. He became chairman of the ruling National Reformation Council following the ouster of Lt. Col. Ambrose Genda on March 27, 1967. The military regime was overthrown on April 19, 1968, by a countercoup to restore civilian government. Juxon-Smith was arrested and charged with treason. He was convicted and sentenced to death the following year, but was granted a reprieve in 1972.

PATRICK CONTEH (Head of State, April 19, 1968–April 22, 1968). Patrick Conteh was named chairman of the National Interim Council on April 19, 1968, following the ouster of the ruling National Reformation Council military regime by a group of officers calling themselves the Anticorruption Revolutionary Movement. Conteh turned over the government to civilian leaders on April 22, 1968.

BANJA TEJAN-SIE (Governor General, April 22, 1968–March 31, 1971). Banja Tejan-Sie was born in Moyamba on August 7, 1917. He was educated locally and worked as a nurse from 1940 until 1946. He continued his education graduated from the London School of Economics in 1951. Tejan-Sie returned to Sierra Leone and joined the Sierra Leone People's party. He served as vice president of the party from 1953 until 1956. He subsequently served as a police magistrate until 1958. Tejan-Sie attended the London conferences con-

cerning his country's independence in 1959. He served as a senior police magistrate in 1961. Tejan-Sie was elected Speaker of the Sierra Leone House of Representatives in 1962. He became chief justice of the Supreme Court in April of 1967 and was selected as acting governor-general on April 22, 1968. He was confirmed as governor-general on September 29, 1970. Tejan-Sie was dismissed from office on March 31, 1971, after a coup attempt against the government of Siaka Stevens.

CHRISTOPHER OKORO COLE (Governor General, March 31, 1971– April 19 1971. Acting President, April 19, 1971–April 21, 1971). Christopher Okoro Eluathan Eustace Cole was born in Waterloo Village on April 17, 1921. He attended local mission schools before studying at the London School of Economics. He received a degree in law in the mid-1940s. Cole returned to Sierra Leone, where he rose through the ranks of the judicial system. He was appointed as a judge on the Supreme Court in December of 1960 and served as chief justice on several occasions in the 1960s. He was named Sierra Leone's permanent representative to the United Nations and ambassador to the United States in January of 1967. Cole returned to Sierra Leone in 1970 and was appointed chief justice of the Supreme Court. He was named acting governor-general on March 31, 1971. He became the first president of the Republic of Sierra Leone on April 19, 1971. Cole served for three days until April 21, 1971, when Prime Minister Siaka Stevens assumed the office.

SIAKA STEVENS (President, April 21, 1971–November 28, 1985). Siaka Probyn Stevens was born in the Moyamba District on August 24, 1905. He was educated locally and joined the police in 1923. He rose to the rank of sergeant before leaving the force in 1930. Stevens then worked as a railway construction worker. He became a station manager at the Marampa mine, where he founded the United Mineworkers' Union in 1943. He remained involved in trade union activities and was elected to the Legislative Council in Freetown in 1951. He was a member of the Sierra Leone People's party and served in the government of Sir Milton Margai as minister of lands, mines, and labor. Stevens was defeated for reelection in 1957 and subsequently joined the People's National party, which was led by Margai's brother, Albert. Stevens was expelled from the party following a disagreement with the leadership concerning elements of the constitutional conference agreement signed in London in April of 1960. He formed the All People's Congress (APC) and became leader of the opposition following Sierra Leone's independence in April of 1961. He was elected Mayor of Freetown in 1964. The APC achieved a narrow victory in general elections in March of 1967, and Stevens prepared to take office as prime minister. A military coup led by Brig. David Lansana seized control of the country on March 21, 1967, and Stevens was placed under house arrest. He was allowed to go into exile in Guinea. He was called to return to Sierra Leone to lead the government following another military coup on April 26, 1968. New elections were held in November of 1968 and Stevens was returned to office. He was forced to declare a state of emergency later in the month when violence broke out between his supporters and the opposition. Stevens's government was threatened by a new opposition party in 1970, and he responded by arresting the leaders of the opposition in October of 1970 in anticipation of a coup attempt. Stevens survived two separate assassination attempts and a military coup on March 23, 1971. Sierra Leone was declared a republic the following month, and Stevens became its president on April 21, 1971. Further violence erupted following elections in 1973, and Stevens ordered the arrest of numerous political opponents the following year, many of whom were executed. Economic problems led to student demonstrations against the government in 1977 that resulted in Stevens again declaring a state of emergency. A new constitution was promoted in 1978 that established Sierra Leone as a one-party state. Stevens was reelected president later in the year. He formed a new government following parliamentary elections in May of 1982. Sierra Leone's economy continued to deteriorate, and Stevens announced his intentions to resign in 1985. He presided over the selection of Maj. Gen. Joseph Momoh as his successor and stepped down from office on November 28, 1985. Relations between Stevens and Momoh became strained following an unsuccessful coup attempt in 1987. Stevens died in Freetown at the age of 82 on May 29, 1988, after a brief illness.

JOSEPH SAIDU MOMOH (President, November 28, 1985–April 29, 1992). Joseph Saidu Momoh was born in Binkolo, in the Northern Province, on January 26, 1937. He worked in the civil service until 1958, when he attended military schools in Ghana, Great Britain, and Nigeria. He joined the Royal Sierra Leone Military Forces in 1963. Momoh rose through the ranks to become a major in 1966. He was arrested following the coup that returned Sierra Leone to democratic rule in 1968. After his release from detention seven months later, he returned to the army. He was promoted to colonel in 1970 and to brigadier in 1973. Momoh also served as a member of Parliament and as minister of state from 1973 until 1985. He was promoted to brigadier general in 1983, and following the retirement of President Siaka Stevens, he was chosen to succeed Stevens as president. Momoh took office on November 28, 1985. He made an effort to stamp out corruption in the government and survived a coup attempt in March of 1987. Momoh promoted a new constitution in September of 1991 that allowed for multiparty elections. His government was faced with a military revolt in eastern Sierra Leone over lack of adequate pay in early 1992. Momoh was ousted in a military coup on April 29, 1992, and went into exile in Guinea.

VALENTINE STRASSER (President, May 1, 1992–   ). Valentine E. M. Strasser served in the Sierra Leone military, where he rose to the rank of captain. He led the coup that overthrew the government of President Joseph Momoh on April 29, 1992. Strasser was named chairman of the National Provisional Ruling Council on May 1, 1992.

HEADS OF GOVERNMENT

SIR MILTON MARGAI (Prime Minister, April 27, 1961–April 28, 1964). Milton Augustus Strieby Margai was born in Gbangbatoke on December 7, 1895. He attended local mission schools before entering King's College in England. He received a degree in medicine in 1926 and returned to Sierra Leone the following year to practice medicine. Margai served in the government as a medical officer from 1928 and was chief medical officer in Bo until his retirement in 1950. He also became involved in politics and was elected to the District Council. He formed the Sierra Leone People's Party (SLPP) in 1949 and served as its leader. The SLPP was victorious in general elections in November of 1951, and Margai headed the Departments of Health, Agriculture, and Forestry. He was elected chief minister in June of 1954. He was challenged for leadership of the party by his brother, Albert, in 1958. Albert Margai subsequently left the SLPP and went into opposition. Sierra Leone adopted a new constitution on August 14, 1958, and Milton Margai became premier. He was knighted in 1959. He led the country to independence on April 27, 1961, and became prime minister. General elections were held in 1962, and Margai was returned to office. He remained prime minister until his death after a brief illness in Freetown at the age of 68 on April 28, 1964.

ALBERT M. MARGAI (Prime Minister, April 29, 1964–March 17, 1967).

Albert Michael Margai was born in Gbangbatoke on October 10, 1910. He was educated locally and worked as a nurse from 1932. He went to Great Britain to study law in 1944 and qualified as a lawyer in 1947. Margai returned to Sierra Leone the following year to establish a legal practice. He was elected to the Protectorate Assembly in 1949 and joined the Sierra Leone People's party (SLPP) led by his brother, Milton Margai. He headed the Departments of Education and Welfare on the Legislative Council. Albert Margai broke with his brother in 1958 and challenged him for the leadership of the SLPP. He narrowly defeated his brother, but declined to take the leadership of the party and instead formed the People's National party. He rejoined the SLPP in a coalition government in 1960 and was named minister for national resources. Albert Margai remained in the cabinet as minister of finance following independence in April of 1961. He succeeded his brother as party leader and prime minister on April 29, 1964, after Milton Margai's death. Sierra Leone's economy was faltering, and Margai was challenged by Siaka Stevens's All People's Congress in general elections in March of 1967. The results were inconclusive, and Stevens was asked to form a government. Brig. David Lansana, a supporter of Margai, led a military coup on March 21, 1967, to keep Stevens from heading the government. Leaders of a countercoup ousted Lansana and formed a military government. Margai was briefly placed under house arrest before being allowed to go into exile in England. He remained in exile until his death on December 18, 1980, at the age of 70 while on a visit to Washington, D.C.

DAVID LANSANA (Head of Government, March 21, 1967–March 23, 1967). *See entry under Heads of State.*

AMBROSE GENDA (Head of Government, March 23, 1967–March 27, 1967). *See entry under Heads of State.*

ANDREW JUXON-SMITH (Prime Minister, March 27, 1967–April 19, 1968). *See entry under Heads of State.*

JOHN N. BANGURA (Head of Government, April 20, 1968–April 26, 1968). John N. Bangura was educated locally and at the Sandhurst Royal Military Academy in Great Britain. He served as an officer in the Sierra Leone army and rose to the rank of brigadier. He was arrested in 1967 on charges of insurrection. Bangura was released later in the year and given a diplomatic assignment in Washington, D.C. He returned to Sierra Leone following the military coup that had ousted the civilian government in March of 1967. Bangura was named head of an interim government on April 20, 1968, following the ouster of the National Reformation Council's military regime. He presided over the restoration of a civilian government, and Siaka Stevens was allowed to become prime minister on April 26, 1968. Bangura was named commander of the army. When he led an abortive military coup in March of 1971, he was captured and charged with treason. Bangura was executed by hanging at the Pademba Road Prison in Freetown in 1971.

SIAKA STEVENS (Prime Minister, April 26, 1968–April 21, 1971). *See entry under Heads of State.*

SORIE IBRAHIM KOROMA (Prime Minister, April 21, 1971–July 8, 1975). Sorie Ibrahim Koroma was born in Port Loko on January 30, 1930. He was educated in Nigeria and was employed in private industry until 1962, when he was elected to Parliament. He was also elected deputy mayor of Freetown in 1964. Koroma served as minister of trade and industry from 1968 until 1969. He served as minister of agriculture and natural resources from 1969 until 1971, when he was named vice president. He was also appointed prime minister on April 21, 1971. Koroma resigned as prime minister to become minister of finance on July 8, 1975. He served until 1978, when he became minister of state enterprises until 1979. Koroma served as first vice president from 1981 until 1986.

CHRISTIAN A. KAMARA-TAYLOR (Prime Minister, July 8, 1975–June 14, 1978). Christian Alusine Kamara-Taylor was born in Kahanta on June 3, 1917. He was educated locally and received a business degree from the London School of Accountancy. He worked as a clerk in the Sierra Leone Development Company from 1937. Kamara-Taylor joined the army in 1940 and rose to the rank of sergeant. He served in Nigeria, India, and Burma during World War II. He returned to Sierra Leone in 1945 and worked with the United African Company. Kamara-Taylor entered politics in 1960 and joined Siaka Stevens's All People's Congress. He served as secretary-general of the party and was elected to Parliament in 1962. He remained in office until the military coup in 1967. Kamara-Taylor returned to the government in April of 1968 when civilian rule was restored. He was named to Siaka Stevens's cabinet as minister of lands, mines, and labor. He was appointed minister of finance in May of 1971. Kamara-Taylor survived an assassination attempt in 1974 when his house was bombed by rebels. He exchanged positions with

Prime Minister Sorie I. Koroma on July 8, 1975. He remained head of government until the position of prime minister was abolished on June 14, 1978. Kamara-Taylor remained in the government as second vice president until his retirement for reasons of health on May 9, 1984. He died at the age of 67 on March 28, 1985.

Singapore, Republic of
(Republik Singapura)

Singapore is an island country off the southern Malay peninsula in southeast Asia. It was granted independence from Malaysia on August 9, 1965.

HEADS OF STATE

YUSOF BIN ISHAK (President, December 3, 1959–November 23, 1970). Yusof Bin Ishak was born in Padang Gajah, Perak, North Malaya, on August 12, 1910. He accompanied his parents to Singapore in 1923. He worked as a journalist and founded the newspaper *Utusan Melayu*, which supported Singapore's independence in the 1950s. Yusof Bin Ishak was chosen by the Legislative Assembly to serve as president following a new constitution granting Singapore self-rule. He took office on December 3, 1959, and remained head of state while Singapore was a member of Malaysia. Singapore withdrew from Malaysia on August 9, 1965, and became an independent republic. Yusof was reelected to the ceremonial position in 1967. He retained office until his death of a heart attack at the age of 60 on November 23, 1970.

YEOH GHIM SENG (President, November 23, 1970–January 2, 1971). Yeoh Ghim Seng was born in Ipoh on June 22, 1918. He was educated locally and at Cambridge, England, where he studied medicine. He returned to Singapore to work in the Government Medical Service from 1951 until 1955.

Yeoh then served as a professor of surgery at the University of Singapore until 1962. He entered politics and became a member of the People's Action party of Lee Kuan Yew. He was elected to Parliament in 1966 and became Deputy Speaker two years later. Yeoh was elected Speaker of the Parliament in 1970 and succeeded as acting president when Yusof Bin Ishak died on November 23, 1970. He retained office until January 2, 1971, following Benjamin Sheares's election to the position by Parliament. Yeoh again became acting president when Sheares died in office on May 12, 1981. He relinquished office to Chengara Veetil Devan Nair on October 24, 1981. He again served as acting president following the resignation of Devan Nair on March 28, 1985. Yeoh retained office until the selection of Wee Kim Wee as president on September 3, 1985.

BENJAMIN H. SHEARES (President, January 2, 1971–May 12, 1981). Benjamin Henry Sheares was born in Singapore on August 12, 1907. He was educated in Singapore and Great Britain, where he received a degree in medicine. He was a renowned gynecologist who developed a widely used gynecological operation named for him. He served as a professor at the University of Malaya before he was unanimously elected to the largely ceremonial position of president. Sheares took office on January 2, 1971. He was reelected to the position in 1975 and 1979. He retained office until his death from a cerebral hemorrhage at the age of 73 on May 12, 1981.

YEOH GHIM SENG (President, May 12, 1981–October 24, 1981). *See earlier entry under Heads of State.*

CHENGARA VEETIL DEVAN NAIR (President, October 24, 1981–March 28, 1985). Chengara Veetil Devan Nair was born in Malacca on August 5, 1923. He was educated in Singapore and became a teacher. He served as general secretary of the Teachers' Union from 1949 until his arrest in 1951. He remained in detention until 1953. The following year Devan Nair was a founder of the People's Action party and served as secretary of the Factory and Shopworker's Union. He was again arrested in 1956 and remained imprisoned until 1959. He subsequently worked in the Ministry of Education. Devan Nair was elected to the Malaysian House of Representatives in 1964. He also founded the Democratic Action party in 1964 and served as its president until 1969. He was active in the National Trades Union Congress and served as its secretary-general from 1969 until 1979

and as its president from 1979 until 1981. Devan Nair was also elected to Parliament in 1979. Following the death of President Benjamin Sheares in May of 1981, Devan Nair was elected to succeed him as president and took office on October 24, 1981. He resigned from office on March 28, 1985, when Prime Minister Lee Kuan Yew revealed to Parliament that Devan Nair suffered from alcoholism. Devan Nair subsequently served as a consultant to the AFL-CIO.

YEOH GHIM SENG (President, March 28, 1985–September 3, 1985). *See earlier entry under Heads of State.*

WEE KIM WEE (President, September 3, 1985–   ). Wee Kim Wee was born on November 4, 1915. He worked as a clerk in a Japanese military establishment during the occupation. Following World War II he worked as a journalist and reported from such hot spots as the Belgian Congo and Indochina. He was appointed high commissioner to Malaysia in 1973, where he remained until 1980. In 1977 he was also appointed a member of the Singapore delegation to the United Nations General Assembly. Wee Kim Wee served as ambassador to Japan from 1980 until 1984. He also served as ambassador to the Republic of Korea from 1981 until 1984. Wee Kim Wee became president of Singapore on September 3, 1985. He was named to a second term in September of 1989.

HEADS OF GOVERNMENT

LEE KUAN YEW (Prime Minister, June 5, 1959–November 28, 1990). Lee Kuan Yew was born in Singapore on September 16, 1923. He was educated locally and at Cambridge in England, where he received a degree in law in 1950. He returned to Singapore to serve

as a legal advisor to several trade unions. Lee founded the People's Action party and was elected to the Legislative Assembly in April of 1955. He was an advocate of self-government for Singapore. He accompanied Chief Minister Lim Yew Hock to constitutional conferences in London in 1957. The People's Action party was victorious in elections under a new constitution granting Singapore the status of a self-governing state within the British Commonwealth in May of 1959. Lee was sworn in as prime minister on June 5, 1959. Lee led Singapore into a federation with Malaya, Sarawak, and Sabah to form Malaysia on September 16, 1963. Rivalry and conflicts between Lee and Malaysian prime minister Tunku Abdul Rahman resulted in Singapore withdrawing from Malaysia on August 9, 1965, and becoming an independent republic. Lee remained prime minister and his party retained power in general elections in 1968. The People's Action party maintained complete control of the legislature in elections in 1972, 1976, and 1980. Support for the party declined slightly, and the opposition won several seats in general elec-

tions in 1984. In October of 1988 Lee announced his intentions to step down. He relinquished office to Goh Chok Tong on November 28, 1990. Lee remained leader of the People's Action party.

GOH CHOK TONG (Prime Minister, November 28, 1990–   ). Goh Chok Tong was born in Singapore on May 20, 1941. He was educated in Singapore and the United States. He worked with the Neptune Orient Lines from 1969 and was elected to Parliament in 1976. Goh served in the Finance Ministry from 1977 until 1979, when he was appointed minister for trade and industry. He was named minister for health in 1981 and became minister of defense in 1982. He also served as first deputy prime minister from 1985. Goh succeeded Lee Kuan Yew as prime minister on November 28, 1990.

Slovenia, Republic of

(Republika Slovenije)

Slovenia is a country in southeastern Europe. It declared its independence from Yugoslavia on June 25, 1991.

HEAD OF STATE

MILAN KUČAN (President, May, 1990–   ). Milan Kučan was born in Krizevci on January 14, 1941. He joined the Yugoslav Communist party in 1958 and was elected to the Central Committee of Slovenia in 1968. Kučan served as president of the Central Committee of

the Slovenian League of Communists from 1986. He was elected president of Slovenia on April 22, 1990, and took office the following month. Slovenia declared its independence from Yugoslavia on October 8, 1991, with Kučan remaining as president.

HEADS OF GOVERNMENT

LUJZE PETERLE (Premier, May 16, 1990–May 14, 1992). Lujze Peterle, a member of the Christian Democratic

party, was selected as premier of Slovenia in the first non–Communist government on May 16, 1990. He was forced to resign on May 14, 1992, following criticism of his government's slow economic reforms.

JANEZ DRNOVŠEK (Premier, May 14, 1992–). Janez Drnovšek was born in Slovenia in 1950. He was a leading economist and a member of the federal presidency of Yugoslavia. He became president of Yugoslavia on May 15, 1989, and was the youngest person to hold the position. He retained that office until May 15, 1990. Following the breakup of Yugoslavia, Drnovek became a member of the Liberal Democratic party of Slovenia. He was named by the Slovenian Assembly to form a government as president of the Executive Council on April 22, 1992. He took office on May 14, 1992.

Solomon Islands

The Solomon Islands are an archipelago in the South Pacific Ocean. The country was granted independence from Great Britain on July 7, 1978.

HEADS OF STATE

SIR BADDELY DEVESI (Governor-General, July 7, 1978–July 1988). Baddely Devesi was born in Guadalcanal on October 16, 1941. He was educated in the Solomon Islands and New Zealand and became a teacher in 1965. He was elected to the British Solomon Islands Legislative and Executive Councils in 1967 and served until 1968. Devesi served in various government ministries during the 1970s and was appointed the Solomon Island's first governor-general following independence on July 7, 1978. He also served as chancellor of the University of the South Pacific from 1980 until 1983. He remained governor-general until July of 1988. Devesi subsequently served as minister of foreign affairs and trade relations until 1991. He also served as deputy prime minister and minister of home affairs from 1990.

SIR GEORGE LEPPING (Governor-General, July 1988–). George Dennis Geria Lepping was born on November 22, 1947. He was educated locally and entered the civil service of the Solomon Islands. He worked with the Department of Agriculture from 1968 and served as undersecretary of agriculture from 1979 until 1980. Lepping served in the Ministry of Home Affairs from 1981 until 1984. He was chosen to succeed Sir Baddeley Devesi as governor-general in July of 1988. The high court of the Solomon Islands ruled in May of 1989 that Lepping's appointment was unconstitutional because he was still employed in the civil service when the appointment was made. The government of Solomon Mamolini reappointed Lepping to conform with the ruling.

HEADS OF GOVERNMENT

PETER KENILOREA (Prime Minister, July 7, 1978–August 31, 1981). Peter Kenilorea was born in Takataka, Malaita, on May 23, 1943. He was educated in New Zealand and became a teacher. He worked in the Department of Finance in 1971 and became deputy secretary to the chief minister and cabinet in 1974. Kenilorea was elected to the Legislative Assembly and became chief minister in 1976. He subsequently became the first prime minister of the independent Solomon Islands on July 7, 1978, and served until August 31, 1981. Kenilorea again served as prime minister of a coalition government from November 19, 1984. The Solomon Islands were hit by Typhoon Namu in May of 1986, and Kenilorea was accused of favoring his home village with relief assistance. Much of his cabinet resigned, and he narrowly averted defeat in a vote of no confidence. He resigned office on November 17, 1986. Kenilorea served as deputy prime minister in the subsequent government of Ezekial Alebua until 1989. He also served as foreign minister from 1988 and added the trade relations portfolio in October of 1990.

SOLOMON MAMOLINI (Prime Minister, August 31, 1981–November 19, 1984). Solomon Mamolini was a leader of the People's Progressive party (PPP). He served as chief minister of the Solomon Islands in 1976. The PPP merged with several others parties to form the People's Alliance party (PAP) in 1979. Mamolini led the coalition to victory in general elections in 1981 and replaced Peter Kenilorea as prime min-

ister on August 31, 1981. He stepped down following inconclusive elections in 1984 and relinquished office to Kenilorea on November 19, 1984. Mamolini was reelected prime minister on March 28, 1989, with the assistance of independent support. He resigned from the PAP in October of 1990 to form a national unity government that included members of the opposition. He was faced with growing economic difficulties in the country and introduced an austerity budget in November of 1991.

PETER KENILOREA (Prime Minister, November 19, 1984–December 1, 1986). *See earlier entry under Heads of Government.*

EZEKIAL ALEBUA (Prime Minister, December 1, 1986–March 28, 1989). Ezekial Alebua served as deputy prime minister of the Solomon Islands under Peter Kenilorea. He succeeded Kenilorea as prime minister on December 1, 1986. He retained office until Solomon Mamolini was elected prime minister on March 28, 1989. Alebua remained the leader of the opposition Solomon Islands United party.

SOLOMON MAMOLINI (Prime Minister, March 28, 1989–). *See earlier entry under Heads of Government.*

Somalia (Somali Republic)

(Jamhuuriyada Soomaaliyeed)

Somalia is a country on the east coast of Africa. It was granted independence from Great Britain on July 1, 1960.

HEADS OF STATE

ADEN ABDULLAH OSMAN DAAR (President, July 1, 1960–July 10, 1967). Aden Abdullah Osman Daar was born in Beledwin in 1908. He was educated at local government schools. He served in the Italian Administration from 1929 until 1941. Osman Daar joined the Somali Youth League in 1949 and was elected leader of the league in 1953. In 1956 he was elected president of the National Assembly, and he served until 1960, when he became president of the Constituent Assembly. On July 1, 1960, he became the first president of independent Somalia. Osman Daar was reelected in July of the following year. He stepped down from office after completing his term on July 10, 1967. He was elected to the National Assembly, where he served until the military coup in October of 1969. Osman Daar was arrested by the military government and was detained until April of 1973.

ABDIRASHID ALI SHERMARKE (President, July 10, 1967–October 15, 1969). Abdirashid Ali Shermarke was born in Harardera on October 16, 1919. He was educated locally and worked in the British administration civil service. He was active in the Somali Youth League and continued his studies at Rome University, where he received a degree in political science in 1958. Shermarke was elected to the National Assembly the following year and was chosen as prime minister of independent Somalia on July 12, 1960. The ruling Somali Youth League retained power in general elections in 1964, but President Aden Abdullah Osman replaced Shermarke as prime minister with Abdirizak Haji Husain on June 14, 1964. Shermarke was a candidate for the presidency in 1967 and was elected to a six-year term. He took office on July 10, 1967. He was successful in negotiating a settlement for border disputes with neighboring Kenya and Ethiopia. Shermarke remained president until his assassination in Mogadiscio by Somali police officers on October 15, 1969.

MOHAMMED SIAD BARRE (President, October 21, 1969–January 26, 1991). Mohammed Siad Barre was born in Garbaharrey in 1912. He was educated in Somalia and the military academy in Italy. He returned to Somali and served in the police force until 1960. Siad Barre subsequently joined the Somali army, where he rose to the rank of major general and became commander in chief of the armed forces in 1966. Following the assassination of President Abdirashid Ali Shermarke on October 15, 1969, Siad Barre led a coup against the government of Prime Minister Mohammed Ibrahim Egal. He served as president of the Supreme Revolutionary Council and head of state of Somalia from October 21, 1969. He also served as prime minister until January 30, 1987. Siad Barre was seriously injured in an automobile accident in May of 1986. Somalia faced severe economic and political problems in the late 1980s. Much of the country was controlled by rebel factions when Siad Barre fled the country on January 26, 1991. He went into exile in Kenya before settling in Nigeria in 1992.

ALI MAHDI MUHAMMAD (President, January 29, 1991–). Ali Mahdi Muhammad was a prominent businessman and a leading financial backer of the rebel United Somali Congress (USC). President Mohammed Siad Barre was forced to flee the country and the USC named Mahdi Muhammad as interim president of Somalia on January 29, 1991. His government was unable to unite the various rebel groups in the country, and the Somali National Movement declared an independent Somaliland Republic with Abd ar-Rahman Ahmad Ali Tur as president in May of 1991. A conference was held in July of 1991 that confirmed Mahdi Muhammad as president. General Muhammad Farah Aydid, the chairman of the USC, boycotted the conference and further fighting developed between government troops and forces loyal to Aydid. The country was also faced with continuing repercussions from a severe drought. The ongoing violence between rival clans made the delivery of humanitarian aid to the country extremely difficult. The United Nations sponsored a cease-fire in Somalia in February of 1992, and United Nations forces were deployed to deliver relief supplies and preserve the peace. The United Nations presence was denounced by General Aydid, who continued to battle against the government. The United States sent ground troops to Somalia in December of 1992 to provide protection for United Nations officials and to insure that humanitarian aid was allowed to reach the people without impediment.

HEADS OF GOVERNMENT

MOHAMMED IBRAHIM EGAL (Prime Minister, June 26, 1960–July 12, 1960). Mohammed Haji Ibrahim Egal was born in Berbera on August 15, 1928. He was educated in Somalia and Great Britain. He joined the Somali National League party in 1956 and became secretary-general in 1958. Egal was selected as prime minister on June 26, 1960, and served as the first prime minister of independent Somalia. He was replaced by Abdirashid Ali Shermarke on July 12, 1960. He subsequently served as minister of defense until 1962, when he was named minister of education. Egal resigned from the cabinet in 1963 to lead the Opposition in Parliament until 1965. He subsequently joined the Somali Youth League party and again served as prime minister from June 10, 1967. Following the assassination of President Shermarke, the government was ousted in a military coup led by Mohammed Siad Barre on October 21, 1969. Egal and his cabinet were arrested and charged with corruption. He remained in detention until July of 1976. He was then named ambassador to India, but was rearrested the following October. Egal was again released in February of 1982. He subsequently became chairman of the Somali Chamber of Commerce, Industry, and Agriculture.

ABDIRASHID ALI SHERMARKE (Prime Minister, July 12, 1960–June 14, 1964). *See entry under Heads of State.*

ABDIRIZAK HAJI HUSAIN (Prime Minister, June 14, 1964–June 10, 1967). Abdirizak Haji Husain was born in Galcaio District in 1924. He was educated locally and entered politics at an early age. He was a founder of the Somali Youth League and was a leading advocate of independence for the country. Haji Husain was elected president of the Somali Youth League in 1956, but left the party to form the Greater Somalia League in 1958. He was briefly arrested following violence during parliamentary elections in 1959, but was released to serve in the Parliament. He was named minister of interior following Somalia's independence in July of 1960. Haji Husain subsequently served as minister of communications and public works. His party was victorious in general elections in 1964, and he replaced Abdirashid Ali Shermarke as prime minister on June 14, 1964. Shermarke was elected president in 1967 and dismissed Haji Hussein from office on June 10, 1967. He formed the opposition Popular Movement for Democratic Action, which was badly defeated in general elections in March of 1969. He was arrested following the coup led by Mohammed Siad Barre in October of 1969 and remained imprisoned until April of 1973. Haji Husain was subsequently appointed Somalia's ambassador to the United Nations, where he remained until 1980.

MOHAMMED IBRAHIM EGAL (Prime Minister, June 10, 1967–

October 21, 1969). *See earlier entry under Heads of Government.*

MOHAMMED SIAD BARRE (Prime Minister, October 21, 1969–January 30, 1987). *See entry under Heads of State.*

MUHAMMAD ALI SAMATAR (Prime Minister, January 30, 1987–September 3, 1990). Muhammad Ali Samatar was born in Chisimaio in 1931. He was educated at the military academy in Rome and in Moscow. He returned to Somalia to command the Somali Police in 1956. Ali Samatar subsequently joined the army and rose to the rank of major general in 1973. He served as secretary of state for defense from 1971 until 1976. He also served as commander in chief of the armed forces from 1971 until 1978. Ali Samatar served as minister of defense from 1976 until 1981 and again from 1982 until 1989. He was appointed first vice president of the Supreme Revolutionary Council in 1982. He was also appointed prime minister of Somalia on January 30, 1987 and served until his dismissal on September 3, 1990.

MUHAMMAD HAWADIE MADAR (Prime Minister, September 3, 1990–January 24, 1991). Mohamed Hawadie Madar was a member of President Mohammed Siad Barre's Somali Revolutionary Socialist party. He was appointed by President Barre to replace Muhammad Ali Samatar as prime minister on September 3, 1990. He left office on January 24, 1991, as rebel forces advanced on the capital.

UMAR ARTEH GHALIB (Prime Minister, January 24, 1991–). Umar Arteh Ghalib was born in Hargeisa in 1930. He was educated in England before returning to Somalia as a teacher in the late 1940s. He remained in education and public administration until he was assigned to the Somali Embassy in Moscow as first secretary. Arteh Ghalib retained that position until 1962. He served as a counsellor with the Somali delegation to the United Nations in 1964 and was named ambassador to Ethiopia in 1965. He returned to Somalia in 1968 and was elected to the Somali National Assembly the following year. Arteh Ghalib served as secretary of state for foreign affairs from 1969 until 1976 and was minister of culture and higher education from 1976 until 1978. He was elected Speaker of the People's Assembly in 1982 and served until his selection as prime minister on January 24, 1991.

South Africa, Republic of

(Republiek van Suid-Afrika)

South Africa is a country in southern Africa. It was granted independence from Great Britain on May 31, 1910.

HEADS OF STATE

NICOLAS JACOBUS DE WET (Acting Governor-General, August 23, 1943–December 31, 1945). Nicolas Jacobus De Wet was born in Aliwal North on September 11, 1873. He was educated at Victoria College and Cambridge University and returned to South Africa to practice law. He was elected to the Transvaal Legislative Assembly in 1907 and served until 1910. De Wet was appointed to Louis Botha's government as minister of justice in 1913. He left the government in 1924. He had been elected to the Senate from Transvaal in 1921, and he remained in the upper house until 1929. De Wet was appointed to the Court of Appeal in 1932 and became chief justice of South Africa in 1939. He became acting governor-general as officer administering the government on August 23, 1943, following the death of Sir Patrick Duncan. He retained that position until December 31, 1945. De Wet died in Hatfield at the age of 86 on March 16, 1960.

GIDEON BRAND VAN ZYL (Governor-General, December 31, 1945–September 20, 1950). Gideon Brand van Zyl was born in Sea Point, Cape Province, on June 3, 1873. He attended Normal College and South Africa College in Cape Town. He became an attorney in 1898 and was subsequently elected to the Cape Provincial Council. Van Zyl was later elected to the Parliament, where he rose to the position of Deputy Speaker. In 1942 van Zyl was appointed administrator of the Cape. He was selected as governor-general of the Union of South Africa and took office on December 31, 1945. Van Zyl served until September 20, 1950. He died on November 1, 1956, after a brief illness.

ERNEST GEORGE JANSEN (Governor-General, January 1, 1951–November 25, 1959). Ernest George Jansen was born in Strathearn on August 7, 1881. He practiced law in Natal before entering politics. He joined the Nationalist party in 1915 and was defeated for Parliament that year. Jansen ran again in 1921 and was elected. He served as Speaker of the Assembly in 1924, and in 1929 he was appointed to the cabinet as minister of native affairs. He returned to the Speakership in 1933 and

remained until 1943, when he lost his seat in Parliament. Jansen returned to Parliament in 1947 and again served as minister of native affairs from 1948 to 1950. He was appointed governor-general and assumed office on January 1, 1951. He retained that position until his death in Pretoria on November 25, 1959.

CHARLES R. SWART (Governor General, January 12, 1960–May 18, 1961. President, May 31, 1961–June 1, 1967). Charles Roberts Swart was born in Winburg, Orange Free State, on December 5, 1894. He was interned in a British concentration camp during the Boer War when he was six years old. He later attended Grey University College in Bloemfontein, where he received a law degree. Swart was arrested briefly in 1914 for protesting South Africa's entry into World War I on the side of the British. He interrupted his law career in 1921 to travel to the United States, where he studied journalism at Columbia University in New York City. Before he returned to South Africa in 1922, he spent some time in Hollywood, where he played bit parts in several cowboy films. Swart was elected to Parliament in 1923 on the Nationalist party ticket and became a prominent figure in party affairs. He remained in Parliament until 1938, when he was defeated for reelection. He returned to office in 1941 and was named to Daniel Malan's cabinet as minister of education, arts, and science in 1948. Swart was subsequently named minister of justice and was responsible for the drafting and passage of many of the repressive apartheid laws in that position. In 1954 he was named deputy prime minister as well as minister of justice in the cabinet of Johannes Strijdom. Swart briefly served as acting prime minister from August 23, 1958, shortly before Strijdom's death. He ran unsuccessfully for the party leadership but was defeated by Hendrik Verwoerd, who took office as prime minister on

September 3, 1958. Swart was reappointed minister of justice and also served as leader of the House of Assembly. He retained these positions until the death of governor-general Ernest Jansen in November of 1959. Swart was appointed to fill the vacancy and took office on January 12, 1960. He became president of South Africa when the country left the British Commonwealth and became a republic on May 31, 1961. He retired from the largely ceremonial position on June 1, 1967, a year before his term was scheduled to expire. Swart died in Bloemfontein on July 16, 1982.

JOZUA NAUDE (Acting President, June 1, 1967–April 10, 1968). Jozua Francois "Tom" Naude was born in Middleburg on April 15, 1889. He practiced law and served on the Pietersburg town council before entering Parliament in 1920. He was a member of the Nationalist party, and when the party came to power in 1948, he was elected Speaker of the House of Assembly. Naude served in various cabinets as minister of health in 1956, minister of finance from 1956 to 1958, and minister of the interior from 1958 to 1960. In 1960 he was elected president of the Senate. He served as acting president from June 1, 1967, until April 10, 1968, when President-Elect Theophilius Donges was unable to assume the office after suffering a stroke. Naude remained Speaker of the Senate until he suffered a cerebral thrombosis in May of 1969. He died in a Capetown hospital without regaining consciousness on May 31, 1969.

JACOBUS J. FOUCHE (President, April 10, 1968–February 21, 1975). Jacobus Johannes Fouche was born in Wapener in the Orange Free State on June 6, 1898. He was educated in South Africa and worked as a farmer, breeding cows and sheep. He was elected to Parliament as a Nationalist in 1941. Fouche served as administrator

of the Orange Free State from 1951 until 1959. He was then appointed minister of defense in the government of Prime Minister Hendrik Verwoerd. Fouche was transferred to the Ministry of Agricultural Technical Services and Water Affairs by Prime Minister John Vorster in April of 1965. Fouche was elected president of South Africa when President-Elect Theophilus Donges was unable to assume the office due to ill health. He was sworn in on April 10, 1968. Fouche completed his term on February 21, 1975, and retired from politics. He died in a Cape Town hospital from a lung infection on September 23, 1980.

NICOLAAS J. DIEDERICH (President, April 19, 1975–August 21, 1978). Nicolaas J. Diederich was born in Lady Brand in the Orange Free State on November 17, 1903. He was educated in South Africa and Germany. He returned to South Africa to teach economics at the University of the Orange Free State. Diederich was elected to Parliament in 1948, where he chaired the Tax Committee. He was appointed minister of economic affairs in December of 1958. He became minister of mines in 1961 and in 1967 was appointed minister of finance. In this position Diederich sought to keep gold as the world monetary standard and thus earned the nickname of "Mr. Gold." He was elected to the largely ceremonial position of president and was sworn in on August 19, 1975. Diederich remained in office until he suffered a major heart attack on August 13, 1978. He died in a Cape Town hospital after suffering a second heart attack on August 21, 1978.

JOHN VORSTER (President, September 29, 1978–June 4, 1979). Balthazar Johannes "John" Vorster was born in Jamestown, Cape Province, on December 13, 1915. He graduated with a law degree in 1938. He became involved in the Afrikaner nationalist movement and founded a militant anti-British organization during World War II. Vorster was arrested for anti-government activities in 1942 and remained imprisoned until 1944. He resumed his law career after the war and lost an election to Parliament in 1948 on the Afrikaner ticket. He subsequently joined the Nationalist party and was elected to Parliament in 1953. Vorster was active in the selection of Johannes Strijdom as prime minister in 1954 and supported Hendrik Verwoerd as his successor in 1958. He was appointed deputy minister of education in October of 1958 and was instrumental in enforcing apartheid policies in regard to excluding nonwhites from South African universities. Vorster was named minister of justice in August of 1961 and pushed through Parliament legislation that expanded the authority of the security forces in dealing with dissidents. He introduced the policy of banning, which made it illegal for certain individuals to speak on public issues and made it a crime for their statements to be published. Vorster was selected to succeed Verwoerd as prime minister following the latter's assassination on September 6, 1966. Vorster took office on September 12, 1966. While he remained a strong proponent of apartheid, a few racial restrictions were lifted during his term. He also became the first prime minister to meet with South African tribal leaders. Demonstrations by black students protesting the government's educational policies turned violent in the township of Soweto in June of 1976. The rioting spread throughout the country and continued through the following year. In 1978 Vorster's government was beset by a scandal following allegations that millions of dollars in government funds were used to promote South Africa's image without authorization. Vorster resigned for reasons of health on September 28, 1978. He accepted the position of state president, which had been vacant since

the death of Nicolaas Diederich the previous month. The following year, on June 4, 1979, Vorster was forced to resign from office after a commission held that he had been aware of the financial irregularities that had taken place in his government. He retired from politics and died from a lung infection in Cape Town on September 10, 1983.

MARAIS VILJOEN (President, June 4, 1979–September 14, 1984). Marais Viljoen was born in Robertson on December 2, 1915. He graduated from the University of Cape Town and subsequently became a reporter for the Nationalist newspaper *Die Transvaler* in 1937. He became active in the Nationalist party, and in March of 1949 he was elected to the Provincial Council. Viljoen was elected to Parliament in 1953 and was appointed deputy minister of lands and mines in December of 1958. He was appointed to the cabinet as minister of labor and minister of coloured affairs in 1966. He was named minister of labor and the interior in 1970. Viljoenwas appointed minister of posts and telegraphs in 1971 and maintained the labor portfolio as well. He retained these positions until 1976, when he was elected president of the Senate. He was subsequently elected president of the republic and took office on June 4, 1979. Viljoen remained in office until September 14, 1984, when the office of state president was eliminated in favor of an executive state president with the powers of president and prime minister.

PIETER BOTHA (President, September 14, 1984–January 19, 1989). Pieter Willem Botha was born in Paul Roux District in the Orange Free State on January 12, 1916. He attended the University of the Orange Free State, but dropped out in 1935 to work with the National party. He rose through the ranks of the party and became first secretary of the National Youth League in 1946. Botha was elected to the Parliament two years later. He also served as chief secretary of the National party in Cape Province until 1958. He was appointed a deputy minister in the cabinet of Hendrik Verwoerd in October of 1958. He was named minister of coloured affairs and community development in August of 1961. He was also appointed minister of public works in 1964. Botha was promoted to minister of defense in April of 1966 and retained that position in the cabinet of Prime Minister John Vorster. Vorster resigned from office in September of 1978, and Botha defeated Connie Muldar for the position of prime minister. He took office on September 14, 1984. The National party remained in power following elections in April of 1981. Botha promoted a new constitution that provided for a tricameral Parliament that allowed Asians and mixed races to be represented, but excluded blacks. Despite opposition from ultraconservative members of his party, the constitution was approved in September of 1983. The constitution also provided for an executive presidency, and Botha was unanimously elected by the electoral college. He assumed the office on September 14, 1984. He introduced other liberalization policies in the government, including the abandonment of segregationist legislation that prohibited mixed marriages. His reforms were viewed as too little by the black majority and moderate whites and were considered too much by the right-wing extremists. Botha introduced further measures to eliminate the apartheid system in January of 1986, including the termination of the pass laws. The government declared a state of emergency in June of 1986 in anticipation of violence on the tenth anniversary of the Soweto riots. Botha's government continued to institute measures designed to limit the opposition movement, while making small liberal reforms. Botha suffered a stroke on January 18, 1989, and J. Christian Heunis was named

acting president the following day while he recovered. Botha resigned as leader of the National party on February 2, 1989, and was replaced by F. W. deKlerk. Botha refused to step down as president of South Africa and resumed his duties on March 15, 1989. He was finally persuaded to leave office on August 14, 1989. Botha subsequently retired from active politics.

J. CHRISTIAN HEUNIS (Acting President, January 19, 1989–March 15, 1989). J. Christian Heunis was born in Uniondale, Cape Province, on April 29, 1927. He graduated from Stellenbosch University with a law degree in 1948. He entered local politics in 1959 and was elected to Parliament in 1970. Heunis was appointed deputy minister of finance in June of 1972. He served as minister of indian affairs and tourism from 1974 until 1975 and remained in the cabinet as minister of economic affairs from 1975 until 1979. Heunis held other cabinet positions including minister of transport, internal affairs, and planning. He also served as chairman of the National party in Cape Province from 1986 until 1989. Heunis was named acting president on January 19, 1989, when President Pieter Botha suffered a mild stroke. Botha resumed his duties on March 15, 1989.

PIETER BOTHA (President, March 15, 1989–August 14, 1989). *See earlier entry under Heads of State.*

F. W. deKLERK (President, August 15, 1989–). Frederick Willem deKlerk was born in Johannesburg on March 18, 1936. He attended Potchefstroom University for Christian High Education and received a degree in law in 1958. He joined a law firm in Vereeniging in 1961. DeKlerk also became active in National party politics and was elected to Parliament in 1972. He was appointed to Prime Minister Pieter Botha's cabinet as minister of posts and telecommunications in 1978 and served in various other cabinet positions. He was named minister of internal affairs in 1982 and became chairman of the Minister's Council in the House of Assembly in 1985. DeKlerk was elected to succeeded Botha as leader of the National party in February of 1989, following Botha's resignation after suffering a stroke. Botha also stepped down as president on August 14, 1989, and deKlerk was elected to succeed him the following day. He was elected to a full five-year term the following month. DeKlerk continued to introduce reforms in South Africa's political system. He rescinded the bans against the African National Congress (ANC) in February of 1990 and freed ANC leader Nelson Mandela after 27 years of imprisonment. He continued to oppose majority rule for South Africa, but supported the elimination of most remaining apartheid laws. DeKlerk's government abandoned the Lands and Group Areas acts which were intended to create self-governing black homelands within South Africa. Ciskei, Transkei, and Venda, homelands that had been previously granted self-government, began negotiations to rejoin South Africa. The government began negotiations with the ANC and other political organizations to create an undivided and democratic nation.

HEADS OF GOVERNMENT

JAN CHRISTIAN SMUTS (Prime Minister, September 3, 1939–May 26, 1948). Jan Christian Smuts was born in Cape Province on May 24, 1870. He worked on his family's farm and later entered Victoria College in Stellenbosch. In 1891 he attended Cambridge in Great Britain on a scholarship. Smuts studied law and returned to South Africa in 1895. He initially supported Cecil Rhodes's government in Cape Colony before becoming disillusioned with Rhodes following the Jameson Raid. He went to Johannesburg, where he joined the Transvaal government. He was named state attorney in 1898 and worked closely with Paul Kruger in an attempt to prevent a war between the Dutch and British in South Africa. When the Boer War began, Smuts was a leader in the resistance to the British. He took government funds from the banks in Pretoria before the British captured the city and used the money to finance a guerrilla war against the British. His group fought until the end of the war in 1902 and then took part in the peace negotiations. Following the war, Smuts was a founder of the Het Volk party. When the Liberal party came to power in Britain, Smuts assisted in negotiations that returned self-rule to South Africa. The Het Volk party was successful in the elections of 1907, and Smuts became colonial secretary and minister of education in the government led by Louis Botha. Smuts was forced to make a series of unpopular decisions, including the arrest of Mohandas Gandhi. He also broke a miners strike in Johannesburg by imposing martial law and calling in the troops. Smuts was also a leading supporter of South Africa's entry into World War I on the side of the British. He was forced to put down a brief rebellion in October of 1914 by Boer veterans who opposed working with the British. After entering the war, South Africa successfully fought against the Germans in South-West Africa, and Smuts was named commander in chief of the forces in East Africa. After leading successful campaigns against the Germans in Tanganyika, he attended the Imperial War Congress in London in March of 1917. He remained in London as part of the

British war cabinet and took part in the peace conference following the war. Smuts returned to South Africa to become prime minister following the death of Botha in August of 1919. Smuts was faced with another violent mines strike in 1922, and he was unsuccessful in convincing Southern Rhodesia to join the Union of South Africa later in the year. The opposition Nationalist party joined with the Labor party and defeated Smuts's South African party in the election of 1924. He was succeeded by J.B.M. Hertzog as prime minister. While out of office, Smuts wrote *Holism and Evolution*, a philosophical work published in 1926. Following the depression of 1929, economic difficulties forced a coalition between Hertzog's Nationalists and Smuts's South African party in 1933. Smuts joined the cabinet as deputy prime minister. The coalition lasted until the onset of World War II. Smuts advocated South Africa's entry into the war on the side of the British, while Hertzog supported neutrality. The issue was settled in the House of Assembly in favor of Smuts's position, and he became prime minister on September 3, 1939. Smuts also served as commander in chief of the South African armed forces, and he often visited sectors where South African troops served. Following Germany's defeat, Smuts took part in the peace negotiations and assisted in drafting the United Nations charter in 1945. Smuts was less successful in dealing with domestic problems. The government had relaxed the enforcement of segregation policies during the war. The new Nationalist party under Daniel Malan advocated apartheid policies to support white supremacy in South Africa. The Nationalists narrowly defeated Smuts in the elections of 1948. Smuts relinquished the office of prime minister to Malan on June 3, 1948, and became leader of the opposition. He died at his home in Irene, near Pretoria, on September 11, 1950.

DANIEL F. MALAN (Prime Minister, June 3, 1948–November 30, 1954). Daniel Francois Malan was born in Riebeek West, Cape Province, on May 22, 1874. He studied theology at the University of Stellenbosch with the intention of becoming a minister in the Dutch Reform Church. He attended the University of Utrecht in the Netherlands and received a doctorate of divinity in 1904. Malan returned to South Africa and worked as a minister until World War I. He entered politics and served as editor of *Die Burger*, the Nationalist newspaper in Capetown. He was elected to Parliament in 1918. Malan served as minister of the interior, public health, and education in the cabinet of Prime Minister James Hertzog in 1924. He remained in the cabinet until the formation of a coalition cabinet with the South African party under Field Marshal Jan Christian Smuts in 1933. He remained in Parliament, where he led the Opposition. Malan was a member of the Afrikander Broederbond, a quasi-Fascist secret society which advocated the elimination of English-speaking public officials from high office. He supported South African neutrality during World War II, and his party suffered reversals in the elections of 1945. Malan's National party was successful in the election in May of 1948, however, and Malan was sworn in as prime minister and minister of external affairs on June 3, 1948. He appointed a cabinet composed entirely of non–English speaking members, most of whom were members of the Afrikander Broederbond. He initiated the policy of apartheid, which advocated the supremacy of the white Europeans over the native population of South Africa. He also initiated the annexation of the South-West African territory, which had previously been held in trusteeship by the League of Nations. In 1952 Malan's government obtained authority from Parliament to deal harshly with demonstrations led by the African and Indian National congresses against the repressive apartheid rules. Malan's party again received a majority in the elections of 1953. Malan resigned as prime minister due to ill health on November 30, 1954. He died following a stroke in Capetown on February 7, 1959.

JOHANNES G. STRIJDOM (Prime Minister, December 2, 1954–August 24, 1958). Johannes Gerhardus Strijdom was born in Willowmore, Cape Colony, on July 14, 1873. He attended Victoria College and returned to work briefly on his family's ostrich farm. He then attended the University of Pretoria, where he received a law degree in 1917. Strijdom went to Transvaal to practice law, and in 1929 he was elected to the Parliament as a member of the Nationalist party. He rose to the leadership of the party in Transvaal in 1939. When the Nationalists were victorious in the 1948 elections, Strijdom was named minister of lands and irrigation in the government of Daniel Malan. Strijdom was considered the leader of the extremist faction of the party. He defeated Nicolaas Havenga in the Nationalist caucus to succeed retiring Prime Minister Malan on December 2, 1954. Strijdom strongly advocated South Africa becoming a republic. He was also a supporter of apartheid policies, including strict racial segregation and the purging of nonwhites from the voting rolls. South Africa's racial policies were condemned by the United Nations, but the Nationalist party increased its majority in the elections of 1958. Strijdom remained prime minister until his death from heart disease in Capetown on August 24, 1958.

CHARLES R. SWART (Acting Prime Minister, August 23, 1958–September 3, 1958). *See entry under Heads of State.*

HENDRIK F. VERWOERD (Prime Minister, September 3, 1958–September 6, 1966). Hendrik Frensch Verwoerd was born in Amsterdam, Holland, on September 8, 1901. He accompanied his parents to South Africa two years later. He was educated at the University of Stellenbosch and at several universities in Germany. Verwoerd returned to South Africa and became a professor of psychology at the University of Stellenbosch in 1928. He became active in right-wing politics, and in 1937 he became editor of *Die Transvaler*, the Nationalist newspaper in Johannesburg. The newspaper was considered pro-Nazi and anti-British during World War II. The Nationalist party was successful in the elections of 1948, though Verwoerd was defeated for a seat in Parliament. He was elected to the Senate later in the year and became minister of native affairs in the cabinet of Prime Minister Daniel Malan in 1950. In this position he served as the leading planner and enforcer of apartheid. He left the cabinet in April of 1958 and ran successfully for election to the Assembly. Verwoerd, who was known as Oom (Uncle) Henk to his supporters, was selected by the National caucus to serve as prime minister following the death of Johannes Strijdom in August of 1958. He took office on September 3, 1958. The continued suppression of the rights of native South Africans resulted in a series of demonstrations in 1960. At a demonstration in Sharpeville, police fired on the protestors, killing 67 and wounding nearly 200. Two weeks after the Sharpeville massacre an English farmer shot Verwoerd twice in the head in protest of his apartheid policies. Verwoerd rapidly recovered from his wounds. In 1961 he removed South Africa from the British Commonwealth, and South Africa became a republic on May 31, 1961. Verwoerd proceeded with his segregation policies, which included the creation of native homelands that would isolate the majority black South Africans on a small percentage of land. Verwoerd was stabbed to death by a mentally deranged parliamentary messenger while attending a session of Parliament on September 6, 1966.

THEOPHILIUS EBEN DONGES (Acting Prime Minister, September 6, 1966–September 13, 1966). Theophilius Ebenhaezer Donges was born in Klerksdorp, Transvaal, on March 8, 1898. He attended the University of Stellenbosch and received a law degree from London University in 1922. He returned to South Africa, where he became active in the Nationalist party and worked for the party newspaper, *Die burger.* In 1927 he left journalism to pursue a career in law. Donges was an unsuccessful candidate for Parliament in 1938, but was elected to a seat in 1941. He was appointed to Daniel Malan's cabinet in 1948 and served as minister of posts and telegraphs. He later was named minister of the interior and was instrumental in formulating and enforcing legislation that established the repressive apartheid laws. Donges was

appointed minister of finance in 1958 and retained the post until 1966. Following the assassination of Hendrik Verwoerd on September 6, 1966, he served briefly as acting prime minister until John Vorster took office on September 13, 1966. In March of 1967 Donges was selected president to succeed Charles Swart. His scheduled inauguration in May was postponed when he was hospitalized with a brain hemorrhage after suffering a stroke. Donges's condition deteriorated, and he died in a Cape Town hospital on January 10, 1968.

JOHN VORSTER (Prime Minister, September 12, 1966–September 28, 1978). *See entry under Heads of state.*

PIETER BOTHA (Prime Minister, September 28, 1978–September 14, 1984). *See entry under Heads of State.*

Spain (Spanish State)
(Estado Español)

Spain is a country on the Iberian Peninsula in southwest Europe.

HEADS OF STATE

FRANCISCO FRANCO BAHAMONDE (Head of State, August 9, 1939–October 30, 1975). Francisco Paulino Hermenegildo Teódulo Franco y Bahamonde was born on December 4, 1892, in El Ferrol, Galicia. He attended the military academy in Toledo, where he graduated in 1910. He entered the Spanish military and was stationed in Morocco the following year. Franco was wounded in action in 1916 and returned to Spain for three years. He was then assigned to the Spanish

foreign legion in Morocco and served as deputy commander from 1920 until 1923, when he was promoted to commander of the legion with the rank of lieutenant colonel. He was active in the military campaign against Abd-el-Krim, the leader of the Rifs. Franco departed Morocco in 1926, with the rank of brigadier general. He subsequently returned to Spain as the director of the military academy at Saragosa. The academy was abolished with the advent of the Spanish Republic and the ouster of the monarchy in 1931. Franco was sent to the Baleric Islands, where he remained until 1934, when the government recalled him to put down a miners strike. His ruthlessness in dealing with the revolt earned him the nickname "the Butcher." He made contact with other military commanders opposed to the republican government before he was sent into virtual exile in the Canary Islands. Franco returned to Spain to attended the funeral of José Calvo Sotelo, an assassinated rightist leader, in July of 1936. He then joined with a military revolt that the assassination had precipitated and took command of rebel troops in North Africa. He assumed control of all the rebel forces following the death of General José Sanjurjo in a plane crash in July of 1936. Franco was proclaimed generalissimo of the army and leader of the Nationalist government in October of 1936. The bloody civil war raged on for the next three years, with Italy and Germany supporting the Nationalist cause and the Soviet Union backing the republican government. Franco led the assault that captured Barcelona in January of 1938, and the war ended with the fall of Madrid in March of 1939. Franco was officially recognized as head of the Spanish government in August of 1939. He was initially supportive of the Axis powers during World War II. He backed away from his earlier endorsement of Hitler and Mussolini as the Allies advanced through Europe, however, and he proclaimed Spanish neutrality. After the conclusion of the war, Franco's Spain was viewed with distrust and hostility by the victorious Allied powers. Spain was refused membership in the United Nations, and many Western nations, including the United States, withdrew their diplomatic representatives from Madrid. Franco began a quest to restore respectability abroad for his regime. Western governments restored diplomatic relations in late 1950, largely as a result of the cold war. The United States approved a large loan to Spain in 1950 and was granted the use of Spanish air and naval bases in an agreement signed in September of 1953. Spain was admitted to the United Nations in 1955. Franco continued to rule Spain in an authoritarian manner that was often criticized at home and abroad. Spain prospered economically during the 1950s and 1960s, and Franco allowed some liberal reforms to be carried out. His government was faced with a revolt from a militant nationalist organization that demanded autonomy for the Basque region of Spain. Student groups and labor unions also became active in the movement to grant the Spanish people greater freedom. Franco continued to hold firmly on to power and in his later years gave serious consideration to his succession. In July of 1969 he announced his decision to restore the monarchy and named Prince Juan Carlos de Borbon, the grandson of Spain's last king, Alfonso XIII, as heir. Despite the assassination by Basque separatists of his premier, Admiral Luis Carrero Blanco, in a bombing on December 20, 1973, Franco continued to liberalize Spain's political system. He became seriously ill in July of 1974 when he suffered from a severe hemorrhage. Franco allowed Prince Juan Carlos to take the powers of government until he was sufficiently recovered in September of 1974. Franco's health again failed on October 21, 1975, when he was stricken by severe heart disease. His health continued to deteriorate from various ailments, and Prince Juan Carlos again became acting chief of state on October 30, 1975. Franco succumbed to his illnesses at the age of 82 at La Paz Hospital in Madrid on November 20, 1975.

JUAN CARLOS I (King, November 22, 1975–). Juan Carlos Alfonso Victor Maria de Borbón y Borbón was born in Rome on January 5, 1938. He was the son of Don Juan de Bórbon y Battenberg and the grandson of

Alfonso XIII, who was ousted as king of Spain in 1931. The Spanish royal family had gone into exile in Italy following the overthrow of the monarchy. Juan Carlos first came to Spain in 1947 to attend a private school near Madrid. Francisco Franco, the leader of Spain, announced in 1947 that the monarchy would be restored. He bypassed Juan Carlos's father in favor of Juan Carlos as heir presumptive to the throne. Juan Carlos was given a military education and commissioned in the armed services in preparation for ascending the throne. He married Princess Sophia, the daughter of King Paul of Greece, on May 14, 1962. The couple resided in the Zarzuela Palace in Madrid. Juan Carlos officially became heir apparent in 1969 with the approval of the law of succession. He was granted the powers of government in July of 1974, when Franco became ill. Franco recovered the following September, but again became seriously ill in October of 1975. Juan Carlos became acting chief of state on October 30, 1975. Franco died on November 20, 1975, and Juan Carlos was crowned King Juan Carlos I two days later. He instituted a series of political reforms to pave the way for a democratically elected Parliament. Political parties were allowed to organize, political prisoners were granted amnesty, and trade unions were recognized. Parliamentary elections were held in June of 1977. These reforms were met with some opposition by the more conservative members of the government and the military. Members of the Civil Guard staged an attempted military coup on February 23, 1981, when they seized the Parliament and announced their intention to establish a military government. King Juan Carlos personally persuaded wavering military leaders not to join the coup and convinced the rebellious officers to surrender. Juan Carlos attempted to remain as aloof from political issues as possible. He traveled widely throughout the world, presenting himself as a symbol of Spanish democracy.

HEADS OF GOVERNMENT

FRANCISCO FRANCO BAHAMONDE (Premier, August 9, 1939–June 9, 1973). *See entry under Heads of State.*

LUIS CARRERO BLANCO (Premier, June 8, 1973–December 20, 1973). Luis Carrero Blanco was born in Santona, in Santander province, on March 4, 1903. He graduated from the Spanish naval academy and was commissioned an ensign in 1922. He saw active duty in Spain's colonies in North Africa in the early 1920s. Carrero Blanco was promoted to lieutenant in 1926 and was later given command of a submarine. He returned from sea after five years and continued his studies in naval warfare. He was named to the staff of the Spanish naval academy in 1934. Carrero Blanco joined the Nationalist navy during the Spanish Civil War, and following Francisco Franco's victory in 1939, he was named chief of naval operations. He became a close associate of Franco and was appointed undersecretary to the presidency of the government in 1941. He was appointed to the Spanish Parliament, the Cortes, the following year. Carrero Blanco became vice president of the Cortes in 1942. He joined Franco's cabinet in 1951 and remained a key advisor throughout the 1950s and 1960s. He also rose through the ranks of the navy and was promoted to admiral in 1966. Franco appointed Carrero Blanco as vice premier in September of 1967. Franco relinquished his duties as head of government, while retaining the presidency, under a new constitution in June of 1973. Carrero Blanco was appointed premier in the new government on June 8, 1973. He was killed six months later on December 20, 1973, when an explosion hurled the limousine in which he had been a passenger onto the roof of the Madrid church where he had just attended services. The assassination was believed to have been carried out by members of a Basque separatist organization.

TORCUATO FERNÁNDEZ MIRANDA Y HEVIA (Acting Premier, December 20, 1973–December 29, 1973).

Torcuato Fernández Miranda y Hevía was born in Asturias, on November 10, 1915. He attended the University of Oviedo, but was forced to go into hiding near the start of the Spanish Civil War in 1936. He later joined Francisco Franco's Nationalist rebels and completed his studies following the victory of Franco's forces in 1939. Fernández Miranda received a degree in law and became a leader of the right-wing Falangist movement. He served in Franco's cabinet as minister of education and was selected as secretary-general of the Movimiento, Spain's only legal political organization, in 1962. He was appointed vice-premier in the government of Admiral Luis Carrero Blanco in June of 1973. When Carrero Blanco was killed by a car bomb on December 20, 1973, Fernández Miranda became acting premier and served until a new government was named on December 29, 1973. Following the ascension of Juan Carlos I as king of Spain, Fernández Miranda was named president of the Spanish Parliament. Spain was in the process of democratizing the government, and Fernández Miranda strived to insure that such changes were conducted in a constitutional manner. He objected to the liberal constitution that was approved in 1978 and resigned from the Union of the Democratic Centre party in protest. He died in London, England, on June 19, 1980.

CARLOS ARIAS NAVARRO (Premier, December 29, 1973–July 1, 1976).

Carlos Arias Navarro was born in Madrid on December 11, 1908. He attended the Central University of Madrid, where he received a doctorate in law. He entered the civil service and was employed at the Ministry of Justice. Arias Navarro became a public prosecutor in Malaga in 1933. His support for the rebellion led by General Francisco Franco during the Spanish Civil War resulted in his arrest by the republican government in 1936. He was released when the pro-Franco Falangist forces captured the city. He joined the rebel army, and following the victory of insurrectionists, he returned to the civil service. Arias Navarro was appointed governor of the province of Leon in 1944 and held several other provincial governorships before being appointed director general of security in June of 1957. He gained a reputation for his harsh dealings with enemies of the Franco regime. He was appointed mayor of Madrid in February of 1965. Arias Navarro was considered a very able administrator who did much to improve the Spanish capital. He was reappointed to the position by Franco in 1971. Admiral Luis Carrero Blanco was appointed premier of the Spanish government in June of 1973, and Arias Navarro joined his cabinet as minister of the interior. When Carrero Blanco was killed in a terrorist bombing on December 20, 1973, Arias Navarro was appointed to succeed him and took office on December 29, 1973. He was reappointed to the position by King Juan Carlos after Franco's death in November of 1975. Arias Navarro's slow progress in democraticizing Spain resulted in strained relations with the king. He resigned on July 1, 1976, to allow for the transition of the Spanish government to a democracy. He retired to his home in Madrid, where he died of a heart attack at the age of 80 on November 27, 1989.

ADOLFO SUÁREZ GONZÁLEZ

(Premier, July 1, 1976–February 25, 1981). Adolfo Suárez González was born in Cebreros in Avila Province on September 25, 1932. He attended the University of Salamanca and the University of Madrid, where he received a doctorate. He entered government service in the early 1950s by taking a minor position in the administration of Fernando Herrero-Tejedo, the governor of Avila. Suárez's administrative abilities captured the notice of the governor, and he received rapid promotions in the provincial government. Suárez later moved to Madrid, where he again served in minor administrative posts. He was appointed governor of Segovia Province in 1968 and was named director general of the Spanish Broadcasting and Television System in November of the following year. He left this position in 1973 to become chairman of the national tourism commission. Suárez became deputy secretary-general of the National Movement under Herrero-Tejedo in March of 1975. He stepped down three months later after Herrero-Tejedo was killed in an automobile accident. Suárez was a founder and leader of the conservative Democratic Union of the Spanish People in June of 1975. He was chosen as premier by King Juan Carlos on July 1, 1976. The post-Franco government moved to democratize the Spanish government by allowing the formation of political parties and organizing free elections. Suárez led his party to victory in the elections of 1977 and 1979. He was criticized in the Parliament for his handling of Spain's economy. His popularity diminished in the polls, and Suárez announced his resignation as premier on January 29, 1981. He nominated Leopoldo Calvo Sotelo as his successor and relinquished the office on February 25, 1981. He was subsequently made the duke of Suárez by King Juan Carlos. The following year he left the Union of the Democratic Centre party and founded the Democratic and Social Centre party. Suárez was reelected to the Parliament from Madrid. His center-right party lost support in the elections in 1991, and Suárez resigned as leader of the party in May of 1991.

LEOPOLDO CALVO SOTELO Y BUSTELO

(Premier, February 25, 1981–December 2, 1982). Leopoldo Calvo Sotelo y Bustelo was born in Madrid on April 14, 1926. His uncle was José Calvo Sotelo, the rightist leader whose assassination sparked the beginning of the Spanish Civil War in July of 1936. Calvo Sotelo attended Madrid's engineering school and received a doctorate in 1951. He subsequently worked in the Spanish chemical industry, where he rose to become director-general of a leading chemical company in 1963. He was placed in charge of the Spanish railways system in 1967 and served until the following year. Calvo Sotelo was elected to the Spanish Parliament in 1971, where he was a supporter of Juan Carlos's succession to the Spanish throne. Calvo Sotelo was appointed minister of commerce in the cabinet of Carlos Arias Navarro following the death of Franco in 1975. He remained in the cabinet as minister of public works in the government of Premier Adolfo Suárez González. He managed the campaigns of the Union of the Democratic Centre in Spain's first democratic parliamentary elections in June of 1977. Calvo Sotelo returned to the Suárez cabinet in February of 1978, when he was placed in charge of Spain's negotiating team to join the European Common Market. He achieved success in this position, as the Common Market voted to approve Spain's entry to the body within a decade. Calvo Sotelo was named Suárez's deputy premier in September of 1980. He was chosen to succeed Suárez as head of the government following the premier's abrupt resignation in January of 1981. An attempted military coup on February 23, 1981, proved unsuccessful, and Calvo Sotelo's nomination was accepted by the Parliament on February 25, 1981. Calvo Sotelo faced a crisis within his own party when numerous defections, including that of former premier Suárez, threatened his government. Early elections were scheduled for October of 1982, and the Union of the Democratic Centre was decisively defeated by the Socialist party. Calvo Sotelo, who lost his own seat in Parliament, stepped down as premier on December 2, 1982. He was elected as a member of the European Parliament in 1986.

FELIPE GONZÁLEZ MÁRQUEZ (Premier, December 2, 1982–). Felipe González Márquez was born in Seville on March 5, 1942. He was educated at the University of Seville, where he received a degree in law in 1966. He became involved with Socialist political organizations while at the university. His association with the outlawed Socialists resulted in his arrest on several occasions during Franco's regime. González became leader of the largest faction of the Spanish Socialists in 1972 and was elected secretary-general of the Spanish Socialist Workers party two years later. He was subsequently sentenced to eight years in prison for his membership in an illegal organization, but the sentence was never carried out. After the death of Franco and the ascension of King Juan Carlos I to the throne, political parties, including the Socialists, were legalized in Spain. González was elected to the lower house of the Chamber of Deputies in June of 1977, with the Socialist party candidates winning a third of the seats. The Socialists' popularity increased over the next several years and early parliamentary elections were scheduled in October of 1982. The Socialists swept the election, and González took office as premier on December 1, 1982. In the late 1980s and early 1990s, the González government was plagued by a slumping economy and corruption scandals.

Sri Lanka,
Democratic Socialist Republic of
(Ceylon) (Sri Lanka Prajatantrika Samajawadi Janarajaya)

Sri Lanka is an island country off the southeast coast of India in the Indian Ocean. It was granted independence from Great Britain on February 4, 1948.

HEADS OF STATE

SIR HENRY MONCK-MASON MOORE (Governor-General, February 4, 1948–July 6, 1949). Henry Monck-Mason Moore was born on March 18, 1887. He was educated at King's College School and graduated from Jesus College, Cambridge, in 1909. He joined the colonial civil service and was commissioned with the Royal Garrison Artillery in Salonika during World War I. After the war he was appointed Assistant Colonial Secretary for Ceylon. Moore remained with the colonial department and was appointed colonial secretary of Bermuda in 1922. In 1924 he was appointed principal assistant secretary of Nigeria, and he rose to deputy chief secretary in 1927. The following year he was appointed colonial secretary of Kenya, and he remained in that position until 1934, when he was named governor and commander in chief of Sierra Leone. In 1937 Moore was named assistant undersecretary of state at the Colonial Office, and two years later he rose to deputy undersecretary of state for the colonies. Shortly thereafter he was appointed governor of the British Colony and Protectorate of Kenya. In 1944 he was again stationed in Ceylon, as governor and commander in chief. After the conclusion of World War II, the Ceylonese petitioned for independence from Great Britain. Moore and Ceylonese leader Don Senanayake were successful in negotiating a peaceful transfer of power. When Ceylon achieved independence in February of 1948, Moore remained as governor-general. He retired from this position in July of 1949 and settled in South Africa. He died at his home in Cape Town on March 26, 1964.

HERWALD RAMSBOTHAM, VISCOUNT SOULBURY (Governor General, July 6, 1949–July 17, 1954). Herwald Ramsbotham was born on March 6, 1887. He attended University College at Oxford and was called to the bar in 1911. He served in the infantry during World War I. Ramsbotham entered politics as a Conservative and was elected to the House of Commons from Lancaster in 1929. In 1931 he was appointed parliamentary secretary to the Board of Education, a position he held for the next four years. He held other governmental appointments and in July of 1941 was appointed chairman of the Assistance Board and was raised to the peerage as Baron Soulbury. He was appointed to the chairmanship of the Commission on Constitutional Reform for Ceylon in November of 1944 and was instrumental in negotiating the independence of that country.

Shortly after Ceylonese independence, Soulbury was named governor-general of Ceylon to succeed Sir Henry Moore. He retained that position until July 17, 1954. After his return to England, he served as chairman of the National Society and was chairman of the Board of Governors of the Royal Ballet School from 1956 until 1964. Viscount Soulbury died at the age of 83 on January 30, 1971.

SIR OLIVER GOONETILLEKE (Governor-General, July 17, 1954–March 2, 1962). Oliver Ernest Goonetilleke was born on September 20, 1892. He was educated at London University and returned to Ceylon to enter the civil service. He served in the colonial auditing department from 1924 until 1931. Goonetilleke was a member of the Ceylon War Council in 1942 and was named home minister in 1947. He served as Ceylon's high commissioner to Great Britain from 1948 until 1951. He returned to Ceylon to serve in the cabinet as minister of home affairs from 1951 until 1952 and as minister of agriculture from 1952 until 1953. Goonetilleke was appointed minister of finance in 1954. He was named the first native-born governor-general of Ceylon on July 17, 1954, when he succeeded Viscount Soulbury to the position. Goonetilleke resigned on March 2, 1962, following allegations that he was involved in a conspiracy against the government of Prime Minister Sirimavo Bandaranaike. He retired from political affairs and died on December 17, 1978.

SIR WILLIAM GOPALLAWA (Governor-General, March 2, 1962–May 22, 1972; President, May 22, 1972–February 3, 1978). William Gopallawa was born in Dullewe, Matale, on September 16, 1897. He was educated locally and worked as a teacher and an attorney. He entered politics and was elected to the Municipal Councils in Kandy and Colombo. Gopallawa was appointed ambassador to China in 1958 and was named Ceylon's ambassador to the United States in 1961. He returned to Ceylon to succeed Sir Oliver Goonetilleke as governor-general on March 2, 1962. He retained office until Ceylon was declared a republic on May 22, 1972. Gopallawa subsequently served as the nation's first president. He stepped down from office following the election of Junius R. Jayawardene to the presidency on February 3, 1978. He died of a heart attack in Colombo at the age of 83 on January 30, 1981.

JUNIUS R. JAYAWARDENE (President, February 3, 1978–January 2, 1989). Junius Richard Jayawardene was born in Colombo on September 17, 1906. He attended the University of Ceylon and received a degree in law in 1938. He also became involved in politics and joined the Ceylon National Congress in 1938. Jayawardene was elected to the State Council in 1943 and was appointed minister of finance in Ceylon's independent government in 1948. He was shifted to the Ministry of Agriculture and Food in 1953 and retained that position until the United National party lost power in 1956. He returned briefly to the cabinet as finance minister in 1960 in the interim government of Dudley Senanayake. Jayawardene served as deputy leader of the Opposition under Senanayake from 1960 until 1965, when the United National party returned to power. He served as minister of planning and external affairs in Senanayake's government until 1970, when he returned to the Opposition. He succeeded Senanayake as leader of the Opposition to Sirimavo Bandaranaike's government. The United National party won a major victory in parliamentary elections in 1977, and Jayawardene became prime minister on January 23, 1977. He sponsored a new constitution that provided for an executive presidency, and he stepped down as prime minister to become president on February 3, 1978. He was reelected for a second term in

October of 1982. Jayawardene continued to face violent disturbances from the minority Tamil population. Violence continued in the 1980s, and the government of India under Prime Minister Rajiv Gandhi intervened with a peacekeeping force in July of 1987. The Sinhalese extremist organization, the People's Liberation Front, also engaged in guerrilla activities against the government, and Jayawardene narrowly avoided death in a grenade attack on the Parliament in August of 1987. Jayawardene retired from office on January 2, 1989, and was succeeded by his prime minister, Ranasinghe Premadasa.

RANASINGHE PREMADASA (President, January 2, 1989–May 1, 1993). Ranasinghe Premadasa was born to a poor family in Colombo on June 23, 1924. He was educated at St. Joseph College and became active in the trade union movement. He was elected to the Colombo Municipal Council in 1950 and became deputy mayor in 1955. Premadasa joined the United National party in 1956 and was elected to the Parliament in 1960. He held positions in several ministries before being named minister of local government in 1968. He served as chief whip of the Opposition in Parliament from 1970 and was elected deputy leader of the United National party in 1976. Premadasa returned to the cabinet as minister of local government in 1977. He was selected as prime minister to succeed Junius R. Jayawardene on February 6, 1978, after Jayawardene became president. His government was faced with a faltering economy and continuing unrest from Tamil separatists from northern Sri Lanka. Premadasa defeated Sirimavo Bandaranaike in December of 1988 to become president of Sri Lanka. He was sworn into office on January 2, 1989. Premadasa also held other major positions in the government, including the Ministries of Defense and Planning. Violence between

Tamil and Sinhalese extremists continue to plague the country. Lalith Athulathmudali, the leader of the Opposition, was killed by assassins in April of 1993. Premadasa also became a victim of ethnic violence when an explosive-laden bicyclist attacked the president during a May Day parade in Colombo. Premadasa was killed in the explosion on May 1, 1993. He was succeeded by Prime Minister Dingiri Banda Wijetunge, who became acting president until the Parliament could choose a permanent successor.

HEADS OF GOVERNMENT

DON STEPHEN SENANAYAKE (Prime Minister, September 26, 1947–March 22, 1952). Don Stephen Senanayake was born on October 20, 1884. He attended St. Thomas College in Mount Lavina. He was elected to the legislative council in 1924. Senanayake served as minister of agriculture from 1931 until 1947, and he also served as leader of the State Council and vice-chairman of the Board of Ministers from 1942 until 1947. In September of 1947 he was asked to form a government. He became the first prime minister of independent Ceylon on February 4, 1948, when Ceylon received full dominion status. Senanayake also served as minister of defense and external affairs in the government. He traveled extensively during his term of office and hosted the meeting of commonwealth foreign ministers held in Colombo in January of 1950. Senanayake was seriously injured in a riding accident on March 21, 1952, when he was thrown from his horse. He died in Colombo of his injuries at the age of 67 on March 22, 1952.

DUDLEY SENANAYAKE (Prime Minister, March 22, 1952–October 12, 1953). Dudley Shelton Senanayake was born on June 19, 1911. He was educated in Ceylon and Great Britain and received a degree in law from Corpus Christi College, Cambridge, in 1934. He returned to Ceylon to practice law. His father, Don Stephen Senanayake, became Ceylon's first prime minister in September of 1947 and Dudley Senana-

yake was named to the cabinet as minister of agriculture and lands. The younger Senanayake was called upon to succeeded his father as prime minister on March 22, 1952, following Don Senanayake's death in a horseback-riding accident. He called for new elections the following week, and his United National party was returned to power with a large majority. Ceylon was facing food shortages and rising inflation, and leftist opponents staged a violent demonstration against the government in September of 1953. Senanayake was suffering from poor health and could not stand the strain of office. He stepped down on October 12, 1954. His successor, Sir John Kotelawala, brought the United National party to defeat in 1956. Senanayake returned to lead the party in 1958 and was appointed caretaker prime minister on March 21, 1960. Sirimavo Bandaranaike's Freedom party was victorious in subsequent elections, and Senanayake relinquished office on July 22, 1960. He led the opposition to Bandaranaike's government and returned to power as prime minister of a coalition government on March 25, 1965. He sought to improve the status of the minority Tamil community. The Freedom party defeated Senanayake's ruling coalition in general elections in 1970 and Bandaranaike again became prime minister on May 28, 1970. Senanayake stepped down as leader of the United National party and retired from politics. He died in Colombo from a heart ailment at the age of 57 on April 12, 1973.

SIR JOHN KOTELAWALA (Prime Minister, October 12, 1953–April 11, 1956). John Lionel Kotelawala was born in 1897. He was educated locally and at Cambridge University in England. He entered politics and was elected to the Ceylon State Council in 1933. Kotelawala served in the government as minister of agriculture and lands. He was appointed minister of communications and works in 1936 and became minister of transport and works in 1946. Kotelawala was a founding member of the United National party and served as vice president from 1946. He was elected to the House of Representatives the following year and remained in the cabinet following Ceylon's independence in February of 1948. Prime Minister Don Senanayake was killed in an accident in March of 1952 and was succeeded by his son, Dudley. Kotelawala remained in the cabinet until Dudley Senanayake resigned for reasons of health in October of 1953. Kotelawala became prime minister on October 12, 1953. His party was defeated in general elections in 1956, and he relinquished office to S.W.R.D. Bandaranaike on April 11, 1956. Kotelawala retired to Great Britain until the late 1970s, when he returned to Sri Lanka. He died in Colombo at the age of 83 on October 2, 1980.

S.W.R.D. BANDARANAIKE (Prime Minister, April 11, 1956–September 26, 1959). Solomon West Ridgway Dias Bandaranaike was born in Colombo on January 8, 1899. He entered politics in the late 1920s and joined the United National party. He was appointed Ceylon's minister of health following independence in 1948 and served until 1951. Bandaranaike was a leading spokesman for the Buddhist Sinhalese in Ceylon, and in 1951 he founded the socialist Sri Lanka Freedom party. He became the leader of the Opposition in the House of Representatives following elections in 1952. New elections were called in April of 1956, and Bandara-

naike allied his party with several of Ceylon's leftist parties. He took office as prime minister on April 11, 1956. His pro-Sinhalese policies alienated the Indian Tamils in Ceylon and caused widespread rioting and violence. Bandaranaike was shot on September 25, 1959, by a Buddhist monk, who apparently disapproved of the government's attempts to bring Western medical practices to Ceylon. Bandaranaike died of his injuries in Colombo the following day.

WIJEYANANDA DAHANAYAKE (Prime Minister, September 26, 1959–March 21, 1960). Wijeyananda Dahanayake was born in Galle on October 22, 1902. He was educated locally and worked as a teacher. He was elected to the Galle Municipal Council in 1935 and served as mayor of Galle from 1939 until 1941. Dahanayake was a leader of the Ceylonese independence movement and was imprisoned by the British for six months during World War II. He was elected to the State Council in 1944 and became a member of the House of Representatives following independence in 1948. He joined S.W.R.D. Bandaranaike's Sri Lanka Freedom party and was named to the cabinet as minister of education in 1956. Dahanayake was chosen to succeed to the office of prime minister on September 26, 1959, following Bandaranaike's assassination. He was defeated in general elections in March of 1960 and relinquished office to Dudley Senanayake, the leader of the United National party, on March 21, 1960. Dahanayake remained active in government affairs. He returned to the cabinet as minister of home affairs in the government of Dudley Senanayake. He remained in office until 1970. Dahanayake was elected to the National State Assembly in 1972. He subsequently left politics and retired to his home in Galle.

DUDLEY SENANAYAKE (Prime Minister, March 21, 1960–July 22,

1960). *See earlier entry under Heads of Government.*

SIRIMAVO BANDARANAIKE (Prime Minister, July 22, 1960–March 25, 1965). Sirimavo Bandaranaike was born Sirimavo Ratwatte in Balangoda on April 17, 1916. She was educated at Saint Bridget's Convent in Colombo and married S.W.R.D. Bandaranaike in October of 1940. Her husband was a prominent Ceylonese politician, and he founded the Sri Lanka Freedom party in 1951. He led the party to victory in 1956 and became prime minister on April 11, 1956. When S.W.R.D. Bandaranaike was assassinated in September of 1959, Sirimavo Bandaranaike became a leading spokesman for the Freedom party. She was chosen as the party's leader in May of 1960. She led the party in a leftist coalition and defeated the United National party. Bandaranaike was appointed to the Senate by Governor-General Sir Oliver Goonetilleke and assumed the office of prime minister on July 22, 1960. She mandated Sinhalese as the official state language in place of English in January of 1961. She also served in the government as minister of defense and external affairs. The Freedom party was unseated by a coalition led by the United National party in elections in March of 1965, and Bandaranaike relinquished the office of prime minister on March 25, 1965. She led the Opposition to Prime Minister Dudley Senanayake until 1970, when the Freedom party was returned to power by a large margin. She resumed the office of prime minister on May 28, 1970. The extremist Sinhalese organization, the People's Liberation Front, led a violent attempt to overthrow the government in 1971. Ceylon officially became known as Sri Lanka in the early 1970s. Bandaranaike continued to head a leftist coalition government until 1977, when the Freedom party was badly defeated in parliamentary elections. She was replaced as prime minister by United National party leader J. R. Jayawardene on January 23, 1977. She led the Opposition to Jayawardene's government until 1980, when she was expelled from the Parliament and deprived of her political rights for alleged corruption while in office. Bandaranaike was ineligible to participate in presidential elections in 1982, though she remained active in the Freedom party. Her rights were restored in a pardon in January of 1986, and she returned to lead the Opposition. She was defeated by Ranasinghe Premadasa in presidential elections in December of 1988.

DUDLEY SENANAYAKE (Prime Minister, March 25, 1965–May 28, 1970). *See earlier entry under Heads of Government.*

SIRIMAVO BANDARANAIKE (Prime Minister, May 28, 1970–January 23, 1977). *See earlier entry under Heads of Government.*

JUNIUS R. JAYAWARDENE (Prime Minister, January 23, 1977–February 3, 1978). *See entry under Heads of State.*

RANASINGHE PREMADASEA (Prime Minister, February 6, 1978–January 2, 1989). *See entry under Heads of State.*

DINGIRI BANDA WIJETUNGE (Prime Minister, March 3, 1989–). Dingiri Banda Wijetunge was born in Polganranga on February 15, 1922. He joined the United National party in 1948. Wijetunge was named to the cabinet as minister of information and broadcasting in 1977. He subsequently served as minister of power and highways and minister of agricultural development. Wijetunge remained in the cabinet as minister of posts and telecommunications until 1988, when he was selected as governor of the Northwestern Province. He was subsequently elected prime minister of Sri

Lanka and took office on March 3, 1989. He also served in the government as minister of finance. Wijetunge became acting president of Sri Lanka on May 1, 1993, when President Ranasinghe Premadasa was killed in a bomb explosion.

Sudan, Republic of the

(Jumhuriyat al-Sudan)

The Sudan is a country in northeastern Africa. It was granted independence from Egypt and Great Britain on January 1, 1956.

HEADS OF STATE

IBRAHIM ABBOUD (President, November 17, 1958–November 15, 1964). Ibrahim Abboud was born in Mohamed-Gol at the Red Sea on October 26, 1900. He attended Gordon College and the Khartoum Military College and entered the Sudan Defense Force in 1925. He saw action in Eritrea and Ethiopia during World War II. Abboud was promoted to the rank of general and was appointed deputy commander of the Sudanese Army in 1954. He rose to the position of commander in chief of the army in 1956. He led a military coup against the government of Abdullah Khalil on November 17, 1958, and became Sudan's president, prime minister and minister of defense. Abboud attempted to improve the nation's economy and to eliminate corruption in the government. He was unable to bring economic stability to the country, however, and was faced with increasing opposition to his rule. His government was ousted by a civilian coup on November 1, 1964. Abboud remained as figurehead president under the new regime until November 15, 1964. He subsequently retired from public life. Abboud died in Khartoum at the age of 82 on September 3, 1983.

ISMAIL AL-AZHARI (President, June 10, 1965–May 25, 1969). Ismail al-Azhari was born in 1900. He was the grandson of Sayed Ismail al-Azhari, the mufti of the Sudan. He attended Gordon College and the American University in Beirut, Lebanon. Azhari joined the Sudanese Department of Education in 1921. He became involved in the Sudanese nationalist movement and founded the Ashigga, or Brothers, party in 1943. He became president of the National Unionist party in 1952 and led his party to victory in parliamentary elections in the pre-independence government in 1953. Azhari became Sudan's first prime minister on January 9, 1954. The Parliament unilaterally declared the Sudan an independent republic on January 1, 1956, and Azhari remained head of the government. He lost his parliamentary majority later in the year and was replaced as prime minister by Abdullah Khalil. He remained a leader of the Opposition during the military rule of Ibrahim Abboud and was arrested for antigovernment activities in July of 1961. Azhari remained imprisoned until January of 1962. He was active in the coup that ousted Abboud in November of 1964 and served as a member of the ruling Presidential Council. He became head of state as chairman of the council on June 10, 1965. Azhari was ousted in a coup led by Gaafar al-Nimeiry on May 25, 1969.

He was detained by the new government until his death in Khartoum from a heart attack at the age of 69 on August 26, 1969.

GAAFAR AL-NIMEIRY (President, May 25, 1969–April 6, 1985). Gaafar Muhammad al-Nimeiry was born in Wad Nubawi on January 1, 1930. He attended the Khartoum Military College and graduated as a second lieutenant in 1952. He subsequently served in the Sudan Defense Force. Nimeiry was accused of complicity in an unsuccessful coup attempt in 1957 and was placed under house arrest. He was allowed to rejoin the army following General Ibrahim Abboud's coup in November of 1958. He was briefly arrested following Abboud's ouster in November of 1964. Nimeiry received further military training and rose to the rank of colonel. He was appointed commanding officer of the Military College in 1969 and led the military coup that ousted President Ismail al-Azhari on May 25, 1969. He became chairman of the Council of the Revolution and minister of defense. Nimeiry also took the office of prime minister on October 28, 1969. He initially allied the Sudan with the Soviet Union and faced a violent revolt from right-wing Muslim Mahdists in March of 1970. Nimeiry broke with the Soviets and purged Communist sympathizers from the government in November of 1970. Left-wing military officers staged a coup on July 19, 1971, and captured Nimeiry captured but troops loyal to the government restored him to power on July 22, 1971. The coup leaders were tried and executed, and Nimeiry was elected president of the Sudan on September 30, 1971. He subsequently allied his government with Egypt and the United States. He survived a Libyan-supported coup attempt in September of 1975 and a Mahdist rebellion in Khartoum in July of 1976. Nimeiry attempted to reach a compromise with dissidents and allowed democratic reforms in the country. He

stepped down as prime minister on August 9, 1976, and appointed Rashid Bakr as his successor. He was reelected president the following year. He dismissed Bakr on September 11, 1977, and reclaimed the office of prime minister. Nimeiry was again reelected in February of 1983. He adopted the harsh Islamic penal code for the Sudan in September of 1983. The Sudan was plagued with a growing economic crisis compounded by a general strike in 1985. Nimeiry also continued to face rebellion in the southern Sudan. General 'Abd ar-Rahman Siwar ad-Dahab ousted the government in a military coup on April 6, 1985, while Nimeiry was returning from a visit to the United States. He went into exile in Egypt following his ouster.

'ABD AR-RAHMAN SIWAR AD-DAHAB (President, April 9, 1985–May 6, 1986). 'Abd ar-Rahman Siwar ad-Dahab was born in Omdurman in 1934. He attended the military academy and was commissioned into the Sudan Defense Forces as a second lieutenant in 1958. He continued to receive military training in Jordan and the United States. Siwar ad-Dahab rose through the ranks and was a field commander in the southern Sudan against the rebel Sudan National Liberation Movement. He became deputy chief of staff of the armed forces in 1982. When President Gaafar al-Nimeiry stepped down as chief of staff and minister of defense in March of 1985, General Siwar ad-Dahab was selected to replace him. Nimeiry's government was faced with growing opposition, and Siwar ad-Dahab led a military coup to oust the president on April 9, 1985. He formed the Transitional Military Council and served as its chairman. Siwar ad-Dahab's military junta presided over general elections the following year, and he relinquished power to a civilian government on May 6, 1986. He was promoted to the rank of field marshal in 1987.

AHMAD AL-MIRGHANI (President, May 6, 1986–June 30, 1989). Ahmad al-Mirghani was a member of the Democratic Unionist party. He was selected as chairman of the Supreme Council on May 6, 1986, following the restoration of the Sudan to civilian rule. Mirghani retained office until June 30, 1989, when the government was overthrown by a military coup led by General Omar al-Bashir. Mirghani was briefly imprisoned by the new regime, but was released later in the year.

OMAR AL-BASHIR (President, June 30, 1989–). Omar Hassan Ahmad al-Bashir was born in 1944. He served in the Sudanese army and rose to the rank of brigadier. He was an officer in a paratroop division station in south Kurdufan when he led the military coup that ousted the government of Prime Minister Sadiq al-Mahdi on June 30, 1989. Bashir also served as chairman of the National Salvation Revolution Command Council and minister of defense. The civil war against the Sudanese People's Liberation Movement in the southern Sudan continued, despite efforts by Bashir's government to negotiate a settlement. Bashir reestablished Islamic religious law in the Sudan in March of 1991. His government survived several coup attempts in 1991 and 1992.

HEADS OF GOVERNMENT

ISMAIL AL-AZHARI (Prime Minister, January 9, 1954–July 5, 1956). *See entry under Heads of State.*

ABDULLAH KHALIL (Prime Minister, July 5, 1956–November 17, 1958). Abdullah Khalil was born in the western Sudan in 1892. He was educated at the Khartoum Military School and received a degree in engineering. He entered the Egyptian army in 1910 and was commissioned into the Sudan Defense Force in 1915. Khalil rose to the rank of brigadier and saw action in Eritrea and Ethiopia during World War II. He became involved in politics and was a founder of the Umma, or Independence party, in 1945. He served as the party's president and became a member of the executive council of the Legislative Assembly in 1948. Khalil was elected to Parliament in 1953 and served in the cabinet as minister of agriculture. He was named minister of defense following Sudan's independence in January of 1956. Khalil was elected prime minister on July 5, 1956. He remained head of the government until November 17, 1958, when he was ousted in a military coup led by General Ibrahim Abboud. Khalil was subsequently inactive in politics. He died in Khartoum at the age of 78 on August 24, 1970.

IBRAHIM ABBOUD (Prime Minister, November 17, 1958–November 1, 1964). *See entry under Heads of State.*

SIRR AL-KHATIM AL-KHALIFA (Prime Minister, November 1, 1964–June 14, 1965). Sirr al-Khatim al-Khalifa was born in 1917. He was educated at Gordon College and worked at the Ministry of Education from 1938. He taught in various facilities and became director of the Khartoum Technical Institute in 1960. Khalifa also served in the government as deputy undersecretary of education. He was appointed prime minister of the provisional government following the ouster of General Ibrahim Abboud on November 1, 1964. He remained head of the government until June 14, 1965. Khalifa subsequently served as ambassador to Italy until 1968, when he was appointed ambassador to Great Britain. He retired to the Sudan in 1969. He returned to the government as minister of higher education in 1972. Khalifa was appointed minister of education in 1973 and served until 1975.

MUHAMMAD AHMED MAHGOUB

(Prime Minister, June 14, 1965–July 27, 1966). Muhammad Ahmed Mahgoub was born in 1908. He attended Gordon College and received a law degree from the Khartoum School of Law. He served as a member of the Legislative Assembly and was the leader of the opposition Umma Mahdists from 1954 until 1956. Mahgoub served as minister of foreign affairs from 1956 until a military coup ousted the government in 1958. He was an unsuccessful candidate for president of the United Nations General Assembly in 1958. He again served as minister of foreign affairs from 1964 until 1965. Mahgoub was named prime minister in a coalition government of the Umma and National Unionist parties on June 14, 1965. He was voted out of office following a split in his own party on July 27, 1966. He was again selected as prime minister on May 16, 1967. Mahgoub became ill in December of 1968 and spent the next three months in treatment out of the country. He returned to the Sudan but was unable to keep his coalition government from dissolving. He offered his resignation in April of 1968, but retained office until dissatisfaction with the economic and political management of the government resulted in a military coup on May 25, 1969. Mahgoub subsequently left the country to write.

SADIQ AL-MAHDI (Prime Minister, August 4, 1966–May 17, 1967). Sadiq al-Mahdi was born in 1936. He was the son of Siddik El Mahdi and the great-grandson of Abdul-Rahman El Mahdi. He was educated in Khartoum and Oxford. Mahdi helped his father organize the National Opposition Front during the military regime of Ibrahim Abboud.

Mahdi became leader of the Umma Mahdist party in 1961. He was selected as prime minister as head of a coalition government on August 4, 1966, and retained office until May 17, 1967. Mahdi was arrested for treason following the ouster of President Ismail al-Azhari in 1969. He was exiled in April of 1970, but subsequently returned to the Sudan. He was rearrested in February of 1972 and remained in prison until April of 1974. Mahdi was again exiled and was the leader of an unsuccessful coup against President Gaafar al-Nimeiry in July of 1976. He was allowed to return to the Sudan in September of 1977 following a reconciliation with Nimeiry. Mahdi was again arrested in September of 1983 and remained in prisoned until December of 1984. Nimeiry was ousted in 1985, and Mahdi, leading the New National Umma party, won the parliamentary elections in April of 1986. He again served as prime minister from May 6, 1986, until his ouster by a coup on June 30, 1989. He was arrested and remained under house arrest until November of 1989. Mahdi was granted amnesty in May of 1991.

MUHAMMED AHMED MAHGOUB

(Prime Minister, May 16, 1967–May 25, 1969). *See earlier entry under Heads of Government.*

ABUBAKR AWADALLAH (Prime Minister, May 25, 1969–October 28, 1969). Abubakr Awadallah was born in the Blue Nile Province in 1917. He studied law at Gordon College and became a district judge in 1947. He was elected Speaker of the first Sudanese House of Representatives in 1954 and served until 1957, when he was appointed to the Supreme Court. Awadallah became chief justice in 1964 and served until 1969. He subsequently became prime minister and foreign minister on May 25, 1969 and served until October 28, 1969. He remained minister of foreign affairs until 1971

and also served as minister of justice and deputy prime minister until 1971. Awadallah served as first vice president from 1972 until 1973.

GAAFAR AL-NIMEIRY (Prime Minister, October 28, 1969–August 9, 1976). *See entry under Heads of State.*

RASHID BAKR (Prime Minister, August 9, 1976–September 10, 1977). Rashid El Tahir Bakr was born in Karkoj in 1931. He attended the University of Khartoum, where he became involved in politics. He was arrested for his opposition to the government of General Ibrahim Abboud in the late 1950s. Following Abboud's ouster in 1964, Bakr was appointed minister of animal resources and justice the following year. He served as ambassador to Libya from 1972 until 1974. He returned to the Sudan to serve as Speaker of the National Assembly until 1976, when he was named second vice president. On August 9, 1976, Bakr was also appointed prime minister and served in that position until September 10, 1977. He remained second vice president and also served as foreign minister until 1980, when he returned to the National Assembly as Speaker, a post he held

until 1981. Bakr subsequently served as attorney general from 1983 until 1984.

GAAFAR AL-NIMEIRY (Prime Minister, September 11, 1977–April 6, 1985). *See entry under Heads of State.*

AL-JAZULI DAF'ALLAH (Prime Minister, April 22, 1985–May 6, 1986). Al-Jazuli Daf'allah was born in the Blue Nile Province in December of 1935. He was educated at the Khartoum Medical College. He was active in the coup that overthrew President Gaafar al-Nimeiry in April of 1985. Daf'allah was subsequently named prime minister in the military government on April 22, 1985. In April of 1986, parliamentary elections were held, and Daf'allah relinquished the position of prime minister on May 6, 1986.

SADIQ AL-MAHDI (Prime Minister, May 6, 1986–June 30, 1989). *See earlier entry under Heads of Government.*

OMAR AL-BASHIR (Prime Minister, July 9, 1989–). *See entry under Heads of State.*

Suriname, Republic of
(Republiek Suriname)

Suriname is a country on the northeastern coast of South America. It was granted independence from the Netherlands on November 25, 1975.

HEADS OF STATE

JOHAN H. E. FERRIER (President, November 25, 1975–August 15, 1980). Johan Henri Eliza Ferrier was born in Paramaribo on May 12, 1910. He served

in the Suriname Parliament from 1946 until 1948 and headed the Department of Education in Paramaribo from 1951 until 1955. He was prime minister and minister of home affairs from 1955 until 1958. The following year he went to the Netherlands, where he served in the Ministry of Education, Arts, and Science until 1965. Ferrier returned to Suriname and became governor in 1968. He retained that position until Suriname gained independence from the Netherlands on November 25, 1975, with Ferrier as its first president. Ferrier was allowed to remain in office following the military coup led by Desi Bouterse that ousted the government of Prime Minister Henck Arron in February of 1980. The military led another coup on August 15, 1980, and Ferrier was replaced by Prime Minister Hendrick Chin A Sen.

HENDRICK R. CHIN A SEN (President, August 15, 1980–February 4, 1982). Hendrik Rudolf Chin A Sen was born in Albina on January 18, 1934. He studied medicine in the Netherlands before returning to Suriname to practice. He was the founder of the Movement for the Liberation of Suriname, and following a military coup, he was named prime minister on March 15, 1980. A subsequent coup occurred on August 13, 1980, and two days later Chin A Sen was also named president of Suriname. He resigned from both positions on February 4, 1982, following the inability of his government to cope with the economic crisis developing in Suriname. Chin A Sen subsequently went into exile in the Netherlands, but returned to Suriname in 1987.

DESI BOUTERSE (Head of State, February 4, 1982–March 31, 1982). Desi Bouterse was born in 1946. He joined the Surinamese military and rose to the rank of sergeant major. He led the military coup that ousted the government of Prime Minister Henck Arron on February 25, 1980. Bouterse served as leader of the ruling National Military Council and promoted himself to the rank of lieutenant colonel. A second coup deposed President Johan Ferrier

in August of 1980. Bouterse installed Hendrick Chin A Sen as acting president. He forced the resignation of Chin A Sen on February 4, 1982, and the ruling National Military Council took over direct rule of the government. A rightist coup attempt took place on March 21, 1982. The rebel leader, Wilfred Hawker, was captured and executed. Bouterse installed Lachmipersad Ramdut-Misier as acting president on March 31, 1982. Bouterse was a leftist who advocated closer ties with Cuba and Nicaragua. Opposition leaders were detained and shot, allegedly while trying to escape, in December of 1982. The Netherlands suspended economic aid to Suriname as a result of the government's actions. Bouterse formed the National Democratic party in 1987 prior to elections to the National Assembly. The party was unsuccessful in the elections, though Bouterse remained the leader of the military junta. He allowed the selection of Ramsewak Shankar as president in January of 1988. Bouterse remained the commander of the military and came into conflict with Shankar's government in late 1990. He resigned his military position on December 23, 1990. Bouterse's second-in-command, Capt. Iwan Graanoogst, ousted Shankar the following day, and Bouterse returned to lead the military. New elections were held in 1991, and Ronald Venetiaan was selected as president on September 16, 1991. Bouterse remained head of the military until November 20, 1992, when he resigned following allegations of corruption.

LACHMIPERSAD F. RAMDUT-MISIER (President, March 31, 1982–January 25, 1988). Lachmipersad F. Ramdut-Misier was named by Lt. Col. Desi Bouterse to replace Hendrick Chin A Sen as acting president on March 31, 1982. Ramdut-Misier remained president, though Bouterse ruled as head of state as leader of the ruling National Military Council. Ramdut-Misier stepped down on January 25, 1988, following the selection of Ramsewak Shankar as president by the National Assembly.

RAMSEWAK SHANKAR (President, January 25, 1988–December 24, 1990). Ramsewak Shankar was a member of the Progressive Reform party. He served in the government as minister of agriculture. The military regime of Lt. Col. Desi Bouterse allowed elections to be held in November of 1987, and the new National Assembly selected Shankar to serve as Suriname's president. He took office on January 25, 1988. His government faced continued opposition from rebel guerrillas, and Shankar's relationship with Bouterse deteriorated in 1990. Bouterse resigned as military commander in December of 1990, and his successor, Capt. Iwan Graanoogst, led a military coup that ousted Shankar's government on December 24, 1990. Shankar remained a leader of the Progressive Reform party.

JOHAN KRAAG (President, December 30, 1990–September 16, 1991). Johannes Samuel Kraag became acting president of Suriname on December 30, 1990, following a military coup that ousted the government of Ramsewak Shankar. Kraag retained office until Ronald Venetiaan was selected as president by the People's Assembly on September 16, 1991.

RONALD R. VENETIAAN (President, September 16, 1991–). Ronald R. Venetiaan was a member of the Suriname National party. He was named to the cabinet as minister of education, science, and culture in 1988. Venetiaan was elected by the People's Assembly to serve as Suriname's president and took office on September 16, 1991. Venetiaan's government negotiated a cease-fire with the two leading guerrilla groups in May of 1992.

HEADS OF GOVERNMENT

HENCK ARRON (Prime Minister, November 25, 1975–February 25, 1980). Henck Alphonsus Eugene Arron was born in Paramaribo on April 25, 1936. He was employed at the Bank of Amsterdam in the Netherlands and subsequently worked at the Verwuurts Bank in Suriname. He was elected to Parliament in 1963 and became chairman of the National party in 1970. Arron was selected as prime minister and minister of finance in 1973 as leader of the National party Alliance coalition. He remained head of the government following Suriname's independence from the Netherlands on November 25, 1975. Arron was ousted in a military coup led by Desi Bouterse on February 25, 1980. He was arrested in August of 1980 and remained imprisoned until the following year. He returned to the banking industry in 1982. Arron returned to government as vice president and prime minister on January 26, 1988. He was again ousted during a military coup on December 24, 1990. Arron remained active in politics as a leader of the Suriname National party and chairman of the coalition New Front for Democracy and Development.

HENDRICK R. CHIN A SEN (Prime Minister, March 15, 1980–February 4, 1982). *See entry under Heads of State.*

HENRY NEYHORST (Prime Minister, March 31, 1982–December 9, 1982). Henry N. Neyhorst was an economist. He was installed to the restored position of prime minister by the ruling National Military Council on March 31, 1982, and also served in the government as minister of finance. He was forced to resign on December 9, 1982, following a conspiracy against the regime of Lt. Col. Desi Bouterse.

NOTWEN NOSREDNA (Prime Minister, December 9, 1982–December 10, 1982). Notwen Nosredna was born on October 25, 1953. He was a sergeant in Suriname's army and a leader in the military revolt in March of 1980. Nosredna succeeded Henry Neyhorst as prime minister on December 9, 1982. He resigned from office the following day and was charged with conspiring against the government. He fled the country and went into exile in the United States.

ERROL ALIBUX (Prime Minister, February 26, 1983–January 8, 1984). Errol Alibux was a founder and leader of the Progressive Workers' and Farm Laborers' Union. He was named prime minister on February 26, 1983. He resigned on January 8, 1984, following a strike by bauxite and electrical workers protesting the government's austerity measures.

WIM UDENHOUT (Prime Minister, February 3, 1984–July 17, 1986). Willem "Wim" Alfred Udenhout was an advisor in the government of Henck Arron in the late 1970s. He was named prime minister of an interim government on February 3, 1984. He retained office until July 17, 1986, when he resigned to allow the formation of a coalition government under Pretaapnarian Radhakishun. Udenhout remained a leading member of the Suriname National party.

PRETAAPNARIAN RADHAKISHUN (Prime Minister, July 17, 1986–February 12, 1987). Pretaapnarian Radhakishun was a member of the Progressive Reform party. He was named prime minister of a coalition government on July 17, 1986. Radhakishun was forced to resign from office on February 12, 1987, when he lost the support of Lt. Col. Desi Bouterse and the Supreme Military Council.

JULES ALBERT WIJDENBOSCH (Prime Minister, February 12, 1987–January 26, 1988). Jules Albert Wijdenbosch served in the government as minister of the interior and deputy prime minister. He was named to replace Pretaapnarian Radhakishun as acting prime minister on February 12, 1987. He was replaced by Henck Arron on January 26, 1988, following legislative elections the previous November. Wijdenbosch was returned to office as acting prime minister and vice president following a military coup on December 24, 1990. New elections were held, and Wijdensbosch was replaced by Jules R. Adjodhia on September 16, 1991. He remained a member of Lt. Col. Desi Bouterse's National Democratic party.

HENCK ARRON (Prime Minister, January 26, 1988–December 24, 1990). *See earlier entry under Heads of Government.*

JULES ALBERT WIJDENBOSCH (Prime Minister, December 24, 1990–September 16, 1991). *See earlier entry under Heads of Government.*

JULES R. ADJODHIA (Prime Minister, September 16, 1991–). Jules R. Adjodhia was named prime minister and vice president of Suriname on September 16, 1991, following the selection of Ronald Venetiaan as president.

Swaziland, Kingdom of

Swaziland is a country in central southern Africa. It was granted independence from Great Britain on September 6, 1968.

HEADS OF STATE

SOBHUZA II (King, December, 1899–August 21, 1982). Sobhuza was born in Swaziland on July 22, 1899. His father, King Ngwane V, died the following December, and Sobhuza was chosen as king designate by a tribal council. He ruled under a regency headed by his grandmother, Labotsibeni, who was assisted by her son, Prince Malunge. Labotsibeni, who headed the tribal council as idlovukazi, or "great she-elephant," established a school in Zombotze, Swaziland, for Sobhuza's education. He later attended the Lovedale Institute in South Africa from 1916 until 1918. He reached his majority and was crowned king, or ngwenyama, of Swaziland on December 22, 1921. Shortly after becoming king, Sobhuza attempted to gain the return of land belonging to the Swazis that had been seized by the British in 1907. Sobhuza led a delegation to London in December of 1922. His claims were eventually rejected by the British courts. Sobhuza supported the British war effort during World War II. King George VI and the British royal family visited Swaziland in March of 1947. Sobhuza continued to seek Swaziland's independence, which was finally granted on September 6, 1968. He initially ruled under a British-designed constitution, which provided for a constitutional monarchy. Sobhuza promoted a new constitution in April of 1973 which allowed him to rule as an absolute monarch. He encouraged foreign investment in his country and promoted the political and economic stability of Swaziland. He reportedly had as many as 130 wives and 600 children. Sobhuza continued to reign until his death near the capital of Mbabane at the age of 83 on August 21, 1982.

DZELIWE SHONGWE (Regent, August 21, 1982–August 10, 1983). Dzeliwe Shongwe was a senior wife of King Sobhuza II. She became queen regent, or idlovukazi, meaning "great she-elephant," following Sobhuza's death on August 21, 1982. The Swazi prime minister, Prince Bhekimpi Dlamini, announced her dismissal on August 10, 1983.

NTOMBE THWALA (Regent, August 10, 1983–April 25, 1986). Ntombe Thwala was a wife of King Sobhuza II. She was the mother of Prince Makhosetive, who was chosen by the tribal council to become Sobhuza's successor. Ntombe was installed as queen regent following the dismissal of Queen Dzeliwe on August 10, 1983. There were allegations of an attempted coup against Queen Ntombe in December of 1983. She remained head of the Regency Council until April 25, 1986, when Prince Makhosetive reached his majority and was crowned King Mswati III.

MSWATI III (King, April 25, 1986–). Makhosetive was born in Swaziland in 1968. He was the son of King Sobhuza II and Queen Ntombe. He was chosen as king designate following the death of Sobhuza in August of 1982. He was sent to the Sherborne School in Great Britain for his education while a Regency Council, led by his mother, Queen Ntombe, ruled Swaziland. The country was beset by political intrigues and economic difficulties, which prompted the early coronation of Makhosetive at the age of 18. He was crowned King Mswati III on April 25, 1986. He abolished the Regency Council and dismissed Prince Bhekimpi Dlamini, the prime minister, in October of 1986. Mswati brought political and economic stability to the country. His absolute rule was threatened by calls for democracy in the early 1990s. Student strikes and demonstrations turned violent in November of 1990. The king then announced plans for a new constitution and multiparty elections to be held in 1993.

HEADS OF GOVERNMENT

MAKHOSINI DLAMINI (Prime Minister, April 25, 1967–March 17, 1976). Makhosini Dlamini was born at the royal residence near Hlatikulu in 1914. He was the son of King Sobhuza and was educated at the Swazi National School. He subsequently worked as a teacher in South Africa. Dlamini was named principal of the Swazi National High School in Lobamba in 1946. He resigned the following year over a conflict with the colonial authorities. He was named to the Swazi National Council in 1949 and served as a rural development officer. Dlamini served as a member of the various conferences that negotiated Swaziland's independence from Great Britain. He was named by King Sobhuza as leader of the newly formed Imbokodovo National Movement in 1964. He served in the Swazi Parliament and was selected as prime minister on April 25, 1967. He retained that position following Swazi independence on September 6, 1968. He retired from office on March 17, 1976. Prince Makhosini died in Swaziland on April 28, 1978.

MAPHEVU DLAMINI (Prime Minister, March 17, 1976–October 25, 1979). Maphevu Dlamini was born in 1914. He was a member of the royal family and served in the Swazi military. He rose to the rank of major general. He was chosen to succeed Prince Makhosini Dlamini as prime minister on March 17, 1976. Prince Maphevu retained office until his death in Swaziland on October 25, 1979.

BEN NSIBANDZE (Acting Prime Minister, October 25, 1979–November 23, 1979). Ben Nsibandze served as acting prime minister of Swaziland from the death of Maphevu Dlamini on October 25, 1979, until the appointment of Mandabala Fred Dlamini on November 23, 1979.

MANDABALA FRED DLAMINI (Prime Minister, November 23, 1979–March 25, 1983). Mandabala Fred Dlamini was named prime minister of Swaziland on November 23, 1979. He organized the release of Swazi political prisoners in May of 1980. He Queen Dzeliwe became head of the Regency Council following the death of King Sobhuza II in August of 1982, and Prince Mandabala remained prime minister. He advocated progressive change and political reforms. He was dismissed on March 25, 1983, when he opposed a land deal with South Africa. He was later forced to go into exile in South Africa.

BHEKIMPI DLAMINI (Prime Minister, March 25, 1983–October 6, 1985). Bhekimpi Alpheus Dlamini was born in the Hhohho District on November 26, 1924. He was educated locally and in South Africa. He served with the British army from 1937 until 1945 and saw action in North Africa and Italy. He returned to Swaziland after World War II and was named to the Swazi National Council. Dlamini subsequently served as a deputy minister of Local Administration. He served as prime minister from March 25, 1983, under the regency of Queen Ntombe. He was dismissed by King Mswati III on October 6, 1985. Dlamini was arrested in May of 1988 and charged with sedition for his role in political intrigues following the death of King Sobhuza.

SOTSHA DLAMINI (Prime Minister, October 6, 1985–July 13, 1989). Sotsha Dlamini served as assistant police commissioner until 1984. He was appointed prime minister of Swaziland on October 6, 1985, following the coronation of King Mswati. He was dismissed by the king on July 13, 1989, for failing to obey orders.

OBED DLAMINI (Prime Minister, July 13, 1989–). Obed Mfanyana Dlamini was born on April 4, 1937. He was educated locally and worked as a teacher until 1964. He subsequently was employed in private business and become general secretary of the Swaziland Federation of Trade Unions. He was appointed prime minister on July 13, 1989.

Sweden, Kingdom of
(Konungariket Sverige)

Sweden is a country on the Scandinavian peninsula in northwest Europe.

HEADS OF STATE

GUSTAF V ADOLF (King, December 8, 1907–October 29, 1950).Oscar Gustaf Adolf was born in the royal palace of Drottningham, near Stockholm, on June 16, 1858. He was the son of Oscar II, who became king of Sweden in 1872, and Queen Sophia Wilhelmina. He was educated at the University of Uppsala in Sweden and served in the Swedish army. Gustaf was made a general in the Swedish and Norwegian armies in 1898. He served as regent for his father while King Oscar was ill in the early 1900s. Norway voted to succeed from Sweden in 1905. King Oscar died two years later on December 8, 1908, and his son succeeded to the throne as King Gustaf V Adolf. The king was instrumental in maintaining Swedish neutrality during World War I. He also succeeded in keeping Sweden out of World War II when he allowed the German army to cross through the country in 1941. Gustaf suffered from a chronic bronchial condition during the late 1940s. He died in Stockholm after a brief illness at the age of 92 on October 29, 1950.

GUSTAF VI ADOLF (King, October 29, 1950–September 15, 1973). Oscar Fredrik Wilhelm Olaf Gustaf Adolf was born in the royal palace in Stockholm on November 11, 1882. He was the son of Gustav V, who became king of Sweden in 1907, and Queen Victoria. Gustaf Adolf was educated at the University of Uppsala and the University of Christiania in Oslo, Norway. He familiarized himself with the workings of the civil government by serving as a clerk in most major departments. He also served in the Swedish military and attended the War College in Stockholm. He married Princess Margaret of Connaught in July of 1905. Gustaf Adolf became crown prince when his father ascended to the throne in 1907. He made numerous state visits throughout the world and often served as regent for his father when Gustaf V was ill or out of the country. Gustaf Adolf was promoted to general in the Swedish infantry and cavalry in 1932. He was crowned King Gustaf VI Adolf upon the death of his father on October 29, 1950. He was respected and liked by his subjects. Gustaf Adolf was also well known as an archaeologist who spent much time traveling incognito as the count of Gripsholm to unearth Etruscan relics in Italy. He also had a vast collection of Chinese art. His studies in botany earned him membership in the British Royal Academy in 1958. Gustaf Adolf suffered from a rare disorder known as erosive mucosal duodenitis. He died from internal bleeding following stomach surgery at the age of 90 in Helsinborg on September 15, 1973.

CARL XVI GUSTAV (King, September 15, 1973–). Carl Gustaf Folke Hubertus was born at the Haga Castle on April 30, 1946. He was the son of Prince Gustaf Adolf and Princess Sibylla. His father, who was heir to the Swedish throne, died in a plane crash on January 26, 1947. Carl Gustaf became crown prince when his grandfather, Gustaf V Adolf, ascended to the throne in October of 1950. He served in the Swedish military for two years and attended the University of Uppsala in 1968. Carl Gustaf traveled widely and served as regent for his grandfather when Gustaf V Adolf was ill or out of the country. He was formally crowned King Carl XVI Gustaf on September 19, 1973, four days after the death of his grandfather. The new king, who vowed to rule as a modern monarch, was denied some of the powers exercised by his predecessors when a new Swedish constitution went into effect in 1975. Carl Gustaf married Silvia Sommerlath, a West German commoner, in June of 1976.

HEADS OF GOVERNMENT

PER ALBIN HANSSON (Prime Minister, September 23, 1936–October 6, 1946). Per Albin Hansson was born in Scania Province on October 28, 1885. He joined the Social Democratic party at an early age and worked for the party's newspaper. He was elected to the lower chamber of the Swedish Parliament in 1918. Hansson was named to the cabinet of Prime Minister Hjalmar Branting as minister of war and national defense in 1920. He was an antimilitarist and his views led to his resignation in 1926. He was named to the Swedish government Public Debt Commission in 1929. Hansson was selected to lead the Social Democratic party in 1936 and became prime minister on September 23, 1936. He advocated Swedish neutrality during World War II and formed a coalition cabinet in December of 1939. His party received an absolute majority in general elections in 1940, though he continued to lead an all-party wartime coalition government. Hansson dismissed the government after the war and formed a Social Democratic cabinet in July of 1945. He remained prime minister of Sweden until he died from a stroke at the age of 60 while he was riding a tram through Stockholm on October 5, 1946.

TAGE ERLANDER (Prime Minister, October 9, 1946–October 14, 1969). Tage Fritiof Erlander was born in Ransater on June 16, 1901. He was educated locally and graduated from the University of Lund in 1928. He joined the staff of *Svensk Uppslagsbok*, the Swedish encyclopedia, after graduation. Erlander also became involved in politics and was elected to the Lund City Council in 1930. He joined the Social Democratic Labor party and was elected to the lower chamber of the Parliament, or Riksdag, in 1933. He was named to the Ministry of Social Welfare in 1938. Erlander joined Per Albin Hansson's wartime coalition cabinet as minister without portfolio in September of 1944 and was appointed minister of education the following year. He succeeded Hansson as leader of the Social Democrats and became prime minister on October 9, 1946. He became a leading architect of Sweden's social welfare system and maintained the nation's neutrality in foreign affairs. Erlander was also a leading proponent of the United Nations. He remained prime minister in a series of coalition governments until 1968, when the Social Democrats formed a majority government. He retired from government in 1969 and presided over the selection of his successor, Olof Palme. Erlander stepped down from office on October 14, 1969, and retired to his home in Stockholm to write his memoirs. He died after a brief illness in the village of Huddinge, near Stockholm, at the age of 84 on June 21, 1985.

OLOF PALME (Prime Minister, October 14, 1969–September 20, 1976). Sven Olof Jochim Palme was born in Stockholm on January 30, 1927. He was educated locally and attended Kenyon College, in Ohio, in the United States. He graduated in 1948 and returned to Sweden, where he received a degree in law at Stockholm University in 1951. Palme became active in the Social Democratic party and served as personal secretary and speech writer for Prime Minister Tage Erlander from 1954. Palme was elected to the upper house of the Swedish Parliament in 1956 and was named to Erlander's cabinet as minister without portfolio in 1963. He was appointed minister of communications in 1965 and was named minister of education two years later. He was an opponent of the United States involvement in Southeast Asia during the Vietnam War and participated in an antiwar demonstration outside the United States Embassy in Stockholm in 1968. Palme was also a critic of the Soviet Union's invasion of Czechoslovakia later in the year. He was chosen to lead the Social Democratic party following Erlander's retirement and became prime minister on October 14, 1969. He continued his predecessor's policies of social and labor reform. The Social Democrats lost support in general elections in 1970 and 1973. Sweden faced a declining economy and increased labor unrest, and the Social Democrats lost control of the government in elections in September

of 1976. Palme was replaced by Thorbjorn Falldin as head of a center-right coalition government on October 4, 1976. Palme served as leader of the Opposition until October 7, 1982, when he returned to lead a minority Socialist government. On February 28, 1986, Palme was shot and killed by an assassin while walking with his wife down a Stockholm street shortly after having left a movie theatre.

THORBJORN FALLDIN (Prime Minister, October 4, 1976–October 18, 1978). Thorbjorn Nils Olof Falldin was born in Vastby on April 24, 1926. He was raised on a farm and entered the Agrarian party at an early age. The party became known as the Center party in 1958, and Falldin was elected to the lower chamber of the Parliament. He was narrowly defeated for reelection to the Parliament in 1964. Falldin was elected to the Center party's executive council in 1967 and was elected to the upper chamber of the Parliament later in the year. He was named first vice-chairman of the Center party in 1969 and succeeded Gunnar Hedlund as chairman in 1971. He served as leader of the Opposition to the Social Democratic prime minister, Olof Palme. Falldin campaigned against the government's nuclear power plans and high tax rate. He led his party to victory in parliamentary elections in 1976 and replaced Palme as prime minister on October 4, 1976. His continued opposition to nuclear power caused a division in his coalition cabinet, and he was replaced by a minority People's Party government on October 18, 1978. Falldin returned to head the government as leader of a center-right coalition on October 9, 1979. The Social Democrats won a narrow victory in parliamentary elections in 1982, and Olof Palme was returned to office as prime minister on October 7, 1982. Falldin remained in Parliament as leader of the Opposition until 1985, when he stepped down after his party made a poor showing in the general election that year.

OLA ULLSTEN (Prime Minister, October 18, 1978–October 9, 1979). Ola Ullsten was born in Umea on June 23, 1931. He joined the liberal People's party in 1957 and was elected to Parliament in 1965. He served as chairman of the People's party in Stockholm from 1972 until 1976 and then joined the cabinet. Ullsten served as deputy prime minister under Thorbjorn Falldin from March until October of 1978. He replaced Falldin as prime minister on October 18, 1978, and headed a minority People's party government. Falldin returned to office on October 9, 1979. Ullsten subsequently served as minister of foreign affairs and deputy prime minister until 1982. He was named ambassador to Canada in 1983 and stepped down as leader of the People's party the following year. He remained in Canada until 1989, when he was appointed ambassador to Italy.

THORBJORN FALLDIN (Prime Minister, October 9, 1979–October 7, 1982). *See earlier entry under Heads of Government.*

OLOF PALME (Prime Minister, October 7, 1982–February 28, 1986). *See earlier entry under Heads of Government.*

INGVAR CARLSSON (Prime Minister, March 12, 1986–October 30, 1991). Ingvar Gosta Carlsson was born in Boras on November 9, 1934. He was educated at the University of Lund, where he received a degree in economics and political science in 1958. He entered politics as a member of the Social Democratic party and served as an assistant to Prime Minister Tage Erlander. Carlsson was elected to the Swedish Parliament, the Riksdag, in 1964, and was named undersecretary of state in 1967. He was appointed minister of education and cultural affairs in

the government of Olof Palme in October of 1969. He remained in the government as minister of housing and physical planning in 1973. Carlsson remained in the Parliament as a member of the Opposition when the Social Democrats lost power in 1976. He was appointed deputy prime minister to Palme when the Social Democrats returned to power in October of 1982. Carlsson was selected to succeed Palme as prime minister on March 12, 1986, following Palme's assassination. His party was again successful in general elections in September of 1988. Sweden was suffering from a faltering economy, and Carlsson introduced an economic austerity program to assist the country's financial stability. His plan was narrowly defeated, and he resigned from office on February 15, 1990. He returned to office on February 26, 1990, after the Parliament accepted a variation of the plan. This led to the defeat of the Social Democrats in elections the following year, and Carlsson was replaced as prime minister by Conservative party leader Carl Bildt on October 30, 1991. Carlsson continued to serve in the Parliament as leader of the Opposition.

CARL BILDT (Prime Minister, October 3, 1991–). Carl Bildt was born in Hallanning on July 15, 1949. He was educated at Stockholm University and became involved in political affairs. He joined the Conservative party as a political secretary in 1973 and was elected to the Stockholm City Council the following year. Bildt was elected to Parliament in 1979 and was chosen to lead the Conservative party in 1986. He led the moderate coalition to victory in parliamentary elections in 1991 and replaced Social Democrat leader Ingvar Carlsson as prime minister on October 3, 1991. He was an advocate of reduced taxation and a decrease of government interference in private enterprise.

Switzerland (Swiss Confederation)

Switzerland is a country in central Europe.

HEADS OF STATE

EDUARD VON STEIGER (President, 1945). Eduard von Steiger was born in Bern on July 2, 1881. He was elected to the Swiss Federal Council in December of 1940 andserved as head of the Department of Justice from 1941. He served as president of the Federal Council in 1945 and 1951. Von Steiger retired from the government in December of 1951. He died on February 10, 1962.

KARL KOBELT (President, 1946). Karl Kobelt was born in St. Gall on August 1, 1891. He studied engineering in Zurich and served as chief of section in the federal office for hydroeconomy. He entered politics in 1933 and was selected as president of the Council of State for St. Gall in 1936. Kobelt was elected to the Swiss Federal Council in 1941 and served as military department director. He served as president of the Federal Council in 1946 and again in 1952. He remained on the council until his retirement in 1954. He died in Berne at the age of 76 on January 5, 1968.

PHILIPP ETTER (President, 1947). Philipp Etter was born in Menzingen on December 21, 1891. He attended school in Zurich, where he studied law. He served as examining judge in the Canton of Zug from 1917 until 1922. Etter was elected to the District Council in 1923 and served in the education and military departments. He also served as mayor of Zug from 1930 until 1934. He was elected to the Council of State and served as head of the Department of the Interior from 1934 until 1959. Etter first served as president of the Swiss Federal Council in 1939. He was again elected in 1942. Etter was reelected president of the Federal Council for a third time on December 12, 1946, when he defeated the Socialist candidate Ernst Nobs by a wide margin. His final term as president came in 1953. He retired from the Federal Council in 1959 and died in Berne at the age of 86 on December 23, 1977.

ENRICO CELIO (President, 1948). Enrico Celio was born on June 19, 1889. He studied law and subsequently became a member of the Tessin Canton government. He was elected to the Swiss Federal Council in 1940. Celio served as director of the Department of Transport, Communications, and Energy. He also served as president of the Swiss Federal Council in 1943 and 1948. Celio left the Federal Council in 1950 and was subsequently appointed minister plenipotentiary to Rome, where he served until 1956. He died on February 23, 1980.

ERNST NOBS (President, 1949). Ernst Nobs was born in Seedorf on July 14, 1887. He was educated in Berne and worked as a schoolteacher from 1906 until 1912. He joined the Social Democratic party and served as editor of the newspaper *Volksrecht* from 1919. Nobs was also elected to the Swiss Federal Assembly in 1919. He also served as lord mayor of Zurich from 1942 until 1943. He was subsequently elected to the Swiss Federal Council, where he served as minister of finance. Nobs served as president of the Federal Council in 1949. He remained on the Council until his retirement in 1952. Nobs died of a heart attack in Zurich at the age of 71 on March 13, 1957.

MAX PETITPIERRE (President, 1950). Max Petitpierre was born in Neuchâtel on February 26, 1899. He studied law in Zurich, Neuchâtel, and Munich and became a lawyer in 1922. He was elected to the Cantonal Council from Neuchâtel in 1937. Petitpierre served as councillor of state in 1942 and was elected a member of the Swiss Federal Council in 1944. He headed the Department of Foreign Affairs from 1945. Petitpierre also served as president of the Federal Council in 1950, 1955, and 1960. He retired from the Federal Council in June of 1961. He subsequently served as director of the International Committee of the Red Cross. Petitpierre died at his home in Neuchâtel on March 25, 1994.

EDUARD VON STEIGER (President, 1951). *See earlier entry under Heads of State.*

KARL KOBELT (President, 1952). *See earlier entry under Heads of State.*

PHILIPP ETTER (President, 1953). *See earlier entry under Heads of State.*

RODOLPHE RUBATTEL (President, 1954). Rodolphe Rubattel was born in Villarzel on September 4, 1896. He was educated in Switzerland, France, and Austria and received a degree in law from the University of Lausanne. He entered politics in 1933 and was elected to the Cantonal Assembly. Rubattel was a member of the Radical party and was elected to the Federal Parliament in 1944. He became a member of the Swiss Federal Council in 1947. He served as minister of public economy from 1948 and served as president of the Federal Council in 1954. He retired from politics in December of 1954. He died of a heart attack at his home in Lausanne at the age of 65 on October 18, 1961.

MAX PETITPIERRE (President, 1955). *See entry under Heads of State.*

MARKUS FELDMANN (President, 1956). Markus Feldmann was born in Thun on May 21, 1897. He attended the University of Bern and received a degree in law in 1921. He joined the staff of the *Neue Berner Zeitung* newspaper in 1922 and rose to become editor in chief. Feldmann entered politics in 1935 and was elected to the National Council. He was elected to the Swiss Federal Council in December of 1951 and served as director of the Department of Justice and the Police. Feldmann also served as president of the Federal Council in 1956. He remained in the federal cabinet until his death in Bern at the age of 61 on November 3, 1958.

HANS STREULI (President, 1957). Hans Streuli was born in Richterswil on July 13, 1892. He was educated at the Federal Institute of Technology in Zurich and began his career as an architect in 1919. He was elected president of the Communal Council of Richterswil in 1928. He served on the Swiss Federal Council from 1954 until 1959 and was its president in 1957. He died on May 23, 1970.

THOMAS HOLENSTEIN (President, 1958). Thomas Emil Leo Holenstein was born in St. Gall on February 7, 1896. He attended the University of Bern and received a degree in law in 1920. He opened a private practice in St. Gall and also taught at the School of Economics and Public Administration from 1933. Holenstein entered politics and was elected to the Great Council of the St. Gall Canton in 1936. He was elected to the National Council the following year. He became president of the Catholic Conservative party in 1942. Holenstein was elected to the Swiss Federal Council in December of 1954 and served as director of the Department of Economic Affairs. He served as president of the Federal Council in 1958. He retired from the government the following year. Holenstein died in Locarno at the age of 66 on October 31, 1962.

PAUL CHAUDET (President, 1959). Paul Chaudet was born in Rivas on November 17, 1904. He attended agriculture school locally, and he became active in the communal government of Rivaz and served as president. He was elected to the National Council in 1943 and headed the Department of Justice and Police from 1946 until 1948. Chaudet then served as head of the Department of Agriculture, Industry, and Commerce. He was elected to the Swiss Federal Council in 1955 and served as director of the Department of Military Affairs. He also served as president of the Federal Council in 1959 and 1962. Chaudet retired from the Council in December of 1966. He died on August 7, 1977.

MAX PETITPIERRE (President, 1960). *See earlier entry under Heads of State.*

FRIEDRICH WAHLEN (President, 1961). Friedrich Traugott Wahlen was born in Gmeis on April 10, 1899. He was educated in Zurich, where he received a degree in agricultural engineering. He joined the Swiss Department of Agriculture and was stationed in Canada in the early 1920s. Wahlen was commissioner of food production during World War II and was the author of the Wahlen Plan, which aimed at self-sufficiency in food supplies during the war years. He was elected to the Council of State in 1942 and served until 1949. He served as director of the agriculture division from 1949 until 1957. Wahlen was elected to the Federal Council in 1958 and became its president in 1961. He also served as director of the Department of Foreign Affairs until his retirement from the Federal Council in December of 1965. He died in Berne at the age of 86 on November 7, 1985.

PAUL CHAUDET (President, 1962). *See earlier entry under Heads of State.*

WILLY SPUHLER (President, 1963). Willy Spühler was born in Zurich on January 31, 1902. He attended the Universities of Zurich and Paris and received a degree in economics. He subsequently worked in both the public and private sectors. Spühler was elected to the National Council in 1938 and served until 1955. He also served on the Town Council and was served as head of the Sanitary and Economics Departments from 1942 until 1959. He was also a member of the State Council until 1959, when he was elected to the Swiss Federal Council. Spühler served as president in 1963 and 1968. He headed the Department of Foreign Affairs from 1966 until his retirement in January of 1970. He died on May 31, 1990.

LUDWIG VON MOOS (President, 1964). Ludwig von Moos was born in Sachseln on January 31, 1910. He attended the University of Fribourg and served as a clerk in the communal government of Sachseln from 1933. He was elected president of the Commune of Sachseln in 1941 and served until 1946. Von Moos was elected to the Council of States in 1943 and served until 1959. He was a member of the Board of Directors of the Bank of Obswalden from 1946 until 1959 and served as president from 1954. He was elected to the Swiss Federal Council as a member of the Conservative party in 1959. Von Moos served as director of the Department of Justice and the Police and was president of the Federal Council in 1964 and 1969. He retired from the government in December of 1971. Von Moos died in Bern at the age of 80 on November 26, 1990.

HANS-PETER TSCHUDI (President, 1965). Hans-Peter Tschudi was born on October 22, 1913. He was educated at the University of Basel and subsequently taught labor law there. He was elected to the Council of States in 1956, and on December 17, 1959, he became a member of the Swiss Federal Council. Tschudi served as director of the Interior Department and was president of Switzerland in 1965 and 1970. He left the Federal Council on December 31, 1973.

HANS SCHAFFNER (President, 1966). Hans Schaffner was born in Granichen on December 16, 1908. He was educated at the University of Bern, where he received a degree in law. He served as secretary to the High Court in Bern from 1938 until 1941. Schaffner directed the Central Office for War Economy from 1941 until 1945 and was a delegate to the Federal Council for Trade Agreements until 1961. He was elected to the Swiss Federal Council in June of 1961. Schaffner directed the Department of Public Economy and also served as president of the Federal Council in 1966. He retired from the government in December of 1969.

ROGER BONVIN (President, 1967). Roger Bonvin was born in Icogne-Lens on September 12, 1902. He was educated in Zurich and received a degree in civil engineering. He subsequently worked with the local public works department. Bonvin was elected mayor of Sion in 1955 and served until 1962. He also served as a member of the National Council from 1955 until his election to the Swiss Federal Council in 1962. He served as director of the Department of Transport, Communications, and Energy. Bonvin also served as president of the Federal Council in 1967 and 1973. He retired from the council following the completion of his term as president in December of 1973. He died on June 5, 1982.

WILLY SPUHLER (President, 1968). *See earlier entry under Heads of State.*

LUDWIG VON MOOS (President, 1969). *See earlier entry under Heads of State.*

HANS-PETER TSCHUDI (President, 1970). *See earlier entry under Heads of State.*

RUDOLF GNAEGI (President, 1971). Rudolf Gnaegi was born in Schwadernau on August 3, 1917. He was educated as a lawyer and became active in the Burghers' party of Berne. He was elected to the Cantonal Government Council of Berne in 1952, and the following year he was elected to the National Council. Gnaegi was elected to the Federal Council in 1965 and served as head of the Ministry of Transport, Communications, and Power until 1968. He subsequently served as director of the Department of Foreign Affairs. He also served as president in 1971 and 1976. Gnaegi retired in December of 1979 and died of a heart attack in Bern at the age of 67 on April 21, 1985.

NELLO CELIO (President, 1972). Nello Celio was born on February 12, 1914. He was educated at the Universities of Basel and Berne and joined the Cantonal Interior Department in 1941. He was elected to the Council of State in 1946 and served until 1949. Celio joined the National Council in 1963 and was elected to the Federal Council on December 15, 1966. He served as leader of the Radical Democrat party and was director of the Department of Defense until 1968. He served as director of the Department of Finance and Customs from 1968 and became president of Switzerland in 1972. Celio remained on the Federal Council until December 31, 1973.

ROGER BONVIN (President, 1973). *See earlier entry under Heads of State.*

ERNST BRUGGER (President, 1974). Ernst Brugger was born in Bellinzona on March 10, 1914. He was educated in Switzerland, England, and France and then returned to teach in Gossau. He served as mayor of Gossau from 1949 until 1959, when he became director of the Departments of Justice and the Interior in the canton government of Zurich. Brugger retained those positions until 1967 and then headed the Department of Public Economy until 1969. The following year he was elected to the Swiss Federal Council and served as director of the Department of Public Economy. He served as president of the Federal Council in 1974 and retired from public office on January 31, 1978.

PIERRE GRABER (President, 1975). Pierre Graber was born in La Chaux-de-Fonds on December 6, 1914. He was educated at the Universities of Neuchâtel and Vienna and became a lawyer in Lausanne in 1933. He served on the Lausanne Legislative Council from 1933 until 1946 and was mayor of Lausanne from 1946 until 1949. Graber subsequently served as a member of the Lausanne City Council until 1962, when he became finance director for the Canton of Vaud Council. He was elected to the Swiss Federal Council in 1970, where he headed the Foreign Affairs Department. He also served as president of the Federal Council in 1975. Graber retired from the council on January 31, 1978.

RUDOLF GNAEGI (President, 1976). *See earlier entry under Heads of State.*

KURT FURGLER (President, 1977). Kurt Furgler was born in St. Gall, on June 24, 1924. He studied at uUniversities in Zurich, Fribourg,and Geneva and became a lawyer in 1950. He was a member of the National Council from 1955 until 1971. Furgler was elected to the Swiss Federal Council in 1972 and served as the leader of the Christian Democratic party. He directed the Department of Justice and Police from

1972 until 1983 and also served as president of the Federal Council in 1977 and 1981. He was placed in charge of the Department of Public Economy in 1983 and again served as president in 1985. Furgler retired from the Federal Council on December 31, 1986.

WILLI RITSCHARD (President, 1978). Willi Ritschard was born in Deitingen on September 28, 1918. He attended technical school in Switzerland and worked as a mechanic. He was elected to the Cantonal Council in Soleure in 1945 and became mayor of Luterbach in 1946. Ritschard became president of the Cantonal Trade Unions Association in 1954 and was elected to the National Council in 1955. He was elected to the Swiss Federal Council in 1973 and served as president of Switzerland in 1978. He remained on the Council until his death on October 16, 1983.

HANS HÜRLIMANN (President, 1979). Hans Hürlimann was born in Walchwil, Zug, on April 6, 1918. He attended the University of Fribourg and the University of Berne and became a lawyer in 1946. He served as director of the Department of Justice, Police, and Military Affairs of the Zug canton government from 1954 until 1962 and was director of the Department of Education, Culture, and Military Affairs from 1962 until 1973. Hürlimann served on the Federal Council as minister of the interior from 1974 until December 31, 1982, and also served as president of Switzerland in 1979.

GEORGES-ANDRÉ CHEVALLAZ (President, 1980). Georges-André Chevallaz was born in Lausanne, on February 7, 1915. He was educated at the University of Lausanne and taught at the School of Commerce from 1942 until 1955. He served as a member of the National Council from 1959 until 1973, when he was elected to the Swiss Federal Council. Chevallaz directed the Department of Finance and Customs from 1974 until 1979 and served as president of Switzerland in 1980. He subsequently headed the Department of Defense until he left the Federal Council on December 31, 1983.

KURT FURGLER (President, 1981). *See earlier entry under Heads of State.*

FRITZ HONEGGER (President, 1982). Fritz Honegger was born in Bischofzsell on July 25, 1917. He attended the University of Zurich and served on the Zurich Cantonal Council from 1957 until 1975. He also served as a deputy to the Council of States from 1967 until 1978. Honegger was elected chairman of the Radical Democratic party in 1974 and was elected to the Swiss Federal Council in July of 1977. He was head of the Department of Public Economy from 1978 until 1982, when he became president of the Federal Council.

PIERRE AUBERT (President, 1983). Pierre Aubert was born in La Chaux-de-Fonds on March 3, 1927. He studied at the University of Neuchâtel and was elected to the La Chaux-de-Fonds local assembly in 1960, where he served until 1968. From 1971 until 1977 he served as a member of the Council of States. He was elected to the Swiss Federal Council in July of 1977 and served as head of the Department of Foreign Affairs. Aubert served as president of the Federal Council in 1983 and again in 1987.

LEON SCHLUMPF (President, 1984). Leon Schlumpf was born in Felsberg, in Canton Grisons, on February 3, 1925. He attended the University of Zurich, where he received a degree in law. He was elected to the Grisons Cantonal Parliament in 1955 and served until 1974. Schlumpf served on the National Council from 1966 until 1974 and was a member of the Council of States from 1974. He was elected to the Swiss Federal Council in May of 1979 and

was head of the Department of Transport, Communications, and Energy until 1987. Schlumpf also served as president of the Swiss Federal Council in 1984. He remained on the Federal Council until 1987.

KURT FURGLER (President, 1985). *See earlier entry under Heads of State.*

ALPHONS EGLI (President, 1986). Alphons Egli was born in Lucerne on October 8, 1924. He was educated in Switzerland and Italy before returning to Lucerne to practice law in 1952. He was elected to the Lucerne Municipal Council in 1963 and advanced to the Lucerne Cantonal Parliament in 1967. Egli served as a member of the Council of States from 1975 and was elected to the Swiss Federal Council in August of 1982. He directed the Department of the Interior from 1982 until 1985 and served as president of the Federal Council in 1986.

PIERRE AUBERT (President, 1987). *See earlier entry under Heads of State.*

OTTO STICH (President, 1988). Otto Stich was born in Dornach, in the Canton Solothurn, on January 10, 1927. He was educated in Basel, where he taught until 1971. He also served as mayor of Dornach from 1953 until 1965 and was a member of the National Council from 1963 until 1983. Stich was elected to the Swiss Federal Council in August of 1983 and served as head of the Department of Finance from 1984. He was elected president of the Federal Council in January of 1988.

JEAN-PASCAL DELAMURRAZ (President, 1989). Jean-Pascal Delamurraz was born in Paudex, Lausanne, on April 1, 1936. He attended the University of Lausanne and in 1974 was elected mayor of Lausanne. He served as a member of the National Council from 1975, and in July of 1983 he was elected to the Swiss Federal Council. Delamurraz headed the Department of Defense from 1984 until 1986 and directed the Department of Public Economy from 1987. He served as president of the Federal Council in 1989.

ARNOLD KOLLER (President, 1990). Arnold Koller was born on August 29, 1933. He was a university professor before being elected to the Swiss Federal Council in October of 1986. A member of the Christian Democratic party, he headed the Defense Department from 1986 until 1989. He was then elected vice president and head of the Department of Justice and Police. In 1990 Koller was elected president of the Swiss Federal Council. When his term expired in 1991, he returned to the Department of Justice and Police.

FLAVIO COTTI (President, 1991). Flavio Cotti was born in Muralto on October 18, 1939. He was educated at the University of Freiburg and worked as an attorney in Locarno from 1965 until 1975. He also served as a member

of the Locarno Communal Council during this period. Cotti was a member of the government of Ticino from 1975 until 1983, and in October of 1986 he was elected to the Swiss Federal Council as a member of the Christian Democratic People's party. He led the Department of Home Affairs from 1987 until 1991, when he became president of the Federal Council.

RENE FELBER (President, 1992). Rene Felber was born in Biel on March 14, 1933. He worked as a teacher in the 1950s and joined the Social Democratic party in 1958. He was elected mayor of Le Locle in 1964 and served until 1980. Felber also served as a member of Parliament from 1965 until 1976 and was a National Councillor from 1967 until 1981. He served as a member of the regional government of Neuchâtel, where he headed the Department of Finance from 1981 until 1987. In September of 1987 he was elected to the Swiss Federal Council and served as foreign affairs director. Felber was elected vice president of the Federal Council in January of 1991 and became president in January of 1992.

Syria (Syrian Arab Republic)

(al-Jumhuriyah al-'Arabiyah al-Suriyah)

Syria is a country in western Asia. It was granted independence from a League of Nations mandate administered by France on April 17, 1946.

HEADS OF STATE

SHUKRI EL-KUWATLI (President, January 24, 1944–March 30, 1949). Shukri el-Kuwatli was born in Damascus in 1891. He was educated in Damascus and Istanbul, where he studied political science. He became involved in the Arab nationalist movement and

was a leader in the Al Arabiya al Fatat. Kuwatli was imprisoned by the Turks for his nationalist activities during World War I. He participated in the regime of Emir Feisal in Damascus after the war and remained in the country when Feisal was expelled by the

French in 1920. He was a leading opponent of the French occupation and participated in the Druze revolt in 1925. Kuwatli was forced to flee to Egypt, and was sentenced to death in absentia. He was pardoned and returned to Syria in 1931. He became the leader of the Istiqlalists, a radical group in the National Bloc party. Kuwatli served on the Syrian delegation which negotiated the Franco-Syrian Treaty of Friendship and Alliance in Paris in 1936. The National Bloc was victorious in subsequent elections, and Kuwatli was named minister of finance and defense in Jamil Mardam's government. He resigned from the government two years later in opposition to concessions granted to the French by Mardam. He continued his fight for full independence for Syria during World War II, and he again fled the country when British and Free French forces invaded in 1941. Kuwatli returned the following year and was allowed to participate in elections by the French authorities. He was elected president and took office on January 24, 1944. He continued to press for the withdrawal of the French from Syria. Syria faced mounting civil disorder as the French refused to liberate the country. The French responded with a military attack on Damascus and other Syrian towns in May of 1945. Kuwatli requested that the British government intervene, and the fighting stopped when British troops entered the country and confined the French troops to their barracks. The following year the question of Syrian and Lebanese independence was put before the United Nations, and the two countries were granted control of their own lands. Kuwatli ran for reelection in April of 1948, despite a constitutional prohibition of a second term. His actions prompted a wave of popular discontent, and he was forced from office on March 30, 1949, in a military coup led by Husain Zaim. Kuwatli was held prisoner for several months before he was allowed to leave the country for

Switzerland. He went into exile in Egypt in 1949, where he remained for the next five years. Syria underwent several more military coups before Kuwatli was invited to return to the country in August of 1954. He again ran for the presidency and was victorious. He took office on September 6, 1955. Kuwatli led a pro-Egyptian government and tried to establish closer ties to the Soviet Union. In 1957 he advocated a union with Egypt. Kuwatli and President Gamal Abdel Nasser of Egypt announced the union of their two countries as the United Arab Republic on February 1, 1958. Kuwatli stepped down from office, leaving Nasser as president of the unified government. Kuwatli was awarded the honorary title of "First Arab Citizen," but broke with Nasser in 1959. Kuwatli again went into exile and settled in Beirut, Lebanon. He died there of a heart attack at the age of 76 on June 30, 1967.

HUSNI ZAIM (President, June 25, 1949–August 14, 1949). Husni Zaim (Zayim) was born in Aleppo in 1897. He served in the Ottoman army and fought against the Arabians during World War I. He joined the French army in Syria in 1920. During World War II Zaim fought against the Allies as part of the Vichy controlled forces. He was briefly imprisoned by the Allies following the conclusion of the war. After his release he was appointed inspector-general of the Syrian police. Zaim was promoted to colonel in May of 1948 and was appointed chief of staff of the Syrian army after the Palestine War. He led a military coup against the government of Shukri el-Kuwatli on March 30, 1949. On April 7, 1949, Zaim took control of the government as prime minister, minister of defense and minister of the interior. On June 25, 1949, he sponsored a referendum that elected him president of the Syrian Republic, and he resigned as prime minister the following day. He began a number of reforms which were initially popular. Zaim was forced to deal with Syria's troubled financial situation by increasing taxation, however. He tried to model his regime on Kemal Atatürk's of Turkey and this offended Muslim fundamentalists in the country. He also lost much of his support in the military, and on August 14, 1949, he was overthrown and executed by a group of officers led by Colonel Sami Hinnawi.

SAMI HINNAWI (Head of State, August 14, 1949–December 19, 1949). Sami Hinnawi was born in Idlib, near Aleppo, in 1898. He joined the Ottoman army during World War I. He later served in the Syrian army formed by the French and rose to the rank of colonel. Hinnawi led a military coup against the government of Husni Zaim on August 14, 1949. After the ouster and execution of Zaim, Hinnawi declared himself president of the Supreme War Council and head of the Syrian army. He asked Hashim el-Atassi to form a government as prime minister on August 15, 1949. Hinnawi attempted to forge closer ties between Syria and Iraq. He was ousted in another military coup led by Abid es-Shishakli on December 19, 1949. He was arrested by the new government and imprisoned until September 8, 1950, when he was released in an amnesty. Hinnawi went into exile in Beirut, Lebanon, where he was shot and killed by an assassin on October 30, 1950. His murderer was Ahmad al-Barazi, the cousin of Muhsin Barazi, the former prime minister of Syria who had been executed during Hinnawi's coup.

HASHIM EL-ATASSI (President, December 19, 1949–December 2, 1951). Hashim el-Atassi was born in 1875. He attended Istanbul University and was elected to the Syrian General Congress in 1919. He was leader of the first Syrian government when nationalists proclaimed the nation's independence in

March of 1920, but France was given control of Syria under a League of Nations mandate the following month. Atassi was elected president of the Constituent Assembly in 1928, after France allowed the restoration of some political rights in Syria. The Assembly was dissolved two years later. Atassi led a delegation to Paris to negotiate a treaty with the French government. He returned to Syria to become president in September of 1936. He resigned from office and retired from politics in 1939, after France failed to honor the treaty. Atassi returned to the government on August 15, 1949, when he was appointed prime minister following a military coup led by Sami Hinnawi. He became president of the nation when a second coup led by Abid es-Shishakli ousted Hinnawi on December 19, 1949. Shishakli led another coup against Prime Minister Maruf ed Dawalibi in November of 1951, and Atassi resigned as president on December 2, 1951. He was again named president on February 25, 1954, following the ouster of Shishakli. Atassi ordered the restoration of democratic government and stepped down on September 6, 1955, following the election of Shukri el-Kuwatli. Atassi retired from politics at his home in Homs. He died there at the age of 85 on December 5, 1960.

FAWZI SILO (Chief of State, December 3, 1951–July 11, 1953). Fawzi Silo served as an officer in the Syrian army. He supported the coup led by Abid es-Shishakli that deposed Sami Hinnawi in December of 1949. He was promoted to the rank of colonel and named minister of defense in the subsequent government. Silo was also appointed chief of state and prime minister of Syria by Shishakli on December 3, 1951. The government was largely controlled by Shishakli. A new constitution was implemented in July of 1953, and Shishakli was subsequently elected president. Silo stepped down as chief of state on July 11, 1953, and was replaced as prime minister on July 20, 1953. He left Syria on October 18, 1953, to go to Saudi Arabia as a counselor to Crown Prince Saud.

ABID ES-SHISHAKLI (President, July 11, 1953–February 25, 1954). Abid es-Shishakli was born in Hama in 1909. He served in the French army while France ruled Syria under a League of Nations mandate. He deserted to the Syrian army in 1945. Shishakli supported Husni Zaim's military coup in June of 1949, but subsequently broke with Zaim. He was dismissed from the army, but was reinstated following Zaim's ouster by Sami Hinnawi in August of 1949. Shishakli then ousted Hinnawi on December 19, 1949. He allowed the restoration of democratic institutions for several years and took the title of deputy chief of state. When the elected government appeared unable to rule, Shishakli again seized power in a coup. He suspended the Chamber of Deputies and dissolved all political parties in December of 1951. He appointed a supporter, Colonel Fawzi Silo, as chief of state and prime minister, but Shishakli wielded most of the power as deputy prime minister and minister of state. He promoted a new constitution in July of 1953. He formed the Arab Liberation Movement and ran unopposed for the presidency. Shishakli took office on July 11, 1953. He also took the position of prime minister on July 20, 1953. Shishakli became increasingly dictatorial as opposition mounted against his rule. He was ousted by a military coup on February 25, 1954. He fled to Paris and subsequently went into exile in Brazil. Shishakli was convicted in absentia of torture, conspiracy, and treason and sentenced to life imprisonment. He was shot to death on a street in Ceres, Brazil, on September 28, 1964, by a Druze avenging the bombing of the Druze Mountain during his rule.

HASHIM EL-ATASSI (President, February 25, 1954–September 6, 1955).

See earlier entry under Heads of State.

SHUKRI EL-KUWATLI (President, September 6, 1955–February 1, 1958). *See earlier entry under Heads of State.*

NAZIM EL-KUDSI (President, November 20, 1961–March 28, 1962). Nazim el-Kudsi (Qudsi) was born in 1906. He was educated in Syria, Lebanon, and Switzerland and received a doctorate in international law. He returned to Syria as an attorney and entered politics. Kudsi was elected a deputy from Aleppo in 1936. He served as Syria's envoy to the United State from 1944 until 1946. He was appointed prime minister on December 24, 1949, following the coup led by Abid es-Shishakli. He resigned the following day. Kudsi was again appointed prime minister and minister of foreign affairs on June 4, 1950 and served until his resignation on March 27, 1951. He served as president of Parliament from 1951 until 1953, when Shishakli suspended the Parliament. Kudsi returned to that position following Shishakli's ouster in 1954 and served until 1957. He was the leader of the Populist party and retained no office while Syria was a member of the United Arab Republic from 1958 until 1961. He was elected Syrian president on November 20, 1961, following the coup that removed Syria from the United Arab Republic. Kudsi was ousted in a military coup led by Abdel-Karim Zahreddin on March 28, 1962. He was returned to office in a countercoup on April 13, 1962, when the coup leaders could not form a government. Kudsi was ousted by another military coup led by Colonel Louai Atassi on March 8, 1963. He took refuge in the Turkish embassy and withdrew from active politics.

ABDUL KARIM ZAHREDDIN (President, March 28, 1962–April 13, 1962). Abdul Karim Zahreddin served as commander in chief of the Syrian armed forces from September of 1961. He was the leader of the coup that ousted Nazim el-Kudsi as president on March 28, 1962. Zahreddin became chief of state and prime minister until Kudsi was restored to the presidency on April 13, 1962. Zahreddin remained minister of defense until January 13, 1963, when Syrian officers and armored units surrounded the army command in Damascus and demanded his dismissal.

NAZIM EL-KUDSI (President, April 13, 1962–March 8, 1963). *See earlier entry under Heads of State.*

LOUAI ATASSI (President, March 9, 1963–July 27, 1963). Louai Atassi was born in 1926. He attended the Syrian Military Academy and served in the Syrian army. He saw active duty in the Palestine War in 1948. He was a supporter of Syria's union with Egypt as the United Arab Republic in 1958 and opposed the dissolution of the union in 1961. Atassi was promoted to the rank of colonel and served in the Syrian Embassy in Washington, D.C., as a military attaché from 1962 until 1963. He led the military coup that ousted Nazim el-Kudsi on March 9, 1963. He served as president of the Revolutionary Council and commander in chief of the Syrian armed forces until July 27, 1963, when he was replaced by Amin al-Hafiz.

AMIN AL-HAFIZ (President, July 27, 1963–February 25, 1966). Amin al-Hafiz was born in Damascus in 1911. He served in the Syrian army and was a member of the Ba'ath party. He was serving as military attaché in Argentina at the time of the military coup in March of 1963. Hafiz was recalled to Syria to serve as deputy prime minister, minster of the interior, and military governor of Syria in the government that followed the coup from March until July of 1963. He subsequently served

as minister of defense and army chief of staff before winning the power struggle within the revolutionary government. He became president of the Revolutionary Council and commander in chief of the armed forces on July 27, 1963. Hafiz also served as prime minister from November 12, 1963, until May 13, 1964, and from October 4, 1964, until September 3, 1965. He remained chairman of the Presidency Council until his ouster on February 25, 1966. He was wounded during the coup and subsequently imprisoned. Hafiz was released in 1967 and went into exile in Lebanon. He became an outspoken opponent of the Syrian government and a supporter of the Iraqi Ba'athist party. He was tried in absentia in August of 1971 for conspiring against the Syrian government and was sentenced to death.

NUREDDIN EL-ATASSI (President, February 25, 1966–November 13, 1970). Nureddin el-Atassi was born in Homs in 1929. He was educated at Damascus University, where he received a doctorate in medicine. He was a supporter of the military coup in March of 1963 and was named minister of the interior the following August. Atassi served as deputy prime minister in October of 1964 and served on the Presidential Council until December of 1965. He was a member of the hard-line wing of the Ba'ath party and led the coup against Amin al-Hafiz in 1966. He became president of Syria on February 25, 1966. Atassi also became prime minister on October 28, 1968. He retained his positions in a compromise agreement when General Hafez al-Assad, a more moderate Ba'athist, won a power struggle in the government. In September of 1970 Syrian troops entered Jordan to fight on the side of the Palestinian Liberation Army that was engaged in a civil war in that country. The Syrians withdrew after several days of heavy losses. On November 13, 1970, Atassi was deposed in a coup led by Assad, who had opposed the Syrian incursion into Jordan, and he was placed under house arrest. He later was interned in a military prison in Damascus, though was never tried. Atassi suffered a heart attack in April of 1992. He was allowed to leave the country and go to Paris for medical care in November. He died in Paris on December 3, 1992.

AHMED AL-KHATIB (President, November 18, 1970–February 22, 1971). Ahmed al-Khatib was born in Al Suwaydaa in 1933. He was employed as a teacher and later served as the director of the Syrian Teacher Association. He was a member of the Presidential Council from 1965 until 1966. Khatib was named president of Syria following a military coup led by General Hafez al-Assad on November 18, 1970. He resigned on February 22, 1971, to become chairman of the People's Council. He also served as a member of the leadership committee of the Ba'ath party from May of 1971. He was subsequently chosen as president of the Federation of Arab Republics and served until 1975.

HAFEZ AL-ASSAD (President, February 22, 1971–   ). Hafez al-Assad was born in Qardaha in Latakia Province in 1928. He joined the Ba'ath party in 1946 and entered the Homs Military College in 1952. He joined the Syrian air force as a pilot officer in 1955. Assad was stationed in Cairo as a squadron leader in the United Arab Republic air force after the merger of Syria and Egypt in 1958. He opposed the secession of Syria from the United Arab Republic in 1961 and was removed from the military. Assad was a leader of the coup that ousted Nazim el-Kudsi in March of 1963. He was named commander of the Syrian air force and was promoted to general in December of 1964. Assad supported the military coup led by Ba'ath extremists that ousted the moderate Ba'ath government of Amin al-Hafiz in February of 1966. Assad was subsequently named minister of

defense. He also led the Syrian air force during the Six-Day War between Arab nations and Israel in June of 1967. Syria suffered massive losses of its air strength, and Israel seized Syrian territory in the Golan Heights. A power struggle developed between Assad and Maj. Gen. Salah al-Jadid, who favored a Marxist economy for Syria. Assad attempted a coup in February of 1969, but was forced to work out a compromise when the Soviet Union threatened to cut off military aid to Syria if Assad ousted the government. The conflict between Assad and Jadid escalated in September of 1970 when Syria sent military assistance to the Palestinian Liberation Organization against the Jordanian army, despite Assad's objection to the plan. The Syrians were beaten back by the Jordanians, and Assad blamed Jadid and President Nurredin el-Atassi for the defeat. The government attempted to oust Assad, who in turn led a military coup that overthrew Atassi. Jadid was sent into exile, and Assad became prime minister on November 19, 1970. Assad was subsequently elected president of Syria and took office on February 22, 1971. He also remained prime minister until April 3, 1971. He sought to improve Syria's relationship with Egypt and Saudi Arabia. Assad approved the formation of the Federation of Arab Republics with Syria, Egypt, and Libya as members in September of 1971. He also supported Egyptian president Anwar el-Sadat's war against Israel in 1973. Assad proposed a new constitution in 1973 that was opposed by Muslim fundamentalists. He sent the Syrian military to assist in maintaining order in Lebanon in 1976 during that country's civil war. He was reelected president in February of 1978. Assad reportedly suffered from a heart ailment during 1984, but was reelected president in February of 1985. Syria supported Iran in that country's long war against Iraq during the 1980s. Syria again intervened in Lebanon by sending troops to

Beirut in 1987. Assad also attempted to improve relations with the United States and other Western governments. He condemned the Iraqi government's invasion of Kuwait in 1990 and sup- ported the alliance against Iraq that was organized by the United States during the Gulf War. Assad was again reelected president in December of 1991.

HEADS OF GOVERNMENT

FARIS EL-KHOURI (Prime Minister, October 14, 1944–October 2, 1945). Faris el-Khouri was born in Kfeir, near Hasbaya, in 1879. He attended the American University of Beirut and received a degree in law in 1897. He became a lawyer in Damascus in 1908 and was elected to the Ottoman Parliament in 1914. Khouri was arrested and charged with treason the following year, but was acquitted of the charges. He began a career teaching law at the Syrian University in 1919. He served as minister of finance in the government of King Feisal of Iraq, who was proclaimed king of Syria in 1920. Khouri took part in the Druze revolt in 1925 and was banished to Lebanon by the French government. He returned in 1926 and was appointed minister of education. He became a leader of the National Bloc in 1928 and was elected to the Syrian Parliament in 1936. Khouri became Speaker of the Parliament in 1938 and retained his position until Parliament was dissolved in 1939. He served as foreign minister in 1941 before he returned to the Parliament as Speaker in 1943. Khouri was named prime minister on October 14, 1944. He retained office until October 2, 1945, when he resumed the office of Speaker of the Parliament. Khouri was appointed Syria's chief delegate to the United Nations in 1947 and served as president of the United Nations Security Council the following year. He returned to Syria to again serve as prime minister on October 29, 1954. He resigned on February 25, 1955. Khouri died in Damascus at the age of 82 after a long illness on January 2, 1962.

SAADULLAH EL-JABRI (Prime Minister, August 20, 1943–December 28, 1946). Saadullah el-Jabri was born in 1893. He replaced Husny el-Barazy as prime minister on August 20, 1943. He retained office until October 14, 1944. Jabri was again named prime minister on October 2, 1945, and served until December 28, 1946, when he resigned for reasons of health. He died in Aleppo on June 19, 1947.

JAMIL MARDAM (Prime Minister, December 28, 1946–December 1, 1948). Jamil Mardam was born in Damascus in 1888. He was educated in Paris, where he founded the Arab nationalist organization al-Fatat in 1911. He served in the Syrian delegation to the Paris Peace Conference in 1919. Mardam was a leader of the Druze revolt again the French in Syria in 1925. He subsequently was a founder of the National Bloc. He was part of the Syrian diplomatic team that negotiated a treaty with France in 1936. Mardam subsequently served as prime minister until 1939, when his government resigned over France's failure to implement the treaty. He was again named prime minister on December 28, 1946. Mardam's government was forced to resign on December 1, 1948, following public criticism of his economic and financial policies. Mardam retired from politics the following year. He died on March 28, 1960.

KHALED EL-AZAM (Prime Minister, December 16, 1948–March 30, 1949). Khaled el-Azam was born to a wealthy family in Damascus in 1903. He entered politics as an independent and served as prime minister of Syria under the Vichy regime from 1941 until 1942. He was again named prime minister on December 16, 1948. Azam retained office until he was ousted in the coup led by Husni Zaim on March 30, 1949. He was again asked to form a government on December 28, 1949, following the coup led by Abid es-Shishakli. He resigned in May of 1950, but was reappointed on March 27, 1951. Azam was again forced to step down on August 9, 1951, following a government employees strike in opposition of his labor policies. He served as deputy prime minister, minister of defense, and minister of finance from 1955 until 1957. He was politically inactive during Syria's unification with Egypt as part of the United Arab Republic from 1958 until 1961. Azam was defeated by Nazim el-Kudsi in an election for president of Syria in 1961. He was again named prime minister on September 13, 1962. He retained office until March 8, 1963, when he was ousted in a Ba'athist coup. Azam sought asylum in the Turkish Embassy until he was allowed to leave the country. He went into exile in Lebanon. He died in Beirut on February 18, 1965, at the age of 62 from complications from acute diabetes.

MUSHIN BARAZI (Prime Minister, June 26, 1949–August 14, 1949). Mushin Barazi was born in Hama in 1893. He entered politics and served in several cabinets during the 1940s. He served as a personal assistant to President Shukri el-Kuwatli in the late 1940s. Barazi was appointed prime minister on June 26, 1949, following the election of Husni Zaim as president. He was ousted in a coup led by Sami Hinnawi on August 14, 1949. Barazi and Zaim were arrested and tried before a military court. They were sentenced to death and summarily executed on August 14, 1949.

HASHIM EL-ATASSI (Prime Minister, August 15, 1949–December 13, 1949). *See entry under Heads of State.*

NAZIM EL-KUDSI (Prime Minister, December 24, 1949–December 25, 1949). *See entry under Heads of State.*

KHALED EL-AZAM (Prime Minister, December 28, 1949–May 1950). *See earlier entry under Heads of Government.*

NAZIM EL-KUDSI (Prime Minister, June 4, 1950–March 27, 1951). *See entry under Heads of State.*

KHALED EL-AZAM (Prime Minister, March 27, 1951–August 9, 1951). *See earlier entry under Heads of Government.*

HASSAN HAKIN (Prime Minister, August 9, 1951–November 10, 1951). Hassan Hakin was born in 1888. He was an independent member of the Syrian Parliament. He was named to serve as prime minister and finance minister by President Taj-ed Din-el-Hassani on September 20, 1941. Hakin resigned on April 18, 1942. He was again asked to form a cabinet by President Hashim el-Atassi on August 9, 1951. He also headed the Ministry of Finance in the government. He resigned on November 10, 1951, following a dispute with Foreign Minister Faidi al-Attassi over Hakin's support for the Middle East Defense Plan and the United States Mutual Aid Program.

MARUF ED-DAWALIBI (Prime Minister, November 28, 1951). Maruf ed-Dawalibi was born in Aleppo in 1907. He was educated in Damascus and Paris. He was a founder and leader of the Syrian People's party and was elected to Parliament in the 1940s. Dawalibi was appointed minister for economic affairs in 1949 and served until the following year. He was elected president of Parliament in 1951. He was nominated prime minister on November 28, 1951, and also assumed the position of minister of defense. Dawalibi indicated that he planned to control the army and the police, and he was ousted by a military coup led by Abid es-Shishakly eight hours after taking office. Dawalibi supported closer ties with the Soviet Union and was named minister of defense in 1954. He was an opponent of the Ba'ath party and was against Syria's merger with Egypt in 1958. He went into exile in Lebanon until Syria broke away from the United Arab Republic in 1961. Dawalibi was again named prime minister on December 22, 1961, and also served as foreign minister. He retained office until March 28, 1962, when he was ousted in another military coup. He subsequently went to Saudi Arabia, where he served as an advisor to the government.

FAWZI SILO (Prime Minister, December 3, 1951–July 20, 1953). *See entry under Heads of State.*

ABID ES-SHISHAKLI (Prime Minister, July 20, 1953–February 25, 1954). *See entry under Heads of State.*

SABRI EL-ASSALI (Prime Minister, March 1, 1954–June 10, 1954). Sabri el-Assali was born in Damascus in 1903. He was a leader of the Arab nationalist movement and was active in the Druze Revolt against France in 1925. He joined the National Bloc in the 1930s and was elected to the Syrian Parliament in the early 1940s. Assali was a founder of the National party in 1947 and served as secretary-general of the organization. He served in several cabinets in the late 1940s. He was appointed prime minister on March 1, 1954, following the ouster of Abid es-Shishakli. Assali resigned over disagreements in the government concerning defense matters and press control. He again became prime minister on February 25, 1955, after the resignation of Faris el-Khouri. Assali stepped down on September 6, 1955, following parliamentary elec-

tions. He was again appointed prime minister on June 15, 1956. He was involved in the negotiations that led to the unification of Syria with Egypt as the United Arab Republic on February 1, 1958. Assali was subsequently appointed one of the four deputies to United Arab Republic president Gamal Abdel Nasser. He resigned several months later and retired from politics.

SAID EL-GHAZZI (Prime Minister, June 19, 1954–October 14, 1954). Said el-Ghazzi was named head of a nonpolitical caretaker government on June 19, 1954. The government supervised the elections in September of 1954. He stepped down on October 14, 1954, following the selection of a new Parliament. He was again named prime minister on September 13, 1955, after the election of Shukri el-Kuwatli as president. Ghazzi vowed that his government would adhere to the constitution and bring stability and economic development to the nation. He resigned his office on June 15, 1956.

FARIS EL-KHOURI (Prime Minister, October 29, 1954–February 25, 1955). *See earlier entry under Heads of Government.*

SABRI EL-ASSALI (Prime Minister, February 25, 1955–September 6, 1955). *See earlier entry under Heads of Government.*

SAID EL-GHAZZI (Prime Minister, September 13, 1955–June 15, 1956). *See earlier entry under Heads of Government.*

SABRI EL-ASSALI (Prime Minister, June 15, 1956–February 1, 1958). *See earlier entry under Heads of Government.*

MAHMOUN EL-KUZBARI (Prime Minister, September 29, 1961–November 20, 1961). Mahmoun el-Kuzbari was born in Damascus in 1914. He was educated at the University of Lyons in France, where he received a degree in law. He returned to the University of Damascus as a law professor. Kuzbari was appointed to the Syrian judiciary in 1948. He was elected Speaker of Parliament in 1953 and was president of the Arab Liberation Movement, the political party founded by Abid es-Shishakli. Kuzbari declared himself acting president following the ouster of Shishakli in February of 1954, but he was forced to relinquish his claims. He was a member of several cabinets from 1955 until 1958. He was politically inactive while Syria was joined with Egypt as part of the United Arab Republic from 1958 until 1961. Kuzbari was named prime minister on September 29, 1961, after a coup restored Syrian independence from Egypt. He resigned on November 20, 1961, and ran unsuccessfully in the presidential elections. He left the government in March of 1962 following another military coup and retired from politics in 1963 after the Ba'ath takeover of Syria.

IZZAT AL-NUS (Prime Minister, November 20, 1961–December 22, 1961). Izzat al-Nus was born in 1912. He served as minister of education and national guidance in the government of Mahmoun el-Kuzbari following the breakup of the United Arab Republic in September of 1961. He was appointed prime minister of a caretaker cabinet on November 20, 1962, when Kuzbari resigned to run for president. Nus also served as foreign minister and minister of defense in the government. He stepped down on December 22, 1961.

MARUF EL-DAWALIBI (Prime Minister, December 22, 1961–March 28, 1962). *See earlier entry under Heads of Government.*

ABDUL KARIM ZAHREDDIN (Prime Minister, March 28, 1962–April 13,

1962). *See entry under Heads of State.*

BASHIR AL-AZMAH (Prime Minister, April 17, 1962–September 13, 1962). Bashir al-Azmah was born in 1910. He led a transitional government from April 17, 1962, until his resignation on September 13, 1962. He remained deputy prime minister in the government of his successor, Khaled el-Azam.

KHALED EL-AZAM (Prime Minister, September 13, 1962–March 8, 1963). *See earlier entry under Heads of Government.*

SALAH AL-DIN BITAR (Prime Minister, March 9, 1963–November 12, 1963). Salah al-Din Bitar was born in Damascus in 1912. He was educated in Damascus and at the Sorbonne in Paris, where he received a degree in science. He returned to Syria and became a teacher in 1934. Bitar entered politics in 1942 in opposition to the French mandate in Syria. He cofounded the Arab Renaissance, or Ba'ath, party with Michel Aflaq in 1942. He started the party newspaper, *al-Ba'ath*, in 1946 and served as editor. Bitar went into exile in Lebanon in 1953 after being accused of plotting against the government of Abid es-Shishakli. He returned to Syria to organize the merger of the Ba'ath and Socialist parties. Bitar was elected to Parliament following the ouster of the Shishakli government in February of 1954. He was named foreign minister in the government of Sabri el-Assali in June of 1956. He was instrumental in negotiating the merger between Syria and Egypt to form the United Arab Republic in 1958. Bitar subsequently served as minister of state for arab affairs in the United Arab Republic government. He resigned near the end of 1959 in opposition to President Gamal Abdel Nasser's curtailing of Ba'athist influence on the government. A group of rightist army officers led a military coup against the Egyptian-dominated government and withdrew Syria from the United Arab Republic in September of 1961. Bitar fled the country, and went into exile in Beirut, Lebanon. He returned to Damascus and became prime minister on March 9, 1963, following the Ba'athist coup that ousted President Nazim el-Kudsi. Bitar stepped down as prime minister on November 12, 1963, to become vice president of the Revolutionary Council. He was again named prime minister by President Amin al-Hafiz on May 13, 1964 and served until October 4, 1964. He was once again asked to form a government on December 21, 1965. Bitar retained office until February 25, 1966, when the extremist faction of the Ba'ath party ousted the government of al-Hafiz. Bitar was arrested following the coup, but escaped and fled to Lebanon. He was tried in absentia for conspiring against the Syrian government in January of 1969 and sentenced to life imprisonment. He settled in exile in France in 1970, where he served as editor of *Arab Renaissance*, a political journal. Bitar was shot to death by an assassin as he entered his magazine office in Paris on July 21, 1980.

AMIN AL-HAFIZ (Prime Minister, November 12, 1963–May 13, 1964). *See entry under Heads of State.*

SALAH AL-DIN BITAR (Prime Minister, May 13, 1964–October 4, 1964). *See earlier entry under Heads of Government.*

AMIN AL-HAFIZ (Prime Minister, October 4, 1964–September 3, 1965). *See entry under Heads of State.*

YOUSSEF ZOUAYEN (Prime Minister, September 23, 1965–December 21, 1965). Youssef Zouayen (Zeayen) was born in 1931. He was educated at the University of Damascus and attended medical school in London, but returned to Syria in 1963 to enter politics. He served as minister of agrarian reform in 1963 and was a member of the Presidential Council from 1964 until 1965. He was appointed prime minister by President Amin al-Hafiz on September 23, 1965. Zouayen resigned on December 21, 1965, after several army officers were arrested in an abortive military coup. He was again named prime minister on February 25, 1966, following the ouster of the Hafiz government. He retained office until October 28, 1968, when he was replaced by President Nureddin el-Atassi.

SALAH AL-DIN BITAR (Prime Minister, December 21, 1965–February 25, 1966). *See earlier entry under Heads of Government.*

YOUSSEF ZOUAYEN (Prime Minister, February 25, 1966–October 28, 1968). *See earlier entry under Heads of Government.*

NUREDDIN EL-ATASSI (Prime Minister, October 28, 1968–November 13, 1970). *See entry under Heads of State.*

HAFEZ AL-ASSAD (Prime Minister, November 19, 1970–April 3, 1971). *See entry under Heads of State.*

ABDUL RAHMAN KHLEYFAWI (Prime Minister, April 3, 1971–December 21, 1972). Abdul Rahman Khleyfawi was born in Damascus in 1927. He studied at the military college and joined the Syrian Arab army. He served as chief of police in Deraa and was governor of Hama. In 1965 he was posted to the Joint Arab Command in Cairo. Khleyfawi was appointed to the government as minister of the interior by Hafez al-Assad in 1970. He replaced Assad as prime minister on April 3, 1971, and served until December 21, 1972. Khleyfawi was again named prime minister on August 1, 1976, and served until March 27, 1978.

MAHMOUD AYOUBI (Prime Minister, December 21, 1972–August 1, 1976). Mahmoud Ben Saleh al-Ayoubi was born in 1932. He served in the cabinet as minister of education from 1969 until 1971. He was also named deputy prime minister in 1970 and served until 1971. Ayoubi took part in negotiations to form a federation between Syria, Egypt, and Libya. He was named vice president in 1971, and on December 21, 1972, he was also appointed prime minister. Ayoubi resigned as prime minister on August 1, 1976. He subsequently served as a member of the Ba'ath party regional command.

ABDUL RAHMAN KHLEYFAWI (Prime Minister, August 1, 1976–March 27, 1978). *See earlier entry under Heads of Government.*

MOHAMMED ALI AL-HALABI (Prime Minister, March 30, 1978–January 9, 1980). Mohammed Ali al-Halabi was born in Damascus in 1937. He was educated at Damascus University and became a teacher. He joined the Ba'ath party and was elected mayor of Damascus. Halabi was elected to the People's Council and served as Speaker from 1973 until 1978. He was named prime minister on March 30, 1978, and served until January 9, 1980.

ABDUL RAUF AL-KASSEM (Prime Minister, January 9, 1980–November 1, 1987). Abdul Rauf al-Kassem was born in Damascus in 1932. He was educated at the University of Damascus, the University of Istanbul, and the University of Geneva. He received a degree in architecture and taught at the Damascus School of Fine Arts from 1964 until 1970. Kassem headed the Department of Architecture at Damascus University from 1970 until 1979. He served as governor of Damascus from 1979 until 1980 and served on the Ba'ath party regional command from December of 1979. He was appointed prime minister on January 9, 1980. Syria's growing economic crisis resulted in Kassem's dismissal on November 1, 1987.

MAHMOUD ZOUBI (Prime Minister, November 1, 1987–). Mahmoud Zoubi was born in Khirbet Ghazaleh, in the Dar'a Province, in 1938. He worked in the Department of Agriculture from 1963. He was leader of the Ba'ath party from al-Ghab and served as secretary of the Pheasant's Bureau of the Ba'ath party from 1972 until 1973. In 1981 Zoubi was elected Speaker of the People's Assembly. He remained in that position until November 1, 1987, when he formed a government as prime minister.

Tajikistan, Republic of

(Respublika i Tojikiston)

Tajikistan is a country in central Asia. It received independence following the breakup of the Soviet Union on December 25, 1991.

HEADS OF STATE

RAKHMAN NABIYEV (President, September 23, 1991–September 7, 1992). Rakhman Nabiyev was born in Tajikistan in 1930. He was educated at the Tashkent Institute of Irrigation and Agricultural Mechanization and later worked at the institute as an engineer and teacher. He joined the Communist party in 1961 and held several party positions. Nabiyev served as minister of agriculture from 1971 until 1973 and then served as prime minister and minister of foreign affairs from 1973 until 1983. He also served as a deputy to the U.S.S.R. Supreme Soviet from 1974 until 1989. He was elected first secretary of the Central Committee for two years in 1983. Nabiyev was elected president on September 23, 1991, after the resignation of Kadreddin A. Aslonov. He remained in office when Tajikistan gained independence from the Soviet Union the following December. Tajikistan was faced with the threat of civil war from dissident elements in the southern region. In May of 1992 Nabiyev was forced to share power with Islamic fundamentalists and anti-Communist activists. On August 31, 1992, armed militants took control of his official residence in Dushanbe. Two days later Nabiyev was dismissed by the Parliament and cabinet in a vote of no confidence. He subsequently went into hiding, but was seized by opposition demonstrators while trying to flee the capital. He resigned the presidency on September 7, 1992. Nabiyev died of a heart attack in Dushanbe at the age of 63 on April 10, 1993.

AKBAR SHAH ISKANDROV (President, September 7, 1992–November 20, 1992). Akbar Shah Iskandrov served as Speaker of the Parliament. He assumed the duties of president following the resignation of Rakhman Nabiyev. He remained acting president until he was replaced by Imomali Rakhmonov on November 20, 1992.

IMOMALI RAKHMONOV (President, November 20, 1992–). Imomali Rakhmonov was born in the southern Kulyab region. He was a former member of the Communist party. He replaced Akbar Shah Iskandrov as president on November 20, 1992. Presidential rule was abolished in Tajikistan on November 27, 1992, and Rakhmonov took the title of chairman of the Supreme Soviet.

Tanzania, United Republic of
(Jamhuri ya muungano wa Tanzania)

Tanzania is a country that consists of Tanganyika on the eastern coast of Africa and includes the island of Zanzibar in the Indian Ocean. Tanganyika was granted independence from a United Nations trusteeship administered by Great Britain on December 9, 1961. Zanzibar was granted independence from Great Britain on December 19, 1963. The two nations merged to become Tanzania on April 26, 1964.

HEADS OF STATE

SIR RICHARD TURNBULL (Governor General, May 1, 1961–December 9, 1962). Richard Gordon Turnbull was born on July 7, 1909. He was educated at University College in London and at Magdelene College, Cambridge University. He entered the British Colonial Service in 1931 and served as a district officer in Kenya until 1948. Turnbull was then named provincial commissioner until 1953. He was appointed chief secretary of Kenya in 1955 and served until 1958. He was named governor of Tanganyika in 1958 and became independent Tanganyika's first governor-general on May 1, 1961. Turnbull retained that position until Tanganyika became an independent republic on December 9, 1962. He was appointed chairman of the Central Land Board in Kenya the following year. He held that position until 1964. Turnbull was then named high commissioner for Aden in 1965. He retired from the colonial service in 1967.

JULIUS NYERERE (President, November 2, 1962–November 5, 1985). Julius Kambarage Nyerere was born in Butiama in March of 1922. He was educated locally and attended Makerere College in Uganda. He subsequently attended the University of Edinburgh in Great Britain, where he received a degree in history and economics in 1952. Nyerere returned to Tanganyika to teach school. He also became involved in politics and founded the Tanganyika African National Union (TANU) in 1954. He was a leading spokesman for Tanganyikan independence and led TANU to victory in elections in September of 1958 and August of 1960. Nyerere became chief minister when Tanganyika was granted self-government on September 2, 1960. He remained head of the government after Tanganyika achieved independence on December 9, 1961. He stepped down as prime minister on January 22, 1962, to reorganize the party. He was elected the first president of the Tanganyikan Republic and took office on November 2, 1962. Nyerere survived a coup in January of 1964 following the establishment of a revolutionary government on the island of Zanzibar. Tanganyika and the Zanzibar People's Republic merged to form the United Republic of Tanzania on April 26, 1964. Nyerere served as president of the unified government. He was confirmed into office by an election in

September of 1965. He maintained Tanzania's neutrality in East-West relations, but allowed Tanzania to serve as a base of operations for guerrilla organizations dedicated to independence for the Portuguese colonies of Mozambique and Angola. Nyerere was reelected to the presidency unopposed in 1970 and 1975. He merged TANU with the Afro-Zhirazi party (ASP), Zanzibar's ruling party, in February of 1977, thereby forming the Revolutionary party of Tanzania. Nyerere was again reelected in 1980 and announced his intention to step down after completing his term in office. He stepped down on November 5, 1985, and was succeeded by Vice President Ali Hassan Mwinyi. Nyerere remained chairman of the Revolutionary party of Tanzania until August of 1990. He subsequently became an advocate of multiparty elections for Tanzania.

ALI HASSAN MWINYI (President, November 5, 1985–). Ali Hassan Mwinyi was born in Kivure, Kisarwe District, on May 8, 1925. He was educated in Zanzibar and England and returned to Zanzibar to teach in 1945. He became principal of the Zanzibar Teacher Training College, where he remained until 1961. Mwinyi returned to England to continue his education for several years before entering Zanzibar's Ministry of Education in 1964. He served on various government committees during the 1960s before he was named minister of state in President Julius Nyerere's office in 1969. He was named to the cabinet as minister of health in February of 1972. Aboud Jumbe, vice president of Tanzania and chairman of the Zanzibar government, resigned on January 27, 1984, due to widespread sentiment for Zanzibar's separation from Tanzania. Mwinyi was selected to replace him on January 30, 1984. He was chosen to succeed President Julius Nyerere, who retired as head of state of Tanzania on November 5, 1985. Mwinyi consolidated his power and was elected chairman of the ruling Revolutionary party of Tanzania in August of 1990. He was reelected to the presidency in October of 1990 and announced plans to transform Tanzania into a multiparty democracy in the early 1990s.

HEADS OF GOVERNMENT

JULIUS NYERERE (Chief Minister, September 2, 1960–May 1, 1961. Prime Minister, May 1, 1961–January 22, 1962). *See entry under Heads of State.*

RASHIDI KAWAWA (Prime Minister, January 22, 1962–December 9, 1962). Rashidi Mfaume Kawawa was born in the Songea District in 1929. He was educated locally and worked in the Tanganyikan Social Welfare Department. He became involved in the labor movement in Tanganyika and became president of the Tanganyika Federation of Labor in 1957. Kawawa was elected to the Legislative Council in 1958 and was named to the government as minister for local government and housing in 1960. He was a close advisor to Julius Nyerere and was named prime minister on January 22, 1962, when Nyerere stepped down to reorganize the Tanganyika African National Union (TANU). He remained prime minister until the position was abolished on December 9, 1962. Kawawa subsequently served as Nyerere's vice president. He became second vice president following the union of Tanganyika and Zanzibar in April of 1964. He again served as prime minister when the position was reestablished on February 17, 1972. Kawawa stepped down on February 13, 1977, but remained in the government as minister of defense and national service until 1980. He subsequently served as minister without portfolio. Kawawa also served as secretary-general of the Revolutionary party of Tanzania from November of 1982 until August of 1990, when he became vice-chairman of the party.

RASHIDI KAWAWA (Prime Minister, February 17, 1972–February 13, 1977). *See earlier entry under Heads of Government.*

EDWARD SOKOINE (Prime Minister, February 13, 1977–November 5, 1980). Edward Moringe Sokoine was born in Monduli, Masai District, in 1938. He was educated locally and in West Germany and was elected to Tanzania's Parliament in 1965. He served as parliamentary secretary to the Ministry of Communications, Transport, and Labor from August of 1967 and was named minister of state in November of 1970. Sokoine was appointed minister of defense and national service in 1972. He replaced Rashidi Kawawa as prime minister on February 13, 1977. He stepped down from office due to ill health from diabetes on November 5, 1980. President Julius Nyerere reappointed Sokoine as prime minister on February 24, 1983, when Tanzania was suffering from serious economic difficulties. He organized a campaign against black marketeering that led to numerous arrests. Sokoine was viewed as a likely successor to President Nyerere before his death in an automobile accident near Morogoro on April 12, 1984.

CLEOPA DAVID MSUYA (Prime Minister, November 7, 1980–February 24, 1983). Cleopa David Msuya was born in Chomvu Usangi, Mwanga District, on January 4, 1931. He was educated at Makerere College in Uganda. He entered the Tanganyikan civil service in 1956 and became commissioner for community development in 1961. Msuya served as a secretary to various government ministries from 1964 and was appointed minister of finance in 1972. He was shifted to the Ministry for Industries in 1975, where he remained until his appointment as prime minister on November 7, 1980. Tanzania's economic condition deteriorated in the early 1980s, and Msuya was replaced as prime minister by Edward Sokoine on February 24, 1983. He returned to the Ministry of Finance, where he remained until 1989. Msuya was appointed minister for industries and trade in 1990.

EDWARD SOKOINE (Prime Minister, February 24, 1983–April 12, 1984). *See earlier entry under Heads of Government.*

SALIM AHMED SALIM (Prime Minister, April 24, 1984–November 6, 1985). Salim Ahmed Salim was born on Pemba Island, Zanzibar, in January of 1942. He was educated locally and at the University of Delhi. He was appointed ambassador to the United Arab Republic in 1964 following Zanzibar's union with Tanganyika. Salim was named high commissioner to India the following year, where he remained until 1968. He subsequently served as ambassador to the People's Republic of China in 1969. Salim was named to serve as Tanzania's permanent representative to the United Nations in 1970. He also served as president of the United Nations General Assembly in 1979. He returned to Tanzania to serve as minister of foreign affairs in 1980. Salim retained that position until his appointment as prime minister on April 24, 1984. He was replaced by Joseph Warioba on November 6, 1985. He remained in the government as deputy prime minister and minister of defense until 1989. Salim was elected secretary-general of the Organization of African Unity in July of 1989.

JOSEPH SINDE WARIOBA (Prime Minister, November 6, 1985–November 9, 1990). Joseph Sinde Warioba was born in 1940. He was educated at the University of Dar es Salaam. He was elected as a member of the Central Committee of the National Executive Committee of the Chama Cha Mapinduzi, the ruling political party. In 1977 he was appointed minister of justice in the cabinet of Edward Sokoine. Warioba became prime minister and first vice president on November 6, 1985. He was demoted from the office of prime minister on November 9, 1990. The following year he served as minister of regional administration and local government in the cabinet of John Malecela.

JOHN MALECELA (Prime Minister, November 9, 1990–). John William Samuel Malecela was born in 1934. He attended Bombay University and Cambridge and entered the civil service in 1960. He served as a consul to the United States Embassy in 1962 and from 1964 until 1968 was Tanzania's permanent representative to the United Nations. Malecela was then appointed ambassador to Ethiopia. He returned to Tanzania as minister of communication, research, and social services of the East African Community from 1969 until 1972. He held several subsequent cabinet positions, including minister of foreign affairs from 1972 until 1975, agriculture from 1975 until 1980, mines from 1980 until 1981, and transportation and commerce from 1982 until 1986. In 1989 Malecela was appointed high commissioner to Great Britain. He returned to Tanzania in 1990 and was named prime minister on November 9, 1990.

Thailand, Kingdom of

(Prathet Thai)

Thailand is a country in Southeast Asia.

HEADS OF STATE

ANANDA MAHIDOL (King, March 2, 1935–June 9, 1946). Ananda Mahidol was born in Germany on September 20, 1925. He was the son of Prince Mahidol of Songkhim. He was sent to Switzerland for his education following the death of his father in 1928. Mahidol assumed the throne of Siam under a regency council on March 2, 1935, following the abdication of his uncle, King Prajahlipok. He continued his studies at the University of Lausanne in Switzerland. He reached his majority in September of 1945 and returned to Siam the following December to prepare for his coronation. He was found dead from a gunshot wound to the head in his bed in the Royal Palace on June 9, 1946. It was initially announced that the king had been the victim of an accident, though later investigations indicated the likelihood of murder or suicide.

BHUMIBOL ADULYADEJ (King, June 10, 1946–   ). Somdet Phra Chao Yu Hua Bhumibol Adulyadej was born on December 5, 1927, in Cambridge, Massachusetts, where his father, Prince Mahidol, was a student at Harvard Medical School. His father died in 1928, and his uncle, King Prajahlipok of Thailand, sent Bhumibol and his older brother, Ananda Mahidol, to school in Switzerland. Ananda Mahidol became king of Siam when Prajahlipok abdicated in 1935. Bhumibol succeeded his brother to the throne when Ananda Mahidol was found dead from a gunshot on June 9, 1946. A regency council was appointed to rule until he came to his majority. Bhumibol returned to Switzerland to continue his education. He reached his majority in December of 1946, but his coronation was delayed on several occasions. He was seriously injured in an automobile accident in October of 1949. Bhumibol recovered from his injuries and married Mom Rachawong Srikit Kitiyakara on April 28, 1950. Bhumibol was crowned Rama IX on May 5, 1950. His son, Crown Prince Maha Vajiralongkorn, was born in 1952. Bhumibol ruled as a constitutional monarch and was a popular figure in the country. He occasionally intervened in political matters. He indicated his dissatisfaction with Prime Minister Luang Pibul Songgram in 1957 by declining to attend public ceremonies. Pibul Songgram was subsequently ousted in a military coup by Field Marshal Sarit Thanarat. Sarit gave the king a more visible public role. Bhumibol indicated his support for student demonstrators against the government of Thanon Kittakachorn in 1973, forcing Thanon's ouster. Military officers attempted a coup against the government of General Prem Tinsulanond in April of 1981. Prem and the royal family fled to Khorat, where Bhumibol issued statements supporting Prem's government. The king's support prevented the rebels from gaining control of the military, and Prem quickly returned to power. Bhumibol also forced the resignation of General Suchinda Kraprayoon's government following widespread demonstrations in May of 1992.

HEADS OF GOVERNMENT

KHUANG APHAIWONG (Prime Minister, August 2, 1944–August 18, 1945). Khuang Aphaiwong was born in 1902. He was educated in Paris, France, where he studied engineering. He returned to Thailand and entered government service. Khuang worked in the telegraph department, where he rose to the position of director-general. He participated in the coup in 1932 that established Thailand as a constitutional monarchy. He subsequently served in Phahon Phon Phayuha's cabinet. Khuang remained in the government of Luang Pibul Songgram. He was a leader of the Democratic party and served in the House of Representatives as vice president in 1943 and 1944. He replaced Pibul as prime minister on August 2, 1944. Khuang was forced to resign on August 18, 1945, because of his association with the Japanese during World War II. He was again selected as prime minister on January 30, 1946, but his government collapsed on March 18, 1946. He was again named prime minister on November 10, 1947, following a military coup. The Democratic party won a slight majority in elections in January of 1948 and Khuang remained head of the government. He was forced to resign by the military on April 7, 1948. He remained involved in the Democratic party and served as leader of the Opposition from 1955. Khuang withdrew from politics in the 1960s to work with an insurance company. He died of cancer in Bangkok at the age of 66 on March 15, 1968.

THAWI BUNYAKET (Prime Minister, August 18, 1945–September 1, 1945). Thawi Bunyaket was a prominent Thai political figure when he was chosen to serve as prime minister in a caretaker cabinet on August 18, 1945, following the resignation of Khuang Aphaiwong. The government was largely controlled by the regent, Pridi Phanomyong, who voided Thailand's declaration of war against the Allies. Thawi also served in the cabinet as foreign minister and minister of agriculture, welfare, and public instruction. He remained in office until Seni Pramoj was selected as prime minister on September 1, 1945.

SENI PRAMOJ (Prime Minister, September 1, 1945–January 31, 1946). Seni Pramoj was born in Nakhon Sawan Province on May 26, 1905. He was educated in Great Britain, where he received a degree in law. He served as Thailand's ambassador to the United States in 1941. Seni refused to deliver Thailand's declaration of war to United States officials in 1941 and joined the Free Thai movement to oppose the Japanese. When World War II was concluded, Seni became prime minister on September 1, 1945, and he served until January 31, 1946. He helped arrange a satisfactory peace settlement with the Allied powers. Seni resumed his law practice and remained active in politics. He became the leader of the Democratic party in 1968 and was elected to Parliament the following year. He formed a government as prime minister on February 21, 1975. Seni resigned on March 6, 1975, after failing to win a vote of confidence in the Parliament. He was again appointed to the office of prime minister to succeed his younger brother, Kukrit Pramoj, on April 20, 1976. He also served in the government as minister of the interior. Seni was criticized for allowing the return of exiled former prime minister Thanon Kittakachorn in September of 1976. Seni was ousted by a military coup led by Admiral Sangad Chaloryu on October 6, 1976. He served on the committee to draft a new Thai Constitution from 1977 until 1978. He subsequently retired from active politics.

KHUANG APHAIWONG (Prime Minister, January 30, 1946–March 18, 1946). *See earlier entry under Heads of Government.*

PRIDI PHANOMYONG (Prime Minister, March 21, 1946–August 21, 1946). Pridi Phanomyong was born in Ayutthaya on May 11, 1900. He was educated in Paris, France, where he received a degree in law. He returned to Siam to teach law at Chulalongkorn University. Pridi was a leader of the coup that forced King Prajahlipok to install constitutional rule in Siam in 1932. He subsequently served in the government as minister of the interior, foreign affairs, and finance. He was a member of the Regency Council during the minority of King Ananda Mahidol from 1941. Pridi led the underground Free Thai group that supported the Allies during World War II. He was instrumental in forcing the ouster of pro-Japanese Prime Minister Luang Pibul Songgram in August of 1944. Pridi became prime minister on March 21, 1946. King Ananda Mahidol was found dead from a gunshot wound in the Royal Palace in June of 1946. Pridi's opponents accused the prime minister of responsibility for the king's death. He resigned from office on August 21, 1946. A military coup led by Pibul Songgram took control of the country in November of 1947, and Pridi was forced to go into exile. He traveled to Macao, the United States, and China before settling in France in 1970. He died of a heart attack in Paris at the age of 82 on May 2, 1983.

LUANG DHAMRONG NAWASA-WAT (Prime Minister, August 23, 1946–November 9, 1947). Luang Dhamrong Nawasawat was born in 1901. He served in the Thai navy and rose to the rank of rear admiral. He was appointed to the Provisional Senate in July of 1932. Dhamrong was named to the cabinet as minister without portfolio in July of 1933. He was appointed minister of

internal affairs in 1934 and served until 1938. He was then named minister of justice. Dhamrong was a member of the anti–Japanese Free Thai Movement during World War II and resigned from the cabinet in 1944. He was the leader of the Constitutional Front party from 1946 and was named prime minister on August 23, 1946. He was ousted in a military coup led by Luang Pibul Songgram on November 9, 1947, and went into exile. Dhamrong was active in an unsuccessful conspiracy against the government of Pibul in February of 1949. He subsequently retired from political activity.

KHUANG APHAIWONG (Prime Minister, November 10, 1947–April 7, 1948). *See earlier entry under Heads of Government.*

LUANG PIBUL SONGGRAM (Prime Minister, April 9, 1948–September 16, 1957). Luang Pibul Songgram was born near Bangkok on July 14, 1897. He attended military school in Bangkok and joined the Siamese army. He continued his training in France and was promoted to lieutenant in 1926. Pibul was active in the coup in June of 1932 that made Siam a constitutional monarchy. He was named minister of defense in September of 1934 in the government of Phahon Phon Phayuha. He replaced Phahon as prime minister on December 21, 1938. The following year the country's name was officially changed from Siam to Thailand. Pibul entered into a treaty with Japan during World War II and declared war on the Allies. He was forced from office on August 2, 1944. He returned to prominence following the death of King Ananda Mahidol in June of 1946. Prime Minister Pridi Phanomyong was accused of complicity in the king's death, and Pibul was a leader of the coup that overthrew his government. He again became prime minister on April 9, 1948. His government faced opposition from Pridi's supporters and survived several coup attempts in the early 1950s. Thailand entered the South East Asia Treaty Organization (SEATO) in 1955. Pibul remained in office following a general election in February of 1957. His government was charged with electoral fraud, and he was ousted in a military coup led by Field Marshal Sarit Thanarat on September 16, 1957. Pibul went into exile in the United States and Japan. He went to India in 1960 to become a Buddhist monk. He died of a heart attack at his home in Tokyo at the age of 66 on June 11, 1964.

POTE SARASIN (Prime Minister, September 21, 1957–December 27, 1957). Pote Sarasin was born in Bangkok on March 25, 1906. He was educated in the United States and Great Britain and received a degree in law. He returned to Thailand, where he set up a law practice. Pote was an advisor to Prime Minister Luang Pibul Songgram and was appointed to the Senate in 1947. He served as foreign minister in Pibul's cabinet in 1948. Pote was appointed ambassador to the United States and the United Nations in 1952 and served until 1957. He also served as prime minister of an interim government designed to supervise new elections from September 21, 1957, until December 27, 1957. He was selected as the first secretary-general of the Southeast Asia Treaty Organization (SEATO) in 1957 and served until 1963. He was appointed minister of development in the cabinet of Thanon Kittakachorn in 1963. He retired from government service in 1972.

THANON KITTAKACHORN (Prime Minister, December 27, 1957–October 20, 1958). Thanon Kittakachorn was born in Tak Province on August 11, 1911. He was educated locally and attended the Royal Thai Military Academy. He graduated in 1929 and entered the Thai army. Thanon held various military positions and rose to the rank of lieutenant in 1935. He served

as an instructor at the Royal Thai Military Academy until 1938 and was promoted to lieutenant colonel in 1944 and major general in 1951. He was also elected to the Thai House of Representatives in 1951. Thanon was named deputy minister of cooperatives in April of 1956 and deputy minister of defense the following year. He also served as assistant commander in chief of the Thai army under Field Marshal Sarit Thanarat. He was active in the military coup that ousted the government of Luang Pibul Songgram in September of 1957 and served as minister of defense in the provisional government. Thanon was chosen as the Nationalist Socialist party's candidate for prime minister and took office on December 27, 1957. His government was unstable and collapsed on October 20, 1958. Sarit Thanarat staged another military coup the same day, and Thanon was named deputy premier in Sarit's military government. He also retained the position of minister of defense. Sarit died on December 8, 1963, and Thanon succeeded him as prime minister and commander of the armed forces. He was promoted to the rank of field marshal the following year. He instituted a campaign against corruption in the government. Thailand was faced with an increase in Communist guerrilla activities in the mid-1960s. Thanon received financial assistance from the United States to combat the growing Communist threat. He promoted a new constitution in 1968 that provided for a popularly elected House of Representatives. Thanon's United Thai People's party won a plurality in February of 1969, and he remained head of the government. He dissolved the Parliament and banned political parties in November of 1971. He worked closely with General Prapas Charusathira, the army commander, in a military government. Thanon was faced with massive student demonstrations in 1973. He lost the support of King Bhumibol and much of the army. He was forced to resign on October 13,

1973, and went into exile in Singapore. He returned to Thailand in September of 1976 and became a Buddhist monk. His return was met with renewed student demonstrations.

SARIT THANARAT (Prime Minister, October 20, 1958–December 8, 1963). Sarit Thanarat was born in Nakhon Phanom on June 16, 1908. He was educated at the Phra Chula Chom Klao Military Academy and entered the army in 1929. He rose through the ranks and commanded a regiment in World War II that accepted the Japanese surrender in north Siam in August of 1945. Sarot supported Field Marshal Luang Pibul Songgram's military coup in 1947 and was promoted to the rank of general in February of 1949. He served as deputy minister of defense from 1951 and was named commander in chief of the army in June of 1954. He was promoted to field marshal in 1956. Sarit was named minister of defense in August of 1957. Pibul Songgram's government was accused of fraud in elections the previous February, and Sarit led a military coup that ousted the government on September 16, 1957. He served as supreme commander of the armed forces. He was seriously ill with cirrhosis of the liver, and General Thanon Kittakachorn was elected prime minister. Sarit went to the United States to receive medical treatment at Walter Reed Army Hospital. He returned to Thailand after his recovery and led another coup that placed him in charge of the government on October 20, 1958. He was an opponent of Communism and received the support of the United States. Sarit also made efforts to improve the economic condition of Thailand's rural provinces. He was hospitalized in November of 1963 for heart and lung ailments and died at an army hospital in Bangkok at the age of 55 on December 8, 1963.

THANON KITTAKACHORN (Prime Minister, December 8, 1963–October 13,

1973). *See earlier entry under Heads of Government.*

SANYA DHARMASAKTI (Prime Minister, October 14, 1973–February 21, 1975). Sanya Dharmasakti was born in Bangkok on April 5, 1907. He attended Bangkok Law School and continued his education in London before returning to Thailand to practice law. He entered the Thai judiciary and rose to the position of chief justice of the Supreme Court. Sanya retired in 1967, but remained a councillor to King Bhumibol Adulyadej. He was appointed rector of Thammasat University in Bangkok in the early 1970s. Sanya was asked to form a government as prime minister on October 14, 1973, following student demonstrations that forced the resignation of the military regime of Thanon Kittakachorn. Political dissension continued in Thailand, and Sanya announced his resignation in May of 1974. The king persuaded him to return to office, and he presided over general elections in January of 1975. He relinquished office to Democratic party leader Seni Pramoj on February 21, 1975. Sanya served as privy councillor to the king the following year. He became president of the World Fellowship of Buddhists in 1984 and held this office until his retirement in 1988.

SENI PRAMOJ (Prime Minister, February 21, 1975–March 6, 1975). *See earlier entry under Heads of Government.*

KUKRIT PRAMOJ (Prime Minister, March 17, 1975–April 16, 1976). Kukrit Pramoj was born on April 20, 1911. He was educated in Thailand and Great Britain, where he studied finance and politics. He returned to Thailand to work in the Finance Ministry, but left soon after for employment with the Bank of Thailand. Pramoj was elected to Parliament in 1946 and served as deputy minister of finance the following year. He founded the *Sayam Rat* newspaper in 1950. He starred in the 1963 U.S. film *The Ugly American*, playing the prime minister of a fictional Asian country. He opposed the military regime of Thanon Kittakachorn and served as Speaker of the National Assembly following Thanon's ouster in 1973. Kukrit organized the Social Action party in 1975 and became prime minister on March 17, 1975. He lost his legislative seat in elections in April of 1976 and was replaced as prime minister by his older brother, Seni Pramoj, on April 16, 1976. He served on the committee to draft a new constitution from 1977 until 1978. Kukrit's Social Action party received a plurality of votes in general elections in April of 1979, but the government of General Kriangsak Chamand controlled the upper house of Parliament and retained power. The party was again the victor in elections in 1983 and entered into a coalition government with Prem Tinsulanond. Kukrit resigned as leader of the party in late 1985, though he remained a member of the Legislative Assembly. He returned to lead the party in August of 1990 and remained a prominent figure in Thai politics.

SENI PRAMOJ (Prime Minister, April 20, 1976–October 6, 1976). *See earlier entry under Heads of Government.*

SANGAD CHALORYU (Head of State, October 6, 1976–November 23, 1980). Sangad Chaloryu was born in the Suphan Buri Province on March 3, 1915. He attended the Royal Navy Cadet Academy and subsequently joined the Thai navy. He was commander of the Thai fleet that was involved in the Korean War. Sangad served as deputy chief of staff of the navy and was named deputy chief of staff of the armed forces in 1971. He was appointed supreme commander in October of 1975 and retired from the navy in September of 1976. Following his retirement, he was named minister of defense

in the government of Seni Pramoj. Sangad led a military coup to oust Seni's government on October 6, 1976. He served as chairman of the newly formed Administrative Reform Council and installed Thanin Kraivichien as prime minister on October 8, 1976. Sangad served in the cabinet as minister of defense. Thanin was ousted in October of 1977, and Sangad served as chairman of the Revolutionary Council. General Kriangsak Chamanan was named prime minister, and Sangad became chairman of the National Policy Council on November 12, 1977. He retained that position until his death in Bangkok from a heart attack at the age of 65 on November 23, 1980.

THANIN KRAIVICHIEN (Prime Minister, October 8, 1976–October 20, 1977). Thanin Kraivichien was born on April 5, 1927. He was educated at Thammasat University and the University of London, where he received a degree in law. He returned to Thailand and was appointed to the judiciary in 1969. Thanin was appointed to the Supreme Court in 1972 and was also elected to the National Assembly the following year. He was senior judge on the Supreme Court when he was chosen as prime minister by the military government on October 8, 1976. Thanin's government was unpopular with the populace and the military, but he survived a right-wing coup in March of 1977. The ruling Administrative Reform Council under Admiral Sangad Chaloryu forced Thanin's resignation on October 20, 1977. He subsequently retired from political affairs.

KRIANGSAK CHAMAND (Prime Minister, November 12, 1977–February 29, 1980). Kriangsak Chamand was born in 1917. He was educated at the Royal Thai Military Academy and served in the Thai army. He saw action during World War II and the Korean War. Kriangsak rose to the position of chief of staff of the army in 1974. He was appointed deputy supreme commander of the Royal Thai Forces following the military coup led by Admiral Sangad Chaloryu in October of 1976. He served on the ruling Administrative Reform Council and became supreme commander of Thai military forces in September of 1977. Kriangsak was instrumental in the ouster of the government of Thanin Kraivichien the following month. He served as secretary-general of the new National Policy Council and was appointed prime minister on November 12, 1977. Parliamentary elections were held in April of 1979, and Kukrit Pramoj's Social Action party won a major victory. Kriangsak remained as head of the government despite the election results. Thailand's continuing economic difficulties led to a vote of no confidence in Kriangsak's government, and he was forced to resign on February 29, 1980. He organized the National Democracy party in June of 1981 and participated in Prem Tinsulanond's coalition government following elections in 1983. Kriangsak allegedly participated in an unsuccessful coup attempt against the government of Prem Tinsulanond in September of 1985. He was arrested and detained until February of 1986.

PREM TINSULANOND (Prime Minister, March 3, 1980–August 4, 1988). Prem Tinsulanond was born in Songkhla Province on August 26, 1920. He attended the Royal Thai Military Academy in Chula Chom Klao and entered the Thai cavalry in 1941. He rose through the ranks to become commander of the cavalry headquarters in 1968. Prem was appointed commander of the 2d Army in 1974 and was named to Prime Minister Kriangsak Chamand's cabinet as deputy minister of the interior in 1977. He was appointed minister of defense in 1979 and became commander in chief of the army. Prem was elected by Parliament to serve as prime minister of Thailand on March 3, 1980, following Kriangsak's resigna-

tion. His government was threatened by a coup in April of 1981, but he retained power with the support of King Bhumibol Adulyadej. He remained prime minister of a coalition government following elections in April of 1983. Prem survived another coup attempt in September of 1985. He continued as leader of a coalition government after elections in July of 1986 that gave a plurality to the Democrat party. Prem called new elections in July of 1988 and declined reappointment to office on August 4, 1988, when the election produced inconclusive results. He subsequently retired from active politics.

CHATICHAI   CHOONHAVAN (Prime Minister, August 4, 1988–February 23, 1991). Chatichai Choonhavan was born in Bangkok on April 5, 1922. He attended the Royal Thai Military Academy in Chula Chom Klao and entered the Royal Thai Army. Chatichai later served in the diplomatic corps and was Thailand's ambassador to numerous countries, including Argentina, Austria, Turkey, and Yugoslavia. He also represented Thailand at the United Nations. He returned to Thailand in 1972 and was named deputy foreign minister. Chatichai rose to the position of foreign minister in 1975 and was appointed minister of industry in 1976. He was a leader of the Thai Nation Party and served as deputy prime minister to Prem Tinsulanond from 1986. He became prime minister on August 4, 1988, following Prem's retirement. Chatichai also served in the government as minister of defense. He resigned on December 8, 1990, over a dispute with the military, but returned to office the following day. He was ousted by a military junta on February 23, 1991. Chatichai subsequently went into exile. His personal wealth was seized by the government in January of 1992. Chatichai returned to Thailand the following month to form the National Development party.

ANAND PANYARACHUN (Prime Minister, March 7, 1991–April 1992). Anand Panyarachun was born on August 9, 1932. He was educated at Bangkok Christian College and Cambridge University in Great Britain. He returned to Thailand and joined the Ministry of Foreign Affairs in 1955, where he served as secretary to the foreign minister in 1959. He was appointed first secretary to the Thailand Permanent Mission to the United Nations in 1964. Anand served as acting permanent representative to the United Nations and ambassador to Canada from 1967 until 1972. He subsequently was named permanent representative to the United Nations and ambassador to the United States and served from 1972 until 1975. He returned to Thailand to serve as undersecretary of state for foreign affairs from 1975 until 1976, and he was appointed ambassador to West Germany in 1977. Anand again returned to Thailand, where he joined the private sector and worked with various corporations. He was appointed acting prime minister on March 7, 1991, following a military coup that ousted Prime Minister Chatichai Choonhavan. He resigned in April of 1992, but was asked to form a new government on June 10, 1992. Anand took office as leader of the interim government and pledged to organize new elections. He stepped down on September 23, 1992,

after the selection of Chuan Leekpai as prime minister.

SUCHINDA KRAPRAYOON (Prime Minister, April 5, 1992–May 24, 1992). Suchinda Kraprayoon was born in 1938. He served in the Thai army and rose to the position of commander of the army. He took office as leader of a coalition government on April 5, 1992. Suchinda declared a state of emergency following civil unrest on May 18, 1992. He called in troops to break up student demonstrations in Bangkok and many casualties resulted. The brutal repression of the demonstrators led the king to intervene in the situation to seek a compromise between the rival factions. Rioting continued throughout the country, and Suchinda was forced to resign as prime minister on May 24, 1992, after the ruling coalition withdrew its support.

ANAND PANYARACHUN (Prime Minister, June 10, 1992–September 23, 1992). *See earlier entry under Heads of Government.*

CHUAN LEEKPAI (Prime Minister, September 23, 1992–). Chuan Leekpai was a leader of the Democratic party. His party was successful in the elections held in September of 1992, and Chuan was selected as prime minister on September 23, 1992.

Togo, Republic of
(République Togolaise)

Togo is a country off the western coast of Africa. It was granted independence from a United Nations trusteeship administered by France on April 27, 1960.

HEADS OF STATE

SYLVANUS OLYMPIO (President, April 27, 1960–January 13, 1963).

Sylvanus Olympio was born in Agone on September 6, 1902. He was educated at the London School of Economics and was employed by the United African Company in 1926. He entered politics as the leader of the Togolese Unity Committee and was a leading spokesman of the Ewe tribe in French Togoland. Olympio supported the reunification of French and British Togoland and was elected president of the Territorial Assembly in 1946. He was also a proponent of autonomy for French Togoland and was opposed by the French colonial government. The French actively supported Nicolas Grunitzky in elections to the Territorial Assembly in 1955, and Olympio's Togolese Unity Committee boycotted the elections. Olympio's supporters continued to advocate autonomy, and France was forced to grant Togo the status of a republic within the French community in 1956. British Togoland was incorporated into Ghana following a referendum later in the year. Olympio's party was victorious in elections in 1958, and he became prime minister on May 16, 1958. He led his country to complete independence on April 27, 1960, and became the nation's first president. Olympio established Togo as a single-party state the following year. He faced opposition from radicals and was the target of three assassination attempts in 1961. Olympio lost the support of elements of the army by denying entry into the Togo army of veterans of the French military. Olympio was ambushed by a group of ex-soldiers, who pursued the president to the United States Embassy, where he intended to seek asylum. He was shot to death by his pursuers at the gates of the embassy on January 13, 1963.

NICOLAS GRUNITZKY (President, January 16, 1963–January 13, 1967). Nicolas Grunitzky was born in Atakpame on April 5, 1913. He was educated in France, where he received a degree in engineering. He returned to French Togoland and worked as a construction engineer. Grunitzky joined the Free French forces during World War II and was elected to the French National Assembly in 1951. He received the support of the French colonial government in elections in 1956 and became chief minister of French Togoland on September 12, 1956. French Togoland was granted autonomy on April 27, 1958, and Grunitzky remained head of the government. He was subsequently defeated by Sylvanus Olympio's Togolese Unity Committee and stepped down from office on May 16, 1958. Grunitzky went into exile in France and Dahomey, where he remained until Olympio was killed by disgruntled army veterans in January of 1963. He returned to Togo to become president on January 16, 1963. He was successful in forming a coalition government which unified the various elements of the country. Grunitzky survived a coup attempt in November of 1966 after the collapse of his cabinet. He was forced from office by Lt. Col. Etienne Eyadema, the leader of the armed forces, on January 13, 1967. He went into exile in the Ivory Coast, where he was seriously injured in an automobile accident on September 24, 1969. Grunitzky was flown to Paris for medical treatment, where he died of his injuries at the age of 56 on September 27, 1969.

KLÉBER DADJO (President, January 13, 1967–April 14, 1967). Kléber Dadjo was born in Kabre, in central Togoland, on August 12, 1914. He was educated locally and joined the Togo Police Force in 1933. He remained on the force until 1938 and joined the Free French Army in June of 1941. Dadjo was trained in Accra and was posted throughout French West Africa. He was sent to France in August of 1948 and was posted to French Indochina a few months later. He fought with the French forces there until 1955. Dadjo then returned to Togo, where he rose to the rank of major and commander of the Garde Togolaise in 1960. He participated in the coup by French army veterans that ousted and killed President Sylvanus Olympio in January of 1963. He was subsequently promoted to lieutenant colonel. Dadjo was named head of President Nicolas Grunitzky's military cabinet with the rank of colonel in 1965. Grunitzky was ousted in a military coup led by Colonel Etienne Eyadema on January 13, 1967. Dadjo served as chairman of the National Reunification Committee that governed the country until April 14, 1967, when Eyadema took executive power. Dadjo was named to Eyadema's cabinet as minister of justice. He retired from the army and the government in 1969.

GNASSINGBE EYADEMA (President, April 14, 1967–). Etienne Gnassingbe Eyadema was born in Pya on December 26, 1937. He entered the French army in Dahomey in 1953 and saw action in Indochina and Algeria. He and other Togolese veterans of the French army were angered when President Sylvanus Olympio refused them entry into Togo's army after independence in 1960. Eyadema was a leader of the rebels who killed Olympio in January of 1963. He was subsequently admitted into the Togolese army and was promoted to the rank of captain the following year. He was appointed by President Nicholas Grunitzky to succeed Emmanuel Bodjolle as chief of staff of the army in May of 1965. Eyadema was promoted to lieutenant colonel the following October. He supported Grunitzky against a military revolt in November of 1966. Eyadema forced Grunitzky's ouster on January 13, 1967, and served as head of the ruling National Reconciliation Committee. His selection as president was confirmed in a referendum in January of 1972. Eyadema was unopposed in his reelection to the presidency in both December of 1979 and December of 1986. His government was faced with strikes and demonstrations demanding democratic reforms in October of 1990. The political opposition formed the Front of Associations for Renewal in March of 1991 and forced Eyadema to agree to multiparty elections. A National Conference was formed, and Joseph Kokou Koffigoh was elected as prime minister on August 27, 1991. The prime minister was granted most executive powers, though Eyadema remained in the now ceremonial position of president.

HEADS OF GOVERNMENT

NICOLAS GRUNITZKY (Chief Minister, September 12, 1956–April 27, 1958. Prime Minister, April 27, 1958–May 16, 1958). *See entry under Heads of State.*

SYLVANUS OLYMPIO (Prime Minister, May 16, 1958–April 27, 1960). *See entry under Heads of State.*

JOSEPH KOKOU KOFFIGOH (Prime Minister, August 27, 1991–). Joseph Kokou Koffigoh was born in Kpele Dafo in 1948. He was educated in France, where he received a degree in law. He returned to Togo and founded the Togo Bar Association in 1980. Koffigoh was active in the Togo Human Rights Organization and was appointed prime minister on August 27, 1991. He was granted executive powers from President Gnassingbe Eyadema by the National Conference on July 16, 1991.

Tonga, Kingdom of

(Fakatu'i 'o Tonga)

Tonga is a country consisting of a group of islands in the South Pacific Ocean. It was granted independence from Great Britain on June 4, 1970.

HEADS OF STATE

SALOTE TUPOU III (Queen, April 5, 1918–December 15, 1965). Queen Salote Tupou was born in Nukualofa on March 13, 1900. She was the oldest daughter of King George II of Tonga and succeeded him to the throne upon his death on April 5, 1918. She was a well-loved leader who established free educational facilities and health care for her people. Her husband, Prince Tungi, served as her prime minister from 1923 until his death in 1941. Salote Tupou made a public visit to Great Britain in 1953 upon the coronation of Queen Elizabeth II. She was hospitalized in Auckland, New Zealand, in November of 1965 for treatment for cancer and diabetes. Her condition worsened, and she died at the age of 65 on December 15, 1965.

TAUFA'AHAU TUPOU IV (King, December 15, 1965–   ). King Taufa'ahau Tupou IV was born Prince Tungi on July 4, 1918. He was the older son of Queen Salote Tupou III and Prince Uiliami Tupoulahi Tungi. The crown prince was educated locally and in Australia. He was named to the government as minister of education in 1943 and served as minister of health from 1944 until 1949. He served as his mother's prime minister from 1949 and also served as foreign minister and minister of agriculture. He succeeded to the throne following the death of Queen Salote Tupou on December 15, 1965, and was crowned King Taufa'ahau Tupou IV. Tonga remained a British protectorate until June 4, 1970, when independence was proclaimed. The king continued his rule as a constitutional monarch with his brother, Prince Fatafehi Tu'ipelchake, serving as his prime minister. His eldest son, Tupouto'a, was named crown prince. Tonga announced plans to allow greater democracy, and the formation of political parties was begun in the early 1990s.

HEADS OF GOVERNMENT

PRINCE FATAFEHI TU'IPELCHAKE (Prime Minister, June 4, 1970–August 21, 1991). Prince Fatafehi Tu'ipelchake was born in Tonga on January 7, 1922. He was the second son of Queen Salote Tupou III and Prince Uiliami Tungi and the brother of King Taufa'ahau Tupou IV. He was educated in Australia and served as governor of Vava'u from 1952 until 1965. He was named prime minister of Tonga in December of 1965 and remained in office following Tonga's independence on June 4, 1970. Prince Tu'ipelahake suffered from a stroke in 1985 and delegated many of his duties to Baron Vaea. He resigned from office because of ill health on August 21, 1991.

BARON VAEA (Prime Minister, August 21, 1991–). Baron Vaea was the cousin of King Taufa'ahau Tupou IV. He served in the cabinet of Prince Tu'ipelchake as minister of labor, commerce, and industry. He was selected to succeed Tu'ipelchake as prime minister on August 21, 1991.

Transkei, Republic of
(Iriphabliki Yetranskei)

Transkei is made up of three discontiguous areas in South Africa. It was granted independence from South Africa on October 26, 1966.

HEADS OF STATE

CHIEF BOTHA SIGCAU (President, October 26, 1976–December 1, 1978). Monzolwandle Botha Sigcau was born in 1913. He was paramount chief of the Pondo tribe and head of the territorial authority of Transkei when the area was granted some self-government in 1963. Sigcau was instrumental in writing the territory's constitution and became Transkei's first president when the African homeland was granted independence from South Africa on October 26, 1976. He attempted to establish a national identity for all the tribes represented in Transkei. Sigcau remained president until his death of a heart attack in the capital of Umtata at the age of 65 on December 1, 1978.

KAISER D. MATANZIMA (President, February 20, 1979–February 20, 1986). Kaiser Daliwonga Matanzima was born in Qamata in the St. Mark's District of South Africa on June 15, 1915. He was educated at missionary schools and the Fort Hare University College. He served as a member of the United Transkeian General Council from 1942 until 1956. Matanzima served as regional chief of Emigrant Tembuland from 1958 until 1961 and was presiding chief of the Transkeian Territorial Authority from 1961 until 1963. He

became chief minister of Transkei when the territory was granted limited home rule on December 11, 1963. He then became Transkei's prime minister when the country was granted independence from South Africa on October 26, 1976. Matanzima was elected to succeed Chief Botha Sigcau as president of Transkei on February 20, 1979. Matanzima opposed the creation of neighboring Ciskei as an independent state in 1981. His government supported several rebellions against the Ciskei government during the 1980s. Matanzima completed his term on February 20, 1986, and retired from office. Matanzima engaged in a dispute with his brother, Chief George Matanzima, over control of the nomination process for candidates in the Transkei National Independence party in 1987. Kaiser Matanzima formed the Transkei National party in May of 1987. He was then banished by his brother to his home village of Qamata. Both brothers were charged with corruption by Maj. Gen. Bantu Holomisa, who led a coup in September of 1987.

TUDOR NYANGELIZWE VULINO-LELA NDAMASE (President, February 20, 1986–). Paramount Chief Tudor Nyangelizwe Vulinolela Ndamase was elected president by the National Assembly on February 20, 1986, and succeeded the retiring Kaiser D. Matanzima. Ndamase retained office following the military coup led by General Bantu Holomisa on December 30, 1987. He also served as leader of the Transkei National Independence party.

HEADS OF GOVERNMENT

KAISER D. MATANZIMA (Prime Minister, October 26, 1976–February 20, 1979). *See entry under Heads of State.*

GEORGE MATANZIMA (Prime Minister, February 20, 1979–September 24, 1987). Chief George Matanzima was the brother of Chief Kaiser D. Matanzima. George Matanzima was selected to succeeded his brother as prime minister on February 20, 1979, when Kaiser Matanzima relinquished the office to become president. George Matanzima also became leader of the Transkei National Independence party. The brothers engaged in a dispute over candidate selection in the party in September of 1986. George Matanzima remained prime minister under President Nyangelizwe Vulindlela Ndamase. He was ousted in a military coup on September 24, 1987, following allegations of corruption and misuse of state funds. Matanzima was accused of various crimes and fled to South Africa.

BANTU HOLOMISA (Prime Minister, September 24, 1987–October 5, 1987). Harrington Bantubonke Holomisa was born in 1955. He served as a major general in the Transkei armed forces. He led a military coup to force the ouster of Prime Minister George Matanzima on September 24, 1987. He stepped down on October 5, 1987, and was replaced by Stella Sigcau. Holomisa led a second coup on December 30, 1987, and took control of the government as head of a military council. His regime was recognized by South Africa in January of 1988. Holomisa survived a coup attempt in November of 1990. He also considered a referendum to reincorporate Transkei into a democratic South Africa.

STELLA SIGCAU (Prime Minister, October 5, 1987–December 30, 1987). Stella Sigcau was the daughter of Transkei's first president, Chief Botha Sigcau. She served as minister of the interior in the country's first cabinet in 1976. She remained in the government and served as minister of posts and telecommunications in the cabinet of Prime Minister George Matanzima. Sigcau was selected to succeed Matanzima as prime minister following his ouster on October 5, 1987. She also served as leader of the ruling Transkei National Independence party. She was ousted in a military coup led by Maj. Gen. Bantu Holomisa on December 30, 1987.

BANTU HOLOMISA (Prime Minister, December 30, 1987–). *See earlier entry under Heads of Government.*

Trinidad and Tobago, Republic of

Trinidad and Tobago is a country consisting of two islands in the southeastern Caribbean Sea. It was granted independence from Great Britain on August 31, 1962.

HEADS OF STATE

SIR SOLOMAN HOCHOY (Governor-General, August 31, 1962–December, 1972). Soloman Hochoy was born in Jamaica on April 20, 1905. He was educated locally and was employed by the Trinidad Port and Marine Department from 1927. He took a position with the Department of Labor in 1939 and served as commissioner of labor from 1949 until 1955. Hochoy was appointed chief secretary in 1956 and became governor of Trinidad and Tobago in 1960. He became Trinidad and Tobago's first governor-general following independence on August 31, 1962. Hochoy retired from office in December of 1972. He died in Trinidad on November 14, 1983.

SIR ELLIS CLARKE (Governor-General, December, 1972–August 1, 1976. President, August 1, 1976–March 19, 1987). Ellis Emmanuel Innocent Clarke was born in Port of Spain on December 28, 1917. He was educated in Trinidad and London and received a degree in law. He served as solicitor general for Trinidad and Tobago from 1954 until 1956. Clarke was deputy colonial secretary from 1956 until 1957 and served as attorney general from 1957 until 1961. He was appointed ambassador to the United States in 1962 and served until 1973. He also served as permanent representative to the United Nations from 1962 until 1966. Clarke was appointed governor-general in December of 1972. He became the nation's first president when Trinidad and Tobago became a republic on August 1, 1976. He retired from office on March 18, 1987.

NOOR MOHAMMAD HASSANALI (President, March 18, 1987–   ). Noor Mohammad Hassanali was born on August 13, 1918. He was educated in Trinidad and Canada and received a degree in law. He returned to Trinidad and Tobago to begin a law practice. Hassanali was named to the judiciary and became high court judge in 1966. He was named an appeal justice on the Supreme Court in 1978 and retired in 1985. He subsequently served on the Judicial and Legal Service Commission. Hassanali became president on March 18, 1987.

HEADS OF GOVERNMENT

ERIC E. WILLIAMS (Chief Minister, September 25, 1956–August 31, 1962. Prime Minister, August 31, 1962–March 29, 1981). Eric Eustace Williams was born on September 25, 1911. He was educated locally and at Oxford University in Great Britain, where he received a degree in history and political science in 1932. He continued his education and received a doctorate in 1938. Williams came to the United States the following year and joined the faculty of Howard University in Washington, D.C. He also served on the Caribbean Commission from 1943 and was deputy chairman of the Caribbean Research Council from 1948 until 1955. He returned to Trinidad in 1955 and formed the People's National Movement. His party received a majority in Trinidad's legislative council, and Williams was selected as chief minister on September 25, 1956. He also served in the government as minister of finance, planning, and development. Trinidad participated in the short-lived West Indies Federation from 1958 until 1962. Williams became the first prime minister of independent Trinidad and Tobago on August 31, 1962, and also served as foreign minister. Trinidad was faced with a militant black power movement in the early 1970s, and Williams survived an attempted coup by the military in April of 1970. Williams announced his intentions to retire from office in October of 1973, but was persuaded to remain in office. His party was victorious in legislative elections in September of 1976. Williams retained office until his sudden death at his home in St. Anne at the age of 69 on March 29, 1981.

GEORGE CHAMBERS (Prime Minister, March 30, 1981–December 18, 1986). George Michael Chambers was born on Trinidad on October 4, 1928. He became a member of the People's National Movement and was elected to Parliament in 1966. He served as minister of finance from 1971 until 1975 and headed other ministries during the 1970s. Chambers was selected to succeed Eric Williams as prime minister and minister of finance on March 30, 1981, following Williams's sudden death. The People's National Movement was defeated in elections in 1986, and Chambers relinquished office to A.N.R. Robinson on December 18, 1986. He resigned as chairman of the party in 1988 and retired from politics.

A.N.R. ROBINSON (Prime Minister, December 18, 1986–December 7, 1991). Arthur Napoleon Raymond Robinson was born in Calder Hall on December 16, 1926. He was educated in Tobago and Great Britain. He became a member of the Parliament of the West Indies Federation in 1958 and served until 1961. Robinson was Trinidad's minister of finance from 1961 until 1967. He was active in the People's National Movement and served as minister of external affairs from 1967

until 1968. He chaired the Democratic Action Congress from 1971 and was a member of the House of Representatives from 1976 until 1980. Robinson served as chairman of the Tobago House of Assembly from 1980. He broke with the People's National Movement and formed the National Alliance for Reconstruction in 1984. He led the coalition to victory and became prime minister of Trinidad and Tobago on December 18, 1986. Robinson also served as minister of economy, and his popularity diminished when he devalued the currency and raised taxes. A coup attempt was staged by black Muslim radicals on July 27, 1990. The insurgents seized control of the Parliament building, and Robinson and many others were held hostage. Robinson was shot in the leg when he refused to sign a letter of resignation. The rebels surrendered on August 1, 1990, and Robinson was released. His party was defeated in the elections the following year, and he left office on December 7, 1991. He also resigned as leader of the National Alliance for Reconstruction party.

PATRICK MANNING (Prime Minister, December 20, 1991–). Patrick Augustus Mervyn Manning was born in Trinidad on August 17, 1946. He attended the University of West Indies and worked as a geologist for Texaco in Trinidad from 1965 until 1966. He served as a parliamentary secretary from 1971 until 1978. Manning later served in the cabinet as minister of energy from 1981 until 1986. From 1986 until 1990 he was the leader of the opposition National People's Movement. He was elected prime minister following elections on December 16, 1991, and took office on December 20, 1991.

Tunisia, Republic of

(al-Jumhiriyah al-Tunisiyah)

Tunisia is a country on the northern coast of Africa. It was granted independence from France on March 20, 1956.

HEADS OF STATE

MUHAMMAD VIII EL-AMIN (Bey, May 15, 1943–July 25, 1957). Muhammad el-Amin was born on September 4, 1881. He was a descendant of Hussein Bey, who was the first bey of Tunisia in 1705. Muhammad el-Amin was placed on the throne of Tunisia by the French on May 15, 1943. He served as bey of Tunisia under the French colonial government. Tunisia was granted independence on March 20, 1956, and the bey was relegated to the status of a figurehead when Habib Ben Ali Bourguiba became prime minister the following month. The bey was deposed by the National Assembly, and Tunisia was proclaimed a republic on July 25, 1957. He was placed under house arrest until 1960. He died in his small apartment in Tunis at the age of 81 on October 1, 1962.

HABIB BEN ALI BOURGUIBA (President, July 25, 1957–November 7, 1987). Habib Ben Ali Bourguiba was born in Monastir on August 3, 1903. He was educated locally and at the University of Paris, where he received a degree in law. He returned to Tunisia in 1928 to practice law. Bourguiba founded the Neo-Destour, or New Constitution, party in 1933 and became a leading advocate of Tunisian independence. The French colonial authorities banned the Neo-Destour party in 1934, and Bourguiba was arrested. He was released in 1936, but was rearrested two years later. He was held in France until 1942, when he was freed by the Germans during the occupation.

Bourguiba was sent to Rome and was allowed to return to Tunisia in April of 1943. He was rearrested by the French when the Allies entered Tunis the following month. He escaped in March of 1945 and went into exile, where he remained an outspoken proponent of Tunisian independence. Bourguiba returned to Tunisia in September of 1949 and began negotiations with the French colonial authorities. The negotiations were unsuccessful, and he was again arrested in January of 1952. The French ultimately agreed to Tunisian independence in July of 1954, and Bourguiba returned to Tunis in June of 1955. Tunisia was granted independence on March 20, 1956, and Bourguiba led the National Front to victory in elections to the Constituent Assembly. He was elected prime minister on April 10, 1956. The bey of Tunisia was deposed, and the monarchy was abolished on June 25, 1957. Tunisia was declared a republic, and Bourguiba stepped down as prime minister to assume the presidency. He was reelected president in 1959. Bourguiba forced the French to abandon Tunisian naval and air bases in the early 1960s. His leading political rival, Salah Ben Yusuf, was assassinated in exile in August of 1961. Bourguiba was again reelected in 1964 and 1969. He was considered a moderate Socialist, and his policies were criticized as being too cautious by his revolutionary neighbors in Algeria and Libya. Bourguiba was proclaimed president for life by the National Assembly in November of 1974. He suffered from failing health during the 1970s and 1980s, but retained firm control of the country. Various potential successors were dismissed from the government when Bourguiba viewed them as possible rivals. Bourguiba was relieved of his duties following recommendations by a panel of doctors that he was medically unfit for office. He was replaced as president by Prime Minister Zine al-Abidine Ben Ali on November 7, 1987. Bourguiba was placed under house arrest following his removal from office.

ZINE AL-ABIDINE BEN ALI (President, November 7, 1987–). Zine al-Abidine Ben Ali was born near Souse on September 3, 1936. He attended the St. Cyr Military Academy in France and studied electronic engineering at the School of Intelligence and Security in the United States. He served in the Tunisian armed forces and was director of military security from 1958 until 1974. Ben Ali was then posted to Morocco as military attaché until 1977. He returned to Tunisia to serve as head of national security in the Ministry of the Interior until April of 1980, when he was appointed ambassador to Poland. Ben Ali was recalled to Tunisia in October of 1984 to serve as secretary of state for internal security. He was named to the cabinet as minister of National Security in October of 1985 and was appointed minister of the interior in April of 1986. He replaced Rachid Sfar as prime minister on October 2, 1987. President Habib Bourguiba was suffering from poor health and was ruled medically unfit to continue in office on November 7, 1987. Ben Ali was sworn in as president and initiated a series of economic and political reforms. He was reelected to the presidency in April of 1989. His government faced mounting dissent from Islamic fundamentalists in the 1990s.

HEADS OF GOVERNMENT

TAHAR BEN AMMAR (Prime Minister, August 2, 1954–April 10, 1956). Tahar Ben Ammar was born in 1886. He was a moderate nationalist and one of Tunisia's largest land owners. He served as president of the Tunisian Chamber of Agriculture and was chosen by Bey Muhammad VIII el-Amin to serve as prime minister of Tunisia on August 2, 1954. Ben Ammar was not a member of the Neo-Destour party, but was acceptable to the party. He participated in the negotiations that led to Tunisia's independence on March 20, 1956. He continued to serve as prime minister of independent Tunisia until Habib Ben Ali Bourguiba returned to assume the office on April 10, 1956. Ben Ammar was subsequently accused of corruption in office.

HABIB BEN ALI BOURGUIBA (Prime Minister, April 10, 1956– July 25, 1957). *See entry under Heads of State.*

BAHI LADGHAM (Prime Minister, November 2, 1969–November 2, 1970). Bahi Ladgham was born in Tunis on January 10, 1913. He worked in the Department of the Interior from 1933 and later served in the Ministry of Finance. He became secretary-general of the Socialist Desturian party in 1953. Ladgham became secretary of state for the presidency and defense and served from 1956 until 1969. Ladgham was prime minister from November 2, 1969, until November 2, 1970. He served as chairman of the Arab Committee which supervised the peace settlement between the Jordanian government and Palestinian guerillas from September of 1970 until April of 1971. Ladgham resigned from the party and government in 1973.

HEDI NOUIRA (Prime Minister, November 2, 1970–February 26, 1980). Hedi Nouira was born in Monastir on April 6, 1911. He became secretary-general of the Confederation of Tunisian Workers in 1938 and was subsequently arrested. He remained in detention until 1943. Nouira served as secretary-general of the Neo-Destour party from 1942 until 1954. He was minister of commerce from 1954 until 1955 and was minister of finance from 1955 until 1958. He served as director of the Central Bank of Tunisia from 1958 until 1970. Nouira regained the post of secretary-general of the Neo-Destour party in 1969, and on November 2, 1970, he became prime minister. He remained in office until February 26, 1980, when he retired from government after suffering a stroke. Nouira died in Tunis after a long illness on January 25, 1993.

MOHAMMED MZALI (Prime Minister, March 1, 1980–July 8, 1986). Mohammed Mzali was born in Monastir on December 23, 1925. He was educated in Tunis and Paris and returned to Tunisia as a teacher. He headed the Ministry of Education from 1956 until 1958 and was elected to the National Assembly in 1959. Mzali headed several government agencies and was again named minister of education in 1969 and retained the position until 1973. He was then appointed minister of health, and in 1976 he returned to the Ministry of Education, where he served until 1980. He became prime minister on March 1, 1980 and retained the office until July 8, 1986. Mzali subsequently went into exile in Paris. He was tried and convicted in absentia for corruption in 1987.

RACHID SFAR (Prime Minister, July 8, 1986–October 2, 1987). Rachid Sfar was born in Mahdia on September 11, 1933. He was educated in Tunis and Paris and joined the Ministry of Finance on his return to Tunisia. He served as minister of finance from 1973 until 1977 and was minister of mines and energy from 1977 until 1978. Sfar was elected to the National Assembly in 1979. He remained in the cabinet as minister of defense from 1978 until 1980 and served as minister of health from 1980 until 1983. He was minister of national economy from 1983 until 1986. Sfar was named prime minister on July 8, 1986, and served until October 2, 1987. He became president of the Chamber of Deputies in 1988 and served as the Tunisian ambassador to the European Economic Community from 1989 until 1992.

ZINE AL-ABIDINE BEN ALI (Prime Minister, October 2, 1987–November 7, 1987). *See entry under Heads of State.*

HEDI BACCOUCHI (Prime Minister, November 7, 1987–September 27, 1989). Hedi Baccouchi was born in 1930. He was active in the movement for Tunisian independence and was arrested by the French government in 1952. He remained politically active and was named minister of social affairs in 1987. Baccouchi became prime minister on November 7, 1987, and served until September 27, 1989.

HAMED KAROUI (Prime Minister, September 27, 1989–   ). Hamed Karoui was born in Sousse on December 30, 1927. He studied medicine in Paris and became active in the nationalist Destour Movement in 1942. He returned to Tunisia and worked as a doctor at the Sousse Regional Hospital from 1957. Karoui served on the Municipal Council of Sousse from 1957 until 1972 and was also elected to the National Assembly in 1964. He served as vice president of the Chamber of Deputies from 1983 until 1986. He was named to the cabinet as minister of youth and sports in 1986 and served until the following year. Karoui was named minister of justice in 1988 and remained in that position until his selection as prime minister on September 27, 1989.

Turkey, Republic of

(Türkiye Cumhuriyeti)

Turkey is a country in southeastern Europe and western Asia.

HEADS OF STATE

ISMET INÖNÜ (President, November 11, 1938–May 22, 1950). Ismet Inönü was born in Inonu on September 25, 1884. He was educated at the Istanbul Military Academy and entered the Turkish army as a captain upon his graduation in 1906. He was active in the revolutionary movement of Young Turks that ousted Sultan Abdul-Hamid II in 1909. Inönü remained in the army and served in Yemen as chief of the General Staff in 1912 and participated in the Balkan war against Greece, Bulgaria, and Serbia. Inönü commanded Turkish troops in alliance with Germany during World War II. He rose to the rank of major general and became a leading advisor to Turkish nationalist leader Mustafa Kemal Atatürk. He again commanded troops against the Greeks in the early 1920s. Inönü joined the cabinet as minister of foreign affairs in 1922 and became Turkey's first prime minister following the proclamation of the Turkish Republic on October 29, 1930. He worked closely with President Atatürk to reform and modernize Turkey. His relationship with Atatürk became strained, and he stepped down as prime minister on October 25, 1937. Atatürk died the following year, and Inönü was chosen by the Grand National Assembly to serve as Turkey's president on November 11, 1938. He ruled in an authoritarian manner and rigidly controlled the political opposition and the press. Turkey remained neutral until the final months of World War II, when it declared war on the Axis powers. Inönü allowed the formation of opposition political parties after the war, and he was defeated by the Democratic party in Turkey's first two-party election in 1950. He relinquished office to Celâl Bayar on May 22, 1950 and became the leader of the Opposition in the Turkish Parliament. The Turkish military ousted the Democratic party government in 1961, and Inönü was asked to form a coalition government as prime minister on November 10, 1961. He maintained close relations with the United States and was a strong supporter of the North Atlantic Treaty Organization (NATO). His government survived coup attempts in January of 1962 and May of 1963. Inönü's government coalition collapsed on several occasions, but he was able to form new cabinets. His government was forced to resign on February 13, 1965, following the National Assembly's rejection of the budget. Inönü led the Republican People's party in opposition to the Justice party government of Süleyman Demirel. Inönü was replaced as leader of the party by Bülent Ecevit in 1972 and was given the ceremonial position of party chairman. He died of a heart attack at his home in Ankara at the age of 89 on December 25, 1973.

CELAL BAYAR (President, May 22, 1950–May 27, 1960). Mahmut Celâl Bayar was born in Umurbey on May 15, 1884. He was educated locally and worked as a bank clerk in Bursa. He joined the Young Turks movement in 1907 and participated in Mustafa Kemal Atatürk's rebellion that deposed Sultan Abdul Hamid II in 1909. Bayar served as a deputy in the Grand National Assembly after World War I and was named to the cabinet as minister of the economy in 1921. He was named minister of reconstruction in 1922. He left the government to reenter the banking industry in 1924. Bayar returned to the government as minister of national economy in 1932 and instituted programs to improve Turkey's economy. He was named to replace Ismet Inönü as prime minister on October 25, 1937. He retained office following Inönü's election to the presidency after Atatürk's death in November of 1938. Bayar resigned on January 25, 1939, and was replaced by Refik Saydam. He remained in the National Assembly until 1945, when he resigned to form the Democratic party with Adnan Menderes. He was reelected to the National Assembly the following year and served as a leader of the Opposition. The Democratic party was victorious in elections in 1950, and Bayar replaced Inönü as president on May 22, 1950. He pursued an economic policy that encouraged private industry, and he was reelected in 1954 and 1957. The growing authoritarian nature of the Democratic government led to student riots in April of 1960. The military led a coup that ousted Bayar and Prime Minister Adnan Menderes on May 27, 1960. Bayar and other leaders of the Democratic party were arrested by the new regime. Bayar and Menderes were sentenced to death. Menderes was hanged, but Bayar's sentence was commuted to life imprisonment due to his advanced age. He was released in a general amnesty in 1964, and his political rights were restored in 1974. He died in a hospital in Istanbul at the age of 102 on August 21, 1986.

CEMAL GÜRSEL (President, May 27, 1960–March 26, 1966). Cemal Gürsel was born in Erzurum in 1895. He entered the Turkish army in 1914 and served as an artillery officer during World War I. He saw action at Gallipoli

and in Palestine and was taken as a prisoner of war in Egypt in 1916. Gürsel was held prisoner for several years before returning to Turkey. He joined Mustafa Kemal Atatürk's nationalist movement after the war. He subsequently attended the Turkish War College and rose through the ranks of the army. Gürsel held various military positions and was promoted to brigadier general in 1946. He became a full general in 1957 and was named commander in chief of Turkish Land Forces. He opposed the attempts of Prime Minister Adnan Menderes to use the army for political purposes. A military coup ousted Menderes's government on May 27, 1960, and Gürsel headed the military junta, the Committee of National Unity. He served as president, prime minister, and minister of defense in the military regime. Gürsel forced the ouster of the more radical members of the junta in November of 1960 and reestablished a parliamentary government. He was officially confirmed as president of Turkey by the Parliament on October 26, 1961. He stepped down as prime minister on November 10, 1961, and Ismet Inönü assumed the position. Gürsel suffered a series of strokes and was incapacitated on February 2, 1966. He was taken to the United States and entered the Walter Reed Army Hospital in Washington, D.C. He went into a coma several days later and was returned to a military hospital in Ankara. When Gürsel's recovery appeared unlikely, the Turkish Parliament removed him from office on March 26, 1966. He remained in a coma until his death in Ankara at the age of 71 on September 14, 1966.

CEVDET SUNAY (President, March 28, 1966–March 28, 1973). Cevdet Sunay was born in Trabzon on February 10, 1900. He attended the Istanbul Military Academy and joined the army as a second lieutenant in 1917. He saw action in Palestine during World War I and was captured by the

British. Sunay was held prisoner in Egypt until the end of the war. He fought with Mustafa Kemal Atatürk against the Greeks in 1921 and entered the Istanbul War College to continue his education following the establishment of the Turkish Republic. He held various military positions and rose to the rank of brigadier general in 1949. Sunay was named chief of operations of the general staff in August of 1958 and was promoted to full general the following year. He was named commander in chief of Turkish Land Forces in August of 1961, after the military coup that ousted the government of Adnan Menderes. Sunay supported the government during military coup attempts in 1962 and 1963. He became a leading advisor to President Cemal Gürsel. Sunay was chosen by the Grand National Assembly to succeed Gürsel as president on March 28, 1966, after Gürsel suffered a series of crippling strokes. Sunay was a moderate leader who helped to negotiate compromises when the military and the government of Prime Minister Süleyman Demirel clashed. He led an interim military regime after Demirel's government was ousted by the armed forces in February of 1971. He presided over the restoration of democratic rule in 1973 and stepped down from office as president when his term expired on March 28, 1973. He subsequently remained inactive in politics. Sunay died after a long illness in an Istanbul hospital at the age of 82 on May 22, 1982.

FAHRI KORUTÜRK (President, April 6, 1973–April 6, 1980). Fahri S. Korutürk was born in Istanbul in 1903. He attended the Turkish Naval Academy and graduated in 1923. He served in the Turkish Navy and was named to the general staff intelligence department in 1934. Korutürk was appointed military attaché in Berlin in 1935 and was posted to Rome the following year. He again served as military attaché in Berlin during World War II from 1942 until 1943. He rose to the rank of admiral in 1957 and served as commander in chief of the Turkish Navy. Korutürk retired from the navy following the military coup in 1960. He was appointed ambassador to the Soviet Union by the military government. He retained that post until 1964, when he was named ambassador to Spain. Korutürk returned to Turkey in 1965 and was elected to the Senate in 1968. He was elected to succeed Cevdet Sunay as president of Turkey as a compromise choice and took office on April 6, 1973. He was unable to bring political stability to the country, and terrorism increased during his presidency. Korutürk completed his term of office on April 6, 1980, and retired from the government. He died in Istanbul at the age of 84 on October 12, 1987.

IHSAN SABRI CAĞLAYANGIL (Acting President, April 6, 1980–September 12, 1980). Ihsan Sabri Cağlayangil was born in Istanbul in 1908. He was educated at the School of Law. He entered government service and served as governor of Antalya from 1948 until 1953. Cağlayangil subsequently served as governor of Cannakale until 1954 and governor of Bursa from 1954 until 1960. He was elected to the Turkish Senate from Bursa in 1961. He served in the government as minister of labor from February until October of 1965. Cağlayangil was subsequently appointed foreign minister and served until 1971. He resumed his position at the Foreign Ministry in 1975 and served until 1977. Cağlayangil was elected president of the Senate in 1979. He became acting president of Turkey on April 6, 1980, when the Turkish Parliament failed to elect a successor to Fahri Korutürk. He retained office until September 12, 1980, when General Kenan Evren led a military coup against the government. Cağlayangil was detained by the military government for several months in 1983.

KENAN EVREN (President, October 27, 1980–November 9, 1989). Kenan Evren was born in Alasehir in 1918. He graduated from the Turkish Military Academy in Ankara in 1938 and served in the Turkish army. He commanded an artillery regiment during the Korean War and rose to the rank of general in 1964. Evren was named chief of staff of the armed forces in 1978. He led the military coup which ousted the civilian government of Süleyman Demirel in September of 1980. He served as chairman of the National Security Council and head of state from October 27, 1980. He was confirmed as president of Turkey by a referendum in November of 1982. Evren allowed the restoration of democratic rule, and Turgut Ozal was chosen as prime minister in December of 1983. Evren completed his term of office and stepped down on November 9, 1989.

TURGUT OZAL (President, November 9, 1989–April 16, 1993). Turgut Ozal was born in Malatya in 1927. He was educated at Istanbul Technical University. He worked with the State Planning Organization and later with the World Bank. Ozal became undersecretary of state planning in 1979 and was deputy prime minister from 1980 until 1982. The military, who had taken over the country in 1980, allowed parliamentary elections to be held in November of 1983. Ozal formed the conservative Motherland party and led it to victory in the election. He was sworn in as prime minister on December 13, 1983. His government was faced with violence from a secessionist movement by the Kurdish Turks. Ozal was able to negotiate a diplomatic treaty with Greece in the hopes of preventing further confrontations between the two countries. He suffered from heart problems in 1987 and went to the United States to undergo triple bypass surgery. The Motherland party was again victorious in parliamentary elections in November of 1987, and Ozal was returned to office. Ozal announced his candidacy for the presidency of Turkey in 1989, despite a drop in popularity for the Motherland party. He was elected president by the National Assembly and resigned as prime minister and leader of the party on November 9, 1989, to assume the presidency. Although the presidency was a largely ceremonial position, Ozal used his influence to continue to guide Turkey in a pro-Western direction. He was instrumental in allowing the United States-led coalition to use Turkish air bases for bombing runs over Iraq during the Persian Gulf War in 1991. Ozal died of heart problems in Ankara at the age of 66 on April 17, 1993.

HEADS OF GOVERNMENT

SÜKRÜ SARACOĞLU (Prime Minister, July 10, 1942–August 7, 1946). Sükrü Saracoğlu was born in Odemis in 1887. He was educated locally and attended the University of Lausanne, where he received a degree in law. He joined Mustafa Kemal Atatürk's nationalist movement and was elected to the Ottoman Parliament in 1919. Saracoğlu participated in the establishment of the Turkish Republic in 1923 and served as a member of Atatürk's Republican People's party in the Grand National Assembly. He was appointed to the cabinet as minister of finance in 1927 and was a close advisor to President Atatürk and Prime Minister Ismet Inönü. He left the cabinet in 1930 to serve as Turkey's economic emissary to the United States and France. Saracoğlu returned to Turkey to serve as minister of justice in 1932. He was named foreign minister in 1938 and negotiated treaties with Great Britain and France to preserve Turkey's neutrality during World War II. He was selected as prime minister on July 10, 1942, following the death of Refik Saydam. Saracoğlu remained foreign minister in the new government. He served as head of the government when Turkey declared war on the Axis powers near the end of World War II in February of 1945. Saracoğlu was replaced by Recep Peker as prime minister on August 7, 1946. He became president of the Republican People's party in 1947 and was elected president of the Grand National Assembly in 1948. Saracoğlu was defeated for reelection to the Assembly when the Democratic party came to power in general elections in 1950. He retired from politics and died at his home in Istanbul at the age of 66 on December 27, 1953.

RECEP PEKER (Prime Minister, August 7, 1946–September 9, 1947). Recep Peker was born in Istanbul in 1888. He was educated locally and graduated from the Yildiz War Academy in 1907. He saw action in the Balkan War in 1912 and fought against Russian troops in World War I. Peker joined Mustafa Kemal Atatürk's nationalist movement and served as parliamentary secretary to the Grand National Assembly from April of 1923. He became secretary-general of Atatürk's Republican People's party later in the year. He was named to the cabinet as minister of the interior in March of 1924 and became minister of national defense the following year. Peker served until December of 1927 and was named minister of public works in October of 1928. He resigned from the cabinet in March of 1931 to resume the position of secretary-general of the Republic People's party. The position was eliminated in 1936, but Peker remained a parliamentary leader of the party. He returned to the cabinet as minister of the interior in August of 1942. He stepped down for reasons of health in May of 1943. Peker was appointed to replace Sükrü Sara-

coğlu as prime minister on August 7, 1946. Turkish President Ismet Inönü allowed the formation of opposition parties, and Peker abruptly resigned from office on September 9, 1947. He died of a heart attack in Istanbul at the age of 62 on April 2, 1950.

HASAN SAKA (Prime Minister, September 9, 1947–January 16, 1949). Hasan Saka was born in Trabzon in 1886. He was educated at the School of Public Service and continued his education in Paris, where he studied economics. He was elected to the Grand National Assembly in 1920. Saka served in various governmental positions during the 1920s and 1930s and was selected as foreign minister near the end of World War II. He helped convince the Grand National Assembly to enter the war on the side of the Allies in February of 1945. He was selected to succeed Recep Peker as prime minister on September 9, 1947. His government was criticized for its failure to solve Turkey's economic difficulties, and he restructured his cabinet in June of 1948. The economy continued to suffer from rising inflation, and Saka resigned on January 16, 1949. He was politically inactive after the Democratic party's victory the following year. Saka died of cancer at his home in Istanbul at the age of 74 on July 30, 1960.

SEMSETTIN GÜNALTAY (Prime Minister, January 16, 1949–May 22, 1950). Semsettin Günaltay was born in Kiemaliye in 1883. He was educated at the University of Istanbul and was elected a deputy from Bilecik in 1915. He served as a history professor at the University of Istanbul and was active in Mustafa Kemal Atatürk's nationalist movement. Günaltay was elected to the Grand National Assembly in 1923. He was a founder of the Turkish Historical Society in 1931 and became the society's president in 1941. He held various government positions and served as minister of state and vice president of the

National Assembly in the late 1940s. Günaltay was chosen to succeed Hasan Saka as prime minister on January 16, 1949. He initiated economic reforms and introduced a new electoral law that resulted in his party's defeat by the Democratic party in elections in 1950. He was replaced as prime minister by Democratic Party leader Adnan Menderes on May 22, 1950. Günaltay remained in the Parliament as a member of the Opposition until his retirement in 1954. He remained a member of the Republican People's party and was elected to the Turkish Senate in October of 1961. He died of cancer four days later at an Istanbul hospital at the age of 79 on October 19, 1961.

ADNAN MENDERES (Prime Minister, May 22, 1950–May 27, 1960). Adnan Menderes was born in Aydin in 1899. He was educated at the American College in Izmir and received a law degree from the University of Ankara. Menderes became a member of the Republican People's party and was elected to the National Assembly in 1930. He resigned from the Parliament in 1945 to form the Democratic party. He became the leader of the opposition to the government formed by the Republican People's party. Menderes led the Democratic party to victory in general elections in 1950 and was selected as prime minister on May 22, 1950. His government led Turkey into joining the North Atlantic Treaty Organization and served as a sponsor of the Baghdad Pact. His party remained in power in elections in 1954 and 1957. Menderes introduced legislation to control the opposition and the press. The increasingly authoritarian nature of his government led to a military coup on May 27, 1960, and Menderes was deposed as prime minister. He was charged with crimes against the Turkish constitution, including corruption and extravagance. He was convicted and sentenced to death. Menderes attempted suicide by

taking an overdose of sleeping pills after hearing the verdict. He recovered and was executed by hanging on the island of Imrali on September 17, 1961.

CEMAL GÜRSEL (Prime Minister, May 27, 1960–November 10, 1961). *See entry under Heads of State.*

ISMET INÖNÜ (Prime Minister, November 10, 1961–February 13, 1965). *See entry under Heads of State.*

SUAT HAYRI URGÜPLÜ (Prime Minister, February 13, 1965–October 27, 1965). Ali Suat Hayri Urgüplü was born in Damascus, Syria, in 1902. He was educated at the University of Istanbul, where he received a degree in law. He became a magistrate at the Supreme Commercial Court in Istanbul in 1929. Urgüplü entered private practice in 1932. He was elected to the National Assembly in 1939 and served in the government as minister of customs and monopolies from 1943 until 1946. He then resigned from the government and left the Republican People's party. Urgüplü joined the Democratic party and was reelected to the National Assembly in 1950. He served as Turkey's ambassador to West Germany from 1952 until 1955. He was named ambassador to Great Britain in 1955 and served until 1957, when he was posted to the United States. Urgüplü returned to Turkey in 1960 after having served briefly in Spain. He was elected to the Turkish Senate in 1961 and served as Speaker of the Senate until 1963. Urgüplü led a coalition government following the resignation of Ismet Inönü as prime minister on February 13, 1965. He retained office until October 27, 1965, when the Justice party won a landslide victory in general elections. He relinquished office to Süleyman Demirel. Urgüplü again served in the Senate in 1966. He was again designated prime minister by President Cevdet Sunay on April 29, 1972. He was unable to form a government which met with the approval of Turkey's military commanders, however, and he was relieved of his assignment on May 13, 1972. Urgüplü retired from politics and died at the age of 79 on December 26, 1981.

SÜLEYMAN DEMIREL (Prime Minister, October 27, 1965–February 12, 1971). Süleyman Demirel was born in Islamkoy, Isparta Province, on October 6, 1924. He attended the Istanbul Technical University, where he graduated with a degree in civil engineering in 1948. He entered the civil service and worked on various government projects. Demirel was named director of the State Water Board in 1955. He entered politics in 1961 and joined the newly formed Justice party. He was elected to the National Assembly and was elected president of the party following the death of General Ragip Gomuspala in November of 1964. Demirel was appointed deputy prime minister in a coalition cabinet in February of 1965. The Justice party was victorious in general elections later in the year, and Demirel took office as prime minister on October 27, 1965. He attempted to restrain right-wing extremists in his party and to maintain good relations with the army. Turkey forced the removal of Greek troops from Cyprus after rioting between Greek and Turkish Cypriots in 1966. Demirel remained in power following general elections in October of 1969, but his government was faced with student demonstrations and labor strikes in 1970. He declared martial law in June of 1970 because of increasing public disorders. The military forced Demirel's resignation on February 12, 1971. He remained in the National Assembly, and members of his party sat in a series of above-party governments. The Justice party lost support in elections in October of 1973. The Republican People's party, under Bülent Ecevit, formed a coalition government in January of

1974, and Demirel remained leader of the Opposition. Ecevit called early elections later in the year that produced inconclusive results. Neither party was able to form a viable coalition until Demirel entered the Justice party into a four-party coalition with parties of the extreme right. He was again selected as prime minister on March 31, 1975. The Republicans became the majority party following elections in June of 1977, and Demirel stepped down on June 21, 1977. He refused to form a grand coalition with the Republican party, but instead formed a coalition with two smaller parties and took office on July 21, 1977. Demirel was again forced to step down on December 21, 1977, after he receiving a vote of no confidence. He led the Opposition until November 12, 1979, when he formed a minority government. Continuing violence and an unstable government led the Turkish military to oust Demirel in a coup on September 20, 1980. Demirel was arrested following the coup, but was released the following month. He formed the Grand Turkey party in May of 1983. The party was banned shortly after its formation, and Demirel was again imprisoned until September of 1983. He subsequently formed the True Path party, which was unsuccessful in local elections in March of 1984. He was a leader of the Opposition to the government of Turgut Ozal and the True Path party increased its representation in the National Assembly in elections in 1987 and 1991. Demirel formed a coalition government and returned to office as prime minister on November 20, 1991.

NIHAT ERIM (Prime Minister, March 19, 1971–April 17, 1972). Nihat Erim was born in Kandira in 1912. He attended the University of Istanbul and the University of Paris and received a degree in law. He returned to Turkey to serve as a law professor at Ankara University. Erim was appointed to the Ministry of Foreign Affairs as a legal advisor in 1942. He joined the Republican People's party and was elected to the National Assembly in 1945. He served as minister of public works and deputy prime minister from 1948 until 1950. Erim retired from politics in 1950 following the rise of the Democratic party to power. He was again elected to the National Assembly in 1961 and represented the Turkish Parliament at the European Council until 1970. Erim was named prime minister on March 19, 1971, and served as head of a coalition government while Turkey was under martial law. His government outlawed extremist parties on the left and the right and banned poppy-growing in Turkey. He resigned from office on April 17, 1972, when the National Assembly refused his request for extraordinary powers to combat terrorism. Erim subsequently served in the Turkish Senate. He was shot and killed by leftist terrorists at his summer home in Kartal, near Istanbul, on July 19, 1980.

FERIT MELEN (Prime Minister, May 22, 1972–April 15, 1973). Ferit Melen was born in Van in 1906. He was educated at the University of Ankara, where he studied political science. He became an auditor at the Ministry of Finance in 1933 and rose to the position of director-general of incomes in 1943. Melen was elected to the National Assembly in 1950 as a member of the Republican People's party. He was named to the government as minister of finance in 1962. He remained in Ismet Inönü's cabinet until 1965. Melen was a founder of the National Reliance party in 1967 and served as deputy leader. He returned to the government as minister of national defense under Nihat Erim in 1971. He became prime minister of a coalition government on May 22, 1972. Melen stepped down on April 15, 1973. He returned to the cabinet as minister of defense in 1975 and served until 1977. He formed a minor political party in 1986 that advocated closer ties between

Turkey and the United States. Melen died of a heart condition in Ankara at the age of 82 on September 3, 1988.

NAIM TALÛ (Prime Minister, April 15, 1973–January 25, 1974). Naim Talû was born in Istanbul on July 22, 1919. He was educated at Istanbul University, where he studied economics. He was employed by the Central Bank of Turkey in 1946, and became its president in 1967. Talû was appointed minister of commerce in 1971 and served until 1973. He became prime minister of a coalition cabinet with the Justice party and the Republican Reliance party on April 15, 1973. He retained office until January 25, 1974, when he was replaced by Bülent Ecevit. Talû remained in the Turkish Senate until 1976 and then returned to the banking industry.

BÜLENT ECEVIT (Prime Minister, January 25, 1974–November 7, 1974). Bülent Ecevit was born in Istanbul on May 28, 1925. He attended Robert College in Istanbul and received a degree in literature in 1944. He continued his education at Ankara University while serving as a press attaché for the Turkish government. Ecevit was stationed in London from 1946 and studied art history at London University. He became a member of the Republican People's party in 1950 and joined the staff of *Ulus*, the party newspaper. He was elected to the Turkish Parliament in 1957 and served in the assembly that drafted a new constitution in 1960. Ecevit served in Prime Minister Ismet Inönü's cabinet as minister of labor from 1961 until 1965. He was elected secretary-general of the Republican People's party in 1966 and became a leader of the leftist faction of the party. The Turkish military took control of the government in March of 1971. Ecevit challenged Inönü for the party's leadership in May of 1972 and became chairman of the party. He led the party to victory in a general election campaign when the military restored civilian rule to the country. He was unable to form a coalition government until January 25, 1974, when he joined forces with the Islamic National Salvation party. The Greek military government sponsored a coup against Archbishop Makarios III in July of 1974. Ecevit ordered Turkish troops to invade Cyprus to oust the Greek-backed junta, and Turkey controlled nearly half of the island before agreeing to a cease-fire. Ecevit's coalition collapsed due to differences with the National Salvation party in September of 1974. He was unable to form a new government and was replaced by an interim government led by Sadi Irmak on November 7, 1974. The Justice party under Süleyman Demirel formed a government the following March and Ecevit remained the leader of the Opposition. General elections were held in June of 1977 in which no party received a majority. Ecevit was named to lead a minority government on June 21, 1977. He was unable to form a viable coalition and was replaced by Demirel on July 21, 1977. He was called upon to form a minority coalition government on January 1, 1978. The country was plagued by widespread unrest, and Ecevit declared martial law in December of 1978. He was again replaced by Demirel on November 12, 1979. The military ousted the government in September of 1980, and Ecevit was briefly detained by the military government. He was again arrested by the military regime in December of 1981 and was released in February of 1982. He was rearrested the following April and was imprisoned from August until October of 1982. Ecevit was barred from political activity, and his wife, Rahsan, announced the formation of the Democratic Left party in March of 1984. Ecevit became chairman of the party following the restoration of his political rights in September of 1987, but his party received little support in subsequent elections.

SADI IRMAK (Prime Minister, November 17, 1974–March 31, 1975). Sadi Irmak was born in Seydisehir, Konya, on May 15, 1901. He studied medicine at the University of Istanbul and the University of Berlin. He returned to Turkey and taught physiology at Istanbul University. Irmak was elected to the National Assembly in 1943 and served as minister of labor from 1945 until 1947. He was elected to the Senate in 1974 and became prime minister on November 17, 1974. He retained office until March 31, 1975, and remained in the Senate until 1980. Irmak served as president of the Constituent Assembly from 1981 until 1983.

SÜLEYMAN DEMIREL (Prime Minister, March 31, 1975–June 21, 1977). *See earlier entry under Heads of Government.*

BÜLENT ECEVIT (Prime Minister, June 21, 1977–July 21, 1977). *See earlier entry under Heads of Government.*

SÜLEYMAN DEMIREL (Prime Minister, July 21, 1977–December 21, 1977). *See earlier entry under Heads of Government.*

BÜLENT ECEVIT (Prime Minister, January 1, 1978–November 12, 1979). *See earlier entry under Heads of Government.*

SÜLEYMAN DEMIREL (Prime Minister, November 12, 1979–September 20, 1980). *See earlier entry under Heads of Government.*

BÜLENT ULUSU (Prime Minister, September 20, 1980–November 23, 1983). Bülent Ulusu was born in Istanbul on November 20, 1927. He attended the Naval Academy and rose through the ranks to become admiral in 1974. He served as commander of the Turkish Naval Forces until 1980. Ulusu served as undersecretary of the Ministry of Defense. He became prime minister of a military-civilian cabinet on September 20, 1980. A new constitution was approved in November of 1982, and elections were held in November of the following year. Turgut Ozal's Motherland party was victorious, and Ozal replaced Ulusu as prime minister on November 23, 1983. Ulusu was elected to Parliament in 1983 and served until 1987.

TURGUT OZAL (Prime Minister, December 13, 1983–November 9, 1989). *See entry under Heads of State.*

YILDIRIM AKBULUT (Prime Minister, November 9, 1989–June 24, 1991). Yildirim Akbulut was born in Erzincan in 1935. He attended the University of Istanbul and graduated with a degree in law. He was elected to Parliament in 1983 and served as minister of the interior from 1986 until 1987. Akbulut then served as Speaker of the Parliament from 1987 until 1989. He became prime minister on November 9, 1989, but he resigned from office when he was defeated by Mesut Yilmaz for the leadership of the Motherland party. Akbulut relinquished the office of prime minister to Yilmaz on June 24, 1991.

MESUT YILMAZ (Prime Minister, June 24, 1991–November 20, 1991). A. Mesut Yilmaz was born in Istanbul on November 6, 1947. He was educated in Turkey, Great Britain, and France. He worked in private industry and was elected to Parliament in 1983. Yilmaz served as minister of culture and tourism from 1986 until 1987 and was foreign minister from 1987 until 1990. He defeated Prime Minister Yildirim Akbulut for the leadership of the Motherland party in June of 1991 and replaced Akbulut as prime minister on June 24, 1991. He called for an early election, and the Motherland party was defeated by Süleyman Demirel's True Path party. Yilmaz stepped down as prime minister on November 20, 1991.

SÜLEYMAN DEMIREL (Prime Minister, November 20, 1991–). *See earlier entry under Heads of Government.*

Turkmenistan, Republic of
(Tiurkmenostan Respublikasy)

Turkmenistan is a country in central Asia. It became independent following the breakup of the Soviet Union on December 25, 1991.

HEAD OF STATE

SAPARMURAD NIYAZOV (President, October 27, 1990–). Saparmurad Atayevich Niyazov was born in 1940. He attended the Leningrad Polytechnic Institute and joined the Communist party in 1962. He worked as a technical instructor and was active in party organizations. Niyazov served as prime minister of the Turkmen Soviet Socialist Republic in 1985 and was first secretary of the Turkmen Communist party from 1985 until 1991. He was elected chairman of the Supreme Soviet on January 19, 1990, and was elected to the position of president on October 27, 1990. Turkmenistan declared its independence in October of 1991 and joined the Commonwealth of Independent States in December of 1991. Niyazov remained head of state as the first president of independent Turkmenistan. He was reelected to the office on June 21, 1992.

Tuvalu, Constitutional Monarchy of
(Fakavae Aliki-Malo i Tuvalu)

Tuvalu is a country consisting of a group of atolls in the South Pacific Ocean. It was granted independence from Great Britain on October 1, 1978.

HEADS OF STATE

PENITALA FIATAU TEO (Governor-General, October 1, 1978–March 1, 1986). Penitala Fiatau Teo was born on July 23, 1911. He was educated locally and worked as a clerk on Ellice Island. He joined the resident commissioner's office in 1937 and remained in the colonial government. Teo was appointed district commissioner for Ocean Island in 1963 and for Ellice Island in 1967. He became governor-general of Ellice Island when it was granted independence as Tuvalu on October 1, 1978. He retired from office on March 1, 1986.

SIR TUPUA LEUPENA (Governor-General, March 1, 1986–March 1, 1990). Tupua Leupena was born on August 2, 1922. He was educated locally and worked as a clerk from 1945. He became chief clerk in 1953 and worked in the resident commissioner's office from 1957. Leupena became a district official in 1973. He was elected to Tuvalu's Parliament following independence in 1978. He also served as chairman of the Tuvalu Public Service Commission from 1982 until his selection as governor-general on March 1, 1986. Leupena completed his term of office and retired on March 1, 1990.

SIR TOARIPI LAUTTI (Governor-General, March 1, 1990–   ). Toaripi Lautti was born in Papua New Guinea on November 28, 1928. He was educated as a teacher and taught in Tarawa, in the Gilbert Islands, from 1953 until 1962. He served as an executive with the Phosphate Commission for Nauru from 1962 until 1974. Lautti returned to Tuvalu and became chief minister in October of 1975. Following the granting of independence to Ellice Island, which became known as Tuvalu, Lautti became the first prime minister on October 1, 1978. He remained in office until September 8, 1981, when he was defeated by a parliamentary vote following Tuvalu's first general elections. He subsequently served as the leader of the Opposition until March 1, 1990, when he succeeded Sir Tupua Leupena as governor-general.

HEADS OF GOVERNMENT

TOARIPI LAUTTI (Chief Minister, October 1975–October 1, 1978. Prime Minister, October 1, 1978–September 8, 1981). *See entry under Heads of State.*

TOMASI PUAPUA (Prime Minister, September 8, 1981–October 16, 1989). Tomasi Puapua was born on September 10, 1938. He attended the Fiji School of Medicine and the University of Otago in New Zealand and graduated with a medical degree. Puapua was elected prime minister of Tuvalu on September 8, 1981. He also served as foreign minister and minister of civil service. He retained office until October 16, 1989, when he stepped down following the defeat of two cabinet members in parliamentary elections.

BIKENIBEAU PAENIU (Prime Minister, October 16, 1989–). Bikenibeau Paeniu was born in 1956. He served in the Parliament and was selected to succeed Tomasi Puapua as prime minister on October 16, 1989. He also served in the government as foreign minister and minister of economic planning.

Uganda, Republic of

Uganda is a country in central eastern Africa. It was granted independence from Great Britain on October 9, 1962.

HEADS OF STATE

SIR WALTER COUTTS (Governor-General, October 9, 1962–October 9, 1963). Walter Fleming Coutts was born in Aberdeen, Scotland, on November 30, 1912. He was educated at St. Andrew's University and St. John's College, Cambridge. He entered the British Colonial Service in Kenya as a district officer in 1936. Coutts rose to district commissioner in 1947. He served as minister of education, labor, and lands in the Kenyan government from 1956 until 1958 and was chief secretary from 1958 until 1961. Coutts was appointed governor of Uganda in November of 1961. He became the first governor-general of Uganda on October 9, 1962. He relinquished office on October 9, 1963, when Uganda was declared a republic. Coutts retired from the colonial service and settled in Australia. He served as chairman of Pergamon Press from 1972 until 1974. Coutts died at the age of 75 in Perth, Western Australia, on November 4, 1988.

SIR EDWARD MUTESA II (President, October 9, 1963–March 2, 1966). Edward Frederick William Waiugembe Mutebi Tuwangeula Mutesa was born in Makindye on November 19, 1924. He was the only son of Sir Daudi Chwa II, the kabaka of Buganda. He was educated at King's College in Budo and succeeded his father as kabaka in 1939. Mutesa continued his education at Makerere College in Kampala and Magdalene College at Cambridge University in Great Britain, where he became known as "King Freddie." He returned to Buganda after he completed his studies and was active in the nationalist movement. He was deported by Governor Sir Andrew Cohen in October of 1953 for refusing to cooperate with the British colonial government. Mutesa was allowed to return from exile in October of 1955. The British colonial government recognized him as a constitutional monarch, and he took a leading role in constitutional conferences held in London in 1961 and 1962. He joined forces with Ugandan prime minister Milton Obote and became Uganda's first president when the country was declared a republic on

October 9, 1963. Mutesa worked in cooperation with Obote for several years, and Buganda was granted some autonomy by the federal government. The kabaka broke with Obote's government in 1966, and Obote led a coup to overthrow the constitution. He ousted Mutesa as president and captured the Bugandan Palace. The kabaka escaped from federal troops and fled to Burundi, where he was granted asylum. He subsequently went into exile in London. He died of a heart attack in his modest London apartment at the age of 45 on November 21, 1969.

APOLLO MILTON OBOTE (President, March 2, 1966–January 25, 1971). Apollo Milton Obote was born in Akokoro, Lango District, in 1925. He was educated at local mission schools and attended Makerere College until 1950. He was prevented by colonial authorities from accepting a scholarship to study law in the United States. Obote subsequently traveled to Kenya, where he became active in the trade union movement. He joined Jomo Kenyatta's Kenya National Union. Obote returned to Uganda in 1955 to establish the Uganda National Union (UNC) in Lagos. He was elected to the Ugandan Legislative Council in 1958. The following year he became president of the Uganda People's Congress, following a split with the UNC. Obote became leader of the Opposition to the government of Benedicto Kiwanuka following elections in March of 1961. He formed a coalition with the Bugandan Kabaka Yekka (King Only) party and gained a victory in elections to the National Assembly in April of 1962. Obote was sworn in as prime minister on April 25, 1962. Uganda was granted independence on October 9, 1962. Obote was instrumental in the selection of Frederick Mutesa, the kabaka, or king of Buganda, to become Uganda's president in October of 1963. Members of the Opposition charged that Obote and army leader Idi Amin were impli-

cated in smuggling gold from the former Belgian Congo. Parliament demanded Amin's ouster and a government inquiry into the allegations. Obote responded by suspending the constitution and detaining several cabinet members. He was cleared by an independent enquiry, but President Mutesa challenged Obote's right to suspend the constitution. Obote ousted the president on March 2, 1966, and took full control of the government. He was officially sworn in as executive president on April 15, 1966. Uganda was declared a republic in September of 1967 and a new constitution was established that granted vast powers to the president. Obote launched a five-year plan to improve Uganda's economic development in 1966, and he promoted a socialist economic system for the country in 1969. He met with the Uganda People's Congress in December of 1969 and declared Uganda a one-party state. Obote was seriously injured when he was shot in the face by an attempted assassin while leaving a UPC meeting on December 19, 1969. He recovered from his wounds and proceeded with plans to socialize Uganda's economy. Discontent with Obote's government and policies grew throughout the country. Obote attempted to curtail the power of Amin, his army commander in chief, in September of 1970, but Amin was able to maintain the support of the majority of the army. Amin staged a military coup against Obote on January 25, 1971, while the president was in Singapore for a meeting of Commonwealth prime ministers. Obote was granted political asylum in Tanzania by President Julius Nyerere. He was accompanied by a large contingent of loyal troops. Obote launched an unsuccessful attack against Amin's government in September of 1972. Obote denounced Amin as a brutal dictator and remained in Tanzania for the next eight years. Nyerere ordered an attack on Uganda following border clashes between the two countries in

November of 1978. Tanzanian and Ugandan exile troops invaded Uganda in February of 1979, and Amin fled the country the following April. Obote's return to power was opposed by exile leaders and a nonparty government was formed under Yusufu K. Lule. Lule was replaced by Godfrey Binaisa, who was ousted in a pro-Obote coup led by Paulo Muwanga. Obote returned to Uganda to campaign for the presidency. Obote's Uganda People's Congress was the winner in the election, and Obote was again sworn into office as president on December 17, 1980. He tried to establish order in the war-ravaged country, but his government was challenged by dissidents and several guerrilla armies. Obote resumed government oppression of the opposition, but ordered the release of a number of political opponents in an amnesty in 1982. Although he made some gains in improving the country's economic stability, his government continued to be threatened by rebel troops. Obote's government was also threatened by discontent in the army. He was ousted by a military coup on July 27, 1985, and went into exile in Kenya. He later settled in Zambia.

IDI AMIN DADA (President, January 25, 1971–April 11, 1979). Idi Amin Dada was born in Koboko in the Kakwa Region in 1925. He entered the British army in 1943 and saw action in Burma near the end of World War II. He returned to Uganda to assist in the campaign against tribal marauders in 1946. Amin also fought with the British to put down the Mau Mau rebellion in Kenya in the 1950s. He was promoted to sergeant major and returned to Uganda in 1957. He rose to the rank of major in the Ugandan army following his country's independence in 1963. Amin was promoted to colonel in 1964 and was named deputy commander of the Ugandan armed forces. In 1966 he was accused of smuggling gold and ivory from the Congo. President

Milton Obote was also implicated in the action. The president suspended the constitution and ordered Amin to arrest the opposition leaders. Obote appointed Amin commander in chief of the army and air force. Amin initially remained loyal to Obote and rose to the rank of major general in 1968. Obote began to consider Amin a rival to his power and sought to undermine his influence in the army. Amin responded by consolidating his support and ousting Obote in a military coup on January 25, 1971. Amin took control of the government and abolished the Parliament. He was proclaimed president on February 20, 1971. Amin solicited foreign aid from Israel, but when Israeli officials failed to supply him a sufficient amount, he expelled them from the country and allied himself with Libyan president Muammar al-Qaddafi. He also forced Asian merchants from the country in August of 1971. The following month Amin repelled an invasion from Tanzania by supporters of former president Obote. Amin also expelled the majority of British citizens from Uganda in January of 1973 and nationalized British-owned firms. He survived a military coup attempt in March of 1974 following the dismissal and murder of Foreign Minister Lt. Col. Michael Ondoga. The coup, led by Brigadier Charles Arube, was crushed, and Arube and many of his supporters were killed. Amin arrested British lecturer Denis Hills in 1975 in order to use him as a hostage to gain military supplies from Great Britain. Hills was convicted of spying and sentenced to death, but was released following the intervention of President Mobutu Sese Seko of Zaire. Palestinian terrorists hijacked an airplane traveling from Tel Aviv to Paris in July of 1976. The Palestinians landed the plane, with 103 hostages aboard, at Entebbe airport in Uganda. An Israeli commando raid rescued the hostages and destroyed a portion of Amin's air force. Amin continued his reign of brutality and terror and summarily executed anyone suspected of being an opponent of his government. The murder of Anglican archbishop Janani Luwum and two members of the cabinet on February 16, 1977, prompted a harsh rebuke from United States president Jimmy Carter. Amin responded by rounding up American citizens remaining in Uganda. The United States sent a naval force to Mombasa, and Amin released the Americans unharmed. Amin survived another coup attempt in July of 1978, with the assistance of Palestinian troops sent from Libya. Uganda's relationship with neighboring Tanzania had been strained for many years. The two countries became involved in a border war in November of 1978. Tanzanian troops, with the assistance of Ugandan exiles, invaded Uganda and captured the capital of Kampala in April of 1979. Amin fled the country on April 11, 1979, and went into exile in Libya, where he remained until 1980. He then went into exile in Jeddah, Saudi Arabia.

YUSUFU K. LULE (President, April 13, 1979–June 20, 1979). Yusufu Kirolde Lule was born in Kampala on April 10, 1912. He was educated at Makerere College and Fort Hare University College in South Africa. He returned to Uganda to teach in 1940. Lule continued his education in Great Britain after receiving a scholarship in 1948. He graduated from the University of Edinburgh with a master's degree in education in 1951 and returned to Uganda to join the faculty of Makerere College. He was appointed minister of rural development in the colonial government and later served as minister of education. He was named to the Public Service Commission following Ugandan independence in 1961 and became chairman of the commission the following year. He returned to Makerere University in 1964 to become principal. Lule was a critic of President Milton Obote and was forced to resign

his position in 1970. He went to London, where he served on the British Commonwealth secretariat as assistant secretary-general. He became secretary-general of the Association of African Universities in Ghana in 1972. Lule retained that position until 1977 and then returned to London. He became involved with Ugandan refugees and formed the Uganda National Liberation Front in opposition to President Idi Amin. Lule returned to Uganda following Amin's ouster and became provisional president on April 13, 1979. His refusal to allow supporters of Milton Obote to join the government resulted in his ouster on June 20, 1979. Lule was briefly detained by the new government of President Godfrey Binaisa before he was allowed to return to exile in London. He remained an opponent of the government following Obote's return to power in December of 1980. He led the National Resistance Movement from 1981. Lule died in a London hospital at the age of 72 after an operation for kidney failure on January 21, 1985.

GODFREY BINAISA (President, June 20, 1979–May 12, 1980). Godfrey Lukwongwa Binaisa was born in Kampala on May 30, 1919. He was educated in Uganda and at King's College in London, where he received a degree in law in 1955. He returned to Uganda to set up a legal practice the following year. Binaisa joined Milton Obote's Uganda National Union party and served as a legal advisor to Obote's government. He was named attorney general in 1962. He resigned from the government for reasons of health in 1967. Binaisa returned to practice law until 1973, when he fled for his life during the rule of President Idi Amin. He went into exile in London until 1977, when he went to New York to join a law firm. He also founded the Uganda Freedom Union, an exile organization that opposed Amin's government. Binaisa returned to Uganda after Amin's ouster in April of 1979. He was named president of Uganda and head of the provisional government following the ouster of Yusufu K. Lule on June 20, 1979. He was forced from office by the military on May 12, 1980, and placed under house arrest. He was allowed to leave Uganda in January of 1981 and went to Great Britain.

PAULO MUWANGA (President, May 18, 1980–December 17, 1980). Paulo Muwanga was born in Mpigi in 1920. He joined the Uganda People's Congress led by Milton Obote in the 1950s. He entered the Ugandan diplomatic corps after independence and was named ambassador to Egypt in 1964. Muwanga served as chief of protocol from 1969 and was appointed ambassador to Paris in 1971, following President Obote's ouster by Idi Amin. Muwanga went into exile in 1973 and became a leading opponent of the Amin regime. He returned to Uganda after Amin's ouster in April of 1979. Muwanga overthrew the government of Godfrey Binaisa in May of 1980. He emerged as the head of the ruling military commission on May 18, 1980. Obote was returned to power on December 17, 1980, and Muwanga served in the government as minister of defense and vice president. Obote was ousted in a military coup in July of 1985. Muwanga was named prime minister in a provisional government on August 1, 1985, but was dismissed from office on August 25, 1985. He was arrested the following year on charges of kidnapping during Obote's term of office. He was imprisoned until October of 1990, when the government dropped charges against him. Muwanga had suffered a heart attack during his imprisonment, and he died at Nsambya Hospital near Kampala at the age of 70 on April 1, 1991.

APOLLO MILTON OBOTE (President, December 17, 1980–July 27, 1985). *See earlier entry under Heads of State.*

TITO OKELLO (President, July 29, 1985–January 26, 1986). Tito Okello Lutwa was born in Namukora in 1914. He was educated locally and entered the King's African Rifles in 1940. He saw action in Somaliland and Burma during World War II. Okello remained in the British army and returned to Uganda in 1955. He entered the Ugandan army as an officer following independence in 1962. He rose through the ranks and was named army chief of staff in 1970. Okello went into exile in Tanzania the following year after Idi Amin seized power from Milton Obote. Okello was a leading opponent of Amin's regime and led the Uganda National Liberation Army against Amin in 1979. He was reappointed army chief of staff when Obote returned to power the following year. Obote was ousted in a military coup led by Brig. Basilio Okello in July of 1985. Tito Okello was named chairman of the ruling military council on July 29, 1985. He attempted to install a government of national unity, and rebel leader Yoweri Museveni was named vice-chairman of the military council in December of 1986. Museveni's National Resistance Army renewed its assault on the government the following month and drove Okello from the capital on January 26, 1986. Okello surrendered later in the year and was absolved of responsibility for crimes committed by troops under his command during the Obote regime.

YOWERI MUSEVENI (President, January 29, 1986–   ). Yoweri Kaguta Museveni was born in 1944. He was educated at the University College of Dar es Salaam. He served as a research assistant in the office of President Milton Obote from 1970 until 1971. Museveni went into exile in Tanzania following the overthrow of Obote. He was a leading opponent of President Idi Amin and took part in the invasion by Ugandan exiles and Tanzanian troops in 1979. He served as defense minister in the interim government that followed

Amin's ouster. Museveni left the government following Milton Obote's return to power in 1980. He joined with Yusufu Lule to lead the National Resistance Army, which fought a guerrilla war against President Obote. Obote was ousted in a military coup in July of 1985, and Museveni continued to lead his troops against the government of Tito Okello. He agreed to a cease-fire in December of 1985 and joined Okello's government as vice-chairman of the ruling military council. He renewed his activities against the government the following month and forced Okello from office. Museveni was proclaimed president of Uganda on January 29, 1986. He also served in the government as minister of defense. He was successful in restoring political stability to the country. Government troops defeated most of the remaining insurgents in April of 1991.

HEADS OF GOVERNMENT

BENEDICTO KIWANUKA (Chief Minister, July 2, 1961–March 1, 1962. Prime Minister, March 1, 1962–April 25, 1962). Benedicto Kiwanuka was born in Buddu in 1922. He was a member of the Muganda tribe. He was educated locally and served in the army from 1942 until 1946. He continued his education in Basutoland in 1950 and attended University College in London, where he received a degree in law in 1956. Kiwanuka was elected to the Uganda Legislative Council in 1961 and served in the government as minister without portfolio. He was elected chief minister on July 2, 1961, and became prime minister on March 1, 1962, when Uganda was granted self-rule. He lost his seat in the assembly the following month when the Uganda People's Congress led by Milton Obote came to power. Kiwanuka relinquished office to Obote on April 25, 1962. He returned to practice law in Kampala. Kiwanuka was detained after an assassination attempt against President Obote in December of 1969. He was released soon afterwards and was named chief justice of the Ugandan Supreme Court. He was considered an opponent of the regime of President Idi Amin and was murdered by Amin's agents on September 21, 1972.

APOLLO MILTON OBOTE (Prime Minister, April 25, 1962–January 25, 1971). *See entry under Heads of State.*

ERIFASI OTEMI ALLIMADI (Prime Minister, December 13, 1980–July 27, 1985). Erifasi Otemi Allimadi was born in Kitgum on February 11, 1929. He was educated locally and served in the East African Army Medical Corps from 1947 until 1953. He subsequently joined Milton Obote's Uganda National Congress and worked as a party organizer. Allimadi was named to Uganda's mission to the United Nations in 1964 and was appointed ambassador to the United States in 1966. He also served as Uganda's permanent representative to the United Nations from 1967. He was removed from office following the ouster of President Obote by Idi Amin in 1971. Allimadi remained in exile during the Amin regime. He returned to the government as minister of foreign affairs following Amin's ouster in 1979. He was appointed prime minister on December 13, 1980, following Obote's return to power. Allimadi retained office until Obote's ouster in a military coup on July 27, 1985.

PAULO MUWANGA (Prime Minister, August 1, 1985–August 25, 1985). *See entry under Heads of State.*

ABRAHAM WALIGO (Prime Minister, August 25, 1985–January 26, 1986). Abraham Waligo was a member of the Uganda People's Congress led by Milton Obote. He was chosen as prime minister in the military government of Lt. Gen. Tito Okello on August 25, 1985, following the ouster of Obote. He was forced from office when the Okello government fell to Yoweri Museveni's National Resistance Movement on January 26, 1986.

SAMSON KISEKKA (Prime Minister, January 30, 1986–January 22, 1991). Samson Kisekka was born in 1912. He served as the leading spokesman for the National Resistance Movement (NRM) in opposition to President Milton Obote. Kisekka was appointed prime minister on January 30, 1986, following NRM leader Yoweri Museveni's takeover of the government. He suffered from poor health, and Museveni appointed three deputy premiers to assist him in February of 1988. Kisekka was replaced by George Cosmas Adyebo as prime minister on January 22, 1991. He remained in the government as Museveni's vice president.

GEORGE COSMAS ADYEBO (Prime Minister, January 22, 1991–   ). George Cosmas Adyebo was born 1947. He was educated as an economist and served as principal at the Uganda College of Commerce. He was a member of the ruling National Resistance Movement and was appointed by President Yoweri Museveni to the position of prime minister on January 22, 1991.

Ukraine

(Ukraina)

The Ukraine is a country in southeastern Europe. It became independent following the breakup of the Soviet Union on December 25, 1991.

HEAD OF STATE

LEONID KRAVCHUK (President, December 1, 1991–   ). Leonid Makarovich Kravchuk was born on January 10, 1934. He joined the Communist party in 1958 and served as chairman of the Ukrainian Supreme Soviet from July 18, 1990, succeeding Volodymyr Ivashko. He was elected to the new position of president on December 1, 1991. Ukraine declared its independence on December 5, 1991, and subsequently joined the Commonwealth of Independent States.

HEADS OF GOVERNMENT

VITOLD FOKIN (Premier, October 23, 1990–September 30, 1992). Vitold Fokin was the Ukraine's former central planning director. He served as acting chairman of the Council of Ministers of the Ukraine from October 23, 1990, after the resignation of Vitaly Masol. Fokin was confirmed as chairman on November 14, 1990, and remained as prime minister following the restructuring of the Council of Ministers in May of 1991. He resigned under pressure on September 30, 1992, after accusations that he was stalling on economic reforms.

VALENTYN SYMONENKO (Premier, October 2, 1992–October 13, 1992). Valentyn Symonenko was appointed interim premier of the Ukraine on October 2, 1992, after Vitold Fokin's resignation. He retained office until Leonid Kuchma was selected by the Parliament on October 13, 1992.

LEONID KUCHMA (Premier, October 13, 1992–May 20, 1993). Leonid Kuchma was born in 1938. He served as director of Uzhmash, the industrial complex that produced the Soviet Union's tactical missiles. He was selected by the Ukrainian Parliament to serve as premier on October 13, 1992. Kuchma resigned in a power struggle with the Parliament and the president on May 20, 1993.

Union of Soviet Socialist Republics (Soviet Union)

The Soviet Union stretched from eastern Europe through central Asia to the Pacific Ocean. It consisted of fifteen republics that disbanded on December 25, 1991.

HEADS OF COMMUNIST PARTY

JOSEF STALIN (General Secretary, April 1922–March 5, 1953). Josef Stalin was born Josif Vissarionovitch Dzhugashvili in the village of Gori in Georgia on December 21, 1879. He was educated at the Orthodox Church Seminary in Tiflis, where he became active in the revolutionary movement in 1897. He joined the Russian Social-Democratic Workers party in Tiflis in 1898 and was expelled from the seminary for his revolutionary activities the following year. Stalin was active as a strike organizer in the early 1900s. He was forced to go underground in November of 1901 and was arrested in the spring of 1902. He was exiled to Siberia, but escaped after a short time. Stalin subsequently supported Lenin and the Bolsheviks against the Mensheviks in the schism that developed in the Social Democratic party in 1903. He attended several international Socialist conferences and was elected to the Baku party committee in 1907. He was again

arrested and deported in November of 1908. Stalin again escaped, but was re-arrested in March of 1910. He was released in June of 1911 and moved to Petrograd, where he helped to establish the party newspaper *Pravda*. He traveled abroad from 1912 until 1913 and spent some time with Lenin. Stalin was again arrested on his return to Russia in February of 1913. He remained imprisoned until the revolution in February of 1917. He returned to Petrograd, where he assumed the editorship of *Pravda*. Stalin became a member of the Politburo in May of 1917 and was active in the October Revolution that resulted in the Communists taking control of the government. He served as People's Commissar of Nationalities from 1917 until 1923 and also served as a member of the Revolutionary War Council from 1920 until 1923. He was also selected as general secretary of the Central Committee of the Communist party in April of 1922. When Lenin died in January of 1924, Stalin became part of a ruling triumvirate with Grigori E. Zinoviev and Lev B. Kamenev and thus prevented his chief rival, Leon Trotsky, from taking power. Stalin broke with Zinoviev and Kamenev in April of 1925 and joined with Nikolai I. Bukharin, Alexei Rykov, Mikhail P. Tomsky, and the right-wing of the party. He succeeded in expelling Trotsky, Zinoviev, and Kamenev from the party in 1928 and then successfully turned against Bukharin and his supporters. After gaining total control of the government, Stalin embarked on a program to industrialize the Soviet Union. Opposition to his policies was ruthlessly suppressed, and he succeeded in relocating millions of Russian peasants to industrial centers to be trained as factory workers. In 1936 Stalin began the first of the major purge trials to eliminate political opponents in the party and the military. During the next several years, Zinoviev, Kamenev, Bukharin, Rykov, and many others were tried for treason and executed. Trotsky, who was living in exile in Mexico, was tried and sentenced to death in absentia and was assassinated in 1940. Stalin was also concerned with the growing threat posed by Germany under the leadership of Adolf Hitler. After failing to convince the Western powers to enter into an alliance with the Soviets against Germany, Stalin entered into a nonaggression agreement with Hitler in August of 1939, shortly before the start of World War II. Stalin also took the office of premier on May 6, 1941, shortly before Hitler violated the peace pact and attacked the Soviet Union on June 22, 1941. Stalin assumed control of the Soviet military during the war years, and the Soviet army successfully halted Germany's attempt to conquer the country. Stalin participated in the Allied conferences in Teheran and Yalta and agreed to enter the war against Japan at the Potsdam Conference in July of 1945. After the conclusion of the war, Stalin extended the

Soviet sphere of influence throughout Eastern Europe, as most of the countries in that region adopted Soviet-dominated Communist governments. He remained the dominant figure in the Soviet Union and the Communist world until he suffered a brain hemorrhage on March 1, 1953. He died in Moscow five days later on March 5, 1953, at the age of 73.

NIKITA KHRUSHCHEV (General Secretary, September 1953–October 15, 1964). Nikita Sergeyevich Khrushchev was born in Kalinovkov, near the Ukrainian border, on April 17, 1894. He worked as a shepherd and a factory worker as a young man before being drafted into the Russian army during World War I. After the Bolshevik Revolution in 1918, Khrushchev joined the Communist party and fought with the Red Army. He returned to the Ukraine in 1920 to work in the mines. He subsequently attended a Communist party technical school and was made a party leader in Stalino, and later, Kiev. Khrushchev attended the Moscow Industrial Academy in 1929 and graduated two years later. He was then assigned to party work in Moscow. He became a member of the Communist party's Central Committee in 1934 and became first secretary of the Moscow Region the following year. Khrushchev was awarded the Order of Lenin for his work in constructing the Moscow Metro. He was sent back to the Ukraine in 1938 to serve as the party's first secretary there. He became a full member of the Politburo the following year. During World War II Khrushchev served as a lieutenant general and directed guerrilla warfare against the Germans. After the German army was defeated, Khrushchev returned to the Ukraine to serve as first party secretary and chairman of the Council of Ministers. He subsequently conducted purges to eliminate those who had collaborated with the Germans during the war. He returned to the

Moscow region as First Secretary in 1949. Khrushchev served as a leading member of the party secretariat at the time of Josef Stalin's death in March of 1953. He succeeded Stalin as first secretary of the Communist party in September of 1953. Khrushchev attempted to consolidate his power and orchestrated the execution of his leading rival, Stalin's secret police chief, Lavrenti Beria, in December of 1953. He forced the resignation of Georgi Malenkov as prime minister in February of 1955 and subsequently made state visits to India, Burma, and Great Britain. Khrushchev denounced the Stalin regime at the 20th Party Congress in February of 1956. This emboldened nationalist elements in Eastern Europe, and the Communist regime was threatened by a revolt in Hungary. Khrushchev sent Soviet troops to quell the uprising and restore a pro-Soviet government in November of 1956. He further consolidated his power inside the Soviet Union when he orchestrated the purges of Vyacheslav Molotov, Lazar Kaganovich, and Malenkov, who had opposed his reorganization plan for Soviet industry. Khrushchev also dismissed General Georgy Zhukov later in the year, leaving himself in complete control of the Soviet military. He forced the resignation of Nikolai Bulganin on March 27, 1958, and succeeded him as prime minister. Khrushchev held a summit meeting with President Dwight Eisenhower and toured the United States in 1959. The meeting was successful in improving relations between the two nations, but a visit by Eisenhower to the Soviet Union was scuttled when a United States U-2 spy plane was shot down over Soviet territory in May of 1960. The Soviet Union's relationship with the People's Republic of China also deteriorated in the early 1960s. Khrushchev met with United States president John Kennedy in June of 1961, but the two leaders were unable to reach an agreement on the division of Germany.

Khrushchev subsequently ordered the construction of the Berlin Wall to separate West Berlin from Soviet-dominated East Germany. Khrushchev engaged in another confrontation with the United States in October of 1962, when Soviet nuclear missiles were reported to be in Cuba. Following a tense period that threatened to bring the two nations to war, Khrushchev agreed to remove the missiles. He was also faced with domestic problems because his agricultural and industrial policies met with little success. Khrushchev was removed from the leadership of the government and the party on October 15, 1964. He retired to his country home at Petromo-Dalnye, near Moscow, where he lived in seclusion. Khrushchev again was in the news when a book entitled *Krushchev Remembers*, reported to be based on his private memoirs, was published in the West in December of 1970. Khrushchev suffered from heart ailments in his later years. He died on September 11, 1971, at the age of 77 at his home following a heart attack.

LEONID I. BREZHNEV (General Secretary, October 15, 1964–November 10, 1982). Leonid Ilyich Brezhnev was born in Dneprodzerzhinsk, formerly Kamenskoye, the Ukraine, on December 19, 1906. He was educated at the Klassicheskaya Gymnaziya and graduated in 1921. He joined the Communist youth organization, the Komsomol, in 1923. Brezhnev subsequently worked as a land use specialist in Byelorussia and the Urals. He returned to his hometown to study metallurgy in 1931 and received his degree in 1935. Brezhnev became a department head in the regional Communist party in 1938. During World War II he served as a political officer in the army. He rose to the rank of major general in 1944 and was appointed chief of the Carpathian military district after the war. Brezhnev served as Communist party first secretary in the Zaporozhe region in 1946 and in his home territory in 1947. He was named first secretary of the Moldavia province in 1950. He became a member of the party's Central Committee and a candidate member of the Presidium in October of 1952. Brezhnev was dropped from these posts during the political confusion following the death of Josef Stalin in March of 1954. He subsequently served as a party official in the Kazakhstan Province from 1954 until 1956. Brezhnev became an ally of Nikita Khrushchev and was restored to the Central Committee and the Presidium in February of 1956. He became a full member of the Presidium in July of 1957. He was selected to succeed Kliment Voroshilov as chairman of the Presidium of the Supreme Soviet of the U.S.S.R. and thus became the Soviet Union's chief of state on May 7, 1960. Brezhnev was reelected to the post in April of 1962. He resigned as chairman on July 15, 1964, to become more active in Communist party activities. He was involved in the ouster of Khrushchev as Communist party first secretary on October 14, 1964. Brezhnev was chosen by the Central Committee to succeed him as first secretary, and he worked with Alexei Kosygin, the new Soviet prime minister, to improve the economic stability of the country. Brezhnev, whose title was changed to general secretary in 1966, moved firmly to suppress dissent in the Soviet Union and its satellite countries. In the spring of 1968 the Czech Communist party under Alexander Dubček attempted to institute reforms in the Czech government that threatened the Soviet domination of the country. When Brezhnev failed to persuade Dubček to recant from his position, Soviet and Warsaw Pact country armies invaded Czechoslovakia in August of 1968 to preserve Soviet domination. In international matters Brezhnev attempted to normalize relations with the West. A period of détente followed the visit of United States president Richard Nixon to the Soviet Union in 1972. The two leaders signed a strategic arms limitation treaty

(SALT), and Brezhnev traveled to the United States the following year. Brezhnev again became head of state as chairman of the Presidium of the Supreme Soviet of the U.S.S.R. on June 16, 1977, replacing Nikolai Podgorny. Brezhnev met with President Jimmy Carter of the United States in 1979 to sign another strategic arms limitation treaty (SALT II). This treaty failed to be ratified by the United States Senate, however. Relations with the United States continued to deteriorate in December of 1979, when the Soviet Army intervened in the Afghanistan civil war. Brezhnev remained the undisputed leader of the Soviet Union until his death in Moscow on November 10, 1982. The 75-year-old leader had suffered from chronic heart and circulatory problems prior to his death.

YURI ANDROPOV (General Secretary, November 10, 1982–February 9, 1984). Yuri Vladimirovich Andropov was born in Nagutskaya, in the province of Stavropol, on June 15, 1914. He graduated from a technical college in 1936 and attended the Petrozavodsk State University. He joined the Communist youth organization, the Komsomol, and became leader of the Karelian district in 1940. Andropov was an organizer of guerrilla units behind German lines during World War II. He remained active in party organizations and was named party secretary in Karelia in 1947. He went to Moscow in 1951 to serve on the Central Committee staff. Andropov entered the Soviet diplomatic corps in 1953 and was stationed in Budapest. He became ambassador to Hungary the following year. Hungary was in a period of political unrest that led to an uprising in 1956. The Soviet army invaded Hungary later in the year, when the reformist government led by Imre Nagy threatened to pull out of the Warsaw Pact. Andropov was instrumental in the suppression of the nationalist uprising and in securing the leadership of Hungary for Janos

Kadar. Andropov returned to Moscow the following year to lead the Central Committee's department supervising relations with other Communist countries. He was named to the Central Committee in 1961. He was chosen by Communist party leader Leonid Brezhnev to serve as leader of the State Security Committee (KGB) in May of 1967. Andropov was named a candidate member of the Politburo the following month and was promoted to full member status in April of 1973. He stepped down as leader of the KGB in April of 1982. Following the death of Leonid Brezhnev, the Central Committee on November 10, 1982, elected Andropov to become general secretary of the Communist party. He also became the Soviet Union's head of state when he was elected chairman of the Presidium of the Supreme Soviet of the U.S.S.R. on June 16, 1983. Andropov instituted a crackdown on the political corruption that had risen under Brezhnev's leadership. He also attempted to repair relations between the Soviet Union and the People's Republic of China. Andropov suffered from a chronic kidney ailment and diabetes shortly after taking power. He died in Moscow on February 9, 1984, at the age of 69 from heart and vascular problems.

KONSTANTIN CHERNENKO (General Secretary, February 13, 1984–March 10, 1985). Konstantin Ustinovich Chernenko was born in Bolshaya Tes in Siberia on September 24, 1911. He worked on a farm in his youth and joined the young Communist organization, the Komsomol, in 1926. He became a member of the Communist party in 1931, and two years later he became an official in the Krasnoyarsk region. Chernenko rose to the position of regional secretary in 1941. He graduated from the party school in Moscow in 1945 and was appointed first secretary in Penza shortly thereafter. He was sent to Moldavia to head the party's propaganda department there

in 1948. Chernenko became a close associate of Leonid Brezhnev, the party's first secretary in the region from 1950 until 1952. Chernenko went to Moscow in 1956 to lead the Communist party's propaganda department and became Brezhnev's chief aide in 1960. He became a member of the Communist party's Central Committee in 1971 and the Politburo in 1978. He was promoted to the position of chief ideologist for the Communist party in January of 1982. Chernenko was bypassed for the position of Communist party leader in favor of Yuri Andropov when Brezhnev died in November of 1982. Chernenko succeeded Andropov as general secretary of the Communist party on February 13, 1984. He also became the Soviet Union's president on April 11, 1984, as chairman of the Presidium of the Supreme Soviet of the U.S.S.R. Chernenko suffered from ill health from the time he took power. His many bouts with illness prevented him from exercising much power during his term of office. He died in Moscow at the age of 73 on March 10, 1985.

MIKHAIL GORBACHEV (General Secretary, March 11, 1985–August 24, 1991). Mikhail Sergeyevich Gorbachev was born in Privolnoye in Stavropol Province on March 2, 1931. He worked on a state farm and joined the young Communist organization, the Komsomol. He later attended the Moscow State University, where he received a degree in law. Gorbachev joined the Communist party in 1952 and rose through the party ranks in Stavropol. He became party leader of the city in 1966 and of the province four years later. He was elected to the Communist party Central Committee in 1971 and became minister of agriculture on the committee in 1978. Gorbachev became a candidate member of the Politburo in 1979 and a full member the following year. He was selected to succeed Konstantin Chernenko as general secretary of the Communist party on March 11,

1985, following Chernenko's death the previous day. He instituted policies of perestroika (restructuring) and glasnost (openness) to transform the Soviet economy and society. His government faced a crisis in April of 1985 when a reactor at the Chernobyl nuclear power plant exploded and caused international concern over the threat of nuclear contamination. Gorbachev proposed disarmament initiatives to the United States and was visited by President Ronald Reagan in 1988. Gorbachev consolidated his power on the Central Committee in 1988 and replaced Andrei Gromyko as chairman of the Presidium of the Supreme Soviet of the U.S.S.R. on October 1, 1988. He continued his efforts to democratize his country and allowed elections to be held for the new Congress of People's Deputies in 1989. Gorbachev took the new position of president of the Soviet Union on March 15, 1990. Later in the year he was awarded the Nobel Prize for Peace for his contributions to ending the Cold War. Gorbachev also conducted several meetings with President George Bush of the United States and attempted to negotiate a peaceful settlement to the Gulf crisis without success. Gorbachev was faced with growing criticism in the country as his economic policies failed to improve living conditions and led to labor unrest. He was criticized by the left for moving too slowly with his reforms and was threatened by the right for moving away from Communist orthodoxy. His plans for a Russian formation which allowed some autonomy for the Soviet Republics was rejected by the Balkan states of Lithuania, Latvia, and Estonia, who demanded full independence. The Soviet Union was faced with a right-wing coup on August 18, 1991, while Gorbachev was in Foros by the Crimea. Elements of the Communist party and the military took control of the government. The coup was foiled by Russian president Boris Yeltsin, who called on the people and the military to support the government. The coup collapsed on August 21, 1991, and the leaders were arrested. Gorbachev returned to Moscow the following day, but his influence had been eclipsed by Yeltsin. Gorbachev resigned as general secretary of the Communist party on August 24, 1991, but remained a member of the party. He attempted to keep the Soviet Union together, but his efforts were unsuccessful. The twelve remaining Soviet Republics agreed to the dissolution of the Soviet Union and the formation of a Commonwealth of Independent States on December 25, 1991. Gorbachev subsequently retired from public office.

HEADS OF STATE

MIKHAIL I. KALININ (President, March 1919–February 25, 1946). Mikhail Ivanovich Kalinin was born in Verkhnyaya, in the Province of Tver, on November 20, 1875. He worked in a munitions factory and became involved with revolutionary organizations in the 1890s. He was arrested on numerous occasions for anti-government activities and was exiled to Siberia in 1916. Kalinin escaped the following year to take part in the October Revolution. He was appointed chairman of the Petrograd Soviet in 1918 and was elected to the Central Committee of the Communist party the following year. Kalinin became the Soviet Union's second president in March of 1919 when he succeeded Jacob Sverdlov as chairman of the Presidium of the Supreme Soviet of the U.S.S.R. He was a popular figure among the Russian peasants and was awarded the Order of Lenin in 1935. He survived the Stalinist purges in the late 1930s and retained the presidency until he retired for reasons of health on

February 25, 1946. He died several months later at the age of 70 on June 3, 1946.

NIKOLAI M. SHVERNIK (President, February 25, 1946–March 6, 1953). Nikolai Mikhailovich Shvernik was born in St. Petersburg on May 19, 1888. He was employed as a factory worker in his early teens and became active in revolutionary politics. He was active in Bolshevik organizations at the time of the abortive Revolution of 1905. Shvernik was arrested and imprisoned several times over the next decade leading up to the Revolution of 1917. He served in the Red Army from 1918 until 1920. He subsequently served as leader of the metal workers' union until 1930, when he was appointed first secretary of the Soviet Trade Unions' Central Council. He remained in this position until February 25, 1946, when he was named chairman of the Presidium of the Supreme Soviet of the U.S.S.R., a largely ceremonial position equivalent to president. He also served on the Soviet commission to investigate German war crimes after the conclusion of World War II. Shvernik stepped down as president on March 6, 1953, following the death of Josef Stalin. He subsequently returned to his trade union position. He was appointed chairman of the party control commission in 1956 and was placed in charge of handling routine party matters. He was removed from the ruling Politburo in 1966. He died in Moscow at the age of 82 after a long illness on December 23, 1970.

KLIMENTI E. VOROSHILOV (President, March 6, 1953–May 7, 1960). Klimenti Efrimovitch Voroshilov was born in Verkhne, Dnepropetrovsky, on February 4, 1881. He was employed in the mines at an early age. He went to work in a factory in his early teens, but was dismissed after leading a strike. Voroshilov was active in revolutionary politics in the Ukraine from 1900. He went to Lugansky in 1903 and became leader of the local Social Democratic party. He led the local workers in revolt against the government in 1905 and subsequently was imprisoned for several months. Voroshilov was exiled in 1907, but escaped to join Josef Stalin in Baku. He was arrested and exiled on several other occasions prior to the Revolution of 1917. He entered the Red Army after the Revolution and served as chairman of the defense committee of Petrograd. Voroshilov was an organizer of the Bolshevik secret police, the Cheka, and became a close associate of Stalin. He gave up his military command following a dispute with Leon Trotsky in 1918 and was transferred to the Ukraine, where he became commissar for home affairs in the region. He was elected to the Communist party Central Committee in 1921. Voroshilov served in various military positions before being named commissar of war by Stalin in 1925. He became people's commissar of defense in 1934 and was promoted to the rank of marshal of the Soviet Union the following year. He was instrumental in mechanizing the Red Army prior to World War II and helped to maintain the army's loyalty to Stalin during the military purges in 1937. Voroshilov left the War Ministry in May of 1940 to become deputy premier. He was placed in command of the Leningrad front during World War II, but failed to halt the German advance. He later saw action in the Urals and Manchuria. He became a member of the Soviet Politburo in 1946 and remained deputy prime minister until Stalin's death in 1953. Voroshilov was selected as chairman of the Presidium of the Supreme Soviet of the U.S.S.R. on March 6, 1953. While in office, he made state visits to China and India. He was forced to step down from the presidency on May 7, 1960. Voroshilov was expelled from the party central committee in October of 1961, when he was denounced by Nikita Khrushchev as a member of the antiparty group that had attempted to oust Khrushchev in 1957. Voroshilov confessed his involvement and recanted his positions. He was spared the disgrace given to other members of the conspiracy and was reelected to the Presidium the following year. He spent his remaining years out of public life. Voroshilor died in Moscow of arteriosclerosis at the age of 88 on December 3, 1969.

LEONID I. BREZHNEV (President, May 7, 1960–July 15, 1964). *See entry under Other Leaders.*

ANASTAS I. MIKOYAN (President, July 15, 1964–December 9, 1965). Anastas Ivanovich Mikoyan was born in the Armenian village of Sanain on November 25, 1895. He graduated from the Armenian Ecclesiastical Seminary in Tiflis in 1915. He subsequently joined the Bolsheviks and became a member of the Baku party committee following the Revolution of 1917. Mikoyan became a close associate of Josef Stalin in the 1920s and supported him in his leadership struggle against Leon Trotsky. He was selected as a member of the Communist party Central Committee in 1923. He was appointed commissar of trade in 1926, commissar of supplies in 1930, and commissar of food in 1934. Mikoyan became a member of the Politburo in 1935 and was promoted to the post of deputy chairman of the Council of Ministers two years later. He supported the Stalin purge trials in the 1930s and was the Soviet Union's leading trade negotiator. He was placed in charge of procuring supplies for the Red Army during World War II. Mikoyan was minister of domestic and foreign trade until 1955, when he was appointed vice-premier. He supported Nikita Khrushchev's denunciation of Stalin in February of 1958. He was elected chairman of the Presidium of the Supreme Soviet of the U.S.S.R. on July 15, 1964, shortly before the ouster of Khrushchev. Mikoyan was allowed to retain his position by the new leadership, but stepped down on December 9,

1965, citing ill health. He resigned from the Politburo in April of 1966 and remained on the Communist party Central Committee until his retirement in 1976. He died in Moscow on October 21, 1978, at the age of 82 following a long illness.

NIKOLAI V. PODGORNY (President, December 9, 1965–June 16, 1977). Nikolai Viktorovich Podgorny was born in Karlovka on February 18, 1903. He worked in a machine shop in his early teens and became involved with the Communist youth organization, the Komsomol. He joined the Communist party in 1930 and graduated from an engineering college in Kiev the following year. Podgorny subsequently went to work in the Ukrainian sugar industry. He survived the Stalinist purges in the late 1930s and became deputy commissar for the food industry in 1939. He spent much of World War II in Moscow and returned to the Ukraine after the war. Podgorny returned to Moscow to represent the Ukrainian Republic in 1946. He was named head of the Communist party in the Kharkov Province in 1950 and became second secretary of the Ukraine party following the death of Josef Stalin in 1953. Podgorny was elected to the Communist party Central Committee three years later. He was named to the Politburo in 1960 and became national Communist party secretary under Nikita Khrushchev in 1963. After Khrushchev's ouster from power, Podgorny was moved to the largely ceremonial position of chairman of the Presidium of the Supreme Soviet of the U.S.S.R. on December 9, 1965. He served as the least powerful member of the ruling Soviet triumvirate with Communist party leader Leonid Brezhnev and Premier Alexei Kosygin. Podgorny made numerous state visits during his term of office and traveled to Egypt, France, Cuba, and much of Africa. He was replaced on the Politburo in May of 1977 and was removed as Soviet president on June 16, 1977, when Brezhnev took the office. Podgorny remained on the Supreme Soviet until his death in Kiev on January 11, 1983, at the age of 79 after a long illness.

LEONID BREZHNEV (President, June 16, 1977–November 10, 1982). *See entry under Other Leaders.*

VASILY V. KUZNETSOV (Acting President, November 10, 1982–June 16, 1983). Vasily Vasilyevich Kuznetsov was born in Sofilovka on February 13, 1901. He joined the Communist party in 1927 and studied metallurgical engineering at the Leningrad Polytechnical Institute. He continued his studies in the United States in the early 1930s. Kuznetsov worked in the Soviet armaments industry during World War II. He was named chairman of the Central Trade Union Organization in 1944 and was appointed to the Communist party Presidium in 1952. Kuznetsov was assigned to the diplomatic corps after Stalin's death in March of 1953. He served as ambassador to the People's Republic of China until 1955, when he became first deputy foreign minister. He also led the Soviet delegation to the United Nations on several occasions. Kuznetsov served as the Soviet negotiator in talks arranging the withdrawal of nuclear missiles from Cuba in 1962. He also led the Soviet delegation in Geneva that negotiated the nuclear test ban treaty in 1963. Kuznetsov represented Leonid Brezhnev in Czechoslovakia after the Soviet-led invasion of that country in 1968. He was elected a nonvoting member of the Politburo in 1977. He assumed the duties of first vice president in October of 1977 and became acting president of the Soviet Union following Brezhnev's death on November 10, 1982. Kuznetsov retained that position until the election of Yuri Andropov on June 16, 1983. He

returned to his duties as first vice president until he was ousted from the Politburo by Mikhail Gorbachev in 1986. Kuznetsov died in Moscow at the age of 89 on June 5, 1990.

YURI ANDROPOV (President, June 16, 1983–February 9, 1984). *See entry under Other Leaders.*

KONSTANTIN CHERNENKO (President, April 11, 1984–March 10, 1985). *See entry under Other Leaders.*

ANDREI GROMYKO (President, July 27, 1985–September 30, 1988). Andrei Andreyevich Gromyko was born in Starye Gromyki in Belorussia on July 18, 1909. He graduated from a teachers college in 1931 and joined the Communist party. He received a degree from the Moscow Agricultural Institute in 1936 and was subsequently employed by the Academy of Sciences Institute of Economics. Gromyko was appointed a counselor to the Soviet Embassy in Washington, D.C., in 1939. He was promoted to ambassador to the United States and minister to Cuba in 1943. He led the Soviet delegation to the Dumbarton Oaks conference in 1944 to discuss plans for postwar Europe. Gromyko served as the Soviet's first chief delegate to the United Nations from 1946 until 1949, where he often used the Soviet veto to halt matters before the United Nations Security Council. He returned to Moscow as first deputy foreign minister in 1949. He served as ambassador to Great Britain from 1952 until 1953, when he resumed his position in the Foreign Ministry. Gromyko was promoted to the post of foreign minister by Nikita Khrushchev in 1957. He retained this position under the leadership of Leonid Brezhnev and was instrumental in pursuing the policy of détente with the United States in the early 1970s. He was named to the Politburo in 1973 and became deputy chairman of the

Council of Ministers in 1983. Gromyko supported the candidacy of Mikhail Gorbachev as Communist party leader in 1985. He was subsequently replaced as foreign minister and given the position of chairman of the Presidium of the Supreme Soviet of the U.S.S.R. on July 27, 1985. He was replaced by Gorbachev as Soviet president on September 30, 1988, and was also removed from the Politburo. Gromyko died in Moscow of a stroke at the age of 79 on July 2, 1989.

MIKHAIL GORBACHEV (President, October 1, 1988–December 25, 1991). *See entry under Other Leaders.*

HEADS OF GOVERNMENT

JOSEF STALIN (Premier, May 27, 1941–March 5, 1953). *See entry under Other Leaders.*

GEORGI M. MALENKOV (Premier, March 6, 1953–February 8, 1955). Georgi Maximilianovich Malenkov was born in Orenburg on January 21, 1902. He joined the Soviet Red Army in 1919 and became a member of the Communist party the following year. He went to Moscow, where he graduated from the Higher Technical Institute in 1925. Malenkov became an associate of Josef Stalin and was named chairman of the Moscow Communist party Committee in 1930. He served as the party's personnel chairman from 1934 until 1939 and was instrumental in carrying out the Stalinist purges in the late 1930s. He was named to the Communist party Central Committee in 1939. Malenkov served on the State Defense Committee during the war and was placed in charge of production of military supplies during World War II. He was appointed deputy prime minister following the war and was appointed to the Politburo in 1946. Malenkov engaged in a rivalry with Andrei Zhdanov in the late 1940s. He led a purge of his rival's supporters following Zhdanov's death in 1948. Malenkov was selected to succeed Josef Stalin as premier on March 6, 1953, following Stalin's death. Malenkov was instrumental in the downfall and exe-cution of secret police chief Lavrenti Beria later in the year. The leadership of the Communist Party had gone to Nikita Khrushchev following Stalin's death, and a power struggle commenced between the two leaders. Malenkov was forced to resign as Premier on February 8, 1955, when he was unable to garner support for his programs. He remained on the Politburo until 1957 when he, Vyacheslav Molotov, and Lazar Kaganovich attempted to oust Khrushchev. Khrushchev was able to survive the power struggle, and Malenkov and his supporters were removed from positions of influence. Malenkov was sent to the Kazakh Republic in Central Asia to manage a power station until his retirement in 1963. He returned to Moscow, where he lived in obscurity until his death at the age of 86 on January 13, 1988.

NIKOLAI A. BULGANIN (Premier, February 8, 1955–March 27, 1958). Nikolai Alexandrovitch Bulganin was born in Nizhni-Novgorod (later Gorky) on June 11, 1895. He worked in a textile factory before joining the Bolsheviks after the ouster of the czar in February of 1917. He served in the secret police organization, the Cheka, after the Bolsheviks came to power in October of 1917. Bulganin was assigned to the Supreme Council of the National Economy after the conclusion of the civil war in 1922. He became chairman of the Moscow Soviet in 1931 and was named a candidate member of the Communist party Central Committee in 1934. He became premier of the Russian Republic in July of 1937 and was named deputy premier of the Soviet Union and chairman of the State Bank the following year. Bulganin served in the military as a political commissar after Hitler's invasion of the Soviet Union in June of 1941. He was promoted to deputy minister of defense in 1944. He became a candidate member of the Politburo of the Central Committee in 1946 and was promoted to the rank of marshal the following year. Bulganin became a full member of the Politburo in February of 1948 and also was named minister of the armed forces until March of 1949. He was named deputy premier and minister of defense in the government of Georgi Malenkov following Stalin's death in March of 1953. He was an ally of Communist party leader Nikita Khrushchev and was appointed to replace Malenkov as premier on February 8, 1955. The new government attempted to ease the tensions of the cold war, and Bulganin met with United States president Dwight Eisenhower and other Western leaders at a Geneva conference in July of 1955. Bulganin also accompanied Khrushchev on goodwill visits throughout the world. The Bulganin regime was also responsible for the harsh repression of democratic movements in Poland and Hungary in 1956. Bulganin participated with Malenkov and others in the so-called antiparty plot to oust Khrushchev in June of 1957. The plot was unsuccessful and Khrushchev replaced Bulganin as premier on March 27, 1958. He was again appointed as chairman of the State Bank until August of 1958, when he was dismissed from his government and party positions. Bulganin was banished to Stavropol, where he served on an economic council until his retirement in 1960. He subsequently lived as a pensioner near Moscow until his death after a long illness at the age of 79 on February 24, 1975.

NIKITA S. KHRUSHCHEV (Premier, March 27, 1958–October 15, 1964). *See entry under Other Leaders.*

ALEKSEI N. KOSYGIN (Premier, October 15, 1964–October 23, 1980). Aleksei Nikolayevich Kosygin was born in St. Petersburg on February 20, 1904. He joined the Soviet Red Army in 1919 and fought in the civil war. He worked with the Soviet cooperative programs after leaving the army in 1921. Kosygin joined the Communist party in 1927. He was trained as a textile engineer from 1929 until 1935 and then worked in a factory in Leningrad. Kosygin held various party positions from the late 1930s and became people's commissar of the textile industry in January of 1939. He was elected to the party's Central Committee two months later. In April of 1940 he was promoted to deputy premier. He served on the State Committee for Defense following the German invasion of the Soviet Union in the summer of 1941 and was responsible for the evacuation of Leningrad in January of the following year. Kosygin served as chairman of the Council of the Russian Republic from 1943 until 1946. He was appointed an alternate member of the Politburo in 1946 and became a full member two years later. He was also named minister of finance in February of 1948 and served until the following December, when he was appointed minister of light industry. Kosygin survived Stalin's purges of Leningrad party leaders in the late 1940s. He was dropped from the Politburo and removed as deputy premier following Stalin's death in March of 1953, but remained in his position in the cabinet. He was again named deputy premier in December of 1953. Kosygin supported Khrushchev in the attempt to replace him as party leader in June of 1957. Kosygin was named an alternate member of the Presidium for his support. He was named chairman of the State Planning

Commission in March of 1959. He became a full member of the Presidium in May of 1960 and served as Khrushchev's leading economic advisor. Kosygin rose to become first deputy premier in July of 1964. He succeeded Khrushchev as chairman of the Council of Ministers on October 15, 1964, when Khrushchev was stripped of his party and government positions. Kosygin served as part of the ruling Soviet triumvirate with Communist party leader Leonid Brezhnev and President Nikolai Podgorny. Kosygin attempted to reform the Soviet economy by advocating decentralization and an increased production of consumer goods. He was also involved in carrying out Soviet foreign policy. He visited Peking in 1965 in an attempt to ease the Sino-Soviet conflict. Kosygin also attended a summit with United States president Lyndon Johnson in Glassboro, New Jersey, in June of 1967. Kosygin's power in the Soviet leadership was eclipsed by Brezhnev. Kosygin suffered from a series of heart attacks in the 1970s and retired as premier for reasons of health on October 23, 1980. Two months later on December 18, 1980, he died of a heart attack in Moscow at the age of 76.

NIKOLAI A. TIKHONOV (Premier, October 23, 1980–September 27, 1985). Nikolai Aleksandrovich Tikhonov was born in Kharkov, the Ukraine, on May 1, 1905. He worked as a locomotive engineer and graduated from the Dniepropetrovsk Metallurgical Institute in 1930. He was subsequently employed as an engineer and became an industrial manager in 1947. Tikhonov was appointed deputy minister of economics in 1955. He returned to the Ukraine in 1957 to lead the Dniepropetrovsk Economic Council until 1960. He was then named deputy chairman of the State Economic Council. Tikhonov became deputy chairman of the Planning Commission in 1963. He was appointed by Leonid Brezhnev to serve

as deputy premier in 1965 and was elevated to first deputy premier in 1976. Tikhonov became a member of the Politburo in November of 1979. He became premier on October 23, 1980, when Alexei Kosygin resigned from office. Tikhonov remained in office until September 27, 1985, when he was replaced by Nikolai Ryzhkov.

NIKOLAI I. RYZHKOV (Premier, September 27, 1985–January 14, 1991). Nikolai Ivanovich Ryzhkov was born in Donetz on September 28, 1929. He was educated at the Irov Ural Polytechnic Institute and joined the Communist party in 1956. He worked as an engineer from 1965 and was named first deputy minister of heavy and transport machine building in 1975. Ryzhkov was named to the Communist party Central Committe in 1981 and was placed in charge of heavy industry. He was elected to the Politburo in 1985 and also was named premier on September 27, 1985. He retained that position until January 14, 1991, when he was replaced by Valentin Pavlov.

VALENTIN S. PAVLOV (Premier, January 14, 1991–August 24, 1991). Valentin Sergeyevich Pavlov was born in Moscow on September 26, 1937. He was educated at the Moscow Institute of Finance and worked in the Finance Ministry from 1959. He served on the State Planning Committee from 1979 until 1986, when he was transferred to the State Price Committee. Pavlov became minister of finance in 1989, and on January 14, 1991, he was named premier. He was arrested on August 22, 1991, for complicity in the unsuccessful coup d'état against the government of Mikhail Gorbachev. He was charged with conspiring against the government in January of 1992 and was brought to trial in April of 1993.

IVAN SILAYEV (Premier, August 24, 1991–December 25, 1991). Ivan Stepanovich Silayev was born in 1930. He was educated at the Kazan Aviation Institute and joined the Communist party in 1959. He worked as an engineer in Gorky from 1954 until 1974. Silayev served as deputy minister of the aircraft industry from 1974. He became first deputy minister in 1977 and minister in 1981. He was also elected to the Communist party Central Committee in 1981. Silayev served as deputy prime minister from 1985 until 1989. He subsequently served as prime minister of Russia. He was named premier of the Soviet Union on August 24, 1991, following the failed coup against the government. He retained that position until the breakup of the Soviet Union on December 25, 1991. Silayev subsequently served as Russia's permanent representative to the European Community.

United Arab Emirates

(al-Imarat al-Arabiyah al Muttahida)

The United Arab Emirates is a country consisting of seven emirates (Abu Dhabi, Dubai, Sharjah, Ras al-Khaimah, Ajmar, Fujairah, and Umm al-Qaiwain) on the eastern Arabian peninsula. It received independence from Great Britain on December 2, 1971.

HEAD OF STATE

ZAID IBN SULTAN AN-NAHAYAN (President, December 2, 1971–). Zaid ibn Sultan an-Nahayan was born in 1918. He was the brother of Sheikh Shakhbut bin Sultan, who ruled Abu Dhabi from 1928. Sheikh Zaid was named governor of the Eastern District of al-'Ain in 1946. Sheikh Shakhbut was deposed by the Abu Dhabi Royal Council on August 6, 1966, and Sheikh Zaid was placed on the throne. Abu Dhabi joined with the Trucial States of Dubai, Sharjah, Ras al-Khaima, Fujaira, 'Ajman, and Umm al-Qaiwain to form the United Arab Emirates, which received independence on December 2, 1971. Sheikh Zaid was chosen by the Supreme Council of Rulers to serve as president of the Union. The Emirates supported the military forces led by the United States that opposed Iraq during the Gulf War in 1991, and the Emirates contributed several billion dollars to the endeavor. Sheikh Zaid suffered financial difficulties in 1991 when the Bank of Credit and Commerce International (BCCI), in which he was a major shareholder, collapsed after charges of money-laundering and fraud.

HEADS OF GOVERNMENT

SHEIKH MAKTUM IBN RASHID AL-MAKTUM (Prime Minister, December 2, 1971–April 25, 1979). Sheikh Maktum ibn Rashid al-Maktum was born in 1943. He was the son of Sheikh Rashid ibn Said, the ruler of Dubai from 1958. He was active in his father's regime and became the first prime minister of the United Arab Emirates upon independence on December 2, 1971.

Maktum stepped down from office on April 25, 1979, and was succeeded by his father. He remained in the government as deputy prime minister and served as head of the government while his father was ill in the late 1980s. He succeeded his father as ruler of Dubai following Sheikh Rashid's death on October 7, 1990. Maktum also returned to the position of prime minister of the United Arab Emirates on November 20, 1990.

SHEIKH RASHID IBN SAID AL-MAKTUM (Prime Minister, April 25, 1979–October 7, 1990). Sheikh Rashid ibn Said al-Maktum was born in 1914. He was the son of Sheikh Said ibn al-Maktum, who ruled Dubai from 1912. Sheikh Rashid was granted considerable authority by his father in the late 1930s and was instrumental in improving the sheikhdom's economic stability.

Dubai gained its first medical office and post office under his guidance. Sheikh Rashid succeeded his father as ruler of Dubai in 1958. He created a deep-water port for shipping after the discovery of oil in Dubai in 1966. He was a co-founder of the United Arab Emirates and served as vice president of the new nation after independence. His son, Sheikh Maktum, served as prime minister in the new government. Maktum resigned on April 25, 1979, and Sheikh Rashid took over the position of prime minister. Rashid suffered from poor health in the late 1980s after suffering a series of strokes. He died after a long illness on October 7, 1990.

SHEIKH MAKTUM IBN RASHID AL-MAKTUM (Prime Minister, November 20, 1990–). *See earlier entry under Heads of Government.*

United Kingdom (Great Britain)
(United Kingdom of Great Britain and Northern Ireland)

The United Kingdom is in northwestern Europe on the British Isles.

HEADS OF STATE

GEORGE VI (King, December 11, 1936–February 6, 1952). George VI was born Albert Frederick Arthur George in York Cottage at Sandringham in Norfolk on December 14, 1895. He was the second son of George V, who became king of England in May of 1911. He was known as Prince Albert before he ascended to the throne. He attended the Royal Naval College and Dartmouth. Prince Albert served in the navy and saw action during the early years of World War I, but ill health forced an end to his naval career in August of 1917. He recovered after surgery for an ulcer and subsequently

entered the Royal Air Force. He was created duke of York, earl of Inverness, and Baron Killarney on June 3, 1920. He married the Lady Elizabeth Bowes-Lyon in April of 1923. The duke and duchess performed their public duties at home and abroad. King George V died on January 20, 1936, and he was succeeded by his eldest son, who was crowned King Edward VIII. When Edward abdicated the throne to marry Wallis Simpson on December 11, 1936, the duke of York ascended the throne. He was crowned King George VI on May 12, 1937, in Westminster Abbey. The following year the new king paid a state visit to France, and in 1939 he became the first British monarch to visit the United States. England entered World War II shortly after the king's return home. The king helped to maintain the morale of the British people during the war years through radio broadcasts and personal tours of areas that had been damaged by German bombs. He also paid visits to British troops engaged in the fighting. Following the war, the king worked with the Labour government in implementing social reforms in the country. India gained independence from Britain in 1947, and George VI relinquished the title of emperor. The king toured South Africa and Rhodesia in 1947, but was forced to cancel a trip to Australia the following year due to poor health. He successfully underwent surgery in March of 1949. His health again declined in 1951, and he was diagnosed as having lung cancer. He again had surgery in September of 1951. George VI seemed to be recovering from his illness when he died suddenly of a heart attack in Sandringham on February 6, 1952, at the age of 56.

ELIZABETH II (Queen, February 6, 1952–). Elizabeth II was born Elizabeth Alexandra Mary in London on April 21, 1926. She was the elder daughter of the future king George VI. She was educated by tutors, with an emphasis on history. Elizabeth spent most of the war years in Windsor. Following the war, she accompanied her parents on a tour of South Africa in early 1947. On her return to England, she announced her engagement to Philip Mountbatten, whom she married on November 20, 1947. Elizabeth and her husband were in Kenya, en route to a visit to Australia and New Zealand, when her father, King George VI, died on February 6, 1952. She returned to England and was crowned Queen Elizabeth II on June 2, 1953. She subsequently continued her tour of New Zealand and Australia. She made other state visits during the 1950s, including trips to Norway, Nigeria, France, and the United States. Queen Elizabeth II announced the creation of her eldest son, Prince Charles, as prince of Wales in July of 1958. She remained a popular monarch and continued to make state visits and preside over ceremonial occasions during her reign. Prince Charles married Lady Diana Frances Spencer in July of 1981. Their union produced an heir, Prince William of Wales, the following year. The royal family was beset with a series of scandals in the late 1980s and early 1990s culminating in the separation of Charles and Diana in December of 1992. Public disenchantment with the monarchy also brought pressure upon the queen to relinquish the royal family's tax exempt status in 1992.

HEADS OF GOVERNMENT

SIR WINSTON CHURCHILL (Prime Minister, May 11, 1940–July 26, 1945). Winston Leonard Spencer Churchill was born at Blenheim Palace near Woodstock in Oxfordshire on November 30, 1874. He was the son of Lord Randolph Churchill, the former Conservative party leader. He attended the military academy at Sandhurst, where he graduated eighth in his class. In 1895, he was appointed to the Fourth Hussars as a sublieutenant. Churchill served in several expeditionary forces and wrote several histories. He returned to England in 1898 and ran unsuccessfully for a seat in Parliament. He went to South Africa as a journalist during the Boer War, and in November of 1899 he was taken prisoner by Louis Botha, the future South African prime minister. Churchill escaped and wrote several books on his South African experiences. He returned to England and in 1900 was elected to a seat in the House of Commons as a Conservative member. He joined the Liberal party in 1904, and two years later he was named undersecretary for the colonies. Churchill was appointed president of the Board of Trade in the government of Herbert Henry Asquith in 1908 and served until 1910. He was subsequently named home secretary until 1911, when he became first lord of the admiralty. He was replaced in 1915 because of criticism of his handling of the Gallipoli disaster. Churchill left government to join the British military during World War I, but was recalled by Prime Minister David Lloyd-George to serve as minister of munitions in July of 1916. He continued to serve in the postwar cabinet as secretary of state for war and the air from 1918 until 1921 and secretary of state for the colonies from 1921 until 1922. He lost his seat in Parliament in the 1922 elections. Churchill was defeated in several attempts to return to Parliament before he was elected to a seat in the fall of 1924. He rejoined the Conservative party and was subsequently named chancellor of the Exchequer in the cabinet of Stanley Baldwin. He continued his writings following the Labour party victory in 1929. Churchill soon broke with Baldwin and was excluded from a cabinet position when Baldwin again became prime minister in 1935. Churchill was a leading advocate of British rearmament prior to World War II. He was also a critic of the appeasement policies of Baldwin's successor, Neville Chamberlain. When Great Britain declared war on Germany on September 3, 1939, Churchill was named first lord of the admiralty. Chamberlain resigned as prime minister following the German invasion of Belgium in May of 1940. When Churchill was asked to form a government as prime minister on May 10, 1940, he formed a coalition

war cabinet and also served as minister of defense. He was given a unanimous vote of confidence by the House of Commons following a rousing speech on May 13, 1940. He led his country during World War II with courage and determination. The Allied forces defeated Germany in 1945, and Churchill was faced with political problems at home in England. The Labour party defeated the Conservatives in the elections on July 25, 1945, and Churchill was replaced as prime minister by Clement Attlee. Churchill led the Opposition until 1951, when the Conservatives were returned to power. Churchill again became prime minister on October 26, 1951, and also served as first lord of the Treasury. He was awarded the Nobel Prize for Literature in 1953 for his historical writings. He was also knighted in 1953. Churchill retired from office on April 6, 1955, but remained in the House of Commons until 1964. He was made an honorary citizen of the United States by an act of Congress on April 9, 1963. Churchill died of a stroke in London at the age of 90 on January 24, 1965.

CLEMENT ATTLEE (Prime Minister, July 26, 1945–October 26, 1951). Clement Richard Attlee was born in Putney, Surrey, on January 3, 1883. He attended the University College at Oxford, where he received a degree in law. He practiced law from 1906 until 1909, when he moved to London's East End to assist with social problems. Attlee entered the British army in 1914 and saw action in Gallipoli and France. He left the army with the rank of major after the conclusion of World War I. He was elected mayor of Stepney in 1919 and was elected to the House of Commons on the Labour party ticket in 1922. Attlee served as a junior minister in the government of James Ramsay MacDonald from 1930 until 1931. He became George Lansbury's deputy party leader in 1931 and succeeded Lansbury as leader of the Labour party in 1935.

Attlee was considered a moderate on domestic issues and was a staunch supporter of the republicans against Franco's forces during the Spanish Civil War in the late 1930s. Attlee supported the British government's declaration of war on Germany in 1939, but refused to join the government of Neville Chamberlain. This helped insure Chamberlain's removal, which resulted in Winston Churchill becoming prime minister. Attlee served as lord privy seal in the coalition war cabinet. He was named Churchill's deputy prime minister in February of 1942. Attlee and his party left the coalition in May of 1945, and the Labour party won a decisive victory in the subsequent parliamentary elections. Attlee became prime minister on July 26, 1945. His government introduced extensive social legislation, including the establishment of a National Health Service. He also supported the nationalization of the railway, electricity, coal, and gas industries. Attlee also presided over the granting of independence to India in 1947. The Labour party lost seats in the elections in May of 1950 and was narrowly defeated in October of 1951. Attlee was replaced as prime minister by Churchill on October 26, 1951. Attlee remained Labour party leader and leader of the Opposition until his retirement in December of 1955. He was created first Earl Attlee shortly after his retirement. He died in a London hospital at the age of 84 after a long illness on October 8, 1967.

SIR WINSTON CHURCHILL (Prime Minister, October 26, 1951–April 6, 1955). *See earlier entry under Heads of Government.*

ANTHONY EDEN (Prime Minister, April 6, 1955–January 10, 1957). Robert Anthony Eden was born in Windlestone, County Durham, on June 12, 1897. He served in the British army during World War II and rose to the rank of brigade major. He attended Oxford in 1919, after the conclusion of the war, and graduated in 1922. Eden then entered politics and ran unsuccessfully as a Conservative for a seat in the House of Commons. He was elected to the Parliament in a by-election in 1923. He became parliamentary private secretary to Foreign Secretary Sir Austen Chamberlain in 1924 and remained in that position until 1929. Eden was appointed undersecretary of state for foreign affairs in 1931. Three years later he was named to the cabinet and placed in charge of League of Nations affairs. Eden was appointed foreign secretary in the government of Stanley Baldwin in December of 1935. Eden resigned from the government in 1938 in opposition to Prime Minister Neville Chamberlain's intention to recognize Italy's conquest of Ethiopia. He was an outspoken critic of fascism and was returned to the cabinet as secretary for the dominions after the start of World War II in September of 1939. He was again named foreign minister in the government of Winston Churchill in December of 1940. Eden was instrumental in the formation of the Grand Alliance against Germany and the Axis powers during the war. He left the cabinet following the defeat of Churchill's Conservative government in July of 1945. He remained the leader of the Conservative party in the House of Commons. Eden was an advocate of Britain's entry into the United Nations and supported a policy of cooperation with the United States. He was reappointed foreign minister when Churchill again became prime minister in October of 1951. Eden also served in the government as deputy prime minister. He became prime minister when Churchill resigned on April 6, 1955. Eden was also knighted by Queen Elizabeth II in 1955. Eden's government was faced with an international crisis in July of 1956 when President Abdel Gamal Nasser of Egypt nationalized the Suez Canal. Israel invaded Egypt's Sinai Desert in October of 1956.

Great Britain and France then dispatched an invasion force to the canal zone. The invasion was terminated following pressure from the United States, the Soviet Union, and the United Nations. Eden subsequently resigned from office for reasons of health on January 10, 1957. He retired to his country home and wrote his memoirs. Eden was elevated to the peerage as Viscount Eden of Royal Leamington Spa in the County of Warwick and Earl of Avon in 1961. He took his seat in the House of Lords and remained concerned with international affairs. Eden became seriously ill in January of 1977 while visiting American statesman W. Averell Harriman in Florida. He was returned to England, where he died of cancer of the liver at his home in Wiltshire at the age of 79 on January 14, 1977.

HAROLD MACMILLAN (Prime Minister, January 10, 1957–October 19, 1963). Maurice Harold Macmillan was born in London on February 10, 1894. He was educated at Eton and Balliol College, Oxford, where he graduated in 1919. He served in the military during World War I and was wounded in action. Macmillan joined the duke of Devonshire in Canada to serve as an aide to the governor-general in 1919. He returned to Great Britain the following year to become director of Macmillan and Co., Ltd., publishing house. He was defeated for a seat in the House of Commons in 1923, but was successful in the parliamentary elections the following year. Macmillan served as a Conservative member until his defeat in 1929. He returned to represent Stockton on Tees in 1931. Macmillan opposed the government's policy of appeasement toward Adolf Hitler and Benito Mussolini prior to World War II. He served as resident minister at the Allied Headquarters in North Africa during World War II from 1942 until 1945. He lost his seat in the House of Commons in 1945, but was returned

from Bromley later in the year. Macmillan served in the cabinet as minister of housing and local government from 1951 until 1954. He was then named minister of defense and served until April of 1955. He was appointed chancellor of the Exchequer in December of 1955. Macmillan became prime minister on January 10, 1957, following the resignation of Sir Anthony Eden. His government successfully dismantled much of the British Empire by granting independence to most of Britain's colonies in Africa. He tried to negotiate Britain's entry into the European Common Market, but his efforts were thwarted by France's veto. Macmillan was also involved in the negotiations that led to the nuclear test ban treaty between the United States, the Soviet Union, and Great Britain in 1963. Macmillan was suffering from ill health in 1963 when his government was faced with a sex scandal involving his secretary of state for war, John Profumo. Macmillan resigned from office on October 19, 1963. He returned to the Macmillan publishing business after his retirement and wrote his memoirs. He also became chancellor of Oxford University. Macmillan was created the Earl of Stockton by Queen Elizabeth II in 1984. He took his seat in the House of Lords, where he was a critic of the social programs of Prime Minister Margaret Thatcher. He died at his home in Birch Grove, Sussex, from complications from pneumonia at the age of 92 on December 29, 1986.

SIR ALEC DOUGLAS-HOME (Prime Minister, October 19, 1963–October 16, 1964). Alexander Frederick Douglas-Home was born in London on July 2, 1903. He was educated at Eton and Christ Church, Oxford. He became known as Lord Dunglass when his father became the thirteenth Earl of Home in 1918. Douglas-Home entered politics in 1929 and was defeated for a seat in the House of Commons. He was elected to the body two years later as a

Scottish Unionist from South Lanark. Douglas-Home was named parliamentary secretary to the undersecretary of state for Scotland and served until 1935. He then became parliamentary secretary to Neville Chamberlain, and in 1937 he became chancellor of the Exchequer. Chamberlain subsequently became prime minister, and Douglas-Home accompanied him to the conferences in Munich that resulted in the partition of Czechoslovakia prior to World War II. Douglas-Home entered active military service during World War II, but resigned when he became seriously ill in 1943. He resumed his parliamentary duties and served as undersecretary of state for foreign affairs in the government from May until July of 1945. He succeeded his father as the fourteenth Earl of Home in 1951. He entered the House of Lords and served as minister of state for Scotland until 1955. Lord Home served as secretary of commonwealth relations from 1955 until 1960 and also served as the leader of the House of Lords from 1956 until 1960. He was appointed foreign secretary in the government of Harold Macmillan in July of 1960. Lord Home was selected to serve as prime minister on October 19, 1963, following Macmillan's resignation. Lord Home disclaimed his peerage and titles upon taking office and returned to the House of Commons. He led the Conservative government until the party was narrowly defeated by the Labour party in parliamentary elections in October of 1964. Lord Home stepped down as prime minister on October 16, 1964, and was replaced as leader of the Conservatives by Edward Heath in July of 1965. He subsequently served as the Conservative Opposition spokesman for foreign affairs. Douglas-Home returned to the government as secretary of state for foreign and commonwealth affairs in the government of Edward Heath from 1970 until 1974. He was created a life peer as Home of the Hirse, Baron of Coldstream in the county of Berwick, in 1974. Lord Home also served as a chancellor at Edinburgh University following his retirement from active politics.

HAROLD WILSON (Prime Minister, October 16, 1964–June 20, 1970). James Harold Wilson was born in Huddersfield, Yorkshire, on March 11, 1916. He graduated from Oxford University in 1937 and remained at the university as a lecturer in economics. Wilson was drafted into the civil service during World War II, serving as an economic assistant to the war cabinet. He served in the Ministry of Fuel and Power until 1944, when he resigned from the civil service to run for the House of Commons. He was elected to Parliament as a Labour member in July of 1945. Wilson served in the Ministry of Works until 1947, when he was named to the Board of Trade. He became president of the Board of Trade the following year. Wilson resigned from the cabinet in April of 1951 in support of Aneurin Bevan's position in opposition to a fee for the National Health Service. Wilson replaced Bevan on Labour's parliamentary committee in April of 1954, becoming the Opposition spokesman on economic affairs in 1956. Wilson challenged Hugh Gaiskell for the leadership of the Labour party in 1960, but was defeated. Wilson became the Opposition spokesman on foreign affairs in November of 1961. When Gaitskell died in January of 1963, Wilson defeated George Brown to become Labour party leader. Wilson led his party to victory in the elections in 1964 and became prime minister on October 16, 1964. He was successful in improving Britain's economy and advocated an increase in technological development in the country. The Labour party increased its majority in elections in April of 1966. Wilson was accused of being overly concerned with detail rather than the larger picture and gained the hostility of the British press. The Labour party was defeated by the Conservatives in elections in June of 1970, and Wilson was replaced as prime minister by Edward Heath on June 20, 1970. Wilson served as leader of the Opposition until March 4, 1974, when the Labour party returned to power in a minority government. Wilson called for another election in October of 1974, and Labour gained a slight majority. Wilson remained prime minister until April 5, 1976, when he retired from office. Wilson served as chairman of the Committee to Review Functioning of Financial Institutions from 1976 until 1980. He also served as chancellor of the University of Bradford from 1976 until 1985. Wilson was given a life peerage and created Baron Wilson of Rievaulx in 1983.

EDWARD HEATH (Prime Minister, June 20, 1970–March 4, 1974). Edward Richard George Heath was born in Brodstairs, Kent, on July 9, 1916. He attended Balliol College at Oxford on a music scholarship. He became active in Conservative politics and graduated in 1939. He served in the Royal Artillery during World War II and was discharged with the rank of second lieutenant in 1946. Heath entered the civil service after the war, serving in the Ministry of Civil Aviation. He resigned the following year to enter politics and was elected to the House of Commons in February of 1950. He rose through the ranks of the Conservative party, becoming privy councillor and parliamentary secretary in December of 1955. He supported Harold Macmillan's selection as party leader in 1957 and was appointed to Macmillan's cabinet as minister of labour in October of 1959. Heath was appointed lord privy seal in July of 1960. He served as the parliamentary spokesman for the Foreign Ministry and was chief negotiator for Britain's unsuccessful attempt to gain entry into the European Economic Community. He was named secretary of state for Industry, Trade, and Regional Development in the government

of Sir Alec Douglas-Home. He remained in the government until the victory of the Labour party in October of 1964. Heath was chosen as leader of the Conservative Opposition in July of 1965. He led the Conservatives to victory in elections in June of 1970 and replaced Harold Wilson as prime minister on June 20, 1970. Heath led Britain into membership in the European Economic Community in 1972. The Conservatives outpolled Labour in elections in February of 1974, but were unable to gain a parliamentary majority. Heath stepped down as prime minister on March 4, 1974. Heath led the Conservative Opposition, and his party was again defeated in parliamentary elections in October of 1974. Heath was replaced by Margaret Thatcher as Conservative leader in February of 1975. He remained a Conservative member of the House of Commons.

HAROLD WILSON (Prime Minister, March 4, 1974–April 5, 1976). *See earlier entry under Heads of Government.*

JAMES CALLAGHAN (Prime Minister, April 5, 1976–May 4, 1979). Leonard James Callaghan was born in Portsmouth on March 12, 1912. He came from a poor family and was educated at local public schools. He joined the civil service in 1929 and worked as a tax officer. Callaghan became a member of the Labour party in 1931 and left the civil service to work in a trade union office in 1936. He served in the Royal Navy during World War II, rising to the rank of lieutenant. He returned to Great Britain after the war and was elected to the House of Commons from Cardiff South in Wales in 1945. Callaghan served in several minor ministerial positions during the 1950s. He was an unsuccessful candidate for leader of the Labour party following the death of Hugh Gaitskell in 1963. He was appointed chancellor of the Exchequer in the cabinet of Harold Wilson the following year. Callaghan's delay in devaluing the pound damaged Britain's economy. He resigned his position in 1967 when forced to devalue the pound. He remained in the cabinet as home secretary and was largely responsible for British policy in Northern Ireland. He left the cabinet in 1970 when the Labour party was defeated by the Conservatives. The Labour party returned to power in 1974, and Callaghan was appointed foreign minister in the Wilson government. Callaghan was a candidate for leader of the Labour party following the resignation of Wilson in April of 1976. He defeated Michael Foot in the balloting and replaced Wilson as prime minister on April 5, 1976. Callaghan remained prime minister until May 4, 1979, when the Conservatives were victorious in parliamentary elections. He stepped down from leadership of the Labour party the following year. He remained a member of Parliament until 1987, when he was created a life peer as Baron Callaghan of Cardiff. He subsequently took his seat in the House of Lords.

MARGARET THATCHER (Prime Minister, May 4, 1979–November 28, 1990). Margaret Thatcher was born Margaret Hilda Roberts in Grantham on October 13, 1925. She was educated at Somerville College, Oxford University. She became involved in the Oxford Conservative Association and was elected the first female president of the organization in 1946. She graduated the following year and was employed as a research chemist. She was an unsuccessful candidate in parliamentary elections in 1950 and 1951. She married Denis Thatcher in December of 1951 and continued her education. Margaret Thatcher became a lawyer in 1953 and was elected to the House of Commons as a Conservative member from Finchley in 1958. She rose through the ranks of the party and served in the shadow cabinet of Edward Heath while the Conservatives were in Opposition from

1964 until 1970. She was named minister of education and science when Heath became prime minister in 1970. Heath was replaced as prime minister by Labour party leader Harold Wilson in 1974, and Thatcher unseated Heath as leader of the Conservative Opposition in February of 1975. She led the Conservatives to a parliamentary majority in elections in 1979 and took office as prime minister on May 4, 1979. She instituted policies to reduce the government's welfare spending and increased military allocations. Thatcher's popularity dwindled until April of 1982, when Argentina invaded the British colony of the Falkland Islands. The Argentine government claimed the Falklands, and Thatcher sent a naval task force to retake the islands during a brief war in June of 1982. The Conservatives were victorious in parliamentary elections the following month, and Thatcher remained prime minister. She survived a bomb attack by the Irish Republican Army while attending a party conference in Brighton in October of 1985. She was also faced with a lengthy miners' strike during 1984 and 1985. Thatcher was a strong supporter of the United States and backed the decision to bomb Libya in 1986 in retaliation to terrorist actions. Thatcher won a third term of office in June of 1987. Her popularity again dwindled when she sponsored a poll tax in April of 1990. Her refusal to tie the pound to currencies in the European Monetary System brought her into conflict with members of her cabinet. She was challenged by her former Defense Secretary Michael Heseltine for leadership of the Conservative party in November of 1990. She was forced into a runoff against Heseltine and stepped down as party leader and prime minister on November 28, 1990. She remained a member of Parliament until 1992, when she was created Baroness Thatcher.

JOHN MAJOR (Prime Minister, November 28, 1990–). John Roy Major was born in Merton on March 29, 1943. He was the son of a circus trapeze artist and was raised in London. He entered banking and became an executive with the Standard Chartered Bank in 1965. Major was elected to Parliament as a Conservative member for Huntingdon in 1979. He was named minister of social security in the cabinet of Margaret Thatcher in 1986. He was appointed deputy chancellor of the Exchequer the following year and became foreign secretary in July of 1989. Major replaced Nigel Lawson as chancellor of the Exchequer in October of 1989 and was responsible for persuading Thatcher to allow the British pound to be tied to the European Monetary System.

He supported Thatcher in her contest against Michael Heseltine for leadership of the Conservative party in November of 1990. Thatcher stepped down when she failed to win a victory on the first ballot, and Major defeated Heseltine and Douglas Hurd to become party leader and prime minister on November 28, 1990. Major's government supported the United States policy in the Persian Gulf following Iraq's invasion of Kuwait in 1990. British troops participated in the United States-led military operation that drove Iraq from Kuwait in 1991. Major led the Conservatives to a parliamentary victory in April of 1992.

United States of America

The United States of America consists of fifty states. Forty-eight states lie in central North America between the Atlantic and Pacific Oceans, while Alaska is located in the northwest corner of North America and Hawaii is located in the central Pacific Ocean. The United States declared its independence from Great Britain on July 4, 1776.

HEADS OF STATE

HARRY S TRUMAN (President, April 12, 1945–January 20, 1953). Harry S Truman was born in Lamar, Missouri, on May 8, 1884. He attended high school in Independence, Missouri, and joined the Missouri National Guard. He saw active duty in France during World War I. Truman returned to Missouri following the war and married Bess Wallace in 1919. He opened a haberdashery in Kansas City, but the business went under in 1921. Truman entered politics in 1922 and was elected a county court judge. He was supported by the powerful Democratic political machine of Thomas J. Pendergast. Truman remained on the county court and became presiding judge in

1926. He was elected to the United States Senate from Missouri in 1934 was reelected in 1940. Truman served as chairman of the special Senate committee that investigated graft and waste in government in 1941. His work on this committee led to a more prominent position in the Democratic party. He was selected by President Franklin D. Roosevelt to be his vice presidential candidate in the elections of 1944. The Roosevelt-Truman ticket was successful, and Truman took office as vice president early in 1945. He succeeded to the presidency following the death of President Roosevelt on April 12, 1945. Truman was faced with bringing World War II to a successful conclusion. He authorized the dropping of the atomic bomb on the Japanese cities of Hiroshima and Nagasaki in August of 1945, which forced the Japanese surrender. He established the Truman Doctrine in 1947, which provided support to Greece, Turkey, and other countries threatened by Communism. Truman also established the Marshall Plan in 1947, which provided for the economic recovery of postwar Europe. In the presidential elections of 1948, Truman and running-mate Alben Barkley defeated the Republican nominee Thomas Dewey in what was regarded as an upset victory. During Truman's second term the United States also assisted in the creation of the United Nations and joined the North Atlantic Treaty Organization (NATO) in 1949. Truman was the target of an unsuccessful assassination attempt by Puerto Rican nationalists in November of 1950. The United States committed troops to Korea in June of 1950 following the invasion of South Korea by the North Korean army. In the early 1950s the cold war continued to escalate, and the government was subjected to loyalty programs and paranoia about Communism. Senator Joseph McCarthy, a militant anticommunist, began his career as a destroyer of lives and jobs through his red-baiting attacks on liberal activists. President Truman declined to seek the presidential nomination in 1952. The Democratic nominee, Adlai E. Stevenson, was defeated by Dwight D. Eisenhower in the November election, and Truman stepped down from office on January 20, 1953. He retired to Independence, Missouri, where he worked to establish the Truman Library, which was dedicated in 1957. He also remained an active campaigner for Democratic candidates. Truman fell ill in early December of 1972. He was taken to a hospital in Kansas City, where he remained until his death from heart failure at the age of 88 on December 26, 1972.

DWIGHT D. EISENHOWER (President, January 20, 1953–January 20, 1961). Dwight David Eisenhower was born in Denison, Texas, on October 14, 1890. He was raised in Kansas and entered the West Point Military Academy in 1911. He graduated in 1915 and married Mamie Geneva Doud the following year. Eisenhower served at a tank training center during World War I. He graduated from the Army War College in 1928. He served as an aide to General Douglas MacArthur, the army chief of staff, from 1933 until 1935. Eisenhower went with MacArthur to the Philippines in 1935, where he remained until the start of World War II. He returned to the United States to serve on the Army General Staff as chief of staff of the war plans division in February of 1942. Eisenhower was named commanding general in Europe in June of 1942. He was given command for the Allied invasion of French North Africa in November of 1942. He was appointed supreme commander of the Allied Expeditionary Forces in December of 1943 and led the Allied landing at Normandy in June of 1944. Eisenhower was promoted to the rank of general of the army in December of 1944. He accepted Germany's surrender in May of 1945. He returned to Washington, D.C., to serve as army chief of staff in December of 1945. Eisenhower retained that position until February of 1948, when he resigned from active duty to become president of Columbia University. He returned to the military to serve as supreme commander of the North Atlantic Treaty Organization (NATO) in Europe in 1951. Eisenhower's record as a war-hero and his extreme popularity among the American people led representatives of both major political parties to encourage him to enter politics. He resigned from the army in April of 1952 to become a candidate for the Republican nomination for president of the United States. He received the nomination and was victorious over Democratic nominee Adlai E. Stevenson in the election in November of 1952. Eisenhower was sworn into office on January 20, 1953. He concluded the conflict in Korea in July of 1953 and negotiated the South East Asia Treaty Organization (SEATO) in 1954. The Eisenhower administration was noted domestically for its improvement of social security legislation and the interstate highway system. Eisenhower also became an opponent of Joseph McCarthy when the junior Republican senator from Wisconsin continued his attack on Communism in the government with an assault on the army. Eisenhower met with Soviet leader Nikita Khrushchev at a summit conference in Geneva in July of 1955. Eisenhower's health was threatened throughout his presidency. He suffered a major heart attack in September of 1955 and underwent abdominal surgery in June of 1956. He ran for reelection in 1956 and again defeated Adlai Stevenson in November of 1956. Eisenhower was an opponent of racial segregation and was involved in the integration of the public school system. He used federal troops to force Governor Orval Faubus of Arkansas to allow the entry of black students into white high schools in Little Rock in 1957. The United States became involved in conflicts in the Middle East in the late 1950s and sent troops to Jordan in 1957 and to Lebanon in 1958 to assist the governments of those countries. This action took place under the Eisenhower Doctrine, which recommended the use of the United States military to protect countries in the Middle East threatened by Communist aggression. The United States successfully launched an orbital satellite in January of 1958, several months after the Soviet Union had launched Sputnik. The president went on a goodwill tour of South America in March of 1960. His hopes for a treaty with the Soviet Union were dashed when a summit conference in Geneva broke up following the shooting down of a United States U-2 spy plane over the Soviet

Union in May of 1960. Eisenhower was barred by the constitution from seeking a third term in 1960. He supported his vice president, Richard M. Nixon, for the Republican nomination. Nixon was defeated by John F. Kennedy, and Eisenhower stepped down from office on January 20, 1961. He retired to his home in Gettysburg, Pennsylvania. Eisenhower again suffered from heart attacks in 1965 and 1968. He was hospitalized at the Walter Reed Army Medical Center in Washington, D.C., in August of 1968, and his health continued to deteriorate due to problems with his heart and an intestinal blockage. He died there at the age of 78 on March 28, 1969.

JOHN F. KENNEDY (President, January 20, 1961–November 22, 1963). John Fitzgerald Kennedy was born in Brookline, Massachusetts, on May 29, 1917. He was the son of Joseph P. Kennedy, a millionaire businessman who had served as ambassador to Great Britain during the administration of President Franklin D. Roosevelt. John Kennedy served in the United States navy as a P.T.-boat commander during World War II. He was decorated for heroism after the Japanese sank P.T.-boat 109 in August of 1943. Following his discharge from the navy in 1945, Kennedy pursued a political career. He was elected to the United States House of Representatives in 1946, and in 1952 he defeated Republican incumbent Henry Cabot Lodge for a seat in the United States Senate. He married Jacqueline Lee Bouvier shortly before his inauguration. In 1956 Kennedy wrote *Profiles in Courage*, a study of his personal political heroes, and was awarded the 1957 Pulitzer Prize for Biography for his efforts. Kennedy was narrowly defeated for the 1956 Democratic nomination for vice president, but was easily reelected to the Senate two years later. He received the Democratic nomination for the presidency in 1960 and went on to defeat Richard M.

Nixon in the general election later in the year. Kennedy was sworn in as president of the United States on January 20, 1961. His administration was noted for its support of civil rights legislation and the establishment of the Peace Corps. Kennedy's term of office was also marked by difficulties with the Communist-led government of Fidel Castro in Cuba. In 1961 a C.I.A.-sponsored attempt by Cuban exiles to overthrow the Castro regime met with failure in the Bay of Pigs incident. The following year Cuba became the base for Soviet nuclear missiles. In a confrontation known as the Cuban Missile Crisis, Kennedy threatened to blockade the island nation unless the Soviet offensive weapons were removed. After a brief period of international tension, Soviet premier Nikita Khrushchev agreed to the removal of the missiles. Kennedy's term of office was cut short when he was shot and killed by a sniper on November 22, 1963, while traveling in a motorcade in downtown Dallas, Texas. Lee Harvey Oswald was arrested for the murder, but was himself shot and killed by Jack Ruby two days later. Kennedy's assassination was ruled to have been carried out by Oswald, acting alone, but speculation persists that the president was the victim of a conspiracy.

LYNDON B. JOHNSON (President, November 22, 1963–January 20, 1969). Lyndon Baines Johnson was born in Gillespie County, Texas, on August 17, 1908. He was educated at the Southwest Texas State Teachers College and became a teacher upon graduation. He became active in politics and went to Washington, D.C., as an aide to Congressman Richard M. Kleberg in 1932. Johnson married Claudia "Lady Bird" Alta Taylor in 1934. He was elected to the United States House of Representatives as a Democrat from the 10th Congressional District in Texas in 1936. Johnson remained in the House until his election to the United States Senate in 1948. He became Democratic Major-

ity Whip in 1951 and gained a reputation as a skilled negotiator. He was elevated to Senate majority leader in 1955. Johnson declared his candidacy for the Democratic nomination for president in 1960. He was defeated at the Democratic convention by John F. Kennedy. Johnson subsequently accepted the vice presidential nomination and was sworn into office on January 20, 1961, after Kennedy defeated Richard M. Nixon in the presidential election. Johnson succeeded to the presidency when Kennedy was assassinated on November 22, 1963. He succeeded in passing civil rights legislation and established an antipoverty program shortly after taking office. Johnson ran for reelection in November of 1964 and defeated Republican candidate Barry Goldwater by a large margin. He dubbed his domestic program the "Great Society" and introduced legislation that established Medicare and funded the federal Education Act of 1965. Johnson also expanded the United States military presence in Southeast Asia. The war in Vietnam continued to escalate during his term of office and led to the formation of a large and vocal peace movement. The war consumed much of Johnson's later period in the White House. He announced his decision not to seek reelection on March 31, 1968. Political violence claimed the lives of two major American figures shortly after Johnson's announcement. The Rev. Dr. Martin Luther King was assassinated on April 4, 1968, and Senator Robert F. Kennedy, a leading candidate for the Democratic presidential nomination, was shot and killed on June 5, 1968. The Democratic National Convention was held in Chicago in August of 1968, and clashes between antiwar demonstrators and the local police erupted into violence. Johnson's vice president, Hubert H. Humphrey, was chosen as the Democrats' presidential nominee. Humphrey was defeated, and Johnson relinquished the White House to Republican victor Richard M. Nixon on January 20, 1969.

Johnson retired to his ranch near Johnson City, Texas, to write his memoirs. He died of a heart attack at the age of 64 on January 22, 1973.

RICHARD M. NIXON (President, January 20, 1969–August 9, 1974). Richard Milhous Nixon was born in Yorba Linda, California, on January 9, 1913. He attended Whittier College in California and received a degree in law from Duke University in 1937. He then returned to Whittier to begin a law practice. Nixon married Thelma Catherine Patricia Ryan in 1940. He served in the navy during World War II and entered politics after the war. He was elected to the United States House of Representatives as a Republican from California in 1946. Nixon was elected to the United States Senate in 1950 and gained a reputation as an anti-Communist. He was chosen as Dwight D. Eisenhower's vice presidential running mate in 1952. The Republican ticket was victorious in November of 1952, and Nixon was sworn in as vice president on January 20, 1953. He was reelected vice president in 1956. He won the Republican nomination for the presidency in 1960, but was defeated by John F. Kennedy in the November election. Nixon was an unsuccessful candidate for governor of California two years later. He subsequently announced his retirement from politics and opened a legal practice in New York. He reemerged to campaign for Republican candidates in 1964 and 1966 and received the Republican presidential nomination in 1968. Nixon chose Maryland governor Spiro T. Agnew as his running mate and defeated vice president Hubert H. Humphrey, the Democratic nominee, and George C. Wallace, an independent candidate, in the election in November of 1968. He was sworn into office as president of the United States on January 20, 1969. Nixon attempted to withdraw American troops from Vietnam. He also established direct diplomatic communications with the People's Republic of China and improved United States relations with the Soviet Union. His policy of détente with the Soviet Union led to the signing of a strategic arms limitation treaty in 1972. Nixon defeated South Dakota Senator George McGovern in his bid for reelection in November of 1972. Nixon's secretary of state, Henry Kissinger, continued negotiations that led to an end to the United States military presence in South Vietnam. Nixon's second term of office was marred by the political scandal known as "Watergate." A breakin occurred at the Democratic National Committee headquarters at the Watergate office and apartment complex in Washington, D.C., in 1972, and a number of the president's top advisors were implicated in the incident and the subsequent cover-up. Vice President Spiro Agnew was forced to resign due to an unrelated financial scandal in October of 1973, and Nixon nominated Congressman Gerald R. Ford as his successor. A number of Nixon's key advisors were tried and convicted on charges stemming from the Watergate breakin, and Nixon was forced to resign on August 9, 1974, following the passage of three articles of impeachment in the U.S. House of Representatives. He was succeeded by Vice President Ford, who granted an executive pardon to Nixon the following month to prevent Nixon's possible prosecution in the Watergate scandal. Nixon retired to his home in San Clemente, where he wrote his memoirs. He later emerged as an elder statesman on United States foreign policy. Nixon suffered a major stroke on April 18, 1994. He died at a New York hospital on April 22, 1994, at the age of 81.

GERALD R. FORD (President, August 9, 1974–January 20, 1977). Gerald Rudolph Ford, Jr., was born Leslie King in Omaha, Nebraska, on July 14, 1913. His parents were divorced when he was an infant, and his mother moved to Grand Rapids, Michigan. She married

Gerald R. Ford, Sr., who adopted her son and gave him his name. Ford attended the University of Michigan and the Yale University School of Law. He opened a law firm in Michigan before enlisting in the United States Navy in 1942. He served in the navy throughout World War II. Ford returned to Grand Rapids to reestablish his law practice and married Elizabeth "Betty" Bloom in 1948. He was also the Republican candidate for the United States House of Representatives in 1948. He was victorious and took office the following January. Ford retained his Congressional seat in subsequent elections. He was appointed to the Warren Commission by President Lyndon Johnson in 1963 to investigate the assassination of President John F. Kennedy. Ford was elected minority leader of the House in 1965 by the Republican membership. He retained that position until his nomination by President Richard Nixon to succeed to the vice presidency following the resignation of Spiro T. Agnew. Ford was confirmed by the Congress and took office on December 6, 1973. He succeeded to the office of president on August 9, 1974, after Nixon resigned during the Watergate scandal. Ford pardoned Nixon the following month for any crimes that the former president might have committed while in office. He chose former New York governor Nelson Rockefeller to serve as his vice president in December of 1974. The United States was faced with rampant inflation followed by the worst economic recession since World War II. Ford announced his candidacy to retain the office of president and defeated Ronald Reagan for the Republican nomination. He selected Kansas senator Robert Dole as his running mate. Ford was defeated in November of 1976 in a close election by Democratic nominee Jimmy Carter. Ford stepped down as president on January 20, 1977. He was considered as a possible vice presidential running mate when Ronald Reagan gained the Republican nomina-

tion in 1980, but George Bush was chosen instead. Ford retired from active politics to participate on boards of various businesses and industries.

JIMMY CARTER (President, January 20, 1977–January 20, 1981). James Earl Carter, Jr., was born in Plains, Georgia, on October 1, 1924. He attended the United States Naval Academy at Annapolis and graduated in 1946. He married Rosalynn Smith later in the year. Carter served in the navy as a submariner and worked with Admiral Hyman Rickover's nuclear submarine program. He returned to Georgia after his father's death in 1953 and managed the family peanut farm. Carter entered politics in 1962 and was elected to the Georgia State Senate. He was elected governor of Georgia in 1970. Carter completed his term in 1974 and became a candidate for the Democratic nomination for the presidency. He received the nomination in July of 1976 after a series of primary victories. He chose Minnesota senator Walter Mondale as his running mate and defeated incumbent president Gerald Ford in the election in November of 1976. Carter was sworn into office on January 20, 1977. His term of office was marred by poor relations with Congress, and his initial popularity waned when he was unable to enact his social and economic legislation. Carter was a leading proponent of human rights in international relations. He succeeded in negotiating a new treaty that granted Panama sovereignty over the Panama Canal Zone by the year 2000. He was instrumental in assisting Egyptian president Anwar el-Sadat and Israeli prime minister Menachem Begin in negotiating peace between their two countries in the Camp David Accords in 1978. Carter also established diplomatic relations with the People's Republic of China in 1979. The relationship of the United States with the Soviet Union deteriorated following the Soviet invasion of Afghanistan in late 1979. The United States Embassy in Iran was captured by Iranian students in November of 1979, and the government of Iran refused to release American citizens held hostage in the embassy. A rescue mission failed in April of 1980, and the continued holding of the hostages dominated Carter's final years in office. He defeated Massachusetts senator Edward Kennedy for the Democratic renomination, but was defeated in November by Republican nominee Ronald Reagan. Carter relinquished office to Reagan on January 20, 1981. He accepted a professorship at Emory University in 1982. He remained involved in international human rights and led international observer teams in elections in Panama, Nicaragua, and Zambia in the late 1980s and early 1990s. Carter hosted negotiations for a peace settlement in Ethiopia in 1989. He also remained involved as an advocate of social reform in the United States.

RONALD REAGAN (President, January 20, 1981–January 20, 1989). Ronald Wilson Reagan was born in Tampico, Illinois, on February 6, 1911. He was educated at Eureka College in Illinois, where he graduated in 1932. He worked as a radio sports announcer in Iowa before going to Hollywood in 1937. Reagan appeared in nearly fifty films over the next three decades. He married actress Jane Wyman in 1940. They divorced in 1948, and he married actress Nancy Davis in 1952. Reagan was also active in the Screen Actors' Guild and served as its president from 1947 until 1952 and from 1959 until 1960. He became a spokesman for General Electric in the 1950s and hosted "G.E. Theater" on television from 1954 until 1962. Reagan also changed his political affiliation from Democrat to Republican during the 1950s. He became more involved in politics and was elected governor of California in 1966. He was briefly a candidate for the Republican presidential nomination in 1968 and was reelected to a second term

as governor in 1970. Reagan left the governor's office in 1974 and challenged President Gerald R. Ford for the Republican presidential nomination in 1976. He was unsuccessful in his attempt, but received the Republican nomination in 1980. He chose George Bush as his vice presidential running mate and defeated incumbent president Jimmy Carter in the election in November of 1980. Reagan took office as president of the United States on January 20, 1981. He survived an assassination attempt on March 30, 1981, when he was shot and seriously injured by John W. Hinckley, Jr. Reagan recovered from his wounds and embarked on a campaign to reduce nondefense spending and lower taxes. His policies led to a large increase in the national debt. He continued massive spending increases in the military and initiated the Strategic Defense Initiative program in 1983. Reagan also sent United States troops to Grenada in October of 1983 to oust the leftist junta that had taken power there. He defeated Democratic nominee Walter Mondale by a wide margin in his reelection bid in November of 1984. The Reagan administration was involved in a scandal in November of 1986 when allegations were made that members of the administration were involved in supplying weapons to the Islamic fundamentalist regime in Iran in exchange for that government's assistance in gaining the release of American hostages in the Middle East. The incident became known as "Irangate" and subsequent investigations led to the indictment of high-ranking officials on the National Security Council. Reagan remained a popular leader, however, and completed his term of office on January 20, 1989. He continued to be an influential spokesman on conservative issues and supported the election of Republican candidates.

GEORGE BUSH (President, January 20, 1989–January 20, 1993). George Herbert Walker Bush was born in

Milton, Massachusetts, on June 12, 1924. He was the son of Prescott Bush, a former United States senator from Connecticut. Bush graduated from Yale University and served during World War II as a naval carrier pilot. He married Barbara Pierce in 1945. He was the cofounder of Zapata Petroleum Corporation in 1953 and was president of the Zapata Offshore Company from 1956 until 1964. Bush entered politics in 1964, when he ran as the Republican nominee for the United States Senate in Texas. He was defeated in that election by incumbent Senator Ralph Yarborough. He was elected a Republican member of the House of Representatives from Texas in 1966. Bush left the House after waging an unsuccessful campaign against Lloyd Bentsen for the U.S. Senate in 1970. He was subsequently named permanent representative to the United Nations, where he served until 1972. He was named chairman of the Republican National Committee from 1973 until 1974

and served as U.S. liaison officer to the People's Republic of China from 1974 until 1975. Bush served as director of the Central Intelligence Agency from 1976 until 1977. He was an unsuccessful candidate for the Republican presidential nomination in 1980, but was subsequently chosen as running mate to Ronald Reagan. They were victorious in the November elections, and Bush took office as vice president in January of 1981. He was returned to office in the elections of 1984. Bush was elected president of the United States in November of 1988 and took office on January 20, 1989. He achieved a considerable degree of popularity at home and abroad for successfully leading the United States in a war against Iraq for the liberation of Kuwait in 1991. Bush's popularity dwindled the following year over a declining economic situation, however. He was defeated for reelection by Democrat Bill Clinton in the elections in November of 1992 and left office on January 20, 1993.

Uruguay, Oriental Republic of

(República Oriental del Uruguay)

Uruguay is a country on the southeastern coast of South America. It was granted independence from Brazil on August 25, 1828.

HEADS OF STATE

JUAN JOSÉ AMÉZAGA (President, March 1, 1943–March 1, 1947). Juan José de Amézaga was born in 1881. He was educated as a lawyer and served in the government as minister of agriculture and as Uruguay's ambassador to the League of Nations. He was a member of the democratic faction of the

Colorado party and defeated Dr. Luis Alberto de Herrera for the presidency of Uruguay in November of 1942. Amézaga took office on March 1, 1943. He survived a right-wing plot against the government in July of 1946. Amézaga completed his term of office and stepped down on March 1, 1947. He retired from politics and died after a long illness in Montevideo at the age of 75 on August 20, 1956.

TOMÁS BERRETA (President, March 1, 1947–August 2, 1947). Tomás Berreta was born near Arroyo Miguelete on November 22, 1875. He joined the Uruguayan army and was active in the revolutions that took place between 1896 and 1904. He was an ally of President José Batlle y Ordóñez and was appointed chief of the Batllista armed forces. Berreta served as a national deputy from 1922 until 1929, when he was appointed to the National Council of Administration. He remained on the council until 1933, when it was dissolved by President Gabriel Terra. Berreta was a leading opponent of the Terra regime and was briefly forced into exile. He was allowed to return to the Uruguayan capital and resumed his opposition to the government. He was elected to the Council of State in 1942 and was appointed minister of public works. Berreta was nominated for the presidency by the liberal Colorado party in 1946 and defeated Luis Alberto de Herrera. He was sworn into office of March 1, 1947. His administration was beset by a general strike on June 30, 1947. Beretta's health failed shortly thereafter, and he relinquished his duties to his vice president, Luis Batlle Berres, on August 1, 1947. He died following an emergency operation in Montevideo on August 2, 1947.

LUIS BATLLE BERRES (President, August 2, 1947–March 1, 1951). Luis Batlle Berres was born in Montevideo on November 26, 1897. He was a nephew of José Batlle y Ordóñez, who served as Uruguay's president from 1903 until 1907 and from 1911 until 1915. Luis Batlle Berres was elected to the Congress in 1923. He remained in the Chamber of Representatives until 1933 and was returned to office in 1942. He was elected president of the Chamber the following year. Batlle Berres was a member of the Colorado party and took office as vice president under Tomás Berreta in March of 1947. He succeeded to the presidency following Berreta's death on August 2, 1947. He was a proponent of a democratic system, and his term of office maintained Uruguay's economic and political stability. Batlle Berres founded the daily newspaper *Accion* in 1948 to support his faction of the Colorado party. He supported Andrés Martínez Trueba as his successor in elections in 1950 and relinquished office to Martínez Trueba on March 1, 1951. He was named to the National Council of Government when Uruguay adopted an executive council form of government in 1952. Batlle Berres again served as Uruguay's head of state as chairman of the council from March 1, 1954, until March 1, 1956. He was succeeded by his ally, Alberto Zubiria, and remained on the National Council. Batlle Berres died in Montevideo on July 15, 1964, at the age of 66 after suffering a stroke.

ANDRÉS MARTÍNEZ TRUEBA (President, March 1, 1951–March 1, 1954). Andrés Martínez Trueba was born in 1884. He was educated at the University of Montevideo. He entered politics in 1903 as a member of the Colorado party. He became a close advisor to President José Batlle y Ordóñez. Martínez Trueba was elected to the Chamber of Deputies in 1918. He served on the National Administration Council during the 1920s. He was a creator of the Banco Hipotecario and served as its president from 1928 until 1932 and from 1942 until 1946. Martínez Trueba also served as mayor of Montevideo during the early 1940s. He became president of the National Bank in 1946 and served until 1950, when he stepped down to become a candidate for president. He was victorious in the election later in the year and took office on March 1, 1951. Martínez Trueba sponsored a constitutional reform in 1951 that established a nine-man Federal Executive Council. He served as the council's first chairman from March 1, 1952, until March 1, 1954, when he relinquished the chairmanship to Luis Batlle Berres. He subsequently retired from politics. Martínez Trueba died in Montevideo at the age of 75 on December 19, 1959.

LUIS BATLLE BERRES (President, March 1, 1954–March 1, 1956). *See earlier entry under Heads of State.*

ALBERTO ZUBIRIA (President, March 1, 1956–March 1, 1957). Alberto Fermin Zubiria was born in Montevideo on October 9, 1901. He was educated at the National University and received a degree in law in 1925. He entered politics as a member of the Batllista faction of the Colorado party and served as the Montevideo Department Council's legal advisor from 1928 until 1932. Zubiria was elected to the Chamber of Deputies in 1932, but resigned the following year when Gabriel Terra became Uruguay's dictator. Zubiria went into exile in Argentina in 1935. He returned to Uruguay after Terra's ouster and was reelected to the Chamber of Deputies. He was named to the cabinet as minister of industry and labor in 1946 and became minister of the interior the following year. Zubiria left the cabinet in 1950 to accept the position of president of the Bank of the Republic. He was selected to serve on Uruguay's National Council in 1954. Zubiria became head of state as chairman of the council on March 1, 1956. He relinquished the chairmanship to Arturo Lezama on March 1, 1957. Zubiria subsequently retired from politics. He died in Montevideo on October 4, 1971.

ARTURO LEZAMA (President, March 1, 1957–March 1, 1958). Arturo Lezama was a member of the Colorado party. He served on the National Council of Government and was elected chairman of the council on March 1, 1957. He completed his term on March 1, 1958.

CARLOS Z. FISHER (President, March 1, 1958–March 1, 1959). Carlos Z. Fisher served as minister of agriculture in the early 1950s. He was selected to serve on the ruling National Council of Government as a member of the Colorado party. He became chairman of the National Council on March 1, 1958. Fisher completed his term of office on March 1, 1959.

MARTÍN R. ECHEGOYEN (President, March 1, 1959–March 1, 1960). Martín R. Echegoyen was born in 1892. He was a leader of the Nationalist party and was a candidate for vice president of Uruguay on the ticket with Luis Alberto de Herrera in 1946. Herrera was defeated by Tomás Berreta. Echegoyen was elected to the Senate in the 1950s and was elected to the National Council of Government in 1959. He served as president of the National Council from March 1, 1959, when the Blancos gained control of the government. He completed his term on March 1, 1960, and remained on the council until 1963. Echegoyen broke from the Blanco Democratic Union to join the Nationalist Popular Movement in 1966. He was the party's unsuccessful candidate for president that year.

BENITO NARDONE (President, March 1, 1960–March 1, 1961). Benito Nardone was born in Montevideo in 1907. He was educated locally and became a political reporter for a Montevideo newspaper. He later became a popular political broadcaster on radio. Nardone entered politics in 1950, when he formed the Federal League to support his agricultural policies. He became a leading figure in the Conservative Blanco party. He was instrumental in leading the Blanco party to victory over the ruling Colorado party in 1958 and served as a member of the National Council of Government. Nardone became Uruguay's head of state as chairman of the National Council on March 1, 1960. He completed his term of office on March 1, 1961, and was succeeded by Eduardo Victor Haedo. He subsequently left the Blanco party to campaign for the return of an executive presidency in Uruguay. Nardone remained active in politics until his death of cancer in Montevideo at the age of 57 on March 25, 1964.

EDUARDO VICTOR HAEDO (President, March 1, 1961–March 1, 1962). Eduardo Victor Haedo was born in 1898. He was educated at the University of San Marcos in Lima, Peru, and returned to Uruguay to teach literature and history. He was elected to the Chamber of Deputies in 1931 and served until 1935. Haedo served in the cabinet as minister of public education and social welfare in 1936. He was elected to the Senate in 1938 and was a leading member of the Blanco Democratic Union. He was elected to the ruling National Council of Government in 1959 and served as its president from March 1, 1961, until March 1, 1962. Haedo remained on the National Council until March of 1963 and subsequently returned to the Senate. He retired from politics in 1967.

FAUSTINO HARRISON (President, March 1, 1962–March 1, 1963). Faustino Harrison was born in 1900. He was a member of the ruralist faction of the National party. He was elected to the ruling nine-member National Council of Government in 1959 and was selected as its president on March 1, 1962. Harrison completed his term on March 1, 1963. He died of a heart attack in Montevideo at the age of 63 on August 20, 1963.

DANIEL FERNÁNDEZ CRESPO (President, March 1, 1963–March 1, 1964). Daniel Fernández Crespo was born in 1901. He was elected to the legislature in the department of Montevideo in 1928 and served until 1931. He was then elected to the Chamber of Deputies. Fernández was a member of the Blanco party and a leading supporter of Luis Alberto de Herrera. Fernandez was elected to the Senate in 1950 and became a supporter of Eduardo Victor Haedo. He was a founder of the Blanco Democratic Union in 1958. He served on the National Council of Government, and became its president on March 1, 1963. To help reduce Uruguay's trade deficit, Fernández forbade the import of luxury goods. He completed his term on March 1, 1964. He remained on the National Council until his death from a heart ailment in Montevideo at the age of 62 on July 28, 1964.

LUIS GIANNATTASIO (President, March 1, 1964–February 7, 1965). Luis Giannattasio was born in Uruguay in 1895. He was educated at Montevideo University and the Massachusetts Institute of Technology. He worked with the World Health Organization after graduation. Giannattasio entered politics in 1959 and served as minister of public works. His success in that position gained his election to the ruling National Council of Government in 1962. He was a member of the Nationalist party and became Uruguay's head of state as president of the National Council on March 1, 1964. Giannattasio retained office until his death from a heart attack in Punta del Este at the age of 70 on February 7, 1965.

WASHINGTON BELTRÁN (President, February 7, 1965–March 1, 1966). Washington Beltrán was born in Montevideo on April 6, 1914. He served as a member of the House of Representatives in 1946 and 1955. He was a founder of the Blanco Democratic

Union. Beltrán was elected to the Senate in 1959 and served on the National Council of Government. He succeeded to the presidency of the National Council following the death of Luis Giannattasio on February 7, 1965. He completed his term of office on March 1, 1966, and returned to the Senate in 1967. Beltrán was banned from political activities by the military government from 1973 until 1980. He subsequently worked as a journalist.

ALBERTO HÉBER USHER (President, March 1, 1966–March 1, 1967). Alberto Héber Usher was born in 1916. He was a prominent Uruguayan business executive and a member of the Blanco party. He served on the National Council of Government and was chosen its president on March 1, 1966. He completed his term of office on March 1, 1967, when the council was abolished and an executive presidency under Oscar Gestido was reestablished.

OSCAR GESTIDO (President, March 1, 1967–December 6, 1967). Oscar Daniel Gestido was born in Montevideo on November 28, 1901. He received a military education and entered the Uruguayan air force. He rose to the rank of colonel in 1942 and general in 1949. Gestido entered politics in 1963 and was chosen by the Liberal Colorado party to serve on the National Council of Government. He resigned from the council in 1966 to become a candidate for president under a new constitution that replaced the National Council with an executive presidency. He was victorious and took office on March 1, 1967. His government was faced with a declining economy, and he declared martial law in October of 1967. Gestido briefly stepped down as president the following month after challenging former Treasury minister Amilcar Vasconcellos to a duel. A court of honor ruled that there was no

justification for the challenge, and Gestido resumed office. He retained office until his death from a heart attack in Montevideo at the age of 66 on December 6, 1967.

JORGE PACHECO ARECO (President, December 6, 1967–March 1, 1972). Jorge Pacheco Areco was born in Montevideo on April 9, 1920. He was elected vice president under Oscar Gestido and took office in March of 1967. He succeeded to the presidency following Gestido's death on December 6, 1967. Uruguay's increasing economic difficulties led to widespread domestic violence. Pacheco declared a state of siege to combat the activities of the leftist Tupamaro guerrillas. He introduced a referendum to change the constitution to allow his reelection in 1971. The referendum was defeated, however, and he was succeeded by Juan María Bordaberry on March 1, 1972. Pacheco was subsequently named ambassador to Spain, where he remained until 1979. He served as ambassador to Switzerland from 1979 until 1980 and was ambassador to the United States from 1980 until 1982. Pacheco was appointed ambassador to Paraguay in 1988.

JUAN MARÍA BORDABERRY (President, March 1, 1972–June 12, 1976). Juan María Bordaberry Arocena was born to a wealthy family in Montevideo on June 17, 1928. He was educated at the University of Montevideo, but abandoned law school to manage his family's estate after the death of his father. Bordaberry entered politics in the 1950s as a member of the National party. He was elected to the Senate in 1962 and succeeded Benito Nardone as a leader of the rural faction of the Nationalists in 1964. He was a proponent of constitutional reforms to establish an executive presidency in 1966. Bordaberry was appointed to President Jorge Pacheco Areco's cabinet as minister of agriculture in October of 1969. He joined the Colorado party and was elected president in November of 1971 when a constitutional amendment to allow Pacheco to succeed himself was defeated. He was sworn into office on March 1, 1972. Bordaberry continued his predecessor's policy of repression against leftist Tupamaro guerrillas, who were waging a violent campaign against the government. He was successful in crushing the Tupamaro forces later in the year. Uruguay continued to face severe economic difficulties. The military staged a coup in February of 1973 that resulted in a military-dominated National Security Council that took over many of the powers of government. Bordaberry retained office as president and dissolved the Congress in June of 1973. He ruled in a dictatorial fashion with the approval of the military until June 12, 1976, when he was deposed after trying to extend his term of office.

ALBERTO DEMICHELLI (President, June 12, 1976–September 1, 1976). Alberto Demichelli was born in 1894. He was a lawyer and member of the liberal wing of the Colorado party. He supported the military coup that banned political activities in February of 1973. Demichelli became vice president of the Council of State and was installed as interim president when the military forced the resignation of President Juan María Bordaberry on June 12, 1976. Demichelli remained president under the supervision of the military until the selection of Aparacio Méndez Manfredini as president on September 1, 1976. Demichelli died at the age of 84 on October 12, 1980, after suffering a stroke in Montevideo.

APARACIO MÉNDEZ MANFREDINI (President, September 1, 1976–September 1, 1981). Aparacio Méndez Manfredini was born in Rivera in 1904. He was educated as a lawyer and became involved in politics. He was active in

the National party and served as minister of public health from 1961 until 1965. Méndez was named to the Council of State following the military coup in February of 1973. He was named president by the ruling National Security Council on September 1, 1976. Uruguay's government continued to be dominated by the military leaders, and Méndez exercised little power as president. He completed his term of office on September 1, 1981, and retired from politics. The following year he became seriously ill. He died in Montevideo at the age of 84 after a long illness on June 26, 1988.

GREGORIO CONRADO ALVAREZ ARMELINO (President, September 1, 1981–March 1, 1985). Gregorio Conrado Alvarez Armelino was born in Montevideo on November 26, 1925. He attended the Uruguay Military College and served as an officer in the cavalry from 1946. He served as chief of the Republic Guard from 1962 until 1979. Alvarez was promoted to general in 1971 and led the Combined Armed Forces Command. He served as first secretary of the ruling Council of National Security from 1973 until 1974 and was commander in chief of the army from 1978 until 1979. He retired from the military in 1979 and was named president of Uruguay on September 1, 1981. Alvarez led a transitional regime that restored democratic rule to Uruguay. Elections were held in November of 1984, and Alvarez relinquished office to the victor, Julio María Sanguinetti Cairolo, on March 1, 1985.

JULIO MARÍA SANGUINETTI CAIROLO (President, March 1, 1985–March 1, 1990). Julio María Sanguinetti Cairolo was born in Montevideo on January 6, 1936. He was educated locally and joined the Colorado party while in his teens. He worked as a journalist during the 1950s. Sanguinetti subsequently attended the University of Montevideo, where he received a degree in law in 1961. He entered politics and was elected to the Chamber of Deputies in 1962. He served in the cabinet as minister of industry and trade from 1969 until 1972 and as minister of education and culture from 1972 until 1973. Sanguinetti resumed his career as a journalist following the military takeover of the government in February of 1973. He became the leader of the Colorado party in 1981 and was instrumental in negotiations that led to the return of democratic rule to Uruguay. He led his party to victory in elections held in November of 1984 and was sworn into office as president on March 1, 1985. Sanguinetti instituted a number of democratic reforms and released all political prisoners in the country, including captured Tupamaro guerrillas. He completed his term of office on March 1, 1990, but remained the leader of the Colorado party.

LUIS ALBERTO LACALLE (President, March 19, 1990–). Luis Alberto Lacalle Herrera was born in 1941. He was elected to the Legislative Assembly in 1971 and became a senator in 1984. He was the National party's candidate for president in November of 1989. Lacalle was victorious, though his party failed to win a majority in the National Assembly. He was sworn in as president of Uruguay on March 19, 1990, and headed a coalition government which included members of the Colorado party.

Uzbekistan, Republic of

(Ozbekiston Respublikasy)

Uzbekistan is a country in central Asia. It became independent following the breakup of the Soviet Union on December 25, 1991.

HEAD OF STATE

ISLAM A. KARIMOV (President, March 24, 1990–). Islam Abduganiyevich Karimov was born in Samarkand in 1938. He was employed as an engineer at the Tashkent aviation factory and joined the Communist party in 1964. Karimov served as minister of finance in the Uzbek Soviet Socialist Republic from 1983 until 1986. He became first secretary of the Central Committee of the Uzbek Communist party in 1989.

Karimov was elected president of the Uzbek on March 24, 1990. The Republic of Uzbekistan declared its independence following the unsuccessful Soviet coup in August of 1991. Uzbekistan joined the Commonwealth of Independent States in December of 1991, and Karimov was confirmed as president by a popular vote on December 29, 1991.

HEAD OF GOVERNMENT

ABDULHASHIM MUTALOV (Premier, December 29, 1991–). Abdulhashim Mutalov was a member of the People's Democratic party. He was appointed to the office of prime minister by President Islam Karimov on December 29, 1991.

Vanuatu, Republic of

(République de Vanuatu)

Vanuatu is a group of islands in the southwest Pacific Ocean. It was formerly known as the New Hebrides. It was granted independence from France and Great Britain on July 30, 1980.

HEADS OF STATE

ATI GEORGE SOKOMANU (President, July 30, 1980–January 12, 1989). Ati George Sokomanu was born George Kalkoa in 1938. He served as deputy chief minister and minister of the interior of the New Hebrides. He became the first president of independent Vanuatu on July 30, 1980. Sokomanu resigned in February of 1984 after being convicted of failure to pay a road tax. He was reappointed to the presidency the following month. Sokomanu attempted to dissolve Parliament on December 16, 1988, following an election victory by the left-wing Vanua'aku party. He illegally named Barak Tame Sope as head of an interim government. The dissolution was ignored by Prime Minister Walter Lini, who ordered Sokomanu's arrest on December 19, 1988, and charged the president with acting in an unconstitutional manner. Sokomanu was dismissed from office on January 12, 1989. He was tried and convicted and sentenced to six years in prison in March of 1989, but was released the following month.

ONNEYN TAHI (President, January 12, 1989–January 30, 1989). Onneyn Tahi served as acting president following the ouster of President George Ati Sokomanu on January 12, 1989. He retained office until January 30, 1989, when he was succeeded by Fred Timakata.

FRED TIMAKATA (President, January 30, 1989–). Fred Kalamoana Timakata was born on Shepard Island in 1936. He served as Speaker of the Parliament from 1985 until 1988. He was named minister of health in 1988 and served until 1989. Timakata was selected by the electoral college to serve as president of Vanuatu on January 30, 1989.

HEADS OF GOVERNMENT

REVEREND WALTER LINI (Prime Minister, July 30, 1980–September 6, 1991). Walter Hadte Lini was born in Pentecost in 1942. He was educated in the Solomon Islands and New Zealand and studied for the Anglican priesthood. In 1970 he was ordained a priest. He served as deputy chief minister and minister of social services of New Hebrides from January to November of 1979. Lini served as chief minister and minister of justice from November of 1979 until New Hebrides became independent as Vanuatu on July 30, 1980. The Lini government faced a secessionist movement on some of the islands, but most of the insurgents surrendered later in 1980. Lini's Vanua'aku party was returned to power in elections in November of 1983. Lini was a leading spokesman in support of the Pacific as a nuclear-free area. He suffered a stroke in 1987. His party lost support in the elections in November of 1987, but Lini retained office. He suffered a heart attack in May of 1991. He became involved in a leadership struggle in the Vanua'aku party in August of 1991. Lini was ousted from the party leadership and lost a vote of confidence in Parliament. He stepped down from office on September 6, 1991. He subsequently formed the Vanuatu National United party in opposition to Donald Kalpokas's Vanua'aku party.

DONALD KALPOKAS (Prime Minister, September 6, 1991–December 16, 1991). Donald Kalpokas served as minister of education and judicial services in the government of Rev. Walter Lini. He served as secretary-general of the Vanua'aku party and challenged Walter Lini for the leadership of the party in August of 1991. Kalpokas was elected leader of the party and replaced Lini as prime minister on September 6, 1991. He remained prime minister until December 16, 1991, when defections from the Vanua'aku party forced his resignation.

MAXIME CARLOT (Prime Minister, December 16, 1991–). Maxime Korman Carlot served as leader of the Union of Moderate Parties from 1987. Carlot was named deputy prime minister in the illegally named government of Barak Tame Sope in December of 1988. Carlot was charged with sedition, convicted, and sentenced to five years in prison, but his sentence was dismissed in April of 1989. He became prime minister on December 16, 1991, when the Union of Moderate Parties joined in a coalition with Walter Lini's newly formed Vanuatu National United party to force the ouster of Donald Kalpokas.

Vatican City

Vatican City State is located within the city of Rome, Italy. It was granted recognition as an independent country by the Lateran Treaty with Italy in February of 1929 and is ruled by the Supreme Pontiff, or Pope, of the Roman Catholic Church.

HEADS OF STATE

PIUS XII (Pope, March 2, 1939–October 9, 1958). Pius XII was born

Eugenio Maria Giuseppe Giovanni Pacelli in Rome on March 2, 1876. He studied for the priesthood at home and was ordained in 1899. Two years later he joined the Vatican Secretariat of State, where he remained until 1917. He was subsequently named the titular archbishop of Sardis and was appointed nuncio to Berlin in 1918. After being created a cardinal in 1929, he returned to the Vatican the following year. He resumed his duties with the Secretariat of State and was elected Pope on March 2, 1939, succeeding Pius XI. An opponent of Nazism, he was criticized as being too weak in his opposition to Hitler, though he was successful in his attempts to protect the lives of many Jews residing in Italy during World War II. Pius XII organized Catholic Action after the war in opposition to Communism and excommunicated Catholic Communists in 1949. Though considered an autocrat, he liberalized church laws and paved the way for the reforms of the Second Vatican Council under his successor, John XXIII. Pius XII was gravely ill in the winter of 1954, though he recovered to continue his duties. He died at Castel Gandolfo, the Papal summer palace near Rome, on October 9, 1958, after suffering several strokes.

JOHN XXIII (Pope, October 28, 1958–June 3, 1963). John XXIII was born Angelo Roncalli in the village of Sotto il Monte, in northern Italy, on November 25, 1881. He was educated in theology in Rome and was ordained to the priesthood in 1904. He served as private secretary to the Bishop of Bergamo until 1915, when he joined the Italian army, serving as a chaplain at military hospital during World War I. He was called to Rome in 1921 and was named titular archbishop in 1925. He served as an apostolic delegate to Bulgaria from 1931 until 1934, when he was transferred to Turkey. He was named apostolic delegate to France in 1944 and also served as the Vatican's observer at the United Nations Educational, Scientific and Cultural Organi-

zation (UNESCO). He was created a cardinal in 1953 and was appointed Patriarch of Venice. He was selected as a compromise candidate to succeed Pope Pius XII on October 28, 1963. John XXIII was an activist Pope and summoned the first general council of the Roman Catholic Church in nearly 100 years shortly after becoming the head of the church. He also made plans to convoke the Second Vatican Council to modernize the church, which convened in October of 1962. John XXIII became seriously ill from a gastric tumor in May of 1963 and died of peritonitis on June 3, 1963.

PAUL VI (Pope, June 21, 1963–August 6, 1978). Paul VI was born Giovanni Battista Montini in Concesio, Italy, on September 26, 1897. He studied for the priesthood at home and was ordained in 1920. He entered the Vatican Secretariat of State in 1922 and advanced to become prosecretary of the internal business of the church under Pope Pius XII in 1944. He was appointed Archbishop of Milan in 1954 and was created a cardinal in 1958. He was elected to succeed Pope John XXIII on June 21, 1963. Paul continued the reforms of his predecessor, and presided over the Second Vatican Council. The reforms he approved included a revision of the liturgy, replacement of Latin as the language of the Mass, and the removal of abstinance of meat on Fridays. He was also an advocate of social justice and made efforts to internationalize the church and promote world peace. He became the first modern pope to travel outside of Europe, traveling to the United States to address the United Nations General Assembly in October of 1965. Paul VI refused to consider the marriage of priests or the ordination of women to the priesthood and authored a controversial encyclical in the summer of 1968 that rejected the use of artificial birth control. Paul VI remained the leader of the Roman Catholic

Church until his death from a heart attack at the summer residence at Castel Gandolfo, on August 6, 1978.

JOHN PAUL I (Pope, August 26, 1978–September 28, 1978). John Paul 1 was born Giovanni Luciani in the town of Canale d'Agordo in northeastern Italy on October 17, 1912. He decided to become a priest at an early age and studied philosophy and theology at the seminary in Belluno. He was ordained to the priesthood in 1935 and joined the faculty of the Belluno seminary two years later. He was named deputy to the Bishop of Belluno in 1948. He was appointed Bishop of Vittorio Veneto in 1958 by Pope John XXIII and became Patriarch of Venice in 1969. He was named a cardinal by Pope Paul VI in 1974. Cardinal Luciani succeeded Paul VI as Pope on August 26, 1978, after four rounds of balloting by the College of Cardinals. His reign as the Bishop of Rome was the briefest since 1605. John Paul I died suddenly of a heart attack during the night of September 28, 1978, while sleeping in his room at the Vatican.

JOHN PAUL II (Pope, October 16, 1978–   ). John Paul II was born Karol Jozef Wojtyła in Wadowice, Poland, on May 18, 1920. He studied literature at Jagiellonian University in Krakow before deciding to become a priest. He studied for the seminary during the Nazi occupation of Poland in World War II and was ordained to the priesthood in November of 1946. Continuing his studies in Rome, he received a doctorate in theology. He returned to Poland to teach at the Catholic University of Lublin. He was named an Auxiliary Bishop of Krakow in 1948 and became Archbishop of Krakow in 1964, then was elevated to the College of Cardinals by Pope Paul VI in May of 1967. He was considered a moderate reformer and became a symbol of the Roman Catholic Church in Communist-dominated Poland. Following the sudden death of the newly selected Pope John Paul I, Cardinal Wojtyła was elected by the College of Cardinals to succeed to the papacy in the eighth round of balloting on October 16, 1978. He became the first non-Italian Pope in 455 years. He chose the name John Paul II and travelled widely during his first years in office. He returned to Poland as Pope in the Summer of 1979 and visited the United States later in the year. John Paul II was shot and seriously wounded in an assassination attempt on May 13, 1981. He recovered from his injuries after a long period of convalescence. John Paul II resumed his duties and continued to travel widely, pressing the issues of humanitarianism and world peace. He aligned himself with Catholic conservatism in his continued opposition to artificial birth control and priestly marriages. He also rejected the doctrine of liberation theology and forbade members of the clergy to hold political office.

Venda, Republic of

(Republiek van Venda)

Venda is a country consisting of two discontinuous areas in South Africa. It was granted independence by South Africa on September 13, 1979.

HEADS OF STATE

CHIEF PATRICK MPHEPHU (President, September 13, 1979–April 17, 1988). Patrick R. Mphephu was born in 1924. He served as paramount leader of the territory of Venda from 1950 and became chief minister when the territory was granted limited self-rule on February 1, 1973. He became the first president of Venda when the country was granted independence from South Africa on September 13, 1979. Mphephu also led the Venda National party, the only recognized political party in the country. He had the strong support of the tribal chiefs and clan leaders and ruled the nation in an authoritarian manner. He retained office until his death on April 17, 1988.

CHIEF FRANK N. RAVELE (President, April 18, 1988–April 5, 1990).

Frank N. Ravele served as minister of finance in the government of Patrick Mphephu. He was selected to succeed Mphephu as president on April 18, 1988. Ravele's regime was accused of corruption and human rights abuses. Ravele was ousted in a military coup led by Gabriel Ramushwana on April 5, 1990.

GABRIEL RAMUSHWANA (President, April 5, 1990–). Gabriel Ramushwana served in the Venda Defense Force. He rose to the rank of colonel and served as deputy chief of the defense force. He led a military coup against President Frank Ravele on April 5, 1990. Ramushwana agreed to the concept of the reincorporation of Venda into a democratic South Africa.

Venezuela, Republic of
(República de Venezuela)

Venezuela is a country on the northern coast of South America. It was granted independence from Spain on July 5, 1821.

HEADS OF STATE

ISAÍAS MEDINA ANGARITA (President, May 5, 1941–October 18, 1945). Isaías Medina Angarita was born in San Cristobal on July 6, 1897. He attended the Venezuelan Military Academy and served in the army from 1914. He was promoted to captain in 1917 and became a teacher at the military school two years later. Medina returned to active duty in 1927 with the rank of lieutenant colonel. He subsequently served again as a teacher at the Venezuelan Military Academy. He was promoted to colonel in 1935 and was

named chief of staff of the Venezuelan army. Medina subsequently was appointed minister of war and the navy in the government of President Eleazar Lopez Contreras. He achieved the rank of general in 1940. Medina resigned from the cabinet in 1941 to campaign for the presidency. He was elected by the Venezuelan Congress and took office on May 5, 1941. He maintained close relations with the United States and severed diplomatic relations with the Axis powers during World War II. Medina also sought to insure civil rights for Venezuelans and to maintain democratic principles. Venezuela's economic stability was jeopardized by difficulties in the industrial and agricultural industries. Medina was ousted in a military coup led by Rómulo Betancourt on October 18, 1945. He was sent into exile in the United States in December of 1945 and lived in New York for the next seven years. He was invited to return to Venezuela shortly after he suffered a stroke in 1952. Medina died at his home in La Florida at the age of 56 on September 15, 1953, after a long illness.

RÓMULO BETANCOURT (President, October 18, 1945–February 15, 1948). Rómulo Betancourt was born in Gautire, near Caracas, on February 22, 1908. He was educated at the Central University in Caracas, where he formed a leftist student movement. Betancourt was briefly imprisoned in 1928 for his opposition to President Juan Vicente Gómez. He led a rebellion against Gómez in April of 1928 and fled to Colombia when the rebellion failed. He remained an outspoken opponent of Gómez and supported several abortive rebellions against the dictatorship while in exile in various Latin American countries. Betancourt returned to Venezuela after Gómez's death in 1936 and founded the leftist newspaper *Orve*. He was again ordered into exile by President Eleazar Lopez Contreras the following year, but remained in hiding in Venezuela. He was captured in 1939 and was sent into exile in Chile and Argentina. Betancourt was allowed to return to Venezuela in 1941 and founded the Democratic Action party. The party's nominee, Rómulo Gallegos Freire, was defeated by General Isaías Medina Angarita in presidential elections in 1941. Betancourt founded another opposition newspaper, *El Pais*, in 1943. He participated in a coup against Medina Angarita on October 18, 1945. Medina Angarita was ousted, and Betancourt became provisional president as head of the seven-man revolu-

tionary junta. Betancourt promised to allow free elections in 1948, and the Democratic Action party nominee, Rómulo Gallegos, was elected president. Betancourt relinquished office to him on February 15, 1948. Gallegos was ousted in a military coup led by former junta member Marcos Pérez Jiménez in November of 1948. Betancourt was again sent into exile and went to the United States. He remained out of Venezuela for nine years, while he traveled to Cuba, Costa Rica, and Puerto Rico. Betancourt was invited to return to Venezuela following Pérez Jiménez's ouster in January of 1958. He reorganized the Democratic Action party and was the party's nominee for president in elections the following December. Betancourt was victorious and took office on February 13, 1959. He pushed for an agrarian reform program and increased industrial development in the country. He survived an army revolt in April of 1960 and an assassination attempt in June of 1960, when a bomb exploded near his car. Betancourt completed his term of office on December 1, 1963, and relinquished the presidency to his long-time associate Raúl Leoni. Betancourt traveled throughout Europe after leaving office. He settled in Switzerland, where he remained until he returned to Venezuela in 1972. He again became active in Venezuelan political affairs and served as the elder statesman of his party and the democracy movement. Betancourt moved to New York City in the early 1980s to work on his memoirs. He died there of complications from a stroke at the age of 73 on September 28, 1981.

RÓMULO GALLEGOS FREIRE (President, February 15, 1948–November 24, 1948). Rómulo Gallegos Freire was born in Caracas on August 2, 1884. He was educated at the Central University, where he received a degree in philosophy. He was a founder and editor of the magazine *La Alborada* in 1911. Gallegos subsequently pursued a career as a teacher and served as a philosophy professor at Caracas's Andres Bello College from 1912. Gallegos also completed his first novel, *Reinadlo Solar* (*Manor Rule*), in 1920. He rose to become director of his college in 1922. Gallegos wrote his prize-winning novel *Dona Barbara* in 1929. He was subsequently appointed to the Senate by Venezuelan dictator Juan Vicente Gómez. He attended no sessions of the Senate and resigned from the office while visiting the United States in 1931. Gallegos remained in exile and went to Spain to work for the National Cash Register Company. He also continued with his writing and published *Contaclar* in 1934 and *Canaima* in 1935. He returned to Venezuela in 1936 and was elected to the Venezuelan Municipal Council. Gallegos also served briefly as minister of education, until his attempts to ban foreign mission schools in Venezuela forced his ouster. He helped found the Democratic Action party in 1941 and was the party's unsuccessful nominee against Isaías Medina Angarita later in the year. Gallegos was again the leftist party's candidate for president in elections held in December of 1947. He was the victor and was sworn in as Venezuela's first popularly elected president on February 15, 1948. Gallegos faced opposition from conservatives and the military and suspended the constitution to preserve order in November of 1948. Despite labor demonstrations in favor of his administration, he was ousted in a military coup on November 24, 1948. Gallegos was exiled to Havana, Cuba, the following month. He subsequently traveled to Mexico, where he remained until the ouster of the dictatorship of Marcos Pérez Jiménez in January of 1958. Gallegos then returned to Venezuela, where he continued writing and engaging in leftist politics. He was granted a life membership in the Venezuelan Senate after his return. He also worked with the Organization of American States and became chairman

of its Inter-American Committee of Human Rights. Gallegos died in Caracas after a long illness at the age of 84 on April 4, 1969.

CARLOS DELGADO CHALBAUD (President, November 24, 1948–November 13, 1950). Carlos Delgado Chalbaud was born in 1909. He served in the Venezuelan military, where he rose to the rank of lieutenant colonel. He was named minister of defense in the government of President Rómulo Gallegos. Delgado was the leader of the bloodless military coup that ousted Gallegos on November 24, 1948. He became provisional president as leader of the ruling three-man military junta composed of himself, Lt. Col. Marco Pérez Jiménez, and Lt. Col. Luis Llovera Paez Secocin. Delgado was shot and beaten to death in Caracas by a mob of twenty assassins on November 13, 1950. The leader of the assassination squad, retired General Rafael Simon Urbina, was killed the following day when he tried to escape from a prison guard.

GERMAN SUAREZ FLAMERICH (President, November 27, 1950–December 3, 1952). German Suarez Flamerich was born in 1907. He was named provisional president of the ruling junta on November 27, 1950, following the assassination of Lt. Col. Carlos Delgado Chalbaud. Junta member Lt. Col. Marcos Pérez Jiménez remained largely in control of the country while Suarez served as head of state. Suarez relinquished office to Pérez Jiménez on December 3, 1952, following a presidential election. Suarez was sent into exile by the new government later in the year.

MARCOS PÉREZ JIMÉNEZ (President, December 3, 1952–January 23, 1958). Marcos Pérez Jiménez was born in Tachira, on April 25, 1914. He attended military schools in Venezuela and Peru and entered the Venezuelan army. He rose to the rank of lieutenant colonel in the early 1940s and served on the General Staff as a section chief. Pérez Jiménez took part in the military coup that ousted President Isaías Medina Angarita in October of 1945. He was named army chief of staff in the subsequent government of Rómulo Betancourt. Pérez Jiménez supported the ouster of President Rómulo Gallegos in November of 1948. He served as a member of the three-man ruling military junta with Lt. Col. Carlos Delgado Chalbaud and Lt. Col. Luis Felipe Llovera Paez. Pérez Jiménez remained a member of the junta following the assassination of Delgado Chalbaud in November of 1950. The junta allowed general elections to be held in November of 1952. Pérez Jiménez was selected as provisional president by the junta on December 3, 1952. The junta subsequently resigned, and Pérez Jiménez was confirmed as president by the newly elected Constituent Assembly in January of 1952. He ruled in a dictatorial fashion and used police suppression against his political opponents. His government was accused of corruption and mismanagement, and the country suffered from growing unemployment during his administration. Widespread resentment against his regime grew among the civilians and military. Pérez Jiménez held a plebiscite in December of 1957 in an attempt to prolong his term of office. A military rebellion against him on January 1, 1958, was crushed and its leaders were arrested. Dissension increased with demonstrations and rioting against the government. Pérez Jiménez was forced to flee Venezuela on January 23, 1958, and was replaced by a military-civilian junta. He subsequently went into exile in the United States. He was extradited back to Venezuela in August of 1963 on charges of embezzling government funds. Pérez Jiménez remained imprisoned until 1968, when he was elected to the Venezuelan Senate. The Supreme Court ruled that he had not met the legal conditions necessary to be a candidate, and his election was annulled. Pérez Jiménez subsequently went into exile in Madrid, Spain.

WOLFGANG LARRAZABÁL UGUETO (President, January 23, 1958–November 14, 1958). Wolfgang Larrazabál Ugueto was born on March 5, 1911. He was commissioned into the Venezuelan navy in 1933 and rose through the ranks. He served as director of the Navy Academy from 1945 until 1947. Larrazabál subsequently served as commander in chief of the navy until 1949. He was appointed naval attaché in Washington, D.C., in 1949. He returned to Venezuela in 1951. Larrazabál led a military coup against President Marcos Pérez Jiménez on January 23, 1958, and served as leader of the ruling junta. His junta survived a coup attempt in July of 1958 led by the minister of defense. He survived a second coup attempt in September of 1958. Larrazabál stepped down as leader of the junta on November 14, 1958, to contest the presidential election the following month. He was defeated by Rómulo Betancourt and returned to the navy as vice admiral. He also served as Venezuela's ambassador to Chile. Larrazabál was again an unsuccessful candidate for the presidency in 1964 and 1968.

EDGARD SANABRIA (President, November 14, 1958–February 13, 1959). Edgard Sanabria was born in 1911. He was a prominent Venezuelan lawyer and teacher. He was named to the ruling junta in May of 1958. Sanabria replaced Wolfgang Larrazabál Ugueto as leader of the junta when Larrazabál stepped down to campaign for the presidency. Rómulo Betancourt was elected president in December of 1958, and Sanabria relinquished office to him on February 13, 1959.

RÓMULO BETANCOURT (President, February 13, 1959–December 1, 1963). *See earlier entry under Heads of State.*

RAÚL LEONI (President, December 1, 1963–March 11, 1969). Raúl Leoni was born in Upata on April 26, 1905. He was educated at the Central University in Caracas. He became involved in liberal politics and was briefly imprisoned in 1921 for his opposition to President Juan Vicente Gómez. Leoni later joined with Rómulo Betancourt in an unsuccessful coup against Gómez in 1928. The coup leaders were arrested, and Leoni was sent into exile in Colombia. He studied law at the National University of Colombia during his exile. He returned from exile following Gómez's death in 1936. Leoni and Betancourt were founders of the Venezuelan Organization Movement, and Leoni was elected to the National Assembly. Gómez's successor as president, General Elezear Lopez Contreras, annulled the election, and Leoni was again forced into exile. He continued his education and received a degree from the Bogota law school in 1938. He then returned to Venezuela and became active in the labor movement. Leoni again joined with Betancourt to form the National Democratic party in 1941. Betancourt became provisional president in October of 1945, following the ouster of President Isaías Medina Angarita, and Leoni was appointed minister of labor in the revolutionary government. He retained his cabinet position until 1948, but was arrested following the military coup led by Marcos Pérez Jiménez in November of 1948. Leoni was sent into exile the following year and lived in the United States, Costa Rica, and several South American countries before returning to Venezuela after Pérez Jiménez's ouster in January of 1958. Leoni helped to reorganize the Democratic Action party and supported the candidacy of Betancourt in December of 1958. Betancourt was elected president, and Leoni was elected to the Venezuelan Senate. He was elected president of the Senate in January of 1959 and became leader of the Democratic Action party. He stepped down from the Senate to campaign for the presidency in 1963. Leoni was elected and succeeded Betancourt to the office on December 1, 1963. Leoni initiated agrarian reforms and presided over great economic growth in the country. His regime was challenged by student demonstrations in December of 1966, however. He briefly suspended the constitution to put down an attempted insurrection by students from the Central University in Caracas. The Democratic Action party's candidate for president was narrowly defeated by Social Christian party candidate Rafael Caldera in the elections in December of 1968. Leoni completed his term of office on March 11, 1969, and turned over the presidency to Caldera. Leoni suffered from ill health in the early 1970s and went to New York City for medical treatment in June of 1972. He died there of a cerebral hemorrhage at the age of 67 on July 5, 1972.

RAFAEL CALDERA RODRÍGUEZ (President, March 11, 1969–March 12, 1974). Rafael Caldera Rodríguez was born in San Felipe on January 24, 1916. He attended the Central University in Caracas, where he became a leader of the Roman Catholic youth movement. He was employed by the National Library in 1936 and soon joined the National Labor Office. Caldera was elected to the National Congress in 1941. He was named attorney general following the coup that installed Rómulo Betancourt as president in 1945. Caldera resigned the following year after a dispute with the left-wing regime. He formed the center-right Socialist Christian party (COPEI) and was elected to the National Assembly in 1946. He was a candidate for president in the elections in 1947, but was defeated by Rómulo Gallegos. Gallegos was ousted in a right-wing military coup in 1948, and Caldera was allowed to remain in the Congress under the military regime. Caldera advocated the restoration of democratic institutions and was arrested on several occasions after Marcos Pérez Jiménez became president in 1953. Pérez Jiménez again ordered Caldera's arrest in August of 1957. He was ordered to leave Venezuela after several months imprisonment and went to New York City in January of 1958. Pérez Jiménez was ousted in a military coup a few day later, and Caldera returned to Venezuela. Caldera was again a candidate for president in December of 1958, but was defeated by Rómulo Betancourt. Caldera returned to the National Congress, where he served as president of the Chamber of Deputies from January of 1959 until December of 1961. He was again defeated for the presidency by Raúl Leoni in December of 1963. Caldera led the opposition to Leoni's administration as leader of COPEI. He again was his party's candidate for president in elections in December of 1968. Caldera won a narrow victory over Democratic Action party candidate Gonzalo Barrios and was sworn into office on March 11, 1969. Venezuela's economy and oil industry monopolized much of Caldera's administration. His party was defeated in presidential elections in December of 1973, and Caldera stepped down on March 12, 1974. He was named a senator for life after leaving the presidency. He was defeated by Jaime Lusinchi for the presidency in December of 1983. Caldera was again a candidate for president in December of 1987, but was denied the COPEI nomination.

CARLOS ANDRES PÉRES (President, March 12, 1974–March 12, 1979). Carlos Andres Péres Rodriguez was born in Rubio, Tachira State, on October 27, 1922. He was educated locally and studied law at Venezuela's Central University. He entered politics at an early age by joining Rómulo Betancourt's Democratic Action party. Péres was active in the revolt that installed Betancourt as president in October of 1945 and served as the president's private secretary. He was elected to the

Chamber of Deputies the following year. The government was ousted by a right-wing military coup in November of 1948, and Péres was jailed for a year in Caracas. He was then sent into exile, where he remained during the 1950s. He spent time in Colombia, Cuba, and Costa Rica before he returned to Venezuela in January of 1958 after the ouster of Marcos Pérez Jiménez. Péres was reelected to the Chamber of Deputies and was named to the cabinet as minister of the interior in the government of Rómulo Betancourt. He stepped down from the government in August of 1963, though he remained active in the Democratic Action party. He was elected secretary-general of the party's national executive committee in 1968. Péres also remained in the Chamber of Deputies as leader of the opposition to President Rafael Caldera from 1969. Péres received the Democratic Action party's nomination for the presidency in 1973 and defeated Lorenzo Fernandez in December of 1973. He took office on March 12, 1974. He nationalized the steel industry in 1975 and the oil industry the following year. Péres completed his term of office on March 12, 1979. He was returned to office in elections in December of 1988 and took office on February 2, 1989. Venezuela's economic condition continued to deteriorate during his second term. Péres survived an assassination attempt during an unsuccessful coup in February of 1992. He was accused of embezzling and misappropriating government funds in 1992. He was suspended and ordered to stand trial by the Venezuelan Senate on May 21, 1993. Ramon José Velasquez was elected interim president by the Venezuelan Congress on June 5, 1993.

LUIS HERRERA CAMPÍNS (President, March 12, 1979–February 2, 1984). Luis Herrera Campíns was born in Acarigua on May 4, 1925. He was educated in Caracas and at the University of Santiago de Compostela in Spain and received a degree in law. He joined the Social Christian Party (COPEI) in 1946 and led a student strike against the military dictatorship of General Marcos Pérez Jiménez in 1952. Herrera was arrested and imprisoned for several months before going into exile in Europe. He returned to Venezuela after Pérez Jiménez's ouster in 1958. Herrera was subsequently elected to the Chamber of Deputies and became chairman of the COPEI parliamentary group in 1961. He retained that position until 1973, when he was elected to the Venezuelan Senate. He was defeated for COPEI's presidential nomination in 1973. Herrera received the nomination in August of 1977 and defeated Luis Piñerua Ordaz in December of 1978. Herrera was sworn into office on March 12, 1979. Venezuela's oil revenues declined during his administration, and the COPEI candidate was badly defeated in elections in 1983. Herrera relinquished office to Jaime Lusinchi on February 2, 1984, but remained a leader of the Social Christian party.

JAIME LUSINCHI (President, February 2, 1984–February 2, 1989). Jaime Lusinchi was born in Clarenes, Anzoategui State, on May 27, 1924. He attended the Central University of Venezuela, where he studied medicine. He joined the Democratic Action party in 1941. Lusinchi was arrested following the right-wing military coup in November of 1948 and was sent into exile after his release. He traveled throughout South America and lived in Argentina and Chile before continuing his medical studies in the United States. He returned to Venezuela following the ouster of Marcos Pérez Jiménez in January of 1958. Lusinchi was elected to the Chamber of Deputies the following year. He served as leader of the Democratic Action party's parliamentary group from 1968 until 1978. He was an unsuccessful candidate for president in 1977 and was elected to the Senate in 1979. He was selected as leader of the party in 1980. He was the party's presidential nominee in 1983 and defeated former President Rafael Caldera in elections in December of 1983. He was sworn into office as president on February 2, 1984. Venezuela's economic condition continued to deteriorate during Lusinchi's presidency. He completed his term of office on February 2, 1989. He remained a leader of a faction of the Democratic Action party.

CARLOS ANDRES PÉRES (President, February 2, 1989–May 21, 1993). *See earlier entry under Heads of State.*

Vietnam, Republic of (South Vietnam)

The Republic of Vietnam was a country in Southeast Asia. The French granted independence to Vietnam in June of 1954. South Vietnam was absorbed by North Vietnam on April 30, 1975.

HEADS OF STATE

BAO DAI (Emperor, January 1926–August 25, 1945; Head of State, June 14, 1949–October 26, 1955). Bao Dai was born Nguyen Vinh Thuy in Hue on October 22, 1913. He was the son of Khai Dinh, who became emperor of Annam in 1916. Bao Dai was educated in Paris. He returned to Annam and ascended to the throne in January of 1926, following the death of his father. A regency council was established to rule until he reached his majority, and Bao Dai returned to France to continue his education. He returned to Annam to take the throne of the French protectorate in September of 1932. He ruled under the French colonial government until 1940, when the Japanese invaded Indo-China. The French were expelled in March of 1945, and Bao Dai accepted limited independence from the Japanese. Japan was defeated the following August, and Bao Dai was forced to abdicate by the Viet Minh on August 25, 1945. He cooperated briefly with Ho Chi Minh, the president of the newly established Democratic Republic of Vietnam. He subsequently went into exile in Hong Kong in July of 1946. The French attempted to reestablish colonial authority in Indo-China and engaged in a war with the Viet Minh. The French entered into negotiations with Bao Dai, and the autonomous Associated State of Vietnam was established in March of 1949. Bao Dai became the chief of government and took office in Saigon on June 14, 1949. The French continued to battle Ho Chi Minh's troops until suffering a major defeat at Dien Bien Phu in July of 1954. A treaty was agreed to in Geneva that established two separate countries divided by the seventeenth parallel. Bao Dai remained head of state of South Vietnam. His premier, Ngo Dinh Diem, sponsored a referendum in 1955 to determine the form of government that should rule Vietnam. The plebiscite overwhelmingly endorsed a republic, and Ngo Dinh Diem was selected as president on October 26, 1955. Bao Dai remained in exile in France, where he remained largely uninvolved in Vietnamese political affairs.

NGO DINH DIEM (President, October 26, 1955–November 1, 1963). Ngo Dinh Diem was born in Hue on January 3, 1901. He was the son of Ngo Dinh Kha, who served as a minister in the government of Emperor Thanh Thai. He was educated in Hue and entered the civil service. Ngo Dinh Diem was named chief of the province of Quangtri in 1930 and was appointed minister of the interior in the government of Emperor Bao Dai in 1933. He resigned two months later in opposition to the French colonial government. He declined to accept an appointment as premier under the Japanese occupation of Vietnam during World War II. Ngo Dinh Diem also refused to participate in the leftist government of Ho Chi Minh after the war. He again refused an offer to serve as premier in the Associated State of Vietnam under Bao Dai in 1949. He left Vietnam the following year and traveled to Japan, Belgium, and the United States. Ngo Dinh Diem returned to Vietnam in June of 1954, following the establishment of an independent Vietnam within the French Union. He accepted the position of premier in Bao Dai's government on June 19, 1954. He consolidated his power in the government and sponsored a referendum that led to Bao Dai's ouster in October of 1955. Ngo Dinh Diem became the first president of the new Republic of Vietnam on October 26, 1955. He governed South Vietnam with the support of the United States, though his failure to initiate promised land reforms increased opposition to his regime. He survived a coup attempt in November of 1960 and was reelected to a second term the following year. His regime became more repressive in the face of growing unrest, and Buddhist leaders in the country went into active opposition to the government. He moved against the Buddhists in May of 1963, claiming they were inspired by the Communist regime in North Vietnam. His actions led to dissatisfaction in the Vietnamese military, which ousted Ngo Dinh Diem in a coup on November 1, 1963. He and his brother, Ngo Dinh Nhu, were murdered the following day on November 2, 1963.

DUONG VAN MINH (President, November 1, 1963–January 30, 1964). Duong Van Minh was born in My Tho on February 19, 1916. He received a military education in France and served in the French colonial army. He fought with the French against the Viet Minh in the early 1950s and earned the nickname "Big Minh." Minh became a leader of the Vietnamese army following the establishment of the Republic of Vietnam in 1955. He was removed from military command by President Ngo Dinh Diem and was a leader of the coup that ousted Diem on November 1, 1963. He led the ruling military junta until January 30, 1964, when he and the junta were deposed in a coup led by General Nguyen Khanh. Minh was restored to the position of head of state on February 8, 1964, though he was largely a figurehead as Nguyen Khanh retained power. He was removed as head of state on August 16, 1964, when Nguyen Khanh became president. Minh was named a member of a three-man ruling junta with Nguyen Khanh and Lt. Gen. Tran Thien Khiem on August 27, 1964. He was selected to lead the junta on September 3, 1964, and remained chief of state until October 25, 1964, when a civilian government under Phan Khac Suu was installed. Minh went into exile in Thailand, where he remained until 1968. He was then allowed to return to South Vietnam by President Nguyen Van Thieu. He announced his opposition to Thieu the following year but declined to become a presidential candidate in 1971. Minh became president of an interim government on April 28, 1975, in the hopes of negotiating conciliatory terms from North Vietnam following the collapse of the South Vietnamese army. He was forced from office on April 30, 1975, and was detained following the Communist takeover of Saigon. He was allowed to emigrate to France in 1983.

NGUYEN KHANH (President, January 30, 1964–February 8, 1964). Nguyen Khanh was born in 1927 and was educated at the Vietnam Military Academy. He was also educated in France and the United States and joined the French Colonial Army in 1954. He joined the Vietnamese army later in the year. Nguyen Khanh served as chief of staff to General Duong Van Minh from 1955 and was active in the coup that ousted President Ngo Dinh Diem in November of 1963. Nguyen Khanh led another coup to purge the ruling military junta on January 30, 1964. He served as head of state until February 8, 1964, when he took the position of premier. He stepped down as premier to become president on August 16, 1964. Nguyen Khanh installed a three-man junta under Duong Van Minh on August 23, 1964, and resumed the position of premier on September 30, 1964. He stepped down as premier on October 30, 1964, but continued to serve as chairman of the Armed Forces Council. He was ousted from power by another military coup. Nguyen Khanh subsequently was sent into diplomatic exile as an ambassador-at-large. He joined the Communist party following the victory of North Vietnam in 1975. He was appointed vice-premier and general secretary of the Council of Ministers in February of 1987.

DUONG VAN MINH (President, February 8, 1964–August 16, 1964). *See earlier entry under Heads of State.*

NGUYEN KHANH (President, August 16, 1964–August 23, 1964). *See earlier entry under Heads of State.*

DUONG VAN MINH (Head of State, September 3, 1964–October 25, 1964). *See earlier entry under Heads of State.*

PHAN KHAC SUU (President, October 25, 1964–June 14, 1965). Phan

Khac Suu was born in Mytho in 1905. He was educated in Paris, France, where he studied agricultural engineering. He returned to Saigon in 1930 and worked for the colonial government as an engineer. Phan Khac Suu became active in the Vietnamese nationalist movement and was arrested by the French in 1940. He remained imprisoned during World War II and returned to Saigon in 1945. He became the leader of the Social Democratic party and was named to the government as minister of agriculture and director-general of land reforms in the government of Ngo Dinh Diem in 1954. Phan Khac Suu subsequently broke with Diem's policies and participated in an unsuccessful coup against the president in 1960. He was arrested and put in prison, where he remained until Diem's ouster in November of 1963. Phan Khac Suu was installed by General Nguyen Khanh as president of a civilian government on October 25, 1964. His government's inability to deal with South Vietnam's numerous problems led to his ouster in a military coup on June 14, 1965. Phan Khac Suu served as president of the Constituent Assembly from 1966 until 1967. He was an unsuccessful candidate for president of South Vietnam in 1967 and became a critic of the United States military involvement in the country. He died in Saigon at the age of 65 after a brief illness on May 24, 1970.

NGUYEN VAN THIEU (President, June 14, 1965–April 21, 1975). Nguyen Van Thieu was born in Ninh Truan, Phan Rang Province, on April 5, 1923 (some sources indicate November of 1924). He was educated in Saigon and Hue. He worked in his family's rice fields during the Japanese occupation from 1942 until 1945. Thieu joined Ho Chi Minh's Communist Viet Minh forces after World War II. He became disillusioned with the Communists, however, and defected from the Viet Minh in 1946. He entered the Viet-

namese National Military Academy in Dalat and was commissioned as a second lieutenant in 1949. Thieu rose through the ranks and became commandant of the National Military Academy following the establishment of the Republic of Vietnam in 1955. He received further military training in the United States and commanded the First Infantry Division as a colonel in the early 1960s. He participated in the coup that ousted President Ngo Dinh Diem in November of 1963 and served on the ruling Military Revolutionary Council. Thieu supported the military coup in December of 1964 and was appointed deputy premier and minister of national defense in February of 1965. He was promoted to major general and replaced Nguyen Khanh as chairman of the Armed Forces Council in March of 1965. He was a leader of the coup that ousted the civilian government on June 14, 1965, and he became the leader of the ruling military junta. Nguyen Cao Ky served in the government as premier, and the two men jointly ruled South Vietnam. Thieu promoted a new constitution in April of 1967 and was elected president in September of 1967. He was sworn into office on October 31, 1967. South Vietnam continued to be besieged by revolutionary forces supported by the Communist government of North Vietnam. Thieu attempted to bring stability to the government with the assistance of United States military and economic aid. He was reelected to office without opposition in 1971. He opposed the Paris Peace Agreement signed by the United States in January of 1973. Although the United States began the withdrawal of military forces from Vietnam, fighting resumed between the South Vietnamese and the Communists, and South Vietnamese troops were overrun by a major military offensive by the North Vietnamese and the Viet Cong in early 1975. Thieu was forced to leave the country on April 21, 1975, as the Communist forces approached Saigon. He went into exile in Thailand and later settled in Surrey, England.

TRAN VAN HUONG (President, April 21, 1975–April 28, 1975). Tran Van Huong was born in Vinh Long Province on December 1, 1903. He worked as a schoolteacher and a school inspector before entering government administration. He briefly served as governor of Saigon in 1954 before being named secretary general of the Vietnamese Red Cross. Tran Van Huong retained that position until 1960. He was a critic of President Ngo Dinh Diem and served on a government advisory council following Diem's ouster in 1963. He was named premier in a civilian government installed by General Nguyen Khanh on October 30, 1964. A military coup ousted the government on January 27, 1965. Tran Van Huong was an unsuccessful candidate for the presidency in 1967. He was again named premier by President Nguyen Van Thieu on May 25, 1968. Tran Van Huong's inability to cope with South Vietnam's economic problems led to his resignation on August 23, 1969. He accepted the position of Nguyen Van Thieu's running mate in the 1971 presidential election and was confirmed as vice president without opposition. He briefly succeeded to the presidency when Thieu fled Saigon on April 21, 1975. Huong relinquished power to General Duong Van Minh on April 28, 1975.

DUONG VAN MINH (President, April 28, 1975–April 30, 1975). *See earlier entry under Heads of State.*

HUYNH TAN PHAT (President, April 30, 1975–July 2, 1976). Huynh Tan Phat was born in My Tho in 1913. He was educated at the University of Hanoi, where he received a degree in architecture. He worked as an architect in Saigon in the 1940s and became involved with the Indo-Chinese Communist party. Huynh Tan Phat was an opponent of the regime of President Ngo Dinh Diem following the establishment of the Republic of Vietnam in 1955. He was arrested on several occasions for his antigovernment activities. He went underground to work with the National Liberation Front and served as its secretary-general. Huynh Tan Phat was named prime minister of the Provisional Revolutionary Government by the Communist insurgents in 1969. He took power in Saigon following the collapse of the republican government on April 30, 1975. He led South Vietnam into reunification with the North, and the new Socialist Republic of Vietnam was established on July 2, 1976. He continued to serve in the government as a vice-premier and chairman of the State Commission for Capital Construction. He was named vice-chairman of the State Council in 1982. He died in Ho Chi Minh City (formerly Saigon) at the age of 76 on September 30, 1989.

HEADS OF GOVERNMENT

BAO DAI (Premier, June 30, 1949–January 1950). *See entry under Heads of State.*

NGUYEN PHAN LONG (Premier, January 1950–April 27, 1950). Nguyen Phan Long was born in Hanoi in 1889. He worked as a customs official in Cochin China before becoming a jour-

nalist. He founded the newspaper *L'Echo Annamité* in 1920. He was active in the moderate Constitutionalist party in Saigon in the 1920s. Nguyen Phan Long supported Vietnam's independence from France and joined the government of the Associated State of Vietnam as Foreign Minister in 1949. He was named premier in January of

1950. He failed to gain economic assistance from the United States and resigned on April 27, 1950. Nguyen Phan Long went into exile in 1955 and died on July 16, 1960.

TRAN VAN HUU (Premier, April 27, 1950–June 1952). Tran Van Huu was born in 1896. He was educated as an agricultural engineer and served in the French colonial government from the 1920s. He became a wealthy landowner and supported the return of Bao Dai as leader of the Associated State of Vietnam in June of 1949. Tran Van Huu was named governor of South Vietnam by Bao Dai and was appointed to succeed Nguyen Phan Long as premier on April 27, 1950. He also served in the government as minister of defense and foreign affairs. He was an advocate of greater independence from France and sought the support of the United States and Great Britain in the struggle against the Communist Viet Minh. Tran Van Huu was unable to unite the country and was dismissed from office in June of 1952. He went into exile in Paris, France, after the establishment of the Republic of Vietnam in 1955. He was politically inactive during his exile and died in a military hospital in Paris at the age of 87 on January 17, 1984.

NGUYEN VAN TAM (Premier, June 1952–December 17, 1953). Nguyen Van Tam was born in Tay Ninh Province in 1895. He served in the French colonial government in Vietnam as a police official before World War II. He joined the government of the Associated State of Vietnam as minister of the interior in 1950. Nguyen Van Tam was named governor of North Vietnam in November of 1951 and was appointed premier in June of 1952. He led a reformist government that attempted to eliminate corruption and institute land reform measures. He met with little success and was dismissed from office on December 17, 1953. Nguyen Van Tam

went into exile in Paris following the establishment of the Republic of Vietnam in 1955. He subsequently remained inactive in Vietnamese politics. He died in Paris at the age of 95 on November 23, 1990.

PRINCE BUU LOC (Premier, January 12, 1954–June 15, 1954). Buu Loc was born in 1915. He was a cousin of Emperor Bao Dai. He was educated at the University of Hanoi and the University of Paris. Buu Loc represented Bao Dai as leader of the Vietnamese delegation in independence negotiations with the French in 1949. These talks led to the establishment of the semiautonomous Associated State of Vietnam in 1950. He continued to represent Vietnam in France and served as ambassador from 1952 until 1954. Buu Loc was named premier and minister of the interior in Bao Dai's government on January 12, 1954. He resigned his position on June 15, 1954, and was replaced by Ngo Dinh Diem.

NGO DINH DIEM (Premier, June 19, 1954–November 2, 1963). *See entry under Heads of State.*

NGUYEN NGOC THO (Premier, November 4, 1963–January 30, 1964). Nguyen Ngoc Tho was born in Long Xuyen province on May 26, 1908. He entered the French civil Service in 1930 and held various positions in the colonial government. He was chosen as minister of the interior in Ngo Dinh Diem's cabinet in 1956 and became vice president under Diem later in 1956. Nguyen Ngoc Tho was chosen by the ruling junta as prime minister and minister of economic affairs on November 4, 1963, following the ouster and murder of Diem. He retained office until January 30, 1964, when General Nguyen Khanh established a military government.

NGUYEN KHANH (Premier, February 8, 1964–August 16, 1964). *See entry under Heads of State.*

NGUYEN XUAN OANH (Premier, August 29, 1964–September 30, 1964). Nguyen Xuan Oanh was educated at Harvard University, where he received a degree in economics. He served in Nguyen Khanh's government as vice-premier from February of 1964. He became acting premier on August 29, 1964, and served until Nguyen Khanh resumed the position on September 30, 1964. Nguyen Xuan Oanh served as deputy premier from November of 1964 until January of 1965, when he was demoted to third deputy premier. He was again named acting premier on January 27, 1965, following the ouster of Tran Van Huong's government. He retained office until February 16, 1965, when a new government was formed by Phuy Huy Quat. Nguyen Xuan Oanh subsequently served as director of South Vietnam's National Institute of Economic Development.

NGUYEN KHANH (Premier, September 30, 1964–October 30, 1964). *See entry under Heads of State.*

TRAN VAN HUONG (Premier, October 30, 1964–January 27, 1965). *See entry under Heads of State.*

NGUYEN XUAN OANH (Premier, January 27, 1965–February 16, 1965). *See earlier entry under Heads of Government.*

PHUY HUY QUAT (Premier, February 16, 1965–June 12, 1965). Phuy Huy Quat was born in 1909. He was educated at the Hanoi School of Medicine. He served in the government as minister of education from 1949 until 1953 and also served as minister of defense in the early 1950s. Phuy Huy Quat briefly served as acting premier in 1954. He was involved in an unsuccessful coup attempt against President Ngo Dinh Diem in 1960 and was imprisoned until Diem's ouster in 1963. He returned to the government as minister of foreign affairs in 1964. Phuy Huy Quat

was installed as premier of a civilian government on February 16, 1965. Vietnamese Roman Catholics demanded his resignation and accused him of favoring Buddhists. He resigned on June 12, 1965, and a military junta under Nguyen Van Thieu took power. He died on April 27, 1979.

NGUYEN CAO KY (Premier, June 19, 1965–October 31, 1967). Nguyen Cao Ky was born in Son Tay in Tonkin Province on September 9, 1930. He was educated locally and entered the French Nam Dinh Reserve Officers' School. He graduated in 1952 and continued his military education at aviation schools in French North Africa and in France. Ky entered the French air force in September of 1954 and transferred to the South Vietnamese air force the following December. He rose through the ranks of the air force and received further training in the United States in the late 1950s. He flew numerous military missions against the North Vietnamese and the Viet Cong in the early 1960s. Ky supported the military coup that ousted President Ngo Dinh Diem in November of 1963, and he was promoted to the rank of general. He was named commander of the air force by General Duong Van Minh and continued to participate in military missions. He was active in Maj. Gen. Nguyen Khanh's military coup in January of 1964 and supported Khanh when a military rebellion attempted to depose him in September of 1964. Khanh stepped down as premier the following month and installed a civilian government. Ky was named to Premier Tran Van Huong's cabinet as minister of youth and sports in December of 1964. Khanh ousted the civilian government in January of 1965, but was forced to relinquish power the following month. A new civilian regime took power until June of 1965, when the military, under Maj. Gen. Nguyen Van Thieu, took control of the country. Ky served in the ruling military junta and became premier of the war cabinet on June 19, 1965. He instituted rigid controls on the government and officially declared South Vietnam to be in a state of war. He led South Vietnam's government in its fight against the Viet Cong insurgents. Ky consolidated his power and eliminated his leading rival, Lt. Gen. Nguyen Chanh Thi, from the National Leadership Committee in March of 1966. Buddhist supporters of Thi held demonstrations against the government in Da Nang, and Ky was forced to negotiate a number of political reforms with the Buddhist leaders. Elections to a Constituent Assembly were held in September of 1966, and a presidential election took place the following year. Ky was elected vice president under Nguyen Van Thieu and stepped down as premier to accept the office on October 31, 1967. His political power eroded and his relationship with President Thieu became strained. He was barred from entering the presidential election in 1971. Ky subsequently retired from politics. He fled South Vietnam in April of 1975 as Communist troops approached the capital. He settled in California in the United States, where he opened a chain of liquor stores.

NGUYEN VAN LOC (Premier, October 31, 1967–May 18, 1968). Nguyen Van Loc was born on February 24, 1922. He was educated at the University of Montpellier, where he received a degree in law. He returned to Saigon to practice law and was a teacher at the National Institute of Administration. Nguyen Van Loc served as chairman of the People and Armed Forces Council Political Committee in 1966. He was named premier by President Nguyen Van Thieu on October 31, 1967. Nguyen Van Loc's cabinet resigned on May 18, 1968.

TRAN VAN HUONG (Premier, May 25, 1968–August 23, 1969). *See entry under Heads of State.*

TRAN THIEN KHIEM (Premier, September 1, 1969–April 4, 1975). Tran Thien Khiem was born in Saigon on December 15, 1925. He served in the Vietnamese army, where he rose to the rank of lieutenant general. He supported President Ngo Dinh Diem in the coup attempt against the government in 1960, but became disillusioned with Diem and participated in his ouster in November of 1963. Tran Thien Khiem supported Nguyen Khanh's coup against the military junta of Duong Van Minh in January of 1964. He was named minister of defense and commander in chief of the armed forces and served on the ruling military junta. He was removed from the junta and named ambassador to the United States in October of 1964. Tran Thien Khiem was appointed ambassador to the Republic of China in October of 1965 and served in that position until May of 1968. He then returned to Vietnam to serve in the government as minister of the interior. He was also named deputy prime minister in March of 1969. Tran Thien Khiem replaced Tran Van Huong as premier on September 1, 1969. He also served in the government as minister of defense from 1972. The rebels supported by North Vietnam continued to score victories in South Vietnam, and Tran Thien Khiem was removed from office on April 4, 1975. He fled to Taiwan as the rebel troops approached the capital.

NGUYEN BA CAN (Premier, April 4, 1975–April 23, 1975). Nguyen Ba Can served as speaker of South Vietnam's lower house of representatives. He was named to head a war cabinet of national union on April 4, 1975. He resigned from office on April 23, 1975, as Communist troops approached Saigon.

VU VAN MAU (Premier, April 28, 1975–April 30, 1975). Vu Van Mau was born in South Vietnam on July 25, 1914. He was educated at the University of Hanoi and the University of Paris. He returned to Hanoi as a lawyer in 1949. Vu Van Mau was appointed secretary of state for foreign affairs in 1953. He also served on the University of Saigon's Faculty of Law from 1955 until 1958. He resigned as foreign minister in August of 1963 in protest of President Ngo Dinh Diem's brutal repression of Buddhist dissidents. He rejoined the foreign ministry in 1964, after the ouster of Diem, and served as ambassador to the United Kingdom, Belgium, and the Netherlands. Vu Van Mau served as a member of the Senate from 1970 until 1975. He was appointed premier on April 28, 1975, and served for three days until the South Vietnamese government fell to the Communists on April 30, 1975.

Vietnam, Socialist Republic of

(Công-Hòa Xã-Hôi Chu-Nghĩa Viêt Nam)

Vietnam is a country in Southeast Asia. It declared independence from France on September 2, 1945, and was recognized as the independent Democratic Republic of Vietnam on July 21, 1954. It annexed South Vietnam to become the unified Socialist Republic of Vietnam on July 2, 1976.

HEADS OF STATE

HO CHI MINH (President, September 2, 1945–September 3, 1969). Ho Chi Minh was born Nguyen That Thanh in Hoang Tru on May 19, 1890. He was educated at a French school in Hue and worked as a teacher from 1907. He traveled to France as a ship's steward in 1912. Ho also spent time in London and the United States before settling in Paris in 1917. He became active in socialist politics and was an advocate of Indo-Chinese independence. He was a founding member of the French Communist party in 1920. Ho worked as a journalist for the party newspaper and also wrote several plays in the 1920s. He received training in the Soviet Union from 1923 until 1925, when he went to China to form the Vietnamese Revolutionary Youth League. He was forced to flee China following Chiang Kai-shek's break with the Communists in 1927, and he returned to the Soviet Union. Ho traveled throughout Asia and formed the Vietnamese Commu-nist party in Hong Kong in 1930. He remained involved in the revolutionary movement during the 1930s, though his activities during this period remain shrouded in mystery. He returned to China to form the Viet Minh in 1941 and was arrested by the Nationalists later in the year. Ho spent a year in prison before being released to assist the Allies against the Japanese during World War II. It was during this period that he adopted the name Ho Chi Minh. Ho declared the independent Democratic Republic of Vietnam on September 2, 1945, and was elected president on January 6, 1946. The French colonial forces returned to Indo-China in 1946, and the Viet Minh engaged in a war of resistance against the French troops. The guerrilla war continued until the French were defeated at Dien Bien Phu in July of 1954. A cease-fire was signed in Geneva that divided Vietnam at the seventeenth parallel. Ho remained president and premier of North

Vietnam until September 20, 1955, when he relinquished the premiership to Pham Van Dong. Ho consolidated his power in the government and the party and instituted a number of drastic agrarian reform measures. He resumed the position of general secretary of the Vietnamese Workers' party in 1956 and was reelected president in 1960. He supported the Viet Cong resistance movement in South Vietnam against the government of President Ngo Dinh Diem. South Vietnam received military support from the United States, and North Vietnam sent troops to fight with the Viet Cong in 1964. He remained the undisputed leader of North Vietnam until his death from a heart attack in Hanoi at the age of 79 on September 3, 1969.

TON DUC THANG (President, September 24, 1969–March 30, 1980). Ton Duc Thang was born in My Hoa Hung, Long Xuyen Province, on August 20, 1888. He was educated in Saigon and became a schoolteacher. He became active in the Indo-Chinese nationalist movement and was forced into exile in France in 1912. Ton Duc Thang entered the French navy during World War I. He participated in a mutiny of French sailors at Sevastopol on the Black Sea in April of 1919 and was dismissed from the navy. He returned to Paris and worked as an automotive mechanic until 1927. Ton Duc Thang then returned to Vietnam and joined Ho Chi Minh's Revolutionary Youth League. He was arrested by the French colonial authorities for sedition and conspiracy to murder in 1929. He was imprisoned on the prison island of Paulo Condore until the end of World War II in 1945. Ton Duc Thang then joined the government of the newly formed Democratic Republic of Vietnam and served as inspector general for political and administrative affairs. He was named vice-premier of North Vietnam in 1960 and succeeded to the presidency on September 24, 1969, following the death of Ho

Chi Minh. He retained the largely ceremonial position following the official reunification of North and South Vietnam in July of 1976. Ton Duc Thang continued to serve as president until his death from a heart attack in Hanoi at the age of 91 on March 30, 1980.

NGUYEN HUU THO (Acting President, March 30, 1980–July 4, 1981). Nguyen Huu Tho was born in Cholon on July 10, 1910. He was educated in France and became a lawyer in Cochin China in the 1930s. He was a member of the French Socialist party and became active in the war for independence against the French. Nguyen Huu Tho was arrested in 1950 and remained under detention until 1952. He supported the 1954 Geneva agreements on Indo-China and founded the Saigon-Cholon Peace Movement. He was arrested for his opposition to the government of President Ngo Dinh Diem later in 1954 and remained imprisoned until his escape in 1961. Nguyen Huu Tho was named chairman of the National Liberation Front Central Committee in 1962. He was the chairman of the Consultative Council of the Provisional Revolutionary Government of the Republic of South Vietnam from 1969 until the absorption of South Vietnam in July of 1976. He then became vice president of the Socialist Republic of Vietnam. Nguyen Huu Tho served as acting president of Vietnam following the death of Ton Duc Thang on March 30, 1980, and retained the office until July 4, 1981. He served as vice president of the Council of State from 1981 until 1984 and again from 1986. He was awarded the Lenin Peace Prize in 1985.

TRUONG CHINH (President, July 4, 1981–June 18, 1987). Truong Chinh was born Dang Xuan Khu in Hu Nam Hinh Province in 1907. He was educated at Hanoi's College of Commerce and became involved in the nationalist movement. He joined Ho Chi Minh's Revolutionary Youth League and was a founder of the Indo-Chinese Communist party in 1930. Truong Chinh was arrested by the French colonial authorities the following year and remained imprisoned in Son La until 1936. He adopted the name Truong Chinh, meaning "Long March," while imprisoned. He returned to Hanoi after his release and worked as a journalist, using the pen name Qua Ninh. Truong Chinh became chairman of the Communist Party Regional Committee in North Vietnam in 1940 and was elected general secretary of the Indo-Chinese Communist party in 1941. He went underground during World War II while the party was banned. He served as a leading propagandist in the party following the establishment of the Democratic Republic of Vietnam in 1946. Truong Chinh was removed as general secretary in 1956 due to the failure of his land reform program. He remained on the Politburo and was appointed vice-premier in 1958. He also served as chairman of the Scientific Research Council and was elected president of the National Assembly. Truong Chinh was appointed president of the Council of State of the Socialist Republic of Vietnam on July 4, 1981, and succeeded Le Duan as general secretary of the Vietnamese Communist party on July 10, 1986. He resigned as general secretary on December 18, 1986, and stepped down as president of the State

Council on June 18, 1987. Truong Chinh remained an advisor to the Communist party Politburo until his death in Hanoi from an accidental fall at the age of 80 on September 30, 1988.

VO CHI CONG (President, June 18, 1987–September 23, 1992). Vo Chi Cong was born near Da Nang in central Vietnam in 1912. He became involved with the Communist party in the 1930s and was imprisoned during World War II. He resumed his revolutionary activities after the war and held various positions in the party and the government. Vo Chi Cong was named to the Politburo in 1961. He served as secretary of the Southern People's party and as a leader in the National Liberation Front during the Vietnam War. He served as vice president of the Council of Ministers from 1976 until 1982. Vo Chi Cong also served in the cabinet as minister of fisheries from 1976 until 1977 and minister of agriculture from 1977 until 1978. He succeeded Truong Chinh as president of Vietnam on June 18, 1987. Vo Chi Cong was replaced by General Le Duc Anh on September 23, 1992.

LE DUC ANH (President, September 23, 1992–   ). Le Duc Anh was born in 1920. He served in the Vietnamese army, where he rose to the rank of general. He served as minister of foreign affairs, defense, and internal security before being named president on September 23, 1992.

HEADS OF GOVERNMENT

PHAM VAN DONG (Premier, September 1955–June 18, 1987). Pham Van Dong was born in the Quang Nam Province of South Vietnam on March 1, 1906. He joined the Communist Revolutionary Youth League in Canton in 1926. Pham Van Dong was arrested by the French authorities in 1929 and remained imprisoned until 1937. He was

a founder of the Revolutionary League for the Independence of Vietnam in 1941. He was named to the government of the Democratic Republic of Vietnam as minister of finance in 1946. Pham Van Dong was dismissed from the government in June of 1947 and represented Ho Chi Minh in South Vietnam. He returned to the government in August of

1949 as president of the Superior Council for National Defense. He was appointed foreign minister in August of 1954 and represented North Vietnam at the peace negotiations with France in Geneva, Switzerland. Pham Van Dong was appointed premier in September of 1955. He attempted to normalize relations with President Ngo Dinh Diem's regime in South Vietnam and opposed the growing military presence of the United States in Vietnam. He remained as head of the government throughout the war with South Vietnam and continued to head the unified government of the Socialist Republic of Vietnam from July of 1976. Pham Van Dong's failing health and eye problems led to his resignation from the Politburo in December of 1986. He was replaced as premier by Pham Hung on June 18, 1987.

PHAM HUNG (Premier, June 18, 1987–March 10, 1988). Pham Hung was born in Vinh Long Province on June 11, 1912. He was a founding member of the Indo-Chinese Communist party in 1930. He was arrested by the French colonial authorities the following year and sentenced to death. His sentence was commuted to life imprisonment, however, and he was held on the prison island of Paulo Condore until the end of World War II in 1945. He fought against the French during the Indo-Chinese War and served as a deputy to Le Duan in South Vietnam. He returned to Hanoi following the defeat of the French at Dien Bien Phu in 1954 and the subsequent treaty signed in Geneva that divided Vietnam at the seventeenth parallel. Pham Hung was named to the Politburo in 1956. He became deputy premier of North Vietnam in 1958. He returned to South Vietnam in 1967 to lead the Central Office of South Vietnam and was the political leader of the Viet Cong guerrillas. Pham Hung became deputy premier in the unified government in 1976 and was named minister of the interior in 1986. He

replaced Pham Van Dong as premier on June 18, 1987. He remained head of the government until his death from a heart attack at the age of 75 in Ho Chi Minh City on March 10, 1988.

VO VAN KIET (Premier, March 10, 1988–June 22, 1988). Vo Van Kiet was born in South Vietnam in 1922. He joined the Indo-China Communist party in the 1930s. In 1958 he became a member of the Central Committee of the Lao Dong party. Vo Van Kiet later served as a member of the Politburo of the Communist party of Vietnam. From 1982 until 1991 he served as vice-chairman of the Council of Ministers. During much of this time, he also served as chairman of the State Planning Commission. He briefly succeeded Pham Hung as acting prime minister on March 10, 1988, and served until June 22, 1988. Vo Van Kiet again became prime minister on August 8, 1991, when he succeeded Do Muoi.

DO MUOI (Premier, June 22, 1988–August 8, 1991). Do Muoi was born in Hanoi in 1917. He was active in the Indo-China independence movement against the French from 1936. He was imprisoned by the French, but escaped in 1945. Do Muoi was a leader in the war for the liberation of Vietnam that was fought against the French from 1951 until 1954. He subsequently served as an official in the Vietnam Communist party. He also served as a deputy to the National Assembly and was minister of commerce in 1969. Do Muoi was named deputy prime minister and minister of building in 1976 and retained the post until 1987. He became prime minister on June 22, 1988, and served until August 8, 1991. He also served as vice-chairman of the National Defense Council from December of 1989.

VO VAN KIET (Premier, August 8, 1991–). *See earlier entry under Heads of Government.*

OTHER LEADERS

TRUONG CHINH (General Secretary, 1941–1956). *See entry under Heads of State.*

HO CHI MINH (General Secretary, 1956–September 3, 1969). *See entry under Heads of State.*

LE DUAN (General Secretary, September 3, 1969–July 10, 1986). Le Duan was born in Quang Tri Province on April 7, 1908. He joined Ho Chi Minh's Revolutionary Youth League in 1928, and was a founding member of the Indo-Chinese Communist party two years later. He was arrested by the French colonial authorities in 1931 and was imprisoned until 1936. Le Duan continued his activities with the Communist party and was rearrested in 1940. He was held on the prison island of Paulo Condore until 1945. He was then named by Ho Chi Minh to serve as the Viet Minh's political commissar in South Vietnam. Le Duan remained in the south after the French withdrew from Indo-China in 1954. He returned to Hanoi in 1957 and entered the Politburo. He remained a leading aide to Ho Chi Minh and was instrumental in directing the guerrilla war against the government of South Vietnam. Le Duan became the leading figure in North Vietnam following the death of Ho Chi Minh on September 3, 1969. He replaced Ho as general secretary of the North Vietnamese Workers' party and accepted the peace agreement in January of 1973 that led to the withdrawal of United States troops from Vietnam. He continued the war against South Vietnam that ended in the collapse of the Saigon government in April of 1975. Le Duan presided over the reunification of the north and south as the Socialist Republic of Vietnam. He entered Vietnam into an alliance with the Soviet Union, which led to

disputes with the People's Republic of China. Vietnam invaded neighboring Cambodia in 1978, and Chinese troops invaded northern Vietnam in response in February of 1979. Border clashes between the two countries continued into the 1980s. Le Duan suffered from poor health in the 1980s, but remained the leader of the Vietnamese Communist party until his death from lung and kidney ailments in Hanoi at the age of 79 on July 10, 1986.

TRUONG CHINH (General Secretary, July 10, 1986–December 18, 1986). *See entry under Heads of State.*

NGUYEN VAN LINH (General Secretary, December 18, 1986–). Nguyen Van Linh was born Nguyen Van Cuc in Hanoi in 1913. He was raised in South Vietnam, where he became active in revolutionary politics. He was arrested in 1930 and remained imprisoned until 1936. Nguyen Van Linh joined the Communist movement in Cochin China and was again imprisoned in 1941. He was released after World War II and became a leader in the revolutionary movement in South Vietnam. He served as director of the Central Office for South Vietnam from 1961 until 1964 and then served as deputy director for the remainder of the war. Nguyen Van Linh was elected a member of the Politburo of the Communist party of Vietnam following the reunification of North and South Vietnam in 1976. He was dismissed from his position in March of 1982. He was reappointed to the Politburo in 1985 and served as permanent secretary to the Central Committee. Nguyen Van Linh was selected to succeed Truong Chinh as general secretary of the Communist party on December 18, 1986.

West Indies Federation

The West Indies Federation was a group of islands in the Caribbean. It was created from British colonial interests in the Caribbean on January 3, 1958, and was disbanded on May 31, 1962.

HEAD OF STATE

PATRICK G. T. BUCHAN-HEPBURN, FIRST BARON HAILES (Governor-General, January 3, 1958–May 31, 1962). Patrick George Thomas Buchan-Hepburn was born in England on April 2, 1901. He was educated at Trinity College, Cambridge. He became private secretary to Winston Churchill and was elected to Parliament in 1929. He became a Conservative whip in 1939 and was named a lord commissioner of the Treasury soon afterwards. He served in the military during World War II and became deputy chief whip in 1945. He rose to the position of chief whip in 1948 and served until 1955. He was elevated to the peerage as the first Baron Hailes in 1957. He was appointed governor-general of the newly formed West Indies Federation and took office on January 3, 1958. The federation failed due to the incompatibility of its member states and was dissolved on May 31, 1962. Lord Hailes returned to England to serve as chairman of the Historic Buildings Council until 1973. He died at the age of 73 on November 5, 1974.

HEAD OF GOVERNMENT

SIR GRANTLEY ADAMS (Prime Minister, January 3, 1958–May 31, 1962). Grantley Herbert Adams was born in Barbados on April 28, 1898. He was educated locally before attending Oxford University in England, where he received a degree in law in 1923. He returned to Barbados to practice law and became involved in politics. Adams was elected to the Barbados House of Assembly in 1934 and became a spokesman for the island's sugar plantation workers. He led the workers in a strike in 1937 and founded the Barbados Progressive League the following year. He was named to the Assembly's Executive Committee in 1941 and also founded the Barbados Workers' Union and served as its president. Adams was an advocate of a federation among Britain's colonies in the West Indies. He continued to lead the majority Labor party in the Assembly and became Barbados' first premier in 1954. He continued to promote the establishment of a union among Britain's dependencies which led to the formation of the West Indies Federation on January 3, 1958. The federation consisted of Jamaica, Trinidad-Tobago, Barbados, the Windwards Islands, and the Leeward Islands, but excluded the British Virgin Islands. Adams became the federation's first prime minister when Jamaica's Norman Manley refused to seek the position. The federation proved unsuccessful, as the various member states were unable to agree on policy. Jamaica announced its withdrawal from the union in 1961, and the West Indies Federation was dissolved on May 31, 1962. Adams retired from active politics and returned to his law practice in Barbados. He died in Bridgetown at the age of 73 on November 28, 1971.

Western Samoa, Independent State of

(Sa'oloto Tuto'atasi o Samoa i Sisifo)

Western Samoa consists of two large islands and several small islands in the South Pacific Ocean. It was granted independence from a United Nations trusteeship administered by New Zealand on January 1, 1962.

HEADS OF STATE

MALIETOA TANUMAFILI II (Co-president, January 1, 1962–April 8, 1963; President April 8, 1963–). Malietoa Tanumafili II was born on January 4, 1913. He was educated as Wesley College in New Zealand and returned to Samoa to serve as an advisor to the government in 1940. He was a member of the New Zealand delegation to the United Nations in 1958 and subsequently served as a member of the Council of State. Tanumafili served with Tupua Tamasese Meaole as joint head of state for life following Western Samoa's independence on January 1, 1962. When Tamasese died in April of 1963, Tanumaîli remained as Western Samoa's head of state.

TUPUA TAMASESE MEA'OLE (Co-president, January 1, 1962–April 8, 1963). Tupua Tamasese Mea'ole was chosen as Western Samoa's joint head of state for life with Malietoa Tanumafili II following independence on January 1, 1962. Tamasese retained office until his death after a long illness on April 8, 1963.

HEADS OF GOVERNMENT

FIAME MATA'AFA FAUMUINA MULINU'U II (Prime Minister, 1959–February 1970). Fiame Mata'afa Faumuina Mulinu'u II was born in 1921. He was chosen as prime minister of Western Samoa in 1959 and remained head of government following independence on January 1, 1962. Mata'afa stepped down from office in February of 1970 and was replaced by Tupua Tamasese Lealofi VI. He returned to office in December of 1973 and remained prime minister until his death on May 20, 1975.

TUPUA TAMASESE LEALOFI VI (Prime Minister, February 1970– December 1973). Tupua Tamasese Lealofi VI was born in 1922. He was selected as prime minister in February of 1970 and retained office until December of 1973. Tamasese again became prime minister on May 21, 1975, following the death of Fiami Mata'afa Faumuina Mulinu'u II. He completed Mata'afa's term and stepped down on March 24, 1976. Tamasese died on July 1, 1983.

FIAMI MATA'AFA FAUMUINA MULINU'U II (Prime Minister,

December 1973–May 20, 1975). *See earlier entry under Heads of Government.*

TUPUA TAMASESE LEALOFI VI (Prime Minister, May 21, 1975– March 24, 1976). *See earlier entry under Heads of Government.*

TAISI TUPUOLA EFI (Prime Minister, March 24, 1976–April 13, 1982). Taisi Tupuola Efi was born in Western Samoa in 1938. He was educated at St. Joseph's College in Western Samoa and at Victoria University in Wellington, New Zealand. He was elected to the Western Samoan Parliament in 1965. In 1970 he was appointed minister of works, civil aviation, marine, and transport in the government of Tupua Tamasese Lealofi VI. Efi remained in the cabinet until 1973. He was selected as prime minister of Western Samoa on March 24, 1976. He was replaced by Va'ai Kolone on April 13, 1982. Efi returned to office following Kolone's defeat on September 18, 1982. He was unable to form a coalition government and resigned following the rejection of his budget bill on December 30, 1982.

VA'AI KOLONE (Prime Minister, April 13, 1982–September 18, 1982). Va'ai Kolone was a leader of the Human Rights Protection party and led the party to victory in elections in February of 1982. He was sworn into office as prime minister on April 13, 1982. The party lost its majority following the ouster of a member in June of 1982,

and Kolone was removed from the Parliament on September 18, 1982. He relinquished the leadership of the party to Tofilau Eti Alesna. Kolone joined the opposition Samoan National Development party in December of 1985. He became the head of a coalition government in January of 1986. Kolone retained office until April 8, 1988, when the Human Rights Protection party again came to power.

TAISI TUPUOLA EFI (Prime Minister, September 18, 1982–December 30, 1982). *See earlier entry under Heads of Government.*

TOFILAU ETI ALESNA (Prime Minister, December 1982–December 27, 1985). Tofilau Eti Alesana was born in 1924. He replaced Va'ai Kolone as the leader of the Human Rights Protection party in September of 1982 and formed a government as prime minister in December of 1982. His government collapsed on December 27, 1985, however, following the defection of members of his party to the opposition. Alesana again led the Human Rights Protection Party to a narrow victory in elections in February of 1988 and was selected as prime minister on April 8, 1988.

VA'AI KOLONE (Prime Minister, January 1986–April 8, 1988). *See earlier entry under Heads of Government.*

TOFILAU ETI ALESANA (Prime Minister, April 8, 1988–   ). *See earlier entry under Heads of Government.*

Yemen, People's Democratic Republic of

(South Yemen)

The People's Democratic Republic of Yemen was a country on the southern coast of the Arabian Peninsula. It was granted independence from Great Britain on November 30, 1967. It merged with the Yemen Arab Republic, or North Yemen, to form the Republic of Yemen on May 22, 1990.

HEADS OF STATE

QAHTAN MUHAMMAD AL-SHAABI (President, November 30, 1967–June 22, 1969). Qahtan Muhammad al-Shaabi was born in Lahej, in the western province of Southern Yemen, in 1925. A graduate of the University of Khartoum in the Sudan, he served as an agriculture inspector in Lahej. In the late 1950s he defected with government funds and joined the South Arabian League. In January of 1963, al-Shaabi became the leader of the National Liberation Front (NLF) of Southern Yemen. The front, which initially had the backing of Egypt's president Gamal Abdel Nasser, had been created to oppose the establishment of a British-backed Federation of South Arabia. The National Liberation Front, under al-Shaabi, was responsible for many acts of terrorism, including grenade attacks on Aden in 1964. In January of 1966 al-Shaabi was placed under house arrest in Cairo after a disagreement with Nasser over the unification of the NLF with Abdul Qawi Makkawi's Front for the Liberation of South Yemen (FLOSY), another nationalist group which had gained the backing of Nasser. Al-Shaabi was released the following year after the defeat of the United Arab Republic in the 1967 war with Israel. The British then began negotiations with the NLF, which had gained control of most of Southern Yemen. Al-Shaabi headed the NLF delegation at the final negotiations in Geneva, with Lord Shackleton representing the British. Immediate independence was granted on November 30, 1967, and al-Shaabi served as the first president and premier of the People's Republic of Southern Yemen. Al-Shaabi's administration was beset by several leftist rebellions in its first year. He conducted a purge of the leftists on March 10, 1968, and reformed his cabinet the following month, removing Ali Salim al-Baydh as minister of defense.

On April 6, 1969, al-Shaabi relinquished the position of prime minister to his cousin, Faisal Abdul Latif al-Shaabi, and attempted a reconciliation with the leftists. In June of 1969 al-Shaabi dismissed the popular interior minister, Muhammad Ali Haitham, after a quarrel during a cabinet meeting. Haitham, who had strong support in the Yemeni army, denounced al-Shaabi, who was subsequently deposed as president during a bloodless coup on June 22, 1969. He was replaced by a five-man Presidential Council which included Salem Ali Rubayyi as chairman, Haitham, and Abd-al Fattah Ismail. Al-Shaabi was arrested, and in November he was expelled from the NLF. He was later released and lived in Aden in relative obscurity until his death from a heart attack at the age of 61 on July 7, 1981.

SALEM ALI RUBAYYI (President, June 22, 1969–June 26, 1978). Salem Ali Rubayyi was born in 1934. He was employed as a school teacher and became active in the Front for the Liberation of South Yemen (FLOSY) in 1963. He was involved in a revolt against President Qahtan Muhammad al-Shaabi in 1967 and was sent into exile. Rubayyi returned following Shaabi's ouster and took office as chairman of the Presidential Council on June 22, 1969. He also served as commander of the armed forces. He was the leader of the pro–Chinese faction on the council. Rubayyi initiated negotiations to discuss the unification of North and South Yemen. He also attempted to improve South Yemen's relations with Saudi Arabia and the United States. His actions were opposed by Abd-al Fattah Ismail, the Marxist leader of the pro–Soviet faction on the Presidential Council. Ismail was reportedly involved in the bombing assassination of North Yemeni president

Ahmed al-Ghashmi on June 24, 1978. Rubayyi attempted to purge Ismail and his supporters from the government, and a brief civil war erupted. Ismail's People's Militia defeated Rubayyi's government troops. Rubayyi was captured by the insurgents and executed by a firing squad on June 26, 1978.

ALI NASSIR MUHAMMAD HUS-SANI (President, June 27, 1978–December 27, 1978). Ali Nassir Muhammad Hussani was born in 1939. He worked as a teacher before entering politics. Muhammad was named governor of several islands in the Red Sea in the 1960s. He became governor of the Second District of South Yemen in 1968 and was appointed minister for local government later in the year. He was appointed minister of defense in 1969. He was named to head the government as prime minister on August 2, 1971. Muhammad became chairman of the Presidential Council on June 27, 1978, following the ouster of Salem Ali Rubayyi. He relinquished the chairmanship to Ismail on December 27, 1978, but returned to lead the Supreme People's Council on April 2, 1980. He stepped down as prime minister on February 14, 1985, though he retained the office of president. Muhammad engaged in a bloody feud with Yemeni Socialist party leader Abd-al Fattah Ismail in January of 1986. Ismail and Defense Minister Salih Muslih Qasim were killed in the fighting. Muhammad was forced from office on January 24, 1986, and went into exile in Northern Yemen. He became the leader of the Democratic Unionist party following the merger of North and South Yemen in 1990.

ABD-AL FATTAH ISMAIL (President, December 27, 1978–April 2, 1980). Abd-al Fattah Ismail was born in 1939. He worked in an oil refinery and became a proponent of Marxism. He became the leader of the pro-Soviet faction of the National Front and served on the three-member Presidential Council from August of 1971. Ismail opposed Salem Ali Rubayyi's negotiations with North Yemen over the question of Yemeni unification and was implicated in the bombing assassination of President Ahmed al-Ghashmi of North Yemen. Rubayyi attempted to arrest Ismail for complicity in the murder, and Ismail's supporters ousted Rubayyi as chairman of the Council in June of 1978. Ismail remained on the Presidential Council and succeeded Ali Nassir Muhammad Hussani as head of state as chairman of the newly formed Supreme People's Council on December 27, 1978. Ismail reportedly stepped down from office for reasons of health on April 2, 1980, and Muhammad again became head of state. He returned to chair the Yemeni Socialist party in February of 1985. President Muhammad purged Ismail's supporters in the government, and Ismail was killed on January 13, 1986.

ALI NASIR MUHAMMAD HUSSANI (President, April 2, 1980–January 24, 1986). *See earlier entry under Heads of State.*

HAIDAR ABU BAKR AL-ATTAS (President, January 24, 1986–May 22, 1990). *See entry under Yemen, Heads of Government.*

HEADS OF GOVERNMENT

QAHTAN MUHAMMAD AL-SHAABI (Premier, November 30, 1967–April 6, 1969). *See entry under Heads of State.*

FAISAL ABDUL LATIF AL-SHAABI (Premier, April 6, 1969–June 24, 1969). Faisal Abdul Latif al-Shaabi was born in 1937. He was a disciple of Palestinian nationalist leader George Habash and a founder of the National Liberation Front (NLF), the Aden branch of the Arab Nationalist Movement. He had previously worked in the Federal Ministry of Commerce and Industry. Al-Latif had served as the leading spokesman for the NLF while his cousin, Qahtan al-Shaabi, remained under house arrest in Egypt in 1966. Following the establishment of the independent People's Republic of South Yemen in November of 1967, al-Latif served in several cabinets. On April 6, 1969, he was named as premier, replacing Qahtan al-Shaabi. One of his first official acts was a state visit to Kuwait, which resulted in aid for South Yemen. Al-Latif's term of office was brief. He was deposed with his cousin on June 22, 1969, and placed under arrest. It was announced on April 3, 1970, that al-Latif had been shot to death while attempting to escape from a detention camp.

MUHAMMAD ALI HAITHAM (Premier, June 24, 1969–August 1, 1971). Muhammad Ali Haitham was born in Dathina, Southern Arabia, in 1940. He worked as a teacher until he was appointed minister of the interior in 1967. He was instrumental in the ouster of President Qahtan Muhammad al-Shaabi in 1969 and served as premier from June 24, 1969. He was also named a member of the three-man Presidential Council in December of 1969. He served as deputy chairman of the council from September of 1970 and was named foreign mininster in January of 1971. Haitham was removed from the government on August 1, 1971, and went into exile in Cairo, Egypt.

ALI NASIR MUHAMMAD HUSSANI (Premier, August 2, 1971–February 14, 1985). *See entry under Heads of State.*

HAIDAR ABU BAKR AL-ATTAS (Premier, February 14, 1985–February 8, 1986). *See entry under Yemen, Heads of Government.*

YASIN SAID NUMAN (Premier, February 8, 1986–May 22, 1990). Yasin Said Numan served in the cabinet as deputy prime minister and minister of fisheries. He was appointed minister of labor and civil service in 1986. He was named premier on February 8, 1986, and remained in office until the merger of North and South Yemen on May 22, 1990. Numan subsequently served as Speaker of the House of Representatives.

Yemen, Republic of

(al-Jumhuriyah al-Yamaniyah)

The Republic of Yemen is a country on the southern coast of the Arabian Peninsula. It was formed by the merger of the Yemen Arab Republic and the People's Democratic Republic of Yemen on May 22, 1990.

HEAD OF STATE

ALI ABDULLAH SALEH (President, May 22, 1990–   ). Ali Abdullah Saleh was born in 1942. He was active in the military coup in June of 1974 and served as security chief of the Taiz Province until June of 1978. He became president and commander in chief of the armed forces of the Yemen Arab Republic on July 17, 1978, following the assassination of Ahmed al-Ghashmi. Saleh survived several revolts against his government later in the year. He reopened talks with the People's Democratic Republic of Yemen which led to the eventual reunion of the Yemens. Saleh was reelected president in May of 1983. When the unified Republic of Yemen was established on May 22, 1990, Saleh served as president of the unified government.

HEAD OF GOVERNMENT

HAIDAR ABU BAKR AL-ATTAS (Prime Minister, May 24, 1990–   ). Haidar Abu Bakr al-Attas served as minister of construction of the People's Democratic Republic of Yemen. He became premier on February 14, 1985, and rose to the presidency following the ouster of Ali Nassir Muhammad on January 24, 1986. Attas relinquished the premiership on February 8, 1986. He became prime minister of the Republic of Yemen following the merger of the People's Democratic Republic of Yemen (South Yemen) and the Yemen Arab Republic (North Yemen) on May 24, 1990.

Yemen Arab Republic
(North Yemen)

The Yemen Arab Republic is a country on the southern coast of the Arabian Peninsula. It was granted independence from the Ottoman Empire in November of 1918. It merged with the People's Democratic Republic of Yemen, or South Yemen, to form the Republic of Yemen on May 22, 1990.

HEADS OF STATE

YAHYA IBN MUHAMMAD IBN HAMID AL-DIN (Imam, 1911–February 17, 1948). Yahya ibn Muhammad ibn Hamid al-Din was born in 1876. In 1904 he succeeded his father as the head of the Zaidi sect of the Shi'ite Moslems, thus becoming the hereditary monarch of Yemen. Yahya was initially opposed to the Turkish occupation of Yemen, but in 1911 he reached an accommodation with the sultan which resulted in the independence of Yemen. After the collapse of the Turkish empire following World War I, Yahya became embroiled in several territorial disputes with Great Britain which were not settled until the signing of the Anglo-Yemini treaty in 1934. Later the same year Yahya engaged in a brief and unsuccessful war with Saudi Arabia. Yemen became more involved in regional and international affairs following World War II and joined the Arab League in 1945 and the League of Nations in 1947. There was a premature report of the imam's death by natural causes in January of 1947, and his announced successor was Sayyid

Abdullah Ibn Ahmed Al-Wazir. Yahya was assassinated the following month on February 17, 1948.

SAYF ABDULLAH IBN AHMED AL-WAZIR (Imam, February 17, 1948–March 13, 1948).

Sayf Abdullah ibn Ahmed al-Wazir was born in 1912. He proclaimed himself the new imam of Yemen following the assassination of Imam Yahya on February 17, 1948. A brief civil war broke out, and two of Yahya's sons were killed in street fighting. Imam Yahya's eldest son, Crown Prince Ahmed, raised an army of royalist supporters and deposed Imam Sayf Abdullah on March 13, 1948. Sayf Abdullah was tried and executed by hanging in Hogga on April 8, 1948.

AHMED IBN YAHYA HAMID AL-DIN (Imam, March 13, 1948–September 18, 1962).

Ahmed ibn Yahya Hamid al-Din was born in San'a in 1891. He was the eldest surviving son of Imam Yahya. He was proclaimed crown prince in 1927 and was appointed governor-general of Southern Yemen. Imam Yahya was assassinated in February of 1948, and Abdullah al-Wazir was proclaimed head of a reformist government. Ahmed joined with several of his brothers to lead a army of tribesmen against Abdullah and took control of the government on March 13, 1948. Ahmed approved some reforms in the country and continued to insist that the British Protectorate of Aden was a legal part of Yemen. Ahmed's brothers, Abdullah and Abbas, led a revolt against the government in April of 1955. Ahmed was imprisoned and forced to abdicate. He escaped from his captors, however, and was reinstated as imam by loyalist forces. Abdullah and Abbas were imprisoned and executed. Ahmed appointed his son, Badr, as prime minister and crown prince. Imam Ahmed suffered from poor health during the late 1950s and was shot and seriously wounded on March 27, 1961. Ahmed's injuries and failing health led to his death at the age of 71 on September 18, 1962.

MOHAMMED AL-BADR (Imam, September 18, 1962–September 27, 1962).

Mohammed al-Badr Saif al-Islam was born in 1928. He was the eldest son of Imam Ahmed and was instrumental in restoring his father to the throne following a rebellion in April of 1955. He served in his father's government as foreign minister and minister of defense. Mohammed was appointed crown prince in 1962 and succeeded as imam following the death of his father on September 18, 1962. He was forced from the throne by a rebellion on September 27, 1962. He was initially reported to have been killed, but reemerged the following month to lead the royalist forces in a civil war against the republican government in San'a. Mohammed suffered from poor health in 1966 and went to Saudi Arabia for treatment. He returned to Yemen to resume the leadership of the royalists in 1969. The royalists reached a reconciliation with the republican government in 1970, though Imam Mohammed was excluded from the negotiations. He fled Yemen in February of 1970 and went to London the following May. He subsequently went into exile in Saudi Arabia.

ABDULLAH AL-SALLAL (President, September 27, 1962–November 5, 1967).

Abdullah al-Sallal was born in 1917. He was educated at the Baghdad Military College in Iraq. He graduated in 1938 and entered the Yemeni military. Sallal supported Sayyid Abdullah Ibn Ahmed Al-Wazir's unsuccessful coup in 1948 and was imprisoned. He was released in the early 1950s and became the commander of the personal guard of Crown Prince Mohammed al-Badr. He also served as governor of Hodeida from 1959 until 1962. Mohammed al-Badr became imam in 1962, and Sallal was appointed commander in chief of the army. He led a revolt against the monarchy in September of 1962 and was declared president of the ruling Revolutionary Council on September 27, 1962. He also took the post of prime minister and from 1963 until 1964 was minister of foreign affairs. Sallal stepped down as prime minister on April 29, 1964. His powers were restricted following the establishment of a Presidential Council in 1965. He led a pro–Egyptian government and remained in Cairo from April of 1965 until September of 1966. Sallal remained president of the Yemen Arab Republic until November 5, 1967, when he was ousted in a coup following the withdrawal of Egyptian troops from Yemen. He went into exile in Baghdad following his ouster.

ABDUL RAHMAN AL-IRYANI (President, November 5, 1967–June 13, 1974). Sayyid Abdul Rahman al-Iryani was born on July 18, 1917. He received a religious education and became an Islamic judge. He was active in the unsuccessful revolt against Imam Ahmed in 1948 and was imprisoned until 1954. Iryani was a leader of the Zaidi Community of Shi'a Muslims and was active in the attempt to overthrow the imam in 1955. He served as a member of the Yemen Revolutionary Council following the ouster of Imam Mohammed in 1962. He served as minister of justice from 1962 until 1963 and was vice president of the Executive Council from 1963 until 1964. Iryani became president of the Revolutionary Council following the ouster of President Abdullah al-Sallal on November 5, 1967. He remained as head of state as chairman of the Presidential Council from 1969 until he was ousted by a military coup on June 13, 1974. Iryani remained in exile until 1981.

IBRAHIM AL-HAMDI (President, June 13, 1974–October 11, 1977). Ibrahim Muhammad al-Hamdi was born in 1943. He served in the Yemeni military, where he rose to the rank of lieutenant colonel. He was a leader of the military coup that ousted the government of Sheikh Abdul Rahman al-Iryani on June 13, 1974. Hamdi led the ruling Military Command Council. He established a strong central government and led Yemem to close relations with Saudi Arabia. He also improved ties with the United States. Hamdi was preparing to go on a state visit to the People's Democratic Republic of Yemen when he and several of his leading advisors were assassinated in Sana by unknown gunmen on October 11, 1977.

AHMED HUSSEIN AL-GHASHMI (President, October 11, 1977–June 24, 1978). Ahmed Hussein al-Ghashmi was born in 1939. He served in the Yemeni military, rising to the rank of lieutenant colonel. He served as commander of the armed forces and became chairman of the Military Command Council following Ibrahim al-Hamdi's assassination on October 11, 1977. Ghashmi was appointed president of the Yemen Arab Republic by the Constituent Assembly in April of 1978. Ghashmi was killed on June 24, 1978, when an envoy from the Yemen People's Democratic Republic delivered a bomb to his military headquarters in San'a.

ALI ABDULLAH SALEH (President, July 17, 1978–May 22, 1990). *See entry under Yemen, Heads of State.*

HEADS OF GOVERNMENT

ABDULLAH AL-SALLAL (Premier, September 27, 1962–April 29, 1964). *See entry under Heads of State.*

MAHMOUD AL-GAYIFI (Premier, April 29, 1964–January 5, 1965). Mahmoud al-Gayifi was born in 1918. He replaced Abdullah al-Sallal as premier of a reformist government on April 29, 1964. He resigned from office on January 5, 1965, and was replaced by Hassan al-Amri.

HASSAN AL-AMRI (Premier, January 5, 1965–April 20, 1965). Hassan al-Amri (Umri) was born in 1916. He attended the Baghdad Military Academy and joined the Yemeni army. He was active in the revolution of 1962 and served as minister of transport in the subsequent republican government from September until October of 1962. Amri was subsequently appointed minister of communications and served until 1963. He was vice president of Yemen from 1963 until 1966. He also served as premier from January 5, 1965, until April 20, 1965. Amri again served as premier from December 18, 1967, until July 8, 1969, and also served as military governor general and commander in chief of the army during that period. He served as premier of a center-left cabinet from August 24 until August 29, 1971. He was subsequently arrested and went into exile in Lebanon, where he remained until his return to Yemen in January of 1975.

AHMED MOHAMMED NU'MAN (Premier, April 20, 1965–July 6, 1965). Ahmed Mohammed Nu'man was born in 1910. He graduated from the Islamic University of al-Azhar in Cairo, Egypt, in 1941. He supported the revolt against Imam Ahmed in 1955 and went into exile in Egypt following the revolt's collapse. A republican government was established in September of 1962, and Nu'man served as representative to the Arab League until 1964. He returned to Yemen as deputy chairman of the Executive Council and was appointed premier on April 20, 1965. He resigned from office on July 6, 1965, but remained on the Presidential Council until September of 1966. Nu'man was detained in Egypt until October of 1967. He sub-

sequently refused an offer to return to the Presidential Council. He advocated a reconciliation between the government and the royalist rebels. Nu'man was again named premier on May 1, 1971, and served until his resignation on July 20, 1971. He was an advisor to the Presidential Council from January of 1972 until February of 1973.

ABDULLAH AL-SALLAL (Premier, July 6, 1965–July 18, 1965). *See entry under Heads of State.*

HASSAN AL-AMRI (Premier, July 18, 1965–November 5, 1967). *See earlier entry under Heads of Government.*

MOHSIN AL-AINI (Premier, November 5, 1967–December 18, 1967). Mohsin al-Aini was born in Bani Bahloul on October 20, 1932. He was educated at Cairo University and the Sorbonne in Paris. He returned to Yemen where he taught. Aini served as minister of foreign affairs from September until December of 1962. He was appointed permanent representative to the United Nations in 1962. He returned to Yemen as foreign minister briefly in 1965 and then resumed his post at the United Nations. Aini was appointed prime minister on November 5, 1967 and served until December 18, 1967. He then returned to the United Nations, where he remained until 1969. He also served as ambassador to the Soviet Union from 1968 until 1970. Aini was reappointed prime minister on February 5, 1970, and held office until February 25, 1971. He served as ambassador to France in 1971 and again served as prime minister from September 18, 1971, until December 28, 1972. He was named ambassador to Great Britain in 1973 and served until he was reappointed premier on June 22, 1974. Aini served until January 16, 1975. He was renamed ambassador to France from 1975 until 1976. He was appointed permanent representative to the United Nations again in 1980 and then was appointed ambassador to West Germany the following year. He retained that position until 1984, when he was named ambassador to the United States.

HASSAN AL-AMRI (Premier, December 18, 1967–July 8, 1969). *See earlier entry under Heads of Government.*

ABDULLAH KURSHUMI (Premier, September 2, 1969–February 1, 1970). Abdullah Kurshumi was born in 1932. He was educated as an engineer and served as minister of communications in the cabinet of Hassan al-Amri. He was named premier on September 2, 1969, and attempted to introduce an austerity budget to improve the economy. Kurshumi was unable to devise a budget that was acceptable to the military and resigned from office on February 1, 1970.

MOHSIN AL-AINI (Premier, February 5, 1970–February 25, 1971). *See earlier entry under Heads of Government.*

AHMAD MUHAMMAD NU'MAN (Premier, May 1, 1971–July 20, 1971). *See earlier entry under Heads of Government.*

HASSAN AL-AMRI (Premier, August 24, 1971–August 29, 1971). *See earlier entry under Heads of Government.*

MOHSIN AL-AINI (Premier, September 18, 1971–December 28, 1972). *See earlier entry under Heads of Government.*

KADHI ABDULLAH AL-HAGRI (Premier, December 30, 1972–March 3, 1974). Kadhi Abdullah al-Hagri was born in 1912. He served as minister in ima Ahmed's government in the

1950s. He remained a royalist and was a personal friend of King Faisal of Saudi Arabia. Hagri was named premier of a conservative cabinet on December 30, 1972. He retained office until March 3, 1974, when he stepped down for reasons of health. Hagri was subsequently appointed deputy chief of Yemen's Supreme Court. He accompanied his wife to London for medical treatment in February of 1977. He and his wife were shot to death by an unknown assassin outside the Hyde Park Hotel in London on April 10, 1977.

MOHAMMED HASSAN MAKKI (Premier, March 3, 1974–June 13, 1974). Mohammed Hassan Makki was born on December 22, 1933. He was educated in Italy and then returned to Yemen to work in the Ministry of Economics. He became minister in 1963 and served until 1964. Makki was minister of foreign affairs from April until September of 1966 and again from 1967 until 1968. He served as ambassador to Italy from 1968 until 1970 and was ambassador to West Germany from 1970 until 1972. He served as deputy prime minister from 1972 until he became prime minister on March 3, 1974. Makki served until June 13, 1974. He served as permanent representative to the United Nations from 1974 until 1976 and also served as ambassador to the United States from 1975 until 1976. He was reappointed ambassador to Italy in 1977 and remained in that post until 1979. Makki served as deputy prime minister for economic affairs from 1980 until 1985 and was deputy prime minister of Yemen from 1985 until 1990. He became deputy prime minister of the Republic of Yemen after the merger of North and South Yemen in 1990.

MOHSIN AL-AINI (Premier, June 22, 1974–January 16, 1975). *See earlier entry under Heads of Government.*

ABDUL-AZIZ ABDEL-GHANI (Premier, January 25, 1975–October 15, 1980). Abdul-Aziz Abdel-Ghani was born in Haifan, Taiz, on July 4, 1939. He was educated in Aden and the United States. He served as minister of health in Sana'a from 1967 until 1968 and was minister of the economy from 1968 until 1969. Abdel-Ghani was governor of the Central Bank of Yemen from 1971 until 1975. He was named premier on January 25, 1975, and served until October 15, 1980. He then served as vice president until 1983. Abdel-Ghani was again named premier on November 13, 1983, and served until May 22, 1990. Abdel-Ghani subsequently served on the Presidential Council.

ABDEL KARIM AL-IRYANI (Premier, October 15, 1980–November 13, 1983).

Abdel Karim al-Iryani was educated at Yale University, where he received a doctorate. He was a nephew of Abdul Rahman al-Iryani, the president of Yemen from 1967 until 1974. Abdel Karim al-Iryani returned to Yemen to direct the Wadi Zabid agriculture project in 1968. He was appointed the first chairman of the Central Planning Organization in January of 1972. He replaced Abdul-Aziz Abdel-Ghani as premier on October 15, 1980, and retained office until November 13, 1983, when he was appointed to organize reconstruction necessitated by the damage caused by a major earthquake.

ABDUL-AZIZ ABDEL-GHANI (Premier, November 13, 1983–May 22, 1990). *See earlier entry under Heads of Government.*

Yugoslavia, Federal Republic of

(Federativna Republika Jugoslavija)

Yugoslavia is a federation of republics in southeastern Europe. It consists of the republics of Serbia and Montenegro. The republics of Croatia, Bosnia-Hercegovina, Macedonia, and Slovenia declared their independence from the federation in 1991.

HEADS OF STATE

PETER II (King, October 11, 1934–November 29, 1945). Peter Karageorgevich was born on September 6, 1923. He was the oldest son of King Alexander and Queen Marie of Yugoslavia. He succeeded his father as king of Yugoslavia following Alexander's assassination in France on October 9, 1934. King Peter II was eleven years old at the time of his ascension to the throne and ruled under a regency coun-

cil headed by his cousin, Prince Paul. Peter reached the age of majority in 1941 and ruled briefly, leading a revolt against the pro–Nazi Prince Paul before being ousted by the German occupation forces. He went into exile in Great Britain and headed a Yugoslav government-in-exile. During the war he flew combat missions with the Royal Air Force. He also supported the Yugoslavian Resistance forces led by

General Draga Mikhailovich during World War II. A rival Resistance force was led by Communist partisan Marshal Tito. Tito's forces captured General Mikhailovich and executed him. Marshal Tito set up a Communist government after the liberation from the Germans, and King Peter was formally deposed on November 29, 1945. Peter remained in exile and was employed by a public relations firm in New York in the 1950s. He worked for the Sterling Savings and Loan Association of California, where he served as chairman of their international advisory board from 1967. He died in Los Angeles from complications from pneumonia on November 3, 1970.

IVAN RIBAR (President, February 2, 1946–January 13, 1953). Ivan Ribar was born in Vukmarnic on January 21, 1881. He was educated as a lawyer and entered politics. He was elected president of the first Constitutional Assembly in 1919. Ribar was active with the Resistance during World War II and was a close aide to Marshal Tito. Following the war, Ribar became president of the Presidium of the National Assembly on February 2, 1946, and served as head of state. He held the position until he was replaced by Marshal Tito on January 13, 1953, when, following changes in the constitution, the post evolved into an executive presidency. Ribar went into political retirement. He died in Zagreb at the age of 87 on February 2, 1968.

TITO (President, January 13, 1953–May 4, 1980). Josip Broz was born in Kumrovec, Croatia, on May 7, 1892. He served in the Austro-Hungarian army during World War I. He was captured by the Russians in March of 1915 and became a Communist three years later. He returned to Croatia, which was now part of the new Kingdom of Serbs, Croats, and Slovenes, and he was active in the Communist party there. He was arrested in 1928 and

sentenced to five years in prison. When he was released, he went to Moscow to meet with the Comintern. During the 1930s he also adopted the name Tito as a cover for his Communist activities. He was active as a recruiter for the republican cause during the Spanish Civil War in 1936. Tito became secretary-general of the Yugoslav Communist party the following year. After the German occupation of Yugoslavia in April of 1941, Tito became the leader of the Partisan Resistance. His forces were successful in driving the Germans out of large portions of Yugoslavia, and his successes were recognized by the Allied forces. Tito entered Belgrade on October 20, 1944, and began the transformation of Yugoslavia into a Communist state. He was recognized as prime minister on March 6, 1945. Tito broke with the Soviet Communists and Josef Stalin in 1948 following an attempt by the Soviets to oust him. This began a feud between Tito and Stalin which lasted until the Soviet dictator's death in 1953. Tito sponsored a new constitution in 1953 that gave more power to an executive presidency. He was elected president on January 13, 1953. Tito was also a leader of the nonaligned nations movement and served as host to the first conference in 1961. He remained prime minister until June 29, 1963, when he relinquished the position. Tito remained the predominant force in Yugoslavian politics throughout his life. He was named president for life in 1974. Tito became seriously ill in January of 1980 when his left leg was amputated because of a blood vessel blockage. He remained hospitalized in Ljubljana until his death from heart failure on May 4, 1980.

LAZAR KOLIŠEVSKI (President, May 4, 1980–May 15, 1980). Lazar Koliševski was born in Macedonia on February 12, 1914. He joined the Yugoslav Communist party in 1935 and fought with the Resistance during

World War II. He was captured in Bulgaria and imprisoned from 1941 until 1944. Koliševski was president of the government of Macedonia in 1945. He was active with the Communist party in Macedonia and served on the Executive Committee of the League of Communists of Yugoslavia from 1952. He served as a member of the Council of Federation from 1967 until 1972. Koliševski was a member of the Collective Presidency of Yugoslavia from 1972 and served as vice president from 1979 until 1980. He succeeded Marshal Tito as president on May 4, 1980, and served until May 15, 1980. He remained a member of the Collective Presidency until 1984, when he returned to serve as a member of the Council of Federation.

CVIJETIN MIJATOVIĆ (President, May 15, 1980–May 15, 1981). Cvijetin Mijatović was born in Lopare in 1912. He joined the Yugoslav Communist party in 1933 and was active in Bosnia-Hercegovina and Serbia. He fought with the Resistance during World War II and served as general of the Yugoslav army. Mijatović later served as deputy prime minister of Bosnia-Hercegovina and ambassador to the Soviet Union. He was Bosnia-Hercegovina's representative to the Collective Presidency of Yugoslavia from 1974. He served as president from May 15, 1980, until May 15, 1981, and remained on the Collective Presidency until 1984.

SERGEJ KRAIGHER (President, May 15, 1981–May 16, 1982). Sergej Kraigher was born in Postonja, Slovenia, on May 30, 1914. He attended Zagreb University and Ljubljana University, where he joined the Communist party. He was arrested and jailed from 1934 until 1936. Kraigher fought with the Resistance during World War II. Following the war, he served as president of the Planning Commission of Slovenia from 1946 until 1950, and he was vice president of Slovenia in

1951. He was director of the National Bank from 1951 until 1953 and served in various government agencies throughout the 1950s and 1960s. Kraigher was elected president of the Assembly of Slovenia in 1967 and served until 1974. He was president of Slovenia from 1974 until 1979. He was a member of the Collective Presidency of Yugoslavia from 1979 and served as vice president from 1980 until 1981. Kraigher was president of Yugoslavia from May 15, 1981, until May 16, 1982. He remained a member of the Collective Presidency until 1984.

PETER STAMBOLIĆ (President, May 16, 1982–May 13, 1983). Peter Stambolić was born in Serbia on July 12, 1912. He attended the University of Belgrade and joined the Communist party in 1935. He was active in the Resistance in Serbia during World War II. Stambolić held numerous government offices in Serbia and served as president of the Executive Council from 1948 until 1953. He was president of the Serbian Assembly from 1953 until 1957 and president of the Federal People's Assembly from 1957 until 1963. He was named prime minister on June 29, 1963, and served until May 18, 1967. Stambolić was a member of the Collective Presidency of Yugoslavia from 1974 and served as vice president from 1974 until 1975 and from 1981 until 1982. He became president of Yugoslavia on May 16, 1982, and served until May 13, 1983. He retired from the Collective Presidency the following year.

MIKA SPILJAC (President, May 13, 1983–May 15, 1984). Mika Spiljak was born in Odra, Croatia, on November 28, 1916. He fought with Marshal Tito in the Resistance during World War II. He was a member of the Communist party and rose through the party ranks. Spiljak became a member of the Central Committee in 1952 and served on the Zagreb City Committee. He became prime minister of the Executive Council of Croatia in 1963 and retained that position until May 18, 1967, when he became prime minister of the federal government. He was replaced by Mitja Ribicic on May 17, 1969. Spiljac subsequently served as president of the Chamber of Nationalities of the Federal Assembly until May of 1974. He was then named president of the Confederation of Trade Unions of Yugoslavia. He served on the Collective Presidency of the Federal Republic and became president of Yugoslavia on May 13, 1983. He completed his term and relinquished office to Vselin Djuranovic on May 15, 1984.

VESELIN DJURANOVIC (President, May 15, 1984–May 15, 1985). Veselin Djuranovic was born in Martinici, Montengro, on May 17, 1926. He fought against the occupation forces during World War II and was active in the Communist party. He held various party positions after the war. Djuranovic served as president of the Central Council of the Socialist Alliance of Working People of Montenegro from 1962 until 1963. He was prime minister of Montenegro from 1963 until 1966 and chairman of the Communist party in Montenegro from 1969 until 1977. He was named prime minister of Yugoslavia on February 14, 1977, following the death of Dzemal Bijedic. Djuranovic was reelected by the Assembly the following year and completed his term on May 16, 1982. He served as president of Montenegro from 1982 until 1984. He became president of Yugoslavia on May 15, 1984, and served until May 15, 1985. Djuranovic remained a member of the Collective Presidency of the Federal Republic until 1989.

RADOVAN VLAJKOVIC (President, May 15, 1985–May 15, 1986). Radovan Vlajkovic was born in Budjanovci, Vojvodina, on November 18, 1922. He joined the Worker's Movement in 1940 and became a member of the Communist party of Yugoslavia in 1943. He served as a member of the Central Committee of the League of Communists in Serbia from 1959 until 1968. Vlajkovic also served as president of the Assembly of Vojvodina in 1963. He was elected a deputy to the Chamber of Nationalities of the Federal Assembly in 1969, where he remained until 1974. He was subsequently elected president of the Collective Presidency of Vojvodina. He remained in that position until 1981 when he became the member from Vojvodina to the Collective Presidency of Yugoslavia. On May 15, 1985, Vlajkovic assumed the rotating presidency and served until May 15, 1986.

SINAN HASANI (President, May 15, 1986–May 15, 1987). Sinan Hasani was born in Pozaranju, Kosovo, in 1922. He fought with the Resistance during World War II. He was a member of the Communist party and served as president of the Assembly of Serbia. Hasani was named ambassador to Denmark during the 1970s. He was active in the Communist party in Kosovo and served as a member of the Collective Presidency of Yugoslavia from 1984 until 1989. He was president of Yugoslavia from May 15, 1986, until May 15, 1987.

LAZAR MOJSOV (President, May 15, 1987–May 15, 1988). Lazar Mojsov was born in Negotino, in Macedonia, on December 19, 1920. He attended Belgrade University and fought with the resistance during World War II. He served as minister of justice in Macedonia from 1948 until 1951 and was president of the Macedonian Supreme Court in 1953. Mojsov was appointed ambassador to the Soviet Union in 1958 and served until 1961. He was ambassador to Austria from 1967 until 1969 and was Yugoslavia's permanent representative to the United Nations from 1969 until 1974. He was elected chairman of the United Nations Security Council in 1973. Mojsov returned to Yugoslavia to serve as deputy foreign minister from 1974 until 1978. He was also elected president of the United Nations General Assembly in 1977. He served as president of the Presidium of the Yugoslav Communist party from October 20, 1980, until October of 1981. Mojsov served as a member of the Collective State Presidency of Yugoslavia from 1984 until 1989. He was vice president of Yugoslavia from 1986 until 1987 and served as president from May 15, 1987, until May 15, 1988.

RAIF DIZAREVIĆ (President, May 15, 1988–May 15, 1989). Raif Dizarević was born in Fojnica in 1926. He fought against the occupation forces during World War II and joined the Communist party in 1945. He served in the Ministry of Foreign Affairs from 1951 and worked in embassies in Bulgaria, the Soviet Union, and Czechoslovakia. Dizarević served as president of Bosnia-Hercegovina from 1978 until 1982 and was minister of foreign affairs from 1985. He served as president of Yugoslavia from May 15, 1988, until May 15, 1989.

JANEZ DRNOVŠEK (President, May 15, 1989–May 15, 1990). Janez Drnovšek was born in 1950. He was a leading economist and a member of the Collective Presidency. He became president on May 15, 1989, and was the youngest person to hold the position. Drnovšek retained office until May 15, 1990. Following the breakup of Yugoslavia, Drnovšek served as premier of Slovenia from May 14, 1992.

BORISAV JOVIĆ (President, May 15, 1990–May 15, 1991). Borisav Jović was born in 1918. He represented Serbia on the Collective Presidency. He was an ally of Serbian president Slobodan Milosevic. Jović became vice president in May of 1989 and succeeded in the rotating presidency on May 15, 1990.

He retained the position until May 15, 1991.

STIPE MESIC (President, July 1, 1991–December 5, 1991). Stipe Mesic succeeded Stipe Suvar as Croatia's representative to the Yugoslav Collective Presidency. As vice president, he was scheduled to take over the presidency on May 15, 1991, but he was blocked from assuming the office by Serbia and its allies. He unilaterally declared himself head of state on May 20, 1991, but was not recognized. Mesic was allowed to take office on July 1, 1991, following a cease-fire treaty between Croatia and Serbia that resulted in Croatia and Slovenia suspending their independence declarations for a period of three months. Mesic was prevented from exercising his executive powers by the pro–Serbian factions in the government, and he resigned on December 5, 1991.

BRANKO KOSTIC (President, December 5, 1991–June 15, 1992). Branko Kostic was Montenegro's representative on the Collective Presidency. He became acting president of Yugoslavia following the resignation of Stipe Mesic on December 5, 1991, and retained the position until Dobrica Cosić was selected on June 15, 1992.

DOBRICA COSIĆ (President, June 15, 1992–May 31, 1993). Dobrica Cosić was born in 1921. He was a prominent Serbian novelist and an ally of Serbian president Slobodan Milosevic. He became president of Yugoslavia on June 15, 1992. He supported the government of Prime Minister Milan Panic and opposed the attempt to oust him in September of 1992. Cosić was accused by rightist members of the Parliament of violating the constitution by delaying the nomination of a prime minister and Supreme Court justices. He was ousted by the National Assembly on May 31, 1993.

HEADS OF GOVERNMENT

TITO (Prime Minister, March 6, 1945–June 29, 1963). *See entry under Heads of State.*

PETER STAMBOLIĆ (Prime Minister, June 29, 1963–May 18, 1967). *See entry under Heads of State.*

MIKA SPILJAK (Prime Minister, May 18, 1967–May 17, 1969). *See entry under Heads of State.*

MITJA RIBICIC (Prime Minister, May 17, 1969–July 30, 1971). Mitja Ribicic was born in Trieste in 1919. He attended the University of Ljubljana and joined the Communist party in 1941. He succeeded Mika Spiljak as prime minister on May 17, 1969, and served until July 30, 1971. Ribicic served as a member of the Collective Presidency of the Federal Republic from 1971 until 1974 and was vice president from 1973 until 1974. He was active in the Communist party in Slovenia and served as president of the Socialist Alliance of Working People of Slovenia from 1974 until 1982. He was elected president of the Central Committee of the Yugoslav Communist party on June 29, 1982, and served until June 3, 1983.

DŽEMAL BIJEDIĆ (Prime Minister, July 30, 1971–January 18, 1977). Džemal Bijedić, the son of Muslim shopkeepers, was born in Mostar on April 12, 1917. He became active in the Yugoslav Communist party in 1939 and was arrested by the prewar government on numerous occasions. He attended Belgrade University, where he received a degree in law. Bijedić was active in the Resistance during World War II. Following the war, he was active in the government and Communist party in Bosnia-Hercegovina. He rose to become chairman of Bosnia-Hercegovina's Assembly

in 1967. Bijedić was named prime minister of the federal government on July 30, 1971. He was also elected to the Presidium of the League of Communists in 1974. He remained prime minister until he and his wife were killed on January 18, 1977, when the executive jet they were passengers aboard crashed near Sarajevo.

VESELIN DJURANOVIC (Prime Minister, February 14, 1977–May 16, 1982). *See entry under Heads of State.*

MILKA PLANINC (Prime Minister, May 16, 1982–May 15, 1986). Milka Planinc was born in Drnis, Croatia, on November 21, 1924. She joined the Communist party in 1941 and was active with the Resistance during World War II. She served in various party and governmental agencies in Croatia and became the leader of the Croatian Communist party in the early 1970s. Planinc was nicknamed the "Iron Lady of Yugoslavia" following her nomination as president of the Federal Executive Council, or prime minister, in January of 1982. She assumed the office on May 16, 1982, and served until May 15, 1986.

BRANKO MIKULIC (Prime Minister, May 15, 1986–March 16, 1989). Branko Mikulic was born in Gornji Vakuf, Bosnia-Hercegovina, in 1928. He was a member of Marshal Tito's National Liberation Army during World War II and was active in the Communist party after the war. He was a party and government official in Bosnia-Hercegovina and served as secretary of the Central Committee in 1964. Mikulic was president of Bosnia-Hercegovina from 1969 until 1974. He was chairman of the organizing committee for the 1984 Winter Olympic Games held in Sarajevo. He was a member of the Collective Presidency of

Yugoslavia in 1984 and served as prime minister of Yugoslavia from May 15, 1986, until March 16, 1989.

ANTE MARKOVIC (Prime Minister, March 16, 1989–December 20, 1991). Ante Markovic was born in Konjic on November 25, 1924. He attended Zagreb University and worked as an engineer. He was prime minister of Croatia from 1982 until 1986 and president of Croatia from May of 1986 until 1988. Markovic served as Yugoslavia's prime minister from March 16, 1989, until his resignation on December 20, 1991.

MILAN PANIC (Prime Minister, July 2, 1992–December 29, 1992). Milan Panic was born in Belgrade on December 20, 1929. He was educated in Belgrade and Heidelberg, Germany, before emigrating to the United States in 1956. He then attended the University of Southern California, where he received a degree in chemistry. Panic worked as a metallurgist and chemist for several corporations. He was the founder and president of the International Chemical and Nuclear Company in 1961. He became a naturalized citizen in 1963. Panic remained head of the company, which became known as the ICN Pharmaceuticals Company, until July of 1992, when he was asked to return to Yugoslavia after a forty year absence to serve as prime minister. He received permission from the United States government to travel to Yugoslavia on July 2, 1992, and accepted the position of head of government. He vowed to bring order to Yugoslavia and was a critic of attacks by Serbs on Bosnia and Hercegovina. Panic challenged Slobodan Milosevic for the Serbian presidency in December of 1992, but was defeated by a wide margin. The Yugoslav Federal Parliament overwhelmingly passed a vote of no confidence against Panic's government on December 29, 1992. Radoje Kontic was named to head an interim government. Panic remained in Yugoslavia to organize opposition to Serbian president Milosevic.

RADOJE KONTIC (Prime Minister, December 29, 1992–). Radoje Kontic served as deputy prime minister in the government of Milan Panic. He was chosen by the Parliament to serve as interim prime minister when Panic was ousted on December 29, 1992.

OTHER LEADERS

TITO (Communist Party Chairman, 1937–May 4, 1980). *See entry under Heads of State.*

STEVAN DORONJSKI (Communist Party Chairman, May 4, 1980–October 20, 1980). Stevan Doronjski was born in the province of Vojvodina in Serbia in 1919. He studied veterinary medicine in Belgrade before joining the Communist Youth League in 1937. He was active in opposing the Fascists in Serbia during World War II. Doronjski was active in the Communist party following the war and served as secretary of the Serbian party and secretary of the Belgrade party committee. He was selected as Serbia's representative to the Collective Presidency in 1974. Doronjski succeeded Marshal Tito as chairman of the Yugoslav Communist party on May 4, 1980, and served until October 20, 1980. He died on August 13, 1981.

LAZAR MOJSOV (Chairman, October 20, 1980–October 1981). *See entry under Heads of State.*

DUSAN DRAGOSAVAC (Chairman, October 1981–June 29, 1982). Dusan

Dragosavac was elected president of the Central Committee of the Yugoslav Communist party in October of 1981. He relinquished office to Mitja Ribici on June 29, 1982.

MITJA RIBICIC (Chairman, June 29, 1982–June 3, 1983). *See entry under Heads of Government.*

DRAGOSLAV MARKOVIC (Chairman, June 3, 1983–June 26, 1984). Dragoslav Markovic was a Serbian who fought with the Resistance during World War II. He joined the Communist party in 1948 and was named to the Central Committee in May of 1974. He became president of the Presidium of the League of Communists on June 3, 1983. Markovic completed his term and relinquished office to Ali Sukrija on June 26, 1984.

ALI SUKRIJA (Chairman, June 26, 1984–June 25, 1985). Ali Sukrija was born in Kosovska Mitrovica, Albania, on September 12, 1919. He joined the Communist party of Yugoslavia in 1939 and fought with the Resistance during World War II. Following the war, he served on various government agencies. Sukrija was a member of the Collective Presidency of the Federal Republic in 1974 and 1978. He was president of the province of Kosovo from 1981 until 1982. He was elected chairman of the Yugoslav Communist party on June 26, 1984, and served until June 25, 1985.

VIDOJE ZARKOVIC (Chairman, June 25, 1985–June 28, 1986). Vidoje Zarkovic was born in Nedajno on June 10, 1927. He fought with the partisans during World War II. Following the liberation, he served in staff positions in the Yugoslav army. He attended the Djuro Djakovic Higher School of Politics, and upon graduation, he taught political science there. Zarkovic was elected president of the Executive Council of Montenegro, and

in 1974 he was elected to the presidium of the League of Communists of Yugoslavia. He became a member of the Collective Presidency of the Socialist Federation of the Republic of Yugoslavia in 1974. He served as vice president from 1976 until 1977 and again from 1983 until 1984. Zarkovic became chairman of the Yugoslav Communist party on June 25, 1985, for a one-year term and left office on June 28, 1986.

MILANKO RENOVICA (Chairman, June 28, 1986–June 30, 1987). Milanko Renovica was born in Sokolac in 1928. He studied law and served as president of the Bosnia-Hercegovina Executive Council from 1974 until 1982. He was president of Bosnia-Hercegovina from 1983 until 1985. Renovica was elected chairman of the Yugoslav Communist party on June 28, 1986, and served until June 30, 1987.

BOSKO KRUNIC (Chairman, June 30, 1987–June 30, 1988). Bosko Krunic was a hard-line member of the Communist party. He succeeded Milanko Renovica as president of the Presidium of the League of Communists on June 30, 1987. He completed his term and relinquished office to Stipe Suvar on June 30, 1988.

STIPE SUVAR (Chairman, June 30, 1988–May 17, 1989). Stipe Suvar was born in 1946. He served as chairman of the Yugoslav Communist party from June 30, 1988, until May 17, 1989. He was subsequently selected as Croatia's representative to the Yugoslav Collective Presidency. He was elected vice president in May of 1990.

MILAN PANCEVSKI (Chairman, May 17, 1989–September 1989). Milan Pancevski was born in 1935. He represented Macedonia on the Central Committee of the League of Communists. He was selected as chairman of the Communist party on May 17,

1989. Pancevski was an ally of Serbian interests on the Central Committee, which proposed to end the party's system of collective leadership on September 11, 1989.

Zaire, Republic of

(République du Zaïre)

Zaire is a country in central Africa. It was granted independence from Belgium on June 30, 1960.

HEADS OF STATE

JOSEPH KASAVUBU (President, June 24, 1960–November 25, 1965). Joseph Kasavubu was born in the village of Kuma-Dizi, though some sources indicate the village of Tshela, in 1913 (sources also indicate 1910 or 1917). His grandfather was a Chinese worker who wed a Bakongo tribewoman. Kasavubu was educated in Catholic missionary schools with the intention of becoming a priest, but became a lay teacher instead. He was employed as a clerk in the colonial government in 1942. He entered politics in the 1950s and became president of the Abako, a political and cultural society of the Bakongo, in 1955. Kasavubu was a proponent of independence for the Belgian Congo and was briefly imprisoned in January of 1959 for nationalist activities. He participated in negotiations with the Belgian colonial authorities on Congolese independence in 1960. Elections in May of 1960 resulted in a stalemate between Kasavubu's supporters and followers of Patrice Lumumba. A coalition government was formed with Lumumba as prime minister and Kasavubu as head of state. Kasavubu became president of the Congo when independence was declared on June 30, 1960. The Congo was beset with civil disorders and tribal violence after independence. The Katanga Province under Moise Tshombe declared its secession the following month, and the Congolese army mutinied. United Nations troops were sent to the Congo to restore order. Kasavubu dismissed Premier Lumumba in September of 1960, but Lumumba's supporters challenged Kasavubu's authority. The issue was settled by a military coup led by Colonel Joseph Mobutu on September 14, 1960. Lumumba was arrested, and Kasavubu was allowed to remain president. Kasavubu recalled exiled Katangan leader Moise Tshombe to the capital to serve as prime minister in July of 1964. Relations between the two leaders were strained, however, and Kasavubu dismissed Tshombe in October of 1965. A period of political instability followed and Mobutu led another coup that removed Kasavubu from office on November 25, 1965. Kasavubu retired from active politics and died of a brain hemorrhage at a Boma hospital at the age of 56 on March 24, 1969.

MOBUTU SESE SEKO (JOSEPH MOBUTU) (Head of State, September 14, 1960–September 20, 1960).

Mobutu Sese Seko Kuku Ngbendu Wa Za Banga was born Joseph Desiré Mobutu in Linsala, Equateur Region, on October 14, 1930. He was educated locally and at the Institut Supérieur d'Etudes Sociales in Brussels, Belgium. He joined the colonial army in 1949 and rose to the rank of sergeant major before his discharge in 1956. Mobutu subsequently worked as a journalist and became involved with the Congolese National Movement under Patrice Lumumba. Mobutu participated in negotiations with Belgian colonial authorities which led to the Congo's independence in June of 1960. He was named secretary of state for national defense. He returned to the army several weeks after independence when the army mutinied. Mobutu was given the rank of colonel and was successful in restoring order in the armed forces. President Joseph Kasavubu attempted to dismiss Premier Patrice Lumumba in September of 1960, and a period of political instability followed. Mobutu led a military coup to oust the government on September 14, 1960. He ordered the arrest of Lumumba and expelled Communist advisors from the country. He established a College of High Commissioners led by Justin Bomboko on September 20, 1960. Mobutu reinstated Kasavubu as president, but retained power as commander of the armed forces with the rank of major general. He again seized power following a power struggle between President Kasavubu and Premier Moise Tshombe on November 25, 1965. He assumed the position of president. Mobutu consolidated his power and reduced the influence of the Parliament. He nationalized the copper mines in the Congo in 1966 and introduced economic reforms in the country. He instituted a new constitution and formed the Popular Movement for Renewal. The Congo became a one-party state, and Mobutu was reelected to the presidency without opposition in October of 1970. He introduced an Africanization movement in the country in 1971 and renamed the Congo as Zaire on October 27, 1971. He adapted the name Mobutu Sese Seko Kuku Ngbendu Wa Za Banga for himself. The government was faced with an invasion in the Shaba Region by the rebel Congolese National Liberation Front in March of 1977. Mobutu was reinstalled as president in December of 1977 and was again elected without opposition in July of 1984. The government was faced with demands for liberalization in the late 1980s. He announced plans to establish a multiparty system of government in April of 1990. Mobutu continued with his repressive policies, and a violent student demonstration took place the following month. He formed a coalition government with members of the opposition in July of 1991. Political instability and domestic violence continued in 1992.

JUSTIN BOMBOKO (Chairman, High Commission, September 20, 1960–February 9, 1961). Justin-Marie Bomboko was born in Boleke on September 22, 1928. He was educated locally and in Belgium, where he studied political science. He returned to the Belgian Congo shortly before independence. He served as chairman of the High Commission that governed the Congo from September 20, 1960, until February 9, 1961, when a power struggle between President Joseph Kasavubu and Prime Minister Patrice Lumumba reached a stalemate. Bomboko subsequently served as foreign minister in the governments of Joseph Illeo and Cyrille Adoula. He was replaced in the cabinet of Moishe Tshombe, but returned as foreign minister in 1965 and served until 1969. He was then appointed ambassador to the United States, where he served until 1970. Bomboko was arrested the following year, and after his release he remained politically inactive for the next decade. He adopted the name Lokumba is Elenge Bomboko and briefly served as deputy prime minister in 1981.

MOBUTU SESE SEKO (President, November 25, 1965–). *See earlier entry under Heads of State.*

HEADS OF GOVERNMENT

PATRICE LUMUMBA (Prime Minister, June 2, 1960–September 5, 1960). Patrice Lumumba was born in Sankuru in Kasai Province on July 2, 1925. He was a member of the Batetele tribe and was educated locally. He was employed by the post office in Stanleyville in the mid-1940s. Lumumba remained with the post office until 1955, when he was convicted of embezzlement. He subsequently spent two years in prison. After his release he moved to Leopoldville, where he was employed by a Belgian brewery. He became active in nationalist politics in 1958 and formed the Mouvement National Congolais. Lumumba was arrested in November of 1959 for his role in civil disturbances in Stanleyville. He was released in January of the following year to attend the Belgian conference on the Congo in Brussels. His party was victorious in elections held in May of 1960, and Lumumba became prime minister on June 2, 1960. He was dismissed on September 5, 1960, by President Joseph Kasavubu, but his dismissal was overturned by the Chamber of Representatives several days later. Lumumba was forced from office on September 14, 1960, following a military coup led by Colonel Joseph Mobutu. Lumumba was given protection by United Nations troops at his home in Leopoldville. He attempted to leave Leopoldville, but was captured by Mobutu's troops on December 1, 1960. He was taken to Elisabethville in January of 1961. Lumumba was murdered there by followers of Katangan president Moise Tshombe on January 17, 1961.

JOSEPH ILLEO (Prime Minister, February 9, 1961–August 1, 1961). Joseph Illeo was born in Leopoldville, now Kinshasa, on September 15, 1921. He was active in the Congolese independence movement and served as an editor of the Catholic newspaper *Conscience Africaine* in 1956. Following independence, he was elected to Parliament as a member of the Mouvement National Congolais party. Illeo was named to succeed Patrice Lumumba as prime minister in September of 1960. He was unable to take office because of the constitutional crisis caused by the clash between Lumumba and President Joseph Kasavubu. Illeo's second attempt to form a government was stymied when Joseph Mobutu seized control of the government. Illeo was finally able to become head of the government on February 9, 1961, following the dissolution of the College of Commissioners. He was unable to bring the various secessionist factions together, however, and resigned office on August 1, 1961. He served as minister of information in the subsequent government of Cyrille Adoula and served as minister of Katangan affairs until 1964. Illeo adopted the name Ileo Songoamba and served as a member of the Political Bureau in the government of Mobutu Sese Seko from 1975.

CYRILLE ADOULA (Prime Minister, August 1, 1961–July 10, 1964). Cyrille Adoula was born in Leopoldville, now Kinshasa, on September 13, 1921. He was active in the trade union movement and was an early leader of the Mouvement National Congolais political party. Adoula was elected to the Senate in May of 1960 and tried to serve as a conciliator between various political factions. He was also an opponent of the authoritarian tendencies of post-independence governments and a defender of human rights. He served as minister of the interior in the government of Joseph Illeo before he was named prime minister on August 1, 1961, after he had brought the followers of Patrice Lumumba into the government. Adoula subsequently sought to restore the secessionist areas of the Congo to the central government. He traveled to Stanleyville, where Antoine Gizenga, deputy prime minister under Patrice Lumumba, had set up a Soviet-backed government. Adoula offered Gizenga a cabinet position, which he refused. Gizenga was subsequently arrested by local troops loyal to the Adoula government. Adoula then brought South Kasai, which was under the control of Albert Kalonji, under federal control. The government required the assistance of United Nations troops in dealing with the Katangan secessionists led by Moise Tshombe. Adoula was dismissed by President Kasavubu on July 10, 1964, and replaced by Tshombe. Adoula subsequently went into exile, but returned following Joseph Mobutu's successful coup. He was named ambassador to Belgium and later was named to the United States. He returned to the Congo to serve as foreign minister in August of 1969, but held the position for only a short period of time. Adoula spent the remainder of his life out of the political limelight. He suffered a heart attack in 1978 and went to Lausanne, Switzerland, for treatment. He died there at the age of 56 on May 24, 1978.

MOISE TSHOMBE (Prime Minister, July 10, 1964–October 13, 1965). Moise-Kapenda Tshombe was born in Musumba, Katanga Province, on November 10, 1919. He was educated at local mission schools and became the manager of his family's business interests. He became a member of the Katanga Provincial Council in 1951. Tshombe served on the Government Council

from 1954 and became president of the Confederation of Mutual Associations of the Lunda Empire two years later. He founded the Conakat party in July of 1959 and served as its president. He attended independence talks with the Belgian colonial authorities in 1960. The Congo became an independent nation on June 30, 1960, and Tshombe announced the secession of the Katanga Province on July 11, 1960. The province was the scene of tribal violence, and the United Nations sent a peacekeeping force to the region to try and restore order. Tshombe used foreign mercenaries to retain power in Katanga until January of 1963, when United Nations troops routed his mercenary army. He fled to Spain, where he remained until June of 1963. He then returned to the Congo and was installed as premier by General Joseph Mobutu on July 10, 1964. Tshombe became involved in a power struggle with President Joseph Kasavubu, who dismissed him on October 13, 1965. He returned to exile in Spain after a military coup the following month. He was tried in absentia for treason in March of 1967 and sentenced to death. Tshombe was kidnapped on June 29, 1967, when the aircraft he was flying in from Majorca to Barcelona was hijacked. He was taken to Algeria, where he was imprisoned near Algiers. He remained imprisoned until his death from heart failure at the age of 49 on June 29, 1969.

EVARISTE KIMBA (Prime Minister, October 13, 1965–November 25, 1965). Evariste Kimba was born in Katanga on July 16, 1926. He was a supporter of Moise Tshombe and served as foreign minister in Tshombe's secessionist Katanga Republic from 1960 until 1963. He was named by Joseph Kasavubu to succeed Tshombe as prime minister of the Democratic Republic of the Congo on October 13, 1965. Tshombe's supporters in the Parliament prevented Kimba from forming a government. Joseph Mobutu led a military coup on

November 25, 1965, and ousted the civilian government. Kimba was arrested in May of 1966 and charged with plotting against Mobutu's government in what was called the "Pentecost Plot." Kimba and several former ministers were found guilty and were hanged in Kinshasa on June 2, 1966.

MULAMBA NYUNYI WA KADIMA (Prime Minister, November 28, 1965–October 26, 1966). Mulamba Nyunyi wa Kadima was born Leonard Mulamba in Kananga, formerly Luluabourg, in 1928. He attended military school and joined the army in 1954. He was promoted to colonel in 1964 and served as chief of staff and commander of the Eastern Province. Kadima was named prime minister on November 28, 1965, and served until October 26, 1966. He served as ambassador to India from 1967 until 1969, when he was named ambassador to Japan, where he served until 1976. He served as ambassador to Brazil from 1976 until 1979, when he returned to Zaire as general of the army.

MOBUTU SESE SEKO (Prime Minister, October 26, 1966–July 6, 1977). *See entry under Heads of State.*

MPINGA KASENGA (Prime Minister, July 6, 1977–March 6, 1979). Mpinga Kasenga was born in Tshilomba on August 30, 1937. He was educated in the Congo and France. He returned to the Congo, where he worked as a professor at Lovanium University from 1966. Mpinga was active in politics and served as prime minister from July 6, 1977, until March 6, 1979.

BO-BOLIKO LOKONGA (Prime Minister, March 6, 1979–August 27, 1980). Bo-Boliko Lokonga Monse Mihomo was born Andre Bo-Boliko in Lobamiti, Bandundu, on August 15, 1934. He was educated in the Congo and Belgium. He was active in the trade union movement in Zaire and served as secretary-general of the National Union of Zairian Workers from 1967 until 1980. Bo-Boliko was elected president of the National Assembly in 1970 and became first state commissioner, or prime minister, on March 6, 1979. He served until August 27, 1980.

NGUZA KARL-I-BOND (Prime Minister, August 27, 1980–April 23. 1981). Nguza Karl-i-Bond was born in Musumba in 1938. He was educated in the Congo and Belgium and worked as a radio announcer from the late 1950s. He served in the cabinet of prime minister Moise Tshombe in 1964 and was stationed as a counselor at the embassy in Belgium from 1964 until 1966. Nguza Karl-i-Bond served with the Congolese delegation to the United Nations from 1966 until 1968. He was appointed ambassador to the United Nations office in Geneva in 1970 and served until 1972. He was foreign minister from 1972 until 1974 and from 1976 until 1977. Nguza Karl-i-Bond was arrested for treason and sentenced to death in September of 1977. His sentence was commuted to life imprisonment, and he was pardoned in March of 1979. He was again named foreign minister and served until 1980. He served as prime minister from August 27, 1980, until April 23, 1981, when he resigned while in Belgium. Nguza Karl-i-Bond called for the overthrow of President Mobutu Sese Seko and remained in exile until 1985. He was appointed ambassador to the United States in 1986, where he served until 1988. He again broke with Mobutu and formed an opposition party, the Federal Union of Independent Federalists and Republicans. He remained a leading critic of the government. Mobutu again named him prime minister on November 25, 1991, in order to diffuse criticism of the government. Nguza Karl-i-Bond clashed with the president on numerous occasions and announced his own candidacy for the presidency in the general elections. He was replaced as prime minister on August 14, 1992.

N'SINGA UDJUU (Prime Minister, April 23, 1981–November 5, 1982). N'Singa Udjuu Ongwabeki Untubwe was born Joseph N'Singa in Bandundu on October 29, 1934. He served as minister of justice from 1966 until 1969. He served briefly as minister of state for home affairs before being named minister of the interior in 1969. N'Singa was appointed minister of state at the presidency until his dismissal in September of 1970. He was appointed prime minister on April 23, 1981, and served until November 5, 1982. He served as state commissioner for justice from 1986 until 1990.

KENGO WA DONDO (Prime Minister, November 5, 1982–October 31, 1986). Kengo wa Dondo was born in 1935. He served as minister of justice from 1979 until 1980, when he was appointed ambassador to Belgium. He returned to Zaire to serve as prime minister from November 5, 1982, until October 31, 1986. Kengo wa Dondo served as foreign minister from 1986 until 1987. He was again named prime minister on November 26, 1988, and served until May 4, 1990.

MABI MULUMBA (Prime Minister, January 22, 1987–March 7, 1988). Mabi Mulumba was a leading Zairian economist and professor. He was appointed to serve as minister of finance in October of 1986. He succeeded Kengo Wa Dondo as prime minister on January 22, 1987. Mabi was dismissed on March 7, 1988, and replaced by Sambwa Pida Nbagui.

SAMBWA PIDA NBAGUI (Prime Minister, March 7, 1988–November 26, 1988). Sambwa Pida Nbagui was selected as prime minister of Zaire on March 7, 1988. He retained office until November 26, 1988, when Kengo wa Dondo was renamed to the position.

KENGO WA DONDO (Prime Minister, November 26, 1988–May 4, 1990). *See earlier entry under Heads of Government.*

LUNDA BULULU (Prime Minister, May 4, 1990–April 1, 1991). Lunda Bululu was the secretary-general of the Economic Community of Central African States. He was named by President Mobutu Sese Seko to serve as prime minister of a transitional government on May 4, 1990. He resigned from office on April 1, 1991.

MULUMBA LUKEJI (Prime Minister, April 1, 1991–September 29, 1991). Mulumba Lukeji was named prime minister by President Mobutu Sese Seko on April 1, 1991, but was unable to control the opposition forces against the government. He was ousted by Mobutu on July 22, 1991, but was reinstated two days later after Etienne Tshisekedi wa Malumba refused to accept the position. Lukeji was again removed as prime minister on September 29, 1991.

ETIENNE TSHISEKEDI WA MALUMBA (Prime Minister, September 29, 1991–October 20, 1991). Etienne Tshisekedi wa Malumba was a leading opponent of President Mobutu Sese Seko. He was imprisoned for nine years during the 1980s. He went into exile, where he remained a vocal critic of Mobutu's regime. Tshisekedi served as the leader of the opposition Union for Democracy and Social Progress and was the leading spokesman for the Sacred Union, a coalition of opposition groups. Tshisekedi returned to Zaire on February 24, 1991, following Mobutu's offer of a general amnesty for all Zairian exiles. Mobutu offered him the position of prime minister on July 22, 1991, but Tshisekedi rejected the offer the following day. He was again offered the post on September 29, 1991, and he accepted the position as head of a coalition cabinet. He clashed often with Mobutu over the composition of the cabinet and the division of powers. Tshisekedi was dismissed by the president on October 20, 1991, and returned to his role as a critic of Mobutu's government. Tshisekedi was elected prime minister of the High Council of the Republic in August of 1992 and returned to the office on August 15, 1992. He continued to clash with President Mobutu. Mobutu dissolved the High Council in December of 1992, but Tshisekedi claimed the president acted illegally and refused to abandon his position.

BERNARDIN MUNGUL DIAKA (Prime Minister, November 1, 1991– November 25, 1991). Bernardin Mungu Diaka was the leader of a small opposition party that was part of the Sacred

Union, a coalition of opposition groups. He was named prime minister by President Mobutu Sese Seko on November 1, 1991. He was branded a traitor by other opposition leaders, who boycotted his government. Massive unrest continued during his brief term of office. Diaka was removed as prime minister on November 25, 1991, and subsequently was named minister of state.

NGUZA KARL-I-BOND (Prime Minister, November 25, 1991–August 14, 1992). *See earlier entry under Heads of Government.*

ETIENNE TSHISEKEDI WA MALUMBA (Prime Minister, August 15, 1992–). *See earlier entry under Heads of Government.*

Zambia, Republic of

Zambia is a country in southern central Africa. It was granted independence from Great Britain on October 24, 1964.

HEADS OF STATE

KENNETH KAUNDA (President, October 24, 1964–November 2, 1991). Kenneth David Kaunda was born in Lubwa on April 28, 1924. He was educated locally and became a teacher in 1943. He formed a farming cooperative in 1949 and became a founder of the Northern Rhodesia African National Conference (ANC). Kaunda worked as a district organizer and became secretary-general of the ANC in August of 1953. He was arrested for nationalist activities in January of 1955 and spent several months in prison. He broke with ANC leader Harry Nkumbula in October of 1958 and formed the Zambian National Congress. He was again arrested by the colonial authorities in March of 1959. Kaunda remained

imprisoned until January of 1960. He then continued to campaign for Northern Rhodesia's independence and formed the United National Independence party. Kaunda became minister of local affairs in a coalition government with Nkumbula following elections in Northern Rhodesia in October of 1962. Northern Rhodesia withdrew from the Central African Federation on December 31, 1963, and Kaunda was elected prime minister under a new constitution the following month. He took office on January 22, 1964. Kaunda was elected president in August of 1964, and Northern Rhodesia was granted full independence on October 24, 1964, and became the Republic of Zambia. Kaunda was reelected to the presidency in 1968. Kaunda's vice president, Simon Kapwepwe, resigned from office in 1969 and went into opposition, forming the United Progressive party two years later. The party was banned in February of 1972 when Zambia was declared a single-party state. Kaunda was unopposed for reelection in 1973 and 1978 when all other candidates were disqualified. He was again reelected without opposition in 1983 and 1988. Kaunda agreed to proposals to democratize the government in 1990. He allowed the formation of political parties and released political prisoners. He allowed multiparty elections in October of 1991, and he and his party were defeated in the balloting. Kaunda relinquished office to Frederick Chiluba on November 2, 1991. He resigned as leader of the United National Independence party in January of 1992, but returned to lead the party the following May.

FREDERICK CHILUBA (President, November 2, 1991–). Frederick Jacob Titus Chiluba was born in Wusakile. He served as chairman of the Zambian Congress of Trade Unions and was a member of Parliament from Nkana. Chiluba was elected president of the Movement for Multiparty Democracy following Zambia's abolishment of the one-party system. Chiluba's party defeated President Kenneth Kaunda's United National Independence party in October of 1991. Chiluba was sworn in as president on November 2, 1991.

HEADS OF GOVERNMENT

KENNETH KAUNDA (Prime Minister, January 22, 1964–October 24, 1964). *See entry under Heads of State.*

MATHIAS MAINZA CHONA (Prime Minister, August 28, 1973–May 27, 1975). Mathias Mainza Chona was born in Nampeyo, Monze, on January 21, 1930. He was educated locally and worked as a court clerk in Livingstone from 1951 until 1955. He received a scholarship to Gray's Inn in London and received a degree in law in 1958. When Chona returned home, he became active in Kenneth Kaunda's United National Independence party. He served as vice president from 1960 until 1961 and was general secretary until 1969. He was elected to Parliament after independence in 1964 and served in Kaunda's cabinet as minister of justice. Chona also served as minister of home affairs from 1964 until 1966 and minister for presidential affairs in 1967. In 1969 he was appointed ambassador to the United States. He returned to Zambia in 1970 to serve as vice president. Chona was named prime minister on August 28, 1973, and served until May 27, 1975. He served as attorney general from 1975 until July 20, 1977, when he was reappointed prime minister. He retained office until June 16, 1978. Chona was appointed ambassador to the People's Republic of China in 1984 and served until 1989.

ELIJAH MUDENDA (Prime Minister, May 27, 1975–July 20, 1977). Elijah Haatukali Kaiba Mudenda was born on June 6, 1927. He attended school in Uganda, South Africa, and Great Britain. He was elected to Zambia's Legislative Assembly in 1962 and served in the Zambian Parliament from 1964. Mudenda served as minister of agriculture from 1964 until 1967 and was minister of finance from 1967 until 1968. He was then named minister of foreign affairs and served until 1969, when he was appointed minister of development and finance. In 1970 he was again named foreign minister and served until 1973. Mudenda was prime minister of Zambia from May 27, 1975, until July 20, 1977. He remained a leader in Parliament and chaired numerous subcommittees.

MATHIAS MAINZA CHONA (Prime Minister, July 20, 1977–June 16, 1978). *See earlier entry under Heads of Government.*

DANIEL LISULO (Prime Minister, June 16, 1978–February 18, 1981). Daniel Lisulo was born in Mongu on December 6, 1930. He was educated in India and was active in the independence movement from 1953 until 1963. He was named director of the Bank of the Zambia in 1964 and was active with the United National Independence party. Lisulo was elected to the National Assembly in 1977 and served as Zambia's attorney general from 1977 until 1978. He served as prime minister from June 16, 1978, until February 18, 1981. He remained active in political affairs and served as vice president of the World Peace Council from 1986 until 1989.

NALUMINO MUNDIA (Prime Minister, February 18, 1981–April 24, 1985). Nalumino Mundia was born in 1926. He was appointed prime minister by President Kenneth Kaunda on February 18, 1981, and retained office until April 24, 1985. Mundia was subsequently appointed Zambia's ambassa-

dor to the United States and other countries in South America. He retained his diplomatic position until his death from a heart attack in La Paz, Bolivia, at the age of 62 on November 8, 1988.

KEBBY MUSOKOTWANE (Prime Minister, April 24, 1985–March 15, 1989). Kebby Sililo Kambulu Musokotwane was born in Musokotwane on May 5, 1946. He was educated in Zambia and became a teacher. He was elected to Parliament in 1973 and served as minister of water and natural resources from 1977 until 1978. Musokotwane served as minister of youth and sports in 1979 and was minister of finance from 1979 until 1983. He was named education and culture minister in 1983 and served until his selection as prime minister on April 24, 1985. He left office on March 15, 1989. Musokotwane was appointed high commissioner to Canada in 1990. He also served as secretary-general of the United National Independence party.

MALIMBA MASHEKE (Prime Minister, March 15, 1989–August 31, 1991). Malimba Masheke served as a general in the Zambian army. He was appointed minister of defense in 1985 and was named minister of home affairs in 1988. He became prime minister on March 15, 1989. When Masheke left office on August 31, 1991, the position of prime minister was abolished.

Zanzibar

Zanzibar is an island in the Indian Ocean. It was granted independence from Great Britain on December 9, 1963. Zanzibar merged with Tanganyika to form Tanzania on April 26, 1964.

HEADS OF STATE

KHALIFAH BIN HARUB SEYYID (Sultan, December 9, 1911–October 9,

1960). Seyyid Khalifah bin Harub bin Thuwaini bin Said was born in Muscat,

Arabia, on December 9, 1879. He ascended to the throne of Zanzibar following the abdication of Sultan Ali on December 9, 1911. He ruled as a constitutional monarch and was a loyal ally of Great Britain. Khalifah supported the Allies during World War I and called upon all Muslims in East Africa to do likewise. He remained loyal to Great Britain during World War II. He attended the coronation of Queen Elizabeth II in London in 1952. The British colonial authorities allowed the organization of political parties in 1955, and a growing independence movement developed in the late 1950s. Sultan Khalifah remained Zanzibar's monarch until his death in the royal palace at the age of 81 on October 9, 1960.

ABDULLAH BIN KHALIFAH (Sultan, October 17, 1960–June 30, 1963). Abdullah bin Khalifah bin Harub was born on February 12, 1910. He was the eldest son of Sultan Khalifah and succeeded to the throne of the British protectorate upon the death of his father on October 17, 1960. He was accused of supporting the Zanzibar Nationalist party over the Afro-Shirzi party as Zanzibar approached self-rule. The sultan suffered from poor health and was hospitalized in June of 1963 for circulatory disorders. He died at the age of 52 following the amputation of both of his legs on June 30, 1963.

JAMSHID BIN ABDULLAH (Sultan, June 30, 1963–January 12, 1964). Jamshid bin Abdullah bin Khalifah was born in 1930. He was the eldest son of Sultan Abdullah. He succeeded to the throne of Zanzibar following his father's death on June 30, 1963. He was viewed as a modern monarch and supported Zanzibar's independence. Zanzibar was granted independence on December 9, 1963. A revolution erupted on January 12, 1964, and the sultan was dethroned. A revolutionary committee was established and the monarchy was abolished. Sultan Jamshid was allowed to go into exile and settled in London, England.

ABEID AMANI KARUME (President, January 12, 1964–April 26, 1964). Abeid Amani Karume was born in 1906. He worked as a sailor on cargo boats while in his teens. He returned to Zanzibar in 1938 and founded a shore launch service. Karume became active in politics and was elected to the town council in 1954. He led the African Association into a merger with the Shirazi Association to form the Afro-Shirazi party in 1957. Karume led the party in subsequent elections, but although he received a slight plurality, he was unable to form a government. A violent revolution led by John Okello overthrew the monarchy and ousted the government on January 12, 1964. Karume was selected as head of state. Relations between the new government and Okello deteriorated, and he was expelled from Zanzibar several months after leading the revolution. Karume negotiated a union between the island of Zanzibar and its neighbor on the mainland, Tanganyika, and the two nations merged to form Tanzania on April 26, 1964. Karume became first vice president of the United Republic of Tanzania and retained power on Zanzibar. He was regarded as a despot and ruled the island as a one-party state. He ruthlessly crushed opposition and eliminated potential rivals from the government. Karume remained in power until he was assassinated by four gunmen during a meeting of the Afro-Shirazi party on April 7, 1972. He was succeeded by Aboud Mwinyi Jumbe as Tanzaniza's first vice president and leader of Zanzibar.

HEADS OF GOVERNMENT

MUHAMMAD SHAMTE (Prime Minister, June 24, 1963–January 12, 1964). Muhammad Shamte Hamadi was a member of a wealthy Shirazi landowning family. He was the owner of a large clove plantation on the island of Pemba. He was active in the formation of political parties in Zanzibar and joined the Afro-Shirazi party in 1957. Shamte left the party to form the Zanzibar and Pemba People's party in December of 1959. He was elected to the Legislative Council and served as minister for Pemba affairs. He joined in a coalition with the Zanzibar Nationalist party and was selected as chief minister following the elections in June of 1961. Shamte became Zanzibar's first prime minister following the establishment of self-government on June 24, 1963. The ruling coalition retained its majority following elections in July of 1963. Zanzibar was granted independence on December 9, 1963, and Shamte remained head of the government. He was ousted, however, by a coup led by John Okello on January 12, 1964. Shamte was sent into exile by the revolutionary government and settled in London.

ABDULLAH KASSIM HANGA (Prime Minister, January 14, 1964). Abdullah Kassim Hanga was born in Zanzibar in 1932. He was educated locally and later studied economics in Great Britain and at Lumumba University in Moscow. He became active in the Afro-Shirazi party and served as deputy general secretary when Zanzibar was granted independence in December of 1963. Hanga was named prime minister of Zanzibar following the revolution on January 14, 1964. The post was abolished a few hours later, and Hanga remained in the government as vice president of the Zanzibar Republic. He subsequently served in the cabinet as minister of industries, mineral resources, and power. He became minister of state following the merger of Zanzibar with Tanganyika in April of 1964. Hanga subsequently fled Zanzibar when he was charged with plotting against the government of Abeid Amani Karume. He went into exile in Guinea until 1967, when he returned to mainland Tanzania after being given a promise of safety by President Julius Nyerere. Hanga was arrested in September of 1969. He and several other Zanzibari political figures were returned to Zanzibar, where they were executed for conspiracy against the government in September of 1969.

Zimbabwe, Republic of

Zimbabwe, formerly known as Rhodesia, is a country in central southern Africa. It declared independence from Great Britain on November 11, 1965. Independence was officially granted on April 17, 1980.

HEADS OF STATE

SIR HUMPHREY V. GIBBS (Governor, December 28, 1959–August 21, 1969). Humphrey Vicary Gibbs was born in London on November 22, 1902. He settled in Southern Rhodesia in 1928 and began farming in Bulawayo. He was elected to the Legislative Assembly in 1948 and served until 1953. Gibbs was selected to succeed P. William-Powlett as governor of Southern Rhodesia on December 28, 1959. He also served as acting governor general of the Federation of Rhodesia and Nyasaland before the federation was disbanded on December 31, 1963. The government of Ian Smith proclaimed a unilateral declaration of independence on November 11, 1965. Claiming that the government had acted illegally, Gibbs unsuccessfully attempted to dismiss Smith. Gibbs remained in Government House as governor, though the Smith government ignored his position and tried to force his removal by cutting off all utilities to the official residence. Gibbs left Rhodesia on August 21, 1969, following the establishment of Rhodesia as a republic. He returned to Great Britain, where he was knighted. He subsequently returned to his farm in Rhodesia, where he remained until 1983. Gibbs then moved his family to Harare. He died there at the age of 87 of complications from influenza on November 5, 1990.

CLIFFORD W. DUPONT (President, April 16, 1970–January 14, 1976). Clifford Walter DuPont was born in London on December 6, 1905. He was educated at Cambridge University and began practicing law in 1928. He served in the British army during World War II and rose to the rank of major. DuPont emigrated to Southern Rhodesia in 1948 and became a wealthy tobacco farmer. He entered politics following the death of his wife and children in a plane crash in 1957. He was elected to the Rhodesian Federal Parliament and was a founder of the Rhodesian Front. DuPont was named to Premier Winston Field's cabinet as minister of justice and law in December of 1962. He stepped down as justice minister in June of 1964, but remained in the cabinet as minister without portfolio. He became deputy prime minis-

ter and minister of external affairs in August of 1964. DuPont defeated former prime minister Roy Welensky in a parliamentary election later in the year. DuPont was suffering from poor health and underwent surgery in February of 1965. He resigned from the cabinet in November of 1965 and was given the position of officer administering the government following Rhodesia's unilateral declaration of independence. He moved into Government House following the retirement of Governor Sir Humphrey Gibbs on June 24, 1969. DuPont was sworn in as president of Rhodesia on April 16, 1970. He continued to suffer from poor health and resigned from office on January 14, 1976. He died in Salisbury at the age of 72 on June 28, 1978, after a long illness.

JOHN J. WRATHALL (President, January 14, 1976–August 31, 1978). John James Wrathall was born in Lancaster, England, on August 28, 1913. He was educated as an accountant and emigrated to Rhodesia in September of 1936. He was employed by the Salisbury Tax Department until 1946, when he became a charter accountant. Wrathall entered politics in 1954 and was elected to the Federal Parliament as a member of the United Rhodesia party. He declined to seek reelection in 1958, but returned to the Parliament as a founding member of the Rhodesian Front party in 1962. He was named to Winston Field's cabinet as minister of african education in December of 1962. Wrathall was also named minister of European education and health the following year. He served as minister of finance in the government of Ian Smith from April of 1964 and became deputy prime minister in September of 1966. Wrathall was elected to the Senate in 1974 and was appointed to succeed Clifford DuPont as president of Rhodesia on January 14, 1976. He retained office until his death from a heart attack in Salisbury at the age of 65 on August 31, 1978.

HENRY EVERARD (Acting President, August 31, 1978–November 2, 1978). Henry Everard was born in 1897. He was a retired Rhodesian Railways commissioner and became acting president of Rhodesia on August 31, 1978, following the death of John Wrathall. He retained office until November 2, 1978, when he stepped down because of poor health.

JACK PITHEY (Acting President, November 2, 1978–May 23, 1979). Jack Pithey was born in South Africa in 1904. He served in the civil service and was minister of justice in Ian Smith's Cabinet. He succeeded Henry Everard as acting president of Rhodesia on November 2, 1978. Pithey retained office until Josiah Zion Gumede was elected president of Rhodesia by the Senate on May 23, 1979.

JOSIAH ZION GUMEDE (President, May 23, 1979–December 7, 1979). Josiah Zion Gumede was born in 1920. He was a member of the Zulu tribe and was educated in South Africa. He subsequently settled in Rhodesia and served in the Foreign Ministry of the Federation of Rhodesia and Nyasaland in the late 1950s and early 1960s. Gumede remained active in politics and served in the municipal government of a township. He was elected president of the Rhodesian Parliament on May 23, 1979, and served as head of state. He retained office until December 7, 1979, when Rhodesia temporarily reverted to its British colonial status under Lord Soames as governor. Gumede died on March 28, 1989.

CHRISTOPHER SOAMES, BARON OF FLETCHING (Governor, December 7, 1979–April 17, 1980). Arthur Christopher John Soames was born in Penn, Buckinghamshire, England, on October 12, 1920. He attended the Royal Military College at Sandhurst and was commissioned into the Coldstream Guards as a second lieutenant in 1939. He served during World War II as a liaison officer to the Free French forces in North Africa. He served in military intelligence later in the war. Soames married Mary Spencer Churchill, the youngest daughter of Winston Churchill, in 1947. He was elected to the House of Commons as a member of the Conservative party in 1949. He became parliamentary private secretary to Churchill in 1952. Soames served in several ministries during the 1950s before being named minister of agriculture, fisheries, and food in 1960 in Harold Macmillan's cabinet. He served as Opposition spokesman for agriculture and later defense when the Labor party came to power in November of 1964. He was defeated for reelection to the Parliament in March of 1966 and entered private business. Soames returned to the government as ambassador to France in 1968 and represented Great Britain's entry into the European Economic Community (EEC). He was knighted in 1972 and appointed as an EEC commissioner. He returned to private business in 1976 and was created a life peer as Baron of Fletching in 1978. Soames became the leader of the House of Lords the following year. Britain agreed to resume authority for administering Rhodesia following negotiations in 1979. Lord Soames was appointed governor of Rhodesia on December 7, 1979. He attempted to end the guerrilla warfare that had plagued the country for nearly a decade. He presided over Rhodesia's transition to majority rule until the nation was granted independence as Zimbabwe on April 17, 1980. Lord Soames returned to England to resume his role as leader of the House of Lords until September of 1981, when he was dismissed by Prime Minister Margaret Thatcher. Soames suffered from poor health during the 1980s. He underwent abdominal surgery early in 1987 and died at his home in Hampshire on September 16, 1987, at the age of 66, from a heart ailment.

CANAAN BANANA (President, April 17, 1980–December 31, 1987). Canaan Sodindo Banana was born in Esiphezini, in the Essexvale District, on March 5, 1936. He was educated in Rhodesia, Japan, and at the Wesley Theological Seminary in the United States. He returned to Rhodesia in 1965 and was ordained a Methodist minister at Epworth the following year. Banana served as vice president of the African National Council (ANC) from 1971 until 1973 and served as the ANC representative to the United Nations and the United States from 1973 until 1975. He was detained in Rhodesia from 1975 until 1976. In 1976 he attended the Geneva Conference on Rhodesia. Robert Mugabe became prime minister of Rhodesia, now called Zimbabwe, on March 4, 1980, and Banana was chosen as president. During President Banana's term of office, a law was passed making it illegal for anyone to make fun of his name. He remained in office until Mugabe became Executive President on December 31, 1987. Banana also served as chancellor of the University of Zimbabwe from 1983 until 1988. He subsequently served as professor of classics, religious studies, and philosophy at the University of Zimbabwe.

ROBERT MUGABE (President, December 31, 1987–). Robert Gabriel Mugabe was born in Kutama on February 21, 1924. He was a member of the Shona tribe and was educated at local mission schools. He became a teacher in 1942 and continued his education at the University of Fort Hare in South Africa in 1950. Mugabe returned to Rhodesia in 1952 and went to Ghana to teach at St. Mary's Teachers Training College in 1956. He returned to Southern Rhodesia in 1960 and became active in the nationalist movement. He joined Joshua Nkomo's National Democratic party (NDP). Mugabe opposed the constitution of 1961, and the NDP was banned in December of 1961. Mugabe then joined

the Zimbabwe African People's Union (ZAPU), which was banned the following year. He was arrested in September of 1962 and imprisoned for several months. He went to Northern Rhodesia after his release, where he was again arrested in March of 1963. Mugabe escaped and went to Tanzania, where he broke with Nkomo and joined Ndabaningi Sithole's newly formed Zimbabwe African National Union (ZANU). He became secretary-general of ZANU and campaigned for majority rule in Rhodesia. He was again arrested in August of 1964. Ian Smith's government in Rhodesia unilaterally declared independence from Great Britain in November of 1965. Mugabe remained imprisoned until December of 1974, when he was freed in an amnesty. He went into exile and defeated Sithole for the leadership of ZANU. He became the leader of the main guerrilla group challenging the white-dominated government of Rhodesia. Mugabe opposed the settlement reached by Ian Smith's government with the moderate black leadership and joined with Nkomo to form the Patriotic Front. Their supporters boycotted the elections held in April of 1979 that resulted in Abel Muzorewa's selection as prime minister. Mugabe's guerrilla forces continued to fight against the government. The Patriotic Front agreed to a ceasefire in September of 1979, when Great Britain agreed to temporarily renew control over the country in anticipation of democratic elections. Mugabe's ZANU won a majority in the House of Assembly, and he was named prime minister on March 4, 1980. Friction continued between Mugabe and Nkomo, who was dismissed from the government in February of 1982. He went into opposition, and violent confrontations between supporters of ZANU and ZAPU took place throughout the country. Nkomo and Mugabe agreed to a merger of their parties in 1987. The position of prime minister was eliminated on December 31, 1987, and Mugabe became executive president of Zimbabwe. He was reelected in March of 1990, and an amendment was passed that abolished the Senate. Mugabe attempted to have the country declared a one-party state in August of 1990, but the party politburo rejected the plan. A major drought led to serious difficulties in Zimbabwe's economic stability in the early 1990s and resulted in widespread shortages of food. Mugabe retained the leadership of the country despite increased opposition to his government.

HEADS OF GOVERNMENT

IAN D. SMITH (Prime Minister, October 24, 1964–May 23, 1979). Ian Douglas Smith was born in Seluwke, Southern Rhodesia, on April 8, 1919. He was educated locally and attended Rhodes University in South Africa. He entered the Royal Air Force in 1939 and saw action as a fighter pilot during World War II. Smith was seriously injured when his plane was shot down over North Africa. He returned to active duty after recovering and was again shot down over Italy. He fought with partisans behind the German lines for five months before rejoining the British forces. Smith completed his education after the war and received a degree in commerce. He returned to Rhodesia and entered politics. He was elected to the Southern Rhodesia Legislative Assembly as a member of the right-wing Liberal party in 1948. Smith was elected to the Federal Parliament in 1953 and served as chief party whip for the United Federal party. He resigned from the Parliament in 1961 in opposition to the acceptance of a new constitution that allowed representation for black Rhodesians. He formed the Rhodesian Front party to support the continuation of a white minority government in an independent Rhodesia. Smith became deputy prime minister under Winston Field in December of 1962. When Field was forced to resign on April 13, 1964, Smith became prime minister. He engaged in negotiations with the British government over the issue of independence. His refusal to consider sharing power with the black majority led to a stalemate in the negotiations. Smith's government unilaterally declared independence on November 11, 1965. Britain repudiated the declaration and imposed economic sanctions on Rhodesia. A new constitution was approved in June of 1969 that supported Smith's actions, and Rhodesia was formally declared a republic on March 2, 1970. He continued to seek a negotiated settlement with the British government as rebel insurgents waged a guerrilla war against the government. He agreed to meetings with the leaders of the African National Conference in 1975. Discussions with the rebel leaders produced no solid results, and fighting continued in the country. An agreement was reached in March of 1978 with some members of the opposition that led to majority rule. A new constitution was enacted in January of 1979, and parliamentary elections were held the following April. Bishop Abel Muzorewa replaced Smith as prime minister on May 29, 1979. He was elected to the Parliament the following year and remained a leader of the opposition Republican Front. He was suspended from Parliament in October of 1987, when the guaranteed white minority seats were eliminated.

ABEL MUZOREWA (Prime Minister, May 29, 1979–December 11, 1979). Abel Tendekayi Muzorewa was born in Old Umtali on April 14, 1925. He was educated locally and at Central Methodist College in Fayette, Missouri, and Scarritt College in Nashville, Tennessee.

He returned to Rhodesia in 1963 and served as pastor at the Old Umtali Mission. In 1968 he was named Resident Bishop for the United Methodist Church for Rhodesia. Muzorewa was elected president of the African National Council in 1971 and attended the Geneva Conference on Rhodesia in 1976. He served on the transitional council from 1978 to 1979 prior to the transfer of power to majority rule in Rhodesia. He served as prime minister of Rhodesia from May 29, 1979, until December 11, 1979, when Great Britain temporarily renewed its authority in the country. Muzorewa was detained from November of 1983 until September of 1984. He went into exile in the United States the following year, but returned to Zimbabwe in November of 1986.

ROBERT MUGABE (Prime Minister, March 4, 1980–December 31, 1987). *See entry under Heads of State.*

Index